VISUAL PROGRAMMING ENVIRONMENTS: PARADIGMS AND SYSTEMS

Visual
Programming
Environments
Paradigms and Systems

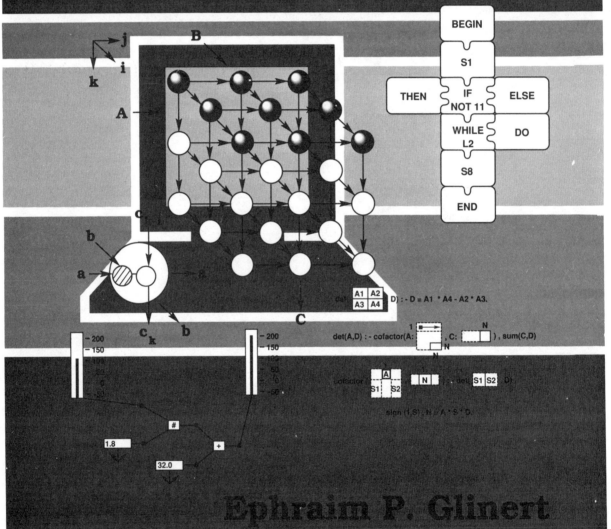

Ephraim P. Glinert

IEEE Computer Society Press Tutorial

VISUAL PROGRAMMING ENVIRONMENTS:
PARADIGMS AND SYSTEMS

Ephraim P. Glinert, Editor

Computer Science Department
Rensselaer Polytechnic Institute
Troy, NY 12180

E–mail: glinert@turing.cs.rpi.edu

IEEE Computer Society Press
Los Alamitos, California

Washington ● Brussels ● Tokyo

Published by

IEEE Computer Society Press
10662 Los Vaqueros Circle
P.O. Box 3014
Los Alamitos, CA 90720-1264

IEEE Computer Society Press Order Number 1973
IEEE Catalog Number EH0324-4
ISBN 0-8186-8973-0 (case)
ISBN 0-8186-5973-4 (microfiche)
SAN 264-620X

Additional copies can be ordered from:

IEEE Computer Society Press
Customer Service Center
10662 Los Vaqueros Circle
P.O. Box 3014
Los Alamitos, CA 90720-1264

IEEE Computer Society
13, Avenue de l'Aquilon
B-1200 Brussels
BELGIUM

IEEE Computer Society
Ooshima Building
2-19-1 Minami-Aoyama,
Minato-Ku
Tokyo 107, JAPAN

IEEE Service Center
445 Hoes Lane
P.O. Box 1331
Piscataway, NJ 08855-1331

THE INSTITUTE OF ELECTRICAL AND ELECTRONICS ENGINEERS, INC.

□□□   □□□   **For Rinat, Eitan and Keren**

Table of Contents

 # Introduction and Tutorial Overview

In the beginning, all human–computer communication was, for technical reasons, constrained to be one–dimensional. Programs as well as commands to the operating system were all linear text strings. For many years, these text strings were either typed in via operators' consoles or broken into segments and keypunched on cards. Eventually, these media of expression were replaced by glowing phosphor behind the glass face of a CRT.

In those early days of computing, classification of programming languages was a relatively simple matter. The imperative procedural paradigm, in which one tells the computer what to do and how to do it, often in excruciating detail, was essentially the sole style of programming available. It remained to determine just the *applications domain*, which could consist of scientific "number crunching" or commercial "data processing," and the *language level*, which was assumed to be roughly inversely proportional to the amount of detail with which the desired computations had to be specified. There were low level languages (e.g., machine language and assembler), higher level languages (e.g., FORTRAN and COBOL), and very high level languages for special domains (e.g., packages such as SPSS and BMDP).

That state of affairs, which reigned supreme for over a quarter century, came to an abrupt end in 1975 with the publication of David Canfield Smith's landmark dissertation *Pygmalion: A Creative Programming Environment*. Smith's research heralded a new era in programming, in which the increased power of computing engines, together with their graphics capabilities, made it possible to utilize the two–dimensional CRT screen as more than a mere backdrop for linear text string wrap–around. Smith introduced a new yardstick for assessing programming languages, namely, *the nature of the human–computer interface, during programming and at run time*. Environments, programming language(s) within the context of an integrated set of software support tools and appropriate hardware (most importantly I/O devices), became the focus of attention. Two new styles of human/computer interaction resulted: *visual environments*, in which graphical elements play prominent roles alongside text, and *iconic environments*, in which users interact with the machine primarily by defining, pointing at, juxtaposing, overlapping and otherwise manipulating postage–stamp size images commonly referred to as icons.

The past decade has witnessed the accumulation of an impressive body of evidence that visual and iconic environments often prove highly beneficial, both to computer–users in general and to programmers in particular. The computer's ability to represent in a visible manner normally abstract and ephemeral aspects of the computing process such as recursion, concurrency, and the evolution of data structures has had a remarkable and positive impact on both the productivity of programmers and their degree of satisfaction with the working environment. Iconic environments are especially intriguing, because they hold out the promise of enabling programmers to employ what were formerly considered merely graphical aids to compose their programs through a process Shneiderman has dubbed "direct manipulation."

It is now universally accepted that graphics can play a significant role in human/computer communication in general. Two examples of areas where the application of graphics has already proven particularly successful are the operating systems associated with certain personal computers, and the visualization of the output generated by large–scale scientific computations. Where programming languages are concerned, however, we remain unable, despite all of the progress that has undeniably been achieved, to bridge the chasm that continues to separate:

The way we, as human beings, conceive of solutions to problems

from:

The way that we now must program these solutions for our computers.

If we could do so, would it not be more pleasant and productive to work in multiparadigm environments which could support, within a single program, both textual and graphical representations for all sorts of computing objects, and which would allow us to fashion our programs as logically structured multidimensional pictures, using a variety of software tools and I/O devices? With the dawn of a new millenium just around the corner, maybe even this vision is too restrained.

Much as we would like to do so, it would be premature to claim that visual or iconic programming is the panacea we seek. This is because of the many open problems which remain, many of a truly fundamental nature. As Stu Schaffner has pointed out in a recent letter, what we normally think of as a programming language definition really consists of two separate parts: an *abstract language*, which determines a domain (e.g., data cells) along with sets of operations and constraints on the elements of that domain, and a *concrete language* which provides a representation (e.g., as strings of ASCII characters) for the abstract language. Where textual languages are concerned, it may not be important to keep the abstract and concrete parts of a language definition separate. However, when we study visual and iconic programming languages we must take care to do so. In particular, it is of paramount importance to investigate how the nature of the concrete parts of these languages may affect their abstract components.

But there is hope. We nowadays view as quaint, humorous or even downright bizarre many of the artifacts prized by previous generations, and which can now be found only in museums and as props on television shows set in bygone eras. The iron machines with their huge wheels, the outdated means of transportation and lighting, the ineffectual drugs and outlandish medical procedures, the punched card equipment, slide rules and mechanical typewriters which not so long ago were ubiquitous—considered in their heydays thoroughly modern and the ultimate to which one could aspire, now they are but memories and collectibles.

Under the circumstances, only the naive or foolhardy would be so bold as to proclaim that programming as it is now commonly practised will still be the norm 50 or 100 years down the road. On the contrary, tomorrow's programming environments will surely be vastly different from anything available today.

As in all areas of scientific endeavor, the future must evolve from and be built upon the present. This does not preclude, however, the possibility that the study of main–line textual languages may have reached the point where only minor, evolutionary advances may be expected. Tomorrow's reality will be fashioned from the dreams of today. Perhaps programming will be three–dimensional rather than "flat" as at present. Artificial intelligence may hold some of the answers. The revolutionary approaches which will endure, and those which will prove to be dead ends to be unceremoniously buried in the dust of history, will unfold in time.

The reprints and original contributions collected in the two volumes which comprise our tutorial on visual programming environments represent some of the best efforts to date to explore the visual alternatives. As such, they should provide the reader with much stimulating food for thought. We begin the volume *"Paradigms and Systems"* in Chapter 1 with an overview of basic concepts and some definitions, along with a brief glance at and comparison of many important systems which will be examined later in more detail. Graphical aids for program design have been around since the earliest days of computing; the most famous (perhaps infamous would be a better adjective in this case) exmaple is, of course, the flowchart. In Chapter 2 we survey both the classical (that is, well known) representations and some which, although more obscure, are nonetheless interesting. Promising recent innovations that attempt to overcome the oldtimers' shortcomings are also given their due.

Chapter 3 focuses on the pioneering visual and iconic systems that were published in the professional literature, including Smith's work to which we referred above. Although these early efforts may seem crude by today's standards, at the time they had a significant impact on research in this area. The reader should carefully note that there were numerous unpublished efforts which preceded those covered in this chapter. For instance, George Nagy has recently brought to our attention the M.Sc. thesis of his student Ed Anson, entitled *"Interactive Creation of Structured Programs by Means of Step-Wise Refinement,"* which describes a rudimentary NSD–based editor for PL/I programs implemented at the University of Nebraska, Lincoln, before August of 1975. This example is by no means unique. Indeed, the last segment of issue 13 of the *SIGGRAPH Video Review* hints that researchers at M.I.T. were exploring interactive programming by means of flowcharts on a graphics display in the late 1960's.

Chapter 4 considers visual extensions to main–line textual languages; examples are given for Pascal, C, Lisp and Prolog. Steve Reiss' research at Brown University has played and continues to play a central role in the development of visual programming, despite the lack of publications in the early years of his career. Steve's work forms the topic of Chapter 5. Chapter 6 discusses six visual systems which make use of novel paradigms and metaphors to accomplish marvelous things. One of these new design approaches involves the use of constraints, to which the next two chapters are devoted in their entirety. Although the most commercially successful example of this paradigm is the spreadsheet, there are noteworthy systems which employ it in other ways. The on–going and seminal work by Alan Borning and his students forms the topic of Chapter 7, while additional constraint-based systems of interest are examined in detail in Chapter 8.

We conclude the volume *"Paradigms and Systems"* in Chapter 9, with a discussion of visual parallel and distributed computing environments. In your editor's assessment, this is an area where the visual approach may prove especially successful in years to come, because in these brave new worlds there is little or no inertia to overcome to get people to abandon old and trusted ways of doing things, and because even a cursory glance at the papers published by researchers in this field reveals that words routinely fail to adequately describe the architecture(s) under consideration, so that it becomes necessary to resort to a profusion of diagrams (e.g., of 2-D and even 3-D processor meshes) to get the desired point across.

We begin the volume "*Applications and Issues*" by surveying, in Chapter 1, a variety of the most exciting iconic systems which have been implemented in recent years (recall that iconic environments are a subclass of the visual environments where the interaction has a special flavor). Chapter 2 turns to a consideration of systems which support visualization of programs, processes and more. These systems provide the user/viewer with a concrete representation for some aspect(s) of what goes on "behind the scenes" when a program executes. Chapter 3 presents several papers which trace the evolution of Marc Brown's BALSA, undoubtedly the most famous program visualization system developed to date. Chapter 4 looks at the realm of commercial data processing. Not surprisingly, we find that the office of the future is going to be an integral part of the visual world.

Nowadays, it seems that everybody wants to design visual systems. It isn't easy, however, to properly design icons. The papers in Chapter 5 explain some of the issues and point out potential pitfalls. Certain ground rules must also be kept in mind if a visual computing environment is to be successful as a whole; these matters are discussed in Chapter 6. Is the visual approach always the right choice? When should graphics be preferred over text, and when are they of little value, even counterproductive? The papers which comprise Chapter 7 delve into this crucial issue, which has baffled many researchers and often sets nasty traps for the unwary.

One aspect of the visual approach which has received far too little attention to date is that it may be both a blessing and a curse to handicapped people. In part, this is because there are so many different kinds of handicaps. More to the point, however, is the fact that visual systems are, for the most part, designed by and for people who are themselves not handicapped. New United States government guidelines on computer accessibility may soon radically alter (and, it is to be hoped, improve) this situation. In Chapter 8 we look at some handicapped-related issues of which all who work in the field of visual computing should be aware. There is even a paper that presents a system for blind users, for whom the "visual" approach is clearly not going to provide much assistance—unless we expand that term to mean something more than it does at present!

One of the major obstacles preventing full realization of the visual approach's potential is the present dearth of formal underpinnings for the field. Even seemingly simple things such as good notations analogous to the BNF which has traditionally been used to precisely and unambiguously describe textual programming languages seem hard to come by in the visual and iconic cases. The best of the work to date in this area is surveyed in Chapter 9. Finally, Chapter 10 contains several papers which reflect your editor's subjective view of where the field of visual programming is headed: visual programming-in-the-large as currently practised in Japan (where, as in much of the orient, interest in visual systems is keen, perhaps because of the ideographic nature of written languages in that part of the world), visual programming in 3-D, and using the audio channel to complement the visual. A couple of these papers are admittedly lacking in hard results and tend to simply explore new directions; nevertheless, we feel that the ideas discussed are important enough to warrant their inclusion in this collection.

Our goal in undertaking to organize this tutorial for the IEEE Computer Society Press has been to make available in one place a well-balanced and comprehensive exposition of the best research to date relating to visual and iconic programming. Despite (or perhaps because of) the size of this collection, we have unfortunately been forced to omit much interesting material for lack of space. The original plan was to produce just a single volume, but as the project progressed it quickly became clear that this was an impossible task. So, if your favorite paper isn't here, we apologize. Also, we realize that there are alternative ways in which the material could have been organized, both within and across chapters. For example, the paper by Kramlich et al. in Chapter 4 of *"Paradigms and Systems"* could have been included in Chapter 2 of *"Applications and Issues."* Similarly, Harel's paper in Chapter 2 of *"Paradigms and Systems"* might instead have been put into Chapter 9 of *"Applications and Issues."* We hope we've made the right decision, at least most of the time. Thus, Harel's paper is where it is because its primary contribution, in your editor's opinion, is the graphical representation rather than the "formalisms" to which the title alludes. Be this as it may, comments and feedback from you, dear reader, will always be most welcome.

Numerous friends and colleagues have assisted us in preparing this work. Special thanks to Mike Graf, Dan Kimura and Clayton Lewis for their original contributions. Thanks also to Alfs Berztiss, Meera Blattner, Shi-Kuo Chang, Robert Duisberg, Steve Tanimoto, the anonymous referees for the IEEE CS Press, and the many others who provided encouragement, helpful comments and suggestions along the way. The beautiful cover artwork was created at the capable hands of Ronald K. Le Van, and through the courtesy of Alan Borning and Ricky Yeung. A very special thank-you to Margaret Brown and her industrious staff at IEEE CS Press. Last but certainly not least, thanks to Joaquim Jorge, David W. McIntyre, Todd Moyer, Charles D. Norton and Arturo Sanchez-Ruiz, without whose invaluable assistance these volumes would most likely never have been completed!

And now, Happy Reading!

— *Ephraim P. Glinert*
June, 1990

□□□ 1 □□□ Classification of Programming Environments

S.-K. Chang. "Visual Languages: A Tutorial and Survey." *IEEE Software*, 4(1):29–39, January 1987.

A.L. Ambler and M.M. Burnett. "Influence of Visual Technology on the Evolution of Language Environments." *IEEE Computer*, 22(10):9–22, October 1989.

B.A. Myers. "Visual Programming, Programming by Example and Program Visualization: A Taxonomy." In *Conference Proceedings, CHI'86: Human Factors in Computing Systems*, Boston, Mass., pages 59–66, April 13-17, 1986. ACM Press, New York.

N.C. Shu. "Visual Programming Languages: A Perspective and a Dimensional Analysis." In *Visual Languages* (S.-K. Chang, T. Ichikawa and P.A. Ligomenides, editors), pages 11–34, 1986. Plenum, New York.

Reprinted from *IEEE Software*, January, 1987, pages 29-39.
Copyright © 1987 by The Institute of Electrical and Electronics
Engineers, Inc. All rights reserved.

Visual Languages: A Tutorial and Survey

KEVIN REAGAN

Shi-Kuo Chang, University of Pittsburgh

Research into visual languages is varied, and growing in popularity. The concept of generalized icons is a framework for the design of the next generation of visual languages.

Low-cost systems that use visual languages to create, transmit, display, manipulate, and retrieve visual information are now feasible. Research into these information systems is spurred by the convergence of new technology in the fields of graphics, image processing, video, and microelectronics, and by the growing interest in multimedia communications.

However, the term *visual language* means different things to different people. To some, it means that the objects handled by the language are visual — a *language for processing visual information* or a *visual information processing language*. To others, it means the language itself is visual — a *language for programming with visual expression* or a *visual programming language*.

The first type, what I call *visual information processing languages*, usually deals with objects that have an inherent visual representation — pictorial objects that are associated with a certain logical interpretation. The languages themselves, however, may not have a visual representation. Usually, these are traditional linear languages that have been enhanced with library subroutines or software packages to deal with visual objects. Visual information processing languages are used in applications like image processing, computer vision, robotics, image database management, office automation, and image communications.

The second type, what I call *visual programming languages*, usually deals with objects that do not have an inherent visual representation. This includes traditional data types such as arrays, stacks, and queues and application data types such as forms, documents, and databases. Presenting these objects visually is helpful to the user. For the same reason, the languages themselves should be presented visually. In other words, both programming constructs and the rules to combine these constructs should be presented visually. Visual programming languages are used in applications like computer graphics, user interface design, database interface design, form management, and computer-aided design.

These two types do not exhaust all the possibilities. The objects dealt with by a visual language can be inherently visual, or

7

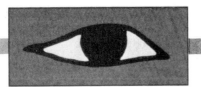

inherently nonvisual but with imposed visual representation. The programming language constructs can be visual or linear. Therefore, there are four types of visual langages, which are summarized in Table 1.

This classification is consistent with the classification of Shu,[1] who distinguishes three types of visual languages, those that (1) support visual interaction, (2) allow programming with visual expressions, and (3) process visual information. The fourth category, not present in Shu's classification, is the visual language that deals with visual objects and is itself visually represented. I call this the *iconic visual information processing language*.

Generalized icons

While the four types of visual languages are indeed different, they all deal with generalized icons. Generalized icons are either *object icons* or *process icons*.

An object icon is a two-part representation of an object, written as (Xm, Xi). Xm is the logical part (the meaning) and Xi is the physical part (the image). Visual programming languages deal with objects that have logical meaning, but no visual image: (Xm, e), e denoting a null object. When the visual representation is imposed, we transform (Xm, e) into $(Xm, X'i)$ so it can be visualized. Visual information processing languages deal with objects that have a visual image, but no logical meaning: (e, Xi). Again, when we impose the logical meaning, we transform (e, Xi) into $(X'm, Xi)$. The third column of Table 1 summarizes the transformations of object icons. Thus, objects handled by a visual language are object icons, or icons with a logical and physical part that represents an object.

Similarly, a process icon represents an action, or a computational process. Language constructs handled by a visual language are process icons, or icons with a logical and physical part that represents a computational process.

The distinction between an object icon and a process icon depends both on context and interpretation. For example, the road sign of a diagonal line inside a circle can be interpreted as a stop sign by a computer vision system, in which case it is an object icon. But the same sign could be interpreted as a halt command by a mobile robot, in which case it is a process (action) icon.

The concept of generalized icons is the basis for designing visual languages. When designing visual languages, we first ask the question: How can we represent visual objects logically and logical objects visually? This question leads to the concept of object icons. We then ask the question: How can we represent programming constructs visually and specify algorithms in a visual language? This question leads to the concept of process icons.

Visual programming languages

In Shu's excellent introduction and survey of visual languages, she proposes a three-dimensional framework to characterize and compare visual languages. To evaluate if the visual language approach is adequate for an intended application with a certain type of user, three questions should be asked:

(1) Is it adequate for visualization?

(2) Is it adequate for representing processes?

(3) Is it adequate for representing objects?

These three questions correspond to the three dimensions in Shu's classification, as shown in Figure 1:

(1) Visibility (adequacy in visualization).

(2) Language level (adequacy in

Table 1.
The four types of visual languages.

	Objects to be dealt with	Transformation of objects	Languages' visibility
Languages that support visual interaction	logical objects with visual representation	$(Xm, e) \rightarrow$ $(Xm, X'i)$	linearly represented constructs
Visual programming languages	logical objects with visual representation	$(Xm, e) \rightarrow$ $(Xm, X'i)$	visually represented constructs
Visual information processing languages	visual objects with imposed logical representation	$(e, Xi) \rightarrow$ $(X'm, Xi)$	linearly represented constructs
Iconic visual informaton processing languages	visual objects with imposed logical representation	$(e, Xi) \rightarrow$ $(X'm, Xi)$	visually represented constructs

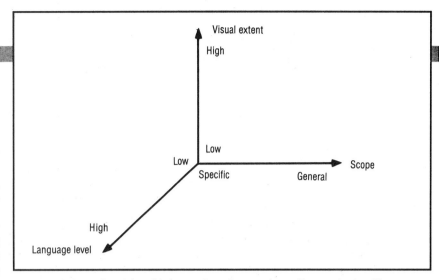

Figure 1. A three-dimensional framework to characterize and compare visual languages.

representing processes by procedural or nonprocedural means).

(3) Language scope (adequacy in representing objects for different applications).

The level of a language is inversely related to the amount of details a user must supply the computer to achieve the desired results. The scope of the language ranges from the general and widely applicable to the specific and narrowly applicable. For example, the Xerox Star system is high in visual content, but low in level and scope. On the other hand, Query-by-Example[2] is low in visual content and scope, but high in language level. The adequacy of visual languages is related to the cognitive aspects in visual information processing, which I discuss later in this article.

Interpreting objects. When generalized icons are used in communication, their meaning is interpreted with respect to the visual language. Lakin[1] explores the parsing and interpretation of visual sentences — or visual communication objects — in visual languages. The objects dealt with are logical objects with visual representation. An analysis of their spatial arrangement reveals the underlying syntactic structure, which could denote a computation process or a complex structure that is subject to further interpretation. Lakin calls this approach *executable graphics*.

In my classification, spatial parsing is applicable to both visual programming languages and iconic visual information processing languages, although Lakin's work is more closely related to the former. For example, in VennLisp, a visual Lisp developed by Lakin, visual objects are used not only to direct computation, but also to represent the results of the computation, as Figure 2 shows. In a VennLisp diagram, spatial enclosures denote the nesting of function calls. Therefore, the spatial parser will first find the spatial enclosing relations among visual objects (using an up-left-first ordering rule), and then construct the corresponding parsing tree.

Another parsing example is illustrated in Figure 3, which shows a visual sentence written in Vic, a visual language for aphasics. Because the Vic sentence is almost linear, the parser will recognize the

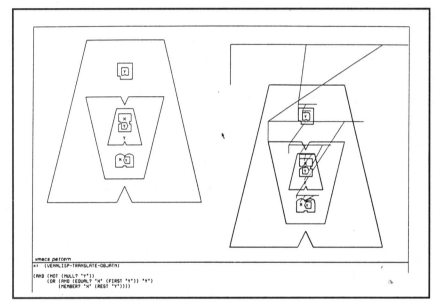

Figure 2. A VennLisp diagram and its parsed version.

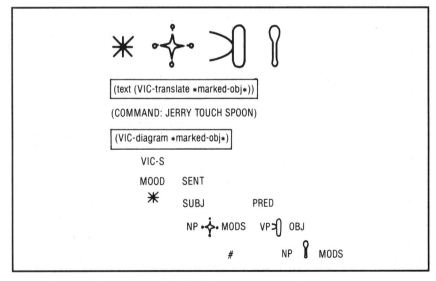

Figure 3. A visual sentence written in Vic.

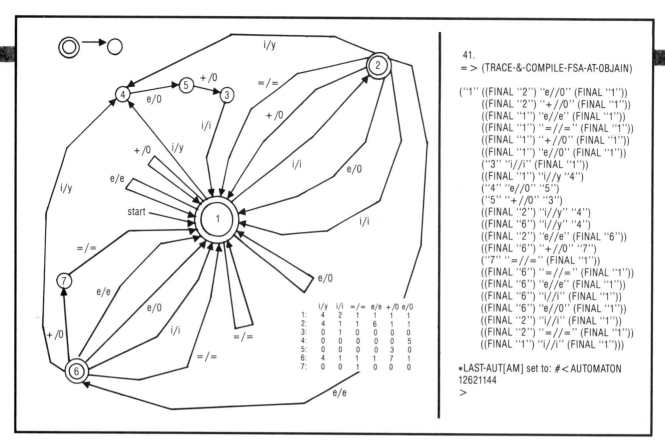

Figure 4. Parsing a finite-state diagram.

The following code appears in the right portion of Figure 4:

```
41.
= > (TRACE-&-COMPILE-FSA-AT-OBJAIN)

("1" ((FINAL "2") "e//0" (FINAL "1"))
     ((FINAL "2") "+//0" (FINAL "1"))
     ((FINAL "1") "e//e" (FINAL "1"))
     ((FINAL "1") "=//=" (FINAL "1"))
     ((FINAL "1") "+//0" (FINAL "1"))
     ((FINAL "1") "e//0" (FINAL "1"))
     ("3" "i//i" (FINAL "1"))
     ((FINAL "1") "i//y "4")
     ("4" "e//0" "5")
     ("5" "+//0" "3")
     ((FINAL "2") "i//y" "4")
     ((FINAL "6") "i//y" "4")
     ((FINAL "2") "e//e" (FINAL "6"))
     ((FINAL "6") "+//0" "7")
     ("7" "=//=" (FINAL "1"))
     ((FINAL "6") "=//=" (FINAL "1"))
     ((FINAL "6") "e//e" (FINAL "1"))
     ((FINAL "6") "i//i" (FINAL "1"))
     ((FINAL "6") "e//0" (FINAL "1"))
     ((FINAL "2") "i//i" (FINAL "1"))
     ((FINAL "2") "=//=" (FINAL "1"))
     ((FINAL "1") "i//i" (FINAL "1")))

*LAST-AUT[AM] set to: #<AUTOMATON
12621144
>
```

The transition table within Figure 4:

	i/y	i/i	=/=	e/e	+/0	e/0
1:	4	2	1	1	1	1
2:	4	1	1	6	1	1
3:	0	1	0	0	0	0
4:	0	0	0	0	0	5
5:	0	0	0	0	3	0
6:	4	1	1	1	7	1
7:	0	0	1	0	0	0

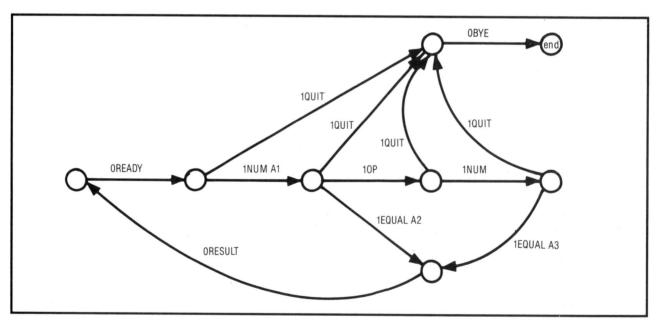

Figure 5. A finite-state diagram of a simple desk calculator.

individual icons and then construct the parsing tree.

A third example, parsing a finite-state diagram, is illustrated in Figure 4. In this example, parsing amounts to constructing an arc-node list by tracing arcs in a directed graph. I have described[3] more sophisti-

cated parsing techniques for spatial arrangement of objects using picture grammars and picture precedence grammars.

Representing abstractions. Jacob also uses a visual programming language to represent an abstract computation that does

not have a direct graphical image.[4] In his approach, the state transition diagram is used as a visual programming language to design and specify user interfaces. Figure 5 shows the state diagram description of a simple desk calculator, where the 1 prefix indicates input, the 0 prefix indicates output, and A1 indicates an action that must be executed by the desk calendar (actions are defined in a separate program specification). Jacob emphasizes that the choice of an adequate visual representation improves human performance.

Programming by rehearsal. The Programming-by-Rehearsal system[7] is a visual programming environment implemented in Smalltalk-80 on the Xerox Lisp Machine. It provides a powerful metaphor for visual programming. A rehearsal world is created by (1) auditioning the available performers by selecting their cues and observing their responses, (2) copying the chosen performers and placing them on the stage, (3) blocking the production, (4) rehearsing the production by showing each performer what actions it should take in response to a cue or user input, and (5) storing the production for later retrieval and execution.

Each performer corresponds to a process icon, and is grouped in a troupe in different windows on the display, as Figure 6 shows. This system is high in visual content, but low in level and scope because only icons on the screen can be manipulated. However, the program design process is quick, easy, and enjoyable; a simple program can be created in less than 30 minutes.

Pict/D. An interactive graphical programming environment developed by Glinert and Tanimoto,[8] Pict/D relies on icons for visual programming. Once the system is initialized, Pict/D users never touch a keyboard. Instead, they draw programs with an input device like a joystick. The prototype Pict/D system lets the user compose programs that do simple numeric calculations.

Figure 7 shows a partial scenario of Pict/D programming, which uses a flowchart metaphor. The subsystems represented are programming (a flowchart icon), erase (a hand holding an eraser), icon editor (a hand holding a pen), and user library (a shelf of books). The user can program an icon, edit it, or run its associated program. The resultant program can be denoted by a new icon, created by the user with the icon editor, that is stored

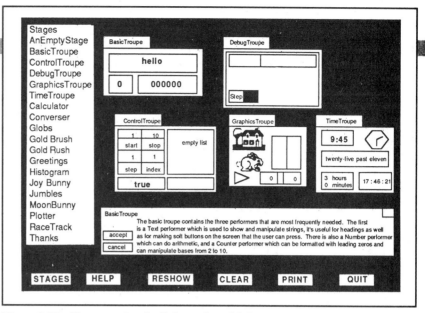

Figure 6. The Programming-by-Rehearsal world theater.

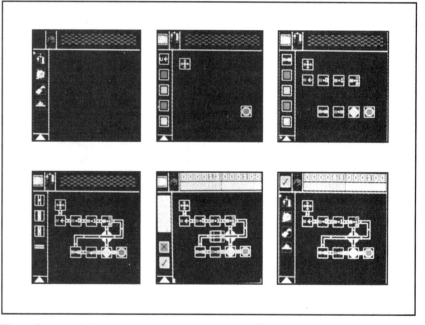

Figure 7. A partial scenario of programming in Pict/D.

in the library for future use.

As it stands, Pict/D is quite suitable for novices, but its language level and scope must be expanded significantly to satisfy the expert user. Interestingly, user acceptance of Pict/D seems to be a function of sex and age — responses from female students were consistently more favorable than male responses, and the youngest third of the students gave consistently more favorable responses than the oldest third.

Languages supporting visual interaction

Recent applications have used graphical (iconic) representations in software design and implementations[5] such as dataflow diagrams, HIPO charts, action diagrams, and Nassi-Shneiderman diagrams. Most of these are written with languages that support visual interaction. For example, the NS diagram[6] uses a two-dimensional rep-

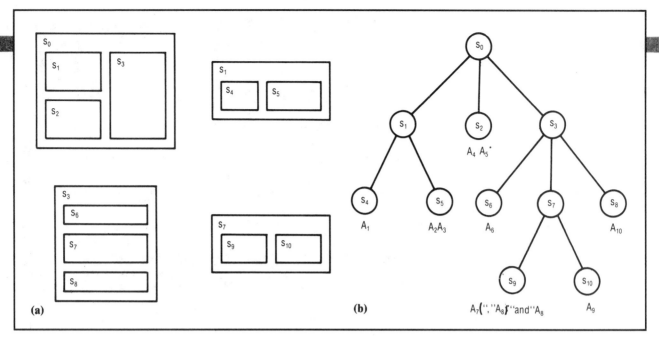

Figure 8. (a) Visual templates of a structured form and (b) their visual sheme.

resentation of three programming constructs: sequence, iteration, and selection. However, the program statements are still written in a conventional programming language. So the NS diagram application is in a language supporting visual interaction. The same is true of the Boxer system, where the list data structures are manipulated graphically by creating and destroying boxes containing list elements.

Special-purpose languages. Two special-purpose visual programming languages

with limited scope have been designed to handle two types of logical objects, forms and databases.

Yoshida and his coworkers[1] describe a form-definition and form-manipulation language that treats forms like objects. Essentially, forms are logical objects with an imposed visual representation. The form-definition language describes the visual structure of a form with templates (Figure 8a) and the logical structure of a form with a corresponding regular expression, or

scheme (Figure 8b). The nonprocedural form-manipulation language creates, retrieves, modifies, and browses forms.

Larson[1] describes a system that uses entity-relationship diagrams to describe a database, as Figure 9 shows. The user can manipulate this graph to create different templates displaying various types of data from the database. The user also queries the database by manipulating the command graph, as shown in Figure 10.

Since both of these languages use linear constructs, they are classified as languages that support visual interaction.

Iconic and visual information processing languages

Iconic languages are visual languages that use icons extensively or exclusively. An iconic language could be any of the four types of visual languages.

Webster's dictionary defines an icon as "an image; figure; representation; picture." Historically, the term icon has been associated primarily with religious images. In computing, it means a symbolic representation that can be used to direct data manipulation operations.

The Korfhages[1] have explored the role of an iconic system as a user-computer interface. They define an *iconography* as a finite set of icons, a *pictograph* as a structured set of related icons (such as icons for hotel or restaurant and action signs such as arrows), and an *iconic sentence* as an iconic

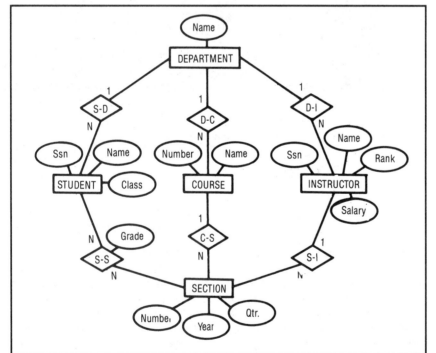

Figure 9. Entity-relationship diagram of a database.

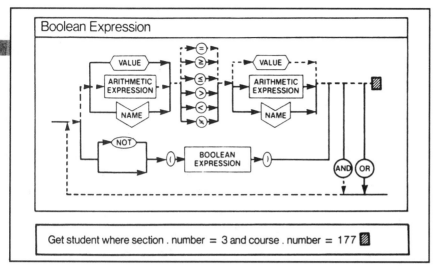

Figure 10. A command graph used to query a database.

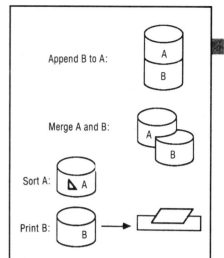

Figure 13. Construction of iconic sentences.

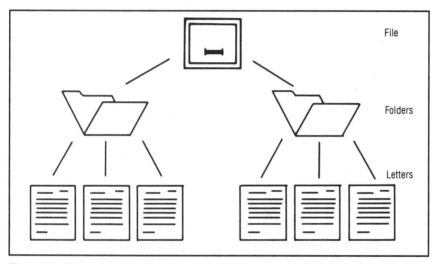

Figure 11. Hierarchical relationships among icons.

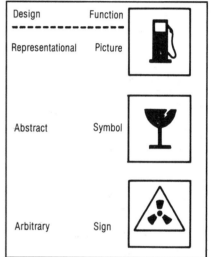

Figure 14. A taxonomy of icons.

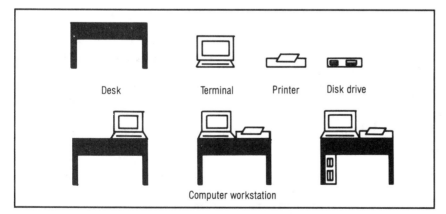

Figure 12. Combining icons to construct complex object icons.

structure formed according to specific linguistic rules. An iconic sentence has definite syntatic rules governing its construction and definite semantic rules governing its interpretation. Finally, an *iconic language* is composed of these iconic sentences.

The Korfhages found that business-oriented iconographies are richer in object icons with strong textual elements, while graphics-oriented iconographies have a better stock of process icons.

Iconographies can handle hierarchical relationships easily, as Figure 11 shows.

They should also allow the user to combine icons into more complex icons, as in Figure 12, and construct new iconic sentences, as in Figure 13. The user of an iconic language also needs the ability to define several levels of descriptive detail, including what information appears or disappears as the levels are changed. In addition, the user should be allowed to define several interlocking hierarchies of iconographies.

Icon design. Icon communication uses images to convey ideas or actions (commands) nonverbally. Lodding's taxonomy of icons classifies them by design and function.[9] By this taxonomy, there are three types of icons, illustrated in Figure 14: representational, abstract, and arbitrary.

An icon image is chosen to relate to the idea or action either by resemblance (picture), by analogy (symbol), or by being selected from a previously defined and learned group of arbitrary images (sign).

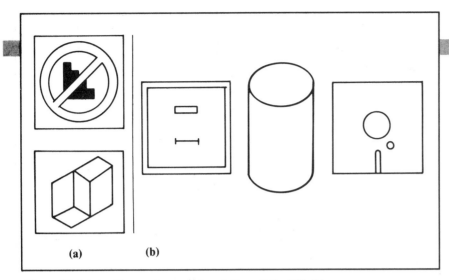

Figure 15. (a) Ambiguous icons; (b) evolution of the "file" icon.

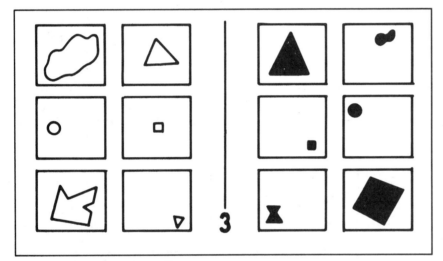

Figure 16. Bongard problem #3.

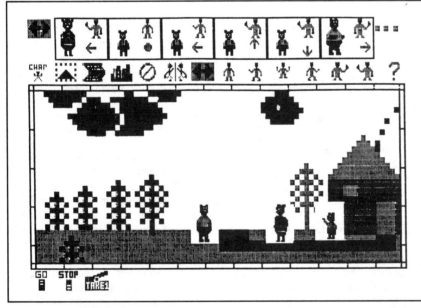

Figure 17. Iconic sentences in Play.

To ensure the correct interpretation of an icon, we must carefully consider the design of the image, the caption associated with the image, and the context in which the icon appears.

Iconic languages have drawbacks. As Lodding points out, some icons are inherently ambiguous and others can only be interpreted within a certain context, as Figure 15a shows. And, as the Korfhages point out, icons evolve, since there is no universally accepted set of icons. Figure 15b shows the evolution of the "file" icon. Therefore, an icon must be designed with care. Lodding suggests dividing the design process into three steps: (1) choosing the representation, (2) rendering the design, and (3) testing the icon.

Montalvo investigates the issue of icon design from a different angle.[10] The central problem, according to Montalvo, is how to symbolically describe visual objects with concepts that are natural to people. To discover and validate the symbolic description of visual properties, Montalvo suggests that we (1) focus on the conversation between the user and the system to validate the *denotation* between symbolic descriptions and visual properties, and (2) use the Bongard diagrams to discover a natural and rich set of visual primitives.

Figure 16 shows a Bongard diagram. The problem is to find the minimal description that distinguishes the figures on the left from the figures on the right. Once the visual properties have been isolated and made explicit, compositional operators are used to construct understandable, complex diagrams.

In my conceptual framework, Montalvo's denotation is the correspondence between Xm and Xi in a generalized icon. What she proposes is a methodology to verify the natural correspondence between Xm and Xi, and to isolate the properties of Xm. Although the compositional operators are not yet fully understood, research in this direction will lead to a better understanding of icon semantics.

The Play system. Tanimoto and Runyan[1] describe an interesting iconic programming system for children called Play. Play is an experimental computing

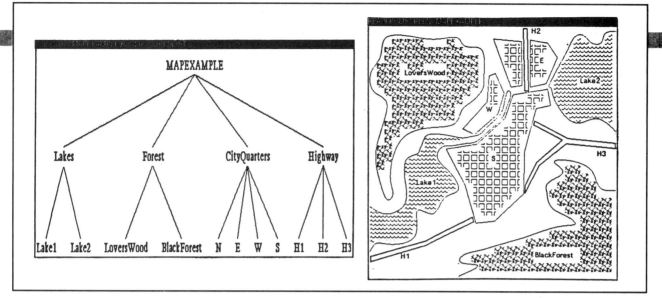

Figure 18. Image database design using Vicon.

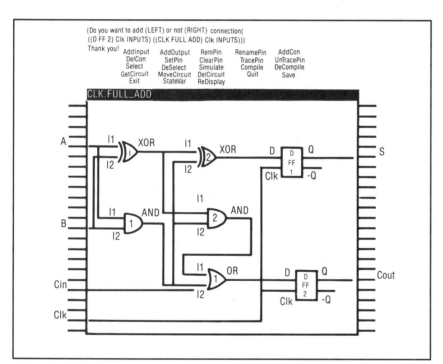

Figure 19. VLSI design using Vicon.

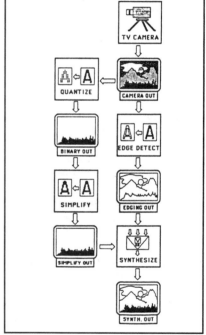

Figure 20. A program in Hi-Visual.

environment that lets children design and move characters and backgrounds, make up plays, and view animated performances. Each play is represented graphically by a script. The script, which looks like a comic strip, consists of a sequence of iconic sentences. Figure 17 shows a screen from Play.

In Play, an iconic sentence can be either an action sentence or a background-loading command. An action sentence has three parts, an icon designating a plaything, an icon designating an action, and a modifier, which usually specifies a direction. The action sentence, with its fixed

syntax and semantics, corresponds to Lakin's visual sentence, the Korfhages' iconic sentence, and Rohr's visual concept.

Vicon. Clarisse and Chang[1] have described Vicon, an approach for designing icon-oriented software systems on a Lisp machine. Vicon's design is based on generalized icons. A generalized icon is implemented as an object with two types of attributes, *aspect* and *relation*. Aspect attributes include icon name, bitmap name, window name, menu, and built-in functions associated with the menu. Relation attributes include pointers to the par-

ent, sibling, and child icons. An icon editor is provided to edit the generalized icons.

This icon-oriented approach is ideally suited to the design of high-level, structured, graphic interfaces. Potential applications include image database design (Figure 18), computer-aided design of integrated circuits (Figure 19), expert system design, office information system prototyping, and robotics.

Icon-oriented software need not be restricted to the design of efficient user interfaces — Vicon can be used as a tool in many applications. Vicon demonstrates that an iconic language may be transformed into a high-level visual programming language or iconic visual information processing language by constructing the proper object icons and process icons in a generalized icon data structure.

Hi-Visual. The Hi-Visual language developed at Hiroshima University by Ichikawa and his coworkers[1] employs icons to represent objects of an application domain, as well as the computation processes they perform, as Figure 20 shows. In other words, Hi-Visual uses both object and process icons for visual interaction. In my classification scheme, therefore, Hi-Visual is an iconic visual information processing language. An earlier version dealt mostly with logical objects such as forms and documents, and is therefore classified as a language supporting visual interaction.

The efforts of Clarisse, Chang, and Ichikawa and his coworkers are part of an international project to design a prototype, general-purpose iconic visual information processing language called IPL.

SDMS and ISQL. Other researchers are exploring the design approaches of visual information processing languages. The Spatial Data Management System lets the user create graphic objects and associate them with individual objects or classes of objects. Parent icons and subicons can be created in a hierarchy, and the user can then zoom in and out of a database visually.[11]

Hoehne and his coworkers[1] describe an extension of the SQL database language, ISQL, that provides tools for handling images in an interactive environment. It is implemented in a prototype image information system for radiology.

Cognitive aspects

Cognitive aspects are important in evaluating whether visual languages are adequate for man-machine interaction.

Humans vs. computers. Weber and Kosslyn[1] compared human imagery with computer graphics systems with a two-fold purpose. First, they wanted to explore how graphics systems could better externalize mental imagery. They also wanted to discover how human imagery might be enhanced by using ideas from computer graphics.

Their research indicates that mental imagery has features that are not now available in computer graphics, including (1) flexible conversion between object and large bitmap representations, (2) zooming and extensive image editing capabilities, and (3) other complex functions:

(1) There is firm evidence that both the "deep," long-term memory representations and the "surface," short-term memory representations are object-oriented. However, the human imagery system seems to be capable of handling both object and bitmapped representations within the same display.

(2) There is also firm evidence that the human imagery system has the capability for continuous-size scale changes (zooming), and extensive editing capability seems to exist for any image size, except where the image becomes so small that resolution is lost.

(3) Human imagery's most obvious advantage over graphics systems is in complex functions such as learning, programming, self-diagnosis, and repair. Also, the integration of imagery with semantic information is remarkable in the human imagery system.

Conversely, computer graphics systems have features that would enhance the capability of human imagery. The large capacity of computer graphic systems and their long retention probably is unattainable by the human imagery system. Therefore, properly designed systems that combine the features of computer graphics, image, and video technology could enhance the humam imagery system and contribute to better visual communication.

Encoding principles. Studies by Rohr[1] demonstrate there is a strong relationship between the degree of abstraction of an icon and its type of use. In general, object icons tend to be strongly pictorial, with the picture of the object reduced to its simplest elements. Process icons (or action icons) tend to be more abstract.

Rohr discusses the adequacy of visual languages from the viewpoint of cognitive psychology. To decide whether visual languages can help, she analyzed how people represent different aspects of the reality, what basic concepts they generally deal with, and what enables them to learn new concepts.

She concludes that there is a real difference in the encoding of visual and linguistic information. Visual information encoded as spatial relations between objects leads to visual concepts, which are helpful in dealing with spatial functions and property transformations. However, highly abstract concepts such as existential functions are too complex to be expressed visually.

Therefore, it is important to provide a specification language for iconic system structure description so we can decide how icons can be used to express effectively such system components.

Definitions

This survey of current research indicates that the concept of generalized icons is an adequate framework for the design of visual languages. The concept of generalized icons, in turn, is based on the following concepts:

• An *iconic system* is a structured set of related icons. A complex icon can be composed from other icons in the iconic system, and therefore can express a more complex visual concept.

• An *iconic sentence* is a spatial arrangement of icons from an iconic system.

• A *visual language* is a set of visual sentences constructed with a given syntax and semantics.

• The *syntactic analysis of visual language* (spatial parsing) is the analysis of visual sentences to determine the underlying syntactic structure.

• Finally, the *semantic analysis of visual language* (spatial interpretation) is the interpretation of a visual sentence to determine its meaning.

Two major software tools are required to implement an iconic system and a visual language: (1) an icon editor to edit a generalized icon, and (2) an icon interpretor to perform syntactic and semantic analysis.

V isual languages introduce a new dimension to man-machine communications and add to our ability to design a multimedia, man-machine communication system.

New programming paradigms invented by designers of visual languages could enrich or even one day replace classical programming languages. But many issues must be explored.

For example, few research projects have considered *dynamic icons*, which are complex icons whose constituent icons have a time-of-appearance attribute. A blinking traffic light signal is an example of a dynamic icon. Another topic to be considered is *icon dynamics*, or the time-sequenced interpretation of an iconic system. Icon dynamics can enhance a system's ability to provide a dynamic system trace, debugging aids, and prototype simulations (for example, a robot icon, a car icon, simulation of a VLSI icon, simulation of a flow-chart icon).

We also need to investigate the effectiveness and the limits of visualization. Rohr has demonstrated that different types of people, called "visualizers," "formalizers," and "verbalizers," have different acceptance levels for visual languages. How will visualization benefit an experienced programmer? How can we visualize more abstract programming concepts such as recursion?

These and many other questions remain. As visual languages mature, there will be an increasing need to empirically study and evaluate these languages in terms of usability (ease of use), degree of meeting the requirements from the intended users, and productivity improvement.

Visual languages and the concept of generalized icons can be studied fruitfully from many different perspectives, including computer graphics, formal language theory, educational methodology, cognitive psychology, and visual design. Interdisciplinary research efforts can lead to a better understanding of the visual communication process, and the development of an effective methodology to design the next generation of visual languages. □

Acknowledgment
This research was supported in part by National Science Foundation grant DMC-8510804 and a research grant from Digital Equipment Corp.

References
1. *Visual Languages*, Shi-Kuo Chang, ed., Plenum Publishing, New York, 1986.
2. M.M. Zloof, "QBE/OBE: A Language for Office and Business Automation," *Computer*, May 1981, pp. 13-22.
3. Shi-Kuo Chang, "Picture Processing Grammar and its Applications," *Information Sciences*, Vol. 3, 1971, pp. 121-148.
4. Robert J.K. Jacob, "A State Transition Diagram Language for Visual Programming," *Computer*, Vol. 18, No. 8, Aug. 1985, pp. 51-59.
5. J. Martin and C. McCure, *Diagraming Techniques for Analysts and Programmers*, Prentice-Hall, 1985.
6. B. Shneiderman, "Direct Manipulation: A Step Beyond Programming Languages," *Computer*, Vol. 16, No. 8, Aug. 1983, pp. 57-69.
7. W. Finzer and L. Gould, "Programming by Rehearsal," *Byte*, Vol. 9, No. 6, June 1984, pp. 187-210.
8. E.P. Glinert and S.L. Tanimoto, "Pict: An Interactive Graphical Programming Environment," *Computer*, Vol. 17, No. 11, Nov. 1984, pp. 7-25.
9. K.N. Lodding, "Iconics — A Visual Man-Machine Interface," *Proc. Nat'l Computer Graphics Assoc.*, NCGA, Fairfax, Va., 1982, Vol. 1, pp. 221-233.
10. F.S. Montalvo, "Diagram Understanding: Associating Symbolic Descriptions with Images," *Proc. of Second IEEE Workshop on Visual Languages,* Dallas, June 1986.
11 C.F. Herot, "Spatial Management of Data," *ACM Trans. Database Systems*, Vol. 5, No. 4, 1980, pp. 493-514.

Shi-Kuo (S.K.) Chang is a professor and chairman of the Department of Computer Science at the University of Pittsburgh. His research interests are in visual languages, image databases, intelligent database systems, office information system modeling and analysis. He has published more than 100 papers and has recently edited a book on visual languages, published by Plenum.

Chang received a BS in electrical engineering from National Taiwan University in 1965, and the MS and PhD degrees in electrical engineering and computer science from the University of California at Berkeley in 1966 and 1969, respectively.

He has also published 10 novels and 4 collections of short stories in Chinese. His novel, *Chess King*, has been translated into English and was recently published in Singapore. A musical based on the novel will be staged in Taiwan this spring.

Influence of Visual Technology on the Evolution of Language Environments

Allen L. Ambler and Margaret M. Burnett

University of Kansas

With the availability of graphic workstations has come the increasing influence of visual technology on language environments. In this article we trace an evolution that began with the relatively straightforward translation of textual techniques into corresponding visual techniques and has progressed to uses of visual techniques that have no natural parallel using purely textual techniques. In short, the availability of visual technology is leading to the development of new approaches that are inherently visual.

Terminology. In the seventies, much of the research on software development technology concentrated on the development of loosely integrated tools for supporting various phases of the software development and maintenance process. The Unix development environment is an example of such a *software support environment*.

Subsets of software support environments directly relate to the programming process of a single programmer. These subsets, or *programming environments*, distinguish facilities for designing, coding, editing, documenting, and debugging indi-

> Since the advent of language environments, use of visual technology has evolved from visualization of existing textual approaches to inherently visual new approaches. We survey this evolution here.

vidual programming tasks from facilities required for planning, tracking, and managing entire software projects. Programming environments may encourage particular programming methodologies and particular languages. Some, referred to as

language environments, are tightly integrated around a single language. Such tightly integrated, language-specific environments are the focus of this article.

One of the first language environments was Interlisp.[1] Developed in the early seventies, Interlisp provided the basic functionality we associate with a language environment: a fully integrated, language-specific environment with its own user interface, editor, interpreter, and symbolic debugger. More recent language environments have adopted and further refined many of Interlisp's features. In some cases, Interlisp's original ideas still represent the state of the art.

At the time language environments were first developed, computer technology was in a more primitive state. Bit-mapped graphics and even CRTs were less common than the standard Teletype terminal. In such an environment, the "friendliest" user interface was the briefest user interface. Therefore, language environments for many years were strictly command-driven. But the advent of visual technology brought dramatic changes in language environment user interfaces.

Layout and operation of the Smalltalk user interface

The Smalltalk environment assumes a high-resolution bitmap display, a keyboard, and a mouse with three buttons. The three mouse buttons are indicated by the appendage to the screen labelled (10, 11, 12).

We should note here that, in Smalltalk terminology, a window is a virtual screen large enough to contain an entire object. To accommodate physical screens, a window is viewed through a potentially smaller rectangular area that can be moved about on the surface of the window. Only this rectangular area, called a view, is actually displayed on the physical screen. By moving the view (a process called scrolling), you can view any portion of the window. In common usage, this distinction between a window and a view into it is often lost, with the term window

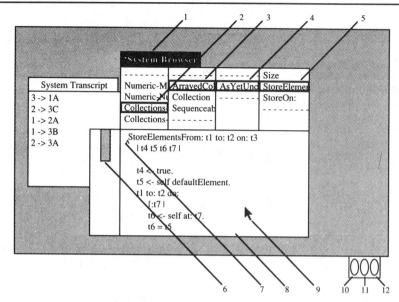

used to refer to the physical window rather than the virtual window. We use "window" to refer to the physical window.

The System Browser window, identified by the tab (1), consists of the body (8) of a method "StoreElementsFrom:to:on:" (5) of object "AsYetUnclassified" (4) of object "ArrayedCollection" (3) of object "Collec-

Visual user interfaces

Multiple windows. Smalltalk[2] introduced not only a new language extending the object-oriented approach of Simula 67, but also a new and highly visual user interface. Alan Kay pioneered the research leading to Smalltalk-76's programming environment. He devised a user-interface paradigm he called overlapping windows. Kay's paradigm allowed for arbitrarily large virtual windows with modeless switching between windows and therefore between functions. (An interface with modes interprets commands with differing results depending upon the current mode. Typically, getting from one mode to another requires some definitive action, such as entering a key sequence.)

The fundamental aspects of Kay's paradigm were

- displays associated with several user tasks could be viewed simultaneously;
- switching between tasks would be done with the press of a button;
- no information would be lost in the process of switching; and
- screen space would be used economically.

The paradigm would serve as the basis for what Kay called an "integrated environment," in which the distinction between

the operating system and an application would fade until every capability of any piece of software would apply to any piece of information. His paradigm contains the foundations for current user-interface paradigms not only for language environments, but also for system shells, including that of the now familiar Apple Macintosh.

See the sidebar on Smalltalk for a detailed example of the Smalltalk user interface.

An alternative windowing paradigm was introduced in Cedar,[3] a language synthesizing many of the same language environment concepts to produce an environment for an Algol-family language. This tiling paradigm is functionally similar to that of Smalltalk, differing primarily in detail and philosophy. See the sidebar on the sample Cedar screen for a description.

Multiple views. With Smalltalk came the concept of multiple windows; with Pecan[4] came the concept of multiple views. The distinction is that multiple views share a common internal data representation of the same data. Whenever any aspect of that data changes, then all views change simultaneously to reflect that change. The idea is that by representing data simultaneously in several ways, an individual user can choose those views that are most useful at a particular time.

In Pecan an internal abstract syntax tree supports concurrent views. The user never

views this internal abstract syntax tree directly, but its information is available through various views. For example, the editor provides a program listing view; the declaration editor provides a separate view of the program's declarations; and the structured flow graph view provides a view of the program as a structured flow graph. Whenever any modification is made to the abstract syntax tree, via any view, all active views are notified of the change. The incremental compiler is treated as an undisplayed view; it receives notifications of any updates and recompiles the appropriate part of the code. The same approach is taken with the execution environment. The sidebar on Pecan shows several sample views.

Software through Pictures[5] is another graphically oriented language environment with a family of graphic editors and a centralized database for information about the system under development. Each editor supports a particular methodology of design or analysis developed in recent years. The major editors in Software through Pictures are the Dataflow Diagram Editor, which supports structured systems analysis; the Entity-Relationship Editor, which supports the entity-relationship data modeling approach; the Transition Diagram Editor, which supports the user software engineering (USE) methodology; the Data Structure Editor, which supports data structure definition; and the Structure

tions-Abstract" (2). The bold-lined boxes in each case indicate the selected item. To select a different item within the class hierarchy, you would use the pointer (9) to point to the new selection and click the left button (10). Given the hierarchical ordering (from left to right), selecting a new item in any of panes (2, 3, 4) deselects the selections for all panes to the right of the new selection. You can scroll each selection pane should there be too many entries to fit.

Whenever the pointer (9) is within the System Browser window and within one of the five panes (2, 3, 4, 5, 8), a scroll box (6) appears along the left side of the containing pane. The scroll box lets you scroll the text of the corresponding pane by moving the pointer into the scroll box and either grabbing and dragging the gray slider up or down within the scroll box to indicate the relative position desired within the corresponding pane or by moving the pointer within the scroll box slightly to the left or right of the slider and clicking it to

move down (left of the slider) or up (right of the slider) one pane of information.

The caret marker (7) indicates the current position within the text where, if you typed, characters would be inserted. You can move this marker arbitrarily by pointing and clicking with the left button. In addition, you can select sections of text by pointing at one end of a desired selection, depressing and holding the left button while moving the pointer to the other end, and releasing the left button. While you make the selection and until you deselect it (by the next click of the left button), the selected text appears in reverse video. You can copy or delete selected text by choosing copy or cut from a pop-up menu associated with the center button (11). You can subsequently paste (insert) it by moving the pointer to a new location and choosing paste from the same pop-up menu.

A pop-up menu appears whenever you depress the center or right buttons. It contains a vertical list of possible opera-

tions applicable in the current context. You select an operation by using the pointer and clicking the left button when the appropriate operation appears in reverse video. After you select an operation, the pop-up menu disappears. The list of possible operations associated with a pop-up menu changes from one pane to another, making the choice of operations sensitive to context.

The right button (12) can also be used for pop-up menus. The convention in Smalltalk is that the center button invokes operations appropriate to the current pane, while the right button invokes commands relating to the window in relationship to all other windows. Typical right-button commands allow closing, reframing (changing a frame's size, shape, and screen position), or overlaying windows. As you can see in the figure, more than one window can be open at any time, with the active window indicated by having its tab (1) distinguished (by a reverse video title).

Sample Cedar screen

In Cedar, windowing features, although similar to those in Smalltalk, are enhanced and have several added features, including icons and buttons. A physical window is called a *viewer*, and viewers are tiled, rather than overlapped as in Smalltalk. Tiling is a method of placing viewers adjacent to one another to cover the entire screen without covering any viewer, partially or totally, with any other viewer.

Tiling versus overlapping has generated considerable discussion. With tiled viewers the system automatically handles sizing and placement of the viewers, but the viewers are therefore not likely to conform to their contents in a way that maximizes the visibility of those contents. With overlapping viewers, the opposite is true: you must handle sizing and placement manually. This allows you to make each viewer conform to its contents.

An open viewer occupies screen space. When a viewer is closed, it yields its screen space and appears only as an icon found at the bottom of the screen. When you reopen the iconic representation of a viewer by selecting and clicking its icon, the viewer is reallocated space on the screen. While a viewer is closed, it is suspended, but not terminated. Resizing a viewer has the effect of resizing at least one other viewer unless it was the only viewer, in which case it cannot be resized.

Within a viewer, other special viewers are possible. In particular, buttons are a

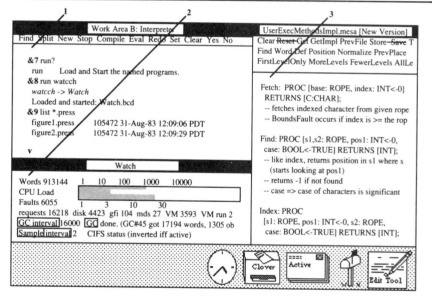

special group of viewers used only for invoking procedures. Buttons are represented as text, possibly surrounded by a small box, or as icons. Selecting a button has the effect of invoking a procedure. This procedure typically performs some action on the associated viewer. Often buttons are arranged in menus and displayed just below the caption bar, but they may be placed arbitrarily within another viewer.

Unique to Cedar is a *guarded* button, displayed as a single line drawn through the normal button representation. It indicates a command with a potentially destructive effect. To invoke a guarded but-

ton, you must click it twice within a short time interval.

The Cedar interpreter viewer shown here shows an instance in which the DWIM (Do What I Mean) facility has corrected a command error (1). This screen also has the performance measurement tool active (2) and shows the on-line documentation (3). In the documentation viewer, the buttons Reset and Save are examples of the guarded button feature.

We adapted this figure from information provided in W. Teitelman's "A Tour Through Cedar," published in the April 1984 issue of *IEEE Software*.

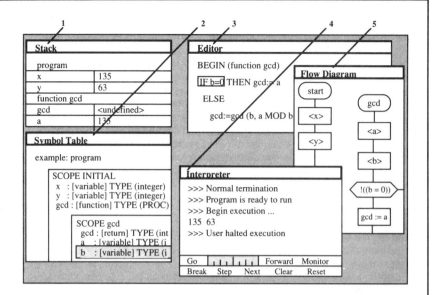

Sample views in Pecan

The stack view (1) shows the values of the variables defined at the current point of execution. The two variables *x* and *y* are part of the INITIAL block, which includes the function gcd. The symbol table view (2) illustrates the scope of each symbol, including *x*, *y*, and gcd, as well as gcd's formal parameters *a* and *b*. The editor view (3) shows the section of code currently being executed, namely the if *b*=0 statement within the gcd function. The interpreter view (4) displays the execution status and user inputs and outputs. The bottom portion of the interpreter view contains the ruler bar and several command selections (Go, Break, Step, etc.) that allow you to control the speed and manner of execution. The flow diagram view (5) shows the diagrammatic version of the section of code currently being executed (the gcd function), with

the current statement (if *b*=0) highlighted.

We adapted this figure from Reiss' ar-

ticle, "Graphical Program Development with Pecan Program Development Systems," published in the May 1984 issue of *ACM SIGPlan Notices*.

Chart Editor, which supports structured design. Each editor can automatically add information to the centralized database as it is generated and modified.

Beyond the visualization of textual languages. From experience with Pecan and generating systems to provide graphical views of otherwise textual languages, Reiss observed that users were limited by the inherent one-dimensionality associated with the underlying textual languages.[6] He concluded that effective use of the two-dimensional capabilities of graphical views required working with languages whose natural expression was graphical, not textual. Reiss responded by developing the Garden[6] system to accept descriptions of visual as well as textual programming objects. Others, making this same observation, have worked on new approaches to visual languages (see "Visual languages" below).

Like Pecan, Garden uses a common internal representation model, in this case an object-oriented environment complete with inheritance. New conceptual models are described by defining new objects that represent the fundamental objects of the new conceptual model, then by defining the interpretation of manipulations to these new objects. Each of these new objects can be given a visual representation as well as a textual representation. The interpretation

of visual manipulations can be described as well. To simplify the process, Garden provides an extensive library of database, process management, user-interface, dynamic display, debugging, and editing facilities usable in defining and testing new conceptual models.

See the sidebar on Garden for a description of the process of defining a new conceptual model.

Visual editing

Syntax-directed editing. One of the more prevalent visual editing techniques to appear in language environments is syntax-directed editing. Here, the editor is aware of the language's syntax and can thus either give the programmer immediate feedback whenever a syntax error is typed in or prevent such errors completely by forcing the programmer to use a template based upon the language syntax.

As with windowing systems above, whole papers discuss syntax-directed editors in detail. We will just touch on a few of the more prominent features as they have appeared in language environments. The two syntax-directed editors discussed, the Cornell Program Synthesizer editor and the Aloe editor used in Gandalf, follow the philosophy that if a portion of the program is created based on some template, then the

structure created by that template must be preserved during editing. This philosophy allows the use of visual hierarchical traversal techniques based on a program's structure. The examples shown in the accompanying sidebars on the Cornell Program Synthesizer and the Aloe editor illustrate the visual techniques used in traversing and editing programs using the two editors.

The Cornell Program Synthesizer[7] is a language environment for a subset of PL/1 called PL/CS. PL/CS programs are constructed through a syntax-directed editor that uses program-structure-based editing. Structural aspects of PL/CS programs, such as blocks and statements, are entered and edited through a special set of language-specific commands. These language-specific commands generate templates that outline the language's syntactic structure and provide a preformatted, properly indented, parentheses-matched form with place-holders to be filled in by the programmer. Non-structure-based phrases, such as expressions, comments, and identifier lists, are entered using conventional text-based editing commands, which are only available for such nonstructural phrases.

The programmer is similarly restrained from modifying a statement. Text entered to replace a place-holder must continue to match the syntactic part specified by the

Defining a new conceptual model in Garden

In Garden, a new conceptual model can be described in three steps. The type structure is specified, the semantics for each type is specified, and the syntax (textual and/or visual) is specified. Three types are needed for the finite state automaton in the figure: one describing a state, one describing a transition, and one describing the complete automaton.

The type editor window (1) shows the type definition and visual syntax for a state. It has no Super Types (2), includes the data fields id and accept (3), and includes the constant field Picture (4), which maps a state to a basic visual object (5) used to display the id field. All fields of a data structure need not be displayed with the visual syntax. Also, a single data structure can have mappings to more than one visual representation.

In addition to basic visual objects, composition objects are available. For example, a layout object can be used to display more complex or variable data structures than simple fields or records. The complete automaton has been mapped to a layout object composed of the basic object representation for states and several arc objects visually representing the transitions.

After the types are defined, the programmer defines their semantics (not shown in this figure) by writing functions using the textual Lisp-like language currently provided by Garden and other graphical or textual metaphors that have already been defined.

In (6), the programmer is experi-

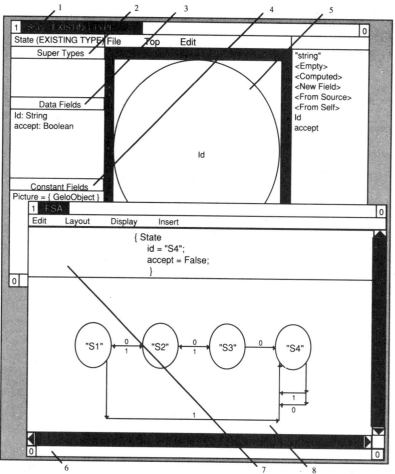

menting with an instance of the automaton type (8). Using this editor, the programmer has created the states using a series of selections, insert commands, and dialogue boxes. Similarly, the transitions have been created by selecting the from and to states, using the connect command, and filling in the values requested in the dialogue boxes. Finally, after several sample

evaluations (not shown), the current state has become "S4" (7).

We adapted this figure from Reiss' "Garden Tools: Support for Graphical Programming," published in *Advanced Programming Environments*, Lecture Notes in Computer Science #244, from Springer-Verlag, New York.

Syntax-directed editing using the Cornell Program Synthesizer

In the Cornell Program Synthesizer, you enter language-specific commands as text, then depress a special function key.

The editor command

.i

would produce the following template:

```
IF ( Condition )
    THEN statement
    ELSE statement
```

where "condition" and "statement" are place-holders. The box around the letter "c," C , shows the placement of the cursor; it denotes that "condition" is to be replaced by user-entered text. When the programmer enters text to replace "condition," the synthesizer will check that the entered text is a Boolean phrase. Should the entered text not match the syntactic part designated by the place-holder, the programmer will be so advised. Similarly, the programmer replaces the two oc-

currences of place-holder "statement" by further language-specific commands, introducing yet more templates.

The use of language-specific commands to generate the more complex syntax of the language PL/CS and the syntactic checking of place-holder replacement text prevents the programmer from entering syntactically incorrect programs. Further, some static semantic checking prevents errors such as referencing an undeclared identifier.

Syntax-directed editing using the Aloe editor

The language-specific command "wh" might be used to cause the place-holder

%stmt

to be replaced by

```
while %cond do
       %stmt
od
```

This template provides the structural parts of a while statement: the required syntactic tokens (while, do, and od) with proper indentation, and place-holders for a conditional expression (%cond) and the statement body (%stmt). The cursor is placed automatically at the first place-holder (%cond). The user may then type in an appropriate Boolean expression, replacing the %cond place-holder or, depending upon the abstract syntax, the user might invoke another constructive command expanding and replacing %cond. For instance, replacing %cond with the template for an and expression yields

```
while ( %expr and %expr ) do
       %stmt
od
```

The abstract syntax can be specified such that all expressions are composed entirely by using constructive commands or by entering a simple variable name or value. When specified in this way, editing, which is required to follow the parse tree, can become very rigid. For instance, to edit $((a + b) + c)$ to be $(a + (b + c))$ requires deleting the syntactic part $(a + b)$ and replacing it with a, followed by replacing c with the syntactic part $(\%expr + \%expr)$, and finally replacing the two occurrences of %expr by b and c. The alternative is an abstract syntax that stops short of generating expressions, that is, there are no syntactic parts specified as replacements for the place-holder %expr. Thus, expressions would be typed and edited as single nodes of the parse tree. Action routines might still be used to check syntactic correctness.

Up and down movement (cursor-previous and cursor-next) corresponds to lateral movement within the parse tree. In and out movement (cursor-out and cursor-in) corresponds to vertical movement within the tree. For instance, in the code shown here, the structural part is shown on the left and the cursor position is identified by a box. If the cursor is initially positioned as (cursor), then up, down, in, or out causes cursor movement as shown.

if %cond then
    %stmt
else
    %stmt
	if eof(input) then
	    done := true;
	else
	    read(ch);
		if eof(input) then
		    done := true;
		else
		    read(ch);
			if eof(input) then
			    done := true;
			else
			    read(ch);
				if eof(input) then
				    done := true;
				else
				    read(ch);
					if eof(input) then
					    done := true;
					else
					    read(ch);

Structural Part	(cursor)	(up)	(down)	(in)	(out)

Graphical representation in Use.It

The binary tree depicts the decomposition of a process for making wooden stools. For each node, represented by a box (1), the input objects are listed on the right of the box and the output objects are listed on the left side of the box. The join control structure (2) decomposes MakeStool into two nodes, MakeParts and Assemble-Parts. Use of join requires that the right node execute before the left node. The right node has the same inputs as its parent, but cannot produce any of the outputs of its parent, only intermediate values. The left node has as inputs only the intermediate values of the right node and must produce as outputs all of the outputs of the parent node.

Next, the include control structure (4) is used to further decompose MakeParts into MakeLegs and Make-Top. Use of the include allows its subnodes to execute in any order or

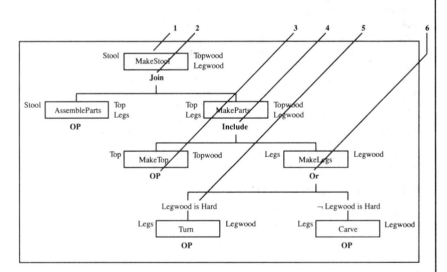

concurrently. The inputs and outputs of each node are disjoint, and the union of the inputs and outputs is exactly the inputs and outputs of the parent node.

Finally, the or control structure (6) is used to decompose MakeLegs into Carve and Turn. Use of the or control structure requires that exactly one of the subnodes be executed depending upon the evaluation of a condition (5). Both nodes have all inputs of the parent node and produce all outputs of the parent node.

We adapted this figure from J. Martin's *System Design from Provably Correct Constructs*, published by Prentice Hall, Englewood Cliffs, N.J., 1985.

place-holder. A syntactic structure entered through language-specific commands must be edited as a structural unit through language-specific commands. The programmer can clip, delete, and insert entire structural units. When a structural unit is clipped or deleted, it is replaced by its place-holder. Likewise, inserted structural units must replace corresponding syntactic parts; they will be reindented and rechecked for syntactic correctness.

The syntactic structure affects cursor movement as well. When the cursor is moved, it will skip over all but text and structural units, permitting itself to be positioned only where modifications are allowed.

A program can be run at any stage of development. Each structural unit is transformed into interpretable code as it is input and checked. Execution is thus immediate. Once begun, execution is suspended when the interpreter encounters either an error or an unexpanded place-holder. Upon detecting an error, the interpreter indicates the error and passes control back to the user, who then may correct the problem or restart. Similarly, when the interpreter encounters an unexpanded place-holder, it will stop, allow the user to insert the required code, and then continue.

The Cornell Program Synthesizer also has a visual tracing capability, a forerunner of program animation. (Program animation refers to the process of displaying the operation of a program through visual representations that dynamically change as the program executes. Selected variables or even entire data structures are displayed, usually graphically, with their contents changing dynamically as the program alters their values. For example, for a program that maintains a binary search tree of customers, the tree of customer names might be displayed graphically. Whenever a node is added or deleted, the display of the tree would be updated on the screen.)

In the Cornell Program Synthesizer, a cursor follows the flow of control through the program during execution. In addition, the synthesizer provides additional windows for monitoring variables and displaying results. The variable monitoring feature dynamically displays variable values using a least-recently modified approach to displaying large numbers of variables in limited screen space.

See the accompanying sidebar for an example of syntax-directed editing using the Cornell Program Synthesizer.

The Gandalf system[8] uses an editor generated by Medina-Mora and Notkin's Aloe editor-generator. Such an editor has a common kernel of editing commands that are language-independent and a set of constructive commands that are language-dependent. Editing commands are used for generic operations such as manipulating parse trees. Typical editing commands delete a construct or move the cursor. Constructive commands use abstract and concrete syntax descriptions to generate templates for each structural part. Cursor movement in building or editing a program parallels movement in the parse tree. In particular, the cursor is moved up, down, in, or out to the appropriate place-holder.

See the accompanying sidebar for an example of syntax-directed editing using the Aloe editor.

Specification-directed editing. The concept of structure-based editing can be extended further by imposing additional rules on the structure of programs and enforcing these rules through the editor. These rules can be used for purposes such as ensuring that only programs provably in accordance with a prescribed set of specifications may be entered. This section discusses two graphically oriented language environments that use such structure-based editors.

Higher Order Software's Use.It[9] takes a formal graphically oriented approach to program construction. Use.It generates code, in a variety of languages, directly from formal specifications, which are entered and edited using a structure-based editor that enforces decomposition based on provably correct design axioms that limit the interactions between modules.

Use.It applications are represented as binary trees known as control maps. Each node of the tree represents a function having a number of input and output objects. In a graphical representation, input objects are listed to the right of the node and output objects are listed to the left. Leaf nodes are typically irreducible low-level primitive functions. Non-leaf nodes are decomposed into subfunctions using the control structures join, include, and or, each of which is consistent with the six axioms on which the methodology relies.

In Use.It, the decomposition of functions into primitive subfunctions is formally specified and rigidly enforced by the graphical editing process. The preciseness of this decomposition ensures the internal consistency of the code generated by Use.It. In particular, Use.It ensures that any decomposition is logically consistent with the six basic axioms describing the structural interfaces between pieces of code. These axioms formally define a reliable system for structured coding.

See the accompanying sidebar for an example of graphical representation in Use.It.

A similar graphical editing technique is employed by PegaSys,[10] a system that uses graphical images to formally represent program design specifications. The emphasis in PegaSys is on the use of formal graphical specifications as documentation and as a means to verify that (user-written) program code meets specifications.

Graphical specifications are referred to as formal dependency diagrams. FDDs are manipulated graphically using editing techniques subject to system-imposed syntactic and semantic constraints. The constraints ensure that certain properties are preserved during the process of designing a program by successive refinement.

This concept of a rigorously controlled decomposition based on a mathematical logic is similar to Use.It, although the rules used and the properties preserved differ for each system.

Once the graphically edited design specifications are complete, they are manually mapped onto the implementation code, developed using PegaSys's structure-oriented Ada editor. Finally, the system formally verifies that the program is consistent with its design specifications.

The sidebar on PegaSys shows two levels in a formal dependency diagram hierarchy.

From visual editing to visually transformed programming. Each of the above visual editing systems is to some degree template-oriented. That is, some portion of a program is identified for replacement, a desired replacement template is selected, and then the replacement is performed as specified by the template, possibly subject to certain rigorously controlled rules. Clearly, this template-oriented approach can be carried to such an extreme that the entire program is constructed by visual editing techniques alone.

The earliest approaches to visual programming consisted of visual editors for traditional imperative textual languages. Often the control flow was given a pictorial or diagrammatic representation, such as a flowchart or Nassi-Schneiderman diagram. Pecan included such views to represent Pascal programs. Later approaches discarded the textual version completely, using the diagram version as

Formal dependency diagram hierarchy using PegaSys

The accompanying figure shows two levels in a formal dependency diagram, or FDD, representing a networking scheme designed using PegaSys. In Level 2 of the figure, the processes Source (1), Destination, H2H_Sndr, H2H_Rcvr, and Data_Link_Protocol are all denoted by ellipses. Dataflow relations are denoted D on the labeled arcs msg (2) and h_pkt, which denote the types of data being passed. The active types msg and h_pkt are also listed at the bottom of the screen (4).

Level 3 is a refinement of Level 2, developed by the user selecting the entity to be refined (5), then, using the appropriate menu commands (3), constructing the replacement entity (6). Note that the dataflow relations D for this entity have also been refined into read relations, denoted R, and write relations, denoted W.

To augment the FDD, PegaSys also includes a facility to associate text with any icon.

We based this figure on Moriconi and Hare's "PegaSys: A System for Graphical Explanation of Program Designs," included in the July 1985 *Proceedings of the ACM SIGPlan 85 Symposium on Language Issues in Programming Environments.*

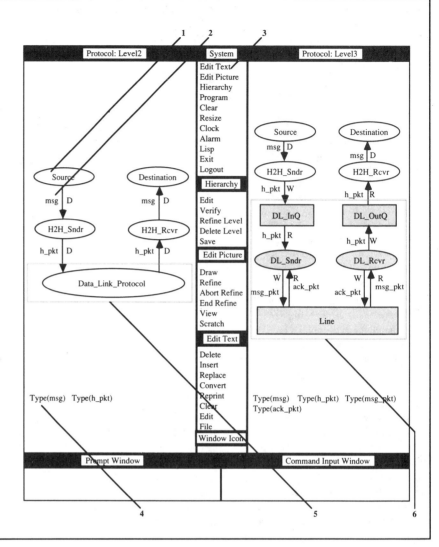

the only representation of the program and graphical editing of the diagram for construction and editing of the program.

A good example of such a system, Pict/D,[11] uses a conventional imperative language paradigm that replaces all keywords with iconic representations. The resulting language creates and manipulates flowcharts with the added ability to create new icons to represent subcharts. Thus, the language semantics are conventional, programming requires conventional concepts and thought processes, and the resulting programs are of equivalent complexity to the corresponding textual programs. Pict/D concentrates on using visual images to improve our ability to comprehend and edit programs.

Reiss's observation about editable views (see "Beyond the visualization of textual languages" above) applies to visual editing as well. Visual editing of an otherwise textual language can severely limit the power and usefulness of visual technol-

ogy. Clearly, enforcing structural decomposition rules still has value, as in Use.It and PegaSys. However, some of the early approaches to visual programming that used graphical technology merely to replace corresponding typing have drawn the criticism that they do little more than force a programmer to use menus and other graphical techniques for operations that can often be typed textually faster. Unfortunately, this criticism has unjustifiably been extended to visual programming in general.

Visual languages

Visual programming uses visual, rather than textual, technology. The development of visual programming languages represents a further step in the evolution toward more visual language environments. Visual languages are generally subdivided into two categories. The first

category, *visually transformed languages,* includes those visual languages that are inherently nonvisual but have superimposed visual representations. These are the visually edited traditional languages discussed in the prior section. They emphasize facilitating our ability to specify and comprehend programs using existing language paradigms.

The second category, *naturally visual languages,* attempts to develop new programming paradigms whose inherent natural expression is visual and for which there may be no strictly textual equivalent. In this section, we survey several divergent naturally visual languages and language environments.

By the very nature of the concept of visual programming, it is often difficult to separate a visual language from its language environment. It is this high degree of integration between the language and its environment that makes naturally visual language technology such an influential

A Celsius-to-Fahrenheit temperature converter constructed in ThingLab

Inserting several instances of previously defined classes into the window (Constant (2), Times (3), and Plus) and entering the constants' values of 1.8 and 32.0 creates the prototype of the TempConverter (4). Connecting two instances of NumberPrinters (1,5) to display the Celsius and Fahrenheit temperatures results in the PrintingConverter as shown in the figure. It works because the constraints placed on Plus and Times force adjustment of one of the Celsius or Fahrenheit temperatures. Whenever the Celsius temperature (1) is edited, the Fahrenheit temperature (5) will be adjusted. Also, because of the multi-way nature of the constraints, editing of the Fahrenheit temperature will result in adjustment of the Celsius temperature.

We based this figure on Borning's "The Programming Language Aspects of ThingLab," published in the October 1981 issue of *ACM Transactions on Programming Languages and Systems.*

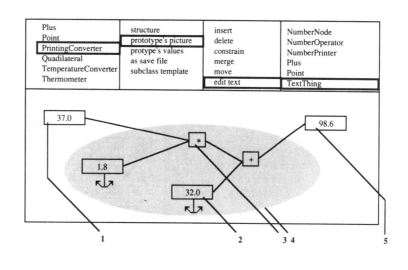

area in language environment research.

Dataflow paradigm. Visual languages based on the dataflow paradigm might be considered visually transformed languages. However, it can be argued that the dataflow paradigm is based on dataflow diagrams, in which a program is composed of functional modules, with connecting paths between inputs and outputs. In textual languages based upon this paradigm, dataflow diagrams are normally drawn first as part of the program design process and then translated into textual syntax. Visual languages based on this paradigm simply omit the translation to text.

Constraint-based paradigms. Many constraint-based programming languages are well suited to a visual representation. The advantage of a visual representation for this paradigm lies in the multi-way nature of constraints. A constraint may affect many variables, which in turn may affect many more; such complicated interrelationships are often easier to see in a diagrammatic representation than in a textual representation.

ThingLab[12] is an experiment in constraint-based programming. Given a set of constraints (rules) describing the invariant properties and relationships of all objects

in a particular problem space, then the set of solutions is the set of values that simultaneously satisfy all constraints. With sufficient constraints, the set of solutions can be made arbitrarily small, thus effecting a solution.

This approach in many respects resembles logic programming, where constraints are analogous to rules and relations and finding a set of values that satisfies all given constraints is analogous to resolving a query. ThingLab is a constraint-oriented simulation language environment that supports the construction of simulation environments using constraints and constraint-inheritance mechanisms. It incorporates inheritance (from the object-oriented paradigm of its underlying implementation language) and allows inheritance of the constraints themselves. This approach has the disadvantage that the inherited constraints may conflict when multiple inheritance is allowed. Still, many recent constraint languages incorporate various forms of inheritance.

Based on Smalltalk and heavily influenced by Sutherland's SketchPad, an early constraint-based graphical communication system that allows the user to directly draw and edit pictures on the screen using a light pen, ThingLab incorporates elements of graphical programming-by-dem-

onstration. Its influence shows in later visual language environments, most notably ThinkPad and Rehearsal World, both described below.

See the sidebar for an example of a Celsius-to-Fahrenheit temperature converter constructed in ThingLab.

Programming-by-demonstration. This is a naturally visual process for which there is no textual equivalent. Programming is done by graphically manipulating the data on the screen, demonstrating to the computer what the program should do. The advantage to this approach is obvious — it is easier for a programmer to perform a process than to describe textually how to perform the process.

ThinkPad is a declarative, graphical, programming-by-demonstration language and environment.[13] To perform programming-by-demonstration, the user graphically manipulates a diagrammatic representation of a data structure to demonstrate the operations on the data. An automatic mapping of the user's manipulations to Prolog code implements the program.

In ThinkPad, the user defines a data structure by drawing its graphical properties. In fact, a single data type can have multiple diagrammatic representations ("forms"), all specified graphically. The

Defining an operation in ThinkPad

A simple example will illustrate the use of ThinkPad. The problem is the insertion of nodes into a binary tree. The first step (not shown) is to define a binary tree, using ThinkPad's data editor. This is done by selecting a shape from the Shapes menu to represent a node (in this example, a rectangle) and resizing and repositioning it to suit. The fields within the node are similarly selected, resized, and repositioned.

The user began by naming the operation INSERT and specifying the type of all parameters and results (1). The system knows from the parameters that two graphical forms, an integer and a tree node, will be needed for the operation, which it automatically displays (3,4).

Next, the function is described by identifying a series of cases and for each case demonstrating the corresponding operation. Each case is distinguished by a unique condition (11). In this case the condition, int 0 < node 1 -> val (10), is entered by sequentially selecting int 0 (3), the less-than symbol (12), and val of node 1 (5).

The user now specifies the results (7) of the INSERT operation by manipulating the forms on the screen to demonstrate the operation for this case. First, the tree node is copied, by depressing the copy button (9) and then selecting

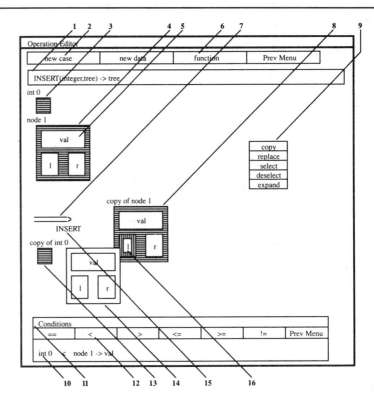

node 1 (4) to create a new node (8).

Next, the function button (6) is pressed and INSERT is selected (15) to indicate a function recursive call. Then, the arguments are indicated by copying int 0 (13) and expanding (9) l (16) of the copy of node 1 (8), giving the structure of the left node (14).

The user has now completely defined

operation INSERT for one case and can continue in the same way for each remaining case (2).

We adapted this figure from "ThinkPad: A Graphical System for Programming by Demonstration," by Rubin, Golin, and Reiss in the March 1985 issue of *IEEE Software*.

---

multiple forms capability allows ThinkPad to support multiple views of a single data type. The user can define operations on the data structure by manipulating the representation on the screen. In addition, the user may specify type constraints that the operations must preserve. Pointing and clicking selects the desired conditions, provided by the condition editor.

Internally, the data structure is represented by a set of Prolog assertions about the data. Relationships in the data structure are also mapped into Prolog assertions, and type constraints are implemented as predicates. All the assertions pertaining to one data structure are grouped into a separate set of Prolog clauses. Graphical specifications are stored in another library, with cross links to the set of Prolog assertions.

Because ThinkPad internally defines operations as transformations from one arrangement of the data structure to another, manipulating the data structures graphically is the equivalent of programming. However, while there is a direct

mapping from the graphical manipulation of the data structures to a program (in this case implemented in Prolog), there is no mapping from the program to the graphical representation of the data structures. Execution and debugging revert to the text-based Prolog code, rather than to the visual interface that exists during the creation of the code.

See the accompanying sidebar for an example of defining an operation in ThinkPad.

Rehearsal World,[14] a visual programming language environment devised for nonprogrammers, is one of the earliest environments to fully support visual programming. Rehearsal World uses a theater metaphor. The basic components, called performers, interact with each other on a stage (the screen) by sending cues. The screen is the stage upon which performers (objects) perform the actions the user has taught them for a particular production (program).

Rehearsal World includes several pre-

defined primitive performers, each of which understands a large predefined set of cues. Any existing performer can be copied; thus, each performer acts as a prototype from which other performers can be generated. The use of predefined performers and cues is, in essence, the integration of predefined code segments into the language environment itself.

The actual code generated by Rehearsal World is Smalltalk, but the programming process normally occurs strictly through graphical or visually oriented manipulation; hence, the user does not have to know Smalltalk to program in Rehearsal World. Likewise, code is normally debugged visually, by observing the performers' behavior during rehearsals, although additional lower-level debugging facilities are available.

For a closer look, see the sidebar "The Rehearsal World theater."

In PT, or Pictorial Transformations,[15] programming takes the form of first describing visual data representations, then

The Rehearsal World theater

The user starts by selecting from the menus of available stages (1) and troupes (2). Each troupe contains a set of performers represented as icons. For example, the BasicTroupe consists of a Text performer (3), a Counter performer (4), and a Number performer (5). For each performer, a category menu (7) is available as a pop-up display via a mouse button. This category menu contains certain commonly used cues (in lowercase) and categories of other cues (in uppercase). Most categories are common to all performers; a few (in bold) are unique to an individual performer. Selecting a category gets a cue sheet (6), which lists the cues available and related to the selected category.

The user can audition a performer by selecting a cue and observing its action. For example, a Text performer offers a variety of functions associated with a text editor. The Text performer performs these various operations when sent appropriate cues (by the user or another performer). For example, setText 'good-bye' will cause 'goodbye' to be displayed by the Text performer.

A performer learns by demonstration to send another performer a particular cue. The user initiates this by sending a performer a cue indicating that an ac-

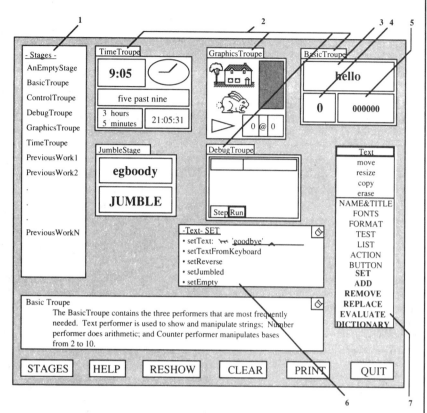

tion is to be defined and telling the system to "watch" the demonstration. A tiny "eye" icon, such as the one in window (6), opens to indicate the system is watching. The user then demonstrates the cues to be sent to other performers by simply selecting those cues from their cue sheets.

We based this figure on Finzer and Gould's "Programming by Rehearsal," in the June 1984 issue of *Byte*.

---

graphically manipulating them to develop program algorithms. Objects in PT, also called *dynamic icons*, consist of tuples of attribute-value pairs (much like association lists in Lisp) and an iconic display function that creates an object's display image as a function of its attribute-value pairs. For instance, its attributes may determine whether or not an object is shaded, where it is located, or how big it is. The value of an attribute may be another object, and thus objects can be hierarchically structured. A graphical object editor allows construction of new object types.

A procedural language, PT uses a film-making metaphor. Programming requires designing graphical objects and using such objects to demonstrate the workings of algorithms. A *picture* is a collection of graphical objects; a *film* (analogous to a procedure or program) is a sequence of manipulations performed on a picture. A programmer first selects a starting picture, then works through pictorial transformations on that picture. The process is re-

corded as one or more films.

By collecting object icons into a picture and filming a sequence of manipulations on objects of this picture, the programmer obtains a visual representation of a program's execution that results from defining the program itself. Thus, the way the programmer selects and modifies objects, plus the dynamic representation of an object based on its attribute values, aids the programmer in designing a program's animation simultaneously with its algorithms.

See the sidebar "Filming in PT."

Form-based paradigms. You can think of form-based programming as a generalization of spreadsheet programming. Even though it uses text, in a spreadsheet the relationships between the data and the expression of the computations are represented as part of the form itself, not described textually. Hence, the spreadsheet is naturally visual. It would be hard to imagine a purely textual version of a spreadsheet as natural to use, partly be-

cause the visual and interactive aspects of spreadsheets play an important role in allowing nonprocedural programming.

The visual representation of a cell matrix allows the omission of the concepts of variables, declarations, and output formatting. In addition, it contributes to the visual image of a large cell matrix wherein each value is normally computed just once per evaluation, with the order of evaluation derived, not specified. The visual interface with its various operational areas allows a modeless operation. Hence, being visual contributes significantly to the success of spreadsheet languages.

Forms[16] extends the spreadsheet paradigm over a larger problem domain. It relies on a visual representation generalized from the spreadsheet representation to minimize required language concepts. The basic "sheet" in Forms is a form, corresponding to a piece of paper on which you can place cell matrices, called *objects*. A cell expression can reference any cell (or cells) in any object within the containing form or within other forms, subject only to the restriction that the resulting derived evaluation must not be made to be circular.

Cell matrices are bounded or unbounded. A bounded cell matrix is one of fixed, known dimensions, whereas an unbounded cell matrix has at least one dimension that is unknown during the specification of the form. However, all objects must have their dimensions fixed prior to evaluation. Values for unbounded objects are specified by generic cell specifications stated in terms of the ijth cell, combined with specific cell specifications for specific fixed cells. A subform is similar in content to a form, but certain objects will inherit their values as parameters. These objects map onto other objects during evaluation. In addition, the value of one or more objects may be returned.

Forms is a declarative language, in that there is no concept of "state." For each evaluation of a form or subform, each cell is evaluated only once. Cyclic evaluation is not allowed. However, iteration and recursion can be accomplished via repeated invocations of a subform, each creating a new instance of the subform. Hence, the set of all forms and subforms used for a given computation provides a

Filming in PT (Pictorial Transformations)

The screen here shows the Pictorial Transformations programming environment during the process of programming a solution to the stable marriage problem. (This problem attempts to match men and women in marriage based on their stated preferences for each other.) In PT, an object is a tuple of attribute-value pairs together with an iconic display function that describes how to display an object based on its attribute-value pairs.

The collection of objects available for use in constructing new objects is displayed in the window at the upper left (1). In this example, several structured objects have already been built. The 6×5 matrix in the center window (2) is a construction of a column of objects, each a row of objects, each a text object. The attribute-value tuple associated with the selected subobject at (3) is displayed in the Attributes window (6).

In this example, an oval shape indicates a female, and a thin contour indicates unmarried. In PT, attributes like contour and shape not only convey information about the visual representation of the algorithm, but also can be tested and used directly in the program solution. Alternatively, these attributes could be named sex or married and might have values such as female and single. An icon has both a logical part and a physical part; hence, the logical values need not be the same as the physical shape.

The iconic display function (not shown) then uses the current set of attribute values to display the object. For instance, the object at (3) is shown to be an unmarried female. When the attribute values of an object change, the object is redisplayed. This has the effect of dynamically animating the execution of a program.

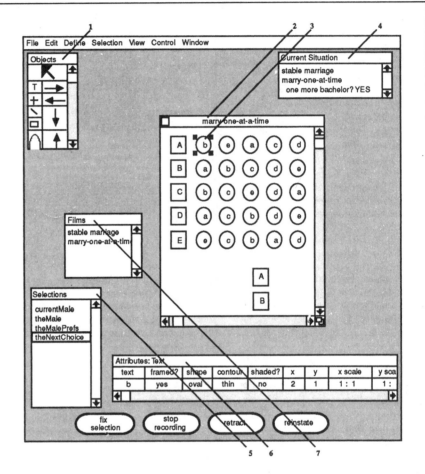

To develop a program, you draw a picture by selecting and placing all objects required in the solution. Series of manipulations to the objects are then recorded as films (analogous to procedures). Current films are listed in the Films window (7). Once initiated, filming proceeds by recording a sequence of selections and actions until terminated.

A selection is an expression that discriminates one or more objects or subobjects of the picture. When completed (fixed), selections can be named for subsequent reuse. The Selection window (5) lists current selections.

Actions transform the values of selected objects. When an action is conditional on the value of a selection, one or more new situations result. During filming, situations are recorded one at a time. Stacked situations are displayed in the Current situation window (4). Since actions may modify an object's attributes, potentially actions might require one or more objects to be redisplayed, thus altering the visual image of the picture. In this way, the picture is animated to follow the execution of the film.

We based this screen on Hsia and Ambler's "Programming through Pictorial Transformations," published in *Proceedings of the 1988 IEEE International Conference on Computer Languages.*

Construction of a subform in Forms

This subform calculates the binomial coefficients for an order *N*-1 equation. Starting from an initially blank form, two objects Coeffs and N are created by selecting icons from the Objects menu (7), dragging them into place, and resizing them as desired. The main cell matrix, named Coeffs, is an unbounded matrix. Both dimensions are unknown and are specified (5) to take the value of the single-cell matrix named N (6) at run-time. Thus, the evaluation of Coeffs will depend on the evaluation of N. This will force N to be evaluated prior to any evaluation of Coeffs.

In this example, the value of N is a parameter, supplied whenever BiCoefficient is instantiated. The computation of BiCoefficient is specified by four expressions (1, 2, 3, 4) that cover the four regions R1C1, R1C*j*, R*i*C1, and R*i*C*j* (for *i,j* > 1). Once the bounds of the matrix are fixed, each cell in each region will be computed using the expression for that region. Cell dependencies will ensure that the matrix will compute correctly starting from R1C1.

When BiCoefficient is to be invoked

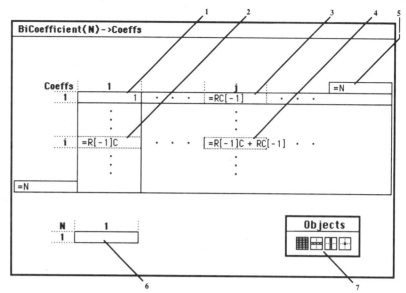

from some other form, a new instance of BiCoefficient is created when you select it from a list of subforms. For this new instance, the object N, which is expected to inherit its value and was previously blank, is now specified to be the value of a cell in the "calling" form from which we are to get the value of N, the matrix order. This has the effect of fixing the dimensions of BiCoefficient.

The result values are bound similarly by selecting the matrix within the "calling" form that is to receive the result values and specifying that their values are to be the contents of the BiCoefficient matrix.

We based this figure on Ambler's "Forms: Expanding the Visualness of Sheet Languages," published in *Proceedings of the 1987 IEEE Workshop on Visual Languages.*

---

complete history of the computation. Consequently, it provides a complete trace of the computation and a naturally visual means of debugging.

The sidebar on Forms shows the construction of a subform.

Trend toward naturally visual. It is too early to say which of these visual language approaches will succeed, but clearly they are moving away from the idea of applying visual transformations to textual approaches and toward the idea of naturally visual approaches. This trend shows general agreement with the observation discussed earlier that visual techniques applied to otherwise textual approaches are limited.

I n the nearly twenty years since the development of Interlisp, the virtues of a visual, highly integrated language environment have become well accepted. In this article we have looked specifically at the influence of visual technology on three elements of language environments: user interfaces, editors, and programming lan-

guages. For each element, we have seen the transition from a strictly textual representation, through relatively straightforward visual representations of otherwise textual technology, and toward new investigations into more naturally visual uses of visual technology. We assert that this trend is also true of other elements associated with language environments, such as debuggers, interpreters, and on-line documentation tools. Perhaps most significantly, visual technology seems to be moving to a convergence between the language itself and the language environment, a convergence that goes beyond the visualization of existing textual approaches, a convergence that is naturally visual.□

Acknowledgments

The authors would like to acknowledge the important contributions made by Phillip G. Bradford, Yen-Teh Hsia, Mike Robinson, and James A. Shelton in the research that led to this article.

References

1. W. Teitelman and L. Masinter, "The Interlisp Programming Environment," *Computer*, Vol. 14, No. 4, Apr. 1981, pp. 25-33.

2. A. Goldberg, *Smalltalk-80: The Interactive Programming Environment*, Addison-Wesley, Reading, Mass., 1984.

3. D.C. Swinehart et al., "A Structural View of the Cedar Programming Environment," *ACM Trans. Programming Languages and Systems*, Vol. 8, No. 4, Oct. 1986, pp. 419-490.

4. S.P. Reiss, "Pecan: Program Development Systems that Support Multiple Views," *IEEE Trans. Software Engineering*, Vol. SE-11, No. 3, Mar. 1985, pp. 276-285.

5. A. Wasserman and P. Pircher, "A Graphical, Extensible Integrated Environment for Software Development," *SIGPlan Notices*, Vol. 22, No. 1, Jan. 1987, pp. 131-142.

6. S.P. Reiss, "Garden Tools: Support for Graphical Programming," in *Advanced Programming Environments*, Lecture Notes in Computer Science #244, R. Conradi, T. Didriksen, and D. Wanvik, eds., Springer-Verlag, N.Y., 1986, pp. 59-72.

7. T. Teitelbaum and T. Reps, "The Cornell Program Synthesizer: A Syntax-Directed Programming Environment," *Comm. ACM*, Vol. 24, No. 9, Sept. 1981, pp. 563-573.

8. A.N. Habermann and D. Notkin, "Gandalf: Software Development Environment," *IEEE Trans. Software Engineering*, Vol. SE-12, No. 12, Dec. 1986, pp. 1,117-1,127.

9. M. Hamilton and S. Zeldin, "Higher Order Software — Methodology for Defining Software," *IEEE Trans. Software Engineering*, Vol. SE-2, No. 1, Mar. 1976, pp. 9-32.

10. M. Moriconi and D.F. Hare, "The PegaSys System: Pictures as Formal Documentation of Large Programs," *ACM Trans. Programming Languages and Systems*, Vol. 8, No. 4, Oct. 1986, pp. 524-546.

11. E.P. Glinert and S.L. Tanimoto, "Pict: An Interactive Graphical Programming Environment," *Computer*, Vol. 17, No. 11, Nov. 1984, pp. 7-25.

12. A. Borning, "Defining Constraints Graphically," *Proc. CHI 86*, Conf. Human Factors in Computing Systems, Apr. 1986, ACM, pp. 137-143.

13. R.V. Rubin, E.J. Golin, and S.P. Reiss, "ThinkPad: A Graphical System for Programming by Demonstration," *IEEE Software*, Vol. 2, No. 2, Mar. 1985, pp. 73-79.

14. W. Finzer and L. Gould, "Programming by Rehearsal," *Byte*, Vol. 9, No. 6, June 1984, pp. 187-210.

15. Y.-T. Hsia and A. Ambler, "Programming through Pictorial Transformations," *Proc. 1988 IEEE Int'l Conf. Computer Languages*, Oct. 1988, CS Press, Los Alamitos, Calif., Order No. FJ874, pp. 10-16.

16. A.L. Ambler, "Forms: Expanding the Visualness of Sheet Languages," *Proc. 1987 Workshop on Visual Languages*, Tryck-Center, Linkoping, Sweden, Aug. 1987, pp. 105-117.

Supplemental readings on visual programming

Due to space limitations, we could not discuss many important visual languages. The following reading list provides sources for additional information.

General surveys

Ambler, A.L., et al., "Integrated Programming Environments: A Survey of Milestones," Univ. of Kansas Computer Science Tech. Report 88-6, Lawrence, Kan., 1988.

Raeder, G., "A Survey of Current Graphical Programming Techniques," *Computer*, Vol. 18, No. 8, Aug. 1985, pp. 11-25.

Shu, N.C., *Visual Programming*, Van Nostrand Reinhold Co., N.Y., 1988.

Visual environments and languages

Halbert, D.C., *Programming by Example*, PhD thesis, Computer Science Div., Dept. of EE and CS, University of California at Berkeley, 1984.

Hirakawa, M., et al., "A Framework for Construction of Icon Systems," *Proc. 1988 IEEE Workshop on Visual Languages*, Oct. 1988, CS Press, Los Alamitos, Calif., Order No. FX876, pp. 70-77.

Kimura, T.D., J.W. Choi, and J.M. Mack, "Show and Tell: A Visual Programming Language," to appear in *Visual Computing Environments*, E.P. Glinert, ed., CS Press, Washington, D.C., 1989.

Kozen, D., et al., "Alex — An Alexical Programming Language," *Proc. 1987 Workshop on Visual Languages*, Tryck-Center, Linkoping, Sweden, Aug. 1987, pp. 315-329.

Ludolph, F., et al., "The Fabrick Programming Environment," *Proc. 1988 IEEE Workshop on Visual Languages*, CS Press, Los Alamitos, Calif., Order No. FX876, Oct. 1988, pp. 222-230.

Moshell, J., et al., "A Spreadsheet-Based Visual Language for Freehand Sketching of Complex Motions," *Proc. 1987 Workshop on Visual Languages*, Tryck-Center, Linkoping, Sweden, Aug. 1987, pp. 94-104.

Pong, M.C., and N. Ng, "PIGS — A System for Programming with Interactive Graphical Support," *Software — Practice and Experience*, Vol. 13, No. 9, Sept. 1983, pp. 847-855.

Smith, D.C., "Pygmalion: A Computer Program to Model and Stimulate Creative Thought," PhD dissertation, Stanford University, Stanford, Calif., 1975.

Smith, D.N., "Visual Programming in the Interface Construction Set," *Proc. 1988 IEEE Workshop on Visual Languages*, CS Press, Los Alamitos, Calif., Order No. FX876, Oct. 1988, pp. 109-120.

Smith, R.B., "The Alternate Reality Kit: An Environment for Creating Interactive Simulations," *Proc. 1986 IEEE Workshop on Visual Languages*, CS Press, Los Alamitos, Calif., Order No. FX722, June 1986, pp. 99-106.

Zloof, M.M., "QBE/OBE: A Language for Office and Business Automation," *Computer*, Vol. 14, No. 5, May 1981, pp. 13-22.

Program animation

Brown, G., et al., "Program Visualization: Graphical Support for Software Development," *Computer*, Vol. 18, No. 8, Aug. 1985, pp. 27-35.

Brown, M., *Algorithm Animation*, published as an ACM distinguished dissertation, MIT Press, Cambridge, Mass., 1987.

Hyrskykari, A., and K. Raiha, "Animation of Algorithms without Programming," *Proc. 1987 Workshop on Visual Languages*, Tryck-Center, Linkoping, Sweden, Aug. 1987, pp. 40-54.

Allen L. Ambler is an associate professor in the Department of Computer Science at the University of Kansas. His research interests include visual programming languages, programming language design, software development environments, and functionally distributed software architectures. He has been a senior architect for Amdahl Corp. and vice president of software development for Dialogic Systems Corp.

Ambler is a reviewer for *IEEE Software* and has served as Executive Committee member-at-large of ACM SIGPlan and as a reviewer for *ACM Computing Reviews*. He is a member of IEEE and ACM.

Ambler received his undergraduate degree in mathematics from the University of Kansas and his MA and PhD in computer science from the University of Wisconsin at Madison.

Margaret M. Burnett is a PhD candidate in computer science at the University of Kansas. Her research interests include visual programming, software development environments, and computer-human interaction. She has been a lecturer for the University of Kansas, a consultant and systems analyst, and a systems engineer for Procter and Gamble.

Burnett holds an MS in computer science from the University of Kansas and a BA in mathematics from Miami University of Ohio.

Readers may contact the authors at 110 Strong Hall, University of Kansas, Lawrence, KS 66045.

Visual Programming, Programming by Example, and Program Visualization: A Taxonomy.

Brad A. Myers

Dynamic Graphics Project
Computer Systems Research Institute
University of Toronto
Toronto, Ontario, M5S 1A4
Canada

ABSTRACT

There has been a great interest recently in systems that use graphics to aid in the programming, debugging, and understanding of computer programs. The terms "Visual Programming" and "Program Visualization" have been applied to these systems. Also, there has been a renewed interest in using examples to help alleviate the complexity of programming. This technique is called "Programming by Example." This paper attempts to provide more meaning to these terms by giving precise definitions, and then uses these definitions to classify existing systems into a taxonomy. A number of common unsolved problems with most of these systems are also listed.

CR Categories and Subject Descriptors: D.1.2 [**Software Engineering**]: Automatic Programming; D.2.2 [**Software Engineering**]: Tools and Techniques-*Flowcharts*; D.2.5 [**Software Engineering**]: Testing and Debugging-*Debugging Aids*; D.3.2 [**Programming Languages**]: Language Classifications; I.2.2 [**Artificial Intelligence**]: Automatic Programming-*Program Synthesis*. I.3.6 [**Computer Graphics**]: Methodologies and Techniques-*Languages*.

Additional Key Words and Phrases: Visual Programming, Program Visualization, Programming by Example, Inferencing.

General Terms: Documentation, Languages.

1. Introduction

As the distribution of personal computers and the more powerful personal workstations grows, the majority of computer users now do not know how to program. They buy computers with packaged software and are not able to modify the software even to make small changes. In order to allow the end user to reconfigure and modify the system, the software may provide various options, but these often make the system more complex and still may not address the users' problems. "Easy-to-use" software, such as the "Direct Manipulation" systems [Shneiderman 83] actually make the user-programmer gap *worse* since more people will be able to use the software (since it is easy to use), but the internal program code is now much more complicated (due to the extra code to handle the user interface). Therefore, systems are moving in the direction of providing end user programming. It is well-known that conventional programming languages are difficult to learn and use [Gould 84], requiring skills that many people do not have. In an attempt to make the programming task easier, recent research has been directed towards using graphics. This has been called "Visual Programming" or "Graphical Programming". Some Visual Programming systems have successfully demonstrated that non-programmers can create fairly complex programs with little training [Halbert 84].

Another motivation for using graphics is that it tends to be a higher-level description of the desired actions (often de-emphasizing issues of syntax and providing a higher level of abstraction) and may therefore make the programming task easier even for professional programmers. This may be especially true during debugging, where graphics can be used to present much more information about the program state (such as current variables and data structures) than is possible with purely textual displays. This is one of the goals of Program Visualization. Other Program Visualization systems use graphics to help teach computer programming.

Programming-by-Example is another technology that has been investigated to make programming easier, especially for non-programmers. It involves presenting to the computer examples of the data that the program is supposed to process and using these examples during the development of the program. Many, although not all, Programming-by-Example systems have also used Visual Programming, so these two technologies are often linked.

Recently, there has been a large number of articles about systems that incorporate some or all of these features [Grafton 85][Raeder 85]. Unfortunately, the terms have been used imprecisely[1], and there has not been a comprehensive taxonomy that classifies these systems. This paper attempts to fill this gap in the literature. First, the important terms are defined in a precise manner, and then these definitions are used to differentiate the various systems. Finally, a number of common unsolved problems with these systems are delineated.

There are many systems that could be included in this paper in the various categories, but no attempt has been made to be comprehensive. It is hoped that the selection of systems listed will help the reader understand the intent of the classification system.

2. Definitions.

Programming   What is meant by computer "programming" is probably well understood, but it is important to have a definition that can be used to eliminate some limited systems. In this paper, "program" is defined as "a set of statements that can be submitted as a unit to some computer system and used to direct the behavior of that system" [Oxford 83]. While the ability to compute "everything" is not required, the system must include the ability to handle conditionals and iteration, at least implicitly.

Interactive vs. Batch   Any programming language system may either be "interactive" or "batch." A batch system has a large processing delay before statements can be run while they are compiled, whereas an interactive system allows statements to be executed when they are entered. This characterization is actually more of a continuum than a dichotomy since even interactive languages like LISP typically require groups of statements (such as an entire procedure) to be specified before they are executed.

Visual Programming   "Visual Programming" (VP) refers to any system that allows the user to *specify* a program in a two (or more) dimensional fashion. Conventional textual languages are not considered two dimensional since the compiler or interpreter processes it as a long, one-dimensional stream. Visual Programming includes conventional flow charts and graphical programming languages. It does not include systems that use conventional (linear) programming languages to define pictures. This eliminates most graphics editors, like Sketchpad [Sutherland 63].

Program Visualization   "Program Visualization" (PV) is an entirely different concept from Visual Programming. In Visual Programming, the graphics is the program itself, but in Program Visualization, the program is specified in the conventional, textual manner, and the graphics is used to illustrate some aspect of the program or its run-time execution. Unfortunately, in the past, many Program Visualization system have been incorrectly labeled "Visual Programming" (as in [Grafton 85]). Program Visualization systems can be divided along two axes: whether they illustrate the *code* or the *data* of the program, and whether they are *dynamic* or *static*. "Dynamic" refers to systems that can show an animation of the program running, whereas "static" systems are limited to snapshots of the program at certain points. If a program created using Visual Programming is to be displayed or debugged, clearly this should be done in a graphical manner, but this would not be considered Program Visualization. Although these two terms are similar and confusing, they have been

widely used in the literature, so it was felt appropriate to continue to use the common terms.

Programming by Example   The term "Programming by Example" (PBE) has been used to describe a large variety of systems. Some early systems attempted to create an entire program from a set of input-output pairs. Other systems require the user to "work through" an algorithm on a number of examples and then the system tries to *infer* the general program structure. This is often called "automatic programming" and has generally been an area of Artificial Intelligence research.

Recently, there have been a number of systems that require the user to specify everything about the program (there is no inference involved), but the user can work out the program on a specific example. The system executes the user's commands normally, but remembers them for later re-use. Bill Buxton coined the phrase "Programming *with* Examples" to more accurately describe these systems. Halbert [84] characterizes Programming with Examples as "Do What I Did" whereas inferential Programming by Example might be "Do What I Mean". The term "Programming by Example" will be used to include both inferencing systems and Programming With Example systems.

Of course, whenever code is executed in any system, test data must be entered to run it on. The distinction between normal testing and "Programming *with* Examples" is that in the latter the system requires or encourages the specification of the examples *before* programming begins, and then applies the program as it develops to the examples. This essentially requires all Programming-*with*-Example systems (but not Programming-by-Example systems with inferencing) to be interactive.

3. Advantages of Using Graphics and Examples.

Visual Programming, Program Visualization, and Programming by Example are very appealing ideas for a number of reasons. The human visual system and human visual information processing is clearly optimized for multi-dimensional data. Computer programs, however, are presented in a one-dimensional textual form, not utilizing the full power of the brain. Two-dimensional displays for programs, such as flowcharts and even the indenting of block structured programs, have long been known as helpful aids in program understanding [Smith 77]. Recently, a number of Program Visualization systems [Myers 80][Baecker 81][Brown 84] have demonstrated that 2-D pictorial displays for data structures, such as those drawn by hand on blackboard, are very helpful. It seems clear that a more visual style of programming could be easier to understand and generate for humans. Smith [77] discusses at length these and other psychological motivations for using more visual displays for programs and data.

It is also well known that people are much better at dealing with specific examples than with abstract ideas. A large amount of teaching is achieved by presenting important examples and having the students do specific problems. This helps them understand the general principles. Programming by Example attempts to extend these ideas to programming. In its most ideal case, the programmer acts like the teacher and just gives examples to the computer and the computer, like an intelligent pupil, intuits the abstraction that covers all the examples.

---

[1] For example, Zloof's Query-By-Example system (see section 4.2) is not a Programming by Example system.

Programming-*with*-example systems require programmers to specify the abstraction, but allow them to work out the program on examples as an aid to getting the program correct. This is motivated by the observation that people make fewer errors when working out a problem on an example (or when directly manipulating data as when editing text or moving icons on the Macintosh [Williams 84]) as compared to performing the same operation in the abstract, as in conventional programming. The programmer does not need to try to keep in mind the large and complex state of the system at each point of the computation if it is displayed for him on the screen. This has been called "programming in debugging mode" [Smith 77]. In addition, these PBE systems may allow the user to specify a program using the actual user interface of the system, which is presumably familiar [Attardi 82].

4. Taxonomy of Programming Systems.

This paper presents two taxonomies. This section discusses one for systems that support programming. Section 5 discusses a one for systems that use graphics *after* the programming process is finished (Program Visualization systems).

A meaningful taxonomy can be created by classifying programming systems into eight categories using the orthogonal criteria of

- Visual Programming or not,
- Programming by Example or not, and
- Interactive or batch.

This taxonomy is original with this paper. Of course, a single system may have features that fit into various categories and some systems may be hard to classify, so this paper attempts to characterize the systems by their most prominent features. Figure 1 shows the division with some sample systems which are discussed in the following sections.

4.1. Not VP, Not PBE, Batch and Interactive

These are the conventional textual, linear programming languages that are familiar to all programmers, such as Pascal, Fortran, and Ada for batch and LISP and APL for interactive.

4.2. VP, Not PBE, Batch

One of the earliest "visual" representations for programs was the flowchart. Grail [Ellis 69] could compile programs directly from computerized flowcharts, but the contents of boxes were ordinary machine language statements. GAL (see Figure 2) is similar except that it uses Nassi-Shneiderman flowcharts [Nassi 73] and is compiled into Pascal [Albizuri-Romero 84]. Another early effort was the AMBIT/G [Christensen 68] and AMBIT/L [Christensen 71] graphical languages. They supported symbolic manipulation programming using pictures. Both the programs and data were represented diagrammatically as directed graphs, and the programming operated by pattern matching. Fairly complicated algorithms, such as garbage collection, could be described graphically as local transformations on graphs[2].

---

[2] It is interesting to note that AMBIT/G, even though it was developed in 1969, used many of the "modern" user interface techniques, including iconic representations, gesture recognition, dynamic menus on the screen, selection from menus, selection of icons by pointing, moded and mode-free styles of interaction, etc. [Rovner 69].

Not Programming by Example

	Batch	Interactive
Not VP	4.1 All Conventional Languages: Pascal, Fortran, etc.	4.1 LISP, APL, etc.
VP	4.2 Grail [Ellis 69] AMBIT/G/L [Christensen 68,71] Query by Example [Zloof 77, 81] FORMAL [Shu 85] GAL [Albizuri-Romero 84]	4.3 Graphical Program Editor [Sutherland 66] PIGS [Pong 83] Pict [Glinert 84] PROGRAPH [Pietrzykowski 83,84] State Transition UIMS [Jacob 85]

Programming by Example

	Batch	Interactive
Not VP	4.4 I/O pairs* [Shaw 75]	4.5 Tinker [Lieberman 82]
VP	4.6 [Bauer 78] traces*	4.7 AutoProgrammer* [Biermann 76b] Pygmalion [Smith 77] Graphical Thinglab [Borning 86] SmallStar [Halbert 81,84] Rehearsal World [Gould 84]

Figure 1.
Classification of programming systems by whether they are visual or not, whether they have Programming by Example or not, and whether they are interactive or batch. The small numbers refer to the section in which the group is discussed. Starred systems (*) have inferencing, and non-starred PBE systems use Programming With Example.

Figure 2.
A Nassi-Shneiderman flowchart program from GAL [Albizuri-Romero 84].

You might think that a system called "Query by Example" would be a "Programming by Example" system, but in fact, according to this classification, it is not. Query by Example (QBE) [Zloof 77] allows users to specify queries on a relational database using two-dimensional tables (or forms), so it is classified as a Visual Programming system. The "examples" in QBE are what Zloof called variables. They are called "examples" because the user is supposed to give them names that refer to what the system might fill into that field, but they have no more meaning than variable names in most conventional languages. The ideas in QBE have been extended to mail and other non-database areas of office automation in Office by Example (OBE) [Zloof 81]. A related forms-based database language is FORMAL [Shu 85] which explicitly represents hierarchical structures.

4.3. *VP, Not PBE, Interactive*

Probably the first Visual Programming system was William Sutherland's [66] which represented programs somewhat like hardware logic diagrams. Some systems for programming with flowcharts have been interactive. PIGS [Pong 83] uses Nassi-Shneiderman flowcharts, and Pict [Glinert 84] uses conventional flowcharts. Pict is differentiated by its use of color pictures (icons) rather than text inside of the flowchart boxes (see Figure 3).

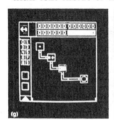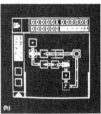

Figure 3.
Three frames from Pict [Glinert 84] showing an implementation of the factorial procedure. The original pictures were in color.

PROGRAPH [Pietrzykowski 83] is another interactive VP system without PBE, but it is distinguished by supporting a functional data flow language. PROGRAPH attempts to overcome some of the problems of this type of language by using a graphical representation that is structured, as shown in Figure 4. Pietrzykowski [84] claims that this alleviates the problem of functional languages where "the conventional representation in the form of a linear script makes it almost unreadable". PROGRAPH is one of the very few truly concurrent Visual Programming systems.

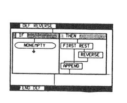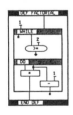

Figure 4.
Two procedures from PROGRAPH [Pietrzykowski 84].

A number of systems for automatically generating user interfaces for programs (User Interface Management Systems) allow the designer to specify the user interface in a graphical manner. An example of this is the state transition diagram editor by Jacob [85] (see Figure 5). Most other UIMSs require that designers specify the programs using some textual representation, so they do not qualify as Visual Programming.

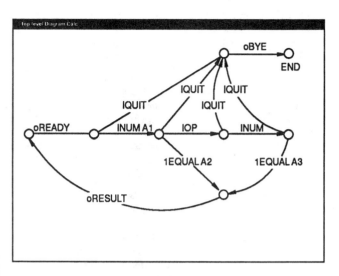

Figure 5.
State diagram description of a simple desk calculator [Jacob 85].

4.4. *Not VP, PBE, Batch*

Some systems have attempted to infer the entire program from one or more examples of what output is produced for a particular input. One program [Shaw 75] can infer simple recursive LISP programs from a single I/O pair, such as (A B C D) = = > (D D C C B B A A). This system is limited to simple list processing programs, and it is clear that systems such as this one cannot generate all programs, or are even likely to generate the correct program [Biermann 76a].

4.5. *Not VP, PBE, Interactive*

Tinker [Lieberman 82] is a "pictorial" system that is not VP. The user chooses a concrete example, and the system executes LISP statements on this example as the code is typed in. Although Tinker uses windows, menus, and other graphics in its user interface, it is not a VP system since the user presents all of the code to the system in the conventional linear textual manner.

4.6. *VP, PBE, Batch*

Inferencing systems that attempt to cover a wider class of programs than those that can be generated from I/O pairs have required the user to choose data structures and algorithms and then run through the computation on a number of examples. The systems attempt to infer where loops and conditionals should go to produce the shortest and most general program that will work for all of the examples. One such system is by Bauer [78], which also decides which values in the program should be constants and which should be variables. It is visual since the user can specify the program execution using graphical traces.

4.7. *VP, PBE, Interactive*

Some of the most interesting systems fall into this final category. Except for AutoProgrammer [Biermann 76b], which is similar to Bauer's system (section 4.6), few attempt to do inferencing.

Pygmalion [Smith 77] was one of the seminal VP and PBE systems. It provides an iconic and "analogical" method for programming: concrete display images for data and programs, called icons, are manipulated to create programs. The emphasis is on "doing" pictorially, rather than "telling". Thinglab [Borning 79 and 81] was designed to allow the user to describe and run complex simulations easily. A VP interface to Thinglab is described in [Borning 86]. Here the user can define new constraints among objects by specifying them graphically (see Figure 6). Also, if a class of objects can be created by combining already existing objects, then it can be programmed by example visually in Thinglab.

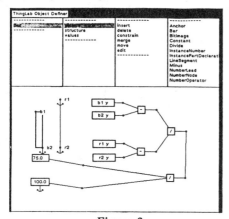

Figure 6.
Creating a constraint graphically to keep a bar graph the same size as the value of a register in Thinglab [Borning 86].

SmallStar [Halbert 81 and 84] uses PBE to allow the end user to program a prototype version of the Star [Smith 82] office workstation. When programming, the user simply goes into program mode, performs the operations that are to be remembered, and then leaves program mode. The operations are executed in the actual user interface of the system, which the user already knows. Since the system does not use inferencing, the user must differentiate constants from variables and explicitly add control structures (loops and conditionals). Halbert reports that Star users were able to create procedures for performing their office tasks with his system.

The goal of Rehearsal World is to allow teachers who do not know how to program to create computerized lessons easily [Gould 84]. Interactive graphics are heavily used to provide a "collaborative, evolutionary and exploratory" environment where programming is "quick, easy and fun." The metaphor presented to the user is a *theater*, where the screen is the *stage* and there are predefined *performers* that the user can *direct* to create a *play* (see Figure 7). The teacher developing the program sees at every point exactly what the student-user of the play will see. In addition, the teacher can have additional performers in the *wings* (so the student will not see them) that provide auxiliary functions such as flow control. Everything is made visible to the teachers, however, which allows their thinking to be concrete, rather than abstract as in conventional programming environments. When a new performer is needed, often its code can be created by example, but when this is not possible, some Smalltalk code must be written. The static representation for all performers is Smalltalk code, which can be edited by those who know how.

Figure 7.
A screen from Rehearsal World [Gould 84] showing the basic menu (on the left) and the standard set of "performers".

5. Taxonomy of Program Visualization Systems.

The systems discussed in this section are not *programming* systems since code is created in the conventional manner. Graphics in these are used to *illustrate* some aspect of the program after it is written. Figure 8 shows some Program Visualization systems classified by whether they attempt to illustrate the code or the data of a program (some provide both), and whether the displays are static or dynamic.

	Static	Dynamic
Code	5.1 Flowcharts [Haibt 59] SEE Visual Compiler [Baecker 86] PegaSys [Moriconi 85]	5.2 BALSA [Brown 84] PV Prototype [Brown 85]
Data	5.3 TX2 Display Files [Baecker 68] Incense [Myers 80,83]	5.4 Two Systems [Baecker 75] Sorting out Sorting [Baecker 81] BALSA [Brown 84] Animation Kit [London 85] PV Prototype [Brown 85]

Figure 8.
Classification of Program Visualization Systems by whether they illustrate code or data, and whether they are dynamic or static. The small numbers refer to the section in which the group is discussed.

5.1. *Static code visualization*

The earliest example of Visualization is undoubtably the flowchart. As early as 1959, there were programs that automatically created graphical flowcharts from Fortran or assembly language programs [Haibt 59]. A modern static system [Baecker 86] has attempted to add multiple fonts, nice formatting, and other graphics to make code easier to read (see Figure 9).

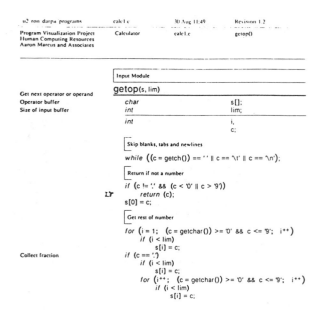

```
u2 ron darpa programs        calc1.c           30 Aug 11:49      Revision 1.2

Program Visualization Project  Calculator      calc1.c          getop()
Human Computing Resources
Aaron Marcus and Associates
```

	Input Module
Get next operator or operand	getop(s, lim)
Operator buffer	char s[];
Size of input buffer	int lim;
	int i,
	c;

```
        Skip blanks, tabs and newlines
        while ((c = getch()) == ' ' || c == '\t' || c == '\n');

        Return if not a number
        if (c != '.' && (c < '0' || c > '9'))
   LT       return (c);
        s[0] = c;

        Get rest of number
        for (i = 1;  (c = getchar()) >= '0' && c <= '9';  i++)
            if (i < lim)
                s[i] = c;
        if (c == '.')
            if (i < lim)
                s[i] = c;
        for (i++;  (c = getchar()) >= '0' && c <= '9';  i++)
            if (i < lim)
                s[i] = c;
```

Collect fraction

Figure 9.
A sample of formatted program code from [Baecker 86].

In PegaSys [Moriconi 85], pictures are formal documentation of programs and are drawn by the user and checked by the system to ensure that they are syntactically meaningful and, to some extent, whether they agree with the program. The program itself, however, must still be entered in a conventional language (Ada).

5.2. *Dynamic code visualization*

Most systems in this class do not animate the code itself, but rather dynamically show what parts of the code are being executed as the program is run using some sort of highlighting. Examples are [Brown 84] and [Brown 85], which are discussed in section 5.4.

5.3. *Static data visualization*

A very early system for the TX-2 computer could produce static pictures of the display file to aid in debugging [Baecker 68]. Incense [Myers 80 and 83] automatically generates static pictorial displays for data structures. The pictures include curved lines with arrowheads for pointers and stacked boxes for arrays and records, as well as user-defined displays (see Figure 10). The goal was to making debugging easier by presenting data structures to programmers in the way that they would draw them by hand on paper.

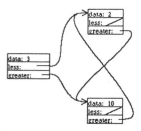

Figure 10.
A display produced automatically by Incense of 3 records containing pointers [Myers 80].

5.4. *Dynamic data visualization*

The first few systems in this class actually fall between dynamic and static. They were computer systems designed to create movies of data structures and algorithms (e.g. sorting) for teaching computer science [Baecker 75][Baecker 81]. The systems did not produce the animations in real time, however, so the movies were made frame by frame. The Balsa system from Brown University [Brown 84] was also designed to teach students about programming, but it produces the illustrations in real time on a personal workstation.

The "PV Prototype" [Brown 85] was designed to aid in debugging and program understanding, and it supports dynamic displays of data and easier construction of user-defined displays. Another system with similar goals, written in Smalltalk, features smooth transitions from one state to another [London 85].

6. Areas for Future Research.

Although these systems are attractive for a number of reasons, and some have been successfully used, they share a number of unsolved problems which are fruitful areas for future research.

6.1. *Visual Programming*

- Difficulty with large programs or large data: Almost all visual representations are physically larger than the text they replace, so there is often a problem that too little will fit on the screen. This problem is alleviated to some extent by scrolling and abstraction.

- Lack of functionality: Many VP systems work only in a limited domain.

- Inefficiency: Most VP systems run programs very slowly.

- Unstructured programs: Many VP systems promote unstructured programming practices (like GOTO). Many do not provide abstraction mechanisms (procedures, local variables, etc.) which are necessary for programs of a reasonable size.

- Static representations of programs that are hard to understand: For flowcharts, AMBIT and similar systems, the program begins to look like a maze of wires. For Rehearsal World and similar systems, the static representation is simply normal linear code.

- No place for comments: An interesting point is that virtually no VP system provides a place for comments.

6.2. *Inferential Programming by Example.*

The major problem with these systems is that the user provides no guidance about the structure of the program so each new example can radically change the program. The programmer often knows, for example, which values are variables and which are constants or where conditionals should go, but there is no way to directly convey this information to these systems. Choosing the correct examples requires great skill, and it is often difficult in these systems to modify programs once they exist.

The generated procedures are often "convoluted and unstructured" [Bauer 78, p. 131] and the user is never sure if the generated procedure is correct unless he reads the code and checks it explicitly. If this is required, however, most of the advantage of PBE is lost since the user must then know how to program in order to check it. In fact, the central idea of this "inductive generalization" programming is directly opposed to the modern software-engineering idea that testing with a few examples can never guarantee that a program is correct. Clearly, generating a program from a few examples has the same problem.

6.3. Programming with Example.

Programming *with* Example systems that do not attempt to do inferencing have been more successful. Most of these are VP systems, so they share the problems listed in section 6.1. Some additional problems with these systems (from [Halbert 84]) include:

- Lack of static representation: These systems often have *no* user-understandable static representation for programs.
- Problem with editing programs: The lack of a static representation makes editing difficult. One alternative is to run a program from the beginning, but this may take a long time. Specifying a change for the middle of a program by example may not be possible without running it from the beginning since the state of the world may not be set up correctly to allow the user to specify the change. Saving periodic snapshots of the system state may alleviate this problem, but there may be a great deal of information to save. In addition, a change may invalidate steps of the program that come afterwards.
- Problem with data description: It is often difficult to specify what the procedures should operate on: constants, user-specified data, or data found somewhere in the system qualified by its type, location, name, etc. Unless there is some explicit mechanism for the user to tell it, the system does not know *why* the user chose some particular data. Also, if the user specifies the same data item in two different places, is this a coincidence, or should the identical item be used in both places?
- Problem with control structure: When specifying a conditional by example, only one branch can be traveled. To go back and travel the other branch, a different example must be given, and the system must be returned to the correct state for the "IF" statement to be re-evaluated. An additional problem is how to specify where in the program the conditionals and loops should be placed.
- Lack of functionality: Many systems only provide Programming with Example for a few data types and a small number of operations. As a patch, some provide escapes to conventional programming languages when PBE is insufficient.
- Avoiding the destruction of real data or other undesirable consequences: In an environment such as the office, where actions in the system may have external consequences, it may be undesirable for the system to actually perform certain actions while the program is being written.

6.4. Program Visualization.

Data Visualization systems have the following problems:
- It is difficult to pick the appropriate picture for a data abstraction.
- After the picture is chosen, it usually requires a great deal of programming to get the system to produce that picture.
- The amount of data is usually large, and it is difficult to fit enough on the screen.
- Related to the above is the layout problem: deciding where to place many differently shaped two-dimensional pictures, which may have arrows and lines connecting them.
- For dynamic data visualization, it is difficult to specify when the displays should be updated. Issues of aesthetics in timing are very important to produce useful animations.

For code, there is a separate set of problems:
- There has not been much work on interesting displays or ways to show progress.
- Like all the other Visual systems, there is the problem of the size of the pictures. Ways must be found to decide what code to display and how to compress procedures to fit on the screen.
- When code and data are animated together, it is difficult for the user to tell what data is being manipulated by what parts of the code, so some way must be found to show the relationships of variables to the displayed data.

7. Conclusion.

Visual Programming, Programming by Example and Program Visualization are all exciting areas of active computer science research, and they promise to improve the user interface to programming environments. A number of interesting systems have been created in each area, and there are some that cross the boundaries. This paper has attempted to classify some of these systems and present the general problems with them in hopes that this will clarify the use of the terms and provide a context for future research.

ACKNOWLEDGEMENTS
For help and support of this article, I would like to thank Bill Buxton, Ron Baecker, Bernita Myers, and many others at the University of Toronto. The research described in this paper was partially funded by the National Science and Engineering Research Council (NSERC) of Canada.

REFERENCES

[Albizuri-Romero 84] Miren B. Albizuri-Romero. "GRASE--A Graphical Syntax-Directed Editor for Structured Programming," *SIGPLAN Notices*. 19(2) Feb. 1984. pp. 28-37.

[Attardi 82] Giuseppe Attardi and Maria Simi. "Extending the Power of Programming by Example," *SIGOA Conference on Office Information Systems*, Philadelphia, PA, Jun. 21-23, 1982. pp. 52-66.

[Baecker 68] R.M.Baecker. "Experiments in On-Line Graphical Debugging: The Interrogation of Complex Data Structures," (Summary only) *First Hawaii International Conference on the System Sciences*. Jan. 1968. pp. 128-129.

[Baecker 75] R.M.Baecker. "Two Systems which Produce Animated Animated Representations of the Execution of Computer Programs," *SIGCSE Bulletin*. 7(1) Feb. 1975. pp. 158-167.

[Baecker 81] Ron Baecker. *Sorting out Sorting*. 16mm color, sound film, 25 minutes. Dynamics Graphics Project, Computer Systems Research Institute, University of Toronto, Toronto, Ontario, Canada. 1981. Presented at ACM SIGGRAPH'81. Dallas, TX. Aug. 1981.

[Baecker 86] Ronald Baecker and Aaron Marcus. "Design Principles for the Enhanced Presentation of Computer Program Source Text," *Human Factors in Computing Systems: Proceedings SIGCHI'86*. Boston, MA. Apr. 13-17, 1986.

[Bauer 78] Michael A. Bauer. *A Basis for the Acquisition of Procedures*. PhD Thesis, Department of Computer Science, University of Toronto. 1978. 310 pages.

[Biermann 76a] Alan W. Biermann. "Approaches to Automatic Programming," *Advances in Computers*, Morris Rubinoff and Marshall C. Yovitz, eds. (15) New York: Academic Press, 1976. pp. 1-63.

[Biermann 76b] Alan W. Biermann and Ramachandran Krishnaswamy. "Constructing Programs from Example Computations," *IEEE Transactions on Software Engineering*. SE-2(3) Sept. 1976. pp. 141-153.

[Borning 79] Alan Borning. *Thinglab--A Constraint-Oriented Simulation Laboratory*. Xerox Palo Alto Research Center Technical Report SSL-79-3. July, 1979.

[Borning 81] Alan Borning. "The Programming Language Aspects of Thinglab; a Constraint-Oriented Simulation Laboratory," *Transactions on Programming Language and Systems*. 3(4) Oct. 1981. pp. 353-387.

[Borning 86] Alan Borning. "Defining Constraints Graphically," *Human Factors in Computing Systems: Proceedings SIGCHI'86*. Boston, MA. Apr. 13-17, 1986.

[Brown 84] Marc H. Brown and Robert Sedgewick. "A System for Algorithm Animation," *Computer Graphics: SIGGRAPH'84 Conference Proceedings*. Minneapolis, Minn. 18(3) July 23-27, 1984. pp. 177-186.

[Brown 85] Gretchen P. Brown, Richard T. Carling, Christopher F. Herot, David A. Kramlich, and Paul Souza. "Program Visualization: Graphical Support for Software Development," *IEEE Computer*. 18(8) Aug. 1985. pp. 27-35.

[Christensen 68] Carlos Christensen. "An Example of the Manipulation of Directed Graphs in the AMBIT/G Programming Language," in *Interactive Systems for Experimental Applied Mathematics*, Melvin Klerer and Juris Reinfelds, eds. New York: Academic Press, 1968. pp. 423-435.

[Christensen 71] Carlos Christensen. "An Introduction to AMBIT/L, A Diagramatic Language for List Processing," *Proceedings of the 2nd Symposium on Symbolic and Algebraic Manipulation*. Los Angeles, CA. Mar. 23-25, 1971. pp. 248-260.

[Ellis 69] T.O. Ellis, J.F. Heafner and W.L. Sibley. *The Grail Project: An Experiment in Man-Machine Communication*. RAND Report RM-5999-Arpa. 1969.

[Glinert 84] Ephraim P. Glinert and Steven L. Tanimoto. "Pict: An Interactive Graphical Programming Environment," *IEEE Computer*. 17(11) Nov. 1984. pp. 7-25.

[Gould 84] Laura Gould and William Finzer. *Programming by Rehearsal*. Xerox Palo Alto Research Center Technical Report SCL-84-1. May, 1984. 133 pages. Excerpted in *Byte*. 9(6) June, 1984.

[Grafton 85] Robert B. Grafton and Tadao Ichikawa, eds. *IEEE Computer*, Special Issue on Visual Programming. 18(8) Aug. 1985.

[Haibt 59] Lois M. Haibt. "A Program to Draw Multi-Level Flow Charts," *Proceedings of the Western Joint Computer Conference*. San Francisco, CA. 15 Mar. 3-5, 1959. pp. 131-137.

[Halbert 81] Daniel C. Halbert. *An Example of Programming by Example*. Masters of Science Thesis. Computer Science Division, Dept. of EE&CS, University of California, Berkeley and Xerox Corporation Office Products Division, Palo Alto, CA. June, 1981.

[Halbert 84] Daniel C. Halbert. *Programming by Example*. PhD Thesis. Computer Science Division, Dept. of EE&CS, University of California, Berkeley. 1984. Also: Xerox Office Systems Division, Systems Development Department, TR OSD-T8402, December, 1984.

[Jacob 85] Robert J.K. Jacob. "A State Transition Diagram Language for Visual Programming," *IEEE Computer*. 18(8) Aug. 1985. pp. 51-59.

[Lieberman 82] Henry Lieberman. "Constructing Graphical User Interfaces by Example," *Graphics Interface'82*, Toronto, Ont. Mar. 17-21, 1982. pp. 295-302.

[London 85] Ralph L. London and Robert A. Druisberg. "Animating Programs in Smalltalk," *IEEE Computer*. 18(8) Aug. 1985. pp. 61-71.

[Moriconi 85] Mark Moriconi and Dwight F. Hare. "Visualizing Program Designs Through PegaSys," *IEEE Computer*. 18(8) Aug. 1985. pp. 72-85.

[Myers 80] Brad A. Myers. *Displaying Data Structures for Interactive Debugging*. Xerox Palo Alto Research Center Technical Report CSL-80-7. June, 1980.

[Myers 83] Brad A. Myers. "Incense: A System for Displaying Data Structures," *Computer Graphics: SIGGRAPH '83 Conference Proceedings*. 17(3) July 1983. pp. 115-125.

[Nassi 73] I. Nassi and B. Shneiderman. "Flowchart Techniques for Structured Programming," *SIGPLAN Notices*. 8(8) Aug. 1973. pp. 12-26.

[Oxford 83] *Dictionary of Computing*. Oxford: Oxford University Press, 1983.

[Pietrzykowski 83] Thomas Pietrzykowski, Stanislaw Matwin, and Tomasz Muldner. "The Programming Language PROGRAPH: Yet Another Application of Graphics," *Graphics Interface'83*, Edmonton, Alberta. May 9-13, 1983. pp. 143-145.

[Pietrzykowski 84] T. Pietrzykowski and S. Matwin. *PROGRAPH: A Preliminary Report*. University of Ottawa Technical Report TR-84-07. April, 1984.

[Pong 83] M.C. Pong and N. Ng. "Pigs--A System for Programming with Interactive Graphical Support," *Software--Practice and Experience*. 13(9) Sept. 1983. pp. 847-855.

[Raeder 85] Georg Raeder. "A Survey of Current Graphical Programming Techniques," *IEEE Computer*. 18(8) Aug. 1985. pp. 11-25.

[Rovner 69] P.D. Rovner and D.A. Henderson, Jr. "On the Implementation of AMBIT/G: A Graphical Programming Language," *Proceedings of the International Joint Conference on Artificial Intelligence*. Washington, D.C. May 7-9, 1969. pp. 9-20.

[Shaw 75] David E. Shaw, William R. Swartout, and C. Cordell Green. "Inferring Lisp Programs from Examples," *Fourth International Joint Conference on Artificial Intelligence*. Tbilisi, USSR. Sept. 3-8, 1975. 1 pp. 260-267.

[Shneiderman 83] Ben Shneiderman. "Direct Manipulation: A Step Beyond Programming Languages," *IEEE Computer*. 16(8) Aug. 1983. pp. 57-69.

[Shu 85] Nan C. Shu. "FORMAL: A Forms-Oriented Visual-Directed Application Development System," *IEEE Computer*. 18(8) Aug. 1985. pp. 38-49.

[Smith 77] David C. Smith. *Pygmalion: A Computer Program to Model and Stimulate Creative Thought*. Basel, Stuttgart: Birkhauser, 1977.

[Smith 82] David C. Smith, Charles Irby, Ralph Kimball, Bill Verplank, and Erik Harslem. "Designing the Star User Interface," *Byte Magazine*. April 1982. pp. 242-282.

[Sutherland 63] Ivan E. Sutherland. "SketchPad: A Man-Machine Graphical Communication System," *AFIPS Spring Joint Computer Conference*. 23 1963. pp. 329-346.

[Sutherland 66] William R. Sutherland. *On-line Graphical Specification of Computer Procedures*. MIT PhD Thesis. Lincoln Labs Report TR-405. 1966.

[Williams 84] Gregg Williams. "The Apple Macintosh Computer," *Byte Magazine*. 9(2) February 1984. pp. 30-54.

[Zloof 77] Moshe M. Zloof and S. Peter de Jong. "The System for Business Automation (SBA): Programming Language," *CACM*. 20(6) June, 1977. pp. 385-396.

[Zloof 81] Moshe M. Zloof. "QBE/OBE: A Language for Office and Business Automation," *IEEE Computer*. 14(5) May, 1981. pp. 13-22.

VISUAL PROGRAMMING LANGUAGES
A PERSPECTIVE AND A DIMENSIONAL ANALYSIS

NAN C. SHU

Reprinted with permission from *Visual Languages*, edited by S.K. Chang, T. Ichikawa, and P.A. Ligomenides, 1986, pages 11-34.

1. Introduction

In the last few years, the rapid decline of computing costs, coupled with the sharp increase of personal computers and "canned" software, has expanded dramatically the population of the computer user community. More and more people today are using computers. However, to many people, the usefulness of a computer is bounded by the usefulness of the canned application software available for the computer. Application programs written for a mass audience seldom give every user all the capabilities that he/she needs. Those who wish to use the computer to do something beyond the capabilities of the canned programs discover that they have to "program."

Learning to program, unfortunately, is still a time-consuming and oftentimes frustrating endeavor. Moreover, even after the skill is learned, writing and testing a program is still a time-consuming and labor-intensive chore. Many people stay away simply because the time and effort required for programming often outweighs the potential benefits of using the computer as a tool to solve their problems, particularly when the problem to be solved is not of a routine nature. Programming has the tendency to lead to what has been termed "analysis paralysis." "The means become the ends as you forget what you wanted to get out of the computer and become wrapped up in the process of getting it out."[2]

Thus, the real bottleneck in access to computing is in the *ease of programming*. The challenge is to bring computer capabilities simply and usefully to people whose work can be benefited by programming.

This challenge, of course, is not new. For years, people have been trying to design new or improved programming languages for easy use. However, until recently, language design has been evolutionary rather than revolutionary. What is happening in the last few years is the recognition that a radical departure from the conventional programming languages is necessary if programming is to be made more accessible.

Traditionally, the structures of the programming languages are based on one-dimensional, textual (i.e., statement by statement) representations. The linearity is geared toward the internal (computer) representations. It was appropriate because it is an efficient representation suitable for the prevailing serially executing machines. In the foreseeable future, profes-

NAN C. SHU • IBM Academic Information Systems, Los Angeles Scientific Center, Los Angeles, California 90025.

sional programmers will still be using the linear programming languages to construct large software systems on the serial machines where the program efficiency is a primary concern. Nevertheless, to encourage end–user computing, representations more amenable for human comprehension must be considered.

Visual programming language is one such departure from the traditional programming languages. It is stimulated by the following premises:

1. People, in general, prefer pictures over words.
2. Pictures are more powerful than words as a means of communication. They can convey more meaning in a more concise unit of expression.
3. Pictures do not have the language barriers that natural languages have. They are understood by people regardless of what language they speak.

Visual programming has gained momentum in recent years primarily because the falling cost of graphics-related hardware and software has made it feasible to use pictures as a means of communications. However, even though visual related works are now mushrooming in the literature, there is no consensus on what visual programming language is, let alone on a way to assess it.

As the field matures, the need to assess the visual programming language arises. For example, while we agree in general with the premises mentioned above, we do not really know to what extent these assumptions hold in the computational environment. Without a framework, there is no objective way to assess the effectiveness and limitations of using pictures for programming purposes.

The purpose of this paper is twofold: to shed some light on the state of the art in this emerging field, and to propose a framework for dimensional analysis, so that visual programming languages can be examined and compared.

Before we proceed, we have to understand what a visual programming language is. In order to have a common understanding, we start with what is considered visual programming, then narrow it down to our definition of a visual programming language.

2. Visual Programming

The term "visual programming" has been used by many people to mean the use of graphical techniques in connection with programming. It is a very general term, which covers a very broad area.

When we examine the recent work reported in the literature, we see the progression of visual programming along two directions. Along one direction, graphical techniques and pointing devices are used to provide a visual environment for program construction and debugging, for information retrieval and presentation, and for software design and understanding. Along another direction, languages are designed to handle visual (image) information, to support visual interaction, and to "program" with visual expressions. These trends are cataloged in Table 1.

To understand the distinctions among the different categories of visual programming, we draw upon the works reported in the literature. Many systems can be cited for each category. However, since our purpose is to illuminate the distinctions, as opposed to presenting a complete survey, we shall use only one or two examples to illustrate each point. One should keep in mind that the facilities provided by a particular system may cover one or more categories. The use of system A as an example of category X does not necessarily mean that the system A can only be classified

TABLE 1
Categorization of Visual Programming

Visual programming					
Visual environment			Visual languages		
Visualization of Program and Execution	Visualization of Data or information	Visualization of System Design	For processing visual information	For supporting visual interaction	For actually programming with visual expression

into category X. The purpose of the classification is to deepen our understanding by focusing on the functional distinctions. Readers interested in surveys may find extensive bibliographies elsewhere, for example, in Chang,[4] Glinert and Tanimoto,[8] and Raeder.[19]

3. Visual Environment

The first major area of visual programming provides visual environment, meaning the incorporation of graphical techniques in a software environment that supports the program or system development.

One category of work in this area deals with graphical support for the *visualization of a program and its run time environment*. PECAN,[21] developed at Brown University, is such an example. PECAN is a family of program development systems that supports multiple views of the user's program. The views can be representations of a program or of the corresponding semantics. The program is represented internally as an abstract syntax tree. The user sees views or concrete representations of it. One such view is a syntax-directed editor which displays the syntax tree by "pretty-printing it with multiple fonts." Another view of the program is a Nassi–Shneiderman flowchart. A third view of the program is a module interconnection diagram showing how the program is organized. All of these views update their display as the abstract syntax tree changes. The semantic views presented to the user include expressions trees, data type diagrams, flow graphs, and the symbol table.

At execution time, users can follow the program's progress. Each statement is highlighted as it is executed, both in the Pascal source and in an automatically generated corresponding flowchart. The stack data view shows the current state of the execution stack, including each current stack frame, the variables in that frame, and their values. Support for data views that render a graphical representation of a user's data structure is the subject of current research.

In short, PECAN is designed to provide the user with multiple displays that concurrently show different aspects of the program in well-known programming terms. Having access to all this information can give the programmers a good feeling of what is going on, and the system is indeed a powerful debugger. As a program development and testing tool, "many of the facilities provided in PECAN are appropriate to a wide range of languages." Plans are in place "to provide PECAN systems for languages other than Pascal, once the prototype implementation is complete and stable."[21] However, it is not the intention of PECAN to explore the possibilities of new languages other than the well-known traditional (algebraic) programming languages. Graphical support in programming environment is the primary concern of PECAN.

Another category of work in the visual environment area deals with *visualization of data or information*. A spatial data management system (SDMS) developed at Computer Corporation of America and described by C. F. Herot[10] is an example. The information in SDMS is stored internally in relational databases, but it is expressed in graphical form and presented to the user in a spatial framework. This graphical data space (GDS) is viewed through a set of color raster-scan displays. Users traverse the GDS surface or zoom into the image to obtain greater detail with a joystick. This approach permits many types of questions to be answered without the need for a keyboard. In essence, SDMS is devoted primarily to using "direct manipulation" as a means for information retrieval and using graphical view of a database, coupled with zooming capability, for visualization of the information retrieved.

The success of using graphical techniques for visualization of program and data has led to work on the *visualization of system design:*

> Graphics techniques should have a very high payoff in a software environment that supports the whole software life cycle. Requirements, specifications, design decisions, and the finished product would all be captured in graphical form for people who have to use or maintain the system or who have to find out about the system.[9]

For example, the Program Visualization (PV) system,[3,11] an outgrowth of SDMS at the Computer Corporation of America, "supports manipulation of static and dynamic diagrams of computer systems; manipulation of program and documentation text; creation and traversal of multidimensional information space; and reuse and dissemination of tools, which is made possible by a library of diagram and text components (templates, for example)."[3] The diagrams constructed on the PV prototype belong to a set of diagrams that are linked hierarchically. The user can select the zoom-in command, point to a box of interest, and see the module at the next level of detail. To support the viewing of dynamic visualizations, the PV prototype provides both speed control and stepping. For animated visualizations, highlights move through the lines of source code as the corresponding object code is executed. At the same time, graphical depictions of data are changed as the data values are updated.

These three examples represent three different categories of visual programming because they emphasize visualization of three different classes of objects. However, at a higher level, they have two characteristics in common: (1) They all provide a visual environment which "captures the spirit of a completely new way for programmers to interact with software and the programs they construct."[9] (2) They do not contribute to any novel approach to the language aspects of the program constructs. This second characteristic marks the sharp distinction between the two major categories of visual programming: visual environment and visual languages.

We shall now examine the second major area of visual programming, namely, visual languages.

4. Visual Languages

Depending on a person's background and his/her sphere of interest, visual languages mean different things to different people. In order to establish a common understanding, we classify visual languages into three categories.

The first category of visual languages are used for the *processing of visual (or image) information.*

One of the earliest works in this category is the GRAIN (Graphics-oriented Relational Algebraic INterpreter) system reported by S. K. Chang *et al.*[5] In the GRAIN system, pictorial information is represented by both logical and physical pictures. Logical pictures are defined in three relational tables: the picture object table, the picture contour table, and the picture page table. The physical pictures or real images are stored in a separate image store. This distinction of logical pictures from physical pictures leads to the design of an efficient pictorial information system. At the same time, the relational database approach provided a framework for a query facility.

The user can specify his/her image query in the GRAIN language. In addition to the algebraic commands that are available for manipulation of relational tables, GRAIN provides many commands specifically designed for image or line drawing such as PLOT ⟨object-name⟩, SKETCH ⟨picture-name⟩, PAINT ⟨picture-name⟩, etc. For example, to retrieve the image containing major highways through Tokyo, one may use the GRAIN query

Sketch highway; through (cityname is 'Tokyo').[4]

A more recent example of this category was described in a paper entitled "An Introduction to PSQL: A Pictorial Structured Query Language."[22] As stated in its abstract, "This paper introduces a Pictorial Query Language for manipulating pictorial and alphanumeric databases. It is an extension of the System R's SQL language which allows direct reference to pictures and advanced processing of pictorial domains."

A typical simple query in PSQL,

SELECT	city_name, state, population
FROM	cities
ON	us_map
AT	loc COVERED_BY (4+4,11+9)
WHERE	population > 450000

produces a map of the area specified by the AT clause and a table containing city_name, state and population of all cities in that area having population greater than 450000. Names of the cities that met the criteria are also displayed on the map to assist the user to visualize the correspondence.

A quick observation can be made from these two examples: Although the information being handled by the languages (GRAIN and PSQL) do involve pictures, and visualization does come into play in the presentation of results, the languages themselves are textual. They belong to the visual languages of the first category: languages designed for the handling of visual information.

Another category of visual languages are designed for *supporting visual interaction*.

For example, as described earlier under the section on visual environment, SDMS[10] data are stored in a conventional database but presented to the user in a graphical view. In order to construct such a view, the database administrator must first describe to the system how each icon should appear and then instruct the system to create a data surface of icons for selected tuples in the system. To describe the appearance of each icon, one uses the icon-class description language, ICDL, which consists of a series of POSITION, TEMPLATE, SCALE, COLOR, and ATTRIBUTE REGION statements. The POSITION statement determines the placement of the icon on the data surface. The TEMPLATE statement specifies the shape of the icon by selecting among a set of pictures that have previously been drawn by the database administrator. For the ship database, the SCALE statement specifies the size of the icon as a function of the ship; the COLOR statement specifies the color of each ship according to its readiness; and the ATTRIBUTE REGION statements place the values of the ship's name, international radio call sign, and commanding officer's name into the specified locations in the picture. Finally, to create a data surface of icons for selected tuples, one uses the ASSOCIATE statement. All these statements are conventional textual statements.

In the same category, but of a more general nature, is "HI-VISUAL: A Language Supporting Visual Interface in Programming."[16] HI-VISUAL, which derives its name from "Hiroshima Visual," is based on a hierarchical multiple window model. Users use it to define icons and to support operations on icons by statements such as icon_define (D: desk, W: window); append (D: desk, W: window); move (W: window, V: vector); rotate (W: window, A: angle); zoom-in (W: window, R: ratio); etc.

In short, this category of languages is designed to support visual representation or visual interaction, but the languages themselves are textual, not visual.

Still another category of visual languages concentrate on allowing users to actually *program with graphical expressions*. They can be more aptly called the "visual programming languages," which is the focus of discussion for the rest of this chapter.

5. Visual Programming Languages

We shall now concentrate on visual programming languages. A *visual programming language* can be informally defined to be a language which uses some visual representations (in addition to or in place of words and numbers) to accomplish what would otherwise have to be written in a traditional one-dimensional programming language.

Note that this definition imposes no restrictions on the type of data or information. It is immaterial whether the object being operated on or being displayed to a user by a visual language is textual, numeric, pictorial, or even audio. What is important is that, in order to be considered as a visual programming language, the language itself must have some meaningful (i.e., not merely decorative) visual representations as a means of programming.

One may argue whether the use of a pointing device (such as a mouse or a joystick) or functional keys constitutes a visual programming language. In our opinion, they are, in most cases, simply better alternatives to keying. Since keying is not considered as an integral part of a programming language, the mere use of a pointing device or functional keys as an alternative to keying is not construed as a visual programming language. For the same reasoning, we do not include menus or windows as visual programming languages, unless the contents of a menu or window have visual representation as a means of programming.

5.1. Two Important Aspects of Programming Languages

When we attempt to assess a programming language, two important aspects come to mind: the level of the language and the scope of the language.

It is generally agreed that the *level of a language* is an inverse measure of the amount of details that a user has to give to the computer in order to achieve the desired results. A language is nonprocedural (and at the highest level) if users only tell the computer what they want done, but not how to do it. A language is procedural if users need to specify the steps the computer must follow. Number and size of the required steps vary with the procedural languages. To achieve the same result, a highly procedural (low-level) language (e.g., assembler) requires many small detailed steps while a less procedural (higher-level) language (e.g., FORTRAN) requires fewer but larger steps with less details from the user. By this measure, FORTRAN is at a higher level than an assembler.

The *scope of the language,* ranging from the general and widely applicable to the specific and narrowly applicable, depicts how much a language is capable of doing. Using FORTRAN and assembler as examples again, a user might use FORTRAN to perform complicated scientific computations, but he/she would not use FORTRAN for multitasking. An assembler language, on the other hand, can generally be used to do both. Thus, we say that the assembler language has a larger problem domain or a wider scope of applicability than FORTRAN.

Of course, there are other ways to classify or characterize a language. However, for most practical purposes, these two aspects are considered as two of the most fundamental dimensions in assessing programming languages. They are applicable to programming languages in general, regardless of whether the language is visual or not.

5.2. *The Third Dimension of Visual Programming Languages*

In order to put visual programming languages into perspective, we introduce an additional dimension: extent of visual expression.

By *visual expression* we mean the meaningful visual representations (for example, icons, graphs, diagrams, pictures) used as language components to achieve the purpose of programming. As we have mentioned earlier, if there is no visual expression in the language (even though the information being retrieved or displayed has pictures), the third dimension simply does not apply.

6. *Dimensional Analysis of Visual Programming Languages*

We are now ready to propose an analytical approach in a qualitative manner, to assess visual programming languages. In essence, it involves the construction of the *profile of a language* which characterizes the language in the three-dimensional framework. Graphically, it may be represented by the surface determined by the relative measures of the language on the three axes labeled as language level, scope, and visual extent as shown in Figure 1.

Based on the principles of design, most of the visual programming languages reported in the open literature fall into three broad categories:

1. On one extreme, graphics are deliberately designed to play the central role in programming. To borrow a phrase suggested by Lakin,[14] they are "executable graphics." Some of the works belonging to this category include David Smith's Pygmalion,[24] Xerox's Star,[25,18] Finzer and Gould's Programming by Rehearsal,[7] Glinert and Tanimoto's Pict,[8] Raeder's PIP,[20] Lakin's VennLISP,[14] and Jacob's State Transition Diagram Language.[12]

2. On another extreme, graphics are incorporated into the programming environment as an extension to conventional programming languages. Some of the works belonging to this category include Diaz-Herrera and Flude's PASCAL/HSD,[6] Pong and Ng's PIGS,[17] and Belady and Hosokawa's "Visualization of Independence and Dependence for Program Concurrency".[1]

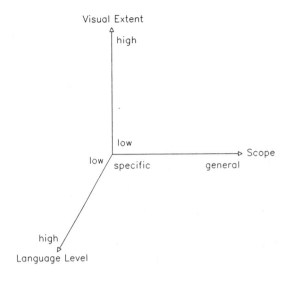

FIGURE 1. Three dimensions of visual programming languages.

3. In the middle, the graphic representations are designed as an integral part of a language. However, unlike the icons in the first category, they are not the "super stars" of the language; and unlike the graphical extensions of the second category, the language cannot function without the graphic representations. Many of the table-based and form-based languages belong to this category (for example, Kitagawa et al.,[13] Luo and Yao,[15] Shu,[23] Yao et al.,[26] and Zloof[27]).

To illustrate our points, we draw upon two examples from each category. They include:

1. In the first category, two iconic systems designed for two distinct classes of "freshman" in the computing world: Xerox Star for office workers,[25,18] and Pict for people learning to program.[8]

2. In the second category, two graphical extensions devised to serve two different purposes: PIGS, which employs Nassi–Shneiderman diagrams as executable program control constructs,[17] and the Belady–Hosokawa proposal, which employs special notations to expose the sequencing and concurrency information.[1]

3. In the third category, two nonprocedural programming languages using tables or forms as visual expressions: QBE[27] for its popularity with nonprogrammers, and FORMAL[23] for its powerful data manipulation and restructuring capabilities.

6.1. The Xerox Star System

We first use Xerox's Star system[25,18] as an example since it is one of the better known systems today and is often credited as the forerunner of the iconic systems.

The Star system was announced by the Xerox Corp. in April 1981. Star uses icons and pointing devices as a means to communicate with the computer. One of the most important principles of the Star interface is to apply the user's familiarity with office objects to the new situation of the computer. Pictures of documents, folders, file drawers, in-baskets, and out-baskets are displayed as small pictures, or icons on the screen. A user can "open" an icon by selecting it (with a mouse) and pushing the OPEN key on the keyboard. When opened, an icon expands into a larger form called a "window." Contents of an icon are displayed in the window. This enables a user to read documents, inspect the contents of folders and file drawers, send and receive mail, etc.

At a finer grain, the Star world is organized in terms of objects that have properties and upon which actions are performed. In order to make properties visible, Star has the notion of property sheets. A few commands can be used throughout the system. They are MOVE, COPY, DELETE, SHOW PROPERTIES, COPY PROPERTIES, AGAIN, UNDO, and HELP.

In terms of the extent of visual expression, Star rates high. Its main emphasis, however, is at the "command" language level. "Calculators" do exist to let a user perform arithmetic calculations. But for more complicated computations, users would have to "escape" to a conventional language called CUSP at some bottom level. As stated in Ref. 18, "Eventually, CUSP will become a full programming language, with procedures, variables, parameters, and a programming environment." Underlying this dichotomy is the dictum: "Simple things should be simple; hard things should be possible."[18] Star was primarily designed for simple things. When CUSP is excluded from the evaluation, Star rates low in terms of the scope of applicability.

As far as giving directives to the computer goes, Star users move the mouse and click the buttons. With some practice, a user can move the cursor to the desired icon and push the appropriate button to select the desired action faster than one can type the commands at a keyboard. However, the tasks are still performed in a step-by-step manner. For computations, "The calculators are user tailorable and extensible. Most are modeled after pocket calculators—business, scientific, four function—but one is a tabular calculator similar to the popular Visicalc program." Pocket calculators require many small steps to perform computations. Rated on the language level, Star is relatively low. Accordingly, the profile of Star in terms of the three-dimensional space is shown in Figure 2.

6.2. The Pict System

Another highly graphical system, developed at the University of Washington, was reported by Glinert and Tanimoto.[8] Unlike Xerox's Star which uses the office as its operational metaphor, Pict is designed to aid program implementation. Its emphasis is to provide a "programming" facility in which computer graphics plays a central role. With Pict, users sit in front of a color graphics display and communicate with the system throughout all phases of their work by pointing (with joystick) to icons in a menu tree:

> With the exception of numerals and short Help messages, users rely totally on nontextual symbols. (Sub)program names and parameter passing modes, data structures, variables, and program operations are represented by icons of various sorts, while control structures such as PASCAL REPEAT-UNTIL or WHILE are represented by colored, directed paths that can actually be seen.

At execution time, Pict uses simple forms of animation to make the drawing "come to life."

Several prototype Pict systems have been implemented at the University of Washington. As a programming language, Pict is "at a language level similar to that of BASIC or simple PASCAL." User programs may be recursive and contain arbitrary chains of subroutine calls. Its capabilities, however, are very limited:

> The main prototype, named Pict/D, allows the user to compose programs that do simple, numeric calculations. . . . Both the types and number of variables are quite restricted in Pict/D, with just four six-digit, nonnegative decimal integers (distinguished by red, green, blue and orange) available in each module (program or subprogram).

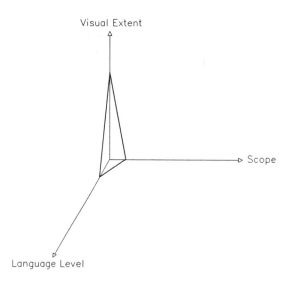

FIGURE 2. A profile of Star.

Compared to Star, Pict has a slightly higher extent of visual expressions (Color is meaningful in Pict but not in Star) and a higher language level. However, owing to the very restricted sizes of the user program modules, the limited set of data types and language constructs, and the extremely small number of variables to which a module can refer, the scope of Pict is not any wider than Star. Taking all three dimensions into consideration, the profile of Pict is shown in Figure 3.

6.3. The PIGS System

Pong and Ng[17] have described an experimental system for Programming with Interactive Graphical Support named PIGS. Like Pict, the system has been designed with the aim of supporting program development and testing in the same graphical environment. The approaches taken by the two systems, however, differ significantly.

In Pict, icons are the essential language elements and play a central role. Programming process is essentially to select and/or compose icons, to place them in proper juxtaposition on the screen, and to connect the icons by paths to indicate the desired flow of control.

PIGS, on the other hand, is a graphical extension to a conventional programming language. Nassi–Shneiderman Diagrams (NSD) are incorporated into PASCAL as the structured control constructs of logic flow. PIGS can interpret a program in NSD chart form, and the execution sequence of the NSD is displayed at a graphical terminal. PIGS also provides interactive debugging and testing aids to support program development. The prototype, implemented at the University of Hong Kong, allows only the use of integers and one-dimensional arrays in NSD programs.

Compared with Pict, PIGS has lower extent of visual expressions but wider scope of applicability. As far as language level is concerned, both of them are at a level of simple PASCAL. Compared with the base language, PIGS has the same scope and level as the base language, but now the surface of the triangle is tilted since the visual extent comes into play. The profile of the PIGS system is shown in solid lines in Figure 4, while its base language is shown in dashed lines.

6.4. The Belady–Hosokawa Proposal

Another proposal on incorporating graphical extension to a conventional programming language has been reported by Belady and Hosokawa.[1] In order to utilize the CRT device's two-dimensional capabilities,

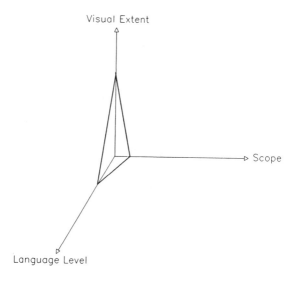

FIGURE 3. A profile of Pict.

a scheme was proposed to permit the explicit indication of a program's potential for parallel execution.

With this scheme, the set of statements to be executed occupies the vertical dimension on the CRT screen, while the sequencing dependencies, if applicable, are represented along the horizontal axis (i.e., axis of time).

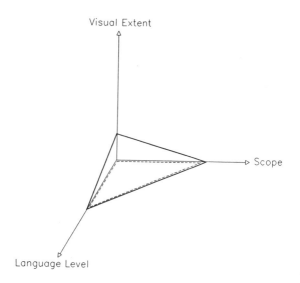

FIGURE 4. A profile of PIGS.

For example, using "o" to indicate the execution sequencing of simple statements, and "L" to indicate the execution sequencing of blocks, the following is an example of a loop:

stmta	o
stmtb	o
stmtc	o
do	LLL
stmtd	Lo
stmte	Lo
stmtf	L o
end do	LLL

51

This represents a program where "stmta" is executed followed by "stmtb" and the loop. Finally, "stmtc" is executed, after the completion of the loop. While the loop is being executed, "stmtd" and "stmte" must be executed before "stmtf." Execution of "stmtd" and "stmte," however, can be parallel since there is no mutual dependence between them.

This two-dimensional specification provides the compiler with sequencing and concurrency information without the need of retrofits such as FORK and JOIN to traditional languages.

At the time of reporting, the proposed scheme was "just an idea." The authors stated that they will soon attempt a quick implementation in the form of a front end to an existing language.

To examine this proposal in the framework of the dimensional analysis, we may conclude that (1) the extent of visual expression is low, as compared to the iconic languages; and (2) regardless of what existing language is chosen as the base language, the scope of the extended language will be wider than the base language while the level of the language will remain the same. Thus, as shown in Figure 5, if the base language is represented by the triangle made of dashed lines, then the profile of the extended language may be represented by the surface enclosed by the solid lines.

6.5. QBE

QBE (Query-By-Example) was released as a product by IBM in 1978 as a query language on relational databases.[27] Over the years, QBE has

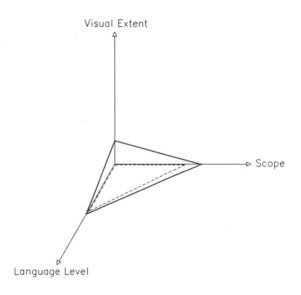

FIGURE 5. A profile of the Belady–Hosokawa proposal.

acquired a reputation as a friendly language. Briefly, the Query-By-Example language allows users to query a database through the use of table skeletons and example elements. For instance, the following query

```
-------------------------------------------------
TRAVEL | NAME | AMOUNT | DATE | F/D |
-------------------------------------------------
         | P.      | P.           |        | F  |
```

instructs the system to display the names and amounts from each record in a table named TRAVEL such that the corresponding F/D field is F. Here "P." stands for print or display, and "F" is a constant element for selection.

The example element concept is used to cover a variety of database operations, such as cross-referencing between fields, formulating conditions on field values, moving data from one object to another, etc. Example elements are underlined or preceded by an underscore so they can be distinguished from constant elements. For example, to construct an output table containing the names, amounts of expenses, trip area (i.e., F/D), and managers of employees who took the domestic trips (i.e., F/D field contains D), the following QBE program is constructed.

```
--------------------------------------------------
TRAVEL | NAME | AMOUNT | DATE | F/D |
---------- |-------- |----------- |------- |----- |
           |  _N    |  _A        |       |  D  |
           --------------------------------------
           EMP | NAME | MGR |
           ------- |-------- | ----- |
                   |  _N    | _MR  |
--------------------------------------------------
EMP1 | NAME | AMOUNT | F/D | MGR  |
-------- |-------- |----------- |----- |------- |
         | P._N   | P._A       | P.  | P._MR |
```

The third table is an output table that the user creates by mapping data from the two base tables (TRAVEL and EMP).

To assess QBE in the three-dimensional framework, we make the following observations: (1) Skeleton tables are used as visual expressions. The extent of visual expressions is not as high as Star or Pict, but it is higher than PIGS or the Belady–Hosakawa proposal. (2) The language is nonprocedural in the sense that the programs do not tell the computer what steps

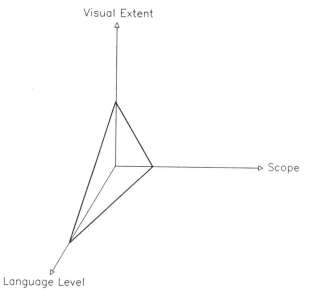

FIGURE 6. A profile of QBE.

53

to take. (3) The scope is wider than either Star or Pict, but it is limited to operations on simple flat tables. The profile for QBE is shown in Figure 6.

6.6. FORMAL

FORMAL[23] is a forms-oriented data manipulation language, implemented at the IBM Los Angeles Scientific Center as an experimental system. The language is not designed to teach would-be programmers the concepts of traditional programming. Rather, it is designed for nonprogrammers to computerize many fairly complex data processing applications without having to learn the intricacies of programming.

FORMAL capitalizes on the user's familiarity with forms in two ways: First, stylized form headings are used as visual representations of data structures which could be very complex (e.g., hierarchical data or nested tables of arbitrary complexity). Second, the structure of the program is also form based. The following is a skeleton FORMAL program:

```
                        |--------------------|
                        |                    |
                        |   (form heading)   |
                        |                    |
          ==============|====================|
          SOURCE        |                    |
          --------------|--------------------|
          MATCH         |                    |
          --------------|--------------------|
          CONDITION     |                    |
          --------------|--------------------|
          ORDER         |                    |
          --------------|--------------------|
```

In using FORMAL, one starts with the visual representation of an output form, and completes a program by specifying a few relevant properties within the outline of a form. Briefly, SOURCE defines the source of data, MATCH specifies the fields to be matched when an output instance is constructed from two input sources, CONDITION describes the criteria for selecting instances from the input(s), and ORDER depicts the desired sequencing of instances within a form or within a group. For instance, to achieve the result of the second example used for QBE, a FORMAL program is shown below. Data processing applications of much more complicated nature can be programmed in a similar manner.

```
VENDPROD:  CREATE VENDPROD

       I-------------------------------------------------------|
       I                     ( VENDPROD )                      |
       I---------------|---------------------------------------|
       I               |                 (PROD)                |
       I    VNAME      |---------------|-----------|-----------|
       I               |  PROD_NO      |   TYPE    |   PNAME   |
========I==============|===============|===========|===========|
SOURCE  I   PRODUCT FORM                                       |
--------I-------------------------------------------------------|
END
```

FIGURE 8. Example of a FORMAL program for the process shown in Figure 7.

54

```
I-------------------------------------------------------------------I
I                          (PRODUCT)                                I
I-------------------------------------------------------------------I
I         |         |       |(SUPPLIER)| (STORAGE)   |              I
I PROD_NO | PNAME   | TYPE  |----------|------|------|PRICE |        I
I         |         |       | VNAME    |BIN_NO| LOC  |      |        I
I=========|=========|=======|==========|======|======|======|       I
I  110    | PIPE    | PVC   | AQUA     | B1   | SJC  | 0.79 |        I
I         |         |       | CHEMTRON | B2   | SJC  |      |        I
I         |         |       |          | B3   | SFO  |      |        I
I-------------------------------------------------------------------I
I  120    | PIPE    | STEEL | ABC      | B4   | SFO  | 4.10 |        I
I         |         |       | CHEMTRON |      |      |      |        I
I-------------------------------------------------------------------I
I  210    | VALVE   | STEEL | AQUA     | B5   | SJC  | 0.45 |        I
I         |         |       | ABC      | B6   | SFO  |      |        I
I         |         |       | CHEMTRON |      |      |      |        I
I-------------------------------------------------------------------I
I  221    | VALVE   | COPPER| ABC      | B7   | SJC  | 1.25 |        I
I         |         |       | CHEMTRON | B8   | SFO  |      |        I
I         |         |       | ROBINSON |      |      |      |        I
I-------------------------------------------------------------------I
                                 |
                                 |
                                 |
                                 |
                                 V
I-------------------------------------------------------------------I
I                          (VENDPROD)                               I
I-------------------------------------------------------------------I
I              |                    (PROD)                          I
I              |-------------------------------------------         I
I    VNAME     |                                                    I
I              | PROD_NO   |    TYPE      |    PNAME                 I
I==============|===========|==============|==============           I
I ABC          |   120     |   STEEL      |   PIPE                   I
I              |   210     |   STEEL      |   VALVE                  I
I              |   221     |   COPPER     |   VALVE                  I
I-------------------------------------------------------------------I
I AQUA         |   110     |   PVC        |   PIPE                   I
I              |   210     |   STEEL      |   VALVE                  I
I-------------------------------------------------------------------I
I CHEMTRON     |   110     |   PVC        |   PIPE                   I
I              |   120     |   STEEL      |   PIPE                   I
I              |   210     |   STEEL      |   VALVE                  I
I              |   221     |   COPPER     |   VALVE                  I
I-------------------------------------------------------------------I
I ROBINSON     |   221     |   COPPER     |   VALVE                  I
I-------------------------------------------------------------------I
```

FIGURE 7. Example of a data processing application.

```
 ----------------------------------------------
|                  (EMP1)                      |
|----------------------------------------------|
|  NAME  |  AMOUNT   |  F/D    |  MGR   |       |
=================================================
 SOURCE  |   TRAVEL            |  EMP   |       |
---------|------------------------------------- |
 CONDITION|          |  'D'    |        |        |
---------|------------------------------------- |
 MATCH   |  TRAVEL.NAME , EMP.NAME               |
---------|------------------------------------- |
```

What sets FORMAL apart from other languages is perhaps its design principle: "What you sketch is what you get." Two important considerations contributed to the effectiveness of this design principle: (1) The formalized visual representation of data structures (known as form headings), and (2) The automatic data transformation or restructuring capabilities given to the compiler.

Data restructuring, often an integral but nontrivial part of an application, is implied in the differences in the output and input headings. For example, the process of transforming PRODUCT form into VENDPROD form (as shown in Figure 7) involves an inversion of a hierarchical structure. A FORMAL program used to achieve the desired result is shown in Figure 8. The transformation is automatically performed by the compiler generated code because the compiler is able to (1) recognize the differences in the formalized visual representations of the input and output data structures, and (2) apply its inferential capabilities to map out a strategy for conforming the input to output. In fact, the responsibility of writing algorithms for such tasks is shifted from the user to the compiler. As a result, without specifying much detail, non-DP professionals are able to use FORMAL to computerize fairly complex data processing applications in a rather simple manner.

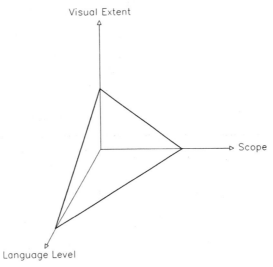

FIGURE 9. A profile of FORMAL.

Let us now compare FORMAL with QBE in the three-dimensional framework. Like QBE, FORMAL is at the middle of the scale for the extent of visual expression. Like QBE, FORMAL is nonprocedural. Users do not tell the computer what steps to follow in order to achieve the results. The language has no prescriptive constructs.

However, because of FORMAL's ability to handle data structures much more complex than the relational tables underlying QBE, FORMAL has a much larger problem domain—a broader scope of applicability—than QBE. The profile of FORMAL is shown in Figure 9.

7. Conclusion

We have, in this chapter, proposed an analytical approach to characterize visual programming languages in a profile expressed in terms of the level of the language, the scope of applicability, and the extent of visual expressions. This approach gives us a means to compare languages in a meaningful (although qualitative) manner. For example, by superimposing the profiles of Pict, PIGS, and FORMAL (as shown in Figure 10), the comparison of the three totally different languages begins to make sense.

Of course, we are only scratching the surface of a wide open area. Many questions need to be answered, and many investigations need to be conducted. For instance, can we use this approach to gauge the distance of a language from a desirable language? The answer depends, more or less, on whether we can postulate the properties of a desired language.

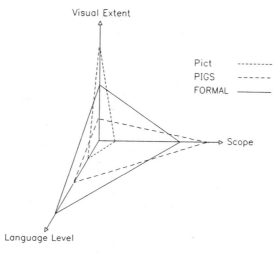

FIGURE 10. A Comparison of Pict, PIGS, and FORMAL.

For example, we generally agree that it is desirable for a programming language to be very high level and have very wide scope. But we cannot agree on (or have no idea), at this stage of development, what is the most desirable extent of visual expression in the programming environment. For example, the use of ill-conceived symbols or over-detailed pictures may be more confusing than informative. Too many visual expressions may produce "spaghetti" effect. It is conceivable that the program development time might be reduced when pictorial representations are used for simple tasks, but there is no evidence of similar payoff for tasks of complex nature. Yet, intuitively, we would like to exploit the potentially powerful pictures as much as possible. Perhaps, the *effectiveness of visual expression* would be a better dimension than visual extent. There are many issues that need to be explored. Empirical studies are barely beginning at this time.

It is to be hoped that as more research is conducted and more experience is gained, we will be able to throw more light on visual programming languages and their related issues. With the speed that the computing technology is progressing, more efforts on visual programming will surely be attempted. We would be better guided for the future direction if our understanding of the visual languages is sharpened and deepened.

References

1. L. A. BELADY, and K. HOSOKAWA, Visualization of independence and dependence for program concurrency, Proceedings of the 1984 IEEE Computer Society Workshop on Visual Languages, Hiroshima, Japan, 1984, pp. 59–63.
2. G. D. BROWN and D. H. SEFTON, The micro vs. the applications logjam, *Datamation* (**Jan.**, 96–104 (1984).
3. G. P. BROWN, R. T. CARLING, C. F. HEROT, D. A. KRAMLICH, and P. SOUZA, Program visualization: Graphical support for software development, *IEEE Comput.* **18**(8), 27–35 (1985).
4. S. K. CHANG, Image information systems, *Proc. IEEE* **73**(4), 754–764 (1985).
5. S. K. CHANG, J. REUSS, and B. H. McCORMICK, Design considerations of a pictorial database system, *Int. J. Policy Anal. Inf. Syst.* **1**(2), 49–70 (1978).
6. J. L. DIAZ-HERRERA and R. C. FLUDE, PASCAL/HSD: A graphical programming system, Proceedings of COMPSAC 80, IEEE Computer Society Press, Los Alamitos, California, 1980, pp. 723–728.
7. W. FINZER and L. GOULD, Programming by rehearsal, *Byte* **9**(6), 187–210 (1984).
8. E. P. GLINERT and S. L. TANIMOTO, Pict: An interactive graphical programming environment, *IEEE Comput.* **17**(11), 7–25 (1984).
9. R. B. GRAFTON and T. ICHIKAWA, Guest editor's Introduction to the special issue on Visual Programming, *IEEE Comput.* **18**(8) 6–9 (1985).
10. C. F. HEROT, Spatial management of data, *ACM Trans. Database Syst.* **5**(4), 493–514 (1980).
11. C. F. HEROT, G. P. BROWN, R. T. CARLING, M. FRIEDELL, D. KRAMLICH, and R. M. BAECKER, An integrated environment for program visualization, in *Automated Tools for Information*

System Design, edited by Schneider and Wasserman (Eds.), North-Holland, Amsterdam, 1982, pp. 237–259.

12. R. J. K. JACOB, A state transition diagram language for visual programming, *IEEE Comput.* **18**(8), 51–59 (1985).

13. H. KITAGAWA, M. GOTOH, S. MISAKI, and M. AZUMA, Form document management system SPECDOQ—Its architecture and implementation, Proceedings of the Second ACM Conference on Office Information Systems, June 1984, pp. 132–142.

14. F. LAKIN, Spatial parsing for visual languages, Chapter 3 of this book.

15. D. LUO, and S. B. YAO, Form operation by example—A language for office information processing, Proceedings of SIGMOD Conference, June 1981, pp. 213–223.

16. N. MONDEN, Y. YOSHINO, M. HIRAKAWA, M. TANAKE, and T. ICHIKAWA, HI-VISUAL: A language supporting visual interaction in programming, Proceedings of the 1984 IEEE Computer Society Workshop on Visual Languages, Hiroshima, Japan, 1984, pp. 199–205.

17. M. C. PONG, and N. NG, PIGS—A system for programming with interactive graphical support, *Software Practice Experience* **13**(9), 847–855 (1983).

18. R. PURVY, J. FARRELL, and P. KLOSE, The design of Star's records processing: Data processing for the noncomputer professional, *ACM Trans. Office Inf. Syst.* **1**(1), 3–24 (1983).

19. G. RAEDER, A survey of current graphical programming techniques, *IEEE Comput.* **18**(8) 11–25 (1985).

20. G. RAEDER, Programming in pictures, Ph.D. dissertation, University of Southern California, Los Angeles, November 1984 (Technical Report TR-84-318, USC, or Technical Report 8-85, Norweigian Institute of Technology).

21. S. P. REISS, PECAN: Program development systems that support multiple views, *IEEE Trans. Software Eng.* **11**(3) 276–285 (1985).

22. N. ROUSSOPOULOS and D. LEIFKER, An introduction to PSQL: A pictorial structured query language, Proceedings of the 1984 IEEE Computer Society Workshop on Visual Languages, Hiroshima, Japan, 1984, pp. 77–87.

23. N. C. SHU, FORMAL: A forms-oriented and visual-directed application system, *IEEE Comput.* **18**(8), 38–49 (1985).

24. D. C. SMITH, Pygmalion: A creative programming environment, Ph.D. thesis, Department of Computer Science, Stanford University, 1975, Technical Report No. STAN-CS-75-499.

25. D. C. SMITH, C. IRBY, and R. KIMBALL, The star user interface: An overview, Proceedings of National Computer Conference, 1982, pp. 515–528.

26. S. B. YAO, A.R. HEVNER, Z. SHI, and D. LUO, FORMANAGER: An office forms management system, *ACM Trans. Office Inf. Syst.* **2**(3), 235–262 (1984).

27. M. M. ZLOOF, QBE/OBE: A language for office and business automation, *Computer* **May,** 13–22 (1981).

□□□ 2 □□□ Graphical Representations for Programs and Systems

L.L. Tripp. "A Survey of Graphical Notations for Program Design: An Update." *ACM SIGSOFT Software Engineering Notes*, 13(4):39–44, 1988.

I. Nassi and B. Shneiderman. "Flowchart Techniques for Structured Programming." *ACM SIGPLAN Notices*, 8(8):12–26, August 1973.

L.A. Belady, C.J. Evangelisti and L.R. Power. "GREENPRINT: A Graphic Representation of Structured Programs." *IBM Systems Journal*, 19(4):542–553, 1980.

R.J.K. Jacob. "A State Transition Diagram Language for Visual Programming." *IEEE Computer*, 18(8):51–59, August 1985.

A.I. Wasserman. "Extending State Transition Diagrams for the Specification of Human–Computer Interaction." *IEEE Trans. on Software Engineering*, SE–11(8):699–713, August 1985.

M. Azuma, T. Tabata, Y. Oki and S. Kamiya. "SPD: A Humanized Documentation Technology." *IEEE Trans. on Software Engineering*, SE–11(9):945–953, September 1985.

D.T. Ross. "Applications and Extensions of SADT." *IEEE Computer*, 18(4):25–34, April 1985.

T.D. Kimura. "Visual Programming by Transaction Network." In *Proc. 21st Hawaii Int. Conf. on System Sciences (HICSS-21)*, Kailua Kona, Haw., Volume 2: Software Track, pages 648–654, January 5-8, 1988. IEEE Computer Society Press, Los Alamitos, Calif.

R.J.A. Buhr. *System Design with Ada* (extended excerpt). Prentice Hall, Englewood Cliffs, N.J., 1984.

M. Moriconi and D.F. Hare. "Visualizing Program Designs Through PegaSys." *IEEE Computer*, 18(8):72–85, August 1985.

D. Harel. "On Visual Formalisms." *CACM*, 31(5):514–530, May 1988.

L. Cardelli. "Two–Dimensional Syntax for Functional Languages." In *Integrated Interactive Computing Systems—Proceedings of a Conference held in Stresa, Italy* (P. Degano and E. Sandewall, editors), pages 107–119, 1983. North Holland, Amsterdam, The Netherlands.

A Survey of Graphical Notations for Program Design–An Update

by

Leonard L. Tripp

Boeing Computer Services

Seattle, Washington

1.0 Introduction

Design can be defined as the process of initiating changes in man-made things [1]. Typically, the design process involves the exchange of information among a variety of people including customers, users, distributors, operators, and the design team. One key to information exchange is the design notation used.

In the design of software, at least two levels can be distinguished, system and program. System design is concerned with the architecture or global design of the software. Program design is concerned with the logic of the software and implementation details. This paper is focused on graphical notations for program design published since 1977. It is an update of earlier papers [2, 3, 4].

In this paper the graphical notations are grouped into three major categories: (1) box and line notations, (2) box notations, and (3) line notations. A box notation is a scheme made up of contiguous boxes with text contained in a box and where a box is typically a rectangle or some other enclosed figure. A line notation is a scheme which consists only of lines and no boxes. A box and line notation is a scheme where boxes are connected by lines in a defined pattern.

The paper compares graphical notations for program design as follows: Section 2 contains a group of five box and line notations; Section 3 contains a second group of three box and line notations; Section 4 contains a group of four box notations; Section 5 contains one example of a line notation; and section 6 contains a group of five notations that were designed for presentation on a computer display. In section 7 in comparing the notations, the three views (functional, structural, and behavioral) as defined in [5] are used. The functional view shows the system as a set of entities performing relevant tasks. This view includes a description of the task performed by each entity and the interaction of the entity with other entities and with the environment. The structural view shows how the system is put together: the components, the interfaces and the flow between them. This view also shows the environment and its interfaces, and information flows between it and the system. The behavioral view shows the way the system will respond to specific inputs: what states it will adopt, what outputs it will produce, what boundary conditions exist on the validity of inputs and states. Figure 1 contains flowcharts of basic control constructs that are used in describing the notations. In presenting some of the notations, T is defined to be a task which is composed of subtasks T1,...,Tn, n ≥ 1.

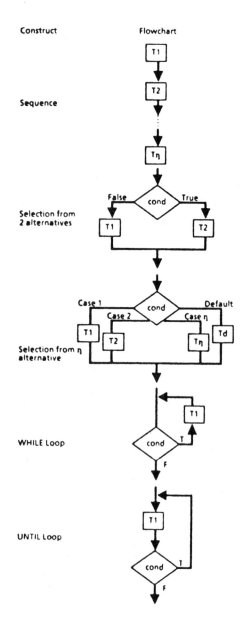

Figure 1. Basic Constructs

2.0 Box and Line Notations - Group 1

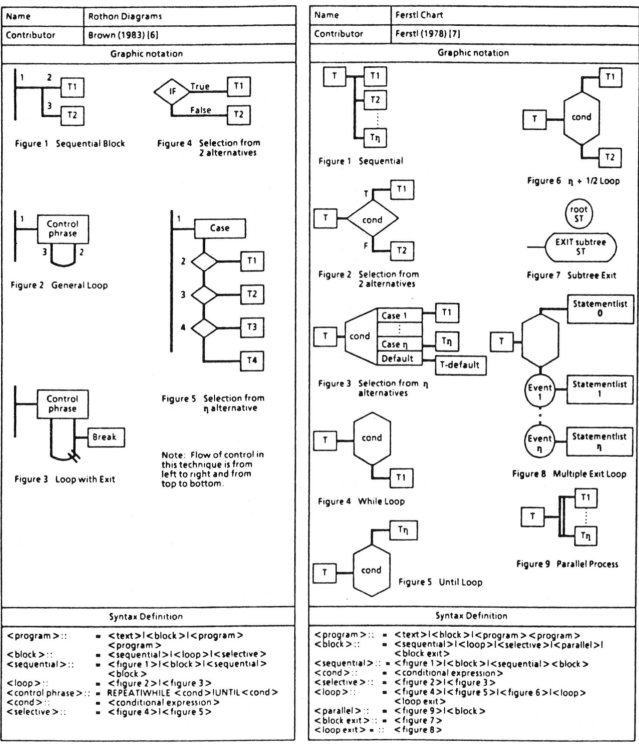

Name	Rothon Diagrams
Contributor	Brown (1983) [6]

Graphic notation

Figure 1 Sequential Block

Figure 4 Selection from 2 alternatives

Figure 2 General Loop

Figure 5 Selection from η alternative

Figure 3 Loop with Exit

Note: Flow of control in this technique is from left to right and from top to bottom.

Syntax Definition

\<program\> ::	= \<text\>l\<block\>l\<program\> \<program\>
\<block\> ::	= \<sequential\>l\<loop\>l\<selective\>
\<sequential\> ::	= \<figure 1\>l\<block\>l\<sequential\> \<block\>
\<loop\> ::	= \<figure 2\>l\<figure 3\>
\<control phrase\> ::	= REPEATIWHILE \<cond\>lUNTIL \<cond\>
\<cond\> ::	= \<conditional expression\>
\<selective\> ::	= \<figure 4\>l\<figure 5\>

Name	Ferstl Chart
Contributor	Ferstl (1978) [7]

Graphic notation

Figure 1 Sequential

Figure 6 η + 1/2 Loop

Figure 2 Selection from 2 alternatives

Figure 7 Subtree Exit

Figure 3 Selection from η alternatives

Figure 4 While Loop

Figure 8 Multiple Exit Loop

Figure 9 Parallel Process

Figure 5 Until Loop

Syntax Definition

\<program\> ::	= \<text\>l\<block\>l\<program\> \<program\>
\<block\> ::	= \<sequential\>l\<loop\>l\<selective\>l\<parallel\>l \<block exit\>
\<sequential\> ::	= \<figure 1\>l\<block\>l\<sequential\> \<block\>
\<cond\> ::	= \<conditional expression\>
\<selective\> ::	= \<figure 2\>l\<figure 3\>
\<loop\> ::	= \<figure 4\>l\<figure 5\>l\<figure 6\>l\<loop\> \<loop exit\>
\<parallel\> ::	= \<figure 9\>l\<block\>
\<block exit\> ::	= \<figure 7\>
\<loop exit\> = ::	\<figure 8\>

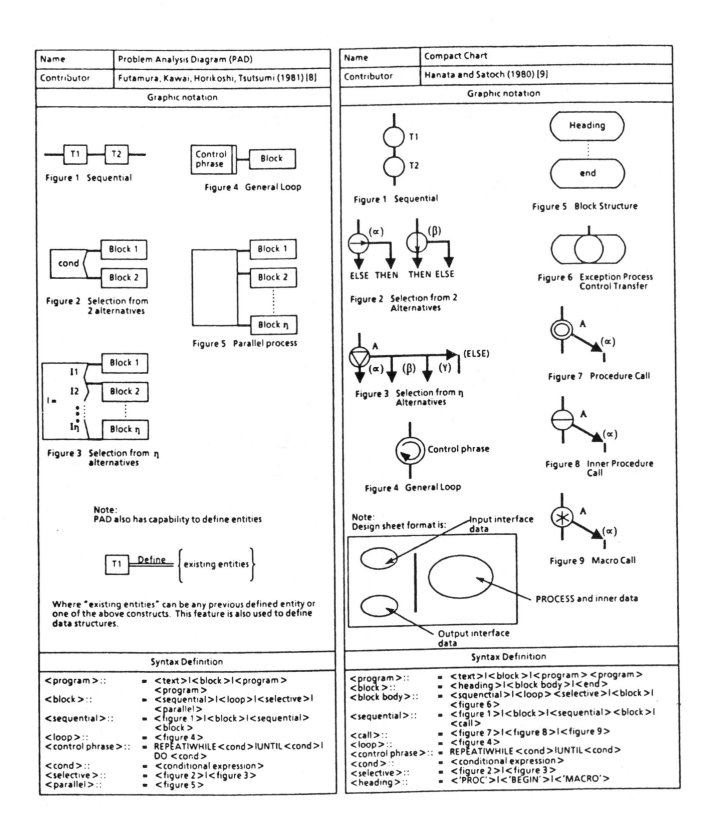

Name	Problem Analysis Diagram (PAD)
Contributor	Futamura, Kawai, Horikoshi, Tsutsumi (1981) [8]

Graphic notation

Figure 1   Sequential

Figure 4   General Loop

Figure 2   Selection from 2 alternatives

Figure 5   Parallel process

Figure 3   Selection from η alternatives

Note:
PAD also has capability to define entities

Where "existing entities" can be any previous defined entity or one of the above constructs. This feature is also used to define data structures.

Syntax Definition

```
<program> ::     = <text>I<block>I<program>
                    <program>
<block> ::       = <sequential>I<loop>I<selective>I
                    <parallel>
<sequential> ::  = <figure 1>I<block>I<sequential>
                    <block>
<loop> ::        = <figure 4>
<control phrase> :: = REPEATIWHILE <cond>IUNTIL<cond>I
                    DO <cond>
<cond> ::        = <conditional expression>
<selective> ::   = <figure 2>I<figure 3>
<parallel> ::    = <figure 5>
```

Name	Compact Chart
Contributor	Hanata and Satoch (1980) [9]

Graphic notation

Figure 1   Sequential

Figure 5   Block Structure

Figure 2   Selection from 2 Alternatives

Figure 6   Exception Process Control Transfer

Figure 3   Selection from η Alternatives

Figure 7   Procedure Call

Figure 4   General Loop

Figure 8   Inner Procedure Call

Note:
Design sheet format is:

Input interface data

PROCESS and inner data

Output interface data

Figure 9   Macro Call

Syntax Definition

```
<program> ::      = <text>I<block>I<program> <program>
<block> ::        = <heading>I<block body>I<end>
<block body> ::   = <squential>I<loop>I<selective>I<block>I
                    <figure 6>
<sequential> ::   = <figure 1>I<block>I<sequential> <block>I
                    <call>
<call> ::         = <figure 7>I<figure 8>I<figure 9>
<loop> ::         = <figure 4>
<control phrase> :: = REPEATIWHILE <cond>IUNTIL<cond>
<cond> ::         = <conditional expression>
<selective> ::    = <figure 2>I<figure 3>
<heading> ::      = <'PROC'>I<'BEGIN'>I<'MACRO'>
```

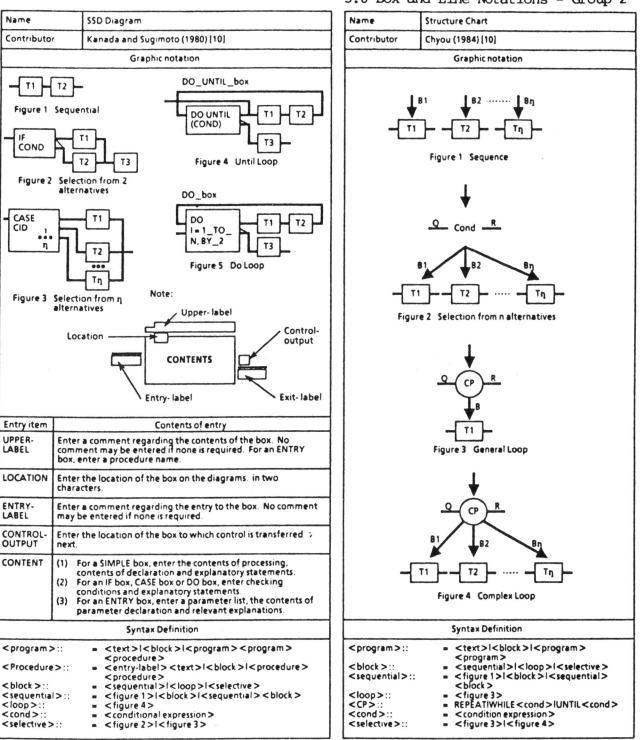

Name	SSD Diagram
Contributor	Kanada and Sugimoto (1980) [10]

Graphic notation

Figure 1 Sequential

Figure 2 Selection from 2 alternatives

Figure 3 Selection from η alternatives

DO_UNTIL_box

Figure 4 Until Loop

DO_box

Figure 5 Do Loop

Note:

Upper-label
Location
Control-output
CONTENTS
Entry-label
Exit-label

Entry item	Contents of entry
UPPER-LABEL	Enter a comment regarding the contents of the box. No comment may be entered if none is required. For an ENTRY box, enter a procedure name.
LOCATION	Enter the location of the box on the diagrams. in two characters.
ENTRY-LABEL	Enter a comment regarding the entry to the box. No comment may be entered if none is required.
CONTROL-OUTPUT	Enter the location of the box to which control is transferred ; next.
CONTENT	(1) For a SIMPLE box, enter the contents of processing, contents of declaration and explanatory statements. (2) For an IF box, CASE box or DO box, enter checking conditions and explanatory statements. (3) For an ENTRY box, enter a parameter list, the contents of parameter declaration and relevant explanations.

Syntax Definition

```
<program>::   = <text>I<block>I<program> <program>
                  <procedure>
<Procedure>:: = <entry-label><text>I<block>I<procedure>
                  <procedure>
<block>::     = <sequential>I<loop>I<selective>
<sequential>::= <figure 1>I<block>I<sequential> <block>
<loop>::      = <figure 4>
<cond>::      = <conditional expression>
<selective>:: = <figure 2>I<figure 3>
```

Name	Structure Chart
Contributor	Chyou (1984) [10]

Graphic notation

Figure 1 Sequence

Figure 2 Selection from n alternatives

Figure 3 General Loop

Figure 4 Complex Loop

Syntax Definition

```
<program>::   = <text>I<block>I<program>
                  <program>
<block>::     = <sequential>I<loop>I<selective>
<sequential>::= <figure 1>I<block>I<sequential>
                  <block>
<loop>::      = <figure 3>
<CP>::        = REPEATIWHILE<cond>IUNTIL<cond>
<cond>::      = <condition expression>
<selective>:: = <figure 3>I<figure 4>
```

63

Name	Doran Chart
Contributor	Doran and Tate (1972) [12]

Graphic notation

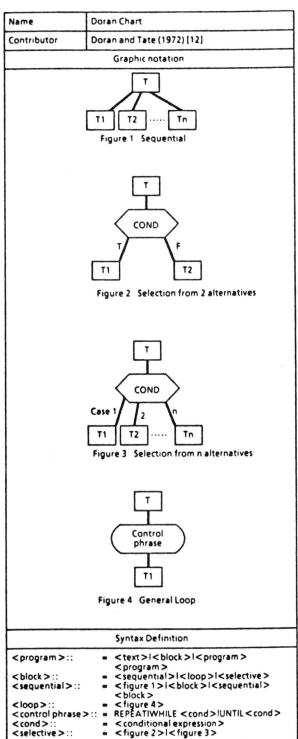

Figure 1   Sequential

Figure 2   Selection from 2 alternatives

Figure 3   Selection from n alternatives

Figure 4   General Loop

Syntax Definition

```
<program> ::      =  <text> I <block> I <program>
                     <program>
<block> ::        =  <sequential> I <loop> I <selective>
<sequential> ::   =  <figure 1> I <block> I <sequential>
                     <block>
<loop> ::         =  <figure 4>
<control phrase> ::  =  REPEATIWHILE <cond> IUNTIL <cond>
<cond> ::         =  <conditional expression>
<selective> ::    =  <figure 2> I <figure 3>
```

Name	Schematic Logic
Contributor	Jensen and Tonies (1979) [13]

Graphic notation

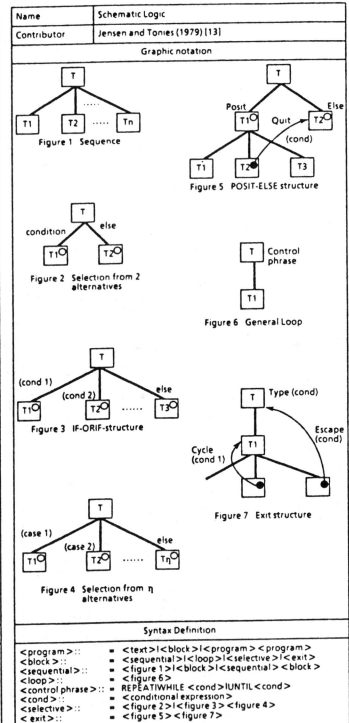

Figure 1   Sequence

Figure 5   POSIT-ELSE structure

Figure 2   Selection from 2 alternatives

Figure 6   General Loop

Figure 3   IF-ORIF-structure

Figure 7   Exit structure

Figure 4   Selection from η alternatives

Syntax Definition

```
<program> ::      =  <text> I <block> I <program> <program>
<block> ::        =  <sequential> I <loop> I <selective> I <exit>
<sequential> ::   =  <figure 1> I <block> I <sequential> <block>
<loop> ::         =  <figure 6>
<control phrase> ::  =  REPEATIWHILE <cond> IUNTIL <cond>
<cond> ::         =  <conditional expression>
<selective> ::    =  <figure 2> I <figure 3> <figure 4>
<exit> ::         =  <figure 5> <figure 7>
```

4.0 Box Notations

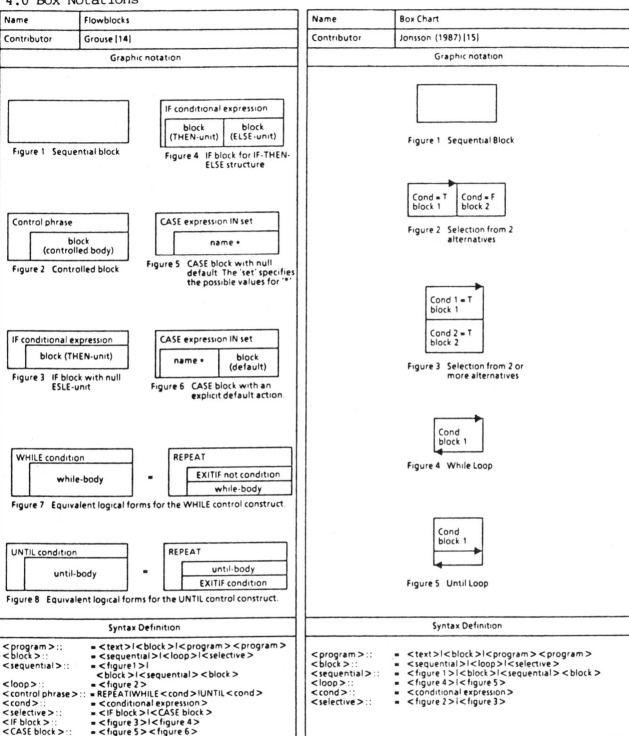

Name	Flowblocks
Contributor	Grouse [14]

Graphic notation

Figure 1 Sequential block

IF conditional expression

| block (THEN-unit) | block (ELSE-unit) |

Figure 4 IF block for IF-THEN-ELSE structure

Control phrase

block (controlled body)

Figure 2 Controlled block

CASE expression IN set

name •

Figure 5 CASE block with null default. The 'set' specifies the possible values for '•'

IF conditional expression

block (THEN-unit)

Figure 3 IF block with null ESLE-unit

CASE expression IN set

| name • | block (default) |

Figure 6 CASE block with an explicit default action.

WHILE condition

while-body

=

REPEAT

EXITIF not condition

while-body

Figure 7 Equivalent logical forms for the WHILE control construct.

UNTIL condition

until-body

=

REPEAT

until-body

EXITIF condition

Figure 8 Equivalent logical forms for the UNTIL control construct.

Syntax Definition

```
<program> ::     = <text>I<block>I<program> <program>
<block> ::       = <sequential>I<loop>I<selective>
<sequential> ::  = <figure1>I
                   <block>I<sequential> <block>
<loop> ::        = <figure 2>
<control phrase> :: = REPEATIWHILE <cond>IUNTIL <cond>
<cond> ::        = <conditional expression>
<selective> ::   = <IF block>I<CASE block>
<IF block> ::    = <figure 3>I<figure 4>
<CASE block> ::  = <figure 5> <figure 6>
```

Name	Box Chart
Contributor	Jonsson (1987) [15]

Graphic notation

Figure 1 Sequential Block

| Cond = T block 1 | Cond = F block 2 |

Figure 2 Selection from 2 alternatives

Cond 1 = T block 1

Cond 2 = T block 2

Figure 3 Selection from 2 or more alternatives

Cond block 1

Figure 4 While Loop

Cond block 1

Figure 5 Until Loop

Syntax Definition

```
<program> ::     = <text>I<block>I<program> <program>
<block> ::       = <sequential>I<loop>I<selective>
<sequential> ::  = <figure 1>I<block>I<sequential> <block>
<loop> ::        = <figure 4>I<figure 5>
<cond> ::        = <conditional expression>
<selective> ::   = <figure 2>I<figure 3>
```

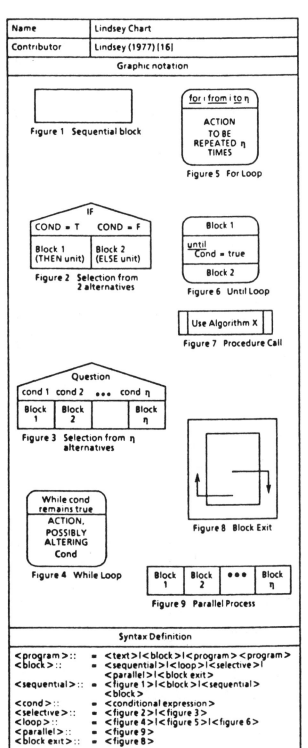

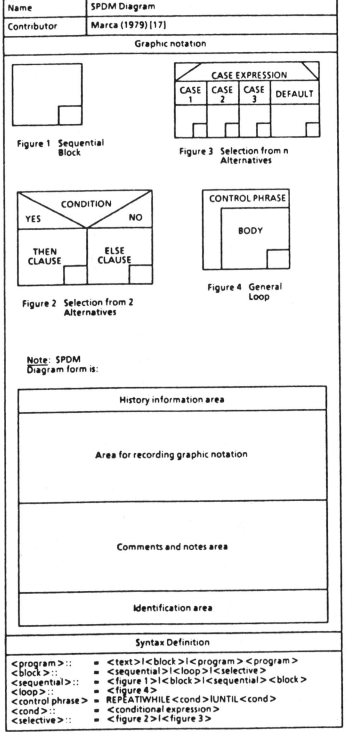

5.0 Line Notations

Name	FP Diagrams
Contributor	Pagan [18]

Graphic notation

In the following description of the functionals, f, f1, f2, etc. stand for arbitrary functions and b, b1, b2, etc. stand for arbitrary objects

(1) The <u>constant</u> functional. The graphical for

represents a function that maps all non-bottom arguments to the object b.

(2) The <u>construction</u> functional. The form

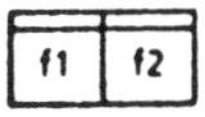

denotes a new function f3 such that;
f3 : b = <f1 : b, f2 : b>

(3) The <u>composition</u> functional. The form

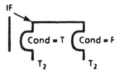

corresponds to f1 • f2 and denotes a new function f3 such that;
f3 : b = f1 : (f2 : b)

(4) The <u>insert</u> functional. The form

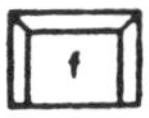

denotes a new function which, when applied to an argument of the form <b1, b2, ... bn>, acts like the ordinary infix expression
b1 f b2 f ... f bn

(5) The <u>apply to all</u> functional. The form

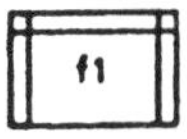

denotes a new function f2 such that;,
f2 : <b1, b2, ..., bn> = <f1 : b1, f1 : b2, ..., f1 : bn>

(6) The <u>condition</u> functional. The form

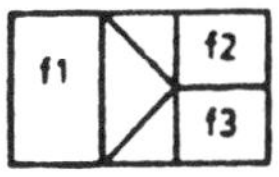

denotes a new function f4 such that;,

f4 : b = { f2 : b, if f1 : b = 'T'
          f3 : b, if f1 : b = 'F'
          bottom, otherwise

Name	Dimensional Flowchart
Contributor	Witty (1977) [19]

Graphic notation

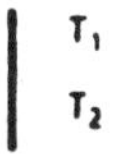

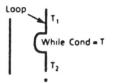

Figure 1   Sequential

Figure 4   General Loop

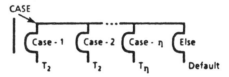

Next task after either T_1 or T_2

Figure 2   Selection from 2 alternatives

Next task after case

Figure 3   Selection from η alternatives

Note:
Scheme can also be used to document data structures.

Syntax Definition

<program> ::	= <text>I<block>I<program><program>
<block> ::	= <sequential>I<loop>I<selective>
<sequential> ::	= <figure 1>I<block>I<sequential><block>
<loop> ::	= <figure 4>
<cond> ::	= <conditional expression>
<selective> ::	= <figure 2>I<figure 3>

6.0 Computer Display Notations

Name	GREENPRINT
Contributor	Belady, Evangelististi, Power (1980) [20]

Name	UFC Diagram
Contributor	Harel, Norvig, Rood, To (1979) [21]

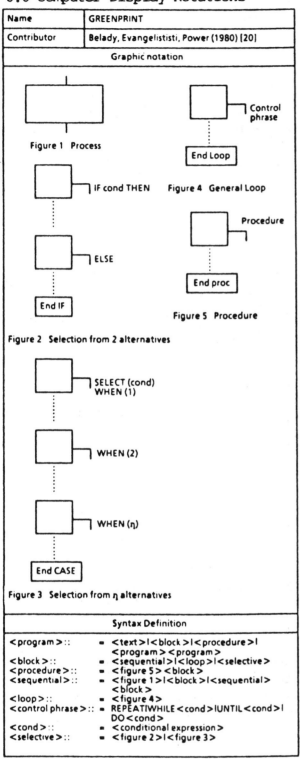

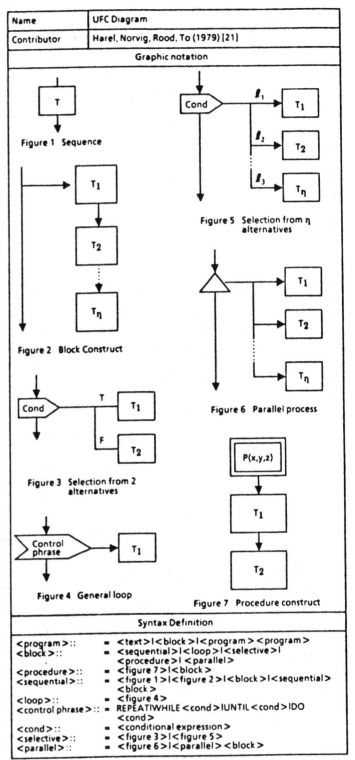

Name	Graphical Structured Flowchart
Contributor	Robillard (1981) [22]

Graphic notation

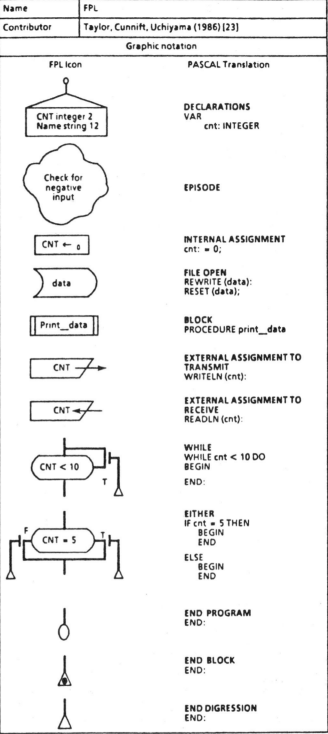

Figure 1   Sequence

Figure 2   Selection from 1 alternative

Figure 3   General Loop

Figure 4   Selection from η alternatives

Note:
After a task is executed, a dash is used to indicate if control is proceeding forward or backward. bottom.

Syntax Definition	
<program> ::	= <test>I<block>I<program> <program>
<block> ::	= <sequential>I<loop>I<selective>
<sequential> ::	= <figure 1>I<block>I<sequential> <block>
<loop> ::	= <figure 3>
<CP> ::	= REPEATIWHILE <Ci>IUNTIL<Ci>
<Ci> ::	= <conditional expression>
<selective> ::	= <figure 2>I<figure 3>

Name	FPL
Contributor	Taylor, Cunnift, Uchiyama (1986) [23]

Graphic notation

FPL Icon   PASCAL Translation

CNT integer 2
Name string 12

DECLARATIONS
VAR
        cnt: INTEGER

Check for negative input

EPISODE

CNT ← 0

INTERNAL ASSIGNMENT
cnt: = 0;

data

FILE OPEN
REWRITE (data);
RESET (data);

Print__data

BLOCK
PROCEDURE print__data

CNT

EXTERNAL ASSIGNMENT TO TRANSMIT
WRITELN (cnt);

CNT

EXTERNAL ASSIGNMENT TO RECEIVE
READLN (cnt);

CNT < 10

WHILE
WHILE cnt < 10 DO
BEGIN

END;

CNT = 5

EITHER
IF cnt = 5 THEN
        BEGIN
        END

ELSE
        BEGIN
        END

END PROGRAM
END;

END BLOCK
END;

END DIGRESSION
END;

7.0 Summary

The notations surveyed in this paper as shown in Figure 2 are similar in capability. Some such as the Rothon Diagram [5] and Compact Chart [9] are distinctive in their graphic formulation. Several such Ferstl [7], Lindsey [16], and Harel [21] handle parallel control structures. The Pagan notation [18] is designed to be a functional programming language. FPL [23] is a set of icons to teach the novice programming is a graphical way how to program. Most of the notations are strongly influenced by the basic control structures of structured programming.

One of the trends observed is the movement toward visual programming capability. This trend is influenced by the common knowledge that the human mind is strongly visually oriented and that people acquire information at a significantly higher rate by discovering relationships in complex pictures than by reading text. See [24] for further information on visual programming.

In the area of graphical program design notations, the only notation to be standardized is the flowchart. There is a need to identify the leading notations and promote efforts to standardize them at the national and international level.

References

1. J.C. Jones, Design Methods: seeds of human futures, Wiley-Interscience, London, 1970.

2. L.J. Peters and L.L. Tripp, "Design Representation Schemes," Proceedings of MRI Symposium on Computer Software Engineering, 1976, pp. 31-56.

3. L.J. Peters, "Software Representation and Composition Techniques," Proceedings of the IEEE, Vol. 68, No. 9, Sept. 1980, pp. 1085-1092.

4. R. Schneyer, "A Survey of Graphic Algorithmic Representation Techniques," Interface, Spring 1984, pp. 38-48.

5. R. Firth, B. Wood, R. Pethia, L. Roberts, V. Mosley, and T. Dolce, "A Classification Scheme for Software Development Methods," Technical Report SEI-87-TR-41, Software Engineering Institute, Carnegie Mellon University, Nov. 1987.

6. E.J. Brown, "On the Application of Rothon Diagrams to Data Abstraction," SIGPLAN Notices, Vol. 18, No. 12, Dec. 1983, pp. 17-24.

Contributor	Functional view			Structural view				Behavioral view			Other		
	Note 1	2	3	4	5	6	7	8	9	10	11	12	13
Brown	●			●				●					
Ferstl	●			●				●	●	●			
Futamura	●			●			●	●					
Hanata		●			●	●	●	●					●
Kanada	●			●		●		●					
Chyou	●				●			●					
Doran	●				●			●					
Jonsen	●				●			●	●				
Grouse	●			●				●					
Jonsson	●			●				●					
Lindsey	●			●		●	●	●	●	●			
Marca	●			●				●			●		
Pagan			●					●					●
Witty	●			●			●	●					
Belady	●					●		●					
Harel	●					●		●		●			
Robillard	●			●				●					
Taylor	●					●		●				●	

Notes:
1. Text description integrated with notation
2. Text separate from graphic notation
3. Syntactic representation of function
4. Implicit structure
5. Explicit structure
6. Procedures
7. Data structures
8. Basis control structure
9. Exit structure
10. Parallel control structure
11. Document preparation conventions
12. Executable specification
13. Functional language support

Figure 2   Comparision of Design Notations

7. O. Ferstl, "Flowcharting by Stepwise Refinement," SIGPLAN Notices, Vol. 13, No. 1, Jan. 1978, pp. 34-42.

8. Y. Futamura, T. Kawai, H. Horikoshi, and M. Tsutsumi, "Development of Computer Program by Problem Analysis (PAD)," Proceedings of 5th International Conference on Software Engineering, 1981, pp. 325-332.

9. S. Hanata and T. Satoh, "COMPACT CHART - A Program Logic Notation with High Describability and Understand-ability," SIGPLAN Notices, Vol. 15, No. 9, Sept. 1980, pp. 32-38.

10. Y. Kanda and M. Sugimoto, Software Diagram Description: SDD and Its Application," Proceedings of COMPSAC-80, 1980, pp. 300-305.

11. S.C. Chyou, "Structure Charts and Program Correctness Proofs," Proceedings of the 7th International Conference on Software Engineering, 1984, pp. 486-498.

12. R. Doran and G. Tate, "An Approach to Structured Programming," Masey University Technical Publication, June 1972.

13. R.W. Jensen and C.C. Tonies, Software Engineering, Prentice-Hall, Englewood Cliffs, N.J., 1979, pp. 267-273.

14. P. Grouse, "FLOWBLOCKS - A Technique for Structured Programming," SIGPLAN Notices, Vol. , No. , 1977, pp. 46-56.

15. D. Jonsson, "Pancode and Boxcharts: Structured Programming Revisited," SIGPLAN Notices, Vol. 22, No. 8, Aug. 1987, pp. 89-98.

16. G.H. Lindsey, "Structure Charts: A Structured Alternative to Flowcharts," SIGPLAN Notices, Vol. 12, No. 11, Nov. 1977.

17. D. Marca, "A Method for Specifying Structure Programs," ACM SIGSOFT Software Engineering Notes, Vol. 4, No. 3, July 1979, pp. 22-31.

18. F.G. Pagan, "A Graphical FP Language," SIGPLAN Notices, Vol. 22, No. 3, March 1987, pp. 21-39.

19. R.W. Witty, "The design and construction of hierarchically structured software," Proceedings of Pragmatic and Sensible Software, Online Ltd, Feb. 1977, pp. 361-388

20. L.A. Belady, C.J. Evangelisti, and L.R. Power, "GREENPRINT: A graphic representation of structured programs,", IBM System Journal, Vol. 19, No. 4, 1980, pp. 542-553.

21. D. Harel, P. Norvig, J. Rood, and T. To, "A Universal Flowcharter," Proceedings of AIAA Computers in Aerospace Conference, 1979, pp. 218-224.

22. P.N. Robillard, "On an Experimental Tool for General Software Development," Proceedings of the 14th Hawaii International Conference on Systems Sciences, 1981, pp. 90-97.

23. R.P. Taylor, N. Cunniff, and M. Uchiyama, "Learning, Research and the Graphical Representation of Programming," Proceedings of 1986 Fall Joint Computer Conference, 1986, pp. 56-63.

24. G. Raeder, "A Survey of Current Graphical Programming Techniques," IEEE Computer, August 1985, pp. 11-25.

Flowchart Techniques for Structured Programming

I. Nassi*
and
B. Shneiderman**

*Digital Equipment Corporation
Maynard, MA 01745

**Dept. of Computer Science
SUNY--Stoney Brook
Stoney Brook, NY 11794

August 1972

SIGPLAN NOTICES 8, 8
August 1973

Abstract: With the advent of structured programming and GOTO-less programming, a method is needed to model computation in simply ordered structures, each representing a complete thought possibly defined in terms of other thoughts as yet undefined. A model is needed which prevents unrestricted transfers of control and has a control structure closer to languages amenable to structured programming. We present an attempt at such a model.

Additional Notes (August 1981)

Since the appearance of our paper, several texts have used structured flowcharts:

- Geller, Dan and Dan Freedman, *Structured Programming in APL*, Winthrop Publishers, Cambridge, Mass., 1976.
- Haskell, Richard, *FORTRAN Programming Using Structured Flowcharts*, Science Research Associates, 1978.
- Keiburtz, Richard—Prentice Hall, Inc., Englewood Cliffs, N.J.

Structured Programming and Problem Solving with ALGOL W, 1975.
Structured Programming and Problem Solving with PL/I, 1977.
Structured Programming and Problem Solving with PASCAL, 1978.

- Merchant, Michael, *FORTRAN 77 Language and Style*, Wadsworth Publishing Co, Belmont, Calif., 1981.
- Orr, Kenneth, *Structured Systems Development*, Yourdon Press, New York, 1977.
- Pollack, Seymour V. and Theodor Sterling, *A Guide to PL/I*, Third Edition, Holt, Rinehart and Winston, New York, 1981.
- Ruston, Henry, *Programming with PL/I*, McGraw-Hill Book Co., New York, 1978.
- Weinberg, Gerald, Workbook and Films on Structured Programming *Edutronics Films*, 1975.
- Yourdon, Ed, Chris Gane, and Trish Sarson, *Learning to Program in Structured COBOL*, Yourdon Press, New York, 1976.

Several other texts using structured flowcharts are in preparation. Articles referencing our ideas and making further contributions include:

*Presently at Apple Cambridge Research Laboratory, 238 Main Street, Cambridge, MA 02142.

**Presently at Dept. of Computer Science, University of Maryland, College Park, MD 20742.

- Brooke, J. B. and K. D. Duncan, "An Experimental Study of Flowcharts as an Aid to Identification of Procedural Faults," *Ergonomics, Vol. 23*, No. 4, 1980, pp. 387-399.

- Brooke, J. B. and K. D. Duncan, "Experimental Studies of Flowchart Use at Different Stages of Program Debugging," *Ergonomics, Vol. 23*, No. 11, 1980, pp. 1057-1091.

- Chen, Thomas L. C., "Reflection on the Implementation of a Software Design," *IEEE Proc. COMPSAC*, 1979, pp. 69-73.

- Friedman, Daniel P. and Stuart C. Shapiro, "A Case for the While-Until," *ACM SIGPLAN Notices*, Vol. 9, No. 7, July 1974.

- Haskell, Boddy, and Jackson, "Use of Structured Flowcharts in Undergraduate Computer Science Curriculum," *ACM SIGCSE Sixth Technical Symposium on Computer Science Education*, ACM, Inc., New York, July 1976.

- Meredith, Carlisle F., "A Structured Graphical Database Modeling Technique," In *The Technology of Data-base Management Systems*, 3rd Ed., R.A. Bassler and J.J. Logan, Editors, College Readings Inc., Alexandria, Va., 1976, pp. 251-264.

- Roy, Patrick, "Linear Flowchart Generator for a Structured Language," *ACM SIGPLAN Notices*, Vol. 11, No. 11, Nov. 1976.

- Van Gelder, Allen, "Structured Programming in COBOL: An Approach for Applications Programmers," *Communications of ACM*, Vol. 20, No. 1, Jan. 1977.

- Witt, Jan, "The COLUMBUS Approach," *IEEE Transactions on Software Engineering*, Vol. SE-1, No. 4, Dec. 1975.

Other articles simply reference our work in their discussion. Through personal contacts, I am aware of extensive use of our structured flowcharts in Burroughs, IBM, GE, ATT, Bell Labs, Siemens, U.S. Navy, and numerous universities.

Now Chapin has made a series of minor variations on the structured flowchart idea and pretentiously christened them Chapin charts. He writes and lectures extensively on this topic.

An excellent review and tutorial article appears in *ACM SIGSOFT—Software Engineering Notes*, Volume 3, Number 5 (November 1978) which contains papers from a "Software Quality and Assurance Workshop" held in San Diego, Calif., November 15-17, 1978. The paper, by Cornelia M. Yoder and Marilyn L. Schrag (both of IBM Endicott), is titled "Nassi-Shneiderman Charts: An Alternative to Flowcharts for Design." This article has been reprinted in the Auerbach Computer Programming Management series.

Graphics based version of structured flowcharts are described in:

- C. Thomas Watson, "Star-Charter: A Design Aid and Documentation Tool for Structured Programs," *IBM Technical Report 07.616*, Sept. 1976.

- Nam Ng, "A Graphical Editor for Programming Using Structured Charts," *IBM Research Report RJ2344*, Sept. 19, 1978, San Jose, Calif.

- H.P. Frei, D.L. Weller, and R. Williams, "A Graphics-Based Programming Support System," *ACM SIGGRAPH*, Vol. 12, No. 3, 1978.

Typically, computer programs go through various phases of formulation and definition. During one of these phases a flowchart may be drawn to describe the program at a level of abstraction somewhere between the problem statement and the code of the completed program. The programmer designs the flowchart in such a way that it can be coded easily into a convenient programming language, yet keeps the underlying algorithm sufficiently transparent to think about in modular terms. Unfortunately the conventional flowchart language has aspects that make it both too powerful and yet too simple a language to model current programming techniques. These techniques tend toward a more restrictive control structure which the flowchart cannot describe nicely. Certain control structures in programming languages, such as iteration, have no direct translation to flowchart language and must be built from simpler control structures, thereby losing the forest in the trees. On the other hand, the power the unrestricted GOTO affords presents problems in logical analysis of programs and program verification, optimization, and debugging. The translation from flowchart to computer program is a one to many relationship whose output ranges over programs only some of which are legible, concise, and efficient.

Top-down programming as defined by Mills[1] (or the *top-down modularization* of Wulf et al.[2]) is the technique of analyzing an idea to form simpler ideas, and recursively applying the technique.

These ideas may take the form of programs, subroutines, macros, lines of code, or other modular forms. Dijkstra's *structured programming*[3] organizes program components into levels which he calls *pearls*, and strings them together into a *necklace* (read "programs"). In addition, Dijkstra proposes abolishing the use of unrestricted GOTOs to help prevent unwieldy programs which are difficult to analyze[4].

The theoretical basis for our representation of structured programs was given by Bohm and Jacopini[5]. They described a flowchart language whose alphabet is as shown in Figure 1 and then proceeded to prove that any program written in that language could also be written in a modified subset of that language whose alphabet consists only of the characters shown in Figure 2 and interpreted processes on a Boolean stack:

$$K(v,w) = w$$

$$T(w) = (t,w)$$

$$F(w) = (f,w)$$

$$W(v,w) = v \quad vc\ \{t,f\}$$

Note that any program in the subset language is a program in the flowchart language, and that no arbitrary transfers of control are permitted or even necessary.

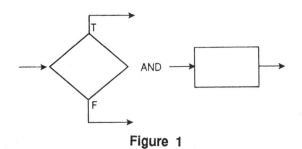

Figure 1

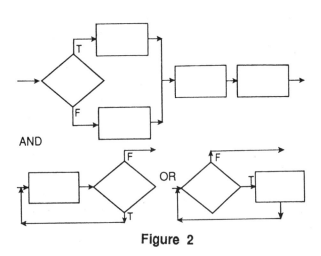

Figure 2

Their method of normalization, although constructive, suffered from the fact that it produced obscure programs due to the introduction of Booleans whose use was strictly overhead. It was argued[4] that this sort of normalization should be an integral part of the thought processes that contribute to writing a program, i.e. it should be done a priori.

With the advent of structured programming, top-down programming, and GOTO-free programming, a method is needed to model computation in simply ordered structures, each representing a complete thought possibly defined in terms of other thoughts as yet undefined.

We propose a flowchart language whose control structure is closer to that of languages amenable to structured programming. Its main advantages over the conventional flowchart language are:

1. The scope of iteration is well-defined and visible.

2. The scope of IF-THEN-ELSE clauses is well-defined and visible; moreover, the conditions on process boxes embedded within compound conditionals can be easily seen from the diagram.

3. The scope of local and global variables is immediately obvious.

4. Arbitrary transfers of control are impossible.

5. Complete thought structures can and should fit on no more than one page (i.e. no off-page connectors).

6. Recursion has a trivial representation.

Any set of flowchart symbols must represent the basic control operations that are available to the programmer. Certainly, the process, iteration, and decision functions are such basic operations. In addition we include a BEGIN-END symbol for representing block structure and for performing some of the functions of the START and END blocks in earlier flowcharting systems. These four symbols provide a notational basis for representing most operations but additional symbols and concepts will be introduced later to improve the practicality and generality of the notation.

Combinations of the four basic symbols may be made to form *structures*, all of which are labeled and are rectangular in shape. The absence of any representation for the branch instruction forces the user to design programs in a structured manner free from branch instructions.

The *process symbol* (Figure 3) is used to represent assignment, input/output statements as well as procedure calls and returns. Additional notation may be introduced to distinguish between these three classes of statements. The shape of the process symbol is rectangular but its particular dimensions may be chosen at the user's convenience. It should be clear that whenever a process symbol occurs, an entire structure could be put in its place. A labeled process symbol standing alone is a structure.

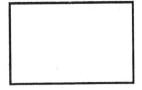

Figure 3

The *decision symbol* (Figure 4) is used to represent the IF-THEN-ELSE statement found in PL/I, ALGOL, and similar languages. The central triangle contains a Boolean expression, the left and right triangles contain a T or an F (or other notation) to represent the possible outcomes and the process symbols contain the sequence of operations to be performed depending on the outcome of the test.

The *iteration symbol* (Figure 5) is used to represent looping statements such as the DO WHILE statement of PL/I or

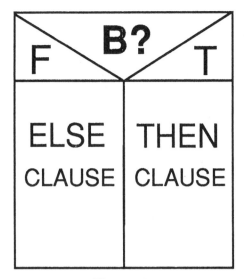

Figure 4

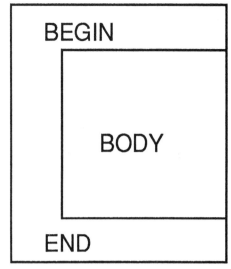

Figure 6

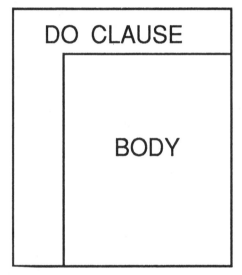

Figure 5

Example 1: The structure in Figure 7 represents a simple program to calculate the factorial of a non-negative integer N using an iterative approach.

Example 2: The complex nesting of a standard matrix multiplication routine is embodied in the structure in Figure 8.

As was mentioned earlier, a process symbol may represent a call to another structure. Recursion may be repre-

the FOR statement of ALGOL. The body of the iteration is a structure of arbitrary complexity. The form of the iteration symbol has the advantage that it clearly shows the scope of the iteration. The left hand portion of the symbol provides a path to follow if the required number of iterations has been completed (or some condition terminates the iteration). Nested iterations are easily represented by nesting the symbol as many times as necessary (see Example 2).

The *BEGIN-END symbol* (Figure 6) is used to represent the BEGIN-END statement pair as found in ALGOL or PL/I. This symbol is akin to the brackets that many programmers draw in the left margin of their programs to indicate nested groups of statements. This technique enables the programmer to easily recognize the scope of his declarations and the logical structures in his program. The body of the BEGIN-END symbol is a structure of arbitrary complexity.

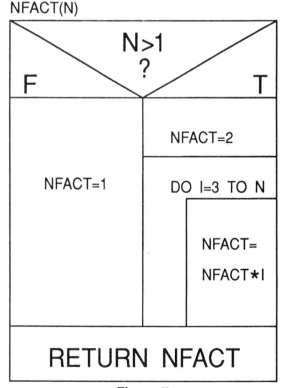

Figure 7

MATMUL

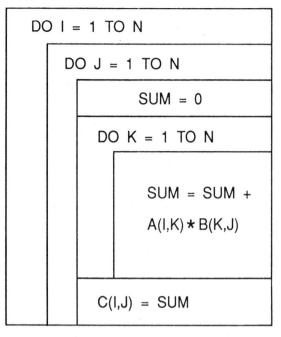

Figure 8

sented quite naturally by a process symbol containing the label of the structure in which the process symbol is located.

Example 3: Figure 9 represents a program to calculate the number of combinations of N items taken K at a time. The main structure refers to another structure for a recursive calculation of factorial.

Example 4: The design of the decision symbol forces the programmer to recognize the significance of compounding IF-THEN-ELSE statements. In this example (Figure 10) the logical conditions that hold for each of the seven process symbols is visually determined:

1. not A
2. not A and not B
3. not A and B
4. A and not C
5. A and not C and not D
6. A and not C and D
7. A and C

Not only does this notation help the programmer to think in an orderly manner, it forces him or her to do so.

The absence of any representation of the GOTO or branch statement requires the programmer to work without it: a task which becomes increasingly easy with practice. Programmers who first learn to design programs with these symbols never develop the bad habits which other flowchart notation systems permit. The development of programs with these symbols forces a structured program and helps prevent the programmer from developing a poorly organized program.

MAIN

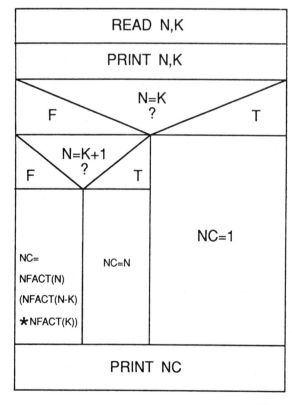

NFACT(N)

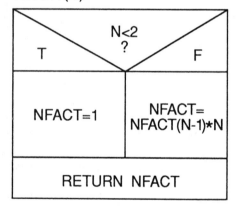

Figure 9

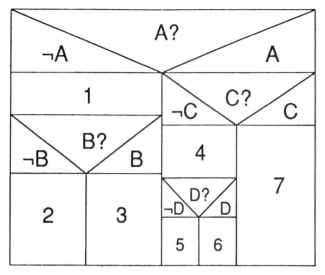
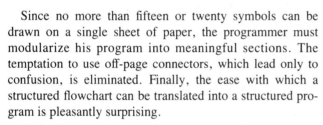

Figure 10

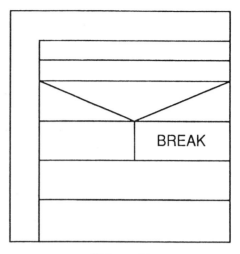

Figure 11

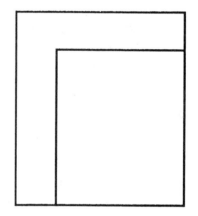

Figure 12

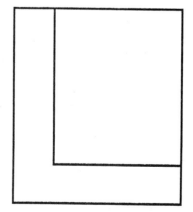

Figure 13

Since no more than fifteen or twenty symbols can be drawn on a single sheet of paper, the programmer must modularize his program into meaningful sections. The temptation to use off-page connectors, which lead only to confusion, is eliminated. Finally, the ease with which a structured flowchart can be translated into a structured program is pleasantly surprising.

We believe that the control structures described above are sufficient to get the flavor of the model. However, there are no strict rules regarding their use. What we have described is for the most part language independent. But in order to make the transition from flowchart to computer program more efficient, we need to express more powerful language constructs in our model.

BLISS[2,6] and BCPL[7] are two languages for systems implementation. There is no GOTO statement in BLISS and its use in BCPL is discouraged. To compensate the desire for some kind of limited forward transfer, BLISS uses a construct whose scope is limited, namely the EXIT construct (e.g. EXITBLOCK, EXITLOOP, etc.). BCPL uses the BREAK statement to terminate the smallest textually enclosing iteration, and the LOOP statement to transfer control to the point just before the test (and possible increment if it is an incremental iteration) in an iteration. To use specific language constructs like these one might write as shown in Figure 11 since a BREAK statement only makes sense in a conditional.

BCPL is rich in convenient control and iteration structures and provides for loop testing at the top (FOR, WHILE, and UNTIL), at the bottom (REPEATWHILE, REPEAT-UNTIL) and at arbitrary points within the iteration (the REPEAT and BREAK combination). The first construct is given in Figure 12. The second, as one might guess is as shown in Figure 13. The third, which is not so natural, is

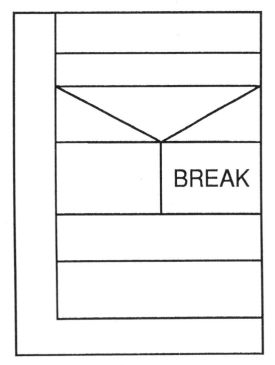

Figure 14

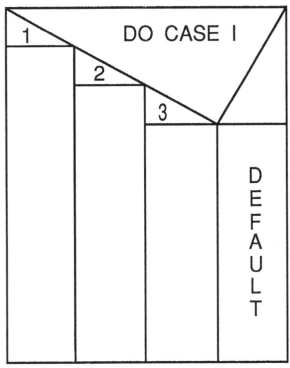

Figure 16

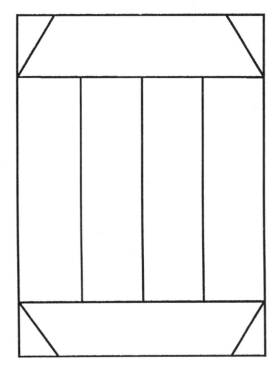

Figure 15

shown in Figure 14. Parallel processing can be represented as shown in Figure 15. The CASE statement can be represented as shown in Figure 16.

The point is that the model is sufficiently powerful to allow the programmer to build his own structure as he identifies patterns of other structures, or as the need arises.

Although we have not made the programmer's job any easier, and in fact more forethought may be required, we believe the benefits in debugging, self-documentation, and maintenance greatly outweigh the additional cost.

Further explorations are revolving about the context-free nature of this language. We also note that while the Contour Model nicely describes ALGOL execution, it is even a nicer description of the execution of programs written from structured flowcharts.[8]

References

1. *Top-Down Programming in Large Systems* by H. Mills. Debugging Techniques in Large Systems (Courant Institute).
2. *Reflections on a Systems Programming Language* by Wulf et al. SIGPLAN Notices Vol. 6 No. 9.
3. *Structured Programming* by E.W. Dijkstra. NATO Science Committee—Software Engineering Techniques April 1970.
4. *GO TO Statement Considered Harmful* by E.W. Dijkstra. CACM Vol. 11 No. 3.
5. *Flow Diagrams, Turing Machines and Languages With Only Two Formation Rules* by C. Bohm and G. Jacopini. CACM Vol. 9 No. 5.
6. *BLISS Reference Manual* by Wulf et al. Carnegie-Mellon Technical Report.
7. *BCPL Reference Manual* by M. Richards.
8. *The Contour Model of Block Structured Processes* by John B. Johnston SIGPLAN Notices Vol. 6 No. 2.

*To improve the readability of programs over existing techniques,
a new program representation termed GREENPRINT has been developed and is discussed in this paper. GREENPRINTs (the name
taken from the phosphor fluorescence of certain display terminals
and paralleling the term blueprints) are tree-structured diagrams
together with source code statements that represent the control
structure of programs. Discussed in this paper are the diagramming conventions, control flow methodology, presentation
graphics, and practical experience with GREENPRINTs.*

GREENPRINT: A graphic representation of structured programs

by L. A. Belady, C. J. Evangelisti, and L. R. Power

Flowcharts are the oldest graphic representations of programs.
The works of Goldstine and von Neumann contain many flowcharts.[1] Largely due to processor speed and storage space limitations, early programs were not structured; branching to common
code was important and occurred frequently. Later, high-level
languages appeared and programs automatically generating flowcharts from program text were developed.[2] At the same time, program structures improved. Nassi-Shneiderman Diagrams (NSDs)
were proposed much later to represent structured programs.[3] In
this form, such program constructs as if-then-else and loop are
represented as nested boxes. With a high level of nesting, these
charts become wide, and their elements vary in size. HIPO charts
attempt to capture the data flow of program segments by focusing
on the representation of input data, process, and output data for
program blocks.[4] Combinations of NSDs and HIPOs can be found
in the literature,[5,6] and in some instances NSDs have been automatically generated.[7]

Further improvement can be achieved by direct input of charts
using interactive graphics. The earliest general-purpose graphics
system was Sketchpad.[8] More specialized approaches include
block diagramming[9] and, more recently, the direct input of
NSDs.[10,11] In the latter case, program text is automatically generated from NSDs. A recent example of the use of graphics in software design is the TELL system,[12] where NSDs are used for detailed program description.

The problem with the above graphics schemes is that source statements in a program listing, as the programmer "normally" views them, do not line up with their associated elements in the graphics representation. Thus, switching attention from one representation to the other can involve a lengthy search for the corresponding entity.

This paper discusses a research effort to study this problem and to try to devise an improved solution. The solution has been called GREENPRINT after the color of the CRT display. GREENPRINT diagrams, the result of the research effort and the subject of this paper, are aligned with formatted source code listings and can be printed side by side with them. Also, GREENPRINTS are suited to inexpensive devices, and can be used for program design or documentation.

GREENPRINTs in general

Just as an engineer studies a blueprint, a programmer may interpret two-dimensional green shapes (if the phosphor is such) at a CRT terminal. A GREENPRINT uses interconnected shapes to show the block structure and the control flow of a program. The detailed program text—the "bill of materials"—completes the part specification.

Many phases of the program development/maintenance process could use GREENPRINTs. During design, detail is suppressed, but an overview of the entire software system is given. Later, program logic is detailed in GREENPRINTs; then program text is written complementing the former. Finally, in maintenance, when more than ever the understanding of programs written by others is crucial, GREENPRINTs, the authors believe, can increase the productivity of program modification.

GREENPRINT was developed as a result of the authors' own difficulty, often frustration, in working with large programs written by others. The current version, which is described here, has evolved gradually. The authors have found it to be a useful tool.

GREENPRINT diagram

A GREENPRINT is a diagrammatic representation of a program drawn next to its program source listing. The diagram consists of only two types of objects—blocks and boxes. Blocks are used to illustrate program control statements and their scope (e.g., IF, DO WHILE); boxes are used to illustrate all other program statements. To represent a program, objects are connected and arranged over a virtual grid that outlines rows and columns. Rows correspond to

Figure 1 GREENPRINT objects

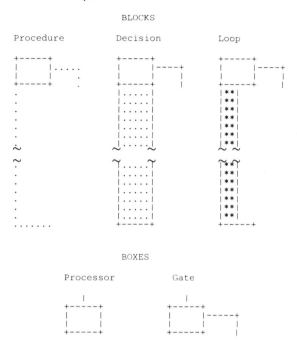

program statements or groups of statements; columns correspond to program block structure nesting.

Figure 1 shows a *procedure block*, a *decision block*, and a *loop block*. Each such block consists of a *pillar* and at least one *gate box* on the top of the pillar (the decision and procedure block may have additional gate boxes along the pillar). Each type of block has a different pillar to distinguish it visually. The figure also shows a *processor box*, distinguished from the *gate box* by the absence of any line to the right. A procedure block defines and spans the contents of a program or subroutine. Decision blocks represent if-then, if-then-else, and case statements. Loop blocks correspond to iterative DO-blocks. A gate box is always part of a procedure block, a decision block, and a loop block; a processor box stands alone. As examples in the paper show, a GREENPRINT representation of a program is a tree where blocks and processor boxes are nodes with the entry at the top and exits at the bottom or on the right. A gate box starts a subtree in the column immediately to its right. Figure 2 shows a GREENPRINT of a procedure with a loop, three types of decision blocks, and processor boxes. (The meaning of the ''<''s on the left of pillars is discussed later.)

program text The processor box represents a segment of sequential statements (straight-line code), and a gate box refers to a predicate (condition) to control either a decision or a loop. The gate at the top of a

Figure 2 GREENPRINT diagram of a procedure block, loop block, three forms of decision
block, and processor boxes

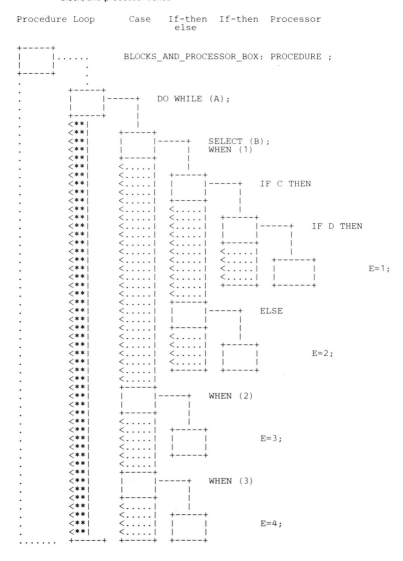

procedure block points to the body of the program. Corresponding text is written immediately to the right of a box. GREENPRINTs are arranged so that there is one box in each row, and the box is the rightmost object in that row. (Extra space may be introduced between rows to accommodate program text.) Figure 3 shows a GREENPRINT with associated text. It can be seen that the right contour of a GREENPRINT follows the indentation of the text and corresponds to the nesting of the program control structures. Since the GREENPRINT diagram is right next to, and in the same order as the program source text, the programmer can easily

IBM SYST J • VOL 19 • NO 4 • 1980   BELADY, EVANGELISTI, AND POWER

Figure 3 A GREENPRINT with indented text

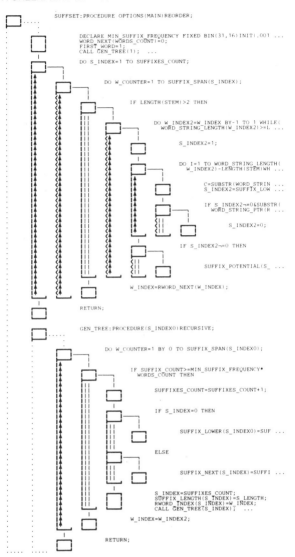

switch attention from diagram to text and back—a great time
saver when studying programs. (The modified appearance of loop
and decision pillars in Figure 3 is discussed later in this paper
under the heading ''Presentation Media.'')

static block structure Processor boxes interspersed with decision blocks and loop
blocks correspond to the static block structure of a program. A
left-to-right scan across a GREENPRINT reveals the decomposition
of blocks and therefore the structure of the program. The procedure block is used to illustrate subroutine nesting. Procedure
blocks always appear on the left, leaving the control flow of the

program displayed on the right. Figure 3 is a moderately complex example of a GREENPRINT. It shows a procedure in column one that consists of a procedure body in the top half of column two and a nested procedure in the bottom half of column two. The procedure body consists of a process box for initialization followed by a doubly nested loop (columns two and three) and a RETURN. The innards of the double loop consist of a decision (column four) to perform another loop (column five) whose body (column six) includes an inner loop and a decision. The decomposition of each block appears in the next column along a left-to-right scan. Notice also that all the processor boxes can be readily seen from the right without any obstruction. The gate boxes, also seen from the right, are partly obscured by right-angle legs exiting from the box. Thus boxes for sequential code and predicates (partly obscured) can be easily seen and discriminated by the user.

The programming language delimiters DO and END, essential for compiling the one-dimensional program text, become redundant because they are implied by the two-dimensional arrangement of blocks and boxes. If a GREENPRINT were used for actual coding, these delimiters could be automatically inserted before compilation for correct language syntax.

Dynamic program execution

Although a GREENPRINT is a tree, it does represent the flow of control of a structured program. While "playing machine" on a GREENPRINT (i.e., tracing control flow), the execution sequence generally progresses downward. Upon each entry to a block, at most one gate forces execution to continue in the next column to the right. The selection of a gate is determined by the truth value of the predicate for the box. An object with no successors beneath it is called a *terminal*. The pillar of a terminal decision block or loop block is tagged with <s on the left edge to facilitate tracing.

Flowcharts explicitly draw all flow of control lines. GREENPRINTs, which accentuate program block structure, omit the flow of control lines from terminal blocks and terminal processor boxes. Instead, the following rule is applied upon completing execution of a terminal object:

1. Move left (as suggested by the <s on terminal blocks) to the next loop block or nonterminal decision block, whichever comes first.
2. If it is a loop block, go up to its gate box to reevaluate its condition. If it is a nonterminal decision block, go down to the next sequential object in the same column.

With a little practice this rule becomes second nature and can be applied at a glance.

nonstructured flow of control

With the above rule, a GREENPRINT defines the flow of control for structured code. Nonstructured flow of control is indicated in a GREENPRINT by special processor boxes. Constructs such as GOTO, CALL, RETURN, and LEAVE are such examples. As opposed to a regular processor box containing possibly many sequential statements, the special version always represents a single statement, which is indicated in the associated text. By drawing these boxes differently (e.g., see the GOTO boxes in Figure 6, shown later) nonstandard flow of control can be highlighted. Auxiliary lines can be added to a GREENPRINT to show the flow of control for simple GOTO statements. This has not been done in the current work, which has concentrated on moderately well-structured code. If GOTO statements are relatively rare, merely highlighting them is adequate, and the diagram remains clean. Also note that the CALL statements in Figures 3 and 6 have not been highlighted by special processor boxes because their highlighting is considered optional.

GREENPRINTs and other charts

We have already shown how GREENPRINTs are related to indented text. Now we show that, as a program tree, GREENPRINT also spans a conventional flowchart. Observe the modified GREENPRINT in Figure 4. Note that it has auxiliary exit lines from the processor boxes drawn for the purpose of explanation. Clearly, the move-left-on-terminal rule previously described is equivalent to these lines. However, the resulting flowchart, thanks to the GREENPRINT drawing rules, highlights the program block structure. If the underlying program is GOTO-free, these rules contain the same information as the auxiliary lines and can therefore be omitted. Again, auxiliary lines can be added to GREENPRINTs to flag nonstructured program flow.

Further, Figure 5 shows transformations of both a flowchart and a Nassi-Shneiderman Diagram (NSD) into a GREENPRINT. The original charts, Figures 5A and 5E, show a loop around an if-then-else. Both transformed charts, Figures 5B and 5D, show blocks and boxes pushed to the right. The resulting GREENPRINT, Figure 5C, is shown with auxiliary control lines added.

Uses of GREENPRINT

There were two goals behind the GREENPRINT study. The first was to draw graphics images of existing program text. Indeed, the very need to understand complex and often obscure code written by others led the authors in the first place to develop GREENPRINT. An experimental program driven by a Backus-Naur Form grammar for PL/I was written to generate data for a drawing pro-

Figure 4 A GREENPRINT with auxiliary control lines added to form a flowchart

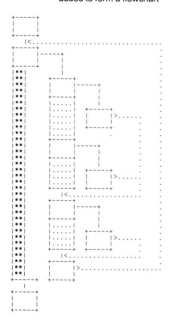

gram that produces a file to be displayed or printed. The best candidates for using these automatically generated GREENPRINTs are likely to be maintainers who must study and modify programs unfamiliar to them.

Secondly, GREENPRINT can be a design tool, a notation to first capture ideas as they emerge. Program design thus becomes drawing GREENPRINTs and entering predicates for gate boxes and sequential statements for process boxes. Since a GREENPRINT is precise, with text associated with each box, manual translation into conventional text is not required. Rather, an automatic transformation of GREENPRINTs and associated text into source statements can precede compilation. As a result, GREENPRINT can be the only program representation, also serving as documentation, whether it represents design or is generated from existing code. One of the authors designed the drawing program by using freehand GREENPRINTs.

GREENPRINT was originally developed specifically for use with IBM 3270 type devices, which are today widely available to programmers. Our current, batch-oriented implementation is used with these terminals and various types of printers. The experimental GREENPRINT drawing program has been parameterized so as to accept user-defined graphics elements corresponding to different source language constructs. This has encouraged user experimentation and led to the introduction of the stylized GOTO-box in Figure 6. Figures 3 and 6, printed on a photocomposer, were generated from the GREENPRINT drawing program by parametrically respecifying the GREENPRINT graphics elements, using an appropriate font. The up-arrow in the loop pillar enhances tracing the flow of control in Figure 3.

An interactive GREENPRINT, which has not been studied, would require only a few commands to support the placing of blocks and boxes at points on a grid. The machine could facilitate this process in several ways. For example, the most recently placed object is terminal by default but changes automatically to nonterminal when a new block or box is suspended from it. The system refuses to accept a second box in the same row, such as a processor box immediately following a processor box (except for special processor boxes) or a stand-alone gate box. Also, as a subtree grows downward, so do all pillars of the enclosing blocks to the left of the subtree, automatically.

To teach programming to a novice, to train programmers, to stimulate insight of designers, or to facilitate the exploration of alternative designs, media other than printers and display terminals come to mind. Imagine, for instance, prefabricated and possibly colored magnetic blocks and boxes placed on a metal board with a marked grid. Programming or its demonstration could then be-

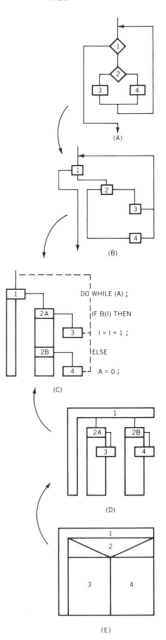

Figure 5 Transformations from a flowchart and an NSD to a GREENPRINT: (A) Flowchart; (B) Transformed flowchart; (C) GREENPRINT; (D) Transformed NSD; (E) NSD

Figure 6　GREENPRINT of a poorly structured program

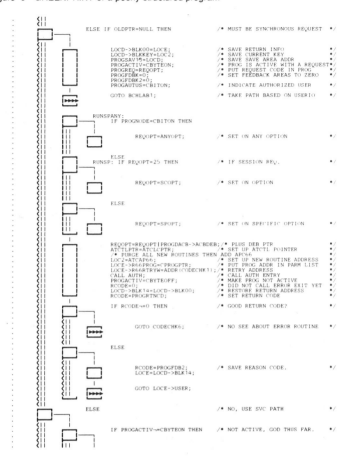

come the exploration of different arrangements of processor boxes, loops, and decisions into trees. This would be similar to a breadboard used in electrical engineering.

GREENPRINT practical experience

In practice, large, complex programs have benefited most from the use of GREENPRINTs. Understanding the flow of control is one of the first steps in understanding a complex program. This can be accomplished by studying a hard copy listing of the GREENPRINT diagram printed beside the source program. The side-by-side, linear correspondence of the GREENPRINT diagram to the source code is a very useful and unique feature of GREENPRINTs. Since the GREENPRINT diagram can be produced directly from a parse of the source code, it would be useful and appropriate for a compiler to optionally append the GREENPRINT diagram to the output listing.

It has been discovered that GREENPRINTs produced from poorly structured source code are of special value. Although GREEN-PRINTs take maximal advantage of the block structuring expressed in source code control structures, they are not restricted to them. Indeed, the desired benefits of block structuring can easily be subverted by a few GOTO statements. Figure 6 is an example of this, being a portion of an actual systems program recognized as a maintenance problem. The GREENPRINT diagram highlights a poorly structured sequence of code that the neatly indented source code hides. Notice the following about the sequence starting at the label RUNSPANY: (a) it can be reached only by a GOTO; (b) it consists of three blocks—a decision block, followed by a processor box, followed by a decision block; and (c) the only way to exit this sequence is via one of the two GOTO statements in the third block. Consequently, this sequence, although nominally embedded within one leg of a decision block, could be moved elsewhere without affecting the logic of the program, thus improving the structure of the code. This flaw in the code was discovered in a few moments by inspecting the GREEN-PRINT. Examination of a traditional, automatically generated flowchart of this same program did not reveal this flaw. The indented source code masked the flaw, and, because it is poorly structured, the program is not expressible as an NSD.

A side issue of user experience concerns source program comments. Although comments are usually a valuable form of program documentation, they often do not describe a program's flow of control. They may instead document data structures, or describe the intent of a program at a more abstract level. Consequently, some users have observed that suppressing comments in a GREENPRINT clarifies the flow of control of a program by eliminating nonessential information primarily concerned with other aspects of the program.

complexity

We propose the following research topic: Deduce certain programming measures from size and shape characteristics of GREENPRINTs. For example, the jaggedness of the right contour could be used to characterize or classify programs with respect to structure, style, or complexity.

A hypothesis could be studied that the average width of a GREEN-PRINT is proportional to the expected reading rate of a programmer or the comprehension complexity of a program based on the following expression:

$$Average\ width = \frac{1}{r_{total}} \sum_{r=1}^{r_{total}} K_r$$

where K_r is the number of occupied columns in row r and r_{total} is the number of rows in the GREENPRINT; and the total complexity C is given by the following equation:

$$C = \frac{S}{r_{total}} \sum_{r=1}^{r_{total}} K_r$$

where S is the total number of program statements. This complexity measure accounts for both the average nesting and the total length of a program. Since the processor box count does not contain the number of sequential statements in the program, the length of the program S is used.

Sometimes an overview of a large program is required at the expense of detail. Two methods are envisioned for this. In the first, which has not been studied in depth, a box or block may stand for an undetailed program segment of any size, and it may contain the name of the segment. In this manner, a subtree can be replaced by a named processor box. Such a facility is important while designing in a top-down fashion. Also, a block, similar to a decision block, can represent a program segment that determines which gate is to receive control. Such a block can be more general in the sense that it gives control to different gates, depending on an algorithm. Figure 7 shows a summary GREENPRINT at the top and detailed GREENPRINTs SUB and DEC below. SUB (for subroutine) illustrates a detailed GREENPRINT and DEC (for decision) represents a program that plays the role of a case-statement predicate. DEC transfers control at exits 1 or 2, thus—at both levels—representing actions to be performed. The pillar of the high-level block is altered to indicate that it is not a standard block. Extending this notion, GREENPRINTs can be used to represent any tree-structured information. By the appropriate design of pillars, boxes, and connectors, the entities and their relations can be depicted graphically.

Figure 7 A high-level GREEN-PRINT with two detailed GREENPRINTS

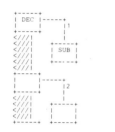

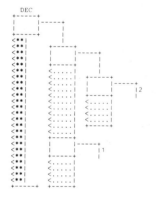

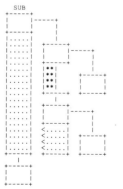

In the second method for overview, as exemplified in Figures 3 and 6, all blocks and boxes can be shrunk horizontally and vertically, even to a single character, thus allowing the display of the control flow of a large program in a smaller area. Figures 3 and 6 were automatically generated and then printed with an appropriately small print font. In addition, some of the program source text was elided in Figure 3.

Concluding remarks

GREENPRINT as a graphics representation of program control structure is unique in that its objects—blocks and boxes—appear from top to bottom in the same order as the associated program text. The two representations can thus be studied and worked with concurrently. Other advantages, some shared by conventional flowcharts and NSDs, include the capability of automatically generating GREENPRINTs from program text and generating control statements from a GREENPRINT. GREENPRINTs can be displayed on inexpensive terminals. In addition, the exactness of GREENPRINTs suggests the possibility of developing program complexity metrics based on purely geometric properties. But this and the extension of the GREENPRINT approach to include structure and flow of data remain interesting research topics at this time.

ACKNOWLEDGMENTS

The authors wish to thank J. Cavanagh for nourishing GREEN-PRINT when it was a seedling, and H. Ellozy for actively using the program and discovering uses in analyzing poorly structured parts of programs.

CITED REFERENCES

1. H. H. Goldstine and J. von Neumann, "Planning and coding problems for an electronic computing instrument," *John von Neumann, Collected Works. Volume V*, A. H. Taub (General Editor), The Macmillan Company, New York (1963), pp. 80–235.
2. L. M. Haibt, "A program to draw multilevel flow charts," *Proceedings of the Western Joint Computer Conference, The Joint IRE-AIEE-ACM Computer Conference*, San Francisco, CA, March 3–5, 1959, published by the Institute of Radio Engineers (now IEEE), New York (1959), pp. 131–137.
3. I. Nassi and B. Shneiderman, "Flowchart techniques for structured programming," *ACM SIGPLAN Notices* **8**, No. 8, 12–26 (August 1973).
4. J. F. Stay, "HIPO and integrated program design," *IBM Systems Journal* **15**, No. 2, 143–154 (1976).
5. N. Chapin, "New format for flowcharts," *Software—Practice and Experience* **4**, No. 4, 341–357 (October-December 1974).
6. K. T. Orr, *Structured Systems Development*, Yourdon, Inc., New York (1977).
7. P. Roy and R. St-Denis, "Linear flowchart generator for a structured language," *ACM SIGPLAN Notices* **11**, No. 11, 58–64 (November 1976).
8. I. E. Sutherland, "Sketchpad, a man-machine graphical communication system," *AFIPS Conference Proceedings, Spring Joint Computer Conference* **23**, 329–346 (1963).
9. L. A. Belady, M. W. Blasgen, C. J. Evangelisti, and R. D. Tennison, "A computer graphics system for block diagram problems," *IBM Systems Journal* **10**, No. 2, 143–161 (1971).
10. N. Ng, *A Graphical Editor for Programming Using Structured Programming*, Research Report RJ2344, IBM Research Laboratory, 5600 Cottle Road, San Jose, CA 95193 (1978).
11. R. Williams and G. M. Giddings, "A picture-building system," *IEEE Transactions on Software Engineering* **SE-2**, No. 1, 62–66 (March 1976).
12. P. G. Hebalkar and S. N. Zilles, *TELL: A System for Graphically Representing Software Designs*, Research Report RJ2351, IBM Research Laboratory, 5600 Cottle Road, San Jose, CA 95193 (1978).

The authors are located at the IBM Thomas J. Watson Research Center, P.O. Box 218, Route 134, Yorktown Heights, NY 10598.

Reprint Order No. G321-5137.

A State Transition Diagram Language for Visual Programming

Robert J. K. Jacob, Naval Research Laboratory

*Visual programming is
about to emerge from its
infancy; graphical
programming languages
are now taking advantage
of its potential even
though few graphical
representations of
abstract objects have been
developed.*

The diagrams, flowcharts, and other iconic representations we have long employed to communicate with other people can now be used directly to describe algorithms to computers. With the availability of graphics-based, personal workstations, these visual modes can eliminate the need to convert algorithms to the linear strings of symbols traditionally required by most computers. Linear, symbolic computer languages have been studied and refined extensively over the past 30 years, but computer language designers now face a new challenge: to provide convenient and natural *visual* programming languages.

Types of languages for visual programming

Languages for visual programming can be divided into two categories. In the first, the object being designed is itself a static graphical object—a menu, a screen layout, an engineering drawing, a typeset report, a font of type. While such objects are frequently designed with symbolic languages (for example, a picture might be programmed as a sequence of calls to Core graphics subroutines), they are obvious candidates for a direct manipulation[1] or "what-you-see-is-

what-you-get" mode of visual programming. A programming environment for such a visual programming language need only simulate the appearance of the final object and provide direct graphical commands for manipulating it. When the designer is satisfied with the graphical simulation, he "saves" it and has thereby "written" a visual program. Such systems combine great power with ease of use, because the visual programming language provides a natural way to describe the graphical object. It is often so natural that the system is not considered a programming language environment at all, but simply a what-you-see-is-what-you-get type of editor. Unfortunately, this approach is possible only where there is a one-to-one correspondence between a visual programming language and the static visual object being programmed.

A more difficult problem arises in the second category of visual programming language, representing something abstract—time sequence, hierarchy, conditional statements, frame-based knowledge. To provide visual programming languages for these objects, we must first devise suitable graphical representations or visual metaphors for them. The powerful what-you-see-is-what-you-get principle is not much help, since the objects are abstract, but

the successful application of the visual programming language paradigm to these situations still depends critically on choosing a good representation. Graphical representation of abstract ideas is a powerful form of communication, but a difficult one. In the absence of an applicable theory of graphical communication, proper use of such representations often requires extensive experimentation.[2]

Choosing a graphical representation. The use of visual programming is in its infancy and few good representations of abstract objects have been developed. It is possible, nonetheless, to adapt representations now being used as a medium for discussing algorithms and to examine how they function in visual programming paradigms.

State transition diagrams have been used widely by computer scientists— albeit with pencil and paper—to describe a variety of algorithms. In particular, they offer a good representation of the user interface of a computer system because of several of their properties:

- In each state, they make explicit the interpretations of all possible inputs.
- They show how to change to a state in which such interpretations would be different.
- They emphasize the temporal sequence of user and system actions in the dialogue.

State transition diagrams have been used in this way for several years[3,4] and have been found preferable to other languages for describing user interfaces.[5,6] It is time to take this pencil-and-paper tool and apply it to the new paradigm of visual programming.

The state transition diagram notation

First, we must consider the static form of the graphical language and how it will be used to describe a user interface. A visual representation chosen for this purpose needs to describe the external (user-visible) behavior of the user interface of a system precisely, leaving no doubt as to the behavior of the system for each possible input. It should separate function from implementation, describing the behavior of a user interface completely, and precisely, without unduly constraining the way it will be implemented. The visual representation should be easier to understand and take less effort to produce than the more conventional symbolic software. Ideally, the overall structure of the visual program should represent the cognitive structure of the user interface. The program should describe the constructs a user will keep in mind when learning about the system—the basic outline around which the user's mental model of the system will be built. Finally, the visual representation must be directly executable in a visual programming environment.

The language illustrated here is an extended version of state transition diagrams. It has been used successfully to specify and directly implement user interfaces for several prototype systems.[7-9] The language is based on the conventional graphical diagrams that describe finite state automata. A diagram consists of a set of nodes (states) and the links between them (state transitions). Each transition is associated with a token in the user input language. From any state, an input language token initiates a transition labeled with that token. A transition may be associated with an output token, which provides output to the user or a processing action that is performed by the system during that transition.

An important feature of the language is the ability of one diagram to call upon another, much as a program makes a procedure call. This feature is analogous to nonterminal symbols in

BNF—invented intermediate constructs that permit the specification to be divided into manageable pieces. Instead of labeling a transition with a single token to be recognized, we can give it the name of a nonterminal symbol. That symbol is then described by a separate state transition diagram. An important criterion for a user interface specification is that its principal constructs—the main nonterminal symbols and states—represent concepts that will be meaningful to users and will help them to construct their own mental models of the system.

One of the principal virtues of state diagram notations is that, by giving the transition rules for each state, they make explicit what the user can do at each point in a dialog and what the effect will be. Feyock[10] makes good use of this property by using a computer-readable representation of the state diagram description of a system as the input to a system help facility. Based on the state diagram and the current state, the system can answer such questions as "What can I do next?" "Where am I?" and "How can I do . . .?"

Other investigators have also found the state transition model helpful in describing a user's mental model of an interactive computer system,[11,12] and some have built diagram interpreters.[13,14] The choice of a state-diagram-based notation is also supported by the empirical observation of Guest,[6] who was surprised to find that programmers preferred for a specification interpreter a state-transition-diagram-based front end to a BNF-based one.

Programming methodology for interfaces

The state transition diagram language used here is part of a methodology for designing and specifying user interfaces. The method is outlined below and described in more detail elsewhere.[7] To reduce the complexity

of the designer's task, the process of designing and programming a user interface is divided into three levels, and a notation suitable for each level is provided. Foley and Wallace[15] introduced the notion of describing an interactive user interface at the *semantic*, *syntactic*, and *lexical* levels. That model[16] is followed here, but the three levels require more precise delineation, particularly with respect to output and to suitable notations for programming them visually.

Semantic level. The semantic level describes the functions performed by the system. The semantic design indicates the information needed for each function and gives the result. It defines "meanings," rather than "forms" or "sequences," which are left to the lower levels. The semantic-level specification provides the high-level model or abstraction of the functions of the system, removing from the graphical description of the user interface syntax details that would obfuscate the structure of the dialog.

In the state transition diagram language, the semantic level manipulates internal variables; no actual input or output operations are described, although the manipulation of values read in as inputs and the generation of values to be displayed as outputs are described. The semantic-level specification consists of descriptions of functions that operate on the internal data—the function parameters, their types, and the effects of the functions. For actual execution, these functions are coded in a conventional programming language. The semantic level also provides dialog independence[17] by permitting the details of the semantic level of the user interface to be partitioned from the syntactic- and lexical-level specifications and treated separately.

Syntactic level. The syntactic level describes the rules by which sequences

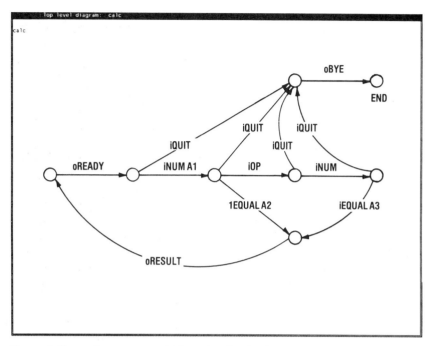

Figure 1. State diagram description of a simple desk calculator.

of words (*tokens*) in the language are formed into proper (but not necessarily semantically meaningful) sentences. The syntactic-level specification describes the sequence of the logical input, output, and semantic operations, but not their internal details. A logical input or output operation is an input or output *token*. Its internal structure is described at the lexical level, while the syntactic level calls it by name, like a subroutine, and indicates when the user may enter it and what will happen next (for an input token) or when the system will produce it (for an output token). A state transition may be associated with an input token or an output token, but not both. Treating outputs as separate tokens on separate transitions (rather than as a special kind of action) at the syntactic-level permits the specification to be more symmetric in the way it describes input and output.

The syntactic-level specification of a simple desk calculator program with this state transition diagram notation

is shown in Figure 1. Each circle corresponds to a state; the start state is at the left; the end state (or states) is named inside its circle. Each transition between two states is shown as a directed arc. It may be labeled with one of the following:

- An input token (lower case *i* followed by upper case, e.g. i NUM);

- An output token (lowercase o followed by upper case; oREADY);

- A nonterminal (all lower case) defined by a separate diagram, called like a subroutine; it must be traversed from start to end to complete the transition;

- An action that calls a semantic-level function; it will be executed if the transition is taken; e.g. A1; or

- A condition, defined in the semantic level, which must be true for the transition to be made.

The details of actions and conditions are shown in numbered footnotes to avoid clutter. Each consists of one or more calls to the semantic functions. The semantic actions called by the digram in Figure 1 are shown in Figure 2, along with their definitions, programmed in C. A prompt (consisting of an output token) may also be associated with a state; whenever that state is reached, its prompt token will be output. The actual value received by an input token (such as the actual number obtained for the token iNUM) is available in a variable named v plus the token name (e.g., viNUM); the actual value to be output by an output token is, similarly, set in a variable named v plus the token name (e.g., voRESULT). Further details and more precise semantics of this form of state transition diagram notation are provided elsewhere.[7]

Lexical level. The lexical level determines how input and output tokens are actually formed from the primitive hardware operations (*lexemes*). It represents the binding of hardware actions to the hardware-independent tokens of the input and output languages. While tokens are the smallest units of meaning with respect to the syntax of the dialog, lexemes are the actual hardware input and output operations that comprise the tokens. The lexical level identifies the devices, display windows, positions with which each token is associated, and the primitive hardware operations that constitute them. All information about the organization of a display into areas and the assignment of input and output tasks to hardware devices is confined to this level. For an input token, the lexical-level description gives the sequence of primitive input lexemes (for example, key presses) and the device for each lexeme that is used to enter the token, as well as any lexical output that is produced. For an output token, the lexical level tells how (that is, with which devices, windows, positions, formats, colors, and the like) the token appears to the user. The actual information to be presented by an output token may have been set by a semantic action or may be constant; the lexical level shows the format of the variable data displayed, but not its contents.

The lexical level is represented in the same state transition diagram notation as the syntactic. It consists of a separate state diagram for each input or

```
char  prevop[100] = "+", preunum[100] -"0"

A1    assign(*savenum1,viNUM);
      /*
       * assign is a built-in function that performs variable assignment
       */

A2    const(*vo RESULTsavenum1);
      /*
       * The function const performs a constant mode calculation
       * Repeats previous peration with new operand num,
       * and returns answer in result
       */
      const(result,num) char **result
          int ians; char strans[100]

          if (STREQ(prevop,"+")) ians=atoi(prevnum)+atoi(num);
          if (STREQ(prevop,"+")) ians=atoi(prevnum)+atoi(num);
          else if (STREQ(prevop,"-")) ians=atoi(num)-atoi(prevnum);
          else if (STREQ(prevop,"*")) ians=atoi(prevnum)*atoi(num);
          else if (STREQ(prevop,"/")) ians=atoi(num)/atoi(prevnum);

          sprint(strans,"%",ians); assign(result,strans);
}

A3    calc(*vo RESULT,savenum1,viOP,viNUM);
      /*
       * The function calc performs calculator operation op
       * on operands num1 and num2, and resulturns answer in result
       */
      calc(result,num1,op,num2) char **result, *num1, *op, *num2; {
          int ians; char strans[100];

          if  (STREQ(op,"+")) {
                  ians=atoi(num1)+atoi(num2);
                  strcpy(prevnum,num1);
          }
          else if  (STREQ(op,"-")) {
                  ians=atoi(num1)-atoi(num2);
                  strcpy(prevnum,num2);
          }
          else if  (STREQ(op,"*")) {
                  ians=atoi(num1)*atoi(num2);
                  strcpy(prevnum,num2);
          }
          else if  (STREQ(op,"/")) {
                  ians=atoi(num1)/atoi(num2);
                  strcpy(prevnum,num2);
          }

          strcpy(prevop,op);
          sprint(strans,%d",ians);  assign(result,strans)
}
```

Figure 2. Actions called by the diagram in Figure 1.

output token, each of which can be called from the syntactic-level diagrams, like other sub-diagrams for nonterminals. In the lexical-level diagrams, output is described by actions on the state transistions that call special functions. Such functions can be called only at the lexical level. At the syntactic level, output is performed only by output token transitions to avoid mixing output actions with input transitions. At the lexical level, all outputs (other than lexical echoes) have already been separated from inputs.

Certain low-level lexical operations are cumbersome to describe. Tracking a mouse with a cursor, highlighting states in reverse video as they are traversed, making font changes, or even echoing characters—these are better described in a more intuitive fashion than in a large state diagram with a very regular structure. As a simple alternative, such operations could be programmed directly into the definitions of the special output functions mentioned above. However they are represented, it is important that such details be captured at and encapsulated in the lexical-level specification. Once they are associated with token names, their specification has no bearing on the specification of the syntax of the dialog or the use of the state-diagram-based notation for that purpose.

Visual programming with the state diagram language

The language described thus far is a static one that has been used to specify the behavior of a variety of user interfaces. In each case, the diagrams were designed, entered as strings of text, then executed by an interpreter. To use this language in a visual programming paradigm, we need a more graphically-oriented and more interactive programming environment. A visual programming environment for this language is cur-

rently being implemented on a SUN workstation. The displays in Figures 3-7 are taken directly from this system, although all of its parts, particularly the interactive editor and the handling of "co-diagram" calls, are not yet fully implemented.

In the visual programming version of the state diagram language, the programmer enters the state diagrams with a graphical editor and affixes the necessary labels and actions. Each nonterminal, token, and lexeme is diagrammed separately in its own window on the display screen so that the individual graphical objects being edited do not become too complicated. Each diagram is given a name by which it may be called from a transition in another diagram. One diagram is designated the top-level diagram. It calls all the rest directly or indirectly.

Semantic actions. While the diagrams are used to describe both the syntactic and lexical levels of the design, the actions called by transitions in them comprise the semantic level. They are currently programmed in a conventional (non-visual) programming language, and their definitions can be shown and edited with a text editor in a separate window for each diagram. Since they are currently written in a compiled language, they must be re-compiled after they are edited. While a similar interpreted language could be used instead, a more interesting possibility is a visual, interpreted language. One approach is to provide a (compiled) library of basic actions (add, subtract, assign, print), then allow the programmer to draw additional state transition diagrams that combine these standard actions to perform the desired functions. This would permit the programmer to remain within the same visual programming language, even when describing the semantic actions of the system. However, the state diagrams were

chosen because they are a good visual metaphor for describing the user interface behavior of a system. As a general-purpose programming language, they are likely to be bulky and obscure for many actions that could be programmed clearly in other languages. Hence they are preferred for programming the syntax but not the semantics. Ideally, the present state diagrams would call the semantic actions by name, as they do now, and these actions would be programmed in a separate, more suitable *visual* programming language. This programming is possible within the present framework, but awaits the invention of a suitable visual metaphor for the action descriptions.

Interactive execution environment. The state diagram notation is an executable language, so that the diagrams can be directly executed after they have been entered. A system for executing such diagrams in a non-visual programming paradigm has been developed[7] and adapted to the interactive visual programming environment. It directly implements the behavior of the user interface as specified in the diagrams. "What you see is what you get" is not a useful maxim in this environment, since the programmer is trying to describe a temporal ordering of events rather than a static visual object. The programming environment has two types of windows. One can be used to demonstrate the user interface being programmed, the other to manipulate the abstract graphical representation of it. As shown in Figure 3, the simulator window on the left shows the newly-designed user interface (of the desk calculator example of Figure 1) as it would appear to the user. When the mouse is pointing to it, it allows the programmer to interact with it in the role of the user. The programming windows on the right show the state diagrams and the action descriptions and allow the programmer

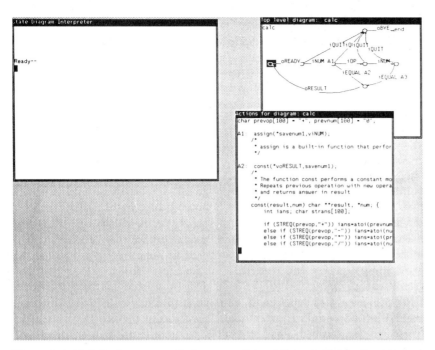

Figure 3. Initial display screen during execution of the calculator diagram.

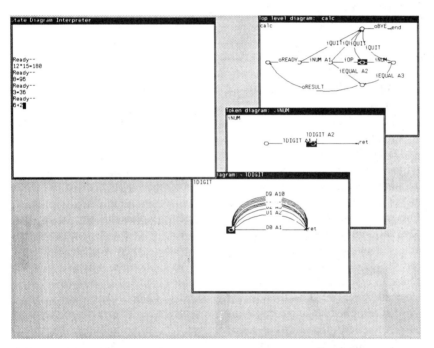

Figure 4. Display screen after execution of the calculator diagram has progressed to the point where subdiagram calls for tokens are pending.

to modify them as desired. This approach does not preclude designing a user interface that, itself, involves several windows; it just requires that the programmer view a picture of it that is small enough to leave room on the screen for the programming windows.

When execution begins in the simulator window, a programming window with the top-level diagram pops up. As

execution of the diagram progresses, the current state in the diagram is highlighted on the screen. As each subdiagram is called for a nonterminal, token, or lexeme, a window containing the diagram pops up. During such calls, the current state of the system consists of a state in the lowest level diagram currently being executed, along with a stack of pending

"subroutine" calls to it from the higher level diagrams. It is displayed as a highlighted state in the lowest level diagram with a pile of windows behind it showing the chain of diagrams that called it. In each window, the state from which the pending call was made is highlighted. Figure 4 shows the display in such a situation (the user has also suppressed the display of the windows with the action bodies in this and subsequent examples).

During execution, the programmer can cause the interpreter to move directly to any state in the diagram by pointing to it. He can cause the interpreter to move to a state via a particular path by pointing to one transition or a sequence of them. (As with other interactive debuggers, the programmer must avoid skipping over a transition that performs an action and subsequently invokes a transition that depends on that action.) He can also edit any of the diagrams with a graphical editor while the system is running. Since the state diagram language is entirely interpreted, the program can be modified arbitrarily while it is running. Of course, if the modification deletes the current state, the programmer will have to point to another state from which execution is to resume.

Nondeterministic programs. It is possible to write a nondeterministic program in this language; there could be several transitions leading from the same state, all accepting the same input token but clarified by subsequent input. In fact, it is possible to write a nondeterministic program inadvertently with calls to sub-diagrams. However, when an interactive system is being described, there cannot be a nondeterministic choice at any point in the diagram involving output. Whenever the interpreter makes a transition that produces output, it is committed to the path with that transition because an interactive system cannot rescind

COMPUTER

outputs that the user has seen or heard. It must produce outputs at the specified points in the dialog. It cannot wait for additional input to select between two transitions. The interpreter itself is a deterministic machine that executes a nondeterministic program by arbitrarily trying one of the possible paths. If it reaches a dead end, it backtracks and tries another. The language permits arbitrary nondeterminism (simulated by backtracking), but the programmer must avoid backtracking over output. The visual programming environment makes this situation easier to see. Whenever there are several possible paths to be taken, the system will show all of them, as separately highlighted target states or, more typically, as separate windows with possible pending subdiagram calls. As soon as user input is sufficient to permit a choice of one of the paths, the rejected options disappear from the display. Figure 5 shows what this nondeterministic choice would look like in a simplified situation. In this state, the user could enter an operator (the token iOP) or an equals sign (iEQUAL) or a quit command (iQUIT). The three subdiagrams for the tokens appear on the screen at this point. In this example, it is easy to see that the very next user input will select from among three clear options (since the three sets of lexemes are disjoint in their current states), and two of the subdiagrams will disappear.

Programming a multi-window user interface

The simplest type of user interface involving several windows has only one context for user interaction. All user input is considered part of one unbroken dialog, with no context switches. Output may appear in various windows for convenience, but it is all part of a single dialog. To describe this with the present tech-

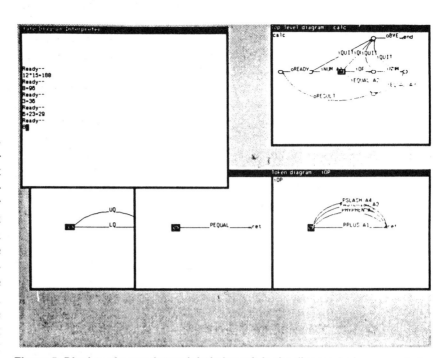

Figure 5. Display of a nondeterministic branch in the diagram being executed.

nique, each output token is tagged with a specific window in its lexical-level diagram, as Shneiderman[18] has done in his extended form of BNF. Several systems with a multi-window user interface have been specified and built with this approach with the state transition diagrams.[7,8]

Concurrent dialogs. A more interesting situation arises when there are several dialogs taking place. Multiple dialogs are typical with more sophisticated display window systems, where one window is associated with each conversation. This use of windows gives rise to a new style of user interface. For example, consider a multi-window user interface for a prototype military message system.[9] It permits manipulation of several different messages, message files, and message file directories concurrently, each in its own window. The user can create display windows for various objects, conduct a separate dialog for viewing or manipulating the objects in each window, and change focus from one window to another at any time without losing the place in any of the dialogs. The user can also change the layout of the windows on the display at any point. Certain input actions are reserved for directives to a window man-

ager for changing the focus of the conversation or the layout of the display. All other inputs are considered input to the "current" dialog, as designated by the most recent command to the window manager. Figure 6 shows a display from such a system.

To describe such a system in a convenient visual notation, it is first necessary to consider the structure of the dialog. Its central concept is the *sequence* of (input and output) events that comprise it, not the layout of the windows on the display (although some logical layout information is provided with the tagged tokens mentioned above). Further programming of the details of the layout are easy to accommodate with a what-you-see-is-what-you-get screen editor, but the main user interface specification should concentrate on the sequence of the dialog.

The syntactic description of a concurrent dialog system thus has two levels. The top level describes the display-arranging commands of the window manager itself. Then, each dialog in each window (such as those for viewing or editing individual message files or other objects) has its own syntax, which is described at a second level although window manager commands can be entered at any time.

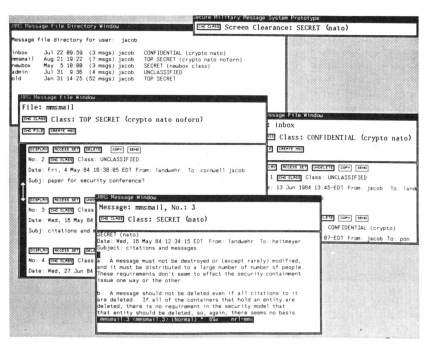

Figure 6. User interface of a prototype multiwindow military message system; the security classifications shown are simulated for demonstration purposes.

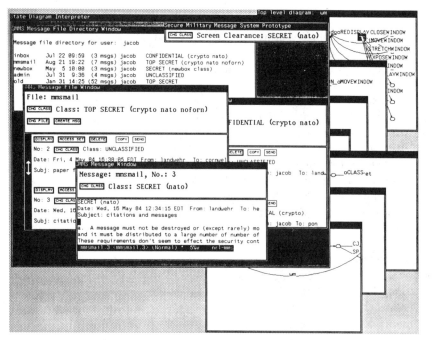

Figure 7. Appearance of the programming environment display when the system being designed (from Figure 6) itself involves several windows.

executed a codiagram call. It is traversed until it makes another codiagram call. For example, if it then called diagram A, A would be resumed at the end state of the transition from which it had called B. Whenever a diagram is entered by a codiagram call, it is resumed with its own stack of pending subdiagram calls intact. If it had made a subdiagram call, it would be resumed within that subdiagram, and upon exit from that subdiagram, it returns to the diagram that called the subdiagram.

With this approach, the syntax for the window manager commands is described in one top-level diagram. Whenever an input other than a window manager command is received, the top-level diagram makes a codiagram call to the syntax diagram for the currently-selected individual dialog. These syntax diagrams are conventional, except that every state permitting escape to the window manager command level is preceded by a transition that makes a codiagram call to the top-level window manager diagram. When the lower-level dialog is resumed after that call, it is ready for user input at the point in its input syntax at which it was interrupted.

Figure 7 shows how such a system might appear while being designed with the visual programming environment. The simulator window shows the entire multiwindow user interface of the prototype military message system (with its windows reduced or truncated), while the programming windows handle the graphical editing of the state diagrams for both the top-level window manager dialog and each of the individual window dialogs.

Use of the visual programming paradigm, particularly for abstract objects, is in its infancy. What-you-see-is-what-you-get types of user interfaces have been highly successful but have no obvious extension for non-graphical objects. To explore the

Such commands will immediately switch the context to the window manager itself, then back to the previous point in the current dialog or to a dialog in another window.

What is the abstract structure of such a multi-window style of dialog? It is really a set of coroutines, and the problem of representing it may be solved by introducing a codiagram call into the present language. This is analogous to the subdiagram call, by which a transition in one diagram is used to call another subdiagram—like a subroutine. When a transition in Diagram A, for instance, makes a codiagram call to Diagram B, Diagram B is entered at the state from which B last

potential for visual programming, a demonstration of a visual programming environment with an already-established graphical language has been presented. To date, only a few suitable graphical representations of abstract objects have been developed for use with the visual programming paradigm. They are typically designed for specific purposes and are not widely applicable. The need now is for more general graphical representations of programming objects. In the long run, a theoretical understanding of visual perception is needed so that a designer can devise natural graphical representations for a wide variety of objects in a more general manner. □

Acknowledgments

This work was supported by the Naval Electronic Systems Command under the direction of H. O. Lubbes. I want to thank the guest editor, Bob Grafton, for encouraging me to think about the possibilities of visual programming.

References

1. B. Shneiderman, "Direct Manipulation: A Step Beyond Programming Languages," *Computer*, Vol. 16, No. 7, July 1983, pp. 57-69.

2. R. J. K. Jacob, "Facial Representation of Multivariate Data," in *Graphical Representation of Multivariate Data*, P. C. C. Wang, ed., Academic Press, New York, 1978, pp. 143-168.

3. D. C. Engelbart and W. K. English, "A Research Center for Augmenting Human Intellect," *Proc. Joint Computer Conf.*, Fall 1968, pp. 395-410.

4. D. L. Parnas, "On the Use of Transition Diagrams in the Design of a User Interface for an Interactive Computer System," *Proc. 24th National ACM Conf.*, 1969, pp. 379-385.

5. R. J. K. Jacob, "Using Formal Specifications in the Design of a Human-Computer Interface," *CACM*, Vol. 26, No. 4, Apr. 1983, pp. 259-264.

6. S. P. Guest, "The Use of Software Tools for Dialogue Design," *Int'l J. Man-Machine Studies*, Vol. 16, No. 3, Mar. 1982, pp. 263-285.

7. R. J. K. Jacob, "An Executable Specification Technique for Describing Human-Computer Interaction," in *Advances in Human-Computer Interaction*, H. R. Hartson, ed., Ablex Publishing Co., Norwood, N.J., 1985, pp. 211-242.

8. R. J. K. Jacob, "Designing a Human-Computer Interface with Software Specification Techniques," *Second Symp. Empirical Foundations of Information and Software Sciences*, 1984, Atlanta, Ga.

9. M. R. Cornwell and R. J. K. Jacob, "Structure of a Rapid Prototype Secure Military Message System," *Seventh DOD/NBS Computer Security Conf.*, Gaithersburg, Md., pp. 48-57.

10. S. Feyock, "Transition Diagram-Based CAI/HELP Systems," *Int'l J. Man-Machine Studies*, Vol. 9, 1977, pp. 399-413.

11. J. Darlington, W. Dzida, and S. Herda, "The Role of Excursions in Interactive Systems," *Int'l J. Man-Machine Studies*, Vol. 18, No. 2, Feb. 1983, pp. 101-112.

12. T. P. Moran, "The Command Language Grammar: A Representation for the User Interface of Interactive Computer Systems," *Int'l J. Man-Machine Studies*, Vol. 15, No. 1, July 1981, pp. 3-50.

13. M. B. Feldman and G. T. Rogers, "Toward the Design and Development of Style-independent Interactive Systems," *Proc. ACM Sigchi Human Factors in Computer Systems Conf.*, 1982, pp. 111-116.

14. A. I. Wasserman and D. T. Shewmake, "The Role of Prototypes in the User Software Engineering (USE) Methodology," in *Advances in Human-Computer Interaction*, H. R. Hartson, ed., Ablex Publishing Co., Norwood, N.J., 1985.

15. J. D. Foley and V. L. Wallace, "The Art of Graphic Man-Machine Conversation," *Proc. IEEE*, Vol. 62, No. 4, Apr. 1974, pp. 462-471.

16. J. D. Foley and A. van Dam, *Fundamentals of Interactive Computer Graphics*, Addison-Wesley, Reading, Mass., 1982, pp. 217-243.

17. T. Yunten and H. R. Hartson, "A Supervisory Methodology and Notation (SUPERMAN) for Human-Computer System Development," in *Advances in Human-Computer Interaction*, H. R. Hartson, ed., Ablex Publishing Co., Norwood, N.J., 1985.

18. B. Shneiderman, "Multi-party Grammars and Related Features for Defining Interactive Systems," *IEEE Trans. Systems, Man, and Cybernetics*, Vol. SMC 12, No. 2, Mar.-Apr. 1982, pp. 148-154.

Robert J. K. Jacob is a computer scientist in the Information Technology Division at the Naval Research Laboratory, Washington, DC, where he is working on man-machine interactions. He is focusing on his work on the formal specifications of user-computer interfaces and on the development of software engineering techniques to simplify program modification by users.

Jacob received his BA, MSE and PhD (EE/CS) from Johns Hopkins University in 1972, 1974, and 1976, respectively. He is currently on the faculty of George Washington University, where he teaches computer science.

Questions about this article can be addressed to Jacobs, Code 7590, Naval Research Laboratory, Washington, DC 20375.

Reprinted from *IEEE Transactions on Software Engineering*, Volume SE-11, Number 8, August 1985, pages 699-713.

Extending State Transition Diagrams for the Specification of Human–Computer Interaction

ANTHONY I. WASSERMAN, MEMBER, IEEE

Abstract–User Software Engineering is a methodology for the specification and implementation of interactive information systems. An early step in the methodology is the creation of a formal executable description of the user interaction with the system, based on augmented state transition diagrams. This paper shows the derivation of the USE transition diagrams based on perceived shortcomings of the "pure" state transition diagram approach. In this way, the features of the USE specification notation are gradually presented and illustrated. The paper shows both the graphical notation and the textual equivalent of the notation, and briefly describes the automated tools that support direct execution of the specification.

This specification is easily encoded in a machine-processable form to create an executable form of the computer–human interaction.

Index Terms–Executable specifications, interactive information systems, rapid prototyping, software development methodology, transition diagrams, user interfaces, User Software Engineering.

I. INTRODUCTION

AN interactive system can be seen as having two components: the user interface to the system and the operations performed by the system. The user interface provides the user with a language for communicating with the system. The interface can take many forms, including multiple choice (menu selection), a command language, a database query language, or natural language-like input. In all cases, however, the normal action of the program is determined by user input, and the program may respond in a variety of ways, including results, requests for additional input, error messages, or assistance in the use of the system.

The user interface is often the principal determinant of system success, especially for those interactive systems where usage (or purchase) is discretionary. Yet for many systems used on alphanumeric terminals, design of the user interface is often an afterthought, with the design based on system-oriented, rather than user-oriented, concerns.[1]

The User Software Engineering project was undertaken in 1975 with the idea of combining concerns about user involvement in the design of interactive information systems with those of software engineering. The outcome of the effort is the creation of a methodology [1], [2] with a set of automated tools to support the methodology [3]-[7]. User participation is very important at the early stages of the meth-

Manuscript received February 8, 1984; revised February 20, 1985. This work was supported by corporate research grants from Nippon Electric Company and from Alcoa Foundation.

The author is with the Section of Medical Information Science, University of California, San Francisco, CA 94143.

[1] Interfaces for graphics-based systems and especially video games are based on the value of pictorial display and interaction. Therefore, more attention is given to the nature of the user interface.

odology, where users (or user surrogates) can provide useful information to help the development process. For example, the initial analysis phase includes not only traditional data and activity modeling, but also identification of user characteristics, e.g., ability to type, intensity of anticipated usage, motivation and education of users, etc. Attention is also given to the environment in which the system will be used, so that the system can fit in with the user's work pattern, and can be tailored to any constraints on terminal types or transmission rates.

The second step of the USE methodology is *external design*, which involves design of the user interface(s) to the proposed system. The analysis step serves to identify major functions and required inputs and outputs, at least at a high level. The concern of external design is to determine how the user can request those functions and how the output will be displayed. Thus, instead of top-down or bottom-up design, the USE methodology uses an "outside-in" design.

The third step is the creation of an executable version of the user interface defined at the previous stage, so that the user and developer can jointly explore, both objectively and subjectively, the usability of the original design, and to make modifications as needed. This ability to rapidly create system prototypes, presenting the user view of the evolving system, is a key aspect of User Software Engineering. Clearly, there is iteration among the first three steps until one or more acceptable interfaces are found.

In the remainder of this paper, we describe the notation used to specify this user interface in the USE methodology. We are not concerned here with the methodological process of defining the user interface, with the succeeding steps of the methodology that lead to a finished system, or with evaluation of the user interface.

II. USER INTERFACE DEFINITION WITH TRANSITION DIAGRAMS

In searching for an appropriate notation for describing user interfaces to interactive systems, we established several requirements, including the following:

1) Formalism: The notation had to serve as a formal definition of the interface.

2) Completeness: The notation had to be self-contained, including user input, system output, and linkage to system operations (application code).

3) Comprehensibility: The notation had to be comprehensible both to system developers and to users (or their representatives).

4) Flexibility: The notation had to accommodate a broad variety of dialog styles. In other words, the notation could not make assumptions about the nature of human–computer interaction, but had to give the designer of the dialog as wide a selection of possibilities as possible. This decision implies the need for a "low-level" approach to dialog specification.

5) Executability: The notation had to be directly executable to support prototyping, development, and testing of interactive information systems.

We observed that the interactive system and its actions are driven by raw or transformed user input. Accordingly, an effective specification technique for programming languages can be used effectively for specifying user interfaces. One can write down the grammar of the user input, and associate program actions with the successful recognition of "words" or "phases" in the grammar.

We decided to adapt transition diagrams for this purpose [8]. Transition diagrams have been used for a variety of language translators, including an early Cobol compiler [9], and are used as the formal specification of the MUMPS programming language [10]. (Transition diagrams have also been selected by others as an appropriate notation for specifying interactive programs [11]–[15].)

A transition diagram is a network of nodes and directed arcs. Each arc may contain a token, corresponding to a character string in the primitive alphabet (such as ASCII), or the name of another diagram. If the path is blank, it will be traversed as the default case, i.e., if all other paths leaving a given node fail. Scanning of the diagram begins at a designated entry point and proceeds until reaching an exit node or a dead end (no successful match on the paths from a given node). An operation may be associated with any path; traversal of the path causes the associated operation to occur.

Intuitively, one can see that paths may contain arbitrary strings and that the state transitions can invoke arbitrary operations. The distinguished inputs then lead to different states from which other input symbols may cause yet additional actions.

We began by using a simple transition diagram model to design and build several small interactive systems. This model contained just three different symbols, as follows:

1) node—shown by a circle, representing a stable state awaiting some user input. Each node within a diagram has a unique name, and an output message may be displayed when a node is reached. One node is designated the *starting node*, designated by two concentric circles, and there is a single exit point.

2) arc—shown by an arrow, connecting nodes to one another. Each arc represents a state transition based on some input. The input is designated either by a string literal, such as "quit," or by the name of another diagram, enclosed within angle brackets, such as <diag2>. One arc emanating from each node may be left blank, in which case it becomes the *default* transition, and is taken only when the input fails to match that specified on any of the other arcs. We shall assume for the moment that there is no ambiguity concerning which arc to take for a given input at a given node.

3) operation—shown by a small square with an associated integer. An action may be associated with a transition to represent an operation that is to be performed whenever a spe-

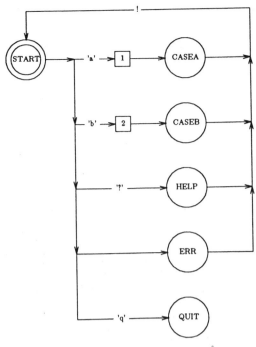

node START
   '   RAPID/USE Tutorial Example Program',
   '   Please choose: ',
   '   a - Case a',
   '   b - Case b',
   '   ? - Help',
   '   q - Quit',
   '   Your choice: '

node HELP
        'Valid commands are "a" and "b"',
        'Press any key to continue'

node CASEA
        'You are at CASEA',
        'Press any key to continue'

node CASEB
        'You are at CASEB',
        'Press any key to continue'

node ERR
        'Sorry, but you made an error -- please try again.',
        'Press any key to continue'

node QUIT
        'Thank you -- good bye'

Fig. 1. A USE transition diagram.

cific arc is traversed. The same action may be associated with more than one arc.

A very simple diagram is shown in Fig. 1. The diagram begins at START, where it waits for input. Input is a string terminated by a carriage return. There is a transition to one of five nodes based upon the input. The input of "a" causes action 1 to be performed during the transition to CASEA; the input of "b" causes action 2 to be performed during the transition to CASEB, the input of "?" causes a transition to HELP, and the input of "q" causes a transition to QUIT; anything other than "a", "b", "q", or "?" causes a transition to ERR.

The text beneath Fig. 1 shows the message displayed when a transition is made to that node. Thus, this figure is a very simple instance of a menu-selection dialog, with the START node used to present a menu, and the five other nodes representing two system commands, a quit command, a help command, and an error case.

We quickly recognized some significant shortcomings with this simple model, including the following.

1) Output Specification: It was important to specify formatting and layout of system output, rather than just describing the message itself.

2) Display of Input Information: It was not possible to include as part of an output specification any text that had been recognized as input from the user. Yet such display is a major component of many interactive programs.

3) Input Processing: Some interactive dialogs accept a line of user input, followed by a terminator, such as a carriage return, before performing an operation or making a transition, while others respond on a single key stroke or the recognition of a specific key, such as a function key. The simple model we were using accepted only a variable length string, followed by a carriage return.

4) Diagram Complexity: Complex dialogs result in very complex diagrams, greatly reducing their comprehensibility and increasing the likelihood of errors in drawing or maintaining the diagrams.

5) Alternative Displays Based on Operations: The logical flow of an interactive program is often dependent upon the result of an operation, e.g., success or failure in a table lookup. Such a situation could not be represented with the simple transition diagram model.

6) Time Limits: It was not possible to make a transition after a fixed amount of time as needed to produce a remainder message.

We therefore sought to develop a transition diagram-like notation that would overcome these shortcomings. We also wanted to define a textual representation of these diagrams to facilitate their encoding for creating an executable version of the user interface. We shall henceforth refer to these diagrams as USE transition diagrams.

We now take up the approaches to these shortcomings that were introduced in USE transition diagrams.

III. OUTPUT SPECIFICATION

A node is used to display a message. In its simplest form, a message may simply be a text string, such as shown in Fig. 1. In practice, though, more power is needed for output specification.

A. Cursor Control

First, it is useful to take advantage of screen-oriented displays, specifying the exact or relative position on a screen at which a message should be placed. Thus, one might want to specify that the message begin on row 12 at column 25, or that it begin two lines below the previously written message. We can specify the message as

r12, c25, 'Good morning, fearless leader'

It is often desirable to center a message on a line. Rather than counting spaces to find the correct starting point, the symbol "c_" may be used to denote the center, so that the specification

r12, c_'Good morning, fearless leader'

would cause the message to be centered on line 12.

We adopt the convention that the upper left hand corner of the screen is (0, 0) and the last row and column are each designated by "$". Thus, a message to be written at the beginning of the last line could be addressed with r$, c0. A relative movement is designated with "+" and "−," so that one could write

r + 2, c25, 'Your request...'

In many cases, a message may contain an entire screen full of information, so that the message could contain an arbitrary mixture of text and positioning directives. One could write, then,

cs, r5, c5, 'Please choose one of the following:',
r + 2, c10, '1) deposit',
r + 2, c10, '2) withdraw',
r + 2, c10, '3) help',
r + 2, c10, '4) quit',
r$, rv, 'Your choice...', sv

to specify a screen filled with text.

Note that screen-oriented directives are used in this example.

cs	clear screen and go to home position (r0, c0)
rv	use reverse video (if available)
sv	return to standard video

Additional screen-oriented directives provide needed cursor control. In all cases, these directives may be included in an output specification.

hm	go to home position (0, 0)
nl	start a new line (r + 1, c0),
cl	clear to end of line on current row
ce	clear to end of screen from current line
dc	delete the character at the current position, then shift subsequent characters on line to left
dl	delete entire line (current row) and scroll lower lines (if any) upward
is_'text'	insert the text beginning at the current position
il	open a blank line at the current position and move lower lines down

B. Reuse of Messages

Second, we may want to reuse a message. Common examples of this situation are error messages, screen headings, and on-line assistance. The structure of a message is identical to that of a node specification, so that a message may include cursor movement information, text strings, and variable names. We define a message name, then refer to it by that name whenever we want to display that message. Conceptually, we would define

message prompt
    r$, rv, 'Your choice...', sv

and we then write

cs, r5, c5, 'Please choose one of the following:',
r + 2, c10, '1) deposit',
r + 2, c10, '2) withdraw',
r + 2, c10, '3) help',
r + 2, c10, '4) quit',
prompt

The appearance of the message name "prompt" causes the substitution of the text associated with the message definition of "prompt."

C. Tab Settings

The layout of the previous example is dependent upon the alignment of four lines of text, requiring the inclusion of the directive "c10" in four different places. Changing the placement of these lines requires changing four occurrences of the column directive in this message, and potentially other dependent column directives in other messages that might be concurrently displayed. Flexibility and the ability to modify layouts rapidly suggests the need to associate *tabs* with column settings.

We introduce the tab definition and allow a column to be associated with a specific tab declaration, as follows.

```
tab t_0 5
tab t_1 10

cs, r5, t_0, 'Please choose one of the following:',
r + 2, t_1, '1) deposit',
r + 2, t_1, '2) withdraw',
r + 2, t_1, '3) help',
r + 2, t_1, '4) quit',
prompt
```

In this way, the alignment may be changed with only one change to the definition, namely the column associated with the tab definition.

D. Partitioned Screens

Another problem in controlling a display is to be able to partition the screen into two or more parts and to move freely between them. For example, we may wish to use the bottom two lines of the screen for error messages, regardless of what has been placed on the remainder of the screen. In that case, we would like to "mark" a position on the screen, move to another position, and then return to the marked position.

The directives "mark" and "tomark" provide part of this capability. The upper and lower case letters may be used as names of marks and then referenced. Named marks may be included as part of the output specification. The nodes

```
node one
     r + 1, 'Your reply: ', mark_A

node error
     tomark_A, cl,
     r$, mark_E, rv, 'Please type a number from 1 to 5',
     sv, tomark_A
```

allow an erroneous reply to be cleared, and an error message to be displayed on the bottom line (in reverse video), after which the cursor returns to the point at which the reply is wanted. Note also that mark_E is set to the beginning of the error line so that some other node could be defined

```
node clean_err
     mark_B, tomark_E, cl, tomark_B
```

to remove the error message at a subsequent point. The removal should not be done in node one, since it would disappear from the screen before the user had a chance to read it.

This screen partitioning is a first step toward the multiple window interfaces employed in systems such as Smalltalk-80 and Interlisp [16], [17]. We return to this point later.

IV. VARIABLES IN DIAGRAM SPECIFICATION

Output messages are often dependent upon previous input or upon computed results. Data entry systems must display and/or reformat information input by a user, as well as passing that data to operations. Programs involving multiple screens typically redisplay data given on one screen on a subsequent display. For example, a bank teller program may obtain account information, and then display the account holder's name or account number later in the interactive dialog. Thus, the limitation of fixed text in the output specification is inadequate, and we must introduce *variables*. We adopt the convention that a variable may be assigned the string received on a specific input, or be assigned a value as the result of an action. The variable name is shown on one or more arcs in a diagram. When such an arc is traversed, the input string is assigned to that variable.

Thus, the appearance of a variable name on an arc emanating from a node means that the input is assigned to that variable.

If there were a message such as

```
cs, r10, c10, 'Please type your name:'
```

the resulting input could be assigned to a variable called "name," and could subsequently be displayed as follows:

```
r0, c40, 'User--', name
```

within a node or another message.

As with variables in programming languages, we wish to define constraints on their values. We define four kinds of constraints:

1) data type: string, integer, float, scalar, date, time
2) string length: minimum and maximum length (both optional)
3) range of values: lexicographic or numeric ranges, depending on type (both optional)
4) display format: used as default format for displaying values of the variable.

Thus, all of the following are variable definitions:

```
string name
string licenseplate [1:7]
string longstring [50:*]
string a_to_c_word range 'a'..'c'
integer count
integer testresult [2:2] range 30..50
scalar weekday (monday, tuesday, wednesday, thursday,
     friday)
float flt display ("r7.2")
date sunbday init '19820222
time lunch init @123000
```

The numbers in square brackets delimit the length of the input in characters. The range constraint specifies a restriction on the *value* of the variable, where the range for "integer" is given by integer values and the range for "string" is given by the ASCII collating sequence. An asterisk "*" may be used to denote the absence of a fixed limit. The syntax for the display format is similar to that used for the *printf* function in the Unix™ standard I/O library, and has been extended to support the display of scalars, month (numeric and text), day, year, weekday, hours, minutes, and seconds, as well as left, right, and center adjustment of displayed variables.

Variables may be assigned by appearing on a transition, so that user input meeting the constraint(s), if any, causes the transition and makes the assignment. In Fig. 2, the transition from step1 to step2 causes the variable "restname" to be assigned the user input string.

Once a variable has been assigned a value, it may subsequently be used in messages and in actions. As with variables in other programming notations, it may also be assigned a new value.

V. INPUT PROCESSING

The basic transition diagram model assumes that the input to determine transitions along an arc is a variable length string terminated by a carriage return. Also, there *must* be some input to cause a transition. All of these assumptions are unnecessarily restrictive, in addition to being unrealistic for the practical design of interactive systems. Therefore, extensions to the transition diagram model are needed for these cases.

First, though, we observe that the input character set must be extended beyond the typical set of 95 ASCII printable graphics, to accommodate control characters, function keys, and other inputs that may be received from a modern terminal keyboard. We use the following symbols to represent the extended input character set.

esc	escape
cr	carriage return (default)
bs	backspace
lf	line feed
del	delete
tab	tab character (ctl_i)
ctl_{A-Za-z}	any control character, such as ctl_D, for any letter
f{0-9}	function keys f0 through f9
↑	up arrow
↓	down arrow
←	left arrow
→	right arrow
home	home key

Thus, in the same way that one can write a string literal on an arc, one can write any of these symbols, treating them as "reversed words" and prohibiting the use of variables with these names.

A. Buffered versus Unbuffered Input

As noted, the assumption of inputs terminated by carriage returns is very restrictive, and fails to represent many of the most common uses of interactive systems. While we use that assumption as a default, we need mechanisms for overriding that case.

First, a single keystroke may be used to determine the appropriate branch, without a terminating character. This ap-

™Unix is a trademark of AT&T Bell Laboratories.

Fig. 2. Assignment to a variable.

proach is commonly found in multiple-choice (menu selection) applications, not only with keyboard input, but also with touch screens and mouse input. Indeed, single keystroke (or equivalent) processing is a key aspect of many highly interactive systems. Rather than buffering the input, it must be processed immediately.

Thus, the two forms of input processing must be distinguished, which cannot be done with the simple model of transition diagrams. We introduce the "!" symbol to denote this immediate transition, which we term a *single key* transition. The appearance of the "!" followed by a character on an arc means that a single "character" input is used to cause a transition. Fig. 3 gives an example of this case.

B. Specific Character Recognition

A similar problem arises when it is desired to make a transition based on the recognition of a particular character, whenever it appears in the user input. This is termed a *special key* transition, and is shown by preceding the key with an ampersand ("&") on the arc. The ampersand indicates the immediate transition, without waiting for a terminator, rather than accepting input until a terminator is received.

Note that "single key" and "special key" transitions are difficult. In a command-oriented system, it may be possible to interrupt a command or any other input by typing a specific key, such as control-C or "?". It is only the "special key" concept that permits this interruption, unless *all* input is handled as "single key."

We have also considered the case in which a specific key, such as an escape or a function key, can be globally used to terminate a diagram and perhaps return to a specific node in a specific diagram. From a notational standpoint, it is necessary to have an explicit arc from every node where such an input could be received. (It is straightforward to implement this idea in software, though.) Without such an explicit arc, a diagram (or, as we shall see, a set of diagrams) may have unconstrained flow of control (the *goto* problem); furthermore, such branching in a set of diagrams raises traditional programming language questions about the scope of variables.

C. Truncating Input String Length

The default case in transition diagrams is to accept a string of any length until a carriage return is received. We wish first to consider strings of fixed length (frequently length 1), and also strings terminated by something other than a carriage return. Consider the very common case of asking a user for a "yes" or "no" response. The decision can normally be made by examining the first character of the user input, so that a variety of different response can be handled similarly. Even in this simple case, the truncation greatly simplifies the problem of decoding input, which might be any of "N," "n," "NO," "No," or "no," excluding numerous possibilities from languages other than English. Note that the *length* option is different from the single_key option in that the length trun-

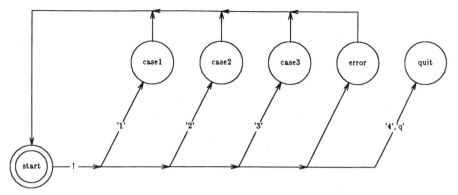

Fig. 3. Transition diagram illustrating immediate transition.

cation is only applied after the input termination character (normally the carriage return) is received.

D. Nonstandard Terminators

The carriage return default may be overridden with the *until* option. In the *vi* text editor for the Unix operating system, for example, insertion mode is terminated with the "escape" character. In other applications where the input may extend over several lines, the carriage return must be treated as a normal input character, with the terminator switched to a different character. Thus, one might wish to describe that all input received prior to an escape character will be assigned to a variable named inputstr.

The until feature may be combined with the length feature, so that an input string may be truncated to a fixed length regardless of the terminator. Fig. 4 illustrates the notation used in the USE transition diagram for nonstandard terminators and/or fixed length strings. This information precedes the input string(s) and is denoted by the slash symbol "/". A list of zero or more alternative terminators is given to the left of the "/" and the length, if fixed, is given to the right. The fragment of the diagram shown in Fig. 4 indicates that input is read until an escape or a tab character is received, and then truncated to eight characters. The resulting string is assigned to variable instring. These extensions to input processing, the extended character set, single key input, special key transitions, alternate terminators, and input string truncation, allow the description of a much greater set of interactive dialogs than was previously possible.

VI. DIAGRAM DECOMPOSITION

The added expressiveness given by the output specification notation, the inclusion of variables, and the extensions to input processing made it possible to describe most interactive systems using alphanumeric display terminals. The USE transition diagrams could be used with a means for specifying the actions, and thereby serve as a specification method.

One important aspect of specifications, though, is comprehensibility. We found that it was very easy to create large complex diagrams that could not easily be written or understood. Diagram complexity arose initially from the desire to provide error handling and help facilities in the interactive dialog. By following our own guidelines for designing inter-

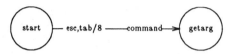

Fig. 4. Nonstandard terminators in USE transition diagrams.

active systems [18], we were led to provide a help arc and an error arc from each node where user input could occur (virtually all). Accordingly, the number of nodes and arcs proliferated. The situation was even worse if one wanted to provide a *different* message on the second occurrence of an error than on the first.

At first, we simply adopted the strategy of drawing a set of diagrams with no error handling and no interactive help facilities so that the diagram presented the "normal" flow of dialog. Yet this was also inadequate as we attempted to model increasingly complex dialogs and systems.

A. Subconversations

The solution taken was to introduce a hierarchy of diagrams, so that any diagram could "invoke" another diagram. A connected set of nodes could be named, and could be "called" from another diagram. This idea of a "subconversation" was useful because it also modeled a commonly occurring situation in interactive systems: a set of "transaction types." Accordingly, a fourth symbol was added to the node, arc, and action:

4) subconversation—shown by a rectangular box, with an associated diagram name. When an arc enters a subconversation box, traversal of that diagram is suspended, and control is transferred to the starting node of the diagram named in the subconversation box. The new diagram is then traversed until its exit point is reached, at which point control returns to the "calling" diagram, and the subconversation box is exited.

A simple example of this situation is shown by the diagram structure of Fig. 5, where there are subconversations for "deposit," "withdraw," and "balance." The capability for any node to have multiple exits is retained in the subconversation by permitting a diagram to return a value to the invoking diagram so that the branch upon exit from the subconversation may be determined by the return value. The returned value is denoted by a nonnegative integer preceded by the "#" symbol in the invoked diagram. If more than one arc emanates from a subconversation box, the associated return value used to determine the branch can appear on each arc. We adopt

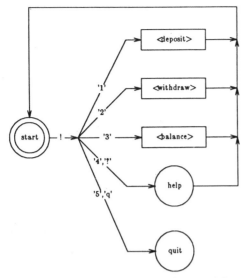

Fig. 5. The use of subconversations for transactions.

Fig. 6. Returning values from subconversations.

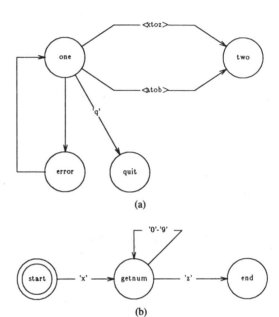

Fig. 7. (a) Using diagram names for arc traversal. (b) Use of a subconversation for string recognition.

the convention that such values may only be returned to the immediate caller, i.e., one level of invocation. This use is shown in Fig. 6.

B. Transitions Described by Diagrams

Until now, we have assumed that all inputs are described either by a string literal (a directly named sequence of characters) or by an input string that is immediately assigned to a variable. In some cases, though, it is useful to use a diagram to describe the syntax that causes a transition. Rather than using a string literal or a variable name on an arc, one can use the name of a diagram. That diagram, and any additional levels invoked from that diagram, must be successfully traversed to cause the given arc to be traversed. This situation is shown in Fig. 7; in Fig. 7(a), the diagram name <xtoz> is associated with an arc connecting nodes "one" and "two," while Fig. 7(b) shows the diagram xtoz. Note that <atob> is another possibility for the traversal from "one" to "two," which can also be tried.

This use of subconversations allows recognition of a string composed of several components, possibly of indeterminate length, without overly complicating the higher level diagram. As before, the called diagram could be inserted into the higher level diagram, without altering the effect. In this case, though, it becomes possible to hide the structure of the recognized string. This construct is also useful for allowing several different strings to cause the same transition, which is frequently needed for dialogs supporting novice and expert interfaces, for example.

C. Decomposing Messages and Actions

Another important option is the ability to decompose messages and/or actions. Suppose that we want to perform action 2 on one arc, actions 2 and 3 in response to another input, and actions 1 and 2 in response to yet another input. To do so, one must create an intermediate node to permit the actions to be specified independently. Yet we do not want to require additional input to cause the second action to occur. Simi-

larly, one may wish to display two separate messages in response to a single input without waiting for additional input from the user.

In both of these cases, one must make an automatic transition from one node to another. This case, called the *skip* case, is denoted by a "+" on an arc; of course, no string, return value, or diagram name can appear on such an arc.

D. User Interfaces as a Hierarchy of USE Transition Diagrams

The use of subconversations is both an aid to diagram decomposition and a notational convenience. There are, however, several distinct advantages to their use.

1) Any diagram may be referenced from other diagrams in a dialog and thereby reused; this supports the creation of libraries of diagrams that can be integrated into systems.

2) A higher level diagram can often be designed without making decisions about the actual input text; this approach allows decisions about the dialog to be deferred and isolated, and therefore changed easily.

3) Subconversations help to break up a diagram that has a large number of nodes; to aid comprehension, diagrams should contain fewer than 10 nodes.

4) Subconversations help to illustrate the structure of a dialog; many dialogs are naturally hierarchical and the subconversation mechanism allows this hierarchy to be shown in the diagrams.

VIII. Semantic Aspects of USE Transition Diagrams

Until now, transitions between nodes in diagrams have been driven by the *syntax* of the user input. The extensions have either been structural, e.g., subconversations, or directed to finer input control, e.g., unbuffered input. Even the introduction of variables into diagrams did not alter this situation. However, it now becomes necessary to introduce *semantic* dependencies into USE transition diagrams.

A. Returning Values from Actions

We previously noted that the direction of a dialog is often dependent upon the result of an action. For example, in a banking system, the user (a teller) would be asked to input a customer account number. A subsequent action would be to look up this account number in the bank's customer account database. The next message presented to the teller would depend on the success of the search.

To achieve this effect, it is necessary to associate a return value with the *action*, and then to branch on that value. This is easily accomplished in our notation by indicating one or more arcs emerging from an action box, with arcs labeled with alternate return values, following the same approach used for subconversations. This situation is shown in Fig. 8. One path, labeled 1, leads to node found, while the other path, labeled 2, leads to node notfound. Note that the continuation from an action may be either unconditional, as we have previously seen, or conditional based on a return value. In the unconditional case, there may be a returned value, but it will not affect the transition following the action.

B. Time Limits

In modeling interactive systems with state transition diagrams, we found no convenient way to express time, since transitions are linked to user input. In practice, though, one often expects user input within a fixed amount of time, with an unexpected delay indicating a problem. Thus, it is desirable to be able to effect a transition on the expiration of a predefined time limit. In this way, it is possible to branch to another node, from which a reminder or help message can be displayed.

We thus introduce the *alarm* transition, and denote that transition by writing the time limit on the appropriate arc, e.g., 30″. The alarm transition is made if no input is received from the user before the time limit expires.

VIII. An Extended Example

To this point, all of the examples of the USE transition diagram specification method have dealt with "toy" examples, intended to denote the overall style and scope of the specification method. In this section, we show a small part of a much larger example, a data dictionary system to support a variant of Structured Systems Analysis [19]. This example not only shows a broad range of the features of the USE specification method for interactive systems, but represents a running application system in everyday use. Because of space limitations, though, only three of the 31 diagrams representing the system are shown, and the display is limited to the diagrams themselves (with the associated text and action calls),

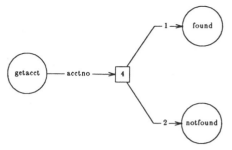

Fig. 8. Branch determined by value returned from action rules.

omitting the description of the actions on which they operate.

The data dictionary is represented by a set of relations, specified in the Troll/USE data definition and manipulation language, and shown in Fig. 9 [5], [20].

The first diagram, the main diagram for the data dictionary system, is shown in Fig. 10(a). Three features are worth noting in this diagram.

1) The action box numbered "2" is a call to the database script "startup." If this action succeeds (return "ok"), then control flows to node "start;" otherwise, control flows to "nodb" and "x" and the program terminates.

2) The center of activity is node "select," which provides a menu-like interface to the user, providing the user with the ability to enter the subconversations "add," "modify," "delete," and "query." The "select" node also provides for terminating the program, asking for help, and handling unexpected input (the "error" node).

3) The structure found in this diagram is generic for transaction-oriented interactive programs. Many interactive information systems exhibit the same structure, and this diagram can be easily modified to suit other applications. (Note the similarity to Fig. 5.)

The subconversation "add" is shown in Fig. 10(b), and has much the same structure as does the top-level diagram, asking the user to specify the type of entry to be placed in the data dictionary. (Clearly, this dialog has been designed to minimize typing and to present a screen-oriented interface to the user.)

Note that the subconversations "add_element" through "add_message" all return the value 0 if the item is successfully inserted in the data dictionary. This return value is used to direct control flow to node "inserted," which displays the message "successful insertion" before prompting the user for another entry.

The "add" subconversation then invokes "add_process" when the user wishes to define a new process and store information about that process in the data dictionary. Several aspects of the diagram shown in Fig. 10(c) are worth noting.

1) Three different kinds of actions are performed in this diagram. The actions "checkpro," "inspro," and "delparams" operate on the database shown in Fig. 9, as indicated by the use of the "call" to the actions. The action "CallEdit" is to an executable program, to be written in a high level programming language; it is, in fact, a call to the *vi* editor for a file to hold the process description for the given process. Finally, there is a case statement, denoted by the "cs" action box, which controls branching after the "checkpro" action is per-

```
relation data_element [key name] of
    name: string;
    el_descrip1,el_descrip2,el_descript3,el_descrip4,el_descrip5: string;
    el_type: string;
    el_constraints: string;
    el_notes: string;
    el_count: integer;
end;

relation data_store [key name] of
    name: string;
    store_notes: string;
    store_count: string;
end;

relation data_flow [key name] of
    name: string;
    flow_notes: string;
    flow_count: integer;
end;

relation process [key name] of
    name: string;
    proc_module: string;
    proc_notes: string;
end;

relation proc_params [key name, param_name] of
    name: string;
    param_name: string;
    param_type: scalar(inparam,outparam);
end;

relation message [key name] of
    name: string;
    msg_descript: string;
    msg_number: integer;
end;

relation allnames [key name] of
    name: string;
    name_type: scalar (element,store,flow,proc,msg);
end;

relation flow_parts [key name, component] of
    name, component: string;
end;

relation store_parts [key name, component] of
    name, component: string;
end;
```

Fig. 9. Relational database schema for data dictionary.

formed. The USE transition diagram notation does not allow two consecutive action boxes, so it is necessary to interject the dummy node "hack1" between the call to "checkpro" and the case statement.

2) Three different values may be returned to "add," representing successful insertion of the information (0), an error in insertion (1), or user cancellation of the insertion (2). Referring back to Fig. 10(b), we note that the "add" diagram does not presently distinguish between the latter two cases.

3) The arc "skip" feature, denoted by "+", is used several times, when actions and/or displays are performed without intervening user input. Without the skip feature, it would be necessary to combine information that is logically separate or to require user input in the interim.

4) The message "main.lastline" is used, allowing the dialog designer to define some standard message formats in the main diagram and then use them throughout the dialog. This feature improves consistency of the interface design for the user.

IX. EXECUTABLE SPECIFICATIONS

As described in the introduction, a critical step in applying the User Software Engineering methodology is to create an executable version of the user interface. To this end, we have designed and built a system called RAPID/USE, which consists

of two components: the transition diagram intepreter (TDI) and the action linker [3], [21]. The TDI was designed to accept an encoding of the USE transition diagrams that resembles the diagrams and messages as much as possible.[2] This encoding, called a *dialog description* or a *script*, is transformed into tables by TDI. In this way, one can draw the diagrams and quickly transform them to an executable form. The encoding may be achieved either by editing the textual representation of the diagrams, or by using a graphical tool, the transition diagram editor [22], to draw the USE transition diagrams interactively, and to have the TDI dialog description generated automatically.

Input to TDI consists of one or more diagram descriptions, each representing a transition diagram. Each diagram may have five types of statements.

1) Diagram name statement—identifies the diagram, its entry node and exit node.

2) Variable definition statements—permit the use of names to describe strings of alphanumeric or numeric characters, along with range constraints on their values.

3) Message definition statements—permit the use of names to describe messages that are to be called from multiple points in the diagram.

4) Node definition statements—define the node names for the diagram, along with the associated messages and screen control for each node.

5) Arc statements—describe the structure of the diagram and its transition conditions.

The Action Linker part of RAPID/USE allows programmed actions to be associated with the transitions. Routines may be written in C, Fortran 77, or Pascal. (Linkage to other languages can also be provided.)

The syntax for the nodes is virtually identical to that shown in Fig. 10(a)–(c). The description for the arcs is given by the name of the starting node, followed by all of the possible branches and actions emanating from that node. Fig. 11 shows the TDI text for the diagram shown in Fig. 10(a). An inspection of this text will show that it is a direct encoding of the diagram itself. This encoding is done automatically by the transition diagram editor, and may also be done manually by someone without access to the graphical editor. Thus, RAPID/USE is used both for building and validating user interfaces (TDI) and for building functioning systems (TDI + Action Linker).

X. FURTHER EXTENSIONS TO DIALOG SPECIFICATIONS

The USE transition diagrams, as described so far, cover a very broad range of the interactive dialogs that are suitable for user interfaces on "intelligent" alphanumeric display terminals. Furthermore, both the diagrams and the accompanying TDI notation are independent of the physical characteristics of any specific terminal. Thus, these diagrams may serve as a general descriptive technique for interactive systems.

With recent advances in computer terminals and worksta-

---

[2] The present distribution of RAPID/USE supports all of the transition diagram features described in Sections III–VII except for some restrictions on transitions described by diagrams (Section VI-B).

main

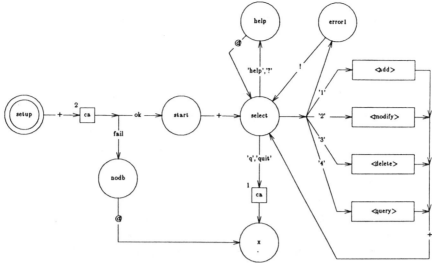

Actions

1   call shutdown
2   call startup

diagram main entry setup exit x

database 'usedddb'
library '../scripts'

tab t_0 15
tab t_1 20

message header
  cs,r2,c0,c_'USE Data Dictionary'

message lastline
  r$,c0,'Hit any character to continue.'

node setup

node select
        tomark_A,ce,r+3,t_0,'Please choose ',
        r+2,t_1,'1: Add a dictionary entry.',
        r+2,t_1,'2: Modify a dictionary entry.',
        r+2,t_1,'3: Delete a dictionary entry.',
        r+2,t_1,'4: Query data dictionary',
        r+2,t_1,'help: Information on use of program',
        r+2,t_1,'quit: Exit USE/Data Dictionary',
        r+2,t_0,'Your choice: '

node help
        cs,r$-3,c0,'For more information about a command, enter',
        r$-2,c0,'the command number, press return and then type "help" or "?" ',
        r$,c0,'Hit any key to continue'

node nodb
        cs,r$,c0,'Could not open database directory'

node start
        header,mark_A

node x
        cs

node error1
        r$-1,c0,rv,bell,'Please type a number from 1 to 4.',sv,
        lastline

(a)

Fig. 10. (a) Top-level USE transition diagram of data dictionary system.

add

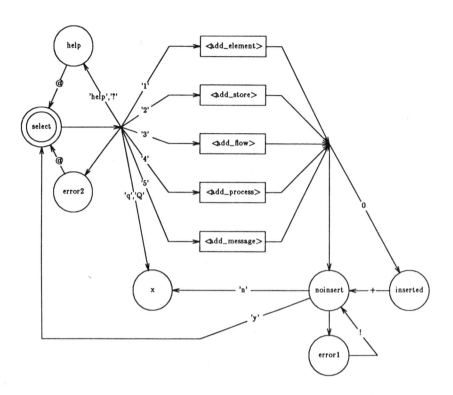

diagram add entry select exit x

tab t_0 10
tab t_1 15

node error1
        r$,c0,rv,'Please type "y" or "n"',sv,tomark_E

node select
        main.header,
        r4,c0,c_'Add entry to dictionary',
        r+2,t_0,'Please select type of data entry: ',
        r+1,t_1,'1: data element',
        r+1,t_1,'2: data store',
        r+1,t_1,'3: data flow',
        r+1,t_1,'4: process',
        r+1,t_1,'5: message',
        r+2,t_0,'Your choice (1-5): '

node help

        cs,r0,c0,c_'USE/Data Dictionary',
        r12,c0,c_'Add new entry',
        main.lastline

node x

node inserted
        r$-4,c0,'Successful insertion'

node error2
        r$-1,cs,rv,bell,'Please type a number from "1" to "5"',sv,
        r$,c0,'Hit any character to continue.'

node noinsert
        r+2,c0,'Another entry (y/n)? ', mark_E

(b)

Fig. 10. (*Continued.*) (b) The "add" subconversion of data dictionary system.

add_process

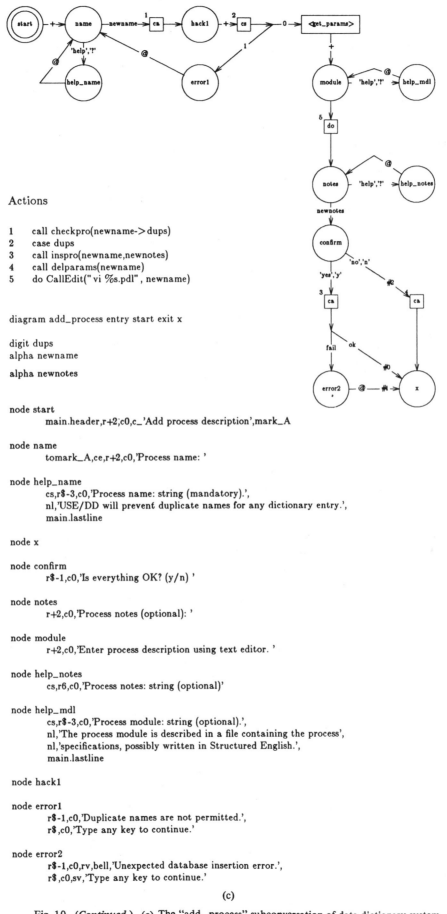

Actions

1   call checkpro(newname->dups)
2   case dups
3   call inspro(newname,newnotes)
4   call delparams(newname)
5   do CallEdit(" vi %s.pdl" , newname)

diagram add_process entry start exit x

digit dups
alpha newname

alpha newnotes

node start
     main.header,r+2;c0,c_'Add process description',mark_A

node name
     tomark_A,ce,r+2,c0,'Process name: '

node help_name
     cs,r$-3,c0,'Process name: string (mandatory).',
     nl,'USE/DD will prevent duplicate names for any dictionary entry.',
     main.lastline

node x

node confirm
     r$-1,c0,'Is everything OK? (y/n) '

node notes
     r+2,c0,'Process notes (optional): '

node module
     r+2,c0,'Enter process description using text editor. '

node help_notes
     cs,r6,c0,'Process notes: string (optional)'

node help_mdl
     cs,r$-3,c0,'Process module: string (optional).',
     nl,'The process module is described in a file containing the process',
     nl,'specifications, possibly written in Structured English.',
     main.lastline

node hack1

node error1
     r$-1,c0,'Duplicate names are not permitted.',
     r$,c0,'Type any key to continue.'

node error2
     r$-1,c0,rv,bell,'Unexpected database insertion error.',
     r$,c0,sv,'Type any key to continue.'

(c)

Fig. 10. (*Continued.*) (c) The "add_process" subconversation of data dictionary system.

```
arc setup
    skip call startup
        when ok to start
        when fail to nodb

arc select
    on 'q','quit' call shutdown to x
    on '4' to <query>
    on '2' to <modify>
    on '3' to <delete>
    on '1' to <add>
    on 'help','?' to help
    else to error1

arc help noecho single_key
    else to select

arc <modify>
    skip to select

arc <delete>
    skip to select

arc nodb noecho single_key
    else to x

arc start
    skip to select

arc <add>
    skip to select

arc <query>
    skip to select

arc error1 single_key
    else to select
```

Fig. 11. Fragment of dialog description syntax from Fig. 10(a) using RAPID/USE syntax.

tions, one is naturally drawn to determine if these ideas can be extended to such devices. Many such extensions seem feasible; in this section, we sketch out suitable strategies for these extensions. Since all of them now become minor refinements of previously discussed concepts, the treatment here is brief.

Modern bit-mapped displays are capable of displaying both textual and graphical output, of partitioning the display into two or more (possibly overlapping) regions (windows), and of either monochromatic or color display. Such displays often have a special pointing device, such as a mouse, that allows "picking" (selecting one of several buttons) and cursor movement.

One can immediately see that the notion of output specification, as associated with nodes in USE transition diagrams, may be extended to accommodate many of these concepts. For example, many pictures may be drawn by using a graphical language such as PIC [23] and simply allowing the output specification language for transition diagrams to include calls to PIC. Similarly, color definitions (or pixel values) can be associated with output nodes or with items displayed within a node, just as reverse video and standard video were used in Section III.

The problem with respect to drawing objects is not so much to draw them, but rather to be able to refer to them subsequently. Graphical interaction often involves the selection of an item, command, or icon with a pointing device. Thus, any object that might be referenced by such a device must be identifiable.

A transition diagram based strategy can only succeed if there is a way to associate placement of objects on the display with the placement of the pointing device. To achieve this, the pointing device must transmit more information than the input signal alone.

For a mouse, the "pick" buttons on top of the device may be specified and handled in the same manner as for a function button or any other single key input, as described in Section V. In other words, one could write "pick(1)" on an arc to indicate a transition from one node to another on receipt of that input. However, that transition would also require an action routine which would need information concerning the current screen position of the pointing device. This information is necessary to associate the pointing device with a displayed object, or to indicate a position at which text or additional objects should be placed.

Extension to multiple windows can also be accomplished. Windows may be edfined independently of the diagrams, and then any transition diagram may be associated with a specific window. When a subconversation is invoked, that may cause the appearance of a new window, either at a predetermined place or at a place indicated by the location of a pointing device on the screen. This approach can work for both "persistent" windows and for "popup" windows.

Once multiple windows are introduced, then the extension to multiple concurrent dialog is also possible. This extension is handled most easily by using the location of the pointing device to determine the active dialog, but other possibilities exist as well.

In general, then, many extensions for bit-mapped graphics, multiple windows, pointing devices, and concurrency can be made within the framework of USE transition diagrams as described here. Such extensions would provide a formal basis for describing a yet larger class of interactive systems.

It is clear, though, that there are practical limits to these extensions. Even with the extensions described here, the notations would be tedious. Many sophisticated users would prefer to do "reverse specification," interactively designing the windows, icons, and user interface, and to generate the formal specification of the interaction from there.

It is important to note that transition diagrams represent a sequence of finite states, so that they become unsuitable as a representation scheme when one attempts to describe continuous input devices, such as found in many video games and drawing systems. Alternative approaches must be devised to represent continuous input.

XI. EVALUATION

In Section II, five requirements were established for a user interface notation: formalism, completeness, comprehensibility, flexibility, and testability. We conclude by evaluating USE transition diagrams against these requirements.

Formalism: Transition diagrams are a specification method for formal grammars, and have long served as a means for unambiguous specification of programming languages. The extensions made for USE transition diagrams retain that formalism, yielding an unambiguous method for dialog specification. When used in combination with formal specifications for the related actions, e.g., preconditions and postconditions, one has a formal specification methodology.

Completeness: The basic form of transition diagrams, while complete from the standpoint for specifying a formal grammar, was far from complete for specifying interactive dialogs. The extensions described here greatly extend the scope of user interaction that can be described with the diagrams, and are quite thorough for dialogs involving alphanumeric keyboards and displays, including special purpose keys and screen-oriented display. We have sketched out approaches for additional extensions that are appropriate for a broader range of terminal, yet even these extensions are incomplete. We continue to search for effective descriptive techniques for broader classes of dialogs.

Comprehensibility: Transition diagrams were selected in preference to Backus–Naur form as a notation for dialog description largely on the basis of relative comprehensibility. Our own empirical evidence supports this decision. At the same time, though, additional extensions to the notation would have a negative effect upon comprehensibility. Furthermore, we have observed that understandability of the diagrams is enhanced by the use of sample screens, either using TDI or hand drawn screens, to show the typical displays from specific nodes.

Flexibility: There are three major "styles" of interactive dialogs on alphanumeric terminals: command oriented, menu selection (multiple choice), and natural language. We found that all three of these styles were easily handled with USE transition diagrams. Furthermore, we saw that we could define *multiple interfaces* to the *same* set of actions. Thus, one could build a menu selection *and* a command oriented interface to a system, where the menu selection might be more appropriate for the novice user, with the command approach designed for the experienced user. Similarly, one could build multilingual programs, carrying out the same set of computations in each case, but providing the user interface in two or more different languages, such as French and English.

The flexibility of the USE transition diagrams comes with a tradeoff against simplicity. Many interactive dialogs are "forms-oriented," in which the user fills in one or more entries on a screen designed to look like a form. Such systems are often specified with a "what-you-see-is-what-you-get" form layout program, as found in numerous commercially available user interface management and application generation systems. The USE transition diagram notation for such a form can be quite complex, involving a node, a transition, and possibly an action for every user input on the form.

The reason for this complexity is that the creators of the forms design system have made numerous standard decisions about the nature of the interface for their users, and hence do not need the generality provided by the USE specification method. The low-level degree of control available with the transition diagram approach is "overkill" for this class of interface, and thus requires the developer to specify in detail many features that are implicit in the form-oriented approach.

As a practical matter, we have designed and written a forms-oriented program to provide a general interface to a Troll/USE relational database. It is instructive to note that this forms-oriented program *generates* the transition diagram language used by the Transition Diagram Interpreter, from which an executable program is created. Thus, the transition diagram

notation is sufficiently flexible to handle the forms-oriented approach.

Executability: The ease of machine processing of the USE transition diagrams allows informal testing of a set of alternative interfaces, so that potential system users may be presented with an executable version of an interface design and the users and dialog designers can jointly evaluate the design. The structure of RAPID/USE allows direct linkage of the executable dialog with programmed actions, so that the prototype of the dialog can be directly extended to produce a fully operational system. Thus, RAPID/USE serves the needs for prototyping *and* development.

Much of the work in program testing is based on coverage of program paths; these notations are easily carried over into interface testing by describing coverage of dialog paths. The formal description of the input language, as given by the USE transition diagrams, is most useful for defining a set of test cases that allow testing of the user interface. Indeed, RAPID/ USE contains logging facilities that support analysis of dialog designs, and includes the "rapsum" subsystem to generate summaries of a session with TDI.

In summary, the USE transition diagram method is a general method for the specification of human–computer interaction. It can be viewed as a pictorial programming language, encompassing many of the issues of control flow and scope of variales found in traditional programming languages. When combined with the use of the Transition Diagram Interpreter to create executable and easily modifiable versions of user interfaces, one can quickly iterate on designs of a user interface, yielding a design that is satisfactory from the user standpoint, while formalizable and implementable from the developer standpoint. The USE transition diagrams can thereby provide effective methods and tools for the engineering of interactive systems.

ACKNOWLEDGMENT

I am grateful to my colleagues who have contributed to the ideas presented in this paper. S. Stinson validated the basic ideas of using state transition diagrams for modeling interactive information systems. D. Shewmake and P. Pircher built the Transition Diagram Interpreter and the RAPID/USE system. C. Mills and P. Pircher built the Transition Diagram Editor used as a front-end to RAPID/USE. M. Kersten built the Troll/ USE relational database management system. Their help has been invaluable.

REFERENCES

[1] A. I. Wasserman, "The user software engineering methodology: An overview," in *Information System Design Methodologies— A Comparative Review*, A. A. Verrijn-Stuart, Ed. Amsterdam, The Netherlands: North-Holland, 1982, pp. 591–628.
[2] ——, "USE: A methodology for the design and development of interactive information systems," in *Formal Models and Practical Tools for Information System Design*, H.-J. Schneider, Ed. Amsterdam, The Netherlands: North-Holland, 1979, pp. 31–50.
[3] A. I. Wasserman and D. T. Shewmake, "Rapid prototyping of interactive information systems," *ACM Software Eng. Notes*, vol. 7, no. 5, pp. 171–180, Dec. 1982.
[4] A. I. Wasserman, D. D. Sherertz, M. L. Kersten, R. P. van de Riet, and M. D. Dippé, "Revised report on the programming language

PLAIN," *ACM SIGPLAN Notices*, vol. 16, no. 5, pp. 59-80, May 1981.

[5] M. L. Kersten and A. I. Wasserman, "The architecture of the PLAIN data base handler," *Software—Practice and Experience*, vol. 11, no. 2, pp. 175-186, Feb. 1981.

[6] A. I. Wasserman, "The unified support environment: Support for the user software engineering methodology," in *Proc. IEEE Comput. Soc. SoftFair Conf.*, July 1983, pp. 145-153.

[7] A. I. Wasserman and M. L. Kersten, "A relational database environment for software development," Lab. Medical Inform. Sci., Univ. California, San Francisco, Tech. Rep. 65, 1983.

[8] A. I. Wasserman and S. K. Stinson, "A specification method for interactive information systems," *Proc. IEEE Comput. Soc. Conf. Specification of Reliable Software*, 1979, pp. 68-79.

[9] M. E. Conway, "Design of a separable transition-diagram compiler," *Commun. ACM*, vol. 6, no. 7, pp. 396-408, July 1963.

[10] J. T. O'Neill, Ed., *MUMPS Language Standard*, ANSI Standard XII.1, Amer. Nat. Standards Inst., 1977.

[11] D. L. Parnas, "On the user of transition diagrams in the design of a user interface for an interactive computer system," in *Proc. 24th Nat. ACM Conf.*, 1969, pp. 379-385.

[12] B. E. Casey and B. Dasarathy, "Modeling and validating the man–machine interface," *Software*, vol. 12, no. 6, pp. 557-569, June 1982.

[13] R. J. K. Jacob, "Using formal specifications in the design of a human–computer interface," *Commun. ACM*, vol. 26, no. 3, pp. 259-264, Mar. 1983.

[14] P. Bieleski, "Flowcharting revisited (obsolete techniques vs. unexploited techniques)," in *Conference Papers: 8th New Zealand Comput. Conf.*, 1983, pp. 123-139.

[15] D. Kieras and P. Polson, "A generalized transition network representation for interactive systems," in *Proc. CHI '83 Human Factors in Comput. Syst.*, 1983, pp. 103-106.

[16] A. Goldberg and D. Robson, *Smalltalk-80: the Language and its Implementation*. Reading, MA: Addison-Wesley, 1983.

[17] W. Teitelman and L. Masinter, "The INTERLISP Programming Environment," *Computer*, vol. 14, no. 4, pp. 25-33, Apr. 1981.

[18] A. I. Wasserman, "User software engineering and the design of interactive systems," in *Proc. 5th Int. Conf. Software Eng.*, 1981, pp. 387-393.

[19] T. DeMarco, *Structured Analysis and System Specification*. Englewood Cliffs, NJ: Prentice-Hall, 1979.

[20] M. L. Kersten and A. I. Wasserman, *Troll/USE Reference Manual*, Lab. Medical Inform. Sci., Univ. California, San Francisco, 1984.

[21] A. I. Wasserman and D. T. Shewmake, "The role of prototypes in the user software engineering (USE) methodology," in *Advances in Human-Computer Interaction*, H. R. Hartson, Ed. Norwood, NJ: Ablex, 1985, pp. 191-210.

[22] C. Mills and A. I. Wasserman, "A transition diagram editor," in *Proc. 1984 Summer Usenix Meeting*, June 1984, pp. 287-296.

[23] B. W. Kernighan, "PIC-A language for typesetting graphics," *ACM SIGPLAN Notices*, vol. 16, no. 6, pp. 92-98, June 1981; see also *Proc. SIGPLAN/SIGOA Symp. Text Manipulation*.

Anthony I. Wasserman (M'71) received the A.B. degree in mathematics and physics from the University of California, Berkeley, and the M.S. and Ph.D. degrees in computer sciences from the University of Wisconsin—Madison.

After three years in industry, he joined the University of California, San Francisco, where he is now Professor of Medical Information Science. Since 1970, he has also been Lecturer in the Computer Science Division at the University of California, Berkeley. He is also the founder and President of Interactive Development Environments, Inc. He is the architect of the User Software Engineering methodology and supporting toolset for the specification and design of interactive information systems. His research interests include software development methods, tools, and environments, human interaction with computers, and data management. He is the author of more than fifty papers and an editor of seven books, including *Tutorial: Software Design Techniques* (IEEE Computer Society), with P. Freeman, and *Automated Tools for Information Systems Design* (Amsterdam, The Netherlands: North-Holland), with H.-J. Schneider.

Dr. Wasserman is the Editor-in-Chief of ACM's *Computing Surveys*, and a member of the Editorial Board of several other journals, including the *International Journal of Man-Machine Studies, Information Systems*, and the *Journal of Systems and Software*. He is a member of the Programme Committee for the IFIP Congress '86, Vice-Chairman of IFIP WG 8.1 (Design and Evaluation of Information Systems), and a former chairman of ACM's SIGSOFT. He is a member of the Association for Computing Machinery and the IEEE Computer Society.

Reprinted from *IEEE Transactions on Software Engineering*,
Volume SE-11, Number 9, September 1985, pages 945-953.
Copyright © 1985 by The Institute of Electrical and Electronics
Engineers, Inc. All rights reserved.

SPD: A Humanized Documentation Technology

MOTOEI AZUMA, TETSU TABATA, YOSHIHIRO OKI, AND SUSUMU KAMIYA

Abstract—The SPD (Structured Programming Diagram) is a documentation technology used to design well structured programs. With SPD, designers can easily express functional structure, control structure, and physical layout of a program on one sheet of paper. Its straightforward expression appeals to both document writers and readers. SPD concept and conventions are introduced in this paper. SPD usage is then explained with a program design example. Other documentation technologies used in coordination with SPD are briefly touched upon. Finally, SPD reputation and evolution in the last ten years are reviewed.

Index Terms—Documentation, software development, Structured Programming Design.

I. INTRODUCTION

NOBODY is successful in software development without sufficient documentation. Documentation provides information to support the effective design, management, implementation, and maintenance, and to facilitate the interchange of information. Documentation technology is important in order to accomplish development smoothly and efficiently, and to maximize the return on development investment.

Manuscript received November 7, 1983.
The authors are with the NEC Corporation, 7-15 Shiba, Minatoku, Tokyo 108, Japan.

As a result of software engineering research and development activities up to now, various useful programming technologies have been developed, such as structured programming [1]-[3], stepwise refinement [4], top-down design [5], one page coding [6], structured design [7], [8], composite design [9], modular programming method [10], [11], Warnier programming method [12], M. Jackson programming method [13], etc. Reflecting these technologies, flowchart usefulness was questioned [17], and various documentation techniques which support these programming technologies to be use, have also been developed, such as Warnier-Orr diagram [12], [14], [15], Jackson diagram [13], [16], NS chart [18], [19], Chapin chart [20], HIPO [21], etc. Although these documentation technologies differ in details, they have a common essential characteristic, that is, to represent a hierarchy of program functions and basic control constructs in a comprehensive fashion. This characteristic is the minimum required quality of a documentation technology for a modern programming method.

In order to improve software productivity, one of the best ways is to reuse existing programs. Ironically, it is obvious that the fewer new programs are created, the greater the productivity gained. However, it is very difficult to manage what and

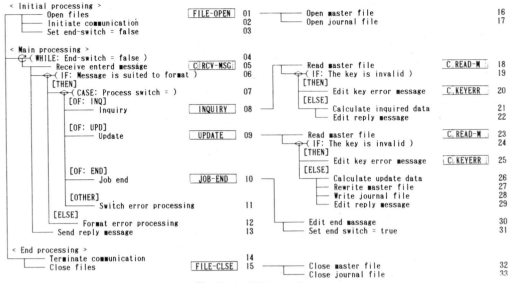

Fig. 1. An SPD example.

where programs have been reused especially in a large software development organization. A documentation technology, specifically designed for this purpose, is the only means to attain managerial visibility.

A documentation technology must not only have an excellent theoretical basis but must also match the organization and development environments, such as methodologies and rules. Moreover, it must have friendliness to its users.

In the beginning, SPD (Structured Programming Diagram) was developed to support structured programming under the effect of Warnier-Orr diagram [11], [14], [15] roughly ten years ago. Since then, it has been improved and matured as a part of STEPS [25], [26] by adopting advice from its users.

SPD is equipped with three important facilities which are necessary to documentation technologies. They are as follows:

1) fitness to the modern programming methods—SPD is positively designed to represent a function hierarchy and control structures.

2) visibility to program reuse—SPD is positively designed to represent physical layout of program modules.

3) friendliness to its users—SPD convention is simple, and its symbols are easy to understand.

Now, SPD is used by many customers in more than 1200 sites including government offices, public offices and private enterprise.

In this paper, the SPD concept and characteristics are outlined, conventions for symbols and notations follow, and then associated documentation technologies are introduced.

II. SPD CONCEPT AND CHARACTERISTICS

An SPD example is shown in Fig. 1. SPD can represent three kinds of structures on one sheet of paper together; functional structures that specify what a program does, control structures that specify the sequence in which each program function is to be executed, and physical structures that specify how the program be assigned to the modules which are often reusable and prepared as standard libraries.

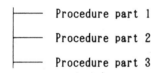

Fig. 2. Sequential construct.

The functional structure means the hierarchy for the functions the program accomplishes. To depict the functional structure, it is desirable that the function description methods possess versatility of describing the hierarchy structures from entirety to details with a function refining pace, step by step. There are several methods for representing hierarchy structures, such as HIPO [21], [22], SADT [23], [24], etc. However, SPD has widely adaptable friendliness because it follows natural styles that a person usually takes, such as an index in a book or a listing in a telephone directory.

It is well known that a program can be composed of only three kinds of constructs: sequential, repetitive, and selective. Each basic construct consists of two parts: a procedure part, which contains one or more operations to be performed, and a control part, which determines the manner in which the procedure part is to be executed. In SPD, a control part is to be represented by the symbol placed on the SPD node. The sequential construct has no special symbol on the node. It determines that the procedure parts are to be executed exactly once. (See Fig. 2.) The control part of either repetitive or selective construct determines explicitly the manner in which the procedure part is to be executed. Typically, it consists of two parts: a directive which determines the consequences of the truth value in its condition part, and a condition part, which is a Boolean expression. Selective and repetitive constructs have special symbols, diamond and circle, respectively, on the SPD node. The diamond has been used and accustomed as a flowchart selective symbol for a long time, and the circle is easy to recognize its meaning. These familiar symbols are learned with no effort. (See Figs. 3 and 4.)

The physical structure specifies the program form at the

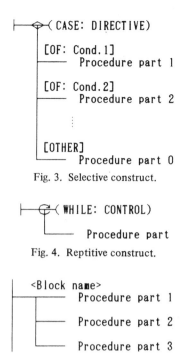

Fig. 3. Selective construct.

Fig. 4. Reptitive construct.

Fig. 5. Blocked functions–description.

Fig. 6. Level description.

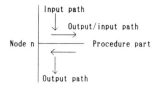

Fig. 7. Node in a level.

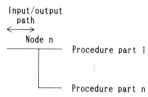

Fig. 8. Node between two levels.

coding level. At the very beginning of a design phase, relevant procedures may be described as one gross block. As the design proceeds, it is refined to more detail functions. However, it is desirable to represent that these functions are being relevant as a whole. Therefore, it is required that documentation technologies can provide the blocked functions description capability. Blocked functions are depicted in Fig. 5.

The one page coding principle is to code relevant functions within the limit of one page, in order to attain source codes readability. According to this, a program may be divided into several hierarchical levels. Items described in a higher level are more abstract than those in a lower level. SPD can specify abstract levels where each module belongs, and their relations. (See Fig. 6.) Besides, procedures that are often used are needed to describe how to assign external modules, i.e., macro, copy library, subroutine, etc. SPD can specify the assignment method and module names as symbols and rectangles on the right side of the function descriptions.

When designing a program using with the SPD, a designer can follow his natural thinking order, rather than the sequence of detail functions. That is, first, he describes main functions. Second, he describes detail functions. Third, he describes control structures. Finally, he refines and describes physical structures.

III. Symbols and Conventions

SPD can represent three kinds of structure (functional, control, and physical) together. Symbols and conventions for each structure are described here.

A. Functional Structure

The only convention is as follows. The functions hierarchy is to be described by indentation. The highest level is described at the left most position on a sheet. The lower the levels are, the farther to the right they are described.

B. Control Structure

In SPD, a vertical course represents the basic process sequence. Conversely, a horizontal course represents the functions hierarchy. Control is transferred by passing a node which is a branching point in the logical control flow. SPD has two different kinds of nodes. One is the node for the transfer of control within a level. The other is the node for the transfer of control between two different levels.

1) Node in a Level: Each node in a level consists of one input, one output, and one output/input path. As control continues along the input path for node *n* and reaches node *n*, the control flow passes first to output/input path. After executing the procedure part, control falls back and continues along the output path. (See Fig. 7.)

2) Node Between Two Levels: In a lower level, one node and one input/output path exist to an upper level. As control is transferred from an upper level to node *n* in a lower level, all procedure parts in the lower level are executed according to the rule within a level. After that, control falls back and continues along the input/output path. (See Fig. 8.)

With this principle, individual basic control constructs, described with using SPD, are depicted in Table I.

In addition to these constructs, connector symbols are specified. Exit and destination for a GO TO statement are depicted as shown in Fig. 9. It is suggested that connector symbols should be used as little as possible. A GO TO connector must not be used for connection to another page. When one SPD is expanded to another page, a continuous connector is used. A vertical connection example is shown in Fig. 10. A horizontal connection example is shown in Fig. 11.

C. Physical Structure

Three symbols are employed to represent physical structure.

1) Module Symbols: The modules assignment is represented by a module symbol. Table II shows a variety of module sym-

TABLE I
SPD Control Constructs

No.	Construct Name	SPD	Flow Chart
1	Imperative	—— P.P.	P.P.
2	Sequential	⊢ P.P.-1 ⊢ P.P.-2	P.P.-1 P.P.-2
3.1	Iterative loop	(WHILE:Cont.) P.P.	Dir. Cond. P.P.
3.2	Repetitive loop	(UNTIL:Cont.) P.P.	P.P. Dir. Cond.
3.3	Continuous loop	(LOOP) P.P.	P.P.
4.1	Monadic choice	(IF:Cond.) [THEN] P.P.	Dir. Cond. P.P.
4.2	Diadic choice	(IF:Cond.) [THEN] P.P.-1 [ELSE] P.P.-2	Dir. Cond.-1 Cond.-2 P.P.-1 P.P.-2
4.3	Multiple exclusive choice	(CASE:Dir.) [OF:Cond.-1] P.P.-1 [OF:Cond.-2] P.P.-2 [OTHER] P.P.-0	Dir. P.P.-1 Cond.-1 P.P.-2 Cond.-2 P.P.-n Cond.-n
4.4	Multiple inclusive choice	(CASE:Dir.) [OF:Cond.-1] P.P.-1 [OF:Cond.-2] P.P.-2 [OTHER] P.P.-0	Dir. P.P.-1 Cond.-1 P.P.-2 Cond.-2 P.P.-n Cond.-n

Legend: P.P. (Procedure Part)
Cont. (Control)
Cond. (Condition)
Dir. (Directive)

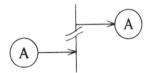

Fig. 9. GO TO connector.

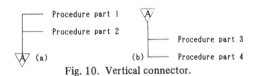

Fig. 10. Vertical connector.

bols and descriptions. If the module is defined at some other place in the same program, the module contents are placed on the lower level, as shown in Fig. 12. If the module is defined externally, only a module symbol is written, as shown in Fig. 13.

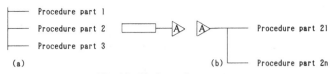

Fig. 11. Horizontal connector.

TABLE II
Module Symbols

No.	Symbol	Description
1	Module name	Module call
2	Module name	Module is standardized
3	E Program name	Program call
4	E Program name	Program is standardized
5	C Macro name	Macro call
6	C Macro name	Macro is standardized

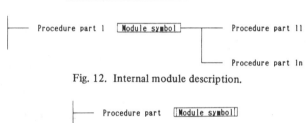

Fig. 12. Internal module description.

Fig. 13. External module description.

2) Block Symbol: A block symbol is employed to clarify block functions. The block symbol is depicted in Fig. 5.

3) Level Symbol: Level symbols can be specified to the abstraction levels, if necessary. The level number is assigned in the abstraction sequence such as Level 1, Level 2, ⋯. A level symbol example is depicted in Fig. 6.

IV. Designing Program Using the SPD

A designing process example, using the SPD, is shown below.

Outline of the Example Program

Receive message from the terminal. The message contains a retrieve key data, process switch value, and, in case of update processing, a new master data. Inquiry or update process is performed according to the condition of the process switch. The reply message displays the processing result to the terminal.

Step 1: List main functions without thinking about control structures. Write in natural style and do not use programming technical terms (Fig. 14).

Step 2: Describe detail functions, considering the basic process sequence. Peculiar program functions (i.e., initiation, termination) are described in this step (Fig. 15).

Step 3: Control structures are described. The most important thing in this step is to clarify control conditions. Level symbols and block symbols are also written (Fig. 16).

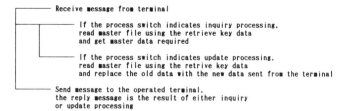

Fig. 14. Step 1.

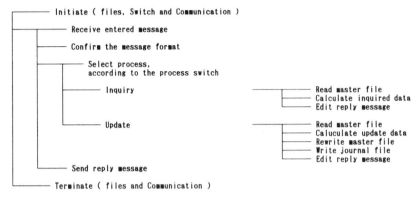

Fig. 15. Step 2.

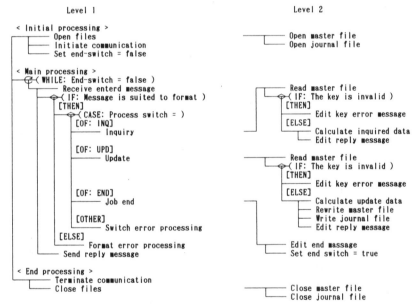

Fig. 16. Step 3.

Step 4: Module assignment methods are investigated and specified as module symbols (Fig. 1).

Summarizing these factors, the following cautions are recommended to enable obtaining good results.

1) Write from left to right and from the top down, with process function abstraction levels.

2) Define abstraction criteria for levels. For example, the top level corresponds to files, the next level corresponds to records within a file, and so on.

3) List functions first. Then describe relations among functions (i.e., control structures).

4) Do not write in too many details.

5) Use other STEPS documentation techniques at the same time. (See Section V.)

6) Number the specification code. (See Section V.)

V. Associated Documentation Technologies

Generally, a system contains many programs. They are consolidated and performed organically to accomplish the required system functions. Therefore, the system must be developed on a step by step basis, such as; divide the whole system into subsystems, the subsystem into programs, and program into modules. However, each step requires a different documentation technology or standard. Therefore, the authors have de-

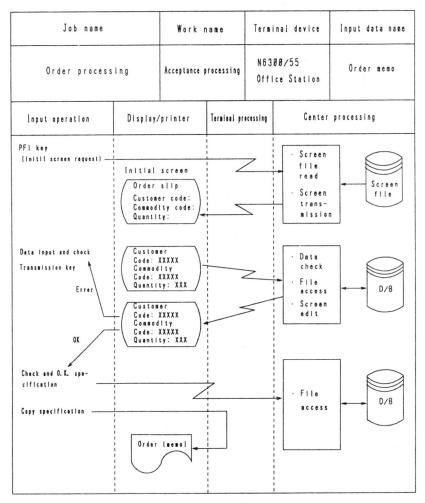

Job name	Work name	Terminal device	Input data name
Order processing	Acceptance processing	N6300/55 Office Station	Order memo

Input operation	Display/printer	Terminal processing	Center processing

Fig. 17. A conversation specification example.

veloped a system for systematic standardization, called STEPS (Standardized Technology & Engineering for Programming Support) to support every development step [25], [26]. STEPS is an integrated standard, covering all the software life cycle. It prepares many kinds of documentation technologies, i.e., to represent a whole system image, relation between subsystems, etc.

SPD is one of the STEPS technologies. It was developed to specify a program structure in the design phase. Since STEPS is indeed an enormous system, the entire system not can be described here. Therefore, some documentation technologies that are recommended for use with SPD are shown in this section. The integration of these documents gives a complete specification for a program.

A. Conversation Specification

When the man–machine system was investigated, process efficiency, accuracy, and operation were effected by conversational format and screen design. Conversation specification can represent screen design, operation at the terminal, and the data processing at the center machine. An example is shown in Fig. 17.

B. Logic Table

Logic Table is employed to clarify the relations between data and each procedure part in SPD. Specification code, procedure part name, input data, procedure part description, and output data are described in an IPO form. In procedure part description fields, a natural language, decision table, SPD, flow chart and so on can be used. A logic table example is shown in Fig. 18.

C. PND (Program Network Diagram)

PND represents data and control flow and the relations between programs and files. SPD is a detail specification of each program in PND. A PND example is shown in Fig. 19. PND symbols are explained in Table III. Besides symbols for data flow by the communication line, terminals, slips, peripheral equipment, connectors, and terminators should utilize the qualified ISO flow diagram symbols.

D. Specification Code

Specification Code specifies the correspondence between SPD and other documents (logic table, decision table, etc.) or between SPD and program list. The code organization may be

Procedure part name	Input data	Procedure part description	Output data
00010 Date set processing	Date from operating system	Accept processing date	Data item for 1st header
00020 Initialize Output file 2	Constant '0'	Initialize page counter	Page counter item (Work area)
00030 Edit Output file 1	Input file 1 .Slip No. .Date .Correspondent code .Commodity code .Quantity .Commodity class code	Posting	Output file 1 .Slip No. .Date .Correspondent code .Commodity code .Quantity .Commodity class code
	Input file 2 .Commodity name .Unit price	Posting	Output file 1 .Commodity name .Unit price
00040 Header edit, print		Execute common sobroutine (HEAD-RTN)	
00050 Edit output file 2		Execute collate-key-match record edit routine (EDIT-MATCH-PR-PROC)	

Fig. 18. A logic table example.

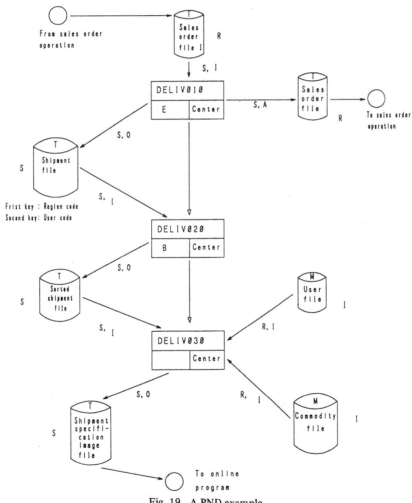

Fig. 19. A PND example.

established by the user. A code organization example is shown in Fig. 20. Specification codes are assigned to all the processing without external call expansion on SPD. An example of specification codes on SPD is shown in Fig. 1.

E. Data Structure

It is desirable to specify data structures easily and clearly throughout a software system development. SPD can also represent hierarchical data structures using with the same

TABLE III
PND Symbols

Symbol	Description
Program name / Pattern name / Partition	Processing symbol: This describes the job step (program) or task. Partition: This indicates that the center processing/terminal processing or human processing is to be enterd.
Data name	Data symbol: This describes the file (record) or memory area. Enter the name of input data, output data, file, record, etc. Do not fail to enter the file classification code (M: Master or T: Transaction) and file organization code (S: Sequential, I: Indexed or R: Relative).
→	Indicates the data flow. Enter the access mode (S: Sequential or R: Random) and processing mode (I: Input, O: Output, A: Aditional or U: Update). If available, do not fail to enter the key item name that would represent the basis of processing like assortment, collating, etc.
▷	Indicates the control flow.

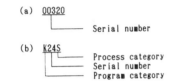

(a) 00320 ———— Serial number

(b) K24S ———— Process category / Serial number / Program category

Fig. 20. A code organization example.

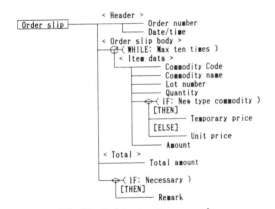

Fig. 21. A data structure example.

convention as program structure representation. A data structure description example is shown in Fig. 21.

VI. Evaluation and Conclusion

In 1974, SPD was introduced as a part of STEPS, an integrated software standard. At first, this method was not accepted smoothly by expert engineers, who had their own design methods. However, those managers and engineers who were interested in software productivity or quality had started using this method. Since then SPD has been accepted and diffused. Engineers who understood the structured programming principle or beginner programmers, who had no knowledge of conventional disciplines, mastered it smoothly. On the contrary, experienced programmers, who could created sophisticated spaghetti programs, tended to resist changing their designing method. Except for those who have never used SPD and refuse to touch it, the authors have never heard that a programmer

who had taken this method once changed to another method or went back to the old method. However, different tales are often reported wherein a group who had used other methods changed to SPD. These factors indicate the SPD predominance.

In the beginning, SPD had no node control symbols and no module symbols. It had only lines and notations. It was recommended to use SPD with logic table and specification code. With the experience gained from using SPD increasing, some shortcomings have been detected and improved. The control symbols are added to the diagram node to represent the control structures. After that, the distinction between the loop in a level and a loop in another level are represented (i.e., in-line perform and usual perform). Further, module symbols are employed to indicate the modules assignment form (i.e., copy library, macro, subroutine, and compile unit). These improvements increased the number of SPD users. Today, there are too many users to trace. Investigation in 1978 showed that SPD was offered to a total of more than 800 companies. So, based on the authors' best guess, SPD may be used in over 1200 companies.

SPD can be easily described by using regular word processors, with the exception of the control symbols. Therefore, SPD documents are easy to maintain. Software tools that generate SPD from source codes had already been developed. Efforts are being made to develop a tool that generates a source code from SPD.

Acknowledgment

The authors wish to thank Dr. Y. Mizuno, Senior Vice President of NEC, who made an important contribution to the initial stage of STEPS development. Thanks are also due to Dr. K. Fujino of the NEC Software Product Engineering Laboratory for his encouragement and helpful comments during this work.

References

[1] E. W. Dijkstra, *A Discipline of Programming.* Englewood Cliffs, NJ: Prentice-Hall, 1976.
[2] ——, "Structured programming," in *Software Engineering: Concepts and Techniques.* 1976, pp. 222–226.
[3] H. D. Mills, "Mathematical foundations for structured programming," IBM Rep. FSC 72-6012, pp. 18–83, Feb. 1972.
[4] N. Wirth, "Program development by stepwise refinement," *Commun. ACM*, Apr. 1971.
[5] E. Yourdon "Top-down design and testing," in *Managing the Structured Techniques.* Yourdon, 1976, pp. 58–87.
[6] H. D. Mills, "Top down programming in large systems," in *Debugging Techniques in Large Systems* (Courant Comput. Sci. Symp. 1), R. Rustin, Ed., New York Univ., New York, 1971, pp. 41–55.
[7] W. P. Stevens *et al.*, "Structured design," *IBM Syst. J.*, vol. 13, no. 2, 1974.
[8] E. Yourdon *et al.*, *Structured Design: Fundamentals of Discipline of Computer Program and System Design.* Englewood Cliffs, NJ: Prentice-Hall, 1979.
[9] G. J. Mayers, "Reliable software through composite design," Petroceli/charter, 1975.
[10] D. L. Parnas, "On the criteria to be used in decomposing systems into modules," *Commun. ACM*, Dec. 1979.
[11] ——, "A technique for software module specification with example," *Commun. ACM*, vol. 15, no. 5, pp. 330–336, May 1972.
[12] J. D. Warnier, *Logical Construction of Programs.* New York: Van Nostrand Reinhold, 1974.
[13] M. A. Jackson, *Principles of Program Design.* New York: Academic, 1975.
[14] D. A. Higgins "Structured programming with Warnier-Orr dia-

gram," in *IEEE Tutorial: Software Design Strategies*, 1979, pp. 60–71.

[15] P. A. Verdgraal *et al.*, "The Warnier–Orr diagram," in *Dig. COMPCON '79*, 1979, pp. 301–306.

[16] M. A. Jackson, "Constructive methods of program design," in *IEEE Tutorial: Software Design Techniques*, 1976, pp. 394–412.

[17] B. Schneiderman *et al.*, "Experimental investigations of the utility of the detailed flowcharts in programming," *Commun. ACM*, vol. 20, no. 6, pp. 373–381, June 1977.

[18] I. Nassi and B. Shneiderman, "Flowchart techniques for structured programming," *SIGPLAN Not.* Aug. 1973.

[19] C. M. Yoder, "Nassi–Schneiderman charts: An alternative flowchart for design," in *IEEE Tutorial on Software Design Techniques*, pp. 386–393, 1978.

[20] N. Chapin, "New format for flowcharts," *Software Practice and Experience*, vol. 4, pp. 341–357, 1974.

[21] J. P. Stay, "HIPO and integrated program design," *IBM Syst. J.*, vol. 15, no. 2, pp. 143–154, (1976).

[22] "HIPO-A design aid and documentation technique," IBM Corp., Rep. 20-1851, 1974.

[23] D. Ross, "Structured analysis (SA): A language for communicating design," *IEEE Trans. Software Eng.*, Jan. 1977.

[24] M. E. Dickover *et al.*, "Software design using SADT," *Structured Analysis and Design*, vol. 2, pp. 101–114, 1978.

[25] M. Azuma and Y. Mizuno, *Software Standardization*. Nippon Keizai Shinbun, 1977.

[26] ——, "STEPS: Integrated software standards and its productivity impact," in *Proc. COMPCON '81*, Washington, Sept. 1981.

Tetsu Tabata graduated from an electric course at Isesaki technical high school.

He is the Senior Researcher of the Software Management Engineering Department, Software Product Engineering Laboratory, NEC Corporation. He is responsible for research and development of software development methodology, software management, and software document standardization to improve software quality and productivity. He joined NEC in 1965, and has been involved in enhancement of Cobol compiler, field support of business systems, and consultation of software development standardization. His research interests include reusable software parts, specification technology, and computer aided engineering for software development and maintenance.

Motoei Azuma received the B.E. degree in industrial engineering from Waseda University.

He has been Manager of the Software Management Engineering Department, Software Product Engineering Laboratory, NEC Corporation, since 1982. He is responsible for improving software quality and productivity at NEC by researching, developing, and transferring software management technologies. He joined NEC in 1963, and has been involved in several computer based system projects as a system and software designer and a software project manager. He was a Visiting Lecturer at Kogakuin University during 1977–1978, and at Waseda University during 1979–1980. His research interests include system analysis, software engineering, and software management, especially requirement analysis, documentation, quality management, and human factors.

He is a member of the IEEE Computer Society, the Information Processing Society of Japan, and Japan Industrial Engineering Society. He has been a COMPSAC Program Committee member since 1983. He has been also involved in software engineering standard activities, as a member of ISO/TC97/SC7.

Yoshihiro Oki received the B.E. degree in industrial engineering from Osaka Prefecture University in 1981.

He is a Researcher in the Software Management Engineering Department, Software Product Engineering Laboratory, NEC Corporation. He joined NEC in 1981, and has been involved in the research and development of software engineering standards, especially software documentation guidelines, programming style standards. His research interests include software engineering framework, software project management, and programming environments.

He is a member of Information Processing Society of Japan.

Susumu Kamiya received the B.S. and M.S. degrees in mathematics from Tohoku University in 1969 and 1971, respectively.

He has been supervisor of the Second Systems Support Department, EDP Marketing Support Division, NEC Corporation, since 1980. His responsibilities consist mainly of improving software quality and productivity at NEC, by researching, developing, and transferring software production technology. He joined NEC in 1971, and has been involved in many projects as a software designer and a chief programmer. His current research interests include software engineering, especially software documentation and software production technology transfer.

Reprinted from *IEEE Proceedings of the 21st Hawaii International Conference on System Sciences (HICSS-21)*, Volume 2: Software Track, 1988, pages 648-654. Copyright © 1988 by The Institute of Electrical and Electronics Engineers, Inc. All rights reserved.

VISUAL PROGRAMMING BY TRANSACTION NETWORK

Takayuki Dan Kimura

Department of Computer Science
Washington University
St. Louis, MO 63130
(314) 889-6122, tdk@wucs2.UUCP

Abstract

This paper introduces a new parallel computation model that is suitable for pursuit of large scale concurrency. Our goal is to develop a semantically clean paradigm for distributed computation with fine-grained parallelism. Our approach is to demote the notion of process as the key concept in organizing large scale parallel computation. We promote, instead, the notion of transaction, an anonymous atomic action void of internal state, as the basic element of computation. We propose to organize a computation as a network, called a *transaction net*, of databases connected by transactions. A transaction, when it is fired, consumes data objects from source databases and produces data objects in target databases as an atomic action. A transaction net is akin to a Petri net, where the token, the place, and the transition corresponds to the data, the database, and the transaction, respectively. The state of computation is represented by the data state without the control state.

An informal definition of the model is given. Solutions are given for well-known programming problems such as sorting, transitive closure, Hamiltonean circuit, shortest path, and the eight queen's problem.

1. Introduction

In the past, a parallel computation was usually modelled by a society of processes communicating with each other, either through shared memory protected by a monitor as in Concurrent Pascal [7], through message passing as in the Actor model [1] and CSP [8], or through remote procedure calls as in Ada [14]. We call the underlying paradigm for these models the send/receive (SR) paradigm because the primary communication primitives are the send and receive operations. We will propose a parallel computation model based on a different set of communication primitives: the consume and produce operations. Thus, we call the underlying paradigm for our model the consume/produce (CP) paradigm.

A process can be arbitrarily complex in terms of local data structures and control sequencing. A process' internal state consists of its control state and its data state. The state of the computation is represented by the Cartesian product of the individual process states. The systolic model and the dataflow model also share the same characteristic of process dominance over data.

There are at least two difficulties in scaling up such process-oriented models. The most significant one is the complexity of algorithm analysis due to the coupling between the control state and the data state. For example, deadlock detection in a CSP program requires information about which process is in what state waiting for what data. Similarly, in systolic algorithm design, data synchronization requires the knowledge about which cell in what state carries what data and is ready to transfer them to which neighbor. Keeping track of both control state transition and data state transformation simultaneously becomes a formidable task when the number of processes increases. Our proposed solution to this problem is to make a process void of internal state and to reduce algorithm analysis to data state analysis.

The second difficulty comes from the management of process identifiers. Since the process name is required for communication through a send/receive protocol even when process names do not contribute to the computation, the programmer must manage a large name space for a large scale concurrent system. This is similar to the label management problem in assembly language programming. With structured programming constructs, programmers seldom need to use a label, while in assembly programming he is forced to use labels. Our proposed solution is to make a transaction anonymous and to replace direct send/receive communication with indirect consume/produce interaction which requires no process identification.

The history of CP paradigm of computation goes back to Post and Markov, even though parallel computation was not an issue for them. It was inherited by Production Systems [17] in AI applications and is adopted by AI programming systems such as OPS83 [4] and KEE [3] as a mechanism for forward chaining. The bridge between the CP paradigm and parallel computation was proposed by the closure statements of associons [15] and generative communication in the Linda project [5]. A recent proposal of Shared Dataspace Language [16] also supports the CP paradigm. However, in all previous known efforts, processes are not necessarily atomic and the database, called the tuple-space or working memory, is the global buffer shared by all processes. In contrast, our transaction is atomic and the database is modularized and distributed to facilitate a higher degree of concurrency.

The Petri Net was originally proposed by Petri as a communication behavior model [12] and later was reintroduced as a concurrent system model by Holt and Commoner [9]. Since then, several attempts have been made to use Petri nets for modelling parallel program behavior. For example, the Colored Petri Net of Zervos [19] defines a colored token to represent an activation of reentrant code (e.g., recursion). However, no known efforts have been made to use a Petri net as a directly executable program statement. There are two major incentives for us to define a programming paradigm based on the Petri Net: a simple and clean formal semantics and a two-dimensional syntax suitable for visualization.

Visual programming is a new concept in software engineering that takes advantage of high resolution graphics capabilities for better software environments [6][13]. While we have demonstrated with the Show and Tell visual programming language design [10] that no textual expressions are needed for programming, our experience suggests that a combination of textual and iconic representations of language constructs would yield better visual languages. A transaction net is a combination of a two dimensional graphic structure and textual expressions.

In the next section we will define the transaction net informally with simple examples. In Section 3 we will construct transaction nets for various programming problems, including sorting, the problems of finding the transitive closure, directed Hamiltonean circuit, shortest paths in a finite digraph, and the eight queen's problem. In the concluding section we will discuss research problems associated with the transaction net.

2. Transaction Net

We will define the transaction net here informally by using simple examples to present the basic concepts. A formal definition will be given elsewhere. Though a transaction net can be defined on any data type, in this paper we will use the integer data type as the basic data objects.

A *transaction net* is a bipartite directed graph of databases (circles) and transactions (boxes) connected by a set of arcs as schematically shown in Figure 1.

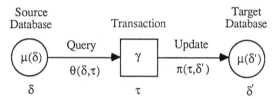

Figure 1: Scheme of Transaction Net

The marking $\mu(\delta)$ of databases δ is a set of *data expressions* each of which consists of constants and parentheses in the form of a well balanced parenthesis expression representing a structured data object (a list of integers, for example). Every arc from database δ to a transaction τ is labelled by a *query expression* $\theta(\delta,\tau)$ consisting of variables and parentheses in the form of well balanced parenthesis expression. The query expression θ specifies the patterns (forms) of data objects to be consumed by τ from δ when τ fires. Similarly every arc from a transaction τ to a database δ' is labelled by an *update expression* $\pi(\tau,\delta')$ in the same form as query expressions with variables and parentheses. The update expression π specifies the data objects to be produced by τ in δ' when τ fires. The transaction box τ may be empty or may contain a *constraint expression* $\gamma(\tau)$ which is a predicate consisting of variables, constants, data operations, and logical operations $\{\wedge, \vee, \neg\}$. The constraint expression γ specifies a condition to be satisfied by all the data objects consumed and produced by a firing of the transaction. The transaction τ is *enabled to fire* when the following condition is satisfied;

> there exists an assignment σ: Variables $\rightarrow$ Constants, a mapping from the set of variables to the set of data expressions, such that for any database δ connected to τ,

(1) $\sigma(\theta(\delta,\tau)) \subseteq \mu(\delta)$,

(2) $(\mu(\delta) - \sigma(\theta(\delta,\tau))) \cap \sigma(\pi(\tau,\delta)) = \phi$ (the empty set),

(3) $\sigma(\gamma(\tau))$ is true,

where $\sigma(\alpha)$ denotes the result of substitution for every occurrence of variables in α by the corresponding constant under σ. For example if $\theta(\delta,\tau) \equiv \{ (x)(y), (x)((y)(x)) \}$, $\sigma(x) \equiv 2$ and $\sigma(x) \equiv 3$, then $\sigma(\theta(\delta,\tau)) \equiv \{ (2)(3), (2)((3)(2)) \}$. Thus, $\sigma(\theta(\delta,\tau))$ and $\sigma(\pi(\tau,\delta'))$ represents in general a set of data objects.

The condition (1) states that the transaction, when it fires with a chosen assignment, should be able to consume all the data objects specified by the query expression under the assignment. The condition (2) states that the data objects to be produced by the transaction should not exist in the database after the data objects to be consumed by the transaction are removed from the database. It follows that the firing condition for a transaction depends upon the markings of both target databases and source databases. This contrasts with the firing rule of the Petri net which states that a transition may fire if all the input places has at least one token, regardless of the contents of the output places. The condition (3) states that the choice of assignment, namely the choice of data objects for productions and consumptions to and from different databases connected to the transaction, must satisfy the condition associated with the transaction.

Among the set of enabled transactions, one transaction, a nondeterministically chosen one, may fire at a time. When the transaction τ *fires*, there exists at least one assignment satisfying the above three conditions, and, with a nondeterministically chosen assignment σ, the marking μ of databases changes to μ' as follows:

> For any database δ,
>
> $\mu'(\delta) = \mu(\delta) - \sigma(\theta(\delta,\tau)) + \sigma(\pi(\tau,\delta))$,
>
> where + denotes the set union operation and - denotes the set difference operation. If there is no arc from δ to τ, then $\sigma(\theta(\delta,\tau)) \equiv \phi$ by definition, and similarly if there is no arc from τ to δ, then $\sigma(\pi(\tau,\delta)) \equiv \phi$.

It is important to note that the above definition of transaction net does not provide a net with the capability of detecting the absence of a particular data object in a particular database. By the same token, there is no direct way of testing whether a particular database is empty. In other words, it is impossible to construct a transaction net in which a particular transaction fires when and only when the database becomes empty. This is parallel with the Petri net's incapability of counting without the introduction of the inhibitor arc.

It is also important to note that, as in the Petri net, the restriction to one firing at a time does not limit the model's capability of specifying concurrent activities in any way. We will discuss this issue further in the next section.

In order to illustrate the syntax and other notations we will use in the next section, we present in Figure 2 a sequence of transaction nets all computing the factorial function. The purpose of this example is not to demonstrate the model's capability for concurrency specification, but to explain different notations and the firing rule defined above.

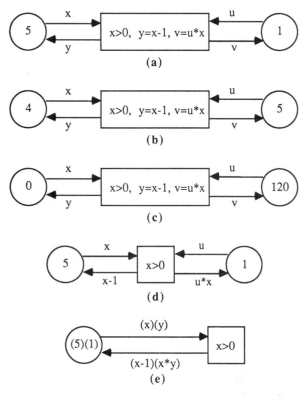

Figure 2: Factorial Functions (a) - (e)

The net (a), which has one transaction and two databases, computes the factorial of 5. The transaction is enabled by the following assignment σ: σ(x) = 5, σ(y) = 4, σ(u) = 1, σ(v) = 5. The firing with this σ will change the marking of (a) to that of net (b). By firing the transaction five times, the net reaches the quiescent marking of net (c).

The net (d) is an abbreviation of net (a). In this abbreviated syntax we allow data operations in update expressions so that constraint expressions can be simplified by reducing the number of variables. The net (d) can be transformed into an equivalent net (e) using the structured data objects. Note that by a similar method any transaction net with n>0 databases can be transformed into an equivalent net with one database containing a set of n-tuples.

The net (f) contains a subnet that represents the factorial function. In this syntax we allow a constant to appear in query expressions and a straight line to represent a transaction as a transition in the Petri net. The transaction Out can fire only when the computation of 5! is completed. Note that this net assumes that at most one number exists in the input database and that firings of the main transaction preserves the following invariant on the markings: $\mu(X)! * \mu(F) = n!$.

3. Concurrent Computations

In this section we will present a few examples of concurrent transaction nets. The factorial examples given in the previous section represent sequential computations in the sense that at all times there exists only one transaction enabled in a net and that at all times there exists at most one data object in each database. We define two enabled transactions to be *concurrent* if they are not in conflict and the order of firings of the two is insignificant. A transaction net is *concurrent* if there exists a reachable marking under which two enabled transactions are concurrent. For example, consider the nets of Figure 3 in the next page.

The net (a) is not concurrent because while A and B are enabled they are in conflict, i.e., the firing of one would block the firing of the other. On the other hand (b) is concurrent because the two transactions are enabled and no conflict exists. The net (c) is an interesting case. According to the above definition, this net is not concurrent because there is only one transaction. However, this net is isomorphic to (b) in the sense that any reachable marking of (b) is also a reachable marking of (c), and vice versa. As a matter of fact, it is easy to show that (c) is isomorphic to any net which has an unbounded number of the identical transactions between the same pair of databases as in (d). Therefore, by considering (c) as an abbreviation of (d), we claim that (c) is a concurrent net. Furthermore we will hereafter consider that every transaction box represents an unbounded, arbitrary number of identical transactions sharing the same source and target databases. With this understanding any net that contains more than one data object in some database is a concurrent net and the degree of concurrency can be measured in general by the number of objects in a database. In the following we will construct transaction net solutions for well known programming problems.

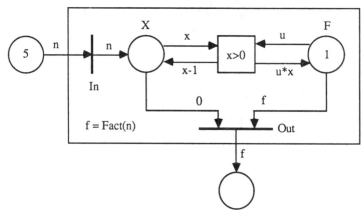

Figure 2: (f)

126

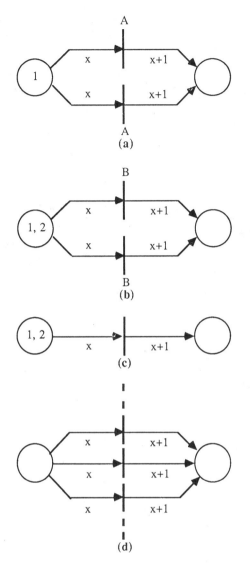

Figure 3: Concurrent Transactions

Concurrent Factorial (Figure 4): The nets presented in Figure 2 compute sequentially the factorial function n! where n>0. The net in Figure 4(a) below generates n! into F in $O(\log(n))$ time at best, but there is no guarantee for such performance due to the nondeterminism about pairing. (Note that we are assuming every transaction is duplicated in unbounded number of times.) In this net and the remaining examples, we will use the abbreviation ',' for ')(' in specifying queries and updates. For example, $(x,y) \equiv (x)(y)$ and $(u(x),v(y)w) \equiv (u(x))(v(y)w)$. However, there should not be any confusion about ',' used for separating two queries. Thus, in (a), the two queries (i,j,x) and (j+1,k,y) are distinct.

$$D = \{ (i,i,i) \mid 1 \le i \le n \}$$

Figure 4 (a): Concurrent Factorial by Pairing

For example, one possible transformation sequence of D for computing 5! is as follows:

$\{ (1,1,1), (2,2,2), (3,3,3), (4,4,4), (5,5,5) \}$

$\{ (1,2,2), (3,3,3), (4,5,20) \}$

$\{ (1,2,2), (3,5,60) \}$

$\{ (1,5,120) \}.$

The net (b) also generates $\{ (k, k!) \mid 1 \le k \le n \}$ into F in $O(\log(n))$ time using the prefix method [18]. It is assumed that n is a power of 2. A double-headed arrow abbreviates two arrows in each direction, i.e., the same objects consumed by the query will be produced back to the same database.

The following condition holds at any time for the database D:

$(i, x, j) \in D \equiv (x * (i - 2^{**}j)! = i!)$ where $n! \equiv 1$ for any integer $n < 1$.

We now show that the condition holds for the initial state of D, and a firing of any transaction in the network preserves the condition; i.e., the condition is an invariant of the network.

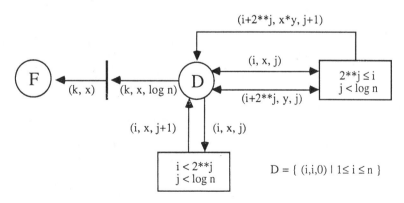

Figure 4 (b): Concurrent Factorial with Prefixing

127

For the initial state: $(i, i, 0) \in D \equiv (i * (i - 2^{*}0)! = i!)$.
Suppose that D satisfies the condition and the transaction on the right fires, producing $(i+2^{**}j, x^{*}y, j+1)$ in D. We want to show that $(x^{*}y) * ((i+2^{**}j) - 2^{**}(j+1))! = (i+2^{**}j)!$, i.e.,
$(x^{*}y) * (i - 2^{**}j)! = (i+2^{**}j)!$.

In order for the transaction to fire, there must be data objects, (i, x, j) and $(i+j^{**}2, y, j)$, in D such that
$$2^{**}j \le i \land j < \log n \land$$
$$x * (i - 2^{**}j)! = i! \land y * ((i+2^{**}j) - 2^{**}j)! = (i+2^{**}j)!.$$
Therefore,
$$y * (x * (i - 2^{**}j)!) = (i+2^{**}j)!, \text{ i.e.,}$$
$$(x^{*}y) * (i - 2^{**}j)! = (i+2^{**}j)!.$$

Suppose that the transaction on the bottom fires, producing $(i,x,j+1)$ in D. We want to show that $x * (i - 2^{**}(j+1))! = i!$. In order for the transaction to fire, there must be a data object, (i, x, j) in D such that $i < 2^{**}j \land j < \log n \land x*(i - 2^{**}j)!=i!$. Since $i < 2^{**}j < 2^{**}(j+1)$, $(i - 2^{**}j)! = (i - 2^{**}(j+1))!$, therefore, $x * (i - 2^{**}(j+1))! = i!$. The transaction on the left does not produce any new data on D, hence no effects on the condition.

As a corollary of the above property the following condition holds for F: $(k,x) \in F \equiv (x = k!)$.

A computation of 8! (i.e., $n = 8$ and $\log n = 3$) will generates the following set of data objects (i, x, j) into D:

i =	1	2	3	4	5	6	7	8
j = 0	1	2	3	4	5	6	7	8
j = 1	1	2	6	12	20	30	42	56
j = 2	1	2	6	24	120	360	840	1680
j = 3	1	2	6	24	120	720	2880	40320

Sorting (Figure 5): For a given array $\{a_i\}$ of $n > 0$ numbers represented by a set of ordered pairs $A \equiv \{(i, a_i) \mid 1 \le i \le n\}$, to construct the sorted array $\{b_j\}$ represented by another set of ordered pairs $B \equiv \{(k, b_k) \mid 1 \le k \le n\}$ such that
if $(i,x), (j,y) \in B$ and $i < j$, then
$x \le y$, and $\{a_i \mid (i, a_i) \in A\} = \{b_k \mid (k, b_k) \in B\}$.

In the sorting net of Figure 5, the database D initially contains a set of ordered pairs A and will contain B when the net terminates. A firing of the transaction reduces the number of inversions in D and the net terminates when no more inversion exists in D. Note that the box in the network represents unbounded arbitrary number of identical transactions.

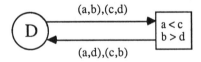

Figure 5: Sorting

Transitive Closure (Figure 6): Find the transitive closure R^+ of a binary relation R. Assuming that the initial database contains the set of ordered pairs representing R, the net in Figure 6 generates the transitive closure in the database.

The net reaches the quiescent state because R^+ is finite when R is finite, and when the transaction tries to produce a pair (x, z) into R where it already exists, the transaction will be disabled according to the definition of the firing rule for a transaction.

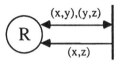

Figure 6: Transitive Closure

The Shortest Path (Figure 7): Find a shortest (minimum cost) path between a pair of vertices in a given directed graph R with the set of vertices $A = (a_1, a_2, \ldots, a_n)$, $n>2$, and the cost function $c: A^2 \to N$ such that for any $x,y \in A$,
$$c(x,y) = 0 \quad \text{if } x = y$$
$$= M \quad \text{if } (x,y) \notin R$$
$$> 0 \quad \text{if } (x,y) \in R \land x \ne y$$
where $M = n * \max\{c(x,y) \mid (x,y) \in R\}$ is an upper-bound of the cost between a pair of vertices.

The net of Figure 7 computes the shortest paths for all pairs of vertices by updating the cost between the vertices x and z whenever a new path through y is found to be less costly. The invariant of the computation is that if $(x,y,c) \in DB$, then c is the shortest path length (the minimum cost) between x and y, known so far. When the net halts the following condition holds: For any vertices x, y, and z; the sum of the shortest length between x and y, and the shortest length between y and z, is always larger than the shortest length between x and z.

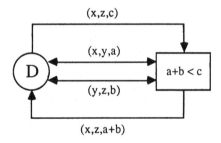

Figure 7: The Shortest Path Problem

Directed Hamilton Circuit (Figure 8): Given a directed graph R with the set of vertices A, to find a cycle containing every element of A. In the net of Figure 8, it is assumed that A is a single object
$$(a_1, a_2, \ldots a_n) \equiv (a_1)(a_2) \ldots (a_n), n > 2,$$
stored in the database A. R is represented by a set of ordered pairs $(a,b) \in R$, stored in the database R. Note that the transaction Compute generates a permutation of $A \equiv (a_1)(a_2) \ldots (a_n)$ as follows: If $(x,y) \in C$, then xy is a permutation of A.

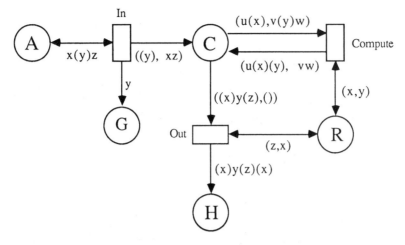

Figure 8: Directed Hamilton Circuit

To see how the algorithm works, consider:

$$R = \{(1,2),(2,4),(2,3),(3,4),(4,1)\}$$

with $A = (1)(2)(3)(4)$.

The transaction IN nondeterministically produces into C the set of all possible starting and remaining vertices as

{ ((1), (2,3,4)), ((2), (1,3,4)), ((3),(1,2,4)), ((4), (1,2,3)) }.

The database G guarantees that the transition IN would not produce redundant lists. The transaction Compute selects a next vertex from the right list and moves to the left, producing lists such as ((1,2), (3,4)) and ((3,4,1), (2)). The final output will be {(1,2,3,4,1), (2,3,4,1,2), (3,4,1,2,3), (4,1,2,3,4)} in H.

The Eight Queen's Problem (Figure 9): Find all configurations of placing eight queens on the chessboard in such a way that no two queens attack each other.

We will represent a solution by a permutation of

(1,2,3,4,5,6,7,8)

satisfying the condition that $|a_i - a_j| \neq |i - j|$ for $1 \leq i < j \leq 8$. One such solution is (1,5,8,6,3,7,2,4). The net given in Figure 9 (next page) generates all possible permutations by sequentially testing the solution condition for each addition of new element into the candidate permutation. Initially the database D contains ((), (1,2,3,4,5,6,7,8)).

Of a list (x, y) in the database R, x represents a partially successful candidate permutation, and y represents a list of available remaining elements. For example, ((3,6,4),(1,2,5,7,8)) in the database shows that (3,6,4) is possibly a part of a solution for the eight queens problem. The transactions Start, Next, and Last select one element from the available pool nondeterministically and try to move it to the candidate list while testing the conflict with already selected candidates. For example, ((3,6,4),(1,2,5,7,8)) in R will be transformed into ((3,6,4,2),(1,5,7,8)) in R as follows:

((3,6,(4,1,2)), (1,5,7,8))	by Start
((3,(6,2,2),4), (1,5,7,8))	by Next
(((3,3,2),6,4), (1,5,7,8))	by Next
((3,6,4,2), (1,5,7,8))	by Last.

The association will be completed into ((3,6,4,2,8,5,7,1), ( )) in R, and then by Out one solution (3,6,4,2,8,5,7,1) will be generated. The purpose of the transaction Catch is to delete superfluous objects which failed the test.

4. Conclusions

As the examples in the previous section show the transaction net is a semantically simple, expressively powerful, visual, and concurrent programming language. Three major issues must be addressed before the concept becomes a significant alternative to the existing process oriented paradigm: the ease of programming, implementability, and possibility of scaling.

The ease of programming in a particular language requires four major supports: software environment, simple semantics, friendly syntax, and a formal method of verification and derivation. Readability is also an important ingredient for programming ease. Our next step in this area is to develop a proof theory for the transaction net. One possible approach is to construct a similar theory developed for the association closure statements by Rem [15]. Another possibility is to translate a transaction net into a set of equations on the database states and to devise a method for finding their fixed-points as suggested by Chandy for the Unity project [2].

The implementability of a transaction net, in essence, can be reduced to that of large scale associative memory, i.e., content addressable memory, and to that of sharing such a resource by a large number of processors. There are two approaches for implementing the required mechanisms. One is to map those capabilities on the existing multi-processor architecture such as the hypercube, the Connection Machine, the Transputer, and the bus-oriented network of computers. The other is to design special purpose VLSI chips for large scale associative memory and for inter-processor communication networks. The Linda project, addressing the same implementation issue, is taking both approaches. Our next step will be to study the first approach with careful performance analysis.

Scaling is a challenging problem for any visual language design. In Show and Tell [10], we introduced two abstraction mechanisms, *naming* and *folding*, for managing graphical complexity of visual programs. We need to study possible adaptation of such mechanisms for Transaction Nets.

Acknowledgement: We thank Dr. Roman and the members of the Concurrent Systems Research Group at Washington University for valuable discussions on the CP paradigm.

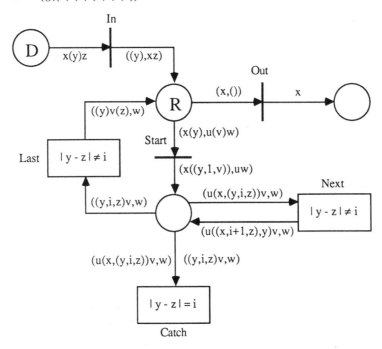

$D = ((),(1,2,3,4,5,6,7,8))$

Figure 9: The Eight Queen's Problem

5. References

[1]   Agha, G., *Actors*, MIT Press,1986.

[2]   Chandy, M., Concurrent Programming for the Masses. Invited Address, 3rd Annual ACM Symposium on Principles of Distributed Computing, Vancouver, August 1984.

[3]   Fikes, R. and Kehler, T., The role of frame-based representation in reasoning. CACM 28(9):904-920, September 1985.

[4]   Forgy, C.L., *The OPS83 Report*, System Version 2.1. Production Systems Technologies, Inc. October 1984.

[5]   Gelernter, D., Generative Communication in Linda. ACM TOPLS, 7(1): 80-112, January 1985.

[6]   Glinert, E.P. and Tanimoto, S.L., Pict: An Interactive Graphical Programming Environment. IEEE *Computer*, 17(11): 7-25, November 1984.

[7]   Brinch Hansen, P., The Programming Language Concurrent Pascal. IEEE Trans. Software Engineering, SE-1: 199-207, June 1975.

[8]   Hoare, C.A.R., Communicating Sequential Processes. CACM, 21(8):666-677, August 1978.

[9]   Holt, A. and Commoner, F., *Events and Conditions*. Applied Data Research, New York, 1970.

[10]   Kimura, T.D., Choi, J.W., and Mack, J.M., Keyboardless Programming in Visual Language. Technical Report WUCS-86-6, Department of Computer Science, Washington University, St. Louis, June 1986.

[11]   Peterson, J. L., *Petri Net Theory and The Modeling of Systems*. Prentice-Hall, 1981.

[12]   Petri, C., Kommunikation mit Automaten. Ph. D. Dissertation, University of Bonn, West Germany, 1962.

[13]   Raeder, G., A Survey of Current Graphical Programming Techniques. IEEE *Computer*, 18(8): 11-25, August 1985.

[14]   *Reference Manual for the Ada Programming Language*. United States Department of Defense, 1982.

[15]   Rem, M., *Associons and the Closure statements*. Mathematical Centre, Amsterdam, 1976.

[16]   Roman, G-C., Language and Visualization Support for Large-Scale Concurrency. Technical Report WUCS-87-20, Department of Computer Science, Washington University, St. Louis, MO 63130, September 1987.

[17]   Rychener, M.D., Production Systems as a Programming Language for Artificial Intelligence Applications. Ph.D. Thesis, Carnegie-Mellon University, 1977.

[18]   Stone, H.S., *Introduction to Computer Architecture*. Science Research Associates, Inc., 1976.

[19]   Zervos, C.R., Colored Petri Nets: Their Properties and Applications. Ph. D. Thesis, University of Michigan, 1977.

System Design with Ada (excerpt)

R.J.A. Buhr

3.2 INTRODUCTION TO PICTORIAL DESCRIPTIONS OF SYSTEM ARCHITECTURES

3.2.1 Pictorial Notation

Figure 3.1 provides the basic pictorial symbols: boxes represent packages and tasks; arrows represent access connections and data flow; and a special oval symbol represents data. It is also useful to have a special cloud symbol for a module whose nature has not yet been defined.

These symbols may be used to construct data flow graphs and/or structure graphs. Data flow graphs identify modules and show data flow interactions among them, without showing the control interactions. Structure graphs show both data flow and control interactions.

The major difference between packages and tasks is symbolized by the different way in which the boxes representing them are drawn. Packages are rectangles. To symbolize their parallel nature, tasks are parallelograms.

The symbols for packages and tasks indicate not only their differences but also their similarities. Boxes are used to symbolize the black-box nature of both packages and tasks. Smaller boxes at the edges are used to symbolize "sockets" which users may use to "plug into" the black boxes. Note that *sockets* is not an Ada term. The term is used to symbolize the common aspects of package and task interfaces. For both packages and tasks, plug compatibility is required. That is, users of packages or tasks as well as bodies of packages or tasks must meet the requirements of the interface specification defining the nature of the sockets.

An access connection from a user to either a package or a task is indicated by an arrow drawn from anywhere on the user box to the appropriate socket of the accessed box. Note that *access* here is a pictorial concept indicating a connection from one module to another. It does not imply use of access variables in the Ada sense.

In both cases, the interface specifications describe only how to connect *to* black boxes. Neither connections *from* black boxes nor identities of users are given in the interface specifications.

Connections to packages may be procedural or nonprocedural. Procedural connections indicate calls to ordinary procedures declared in the package specification. Nonprocedural connections indicate access to other internal aspects of a package, such as internal variables which are declared in the package specification.

Isolated procedures are depicted as rectangular boxes without sockets. They may be visualized as degenerate packages.

Sockets of tasks, known in Ada as entries, behave, from the user's viewpoint, very much like package procedures. Indeed, a task with an interface which is never accessed by more than one other task can be replaced functionally by a package, with procedures replacing the entries. Conversely, a package whose procedures may be accessed by more than one task in a non-overlapping fashion can be replaced functionally by a task, with entries replacing the procedures.

The significant difference between procedural access to packages and entry access to tasks lies, from the user's viewpoint, in mutual exclusivity and timing, not functionality. The rendezvous mechanism requires the calling task to *meet* with the accepting task and then wait while the accepting task services the call. If an accepting task is busy performing its own work or interacting with another task, then it cannot accept a new call. In such circumstances, new callers must wait in a queue associated with the entry. This ensures

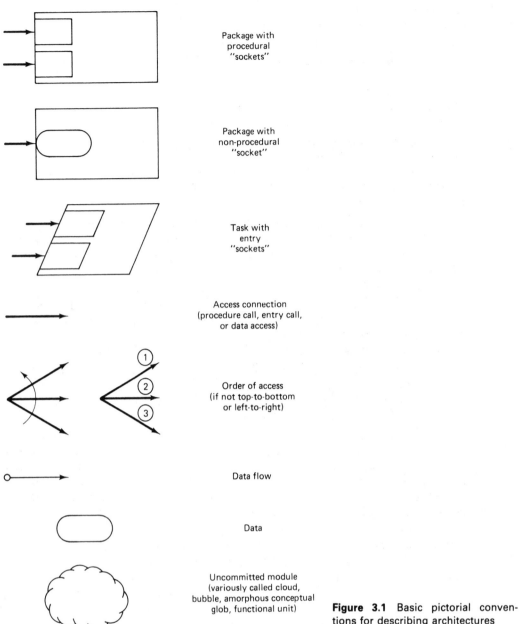

Package with
procedural
"sockets"

Package with
non-procedural
"socket"

Task with
entry
"sockets"

Access connection
(procedure call, entry call,
or data access)

Order of access
(if not top-to-bottom
or left-to-right)

Data flow

Data

Uncommitted module
(variously called cloud,
bubble, amorphous conceptual
glob, functional unit)

Figure 3.1 Basic pictorial conventions for describing architectures

mutually exclusive processing of entry calls from different tasks. It also has timing implications for the caller, who may have to wait for an unpredictable length of time to return from the call.

The symbols of Figure 3.1 are not sufficient for all purposes. In particular, the rendezvous mechanism has a number of options which must be distinguished for design purposes by different symbols.

In what follows, the reader should assume, unless stated otherwise, that all tasks loop forever and never terminate. The calling and accepting patterns shown in the figures then may be interpreted as patterns for one cycle of the loop.

Figures 3.2 and 3.3 illustrate the various rendezvous options and the corresponding pictorial symbols. As illustrated by these figures, entry calls may be unconditional, conditional, or timed, and acceptances of entry calls may be in fixed order, in time order (first-come-first-served), or conditional. As well, the acceptor may time out if no calls occur for a predefined time interval.

With reference to Figure 3.2, we introduce a new symbol with a bent-back arrow to indicate refusal by a caller to wait indefinitely for acceptance. The refusal can take two forms. If no delay is permissible, then the call is said to be conditional, and an alternative action indicated by an *ELSE* statement must be specified. If a delay T is permissible, then the call is said to be timed, and the permissible delay T must be specified in an *OR* statement. In either case an alternative action may be performed.

As shown by Figure 3.3(a), entries accepted in fixed order are indicated pictorially either by an arrow drawn across the access arrows in the structure graph in the fixed order of acceptance or by numbering the arrows in that order. As shown by Figure 3.3(b), a set of entries accepted on a first-arrival basis (in other words in time order) by selective waiting is indicated pictorially by drawing a line around or across the corresponding set of entry sockets. As shown by Figure 3.3(c), entries ignored until a guard is cleared are indicated by a dot adjacent to the access arrow. As shown by Figure 3.3(d), the possibility of timeout from a selective wait condition is indicated by including a delay alternative, as a pseudo-entry socket in this task. Such an alternative is like another entry from the acceptor's point of view. It is effectively an entry called by the run-time system.

In Figure 3.3(b), the selective accept clause indicates that the acceptor task wishes to wait for the first entry call of any of entries A or B; if calls on A and B occur simultaneously, then one of them is to be picked at random. When a call is made and accepted, the rendezvous lasts until the acceptor reaches the END statement. This is the so-called *critical section*. Further processing may be performed by the acceptor relative to an entry after the end of the critical section but before leaving the selective wait clause.

With reference to Figure 3.3(b), it is essential to understand that waiting for an entry call in a selective wait clause is not *busy* waiting. The form of the selective wait clause, with its list of select alternatives separated by *or*, can mislead the reader into thinking that these alternatives are tried one after the other in an iterative fashion until one is found on which a call is pending. Nothing could be further from the truth. In fact, the entire selective wait clause, with all its select alternatives, should be regarded as a primitive instruction to set up a compound waiting condition. During the waiting period, the accepting task is in a suspended state.

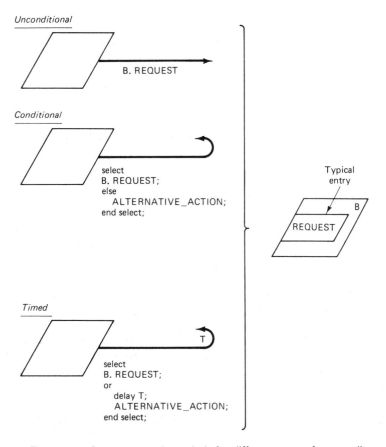

Figure 3.2 Structure graph symbols for different types of entry call

133

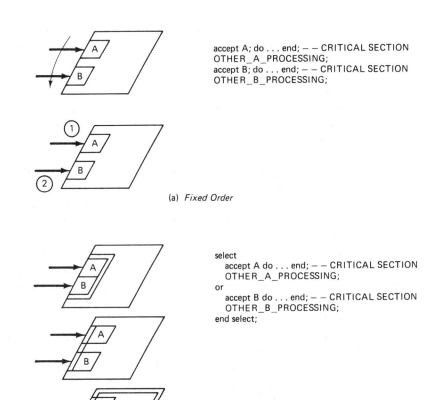

accept A; do . . . end; – – CRITICAL SECTION
OTHER_A_PROCESSING;
accept B; do . . . end; – – CRITICAL SECTION
OTHER_B_PROCESSING;

(a) *Fixed Order*

```
select
   accept A do . . . end; – – CRITICAL SECTION
      OTHER_A_PROCESSING;
or
   accept B do . . . end; – – CRITICAL SECTION
      OTHER_B_PROCESSING;
end select;
```

(b) *Time Order* (*Selective Waiting*)

Note:

Dots indicate guards. Annotated dots indicate entry-closed condition.

x = FALSE

y = FALSE

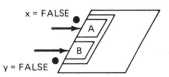

```
select
   when x = >
      accept A do . . . end; – – CRITICAL SECTION
         OTHER_A_PROCESSING;
or
   when y = >
      accept B do . . . end; – – CRITICAL SECTION
         OTHER_B_PROCESSING;
end select;
```

(c) *Conditional*

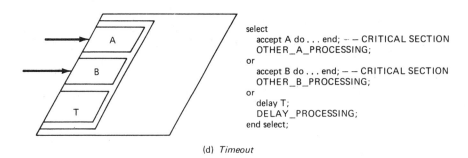

```
select
   accept A do . . . end; – – CRITICAL SECTION
      OTHER_A_PROCESSING;
or
   accept B do . . . end; – – CRITICAL SECTION
      OTHER_B_PROCESSING;
or
   delay T;
   DELAY_PROCESSING;
end select;
```

(d) *Timeout*

In Figure 3.3(c), the *WHEN* statement uses a guard variable X to defer acceptance of a call on entry A until X is true. In practice a guard will be cleared during processing of another entry in the same selective wait statement or as a result of an entry call to another task.

With reference to Figure 3.3(c), it is essential to understand that guards are set when the select clause is invoked and do not change dynamically while the task is waiting.

With reference to any of Figures 3.3(b)–(d), it is essential to understand that only one entry call is accepted in a single invocation of a selective waiting clause. After

134

processing this entry, the acceptor will typically invoke the clause again to wait for another entry call, on the next cycle through its infinite loop.

It will be useful to distinguish the types of delays which can occur in task interactions as follows:

1. A calling or accepting task may experience *structural delays* resulting from either fixed order of acceptance or conditional acceptance. Structural delays depend on the structure of the interactions between tasks. The possibility of their occurrence is visible in the structure graph.

2. A calling task may experience *congestion delays* due to entry queueing. Congestion delays depend on the number of tasks calling a single acceptor and on the frequency of their calls. The possibility of congestion delays is thus also visible in the structure graph.

3. A calling or accepting task may experience *latency delays,* even in the absence of structural delays or congestion delays. This may occur either because the accepting task has not yet reached the point in its internal logic where it accepts an entry which has already been called or because the calling task has not yet reached the point in its internal logic where it calls an entry which has already been accepted. Latency delays must be assumed to be small in any sensibly designed system. Their nature is not visible in the system structure graph.

Figure 3.4 illustrates how some of these symbols may be used to depict systems. Figure 3.4(a) is a *data flow graph*, which shows only data flow between modules. It does not show access connections. It may include any of the module types of Figure 3.1.

Figure 3.4(b) is a *structure graph*, which shows the actual access connections between modules. A structure graph also shows the data flow between modules. It presents a static picture of the structure of the system, including both control and data interactions. It also gives some information about the sequencing of interactions.

To a large extent, packages and tasks may be freely interconnected and nested as illustrated by Figure 3.5. Care must be taken to ensure that where a package is accessed by more than one task, the tasks will not interfere with each other. This is a design problem covered in Section 3.2.

As illustrated by Figure 3.5, it is useful to distinguish between *passive* and *active* packages. A passive package contains no nested tasks. An active package contains nested tasks, which may be hidden by the package interface specification.

Our pictorial notation provides a hardwarelike metaphor for systems as collections of black boxes connected together by plugs and sockets. However, this is primarily a static metaphor, helpful mainly for visualizing relationships.

A dynamic metaphor of system operation is required for visualizing operation of the system as a dynamic entity with possible concurrent activities. This requirement is addressed in Section 3.2.2, following.

3.2.2 Dynamic Metaphor of Ada Tasking: Human Interactions

Our purpose here is to assist the reader in harnessing his or her intuition about human interactions and organizations to develop a dynamic metaphor of Ada tasking.

Think of the structure graph of a system as describing the static, physical structure of a business office. People in offices are connected by corridors and doorways. People correspond to tasks. Corridors correspond to access connections. Offices with their doorways correspond to interfaces of tasks or active packages. Walking down a corridor to

---

Figure 3.3 Structure graph symbols for different types of entry acceptance (*note:* Dots indicate guards. Annotated dots indicate entry-closed condition.)

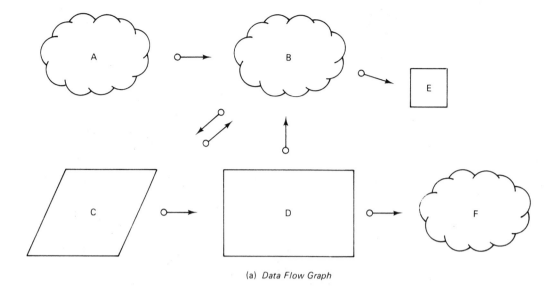

(a) *Data Flow Graph*

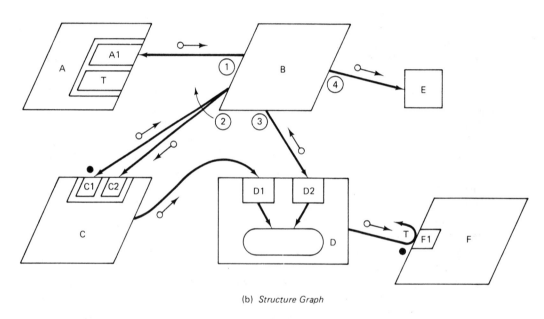

(b) *Structure Graph*

Figure 3.4 Examples of use of pictorial notation

another office corresponds to a task entry call or an active package procedure call. Waiting outside the office for service and then receiving service corresponds to the rendezvous mechanism. Using a passive resource such as a dictaphone, word processor, or filing cabinet corresponds to accessing a passive package.

A small portion of the structure of a business office is depicted by the structure graph of Figure 3.6. Figure 3.6(a) provides an informal view, using stick figures for people, and Figure 3.6(b) provides a corresponding Ada view. This graph shows an incomplete set of possible access and rendezvous relationships among several persons (tasks) and passive black boxes (passive packages) in a typical office environment. Note that this structure is not necessarily a good one; it is simply one of many possible structures. Shown are five persons: the vice president, two managers, a secretary, and an assistant to one of the managers. Also shown are three passive black boxes, all of which are filing cabinets in this particular example. Because, in the sense we shall be developing it, the analogy between black boxes and packages and between persons and tasks is exact, for

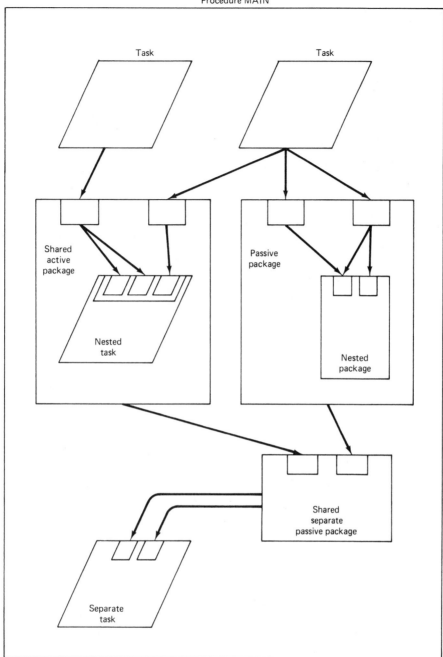

Figure 3.5 Nested, separate, and shared packages and tasks

clarity we shall henceforth refer only to packages and tasks. We shall now proceed to describe the relationships in this figure informally.

First consider the vice-president task. He accesses his private filing cabinet at his own pleasure without any need to coordinate this access with any other task. He may also choose to access a more public filing cabinet, such as the company personnel file, and then perform a rendezvous with one of his managers to hand over control of that file to the manager. The access arrow from the vice-president task to the personnel manager indicates a visit by the vice president to the personnel manager's office to make a rendezvous. Here the rendezvous is used to request the acceptor to perform a service on behalf of the caller. The caller names the service requested, in this case *process personnel file*, and may also pass parameters to the acceptor such as the name of the person whose file is to be processed and the type of processing required. In general a rendezvous may

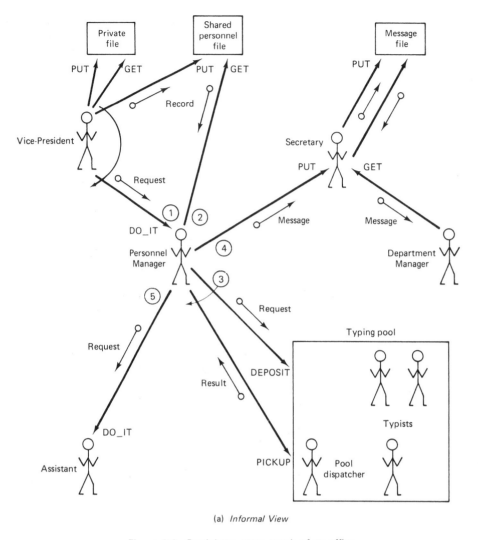

(a) *Informal View*

Figure 3.6 Partial structure graph of an office

be used to pass parameters and data in either direction. While a rendezvous is in progress, the caller waits, and either task may have to wait for the rendezvous to commence. For example, the vice-president may have to wait for the manager to accept his request, or the manager, who may be expecting a request from the vice-president, may have to wait for his request to arrive before it can be accepted.

In this particular example, the vice-president task accesses three modules, namely two passive packages and one task. The structure diagram can give considerable information on the time ordering of these accesses as shown.

An Ada program skeleton for the vice-president task is given in Figure 3.7. The term *skeleton* implies that only the major logical features of the program are given, omitting details. Program skeletons of this kind are sometimes useful design and specification tools. Note in this case, however, how the information contained in the program skeleton is also contained in more compact form in the structure graph.

Now consider the personnel manager. He waits for a call from the vice-president and then processes the named personnel record. Interactions of the type depicted here which involve a shared package are tricky in programming terms, as they are in real life, because control over the shared package must be very carefully handed over from task

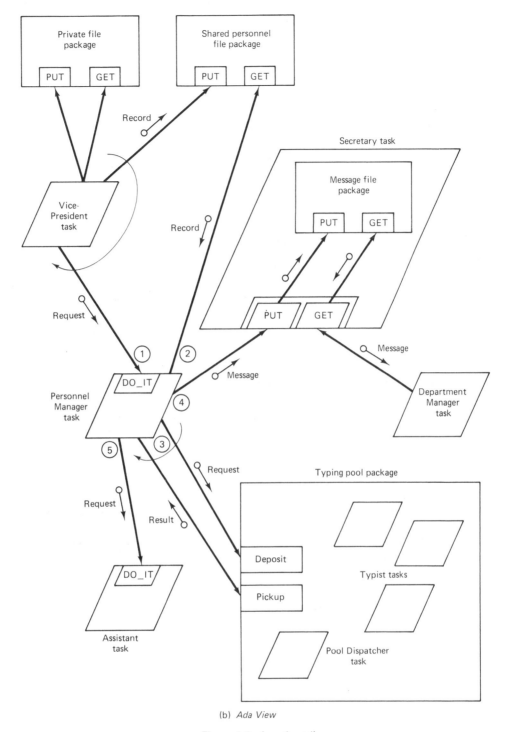

(b) *Ada View*

Figure 3.6 (continued)

to task. For example, the vice-president must be careful not to modify the particular record in the personnel file after he has asked the personnel manager to process it and before the personnel manager has informed him that the work is done.

To process the file, suppose the personnel manager has the following operations to perform: he must pick up the designated record, have a report typed based on the record, pass the report to the manager of the department concerned, and request his own assistant to keep track of further developments. He may be happy to interact directly with the typing pool and with his assistant, knowing they will not keep him waiting, but direct interaction with the departmental manager, who is not always available, may be incon-

```
task body VICE__PRESIDENT is
  . . .
begin
  loop
    . . .
    PRIVATE__FILE.GET ( . . . );
    . . .
    PRIVATE__FILE.PUT ( . . . );
    . . .
    PERSONNEL__FILE.PUT ( . . . );
    PERSONNEL__MANAGER.DO__IT ( . . . );
    . . .
  end loop;
end VICE__PRESIDENT;
```

Figure 3.7 Ada program skeleton for the vice-president task

venient. Therefore he may decide instead to perform a rendezvous with a secretary to deposit a message for the departmental manager. Whether the departmental manager performs a rendezvous with the secretary to pick up messages before the message is deposited or after the message is deposited does not matter to the personnel manager; in either case, the personnel manager expects that the message will get there eventually.

An Ada program skeleton for the personnel manager task is given in Figure 3.8.

The secretary performs message-drop services for a number of managers depositing these messages in a message file as they arrive from some managers and handing them over to other managers as they are requested. The secretary initiates no rendezvous but participates in a number of rendezvous by accepting calls for service.

An Ada program skeleton for the secretary task is given in Figure 3.9.

The assistant to the personnel manager simply waits for orders from the personnel manager and then executes these orders. This execution is not shown.

The departmental manager picks up messages from the secretary by initiating rendezvous with the secretary and then performs his own functions not shown in the structure diagram.

Consider now the interaction of the personnel manager and the typing pool. The personnel manager needs to be able to assign typing of the report to any free typist in

```
task PERSONNEL__MANAGER is
  entry DO__IT( . . . );
end PERSONNEL__MANAGER;

task body PERSONNEL__MANAGER is
  . . .
begin
  loop
    . . .
    accept DO__IT ( . . . ) do . . . end;
    PERSONNEL__FILE.GET ( . . . );
    . . .
    TYPING__POOL.DEPOSIT ( . . . );
    . . .
    TYPING__POOL.PICKUP ( . . . );
    SECRETARY.PUT ( . . . );
    ASSISTANT.DO__IT ( . . . );
    . . .
  end loop;

end PERSONNEL__MANAGER;
```

Figure 3.8 Ada program skeleton for the personnel manager task

```
task SECRETARY is
   entry PUT ( . . . );
   entry GET ( . . . );
end SECRETARY;

task body SECRETARY is
   . . .
begin
  loop
     . . .
        select
           accept PUT ( . . . ) do . . . end;
        or
           accept GET ( . . . ) do . . . end;
        end select;
        . . .
     end loop;

end SECRETARY;
```

Figure 3.9 Ada program skeleton for the secretary task

the pool. Similarly, free typists in the pool need to be able to signify their readiness to do work for users of the pool. There are two approaches to these types of interactions in human organizations:

- third party coordination by another person, acting as a dispatcher for the pool, or
- direct multiway interactions between the multiple persons in the pool and the multiple potential users.

Third-party coordination is easy to describe. The clients and the typists both rendezvous with a pool dispatcher who accepts typing requests and allocates work to free typists. The dispatcher and typists are together regarded by users as a resource with its own office. This resource is an analogy for an active package.

Direct multiway interactions between users of the typing pool and the typists in the pool are more complex to describe. In human terms, a user may walk into the pool and, in effect, broadcast a request to all typists in the pool. This may be done by shouting, ringing a bell, visual scanning and making eye-to-eye contact, or other similar means. If there are many free typists, they will require a method of agreeing among themselves who will volunteer to perform the service. Alternatively, they may all volunteer, and the user will accept one and reject or ignore the rest. In the latter case, typists not explicitly rejected will have to recognize that they have been ignored. If the pool is very busy, then many users may be waiting for service, and a method for matching users to typists is required.

Clearly, the Ada rendezvous mechanism provides a good metaphor for systems as groups of persons interacting on a one-to-one basis. Multiway interactions must be reduced to sets of one-to-one interactions to be described in rendezvous terms. Third-party coordination of multiway interactions is directly and easily described in this way; direct multiway interaction is not.

There are two ways of looking at Ada's restriction to one-to-one interactions between tasks:

- as a welcome application of the KISS (Keep It Simple Stupid) principle, or
- as a limitation.

On the one hand, if Ada provided a mechanism by which a rendezvous could occur with any free member of a selected pool of tasks, then the multiway direct interaction could be more simply described in Ada. There would need to be a method for queueing multiple tasks wishing to avail themselves of this mechanism for the same pool. On the other hand, as was discussed earlier, such a mechanism can be easily specified in Ada by packaging a number of worker tasks and a dispatcher task to form such a pool. Thus there do not appear to be any limitations imposed on design freedom by the one-to-one nature of the rendezvous mechanism.

We defer the detailed consideration of structure graphs and program organizations for active packages and for pools of tasks until Section 3.3.

The relationships shown by the structure graph of Figure 3.6 and the program skeletons of Figure 3.7-3.9, although incomplete, are representative both of real operations in an office and of interactions between program modules in an Ada program. There are a number of aspects omitted from this particular example diagram which give rise to further questions. For example, how, later on, can the vice-president check or be notified that the correct action has been performed? This question and others like it lead, in programming terms as in real life, to a need for multiple rendezvous between the vice-president and the personnel manager and, indeed, between other tasks in the structure diagram. However, we shall leave these questions to Section 3.3.

We now need to examine the rendezvous mechanism in more detail.

3.2.3 Human-Interaction Metaphor for the Ada Rendezvous Mechanism

A metaphor for the rendezvous mechanism in human interaction terms for the simplest type of rendezvous is illustrated in Figure 3.10. The caller leaves his office and goes to the acceptor's office, where he finds the acceptor's door open. He gives a request *form* providing the nature and parameters of the request to the acceptor and then goes to sleep outside the acceptor's office. The acceptor, who has been waiting for a call with his door open, accepts the request form and processes the request while the caller is asleep. At the end of the rendezvous, the acceptor reopens his door and awakens the caller, who then returns to his office.

Life is not always as simple as in Figure 3.10 and in general, either the acceptor must wait with his door open for a call, or the caller must wait outside the closed door for acceptance before rendezvous can begin. Figure 3.11 illustrates both of these cases. In either case the progress of the rendezvous after it begins is the same as shown in Figure 3.10.

Figure 3.12 illustrates the general case. Multiple callers queue in first-in-first-out (FIFO) order outside the acceptor's door (multiple doors symbolize multiple entries). In Ada terms there is a separate entry queue for each entry, organized in first-in-first-out order. Not all doors may be open while the acceptor is waiting; closed doors correspond to closed entries (closed by guards).

Where no parameters are associated with the call of an entry, it is appropriate to think of each request form as simply a token to indicate that the service provided by that entry is required. In general terms, the request form includes input parameters and a tear-off sheet containing spaces to fill in returned parameters. The caller picks up this tear-off sheet from the acceptor before walking away from the rendezvous.

An acceptor may close his door again immediately after terminating a rendezvous, even if someone is waiting outside the door, in order to finish processing the request associated with the terminated rendezvous, or to perform other internal actions.

Structural delays are experienced by callers when a door is closed even when the acceptor is not busy and other doors are open. Congestion delays are experienced when a queue forms in front of a door which the acceptor is servicing as fast as possible. Latency delays are experienced when all doors are closed while the acceptor performs his own internal work even though no guards are set. Note that an acceptor's own internal work might require him to visit other offices. Therefore, when a door is closed, the acceptor might not even be in his office.

Thus, visits to other offices may waste time in unpredictable ways. And while absent from his own office, a person may miss important events. Other things being equal, a person in an office will usually prefer to interact with other persons by being

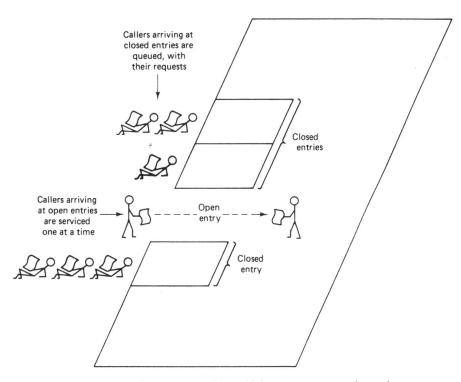

Callers arriving at
closed entries are
queued, with
their requests

Closed
entries

Callers arriving
at open entries
are serviced
one at a time

Open
entry

Closed
entry

Figure 3.12 Rendezvous with multiple-entry queues and guards

visited rather than by making visits. Then there is never any need to waste time waiting for other persons unless there is nothing else to do.

Obviously, this selfish viewpoint would result in no interactions at all if every task adopted it. As we shall see, in Section 3.3, the problems of designing interaction structures for interacting tasks center around deciding which tasks have roles which require minimal interference with their other work. Only in the simplest systems is the rendezvous direction unimportant; for example, if two tasks interact only with each other then it is not important who calls whom.

As a final remark on the rendezvous mechanism, any impression that may have been formed that a rendezvous restricts callers and acceptors from concurrent activities while the acceptor is servicing a request made by an entry call should be dispelled. The restriction on concurrency exists only during the actual rendezvous when the entry call itself is being processed. A rendezvous may be used simply to deposit a request which may require further processing by the acceptor after the rendezvous has terminated. An example is the rendezvous performed by the vice-president with the personnel manager in Figure 3.6, to hand over a file for processing. The vice-president may continue to work independently after the rendezvous has terminated, while the personnel manager processes the file. In this case, the rendezvous itself is used only to pass the request to process the file.

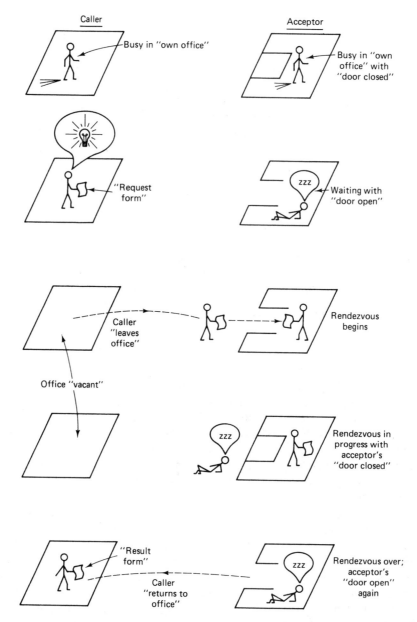

Figure 3.10 Operation of the Ada rendezvous mechanism: simplest case

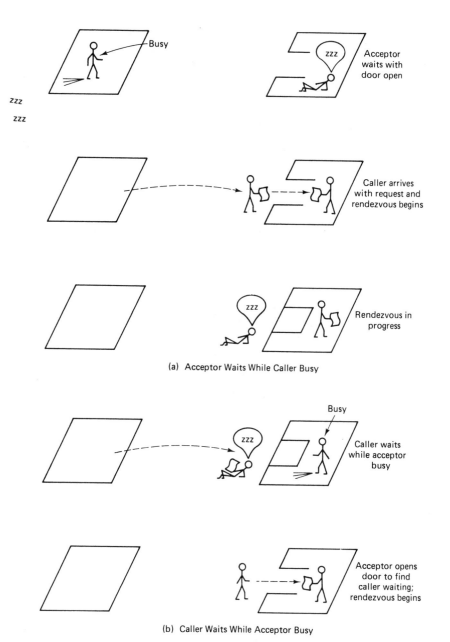

(a) Acceptor Waits While Caller Busy

(b) Caller Waits While Acceptor Busy

Figure 3.11 Some rendezvous examples

Applications and Extensions of SADT

Douglas T. Ross, SofTech, Inc.

*Embodying an organized
discipline of thought and
action, the SADT
methodology has been
successful in many
applications previously
thought too nebulous for
technical treatment.*

At the time the definitive papers on SADT,* SofTech's Structured Analysis and Design Technique, were published in 1977, [1-3] the methodology had been in extensive development and use for several years. Originally introduced as a "system-blueprinting" method for documenting the architecture of large and complex systems, [4] SADT had become a full-scale methodology for coping with complexity through a team-oriented, organized discipline of thought and action, accompanied by concise, complete, and readable word and picture documentation. SADT broke new ground in the areas of problem analysis, requirements definition, and functional specification because it allowed rigorous expression of high-level ideas that previously had seemed too nebulous to treat technically. In the seven years since its introduction, SADT and its derivatives and extensions have been successfully applied to hundreds of major projects in a very broad range of application areas. An overview of this application experience and a look toward the future development of SADT are the subjects of this article.

What is SADT?

SADT consists of two principal parts: (1) the box-and-arrow diagram-

*SADT is a trademark of SofTech, Inc.

ming language of *structured analysis* and (2) the *design technique,* which is the discipline of thought and action that must be learned and practiced if the language is to be used effectively. Both parts are intimately related. Without the simplicity, generality, readability, and rigor of the SA diagramming language, the important ideas of the DT methodology would not be sufficiently visible and tangible to be of any coherent use. But without the DT discipline, those same language features of SA would make it almost useless (so much so that in 1977 Softech laid proprietary claim to its methodology, even while placing all the specifics of the SA language in the public domain). The situation would be much like knowing the rules and notation of algebra (capable of extensive calculation in almost any domain) without having any guidance or experience in translating word problems into properly formulated expressions.

Neither SA nor SADT solves problems. Both are tools that allow people to express, understand, manipulate, and check problem elements in ways previously not possible. All of SADT stems from a single premise: The human mind can accommodate any amount of complexity as long as it is presented in easy-to-grasp chunks that together make the whole. The objective of SADT is to find those chunks,

EH0324-4/90/0000/0147/$01.00 © 1985 IEEE   147

make them and their collective structure visible, and model the relevant relationships concisely enough to achieve some stated purpose.

The graphic language of SA. Everything worth saying, about anything worth saying something about, must be expressed in six or fewer pieces. That is the structured analysis maxim at the heart of SADT. The limitation of six ensures that, in the context of the whole, the meaning of any single part cannot be too difficult to grasp. Any part that is not yet sufficiently easy to grasp must, in turn, be broken further into pieces, according to the maxim. The maxim implies a hierarchical, top-down decomposition of the whole into easy-to-grasp chunks, and in the process, the whole and all of its sub-wholes and parts become more understandable because each whole bounds the context within which its parts are to be understood. This basic idea of the SA part of SADT is simplicity itself.

Equally simple is the graphic language notation of structured analysis. Each one of the six or fewer pieces is uniformly expressed in the form of the *SA box,* whose four sides always mean *input, control, output,* and *mechanism,* as shown in Figure 1. Input is transformed into output under control. The mechanism is what carries out the transformation. An algebraic analogy would be $A * X + B = Y,$ where X (as argument) is input, A and B (as parameters) are control, and Y

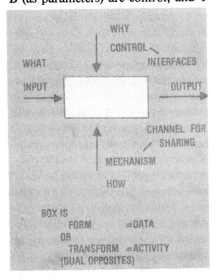

Figure 1. The structured analysis box.

(as result) is output; the arithmetic itself is mechanism (the "$*$" and "$+$" being specific operators), and the formula as a whole is the box. Note that both inputs and controls (collectively called *entries*) participate in the transformation to output.

In all cases except at an atomic level (where the idea is expressed clearly enough that no detail is necessary), the idea-entity whole represented by a box is decomposed into a collection of parts, also represented by the same kind of boxes, drawn on a *detail diagram.* The box being detailed is called the *parent box* and it, in turn, is a part of the *parent diagram.* These boxes are components of a graphical language expressing ideas, and the meanings of the boxes must not overlap. Furthermore, the entire meaning of the parent box whole, but no more than that meaning, must be somewhere in the parts. That is, there must be no gaps and no additions between the whole and its parts. This ensures that the transition from box to diagram is truly a decomposition of the parent box idea.

Input, control, and output are the interfaces between the parts as they compose the whole and are completely different from mechanism. These interfaces are indicated by branching arrows that connect outputs to inputs or controls (and sometimes, mechanisms) so that the result of one transformation can be further transformed by another box or can control (or sometimes, contribute to the means for performing) the transformation of some other input by another box. Thus, SADT can be applied to analyze or design any system composed of objects and actions upon those objects.

Boxes are named and arrow segments are labeled. Boxes are also numbered (arbitrarily) and arrow ends may be tagged with ICOM codes, the letter I, C, O, or M (for input, control, output, or mechanism) followed by the corresponding arrow number (sequential per box, top to bottom or left to right). Parent box ICOM codes must be written on the unconnected ends of external arrows of a diagram so that the matching of the diagram boundary to the parent box boundary is well

defined. Figure 2 shows a box and its detail diagram, including meta-notes (indicated by circled numerals) explaining the diagram but not included in its meaning. ("FEO" for "for exposition only.")

Multiple models. A collection of diagrams interconnected by ICOM codes is called a *model.* One can construct an SA model of any subject whatsoever by choosing the names and labels from any language natural to that subject. We say "M is a model of A if M can be used to answer questions about A." The extent of the questions and the suitability of the answers determine the quality of a model. But every SA model *is* a model by definition.

Names and labels must be dual opposites with respect to the modeled subject. Most SADT practitioners use nouns and verbs for the things and happenings that comprise the complex of ideas of the subject matter and construct *activity models,* in which box names are verb phrases and arrow labels are noun phrases. Thus, the things are transformed by the happenings; i.e., both of the opposites participate in the model. (Figure 2 is an activity diagram.)

Data models result from an opposite approach: box names are noun phrases (describing kinds or states of things), and arrow labels are verb phrases (describing the activities that take place between the things). Again, both things and happenings participate in the model. The most complete modeling of a subject involves creating distinct but complementary activity *and* data models of the same subject and relating them by the *SA tie process,* in which arrow segments in the middle levels of each model are cross-referenced with the corresponding box number (or numbers) from the dual model. The words labeling arrow segments in one model then can be understood in detail when the decomposition of the boxes in the other model is examined. By reading back and forth between the two models, we strengthen our understanding of the subject.

In general, models have arbitrary names, and within a model each box/diagram combination has a *node number*, which is A or D (depending on model type) followed by the box numbers of its ancestry. (The single top-most box, numbered A0 or D0, represents the modeled subject as a whole, and A23 is the third box of the detailing of the second box of the A0 diagram, for example.) Every aspect of a model is open to precise discussion because a reference expression language allows each box and arrow segment to have a unique name composed of model names, box number, and ICOM codes (with special punctuation).

Arrows pointing up into the mechanism side of the SA box are not interfaces but open channels permitting nonhierarchical network interconnections between submodels. An upward-pointing mechanism arrow is called a *support arrow*; it is labeled with the node number of a box, which may occur in an arbitrary, different model. That box is considered the 0-level top of a *support model*, and the support arrow (channel) connection from the box to the supported box (also considered the 0-level top of a submodel)

indicates that portions of the details of the supported model can be shared with the details of the support model. [This corresponds to scope rules of a programming language.] The sharing is indicated by a downward-pointing arrow (referred to as a *call arrow*) from the mechanism side of a detail box somewhere in the supported model. The call arrow is labeled with the box name (node number) of the *called box* (in the support model) to be shared. [This corresponds to a subroutine call in a programming language.] For each such instance of a call, notation conventions establish which interface (and

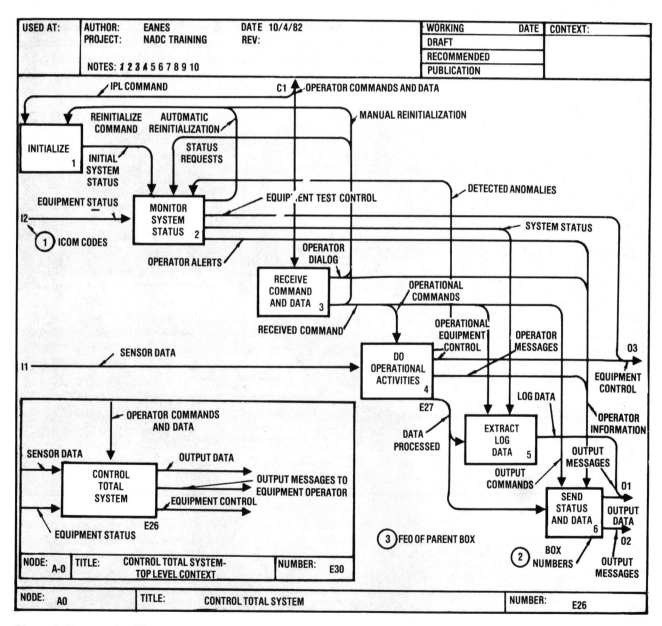

Figure 2. Diagram detailing parent box (activity model).

perhaps mechanism) arrows come from the called or calling context [corresponding to parameter passing in a subroutine call in a programming language]. Conditional, case, iterative, and recursive calls are possible, though rare. Figure 3 illustrates the basic call and support ideas.

Finally, additional notations (not usually taught, and even less often used) indicate whether the entities represented by arrows are consumed or only accessed across the interface to each box transformation, so that event-driven behavior can be constrained and expressed. Using this information, algorithms can transform any collection of diagrams extracted as a submodel into a well-structured loop-with-exits structured program.[5] Thus, the full SA notation system allows complete data flow networks of models to be constructed, modeling both the static relationship and the dynamic behavior of the things and happenings of the subject. In fact, although the source of the SADT acronym is "Structured Analysis and Design Technique," it can also stand for "states, activities, data, transitions," covering the full scope of SA itself. Although it has yet to be formalized, SA as a modeling language is both rigorous and complete. Even the combination of SADT with the RML language of requirements modeling, described by Greenspan,[6] is the association of a particular formal semantics for an interpretation of an SADT model's syntax rather than formalization of SA semantics itself, as Greenspan acknowledges. Formalization of SA itself is very difficult.

The Practice of SADT

At the most fundamental level, structured analysis is a discipline of thought. The SA language and additional notations merely provide a means of expression of rigorously controlled thought processes, which are taught to both "authors" and "readers" of SA models. The most universal principle is *bound the context*. Every subject and every action is to be seen only as part of a larger whole that provides the context for detailed considerations or activities. Authors are taught to state the context and to "shift mental gears" consciously when passing from one context to another. Every SA model has an *orientation*, which includes *context* (with vantage point in the context), *viewpoint* (what is seen—similar to the differing scenes

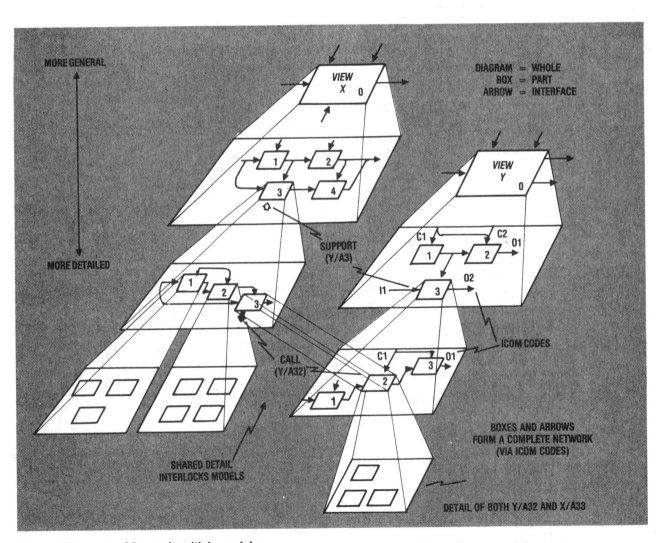

Figure 3. Decomposition and multiple models.

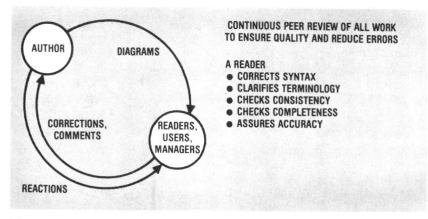

Figure 4. The SADT reader/author cycle.

Text inside figure:
CONTINUOUS PEER REVIEW OF ALL WORK
TO ENSURE QUALITY AND REDUCE ERRORS

A READER
- CORRECTS SYNTAX
- CLARIFIES TERMINOLOGY
- CHECKS CONSISTENCY
- CHECKS COMPLETENESS
- ASSURES ACCURACY

AUTHOR · DIAGRAMS · CORRECTIONS, COMMENTS · READERS, USERS, MANAGERS · REACTIONS

resulting from x-ray, ordinary, or infrared vision—as well as view-boundary limitations), and *purpose* (which determines the structuring of the model by addressing higher priority matters, first, to provide context for details). In general, a subject merits modeling from several orientations, one for each class of user interested in the subject.

The SADT Principle of Limitation of Information takes the most concrete form in the rule that a diagram may contain no more than six boxes, so that the context has a chance to be effective. Other rules and notations cover the addition of meta-notes to diagrams and their use in structured reviews built around the SADT Reader/Author Cycle for systematic quality control checking (see Figure 4). Structured interview techniques, version control, project organization, a project librarian function, and model archiving also are supported by the SADT methodology.

Why SADT works. SADT is a powerful methodology for working out a clear-cut understanding of an initially obscure, complex subject, documenting that understanding, and then communicating it to others (including the user himself in the future, when he wishes to rethink the subject). SADT is completely general and applicable to any situation whatsoever, precisely because it provides no solution to any problem (unlike mathematics or logic —or even programming languages, which ultimately depend on mathe-

matics or logic). SADT notations and thought disciplines are analogous to the content-free punctuation and framework of all natural language. The words of natural language, such as English, are notoriously ambiguous; most dictionary entries list multiple meanings for a single word. And yet (except for puns or errors) most natural-language communication is exact and unambiguous. This is because the communicators both are aware of the intended bounded context, and they use punctuation (or gestures or equivalent tone inflections) to structure and control the various groupings so that only the intended meaning filters through that structure. The punctuation has no meaning of its own, but absolutely controls the meanings of the words embedded in it. Precisely the same is true of SA box-and-arrow conventions. Whatever the subject may be, if the structuring is well formed and complete for the intended purpose, the natural-language names and labels can have only the intended meaning—all the ambiguity is squeezed out. (See Ross,[7] which outlines a demonstration.)

In principle, then, SADT can be used for any purpose and can provide the framework for a problem-solving methodology for any kind of problem. In practice, however, it is thought of primarily as a requirements definition methodology (because in that field it originally had no competitors and it is very effective there) that interfaces well to other design and implementa-

tion methodologies, even though actual applications have been much broader.

Practical limitations of SADT. As a practical problem-solving methodology, SADT has had many resounding successes, but on occasion it also has delivered disappointments. Naturally enough, the successes receive most emphasis in this article, but the failures are in some measure even more instructive for they highlight a basic truth about any methodological tool as distinct from tools in general.

Consider a screwdriver. Clearly it is designed for a special purpose—namely, screwing a screw with a head of a particular size and shape into some appropriate material. If a screwdriver is used as a crowbar and bends and breaks, clearly that is not the fault of the screwdriver but of the user, who chose the wrong tool for the job at hand. Methodological tools don't enjoy such a luxury.

When a methodological tool fails in specific application, the failure signals a flaw or weakness in the tool itself, even if analysis shows that it was applied inappropriately. Just as a good computer program should be complete enough to reject bad data, a good methodological tool should reject improper applications as part of its normal use. There is no room for excuses. A failure of an end result is a failure of the tool, for the user cannot know in advance the bounds of the methodology and should not be allowed to proceed to completion in a failing case.

The limits of a methodology are shown very clearly in the case of SADT, for like the rules and notation of algebra, the SA diagramming language is rigorous, well defined, and essentially complete. The generality of the language and method makes it applicable, in theory, to virtually any kind of problem. If the grammar rules of the graphical language are not violated and if the natural-language words used in the diagrams are reasonably chosen for the problem at hand, every SADT model (collection of diagrams) *is* a model by definition. Hence if a model fails to achieve its stated purpose, i.e., if an SADT project fails, the failure is (again by definition) rooted in the DT portion of the total SADT methodology. That portion is, of course, shared in practice between the individual practitioner of the methodology and the designer of the methodology. But as the above comparison of screwdrivers to computer programs shows, the user's responsibility is overshadowed by the designer's. At the present time, we don't know how to bound or characterize the problems to which SADT is easily applicable, and the ones to which it is not, especially in terms a novice user could work with. In this sense, the DT of SADT must be considered not yet complete. But where worked-out examples are available for emulation, good efforts yield good results.

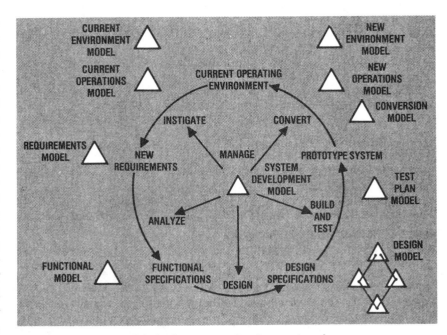

Figure 5. Types of models in the system development cycle.

Application experience with SADT

What does it mean to apply SADT to solve a problem? In applying SADT, the author (skilled in the application of SADT) works with experts in the field of the application to carefully define the problem to be solved and then identifies one or more models to be developed to help solve the problem. The problem to be solved is constantly before the author, guiding how he performs the SADT modeling by dictating which facts to include or exclude in the model so that it provides useful answers to the problem at hand.

SADT is particularly effective in the early and late stages of the system development life cycle. Context analysis; requirements definition; functional specification; hardware, software, and general system architecture; user environments; operating procedures; system design; package design; documentation organization; curriculum design for teaching; and project estimating and management all have been treated effectively. At the present time, SADT has been less effectively used for actual detailed design of software systems, although preliminary design

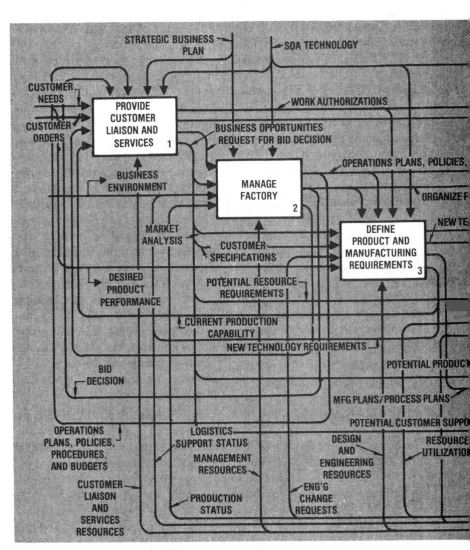

Figure 6. FOF generic functions.

Table 1. Types of SADT applications.

CATEGORY	SADT MODELS	MODEL PURPOSES
Requirements	Present operations	Understand current procedures
	Future operations	Visualize future procedures
	Operational system hardware/software/people	Specify and design
Software systems	User requirements	Include user needs
	Functional specification	Identify system modules and interfaces
	System/subsystem design	Top-level design
Project Management	Project operation	WBS development Task assignment Procedure definition Communications
Simulation	Man-machine interaction	Analyze performance

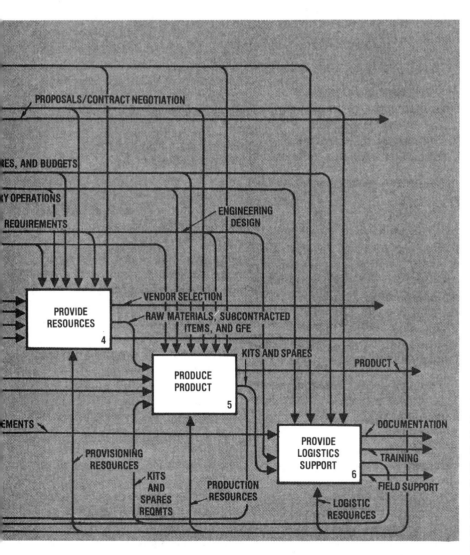

(as cited above) often is supported. In theory, the DT of SADT should encompass such detailed design, but in practice it probably awaits development of automated support tools as described in the closing section of this article. Without such tools, manual methods seem to become swamped.

To properly categorize the current application experience with SADT, it is more informative to list the types of problems solved with SADT (project management, software system specification, etc.) than the types of system where it was applied (real-time, system software, etc.). Under each problem category, SADT has been applied to many types of systems and at many points in the system life cycle.

Four types of problems (see Table 1) have comprised the primary use of SADT to date (although it is impossible to document all uses of the method due to its general problem-solving nature). The following are brief, illustrative examples from SADT application experience:

Developing common understanding: nationwide multicompany project. SADT has been used most extensively in the requirements definition phase of complex, large-scale, technical projects involving people, machinery, computers, and communication—hardware, software, and "fleshware." Essentially the entire scope of SADT activity modeling was adopted as IDEF-0, the ICAM Definition Methodology[8] of the Air Force-led Department of Defense Integrated Computer-Aided Manufacturing Program—a multiyear, heavily funded program to enhance manufacturing technology. Thousands of people from hundreds of organizations working on more than one hundred major projects use the methodology not only for the technical work of system definition and design, but for project management and integration as well (see Figure 5). The ICAM Program Office has cited IDEF as recipient of a Top-of-the-Line Manufacturing Technology Success Story award. The IDEF methodologies are taught in several universities.

A significant showpiece of the ICAM effort has just been completed —The Factory of the Future (FOF) Conceptual Framework "based on. . . detailed studies successfully completed in past ICAM projects." The objective of this project was to create a baseline model for the total system of the aerospace enterprise and its operations valid through the year 1995. Considerations include design, finance, marketing, QA/QC, manufacturing, inventory control, and product support (see Figure 6). Comparison of the "as-is" and the "to-be" systems of models in the needs-analysis document identified more than 400 needs in seven major categories for the future enterprise, and in materials management alone, 22 distinct systems were identified, with 51 required improvements needed to meet the goals of a computer-integrated manufacturing environment. IDEF-1 models for integrated but distributed databases linked through an information processing and communications network complete the framework, which already is being used by several of the contributing coalition firms.

Separation of function and design: office building control system. Using SADT, a large building environment control system manufacturer was able to separate the functional elements of his new product line from specific design detail, so that he could address major new subsystem interaction issues without becoming embroiled in design issues. For example, the coordination of the heating and air conditioning controls with the new environmental energy-saving system needed to be studied, as well as their interactions with the theft-control and daily start-up systems, to prevent one system from issuing signals in conflict with those of another system. Once the functional coordination issues had been decided, the functions could be designed to work on many different physical pieces of equipment.

Uncovering overlooked elements: commercial network definition. SADT has helped numerous project

managers uncover overlooked tasks and bring projects under control. A large software development project was reorganized after its manager had struggled for two years to control it, performing little real management because he had to perform tasks overlooked in the original plan. Also, many of the project record-keeping tasks and communications paths were unclearly defined. The SADT project model was used to lay out a more comprehensive work breakdown structure and to devise well-defined procedures that resulted in customer satisfaction and the completion of the redesigned project ahead of schedule and under budget.

Impact assessment: factory modernization. SADT has been used for many years to assess the impact of a software change before making that change. In factory modernization ef-

---

It's normal for systems requirements algorithms to be refined throughout development, so software requirements are also refined

---

forts, the same concept has been applied to modernization planning. The impacts of shop-floor technical changes are assessed as they relate to engineering, purchasing, quality assurance, shipping, and other departments. Impact analysis has been applied before installing the changes, thus avoiding integration problems.

Focus on details: corporate meetings. A large corporation, which had adopted SADT as a standard methodology, cited one of the "surprise benefits" of the method as a significant reduction in meeting time. Using the SADT product specification and design diagrams for meeting control, participants could address specific issues and make decisions with considerably less effort and time than before using SADT.

Training assistance: new staff orientation. A multiyear project was restructured to improve its quality assurance effort. A new QA manager was hired and two staff members were reassigned to QA tasks. Their duties were laid out on the SADT project model, and specific procedures were developed corresponding to the control arrows of the SADT model. The new QA organization was functioning in a brief period of time, and the final product exceeded the quality goals of the customer.

Management decision baseline: large telephonic system. The customer had spent several months using pure text to describe a planned new telephone switching system. The customer felt lost in the morass of detail, so SADT was applied to the effort. The separation of functional elements and the top-down strata of detail permitted comprehension of the total system and uncovered elements that had been overlooked, as well as providing a solid technical basis for management decision making.

Extensions and enhancements of SADT

Often SADT is interfaced and coupled with other methodologies as part of a total system development process. By choosing model orientations appropriately and doing model decompositions in a specialized style, one can make traceable and manageable connections to various methods for structured design, PDL specifications, simulation, etc. Among such extensions of SADT are the following examples:

In the mid-1970's, ITT Europe selected SADT as a standard for specifying and designing telephonic switching systems of all sizes and varieties in its many companies in many countries of Europe.[9] ITT Europe used SADT for training personnel (including some customers) to specify complex requirements exactly. The firm also designed a companion methodology for generating detailed code specifications from the functional models. SADT also was used to document existing systems for update review and for five-year maintenance and enhancement decisions.

SADT (and recently IDEF-0, as well) has been used extensively in numerous major defense programs, in which entire weapons systems, including command and control structures, mission profiles, and manual and automatic subsystem interaction, were modeled and evaluated from multiple viewpoints. Again, various extensions have been used both to derive PDL specification of programs and to set up extensive simulation.

Similar significant efforts have been carried out in commercial application areas in both the government and the private sector. Financial and transaction models, as well as models of major budget construction, approval, and tracking cycles, have been constructed as part of major system implementations. Often user education needs are modeled and a full, structured curriculum of courses (including models of student characteristics and teacher skills) is developed. All aspects of security (of materials, money, data, communications, and secrets) were studied for a worldwide manufacturer. The only apparent limit to the utility of SADT seems to be the imagination of its users.

In all these application areas, the human element looms large. Unless the right combination of SADT analytic and expressive skill is matched up with human insight into the problem area, the going is rough, for SADT exposes poorly structured thought just as effectively as well-structured ideas. Not everybody has equal analytic talents, but people who have difficulty in the creative side of authoring often make the best technical readers in a project—it is as though they find an outlet for supercritical faculties that block creation in a rigorous environment but are ideal for checking purposes. Once a key person has gained the insight of the (usually multifaceted) viewpoint that cracks a difficult area, others instantly become

productive, emulating their colleague's style and approach.

Finally, the helpful thought discipline and expressive power of SADT works on a personal level as well as on big team projects. Even when they move to a project that does not formally use SADT, many SADT practitioners make sketch models just to organize their thinking, whatever their current task. In particular, the reader/author cycle is often transported to cover any form of memo, letter, or other documentation, because concise input from colleagues always is beneficial.

Most SADT modeling is activity based, but for some applications, data modeling is more appropriate. Thus, SADT has been interfaced not only to various structured methodologies and tools such as PSL/PSA, Yourden, Jackson Method, Warnier-Orr,

---

Methodologies and tools developed for information processing systems are not adequate for embedded computer systems.

HIPO, Nassi-Schneiderman, Petri nets, and various PDL pseudolanguages, but also to Bachman-style, Codasyl, Entity Relation Attribute (ERA), IDEF-1, and Relational database design.

By choosing viewpoint and purpose properly, system designers can use SADT modeling to drive various simulation techniques for dynamic modeling of systems. One of the more successful and complete systems of this sort is SofTech's SADT/SAINT methodology (system analysis of integrated networking of tasks).[10] The system is further being extended to tie to the Navy's A-7E system documentation methodology.[11] IDEF-2 of the ICAM program also allows system scenarios to be studied during the requirements analysis phase.[8]

Need for tool support

At various times, attempts have been made to produce graphic computer support tools for SADT, with varying degrees of success. It turns out that SADT models pack a tremendous amount of finely structured information into very little space, so that even though the graphic requirements are modest, their coupling with standard database techniques for automation of retrieval, checking, and analysis often overburdens the resulting system. In ICAM, the AutoIDEF tool exists on a timeshared CDC 6600, but is lightly used.[12] Other implementations, such as the SPECIF computer-aided specification tool,[13] show promise, and networked micros and minis may be better suited to the task. Both SofTech and the Mitre Corporation have graphics-based efforts under way to link SADT with Ada packages for life-cycle software development environments. Even when economic and efficiency problems are mastered, however, it still is likely that a system-tuning evolution will be needed to make such tools unobtrusive and helpful. Aided by a handy copier and a well-trained project librarian, the manual methods now widely used with SADT will be hard to replace.

If multiple model orientations are properly chosen, SADT can be used for every aspect of life-cycle system development and maintenance, including detailed design, performance analysis, rapid prototyping, simulation, and optimization. To date, these areas have been handled by coupling SADT with other methodologies as described above. But if the sound, uniform concept-engineering principles and methods of SADT were used directly to build support tools for every aspect of an integrated development environment, even greater benefits could be anticipated. Then the shortcomings of the DT of SADT cited earlier could be overcome by the built-in features of the integrated tools. Learning to use the environment productively would steer users away from inappropriate applications and guide their steps toward success. At that stage SADT could be said to have reached its full maturity. □

References

1. D. T. Ross, "Reflections on Requirements," guest editorial, *IEEE Trans. Software Engineering,* Vol. SE-3, No. 1, Jan. 1977, pp. 2-5.

2. D. T. Ross, "Structured Analysis (SA): A Language for Communicating Ideas," *IEEE Trans. Software Engineering,* Vol. SE-3, No. 1, Jan. 1977, pp. 16-34.

3. D. T. Ross, and K. E. Schoman, "Structured Analysis for Requirements Definition," *IEEE Trans. Software Engineering,* Vol. SE-3, No. 1, Jan. 1977, pp. 6-15.

4. D. T. Ross, *Modularity Methods for AFCAM Architecture,* SofTech, Inc., 460 Totten Pond Rd., Waltham, MA 02154, May 25, 1973.

5. D. T. Ross, "Sequencing for Code Specification," SofTech document 9022-67.1, SofTech, Inc., 460 Totten Pond Rd., Waltham, MA 02154, Jan. 1975.

6. S. J. Greenspan, "Requirements Modeling: A Knowledge Representation Approach to Software Requirements Definition," Univ. of Toronto technical report CSRG-135, Mar. 1984; see also Borgida, Mylopoulos, and Greenspan in this issue, pp. 82-91.

7. D. T. Ross, "Removing the Limitations of Natural Language," in *Software Engineering,* H. Freeman and P. Lewis, eds., Academic Press, New York, Oct. 1979.

8. S. R. LeClair et al., "Integrated Computer-Aided Manufacturing (ICAM) Architecture Part II," Vol. I-VI, NTIS B062454-B052459, June 1981.

9. D. Combelic, "User Experience with New Software Methods (SADT)," *Proc. NCC,* Vol. 47, 1978, pp. 631-633.

10. R. F. Bachert, K. H. Evers, and P. R. Santucci, "SADT/SAINT Simulation Technique," *National Aerospace and Electronics Conf. Proc.,* 1981.

11. "DWS/CS Emergency Preset Extensions to the A-7E Methodology," SofTech, Inc., TP 150, 460 Totten Pond Rd., Waltham, MA 02154, Mar. 1983.

12. D. G. Smith, "Integrated Computer-Aided Manufacturing (ICAM) Architecture Part II—Automated IDEF-0 Development," NTIS B062454-B052459, Aug. 1981.

13. "SPECIF (Computer-Aided Specification Tool)," Institut de Genie Logiciel, Toulouse, France, 1984.

Douglas T. Ross is chairman of SofTech, Inc., and part-time lecturer in the Department of Electrical Engineering and Computer Science at MIT. His current interests include all aspects of the software development process, including theory, methodologies, languages, and tool development for requirements, specification, design, production, documentation, education, and maintenance in unified, distributed environments. Before founding SofTech in 1969, he was head of the Computer Applications Group in the Electronic Systems Laboratory at MIT. Originator of the international standard APT language for numerically controlled machine tools and leader of MIT's early work in computer-aided design and computer graphics, he has received several awards for his papers and work.

Ross is a member of the ACM, the IEEE Computer Society, AAAS, Sigma Xi, and the IFIP WG 2.3 (programming methodology). He received a BS in mathematics from Oberlin College in 1951 and an MS from MIT in 1954.

Ross's address is SofTech, Inc., 460 Totten Pond Rd., Waltham, MA 02154.

Visualizing Program Designs Through PegaSys

Mark Moriconi and Dwight F. Hare, SRI International

PegaSys is concerned more with explaining program design than describing programs, and offers more extensive support to programming in the large than other graphical systems.

This article is an introduction to many of the interesting features of PegaSys,* an experimental system that encourages and facilitates extensive use of graphical images as formal, machine-processable documentation. Unlike most other systems that use graphics to describe programs, the main purpose of PegaSys is to facilitate the explanation of program designs.

A program design is described in PegaSys by a hierarchy of interrelated pictures. Each picture describes data and control dependencies among such entities as "subprograms," "processes," "modules," and "data objects," among others. The dependencies include those represented in flowcharts, structure charts, dataflow diagrams, and module interconnection languages. Moreover, new abstractions can be defined as needed.

What is particularly interesting about PegaSys is its ability to: (1) check whether pictures are syntactically meaningful, (2) enforce design rules throughout the hierarchical decomposition of a design, and (3) determine whether a program meets its pictorial documentation. Much of the power of PegaSys stems from its ability to represent and reason about different kinds of pictures within a single logical framework. This framework is transparent to PegaSys users in the sense

that interactions are in terms of icons in pictures. For example, formal properties of a program are described by standard graphical operations on icons rather than by sentences written in a formal logic.

Excerpts from a working session with PegaSys are used to illustrate the basic style of interaction as well as the three PegaSys capabilities.† We describe the key ideas behind PegaSys elsewhere.[2,3]

Background and related work

Pictures have been used extensively by computer scientists in textbooks, professional publications, and on blackboards to explain dependencies in programs. Although pictures may be quite perspicuous, they have tended to be inadequate as a means of documentation. One reason is the use of imprecise concepts that result in pictures that are confusing and easily misinterpreted. For example, the same graphic symbol is often used to represent a process, a subprogram, and a data structure, all in the same picture. Similarly, an undifferentiated arrow might represent the flow of data to a process, the flow of control between subprograms, or the writing of data

---

* Programming Environment for the Graphical Analysis of SYStems.

†This article is a condensed version of a paper contained in a technical report.[1] Because of space limitations, we have removed many of the pictures that describe the design of the example system developed during the session.

into a data structure, all quite distinct concepts.

While formal documentation does not suffer from this imprecision, its advantages have tended to be outweighed by the difficulty of constructing and understanding it. Moreover, formal documentation has inadequately captured dependencies among components of the program it is intended to describe. An understanding of such dependencies is crucial throughout the software life cycle, especially during maintenance, and becomes increasingly more difficult to glean from a program as it increases in size and complexity.

In light of these observations, PegaSys attempts to take advantage of pictorial communication in describing data and control dependencies while, at the same time, maintaining the advantages of mathematical rigor. PegaSys is differentiated from previous graphical systems by its wider range of representation and analysis and its more extensive support for programming in the large. Previous work most closely related to PegaSys is concerned with representation and analysis techniques. We review this work and then describe related systems.

For a system to perform any sort of meaningful analysis of a picture, it must maintain a logical representation of the picture. A number of formalisms have been developed that have, or easily could have, a pictorial rendering. Examples are flowcharts,[4] structure charts,[5] pictographs,[6] dataflow diagrams (surveyed in Davis and Keller[7]), plans,[8] and module interconnection languages.[9-12] All of these formalisms capture data and control dependencies, typically down to executable program fragments. Pictures in PegaSys describe what we believe to be the important design concepts in these formalisms, plus other concepts as well.

The presence of a logical representation for a picture provides a basis for reasoning about the picture. In addition to checks for syntax errors, two other sorts of syntactic analysis of pictures have been performed by previous systems. The first involves the hierarchical refinement of a picture. If we think of a picture as a graphlike diagram, a node in a diagram may be replaced by a diagram provided that the replacement preserves the connectivity of the original diagram. Example uses of this idea can be found in Davis and Keller[7] and Rich and Shrobe.[8] The second sort of analysis concerns the relationship between a picture and

---

Pictures in PegaSys describe how algorithms and data structures fit together to form the design of a larger program.

---

the program it is intended to describe. If a picture is not executable, it is important to verify whether it accurately describes the program. For example, the flow of control in a program can be determined purely syntactically if we assume that conditional control paths may always be executed. Similarly, the "uses" and "requires" relations in module interconnection languages can be verified using type-checking techniques.[12] In contrast, PegaSys additionally places semantic constraints on design refinements and programs.

One such constraint deals with the logical consistency between a picture and the program it is intended to describe. Traditionally, program verification efforts have employed general methods for establishing the logical consistency between a formal specification and a program.[13] The PegaSys verification procedure is more specialized and simpler, and does not have

the practical drawbacks of traditional approaches.

A related system that deals with program dependencies is the PECAN system.[14,15] PECAN provides multiple "views" of a program by extracting dependencies directly from a program and then displaying them graphically. A similar, albeit nongraphical, approach at the level of specifications is described in Swartout.[16] The approach taken by PegaSys differs in that the program designer is responsible for describing a program in terms of the abstractions used in its conceptualization. This approach is based on our belief that it is difficult, if not impossible, to generate these abstractions from the final program.

Other related systems that make extensive use of graphics to describe aspects of programs fall into two major categories. First, there are a number of systems for "animating" dynamic program execution, a good example of which is the Balsa system.[17] Balsa creates simulations in which sophisticated graphical representations of an algorithm and its data structures are continually updated throughout the execution of the algorithm. There are other examples of animation systems.[17-22] The second category is concerned with "visual programming," i.e., programming by spatial arrangement of icons.[23-27] Both kinds of systems have tended to focus almost exclusively on programming in the small—that is, on individual algorithms and data structures. Pictures in PegaSys, on the other hand, describe how algorithms and data structures fit together to form the design of a larger program.

Getting started

Figure 1 shows a bitmap display connected to a Xerox personal computer.* Screen real estate is divided

---

*PegaSys is implemented in Interlisp-D and runs on Xerox 1100-series personal computers.

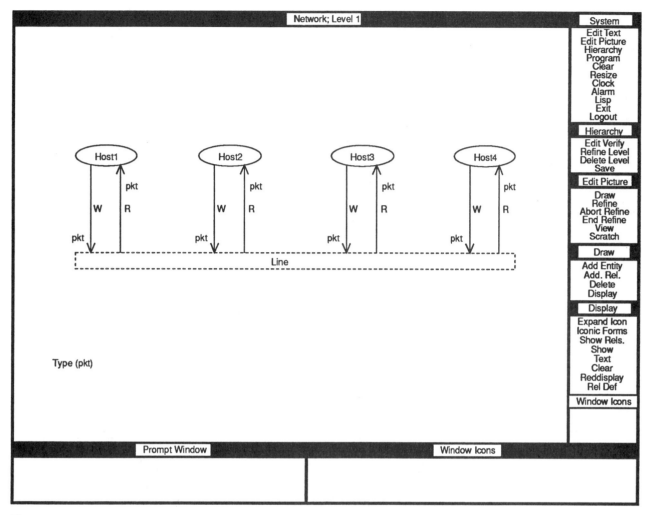

Figure 1. First level in broadcast network documentation hierarchy.

into adjacent, nonoverlapping rectangular areas called *windows*.* Screen layout will be adjusted throughout the scenario in an attempt to make maximal use of screen real estate. This is done by pointing with the mouse. The small windows down the right-hand side are *menus* containing commands, each of which may be selected by pointing at it with the mouse. The black strip at the top of each window contains the window's name. The name of a window is intended to be suggestive of its contents. For example, the name "Network:Level1" indicates that the contents of the associated window is

the first level of the picture hierarchy for a network.

For the most part, arguments to commands are selected or constructed by pointing, and pictures are manipulated by pointing as well. On-line help and feedback on errors appear in the prompt window in the lower-left corner of Figure 1.

The example session used to illustrate aspects of PegaSys is concerned with the development of a realistic broadcast network. It is not necessary to understand the details of the network or its implementation in order to get a "feel" for the capabilities being demonstrated. Particularly germane aspects of the example network are explained as needed. As the session pro-

gresses, details of the network are omitted so as to focus attention on the aspect of PegaSys being described.

The session begins with the design of the overall broadcast network down to the host level. It then focuses on the development of a single host, whose multilevel design and implementation is reused several times in the overall network. The network was implemented in the Ada programming language[29] (using PegaSys) and subsequently run on a Data General MV/10000 computer.

The meaning of a picture

A crucial aspect of the PegaSys design is its treatment of a picture as

---

*Our display management strategy is patterned directly after the *tiling* strategy used in Cedar.[28]

both a graphical and a logical structure. These structures affect user interaction with PegaSys in several important ways.

Dual interpretation of pictures. A picture is represented as a graphical structure composed of icons and their properties, such as size and location. Icons in a picture correspond to predicates in the underlying logical representation of the picture. This logical structure captures the computational meaning of a picture; each predicate in this structure denotes a computational concept expressed by the picture.

The picture shown in Figure 1 contains several icons: four ellipses, a rectangle, several arrows, and several character strings.* These icons denote several concepts about the example network. Each of the four hosts in the network is modeled as a process (indicated by an ellipse); the communication line by a module (indicated by a dashed rectangle); and a packet of data by a type (indicated by a label on arcs).† Interrelationships among hosts, packets, and the line are described by the "write" relation (denoted by the letter W on arrows) and the "read" relation (denoted by R).

At a first approximation, the picture says that the broadcast network consists of four hosts that communicate by means of a line. More precisely, processes named Host1,...,Host4 write values of type pkt into a module called

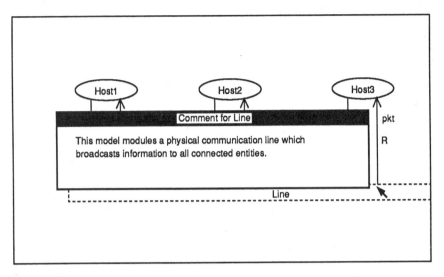

Figure 2. Explanatory text may be associated with computationally meaningful icons.

Line and read values of the same type from the Line module.

This statement about the network is represented in PegaSys by a conjunction of the predicates

process (*Host1*), *process* (*Host2*),
process (*Host3*), *process* (*Host4*),
module (*Line*), *Type* (*pkt*),
write (*Host1, Line, pkt*),
Read (*Host1, Line, pkt*)

with similar *Write* and *Read* predicates involving *Host2, Host3,* and *Host4.* Notice that every predicate corresponds to a different icon in Figure 1. Purely cosmetic changes to a picture, such as an adjustment to the size or location of an icon, do not require updates to the logical representation of the picture.

The logic in which pictures are represented is called the *form calculus.* A syntactically correct picture is said to describe the *form of a program* and is represented by a well-formed formula of the form calculus.

The following terminology will be adopted to refer to components of a picture. *Active entities* may initiate actions that create, destroy, or transform data objects (variables); the data objects themselves are called *passive entities.* The existence of an active or

passive entity is determined by its membership in a defining relation. An example of an active entity is *process* (*Host1*), and an example of a passive entity is *Type* (*pkt*). The term *entity* refers to both kinds of entities. A relationship among entities, such as specified by the *Write* relation, is called an *interaction.*

Entities and interactions specified in pictures correspond to either primitives of the form calculus or predicates defined in terms of the primitives. The primitives were carefully chosen to facilitate the definition of new concepts.[2]

A brief summary of the primitives will suggest the general kinds of concepts that can be expressed by pictures in PegaSys. Active entities are specified by "subprogram," "process," and "module" relations. We have chosen this relatively course grain in an attempt to capture the salient aspects of the design of a program, as opposed to the details of particular algorithms. Passive entities are specified by a "name" relation and by "simple type" and "structured type" relations. A name is used to refer to the object and a type to denote a (possibly structured) value set. The manipulation

---

*Note that type pkt is represented by text in the lower left of the picture rather than by an icon. If PegaSys does not have an appropriate icon for a concept, the convention is to display its logical representation as text.

†A *process* sequentially executes a series of actions that may proceed in parallel with actions of other processes; a *module* is a collection of one or more logically related entities; and a *type* is a, possibly structured, value set. The line is not modeled as a process because its actions are initiated by hosts.

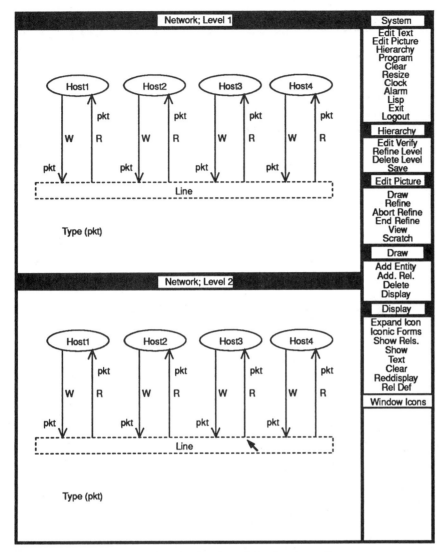

The following are menu labels shown in the figure:

Network; Level 1
System
Edit Text
Edit Picture
Hierarchy
Program
Clear
Resize
Clock
Alarm
Lisp
Exit
Logout
Hierarchy
Edit Verify
Refine Level
Delete Level
Save
Edit Picture
Draw
Refine
Abort Refine
End Refine
View
Scratch
Draw
Add Entity
Add. Rel.
Delete
Display
Display
Expand Icon
Iconic Forms
Show Rels.
Show
Text
Clear
Reddisplay
Rel Def
Window Icons

Figure 3. Creation of a level and selection of the line for refinement.

and sharing of data objects are specified by means of primitive interaction relations that capture general notions of data object declaration, data object visibility, aliasing of names, modification of the value of a data object, and accessing the value of a data object. There are also primitives for modeling (synchronous and asynchronous) interprocess communication and ordinary transfer of control. See reference 3 for details.

Finding out about what is not in a picture. A picture may be augmented with explanatory text. In particular, text may be associated with any computationally meaningful icon. If the user points at an icon and presses a button on the mouse, the associated pop-up comment will appear on the display until the user releases the button. Figure 2 shows the *pop-up comment* for the line module. Given this and related features of PegaSys, the best way to gain an understanding of the pictures presented here is by means of an interactive dialog with PegaSys.

Manipulation of pictures

Interactions with PegaSys are in terms of icons. However, graphical operations on pictures are restricted by logical constraints imposed by the form calculus. These constraints are intended to ensure that graphical operations make sense computationally.

Graphical manipulation of pictures. Graphical manipulation of a picture depends upon a one-to-one mapping between computationally meaningful icons and predicates. An icon and its associated predicate denote the same concept.

Perhaps the simplest example of how PegaSys takes advantage of this mapping concerns the selection of a concept, which is done by pointing at the appropriate icon. For example, positioning the mouse to point at the ellipse labeled Host1 in Figure 1 and clicking (depressing and releasing) a button on the top of the mouse results in selection of the predicate *process (Host1)*.

Another example concerns the construction of pictures. Pictures are constructed by using a series of graphical operations on the display that have the twofold effect of building a graphical structure and a corresponding formula in the form calculus. Each operation involves the selection of a concept from a menu followed by its placement at a location on the screen. An icon is associated automatically with most concepts. If a concept must be named, the user must enter a name for it and PegaSys will size the associated icon relative to the size of the name. Placement is done by pointing. Layout adjustments may be made by pointing at the desired icon (selection), pointing at the destination location, and clicking a button on the mouse. PegaSys repositions the selected icon at the specified location, readjusting related icons (such as connected arrows) as best it can.

Logical constraints on graphical manipulations. Both syntactic and semantic constraints are placed on graphical manipulations. An example of the former concerns the construction of pictures. While pictures are constructed by means of standard graphical operations, the form calculus guides the entire process. PegaSys

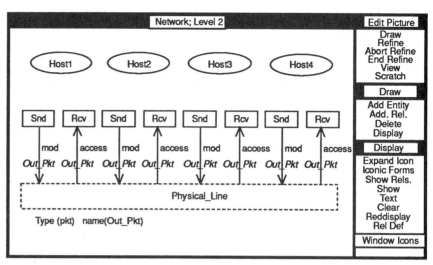

Figure 4. Constructing a replacement for the line.

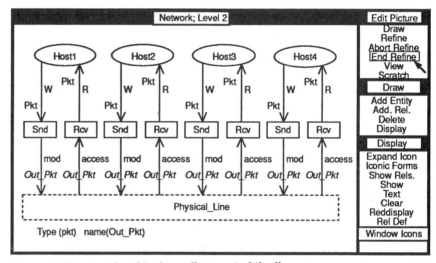

Figure 5. Picture at level 2 after refinement of the line.

uses the *grammar* of the form calculus to guide the construction of pictures in much the same way that a structure-oriented editor uses the grammar of a programming language to guide the construction of programs. Pictures may contain only concepts that are primitive in the form calculus or that have been defined in terms of the primitives. PegaSys uses the *type constraints* on predicates to prevent a nonsensical composition of concepts. For example, if a predicate has been defined to take two processes as its arguments, PegaSys ensures that both arguments are provided and, moreover, that both are processes. If not, a type error is signaled.

Semantic constraints are needed to restrict picture refinements and to analyze the relationship between a picture hierarchy and the program it is intended to describe. In both instances, it is necessary to prove logical formulas in the form calculus. However, this can be done quickly and without user interaction (due in part to the decidability of the form calculus).

Hierarchical decomposition of pictures

A hierarchy of pictures related according to the PegaSys design rules is said to describe the design of a program.

Creating a new level in a hierarchy. Each level in a picture hierarchy is a description of a program at a particular level of detail. A level is formed by a sequence of refinements to the immediately preceding level in the hierarchy. A refinement adds detail to an existing concept and is not allowed to delete concepts from a picture. Therefore, a concept cannot appear at any level in a hierarchy (except the top one) unless it is a refinement of a more abstract concept.

The procedure for building a new

level in a hierarchy is as follows. As soon as the user indicates a desire to create a new level, PegaSys makes a copy of the immediately preceding level. The new level is formed by a sequence of refinements to this copy. An individual refinement involves the following three steps: (1) selection (by pointing) of the relation to be refined, (2) construction or selection of its replacement, and (3) selection of the appropriate menu command.* PegaSys checks whether the refinement satisfies its design rules.

---

*This is a good example of the modeless style of interaction supported by PegaSys in that argument selection precedes command selection. See Tesler's discussion of this approach to man-machine interfacing.[30]

Refinement of an active entity. Recall that an active entity is an entity that has the ability to manipulate data. The active entities in Figure 1 are the host processes and the line module. The next step in the scenario illustrates a refinement technique called *active entity refinement*—the first, and simplest, of three refinement techniques employed in the network development.

Provided the replacement preserves interactions involving the replaced entity, PegaSys allows an active entity to be replaced by a picture. The three steps in an active entity refinement are illustrated by Figures 3 through 5. The window at the bottom of the display (see Figure 3) contains a copy of level 1, where the Line module has been se-

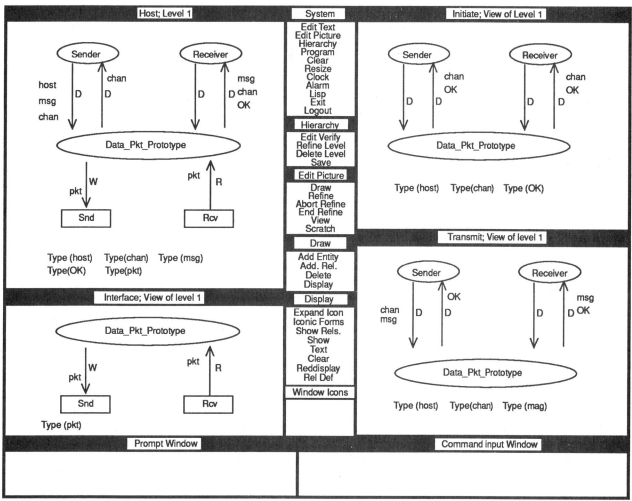

Figure 6. Level 1 of protocol hierarchy for a host computer. The upper-left window contains a picture of the entire level, which is explained by the views in the other three windows. This figure is read starting with (a) for the upper-left window and progressing clockwise for windows (b) through (d).

lected for refinement (indicated by boldface highlighting). The user next constructs a replacement for the line, as shown in Figure 4. Solid-lined rectangles denote "subprograms" that are intended to specify the interface to the line; Out_Pkt is a variable modified by these subprograms.* Finally, the user indicates (by pointing) its exact connection between the replacement for the line and the hosts (see Figure 5). This completes the refinement, and

PegaSys checks that interactions at level 1 are preserved at this level and that the entire picture at level 2 satisfies the type constraints imposed by the form calculus. (PegaSys accepts only well-formed pictures and, therefore, requires that type errors be removed before it attempts any further analysis of the offending picture.)

Figure 5 also illustrates a useful aspect of picture layout in PegaSys. Even though the Snd and Rcv entities appear four times each at level 2, they describe only one interface to the line and, therefore, appear only once in the internal logical representation of the

picture. In general, duplication is a good technique for avoiding crossover and curved lines.

Views are used to manage complexity. We are now ready to design the hosts in the network. Rather than designing four separate hosts, our strategy will be to design *one* host and then "replicate" it four times at level 2 of the network hierarchy (see Figure 5).

Figure 6a shows the first level in the design hierarchy for a host. This picture is not particularly perspicuous because it mixes several important properties of a host. These properties may be separated by means of three

---

*The access and mod relations in Figure 4 require Out_Pkt to be a variable belonging to the physical line module.

views (explained below), obviating the need to study Figure 6a.

In general, multiple views of the same picture are used to manage complexity or to emphasize particular aspects of a picture. A *view* in PegaSys is a single grouping of logically related icons from a picture. Views are presently constructed interactively by structured selection and positioning of related icons. A more sophisticated view mechanism, based on relational database technology, is planned.

Two of the views describe the two steps in interhost communication—namely, establishment of a communication link (i.e., a channel) between hosts (Figure 6b) and transmission of an actual message (Figure 6c). In Figure 6b, a sender process asks a data packet protocol to open a channel between it and another host. (A single host may have multiple open channels.) If the channel is successfully opened, the variable OK has the value true and chan contains the name of the open channel. If the attempt to initiate a connection fails, OK has the value false. The receiver opens a channel in the same manner.

Figure 6c describes message transmission. The sender sends a message (msg) over the open channel (chan) and receives back an indication as to whether the transmission was successful. The receiver, on the other hand, tells the data packet protocol that the channel called *chan* is open and awaits the arrival of a message.

The third view, shown in Figure 6d, describes the interface between a host and an external network backbone. This view says that a host reads and writes packets by means of subprograms Rcv and Snd, respectively. This interface would be suitable for a variety of network configurations, including the line interface in Figure 5. We will say more about this interface later when we "paste" the completed host design into our network.

Refinement of an interaction. We have seen one example of how refinements add detail to an existing design concept. In particular, a refinement of an active entity adds detail in the sense that it syntactically elaborates the entity and preserves interactions in the

design. (Pictures only suggest the semantics of entities by means of mnemonic entity names. It is expected, but in no way enforced, that the refinement of an entity provide a more detailed description of the computation suggested by the entity name.) For refinements of interactions, it is possible to enforce stringent logical requirements—in particular, a refinement of an interaction must be a more detailed description of the interaction. For example, if a picture says that an entity "writes" into a particular data object, then refinements of the notion of writing must specify one of the possible ways in which writing may occur.

The sequence of steps performed in refining an interaction are illustrated in Figures 7 through 10. The user first selects a dataflow relation D (see Figure 7). Its replacement is constructed by selecting the menu command for adding a relation and then the Write relation from a pop-up menu (see Figure 8). Note that the dataflow relation has disappeared while it is being refined. The Write relation takes three arguments, two of which are selected in Figure 8. The two selections

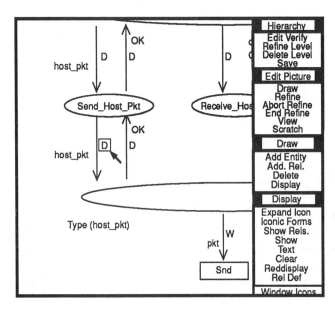

Figure 7. Selection of an interaction relation for refinement. The letter *D* is an abbreviation for a dataflow relation.

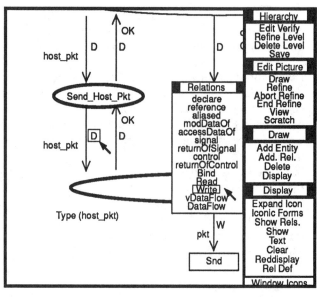

Figure 8. Selection of the Write relation from a pop-up menu to replace the dataflow relation selected in Figure 7.

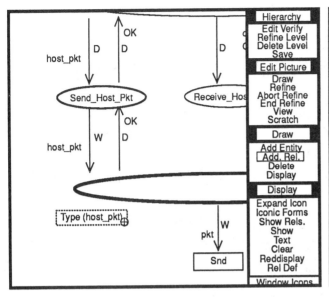

Figure 9. Selection of an argument to the Write relation. The cursor has changed to prompt for a selection.

Figure 10. The dataflow relation of Figure 7 has been replaced by the Write relation (abbreviated as W). Validation of this refinement required a logical proof.

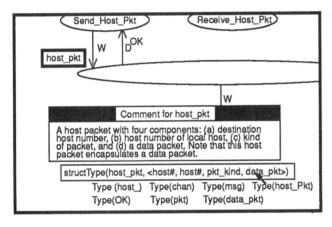

Figure 11. Selection of passive entity host__pkt with a pop-up comment explaining its selected refinement.

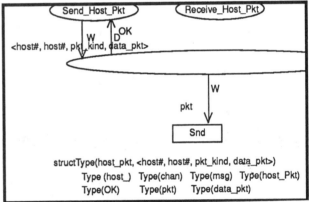

Figure 12. The result of the refinement started in Figure 11.

are the bold ellipse (whose name Line_Pkt_Protocol is occluded by menus) and Send_Host_Pkt. The third argument is selected in Figure 9. (The cursor has changed to let the user know that a selection is required.) The final result is seen in Figure 10, which specifies that a data object of type host_pkt is written from Send_Host_Pkt to Line_Pkt_Protocol.

PegaSys allowed the replacement of the DataFlow relation by the Write relation because it was able to prove a certain logical relationship between them. Roughly speaking, the refinement of an interaction is said to add detail if the interaction is a logical consequent of its refinement. This logical relationship is verified by means of a (fully automatic) logical proof.*

---

*This procedure applies to any derived relation, while the active entity refinement strategy applies only to primitive active entities.

Refinement of a passive entity. Recall that a passive entity is a data object manipulated by active entities. A data object is characterized by a name (which is used to refer to the object) and a simple or structured type (which denotes a set of possible values). A passive entity refinement, unlike refinements described earlier, does not necessarily replace an existing relation; it usually augments a *partial characterization* of a data object. The simplest example is the addition of a miss-

COMPUTER

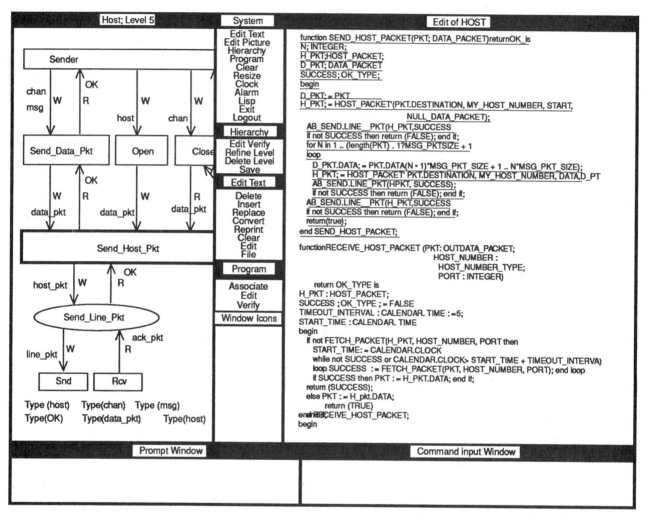

Figure 13. Associating entities in pictures with program text.

ing name or type to a data object. A more complex example involves the specification of the structure of a global type. (All types are global.) It is often convenient to specify different *instances* of the *same* type differently. In particular, only the relevant components of a structured data object need be specified for each instance of the object.

The refinement of a single instance of a type is illustrated in Figures 11 and 12. In Figure 11, the user has selected the type host_pkt (indicated by the bold rectangle), constructed the refined structure (the structType relation at the present position of the cursor), and entered the pop-up comment explaining the relation. Figure 12 shows the completed refinement. This refinement of host_pkt into a four-tuple applies only to the selected instance of type host_pkt. Components of the host_pkt structured type, such as host# and pkt_kind, can be further refined into structures and substructures using the structType relation.*

Sometimes it is convenient to refine an instance of a simple type into another simple type, rather than a struc-

---

*In order to avoid clutter on the display, simple types are not actually replaced by structured types in pictures. For example, *host__pkt* was not actually replaced in the picture by the four-tuple describing its structure. However, if the user points at host__pkt (on the arc between Send__Host__Pkt and the partially occluded ellipse) and presses a button on the mouse, the specified structure is displayed (see Figure 12).

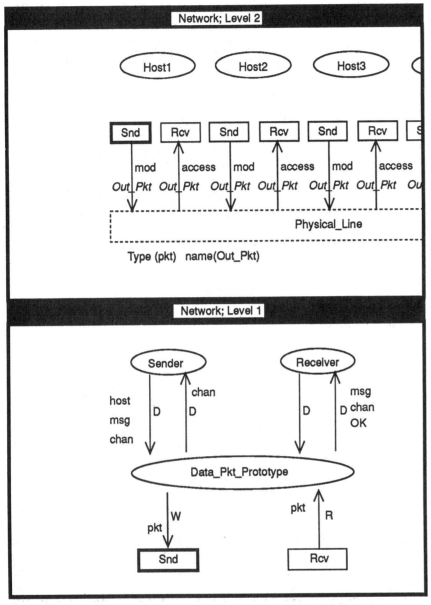

Figure 14. A design is shared through its interface entities, which are connected to another design by pointing.

tured type. This is done if a single type is used to denote a *union of types*. For example, we use the type pkt in our network as an abstraction for two different kinds of packets, a line packet and an acknowledgment packet. PegaSys allows us to replace pkt by line_pkt in one refinement and by ack_pkt in another. (Eventually, line packet line_pkt is refined into < host#, host#, seq, host_pkt >. This packet en-

capsulates host packets and contains an acknowledgment bit (of type seq) required by the line-level protocol. An acknowledgment packet is refined into < host#, host#, seq >.)

Reasoning about programs

We omit the development of the remaining levels in the host hierarchy

(which are described in reference 1) and rejoin the session. We are now ready to implement the host in Ada and to verify that its implementation is logically consistent with the host design. Programs are written interactively using the PegaSys structure-oriented editor; the verification process does not require human intervention except to establish the correspondence between entities in a picture and program constructs.

Each correspondence is specified by two structured selections, one from a picture and one from a program. This is illustrated in Figure 13, where the user has selected an entity called Send_Host_Pkt (indicated by the bold rectangle) and an Ada program unit called SEND_HOST_PACKET (indicated by the underlined text). Issuing the Associate menu command (see the cursor) causes PegaSys to record the specified association.

PegaSys requires that each *atomic entity*—i.e., one that is not refined— must be associated with exactly one program construct. Active entities must be associated with program units (in the case of Ada, a subprogram, package, task, or generic) and passive entities with data object or type declarations. The kind of an entity determines what it can be associated with. This association may occur at any stage of the development and at any level in a design hierarchy.

Nonatomic entities are not allowed to be associated with program constructs. We just saw that the type abstraction called pkt was replaced by line_pkt and ack_pkt. It does not make sense to require type pkt to be represented in the program, only that line_pkt and ack_pkt be represented. However, in general, there are situations in which it would be desirable to associate nonatomic entities with program constructs. The association would have to be restricted based upon properties of the refinement history. PegaSys maintains this history but

does not as yet provide this capability.

Once a program construct has been associated with every atomic entity in a hierarchy, PegaSys can attempt to prove that the program and the hierarchy are logically consistent. That is, PegaSys proves that the *lowest level* in a hierarchy is logically consistent with the program it is intended to describe. (This does not mean that an entire hierarchy is consistent with a program. PegaSys shows that every level in a hierarchy follows from the immediately preceding level by valid applications of our refinement rules and that the lowest level is consistent with the program it is intended to describe.) The PegaSys proof procedure has the following two important characteristics: (1) properties of nested program units are inherited by their parents and (2) specified interactions can be satisfied in a variety of ways by an implementation.[2] Without these considerations, impractical constraints would be placed on an implementation.

It should be pointed out that PegaSys is actually proving that a picture is logically consistent with a program under a *reasonable interpretation* of the program. PegaSys presently assumes that the consistency between a picture and the program it is intended to describe does not depend upon certain properties of its implementation. For example, it assumes that consistency does not depend upon "dead" control paths or aliasing of names in the same context. For the sorts of properties described by pictures in PegaSys, the assumptions appear to be reasonable and to coincide directly with our *intuitive model* of what such proofs should mean. These assumptions, together with the decidability of the form calculus, enable PegaSys to fully mechanize consistency proofs.

Reuse of a hierarchy

Having completed the host (its design, implementation, and verifica-

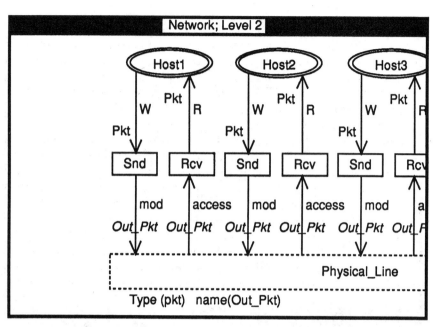

Figure 15. Hosts are marked to indicate reuse of an extant development.

tion), we would like to reuse it four times in Figure 5 with minimal reduplication of previous work. Below, we refer to the presently active development as the *primary* one and the development that we intend to reuse as the *secondary* one. At this stage of our example, the network is primary and the host secondary. We first consider reuse of the host design then its implementation.

There is a simple, yet useful, way to connect primary and secondary designs. An *atomic* active entity in a primary hierarchy may be replaced by an entire secondary hierarchy provided that (1) the atomic active entities that serve as interface to the secondary hierarchy are "matched up" with active entities of the primary hierarchy and (2) interactions with the replaced entity of the primary design are preserved (in the same sense as with active refinements).

This procedure is illustrated in Figure 14. The top window shows the lowest level of the network hierarchy, and the bottom one shows the highest level of the host hierarchy. We want to replace each of the host entities in the network (which are atomic) with the entire host hierarchy. Recall from Figure 6d that a host interfaces with a network backbone by means of the atomic Snd and Rcv entities. The Snd and Rcv entities of the host are associated (by pointing) with Snd and Rcv of the network, respectively. This pairing is done four times, once for each reuse of the host. In Figure 14, the user has started the series of pairings by selecting the leftmost Snd subprogram of the network and the Snd subprogram of the host interface.* Figure 15 shows the final result. A double-ringed ellipse has been drawn around the network hosts to indicate their connection to another design hierarchy.

Reusability of an implementation is achieved by direct sharing of interface

---

*Things do not always work out as fortuitously as in this example. In particular, interfaces between designs do not always have identical interactions. In this event, it is sometimes possible to introduce a "dummy" entity that serves as an interface between the two designs.

code. For example, the implementation of Snd for the host must be identical, possibly with renaming, to the implementation of Snd for the network.* This is not as restrictive as it might sound. Most often, the interface of the secondary reusable implementation consists of code skeletons involving only headers for program units needed in the verification of the secondary design. Note that, under this condition, reverification of the secondary implementation is unnecessary.

At this point, the reader should not be misled into thinking that PegaSys always avoids unnecessary work. In fact, PegaSys presently is not incremental and duplicates work in many commonly occurring situations. In this example, the secondary host design and implementation are reused *before* the network has been implemented and verified. PegaSys would have to reverify the entire network (except for the host) if the network had been verified before reuse of the host. Our first priority has been to develop the basic capabilities of PegaSys, and we are now beginning to consider the problems of incremental analysis.

Having completed the host and reused it in the development of the network, the remaining task is to design and implement the physical line module. As the rest of the session follows the pattern of development already described, we omit it here.

PegaSys is an experimental system that we plan to extend in a number of ways. One area in which it is presently lacking involves the representation of persistent data and data dependencies, both of which arise in database applications. We expect to add several new capabilities, such as incremental analysis of changes, a sophisticated view mechanism, and a dynamic animation and testing facili-

ty. Animations would display particular execution states in terms of hierarchical pictures of the program design. In Figure 5, for example, we might show a packet flow from a host to the line whenever the "write" relation is satisfied.

While the precision and descriptive capability of pictures has legitimately been questioned in the past, PegaSys seems to suggest that it is possible to profitably combine both graphics and logic for a rich domain. Our limited experience suggests that PegaSys makes techniques more palatable to program developers. It is our expectation that such uses of graphics will lead to the utilization of formal documentation and analysis techniques by a wide, possibly mathematically unsophisticated audience. ☐

Acknowledgment

This research was supported by the Office of Naval Research under Contract N00014-83-C-0300, by the Naval Electronics Systems Command under Contract N00039-82-C-0481, and by the Defense Advanced Research Projects Agency under Contract F30602-81-K-0176 (monitored by Rome Air Development Center).

---

*The present implementation requires identical names.

References

1. "PegaSys: A Graphical Program Design Environment, Three Papers," tech. report CSL-145, Computer Science Laboratory, SRI International, June 1985.

2. M. Moriconi and D. F. Hare, "PegaSys: A System for Graphical Explanation of Program Designs," *Proc. ACM SIGPLAN 85 Symp. Language Issues in Programming Environments,* Seattle, Washington, June 1985, pp. 148-160. Also in tech. report CSL-145, Computer Science Laboratory, SRI International, June 1985.

3. M. Moriconi, "A Logical Basis for Graphical Description of Program Designs," tech. report CSL-145, Computer Science Laboratory, SRI International, June 1985. Submitted for publication.

4. I. Nassi and B. Shneiderman, "Flowchart Techniques for Structured Programming," *SIGPLAN Notices,* Vol. 8, No. 8, Aug. 1973, pp. 12-26.

5. E. Yourdan and L. L. Constantine, *Structured Design: Fundamentals of a Discipline of Computer Program and Systems Design,* Prentice-Hall, Inc., Englewood Cliffs, N.J., 1979.

6. M. L. Powell and M. A. Linton, "Visual Abstraction in an Interactive Programming Environment," *Proc. ACM SIGPLAN 83 Symp. Programming Language Issues in Software Systems,* June 1983, pp. 14-21.

7. A. L. Davis and R. M. Keller, "Data Flow Program Graphs," *IEEE Computer,* Vol. 15, No. 2, Feb. 1982, pp. 26-41.

8. C. Rich and H. Shrobe, "Initial Report on a Lisp Programmer's Apprentice," *IEEE Trans. Software Eng.,* Vol. SE-4, No. 6, Nov. 1978, pp. 456-466.

9. L. W. Cooprider, "The Representation of Families of Software Systems," PhD thesis, Computer Science Dept., Carnegie-Mellon University, April 1979.

10. F. DeRemer and H. H. Kron, "Programming-in-the-large Versus Programming-in-the-small," *IEEE Trans. Software Engineering,* Vol. SE-2, No. 2, June 1976, pp. 80-86.

11. H. C. Lauer and E. H. Satterthwaite, "The Impact of Mesa on System Design," *Proc. 4th Int'l Conf. Software Engineering,* Sept. 1979, pp. 174-182.

12. W. F. Tichy, "Software Development Control Based on Module Interconnection," PhD thesis, Computer Science Dept., Carnegie-Mellon University, Jan. 1980.

13. R. L. London, "Perspectives on Program Verification," R. T. Yeh (ed.), in *Current Trends in Programming Methodology,* Vol. 2, pp. 151-172, Prentice-Hall, Inc., Englewood Cliffs, N.J., 1977.

14. S. P. Reiss, "Graphical Program Development with PECAN Program Development Systems," *Proc. ACM SIGSOFT/SIGPLAN Software Engineering Symp. Practical Software Development Environments,* April 1984, pp. 30-41.

15. S. P. Reiss, "PECAN: Program Development Systems that Support Multiple Views," *IEEE Trans. Software Eng.,* Vol. SE-11, No. 3, March 1985, pp. 30-41.

16. W. Swartout, "The Gist Behavior Explainer," *Proc. 3rd Nat'l Conf. Artificial Intelligence,* Aug. 1983, pp. 402-407.

17. M. H. Brown and R. Sedgewick, "Techniques for Algorithm Animation," *IEEE Software,* Vol. 2, No. 1, Jan. 1985, pp. 28-39.

18. R. Baecker, *Sorting Out Sorting,* 16mm color sound film, 25 min., 1981. (SIGGRAPH 1981, Dallas, Texas.)

19. R. M. Balzer, "EXDAMS—Extendable Debugging and Monitoring System," *Proc. AFIPS Spring Joint Computer Conf.,* 1969, pp. 567-580.

20. H. Lieberman, "Seeing What Your Programs Are Doing," tech. report 656, Artificial Intelligence Laboratory, Massachusetts Institute of Technology, Feb. 1982.

21. R. L. London and R. A. Duisberg, "Animating Programs Using Smalltalk," tech. report CR-84-30, Computer Research Laboratory, Tektronix, Inc., Beaverton, OR, Dec. 1984.

22. B. A. Myers, "Displaying Data Structures for Interactive Debugging," tech. report CSL-80-7, Xerox Palo Alto Research Center, Palo Alto, CA, June 1980.

23. A. Borning, "The Programming Language Aspects of ThinkLab, a Constraint-oriented Simulation Laboratory," *ACM Trans. Programming Languages and Systems,* Vol. 3, No. 4, Oct. 1981, pp. 353-387.

24. H. P. Frei, D. L. Weller, and R. Williams, "A Graphics-based Programming-support System," *Computer Graphics,* Vol. 12, No. 3, Aug. 1978, pp. 43-49.

25. R. V. Rubin, E. J. Golin, and S. P. Reiss, "ThinkPad: A Graphical System for Programming by Demonstration," *IEEE Software,* Vol. 2, No. 2, March 1985, pp. 73-79.

26. I. E. Sutherland, "SKETCHPAD: A Man-Machine Graphical Communication System," tech. report 296, MIT Lincoln Laboratory, Jan. 1963.

27. M. Wolfberg, "Fundamentals of the AMBIT/L List-processing Language," *SIGPLAN Notices,* Vol. 7, No. 10, Oct. 1972, pp. 66-76.

28. W. Teitelman, "A Tour Through Cedar," *IEEE Software,* Vol. 1, No. 2, April 1984, pp. 44-73.

29. *Reference Manual for the Ada Programming Language,* ANSI/MIL-STD-1815A-1983, Dept. of Defense, US Govt. Print. Off., Washington, D.C., Jan. 1983.

30. L. Tesler, "The Smalltalk Environment," *BYTE,* Vol. 6, No. 8, Aug. 1981, pp. 90-146.

Mark Moriconi is a program director in the Computer Science Laboratory at SRI International. His research interests span the fields traditionally called "programming environments" and "program verification." He is especially interested in the construction of systems that effectively support and rigorously analyze software life-cycle activities. Moriconi's research activities have included the development of program verification systems, novel verification system components for analyzing incremental changes and for generating axiomatic semantic proofs from suitable tables, and, more recently, the PegaSys environment that accepts and reasons about pictures as formal documentation.

Moriconi holds a PhD degree in computer science from the University of Texas at Austin.

Dwight Hare is a researcher in the Computer Science Laboratory at SRI International. He has been involved in the design and construction of programming environments that involve the analysis of programs. He has designed and built a verification system using HDM (Hierarchical Development Methodology), which was used to prove properties of a fault tolerant operating system. He has contributed to the design and has been primarily responsible for the implementation of the PegaSys system.

Hare has a Master's degree in computer science from the University of Texas at Austin.

Questions about this article can be addressed to either author at the Computer Science Laboratory, SRI International, 333 Ravenswood Avenue, Menlo Park, CA 94025.

"On Visual Formalisms" by D. Harel from *Communications of the ACM*, Volume 31, Number 5, May 1988, pages 514-530. Copyright 1988, Association for Computing Machinery, Inc., reprinted by permission.

ON VISUAL FORMALISMS

The higraph, a general kind of diagramming object, forms a visual formalism of topological nature. Higraphs are suited for a wide array of applications to databases, knowledge representation, and, most notably, the behavioral specification of complex concurrent systems using the higraph-based language of statecharts.

DAVID HAREL

Visualizing information, especially information of complex and intricate nature, has for many years been the subject of considerable work by many people. The information that interests us here is nonquantitative, but rather, of a structural, set-theoretical, and relational nature. This should be contrasted with the kinds of quantitative information discussed at length in [43] and [46]. Consequently, we shall be interested in diagrammatic paradigms that are essentially topological in nature, not geometric, terming them *topovisual* in the sequel.

Two of the best known topo-visual formalisms have their roots in the work of the famous Swiss mathematician Leonhard Euler (1707–1783). The first, of course, is the formalism of graphs, and the second is the notion of *Euler circles*, which later evolved into *Venn diagrams*. Graphs are implicit in Euler's celebrated 1736 paper, in which he solved the problem of the bridges of Königsberg [12]. (An English translation appears in [3].) Euler circles first appear in letters written by Euler in the early 1760s [13], and were modified to improve their ability to represent logical propositions by John Venn in 1880 [48, 49]. (See [19, chap. 2] for more information.[1])

A graph, in its most basic form, is simply a set of points, or nodes, connected by edges or arcs. I*t*s role is to represent a (single) set of elements S and some binary relation R on them. The precise meaning of the relation R is part of the application and has little to do with the mathematical properties of the graph itself. Certain restrictions on the relation R yield special classes of graphs that are of particular interest, such as ones that are connected, directed, acyclic, planar, or bipartite. There is no need to elaborate on the use of graphs in computer science—they are used extensively in virtually all branches of the field. The elements represented by the nodes in these applications range from the most concrete (e.g., physical gates in a circuit diagram) to the most abstract (e.g., complexity classes in a classification schema), and the edges have been used to represent almost any conceivable kind of relation, including ones of temporal, causal, functional, or epistemological nature. Obviously, graphs can be modified to support a number of different kinds of nodes and edges, representing different kinds of elements and relationships.

A somewhat less widely used extension of graphs is the formalism of *hypergraphs* (see, e.g., [1]), though these are also finding applications in computer science, mainly in database theory (see [14], [15], and [31]). A hypergraph is a graph in which the relation being specified is not necessarily binary; in fact, it need not even be of fixed arity. Formally, an edge no longer connects a pair of nodes, but rather a subset thereof. This makes hypergraphs somewhat less amenable to visual representation, but various ways of overcoming this difficulty can be conceived (see Figure 1). In analogy with graphs, several special kinds of hypergraphs are of particular interest, such as directed or acyclic.

It is important to emphasize that the information

---

[1] Interestingly, both these topo-visual achievements of Eu' ere carried out during the period in which he could see with one eye only. ᵢuler lost sight in his right eye in 1735, and in the left around 1766.) It is tempting to attribute this in part to the fact that the lack of stereoscopic vision reduces one's ability to estimate size and distance, possibly causing a sharper awareness of topological features.

Part of this work was carried out while the author was at the Computer Science Department of Carnegie-Mellon University. Pittsburgh. Pennsylvania.

conveyed by a graph or a hypergraph is nonmetric and captured by the purely topological notion of *connectedness* (a term taken from [18]); shapes, locations, distances, and sizes, for example, have no significance.

Although not quite as widely used as graphs, Euler circles, or Venn diagrams, are often used to represent logical propositions, color charts, etc. (see Figure 2). The basic idea is to appeal to the two-dimensional case of the Jordan curve theorem (e.g., [11, 30]), which establishes that simple closed curves partition the plane into disjoint inside and outside regions. A set is then represented by the inside of such a curve,[2] giving the topological notions of *enclosure*, *exclusion*, and *intersection* of the curves their obvious set-theoretic meanings: being a subset of, being disjoint from, and having a nonempty intersection with, respectively.[3]

The bottom line is that, whereas graphs and hypergraphs are a nice way of representing a set of elements together with some special relation(s) on them, Euler/Venn diagrams are a nice way of representing a *collection* of sets, together with some *structural* (i.e., set-theoretical) relationships between them. The difference between the two types of relationships is obvious. The structural ones are uniformly interpreted in the obvious set-theoretic fashion, in much the same way as the = symbol in logical formalisms is uniformly interpreted as the equality predicate, whereas the edge relations of graphs and hypergraphs attain different meanings in different applications.

The main observation motivating the present work is that in numerous computer-related applications the complexity of the objects, systems, or situations under consideration is due in large part to the fact that *both* capabilities are needed. We have a (usually large) number of sets that are interrelated in nontrivial set-

theoretic ways, but they are also related via one or more additional relationships of special nature, depending on the application at hand. Furthermore, among the structural, set-theoretic relationships it is often desirable to identify the *Cartesian product* of some of the sets—an action that can be crucial in preventing certain kinds of representations from growing exponentially in size. In line with these observations, which will be supported by examples in the sequel, the purpose of this article is to extend and combine Euler's two topo-visual formalisms into a tool suitable for dealing with such cases.

In the next section, we introduce *higraphs*,[4] first modifying Euler/Venn diagrams somewhat, then extending them to represent the Cartesian product, and finally connecting the resulting curves by edges or hyperedges. (The appendix contains the formal syntax and semantics of simple higraphs.) We will then illustrate the power of the formalism by briefly discussing higraph-based versions of such graphical languages as entity-relationship diagrams, semantic and associative networks, and dataflow diagrams. Later we will detail a less obvious application called *statecharts* [21], which are essentially a higraph-based version of finite-state machines and their transition diagrams.

HIGRAPHS
Let us start with a simple example of Euler circles (Figure 3). As can be seen, we prefer to use rounded rectangles, or rounded rectilinear shapes (*rountangles?*), rather than circles or unrestricted curves, and shall call the areas, or zones, they enclose *blobs* in the sequel. Second, as the formal definition supplied in the appendix shows, we regard each blob as denoting a certain kind

---

[2] Venn himself was not always consistent in this respect; see [49, p. 117] or [19, p. 43] for a description of his five-set diagram.

[3] The topological paradigm used here is termed *insideness* in [18].

[4] This is not a particularly successful choice of term, but was chosen nevertheless to be reminiscent of *high graphs* or *hierarchical graphs*, though our diagrams are not limited to being stratified in the way the word *hierarchical* might imply.

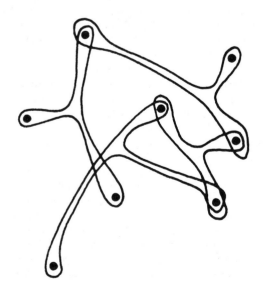
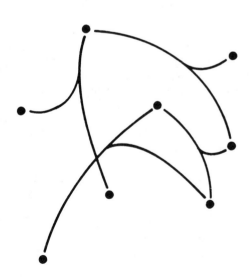

FIGURE 1. Graphical Representation of Hypergraphs

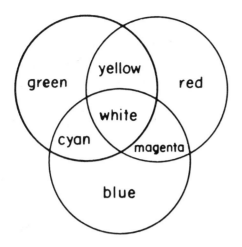

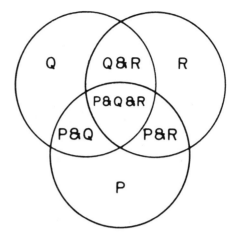

FIGURE 2. Applications of Euler Circles, or Venn Diagrams

of set, with the nesting of curves denoting set inclusion, not set membership. Thus, Figure 3 can be seen to contain several cases of inclusion, disjointness, and intersection of sets.

For our first real departure from Euler and Venn's treatment, we now require that every set of interest be represented by a unique blob, complete with its own full contour. One of the reasons for this is the desire to provide every set with its own area (e.g., for naming or labeling purposes). For example, does the A in Figure 3 represent the difference between the sets represented by the two large blobs, or the entire set on the upper left? The answer, following Venn's notational conventions, would appear to be the former; but then how do we label the upper set itself?

Our solution is illustrated in Figure 4, where the two large intersecting blobs are clearly labeled A and D, the intersection $A \cap D$ is labeled C, and the difference $A - D$ is called B. In fact, had we left out B and its contour we could not refer to $A - D$ at all. More pre-

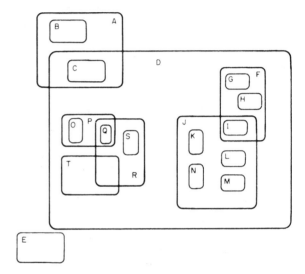

FIGURE 4. Adding Unique Contours for All Identifiable Sets

cisely, with this "unique-contour" convention, the only real, identifiable sets are the *atomic* sets, that is, those represented by blobs residing on the bottom levels of the diagram, containing no wholly enclosed blobs within. Any other blob merely denotes the compound set consisting of the union of all sets represented by blobs that are totally enclosed within it. The atomic blobs of Figure 4 are thus B, C, E, G, H, I, K, L, M, N, O, Q, S, and, significantly, also T. The fact that T, as a Jordan curve, intersects R in Figure 4 does not necessarily mean that the sets represented by[5] T and R really intersect or that $T - R$ is nonempty. In fact, in our formalism, the intersection of two curves does not, in itself, mean anything since unless internal blobs appear in the appropriate places neither the difference nor the intersection of the sets they represent is itself identifiable. Thus, as far as the information present in Figure 4, T could just as well have been drawn completely dis-

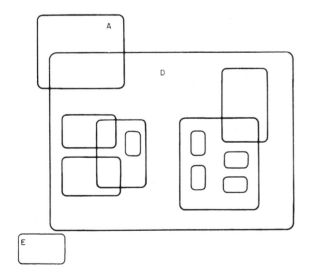

FIGURE 3. Simple Blobs

---

[5] In the sequel, we shall often blur the distinction between a curve, its associated blob, and the set it depicts.

joint from R, since R is defined by the figure to be the union of Q and S, whether T's curve intersects it or not. Of course, if T had been entirely enclosed within R, things would have been quite different, with R then being the union of Q, S, and T. All this might sound a little strange, but it is not really restrictive, since one can always let T and R intersect and simply add extra blobs representing $T \cap R$ and $T - R$, as is done in Figure 5.

Thus, one might say that empty space in our diagrams always represents nothing at all, except if it is the area of an atomic blob, which is one that contains no enclosed blobs. An atomic blob always represents some identifiable set, though clearly such a set might just happen to be an empty one.

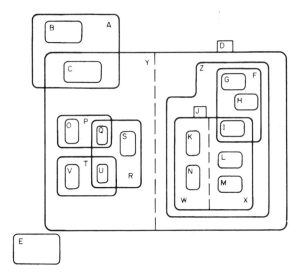

FIGURE 5. Adding Cartesian Products

We now add the ability to represent the *Cartesian product*. Figure 5 shows the notation used—a *partitioning* by dashed lines. In it J, for example, is no longer the union of K, N, I, L, and M, but, rather, the product of the union of the first two with the union of the last three. Symbolically,

$$J = W \times X = (K \cup N) \times (I \cup L \cup M).$$

We shall call the operands of the product, W and X in this case, the *orthogonal components* of blob J. Actually, the Cartesian product is *unordered*, in the sense that $A \times B$ is always the same as $B \times A$, so that J is really a set of unordered pairs of elements. Thus, our $\times$ operator is symmetric, and in fact, in the appendix we use the symbol $\otimes$, instead of $\times$, to denote it. Another consequence of this, and of our previous convention regarding set inclusion versus set membership, is that the product is also associative. In this way, if $c \in C$, $k \in K$, and $m \in M$, then the unordered triple $\{c, k, m\}$ would be a legal element of the set D of Figure 5, without the need to distinguish it from $\{c, \{k, m\}\}$. To make this idea work, it helps to assume that all atomic sets are pairwise disjoint (i.e., no element appears in any two of these sets).

Decomposing a blob into its orthogonal components by topologically partitioning the inner area of a Jordan curve yields a unique unambiguous area for each such component. Thus, the labels Y, W, and X in Figure 5 label the appropriate components unambiguously. On the other hand, as we shall see, there is another reason for wanting sets to have their own blob contours, and if so desired an orthogonal component can be enclosed in one of its own, as is Z in Figure 5. Notice the somewhat awkward location for the labels D and J. There are a couple of other possibilities for locating the label of a product blob, among which is the one illustrated in Figure 6, but we shall remain with that of Figure 5.

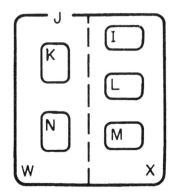

FIGURE 6. An Alternative for Labeling Partitioned Blobs

Now that we have a formalism for representing the sets we are interested in and their structural, set-theoretic relationships, it is time to add edges. A *higraph* is obtained by simply allowing edges, or more generally, hyperedges, to be attached to the contour of *any* blobs. As in graphs, edges can be directed or undirected, labeled or unlabeled, of one type or of several, etc. In Figure 7 we have allowed for a single kind of unlabeled directed hyperedge of arity between 2 and 3. Most of the arrows in the figure are simple binary edges, such

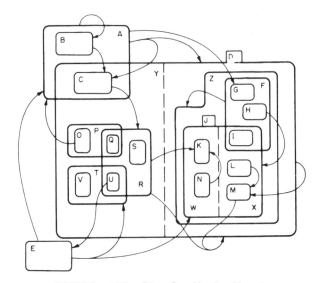

FIGURE 7. Adding Edges Resulting in a Higraph

as the very high-level one connecting E to A, the very low-level one connecting N to K, and the interlevel one connecting U to E. Others are directed three-way hyperedges, such as the one connecting E to both J and T, and the one connecting both R and M to D. Clearly, there is nothing to prohibit self-directed or partially self-directed edges, such as the one connecting A to its subblob B. The formal meaning of such edges (see the appendix) in the graph-theoretic spirit simply associates the target blobs with the source blobs via the particular relationship the edges represent. Here, then, is the other reason for wanting each set of interest to have its own contour: to enable it to be connected to others via the edges.

In the sequel the term *higraph* will be used in a very liberal sense, making no real distinction between the various possibilities, for example, the edge-based or hyperedge-based cases.

we are free to attach any meaning at all to the relationship itself and to the way (if any) that it extends downwards to the elements of those sets. Thus, if we take the relationship R represented by ordinary arrows in a higraph to mean "each element in the source set is related to *some* element in the target set by relationship T," then the information conveyed by Figure 9, for example, cannot really by captured by an ordinary graph with T-edges, since one would be forced to decide which element in the target set is meant, thus causing an overspecification.

The computer science literature is full of uses of graphs, and it appears that many of these can benefit from the extensions offered by higraphs. Consider the *entity-relationship (E-R) diagrams* used in the conceptual specification of databases [7]. These are really hypergraphs with a single type of node that is depicted by a rectangle and denotes an entity in the described pool of

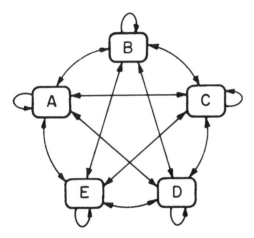

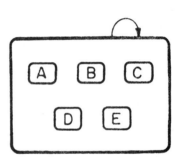

FIGURE 8. Two Representations of a 5-clique

SOME IMMEDIATE APPLICATIONS

The first thing to notice when attempting to apply higraphs is that edges connect sets to sets, not elements to elements as in graphs. The most common way of interpreting a higraph edge is as a collection of regular edges, connecting each element in one set with each element in the other. In this way, for example, it is possible to represent a 5-clique, as in Figure 8. This all-to-all semantics is not mandatory, however, since the bare meaning of a higraph edge is that the relationship it represents holds between the *sets* it connects. Hence,

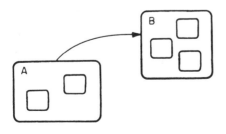

FIGURE 9. A Simple Higraph

data. The hyperedges, whose labels are written in small diamond-shaped boxes (that should not be regarded as nodes), capture the intended relationships between entities. Figure 10 shows a simple example of such a diagram, representing a small part of the data used by an airline company.[6] Its information content is clear: `pilots` can fly `aircraft`, `secretaries` work for `employees`, and `employees` are paid `salaries` on certain `dates` (the latter being a three-way relationship). Notice, however, the `is-a` edges, informing us that `pilots` and `secretaries` are really `employees` too. These are conveying information of a totally different kind. Indeed, they capture precisely the kind of structural, set-theoretic relations discussed earlier. Using the very same "flat" diagrammatic representation for both kinds of relationships can cause a lot of confusion, especially in large and intricate cases, as a glance at some of the examples in the literature shows.

---

[6] Actually, Figure 10 does some injustice to the E-R formalism, as it is sometimes called, by ignoring the additional features that the formalism supports, such as attributes for both entities, and relationships and the classification of relationships as one–one, many–one, etc. Throughout, we shall have to be satisfied with describing only those features of a formalism that are directly relevant to our discussion.

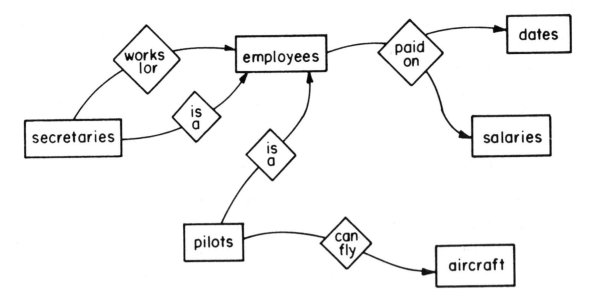

FIGURE 10. A Simple E-R Diagram

Figure 11 shows the way such information can be represented in a higraph-based extension of E-R diagrams. The set of `employees` is divided into the subsets of interest, `secretaries` and `pilots` (with an additional blob for all `others`, if so desired). The `paid-on` edge emanates from the `employees` blob, while the `can-fly` edge emanates from the `pilots` blob only—exactly what one would expect. The `work-for` edge rightly connects the `secretaries` blob with its parent blob—`employees`. The new information has been quite easily added: `aircraft` are now just part of the overall `equipment`, which is related to `years` by the relationship `received-on`, while the `dates` on which `salaries` are received have been specified as consisting of pairs from the orthogonal components `month` and `year`. Moreover, independent divisions can be represented by overlapping blobs, as illustrated in Figure 12, which shows how a new breakup of the `employees` by sex can be added to the previous figure

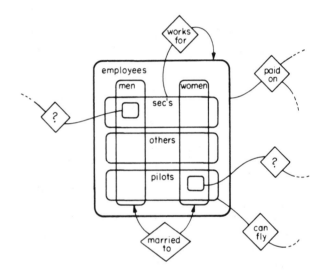

FIGURE 12. Two Breakups of Employees

with a couple of additional details. In it we might have reason to relate the `female pilots` or the `male secretaries` to other entities. In practice, overlaps should probably be used somewhat sparingly, as overly overlapping blobs might detract from the clarity of the total diagram, an observation that is in line with the often-made claim that a hierarchy is by far the way humans prefer to structure things (see [45, chap. 1]. This opinion is not universally accepted, however, so the human-factors aspects of formalisms like higraphs would appear to require careful experimental research, such as those carried out in [18] and [20].

Occasionally, authors have used other labels to capture `is-a` relationships, typically ones that try to describe the special nature of the breakup into subsets. As

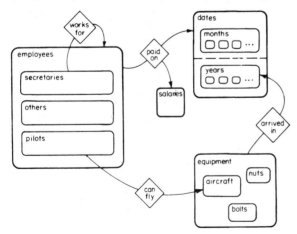

FIGURE 11. A Higraph-Based Version (and extension) of Figure 10

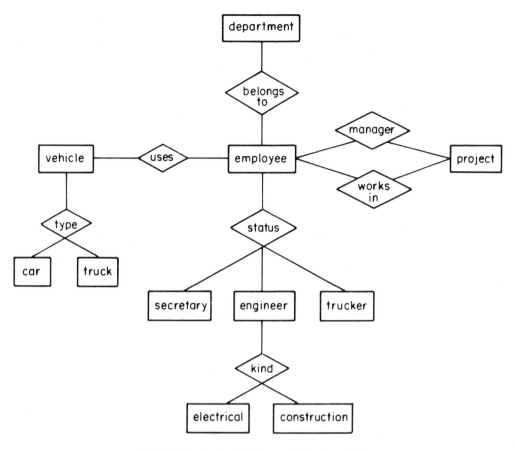

FIGURE 13. Another E-R Diagram (taken from [39])

an example consider Figure 13, which is Figure 9 of
[42] almost verbatim, and our higraph-based Figure 14,
which contains the same information.

A formalism that is very similar to that of E-R diagrams, and actually predated it by a number of years
(see [40]), is that of *semantic*, or *associative*, *networks*.
These graph-based structures are used widely in artificial intelligence for natural language processing and
knowledge representation, and are discussed in numer-

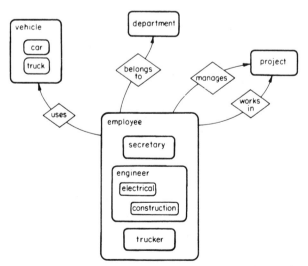

FIGURE 14. A Higraph-Based Version of Figure 13

ous books and papers. (A good survey and history appears in [4], and more examples can be found in [6],
[37], [44], and [50] and in the collection of papers in
[17].) Semantic networks can actually be thought of as
concept-relationship diagrams, with much of the research
in the area concerned with the association of rich semantic meaning with the various types of nodes and
edges. Here, too, is‑a edges are used in abundance
resulting in large, and at times incomprehensible, diagrams. Often, semantic networks contain more than
one distinct type of is‑a edges, corresponding to set
inclusion, set membership, a physical "being-part-of"
relationship, etc.[7] The way higraphs can be used here is
exactly as in E-R diagrams, and the advantages become
all the more significant if such different shades of structural is‑a relationships can be made visually distinct
(see the section called "Possible Variations on the
Theme"). Clearly, it would be naive to claim that the
profound problematics of knowledge representation can
be overcome by diagrammatic considerations alone.
Nevertheless, every little improvement helps.

In both E-R diagrams and semantic networks, people
have observed that often the relationships, not only the
entities and concepts, have to be stratified by levels of

---

[7] A variety of names have been attached to these, such as isa and inst in
[6], SS and EL in [37] (standing for *is a, instance, subset,* and *element,* respectively), and many others elsewhere, such as a‑kind‑of, group‑of,
is‑part‑of, etc.

detail. This is typically done by considering the diamond-shaped relationship labels to be nodes of a second kind, and involving them also in structural is-a relationships with others. Although some people are opposed to this visual blurring of the distinction between entities and relationships, there is nothing to prevent those who are not from transferring this idea to the higraph framework. This would yield a blob structure also for the relationships, with the edges now serving to connect the entities and concepts to their relevant real, nonstructural relationships.

It is noteworthy that the area of the blobs in a higraph can be further exploited in these applications. Full E-R diagrams and semantic networks are typically laden with attributes, or properties, that are attached as additional "stump" nodes to the various entities. These attributes are often of the kind that are "inherited down" the is-a hierarchy, as the phrase goes. (In fact, there are many interesting issues associated with the very notion of inheritance; see [5], [45].) In a higraph-based representation, the area inside a blob would appear to be an ideal place to list, attach, or otherwise identify any properties, attributes, or explanations that are relevant to that blob and anything enclosed therein. Thus, simple inheritance is made possible quite naturally by the insideness approach to representing the subset relationship.

We should remark that some papers on semantic networks and the E-R model have indeed suggested the use of insideness and interblob edges to represent high-level entities and relationships, though the ideas do not seem to have been pursued to their full potential (see [10], [16], [25], [34], and [36]). Also, the idea of basing the decomposition of sets on Cartesian products and OR's is consistent with much of the literature on types. (For example, see [5] where these two features are captured by the notions of a *record* and a *variant*, respectively.)

Among the other graph-based formalisms for which higraphs appear to be useful are data-flow diagrams. A higraph-based version of such diagrams, called *activity-charts*, is one of the graphical languages supported by the STATEMATE system of i-Logix and is described in [24] and [28]. In activity charts the blobs denote functions, or activities, with the subset relation representing the subfunction relationship. The edges denote the possible flow of data. (Cartesian product is not used.) Consider the activity-chart of Figure 15, which is a simple part of the functional decomposition of an automatic teller machine. One of the edges therein means that the customer's account-number might possibly flow (following, perhaps, a read or write instruction) from the identify activity to the update-account activity, or to anywhere in the serve-customer activity, that is, to either (or all) of the deposit, withdraw, or balance-query subactivities. Another of the edges in Figure 15 means that the new amount with which the customer's balance should be adjusted might flow from any one of the deposit or withdraw activities to the update-account activity.

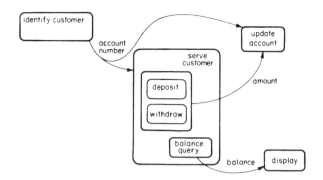

FIGURE 15. A Simple Activity Chart

Higraphs also form the basis of a recent paper [47], in which a visual language for specifying security constraints in operating systems is presented. The formalism represents access rights and exceptions thereof as distinct kinds of edges in a higraph, the blobs of which represent groups of users, files, and other entities. Cartesian product is used to represent the breakup of files into their components. Reference [47] also contains a number of interesting special-purpose extensions to the basic higraph formalism. Another use of higraph-like ideas appears in [32] and [38] in the form of proof diagrams for verifying concurrent programs, and there is a simple way of using higraphs as the basis of a hypertext system rather than conventional graph. In part, many issues that arise in the context of hypertext systems, such as multiple hierarchies, superconcepts, and composite nodes are treated naturally in the higraph formalism. (See [8].) One can also conceive of additional applications in visualizing interrupt-driven flowcharts and certain kinds of model-collapsing constructions in model theory.

STATECHARTS: A LESS OBVIOUS APPLICATION
The previous section notwithstanding, it would appear that the most beneficial application of higraphs lies in extending state-transition diagrams to obtain the *statecharts* of [21]. It was actually in the process of trying to formulate the underlying graphical concepts embodied in (the earlier) statecharts that higraphs emerged. This section contains a brief description of the statechart formalism; the reader is referred to [21] for further details.

To motivate the discussion, there appears to be agreement in the literature on software and systems engineering as to the existence of a major problem in the specification and design of large and complex *reactive systems*. A reactive system (see [22] and [39]), in contrast with a *transformational system*, is characterized by being event driven, continuously having to react to external and internal stimuli. Examples include telephones, communication networks, computer operating systems, avionics systems, VLSI circuits, and the man-machine interface of many kinds of ordinary software. The problem is rooted in the difficulty of describing reactive behavior in ways that are clear and realistic,

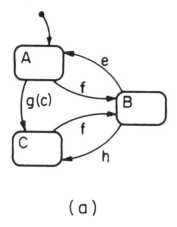 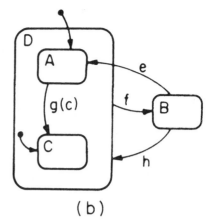

(a)   (b)

FIGURE 16. Depth in State Charts

and at the same time formal and rigorous, in order to be amenable to precise computerized analysis. The behavior of a reactive system is really the set of allowed sequences of input and output events, conditions, and actions, perhaps with some additional information such as timing constraints.

Most notable among the solutions proposed for this problem are Petri nets [41], communicating sequential processing (CSP) [26], the calculus of communicating systems (CCS) [35], the sequence diagrams of [51], ESTEREL [2], and temporal logic [39]. Statecharts constitute yet another attempt at solving this problem, but one that is aimed at reviving the classical formalism of finite-state machines (FSMs) and their visual counterpart, state-transition diagrams, trying to make them suitable for use in large and complex applications. Indeed, people working on the design of really complex systems have all but given up on the use of conventional FSMs and their state diagrams for several reasons:

(1) State diagrams are "flat." They provide no natural notion of depth, hierarchy, or modularity, and therefore do not support stepwise, top-down, or bottom-up development.

(2) State diagrams are uneconomical when it comes to transitions. An event that causes the very same transition from a large number of states, such as a high-level interrupt, must be attached to each of them separately resulting in an unnecessary multitude of arrows.

(3) State diagrams are extremely uneconomical, indeed quite infeasible, when it comes to states (at least when states are interpreted in the usual way as "snapshots" of the situation at a given point in time). As the system under description grows linearly, the number of states grows exponentially, and the conventional FSM formalism forces one to explicitly represent them all.

(4) Finally, state diagrams are inherently sequential in nature and do not cater for concurrency in a natural way.[8]

There have been attempts to remove some of these drawbacks, mostly by using various kinds of hierarchical or communicating state machines. Typically, however, these hierarchies provide little help in reducing the size of the resulting description, as they do not condense any information. Moreover, the communication between FSMs is usually one-to-one, being channel or processor based, and allows for only a single set of communicating machines on the highest level of the description. Furthermore, for the most part such extensions are not particularly diagrammatic in spirit, and hence one loses the advantages a visual medium might offer.

Statecharts are a higraph-based extension of standard state-transition diagrams, where the blobs represent states and arrows represent transitions. (For additional statechart features, the reader is again referred to [21].)[9] As to the basics, we might say that

state charts = state diagrams + depth
  + orthogonality + broadcast communication.

Depth is represented by the insideness of blobs, as illustrated in Figure 16, where 16b may replace 16a. The symbols e, f, g, and h stand for events that trigger the transitions, and the bracketed c is a condition. Thus, $g[c]$ triggers the transition from A to C if and when g occurs, but only if c is true at that time. The fact that A and C do not overlap and are completely inside D means that the latter is the *exclusive-or* (*XOR*) of the former, so that being in D is tantamount to being in either A or C, but not in both. The main point here is that the f-arrow, which leaves the contour of D, applies to both A and C, as in 16a. This simple higraph-based principle, when applied to large collections of states with many levels, helps overcome points (1) and (2) above (flatness and multilevel events). The idea of exploiting this kind of insideness in describing levels in a state-transition diagram appears also in [20]. It should be noted that the small *default arrows* depend on their

---

[8] Here, modeling a highly concurrent system by its global states only is considered unnatural.

[9] Some encouraging experimental evidence as to the appropriateness of statecharts for system description is discussed in [21. sect. 9].

encompassing blobs. In Figure 16a state A is singled out as being the default, or start state, of the three, a fact represented in 16b by the top default arrow. The bottom one, however, states that C is default among A and C if we are already in D and hence alleviates the need for continuing the h-arrow beyond D's boundary.

Orthogonality is the dual of the *XOR* decomposition of states, in essence an *AND* decomposition, and is captured by the partitioning feature of higraphs, that is, by the unordered Cartesian product. In Figure 17b state Y consists of two *orthogonal components*, A and D, related by *AND*: To be in Y is tantamount to being in both A and D, and hence the two default arrows. The intended semantics of 17b is given by its equivalent "flat" version 17a, which represents a sort of automata product. Notice the simultaneity of transitions that takes place when event e occurs in state configuration (B, F), and the merging and splitting transitions that lead to and from Y. Note also the special condition $[in(G)]$ attached to the f-transition from C, and the way it is reflected in Figure 17a. Figure 17 illustrates the heart of the exponential blowup problem, the number of states in the explicit version of Y being the product of the numbers

pearing along a transition in a statechart is not merely sent to the "outside world" as an output. Rather, it can affect the behavior of the state chart itself in orthogonal components. This is achieved by a simple broadcast mechanism: Just as the occurrence of an external event causes transitions in all components to which it is relevant (see Figure 17), if event e occurs and a transition labeled e/f is taken, the action f is immediately activated, and is regarded as a new event, possibly causing further transitions in other components.

Figure 18 shows a simple example of this. If we are in (B, F, J) and along comes the external event m, the next configuration will be (C, G, I), by virtue of e being generated in H and triggering the two transitions in components A and D. This is a *chain reaction* of length 2. If no external event n occurs, the new configuration will be (B, E, J), by virtue of a similar chain reaction of length 3.

This concludes our brief account of the basic features of statecharts, and we now illustrate the formalism with a rather simplified version of the digital watch described in [21]. The watch has four external control buttons, as well as a main display that can be used to

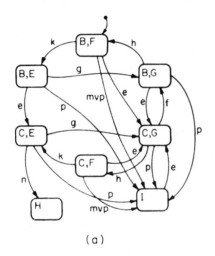

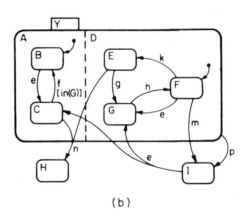

FIGURE 17. Orthogonality in State Charts

of states in the orthogonal components of its higraph version. If orthogonality is used often and on many levels, the state explosion and sequentiality difficulties (points (3) and (4)) are also overcome in a reasonable way. This can be further observed by studying the examples and references in [21].

Figures 16 and 17 do not contain any outputs, and hence, orthogonal components can synchronize so far only through common events (like e in Figure 17) and can affect each other only through $[in(state)]$ conditions. A certain amount of subtlety is added to the way statecharts model concurrency by allowing *output* events. Here, statecharts can be viewed as an extension of Mealy machines (see [27]), since output events, which are called *actions*, can be attached optionally to the triggering event along a transition. In contrast with conventional Mealy machines, however, an action ap-

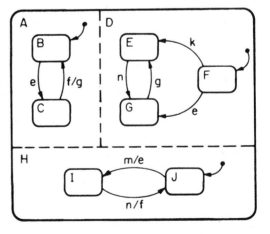

FIGURE 18. Broadcasting in State Charts

show the time (hour, minutes, and seconds) or the date (weekday, day of month, and month). It has a chime that can be enabled or disabled, beeping on the hour if enabled. It has an alarm that can also be enabled or disabled, and beeps for 2 minutes when the time in the alarm setting is reached unless any one of the buttons is pressed earlier. It has a stopwatch with two display modes (regular and lap), a light for illumination, and a weak-battery blinking indication.

Some of the external events relevant to the watch are a, b, c, and d, which signify the pressing of the four buttons, respectively, and b-up, for example, which signifies the release of button b. Another event we shall be using, 2-min, signifies that 2 minutes have elapsed since the last time a button was pressed. (We choose not to get involved here in a syntax for the event expressions themselves. In a language of compound events that includes a time-out construct, such as that of [24] and [28], this last event can be expressed easily.)

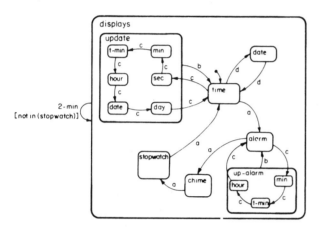

FIGURE 19. Part of the displays State in a Digital Watch

Statecharts can be used to describe the behavior of the watch in terms of its human interface; namely, how the user's operations, such as pressing buttons, influence things. It should be noted, however, that the descriptions that follow do not specify the activities carried out internally by the watch, only their control. Thus, nothing is said here about the time elapsing activity itself, or the technicalities of the beeping, the blinking, or the displays. These aspects of a system can be described using other means, and should be incorporated into the overall specification together with the statecharts. (See [24] for one approach to this incorporation.)

Figure 19 shows the basic displays state of the watch. Notice that time is the default state, and there is a cycle of pressings of a leading from time through the alarm, chime, and stopwatch states back to time. There is a general update state, and a special state for updating the alarm's internal setting. The 2-min event signifies return to time if 2 minutes have elapsed in any state other than stopwatch and no button has been pressed.

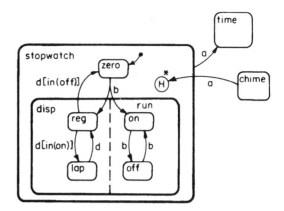

FIGURE 20. The stopwatch State

The specification of the watch contains examples of orthogonal states on various levels. We should first consider the stopwatch state, detailed in Figure 20. It has two substates, zero and {disp, run}, the first being the default. Pressing b takes the stopwatch from the former to the latter causing it to start running with a regular display. Repeatedly pressing b causes it to stop and start alternately. Pressing d can be seen to cause the display to switch to lap and back to reg, or to leave the orthogonal state and return to zero depending, as illustrated, on the present state configuration. The encircled and starred H is one of the additional notations described in [21], and prescribes that, upon entering stopwatch from chime by pressing a, the state actually entered will be the one in which the system was in most recently. Thus, we are entering the stopwatch state by "history"—hence, the H. The default will be used if this is the first time stopwatch is entered, or if the history has been cleared.

The description of the high levels of the watch also uses orthogonality. In Figure 21 the watch is specified as being either dead or alive, with the latter consisting of five orthogonal components. (Notice where the

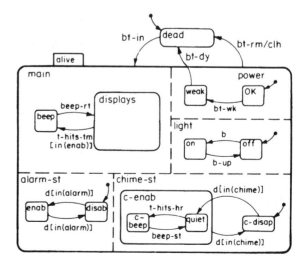

FIGURE 21. A High-Level Description of the Watch

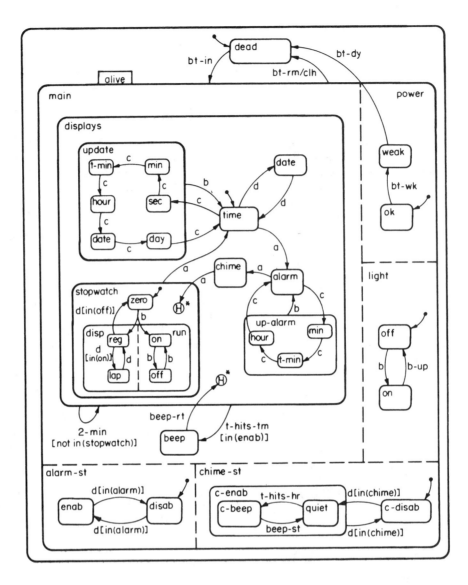

FIGURE 22. A State Chart for the Digital Watch

displays state fits in.) In this figure the events `bt-in`, `bt-rm`, `bt-dy` and `bt-wk` signify, respectively, the insertion, removal, expiration, and weakening (below a certain level) of the battery. We use `t-hits-tm` to signify that the internal time of the watch has reached the internal time setting of the alarm, and `t-hits-hr` to signify that it has reached a whole hour. Also, `beep-rt` occurs when either any button is pressed or 2 minutes have elapsed since entering `beep`, and `beep-st` occurs 2 seconds after entering `c-beep`. (As mentioned, these events should also be written formally as compound event expressions in a language involving time-outs, disjunctions, and so on; see [28].)

The first of the five components in Figure 21, `main`, specifies the transitions between displaying and beeping, where `displays` is simply the state described earlier (see Figure 19). (In actuality, the displaying activities themselves do not shut off when the watch is beeping, but cannot be changed until control returns to the

displays state.) The `alarm-st` component describes the status of the alarm, specifying that it can be changed using d when control is in the `alarm` display state. The `chime-st` state is similar, with the additional provision for beeping on the hour given within. The `power` state is self-explanatory, where the activity that would take place in the `weak` state would involve the displays blinking frantically.

In considering the innocent-looking `light` state, the default is `off`, and depressing and releasing b cause the light to switch alternately between `on` and `off`. What is interesting is the effect these actions might have elsewhere. If the entire statechart for the parts of the watch described so far is contemplated (see Figure 22), one realizes that pressing b for illumination has significant side effects: It will cause a return from an update state if we happen to be in one, the stopping of the alarm if it happens to be beeping, and a change in the stopwatch's behavior if we happen to be working with it. Conversely, if we use b in displays for any one of these things the light will go on, whether we like it or not. These seeming anomalies are all a result of the fact that the light component is orthogonal to the main component, meaning that its scope is very broad. One can imagine a far more humble light component, applicable only in the time and date states, which would not cause any of these problems. Its specification could be carried out by attaching it orthogonally, not to main, but to a new state surrounding time and date, as in Figure 23.

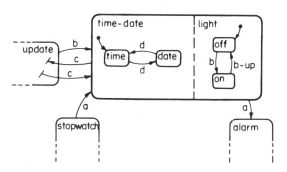

FIGURE 23. A Smaller Scope for the Light

As mentioned earlier, this section has only described the "no-frills" version of the statecharts. A more complete treatment appears in [21], and a formal syntax and semantics appear in [23]. The reader may have noticed that we have not used intersecting states in the statecharts. While intersecting blobs in higraphs do not cause any serious semantic problems (see the appendix), intersecting states in state charts do. In fact, since not all syntactically legal higraphs make sense as statecharts, it is not even clear how to define an appropriate syntax for statecharts with intersecting states (see [21, sect. 6.2]). A preliminary approach to these problems appears in [29].

POSSIBLE VARIATIONS ON THE THEME

The higraph formalism can be enriched and extended in various ways. We shall point to a few of these possibilities briefly and informally.

At times it becomes useful to base a formalism on a three-valued, rather than a two-valued, underlying model. For example, in certain uses of graphs in databases and artificial intelligence there arises a need to state not only that a certain relationship R holds or does not hold between two objects, but also to capture the situation whereby we do not know which of these is the case. One possibility is to reinterpret the absence of an R arrow as denoting the don't-known situation, and have a new kind of arrow representing the *negative information* that R definitely does *not* hold. This simple idea can be adopted in higraphs too, as in Figure 24, which is suppose to indicate that R holds between A and B and does not hold between B and C, and that all

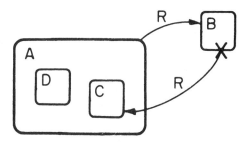

FIGURE 24. Negative Arrows

other possibilities (including whether or not R holds between C and B)[10] are left open.

Often a don't-know option is needed not only for arrows, but for blobs as well. That is, we might want to represent uncertainty as to the presence or absence of identifiable sets, rather than relationships. Accordingly, we can use a new blob notation (e.g., one with a dashed contour) to denote a set that we are not sure actually exists (here one assumes that all regular blobs stand for nonempty sets). Figure 25 asserts our uncertainty as to whether $A - B$ is empty or not, and also states that if it is not empty then the difference is called E and is related to F via relationship R.

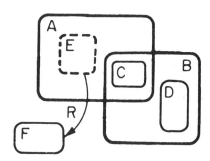

FIGURE 25. "Not-Quite-Sure" Blobs

When higraphs are used in practice (see [21], [24], [28], and [47]), it is useful to be able to "zoom out" of a particular view, suppressing low-level details. A good example would be going from Figure 22, the detailed state-chart description of the watch, to the less detailed Figure 21. In such cases there arises a problem with edges connected to subblobs that are omitted from the new, less detailed view. If we decide to zoom out of the likes of Figure 26 by suppressing blobs B and C, it might be a mistake to consider Figure 27a as the correct new version, since the two are clearly inconsistent. Figure 27b is better, with its stubs that represent relationships to unspecified subblobs. For example, since a state-chart arrow whose target is a high-level state A prescribes entrance to none other than the default substate

---

[10] This is not determined by the arrow from A to B, since, as discussed earlier, the fact that R holds between A and B says nothing about what the case is for A's subsets.

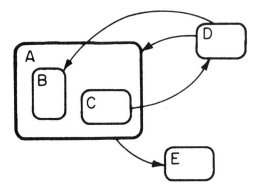

FIGURE 26.   Another Simple Higraph

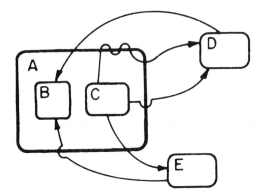

FIGURE 27.   Two Possible Zoom Outs for Figure 26

of *A*, Figure 21 is somewhat inconsistent with Figure 22. In the present context, a better version would have shown the `beep-rt` arrow crossing the contour of the `displays` state and ending with a stub indicating entrance to a substate (as of now unspecified) that is possibly different from the default substate, `time`.

One weakness of the higraph formalism is its inability to specify both set inclusion and set membership. We have chosen to adopt the former as the meaning of blob enclosure, although we could probably have cho-

sen the latter too without causing too many problems. This weakness is all the more apparent when higraphs are contrasted with their graph-based equivalents, in which set inclusion is depicted by `is-a` edges (see Figure 10). In the latter, one need only use an additional type of edge, labeled `elmnt-of`, for instance, to be able to represent set membership. We would like to claim that this is not much more than a notational problem that requires a topo-visual way of distinguishing between two different kinds of insideness. Most of the solutions to this notational problem that come to mind are somewhat unsatisfactory, with the exception of the one that calls for a three-dimensional basis for higraphs, in which the third dimension is responsible for such distinctions (e.g., by having set inclusion take place in the same plane and set membership be reflected by different levels of planes).[11]

An additional possible extension to higraphs is to make arrows mean more than a simple connection between source and target. (We are assuming ordinary directed binary edges here, not, say, hyperedges.) Since higraph arrows in general cut across blob contours, we might want to say something more about the *sequence* of crossovers that the edge takes on its way from the source to the target. This can be achieved trivially by drawing the arrow through the appropriate contours in the desired order (assuming this order is indeed possible, given the basic topology of the blobs). The interesting case occurs when we want to omit from such a sequence one or more of the contours that, topologically speaking, must be crossed by any line from the source to the target. We would like the *D*-to-*B* arrow in Figure 26, for example, to enter *B*, but *not* to enter *A* in the process. State charts with intersections give rise to one interesting motivation for such cases, whereby one wants the system to enter only one of two intersecting

[11] Visual formalisms that are predominantly two-dimensional in nature, but make some use of a third dimension, are far from being out of the question, even if we are not willing to wait for quality holographic workstations to show up. If all we need, as in this case, is the ability to tell when two nested blobs are on the same plane or not, then a simple graphical simulation of a dynamic left–right shift in point of view would do the job.

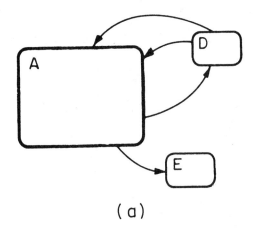

(a)

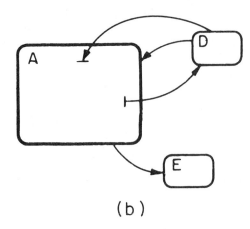

(b)

FIGURE 28.   Skipping and Multiple Crossovers

states; again, the reader is referred to [21, sec. 6.2] for details. This richer notion of an edge can be represented visually by simply allowing arrows to skip edges as in Figure 28. Multiple crossovers, if desired, can also be represented as illustrated in the figure. Clearly, the formal semantics would be more elaborate, since a finite sequence of blobs, rather than an ordered pair, is the interpretation of a directed edge, and a finite set thereof, rather than an unordered pair, is the interpretation of an undirected edge.

CONCLUSION AND FUTURE WORK
Higraphs seem to give rise to several interesting mathematical notions adapted to a large extent from graphs and hypergraphs. For example, one can provide reasonable definitions of connectivity, transitive closure, planarity, and acyclicity in higraphs, as well as a couple of different notions of "hitrees." For each of these, we may ask for upper and lower bounds on the computational complexity of the corresponding algorithmic problems. In some cases algorithms and bounds can be carried over from the work on graphs and hypergraphs, but one gets the feeling that in other cases these bounds can be improved by utilizing the special structure of higraphs. Some of these algorithmic problems have indeed arisen during the implementation of the STATEMATE system [24, 28], which supports three higraph-based formalisms. It would appear that the algorithmics of higraphs forms a fruitful avenue for further research.

The main thesis underlying this paper is that the intricate nature of a variety of computer-related systems and situations can, and in our opinion should, be represented by *visual formalisms*: visual, because they are to be generated, comprehended, and communicated by humans; and formal, because they are to be manipulated, maintained, and analyzed by computers. (This thesis is consistent with the study in [9], which argues for a more visual, nonverbal approach toward mathematics.)

Part of our motivation in stressing this point, despite the fact that it might appear to be so obvious, is the rather different approach that one occasionally finds elsewhere. For example, [33] is a compendium of many computer-related diagrammatic methods (virtually all of which are based on graphs). In our opinion, [33] is quite inadequate, since it accepts the *visual*, but apparently rejects the *formal*. For the most part, the methods and languages appearing in [33] are described in a manner that is devoid of semantics, and can therefore be used at best as informal aids when working with some other, hopefully more rigorous, nonvisual medium.

One of the implicit points we have tried to make in this article is that a considerable amount of mileage can be gotten out of basing such formalisms on a small number of simple diagrammatic notions, first and foremost among which are those that are topological in nature, not geometric. A lot can be gained by using topo-visual formalisms based on insideness, connectedness, and partitioning, with the semantics as given here, before one attempts to attach special significance to, for example, shapes, colors, and sizes.

We are entirely convinced the future is "visual." We believe that in the next few years many more of our daily technical and scientific chores will be carried out visually, and graphical facilities will be far better and cheaper than today's. The languages and approaches we shall be using in doing so will not be merely iconic in nature (e.g., using the picture of a trash can to denote garbage collection), but inherently diagrammatic in a conceptual way, perhaps also three-dimensional and/or animated. They will be designed to encourage visual modes of thinking when tackling systems of ever-increasing complexity, and will exploit and extend the use of our own wonderful visual system in many of our intellectual activities.

APPENDIX.   Formal Definition of Higraphs

In what follows we present a formal (nongraphical) syntax and semantics for higraphs with simple binary directed edges. The reader should have no difficulty in extending the edge set E to represent, say, hyperedges.

A *higraph* is a quadruple

$$H = (B, \sigma, \pi, E),$$

where B is a finite set of elements, called *blobs*, and E, the set of *edges*, is a binary relation on B:

$$E \subseteq B \times B.$$

The *subblob* function σ is defined as

$$\sigma: B \longrightarrow 2^B.$$

It assigns to each blob $x \in B$ its set $\sigma(x)$ of subblobs and is restricted to being cycle free. Thus, if we

define

$$\sigma^0(x) = \{x\}, \qquad \sigma^{i+1}(x) = \bigcup_{y \in \sigma^i(x)} \sigma(y),$$

$$\text{and} \qquad \sigma^+(x) = \bigcup_{i=1}^{\infty} \sigma^i(x),$$

then σ is restricted so that $x \notin \sigma^+(x)$.

The *partitioning* function π is defined as

$$\pi: B \longrightarrow 2^{B \times B},$$

associating with each blob $x \in B$ some equivalence relation $\pi(x)$ on the set of subblobs, $\sigma(x)$. This is really just a rigorous way of specifying the breakup of x into its orthogonal components, which are now defined simply to be the equivalence classes induced by the relation $\pi(x)$. Indeed, for $x \in B$ let us denote these classes by $\pi_1(x), \ldots, \pi_{k_x}(x)$. For the orthogonal division into components to be representable graphically (and in order to make the semantics cleaner), we shall require that blobs in different orthogonal components of x are disjoint. Formally, for each x we require that no two elements y and z of $\sigma(x)$ can intersect—that is, can satisfy $\sigma^+(y) \cap \sigma^+(z) \neq \varnothing$—unless they are in the same orthogonal component—that is, unless the relation $\pi(x)$ renders them equivalent. Clearly, $k_x = 1$ means x is not partitioned into components at all.

This concludes the syntax of higraphs; now for the semantics. Two notations are useful. Given a higraph H, define the set of *atomic blobs* to be

$$A = \{x \in B \mid \sigma(x) = \varnothing\}.$$

(Obviously, the finiteness of B and the cycle-freeness restriction on σ imply A is nonempty.) The *unordered Cartesian product* of two sets S and T is defined as

$$S \otimes T = \{\{s, t\} \mid s \in S, t \in T\}.$$

Given a higraph H, a *model* for H is a pair

$$M = (D, \mu),$$

where D is a set of unstructured elements[12] called

---

[12] We want to avoid situations in which, say, x and $\{x\}$ are both elements of D.

the *domain* of the model M, and μ assigns disjoint subsets of D to the atomic blobs of H. Thus,

$$\mu: A \rightarrow 2^D,$$

where if $x \neq y$ then $\mu(x) \cap \mu(y) = \varnothing$. We now have to show how to extend the association of atomic blobs with sets over D to an association of all blobs with more complex objects over D. Accordingly, extend μ by defining, inductively, for each $x \in B$,

$$\mu(x) = \bigotimes_{i=1}^{k_x} \left(\bigcup_{y \in \pi_i(x)} \mu(y) \right),$$

the intuition being that to calculate the semantics of a blob x we form the unordered Cartesian product of the meanings of its orthogonal components, each of which, in turn, is simply the union of the meanings of its constituent blobs. In particular, of course, if $k_x = 1$, no product is taken, and we really have

$$\mu(x) = \bigcup_{y \in \sigma(x)} \mu(y),$$

as expected.

To complete the semantics, note that the edge set E induces a semantic relation E_M on the $\mu(x)$s, defined by

$$(\mu(x), \mu(y)) \in E_M \qquad \text{iff} \quad (x, y) \in E.$$

Acknowledgments. Thanks are due to Ton Kalker, Doug Tygar, and Jeanette Wing for comments on the appendix, and to an anonymous referee for a very detailed and thoughtful report.

REFERENCES
1. Berge, C. *Graphs and Hypergraphs.* North-Holland, Amsterdam, 1973.
2. Berry, G., and Cosserat, I. The ESTEREL synchronous programming language and its mathematical semantics. In *Seminar on Concurrency*, S. Brookes and G. Winskel, Eds. Lecture Notes in Computer Science, vol. 197. Springer-Verlag, New York, 1985, pp. 389–448.
3. Biggs, N.L., Lloyd, E.K., and Wilson, R.J. *Graph Theory: 1736–1936.* Clarendon Press, Oxford, 1976.
4. Brachman, R.J. On the epistemological status of semantic networks. In *Associative Networks: Representation and Use of Knowledge by Computer*, N.V. Findler, Ed. Academic Press, New York, 1979, pp. 3–50.
5. Cardelli, L.A. Semantics of multiple inheritance in semantics of data types. Kahn, G. et al. Lecture Notes in Computer Science. vol. 173, Springer-Verlag, 1984, pp. 51–67.
6. Charniak, E., and McDermott, D. *Introduction to Artificial Intelligence.* Addison-Wesley, Reading, Mass., 1985.
7. Chen, P.P.-S. The entity-relationship model—toward a unified view of data. *ACM Trans. Database Syst. 1*, 1 (Mar. 1976), 9–36.
8. Conklin, J. Hypertext: An introduction and survey. *IEEE Computer 20*, 9 (Sept. 1987), 17–41.
9. Davis, P.J., Anderson, J.A. Nonanalytic aspects on mathematics and their implication on research and education. *SIAM Review 21*, 1 (Jan. 1979), 112–127.
10. dos Santos, C.S., Neuhold, E.J., and Furtado, A.L. A data type approach to the entity-relationship model. In *Entity-Relationship Approach to Systems Analysis and Design*, P.P. Chen, Ed. North-Holland, Amsterdam, 1980, pp. 103–119.
11. Dugundji, J. *Topology.* Allyn and Bacon, Boston, Mass., 1966.
12. Euler, L. Solutio problematis ad geometriam situs pertinentis. *Comm. Acad. Sci. Imp. Petropol. 8* (1736), 128–140.
13. Euler, L. *Lettres à une Princesse d'Allemagne.* Vol. 2. 1772 (letters 102–108).
14. Fagin, R. Degrees of acyclicity for hypergraphs and relational database schemes. *J. ACM 30*, 3 (July 1983), 514–550.
15. Fagin, R., Mendelzon, A., and Ullman, J. A simplified universal relation assumption and its properties. *ACM Trans. Database Syst. 7*, 3 (Sept. 1982), 343–360.
16. al-Fedaghi, S.S. An entity-relationship approach to modelling petroleum engineering database. In *Entity-Relationship Approach to Software Engineering*, C.G. Davis et al., Eds. Elsevier Science Publishers, Amsterdam, 1983, pp. 761–779.
17. Findler, N.V., Ed. *Associative Networks: Representation and Use of Knowledge by Computer.* Academic Press, New York, 1979.
18. Fitter, M., and Green, T.R.G. When do diagrams make good computer languages? *Int. J. Man-Mach. Stud. 11*, 2 (March 1979), 235–261.
19. Gardner, M. *Logic Machines and Diagrams.* 2nd ed. University of Chicago Press, Chicago, Ill., 1982.
20. Green, T.R. Pictures of programs and other processes, or how to do things with lines. *Behav. Inf. Technol. 1*, 1 (1982), 3–36.
21. Harel, D. Statecharts: A visual formalism for complex systems. *Sci. Comput. Program. 8*, 3 (June 1987), 231–274.
22. Harel, D., and Pnueli, A. On the development of reactive systems. In *Logics and Models of Concurrent Systems*, NATO, ASI Series, vol. 13, K.R. Apt, Ed. Springer-Verlag, New York, 1985, pp. 477–498.
23. Harel, D., Pnueli, A., Schnidt, J.P., and Sherman, R. On the formal semantics of statecharts. In *Proceedings of the 2nd IEEE Symposium on Logic in Computer Science* (Ithaca, N.Y., June 22–24). IEEE Press, New York, 1987, pp. 54–64.
24. Harel, D., Lachover, H., Naamad, A., Pnueli, A., Politi, M., Sherman, R., and Shtul-Trauring, A. STATEMENT: A working environment for the development of complex reactive systems. In *Proceedings of the Tenth IEEE International Conference on Software Engineering* (Singapore, April 13–15). IEEE Press, New York, 1988.
25. Hendrix, G.G. Expanding the utility of semantic networks through partitioning. In *Proceedings of the 4th International Conference on Artificial Intelligence* (Tbilisi, Georgia, USSR, Sept. 3–8). International Joint Council on Artificial Intelligence, Cambridge, Mass., 1975, pp. 115–121.
26. Hoare, C.A.R. Communicating sequential processes. *Commun. ACM 21*, 8 (Aug. 1978), 666–677.
27. Hopcroft, J.E., and Ullman, J.D. *Introduction to Automata Theory, Languages, and Computation.* Addison-Wesley, Reading, Mass., 1979.
28. i-Logic. The languages of STATEMATE. Tech. Rep., i-Logix, Burlington, Mass., 1987.

29. Kahana, C.A. Statecharts with overlapping states. M.S. thesis, Dept. of Mathematics and Computer Science, Bar-Ilan University, Ramat Gan, Israel, 1986 (in Hebrew).
30. Lefschetz, S. *Introduction to Topology.* Princeton University Press, Princeton, N.J., 1949.
31. Maier, D., and Ullman, J.D. Connections in acyclic hypergraphs. In *Proceedings of the ACM Symposium on Database Systems* (Los Angeles, Calif., March 29–31). ACM, New York, 1982, pp. 34–39.
32. Manna, Z., and Pnueli, A. Specification and verification of concurrent programs by ∀-automata. In *Proceedings of the 14th ACM Symposium on Principles of Programming Languages* (Munich). ACM, New York, 1987, pp. 1–12.
33. Martin, J., and McClure, C. *Diagramming Techniques for Analysts and Programmers.* Prentice-Hall, Englewood Cliffs, N.J., 1985.
34. McSkimin, J.R., and Minker. J. A predicate calculus based semantic network for deductive searching. In *Associative Networks: Representation and Use of Knowledge by Computer,* N.V. Findler, Ed. Academic Press, New York, 1979, pp. 205–238.
35. Milner, R. *A Calculus of Communicating Systems.* Lecture Notes in Computer Science, vol. 92. Springer-Verlag, New York, 1980.
36. Nakano, R. Integrity checking in a logic-oriented ER model. In *Entity-Relationship Approach to Software Engineering,* C.G. Davis et al., Eds. Elsevier Science Publishers, Amsterdam, 1983, pp. 551–564.
37. Nilsson, N.J. *Principles of Artificial Intelligence.* Tioga, Palo Alto, Calif., 1980.
38. Owicki, S., and Lamport, L. Proving liveness properties of concurrent programs. *ACM Trans. Program. Lang. Syst. 4,* 3 (July 1982), 455–495.
39. Pnueli, A. Applications of temporal logic to the specification and verification of reactive systems: A survey of current trends. In *Current Trends in Concurrency,* J. W. de Bakker et al., Eds. Lecture Notes in Computer Science, vol. 224, Springer-Verlag, New York, 1986, pp. 510–584.
40. Quillian, M.R. Semantic memory. In *Semantic Information Processing,* M. Minsky, Ed. MIT Press, Cambridge, Mass., 1968, pp. 227–270.
41. Reisig, W. *Petri Nets: An Introduction.* Springer-Verlag, Berlin, 1985.
42. Schiffner, G., and Schuermann, P. Multiple views and abstractions with an extended-entity-relationship model. *Comput. Lang. 4,* 3/4 (1979), 139–154.
43. Schmid, C.F. *Statistical Graphics: Design Principles and Practices.* Wiley, New York, 1983.
44. Shapiro, S.C. A net structure for semantic information storage, deduction, and retrieval. In *Proceedings of the 2nd International Joint Conference on Artificial Intelligence.* 1971, pp. 512–523.
45. Touretzky, D.S. *The Mathematics of Inheritance Systems.* Pitman, London, and Morgan Kaufmann, Los Altos, Calif. 1986.
46. Tufte, E.R. *The Visual Display of Quantitative Information.* Graphics Press, Cheshire, Conn., 1983.
47. Tygar, J.D., and Wing, J.M. Visual specification of security constraints. In *The IEEE Workshop on Visual Languages* (Linköping, Sweden, Aug. 19–21). IEEE Press, New York, 1987.
48. Venn, J. On the diagrammatic and mechanical representation of propositions and reasonings. *Phil. Mag.* (1880), 123.
49. Venn, J. *Symbolic Logic.* 2nd ed. London, 1894. (Reprinted by Chelsea, Bronx, N.Y., 1971.)
50. Woods, W.A. What's in a link? Foundations for semantic networks. In *Representation and Understanding,* D.G. Bobrow and A.M. Collins, Eds. Academic Press, New York, 1975, pp. 35–82.
51. Zave, P. A distributed alternative, to finite-state-machine specifications. *ACM Trans. Program. Lang. Syst. 7,* 1 (Jan. 1985), 10–36.

CR Categories and Subject Descriptors: C.0 [**Computer Systems Organization**]: General—*systems specification methodology*; C.3 [**Computer Systems Organization**]: Special-Purpose and Application-Based Systems—*real-time systems*; D.0 [**Software**]: General; D.2.1 [**Software Engineering**]: Requirements/Specifications; D.2.2]: Tools and Techniques; D.2.10 [**Software Engineering**]: Design; E.0 [**Data**]: General; E.1 [**Data**]: Data Structures—*graphs*; F.1.1 [**Computation by Abstract Devices**]: Models of Computation—*automata*; H.1.0 [**Models and Principles**]: General; I.2.4 [**Artificial Intelligence**]: Knowledge Representation Formalisms and Methods—*semantic networks*
General Terms: Design, Languages, Theory
Additional Key Words and Phrases: Higraph, reactive systems, state charts, visual formalisms

Author's Present Address: David Harel, Department of Applied Mathematics and Computer Science, The Weizmann Institute of Science, Rehovot, Israel 76100.

TWO-DIMENSIONAL SYNTAX FOR
FUNCTIONAL LANGUAGES

Luca Cardelli
Bell Laboratories
600 Mountain Avenue
Murray Hill, NJ 07974, USA

"Two-Dimensional Syntax for Functional Languages" by L.
Cardelli in *Proceedings of Integrated Interactive Computing
Systems*, 1983, pages 107-119. Copyright © 1983 by Elsevier
Science Publishers B.V. All rights reserved.

Introduction

The ideas discussed in this paper developed from some attempts at programming with boxes (Cardelli 82) and other graphical data structures (Cardelli 81). Boxes, intended as rectangles with reference points (Knuth 79),
are interesting data structures for expressing two-dimensional layouts of
text or pictures. They can be composed and moved around by a simple set of
operations, and can be manipulated in a fairly abstract way, often independently of their exact size.

Unfortunately, the programs one writes to compose boxes are not very suggestive of the compound boxes they produce, mostly because an essentially
two-dimensional activity of box composition has to be flattened out in textual format. Is it possible to write these programs on a (high-resolution)
screen in some graphical fashion, so that they can give a feeling of what
they are doing? This can be done easily for non parametric expressions, but
if we look for generality the need for two-dimensionality rapidly spreads to
all the features of the language. One wants to manipulate lists of boxes, to
write functions producing boxes, etc. The problem becomes that of defining a
general purely graphical notation for arbitrary data structures (not just
two-dimensional ones), and involves solving difficult problems like the
graphical interpretation of parameterisation.

This paper is a preliminary attempt at graphical programming (Lakin 80).
Some standard control constructs do not seem to fit in this approach, while
some non standard ones developed for functional languages (noticeably case-
analysis (Burstall 80)) fit particularly well. What we hope to achieve with
this kind of notation is freedom from the keyboard slavery, an intuitive interface for naive users, and an effective way of exploiting high-resolution
screens and pointing devices. Experiments are needed to determine whether
this approach can help in the normal software development activity.

In the following sections, we first examine a simple but complete general
purpose language having a graphical syntax, and then we introduce boxes and
their operations. Examples are given of most of the features of the language,
but they are not intended to be exhaustive; some effort may be required to
see how the examples fit the definitions.

Variables and Simple Data Types

We begin with the graphical interpretation of variables as ellipses; to
distinguish an ellipse from another we may insert some text or symbol into
them. The ellipses surrounding identifiers may sometimes be omitted, especially when the identifiers are in function position. The type of a variable
is inferred from the context of its occurrences; we assume here the poly-
morphic type system of Edinburgh ML (Gordon 79) (ML also inspires many of
the features of the language).

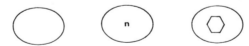

For the purpose of describing the syntax of expressions we need meta-
variables denoting them. We use hexagons for this purpose, noticing that
they are not part of the actual syntax.

Parentheses are drawn as rectangular frames which may contain any expression. Multiple parentheses may be collapsed. An empty parenthesis is inter-

preted as the object <u>nil</u>, the only element of the primitive type <u>null</u>.

Boolean constants and operators are denoted by the following symbols:

We introduce here the syntax for function application, in order to show some boolean expressions. The argument of a function is enclosed in a "dented" box pointing to the function; infix operators with two or more arguments have several argument boxes pointing to them:

Numbers are built from a constant (zero) and two unary operators (succ and pred):

The succ operator is applied by appending it to the left of an existing number or expression, so that succ(zero) looks like one (1!) little square, succ(succ(zero)) like two (2!) squares, and so on. Similarly for pred, which is appended to the right and can form negative numbers. As an abbreviation we also allow to put arabic numerals in number frames:

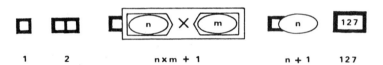

Somebody might worry about graphical ambiguities (like nil and the number 1, which are very similar); we assume that we are always able to disambiguate these situations, e.g. by the thickness of the lines or the absolute size of an object. We shall see later that this is not an important issue because we shall not actually try to parse pictures mechanically, and some ambiguity may be tolerated.

We can now consider some simple compound types. A <u>pair</u> of objects can be formed by a vertical or horizontal bar:

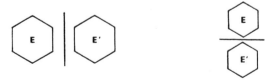

Pairing is a right-bottom-associative operation, so that the following expressions are considered equivalent:

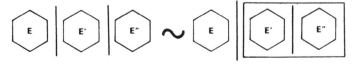

Homogeneous linear <u>lists</u> are obtained by a constant (empty) and a binary operator (cons) having as arguments an object and a list of objects of the same type:

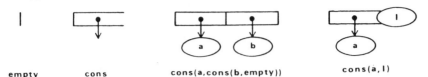

empty   cons   cons(a,cons(b,empty))   cons(a,l)

Finally we introduce objects of disjoint union types by the unary operators of left injection (inleft) and right injection (inright) in the left and right part of a disjoint union:

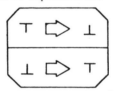

inleft   inright   inleft(inleft(inright(a)))

These operations are used, for example, when we want to write a function returning booleans or numbers: the type of its codomain will be the disjoint union of boolean and number.

Note that we have only defined constructors for our ground and compound types, ignoring selectors and discriminators. This is justified by the introduction of case-analysis (a simple form of pattern matching) in the next section.

Functions and Declarations

Functions are defined by cases on a set of "typical" inputs. For example the boolean <u>not</u> operation can be expressed as:

i.e. <u>not</u> maps true to false and false to true. All the different cases of a function are stacked vertically in an octogonal frame. This frame is to be interpreted as an if-then-else: if the left hand side of the first case matches the input, then the right hand side is evaluated and given as result, else the subsequent cases are considered in turn. If no case matches the input, then we have a run-time failure.

This <u>case analysis</u> may involve the binding of variables to parts of the input: in this situation the bound variables can be used in the respective right hand sides, as in the following function which swaps a pair:

Note that a data constructor on the left hand side of an arrow works like a selector, and that case analysis replaces the use of discriminators.

Functions have a domain and a codomain, hence all the left hand sides of a case analysis must have the same type (the domain type) and all the right hand sides must have the same type (the codomain type). These rules can be checked automatically without explicit type declarations (Milner 78), and they are not restrictive because of the presence of disjoint union types.

To assign names to functions, and in general to any data object, we introduce <u>definitions</u> in the form of left-pointing arrows:

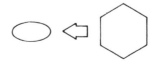

here, the variable on the left hand side of the arrow is bound to the (value
of the) right hand side. In general, a pattern may appear on the left hand
side (just like in case-analysis) and it should match the result of the
right hand side. In the case of function definition we may use an abbreviation exemplified by the not operation:

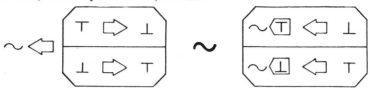

Multiple definitions are organized into declarations. A declaration is
either a single definition, or the composition of simpler declarations. We
use four operators for assembling declarations, which were first described
in (Milne 76); parallel declarations are independent of each other; sequential declarations are the usual cascaded declarations, each of them possibly
using the previous ones; private declarations account for own variables;
recursive declarations allow us to define recursive functions. From a semantic point of view, we are working with a statically scoped language using
call-by-value for parameter passing.

We use triangles as meta-variables for declarations, and round-edged
rectangles to bracket declarations:

To explain the effect of declarations, we say that each declaration
imports some variables, used in the right hand sides of its definitions, and
exports other variables (those being defined), appearing in the left hand
sides of its definitions. A simple definition imports all the free variables
used in its right hand side (i.e. those variables not bound by an inner case-
analysis or declaration), and exports all the variables occurring in its left
hand side (there may be several of them because of pattern matching, but they
must all be distinct).

The simplest form of compound declaration is obtained by parallel composition, represented by the simple juxtaposition of declarations:

The parallel composition of two declarations D and D' exports the union of
the exports of D and D' (there must be no repeated definition), and imports
the union of the imports of D and D'. The exports of D are not imported in
D' and vice versa.

The sequential composition of declarations is represented by the following
right-bottom-associative operator:

The sequential composition of D and D' exports the exports of D' and those
exports of D which are not exports of D', and imports the imports of D and
those imports of D' which are not exports of D. Moreover the exports of D
are imported in D', but not vice versa. Hence D may be used in D' and outside the composition (if it is not "hidden" by D').

The private composition of declarations is represented by another right-
bottom-associative operator:

The _private_ _composition_ of D and D' exports the exports of D' only, and
imports the imports of D and those imports of D' which are not exports of D.
Again, the exports of D are imported in D', but not vice versa. Hence D is
"own" by D' and it is not "known" outside the composition.

Finally, a _recursive_ _declaration_ is represented by a declaration enclosed
in special brackets:

The recursive closure of D exports the exports of D, and imports those imports of D which are not among its own exports. Moreover the exports of D
are imported back into D. Hence D "knows" its own definitions. Recursive
declarations may only contain _function_ definitions, and must not contain
private declarations.

We are now able to draw some interesting examples, starting (of course!)
with the _factorial_ function:

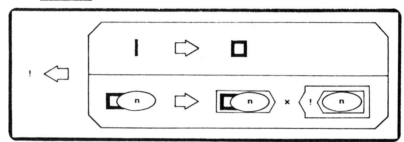

The _append_ function gives a simple example of list manipulation:

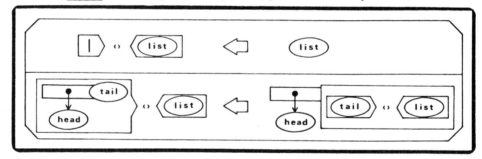

Note how the arrows have been reversed in this example, according to a previously defined abbreviation.

There should be a way of delimiting the scope of declarations. This is
done by inserting a declaration and an expression in a _scope_ _block_; the
expression is then the only part of the program having access to the exports
of the declaration:

An example of scope block is given in the following _split_ function, which
splits a list at a given position, returning the two halves as results. Note
that every function takes a single argument and returns a single value, but
values may be pairs, tuples (i.e. multiple pairs) or lists, simulating the
effect of functions with multiple arguments and results.

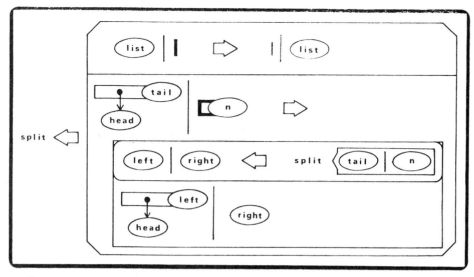

We complete our set of programming constructs with the graphical representation of if-then-else:

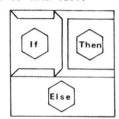 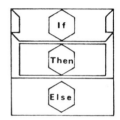

The else part may contain another if-then-else without need to enclose it in a surrounding frame.

Boxes

The notation we have developed becomes particularly interesting when applied to the manipulation of actually two-dimensional data structures. We introduce now a data type box and operations for manipulating boxes.

A box is a rectangle with a reference point ($\oplus$). Boxes always have horizontal and vertical sides, i.e. they cannot be oblique.

There is a set of basic boxes which we assume here to contain characters and graphical symbols. In general, basic boxes may contain very complex pictures, generated by direct graphical interaction, or by an adequate set of graphical functions (e.g. splines).

Furthermore, there is a set of primitive operations on boxes:
- size: takes a box and returns its size as a pair of numbers (x,y);
- refpoint: takes a box and returns a pair of numbers which are the displacement of the reference point from the lower left corner of the box;
- move: takes a box and two numbers, and moves the box with respect to its reference point by the quantity specified by the numbers, e.g.:

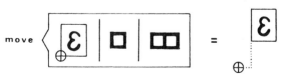

– frame: takes a box and two pairs of numbers, and replaces the rectangle
of the box with the rectangle specified by the four numbers (the first two
are the lower left corner and the second two are the upper right corner):

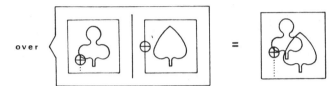

– over: takes two boxes and overlaps them identifying their reference points.
The result is the smallest rectangle enclosing both the argument rectangles,
with reference point in the common reference point, e.g.:

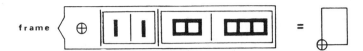

– composition: there are four kinds of compositions of two boxes, denoted
by horizontal and vertical "bumped" bars (see below). Horizontal composition
is obtained by placing the two boxes so that the right side of the first box
is aligned on the same vertical line as the left side of the second box,
with reference points aligned on the same horizontal line. The result is the
smallest box enclosing both arguments, where the reference point is the reference point of the first box if the "right-bumped" composition is used, or
the reference point of the second box if the "left-bumped" composition is
used. Similarly for vertical composition, which connects in the top-to-bottom
direction.

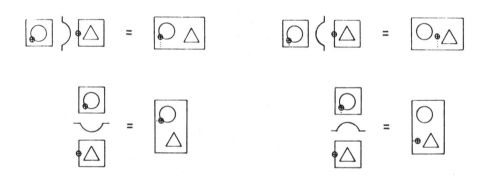

Compositions are not in general associative, hence by convention they associate to the left and to the top. Moreover we use abbreviations like:

These are all the primitive operations we need to manipulate boxes (we
might add rotations and reflections around the reference points, without
affecting the basic ideas). Some useful derived operations can be easily
programmed, such as horseq which builds a horizontal sequence of several
copies of the same box, with resulting reference point to the left (and
similarly for verseq, with resulting reference point to the bottom):

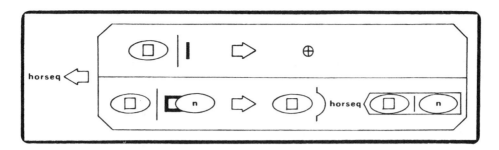

Here is a function, called <u>wrap</u> which puts a frame around a box, leaving the reference point in the lower left corner:

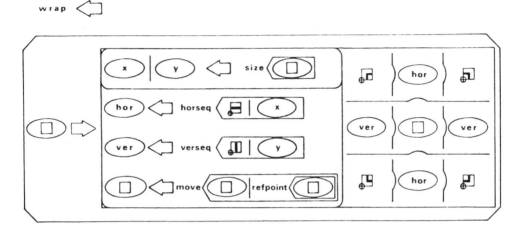

The little basic boxes composing the frame in the figure above have unitary size. Note that the reference point of the argument box has to be renormalized to the lower left corner (to place the frame in the correct position): the result of the refpoint operation is used to move the box.

In order to use case analysis on boxes we adopt the convention that a <u>shaded</u> variable matches any arbitrary <u>basic</u> box. We can then write, for example, the following <u>basics</u> function which builds a list of all the basic components of a (compound) box:

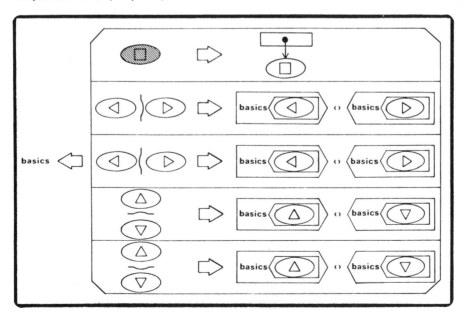

Two-Dimensional Editing

Is it possible to implement an editor for the syntax we have presented, and to create and edit programs in this fashion? We think this is rather easy, provided that we have a high-resolution screen and a pointing device.

However we cannot use traditional parsing techniques, and the task of parsing programs from pictures seems to be rather unfeasible or even hopeless.

Fortunately we do not actually need a parser. The internal representation of programs is still to be done by standard abstract syntax trees, so that the two-dimensionality only appears in the concrete syntax. Hence we can use structure editors working on the abstract syntax (Donzeau-Gouge 80)(Teitelbaum 81) to create and edit our programs. This has also the advantage that we are not forced to draw all the details of our pictures because most of this work will be done for us automatically by the printing routine of the editor.

All we need is then a prettyprinter producing pictures from syntax trees, which might conveniently be written using our box data structures. We might also have a more conventional prettyprinter, producing formatted text, and we could merge the graphical and textual notations according to our taste. However, in the most extreme situation, we would only work on pictures, carefully hiding the abstract syntax representation, so that the user could have the feeling of manipulating pictures directly.

Conclusions

We have described a graphical syntax for a small functional language, avoiding semantic considerations whenever possible. These ideas may be the basis for a programming system using a structure editor to manipulate two-dimensional representations of programs. We have also given an example of a simple graphical data structure (boxes) which can be more effectively manipulated by a graphical notation. More general graphical data structures can be found in (Cardelli 81).

The particular syntax presented here is very experimental and better versions may be found. We think that for some applications a graphical notation is preferable to a textual one, and it is not excluded that the former can also be applied to conventional programming after a period of experimentation and adjustment.

Along with the increasing availability of graphical devices, picture manipulation is becoming a more and more important and widespread activity. We hope that notations on the style of the one we have proposed can help in making it also an easier activity, especially when naive users are concerned.

References

(Burstall 80) R.M.Burstall, D.B.MacQueen, D.T.Sannella: "Hope: an experimental applicative language". Proc. 1980 LISP Conference, Stanford.

(Cardelli 81) L.Cardelli, G.Plotkin: "An algebraic approach to VLSI design". in J.P.Gray (ed.): VLSI 81. Academic Press.

(Cardelli 82) L.Cardelli: "PaperBox: an applicative text formatter". Unpublished program documentation.

(Donzeau-Gouge 80) V.Donzeau-Gouge, G.Huet, G.Kahn, B.Lang: "Programming environments based on structured editors: the Mentor experience". Report 26, INRIA.

(Gordon 79) M.J.Gordon, R.Milner, C.P.Wadsworth: "Edinburgh LCF". Lecture Notes in Computer Science, n.78. Springer-Verlag.

(Knuth 79) D.E.Knuth: "TEX and Metafont". Digital Press.

(Lakin 80) F.Lakin: "Computing with text-graphic forms". Proc. 1980 LISP Conference, Stanford.

(Milne 76) R.E.Milne, C.Strachey: "A theory of programming language semantics". Chapman and Hall.

(Milner 76) R.Milner: "A theory of type polymorphism in programming". JCSS, vol.17, n.3.

(Teitelbaum 81) T.Teitelbaum, T.Reps, S.Horwitz: "The why and wherefore of the Cornell Program Synthesizer". Proc. of the ACM symposium on Text Manipulation.

☐☐☐ 3 ☐☐☐   Environments I:
The Pioneering Efforts

I.B. Sutherland. "SKETCHPAD, A Man–Machine Graphical Communication System." In *Proc. Spring Joint Computer Conference*, pages 329–346, 1963. AFIPS Press, Reston, Va.

D.C. Smith. *PYGMALION: A Creative Programming Environment* (extended excerpt). PhD Thesis, Dept. of Computer Science, Stanford University, Stanford, Calif., 1975.

H.P. Frei, D.L. Weller and R. Williams. "A Graphics–Based Programming–Support System." *ACM Computer Graphics* (*Proc. SIGGRAPH'78*, Atlanta, Ga.), 12(3):43–49, August 1978.

M.C. Pong and N. Ng. "PIGS: A System for Programming with Interactive Graphical Support." *Software—Practice & Experience*, 13(9):847–855, September 1983.

E.P. Glinert and S.L. Tanimoto. "PICT: An Interactive, Graphical Programming Environment." *IEEE Computer*, 17(11):7–25, November 1984.

SKETCHPAD

A MAN-MACHINE GRAPHICAL COMMUNICATION SYSTEM*

Ivan E. Sutherland
*Consultant, Lincoln Laboratory***
Massachusetts Institute of Technology

I. INTRODUCTION

The Sketchpad system makes it possible for a man and a computer to converse rapidly through the medium of line drawings. Heretofore, most interaction between man and computers has been slowed down by the need to reduce all communication to written statements that can be typed; in the past, we have been writing letters to rather than conferring with our computers. For many types of communication, such as describing the shape of a mechanical part or the connections of an electrical circuit, typed statements can prove cumbersome. The Sketchpad system, by eliminating typed statements (except for legends) in favor of line drawings, opens up a new area of man-machine communication.

AN INTRODUCTORY EXAMPLE

To understand what is possible with the system at present let us consider using it to draw the hexagonal pattern in Figure 4. We will issue specific commands with a set of push buttons, turn functions on and off with switches, indicate position information and point to existing drawing parts with the light pen, rotate and magnify picture parts by turning knobs, and observe the drawing on the display system. This equipment as provided at Lincoln Labora-

tory's TX-2 computer[1] is shown in Figure 1. When our drawing is complete it may be inked on paper, as were all the drawings in this paper, by a PACE plotter.[15]

If we point the light pen at the display system and press a button called "draw," the computer will construct a straight line segment which stretches like a rubber band from the

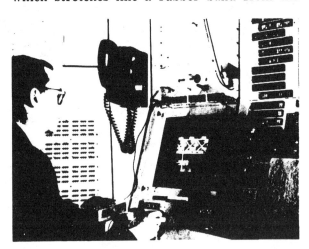

Figure 1. TX-2 operating area—Sketchpad in use. On the display can be seen part of a bridge similar to those of Figure 15. The Author is holding the light pen. The push buttons "draw," "move," etc., are on the box in front of the Author. Part of the bank of toggle switches can be seen behind the Author. The size and position of the part of tne total picture seen on the display are controlled by the four black knobs just above the tables.

---

* This paper is based in part on a thesis submitted to the Department of Electrical Engineering, M.I.T., in partial fulfillment of the requirements for the Degree of Doctor of Philosophy.

** Operated with the support of the U.S. Army, Navy, and Air Force.

initial to the present location of the pen as shown in Figure 2. Additional presses of the button will produce additional lines, leaving the closed irregular hexagon shown in Figure 3A.

To make the hexagon regular, we can inscribe it in a circle. To draw the circle we place the light pen where the center is to be and press the button "circle center," leaving behind a center point. Now, choosing a point on the circle (which fixes the radius) we press the button "draw" again, this time getting a circle arc whose angular length only is controlled by light pen position as shown in Figure 2.

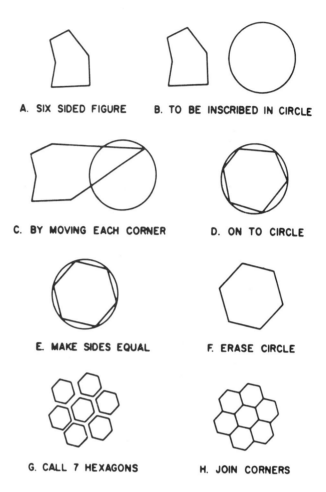

A. SIX SIDED FIGURE B. TO BE INSCRIBED IN CIRCLE

C. BY MOVING EACH CORNER D. ON TO CIRCLE

E. MAKE SIDES EQUAL F. ERASE CIRCLE

G. CALL 7 HEXAGONS H. JOIN CORNERS

Figure 3.   Illustrative example, see text.

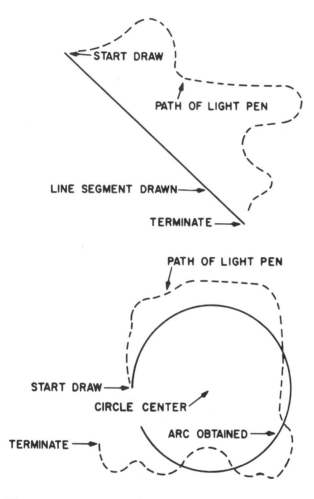

Figure 2.   Steps for drawing straight lines and circle arcs.

Next we move the hexagon into the circle by pointing to a corner of the hexagon and pressing the button "move" so that the corner follows the light pen, stretching two rubber band line segments behind it. By pointing to the

circle and terminating, we indicate that the corner is to lie on the circle. Each corner is in this way moved onto the circle at roughly equal spacing as shown in Figure 3D.

We have indicated that the vertices of the hexagon are to lie on the circle, and they will remain on the circle throughout our further manipulations. If we also insist that the sides of the hexagon be of equal length, a regular hexagon will be constructed.

With Sketchpad we can say, in effect, make *this* line equal in length to *that* line, pointing to the lines with the light pen. The computer satisfies all existing conditions (if it is possible) whenever we turn on a toggle switch. This done, we have a complete regular hexagon inscribed in a circle. We can erase the entire circle by pointing to any part of it and pressing the "delete" button. The completed hexagon is shown in Figure 3F.

To make the hexagonal pattern in Figure 4 we wish to attach a large number of hexagons together by their corners, and so we designate the six corners of our hexagon as attachment points by pointing to each and pressing a button. We now file away the basic hexagon and begin work on a fresh "sheet of paper" by changing a switch setting. On the new sheet we assemble, by pressing a button to create each hexagon as an "instance" or subpicture, six hexagons around a central seventh in approximate position as shown in Figure 3G. A subpicture may be positioned with the light pen, rotated or scaled by turning the knobs, or fixed in position by a termination signal, but its internal shape is fixed.

By pointing to the corner of one hexagon, pressing a button, and then pointing to the corner of another hexagon, we can fasten those corners together, because these corners have been designated as attachment points. If we attach two corners of each outer hexagon to the appropriate corners of the inner hexagon, the seven are uniquely related, and the computer will reposition them as shown in Figure 3H. An entire group of hexagons, once assembled, can be treated as a symbol. An "instance" of the entire group can be called up on another "sheet of paper" as a subpicture and assembled with other groups or with single hexagons to make a very large pattern.

INTERPRETATION OF INTRODUCTORY EXAMPLE

In the introductory example above we used the light pen both to position parts of the drawing and to point to existing parts. We also saw in action the very general *subpicture, constraint,* and *definition copying* capabilities of the system.

Subpicture:

The original hexagon might just as well have been anything else: a picture of a transistor, a roller bearing, or an airplane wing. Any number of different symbols may be drawn, in terms of other simpler symbols if desired, and any symbol may be used as often as desired.

Constraint:

When we asked that the vertices of the hexagon lie on the circle we were making use of a basic relationship between picture parts that is built into the system. Basic relationships (atomic constraints) to make lines vertical, horizontal, parallel, or perpendicular; to make points lie on lines or circles; to make symbols appear upright, vertically above one another or be of equal size; and to relate symbols to other drawing parts such as points and lines have been included in the system. Specialized constraint types may be added as needed.

Definition Copying:

We made the sides of the hexagon be equal in length by pressing a button while pointing to the side in question. Had we defined a composite operation such as to make two lines both parallel and equal in length, we could have applied it just as easily.

IMPLICATIONS OF INTRODUCTORY EXAMPLE

As we have seen, a Sketchpad drawing is entirely different from the trail of carbon left on a piece of paper. Information about how the drawing is tied together is stored in the computer as well as the information which gives the drawing its particular appearance. Since the drawing is tied together, it will keep a useful appearance even when parts of it are moved. For example, when we moved the corners of the hexagon onto the circle, the lines next to each corner were automatically moved so that the closed topology of the hexagon was preserved. Again, since we indicated that the corners of the hexagon were to lie on the circle, they remained on the circle throughout our further manipulations.

As well as storing how the various parts of the drawing are related, Sketchpad stores the structure of the subpictures used. For example, the storage for the hexagonal pattern of Figure 4 indicates that this pattern is made of smaller patterns which are in turn made of smaller patterns which are composed of single hexagons. If the master hexagon is changed, the entire appearance but not the structure of the hexagonal pattern will be changed. For example, if we change the basic hexagon into a semicircle, the fish scale pattern shown in Figure 4 instantly results.

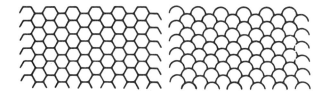

Figure 4. Hexagonal lattice with half hexagon and semicircle as basic elements.

SKETCHPAD AND THE DESIGN PROCESS

Construction of a drawing with Sketchpad is *itself* a model of the design process. The locations of the points and lines of the drawing model the variables of a design, and the geometric constraints applied to the points and lines of the drawing model the design constraints which limit the values of design variables. The ability of Sketchpad to satisfy the geometric constraints applied to the parts of a drawing models the ability of a good designer to satisfy all the design conditions imposed by the limitations of his materials, cost, etc. In fact, since designers in many fields produce nothing themselves but a drawing of a part, design conditions may well be thought of as applying to the drawing of a part rather than to the part itself. When such design conditions are added to Sketchpad's vocabulary of constraints, the computer will be able to assist a user not only in arriving at a nice looking drawing, but also in arriving at a sound design.

PRESENT USEFULNESS

As more and more applications have been made, it has become clear that the properties of Sketchpad drawings make them most useful in four broad areas:

For Storing and Updating Drawings:

Each time a drawing is made, a description of that drawing is stored in the computer in a form that is readily transferred to magnetic tape. A library of drawings will thus develop, parts of which may be used in other drawings at only a fraction of the investment of time that was put into the original drawing.

For Gaining Scientific or Engineering Understanding of Operations That Can Be Described Graphically:

A drawing in the Sketchpad system may contain explicit statements about the relations between its parts so that as one part is changed the implications of this change become evident throughout the drawing. For instance, Sketchpad makes it easy to study mechanical linkages, observing the path of some parts when others are moved.

As a Topological Input Device for Circuit Simulators, etc.:

Since the storage structure of Sketchpad reflects the topology of any circuit or diagram, it can serve as an input for many network or circuit simulating programs. The additional effort required to draw a circuit completely from scratch with the Sketchpad system may well be recompensed if the properties of the circuit are obtainable through simulation of the circuit drawn.

For Highly Repetitive Drawings:

The ability of the computer to reproduce any drawn symbol anywhere at the press of a button, and to recursively include subpictures within subpictures makes it easy to produce drawings which are composed of huge numbers of parts all similar in shape.

II. RING STRUCTURE

The basic n-component element structure described by Ross[10] has been somewhat expanded in the implementation of Sketchpad so that all references made to a particular n-component element or block are collected together by a string of pointers which originates within that block. For example, not only may the end points of a line segment be found by following pointers in the line block (n-component element), but also all the line segments which terminate on a particular point may be found by following a string of pointers which starts within the point block. This string of pointers closes on itself; the last pointer points back to the first, hence the name "ring." The ring points both ways to make it easy to find both the next and the previous member of the ring in case, as when deleting, some change must be made to them.

BASIC OPERATIONS

The basic ring structure operations are:
1. Inserting a new member into a ring at

some specified location on it, usually first or last.

2. Removing a member from a ring.

3. Putting all the members of one ring, in order, into another at some specified location in it, usually first or last.

4. Performing some auxiliary operation on each member of a ring in either forward or reverse order.

These basic ring structure operations are implemented by short sections of program defined as MACRO instructions in the compiler language. By suitable treatment of zero and one member rings, the basic programs operate without making special cases.

Subroutines are used for setting up new n-component elements in free spaces in the storage structure. As parts of the drawing are deleted, the registers which were used to represent them become free. New components are set up at the end of the storage area, lengthening it, while free blocks are allowed to accumulate. Garbage collection periodically compacts the storage structure by removal of the free blocks.

GENERIC STRUCTURE, HIERARCHIES

The main part of Sketchpad can perform basic operations on any drawing part, calling for help from routines specific to particular types of parts when that is necessary. For example, the main program can show any part on the display system by calling the appropriate display subroutine. The big power of the clearcut separation of the general and the specific is that it is easy to change the details of specific parts of the program to get quite different results without any need to change the general parts.

In the data storage structure the separation of general and specific is accomplished by collecting all things of one type together in a ring under a generic heading. The generic heading contains all the information which makes this type of thing different from all other types of things. Thus the data storage structure itself contains all the specific information. The generic blocks are further gathered together under super-generic or generic-generic blocks, as shown in Figure 5.

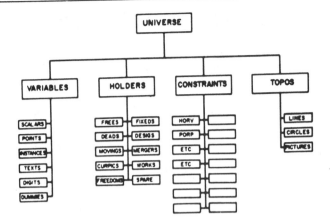

Figure 5. Generic structure. The n-component elements for each point or line, etc., are collected under the generic blocks "lines," "points," etc., shown.

EXPANDING SKETCHPAD

Addition of new types of things to the Sketchpad system's vocabulary of picture parts requires only the construction of a new generic block (about 20 registers) and the writing of appropriate subroutines for the new type. The subroutines might be easy to write, as they usually are for new constraints, or difficult to write, as for adding ellipse capability, but at least a finite, well-defined task faces one to add a new ability to the system. Without a generic structure it would be almost impossible to add the instructions required to handle a new type of element.

III. LIGHT PEN

In Sketchpad the light pen* is time shared between the functions of coordinate input for positioning picture parts on the drawing and demonstrative input for pointing to existing picture parts to make changes. Although almost any kind of coordinate input device could be used instead of the light pen for positioning, the demonstrative input uses the light pen optics as a sort of analog computer to remove from consideration all but a very few picture parts which happen to fall within its field of view, saving considerable program time. Drawing systems using storage display devices of the Memotron type may not be practical because of the loss of this analog computation feature.

* The reader unacquainted with light pens should refer to the paper on Man-Machine Console Facilities by Stotz[12] in this issue.

PEN TRACKING

To initially establish pen tracking,* the Sketchpad user must inform the computer of an initial pen location. This has come to be known as "inking-up" and is done by "touching" any existing line or spot on the display, whereupon the tracking cross appears. If no picture has yet been drawn, the letters INK are always displayed for this purpose. Sketchpad uses loss of tracking as a "termination signal" to stop drawing. The user signals that he is finished drawing by flicking the pen too fast for the tracking program to follow.

DEMONSTRATIVE USE OF PEN

During the 90% of the time that the light pen and display system are free from the tracking chore, spots are very rapidly displayed to exhibit the drawing being built, and thus the lines and circles of the drawing appear. The light pen is sensitive to these spots and reports any which fall within its field of view. Thus, a table of the picture parts seen by the light pen is assembled during each complete display cycle. At the end of a display cycle this table contains all the picture parts that could even remotely be considered as being "aimed at."

The one-half inch diameter field of view of the light pen, although well suited to tracking, is relatively large for pointing. Therefore, the Sketchpad system will reject any seen part which is further from the center of the light pen than some small minimum distance; about $\frac{1}{8}$ inch was found to be suitable. For every kind of picture part some method must be provided for computing its distance from the light pen center or indicating that this computation cannot be made.

After eliminating all parts seen by the pen which lie outside the smaller effective field of view, the Sketchpad system considers objects topologically related to the ones actually seen. End points of lines and attachment points of instances (subpictures) are especially important. One can thus aim at the end point of a line even though only the line is displayed. Figure 6 outlines the various regions within which the pen must lie to be considered aimed at a line segment, a circle arc, their end points, or their intersection.

PSEUDO PEN LOCATION

When the light pen is aimed at a picture part, the exact location of the light pen is ignored in favor of a "pseudo pen location" exactly on the part aimed at. If no object is aimed at, the pseudo pen location is taken to be the actual pen location. The pseudo pen location is displayed as a bright dot which is used as the "point of the pencil" in all drawing operations. As the light pen is moved into the areas outlined in Figure 6 the dot will lock onto the existing parts of the drawing, and any moving picture parts will jump to their new locations as the pseudo pen location moves to lie on the appropriate picture part.

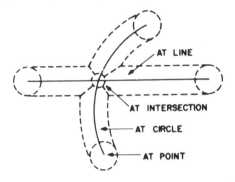

Figure 6. Areas in which pen must lie to "aim at" existing drawing parts (solid lines).

With just the basic drawing creation and manipulation functions of "draw," "move," and "delete," and the power of the pseudo pen location and demonstrative language programs, it is possible to make fairly extensive drawings. Most of the constructions normally provided by straight edge and compass are available in highly accurate form. Most important, however, the pseudo pen location and demonstrative language give the means for entering the topological properties of a drawing into the machine.

IV. DISPLAY GENERATION

The display system, or "scope," on the TX-2 is a ten bit per axis electrostatic deflection system able to display spots at a maximum rate of about 100,000 per second. The coordinates of the spots which are to be seen on the display are stored in a large table so that computation and display may proceed independently. If, instead of displaying each spot successively, the display program displays them in a random order or with interlace, the flicker of the display is reduced greatly.

MARKING OF DISPLAY FILE

Of the 36 bits available to store each display spot in the display file, 20 give the coordinates of that spot for the display system, and the remaining 16 give the address of the n-component element which is responsible for adding that spot to the display. Thus, all the spots in a line are tagged with the ring structure address of that line, and all the spots in an instance (subpicture) are tagged as belonging to that instance. The tags are used to identify the particular part of the drawing being aimed at by the light pen.

If a part of the drawing is being moved by the light pen, its display spots will be recomputed as quickly as possible to show it in successive positions. The display spots for such moving parts are stored at the end of the display file so that the display of the many nonmoving parts need not be disturbed. Moving parts are made invisible to the light pen.

MAGNIFICATION OF PICTURES

The shaft position encoder knobs below the scope (see Figure 1) are used to tell the program to change the display scale factor or the portion of the page displayed. The range of magnification of 2000 available makes it possible to work, in effect, on a 7-inch square portion of a drawing about $\frac{1}{4}$ mile on a side.

For a magnified picture, Sketchpad computes which portion(s) of a curve will appear on the display and generates display spots for those portions only. The "edge detection" problem is the problem of finding suitable end points for the portion of a curve which appears on the display.

In concept the edge detection problem is trivial. In terms of program time for lines and circles the problem is a small fraction of the total computational load of the system, but in terms of program logical complexity the edge detection problem is a difficult one. For example, the computation of the intersection of a circle with any of the edges of the scope is easy, but computation of the intersection of a circle with all four edges may result in as many as eight intersections, some pairs of which may

be identical, the scope corners. Now which of these intersections are actually to be used as starts of circle arcs?

LINE AND CIRCLE GENERATION

All of Sketchpad's displays are generated from straight line segments, circle arcs, and single points. The generation of the lines and circles is accomplished by means of the difference equations:

$$x_i = x_{i-1} + \Delta x \qquad y_i = y_{i-1} + \Delta y \qquad (1)$$

for lines, and

$$
\begin{aligned}
x_i &= x_{i-2} + \frac{2}{R}\,(y_{i-1} - y_c) \\
y_i &= y_{i-2} - \frac{2}{R}\,(x_{i-1} - x_c)
\end{aligned}
\qquad (2)
$$

for circles, where subscripts i indicate successive display spots, subscript c indicates the circle center, and R is the radius of the circle in Scope Units. In implementing these difference equations in the program, the fullest possible use is made of the coordinate arithmetic capability of the TX-2 so that both the x and y equation computations are performed in parallel on 18 bit subwords. Even so, about $\frac{3}{4}$ of the total Sketchpad computation time is spent in line and circle generation. A vector and circle generating display would materially reduce the computational load of Sketchpad.

For computers which do only one addition at a time, the difference equations:

$$
\begin{aligned}
x_i &= x_{i-1} + \frac{1}{R}\,(y_{i-1} - y_c) \\
y_i &= y_{i-1} - \frac{1}{R}\,(x_i - x_c)
\end{aligned}
\qquad (3)
$$

should be used to generate circles. Equations (3) approximate a circle well enough and are known to close exactly both in theory and when implemented, because the x and y equations are dissimilar.

DIGITS AND TEXT

Text, to put legends on a drawing, is displayed by means of special tables which indicate the locations of line and circle segments to make up the letters and numbers. Each piece of text appears as a single line of not more than 36 equally spaced characters which can be changed by typing. Digits to display the value of an indicated scalar at any position and in any size and rotation are formed from the same type face as text. It is possible to display up to five decimal digits with sign; binary to decimal conversion is provided, and leading zeros are suppressed.

Subpictures, whose use was seen in the introductory example above, are each represented in storage as a single *n*-component element. A subpicture is said to be an "instance" of its "master picture." To display an instance, all of the lines, text, etc. of its master picture must be shown in miniature on the display. The instance display program makes use of the line, circle, number, and text display programs and *itself* to expand the internal structure of the instance.

DISPLAY OF ABSTRACTIONS

The usual picture for human consumption displays only lines, circles, text, digits, and instances. However, certain very useful abstractions which give the drawing the properties desired by the user are represented in the ring structure storage. For example, the fact that the start and end points of a circle arc should be equidistant from the circle's center point is represented in storage by a "constraint" block. To make it possible for a user to manipulate these abstractions, each abstraction must be able to be seen on the display if desired. Not only does displaying abstractions make it possible for the human user to know that they exist, but also makes it possible for him to aim at them with the light pen and, for example, erase them. To avoid confusion, the display for particular types of objects may be turned on or off selectively by toggle switches. Thus, for example, one can turn on display of constraints as well as or instead of the lines and circles which are normally seen.

If their selection toggle switch is on, constraints are displayed as shown in Figure 7. The central circle and code letter are located at the average location of the variables constrained. The four arms of a constraint extend from the top, right side, bottom, and left side of the circle to the first, second, third, and fourth variables constrained, respectively. If fewer than four variables are constrained, ex-

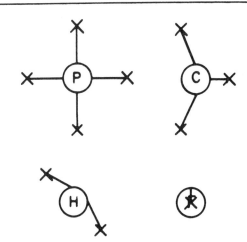

Figure 7. Display of constraints.

cess arms are omitted. In Figure 7 the constraints are shown applied to "dummy variables," each of which shows as an X.

Another abstraction that can be displayed if desired is the value of a set of digits. For example, in Figure 8 are shown three sets of digits all displaying the same scalar value, -5978. The digits themselves may be moved, rotated, or changed in size, without changing the value displayed. If we wish to change the value, we point at its abstract display, the # seen in Figure 8. The three sets of digits in Figure 8 all display the same value, as indicated by the lines connecting them to the #; changing this value would make all three sets of digits change. Constraints may be applied independently to either the position of the digits or their value as indicated by the two constraints in the figure.

V. RECURSIVE FUNCTIONS

In the process of making the Sketchpad system operate, a few very general functions were developed which make no reference at all to the specific types of entities on which they oper-

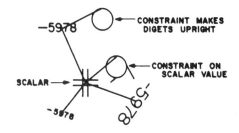

Figure 8. Three sets of digits displaying the same scalar value.

ate. These general functions give the Sketchpad system the ability to operate on a wide range of problems. The motivation for making the functions as general as possible came from the desire to get as much result as possible from the programming .effort involved. For example, the general function for expanding instances makes it possible for Sketchpad to handle any fixed geometry subpicture. The power obtained from the small set of generalized functions in Sketchpad is one of the most important results of the research.

In order of historical development, the recursive functions in use in the Sketchpad system are:

1. Expansion of instances, making it possible to have subpictures within subpictures to as many levels as desired.
2. Recursive deletion, whereby removal of certain picture parts will remove other picture parts in order to maintain consistency in the ring structure.
3. Recursive merging, whereby combination of two similar picture parts forces combination of similarly related other picture parts, making possible application of complex definitions to an object picture.

RECURSIVE DELETING

If a thing upon which other things depend is deleted, the dependent things must be deleted also. For example, if a point is to be deleted, all lines which terminate on the point must also be deleted. Otherwise, since the n-component elements for lines contain no positional information, where would these lines end? Similarly, deletion of a variable requires deletion of all constraints on that variable; a constraint must have variables to act on.

RECURSIVE MERGING

If two things of the same type which are independent are merged, a single thing of that type results, and all things which depended on either of the merged things depend on the result* of the merger. For example, if two points are merged, all lines which previously terminated on either point now terminate on the single resulting point. In Sketchpad, if a thing is being moved with the light pen and the termination flick of the pen is given while aiming at another thing of the same type, the two

things will merge. Thus, if one moves a point to another point and terminates, the points will merge, connecting all lines which formerly terminated on either. This makes it possible to draw closed polygons.

If two things of the same type which do depend on other things are merged, the things depended on by one will be forced to merge, respectively, with the things depended on by the other. The result* of merging two dependent things depends, respectively, on the results* of the mergers it forces. For example, if two lines are merged, the resultant line must refer to only two end points, the results of merging the pairs of end points of the original lines. All lines which terminated on any of the four original end points now terminate on the appropriate one of the remaining pair. More important and useful, all constraints which applied to any of the four original end points now apply to the appropriate one of the remaining pair. This makes it possible to speak of line segments as being parallel even though (because line segments contain no numerical information to be constrained) the parallelism constraint must apply to their end points and not to the line segments themselves. If we wish to make two lines both parallel and equal in length, the steps outlined in Figure 9 make it possible. More obscure relationships between dependent things may be easily defined and applied. For example, constraint complexes can be defined to make line segments be collinear, to make a line be tangent to a circle, or to make the values represented by two sets of digits be equal.

RECURSIVE DISPLAY OF INSTANCES

The block of registers which represents an instance is remarkably small considering that it may generate a display of any complexity. For the purposes of display, the instance block makes reference to its master picture. The instance will appear on the display as a figure geometrically similar to its master picture at a location, size, and rotation indicated by the four numbers which constitute the "value" of the instance. The value of an instance is considered numerically as a four dimensional vector. The

---

* The "result" of a merger is a single thing of the same type as the merged things.

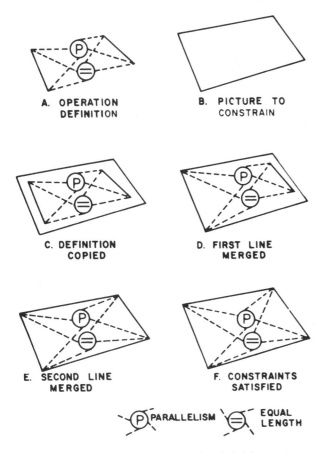

A. OPERATION
   DEFINITION

B. PICTURE TO
   CONSTRAIN

C. DEFINITION
   COPIED

D. FIRST LINE
   MERGED

E. SECOND LINE
   MERGED

F. CONSTRAINTS
   SATISFIED

(P) PARALLELISM   (=) EQUAL
                         LENGTH

Figure 9. Applying a two-constraint definition to turn
a quadrilateral into a parallelogram.

components of this vector are the coordinates of the center of the instance and its actual size as it appears on the drawing times the sine and cosine of the rotation angle involved.

In displaying an instance of a picture, reference is made to the master picture to find out what picture parts are to be shown. The master picture referred to may contain instances, however, requiring further reference, and so on until a picture is found which contains no instances. At each stage in the recursion, any picture parts displayed must be relocated so that they will appear at the correct position, size and rotation on the display. Thus, at each stage of the recursion, some transformation is applied to all picture parts before displaying them. If an instance is encountered, the transformation represented by its value must be adjoined to the existing transformation for display of parts within it. When the expansion of an instance within an instance is finished, the transformation must be restored for continuation at the higher level.

ATTACHERS AND INSTANCES

Many symbols must be integrated into the rest of the drawing by attaching lines to the symbols at appropriate points, or by attaching the symbols directly to each other. For example, circuit symbols must be wired up, geometric patterns made by fitting shapes together, or mechanisms composed of links tied together appropriately. An instance may have any number of attachment points, and a point may serve as attacher for any number of instances. The light pen has the same affinity for the attachers of an instance that it has for the end point of a line.

An "instance-point" constraint, shown with code T in Figure 10C, is used to relate an instance to each of its attachment points. An instance-point constraint is satisfied only when the point bears the same relationship to the instance that a master point in the master picture for that instance bears to the master picture coordinate system.

Any point may be an attacher of an instance, but the point must be designated as an attacher in the master drawing of the instance. For example, when one first draws a resistor, the ends of the resistor must be designated as attachers if wiring is to be attached to instances of it. At each level of building complex pictures, the attachers must be designated anew. Thus of the three attachers of a transistor it is possible to select one or two to be the attachers of a flip-flop.

VI. BUILDING A DRAWING, THE COPY FUNCTION

At the start of the Sketchpad effort certain ad hoc drawing functions were programmed as the atomic operations of the system. Each such operation, controlled by a push button, creates in the ring structure a specific set of new drawing parts. For example, the "draw" button creates a line segment and two new end points (unless the light pen happens to be aimed at a point in which case only one new point need be created). Similarly, there are atomic operations for drawing circles, applying a horizontal or vertical constraint to the end points of a line aimed at, and for adding a "point-on-line" constraint whenever a point is moved onto a line and left there.

The atomic operations described above make it possible to create in the ring structure new picture components and relate them topologically. The atomic operations are, of course, limited to creating points, lines, circles, and two or three types of constraints. Since implementation of the copy function it has become possible to create in the ring structure any predefined combination of picture parts and constraints at the press of a button. The recursive merging function makes it possible to relate the copied set of picture parts to any existing parts. For example, if a line segment and its two end points are copied into the object picture, the action of the "draw" button may be exactly duplicated in every respect. Along with the copied line, however, one might copy as well a constraint, Code H, to make the line horizontal as shown in Figure 10A, or two constraints to make the line both horizontal and three inches long, or any other variation one cares to put into the ring structure to be copied.

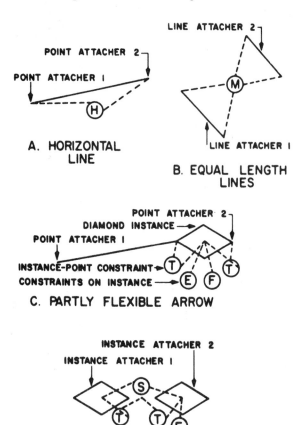

A. HORIZONTAL LINE

B. EQUAL LENGTH LINES

C. PARTLY FLEXIBLE ARROW

D. PRE-JOINED INSTANCES

Figure 10. Definition pictures to be copied, see text.

When one draws a definition picture to be copied, certain portions of it to be used in relating it to other object picture parts are designated as "attachers." Anything at all may be designated: for example, points, lines, circles, text, even constraints! The rules used for combining points when the "draw" button is pressed are generalized so that:

For copying a picture, the last-designated attacher is left moving with the light pen. The next-to-last-designated attacher is recursively merged with whatever object the pen is aimed at when the copying occurs, if that object is of like type. Previously designated attachers are recursively merged with previously designated object picture parts, if of like type, until either the supply of designated attachers or the supply of designated object picture parts is exhausted. The last-designated attacher may be recursively merged with any other object of like type when the termination flick is given.

Normally only two designated attachers are used because it is hard to keep track of additional ones.

If the definition picture consists of two line segments, their four end points, and a constraint, Code M, on the points which makes the lines equal in length, with the two lines designated as attachers as shown in Figure 10B, copying enables the user to make any two lines equal in length. If the pen is aimed at a line when "copy" is pushed, the first of the two copied lines merges with it (taking its position and never actually being seen). The other copied line is left moving with the light pen and will merge with whatever other line the pen is aimed at when termination occurs. Since merging is recursive, the copied equal-length constraint, Code M, will apply to the end points of the desired pair of object picture lines.

COPYING INSTANCES

As we have seen above, the internal structure of an instance is entirely fixed. The internal structure of a copy, however, is entirely variable. An instance always retains its identity as a single part of the drawing; one can only delete an entire instance. Once a definition picture is copied, however, the copy loses all identity as a unit; individual parts of it may be deleted at will.

One might expect that there was intermediate ground between the fixed-internal-structure instance and the loose-internal-structure copy. One might wish to produce a collection of picture parts, some of which were fixed internally and some of which were not. *The entire range of variation between the instance and the copy can be constructed by copying instances.*

For example, the arrow shown in Figure 10C can be copied into an object picture to result in a fixed-internal-structure diamond arrowhead with a flexible tail. As the definition in Figure 10C is set up, drawing diamond-arrowheaded lines is just like drawing ordinary lines. One aims the light pen where the tail is to end, presses "copy," and moves off with an arrowhead following the pen. The diamond arrowhead in this case will not rotate (constraint Code E), and will not change size (constraint Code F).

Copying pre-joined instances can produce vast numbers of joined instances very easily. For example, the definition in Figure 10D, when repetitively copied, will result in a row of joined, equal size (constraint Code S) diamonds. In this case the instances themselves are attachers. Although each press of the "copy" button copies two new instances into the object picture, one of these is merged with the last instance in the growing row. In the final row, therefore, each instance carries all constraints which are applied to either of the instances in the definition. This is why only one of the instances in Figure 10D carries the erect constraint, Code E.

VII. CONSTRAINT SATISFACTION

The major feature which distinguishes a Sketchpad drawing from a paper and pencil drawing is the user's ability to specify to Sketchpad mathematical conditions on already drawn parts of his drawing which will be automatically satisfied by the computer to make the drawing take the exact shape desired. The process of fixing up a drawing to meet new conditions applied to it after it is already partially complete is very much like the process a designer goes through in turning a basic idea into a finished design. As new requirements on the various parts of the design are thought of, small changes are made to the size or other properties

of parts to meet the new conditions. By making Sketchpad able to find new values for variables which satisfy the conditions imposed, it is hoped that designers can be relieved of the need of much mathematical detail. The effort expended in making the definition of constraint types as general as possible was aimed at making design constraints as well as geometric constraints equally easy to add to the system.

DEFINITION OF A CONSTRAINT TYPE

Each constraint type is entered into the system as a generic block indicating the various properties of that particular constraint type. The generic block tells how many variables are constrained, which of these variables may be changed in order to satisfy the constraint, how many degrees of freedom are removed from the constrained variables, and a code letter for human reference to this constraint type.

The definition of what a constraint type does is a subroutine which will compute, for the existing values of the variables of a particular constraint of that type, the error introduced into the system by that particular constraint. For example, the defining subroutine for making points have the same x coordinate (to make a line between them vertical) computes the difference in their x coordinates. What could be simpler? The computed error is a scalar which the constraint satisfaction routine will attempt to reduce to zero by manipulation of the constrained variables. The computation of the error may be non-linear or time dependent, or it may involve parameters not a part of the drawing such as the setting of toggle switches, etc.

When the one pass method of satisfying constraints to be described later on fails, the Sketchpad system falls back on the reliable but slow method of relaxation[11] to reduce the errors indicated by various computation subroutines to smaller and smaller values. For simple constructions such as the hexagon illustrated in Figure 3, the relaxation procedure is sufficiently fast to be useful. However, for complex systems of variables, especially directly connected instances, relaxation is unacceptably slow. Fortunately it is for just such directly connected instances that the one pass method shows the most striking success.

ONE PASS METHOD

Sketchpad can often find an order in which the variables of a drawing may be re-evaluated to completely satisfy all the conditions on them in just one pass. For the cases in which the one pass method works, it is far better than relaxation: it gives correct answers at once; relaxation may not give a correct solution in any finite time. Sketchpad can find an order in which to re-evaluate the variables of a drawing for most of the common geometric constructions. Ordering is also found easily for the mechanical linkages shown in Figures 13 and 14. Ordering cannot be found for the bridge truss problem in Figure 15.

The way in which the one pass method works is simple in principle and was easy to implement as soon as the nuances of the ring structure manipulations were understood. To visualize the one pass method, consider the variables of the drawing as places and the constraints relating variables as passages through which one might pass from one variable to another. Variables are adjacent to each other in the maze formed by the constraints if there is a single constraint which constrains them both. Variables are totally unrelated if there is no path through the constraints by which to pass from one to the other.

Suppose that some variable can be found which has so few constraints applying to it that it can be re-evaluated to completely satisfy all of them. Such a variable we shall call a "free" variable. As soon as a variable is recognized as free, the constraints which apply to it are removed from further consideration, because the free variable can be used to satisfy them. Removing these constraints, however, may make adjacent variables free. Recognition of these new variables as free removes further constraints from consideration and may make other adjacent variables free, and so on throughout the maze of constraints. The manner in which freedom spreads is much like the method used in Moore's algorithm[8] to find the shortest path through a maze. Having found that a collection of variables is free, Sketchpad will re-evaluate them in reverse order, saving the first-found free variable until last. In re-evaluating any particular variable, Sketchpad uses only those constraints which were present when that variable was found to be free.

VIII. EXAMPLES AND CONCLUSIONS

The examples in this section were all taken from the library tape and thus serve to illustrate not only how the Sketchpad system can be used, but also how it actually has been used so far. We conclude from these examples that Sketchpad drawings can bring invaluable understanding to a user. For drawings where motion of the drawing, or analysis of a drawn problem is of value to the user, Sketchpad excels. For highly repetitive drawings or drawings where accuracy is required, Sketchpad is sufficiently faster than conventional techniques to be worthwhile. For drawings which merely communicate with shops, it is probably better to use conventional paper and pencil.

PATTERNS

The instance facility enables one to draw any symbol and duplicate its appearance anywhere on an object drawing at the push of a button. This facility made the hexagonal pattern we saw in Figure 4 easy to draw. It took about one half hour to generate 900 hexagons, including the time taken to figure out how to do it. Plotting them takes about 25 minutes. The drafting department estimated it would take two days to produce a similar pattern.

The instance facility also made it easy to produce long lengths of the zig-zag pattern shown in Figure 11. As the figure shows, a single "zig" was duplicated in multiples of five and three, etc. Five hundred zigs were generated in a single row. Four such rows were plotted one-half inch apart to be used for producing a printed circuit delay line. Total time taken was about 45 minutes for constructing the figure and about 15 minutes to plot it.

A somewhat less repetitive pattern to be used for encoding the time in a digital clock is shown in Figure 12. Each cross in the figure marks the position of a hole. The holes are placed so that a binary coded decimal (BCD) number will in-

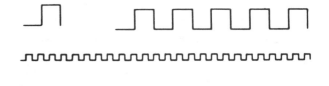

Figure 11. Zig-Zag for delay line.

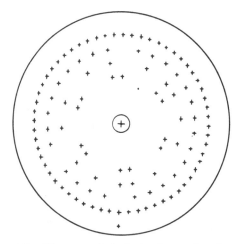

Figure 12. Binary coded decimal encoder for clock. Encoder was plotted exactly 12 inches in diameter for direct use as a layout.

dicate the time. Total time for placing crosses was 20 minutes, most of which was spent trying to interpret a pencil sketch of their positions.

LINKAGES

By far the most interesting application of Sketchpad so far has been drawing and moving linkages. The ability to draw and then move linkages opens up a new field of graphical manipulation that has never before been available. It is remarkable how even a simple linkage can generate complex motions. For example, the linkage of Figure 13 has only three moving parts. In this linkage a central ⊥ link is suspended between two links of different

Figure 13. Three bar linkage. The paths of four points on the central link are traced. This is a 15 second time exposure of a moving Sketchpad drawing.

lengths. As the shorter link rotates, the longer one oscillates as can be seen in the multiple exposure. The ⊥ link is not shown in Figure 13 so that the motion of four points on the upright part of the ⊥ may be seen. These are the four curves at the top of the figure.

To make the three bar linkage, an instance shaped like the ⊥ was drawn and given 6 attachers, two at its joints with the other links and four at the places whose paths were to be observed. Connecting the ⊥ shaped subpicture onto a linkage composed of three lines with fixed length created the picture shown. The driving link was rotated by turning a knob below the scope. Total time to construct the linkage was less than 5 minutes, but over an hour was spent playing with it.

A linkage that would be difficult to build physically is shown in Figure 14 A. This link-

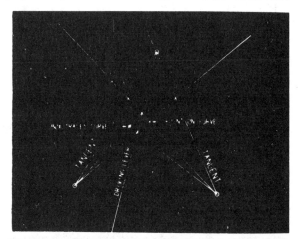

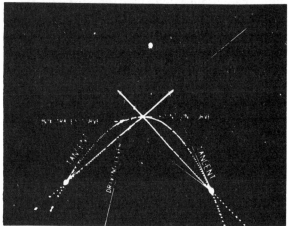

Figure 14. Conic drawing linkage. As the "driving lever" is moved, the point shown with a box around it (in A) traces a conic section. This conic can be seen in the time exposure (B).

age is based on the complete quadrilateral. The three circled points and the two lines which extend out of the top of the picture to the right and left are fixed. Two moving lines are drawn from the lower circled points to the intersections of the long fixed lines with the driving lever. The intersection of these two moving lines (one must be extended) has a box around it. It can be shown theoretically that this linkage produces a conic section which passes through the place labeled "point on curve" and is tangent to the two lines marked "tangent." Figure 14 B shows a time exposure of the moving point in many positions. At first, this linkage was drawn and working in 15 minutes. Since then we have rebuilt it time and again until now we can produce it from scratch in about 3 minutes.

DIMENSION LINES

To make it possible to have an absolute scale in drawings, a constraint is provided which forces the value displayed by a set of digits to indicate the distance between two points on the drawing. This distance-indicating constraint is used to make the number in a dimension line correspond to its length. Putting in a dimension line is as easy as drawing any other line. One points to where one end is to be left, copies the definition of the dimension line by pressing the "copy" button, and then moves the light pen to where the other end of the dimension line is to be. The first dimension line took about 15 minutes to construct, but that need never be repeated since it is a part of the library.

BRIDGES

One of the largest untapped fields for application of Sketchpad is as an input program for other computation programs. The ability to place lines and circles graphically, when coupled with the ability to get accurately computed results pictorially displayed, should bring about a revolution in computer application. By using Sketchpad's relaxation procedure we were to demonstrate analysis of the force distribution in the members of a pin connected truss.

A bridge is first drawn with enough constraints to make it geometrically accurate. These constraints are then deleted and each member is made to behave like a bridge beam.

A bridge beam is constrained to maintain constant length, but any change in length is indicated by an associated number. Under the assumption that each bridge beam has a cross-sectional area proportional to its length, the numbers represent the forces in the beams. The basic bridge beam definition (consisting of two constraints and a number) may be copied and applied to any desired line in a bridge picture by pointing to the line and pressing the "copy" button.

Having drawn a basic bridge shape, one can experiment with various loading conditions and supports to see what the effect of making minor modifications is. For example, an arch bridge is shown in Figure 15 supported both as a three-hinged arch (two supports) and as a cantilever (four supports). For nearly identical loading conditions the distribution of forces is markedly different in these two cases.

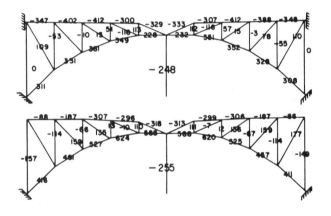

Figure 15. Cantilever and arch bridges. The numbers indicate the forces in the various members as computed by Sketchpad. Central load is not exactly vertical

ARTISTIC DRAWINGS

Sketchpad need not be applied exclusively to engineering drawings. For example, the girl "Nefertite" shown in Figure 16 can be made to wink by changing which of the three types of eyes is placed in position on her otherwise eyeless face. In the same way that linkages can be made to move, a stick figure could be made to pedal a bicycle or Nefertite's hair could be made to swing. The ability to make moving drawings suggests that Sketchpad might be used for making animated cartoons.

Figure 16. Winking girl, "Nefertite," and her component parts.

ELECTRICAL CIRCUIT DIAGRAMS

Unfortunately, electrical circuits require a great many symbols which have not yet been drawn properly with Sketchpad and therefore are not in the library. After some time is spent working on the basic electrical symbols it may be easier to draw circuits. So far, however, circuit drawing has proven difficult.

The circuits of Figure 17 are parts of an analog switching scheme. You can see in the figure that the more complicated circuits are made up of simpler symbols and circuits. It is very difficult, however, to plan far enough ahead to know what composites of circuit symbols will be useful as subpictures of the final circuit. The simple circuits shown in Figure 17 were compounded into a big circuit involving about 40 transistors. Including much trial and error, the time taken by a new user (for the big circuit not shown) was ten hours. At the end of that time the circuit was still not complete in every detail and he decided it would be better to draw it by hand after all.

CONCLUSIONS

The circuit experience points out the most important fact about Sketchpad drawings. It is only worthwhile to make drawings on the computer if you get something more out of the drawing than just a drawing. In the repetitive

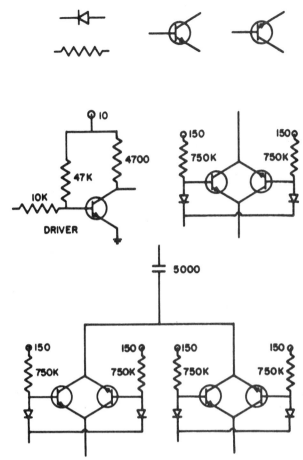

Figure 17. Circuit diagrams. These are parts of the large circuit mentioned in the text.

patterns we saw in the first examples, precision and ease of constructing great numbers of parts were valuable. In the linkage examples, we were able to gain an understanding of the behavior of a linkage as well as its appearance. In the bridge examples we got design answers which were worth far more than the computer time put into them. If we had had a circuit simulation program connected to Sketchpad so that we would have known whether the circuit we drew worked, it would have been worth our while to use the computer to draw it. We are as yet a long way from being able to produce routine drawings economically with the computer.

FUTURE WORK

The methods outlined in this paper generalize nicely to three dimensional drawing. In fact, the work reported in "Sketchpad III" by Timothy Johnson[3] will let the user communicate solid objects to the computer. Johnson is completely bypassing the problem of converting several two dimensional drawings into a three dimensional shape. Drawing will be directly in three dimensions from the start. No two dimensional representation will ever be stored.

Work is also proceeding in direct conversion of photographs into line drawings. Roberts reports a computer program[9] able to recognize simple objects in photographs well enough to produce three dimensional line drawings for them. Roberts is storing his drawings in the ring structure described here so that his results will be compatible with the three dimensional version of Sketchpad.

Major improvements to Sketchpad of the same order and power as the existing definition copying capability can be foreseen. At present Sketchpad is able to add defined relationships to an existing object drawing. A method should be devised for defining and applying changes which involve removing some parts of the object drawing as well as adding new ones. Such a capability would permit one to define, for example, what rounding off a corner means. Then, one could round off any corner by pointing to it and applying the definition.

ACKNOWLEDGEMENTS

The author is indebted to Professors Claude E. Shannon, Marvin Minsky and Steven A. Coons of the Massachusetts Institute of Technology for their help and advice throughout the course of this research.

The author also wishes to thank Douglas T. Ross and Lawrence G. Roberts for their help and answers to his many questions.

BIBLIOGRAPHY

1. CLARK, W. A., FRANKOVICH, J. M., PETERSON, H. P., FORGIE, J. W., BEST, R. L., OLSEN, K. H., "The Lincoln TX-2 Computer," Technical Report 6M-4968, Massachusetts Institute of Technology, Lincoln Laboratory, Lexington, Mass., April 1, 1957, *Proceedings of the Western Joint Computer Conference*, Los Angeles, California, February 1957.

2. COONS, S. A., *Notes on Graphical Input Methods*, Memorandum 8436-M-17, Dynamic Analysis and Control Laboratory, Massachusetts Institute of Technology, Department of Mechanical Engineering, Cambridge, Mass., May 4, 1960.

3. JOHNSON, T. E., "Sketchpad III, Three Dimensional Graphical Communication with a Digital Computer," *Proceedings of the Spring Joint Computer Conference*, Detroit, Michigan, May 21-23, 1963, (this issue).

4. JOHNSTON, L. E., *A Graphical Input Device and Shape Description Interpretation Routines*, Memorandum to Prof. Mann, Massachusetts Institute of Technology, Department of Mechanical Engineering, Cambridge, Mass., May 4, 1960.

5. LICKLIDER, J. C. R., "Man-Computer Symbiosis," *I.R.E. Trans. on Human Factors in Electronics*, vol. HFE, pp. 4-10, March 1960.

6. LICKLIDER, J. C. R., and CLARK, W., "On-line Man-Computer Communication," *Proceedings of the Spring Joint Computer Conference*, San Francisco, California, May 1-3, 1962, vol. 21, pp. 113-128.

7. LOOMIS, H. H. JR., Graphical Manipulation Techniques Using the Lincoln TX-2 Computer, Group Report 51G-0017, Massachusetts Institute of Technology, Lincoln Laboratory, Lexington, Mass., November 10, 1960.

8. MOORE, E. F., "On the Shortest Path Through a Maze," *Proceedings of the International Symposium on the Theory of Switching*, Harvard University, Harvard Annals, vol. 3, pp. 285-292, 1959.

9. ROBERTS, L. G., *Machine Perception of Three Dimensional Solids*, Ph.D. Thesis, Massachusetts Institute of Technology, Electrical Engineering Department, Cambridge, Mass., February 1963.

10. ROSS, D. T., RODRIGUEZ, J. E., "Theoretical Foundations for the Computer-Aided Design System," *Proceedings of the Spring Joint Computer Conference*, Detroit, Michigan, May 21-23, 1963, (this issue).

11. SOUTHWELL, R. V., *Relaxation Methods in Engineering Science*, Oxford University Press, 1940.

12. STOTZ, R., "Man-Machine Console Facilities for Computer-Aided Design," *Proceedings of the Spring Joint Computer Conference,* Detroit, Michigan, May 21-23, 1963, (this issue).

13. VANDERBURGH, A. JR., *TX-2 Users Handbook,* Lincoln Manual No. 45, Massachusetts Institute of Technology, Lincoln Laboratory, Lexington, Mass., July 1961.

14. WALSH, J. F., and SMITH, A. F., "Computer Utilization," *Interim Engineering Report 6873-IR-10 and 11,* Electronic Systems Laboratory, Massachusetts Institute of Technology, Cambridge, Mass., pp. 57-70, November 30, 1959.

15. Handbook for Variplotter Models 205S and 205T, PACE, Electronic Associates Incorporated. Long Branch, New Jersey, June 15, 1959.

Reprinted from *PYGMALION: A Computer Program to Model and Stimulate Creative Thought (extended excerpt)*, by D.C. Smith, 1977, pages 68-153. Published by Birkhaeuser Verlag, 1977.

Principles of Iconic Programming

D.C. Smith

> Graphic communication draws upon the natural resources of its own language, and refers to visual experience as a source of principles and values for designing more articulate form ... [It] is a conceptual logic rather than a technical method; a way of seeing the graphic figure as a visual statement.
>
> -- William Bowman[1]

Summary

The main innovations of PYGMALION are:

(1) a dynamic representation for programs -- an emphasis on *doing* rather than *telling*;

(2) an iconic representation for parameters and data structures requiring less translation from mental representations;

(3) a "remembering" editor for icons;

(4) descriptions in terms of the *concrete*, which PYGMALION turns into the *abstract*.

Part I discussed a model of creative thought, emphasizing visual thinking. The model serves as the basis for the design principles in Part II. Part I may be summarized as follows.

(1) Visual thought processes deal with images that are structurally similar to the features of the concepts being represented. Images are a powerful, flexible and effective metaphor for thought.

(2) Creativity involves the conjunction of two normally-distinct thought contexts.

(3) Communication is concrete. Abstraction (i.e. understanding) occurs in the mind from concrete information.

(4) Creativity and understanding are incremental; large discoveries usually derive from a bisociation of smaller ones.

This chapter utilizes the model in a computer environment. It presents the general form and goals of PYGMALION. Most of the specific implementation details are deferred until the next chapter.

Section A -- Introduction

The main goal of PYGMALION is to *develop a system whose representational and processing facilities correspond to and assist the mental processes that occur during creative thought*. It attempts to make Pygmalions out of people, to provide the average person with a medium for creativity without requiring a substantial recasting of his ideas into terms different from his normal way of thinking. The medium is an environment for writing computer programs. Non-numeric programming primarily involves the manipulation and transformation of structure. In PYGMALION sufficient flexibility is incorporated to permit the programmer to design structures patterned after images in his mind. Part I provides two concrete guidelines for the implementation:

(1) Multi-dimensional representations are superior to one-dimensional for communicating some types of information to a human being. Since the intent is to provide as articulate an interface as possible, the system is founded on visual communication using a graphics display.

(2) Interactive feedback is essential in a creative environment. Interactive text editors are a case in point: they are far easier to use than batch-oriented editors. A text editor is similar to a programming language operating on the restricted domain of text strings. If we generalize the domain to arbitrary data structures, the similarity becomes more apparent. If the editor remembers the editing commands and re-executes them on demand, the two concepts become virtually identical.

The heart of PYGMALION is an interactive, "remembering" editor for iconic data structures exhibited graphically on a display screen. PYGMALION is a visual metaphor for computing. Instead of symbols and abstract concepts, the programmer uses concrete display images, called "icons". The system maps the visual characteristics of icons into corresponding machine semantics. The display screen is equivalent to a document to be edited. Programming involves creating a sequence of display frames, the last of which contains the desired information. Display frames are modified by editing operations. When in "remember mode", the system records the operations as they are done.

PYGMALION is a direct descendant of Kay's FLEX machine[1969] Many of the features of the implementation are derived from FLEX and from conversations with Kay. Perhaps the simplest description of PYGMALION is to say it is just Radia Perlman's button box "grown up" (cf. Chapter 3-E). Though developed independently, they are similar in design. Instead of the elemental turtle operations like "go forward", PYGMALION incorporates general-purpose programming operations like "store value". But the instant-response, visually-oriented, "teaching," error-free characteristics and philosophy are the same.

I want to emphasize that PYGMALION is not a graphical programming language in the traditional sense. Graphical programming languages have all attempted to find two-dimensional ways to *tell* programs what to do. This inherently involves the manipulation of formal representations of data. PYGMALION has no representation for *telling* a program anything; PYGMALION is an environment for *doing* computations. If the system happens to remember what is done, then a program is constructed as a side effect. But the goal of the programmer is to *do a computation once*. This is helpful for understanding in any case: *a good way to understand a complicated algorithm in any language is to work through it with representative values*. Instead of using the medium of paper or blackboard, the PYGMALION programmer uses the display screen.

Section B -- The PYGMALION Philosophy

The overall philosophy of PYGMALION is summarized in the following list. These are the design principles guiding the implementation. The individual principles derive from the model of thought in Part I.

(1) VISUAL: The system is visually oriented.

(2) CONCRETE: Since for many subjects concrete information is easier to deal with than abstract concepts, the form of information manipulated is explicitly represented, rather than implicitly described. Arguments and values of functions are analogical.

(3) PARTIAL: Since people deal with selected, incomplete fragments of memory images, data structures may be left partially instantiated and routines partially specified, with traps on incomplete paths.

(4) LEVELS OF DETAIL: Since the quantity of information a person can handle comfortably (his short term memory) is limited, the system incorporates a detail suppression control. A structure may be displayed at any level of detail, including a symbolic (i.e. string) representation.

(5) MULTIPLE ROLES: Icons are capable of assuming different roles, corresponding to the functions which images serve in thought. Variables may be signs, symbols or pictures of their values. An icon representing a program may simultaneously be a part of a picture or data structure.

(6) SCHEMATA: In order to provide schemata for problem solving, generic prototypes of common operations are provided, such as conditionals, subroutines, iteration, recursion, sequentiality, subgoal hierarchies, and classes and subclasses. In addition, a rectangular shape representing a cell for storing information is provided as the default iconic shape.

(7) INCREMENTAL: Since creativity is incremental, programming proceeds in a step-by-step, interactive fashion, much as one uses an editor to change a body of text.

(8) TIME DEPENDENT: Information is capable of a time-dependent readout, since it is stored sequentially. The proper representation of a PYGMALION program is a *movie*.

(9) CONTEXT DEPENDENT: Since a person *projects* his internal models during perception, the system does likewise. It forms expectations about its input and interprets the

input in light of those expectations. For example, the mouse buttons are context dependent.

(10) COMPUTABILITY: The system is a general purpose programming language, capable of computing anything computable (i.e. equivalent to a Turing machine).

Section C -- Iconology

> The mysterious way in which shapes and marks can be made to signify
> and suggest other things beyond themselves ...
>
> -- E.H.Gombrich[2]

Webster defines "*icon*" as "a pictorial representation, a vivid or graphic representation or description, something introduced to represent something else that it strikingly resembles or suggests, a reproduction or imitation of the form of a thing."[3] PYGMALION icons are two-dimensional, visual, analogical, concrete descriptions of concepts. They can be used to represent anything that can be drawn on a blackboard. (This is not suggesting that icons may only represent concrete concepts or that they must look like the concepts. Icons, like mental images, may be classified as "mimetic" or "non-mimetic" depending on whether they resemble objects or concepts in physical appearance.) Visual images are a powerful medium for portrayal in the mind. Except for the restriction to two dimensions, PYGMALION icons retain all the expressive power of mental images. Icons form the communication interface: person ↔ PYGMALION ↔ computer.

The primary entity used for computing in PYGMALION is the ICON.

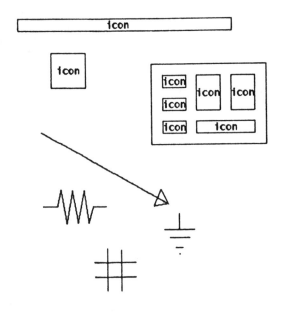

Examples of Icons

Programming in PYGMALION is a process of *designing and editing icons*. The PYGMALION programmer is an "*iconographer*" -- "a maker or designer of figures or drawings."[Webster[4]] The programmer of the future will be as well skilled in design as architects and artists today. Icons define the "PYGMALION machine". Everything that can be done to information is done through icons. Icons provide the mechanism for storing and retrieving information and for representing procedures. Icons exist on a variety of conceptual levels. On the most primitive level, an icon may simply be a picture, a piece of data consisting of line drawings. On a symbolic level, an icon may represent a single machine bit, and the contents of that icon represent the state of the bit, either 0 or 1. On higher levels an icon may represent a machine word, a sequence of words, an arbitrary data structure, the state of the computation, all of memory, the entire computer, or indeed anything which can be simulated. Icons may also represent dynamic processes: functions, coroutines, interrupts. The virtue of PYGMALION lies in being able to use icons as metaphors for the objects to be manipulated. Every operation on icons affects the display state as well as the internal machine state. The programmer need interact with the system only on the display level, with the images he has created. The artist Alexander Cozens

218

taught his students to project their ideas onto random blots of ink, much as Rorschach did a century later. The inkblots became a *source* of ideas to the artists. PYGMALION as an iconic programming language attempts to fulfill the same role. Icons provide an alternative representation which stimulates creative thought in the programmer.

Suppose, as an example, we want to design a controller for "spacewar" space ships. The display screen might contain the following:

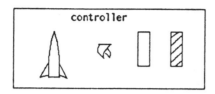

A Controller for Space War

This indicates there are four arguments to "controller": an object of type "ship", an object of type "thrust", an object of type "empty torpedo tube", and an object of type "full torpedo tube". This is far more descriptive than:

PROCEDURE CONTROLLER (SHIP S; THRUST T;
    EMPTY TORPEDO TUBE T1; FULL TORPEDO TUBE T2),

even assuming the programming language used permitted the above data types to be defined, which most languages do not. Some extensible languages, like SMALLTALK or LISP70 [Tesler,Enea,Smith[1973]], permit conceptual entities like "ship" to be easily defined and manipulated. But imagine trying to manipulate a ship represented as an array of numbers in FORTRAN. The amount of translation required from the mind's representation is enormous!

Icons have several "properties" or "attributes", some governing the visual (display) state and some governing the internal (machine) state. The total collection of attributes constitutes the "state" of an icon. Each attribute will be discussed in detail later in the paper where it is relevant. A complete listing follows.

Attributes of Icons

NAME	-- a string
VALUE	-- any object
SHAPE	-- code to generate the shape
BODY	-- code representing the functional semantics
DISPLAYED	-- one of {FALSE, NAME, VALUE, SHAPE}
CONTAINER	-- an icon
RUNCODE	-- code executed when the icon is told to "RUN"
FRAME	-- a display frame (a Smalltalk class); the entire rectangular boundary of the icon
IX	-- a number, the X coordinate of the upper left corner of the boundary
IY	-- a number, the Y coordinate of the upper left corner of the boundary
IWD	-- a number, the width of the boundary
IHT	-- a number, the height of the boundary
FETCHER	-- code to retrieve an attribute of an icon
STORER	-- code to store a value into an attribute of an icon

Icons also respond to several queries and commands. (In Smalltalk parlance, they respond to "messages".) The most important messages are "has", "run", "fetch" and "store":

<icon> has x y

<icon> run

<icon> fetch <attribute>

<icon> store <attribute> <value>

"Has" and "run" are discussed in Chapter 5-F. "Fetch" and "store" are generic access paths to the iconic state. Every icon responds to the messages "fetch" and "store", but the actions taken are icon-specific. In fact, the semantics of "fetch" ("store") are: (a) bind some internal variables to the rest of the message, then (b) execute the code in the FETCHER (STORER) attribute. This has great potential power, but it has been largely unexploited in the initial implementation of PYGMALION. See Chapter 5-C for the chief application.

Section D -- Text Editors as Programming Languages

The actual implementation of PYGMALION is founded upon the following observation: People using interactive text editors on a computer, even untrained people, rarely make permanent-type mistakes in which they attempt to correct a line, fail to do so, and exit from the editor with the line still wrong. Since the editor is interactive, the user (if he is paying attention) will see that the line is still wrong and will simply edit it again until he corrects it. Thousands of people have used interactive text editors, many of them untrained in computer programming. Secretaries and office workers are beginning to use them because it is so easy to create documents, correct mistakes, and change words. But many of these same people shy away from programming because it is "too difficult".

Text editors begin to lose their error-free characteristics when they become batch oriented or when they employ complicated macros (for example, string-substitution macros) that operate on large sections of the text before they show the results. With these types of editors, changes are sometimes made that were undesired and are not detected until later.

Let's examine the nature of text editors a little more closely. Without too much difficulty, we should be able to see that *text editors resemble programming languages operating on a restricted domain.* Their operations, though restricted to text strings, have a functional similarity to operations in programming languages. For example, changing a character in a text string is similar to changing the value of a variable. I'm not going to belabor this point; the reader will be able to find numerous similarities. Instead, note that one difference between the two is that text editors *forget* their operations as soon as they have executed them. A typical cycle is (1) prompt for a command, (2) execute the operation, (3) display the result, (4) go to 1. In a program one wants the operations remembered, so that the program may be run as many times as desired. If, instead of forgetting, text editors *remembered* the operations as they were done, then the similarity with programming languages would become even closer. With such a "remembering" editor, we would not only be editing a body of text; we would also be *writing a program* that, given the same body of text containing the same errors, would automatically correct it. Furthermore, we could be sure that if we correctly edited the text once, every subsequent processing of the same text would also be correct! Of course this is seldom necessary, but some editors do maintain transaction files in case of machine crashes. At the heart of such editors is a powerful idea that may radically change the way software is written. For suppose that instead of limiting our editor to text, we expand its domain to include *arbitrary data structures.* And suppose we also expand its set of operations to include arithmetic, conditionals, subroutines, etc. Then we find our once-meek editor assuming all the capabilities of a general-purpose programming language. And the motivation for doing this is our claim that *it is a far easier programming language to use.*

> BASIC PYGMALION METAPHOR: a program is a series of EDITING CHANGES to a DISPLAY DOCUMENT. Input to a program is an initial display document, i.e. a display screen containing images. Programming consists of editing the document. The result of a computation is a modified document containing the desired information.

PYGMALION uses a remembering editor operating on iconic data structures. PYGMALION differs from all other programming languages in that there is *no static representation* for a program. One programs in PYGMALION by *doing* the operations on data structures directly, rather than by *telling* the program how to do them. When I first began this project, I spent a great deal of time trying to decide what is a good representation for communicating with a machine. Should it be at machine-language level, or higher level? Linear or multi-dimensional? Procedural or descriptive? Pattern-matching or imperative? Because of the reasons in Part I, I chose a two-dimensional representation for objects. But all two-dimensional languages I considered suffer from the same deficiency: they are too complex when representing the dynamic aspects of programming -- the semantics of operations and the flow of control. The representation had to be *articulate.* It had to correspond to representations in the mind. However I don't believe the current state of knowledge permits one to claim that some fixed notation is *the* mind's representation for *any* problem, let alone for *all* problems. In fact I believe that a myriad of representations are used in everyone's mind. The question then arises: why bother to have a predefined representation at all? The important thing is that the *mind* have a representation for a problem. Why not just solve the problem and let the computer "take notes"? The answer, which rather surprised me, is that *there is no need for an intermediate, predefined level of representation between the mind and the computer*. Any intermediate level is just extra work. The reason interactive editors like Engelbart's "NLS" and Swinehart's "TV" are so easy to use is that they don't interpose an intermediate level of work between a person's intention to do a task and the task itself.

Section E -- The PYGMALION Machine

> In computer-aided design these relationships, between the aesthetic and technical side, must be made explicit, must be clearly and precisely formulated. There are two aspects of design to be considered: the visual and physical aspects of design as understood by the designer; and the mathematical representation of the design and associated information which is the form it takes inside the computer.
>
> -- Anthony Hyman[5]

Hardware

Display with Keyboard and Mouse

To use PYGMALION, the designer sits in front of a television-like *display screen*. The one shown is capable of displaying both text and graphics. In front of the display is a typewriter-like *keyboard* and a *"mouse"*. A mouse is a small device originally developed at SRI which has an X-Y tracking capability and three buttons on top that can be read under program control as three binary digits. Pressing a mouse button changes the corresponding binary digit from 0 to 1; releasing it changes the digit back to 0. Associated with the mouse is a *cursor* on the display screen; moving the mouse on the table moves the cursor correspondingly on the display. The cursor instantaneously follows mouse movements; mouse tracking is done in machine language. An interactive computer, a graphics display and a pointing device such as a mouse or light pen are the essential hardware elements of PYGMALION

Software

When a programmer starts to use the system, the display screen shows the basic PYGMALION design environment. This provides a visual *schema*, an initial design metaphor. The basic environment consists of six icons and an empty area called the "design space". The initial icons are named (1) "world", (2) "menu", (3) "mouse", (4) "mouse value", (5) "remembered", and (6) "smalltalk".

(1) Icon "world"

Every icon is an instance of the Smalltalk class ICON. Two of the attributes possessed by every icon are a BOUNDARY and a CONTAINER.

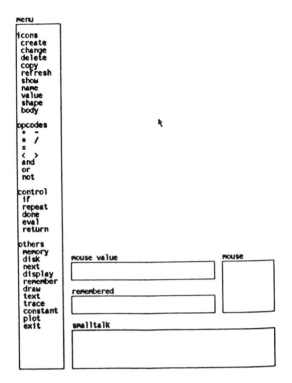

PYGMALION Design Environment

BOUNDARY

The BOUNDARY of an icon is a rectangular area of the display screen. An icon is capable of detecting when the mouse cursor is within its boundary. The boundary of the "world" encompasses the entire display screen; therefore *all icons shown on the display lie within the boundary of the "world" icon.* This sets up a correspondence between the physical and logical characteristics of the display. The *upper left corner* of the boundary is called the *"origin"*. All coordinates used by icons are relative to this point. When a PYGMALION operation positions an icon on the display, it asks for a location for the origin. The origin of the "world" icon is location (0,0) on the display.

CONTAINER

"Containment" is a natural characteristic of images. The rule is:

> The container of an icon "I" is the most recent icon created and currently being displayed whose boundary physically encloses I's origin.

The reason for this particular convention is related to the notion of "iconic context" and is explained in Chapter 5-F. Ordinarily physical containment is the same as logical containment; i.e. if the boundary of icon A encloses icon B on the display screen, then icon A is B's CONTAINER. In the top two pictures below, icon A contains icon B; in the bottom two pictures neither icon contains the other, because neither contains the other's upper left corner.

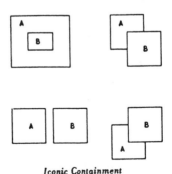

Iconic Containment

An exception to the containment rule is provided by the "change container" command. (Individual operations are explained in detail in the next chapter.) It is occasionally useful for icons to be logically connected while physically separate. The change container command explicitly sets the containment relationship between two icons. In the example above, icon A could explicitly be made the container of B, or vice versa, by using this command.

Iconic Structures

The container attribute is an integral part of the internal semantics of icons. It is used to organize icons into hierarchical structures. The container of an icon is itself an icon. Every icon has a unique container, and every icon may, but need not, contain other icons. If an icon does contain other icons, its VALUE attribute (discussed later) is said to be an "iconic structure". The VALUE of the "world" is an iconic structure containing all the top level icons.

An Icon Containing Three Sub-Icons

An *iconic structure* is a collection of icons. The purpose of iconic structures is to provide a symbolic way to access all the icons on the display. Every icon is a member of some iconic structure. Internally iconic structures are organized as queues. New icons may be added only to the back of the queue, but icons can be deleted from any position. Internal descriptions of icons are in the form of *index lists*, in which each index is an offset from the front of a queue. Since the boundary of the "world" icon encompasses the entire display screen, all index lists begin with an offset in the "world's" queue. Icons are recursively organized. In addition to being a member of some iconic structure, every icon may contain its own iconic structure. The "world" is the root of the tree; it is the top-level structure that provides access to all the other icons. The index list (6 3 5) refers to the sixth icon (call it "A") in the "world's" iconic structure, then to the third icon (call it "B") in A's iconic structure, and finally to the fifth icon in B's iconic structure. While (6 3 5) is a Fregean representation internally, it is created analogically by pointing to the icon with the mouse cursor (see icon "mouse" below).

Since each icon has exactly one container, it follows that each icon must be unique. Making a COPY of an icon creates a new icon, with its own unique container. The container attribute may be changed by

(a) CREATEing an icon;

(b) FETCHing an icon from memory (core or disk).

(c) COPYing an icon;

(d) CHANGEing an icon's position;

(e) CHANGEing an icon's container explicitly;

(2) Icon "menu"

As mentioned, PYGMALION uses an interactive remembering editor operating on iconic representations of data. On the left of the display screen is a list called the "menu" of the editing operations and submodes that are currently available. An interesting aspect of PYGMALION is the scarcity and simplicity of its operations. The trend among high-level languages is to include more and more esoteric operations. PYGMALION runs counter to this trend. There are only a few basic operations, and they are grouped into four categories:

> *structure* -- operations which create and edit icons themselves
>
> *opcodes* -- arithmetic and boolean operations on values
>
> *control* -- operations which affect the flow of control in a program (conditional, iteration, subroutine)
>
> *others* -- miscellaneous operations to save icons in memory, turn remember mode on or off, draw a shape, etc.

The principle *structure* operations are CREATE, DELETE and COPY icons; CHANGE the size or position of icons; SHOW and REFRESH different levels of iconic structure; and fetch from and store into the NAME, VALUE, SHAPE or BODY attributes of icons. Fetching and storing attributes are comparable to fetching and storing the contents of a cell in memory -- the most primitive machine operations. The *opcodes* provide the standard arithmetic and boolean functions on values. The *control* operations provide conditional branching (IF), iteration (REPEAT, DONE), and subroutine invocation (EVAL, RETURN). The *miscellaneous* operations provide various other facilities that have been added from time to time: operations to save icons in memory (MEMORY, DISK), make line drawings (DRAW, TEXT), step through iconic structures (NEXT), turn display and remember modes on and off (DISPLAY, REMEMBER), trace the execution of iconic functions (TRACE), fetch constant values (CONSTANT), make a hard copy of the display screen (PLOT), and leave the PYGMALION environment (EXIT). No claim is made that this is a necessary, complete or even the most useful set of operations. PYGMALION is intended to demonstrate how a set of operations (a display metaphor) can be implemented iconically. The reader should be able to define his own set given the formalism presented in this report. Additional operations can be added to the menu at any time. In fact, the only difference between menu operations and iconic functions is that the names of the menu operations appear in the menu. The reason names (a Fregean representation) are used in the menu is that there is not enough space to display all the operations graphically. However iconically-displayed operations *can* be created, and Chapter 5-B has an example of an iconic menu.

```
menu

icons
 create
 change
 delete
 copy
 refresh
 show
 name
 value
 shape
 body

opcodes
 + -
 * /
 =
 < >
 and
 or
 not

control
 if
 repeat
 done
 eval
 return

others
 memory
 disk
 next
 display
 remember
 draw
 text
 trace
 constant
 plot
 exit
```

Hyman has a perceptive comment on the use of menus:

> The presentation of a menu of choice is a powerful working tool. With a well designed system a teaching manual is largely redundant: the system incorporates a sort of programmed learning as a part of the design system. It may be held that the rhetoric of a subject is not to be learned that way, but it will serve well enough for the three Rs. It would also be of help to a designer transferring from one automated design to another. When the designer is freed from the burden of attention to detail, which grows enormously in a real production system, his attention is freed for creative design.[6]

A menu provides constant reinforcement about the capabilities of the system. It relieves the short term memory from constantly having to recall the available operations.

The programmer should quickly attain a high degree of confidence in the system because

(a) each operation is simple and easy to understand;

(b) its effect is immediately displayed;

(c) mistakes can usually be undone without harmful side effects.

A menu operation may be "*executed*" by pointing to it with the mouse cursor and pressing the top (DOIT) mouse button.

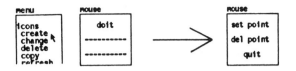

Executing a Menu Operation (note change in mouse state)

This typically sets up a new context in which subsequent commands are interpreted. One effect is to *project* an interpretation onto the mouse buttons.

(3) Icon "mouse"

The mouse is the primary input and control device in PYGMALION. The two main uses of the mouse are to:

(a) designate an icon

(b) accept button commands.

An icon is said to be "*designated*" when the mouse cursor is within its boundary.

Designating an Icon with the Mouse Cursor

Only icons currently on the display screen can be designated, and only designated icons can be affected by menu operations. What you see is what you get. This is a simulation of the principle that only images in the brain's short term memory are operated on by conscious thought. The display screen corresponds to short term memory. Icons not on the display must first be brought to display level by creating them or retrieving them from storage. Core and disk memory simulate the brain's long term memory. There is a fairly accurate correspondence:

The Mind		The Computer
short term memory	↔	display screen
long term memory	↔	core and disk memory
conscious thought	↔	operations on icons

(The simulation breaks down at the interface between short and long term memory. In PYGMALION icons are retrieved from memory by referring to their symbolic names, e.g. "factorial" or "resistor", under the control of a (conscious) menu operation. In the mind that would correspond to bringing everything into short term memory under the control of conscious thought, which is certainly not the case. As pointed out in Chapter 2, creative retrieval is often subconscious and involuntary. However, the rest of the simulation is as faithful as I can make it.)

Actions are initiated by pointing to an icon with the mouse and pressing one of the mouse buttons. The mouse is context sensitive; the mouse buttons have different interpretations depending on which icon the cursor is in and which operation is currently being executed. The "mouse" icon acts as a prompt, displaying the current interpretation. Descriptions of the interpretations are represented in this paper by the following picture.

Explanation of the buttons

top button

middle button

bottom button

For the menu, the interpretation is:

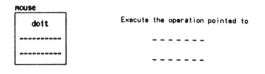

Execute the operation pointed to

(4) Icon "mouse value"

```
mouse value
┌─────────────────────────────────────┐
│                                     │
└─────────────────────────────────────┘
```

In PYGMALION, the mouse has a *value* associated with it, in addition to its cursor and its buttons. Several operations like NAME and VALUE use the mouse value. Fetching an attribute from an icon may be thought of as *attaching* it to the mouse. The value may then be *deposited* in some other icon. The "mouse value" icon shows the current value attached to the mouse.

(5) Icon "remembered"

```
remembered
┌─────────────────────────────────────┐
│                                     │
└─────────────────────────────────────┘
```

In "remember" mode (explained later) the system keeps track of operations as they are done and inserts them in a code list. The last operation or two remembered (i.e. in the current code list) is displayed in the "remembered" icon.

(6) Icon "smalltalk"

```
smalltalk
┌─────────────────────────────────────┐
│                                     │
│                                     │
│                                     │
└─────────────────────────────────────┘
```

This icon is for communicating with Smalltalk. When the mouse cursor is in this icon, Smalltalk expressions may be typed and evaluated. In addition, other information about the state of the system is periodically displayed in this icon.

The Design Space

The rest of the screen is a large area called the "design space", available for displaying iconic data and program. The design space lies within the "world's" boundary, of course. The programmer performs computations in this environment by pointing with the mouse cursor to operations in the menu and then selecting operands from the data structures in the design space. At times an operation may request linear data, e.g. a number or string, which may be input from the keyboard. The result of every operation is immediately displayed; if it is not what was intended, other operations can be executed until the desired state is achieved.

Routines are written by editing actual data structures and performing operations on actual operands. It is programming by example. Instead of trying to *imagine* what data objects are being passed around, the PYGMALION designer manipulates the *actual* objects. And instead of *telling* the machine the sequence of operations to perform by putting them down on paper, the PYGMALION designer *does* them himself, and the machine records them. With very few exceptions, programming languages have required programs to be written with formal arguments. This additional level of abstractness obscures the meaning of routines and is the single most important source of programming errors. In PYGMALION even formal arguments can be visual images of structures. For example, the structure of a data object can be concretely described while the values of the fields are formally represented. The following is an example of an iconic structure that might be used to represent the concept "person" in varying degrees of tangibility. Even more concrete information could, of course, be shown; the degree is up to the designer. The child "Bobby" below may itself be a reference to an instance of PERSON, and it could be displayed to the same level of detail if desired.

Modes of Execution

There are two modes of execution in PYGMALION:

(1) Display mode

(2) Remember mode.

Every operation has a well-defined meaning in each of the modes, but not every operation does something in each mode.

(1) *Display mode* provides a means for communicating the semantics of operations visually. In display mode each operation shows iconically the results of its execution. This permits the user to remain in the display metaphor without having to deal with the internal semantics of operations. Display mode is usually on while a program is being written. It is also turned on when an iconic trace of a program is desired. Display mode may be turned

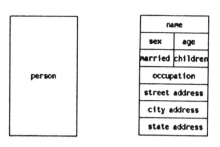

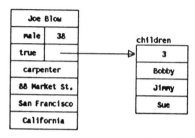

Degrees of Representation of the Concept "PERSON"

off to gain additional speed of execution, since the display code in each operation will then not be executed.

(2) *Remember mode* is for writing programs. In this mode the designer *does* the computation and the machine *remembers* each operation as it is done. The operations place themselves in a *"code list"*. When the computation is complete, the designer executes "stop remembering" and assigns the code list to the BODY or SHAPE attribute of an icon. Programming in remember mode corresponds closely to the debugging process in most languages. Remember mode is similar to an interactive, display-oriented debugger that permits operations to be inserted and deleted in the code and that permits execution to be initiated from any point.

PYGMALION routines may be partially written and run while only partially specified; the specification has to be completed only when the code is about to be executed. This is frequently done with conditionals. When a program is written using actual data, only one branch of a conditional will be taken, with the other branch being left until (and if) it is entered. Every code list ends with a trap to the user asking for more instructions. If the list is completely specified (i.e. terminated with "stop remembering"), the trap is removed. Only if the trap on a partially specified branch is encountered will the programmer have to give additional instructions.

An unusual aspect of PYGMALION's remember mode is that it does not involve a compiler from the display-level actions to the machine-level actions. Rather *each operation is its own compiler*. Each operation is responsible

(a) for accomplishing a given internal machine task -- the machine "semantics" of the operation;

(b) in display mode, for generating a representative visual action;

(c) in remember mode, for adding onto the current code list the operation(s) necessary to reproduce itself.

The operations added are "primitive" in the sense that they are not built up out of other operations available to the program designer. (An exception might be a macro-operation added by the designer to do some commonly-repeated task.) Thus the product of remember mode is a code sequence of the lowest-level operations possible. Ideally all or parts of these operations would be coded in machine language or microcode. In the current implementation they are coded in Smalltalk.

This concludes the basic hardware and software elements in the "PYGMALION machine".

Section F -- Characteristics of Programming in PYGMALION

Using PYGMALION causes several changes in the way software is constructed:

(1) *One may expect to write error-free programs the first time.* This is not the usual case with programming languages, where a great amount of theory and effort has been

227

spent on the debugging process. It *is* the case with interactive text editors. The relevant characteristics are: (a) The system is highly interactive. *The results of operations are immediately visible, and mistakes immediately correctable.* (Therefore PYGMALION must be implemented on a computer that permits interaction, for example on a time-sharing system or mini-computer.) (b) *Operations are primarily concrete rather than abstract.* Some operations are inherently abstract, such as evaluating a subroutine or iterating over the "ith" element of a structure. But most operations are explicitly represented and their consequences immediately displayed. This concreteness simplifies the model-building (understanding) of the programmer. (c) *Data and program are visually represented.* Programs are display documents that can be visually examined and changed until they contain the desired information.

(2) *The standard mode for writing programs is what other systems consider to be debugging mode.* In the traditional writing mode, one works out the logic of a program and organizes the operations that will implement that logic. In debugging mode, one observes the step-by-step execution of operations on actual data, interrogates key values at certain times, and corrects (or at least notes) those operations that are in error. In PYGMALION there is no difference between the two modes. Designers of large systems, such as operating systems and programming languages, are beginning to realize that debugging tools should be designed and implemented *first*, as an integral part of the project. The more complex a system is, the stronger is the need to *see* what is going on. PYGMALION extracts the useful features of debuggers and integrates them directly into the programming process.

(3) *The human programmer is considered to be part of the execution of the program.* A program need not be completely specified in machine-executable terms. At certain points the human may be called upon to guide the machine through more operations, with the machine remembering what the human does. Thus there is a distinction between two kinds of programs in PYGMALION: *"open"* programs and *"closed"* programs. An *open* program consists of one or more machine-executable operations, of which one or more are requests for human intervention; a *closed* program consists of one or more machine-executable operations, none of which are requests for human intervention. The program is "closed" in the sense that the human has told it everything it has to be told. With few exceptions, conventional programming languages require closed programs. Production software (i.e. intended for use by other people without the writer being present) should be closed. But software in development may, and in fact *should*, be "open", since such software is far easier to create.

(4) *No additional medium besides the computer is used in designing software*: no paper listings, no punched cards, no scratch paper. Routines are specified dynamically rather than statically, by *doing* rather than by *telling*. There has been no attempt to make a static representation for a dynamic process. A listing of a PYGMALION routine is a *movie*, a sequence of display frames. Examples of such movies are found in Chapter 6.

Section G -- PYGMALION versus Automatic Programming

> It is characteristic of computers that each time they intrude into a new subject they force practical decisions on questions which have hitherto been considered of a philosophical character, more suited to meandering discussions over cups of coffee far into the night than to the prosaic daylight world of industrial practice.
>
> -- Anthony Hyman[7]

The goals of PYGMALION are quite different from those of automatic programming. The general goal of automatic programming is to automate some of the programming process. In the ideal system, the human specifies the goal of the program in the form of input/output relations. The computer chooses internal representations, organizes the logic, maintains consistency, verifies correctness, and so on. Such tasks are problem-independent; they involve techniques that programmers learn from experience and apply to many different programs. By extracting problem-independent aspects, automatic programming hopes to make the process of programming easier. Balzer[1973] presents an example of a person communicating the semantics of an airline reservation system to a hypothetical automatic programming system. It is evident that such a system would require less superfluous detail than would conventional programming languages.

However there is a danger in this, if carried too far. By making the computer into a "black box" that does the actual programming, the user has to think less about the logical structure of the problem. Furthermore, the user's interaction with the computer is on a verbal level. Verbal communication is Fregean and inhibits understanding the developing program. The questions that Balzer has his hypothetical system ask often seem obscure, since the user does not know what logical relationships the computer is forming. The computer may even ignore the user's recommendations, for example on internal representation, if it thinks it knows better. If successful, automatic programming systems

228

will replace some fairly high-level thinking processes in humans. *Instead of encouraging humans to do more and better thinking, automatic programming may encourage humans to do less and poorer thinking.* At any rate, automatic programming is unlikely to stimulate the development of new problem-solving techniques in the user.

On the other hand, Kay and Papert have shown that learning to program can actually improve children's thinking and learning skills. The notion of debugging is particularly fruitful in giving children new learning strategies. Programming can serve as a catalyst for creativity; knowing how to program can provide the schemata necessary to solve problems, just as knowing how to play chess is frequently useful in real-world situations. With an articulate interface, computers can form a symbiotic relationship with a person which will vastly increase his thinking power. PYGMALION and systems such as those mentioned in Chapter 3 are attempts to provide such an interface.

The Internal Structure of PYGMALION

Summary

   (a) Icons can exist on a variety of conceptual levels: as pictures, symbols or signs.

   (a) PYGMALION is a remembering editor for icons. Operations are provided to deal with icons on each of their levels.

Section A -- Smalltalk

PYGMALION is implemented in Smalltalk, a language designed by Alan Kay and implemented at Xerox PARC by his Learning Research Group. I highly recommend Kay's "personal dynamic media" and Smalltalk papers[1972(a),1972(b),1975] for an enjoyable reading experience. Smalltalk is an interactive symbol-processing language with flexible display primitives. Smalltalk, like LISP, is an interpreted language, with an evaluator for implicitly and explicitly evaluating objects. The dominant characteristics of Smalltalk are its notions of *"class"* and *"intrinsic semantics"*. In Smalltalk every object is an instance of a class. Classes themselves are instances of the class CLASS. This provides an elegant and consistent internal structure, even more consistent than pure LISP.

Communication between instances is done with *"messages"*. A message is a sequence of symbols. The set of messages that a class can handle, together with the responses to those messages, constitute the *"semantics"* of the class. (Hewett[1973] has derived a similar concept called "actors" from these Smalltalk ideas.) Since the code for processing messages is internal to the definition of each class, the semantics are said to be *"intrinsic"* to the class. Neither the evaluator nor other classes know about the internal workings of a particular class; they know only to what messages the class will respond and what form the responses will take. The class NUMBER responds to the message "+" by performing an addition, but how it manages to accomplish the addition is usually not of interest. This differs from most other systems in which the semantics of objects are represented "extrinsically". In compilers the semantics of data types are represented by the code the compiler produces for them. Data types themselves have no intrinsic meaning; their meaning is distributed among the code generators. Having the semantics localized in a single definition is a significant aid to understanding and modifying data types.

Classes and Subclasses

Smalltalk is a descendant of the original SIMULA [Dahl[1966]] and FLEX[Kay[1969]]. Unlike SIMULA-67[Dahl[1970]], however, Smalltalk classes normally exist on the same conceptual level; that is, one does not normally think of Smalltalk classes as being subclasses of other classes (except class CLASS). Here we will briefly discuss the concept of hierarchical classes, since iconic data structures (cf. section D) are hierarchically organized. Hierarchical classes are not currently in Smalltalk, though they can be simulated.

The key principle of hierarchical classes is that a subclass is an *instance of an instance*. Currently Smalltalk objects are classes, instances of classes, and activations of instances. The notion of "subclass" involves a new kind of object: an instance of an instance. One creates an instance of a class, as before, and gives it instance-specific state information. Then one makes a copy of it, preserving all the filled-in state. Additional information is then added to the new instance, making it a subclass of the original instance. Subclasses are recursive; a subclass can itself have subclasses, forming a tree structure. To implement hierarchical classes, Smalltalk would need the additional capability of *dynamically adding attributes to instances*. This is necessary if changes to attributes at a subclass level are not to alter its superclasses. PYGMALION's iconic classes provide this capability since additional icons can be added to iconic structures at any time.

There are two kinds of behavior that subclasses can exhibit:

(1) *Upward Mobility*

(2) *Downward Mobility*

These refer to the information (and hence control) paths between class and subclass.

(1) In "upward mobility", each subclass can access all of the knowledge of all of its superclasses. In addition each subclass has some information of its own which causes it to be distinguished from its immediate superclass. For example, the class HUMAN might be discriminated into subclasses MAN and WOMAN based on the additional information, SEX.

This additional state may involve changes in the values of superclass attributes, or it may be entirely new attributes not present in a superclass. Changes made at the subclass level do not affect its superclasses. For example, if subclass MAN changes the attribute HAIR-LENGTH to SHORT, the change occurs at the subclass (MAN) level, not at the superclass (HUMAN) level.

The key aspect of upward mobility is the *access method* that subclasses use to retrieve information. In what we might call "*dynamic upward mobility*", a request for the value of an attribute begins at the level making the request and searches up the tree of superclasses until it find the first occurrence of the attribute. This is the most general form. SIMULA-67 uses a more restricted form, which we might call "*static upward mobility*". SIMULA copies superclass information into each subclass, so a subclass can access only the information that exists in its superclass *at the time the subclass is created*. No new knowledge can be added dynamically. (Actually creating subclasses is a compile-time action in SIMULA; at run-time SIMULA does not even remember the class-subclass relationship.)

(2) In "downward mobility", any change in a superclass is reflected in all of its subclasses. Again we might further discriminate this behavior into "*dynamic downward mobility*" and "*static downward mobility*". Suppose the class HUMAN possesses an attribute called NUMBER-OF-LEGS, and suppose its value suddenly changes from 2 to 1. In the dynamic form, all the subclasses of HUMAN (i.e. MAN, WOMAN) are immediately updated. In particular, any instance of HUMAN drawn on the display screen would now be drawn with only one leg. In the static form, the change will be observed by the subclasses if they ever ask for the value of the NUMBER-OF-LEGS attribute, but otherwise they will never know. Static downward mobility is equivalent to dynamic upward mobility.

Dynamic upward mobility requires that there be a link from each subclass to at least its immediate superclass and that the access method for attributes search back through the tree. Dynamic downward mobility requires that each superclass have links to all of its subclasses and that the "change attribute" operation be monitored, so that changes in a superclass can be broadcast to the subclasses. Static upward mobility as in SIMULA does not require the presence of links, but it has the unfortunate trait that each subclass must be larger than its superclass, since the superclass information is copied into it. By the time one gets to the leaves of the tree, the subclasses might be quite large.

Smalltalk has proven to be an exceptionally flexible language in which to implement PYGMALION, as well as a fascinating language in its own right. The SIMULA notions of subclasses have also proven useful.

Section B -- Icons as Pictures

Icons derive their power of expression from the fact they are abstract in content but concrete in shape. The virtue of abstraction is that many different instances can be handled within one framework. The virtue of concreteness is that it provides a schema for organizing thought and reduces the possibility of mistakes. Arnheim points out that mental images can assume different functions: they can be signs, symbols or pictures of their values. PYGMALION icons can also assume any of these functions. This section deals with their most concrete use, as pictures. The operations described here all deal with the visual properties of icons themselves, as they appear on the display screen. The picture operations are:

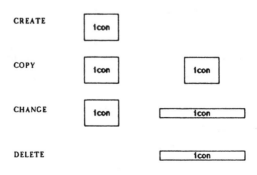

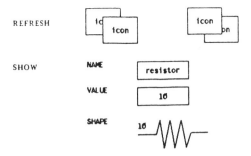

The user interface is basically the same for all of these, so we will only describe CREATE in detail. Executing the CREATE operation in the menu establishes a context for the mouse. The mouse icon will show that the user can now

mouse

set point	Set a point (a corner of an icon)
del point	Delete the last point set
quit	Quit

The user moves the mouse cursor into the design area and presses the top button. This fixes one corner of the rectangular *boundary* of an icon. As the mouse is moved around, the opposite corner follows the cursor, dynamically changing the shape of the rectangle. The middle button may be pressed to start over. Once an icon is started, pressing the top button a second time fixes the opposite corner. This completely defines the boundary of an icon. Each icon starts off with its boundary as its shape, but it can be given a fancier shape. The DELETE operation is the inverse of CREATE. The CHANGE operation can be used to change the position of an icon, the size of its boundary, or its CONTAINER attribute.

The CREATE, CHANGE and DELETE operations have internal semantics in addition to their display actions. As explained in Chapter 4-E, every icon is a member of exactly one iconic structure, and every icon can (but need not) contain its own iconic structure. The CREATE operation adds the created icon to the structure which contains its origin. If no icon encompasses its origin, it is added to the "world's" iconic structure. Similarly for DELETE; the deleted icon is removed from the structure in which it occurred. Normally physical containment and logical containment are the same: an icon logically contains another icon if it physically encloses the other icon's origin. The CHANGE operation can be used to explicitly change the container, and thus the structure containing, any icon. This enables icons to be logically linked while physically separate on the display screen.

(Aside: Most icons are pointed to only once, but multiple references to icons may be created if iconic structures are treated as values. For example, if the value of an icon is an iconic structure, and its value is "fetched" and then "stored" in another icon, there will now be two references to all of the icons in the structure. This is dangerous and not recommended. However it is sometimes done by the system in controlled circumstances.)

The COPY operation gives icons class/subclass characteristics. An icon can be constructed which represents a template of a class. For example, the following is an iconic menu of classes of circuit elements. The elements are all icons which have been given various pictorial and internal properties. The COPY operation can be used to create instances of each class. All properties are copied by value, not by reference. Thus iconic subclasses display *static upward mobility* (cf. section A) in the current implementation. With the COPY operation items can be selected and positioned on the display without leaving the iconic metaphor -- that is, without having to refer to them symbolically.

The SHOW and REFRESH operations cause different levels of iconic representation to be displayed. The REFRESH operation simply redraws an icon at its current level. This is useful if it has been obscured by other drawings. The SHOW operation sets up the following mouse context.

mouse

show name	Show the NAME of an icon
show value	Show the VALUE of an icon
show shape	Show the SHAPE of an icon

Usually pressing any of these buttons simply causes the corresponding attribute of the designated icon to appear on the display. However there are several special cases. If the NAME of an icon (see the next section) is already being displayed when the "show name" button is pushed, the effect is that (a) the name of the icon's *container* is displayed, and (b) all of the icons in the container's iconic structure are erased. If the VALUE of an icon (see the next section) is an iconic structure, then pressing the "show value" button causes all of the icons in the structure to display themselves. The "show name" and "show value"

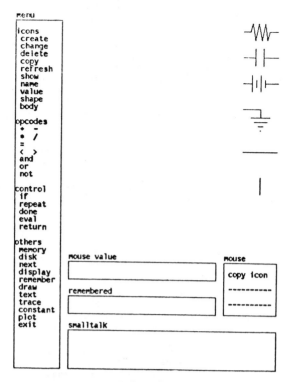

An Iconic Menu

buttons can thus be used to move up and down in iconic structures, selectively displaying or suppressing structure. If an icon has a shape routine defined for it, then pushing the "show shape" button causes the shape routine to be evaluated.

SHAPE Attribute and Operation

The main pictorial attribute of icons is:

SHAPE -- code to draw the icon

The initial shape for an icon consists of the rectangular boundary with its name inside it. The default name is "icon".

Default Iconic Shape

The default shape emphasizes the concept of "container": an icon is a cell which can hold information. It also indicates that the cell has a name and can be referenced symbolically.

However icons are not limited to rectangular shapes. In general the value of an icon's SHAPE attribute is a user-definable routine which displays the icon's surface-level structure. A shape may be any display image that can be generated by a routine. This flexibility allows the iconographer to *design* his metaphors. He may give them whatever shape he considers appropriate to their meaning. This is another example of PYGMALION's attempt to program in the language of thought.

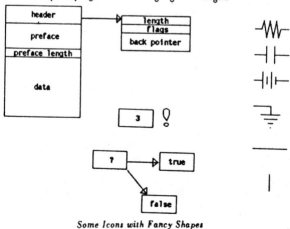

Some Icons with Fancy Shapes

Any icon can be given a fancy shape, regardless of its intended use: picture, variable, function, data type, etc. The value of the shape in communicating semantic intent is entirely dependent on the user's skill in designing images. It is the task faced by artists in communicating with the public. PYGMALION presents an empty canvas with only a few pre-defined icons and operations. A suggestion for the future (Chapter 7) is to develop within the PYGMALION paradigm a more extensive graphic vocabulary to serve as schemata for the user. But the initial system presents just the tools and not the patterns for designing icons. (For those who can't draw, PYGMALION does provide tools for defining rectangular shapes: CREATE, COPY, CHANGE.) Defining a shape routine is exactly like defining an iconic function, except that the code assembled is put in the SHAPE attribute instead of the BODY attribute. Shape code is evaluated with the "show shape" button in the SHOW operation. (Function code is evaluated with the EVAL operation.) The SHAPE operation is used to define shape routines. The procedure is to put the system in "remember" mode, and then execute menu operations which draw the shape. This is discussed extensively in the section on icons as functions, section E. While any menu operation can be "remembered", the two most useful ones for shapes are DRAW and TEXT.

DRAW Operation

The DRAW operation is used for making line drawings. It sets up the following mouse context.

mouse	
start line	Start a new line
stop line	End the current line
quit	Quit

Pressing the top mouse button causes a new line to be started at the current position of the mouse cursor. As the mouse is moved around, the other end of the line will dynamically follow the cursor (Sutherland's "rubber band" line). When the top button is pressed again, the other end point is fixed at the current cursor position and a new line begun from there. Pressing the middle button causes the end point to be fixed without starting a new line. The bottom button leaves the mouse context. The lines are all relative to the origin of an icon designated by the user; if the icon changes position, the lines move with it.

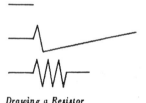

Drawing a Resistor

TEXT Operation

Text strings can be included in pictures with the TEXT operation. Executing it (a) first asks the user to type a string in the "smalltalk" icon, (b) then asks him to designate an icon to use as a base position, and (c) finally asks him to position the text on the screen. The text is positioned relative to the origin of the designated icon. As with line drawings, if the icon moves, the text moves also, maintaining the same relative position to the icon's origin.

Section C -- Icons as Variables

The mathematical concept of "variable" has the attributes NAME and VALUE associated with it. These attributes are preserved in PYGMALION because icons can serve as variables:

NAME -- a string

VALUE -- any object; e.g. number, string, vector, icon, iconic structure

But PYGMALION variables can have an additional attribute not usually possessed by variables, a SHAPE. For example, a variable which is to be bound to resistors might be represented by an icon having the following attributes:

NAME — "R"

VALUE — unbound

SHAPE — —⋀⋀⋏—

NAME Attribute and Operation

The NAME attribute is an ordinary string of characters and is one way to refer to an icon. Names are used to suppress detail when complex structures are being manipulated. They can refer to icons without causing their shapes to be displayed. Names serve the same functions in PYGMALION that words serve in conscious thought: they provide a reference to other structures without exhibiting the full detail of the structures. Just as the *referents* of words, not words themselves, are used in thinking, the *referents* of names (i.e. icons) are used in computations in PYGMALION. This correspondence is another of the ways in which PYGMALION attempts to bring programming closer to thinking.

Examples of names:
```
"x"
"alongname"
"a multi-word name"
"a strange e!12$3+._,& name"
"UPPER AND lower case LETTERS"
```

The name of an icon can be changed by using the NAME operation in the menu. Executing the NAME operation sets up the following mouse context.

fetch name	Fetch the name attribute
store name	Store the name attribute
quit	Quit

The top button attaches the name attribute of the designated icon to the mouse. The middle button deposits the mouse value in the name attribute of the designated icon. The bottom button leaves this context. With these buttons the user can point to icons and manipulate their NAME attributes. The effect of the buttons depends on the icon designated; it is not the same for every icon. "Fetching" a name from the "smalltalk" icon causes a "read" to happen; the user may then type in a name or something which evaluates to a name. "Storing" into the "smalltalk" icon causes the value attached to the mouse to be printed. "Storing" into any of the other initial icons ("menu", "mouse", "mouse value", "remembered" or "world") is illegal.

VALUE Attribute and Operation

The VALUE attribute and VALUE operation are identical to the NAME attribute and operation, except that the VALUE attribute can be any object in the system, not just a string as with the NAME attribute. Since the VALUE of an icon can be any object, in particular it can be an iconic structure. (Recall that an iconic structure is an ordered collection -- a queue -- of icons.) Each of the icons in the structure can be used as a variable, so that any icon can effectively have more than one value. Indeed any sub-icon can have its own iconic structure as its VALUE, and so on indefinitely. In this way entire structures can be built up and manipulated.

Examples of values:
```
atom
193
"a string"
(a vector)
```

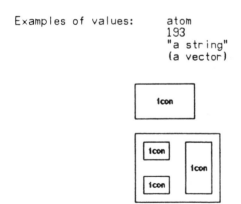

Note that the NAME and VALUE operations, like the picture operations described in the last section, are perceived by the user as *editing operations on display images*. They change the contents of the display screen as part of their execution. They also change the internal state, of course, but the mapping between this state and the display screen permits the user to deal with them on the display level, without bothering about the internal implementation. He perceives his task as *editing the display screen until it contains the desired information*.

As mentioned in the previous section, an icon can have an iconic structure as its value. In that case we say the icon "contains" the iconic structure. That terminology derives from the fact that the iconic structure usually occurs physically within the boundary of the icon, as is the case with the example presented below:

An Iconic Structure Consisting of Three Sub-Icons

Since sub-icons can themselves contain other icons, structures of any degree of complexity can be built. The structure may be a single level deep, as in the array below,

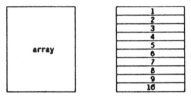

An Iconic Structure Representing an ARRAY

or the structure can have nested sub-levels.

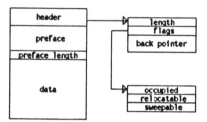

Nested Iconic Structure

Classes of objects can be constructed by creating an iconic structure containing the desired number of sub-fields, filling in the relevant sub-fields with type-dependent information, and then saving it in memory or on the disk. This provides a *visual template* for the data type. The following are steps defining a class of 10 ohm resistors.

If we wanted arbitrary (instead of 10 ohm) resistors, we could simply leave the VALUE attribute unspecified. This is a very simple definition, involving no substructure. A more realistic simulation of resistors might have sub-icons containing current flow, connectivity information, and other model-specific details. The design flexibility and the visual concreteness of iconic structures permit the programmer to use them effectively to represent his ideas. They serve as *schemata in thought*.

235

Another attribute possessed by every icon is:

BODY -- code for functional semantics

This permits icons to represent functions. The BODY of an icon can be evaluated at any time by executing the EVAL menu operation and then pointing to the icon to be evaluated.

Since the EVAL operation, like all operations, can be "remembered", subroutine calls to iconic functions can be included in a function's definition. An iconic function can EVAL itself, so that recursion is possible. This is similar to Radia Perlman's Button Box, but PYGMALION includes conditional and iteration operators for execution control. (Recall that Perlman's procedures had no way to terminate recursion.)

Defining Iconic Functions

Iconic functions can be defined in PYGMALION by executing the BODY operation in the menu. Basically this entails *putting the system in "remember" mode and then doing the calculation to be performed by the function*. This is precisely the "dynamic programming" philosophy of the Unimate robot, HP-65 calculator and Perlman Button Box: the programmer "teaches" the machine a procedure by *doing it once*. The following are the steps necessary to completely define a function.

(1) Create an icon. This is called the "function's icon" and serves as the framework for the definition. The code for the function will be put in the icon's BODY attribute.

(2) Give the icon a symbolic name. Symbolic names are used to invoke functions that are not on the display screen (i.e. that are in memory or on the disk). The function need not have a name if it will never be invoked symbolically, in which case it is like an unlabeled LAMBDA expression in LISP.

(3) Create sub-icons in the function's icon to hold individual arguments to the function. This makes the function's icon into a formal "argument icon". This need not be done if the function takes no arguments.

(4) START REMEMBERING.

(5) DO THE COMPUTATION ONCE.

(6) Create sub-icons in the function's icon to hold the values computed. This makes the function's icon into a "value icon". This need not be done if the function returns no values. Frequently the same structure can be used both as argument icon and as value icon.

(7) STOP REMEMBERING

The argument icon and the value icon provide the communications interface between routines. Anything in the argument icon when a function is EVALed may be used by the body of the function. Anything in the value icon when the function returns may be used by the caller. It is easily seen that functions in PYGMALION can take zero or more arguments (the contents of the argument icon) and return zero or more values (the contents of the value icon). So we get multi-valued functions easily. The argument and value icons can be any size. In particular they can cover the entire design area. In that case everything on the display screen is passed to and returned from the function.

As with iconic data structures, the argument and value icons correspond to the *schemata* used in thought. Once the argument icon is displayed, the designer fills it in with actual values. This eases the problem of interfacing procedures since the called procedure can display the structure of the arguments that it wants. It eliminates a major source of bugs: calling a procedure with the wrong number or type of arguments. Similarly the value icon helps to reduce confusion about the values functions return. A cleverly designed value icon can be of substantial assistance in keeping values straight. In a large program with many procedures, it is a difficult task to remember the calling/returning conventions. Fregean descriptions of parameters (e.g. "ARRAY X", "LIST L") provide little help. One of the aspects of PYGMALION I like best is the very real assistance provided by concrete, analogical argument/value icons.

Icons representing functions can, of course, have any of the other attributes of the class ICON, such as a SHAPE routine.

236

"*Remember*" mode is one of the two modes in which PYGMALION can operate. (The other is "*display*" mode.) Remember mode is entered by evaluating either the BODY or the SHAPE operation in the menu, depending on whether the user wants to define a function body or an iconic shape. (Actually the difference between the two is purely a matter of convention; the SHAPE attribute could be used to hold a second function body if the programmer so desires. Both attributes use the same set of operations.) When the BODY or SHAPE operation is executed, an empty "code list" is placed in the corresponding attribute of the designated icon. A "code list" is a sequence of operations. A reference to the code list is also placed in the "remembered" icon. The code list in the "remembered" icon is called the "*current code list*". As mentioned in Chapter 4, each operation in the menu is capable of adding itself to the current code list. An internal flag called REMEMBERMODE controls this: when true, operations execute and add themselves to the current code list; when false, the operations simply execute. The BODY and SHAPE operations set REMEMBERMODE to true. The "stop remembering" option of the REMEMBER operation sets it to false when the computation is complete.

There are several display indications that the system is in remember mode. The notation "remembering..." appears at the top of the screen. The last operation or two done is shown in symbolic form in the "remembered" icon. The picture above shows that the user has just fetched the value 9999 from the fifth icon ("smalltalk") and stored it in the sixth icon (in the middle of the screen). Then the REMEMBER operation was executed to display the "remember" options available: remembermode can be temporarily suspended and then resumed, or stopped altogether. The suspend/resume option is useful to make adjustments to the display screen without having the operations remembered.

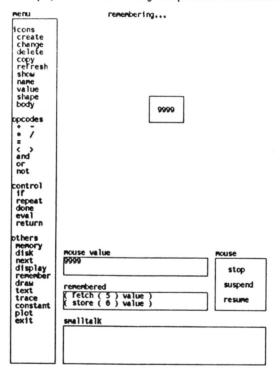

Calling Iconic Functions -- Iconic Contexts

Each iconic function carries with it an "*iconic context*". An iconic context is an image of the display screen -- the state of the display that exists when the function is first defined. Internally an iconic context is just a copy of the "world's" iconic structure, in which the icons are copied into a new iconic structure *by reference*. Iconic contexts are necessary to insure that the display screen looks the same when a function is *evaluated* as when it was *defined*. (This is explained further at the end of the next section.) The following are the steps involved in calling an iconic function; the steps marked with an asterisk (*) are done by the user.

(1*) The argument icon for the function is brought to display level. Recall that the argument icon is an iconic structure containing cells for all the parameters to be passed to the function. The icon is displayed by retrieving it from memory, from the disk, or by making a copy of an icon already on the display screen. The parameter cells are then filled in with actual values.

(2*) When its argument icon is sufficiently (not necessarily completely) instantiated, the function is evaluated with the EVAL operation.

237

(3) The display screen is set to the function's iconic context. The display screen now contains the same number and types of icons as it did when the function was defined, except that the newly-instantiated argument icon replaces the argument icon used when the function was written.

(4) The BODY of the function is executed. Recall that the BODY attribute of an icon contains a list of menu operations. Some of the operations must place the values to be returned into the argument icon, turning it into a value icon.

(5) The display screen is restored to its state before step (3), except that the function's value icon now appears where its argument icon used to be.

(6a) The values in the value icon are attached with the mouse and deposited in other argument or value icons, for use in further computations.

Normally iconic functions should be defined with no superfluous icons on the screen. However some interesting effects can be acheived through the judicious choice of "permanent" icons, icons which remain on the screen across function boundaries. They can provide an alternative means of communicating between functions, similar to global variables in other languages. The following is an iconic context with a four-icon interrupt vector in one corner of the display screen. This can remain on the screen, and thus appear in iconic contexts, for a number of functions. Any of the functions can set or interrogate the icons. The icons themselves can be iconic functions that the user evaluates after he fetches or stores their values. This is an iconic version of *software interrupts*.

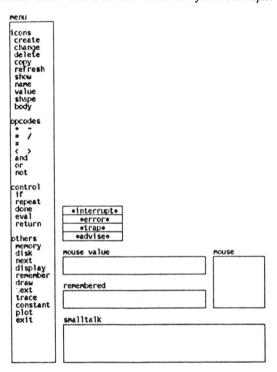

A Shared Structure: An Iconic Interrupt Vector

Another possibility is to create a set of shareable cells for use as global variables. The picture below shows a four-cell structure similar to a FORTRAN "COMMON" area, of which three are taken by the (global) variables X, Y and Z. If more cells are needed, the user can always add additional icons to the iconic structure. The cells then be used to hold information for later access by other functions.

Local variables are easy to create and a very natural concept in this environment. A variable is just a cell for holding information. Since icons can have values, to create a new local variable the user has only to create a new icon. (The CREATE operation can be remembered.) The normal procedure is to position the icon in the design area so that it becomes part of the "world's" iconic structure, but it could be placed inside some other icon. The icon's VALUE attribute can then be set and retrieved using the mouse. Local variables can be created and deleted at any time as part of the definition of a function. The number of variables is limited only by the size of the display screen. Using the detail-suppression techniques of the last section, even physical size presents little constraint.

238

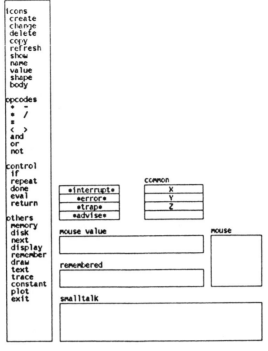

```
menu

icons
  create
  change
  delete
  copy
  refresh
  show
  name
  value
  shape
  body

opcodes
  +    -
  *    /
  =
  <    >
  and
  or
  not

control
  if
  repeat
  done
  eval
  return

others
  memory
  disk
  next
  display
  remember
  draw
  text
  trace
  constant
  plot
  exit
```

```
                          common
                            X
•interrupt•                 Y
 •error•                    Z
 •trap•
 •advise•

mouse value               mouse


remembered



smalltalk


```

Two Shared Structures: An Interrupt Vector and a Common Area

OPCODES

We will illustrate the execution of iconic functions with some simple functions called "opcodes". (An illustration of the execution of FACTORIAL is presented in Chapter 6-B.) Opcodes are operations on values that are so frequently used that it is convenient to include their names in the menu. The semantics of opcodes are identical to those of iconic functions with one exception since its name is in the menu, an opcode can be invoked -- that is, its argument icon brought to display level -- by simply executing its menu entry. Other functions are invoked by fetching them from storage using the MEMORY or DISK operation. As with all iconic functions, the body of the opcode may be evaluated as soon as the argument icon is sufficiently instantiated. The value icon replaces the argument icon when the execution is complete. The opcodes presently available are

```
Arithmetic opcodes:    +      add
                       -      subtract
                       *      multiply
                       /      divide


Boolean opcodes:       =      equal
                       <      less than
                       >      greater than
                       and    logical and
                       or     logical or
                       not    logical not
```

Since these all work the same way, we will only discuss "+" here. Executing the "+" operation in the menu initiates the following process.

(1) The argument icon for "+" is brought to display level and positioned where designated by the mouse cursor. The "+" process then suspends.

(2) "+" has two formal icons for holding the addend and augend. They may be given values.

(3) As soon as both values are present, the body of "+" may be evaluated with EVAL. In this case the body simply computes the sum of the two values; i.e. 3 + 2.

239

(4) When the body finishes executing, the value icon is displayed. In this case it is simply a rectangle containing the number which is the sum.

Actually, the value returned by "+" need not be a number at all. To be completely acccurate, the value is the result returned by passing to the first argument the message "+" together with the second argument. The position taken by most extensible languages, Smalltalk included, is that symbols like "+" have no intrinsic meaning. Symbols are defined by the rules which use them. For example, the rule

<INTEGER> + <INTEGER> → ...

might be used to define "+" to be integer addition, but another rule

<REAL> + <REAL> → ...

might be used in the same translator to define "+" to be addition of real numbers. In Smalltalk, *classes* have intrinsic meaning, not symbols. The symbol "+" has meaning only insofar as classes know how to deal with it. For example, Smalltalk objects of class NUMBER (e.g. 3) contain code to handle messages containing "+", understanding it to mean ordinary addition. Objects of class STRING (e.g. "abc") can also handle "+", but in this case it is interpreted to mean "concatenate". The semantics of classes are intrinsic in Smalltalk; the semantics of symbols are extrinsic. This distinction is preserved in PYGMALION.

The body of opcodes [step (3) above] may now be more accurately described as follows:

(3') As soon as both values are present, the body of "+" may be EVALed. The body passes to the first value the message "+" together with the second value; e.g.

<value 1> + <value 2> .

The first value must be an object that knows how to handle the message "+"

IF Operation

Conditionals are provided by the IF menu operation. Executing it brings the following argument icon to display level.

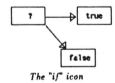

The "if" icon

The "if" icon contains three sub-icons. Only the value of the sub-icon named "?" is of interest. It must be assigned a value before the "if" icon is EVALed. The BODY of the "if" icon tests the value of the "?" icon and depending on the result evaluates the BODY of either the "true" icon or the "false" icon. Initially the BODYs of these icons consist of code lists containing only a trap to the user asking for more instructions. When the trap is encountered, the system is automatically put in remember mode. The BODY can then be defined in the usual way.

REPEAT Operation

Iteration is provided by the REPEAT menu operation. The "repeat" icon has the following shape.

The "repeat" icon

The "repeat" icon has one sub-icon named "loop". It has the same flavor as the "if" icon, except that its semantics are: successively evaluate the BODY of the "loop" icon until the DONE operation is encountered. The DONE operation is for terminating repeat-loops. As with the "true" and "false" icons above, the "loop" icon's BODY initially consists only of a trap to the user asking for more instructions.

EVAL Operation

Subroutines are called with the EVAL menu operation. It may be used to evaluate the BODY of any icon. The icon must be displayed before it can be evaluated. This means that invoking an iconic function is a three stage process:

(1) Bring the function's icon to display level.

(2) Instantiate its argument icon with values.

(3) Evaluate its BODY with EVAL.

Section F -- Icons as Processes

The key to associating actions with icons on the display screen is a set of attributes possessed by icons:

```
DISPLAYED -- a data attribute

HAS       -- a procedure attribute

RUN       -- a procedure attribute
```

RUN

The RUN attribute is said to be a "procedure" attribute because a procedure, instead of a piece of data, is associated with it. (In precise Smalltalk terms, RUN is a *message* rather than an *attribute* of icons; but in this case there is no difference in the user's perception of the two.) PYGMALION is organized as a process structure. Each icon is an independent process. An icon *gains control* by being internally told to RUN and by the mouse being within its boundary. It will retain control so long as the mouse remains within the boundary. The mouse, then, serves as a dynamic control manipulator. The user transfers control between icons by moving the mouse from one to the other. (An exception occurs if an icon, by error or design, does not give up control based on mouse movements. This is sometimes necessary to insure that a task gets completed before control is transferred.) The code associated with the RUN attribute for user-defined icons usually just invokes the VALUE menu operation. The "smalltalk" icon has run-code that waits for a character to be typed on the keyboard and then evaluates the subsequent Smalltalk expression. The "menu" icon's run-code executes menu operations. The "remembered" icon's run-code is an editor for code lists.

Process control derives from the "world" icon. The run-code for the "world" is: repetitively ask each icon if the mouse cursor is within its boundary; if it is, tell the icon to RUN. The "world" can access each icon because its value contains pointers to all of the top-level icons on the display screen. These in turn contain pointers to lower level icons.

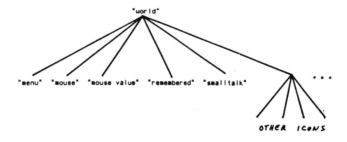

241

DISPLAYED

The HAS and DISPLAYED attributes are the primitives used by PYGMALION to control the "aesthetic" and "technical" elements in design. The programmer/designer can manipulate only those icons that he can see, that are on the display screen. The DISPLAYED attribute can have any of the following values:

```
false - the icon is not currently being displayed.

name  - the name (and boundary) of the icon are
        currently being displayed.

value - the value of the icon is currently being
        displayed.

shape - the shape of the icon is currently being
        displayed.
```

Only those icons having a non-false DISPLAYED attribute can be designated with the mouse. And only designated icons can be the object of menu operations. The result is that only icons displayed in some form are accessible to the user.

HAS

Like RUN, the HAS attribute is said to be a "procedure" attribute because a procedure is associated with it. The procedure takes two parameters, an X coordinate and a Y coordinate. An icon can be asked if it "has" a particular value of X and Y; e.g.

```
i has mousex mousey .
```

The procedure checks if the X-Y values given are within the boundary of the icon. In the example above, the icon "i" is being asked if the mouse is currently within its boundaries. HAS first checks if the DISPLAYED attribute is false, returning false if it is. Therefore, an icon will respond that it "has" an X-Y value only if it is currently being displayed in some form and the X-Y pair is within its boundaries.

Abstract Designation of Icons

There is no difficulty in designating icons when operations are first done. The programmer merely points to an icon with the mouse and executes a command (such as "fetch value") by pushing a mouse button. The command then operates on the icon to which the mouse is pointing. But suppose we are defining a program. With PYGMALION's "remembering editor" every operation done is added to a code list that eventually becomes the BODY or SHAPE of some icon. When the program is run, the operations will be re-executed, probably without the programmer even being present. It is impossible (and, in any case, undesirable) to require the programmer to point with the mouse to every icon to be operated on. He should have to designate the icons only while he is *writing* the program; thereafter the program must automatically act on corresponding icons. The problem is: how are "corresponding " icons to be identified without using the mouse? Three solutions:

(1) One solution might be to specify an icon by its X-Y coordinate location -- its two-dimensional "address" on the display. This is the two-dimensional analogue of absolute addressing, in which symbolic variables (like "X") in a program are mapped to absolute locations in memory during compilation. However, absolute addressing has several drawbacks, such as making recursion and relocation difficult. Recursive calls on a function would have to display the function's icons in the same place every time, overlaying and obscuring earlier calls. Furthermore, one might wish to rearrange the icons on the display screen for aesthetic reasons (permitted since PYGMALION's philosophy is that one *designs* a program, and designing involves aesthetics). It seems unreasonable either to prohibit rearranging icons or to have it invalidate code written earlier. (As Ivan Sutherland pointed out, the representations of images in human visual memory are invariant over size and position changes.)

A variation on absolute addressing might be to order the icons on the display topologically. But again one might wish to rearrange them for aesthetic reasons, which should not invalidate code.

(2) Another solution might be to specify icons by a unique label. We could give every icon in the system its own unique identifying symbol (such as a LISP "gensym") and use those symbols when dealing with icons. But again recursion causes difficulties. There is no way to tell at program-writing time what names will be used in recursive calls to a function at execution time. If recursion is permitted, the method of accessing icons must itself be recursive.

(3) The solution adopted by PYGMALION is a two-dimensional analogue of dynamic addressing. Some programming languages, e.g. ALGOL and LISP, use a stack to allocate space for variables. Every time a function is entered, a fresh cell is created on the stack for each local variable. This simplifies recursion at a slight cost in execution speed.

As mentioned earlier, in PYGMALION iconic structures are actually *queues*. Whenever an icon is created on the display screen, it is added to the end of the queue of the iconic structure which contains it. There is a top-level icon called the "world" whose boundary encloses the entire display; so *every icon occurs within some iconic structure*. This queue structure establishes a *time sequential* access: icons which are put on the screen first occur "earlier" in an iconic structure than later entries; i.e. they are towards the front of the queue. Since each icon is contained in exactly one iconic structure, we can uniquely describe it by its queue index. The complete representation is a list of queue indices beginning with the outermost structure (the "world"). For example, the sixth icon on the display is represented by (6). This description is recursive. If the sixth icon on the display contains an iconic structure, then we may specify the second icon in the structure by (6 2). There is no theoretical limit to the depth of this nesting. This was discussed in Chapter 4-E.

Time sequential accessing is important to the "remembering editor" aspect of PYGMALION. Editing operations are done to actual icons on the display screen using the mouse; the icons are translated by the system into queue offsets when the operations are remembered. Concrete, aesthetic display images are transformed into abstract, technical queue offsets. However there is a difficulty. With the time sequential access method described, the same environment must exist when a function is *executed* as when it was *written*, or at least the same number and types of icons must be present on the display screen. Otherwise a queue representation like (6 2) may be invalid -- there may not even *be* a sixth icon on the screen. To permit the PYGMALION programmer to use functions written by others without requiring him to know in detail their environments, each iconic function carries with it an *iconic context* (cf. section E). When the function is evaluated, the screen is set to the state that existed when the function was defined, and restored after execution is complete. The function's argument/value icon is the primary means of communicating between the two contexts.

Examples of Purely Iconic Programming

This chapter imitates the branch of ancient Indian geometry that used only one word "BEHOLD" in its proofs (Chapter 1-G). The reasoning was done iconically. In this chapter sequences of display images are presented with a minimum of text accompanying them.

Section A -- LISP70 Memory Organization

The first example is an iconic description of the LISP70 [Tesler,Enea,Smith[1973]] memory organization. Memory consists of a series of structured "blocks" of consecutive words of core. The block structure is presented here in various levels of detail. The purpose of this example is to demonstrate the expository capacity of icons and the detail suppression facilities in PYGMALION.

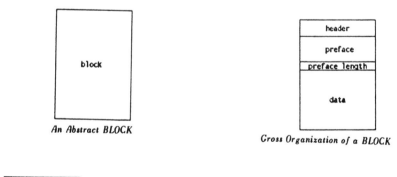

An Abstract BLOCK

Cross Organization of a BLOCK

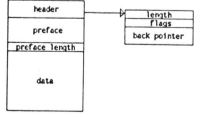

Structure of a BLOCK HEADER   *Structure of the FLAGS field in a BLOCK HEADER*

Section B -- Factorial

This example presents an iconic trace of the execution of the function FACTORIAL on the argument 6. On the display screen these frames appear in sequence, forming a movie of the execution. For completeness and to demonstrate that there is a static representation for PYGMALION functions, the code list assembled by these operations is included at the end. But this is not the most articulate notation. *The proper representation of a PYGMALION function is a movie.*

This example presents the iconic versions of these concepts in the context of a familiar function, FACTORIAL. While FACTORIAL is not a particularly iconic function, mapping numbers into numbers, it does exhibit several powerful programming concepts:

(a) the concept of "variable", and fetching from and storing into variables;

(b) the concept of "conditional";

(c) the concept of "recursion";

(d) arithmetic and boolean operations (+ - * =);

Note: the dashed lines in the following pictures are NOT part of the definition. They have been added by hand to clarify the movement of values. In actual use such clarification is unnecessary, as the movements of the mouse cursor adequately indicate which icons are affected.

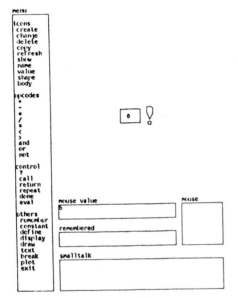

The BODY of FACTORIAL with the VALUE 6 is evaluated with the EVAL operation

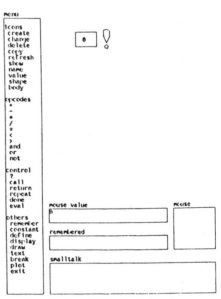

The display screen is set to FACTORIAL's iconic context (no superfluous icons)

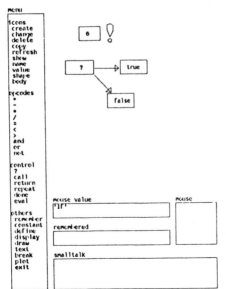

A conditional icon is brought to display level

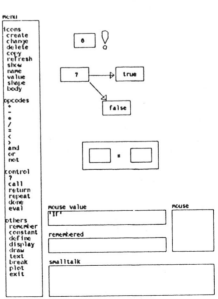

An icon for testing equality is invoked

244

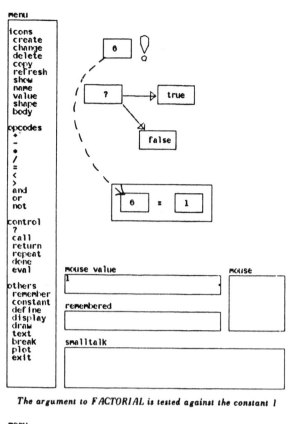

The argument to FACTORIAL is tested against the constant 1

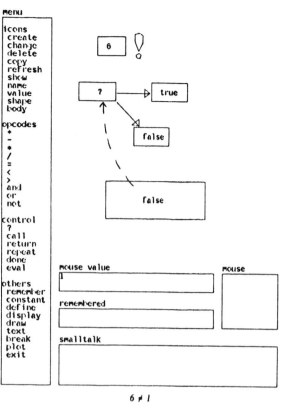

6 ≠ 1

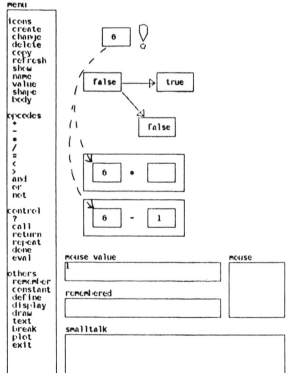

*The "false" icon causes 6 * FACTORIAL(6 - 1) to be computed*

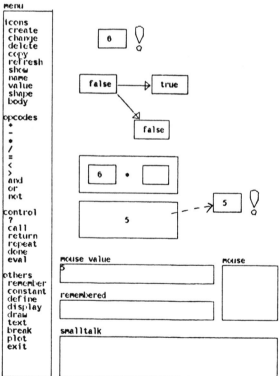

Preparing for a recursive call on FACTORIAL

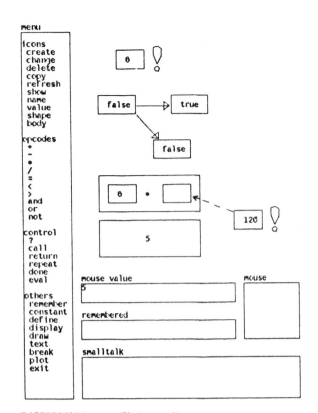

FACTORIAL(5) = 120 (The intermediate steps have not been shown.)

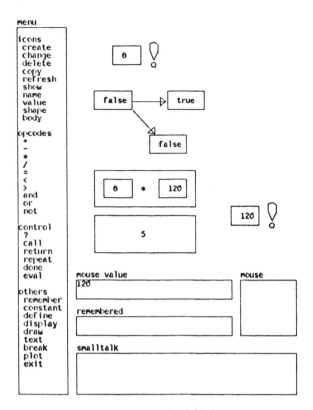

The value 120 has been placed in the other half of the multiplication icon

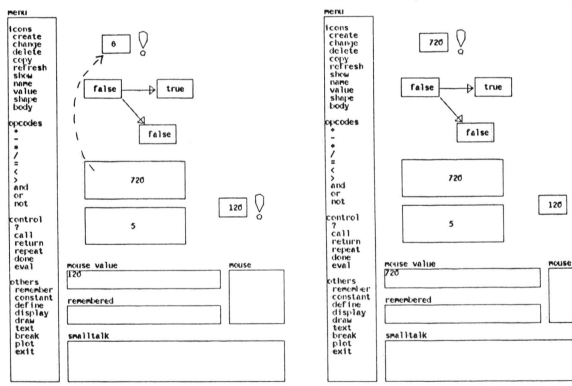

6 ∗ 120 = 720

The value 720 is placed in FACTORIAL's argument icon, turning it into a value icon

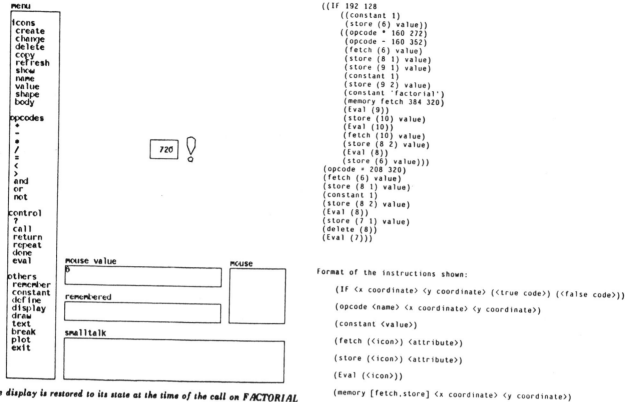

```
menu

icons
 create
 change
 delete
 copy
 refresh
 show
 name
 value
 shape
 body

opcodes
 +
 -
 *
 /
 =
 <
 >
 and
 or
 not

control
 ?
 call
 return
 repeat
 done
 eval

others
 remember
 constant
 define
 display
 draw
 text
 break
 plot
 exit
```

720

mouse value
6

mouse

remembered

smalltalk

The display is restored to its state at the time of the call on FACTORIAL

```
((IF 192 128
     ((constant 1)
      (store (6) value))
     ((opcode * 160 272)
      (opcode - 160 352)
      (fetch (6) value)
      (store (8 1) value)
      (store (9 1) value)
      (constant 1)
      (store (9 2) value)
      (constant 'factorial')
      (memory fetch 384 320)
      (Eval (9))
      (store (10) value)
      (Eval (10))
      (fetch (10) value)
      (store (8 2) value)
      (Eval (8))
      (store (6) value)))
 (opcode = 208 320)
 (fetch (6) value)
 (store (8 1) value)
 (constant 1)
 (store (8 2) value)
 (Eval (8))
 (store (7 1) value)
 (delete (8))
 (Eval (7)))
```

Format of the instructions shown:

    (IF <x coordinate> <y coordinate> (<true code>) (<false code>))

    (opcode <name> <x coordinate> <y coordinate>)

    (constant <value>)

    (fetch (<icon>) <attribute>)

    (store (<icon>) <attribute>)

    (Eval (<icon>))

    (memory [fetch,store] <x coordinate> <y coordinate>)

    (delete (<icon>))

The code assembled as a side effect of computing FACTORIAL

Section C -- Circuit Simulator

Iconic menus are possible, and in fact encouraged. The initial menu is symbolic (contains names) to save display space. Below is a menu of electronic circuit elements. The COPY operation is used to select icons from the menu. Each icon has a semantically descriptive SHAPE attribute. In addition, each icon contains an iconic structure representing the electronic characteristics that are being modeled. The structure of the "power supply" icon is shown in one picture. The choice of structure is entirely up to the user.

The definition and execution of operations are not shown here; they are similar to the FACTORIAL example. The fact that the operations modify icons having fancy shapes instead of mere rectangles has little significance internally. Programming the semantics of a circuit simulation proceeds in the same way as programming any function. The difference between using PYGMALION and using a one-dimensional programming language is that no additional media (scratch paper, blackboard) need be employed. The display screen can be used to sketch out ideas.

247

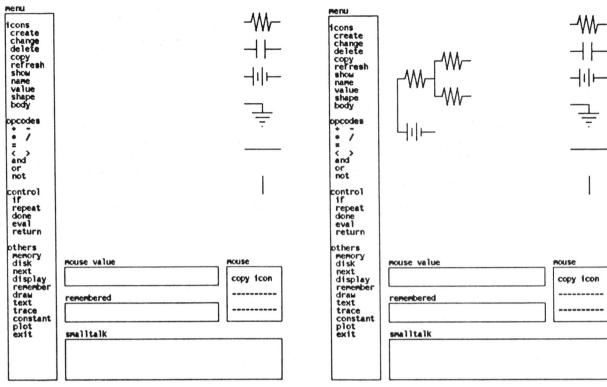

The COPY operation and a menu of electronic circuit elements	Several icons are copied from the menu and assembled into a circuit

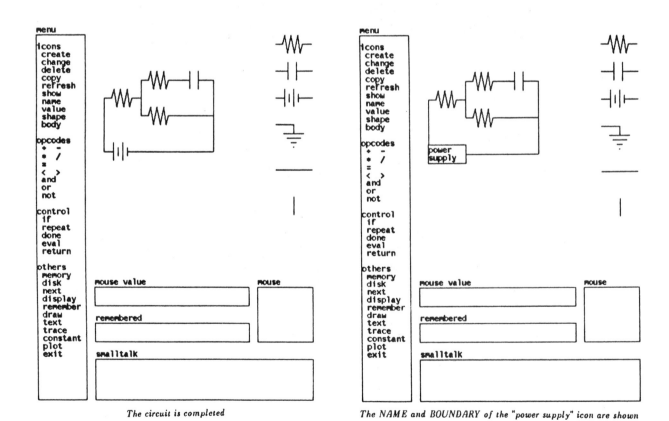

The circuit is completed	The NAME and BOUNDARY of the "power supply" icon are shown

248

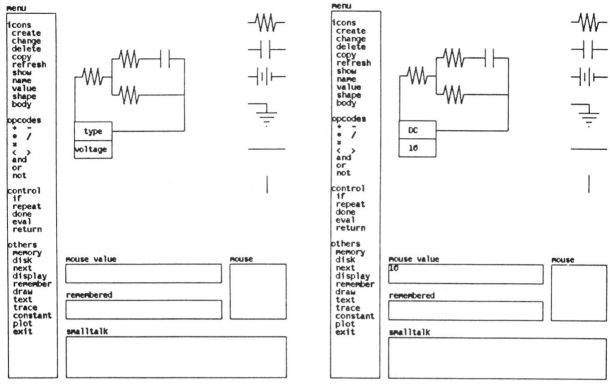

The iconic structure of the "power supply" icon is shown   *The power supply is set to 10 volts, direct current*

Section D -- Smalltalk Evaluator

This example contains part of a simulation of the Smalltalk evaluator. Several stages in the evaluation of a Smalltalk expression are displayed. The first two pictures present the principal memory structures involved: "activation records" (AREC) and "vector messengers" (VMESS). Subsequent frames show the creation and evolution of instances of these structures. The actual operations changing the contents of the fields are not shown, as they were in the FACTORIAL example; just the results of operations on the state of the structures are presented here.

```
to cons : hd tl
  (◁hd⇒
    (◁←⇒
      (⇑☞hd ← :)
    ⇑hd)
  ◁tl⇒
    (◁←⇒
      (⇑☞tl ← :)
    ⇑tl))
```

☞x ← cons 3 4

x hd + x tl

The Smalltalk statements involved are listed above in Smalltalk notation. Briefly, the symbols have the following meanings:

```
eyeball          peek ahead in the message stream for a literal
                     symbol

double right     conditional: evaluate the vector on the right
  arrow              if the expression on the left is true

double up        return the value of the expression on the right
  arrow

hand             quote the following atom

colon            fetch a message evaluated
```

249

The class presented simulates a LISP "cons" pair. It responds to the messages "hd" (head)
and "tl" (tail). The variable "x" is assigned the cons pair (3 . 4). Then the expression "x hd
+ x tl" is evaluated. The display frames describe the execution from this point.

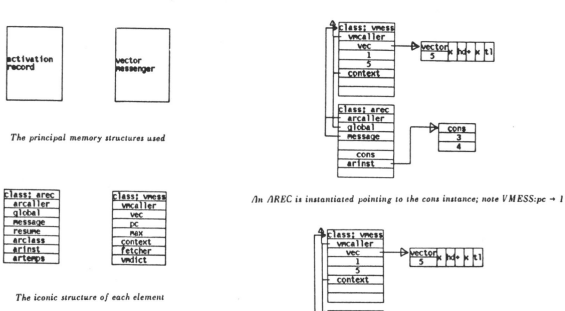

The principal memory structures used

An AREC is instantiated pointing to the cons instance; note VMESS:pc → 1

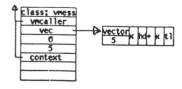

The iconic structure of each element

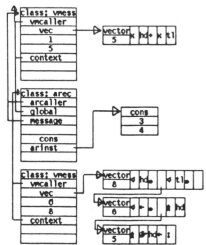

A VMESS is instantiated pointing to the vector (x hd + x tl)

A second VMESS is instantiated pointing to the CONS message handler

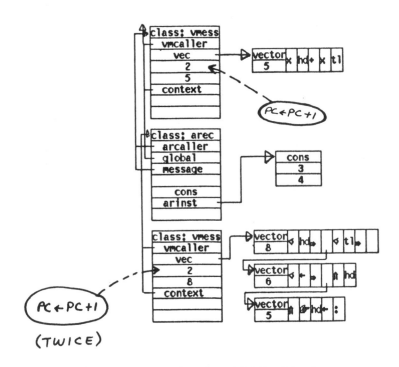

The message is scanned for the symbol "hd", and found

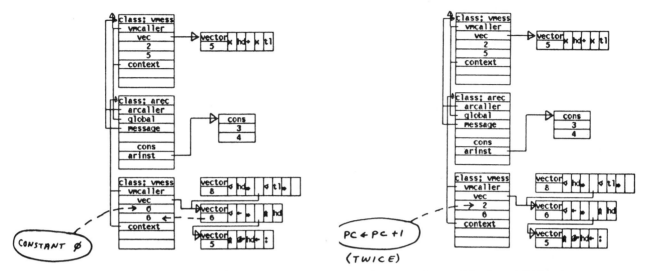

The second VMESS now points to the vector after the conditional arrow

The message is scanned for the symbol "←", and not found

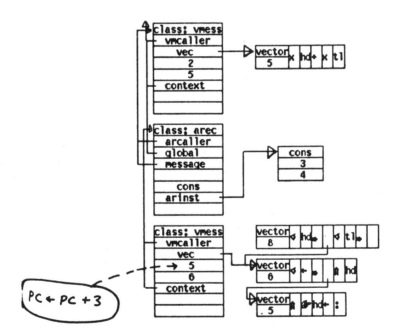

The return up-arrow is evaluated, which instantiates another AREC, etc.

251

A GRAPHICS-BASED PROGRAMMING-SUPPORT SYSTEM

H. P. Frei
D. L. Weller
R. Williams

IBM
Research Division
San Jose, CA.

ABSTRACT

A programming support system using extended Nassi-Shneiderman diagrams (NSD) is described. The aim of the work is to develop techniques for improving the quality and cost of specifying, documenting and producing computer programs. NSD's can be executed interpretively or compiled to produce running code. The system implementation has begun and charts can be drawn on a variety of display devices. The system is being developed using the Picture Building System developed earlier.

KEY WORDS AND PHRASES: interactive computer graphics, Nassi-Sheiderman diagrams, structured programming, program representation

CR CATEGORIES: 4.12, 4.13, 4.22, 4.33, 4.34, 8.2

THE SOFTWARE PROBLEM

During the last decade software systems showed the tendency of growing drastically in both size and complexity. Frequently, the increased size and complexity result in software systems that are unreliable, error prone, and difficult to maintain. Also, studies by the U.S. Navy have shown that in the last 20 years the cost of software for hardware/software systems has grown from less than 20% of the total cost to more than 75% of the total cost [BOE 73]. Many corporations have recognized the severity of this problem and have begun to study the software problem.

Capers Jones [JON 77] reports the deplorable fact that in the traditional world of programming more than half of the total effort expended goes to defect removal activities in the forms of testing and post-release defect repairs. Mills mentions that "some 75 percent of data processing personnel are already taken up with maintenance, not development. And unless radical new methods are found, maintenance will go even higher in its demands and will very nearly stifle further development" [MIL 76]. Documentation also seems to be a problem since Capers Jones indicates that for a large system it would take someone one or two months just to read the documentation [JON 77].

Thus we conclude that there is a great need for a software support system, possible based on existing concepts.

PROGRAM REPRESENTATION

It is our belief that what is needed is a total software support system along with a shift in emphasis in the software development process. The fact "that an application system is maintained indefinitely after a definite period of development" [MIL 76] as well as the tremendous decrease in hardware costs (along with increases in speed), should encourage one to choose reliability and maintainability as the dominant criterion rather than the more traditional execution speed when deciding on appropriate tools for software production. For example, it is much easier to speed up and optimize a neatly designed and reliable piece of software than to debug a fast running unstructured one. A total software support system must support the design, coding, debugging, maintenance, and documentation of software systems.

Most of the new programming techniques, in the literature often referred to as "Structured Programming" [DAH 71] or "Modern Style Programming" [JON 77], can lead to better software development. These techniques include graphic design methods like HIPO and Nassi-Shneiderman diagrams (NSD), top-down and modular programming, and on-line development of programs. It seems to be proved that "Modern Style Programming" is considerably less expensive than "Old Style Programming". Capers Jones even claims that these methods reduce debugging and maintenance costs by over 50% [JON 77]. The problem seems to be supplying a programming support system that supports "Modern Style Programming" and maybe even disallows nonstructured methods.

Graphical representations for design and implementation have been known to be of great value in engineering and many other fields. But many fields have an advantage over programming in that they have what could be called a "natural" graphical representation. By "natural" it is meant that the items of interest already have a two dimensional layout. For example, the formalism of schematic diagrams for electrical circuits just maintains the topology of electrical circuit connections without creating something new. Programming languages lack a "natural" graphical representation. Therefore an artificial graphical representation should be created that can be used for software design and implementation. Such a representation will undoubtedly facilitate the visualization of program structure making understanding of the program easier. The consequence of this is that the programs will be easier to write, debug, and maintain.

A number of graphical representations of programs have been used for a long time, but they have never, to our knowledge, been used in an interactive graphics environment for the purpose of programming. Three existing graphical representations are examined with a view to their possibilities as actual interactive graphical programming languages. The three methods examined are: flow charts, HIPO diagrams [STA 76], and Nassi-Shneiderman diagrams [NAS 73]. A number of people have mentioned structured flowcharts [CHA 74] [LIN 77], but these charts are very similar to Nassi-Shneiderman diagrams and will not be considered separately.

One of the oldest charting methods is the drawing of conventional flow charts. This method was developed originally for supporting the writing of programs in assembly or even machine language. Flow charts consist of very simple and self-explanatory symbols and have the property that they clearly demonstrate the control flow of the programs they represent. On the other hand, flowcharting does not support the modular design of programs, but rather allows the creation of "spaghetti bowl" designs that are difficult to test and correct. Unfortunately, these diagrams also have the tendency of spreading out over large sheets of paper. To overcome this disadvantage, several charts on different pieces of paper are connected together by so-called off-page connectors. It turns out, however, that it is very difficult to recognize the overall structure of a program represented by a large flow chart.

HIPO diagramming is a more recent technique for documenting and programming than flowcharting. Programs are represented by two distinct kinds of diagrams consisting of simple rectangular figures. One kind of diagram breaks a task down into subtasks using task and subtask descriptions in a natural language (e.g. English). The other kind of diagram describes the input, the actual action to be performed, and the output of each rectangular figure. Such an approach certainly supports top-down development of programs and clearly demonstrates the structure of the program in question. (The method was originally developed as a means of program documentation!). On the other hand, the structure and the action of the program are entirely separated. This is the reason that the breaking down of a task into subtasks becomes a rather arbitrary action when this method is employed. In addition, the use of a natural language with all its imprecision is a serious drawback. Furthermore, a HIPO diagram tends to show no context for the part of the program represented by the diagram, which makes it difficult to use as a design or testing vehicle. Needless to say, it does not help to prevent errors committed due to lack of information about the context.

NSDs were developed with the aim of supporting Structured Programming [NAS 73]. Programs are described by a collection of rectangular figures each of which represents a program segment. Such a rectangular figure may contain either a succession of simple statements written in the base language (e.g. PL/I) or other rectangular figures representing structured statements (e.g. IF, DO). It is quite an advantage that there are special NSD figures symbolizing structured statements like IF, DO, and CASE, even though these symbols have to be learned by the user. The size of an individual diagram representing a procedure is somewhat artificially restricted by the size of the sheet of paper. Although this approach greatly encourages modular design and clearly demonstrates both syntax and the logical meaning of each piece of the program, it is questionable as to whether it is also useful for the development of large programs. However, "Endicott programmers report that they prefer Nassi-Shneiderman charts to either flow charts or HIPO diagrams" [JON 77]. The use of NSD has been shown to be cost-effective, whereas the use of HIPO diagrams was shown to be cost-effective only some of the time, and the use of flowcharts was shown to be usually not cost-effective [JON 77]. Two existing partial programming support systems [GEW 77] [VAN 77] which make use of NSD claim to have noticed great advantages for software design and development. Unfortunately, neither of these systems allows a user to interact with an NSD in a graphics mode.

Undoubtedly, the proper use of NSD and HIPO diagrams can greatly support top-down development of programs and the understanding of a complex program structure. On the other hand, developing and drawing charts is a rather cumbersome process and if at a certain point during the design phase alterations to the program structure become necessary, the revision of the already drawn charts causes a great deal of work. Although there exist some interactive systems that support the drawing, charts representing a program are still manually translated into machine executable statements and this translation represents an additional source of errors. Also, an additional checking step becomes necessary. It is widely agreed that the introduction of graphics techniques into many kinds of human activities and in particular into program development is a great help. Usually two reasons are mentioned in this connection. First of all, it is an advantage to simply introduce an additional way of human perception as a supplement to reading. Secondly, graphical figures have proved to be a powerful way of communicating. Methods should be sought to integrate program documentation--often considered to be a secondary job of minor intellectual value--into the program development phase either by entirely automating documentation or by choosing a self-documenting program representation.

It should also be noted that there is convincing evidence to support the idea that the use of interactive systems reduces costs for software development [JON 77] [REA 74] [SAC 68].

Based on the material presented above, it is assumed that a software support system should provide a programming language with a graphical representation clear enough for documentation that can be edited in an interactive graphics fashion and automatically be converted into executable code, and should lead the user towards structured programming.

In order to help people produce correct programs that are self-documenting and easily read and understood by others, we have conceived of and designed a "Programming Support System". The specific goals of the Programming Support System are:

1. To develop both a programming system and techniques for improving the quality of specifying, documenting, and producing computer programs by
a) establishing charting techniques to specify programs in a way that clearly shows their structure and logic;
b) using an interactive graphics system to draw and edit these charts;
c) providing a preprocessor/compiler mechanism to translate charts into executable code;
d) providing self-documentation as a by-product of the program development process;
e) providing better, interactive diagnostics and program development aids than is currently the case using a program interpreter.
2. To evaluate the Programming Support System in real applications.

The Nassi-Shneiderman diagram has been extended in our work to include a data definition section and PL/I embedded statements so that it is possible to make an executable module from it. We refer to these extended Nassi-Shneiderman diagrams from here on and call them NSDs. With our Programming Support System a programmer can create and run NSDs, where an NSD corresponds to a program or procedure. It appears that the goals can be met with a system consisting of the following components:

1) An NSD (program) editor
2) An NSD interpreter
3) An NSD preprocessor/compiler
4) A dialog component for answering questions about NSDs and system commands.
5) A set of utility routines.

It is intended that the system would be run using a graphics terminal. The editor would allow a user to create an NSD graphically, adding and editing structure and program text until he is satisfied with it. A preprocessor could be invoked to produce a program (in PL/I for example) that could be compiled by a normal compiler. Alternatively an interpreter could be invoked to interpretively execute an NSD. The interpreter would provide higher-level diagnostics than would be obtained from the compiler. At any time the user could enter a question answering mode to find out what commands are available, (e.g. editing and compiling commands), or to find out what other NSDs are in the system database. One could also keep a catalog of NSDs together with a description of their function and I/O parameters so that they could be reusable. Various utility routines for copying NSDs etc. would be available also for convenience.

We have started to implement such a software support system using the Picture Building System [WEL 76] which provides a graphics software package, high-level application building tools and a (relational) database, all of which are needed for a Programming Support System.

The programming language is based on the graphical representations used by Nassi and Shneiderman [NAS 73] which we have extended and which we call an "NSD". An NSD is a separately executable module with no internal subroutines, that may contain calls to other NSDs and external subroutines. It seems desirable that the executable code, including general comments and remarks, should not exceed one page. Therefore the size of an NSD will be restricted (but not necessarily to the size of a physical screen).

Each NSD consists of two parts: 1) a data definition header, and 2) NSD constructs with embedded language statements. The data definition header includes the diagram name, a comment about its function, and a definition of the local variables and parameters used by the diagram. In the interest of maintaining a structured programming environment no global variables will be allowed (at least initially).

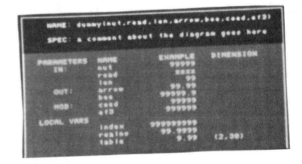

Figure 1. Example data definition header for an NSD.

The actual data definition consists of the declaration of the parameters followed by the declaration of the local variables as shown in the example in Fig. 1. There are three different classes of parameters IN, OUT and MOD, with the following meanings: IN - read-only, OUT - write only, MOD - read-write. Each data declaration is specified by example. The example given specifies the length and type of the variable, for example 999 means an integer with no more than three digits. If a specification is the same as another variable then that variable name can be used instead as in the example shown in Fig. 3, where MAXPOS is the same as n. The different types of data that can be specified are real or integer numbers, characters strings and bit strings. One may specify arrays also, for example: table 9.99(2,30) specifies an array size 2 by 30 of real numbers each of which has at most two decimal digits and one integer digit. Thus the dimension is specified in a manner similar to PL/I.

The executable part of an NSD consists of NSD constructs with embedded language statements for a

Figure can be found printed in color on page 655.

conventional language (e.g. PL/I). The NSD constructs specify the control flow and the language statements specify the actions to be performed. The allowable NSD constructs are: 1) a simple construct, 2) an IF construct, 3) a CASE construct and 4) a DO-LOOP construct. Fig.2 shows the syntax of the NSD programming language by means of two-dimensional flow diagrams. Capitals are used for terminal symbols. The allowable language statements are: 1) assignment, 2) call, and 3) input-output. Also for convenience comments and blank or null lines can be inserted anywhere. Initially the only language statements supported will be PL/I statements. Fig.3 shows an example of an NSD with PL/I language statements. A simple construct consists of a sequence of language statements. A DO-LOOP construct consists of NSD constructs and a conditional expression, which may be at the top, the bottom or anywhere in between. The NSD constructs are executed repeatedly while the condition remains true. An IF construct consists of a conditional expression at the top, NSD constructs on the left to be executed if the condition is true, and NSD constructs on the right to be executed if the condition is false. A CASE construct consists of an expression and several conditional parts, one of which is to be executed depending on the value of the expression. A default part is executed if the expression does not match any of the test values.

It remains to be seen whether restricting the programming language to allow programs that are structured in the sense described in this section and with the limited number of statement types would be accepted by people used to other programming methods.

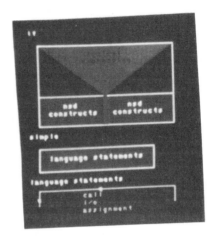

Figure 2. NSD syntax.

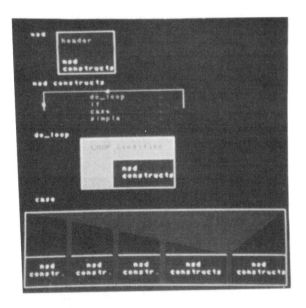

Figure 3. A sample NSD.

USER INTERFACE

Editing program text is a dynamic process and usually performed using an interactive system. Programs are normally designed by applying a succession of refinement steps [WIR 72]. Because of its dynamics, this process is rather difficult to perform by means of pencil and paper, since each refinement step is achieved by adding and/or inserting new material into the existing program. Thus, the ideal way to accomplish this activity is using a highly dynamic environment established by a special purpose interactive system.

Ideally, a user environment should be easy enough to handle that the general user is able to concentrate on the programming task without being distracted by the idiosyncrasies of the interactive system being employed. The interactive system has to be designed in a way that both the experienced and the inexperienced user may employ it with comparative ease. In particular, the user should not have to draw NSD constructs, or explicitly create space on the screen in order to include new constructs. Instead, these actions should be initiated by a high level screen-oriented command language to place and draw constructs.

Taking into account the above ideas, the system we designed displays both NSDs and messages to the user on a color graphics screen. Input is via a keyboard and a graphical pointing device which allows one to point to an arbitrary location on the screen.

The commands available are structured according to the five components mentioned in section 3, namely NSD editing, interpretation, preprocessing and compilation, question answering, and utility. From each of these command sets only commands specific to that set may be invoked. However, these different sets (or states) are interconnected and may be invoked iteratively.

Since editing commands invariably belong to the most frequently used commands of an interactive system, they are treated here in more detail. Note that these commands are not only used to edit, but also to create NSDs. Special attention has been devoted to making the invocation of these commands simple: typing a single letter, mostly in connection with pointing to a location on the screen, performs the desired action. The most important edit commands are:

flip	: flip to NSD header when the constructs are displayed and vice versa;
do loop	: draw a do loop construct;
if	: draw an if construct;
case	: draw a case construct;
simple	: draw a simple construct;
delete	: delete the construct pointed to (this command serves also to delete text lines);
text	: allows to place text within an NSD construct (i.e. to write language statements, conditions, and comments);
end	: leave the editor.

There are also commands which allow one to move a construct on the screen, and some conventional in-line editing commands to change character strings. In addition to that, a command to select the colors used by the system when NSD constructs are drawn is included as a convenience for the user.

Interpretive execution of NSDs will be provided to facilitate the development and debugging of programs. In addition, features will be provided to interpret an NSD step-wise, to stop at break points, to interrupt interpretation at any point of the NSD as well as to display and reset program variables at will. A number of simple commands serve to invoke all these activities.

The first realization of the system where PL/I is used as the embedded language has a preprocessor which translates an NSD into compilable PL/I code. There is only one command necessary to invoke this activity.

The question answerer is a quite important part of the system. It is active at all times and provides information about both the system itself (e.g. a list and a description of active commands) and existing NSDs (e.g. a list of NSDs and the NSDs they call).

Extra flexibility is gained by having utility routines to copy, delete, and rename NSDs.

To develop a program, the user creates an NSD diagram. First, he types in the name of the NSD which causes the system to provide the necessary relation in the underlying database [WEL 76] and to display an essentially empty NSD. (Of course, if an NSD with that name already exists, this NSD is displayed and made ready for editing.) Subsequently, the user is prompted to enter the specification and the declarations for the program to be developed. The specification part describes the action performed by the NSD, and currently is treated and stored as a comment. The specification has no influence on the execution of the program. The declarations, however, are used when the NSD is interpreted or translated into compilable code. It is to be noted that the user may redisplay a previously created declaration part at any time to edit or add declarations. This capability is especially important with respect to local variables which are hardly ever known prior to the development of the program body.

For the purpose of explaining how an NSD may be created, let us assume the following display on the screen:

Pointing near one of the corners between the two displayed constructs and typing L inserts the outline of a do loop construct between the two simple constructs:

Figure can be found printed in color on page 655.

256

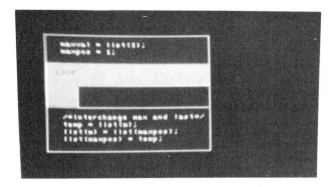

If the user points to the inside of an NSD construct and issues one of the construct drawing commands, the new construct is embedded. The following figures show how the outline of an if construct is embedded into an existing do loop construct:

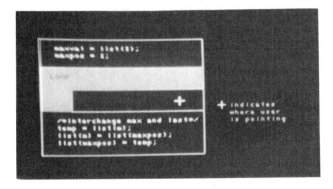

Given the above display and hitting I performs the desired action:

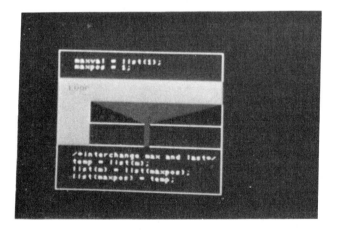

Although it is difficult to convey the flavor of a dialog by a verbal description, it might be seen that the above described commands constitute a highly interactive and flexible environment which is believed to be of great help when programs are being developed. For convenience most of the commands are invoked by a single key stroke.

The most outstanding characteristic of this system is that a graphical program representation is automatically translated into executable code, instead of producing NSDs as an after-effect as in existing systems [GEW 77] [VAN 77].

IMPLEMENTATION

The currently implemented Programming Support System runs on top of the Picture Building System (PBS) which provides a graphics software package, high-level application building tools, and a relational data base [WEL 76]. The Programming Support System is written as a collection of PL/I procedures and contains subroutine calls to both PBS and GXRAM [MOO 76], the graphical interface to the relational data base.

Besides PL/I programs, the Programming Support System consists of a small number of utility relations which hold part of the information necessary to draw the outlines of NSD constructs. For example, there is a distinct database relation for each of the possible NSD constructs and it contains the information about both the graphical appearance and the colors of that construct. Altering data in one of these relations causes all the occurrences of the associated construct to uniformly show up as different geometrical figures and/or to change colors. A number of references to these relations are created when drawing an NSD. Note that these utility relations are not needed when an NSD is interpreted or translated into executable code.

Apart from the database relations belonging to the system, there is a one-to-one correspondence between NSDs and relations in the data base. In other words: a program specified as an NSD is represented by only one ordered relation having the name of that NSD. This name is selected by the user when he creates the NSD and is also employed when the NSD is used. Such a relation contains data about both the action to be performed by the NSD and the NSD's graphical appearance on the screen. In contrast to the utility relations which are provided by the system, these relations are dynamically built up or altered as the user creates or edits the NSD. A relation representing an NSD contains information about the data declaration, the NSD constructs, and the embedded language statements.

The translation of an NSD into executable code is straightforward. In a first phase of the project, PL/I statements are used as embedded language statements (i.e. assignment, input/output, and call statements are written in PL/I). When compiling, NSD constructs will be translated into regular PL/I by a preprocessor. Then, the normal PL/I compiler and run-time system will take care of the further processing when an NSD is to be executed.

CONCLUSIONS

We have shown how a programming support system using extended Nassi-Shneiderman diagrams can be built. The main advantage of this programming support system is that a user works with a two-dimensional, graphical representation of his or

Figures can be found printed in color on page 656.

her programs, instead of a linear text string representation for a conventional programming language. Specifying a program as a two dimensional structure exhibits the meaning of a program more clearly and results in better coding, improved programming productivity and higher quality documentation thus reducing the time and effort (cost) for production and maintenance of software.

ACKNOWLEDGMENT

The authors wish to thank Herbert Weber and Jose Becerril who helped with the initial design of the programming support system presented in this paper.

REFERENCES

[BOE 73] Boehm, B.W. "Software and its Impact: A Quantitative Assessment", Datamation, Vol. 19, No. 9, May 1973.

[CHA 74] Chapin, N. "New Format for Flowcharts", Software Practice and Experience, Vol. 4 No. 4, Oct. 1974.

[DAH 72] Dahl, O.J., Dijkstra, E.W., and Hoare, C.A.R. "Structured Programming", Academic Press, New York, 1972.

[FAG 76] Fagan, M.E. "Design and code inspections to reduce errors in program development", IBM Syst. J., Vol. 15, No. 3, IBM Corporation, 1976.

[GEW 77] Gewald, K., et al. "COLUMBUS – Strukturierte Programmierung in der Praxis", Elektronische Rechenanlagen, 19. Jahrg., Heft 1, pp. 30-34, Feb. 1977.

[JON 77] Jones, C. "Program Quality and Programmer Productivity, IBM Technical Report, TR 02.764, Jan. 1977.

[LIN 77] Lindsay C.H. "Structure Charts – A Structured Alternative to Flowcharts", ACM SIGPLAN Notices, Vol. 12, No. 11, Nov. 1977.

[MAR 73] Martin, J. "Design of Man-Computer Dialogues", Prentice-Hall, Englewood Cliffs, N.J., 1973.

[MIL 76] Mills, H.D. "Software Development", IEEE Transactions on Software Engineering, Vol. SE-2, No. 4, Dec. 1976.

[MOO 76] Moorhead, W.G. "GXRAM, Relational Data Base Interface for Graphics", IBM Research Report RJ 1735, 1976.

[NAS 73] Nassi, I., and Shneiderman, B. "Flowchart Techniques for Structured Programming", SIGPLAN Notices of the ACM, Vol. 8, No. 8, Aug. 1973.

[REA 74] Reaser, J.M., et al "A Production Environment Evaluation of Interactive Programming", National Technical Information Service, AD/A-006 502, Dec. 1974.

[SAC 68] Sackman, H., Erikson, W.J., and Grant, E.E. "Exploratory Experimental Studies Comparing on-line an off-line Programming Performance", CACM, Vol. 11, No. 1, pp. 3-11, Jan. 1968.

[STA 76] Stay, J.F. "HIPO an integrated program design", IBM Syst. J., Vol. 15, No. 2, IBM Corporation, 1976.

[SUT 63] Sutherland, I.E. "Sketchpad, A Man-Machine Graphical Communication System", Proc. Spring Joint Conf., pp. 329-346, Spartan Books, New York, 1963.

[URS 75] Urschler, G. "Automatic Structuring of Programs", IBM J of Research and Development, pp. 181-193, March 1975.

[VAN 77] Van Gelder, A. "Structured Programming in Cobol: An Approach for Application Programmers", CACM, Vol. 20, No. 1, Jan. 1977.

[WEI 71] Weinberg, G.M. "The Psychology of Computer Programming", Van Nostrand, New York, 1971.

[WEL 76] Weller, D., and Williams, R. "Graphic and Relational Data Base Support for Problem Solving", Proc. of Conf. on Computer Graphics, SIGGRAPH-ACM, Vol. 10, No. 2, 1976.

[WIR 71] Wirth, N. "Program Development by Step-wise Refinement", CACM, Vol. 14, No. 4, pp. 221-227, April 1971.

PIGS--A System for Programming with Interactive Graphical Support

M. C. PONG and N. NG

Centre of Computer Studies and Applications, University of Hong Kong, Hong Kong

SUMMARY

This paper describes an implementation of a system for programming using structured charts with interactive graphical support. It provides a graphical editor for the user to interactively build and edit programs using Nassi-Shneiderman diagrams (NSD) as the structured control constructs of logic flow. It can interpret a program in NSD chart form, and the execution sequence of the NSD is displayed at a graphical terminal. On-line debugging and testing facilities are available which allow the user to examine and modify the program under execution. The system has been designed with the aim of supporting the development, debugging, testing, documentation and maintenance of programs in the same environment.

Keywords: Programming support system   Structured programming   Structured charts
             Nassi-Shneiderman diagrams   Graphical editor

INTRODUCTION

From about 1968 to the mid-1970s, there were many discussions on how to tackle the "software crisis" using "structured programming."[2,5] For example, the programming language Pascal[6] was designed with the aim to allow the programmer to formulate his thoughts in terms of abstractions suitable to his problem rather than in terms of facilities offered by his hardware.[7] One of Pascal's innovations was in the introduction of systematic control structures of logic flow.

The structure of the logic flow of a program is basically two-dimensional rather than linear, owing to the presence of selective and repetitive actions. If one has to write a program as a linear sequence of textual statements in a conventional programming language, even with suitable indentation, one loses something in understanding the two-dimensional nature of the logic flow involved. The conventional flowchart has existed for a long time as a means to depict the logic flow of a program, because graphical representation can give the human being a better grasp of the two-dimensional characteristics. It was developed originally for supporting programming in assembly language, which contained no inherent control structure of logic flow. For structured programming, researchers have proposed structured flowchart techniques.[1, 8, 11]

A pitfall using flowcharts (including structured flowcharts!) is that they are not the actual programs that get executed. There is often a discrepancy between the program coding and the flowchart. Special programs (e.g. References 12 and 13), have been produced to convert programs into structured chart format, but they are available only after the original source programs have been developed. It is more desirable if one can use structured charts directly for programming, with supporting tools to aid the process of program development and maintenance.

Frei *et al.*[14] have conceived of a graphics-based programming-support system that supports editing and execution of programs maintained in special chart forms. They proposed the use of Nassi-Shneiderman diagrams (referred to as NSD hereafter) as the structured control constructs of the logic flow of programs, after comparing NSD with conventional flowcharts, HIPO diagrams[15] and structured charts similar to NSD.[8, 9] Since all the NSD constructs are in rectangular form, this gives a neat and compact layout, and shows the scope of each construct clearly. Such a representation will facilitate the visualization of program structure and makes understanding of a program easier. The idea of using NSD for programming has been tested using a graphical editor and preprocessors for programs in NSD

"PIGS: A System for Programming with Interactive Graphical Support", by M.C. Pong and N. Ng, from *Software -- Practice and Experience*, Volume 13, Number 9, September 1983, pages 847-855. Reproduced by permission of John Wiley and Sons Limited.

Received 27 October 1984

0038/0644/83 090847 09$01.00

representation.[16] However, the preprocessor approach imposes another piece of software between the user and the program, and creates various difficulties for the programmer, particularly in debugging.

In this paper, we describe an experimental system for Programming with Interactive Graphical Support[17] (named as PIGS) which aids a programmer to develop, debug, test, document and maintain programs using NSD representation in the same environment. A program developed in PIGS is called an 'NSD program,' which is composed of one or more 'NSD modules' as program segments external to each other. The system provides an editor for a user at a graphics terminal to build and edit NSD programs, an interpreter to execute them and interactive facilities to aid program debugging and testing. Any modification of the program is performed as a modification of the NSD representation. When an NSD program is ready for execution, the documenting flowchart is already available and can be recorded as hard copy for program maintenance.

THE SYSTEM PIGS

The important feature of PIGS is that its interpreter can execute an NSD program in chart form directly. An interpreter rather than a compiler is used because it allows the user to interact with the program flexibly during execution and makes changes to the NSD program. The user can watch and follow the logic flow of an NSD program as execution proceeds. In the course of executing each NSD construct which represents sequential, selective or repetitive control flow, the construct outline and the embedded test are displayed and brightened up at the graphics terminal. Sequential action is visualized as the sequential display of constructs. Selection action is shown as the display of those constructs which are to be executed depending on the selection condition. Repetition action is seen as repeated brightening of the construct until the repetition condition does not hold. The system thus enables the static NSD representation of a program to be executed in the same chart form. This helps a programmer to understand the logic flow of a program and locate areas of erratic behavior more easily.

PIGS also provides interactive debugging and testing aids to support program development. If any syntax error is detected during interpretative execution of a construct, the display will halt and allow the user to correct the error, or to interact with the program by examining or modifying the values of the variables used in the program. Immediately after, execution can start again. Moreover, a user can set a break-point on any construct. On every execution of that construct, the display will halt and allow the user to examine or modify the program. To detect data flow anomaly,[18] the system provides facilities to perform dynamic data flow analysis on all the variables used. These features are described below.

AN IMPLEMENTATION

PIGS has been implemented on an experimental basis at the University of Hong Kong as a Pascal program using the OMSI Pascal-1 Version 1.2 compiler[19] on a PDP-11/70 computer operating under RSTS/E Version 7. The NSD can be displayed on a Tektronix 4010 storage tube graphics terminal. Owing to the limitations of the RSTS/E system, overlaying of programs is necessary for PIGS to run. The organization of PIGS can be divided into three modules. One of these modules is for manipulating the underlying data structure and generating displays of NSD. This module is always resident in the primary memory. The other two modules are the NSD editor and the interpreter. They overlay one another in the same region of primary memory.

An NSD program developed in PIGS consists of a main NSD module which may call other NSD modules as external subroutines. An NSD module consists of a HEADER block and a module body (Figure 1). The NSD module name, formal parameter list, constants, variables and external NSD module names are declared in the HEADER block. Three other NSD constructs are allowed in the module body, namely SIMPLE construct, LOOP construct and IF construct (Figure 2).

In Figure 2, the unshaded area inside a construct is the 'identification area' of the construct. If the user positions the crosshair cursor inside this area and enters a command, PIGS will know that this indicated construct is the one to be operated on and the appropriate action will be taken.

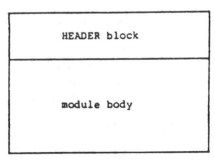

Figure 1. NSD module

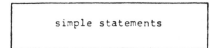

(a)   SIMPLE construct

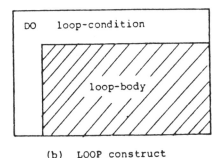

(b)   LOOP construct

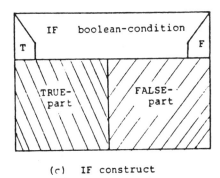

(c)   IF construct

Figure 2 Basic NSD constructs

The LOOP and IF constructs contain inner block(s) (the shaded area shown in Figure 2) which can contain sequence of NSD constructs. As can be seen from the diagram, an IF construct includes a TRUE-part and a FALSE-part, which is equivalent to an IF-THEN-ELSE control structure. A LOOP construct includes a loop-body as the inner block. Figure 2(b) is used as the construct for three types of LOOP structure--DO-WHILE loop, DO-UNTIL loop and DO-FOR loop--instead of using different shapes of construct as originally proposed by Nassi and Shneiderman.[1] Thus PIGS supports all the control structures of the Pascal language with the exception of the CASE and GOTO statements.

At present, PIGS only allows the use of integers and one-dimensional arrays in NSD programs. Text following Pascal syntax rules is to be entered by the user into the identification area of the constructs. External NSD module calls, if any, have to be explicitly declared in the HEADER block. Inside a SIMPLE construct, only assignment, read/write and external NSD module invoking statements are allowed. The IF condition is a boolean expression, so must be WHILE-loop and UNTIL-loop conditions. In the case of a FOR-loop condition, an iteration range must be entered. Since the constructs are easily distinguishable, keywords such as BEGIN and END are not required.

The semantics of NSD programs follow that of Pascal except:

.(a) . Pascal scope rules do not apply. The calling of other NSD modules is treated as invoking external subroutines. They are not nested, but recursive cells are allowed.

.(b) . No global data structure is allowed.

.(c) . All communication between NSD modules are through parameter passing. Parameters may be passed by-value or by-reference except that array parameters must be declared explicitly as passed by-reference.

As an example, the NSD module for an interchange sort program for sorting N numbers in descending order is shown in Figure 3. Notice that the program has a bug because in the IF construct, the boolean condition is incorrectly typed as 'A[I]< = A[I+1]' instead of 'A[I]<A[I+1].' The program will loop infinitely if some input numbers are equal. Since the execution sequence of NSD is displayed on the screen, the user on watching the never-ending display of the DO-UNTIL loop will immediately realize that something is wrong with the program.

The data structure for representing an NSD is a tree. Editing and execution of NSD are made by manipulation and traversal of this underlying tree structure. A node of the tree corresponds to an NSD construct. It contains the physical dimension data for displaying the constructs as well as the embedded text lines. Pointers from the node link it to the inner body of the construct and the next construct that follows.

NSD EDITING

Using the graphical editor, a user can interactively build or edit an NSD. All the editor actions are performed as operations on the underlying tree structure. The editor commands are summarized in the Appendix. Most of the commands operate on constructs. When the crosshair cursor (simply referred to as the cursor hereafter) appears, the user can position it inside the identification area of a construct and type a command. PIGS make use of the cursor co-ordinates to determine which construct is picked and then the appropriate action is taken. Insertion and deletion of constructs are performed as tree node insertion and deletion, respectively. The effect of the delete command is merely observed as crossing out the construct on the screen. Actual node deletion is performed on redrawing the NSD module when the tree structure is traversed. Thus, it is possible to cancel the deletion before redrawing by using a 'cancel delete' command, which is desirable for recovery from a mistake.

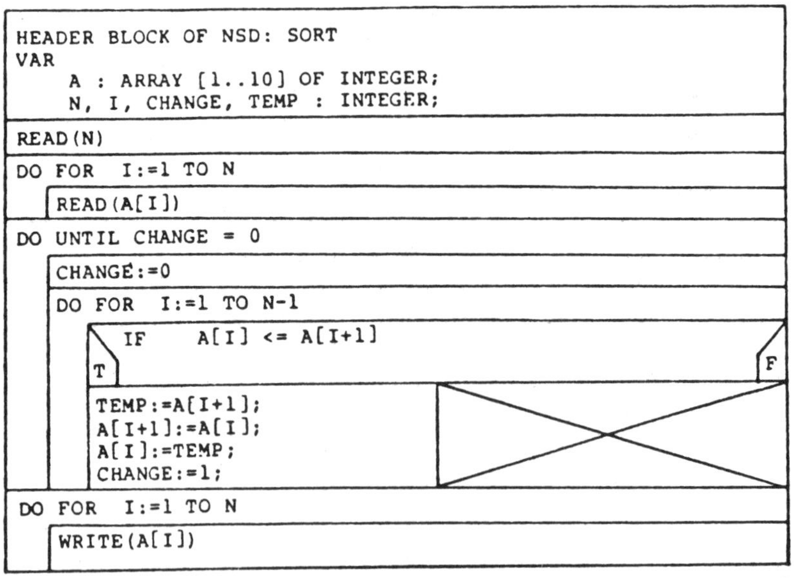

```
┌─────────────────────────────────────────────────────────────────────────────┐
│ HEADER BLOCK OF NSD: SORT                                                     │
│ VAR                                                                           │
│       A : ARRAY [1..10] OF INTEGER;                                           │
│       N, I, CHANGE, TEMP : INTEGER;                                           │
├─────────────────────────────────────────────────────────────────────────────┤
│ READ(N)                                                                       │
├─────────────────────────────────────────────────────────────────────────────┤
│ DO FOR  I:=1 TO N                                                             │
│   ┌───────────────────────────────────────────────────────────────────────┐ │
│   │ READ(A[I])                                                              │ │
├───┴───────────────────────────────────────────────────────────────────────┴─┤
│ DO UNTIL CHANGE = 0                                                           │
│   ┌───────────────────────────────────────────────────────────────────────┐ │
│   │ CHANGE:=0                                                               │ │
│   ├───────────────────────────────────────────────────────────────────────┤ │
│   │ DO FOR  I:=1 TO N-1                                                     │ │
│   │   ┌──────────────────────────────────────────────────────────────────┐│ │
│   │   │╲      IF     A[I] <= A[I+1]                                      ╱││ │
│   │   │ ╲                                                               ╱ ││ │
│   │   │T ╲                                                             ╱ F││ │
│   │   ├───────────────────────────┬──────────────────────────────────────┤│ │
│   │   │ TEMP:=A[I+1];             │╲                                    ╱ ││ │
│   │   │ A[I+1]:=A[I];             │ ╲                                  ╱  ││ │
│   │   │ A[I]:=TEMP;               │  ╲                                ╱   ││ │
│   │   │ CHANGE:=1;                │   ╲                              ╱    ││ │
├───┴───┴───────────────────────────┴──────────────────────────────────────┴┴─┤
│ DO FOR  I:=1 TO N                                                             │
│   ┌───────────────────────────────────────────────────────────────────────┐ │
│   │ WRITE(A[I])                                                             │ │
└───┴───────────────────────────────────────────────────────────────────────┴─┘
```

Figure 3. An interchange sort program for sorting N numbers in descending order (with a bug)

When the NSD module is to be redrawn starting from an indicated construct, the corresponding tree node is located and preorder traversal of the tree starting from this node is carried out. On visiting each node, the construct and its embedded test are displayed on the screen. For a relatively large NSD module (which is not recommended under the guidelines of modular programming), the screen cannot accommodate all of its constructs. Those constructs beyond the screen limits are not shown, but can be seen by scrolling the viewport. The display will start from the desired construct which is drawn to full screen width. Thus a zooming effect on NSD is achieved.

To edit the text lines, i.e. the program statements, inside the constructs, the user can issue the editor command 'T.' PIGS will enter the text-editing mode and display the text of the construct. Text-editing is performed as insertion and deletion operations on the linked list of text lines associated with the tree node. The user uses 'X' to delete or 'S' to substitute the line. When the command 'E' is issued, PIGS exits from the text-editing mode and returns to the NSD editing mode.

INTERPRETATIVE EXECUTION OF AN NSD PROGRAM

The user can request for interpretative execution of an NSD program while the editor is handling the main NSD module of the program. The tree structure of the NSD module is traversed, starting from the root, according to the type of the node being visited. If it is a SIMPLE node, the construct is displayed and then executed. For an IF node, the IF-condition, i.e. a boolean expression, is first evaluated. Then one of the inner blocks of the IF construct is executed depending on the result of evaluating the boolean expression. For a LOOP node, execution follows the semantics of the LOOP types depending on whether it is a DO-WHILE loop, a DO-UNTIL loop or a DO-FOR loop. The LOOP-condition is evaluated and checked on each iteration through the loop. If the iteration condition is true, the LOOP body is traversed.

At the start of interpretation, a symbol table using the declaration information of the HEADER block is built. Then the constructs following the HEADER block are executed one after the other. In executing each construct, its text is processed using Wirth's Pascal implementation methodology.[20] A recursive descent technique is used to parse the text content of an NSD construct. A string of postfix codes is generated, which are then executed via a stack mechanism. If syntax error occurs, PIGS halts. The user can edit the text content of the current construct or that of the HEADER block immediately. The latter is necessary in case an identifier has not been declared in the HEADER block. Of course, any modification of the HEADER block will require interpretation from the beginning of the NSD to effect the declaration.

Before execution starts, the user can request run-time interaction. PIGS will prompt the user to set a break-point at a construct by means of the cursor. The node is remembered. Execution will be halted when this mode is encountered and will be restarted only at the request of the user. Whenever PIGS halts, the user is provided with facilities for interactive debugging. This includes commands for examining and modifying the variables and array elements used in the module, setting or removing a break point and editing the text of the current construct or the HEADER block. The user also has the choice to continue the execution or to abandon and return to the editor.

PIGS supports modular programming by allowing an NSD to invoke other NSD modules directly and recursively. Modules are regarded as external to each other in the current implementation rather than nested according to Pascal scope rules. The main reason for this decision is memory size limitation. If an external NSD module is called, swapping of the calling module and the called module is performed. On entry to an external module, PIGS allows the user to choose to enter the external module or bypass it for direct return. If the direct return option is chosen (say, in the case that the external module has not been created), the actual parameter list in the calling module is not processed, and PIGS halts. At this point, the user can examine or modify the calling module. For example, the user may assign some values to the actual parameters of the module invoking statement before the execution continues. In this way, PIGS allows for top-down program development and testing because a test run of a program can be carried out even if some external modules are not yet developed.

Table 1. State transition table for data flow analysis

| | State | | | |
Action	U	R	D	F
Undefine	U	U	A	U
Reference	E	R	R	F
Define	D	D	A	E
As-For-loop-index	F	F	A	E
Pass-in-by-reference	U	D*	D*	A
Pass-in-by-value	U	D*	D*	D*

N.B. Program variables or array elements may assume the following states:
U--Undefined.
R--Referenced.
D--Defined but not referenced.
F--For-loop-index, to be referenced, but not defined.
A--Abnormal.
E--Error (a kind of anomaly which is fatal).
*Since parameter passing is done by copy-restore mechanism, a variable with a value passed into the called module is regarded as in DEFINED state.

To aid program testing, PIGS automatically performs data flow analysis on an NSD program. Each variable or array element used in the program is associated with a STATUS field which records its state during the course of execution. STATUS may take one of the values UNDEFINED, DEFINED, REFERENCED or FOR-loop-INDEX. It is updated whenever a program action is performed on a variable or an array element. The state transition rules of the various actions on the states used by PIGS for data flow analysis are shown in Table I. Four kinds of data flow anomalies can be identified:

.(a). undefine a DEFINED variable or array element

.(b). define a DEFINED variable or array element

.(c). use a DEFINED variable as a FOR-loop INDEX variable

.(d). use a FOR-loop INDEX variable as passed-by-reference actual parameter, thus the FOR-loop INDEX value may be altered on return from the called NSD module.

When a data anomaly is detected, PIGS will halt as at break-point, display the nature of the anomaly and allow the user to determine the next step. This interactive testing aid thus helps the user to locate and correct possible programming errors.

DISCUSSION

PIGS has been designed to provide interactive support for writing and testing programs in structured chart form. The dynamic as well as static flow of the programs under test can be observed by the user at a graphics terminal. This enables a programmer to understand how the program behaves more clearly. Also, there is no need to worry about discrepancies between the program and the documenting flowchart since they are the same. In fact, the NSD charting facilities provide a structure for hierarchical design of programs. It can also be used to specify functions and control flow, prior to the actual writing of programs. What is written inside the NSD can be pseudo-code or natural language.[21,22] This serves as a bridge in top-down software development between higher-level design block diagrams and lower level implementation coding. Using the graphical editor of PIGS, the NSD developed in the top-down design process can be recorded as the document of detailed design. Thus, PIGS supports the design, development, editing, debugging, testing, documentation and maintenance of NSD programs in the same environment.

If the current implementation of PIGS is enhanced to support more data types and control structures, the system can be used as a production tool in a real world programming environment. We believe that such a programming support system will help to reduce the cost of program development and maintenance.

APPENDIX: SUMMARY OF NSD EDITOR COMMANDS

The NSD editor commands can be classified into three categories. Only some of the functions are described below; details of the commands are given in Reference 17.

The first group is related to insertion and deletion of a construct in the NSD module:

. Cancel deletion (C)--Cancel the deletion of a construct.

. Delete construct (X)--Delete the indicated construct.

. Insert-before (B)--Enter the 'insert-before' mode for inserting a new construct before the indicated construct.

. Insert IF construct (I)--Insert an IF construct at the cursor location.

. Insert LOOP construct (L)--Insert a LOOP construct at the cursor location.

. Insert SIMPLE construct (S)--Insert a SIMPLE construct at the cursor location.

The second group of editor commands is used for displaying the NSD module.

. Redraw (R)--Redraw the NSD module starting from the indicated construct.

. Scroll down viewport (D)--Scroll down the viewport for displaying NSD module.

. Scroll up viewport (U)--Scroll up the viewport for displaying NSD module.

. Vary text length (V)--Vary (shorten) the length of the text lines so that all text can be displayed on the screen.

The last group is miscellaneous commands:

. Abandon editing (A)--Abandon the editing of the current NSD module.

. Execute NSD module E--Start execution of the NSD module.

. Finish editing (F)--Exit the editor.

. Text edit (T)--Enter the text-editing mode for editing text in constructs.

. Help messages (?)--Display the help messages for using the editor commands.

REFERENCES

1. .I. Nassi and B. Shneiderman, "Flowchart techniques for structured programming," *ACM SIGPLAN Notices*, 8 (8), 12-26 (1973).

2. .P. Denning (Ed.), *Computing Surveys '74, The Special Issue on Programming*, 6 (4), (1974).

3. .O.J. Dahl, E.W. Dijkstra and C.A.R. Hoare, *Structured Programming*, Academic Press, London, 1972.

4. .E.W. Dijkstra, "Goto statement considered harmful," *CACM*, 11 (3), 147-148 (1968).

5. .L.H. Weiner, "The roots of structured programming," *ACM SIGCSE Bulletin*, 10 (1), 243-254 (1978).

6. .N. Wirth, "The programming language, Pascal," *Acta Informatica*, 1 (1), 35-63 (1971).

7. .N. Wirth, "Programming languages: what to demand and how to access them," in P.H. Perrott (Ed.), *Software Engineering, Proceedings of a Symposium held at the Queen's University of Belfast 1976*, Academic Press, London, 1977, pp. 155-173.

8. .N. Chapin, "New format for flowcharts," *Software--Practice and Experience*, 7 (5), 553-584 (1977).

9. .C.H. Lindsay, "Structured charts--a structured charts--a structured alternative to flowcharts," *ACM SIGPLAN Notices*, 12 (11), 36-48 (1977).

10. .N.M. Rothon, "Design structure diagrams: a new standard in flow diagrams," *BCS Computer Bulletin, Series 2*, (19), 4-6 (March 1979).

11. R.W. Witty, "Dimensional flowcharting," *Software--Practice and Experience*, 7 (5), 553-584 (1977).

12. J.F. Gimpel, "CONTOUR--a method of preparing structured flowcharts," *ACM SIGPLAN Notices*, 15 (10), 35-41 (1980).

13. .P. Roy, "Linear flowchart generator for a structured language," *ACM SIGPLAN Notices*, 11 (11), 58-64 (1976).

14. .H.P. Frei, D.L. Weller and R. Williams, "A graphics-based programming-support system," *ACM SIGGRAPH*, 12 43-49 (1978).

15. J.F. Stay, "HIPO--an integrated program design," *IBM System Journal*, 15 (2), IBM Corporation, 1976.

16. .N. Ng, "A graphical editor for programming using structured charts," *Digest of Paper, IEEE COMPCON 79*, Spring 1979, pp. 238-243.

17. .M.C. Pong, "A system for programming with interactive graphical support," *M. Phil. thesis*, University of Hong Kong, July 1980.

18. J.C. Huang, "Detection of data flow anomaly through program instrumentation," *IEEE Trans. Software Engineering*, SE-5 (3), 226-236 (1979).

19. .*OMSI Pascal-1 Version 1.2 Language Specification*, Oregon Minicomputer Software Inc., January 1980.

20. *N. Wirth, Algorithm + Data Structures = Programs*, Prentice-Hall, Englewood Cliffs, New Jersey, 1976.

21. .D. Marca, "A method for specifying structured programs," *ACM SIGSOFT Software Engineering Notes*, 4 (3), 21-31 (1979)

22. .C.M. Yoder and M.L. Schrag, "Nassi-Shneiderman charts: an alternative to flowcharts for design," *Proc. Software Quality and Assurance Workshop*, November 1978, pp. 79-86.

Pict:
An Interactive Graphical Programming Environment

Ephraim P. Glinert and Steven L. Tanimoto, University of Washington

More and more people are today finding that they are able to successfully use computers, especially personal and home computers, thanks to an abundance of well-designed "canned" software. Those who wish to progress beyond the canned software stage, however, discover that programming is painstaking work. Worse yet, *learning* to program is, for many, even more forbidding; indeed, the attempt is often eventually abandoned in frustration.

Frustration comes largely from inadequacies in common procedural, text-based programming languages. As Smith has pointed out, "The representation of a problem in most programming languages bears little resemblance to the thought processes that occurred in its solution."[1] Why do programmers—especially novices—often encounter difficulties when they attempt to transform the human mind's *multidimensional, visual,* and often *dynamic* conception of a problem's solution into the *one-dimensional, textual,* and *static* representa-

tion required by traditional programming languages? The groups of italicized antonyms in the preceding sentence may give one hint. Another reason may be that the type and variable names we use in our programs, such as "x" or "root," are *signs* that bear no resemblance to their values (an integer, say, or a pointer to a binary tree of records of some type). Yet another explanation may be that the von Neumann paradigm of procedural programming is inherently unsuitable; some other method of programming, perhaps more functional, might prove easier to assimilate.

Because of this general dissatisfaction, repeated attempts have been made to design "new, improved" programming languages. We believe that a radical departure from current programming styles is necessary if programming is to be made more accessible. Attempts to evolve new varieties of conventional languages will not suffice. With the cost of graphics displays decreas-

ing—and availability, most notably as integral components of personal computers, increasing—we believe it is time to take advantage of the human brain's ability to process pictures more efficiently than text. As Malone said, "Perhaps the best use of sound and graphics...is to represent and convey information more effectively than [is possible] with words or numbers."[2]

In this article we describe our work on developing a programming methodology called Pict that permits humans to use their native intelligence in programming. Our results represent but an imperfect collection of beginnings in a field now in its infancy. Still, our work straddles the interface of several established disciplines, the primary ones being (1) the design and implementation of programming systems (including languages) and (2) the psychology and ergonomics, or human factors, of human-machine communication. Although Pict systems make heavy use of computer graphics, our work did

EH0324-4/90/0000/0265/$01.00 © 1984 IEEE

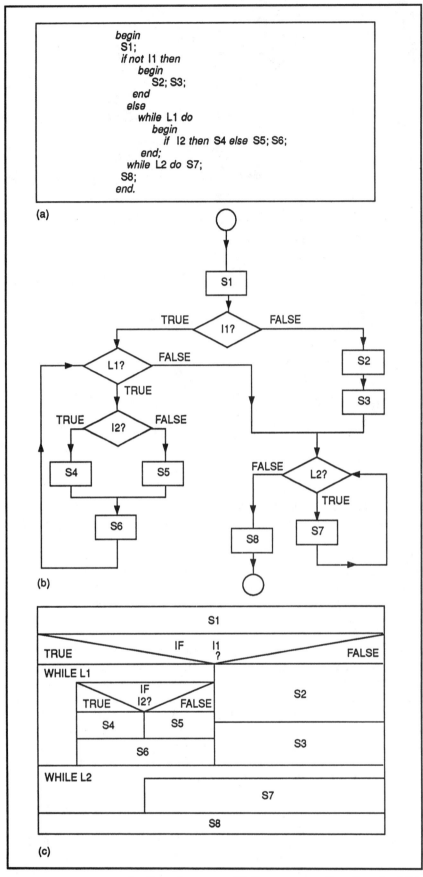

```
        begin
        S1;
        if not I1 then
            begin
                S2; S3;
            end
        else
            while L1 do
                begin
                    if I2 then S4 else S5; S6;
                end;
            while L2 do S7;
        S8;
        end.
```

(a)

(b)

(c)

Figure 1. A segment of a Pascal program (a), its corresponding flowchart (b), and a Nassi-Shneiderman structure diagram (c).

not constitute actual research into this field.

Pict is designed to aid program implementation rather than algorithm design and selection. This approach is appropriate for two reasons. The first is that many people find it hard or even impossible to learn how to use existing programming languages. The second is that, while one can reasonably argue that designing a good, new algorithm is probably harder than overcoming any obstacles to its implementation, the vast majority of programs—and certainly those written by beginning students —actually employ old (familiar) algorithms, perhaps combined in new ways.

The limited domain of programs that our Pict systems are capable of supporting (the data types, for example, are limited to the nonnegative integers in our main system) and the informal methodology employed in our experiments may elicit some criticism. With respect to the first of these issues, we make no claim that the systems implemented are general-purpose programming environments suitable for carrying out large-scale projects. Our systems were intended to serve as experimental prototypes capable of supporting small, but nontrivial, programs similar to those often assigned to students in introductory programming courses. We know that novices and experienced programmers approach programming problems in significantly different ways, and that writing a large program is fundamentally different from writing a small one. Nevertheless, we believe our systems have been successful in providing insights both into questions concerning the design of interactive, graphical programming environments in general and into their acceptance, at least by a specific class of user.

With respect to our experiments, the literature abounds with valid criticisms leveled against imprecise work that lacks proper methodological techniques. We will return to this point later on, but for the time being, suffice it to say that we are

COMPUTER

aware of the problem yet believe that the conclusions drawn from our experiments are warranted and supportable.

Using images in programming

How does one commonly program a computer today? Once the algorithm has been selected, its implementation as a program has four steps:

- Select signs for the data structures and needed variables, trying to use the most meaningful names possible.
- Encode the algorithm as a linear text string that conforms to certain syntactic and semantic rules (those depend on the language used for implementation). Sometimes, in an effort to clarify the logical structure of programs, aids such as indentation or letters of different cases are used to denote various groups of language elements, such as reserved words.
- Run the program and wait for results, regardless of whether the programming environment is batch or interactive.
- If the results seem incorrect, try to figure out where the "bugs" are. Then, modify the program and go back to the previous step.

However, if we could, we might well prefer to program in the following manner, at least for certain types of applications:

- Select images that *visually represent* the data structures and variables needed.
- *Draw* the desired algorithm as a logically structured, multidimensional picture.
- *Watch* the program run and *see* the results being generated.
- If the program isn't doing what is expected, *see where* and *when* the error(s) occur.

This sketch of a graphical approach to programming and interaction with the computer elucidates

what we mean by *iconic programming* and an *interactive, graphical programming environment*. In general, we can classify programming environments as textual (including Pascal, Cobol, Lisp, and the like —clearly of no interest to us here), visual, or iconic, according to the degree to which they employ text as opposed to graphics. These categories are not disjoint, however.[3]

A programming language or system is termed *visual,* as opposed to textual, if one or both of the following conditions hold.

(1) Higher level graphical entities are made available to users as atoms that they may (or perhaps are required to) manipulate in either the programming or runtime environment. Here, higher level graphical entities are geometric objects, such as circles and squares, or any image that does not represent individual characters in the standard programming alphabet ("alphabet" being used in the formal language-theory sense). Higher graphical entities are not the mere ability to reference individual pixels.

(2) Graphical elements (which may contain text and numbers as components) form an integral, not merely decorative, part of the display generated by the system for users in either the programming or runtime environment.

A visual programming system is termed *iconic* if the programming process is essentially to select and/or compose icons and place them in proper juxtaposition on the screen. Icons are images that have associated syntactic and semantic rules allowing them to represent language elements. Since icons can sometimes be placed to partially or completely overlap, we can assume that, like overlay planes for a single frame in an animated cartoon, they are "drawn" on transparent backgrounds.

All environments examined in the following pages are visual or iconic. Note that, according to our criteria the Apple Macintosh Pascal interpreter is *not* a visual system because it employs graphics essentially as decoration.

Most computer users feel that programming and human-machine communication in general ought to be more visual. Of course, the use of flowcharts for program description and documentation has long been established. With the advent of so-called "structured programming," it is common to indent blocks of code in typed programs to highlight their logical interrelation; in addition, Nassi-Shneiderman structure diagrams have been introduced.[4] Figure 1 displays a flowchart and N-S diagram for a segment of Pascal code.

More recently, directed graphs for language syntax specification have

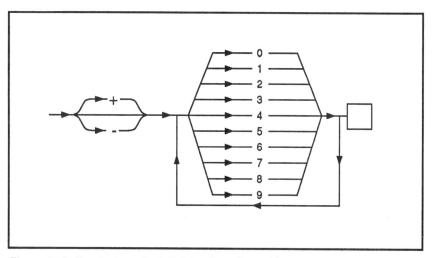

Figure 2. A directed graph definition for a Pascal integer.

become commonplace, as attested to by any modern text on Pascal (Figure 2). Unfortunately, all of the aforementioned graphical aids have traditionally served merely as tools for external program documentation, even in the rare instances when they are computer generated. Because they do not comprise the programs themselves, there are serious drawbacks to their use, primarily during the debugging process when they inevitably cease to represent the code that actually gets executed.

What are some of the features of images that make them potentially powerful and useful tools in the computational environment? First, they provide a natural supplement to other means of communication; in Smith's terminology,[1] the "translation distance" required for image comprehension is often small. For this reason, images often serve as the entire means of communication. Take, for example, international traffic signs. In addition, graphics (and sound) may be able to convey certain information more effectively than words and numbers; witness the impression created by a good graphic representation of a function as opposed to that produced by a long table of floating point numbers.

Second, human image memory and processing capabilities are powerful "parallel processors." Images are often easily learned, retained, and recalled as single units of information. This concept is important, because there appear to be physiological limits to the number of data "chunks" we can concurrently access,[5] whether they are visual or any other kind. Clearly, a single image may contain a wealth of detailed information; however, our brains still treat the entire image as a unit insofar as the "chunk count" is concerned. Thus, images may provide a high bandwidth for human-machine communication.

Third, images may possess a universality that natural languages and their associated programming languages do not. Thus, throughout

Europe we find standardized signs in airports and on restroom doors—signs that can be understood by people who speak many languages.

Finally, the rapidly falling cost of graphics-related hardware coupled with a dramatic increase in performance means that images are becoming more and more suitable for human-machine communication.

Of course, just any use of images is not necessarily beneficial. The use of arbitrary or over-detailed images, for example, may be more confusing than informative (consider the use of

---

Images are easily learned, retained, and recalled as single units of information, often serving as the entire means of communication.

---

flowcharts at the block or subprogram level as opposed to the single-instruction level). We may want to redundantly encode pertinent data, such as when we indent the blocks in our Pascal programs. Whatever images we employ, however, should be easy to revise, as exemplified by Pascal compilers that automatically indent versus those that require the user to reindent at each revision. We do not go as far as Lodding, who cautions, "The single most important point in the actual rendering of an icon is that it should be done by a [professional] graphic designer,"[6] but reasonable care must surely be taken. We will return to this point later, when we discuss our experiences with Pict.

The aforementioned notwithstanding, research into interactive, graphical programming environments seems to have remained rather esoteric until recently, when literature devoted to it began to mushroom. Nevertheless, graphical programming systems of various sorts have been proposed over the years and prototypes have been implemented, albeit usually in an experimental environment.

Past and present systems

Visual programming systems. In this section's essentially chronological history of visual programming systems, we must unfortunately be brief, but interested readers can find more details (along with an extensive bibliography) elsewhere.[3] To facilitate our discussion, we need to define some terms:

(1) *Procedural/nonprocedural programming system.* A programming system is procedural if users need to specify the steps the computer must follow to generate the desired results. A system is nonprocedural if users must tell it what they want done, but not how to go about doing it (that is, the system uses appropriate built-in strategies to decide how to satisfy user requests). Fortran, Pascal, Cobol, and other common languages are procedural; statistical packages such as SPSS and BMDP are simple nonprocedural systems in which the user's request is fulfilled by issuing a subprogram call with appropriate parameters. Borning's *Thinglab,* discussed later, is a more sophisticated example of a nonprocedural system.

(2) *Algorithmic system.* A procedural programming system is algorithmic if users tell the computer how to perform the desired computation without actually computing any values during the instructional process. Thus, programs written algorithmically may be expressed in the second person future (third person present): "Listen to what I am about to tell you; then, when I give the word, do it. First, you will do (one does) this, then you will do (one does) this, then you will do (one does) this..."

(3) *Demonstrational system.* A procedural programming system is demonstrational if users show the computer how to perform the desired computation by actually computing one or more values during the instructional process. Thus, programs written demonstrationally may be expressed in the first person pre-

sent: "Watch what I am about to do; then, when I give the word, repeat what you saw me do. First, I do this, now I do this, now I do this..."

One relatively straightforward approach to incorporating graphics into the programming environment is to devise a graphical extension for a conventional programming language; all such systems clearly fall into the visual, but not the iconic, category. Graphical extensions to Pascal include Diaz-Herrera and Flude's relatively modest Pascal with Hierarchical Structure Diagrams (Pascal/HSD),[7] and Clark and Robinson's Graphical Interacting Program Monitor,[8] and Pong and Ng's Programming with Interactive Graphical Support, or PIGS,[9] both of which employ N-S diagrams to show program structure.

Reiss's Pecan[10] and Schwartz et al.'s Magpie[11] define the state of the art of Pascal extensions, because they provide rich programming and runtime environments offering multiple views of the objects being manipulated. In Pecan, for example, users for the most part indicate the sequence of actions they wish to perform by pointing with a mouse to entries in fixed and/or popup (textual) menus. The built-in editor recognizes Pascal syntax and thus can immediately highlight erroneous statements. Incremental compilation allows users to run programs after writing them or making changes in them without the lengthy delay caused by recompiling. At runtime, users can follow the computer's progress through programs, with each statement being highlighted as it is executed, both in the Pascal source and in an automatically generated corresponding flowchart (Reiss plans to provide N-S diagrams as well in the near future); however, users cannot edit the graphic representation of their programs. Pecan allows users to watch the generation of new values and the behavior of the runtime stack; it can graphically display the data structures being manipulated through the use of Brown and Sedgewick's[12] Balsa subsystem (short for Brown University's Algorithm Simulator and Animator).

An extension to Pascal of a different nature is Magnenat-Thalmann and Thalmann's three-dimensional graphics and animation system, Mira-3D.[13] This preprocessor embodies a new primitive abstract data type for Pascal, called a figure, which, in conjunction with appropriate new operations and a library of about 50 built-in procedures and functions, provides the

> One way to incorporate graphics into programming is to devise a graphical extension to a conventional programming language.

user with powerful tools for working in a graphical domain.

Finally, there are also graphical extensions to C, such as Kramlich et al.'s Program Visualization,[14] and to Lisp, including Teitelman's Display Oriented Programmer's Assistant,[15] Lieberman and Hewitt's Tinker,[16] and Lakin's Pattern Manipulating Systems.[17]

Iconic programming systems. Some iconic systems date back to the 1960's, including Sutherland's Sketchpad,[18] the first significant system that allowed users to build anything interactively by using graphics; Newman's Reaction Handler;[19] Ellis et al.'s Grail;[20] Christensen et al.'s Ambit/G and Ambit/L;[21] and Denert et al.'s Plan-2D.[22]

Four recent systems merit more than just a few words. The first is David Smith's Pygmalion.[1] Smith concluded that three conditions were necessary to the achievement of his goal to develop a system whose representational and processing facilities correspond to and assist the mental processes that occur during creative thought[1]—(1) that the programming environment be based on visual man-machine communication through the use of a graphics display; (2) that the system provide the user with interactive feedback; and (3) that the emphasis in programming be on "doing" rather than "telling" (since many people find it easier to demonstrate what they want done than to describe it). Thus Pygmalion, written in Smalltalk for the Xerox Alto, was designed as a demonstrational system for procedural programming in which the icon concept is central. Programming in Pygmalion is a process of designing and editing icons. Everything that can be done to information is done through icons, and every operation on icons affects the display state as well as the internal machine state. Programmers need to interact with the system only on the display level with the images they have created.[1] With the aid of a mouse, the Pygmalion programmer demonstrates the steps of a computation using sample data values; Pygmalion then replays the exact sequence of operations to perform the desired computation on other values.

A second recent iconic programming system is Gael Curry's Programming by Abstract Demonstration, or PAD.[23] Curry designed an innovative system that embodied a significant extension of the Pygmalion philosophy. The system, —implemented in XPL/G for the Xerox Sigma/5 computer equipped with an IMLAC PDS-1D vector graphics terminal and a light pen— was, like Pygmalion, a demonstrational system for procedural programming. However, unlike Pygmalion, it allowed user demonstrations to be carried out on potentially unbounded ranges of values, which Curry called *abstract data,* rather than actual sample data. Thus, users could merely indicate, if they so wished, that "an integer" was to be input to satisfy a *read* statement; alternatively, the datum could be more precisely specified as "an integer between 15 and 22" or even "19," as in Pygmalion.

Depending on the degree of generalization in the demonstration, PAD could determine various approximations, as Curry termed them, to the values a program would eventually output, such as "an integer," "an integer less than 14," or "2." Thus, PAD provides, at least in theory, a continuum of demonstrational precision, where one end of the spectrum is the completely abstract (only the type of a value is stated, such as "an integer") and the other is the completely concrete (specific values, such as "19," are stated).

In another system, called Thinglab,[24] Alan Borning provides programmers with a set of tools to help them graphically represent experiments in a constraint-oriented simulation laboratory. That is, the elements in displays must conform to some relation that must be continuously maintained. Consequently, altering one value causes any other(s) to immediately change in response according to criteria laid down by the user when the experiment is programmed.

This approach is actually quite similar to what spreadsheet programs such as Visicorp's Visicalc now do, although Thinglab is on a much grander scale, incorporating both graphical and symbolic objects in addition to numeric ones. Implemented in Smalltalk for the Xerox Alto, the system envisages two distinct classes of users: (1) lab instructors, experts in their field as well as programmers proficient in the use of procedural, higher level languages, and (2) students. The lab instructor defines building blocks for a given domain (for example, resistors, batteries, wires, and meters for the simulation of electrical circuits) by drawing the icon that is to graphically represent each entity and specifying the constraint(s) to which the entity is subject. The student then employs these building blocks to construct and explore particular simulations. Thinglab is especially notable for its user-friendly, interactive, and essentially

iconic interface (at least for students).

The fourth recently developed iconic programming system of note was designed by William Finzer and Laura Gould and implemented in Smalltalk on a Xerox Dorado computer. The system, called Programming by Rehearsal,[25] uses the theater as its operational metaphor. Like Thinglab, it assumes that users are either lab instructors or students. Programs are "productions" (in the theatrical sense), and to form one, the instructor selects "performers,"

Some iconic interfaces allow computer-user interaction at the operating system level; others allow programming in a graphical environment.

---

each of which responds to a variety of predefined "cues" and places them on a "stage" (which comes equipped with a "wings" area where things can be intentionally hidden from the student). Performers with similar capabilities are grouped together into "troupes." In addition to the standard data types and programming constructs, Programming by Rehearsal includes among its performers graphical entities like pictures and "travelers," which are pictures that can be made to move; a Logo-type turtle; and more unusual objects such as clocks.

One of the more interesting cues allows an action to be keyed to performer changes. Alternatively, a performer may be told to become a button that will initiate some action whenever the button is "pressed" (pointed at with the mouse). Traveler objects respond to additional cues that determine how and when they are to move about on the screen. Most programming is done by rehearsal, that is, demonstrationally, but the system may also be programmed algorithmically. Algorithmic programming is done either by typing in Smalltalk code directly or by cutting and pasting code that has

already been written for other performers. There is a large on-line Help subsystem that displays its messages in a prompter's box at either the system's or the user's behest.

Finzer and Gould tested their system in July 1983 on two designers of curricula at San Francisco State University. The results were encouraging: Although the subjects were initially skeptical about being able to master Programming by Rehearsal, they were able to actually create a nontrivial prototype activity after just two or three days. Finzer and Gould estimate that these subjects, who had previously seen computer programs written in Basic but who did not know how to program a computer, would have required many months of hard work to achieve a similar result had they been using a conventional programming language.

Iconic systems have also been devised for the office, the home, and for young children. Some iconic interfaces concentrate on allowing users to converse with the computer at the operating system level; examples include the Apple Lisa and Macintosh and the Hewlett-Packard HP-150 (touch screen) home computers and the Xerox Star system for personal workstations in an automated office—all of which work in similar ways. For example, in the Star system, icons represent various functions and data objects commonly found in business environments. Thus, files are identified by icons that resemble file folders; to print a document, the user points with a mouse to a little picture of a printer on the screen.

Still other iconic interfaces concentrate on allowing users to actually program in a graphical environment; examples include DeJong and Zloof's nonprocedural language for the office, called Query by Example,[26] for retrieving information from databases. In this system, users textually fill in blanks in graphical objects that resemble forms, charts, tables, and reports. Although user entries are often quite cryptic in appearance, there is no doubt that Query by Example is much easier for most people to use than, say, Cobol.

Certainly the best known system that uses graphics to help familiarize children with computers is Seymour Papert's Logo. The primary graphics artifact used in the system, the turtle, has undoubtedly contributed immensely to Logo's success, since children can readily understand its capabilities. In contrast, the capabilities of CRT graphics are harder to communicate to children, probably because electronic plotting is more abstract and unreal than the motions of a turtle crawling around on the floor. Researchers have commented on the utility of concrete models when teaching programming to novices,[27,28] and as Fitter has aptly noted,[29] a concrete image is particularly important when teaching programming to children. Logo has definitely proved effective when taught to children old enough to read; we speculate that the use of text is its main limitation when very young children are involved.

The Pict approach

Each of the systems just described provide many features we believe to be important in a graphical programming environment. However, all suffer from one or more of the following undesirable characteristics: (1) users have to employ one of the standard programming languages to code their programs at some bottom level; (2) operations lack functionality or simplicity of operation; (3) users cannot see a complete, static representation of their programs in graphical form; and (4) except for PIGS, the display is monochromatic rather than color. Furthermore, many of the systems were demonstrational —which some believe is the most promising way to make programming accessible to the layman. We disagree. In our opinion, whatever success demonstrational systems may have enjoyed to date is probably due primarily to the interactive and graphical nature of their interfaces,

rather than to their demonstrational features alone.

Our system attempts to provide a new type of algorithmic programming environment in which computer graphics plays a central role. With Pict, users don't write computer programs using letters, digits, and punctuation marks; in fact, users never have to touch a keyboard once the system has started up. Instead, users sit in front of a color graphics display and draw programs using a suitable input device, like a joystick, that controls the movement

---

Pict users never touch a keyboard once the system has started up. Instead, they draw programs using an input device like a joystick.

---

of a cursor on the screen. User drawings are not free-form, but rather have the flavor of one-of-a-kind jigsaw puzzles with juxtaposed, predefined components. Graphics, colors, sound, and animation are used to make user programs appear as multidimensional and concrete as possible. With the exception of numerals and short Help messages, users rely totally on nontextual symbols. (Sub)program names and parameter passing modes, data structures, variables, and program operations are represented by icons of various sorts, while control structures such as the Pascal *repeat-until* or *while* are represented by colored, directed paths that can actually be seen.

Pict provides all tools users need to compose, edit, and run their programs integrated within a simple, consistent command structure. Users communicate with the Pict system throughout all phases of their work by pointing to icons in a menu tree; Pict responds by altering its display in an appropriate manner or, if the user has erred, by presenting a Help message. As a secondary sensory stimulus, Pict also employs simple auditory cues—a single sounding of its bell to confirm acceptance of user

commands, two soundings of the bell in rapid succession to draw attention to an error. User program syntax is checked continuously during the programming process, eliminating syntactic inconsistencies in a (sub)program—even when only partially specified.

User programs may be recursive and contain arbitrary chains of subprogram calls. When users wish to test a program, Pict uses simple forms of animation to make the drawing "come to life," and the execution is displayed step by step unless the user has requested that this feature be suppressed. If users don't like what they see, it is easy to return to the editing subsystem and make revisions. The alternation between composing programs and test-running them may start even before the program has been completely specified; if the Pict runtime supervisor reaches a point where it cannot continue, it will simply halt and tell the user that more programming is required.

Because programming is an iterative process, Pict provides the means to edit programs with a minimum of trouble. Icons may be added to a (sub)program in any order, and they may be replicated and moved about at will. Users may overwrite existing icons with new ones or delete them entirely. When an icon is deleted, Pict automatically deletes all paths leading into or issuing from the icon. Alternatively, individual paths between icons may be deleted and new ones inserted. Some operations require just a single selection with the joystick; those that require several may be abandoned at any time before their completion without penalty. In general, anything may be undone in at most a few extra steps.

A session with Pict/D

Several prototype Pict systems have been implemented in Pascal for the DEC VMS compiler running under Bell Laboratories' Unix on a Vax 11/780. The graphics display used by the prototypes is a Gould-DeAnza Systems 512 × 512 pixel color raster device with a 1024-entry color map. The main prototype, named Pict/D, allows the user to compose programs that do simple, numeric calculations. Figure 3 shows a schematic representation of its display. Pict/D user programs look like flowcharts, and although some professionals have questioned the usefulness of these diagrams, we find much to recommend the flowchart when it is the program itself rather than merely an aid to documenting it. Both the types and number of variables are quite restricted in Pict/D, with just four six-digit, nonnegative decimal integers (distinguished by red, green, blue, and orange) available in each module (program or subprogram). The Pict/D language primitives may be defined as follows:

```
<language primitive> ::=
    <system control>
    | <declarative op>
    | <boolean op>
<system control> ::=
    'start (entry point)'
    | 'stop/return'
<declarative op> ::=
    'add' | 'subtract'
    | 'increment by 1'
    | 'decrement by 1'
    | 'set to 0'
    | 'set to 1'
    | 'assign a copy'
    | 'input from joystick'
    | 'write to disk file'
<boolean op> ::=
    '>' | '=' | '<' | '=0' | '=1'
```

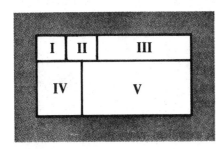

Figure 3. The Pict/D display, where I = (sub)program name, II = subsystem indicator, III = Help bulletin board/ data structure display, IV = system menu/input keypad, and V = user program/easel.

Thus, working in Pict/D is working at a language level similar to that of Basic or simple Pascal, but visually.

We now propose to take you on a tour of Pict/D with the aid of a gallery of color images (see facing page). In what follows, we will often use "module" to mean either a program or subprogram; indeed, the distinction between the two is minimal in Pict/D, since any routine may be either run independently as a program or called as a subprogram from any other (although one or the other of these options may not make sense for a given routine). Image (a) shows the display presented to the user at the beginning of a session. The main system menu displays four icons that denote Pict/D's major subsystems; from top to bottom, these are *programming*, represented by a small flowchart; *erasing*, represented by a hand holding an eraser up to a blackboard; *icon editor*, represented by a hand writing with a pen on a sheet of paper; and *user library*, represented by a shelf of books.

Let's begin with the user program library (b). The library icon is redisplayed in the new menu as the first entry; when the library icon is touched with the cursor, the next four library elements (if they exist) appear. The other menu entries shown in (b) are the names of a short driver routine, two (recursive) routines that calculate binomial coefficients and the factorial function, and a subprogram for natural number multiplication by means of repeated addition. The icon for this last routine (c) is shown blown up on the icon editor's easel; the routine itself is displayed by the library subsystem (d). The Pict/D code shown is equivalent to the Pascal subprogram below. Note how the two call-by-value parameters, the function-return register, and the local variable are specified in the icon that names the routine by the presence or absence of small, downward-pointing triangles. The magnifying glass that appears in its turned-off state along the right edge of the easel in (c)

indicates that at runtime we do not wish to see the details of this routine's execution.

```
type SixDigits = 0..999999;
function Red (Green, Blue :
    SixDigits) : SixDigits;
(*multiply two natural numbers
    by means of repeated
    addition*)
var Orange : SixDigits;
begin
    if Blue>Green then
    begin
        Orange := Blue;
        Blue := Green;
        Green := Orange;
    end;
    Red := 0;
    while Blue>0 do
    begin
        Red := Red + Green;
        Blue := Blue − 1;
    end;
end;
```

The user can program an icon or edit or run its associated program by selecting the icon from the user library so that it is on display in the upper lefthand corner of the screen (area I in Figure 3). In (e) the driver routine is on display; this routine is programmed to read in a value *n* and invoke the factorial subprogram to calculate *n*!. To run this program, we leave the library, going back to the main system menu, and point to any spot in the actual routine (area V in Figure 3). Image (f) shows what happens next. For input, a numeric (soft)keypad is displayed with red "reject" and green "accept" buttons. The four numeric registers in which computations will be performed are also displayed. The keypad, similar to those commonly found in automatic teller machines, flashes different colors to alert the user when a *read* operation is encountered (g). Images (h) through (k) show various steps in the recursive calculation of 7! that now follows; note the blue and red indicator for the runtime stack height at both edges of the main area of the screen. In some of the images, a white box is shown that moves along a flow-of-

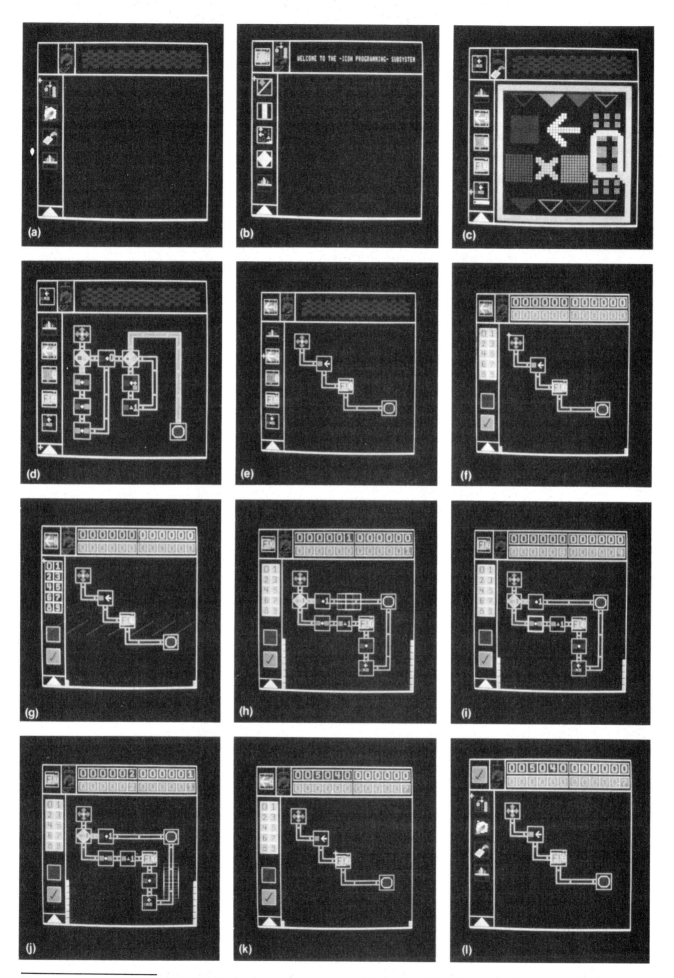

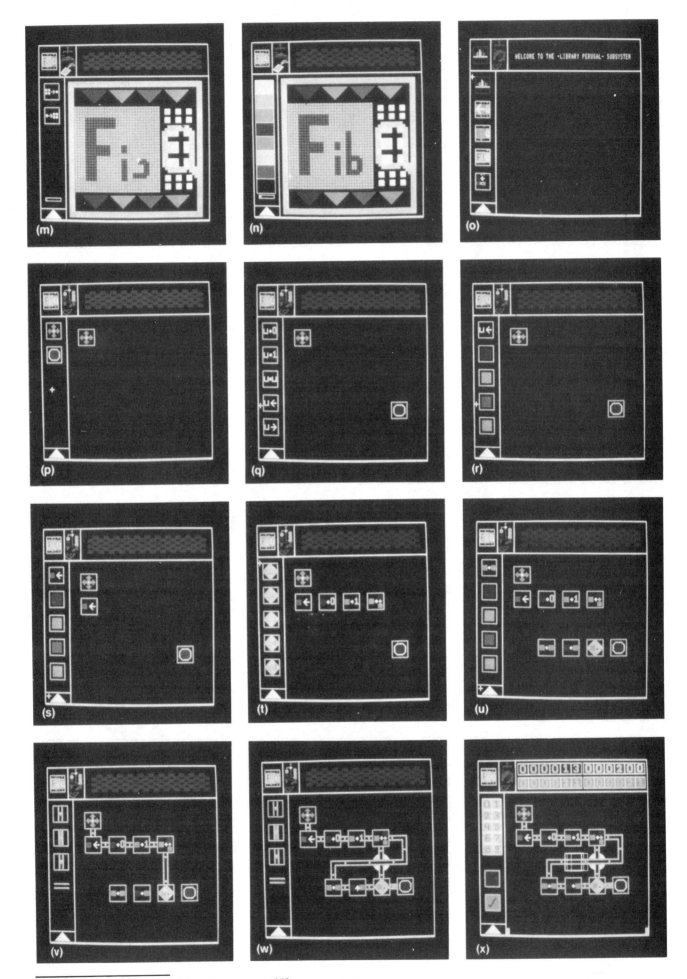

Figures can be found printed in color on page 658.

the runtime stack height at both edges of the main area of the screen. In some of the images, a white box is shown that moves along a flow-of-control path, making explicit and visible Pict/D's progress through the user program as it is being run. Eventually, program execution terminates successfully,* so a green check mark appears in the upper left-hand corner of the display (l).

Now that we've seen how a Pict/D program runs, let's write one, say, a program to calculate the elements in a Fibonacci sequence until the first one is found that is greater than some input value N. Recall that the definition is

$$f_0 = 0, f_1 = 1$$
$$f_i = f_{i-1} + f_{i-2} \quad (i > 1)$$

The first step is to devise an icon for the program. Image (m) shows the beginnings of such a creation using the icon editor; the letters "Fib" have been chosen to name the routine, but they are unaesthetically misaligned. In (n), this deficiency has been rectified. The menus shown in (m) and (n) are for setting the brush width and paint color, respectively.

Now let's write the body of the program. Icons denoting the various operations needed to perform the calculations must be selected and placed in the module [(o) through (u)]; these must then be connected by paths to indicate the desired flow of control [(v) and (w)]. The order in which the icons are chosen is immaterial, but a path can be laid down only between two existing icons. For icons that act on variable(s), we must first choose a *template icon* that indicates what operation we have in mind; then, the system prompts us to enter the specific variable(s). To connect two icons with a flow path, we need only point to the desired endpoints; Pict/D will then find the shortest and straightest path possible between the indicated icons and, if necessary, even redefine and move paths previously laid down. Since Pict/D continuously checks all aspects of program syntax, the flow of control cannot be improperly

specified; for example, two red paths cannot leave a Boolean operation). Image (x) shows a step in the execution of the finished program with input value $N = 200$.

The great flexibility of Pict/D is one of its major assets. If users don't like the way a program runs, they can easily return to the programming or erasing subsystem and change it. Similarly, if users decide they want to improve the appearance of the icon that names a module, they can do so with no problem after writing the program or even in the middle of writing it. Our "tour" of Pict/D represents only a sampling of the system's capabilities, not a complete description of them.

User response to Pict/D

Pict/D was tested on more than 60 undergraduate and graduate students at the University of Washington, all unpaid volunteers. The experiments proved valuable in providing us with feedback about the good and bad aspects of the system, which we could use to modify Pict/D into its present form. In addition, we could identify areas for future work.

Pict/D experiments. All of the undergraduate subjects were students at the University of Washington enrolled in C SCI 241 ("Pascal Programming") during the 1983 autumn quarter and C SCI 201 ("Introduction to Computer Science") during the 1984 winter quarter. The students were, for the most part, freshmen and sophomores, many of whom wanted to major in computer science but whose background and experience in computer use varied widely. Some subjects had had no prior contact with computers, while others had been programming a variety of machines in a multitude of languages for years. We made no attempt to exclude students at either extreme; in fact, we included quite a few who, in despair, ended up dropping the course midway through it. The graduate subjects were working

on advanced degrees in computer science. Statistical data on the subjects is summarized in Table 1.

Each experiment lasted approximately two hours. Subjects were first given a demonstration of the system's capabilities that lasted about 30 minutes. Then, they were asked to implement one or two simple programs; help with designing the algorithms was provided as needed. On the average, each undergraduate subject wrote 1.7 programs, with each program taking 29.3 minutes to write, debug, and run at least once; each graduate subject wrote 1.9 programs, on the average, and took 21.4 minutes for each. Finally, all subjects were asked to fill out a questionnaire. The questions (on pp. 18 and 19) could be answered by circling a value between 1 and 5. Several subjects, graduates as well as undergraduates, felt that they had to qualify what seemed to them to be relatively low answers to question (13) with comments such as "only because Pascal is higher level and this is [my] first time with Pict."

The following are typical undergraduate responses to the last question on the questionnaire, which was merely, "Any comments?" The first two are especially noteworthy, not because they are true (they aren't—the subjects did learn a programming language, as well as a simple editor),

Table 1. Statistical data on the 65 participants in the Pict/D experiments.

CATEGORY	TOTAL
Undergraduate subjects*	55 (84.6%)
Males	40
Females	15
Graduate subjects†	10 (15.4%)
Males	5
Females	5
Subjects ≤20 years	21 (32.3%)
Subjects >20 but ≤22 years	22 (33.8%)
Subjects >22 years	22 (33.8%)
Total No. of Subjects	65

*Male undergraduates were from 19 to 35 years old; female undergraduates, from 19 to 34.
†Male graduates were from 25 to 29 years old; female graduates from 23 to 43.

---

*By this, we mean that the program reached a *stop/return* icon instead of, say, falling off an undefined path; we do *not* mean that the numbers generated are correct.

but because they show the subjects' positive frame of mind after coming into contact with Pict for the first time:

- "Writing up a flowchart is already writing up a program; no computer languages are required [to write] a program"
- "[Pict] would be great for... home computers, [since] people wouldn't need to learn a computer language"
- "[Pict] is very easy to understand and pick up"
- "Most of the time I didn't even need to use the Help function, because most errors were easy to detect without help"

- "I liked 'seeing' the program run"
- "Perhaps the main power of this tool [Pict] is in debugging; seeing [one's] program run should quickly point out where the problems are"
- "At this stage [in my knowledge of programming], Pict [is] more elementary than I need; however, people such as my mother or step-dad would be assisted greatly by it"
- "[Pict] would make a great way to introduce children to programming" (at least half a dozen subjects made similar comments).

Only two undergraduate subjects reacted very unfavorably to the Pict/D system. One of these, the star student in an introductory computer science course, complained, "I am totally verbally, non-visually oriented—a system like this is very difficult for me!" The other subject who disliked the system commented, "I found myself frustrated by my inability to communicate with the machine...unfortunately, I'm accustomed to 'static' programming, [to] sitting down and working problems out before I interact with the [computer]...I like keyboards—I felt restricted by the joystick." These two subjects, both males, were

---

Pict user response

The following questions were asked of Pict users, who were requested to circle numbers from 1 to 5, with "1" corresponding to most negative and "5" to most positive.

(1) In general, how easy did you find it to use the Pict prototype? (5 = Pict very easy)

(2) In general, how much fun did you find it to use Pict? (5 = Pict a lot of fun)

(3) Did you find using a joystick preferable to the use of a keyboard for communicating with the computer? (5 = liked joystick a lot)

(4) Did you like the way the main Pict menu is organized like a tree in which you move up and down? (5 = liked menu tree a lot)

(5) How useful did you find Pict's Help feature? (5 = Help very useful)

(6) How easy did you find it to learn and remember the meanings of the Pict icons? (5 = icons easy to learn)

(7) Did you like the way Pict programs are drawn and displayed as flowcharts? (5 = liked Pict flowcharts a lot)

(8) Do you find it easier to comprehend a Pict flowchart program, as opposed to one displayed textually by, say, Pascal? (5 = Pict programs clearer)

(9) Do you customarily employ flowcharts of some sort to design your computer programs? (5 = use flowcharts a lot)

(10) Did you find it useful to see your program's execution animated and traced step by step? (5 = like execution a lot)

(11) How important an aspect of Pict would you rate the use of color? (5 = color very important)

Undergraduate responses.

QUESTION	ANSWER 1	2	3	4	5	N/A	PERCENTAGE ANSWERING "3" OR BETTER
Pict easy to use?	0	1	5	28	20	1	98.1
Pict fun to use?	1	0	2	22	30		98.2
Like joystick?	2	3	17	18	15		90.9
Like menu tree?	0	1	7	23	24		98.2
Was Help useful?	1	8	27	8	9	2	83.0
Icons easy to learn?	1	2	1	14	35	2	94.3
Like Pict flowcharts?	0	1	5	15	34		98.2
Pict clearer than Pascal?	1	5	5	21	21	2	88.7
Do you use flowcharts?	10	12	7	13	12	1	59.3
Like animated execution?	0	3	7	13	32		94.5
Was color important?	1	1	3	15	35		96.4
Was sound important?	2	10	17	18	8		78.2
Pict programming fast?	8	13	17	9	6	2	60.4
Overall evaluation of system?	0	0	4	31	20		100.0
Want another Pict session?	0	2	2	26	25		96.4
Might prefer Pict in future?	0	5	14	27	8	1	90.7

Graduate responses.

QUESTION	ANSWER 1	2	3	4	5	N/A	PERCENTAGE ANSWERING "3" OR BETTER
Pict easy to use?	0	1	1	6	2		90.0
Pict fun to use?	0	1	3	4	2		90.0
Like joystick?	1	2	2	3	2		70.0
Like menu tree?	1	0	2	3	4		90.0
Was Help useful?	0	3	6	0	0	1	66.7
Icons easy to learn?	0	0	1	4	5		100.0
Like Pict flowcharts?	1	2	2	4	1		70.0
Pict clearer than Pascal?	1	1	3	2	3		80.0
Do you use flowcharts?	3	4	2	1	0		30.0
Like animated execution?	0	2	2	4	2		80.0
Was color important?	1	0	0	3	6		90.0
Was sound important?	1	2	3	4	0		70.0
Pict programming fast?	4	4	0	2	0		20.0
Overall evaluation of system?	0	0	3	3	3	1	100.0
Want another Pict session?	0	1	5	3	1		90.0
Might prefer Pict in future?	2	6	0	2	0		20.0

among the oldest participants in the experiments (born in 1951 and 1954, respectively). We will return to this point later, although it would clearly be unwise to draw any hasty conclusions from such a small sample.

As can be seen from the tables in the box below, graduate students were, as a rule, more critical of Pict/D than undergraduates were. As one put it, "I believe the less you know about conventional programming languages the more natural [Pict/D's] interface seems to be." Even so, many graduates responded favorably; one was pleased to actually be able to "see...recursion being carried out." Another commented, "[Pict/D] would be a good device for teaching children programming...if you [were to] sell [it] I would buy it for my kids." However, few were inclined to use it on a regular basis as a substitute for their favorite textual language(s), except in certain applications such as the visualization of B-tree manipulation. We think results such as these are to be expected, since graduate students have, on the whole, overcome the difficulty associated with learning to program. Indeed, many probably find it easier to write programs than to write descriptions of these programs in English.

Interpreting experimental results. The experiments described in the preceding section can be criticized on the grounds that they lack the methodology commonly used in the behavioral sciences. As Brooks has forcefully stated, "In order to maintain creditability with behavioral researchers in other areas, behavioral researchers in computer science must pay close attention to methodological issues."[30] Novelty most likely played a part in the favorable responses to our system, and the presence of the system's designer (Glinert) during the experimental sessions may similarly have contributed to the high ratings received. With

---

(12) How important an aspect of Pict would you rate the use of sound (the CRT bell)? (5 = sound very important)

(13) Can you estimate how much more time and effort it might have taken you to write the program(s) you just worked on in some "conventional" language such as Pascal? (5 = Pascal more time)

(14) What is your overall evaluation of the Pict concept and prototype? (5 = overall, Pict excellent)

(15) How thrilled would you be if you were asked to participate in another Pict session? (5 = very pleased)

(16) If it were possible to do so (in the future), how would you rate the chances that you would prefer on a regualr basis to use an expanded, Pict-like system to write your computer programs rather than a language such as Pascal? (5 = would prefer Pict)

Average responses for all subjects by age.

QUESTION	AGE <28	20 ≤ AGE ≤ 22	22 <AGE
Pict easy to use?	4.2	4.3	4.0
Pict fun to use?	4.5	4.5	4.0
Like joystick?	4.0	3.7	3.4
Like menu tree?	4.4	4.2	4.1
Was Help useful?	3.5	3.2	2.9
Icons easy to learn?	4.6	4.6	4.3
Like Pict flowcharts?	4.5	4.5	3.9
Pict clearer than Pascal?	4.3	4.1	3.5
Do you use flowcharts?	3.2	2.6	3.0
Like animated execution?	4.4	4.0	4.2
Was color important?	4.7	4.4	4.3
Was sound important?	3.2	3.5	3.2
Pict programming fast?	2.7	3.0	2.4
Overall evaluation of system?	4.4	4.2	4.1
Want another Pict session?	4.3	4.6	3.7
Might prefer Pict in future?	3.8	3.6	3.0

Average undergraduate response by sex.

QUESTION	MALES	FEMALES	TOTAL
Pict easy to use?	4.2	4.5	4.2
Pict fun to use?	4.4	4.6	4.5
Like joystick?	3.8	3.5	3.7
Like menu tree?	4.3	4.3	4.3
Was Help useful?	3.2	3.6	3.3
Icons easy to learn?	4.4	4.7	4.5
Like Pict flowcharts?	4.5	4.5	4.5
Pict clearer than Pascal?	3.9	4.4	4.1
Do you use flowcharts?	3.0	3.4	3.1
Like animated execution?	4.3	4.5	4.3
Was color important?	4.4	4.7	4.5
Was sound important?	3.3	3.4	3.4
Pict programming fast?	2.6	3.4	2.8
Overall evaluation of system?	4.2	4.5	4.3
Want another Pict session?	4.3	4.5	4.3
Might prefer Pict in future?	3.6	3.9	3.7

Average graduate response by sex.

QUESTION	MALES	FEMALES	TOTAL
Pict easy to use?	3.8	4.0	3.9
Pict fun to use?	3.6	3.8	3.7
Like joystick?	3.0	3.6	3.3
Like menu tree?	4.0	3.8	3.9
Was Help useful?	2.4	3.0	2.7
Icons easy to learn?	4.2	4.6	4.4
Like Pict flowcharts?	3.0	3.4	3.2
Pict clearer than Pascal?	3.4	3.6	3.5
Do you use flowcharts?	1.6	2.6	2.1
Like animated execution?	2.8	4.4	3.6
Was color important?	3.8	4.8	4.3
Was sound important?	3.2	2.8	3.0
Pict programming fast?	1.8	2.2	2.0
Overall evaluation of system?	4.3	3.8	4.0
Want another Pict session?	3.8	3.0	3.4
Might prefer Pict in future?	2.0	2.4	2.2

prolonged exposure and the demand that they write more complex programs, the subjects' evaluation of Pict would probably have declined.

Perhaps the major shortcoming of our experiments is the fact that we did not divide our subjects into groups, which we could have then exposed to identical environments, except for a few, intentionally altered factors. Had we been able to carefully control and monitor the environment in this way, we could then have precisely gauged the importance to the Pict environment of changing certain factors by applying widely accepted statistical tools to our data. In this manner, we could have attained two independent objectives: (1) to compare the relative success of novices in mastering the material in an introductory programming course when using Pict as opposed to a conventional programming language like Pascal; and (2) to evaluate how important various features of Pict are to the overall appeal of the system.

The first of these two experiments would, undoubtedly, have been the more intriguing, but to carry it out would have been economically infeasible, for it would have meant teaching two programming courses: a conventional one and one in which the students used the Pict environment for all their work. Unfortunately, in the latter, a sizable number of interactive graphics terminals would have been required, along with appropriate computing power, either individual workstations or a very large mainframe. (We have, however, applied for a grant in the hope of funding such rigorous experimentation during the 1984-1985 year.)

Under the circumstances, we should probably avoid analyzing our data with powerful statistical tools. Nevertheless, we can draw many useful conclusions. Let us first examine the negative reactions, however. Essentially, the only negative remarks recorded during the Pict/D experiments other than those already discussed fell into one of the following three categories: dissatisfaction over bugs in early versions of the system, complaints that the size of each program module and Pict/D's repertoire of operations were too restricted, and displeasure that the response time of the multiuser Vax was sometimes inadequate. The interplay of two distinct factors seems to be responsible for the third points. First, users of interactive graphical systems want response time to be fast; they feel uncomfortable when what Shneiderman[31] calls "the pressure for [short-term memory] closure" is violated as the following

---

Novelty and the presence of Pict's designer during user experiments may have heightened favorable response to the system.

---

events unfold in a time-shared computing environment: (1) part of an object, such as an icon, is displayed, (2) the computer "stutters" as some other processes are run for awhile, and (3) the remainder of the object (icon) is displayed. Worse yet is the variability in response time as a function of machine load. As Miller[32] has reported, this can be even more annoying than a constant, slow response, to the extent that it may cause users to perceive the command structure, speed, and general utility of a system—even the brightness and size of the physical display—as inadequate.

Thus, we clearly have two goals: (1) to implement a Pict-like system on a powerful single-user workstation and (2) to extend the sizes of the user program modules, the set of data types, and the language constructs and to increase the number of variables to which a module may refer.

Designing iconic programming environments

From our experiments, we have identified some of the issues crucial to the design of successful interactive, graphical programming environments.

Alternatives to the flowchart metaphor. Undoubtedly the most basic design decision for an iconic programming system is fixing the graphical representation scheme for user programs. For several reasons, we chose simplified, conventional flowcharts for Pict, despite the well-known controversy over their efficiency. First, people have easily understoood and used these diagrams for more than 30 years. Neither Nassi-Shneiderman diagrams nor any of the numerous, less well-known methods of graphically displaying a program's structure has become widely accepted to date. Furthermore, much of the ill will toward flowcharts (and other external documentation aids) probably arises because they do not comprise the actual programs themselves. Thus, Brooks is quoted by Shneiderman as saying that flowcharts are "a curse," a "space-hogging exercise in drafting," and a "most thoroughly oversold piece of program documentation."[31] In a more restrained tone, Shneiderman explains that a "flowchart is at a disadvantage because it is more spread out (the page flip and off-page connector problems) and it is incomplete (omitting declarations, statement labels, and input/output formats). At best, a detailed flowchart repeats the program syntax."[31] Criticisms of this nature become more muted when the flowchart actually *is* the program. Indeed, a recent article by Gilmore and Smith concludes that even external flowcharts may well be useful, depending on "the nature of the task and the individual programmer characteristics."[33]

A more relevant criticism of flowcharts, which is not valid for, say, N-S diagrams, is that the level of operations they support is too low, corresponding more to Fortran and Basic than to Pascal. We agree that flowcharts may allow the user to generate programs with little "structure" (this concept is commonly understood), but we cannot say that "little structure" is all bad where novice programmers are concerned.[34] Indeed, Smith and Dunsmore[35] and Arblaster[36] published papers with opposite viewpoints just two years ago.

The foregoing notwithstanding, we do not purport to be strong advocates of flowchart utility, nor do we believe they are the ultimate way to depict program structure or that structured programming is a bad practice. Cardelli's novel diagrams[37] are one example of a compact and aesthetically appealing "functional" alternative. At one point, we experimented with a procedural, top-down graphical representation scheme that seemed to hold great promise; unfortunately, the metaphor required significant panning and zooming, making its implementation impractical using the available hardware.

The flowchart metaphor employed by Pict/D was not entirely successful. Whenever too many "disconnected" icons appeared on the screen (icons not yet hooked into the flow of control), some subjects tended to become confused as to the order in which their programs were going to execute instructions. Therefore, future systems that employ this metaphor should probably require that each icon be connected to at least one other immediately after it is laid down in the program plane. The system could automatically propose a path to connect a newly placed icon to, say, that placed previously, and the user could confirm or easily override the proposal.

Allocating limited space. The space available on a single screen is obviously severely limited, yet it must suffice for the display of both user programs and data structures as well as of various menus and subsidiary information. How can we increase this scarce resource, and how can we apportion what we do have? The total space at our disposal is determined by the number of screens, their physical size(s), and their resolution(s), where the "number of screens" is a function of the actual number of monitors and the speed with which these can be refreshed (if this is fast enough, several logical screens could be supported on one physical device).

Increasing any of these parameters unduly may create problems. If there are too many physical screens, users may need to constantly rotate their heads and bodies to look at the proper ones, thus causing muscular strain and discomfort. If we refresh a screen often to show different logical displays, users may become con-

---

Undergraduates tended to be less critical of Pict than graduates, and females at both levels tended to be less critical than males.

---

fused. If we increase the resolution of the device so that it can display more information at one time, individual icons may become too small to be easily seen.

As mentioned earlier, several subjects in our experiments thought Pict's primary usefulness might be to allow them to watch the traversal and manipulations of complex linked data structures such as trees. In Pict/D, however, most of the screen area must be devoted to displaying the user program. One solution is to employ pan and zoom. Alternatively, we could add another screen to the system, one devoted entirely to the display of data objects. Yet a third possibility is to provide users with a "switch," which could help them at runtime to flip back and forth between viewing the program and its data. Clearly, the third solution, in common with the use of frequent scrolling, is only viable if the display can be refreshed quickly enough and in a visually pleasing manner—something that unfortunately was not possible in the environment supporting the Pict prototypes.

All these problems are true of visual systems, in general, not just Pict. Thus, the short videotape demonstration of a prototype of Kramlich et al.'s Program Visualization for C (graciously supplied by Mark Friedell of Harvard University) seems to show the user appearing noticeably uncomfortable as from time to time he swivels his head to look at the proper one of the system's three screens. In addition, demonstrations we have seen of Brown University's Balsa system, Schwartz et al.'s Magpie, and Reiss's Pecan, as well as Kramlich et al.'s PV, indicate that all these systems are subject to "thrashing" when they attempt to highlight the current line of a running program that is too big to fit on the screen. In addition, both Pecan and Apple's Lisa and Macintosh have some icons that are too small to discern easily.

Choosing the input device(s). Subjects new to graphical interaction generally found the joystick quite acceptable, but those with more experience often commented that they would prefer a mouse or trackball as the input device. This finding is in line with current trends, but again, hardware limitations prevented our use of other input devices.

Some subjects commented that they would like a physical keypad for numeric input rather than the graphical softkeys displayed on the screen because they could enter data considerably faster using physical keys. Pict/D does not allow the user to manipulate text, but in an expanded system that did accommodate this data type, a physical keypad would most likely be essential. Alternatively, users could input data by writing on a tablet, which could double as the display, thereby rendering the CRT obsolete and at long last combining input and output devices into a single unit. In the more distant future, speech recognition might replace all manual data entry.

Quite a few subjects were slightly disturbed by Pict/D's tendency to guess where the user might next want the cursor, and then to abruptly move it to the new location. Subjects often tended to believe they still "saw" the cursor in its previous position and sometimes had trouble finding where it had gone. Thus, it would appear that less system intervention here might be a good idea.

Using color. Although some insist that color is unnecessary and even undesirable in the programming environment, its use in Pict/D was very popular with users. Answers to Question (11), "was color important?" indicated that subjects considered color one of Pict/D's most important features. Furthermore, although one of the male undergraduate subjects suffered from red-green color blindness, he did not encounter any special difficulty in the use of the system, aside from an initial slight confusion over the identities of two variables (undoubtedly because squares of solid color were used as variable names).

The use of color is not without potential pitfalls, however. Too many distinct colors is bad because the user may have trouble correctly distinguishing among the various hues. In the Pict prototypes, we used just eight colors, chosen for their sharp contrast; this approach is in line with the guidelines set down by Davis and Swezey[38] and the sources they cite.

The following anecdote may serve to illustrate the unintentional blunders users may make regarding color choices. Originally, the *erasing* icon in Pict/D's root menu was colored according to the scheme

    hand = blue
    background = yellow
    eraser = white
    writing = black

As a result, few realized that the icon was supposed to depict a hand holding an eraser up to a blackboard; indeed, many thought they saw a wrench around a bolt. On the advice of two subjects, the colors were changed to

    hand = orange
    background = black
    eraser = blue
    writing = white

From then on, this icon became the easiest to comprehend. Compare the confusion over the original coloring to that encountered when looking at a negative from which color prints are to be made; the amateur photographer has a hard time deciphering what the image will look like. When we introduced the revised coloring for the *erasing* icon, it was as if the user were suddenly seeing the (positive) print itself. Thus, *proper choice of color is essential*.

Representing data structures and variables with icons

Little work has been published to date on the iconic representation of data structures.[39,40] Should a structure be represented as a collection of generic nodes connected by pointers, or do we perhaps need to see the fields and subfields in each node explicitly? Maybe we need to view the physical, as opposed to the logical, layout of the data structure in certain instances. If the data in the structure is made up of numbers, we may sometimes be interested in the binary values actually stored rather than in their decimal equivalents; at other times, we may need to ascertain only the relative sizes of the data values or their signs. If the data represents a complex document that consists of an amalgam of text, graphical figures, and handwritten material, the possible approaches to developing a structure would be numerous and varied. Our Pict systems have displayed only a small number of integers and simple bidirectionally linked linear lists—display problems could become much more complex.

A closely allied problem is how to determine ways to iconically specify variable names for large quantities of data so that they are easily distinguishable. Pict/D's use of simple squares of solid color will not suffice, in general. McCleary has done some work[41] on the possible integrated use of texture and shape to define what he terms an "effective graphic vocabulary." We believe that a

viable alternative is to integrate text with graphics (even though we also believe that text in the programming environment should be minimized). Thus, icons for variables might indicate graphically the type (in the Pascal sense) and textually the instance (the name of the individual) so that a pointer to a tree might be denoted by a graphical representation of a tree beneath which the user would specify a meaningful name for the pointer.

The menu hierarchy and its display. Several graduate students were dissatisfied because they were not provided an overview of the entire menu tree along with a pointer to their current location in it. Worse yet, numerous subjects disliked the pure tree structure originally used for the system menu, especially when the alternative they wished to choose was already visible on the screen, although technically located on a different branch of the tree. Consequently, the menu structure is now a lattice, so that users can jump "sideways" from branch to branch without first popping a level when changing flow-path color, for example. This change satisfied many users, but others were still unhappy over the need to sometimes pop several levels before they could access the next desired subsystem; the major culprit in this case was the erasing subsystem, located all the way up at the root of the tree. To solve this problem, we could provide links, or special "buttons," in the menu area that the user can push to make "long jumps" to often needed menu elements without regard to the current location. Clearly, all these solutions suffer from their ad hoc nature, and a new and imaginative alternative to the tree is needed. What form it should take, however, is not obvious.

Left- versus right-handedness in the display. An unanticipated problem arose because Glinert is left-handed and designed the *icon editing* icon with the pen clearly in a left hand. This drawing confused right-handed people. Also, the menu area is located at the left edge of Pict/D's screen, and at least two right-handed subjects said they would have preferred to have the menu placed at the right of the screen. Left- or right-handedness is not a factor to be ignored, especially since among computer scientists and programmers, the percentage of left-handed individuals appears to be far higher than that in the general population.

Clear demarcation of screen windows. Originally, the part of the display screen in which users composed their programs was framed by white lines at the top and on the left only. Some subjects had trouble understanding where the logical screen actually ended, however (the physical glass extends a few extra inches to the right, an area inaccessible in practice). Since the problem disappeared when all screen areas were framed on all four sides, we believe that the various screen windows must be clearly and completely outlined.

User acceptance of Pict as a function of sex and age. Responses from both undergraduates and graduate females were consistently more favorable than male responses, even though sometimes by only a small margin (see the tables on p. 19). Malone[2] encountered similar phenomena in his study of video games. A more striking difference in user acceptance of Pict/D is shown in the table that breaks down subjects according to age. The oldest third of the subjects gave consistently less favorable responses than the youngest third.

Ease of use. In general, a good rule of thumb is "if an interactive, graphical programming environment is to win user acceptance, it must appear simple and be fast and versatile." Many programmers seem to expect traditional programming languages to be rather hard to use and somewhat slow, at least for certain applications, but they have no such ex-

pectations with an interactive, iconic system.

In Pict, we can enhance ease of use in two ways. The first is to allow the user to insert a new icon between any two existing ones, in any direction; this ability implies that the system knows how to make "cuts" in the programming surface and insert new strips of program as required (any previous existing paths that crossed the divide would have to be appropriately stretched).

The second is to allow the user to designate blocks of code for naming

---

Pict is appropriate for novices, but to woo the expert user, its capabilities must be significantly expanded.

---

as subprograms after they have already been written as part of an existing routine, as long as the entire block has a single entry and a single exit path. Pict would then remove the block from its current routine, assign it an icon (name), and insert a copy of that icon in the appropriate position in the original routine while closing up any unsightly gaps. The icon assigned to the subprogram could be user-defined (drawn), or it might be automatically generated by the Pict system according to an algorithm based on the statements making up the routine, the names of routines that it calls in its turn, and the variables that it alters.

Pict and the future

As it stands, Pict/D is quite suitable for initiating novices into the world of computer programming. To woo the expert user, however, we must significantly expand the system's capabilities. In addition to the enhancements mentioned already, we might use techniques from artificial intelligence so that the system can guide users in a more

meaningful way than that possible with rudimentary Help messages. Such techniques might also provide Pict systems with what Innocent[42] has termed a "self-adapting user interface" so that the facade presented to users can be tailored to meet their abilities and needs.

Some may argue that we have overdone our emphasis on graphics to the almost total exclusion of text. We feel that the use of text is appropriate in on-line Help systems and for documentation. From our experience, designing an icon that will adequately describe an operation is both difficult and time-consuming, especially for more complex and advanced applications. Therefore, textual documentation should be provided as a complement to the pictorial.

In closing, we note that Pict systems may be of value even to strong advocates of textual programming languages. Novices could be introduced to programming by means of a "pure" Pict system. Then, as they progress, the system could begin to show them automatically generated code in Pascal, say, equivalent to their pictorial programs. At a still later stage, the system could allow the editing of either the graphical or the textual representation of a program while updating the other view to maintain correspondence. Eventually, users could be weaned from the graphical environment to continue their work in a purely textual one.

An interactive, graphically oriented programming environment, Pict, has been proposed as an easier and more natural way for novices to learn programming than conventional, text-based programming languages. Lessons have been learned from experiments conducted with several scores of university students who were exposed to the Pict/D prototype. We believe it noteworthy that some subjects actually believed they had written computer programs without having to first learn a programming language. The use of graphics, color, and simple runtime animation was clearly a factor in this success.

The work reported here is admittedly far from complete. The Pict prototypes clearly lack many desirable features, and future work is needed to correct these deficiencies. Despite the limited scope of our research so far, we can conjecture that even programmers who feel quite comfortable with textual programming languages might soon prefer to do much or all of their work in an interactive, graphical programming environment, at least for special applications whose input and/or output naturally lends itself to graphic representation. □

Acknowledgments

We thank Alan Borning, Alan Shaw, and the anonymous referees of the IEEE Computer Society for their many helpful suggestions and comments on this work. We also express our gratitude to the many University of Washington students who graciously volunteered to participate in our experiments without compensation.

This research was supported in part by the National Science Foundation under grant MCS-8310410. Glinert's work was also supported in part by an IBM graduate fellowship.

References

1. D. C. Smith, *Pygmalion: A Creative Programming Environment,* PhD dissertation, Dept. of Computer Science, Stanford University (tech. report STAN-CS-75-499), 1975.

2. T. W. Malone, *What Makes Things Fun To Learn? A Study of Intrinsically Motivating Computer Games,* PhD dissertation, Dept. of Psychology, Stanford University, Stanford, Calif. (also published by Xerox Palo Alto Research Center, Palo Alto, Calif.), 1980.

3. E. P. Glinert, *PICT: Experiments in the Design of Interactive, Graphical Programming Environments,* PhD dissertation, Dept. of Computer Science, University of Washington, Seattle, Wash. (to be published).

4. I. Nassi and B. Shneiderman, "Flowchart Techniques for Structured Programming," *ACM Sigplan Notices,* Vol. 8, No. 8, Aug. 1973, pp. 12-26.

5. G. A. Miller, "The Magic Number Seven Plus or Minus Two: Some Limits on Our Capacity for Information Processing," *Psychological Review,* Vol. 63, No. 2, 1956, pp. 81-96.

6. K. N. Lodding, "Iconic Interfacing," *IEEE Computer Graphics and Applications,* Vol. 3, No. 2, Mar./Apr. 1983, pp. 11-20.

7. J. L. Diaz-Herrera and R. C. Flude, "PASCAL/HSD: A Graphical Programming System," *Proc. Compsac 80,* IEEE Computer Society Press, Los Alamitos, Calif., 1980, pp. 723-728.

8. B. E. J. Clark and S. K. Robinson, "A Graphically Interacting Program Monitor," *Computer J.,* Vol. 26, No. 3, Aug. 1983, pp. 235-238.

9. M. C. Pong and N. Ng, "PIGS—A System for Programming with Interactive Graphical Support," *Software—Practice and Experience,* Vol. 13, No. 9, Sept. 1983, pp. 847-855.

10. S. P. Reiss, "PECAN: Program Development Systems that Support Multiple Views," tech. report CS-83-29, Dept. of Computer Science, Brown University, Providence, R.I., 1983.

11. N. M. Delisle, D. E. Menicosy, and M. D. Schwartz, "Viewing a Programming Environment as a Single Toll," *Software Engineering Symp. Practical Software Development Environments,* ACM Sigsoft/Sigplan, Apr. 1984.

12. M. H. Brown and R. Sedgewick, "A System for Algorithm Animation," *ACM Computer Graphics,* Vol. 18, No. 3, July 1984, pp. 177-186.

13. N. Magnenat-Thalmann and D. Thalmann, "The Use of High-Level 3-D Graphical Types in the Mira Animation System," *IEEE Computer Graphics and Applications,* Vol. 3, No. 9, Dec. 1983, pp. 9-16.

14. D. Kramlich et al., "Program Visualization: Graphics Support for Software Development," *Proc. 20th Design Automation Conf.,* 1983, pp. 143-149.

15. W. Teitelman, "A Display Oriented Programmer's Assistant," *Int'l J. Man-Machine Studies,* Vol. 11, No. 2, Mar. 1979, pp. 157-187.

16. H. Lieberman and C. Hewitt, "A Session with TINKER: Interleaving Program Testing with Program Design," *Conf. Record 1980 Lisp Conf.,* Stanford University, Stanford, Calif., Aug. 1980, pp. 90-99.

17. F. H. Lakin, "A Structure from Manipulation for Text-Graphic Objects," *ACM Computer Graphics,* Vol. 14, No. 3, July 1980, pp. 100-107.

18. I. B. Sutherland, "Sketchpad, a Man-Machine Graphical Communication System," *Proc. AFIPS Conf.,* Vol. 23, 1963 SJCC, AFIPS Press, Reston, Va., 1963, pp. 329-346.

19. W. M. Newman, "A Graphical Language for Display Programming," *Int'l Computer Graphics Symp.,* Brunel University, Uxbridge, England, Aug. 1968.

20. T. O. Ellis, J. F. Haefner, and W. L. Sibley, "The GRAIL Project: An Experiment in Man-Machine Communications," Rand tech. report RM-5999-ARPA, The Rand Corporation, Santa Monica, Calif., 1969.

21. C. Christensen, M. S. Wolfberg, and M. J. Fisher, "AMBIT/G, Final Report—Task Area I," tech. report AD-720-313, Nat'l Tech. Information Service, Springfield, Va., 1971.

22. E. Denert, R. Franck, and W. Streng, "PLAN2D—Towards a Two-Dimensional Programming Language," *Proc. Fourth Gesellschaft für Informatik Berlin,* 1974, pp. 202-213 (published by Springer-Verlag, Berlin, as Vol. 26 of *Lecture Notes in Computer Science*).

23. G. A. Curry, *Programming by Abstract Demonstration,* PhD dissertation, Dept. of Computer Science, University of Washington, tech. report 78-03-02, Seattle, Wash., 1978.

24. A. Borning, "The Programming Language Aspects of ThingLab, A Constraint-Oriented Simulation Laboratory," *ACM Trans. Programming Languages and Systems,* Vol. 3, No. 4, Oct. 1981, pp. 353-387.

25. W. Finzer and L. Gould, "Programming by Rehearsal," *Byte,* Vol. 9, No. 6, June 1984, pp. 187-210.

26. M. M. Zloof, "A Language for Office and Business Automation," *1980 Office Automation Conf. Digest,* AFIPS Press, Reston, Va., 1980, pp. 249-260.

27. R. E. Mayer, "The Psychology of How Novices Learn Computer Programming," *ACM Computing Surveys,* Vol. 13, No. 1, Mar. 1981, pp. 121-141.

28. F. Mavaddat, "Another Experiment with the Teaching of Programming Languages," *ACM Sigcse Bulletin,* Vol. 13, No. 2, June 1981, pp. 49-56.

29. M. J. Fitter, "Towards More Natural Interactive Systems," *Int'l J. Man-Machine Studies,* Vol. 11, No. 3, May 1979, pp. 339-350.

30. R. E. Brooks, "Studying Programmer Behavior Experimentally: The Problems of Proper Methodology," *Comm. ACM,* Vol. 23, No. 4, Apr. 1980, pp. 207-213.

31. B. Shneiderman, *Software Psychology: Human Factors in Computer and Information Systems,* Winthrop Publishers, Cambridge, Mass., 1980.

32. L. H. Miller, "A Study in Man-Machine Interaction," *AFIPS Conf. Proc.,* Vol. 46, 1977 NCC, AFIPS Press, Reston, Va., 1977, pp. 409-421.

33. D. J. Gilmore and H. T. Smith, "An Investigation of the Utility of Flowcharts During Computer Program Debugging," *Int'l J. Man-Machine Studies,* Vol. 20, No. 4, Apr. 1984, pp. 357-372.

34. B. Shneiderman, "Exploratory Experiments in Programmer Behavior," *Int'l J. Computer and Information Sciences,* Vol. 5, No. 2, June 1976, pp. 123-143.

35. C. H. Smith and H. E. Dunsmore, "On the Relative Comprehensibility of Various Control Structures by Novice Fortran Programmers," *Int'l J. Man-Machine Studies,* Vol. 17, No. 2, Aug. 1982, pp. 165-171.

36. A. Arblaster, "Human Factors in the Design and Use of Computer Languages," *Int'l J. Man-Machine Studies,* Vol. 17, No. 2, Aug. 1982, pp. 211-224.

37. L. Cardelli, "Two-Dimensional Syntax for Functional Languages," *Proc. European Conf. Integrated Interactive Computing Systems,* Sept. 1982, pp. 107-119.

38. E. G. Davis and R. W. Swezey, "Human Factors Guidelines in Computer Graphics: A Case Study," *Int'l J. Man-Machine Studies,* Vol. 18, No. 2, Feb. 1983, pp. 113-133.

39. S. L. Getz, G. Kalligiannis, and S. R. Schach, "A Very High-Level Interactive Graphical Trace for the Pascal Heap," *IEEE Trans. Software Engineering,* Vol. SE-9, No. 2, Mar. 1983, pp. 179-185.

40. B. A. Myers, "Incense: A System for Displaying Data Structures," *ACM Computer Graphics,* Vol. 17, No. 3, July 1983, pp. 115-125.

41. G. F. McCleary, Jr., "An Effective Graphic Vocabulary," *IEEE Computer Graphics and Applications,* Vol. 3, No. 2, Mar./Apr. 1983, pp. 46-53.

42. P. R. Innocent, "Towards Self-Adaptive Interface Systems," *Int'l J. Man-Machine Studies,* Vol. 16, No. 3, Apr. 1982, pp. 287-299.

Ephraim P. Glinert is completing a PhD dissertation on interactive, graphical programming environments. His research interests include programming languages and systems, human factors (especially computers and the handicapped), computer graphics, artificial intelligence, and computer education. He is the author of *Introduction to Computer Science Using Pascal,* published by Prentice-Hall, 1984.

Glinert holds a BSc and MSc in mathematics from Technion, Israel Institute of Technology. He is a member of the ACM and the IEEE Computer Society.

Steven L. Tanimoto is an associate professor in the Dept. of Computer Science at the University of Washington in Seattle. His research interests include image processing (especially pyramid data structures and the languages and parallel algorithms that work with them), computer graphics, artificial intelligence, and the use of pictures and diagrams to program and use computers. He has also been a visiting professor at the Institut de Programmation, University of Paris, and a visiting scientist at the Dept. of Electrical Engineering, Linkoping University, Sweden.

Tanimoto received a BSc from Harvard University in 1971 and a PhD in electrical engineering from Princeton University in 1975. He is a member of the ACM, the IEEE Computer Society, and the American Association for Artificial Intelligence, and is an associate editor of *IEEE Transactions on Pattern Analysis and Machine Intelligence.*

Questions about this article can be directed to either author, Dept. of Computer Science, FR-35, University of Washington, Seattle, WA 98195.

□□□ 4 □□□ Environments II: Visual Front Ends for Main–Line Textual Languages

J.L. Diaz-Herrera and R.C. Flude. "Pascal/HSD: A Graphical Programming System." In *Proc. COMPSAC'80*, Chicago, Ill., pages 723–728, 1980. IEEE Computer Society Press, Los Alamitos, Calif.

D. Kramlich, G.P. Brown, R.T. Carling and C.F. Herot. "Program Visualization: Graphics Support for Software Development." In *Proc. 20th Design Automation Conference*, Miami Beach, Fla., pages 143–149, June 27-29, 1983. ACM Press, New York.

M. Edel. "The TINKERTOY Graphical Programming Environment." In *Proc. COMPSAC'86*, Chicago, Ill., pages 466–471, 1986. IEEE Computer Society Press, Los Alamitos, Calif.

M.E. Kopache and E.P. Glinert. "C^2: A Mixed Textual/Graphical Programming Environment for C." In *Proc. Workshop on Visual Languages*, Pittsburgh, Penn., pages 231–238, October 10-12, 1988. IEEE Computer Society Press, Los Alamitos, Calif.

P.T. Cox and T. Pietrzykowski. "Using a Pictorial Representation to Combine Data–Flow and Object Orientation in a Language–Independent Programming Mechanism." In *Proc. Int. Computer Science Conference, Hong Kong*, pages 695–704, 1988 (available as *Tech]nical Report TR–3–1988*, School of Computer Science, Technical University of Nova Scotia, Halifax, Canada).

PASCAL/HSD: A GRAPHICAL PROGRAMMING SYSTEM

J.L. Diaz-Herrera and R.C. Flude

University of Lancaster. UK

Abstract

New trends in programming methodology have made it
necessary to look for more suitable
representational tools to replace conventional
ones such as flowcharts. A number of diagrammatic
forms for presenting programs have been proposed
in the last decade or so, but they have all been
unsuitable for program development using pencil
and paper. We have developed a diagrammatic
language based on the programming language PASCAL
to be used in CONJUNCTION with interactive
computer graphics to provide an on-line
programming system which implements current
programming methods. A real time animation of the
compilation and interpretation of the user
programs is produced on the graphics display under
interactive control. This feature provides a
powerful facility for teaching both programming
and compiling techniques.

Introduction

PASCAL/HSD is a high-level language programming
system based on and developed from PASCAL/S,[25]
which is in turn a subset of PASCAL/P.[1] PASCAL/HSD
is in fact a diagrammatic version of PASCAL/S in
which constructs take the form of graphical
two-dimensional symbols.[5] The main feature of the
system is its facilities for defining computations
at different levels of detail (abstractions) and
for representing hierarchical information in a
more natural way than is possible with written
text.[8] PASCAL/HSD programs are highly structured
and exist in the form of program charts which can
only be inspected/edited from a computer graphics
work station. Graphical aids appear to be very
useful in problem solving,[12] and they play an
important role in education;[3] moreover, the use of
interactive computer graphics for making this
pictorial representations mobile gives more
insight into the process being modelled.[11,20]

The idea of developing programs with the aid
of interactive computer graphics is not a new
one.[6,9,10,16,18,19] Early systems have been
characterized by the use of terminals in
"interactive programming" simply to provide
graphical input and text-editing facilities aimed
at producing good up-to-date documentation.
PASCAL/HSD represents a new approach to the
problem. PASCAL/HSD has been designed as an
integrated program development system which
includes a compiler, an interpreter, and an
editor-monitor, as opposed to previous systems
which were designed as preprocessors to existing
compilers and interpreters.

The main characteristic of the PASCAL/HSD
compiler and interpreter is a run time
user-interaction facility whereby the progress of
the compilation and of the interpretation can be
selectively displayed at slow speed. The
PASCAL/HSD compiler requires the source to be in
the form of an on-line data base for the program
under development. This data base is constructued
using the editor-monitor which also provides some
assistance in the building of the programs. This
editor-monitor is a table driven parser[26] that
ensures programs are free from syntactical errors.

Our approach has been inspired and motivated
by the fact that programming today requires more
interactive and computer-aided tools for
constructing and debugging correct and structured
software.[17,21] The trend towards online
programming started with the development of
time-sharing systems in the sixties. The advent of
microcomputers has made interactive programming a
necessity. Currently two major complementary
methods for constructing software have been put
forward: structured programming,[4] restricting the
use of control structures; and top-down or
step-wise refinement,[24] to reduce the problem to a
set of more manageable subproblems.

Until now, programming languages have been
the most widely used tools. The difficulty is
however, that although any procedural type of
language is suitable for achieving structured
control flow, the development of programs in a
top-down or step-wise manner is obviously not

possible to do naturally.[14] The problem is to represent the hierarchical structure which is generated when the program is developed; even if we use "scoped" and "indented" comments as abstractions (the extent to which they can be used is limited by the size of normal I/O media) they are usually eliminated and replaced by the corresponding refinements. When eventually all the higher level comments (abstractions) are replaced, the tree-like way in which the program was constructed will have been obscured completely.

Restrictions imposed on the conventional flowchart[2,22,23] and the development of more structured diagrammatical aids[13,15,27] solve some of the problems, but they are inherently manual. We have found that manual tools are quite inadequate for use in top-down step-wise programming. In particular, each stage of refinement usually requires the complete redrawing of the design.

Finally it is also important to stress the idea of minimizing the probability of making errors (especially syntactical ones), and increasing programs reliability. This can be greatly improved by relieving programmers from the most time-comsuming and error-prone tasks so as to enable them to concentrate more on the design.

Hierarchical Structured Diagrams

The use of diagrammatic languages provides a spatial representation of the logic of the programs that visually projects the control flow in a manner that is much more direct than using text indentation. A PASCAL/HSD program exists as a two-dimensional "Hierarchical Structured Diagram" (HSD),[5] which is a representational tool whereby the program's structured control flow and hierarchical levels of detail can be compacted and viewed as a unit.

These diagrams are made up from graphical representations of the basic structured constructs sequence, iteration, and decision together with textual statements written in PASCAL/S. The HSD's are based on two graphical symbols (called statement symbols) which in various combinations are used to represent the language constructs. Text is formatted to lie inside the graphic outline of these symbols.

Statement symbols

A statement symbol is represented by a box enclosing text and describes a specified computation, which can only be of two types,

namely ACTIONS and TESTS, each represeted by a different symbol. Any statement symbol can be recursively expanded to include an inner level chart, in which case its text is treated as a comment, and serves to describe in more general terms the sub-algorithms described by the expansion. A symbol which is not refined or expanded is called a terminal symbol, and its text represent simple statements in PASCAL/S.

ACTION statement symbol (Fig-1a): The text of a terminal ACTION symbol is composed only of PASCAL/S assignement statements and procedure calls separated by semicoloms.

TEST statement symbol (Fig-1b): The expansion of this symbol into a further chart results in the definition of this new chart as a boolean function. The text of a terminal TEST symbol describes test expressions in PASCAL/S. There are three types of test expressions, namely Boolean tests, Case tests, and For tests.

Fig-1 ACTION and TEST statement symbols

Constructs

Constructs are single-entry single-exit building blocks formed from combinations of one or more statement symbols. The permitted combinations are predefined and specified in a syntax table. Constructs fall into one of the two categories simple or compound. A simple construct is just the occurrence of one action symbol, and a compound construct involves a test symbol and one or more action symbols. In what follows we are explaining the constructs implemented in PASCAL/HSD. The semantics of these constructs is as defined for PASCAL/S.

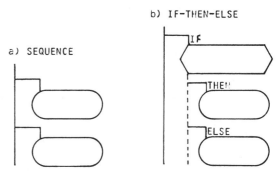

Fig-2 SEQUENCE and IF-THEN-ELSE constructs

SEQUENCE construct (Fig-2a): This construct is represented by one or more action statement symbols.

IF-THEN-ELSE construct (Fig-2b): This construct is formed by a test statement symbol and two action symbols. The TEST symbol holds the boolean expression to be tested, whereas the two ACTION symbols are used to represent the 'THEN' and 'ELSE' clauses. The 'ELSE' clause may be omited.

CASE-OF construct (Fig-3a): It is composed of a test statement symbol and two or more action statement symbols. Each ACTION symbol represets an alternative for the case expression containned in the TEST symbol.

REPEAT-UNTIL construct (Fig-3b): This is an action symbol followed by a test symbol. The dotted line from the TEST symbol which is connected back to the ACTION symbol represents the back jump for the loop. This dotted line is traversed if the result from the boolean expression inside the test symbol is false.

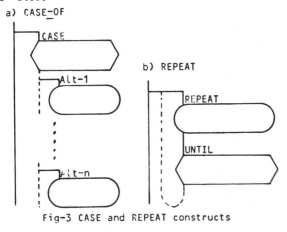

Fig-3 CASE and REPEAT constructs

WHILE-DO (and its variant FOR-DO) (Fig-4): This is a test symbol followed by an action symbol. The inner execution (dotted) line connects back to the TEST symbol after the ACTION symbol is processed, which will be repeated if the outcome of the boolean expression inside the test symbol is true.

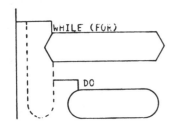

Fig-4 WHILE-FOR constructs

PASCAL/HSD source programs

Programs are built by connecting constructs along a vertical line (execution line) to form an HSD chart representing the source program. An inner level chart is shown to the right of the construct being expanded, thereby allowing the sequence of control flow to be shown from top-to-bottom and hierarchical levels of detail from left-to-right on the charts.

Program execution proceeds by traversing execution lines from the top to the bottom. If in traversing an execution line a construct which has been expanded is reached, then the execution line of the new inner chart is entered (Fig-5). When the last node of this execution line is processed, then the control flow returns to the execution line on the previous outer level at the point of the expansion. This is repeated until the last construct of the outer most execution line has been executed. Backward jumps associated with loops, and decision paths are specified as broken execution lines. A broken line then always follows from a test symbol in any compound construct, and generally means that the control flow might or might not pass through that line.

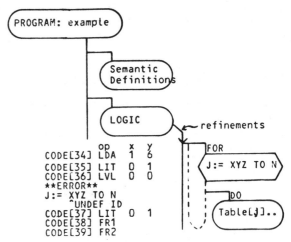

Fig-5 HSD example

System implementation

The system has been implemented using an interactive graphics satellite computer connected to a general purpose host computer (Fig-6). The heart of the system includes the program representation which is described as a display file on the graphics computer, and in a data base on the host computer.

In the data base the program is represented as a binary tree with one link connecting the instances at a given level on the hierarchy, and the other linking the levels. Each instance has the information pertaining to one specific part of the program developed. Thus, associated with the instance there is a record (or node) describing the type of instance, textual content, and the current state of the development process at that point on the program.

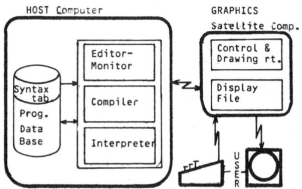

Fig-6 System Design and Implementation

The host computer and the graphics satellite computer communicate to each other through a very simple protocol based on a single ASCII charater language called the User Command Language (UCL). User interaction is carried out through a keyboard attached to the graphics computer, on which the user types UCL instructions. These commands are sent to the host for interpretation, the result of which generates updating of the display file and consequently of the picture seen on the screen.

Portability and transferability has been aimed at throughout the design and implementation of the system. The system is virtually independent of the host computer since the software was written in PASCAL/P.[1] The only machine dependent code written was that for the graphics satellite computer.

Building PASCAL/HSD programs

The PASCAL/HSD system is intended to be used in conjuction with a graphics terminal. The editing process is monitored by a table driven interactive parser. This table describes the commands that the user can issue in the form of a transition table, in which the next valid command depends on the current state of the table. This editor can in general be viewed as a computer aided program development facility which provides a common framework for programming. Thus it guides the user in developing the diagrams so that the final product will be syntactically correct. The syntax table simultaneously represents a definition of the syntax of the language in itself and also a model of this definition[7] which can be

automatically interpreted in order to:

a) Prompt the user to provide the right information (commands) at each stage of the development.
b) Inform the user of alternative constructs available from the current state of development (a HELP mechanism).
c) Respond to queries from the user about the model and hence about the syntax of the language (a teaching tool).

The display screen initially is empty of any diagrammatic information, and could be thought of as a window into a much larger drawing space for the programmer to work. The user proceeds by inserting instances of the diagram's templates (constructs) in the area of the screen currently pointed at by the cursor. Other operations include further refinement of previously entered constructs, deletion of unwanted constructs, insertion of text, and moving the cursor along the execution lines.

Compiling PASCAL/HSD programs

The input to the compiler is the data base built for the program. This tree-like data base is traversed visiting the root first, and then recursively visiting the righthand subtree (inner level chart) followed by the lefthand subtree (subsequent nodes at the current level). Each visited node may be displayed on the graphics terminal showing it's relationships with previous nodes (i.e hierarchy or sequence of control). Terminal nodes are compiled, and other nodes are processed as comments. The code and tables produced are placed in the data base as further levels of detail of the respective terminal nodes. If any errors are detected no code is produced for that node, but the error is recorded and displayed.

Compilation can proceed in three different modes of operartion: automatic, semiautomatic, and manual. In automatic mode no user interaction is allowed and the graphics display is not used; the compiler in this mode behaves like any conventional compiler. Semiautomatic mode neither allows user interaction, but the graphics display is used for showing the progress of the compilation in slow motion. Finally manual mode does allow the user to interactively specify which nodes are required to be seen during the compilation and to what level of detail (this includes the possibility to see the actual CODE produced for a particular statement); this mode also allows the user to enter the Editor (e.g. for correcting errors) and to restart the compilation.

Interpreting PASCAL/HSD programs

The input to this process is the previously generated intermediate code and tables, which are to be found in the data base. Interpretation carries on similarly as for compilation. It starts at the root of the tree structure program data base, traversing it down to the terminal nodes; and it also operates in any of the automatic, semiautomatic, and manual modes.

As for the compiler, the interpreter in automatic mode behaves like any other non-interactive conventional interpreter. In any of the other two modes, the diagrammatic representation attached to each visited node is displayed on the graphics screen, together with its textual information describing either comments (abstractions) or PASCAL/S statements (refinements). When the interpretation is done in the manual mode, the user can interactively choose whether or not to see more detail (refinements) of particular abstractions, and also to provide new data values.

The content of a terminal node in the data base, after compilation, describes the intermediate CODE to be interpreted. This code may be optionally displayed next to the corresponding higher level graphical construct currently being interpreted (Fig-5), and if shown, a pointer indicating the actual instruction about to be interpreted is is also seen. Porgram data is shown by displaying the content of the run-time stack used in the interpretation of PASCAL/S programs.

Conclusions

The general objective of the project has been to explore the capabilities and potentialities of computer graphics at the front end of a computer aided program development system. Specifically the system aims to provide help by:
   a) Making it more "natural" to construct programs, particularly for computer naïve users. Graphical notation has made it unnecessary to use "bracketing" and "closing" keywords, the use of which may lead to arbitrary indentation producing unreadable programs.
   b) Making it easier and less time consuming to construct programs. A lot of "typing-in" is eliminated, and the user is led to develop programs which are syntactically correct.
   c) Enforcing the use of standards and design methods to assist in program development.
   d) Making it easier for users to understand the behaviour of their programs by the use of an interactive real-time interpreter with graphical I/O.

We have developed a new format for representing programs called Hierarchical Structured Diagram, which is intended for use with a graphics terminal to provide a representation of algorithms showing hierarchy together with structured control flow. The diagrams are the only form of the programs seen by the user, and are interactively interpreted at a slow enough speed so as to allow the user to actually see the programs running. This approach allows us to observe at different levels of detail the processes being interpreted and the data being manipulated, thus providing a powerful tool for debugging and program understanding.

The PASCAL/HSD compiler has not been implemented as an incremental compiler. This would have avoided the need for recompiling the whole program when errors are found. However, this approach creates other problems, such as reprocessing context sensitive statements, which are more important than the overhead impossed by recompilation. Good, well-structured languages always contain context-dependent features. These problems are not beyond solution, and most of the proposed ones result in recompiling part of the program.

It seems undesirable to produce a textual version of a program, since this allows the user to change it, making the design and diagrams obsolete. However, it might be desirable, for practical reasons, to provide a preprocessor and a postprocessor to interface the system to other PASCAL source programs and compilers respectively. It is also possible to reproduce the HSD's on a plotting device although it may need to be done selectively.

It is intended to provide at a later date some facilities for the gathering of statistics to be used in the assesment of "program behaviour" and "program quality". For example, run-time statement counts are useful in debugging, testing, and for actual (not just theoretical) algorithm analysis; static information about the program structure will assist in measuring program complexity and in stylistic analysis. It is also desirable to design a semantic definition library (abstraction library) to allow the provision of extensible language facilities, whereby the user could define new constructs, from already existing ones, with a temporal or permanent character.

Improvements can also be made in the graphics facilities providing more general purpose graphics capabilities so that the user could define pictorial forms (for data and/or operations) closer to the problem area, as to produce a more problem oriented animation. The fact that the syntax of the target language is described in a table, and that the drawing routines are contained in separate modules, present the possibility of implementing different "inferred" programming languages and several diagrammatic forms with a minimum of effort.

The system has not as yet been widely used. It is hoped that it will prove to be useful as a teaching aid.

ACKNOWLEDGEMENT

This research has been sponsored by the Venezuelan goverment partially through the scholarship program "Fundacion Gram Mariscal de Ayacucho" in Caracas, the "Universidad Centro Occidental Lisandro Alvarado" , and the 'Empresa Regional de computacion ERCO" both in Barquisimeto, Venezuela.

Authors' address:
J.L. Diaz-Herrera:
Universidad Centro Occidental Lisandro Alvarado, Escuela de Ciencias. Apartado 400, Barquisimeto, Venezuela.
R.C. Flude:
University of Lancaster, Dept. of Computer Studies. Bailrigg LA1 4YN, Lancashire U.K.

REFERENCES

(1) Ammann U., Jensen K., Nageli H.H., and Nori K.V. (1974) "The PASCAL<P> compiler; Implementation notes". ETH Zurich 1974.
(2) Bohm C. and Jacopini G. (1966) "Flowdiagrams, Turing machines, and languages with only two formation rules". C.ACM Vol.9, No.5, pp 366-371.
(3) Bork A. (1975) "Learning through graphics". Ten-year forecast for computers and communications: implications for education. HumRRo conf. Sept. 1975.
(4) Dahl O-J., Dijkstra E.W., and Hoare C.A.R (1972) "Structured programming". Academic Press.
(5) Diaz-Herrera J.L. and R.C. Flude (1980) "Hierarchical Structured Diagrams". Computer Graphics 80, ONLINE Conference, Brighton Aug. 1980, pp535-547
(6) Ellis T.O, Heafner J.F, and Sibley W.L. (1969) "The GRAIL project: an experiment in man-machine commnications". Memo RM-5999-ARPA, Rand corporation, Sept 1969.
(7) Feyock S. (1977) "Transition diagram-based CAI/HELP systems". Intern. J. of Man-machine studies. Vol.9, pp 399-413.
(8) Fitter M. and Green T.R.G. (1979) "When do diagrams make good computer languages?". Intern. J. Man-machine studies. Vol 11, pp 235-261.
(9) Frei H.P., Weller D.L., and Williams R. (1978) "A graphics-based programming-support system". Proc. SIGGRAPH-ACM conf. Aug. 1978. pp43-49.
(10) Goddard G., Whitworth M., and Strovink E. (1978) "JOVIAL structured design diagrammer

(JSDD)". Vol 1,2,3,4. Charles stark Draper Lab. Inc. Cambridge, MA USA. Feb 1978.
(11) Huggings W.H. and Entwisle D.R (1969) "Computer animation for the academic community". AFIPS Spring Joint Conf. 1969, pp 623-627.
(12) Huttenlocher J. (1968) "Constructing spatial images: a strategy in reasoning". Psych. Review 75, 1968.
(13) Jackson M.A. (1975) "Principles of program design". Academic Press. 1975
(14) Meertens L. (1978) "Program text and program structure" Constructing Quality Software, IFIP conference 1978, pp 271-283.
(15) Nassi I. and Shneiderman B. (1973) "Flowchart techiniques for structured programming". SIGPLAN Notices-ACM- Vol.8, No.8, pp 12-26.
(16) Neroth C.C. (1975) "A graphical programming system with speech input". Computer & Graphics, Vol.1, pp 227-231.
(17) Roman G-C. (1977) "An argument in favor of mechanized software production". IEEE trans. on software Eng. Vol.SE-3, No.3, Nov. 1977.
(18) Sutherland W.R.(1966) "On-line graphical specification of computer programs". Tech. report 405, Lincoln Lab. MIT, USA. 1966.
(19) Triance J.M. and Edwards B.J. (1979) "A computer aided program design project". Proc. EURO-IFIP 79, London Sept. 1979. pp 621-626.
(20) Weiner D.D. (1971) "Computer animation: an exiting new tool for educators". IEEE Trans. on Educ. Vol.E-14, No.4.
(21) Winograd T. (1975) "Breaking the complexity barrier again". SIGPLAN Notices, ACM. Vol.10, no.1, pp 13-22
(22) Williams W.H. (1977) "Generating structured flow diagrams : the nature of unstructuredness". The computer Journal. Vol.20, No.1, pp 45-50.
(23) Williams W.H. and Ossher H.L. (1978) "Conversion of unstructured flow diagrams to structured from". The computer Journal. Vol.21, no.2, pp 161-167.
(24) Wirth N. (1971) "Program development by step-wise refinement". C.ACM Vol.14, No.4, pp 221-227.
(25) Wirth N. (1976a) "PASCAL/S" ETH ch-8092. Zurich, march 1976.
(26) Wirth N. (1976b) "Algorithms + data structures = programs". Prentice Hall.
(27) Witty R.W. (1977) "Dimensional flowcharts". Software practice & experience, Vol.7, pp 553-584.

Program Visualization: Graphics Support for Software Development

David Kramlich, Gretchen P. Brown, Richard T. Carling, Christopher F. Herot

Computer Corporation of America
Four Cambridge Center
Cambridge, Massachusetts 02142

Abstract

This paper reports on the design and implementation of a program visualization (PV) environment, intended to offer the user an integrated graphics programming support system. The PV environment will capitalize on recent progress in the graphical representation of information, to provide designers and programmers with both static and dynamic (animated) views of systems. PV is currently being implemented to support programming in C, although large portions of the system are independent of the software development language. In this paper we provide an overview of the PV environment, along with a detailed discussion of the technique used to instrument programs.

KEYWORDS:

programming workstations, graphics, integrated environments, software engineering, computer animation, program instrumentation

1. Introduction

The Program Visualization (PV) System will offer the user an integrated graphics programming support system. It will support the programmer in writing, debugging, and documenting computer programs. A key feature of the system is the ability to monitor running programs in order to display dynamic visualizations of their operation. We expect the PV system to, in effect, "open the side of the machine" so that the user can form an accurate model of the program.

This research was supported by the Defense Advanced Research Project Agency of the Department of Defense and was monitored by the Office of Naval Research under Contract No. N00014-80-C-0683. The views and conclusions contained in this document are those of the authors and should not be interpreted as necessarily representing the official policies, either expressed or implied, of the Defense Department, the Office of Naval Research, or the U.S. Government.

Computer-generated images were used to visualize the dynamic behavior of programs in the early days of computer graphics (e.g.,[3,10,13]), and dynamic visualizations have continued to receive attention (e.g., [1,2,4,5,9,12,15]). Only recently, however, have advances in hardware and software allowed automated production of dynamic (as well as static) illustrations to become cost-effective for a broad range of applications. Significant research still remains to be done in order to identify, represent, and generate a useful range of dynamic visualizations.

In this paper, we describe the goals and status of the PV research effort, which at the time of writing is in the second year of a three-year project. Section 2 presents examples of the types of visualization that we expect the system to include, and Section 3 gives an overview of the PV environment. Section 4 looks at an important technical problem, the instrumentation of programs in order to monitor them while they run. While the PV system is not being designed to monitor real-time systems, it is being designed to support large programs, for which efficient detection of updates is crucial. Finally, the implementation status of the PV system is discussed in Section 5.

2. An Example Program Visualization

When we set out to design and build a graphic programming environment, it was not clear what types of dynamic visualizations should be supported. In the past, graphics for software documentation and demonstration have been tightly constrained by existing graphic production and maintenance tools. As the technology of computer-driven bit-mapped color display-systems removes these constraints, the question remains: What should we display and how should we display it? This problem was addressed in [7], which identified important categories of program visualizations. In this paper, we present a sample pair of integrated visualizations that was developed in collaboration with graphic designers. The example shows some of the possibilities presented by the new technology.

Figure 1 shows an integrated visualization of

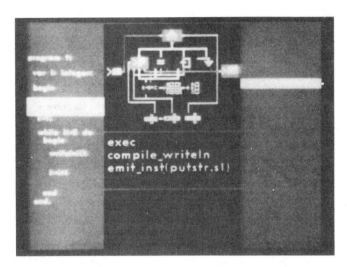

Figure 1. Overview of a running compilation. (Animated mock-up.) Source code is on left, object code appears on right as it is output. Highlights on compiler structure diagram indicate active routines, which are named in the stack trace below the structure diagram.

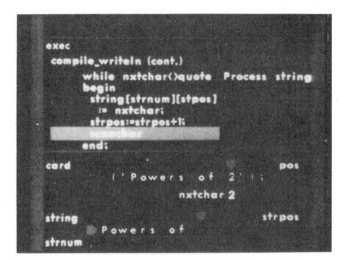

Figure 2. Detailed view of a running compilation. (Animated mock-up.) As highlights move through code, graphical index pointers advance across arrays and the box for the NXTCHAR variable moves along under the CARD array to the appropriate position. The break in the left hand part of the CARD array is used to indicate the existence of initial entries in the array that do not appear in the current display.

a compiler that handles a small subset of Pascal.* The mini-compiler structure diagram in the center of Figure 1 has modules labeled with icons rather than text, an approach that we are exploring as part of the PV project. Icon labels may aid module recognition and discrimination, particularly at small scale. On the left in Figure 1 is the text of a source program, which is highlighted as each line in the source is compiled. Highlights move around the structure diagram to indicate flow of control in the compiler. Below the structure diagram is a stack trace of compiler procedure calls that grows and shrinks appropriately. Object code (in a hypothetical assembly language defined in [8]) appears with highlights on the right as it is generated.

Figure 2 shows another view of the same mini-compiler, this time at a more detailed level. At the top of Figure 2 is the Pascal code of the compiler, at the bottom are illustrations of data structures from the routine being executed. Execution causes highlights to move through the code and data structures to be updated. When

COMPILE_WRITELN copies a substring from the one-dimensional array CARD into the two-dimensional array STRING, the graphic pointers move as the array indices advance. The box for the variable that holds the next character to be processed (NXTCHAR) moves along under the appropriate position of the array.

Figure 2 would be accessible to the programmer by zooming in on the stack trace portion of Figure 1. The top and sides of Figure 2 indicate its context in Figure 1. In addition, the stack trace context is preserved by the bands at the top of the screen, which indicate the depth of procedure calls (in this case, the user is two deep: EXEC and COMPILE_WRITELN). The destination of a particular zoom is up to the diagram builder; the system provides the linking capability.

We are presenting a simple example so that two key ideas will emerge. The first idea is that the programmer should have a choice of level of detail, to complement different problem solving strategies. The user can shift from an overview level to a view that zeros-in on details. The second key idea is the integration of information in a single view. This is illustrated by the combination of code, stack trace, and structure diagram in Figure 1. In Figure 2 this integration consists of the joint display of text and data structures; less immediately obvious is the spatial association between indices, arrays, and the NXTCHAR variable. When watching an animated view of Figure 2 it is relatively easy to determine when indices are being updated correctly and when they are out of phase, a common bug.

---

* Figures 1 and 2 in this section were taken from a videotape that was made to explore different types of program images. The images are mock-ups, in that none of the animation was driven by a program being monitored. The PV implementation has, however, progressed to the point that limited animation is fully supported. (See Sec. 5.) The mini-compiler discussed in this section was adapted from [8], where it was presented for pedagogical purposes. Note that, although the mini-compiler is coded in Pascal, the first PV research prototype will support only C.

The types of program visualizations exemplified in Figure 1 and Figure 2 pose a number of research problems, among them:

1. How the user specifies the static image and the type of animation.

2. How the user instruments the program (i.e., binds parts of the program to the visualization).

3. How the system generates the graphic displays (e.g., how it does the animation).

4. How the user controls the graphic displays (e.g., control of animation speed and motion between different levels of detail).

5. How the system monitors the running program.

The PV project addresses each of these issues. The next section gives an overview of the PV environment, summarizing our approach.

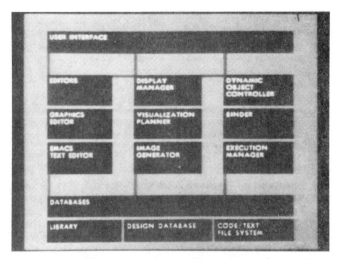

Figure 3. Top level diagram of the Program Visualization system. This diagram was produced using the Graphics Editor of the PV system.

3. Overview of the PV Environment

The current workstation for the Program Visualization system consists of three medium-resolution AED 512 color displays. The user interacts with the system via a combination of data tablet with four-button puck, keyboard, and touch sensitive devices on the displays. The display arrangement is flexible, and we are scheduled to move the PV research prototype to a single high-resolution color display.

A programmer uses the PV system via a menu-oriented user interface that displays diagrams and text in multiple windows on the screen. The current PV window system is in the spirit of [14], which has been widely replicated. We are exploring ways to build more structure into the user interface, so that windows will cluster appropriately, resulting in less window management work for the programmer/user. Information access in the PV system is aided by diagrams acting as spatial navigational aids, in the manner pioneered in [6]. The PV system is being prototyped to support programming in C, although large portions of the system are independent of the software development language. The implementation runs on a VAX 11/780 under Berkeley UNIX.

We intend that programmers use the PV system as a full software development environment. For this reason, the system supports the following:

- Manipulation of static and dynamic diagrams of computer systems

- Manipulation of program and documentation text

- Creation and traversal of multi-dimensional information space

- Reuse and dissemination of tools via a library of diagram and text components (e.g., templates)

The remainder of this section discusses the PV facilities in these four areas. The modules named are illustrated in Figure 3 (produced using the PV Graphics Editor).

1. Manipulation of Static and Dynamic Diagrams of Computer Systems

To create, edit, and view static diagrams, the programmer/user invokes the Graphics Editor. The Graphics Editor provides a high level graphics language and gives the programmer access to prespecified diagram components (e.g., templates and collections of notational symbols) in the Library. The PV system will provide an optional automated visualization planning capability, performing functions such as selecting colors, sizing and positioning objects, and positioning labels. (Because visualization planning is a fundamental open research problem, the PV system will not necessarily perform these functions as well as a human can, but we expect it to perform well enough to save the programmer time in cases where a rough visualization is sufficient.)

To create, edit, and view dynamic diagrams of programs, the programmer uses the Dynamic Object Controller. The creation of dynamic diagrams can be semiautomatic; in particular, the programmer can point to variables in his or her C code and the system will automatically select appropriate diagrams to display them. Alternatively, the user can build or select diagrams and bind diagrams to code with the Binder. In either case, when the programmer finally runs the program, the Execution Manager in the Dynamic Object Controller will monitor the running code to activate the visualization.

All diagrams are stored in the Design Database. The programmer/user will be provided with a diagram of the Design Database structure and its current contents. This diagram can be used as a navigational aid when storing and accessing diagrams.

2. Manipulation of Program and Documentation Text

The programmer can use the PV system to create and manipulate static text and also dynamic text (e.g., highlights moving through code to indicate flow of control).

To create and manipulate static text, the programmer invokes the Text Editor. This text editor is an implementation of EMACS enhanced for the purposes of the PV environment. EMACS was chosen because of its power and extensibility. Labeled keycaps on terminal function keys simplify the use of the text editor. Text (including code) files are stored using the UNIX file system, with the PV system providing additional spatial file access mechanisms.

To create and manipulate dynamic text, the programmer invokes the Dynamic Object Controller. The process of tying dynamic text to code is similar to the process of tying diagrams to code.

3. Creation and Traversal of Multi-Dimensional Information Space

Fundamental to the programmer's ability to use the system is an information integration mechanism that allows convenient access to the quantities of diagrams and documents that are part of a large-scale system development effort. The PV system provides a multi-dimensional information space in which the programmer can establish links: diagram to diagram, text to text, diagram to text, or text to diagram. Links are associated with the whole or with individual parts of the diagrams or text. A user viewing a program structure diagram can, for example, zoom from one level of abstraction to another, ending up at the lowest level with program code.

4. Library of Diagram and Text Components (e.g., Templates)

When the individual programmer, or some group of programmers, identifies a graphic or text component that can be expected to be of repeated utility, then it can be added to the Library. The Library is a network of programming and graphics concepts accessible spatially, via a library structure diagram that acts as a navigational aid. Library components include pictorial and textual building blocks such as programming subroutines; templates which the user "fills in" to complete a graphic, program, or documentation construct; kits of components from which the user can assemble a diagram or textual description; and generator programs which the user can run in order to interactively create a diagram or text construct.

It should be clear from this overview that there are a number of important technical problems that must be solved before graphic software environments become practical. The next section discusses one of them, the need to monitor large running programs to detect the updates to be displayed. This is a critical mechanism for the production of dynamic program visualizations, and it is an area in which the PV implementation is relatively complete as of the writing of this paper.

4. Monitoring Running Programs

The Execution Manager, as its name implies, interacts with and manages the program being monitored. It has two main tasks: determine where the program is currently executing, and monitor user-selected variables for updates.

Our implementation of the Execution Manager makes use of software debugging facilities provided in the UNIX operating system and hardware features used to implement virtual memory. The UNIX environment provides a set of facilities by which one process may manipulate the registers and address space of another process. Several new features were added to allow the monitoring process (Execution Manager) to manipulate the memory mapping of the monitored process (the user's program). In addition, the Portable C Compiler was modified to produce a supplemented symbol table, which the Execution Manager uses to locate variables and code in the user's program.

There were two primary goals in the implementation of the Execution Manager: minimize any special requirements on the monitored program, and make monitoring as efficient as possible.

4.1 Minimizing Special Requirements

The first goal was achieved by placing the burden of program monitoring on the C compiler and the Execution Manager. The modified C compiler produces a complete description of the global variables, procedures, local variables, and source code to machine code mapping. The Execution Manager uses this augmented symbol table to map symbol names into addresses in the monitored process. It should be noted that the C compiler is a modified version of the one distributed by U.C. Berkeley. Berkeley's version produces a very complete symbol table; the compiler was modified to correct the few deficiencies that it had.

In order to monitor a particular program, the only requirements are that it be compiled by the modified C compiler and that it be linked with a special assist routine described below. The code generated by the modified C compiler is identical to that generated by the conventional compiler. That is, there are no performance penalties in using the modified compiler. The only difference is the larger symbol table that is produced.

4.2 Efficiency

The second goal, efficiency in program monitoring, was supported by exploiting applicable hardware characteristics. Two of the characteristics exploited are found on nearly all machines: the single-step execution mode and the breakpoint instruction. The third characteristic is virtual memory, a feature common on new machines.

The single-step mode of execution is used principally to track the execution of the monitored process. After each machine instruction has executed, the process traps to the operating system which then notifies the Execution Manager. The Execution Manager reads the current value of the program counter and maps the value into a file name, procedure name, and line number in the source code using the mapping provided by the compiler in the symbol table. This information then can be used for highlighting a line of code in a source code display or highlighting a procedure invocation on a stack.

The breakpoint instruction also is used to track execution, but at a coarser granularity. Although the user may insert breakpoints anywhere in the code, the most common use of the breakpoint is at the beginning of a procedure that contains local variables to be monitored.

Our use of virtual memory is less self-evident, and we spend the rest of this section discussing it. In order to maintain an accurate display of data structures which the user has selected for viewing, the Execution Manager must detect any updates. There are several ways in which this detection might be done: analyze the executing program for all assignments to the selected data structures; examine each data structure after every instruction for value changes; tag the data structures so that an update will cause an event. These approaches are discussed below.

Code analysis will catch most, but not all, assignments. Programs written in languages that allow indirect references through pointers (as in C) or which allow the dynamic creation of data structures at run-time (through memory allocation routines) may have "hidden" assignments in them. Examining each data structure after every instruction is very inefficient and slows the speed of execution of the monitored process significantly. Tagging the data structures is the most general approach, but it suffers from several limitations: most machines do not allow individual memory locations to be tagged; local variables pose a problem because their locations in memory are not fixed; and register variables usually cannot be tagged.

To overcome these limitations, the PV implementation uses a variation on tagged memory. Instead of tagging individual memory locations, an entire page is tagged. By setting the protection of a page that contains a data structure being monitored to be read-only, a trap will occur whenever a write occurs on that page. The Execution Manager then checks to see whether the address(es) just written include a data structure which it is moni-

toring. If so, the new value is read and displayed.

The process of catching updates works in a straightforward way for global and static variables because their addresses are fixed at load time and do not change. However, variables local to a procedure are allocated space on the stack. Thus their real addresses will vary, depending on the history of procedure invocations. To overcome this problem, the Execution Manager sets a special breakpoint at the beginning of each procedure that contains local variables to be monitored. When one of these breakpoints is executed, the following steps are performed:

1. Record the value of the stack pointer at that point.

2. Copy the current stack frame (corresponding to the procedure just invoked) on the stack to make room for a new interposed stack frame. This new frame represents the context of the special assist routine mentioned earlier and is used during the cleanup after the watched procedure returns.

3. Set the stack page(s) that contain the local variables to be read-only.

4. Resume execution of the interrupted procedure.

Execution continues as in the case of global variables. Traps will occur when the protected stack pages are written to. When the procedure returns, it returns to the special assist routine. The assist routine signals the Execution Manager that a procedure that had local variables being monitored has returned. The Execution Manager then resets the protection on the pages and resumes execution of the monitored program.

The implementation of the Execution Manager has been described. The Execution Manager monitors the status of the executing program in such a way as to minimize the effects of the monitoring on performance. This is achieved by means of modifications to the C compiler used to compile the monitored programs and by extending the UNIX kernel to allow one process access to another process' memory map.

5. PV Implementation Status

As of Fall 1982, the PV research prototype has a base user interface (window management and menus) that accepts input from touch sensitive screen, data tablet, and keyboard. A base Graphic Editor allows the user to create structured objects, label the objects with text or graphic icons, and choose line widths and text fonts. The Graphic Editor also provides a grid system and color mixing facilities. The EMACS text editor has been integrated into the system, and the Design Database and PV Library are supported at a basic level.

In the Dynamic Object Controller, the Execution Manager has been implemented as described.

The Binder currently consists of a collection of special purpose routines, which will be generalized. In the Display Manager, the Image Generator has reached a level sufficient to support Figure 2.

The project's first fully supported visualization is shown in Figure 4. In this visualization, the contents of one array are sorted into a second array as a selection sort routine runs. Work is underway on examples from a variety of graphical and data structure types (tables, trees, networks). We are also working with CCA's Multibase Project to identify the kinds of illustrations that are useful in their design and implementation of a heterogeneous distributed DBMS [11].

In the next phase of the project, we will be upgrading modules already implemented, with emphasis on extending the scope of automated visualization planning. Some redesign of the user interface is also planned for early 1983 when we move from medium resolution graphics to a high resolution Ikonas graphics system.

6. Conclusions

We have described a system that is not only an integrated programming environment, but also an integrated graphics programming environment. Our experience with the PV research prototype to date supports our hypothesis that graphics will have a profound impact on software development. We suggest the analogy with the way that text editing facilities have changed the process of writing papers.

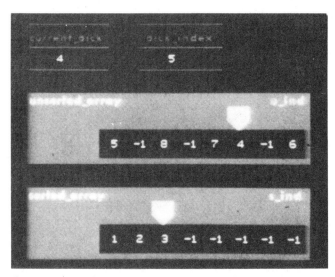

Figure 4. Visualization of a selection sort. (Fully supported example.) The integers are sorted from one array to the other; -1 is used to initialize and to blank array cells. The current_pick variable holds the minimum value at each point in the scan of unsorted_array; pick_index, which holds the index of current_pick, reflects the zero-based addressing in C.

The Program Visualization system is being developed to aid programmers in the formation of clear and correct mental images of the structure and function of programs. With both graphics and text, the programmer will be able to choose the modality most appropriate to a particular task. With the ability to produce dynamic visualizations, the user will be able to "open the side of the machine" to watch programs as they run.

Acknowledgements

Becky Allen, Nancy Flood, Jane Hathaway, Aaron Marcus, and Paul Souza contributed to the concept and graphic design of the visualizations. Ronald Baecker originated the concept of Figure 1. The authors wish to thank Jane Barnett and Diane Smith for helpful comments on drafts of this paper.

7. References

[1] Baecker, R.M., "Sorting Out Sorting," 16mm color, sound, 25 minutes (Dynamic Graphics Project, Computer Systems Research Group, Univ. of Toronto, 1981).

[2] Baecker, R.M., "Two Systems which Produce Animated Representations of the Execution of Computer Programs," ACM SIGCSE Bulletin, 7, 1 (Feb. 1975) 158-167.

[3] Balzer, R.M., "EXDAMS - EXtendable Debugging and Monitoring System," AFIPS Joint Spring Computer Conference (1969) 567-580.

[4] Dionne, M.S. and Mackworth, A.K., "ANTICS: a System for Animating LISP Programs," Computer Graphics and Image Processing, 7 (1978) 105-119.

[5] Galley, S.W. and Goldberg, R.P., "Software Debugging: The Virtual Machine Approach," Proceedings: ACM Annual Conference (1974) 395-401.

[6] Herot, C.F., Carling, R.T., Friedell, M., Kramlich, D., "A Prototype Spatial Data Management System," SIGGRAPH '80 Proceedings: ACM/SIGGRAPH Conference (1980) 63-70.

[7] Herot, C.F., Brown, G.P., Carling, R.T., Friedell, M., Kramlich, D., Baecker, R.M., "An Integrated Environment for Program Visualization," in Schneider, H.J. and Wasserman, A.I. (eds.), Automated Tools for Information System Design, North Holland, Amsterdam, 1982.

[8] Holt, R.C. and Hume, J.N.P., Programming Standard PASCAL, Reston Publishing Co., Reston VA, 1980.

[9] Hopgood, F.R.A., "Computer Animation Used as a Tool in Teaching Computer Science," Proceedings of the 1974 IFIP Congress, Applications Volume, (1974) 889-892.

[10] Knowlton, K.C., "L6: Bell Telephone Laboratories Low-Level Linked List Language," two black and white films, sound (Bell Telephone Laboratories, Murray Hill, New Jersey, 1966).

[11] Landers, T. and Rosenberg, R.L. "An Overview of Multibase," in Schneider, H.J. (ed.), Distributed Data Bases, North Holland, Amsterdam, 1982.

[12] Myers, B.A., "Displaying Data Structures for Interactive Debugging," CSL-80-7, XEROX Corp., Palo Alto Research Center (1980).

[13] Stockham, T.G., "Some Methods of Graphical Debugging," Proceedings of the IBM Scientific Computing Symposium on Man-Machine Communication (1965) 57-71.

[14] Teitelman, W., "A Display Oriented Programmer's Assistant," Fifth International Joint Conference on Artificial Intelligence (1977) 905-915.

[15] Yarwood, E., "Toward Program Illustration," Tech. Report CSRG-84, Computer Systems Research Group, Univ. of Toronto (1977).

THE TINKERTOY GRAPHICAL PROGRAMMING ENVIRONMENT

Mark Edel

Digital Equipment Corporation
75 Reed Rd
Hudson, MA 01749

ABSTRACT

Tinkertoy is a graphic interface to LISP, where programs are "built" rather than written, out of icons and flexible interconnections. It is exciting because it represents a computer/user interface that can easily exceed the interaction speed of the best text-based language editors and command languages. It also provides a consistent framework for interaction across both editing and command execution. Moreover, because programs are represented graphically, structures that do not naturally conform to the text medium can be clearly described, and new kinds of information can be incorporated into programs and program elements.

INTRODUCTION

The appropriate use of graphics can vastly improve the representation of computer languages and the ways in which people interact with computers. Though most people will agree that these statements are true, and though improvements in computer hardware have made graphics practical enough for everyone to use, we are still far from developing software that takes full advantage of the tremendous increase in expressive power graphics can bring. This paper presents a system which successfully applies a new kind of graphical interaction based on icons and flexible links. I developed the Tinkertoy prototype in late 1984 as part of my thesis research at the University of Illinois.

Tinkertoy icons resemble Apple MacIntosh icons (which are descended from the original work on Smalltalk[1] at Xerox PARC). They are small pictures that can be moved around the screen like bits of paper on a desk. They differ in that they have input and output sites on them through which they can be connected together with other icons to build structures. Figure 1. shows some Tinkertoy icons.

(1)   (2)   (3)   (4)   (5)   (6)

Figure 1. Typical Icons

Editing a program with Tinkertoy is similar to using a syntax directed editor since icons represent the syntactically meaningful chunks of the program. Without the unnecessary detail of individual characters, lines and terminators found in other editors, a program can be approached on a higher level. In addition, editing operations themselves are simpler because they mostly involve picking up and moving icons, or are implied by how icons are positioned. Simple, straightforward, and powerful editing operations make for fast editing and a system that is easy to learn.

This same ability to compose and manipulate iconic structures used for editing serves as Tinkertoy's command interface. In an interpreted language like LISP, the same statements that make up a program can be used interactively to communicate with the system. The interactive user executes Tinkertoy icons by pointing at them, so they in turn can activate programs or commands. This traditional way of using icons is extended by Tinkertoy's ability to compose structures, so that commands can be modified and combined into larger commands as in a command language.

Tinkertoy icons, when evaluated, return values that are iconic structures, just as LISP functions return values which are LISP structures. This is of particular interest because the new structures can themselves be manipulated and evaluated and produce further structures.

A Sample Tinkertoy Session

Figure 2 is an example of a simple Tinkertoy session.

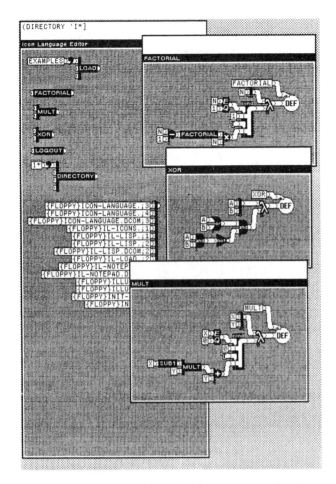

```
(DIRECTORY 'I*]
```

Figure 2. A section of the screen showing
a tall window as a system interface,
and three smaller windows as editors.

When the user types LISP expressions
in the white area above a Tinkertoy window,
the system forms iconic representations for
them, which he can then manipulate by
pointing. The iconic structures can be
broken apart and combined by picking up
pieces, moving them, and snapping them
together.

In the example, the big window is
being used as a system interface with the
three small windows as editors. The first
structure in the big window will load the
file called EXAMPLES whenever it is
evaluated (An icon is evaluated when the
right mouse button is pressed over it).
The next item down is an icon that
calculates the factorial of a number.
Attaching a number to this icon and then
evaluating it will produce an icon
containing the factorial of that number.
The second, third and fourth icons
represent the functions being edited in the
three small windows. These windows were
created by editing the three icons in the
big window. (Pressing the middle mouse
button over an icon produces a pop-up menu
that will contain the item "edit" when
source code exists for that icon.) The

fifth and sixth structures are typical
system functions for logging out of the
system and viewing a directory of files.
The seventh structure is the result of
evaluating the sixth. It consists of a
list icon enclosing several file names.
These file names can be manipulated just
like any other icons and used as arguments
to other functions.

Most editing is done by simply picking
up part of a structure and moving it to
another location. By default, picking up
an icon also picks up its enclosed LISP
structure (the icon's arguments, the
arguments' arguments, etc.). If the
structure is connected to any stationary
structures, the connections become elastic.
Dropping an icon with a site on a mating
site forms a connection between the two.
When an icon site is near a compatible
(mating) site, it "snaps" into position on
that site. While an icon is being carried
by the mouse, connections are made or
broken by clicking the right mouse button.
Figure 3 shows an "EQ" icon with two
arguments. The user: (1) picks up icon
"B," (2) moves it away from EQ and then (3)
severs its connection with EQ. B can now
be used as an argument somewhere else,
deleted, or just dropped somewhere by
itself.

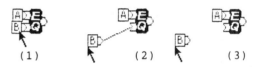

Figure 3. (1) Picking up, (2) pulling
away, and (3) disconnecting an icon.

If an icon has a variable number of
arguments, positioning another argument
between two existing ones, or after or
before the list causes the icon to expand
and accept the new argument at that point.
Figure 4 shows a structure for (AND A C).
To change this to (AND A B C), the user (1)
picks up, copies, or types in the icon B
and (2,3) drops it between A and C.

Figure 4. Changing (AND A C) to (AND A B C)
by dropping the icon B between A and C.

BENEFITS OF A GRAPHIC REPRESENTATION

There are many features and utilities
that can be found only in LISP programming
environments because it is one of the few
languages where the fundamental
representation of a program is not a text
file but a data structure. This makes it
much easier for programs to operate on
other programs and is one of the reasons

for the extensibility (and the popularity) of LISP[2]. A graphical representation further removes the limitations imposed by having to translate programs back to text.

With graphics, it is possible to go even closer to the machine version of a program without compromising readability. In many cases, this is also closer to what the programmer wants to see to understand what his program is doing. In Tinkertoy it is easier to understand flow of control and complicated data structures because the graphic form is more like the list-structure form of the internal representation.

Some concepts that are very difficult to represent textually fall out naturally in a true two dimensional system. Structures that are not tree-like such as connected graphs are one example (though many of these are also difficult to represent in two dimensions).

There are also benefits that come, not from the structure itself, but from additional information that can be attached to it. The appearance of an icon can convey information such as compatibility of data types, number of arguments, names of arguments and functionality. Additional icons can display intermediate values or breakpoints for debugging, program verification information, and comments that point exactly at the structures they describe. Such optional information could also be displayed only as needed, like invisible layers often found in CAD tools, or structures that shrink to tiny icons. Tinkertoy is particularly conducive to piling new information on top of what is already displayed, because things can arbitrarily overlap one another.

INTERACTING WITH GRAPHIC STRUCTURES

Though many of the long term benefits of going from text based systems to systems like Tinkertoy come from the graphic representation, in the short term fast interaction is more important. The representation is less important because people can adapt to even arbitrary representations[3], and refining the presentation of information and adding graphical features can be an incremental process, building on the experience of the first users. People, however, will never begin to use something that is harder to work with than what they have now. Interaction has generally been a problem in other graphical programming environments[4].

The two basic kinds of interaction in Tinkertoy are pointing and typing. The relative merits of the two have been debated at great length in technical publications (some of these arguments are presented in [4]). A Tinkertoy user can do everything a conventional command language user can do, without ever touching the keyboard. Typing is important, however, because it gives the user instant access to icons which might otherwise take many pointing operations to reach.

Typing is generally for presenting new things to the system (icons or structures that are not already displayed on the screen). Tinkertoy will convert any arbitrarily complex LISP expression into iconic form, and visa versa, so text and iconic editing are interchangeable. Icons are generated automatically from atom and function names. Though Tinkertoy users may design their own icons, it is much easier to just use names and let the system take care of it for them (Designing customized icons is more difficult than it may first appear[4] even with the best graphic tools).

In generating an iconic structure from a LISP expression, Tinkertoy gives the user some feedback on the correctness of his expressions. The way that structures snap together also gives feedback because only things that fit together properly will snap together. In a strongly typed language, differently styled sites could show compatibility of data types.

For interaction by pointing, Tinkertoy uses the context of what a user is pointing at in order to decide what to do or what to present as a choice for him to do. The two most important functions, move and evaluate, are accessible immediately through mouse buttons, while other possibilities such as delete, copy, help, and different ways to group icons for the various operations are presented in an intelligent menu that only lists those relevant to that icon. Pointing at window borders and backgrounds also present relevant options. This keeps the size of the menus small without having to resort to any kind of nesting.

OTHER GRAPHICAL PROGRAMMING ENVIRONMENTS

Tinkertoy: A Practical Iconic Programming Environment[4] compares Tinkertoy with other graphical programming environments, program visualization tools, and computer aided design tools. Two additional articles which do not appear in its references are are worth noting: A Survey of Current Graphical Programming Techniques[5] further compares many of the systems mentioned in [4] and discusses the author's own system called PiP (Programming in Pictures). Visual Programming[6] presents a graphical LISP syntax which is strikingly similar to Tinkertoy's.

301

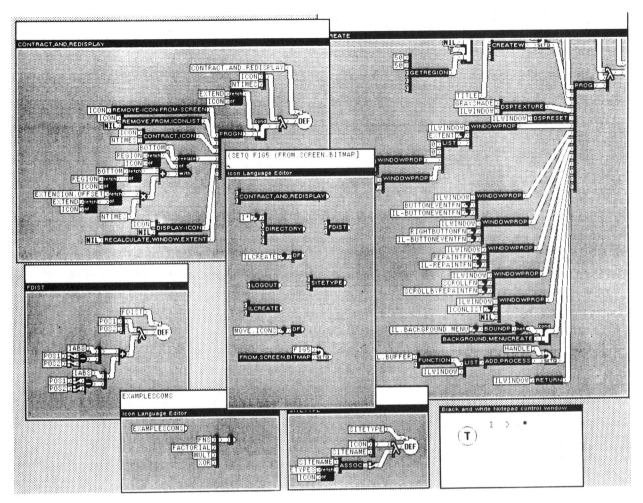

Figure 5. A full screen showing some code from Tinkertoy. The two large functions illustrate the clumsiness of large PROG statements.

PROBLEMS

Compactness is Tinkertoy's worst problem, and one which has plagued most other attempts at graphical programming languages[4]. Tinkertoy programs are larger by about 20% than equivalent text programs. The problem seems to come from interconnections (which do not exist in text languages), from large icons with unused sites, and from oddly shaped layouts that tend to spread out in non-rectangular shapes. Much of the space wasted by interconnections and odd-shaped structures comes from sequencing and iterative functions. Figure 5 shows some source code from Tinkertoy illustrating the kind of structures that arbitrary LISP expressions create. A method with icons that would stretch instead of forcing connections to fan out would help this tremendously. It is also possible that this kind of iterative structure is a relic of traditional programming languages. Often the only reason for using a sequencing function like PROG is that LISP expressions that are nested too deeply are hard to read. A PROG statement, with local variables and SETQs for intermediate results, breaks up the calculation into manageable pieces. In Tinkertoy, deeply nested expressions are as easy to read as sequential ones. Distribution of results would further reduce this need for SETQing intermediate results. The problem of unused sites is mostly a question of whether having a fixed set of sites is beneficial, since fixed icons could easily all be replaced by extendible ones. An intermediate solution might be to collapse unused sites into smaller sites which expand when something is attached to them.

The Tinkertoy prototype does not evaluate iconic structures directly, it first converts them to LISP, then executes the resulting code. This introduces a few peculiarities because there are now two copies of the structures and destructive functions like NCONC will only affect the LISP copies.

Creating an evaluator for the iconic structures themselves presents many new conceptual problems. Unlike a conventional environment where text becomes "dead" after it is executed, in a true iconic environment, displayed structures are still "alive" and should reflect any changes made to them by their own execution or the execution of other programs. This is complicated by the fact that there may be several copies of a particular structure displayed at the same time. The system must have an incremental layout function that knows not only how to initially lay out a structure, but also how to change it, and it must deal with multiple views of the displayed data structures. If all of this can be done properly, it will result in an integrated programming/program visualization tool which would allow users to watch data structures change during execution, and to watch their own programs change as they execute editing functions (which are trivial to write in such a system).

Windows are very important in Tinkertoy because they give the user better control over utilization of screen space and provide visually separate contexts for separate tasks. However, they also present a conceptual problem, because they are barriers requiring special treatment for icons to cross. Right now, a command in the background menu, called "get icon." changes the cursor to a set of forceps (the "get" cursor). The user can then point at a set of icons in another window, and they will be copied into the window from which the "get" was initiated. During the operation, the user has access to all of the window management tools, so that he can get icons from buried windows, or icons that have been scrolled out of view. It would be nicer, however, if this could somehow be integrated into standard icon movement, so that moving icons between windows would not be much different from moving them within a window.

Similarly, the text buffers above Tinkertoy windows are a workable but not ideal solution to the problem of managing type-in and print-out. They take up screen space, separate the user's focus between the window and the buffer, and are not large enough to handle more than one line of text output at a time. A better solution for type-in would be to create iconic structures on the fly as the user types without an intermediate text form, and to use separate pop-up windows for other types of text input and output (such as dialogs).

Though the editing operations available in the Tinkertoy prototype are already very effective, they could be enhanced by duplicating some of the functions available in standard text editors (like search and replace), and by adding some keyboard editing commands to do the same operations as the mouse commands. A more elaborate mouse with more buttons or proportional devices would make for much richer pointing interaction.

THE TINKERTOY PROTOTYPE

The Tinkertoy prototype was developed to the point that I could do some of Tinkertoy's development in Tinkertoy. There were several limiting factors, however. Interlisp has many structures that are long lists of single atoms (comments and iterative statements being the worst) for which the corresponding Tinkertoy structures are very awkward. Unfortunately all of the Tinkertoy code makes heavy use of them. Though it is possible to develop graphic macros for such structures, it was somewhat beyond the scope of this project. The prototype itself was limited in its usefulness as an editor because the layout function (the graphic pretty-printer) was too slow (about 15 seconds for a large function) to be effective in an environment where you are continually opening and closing editing windows (though not for any fundamental reasons).

Though I didn't do much editing with it, the ability to keep frequently used commands around, the ease of modifying those commands, and the ability to use their resulting outputs, put it in constant use as a command interface.

CONCLUSION

Tinkertoy successfully unifies graphical interaction methods with conventional text programming methods. In doing so, it provides a means to expand into other aspects of two dimensional and graphical programming without losing any of the capabilities of traditional systems. Tinkertoy's graphical representation is much more flexible than a textual representation, can present more information, and can clearly represent many constructs that are hard to understand in text form.

Graphical interaction provides many improvements over conventional methods of program editing and command execution. Tinkertoy drastically simplifies editing methods, because programs are manipulated at a higher level and operations are implied naturally by pointing and positioning. The system can exhibit more intelligence than conventional systems because the representation is closer to the machine representation, making it easier to use such things as context to improve interaction.

The computer is one of the most complicated things that man has ever created, and designing and programming better computers is largely a struggle to extend the limits of comprehensibility[7]. A system like Tinkertoy is important because it can reduce the complexity of programming without reducing the expressive power.

This work was sponsored by the U.S. Army Corps of Engineers Construction Engineering Research Laboratory in Champaign Illinois, and is not related to the work I am doing at Digital Equipment Corporation.

REFERENCES

[1] A. Goldberg, Smalltalk-80, The Interactive Programming Environment, Addison Wesley, Reading, Mass. (1984).

[2] P. H. Winston Artificial Intelligence, Addison Wesley, Reading, Mass. (1977).

[3] K. N. Lodding, "Iconic Interfacing," IEEE Computer Graphics and Applications, Vol. 3, No. 2 (1983) pp. 11-20.

[4] M. W. Edel, "Tinkertoy: a Practical Iconic Programming Envirnoment," Masters Thesis, Department of Electrical Engineering, University of Illinois, June 1985.

[5] G. Raeder, "A Survey of Current Graphical Programming Techniques," IEEE Computer, Vol. 18, No. 8 (1985) pp. 11-25.

[6] R. Levien, "Visual Programming," Byte, Vol. 11, No. 2 (1986) pp. 135-144.

[7] T. Winograd, "Breaking the Complexity Barrier Again," SIGPLAN Notices, ACM. Vol. 10, No. 1 (1975) pp. 13-22.

C²:

A Mixed Textual/Graphical Environment for C

Mark E. Kopache*
Ephraim P. Glinert

Department of Computer Science
Rensselaer Polytechnic Institute
Troy, New York 12180

Abstract

A visual programming environment for a subset of the C language is described. The C² environment, as it is called, runs on a personal workstation with high-resolution graphics display. Both conventional textual code entry and editing, and program composition by means of an experimental hybrid textual/graphical method, are supported and coexist side by side on the screen at all times. The built-in text editor incorporates selected UNIX *vi* commands in conjunction with a C syntax interpreter. Hybrid textual/graphical program composition is facilitated by a BLOX-type environment in which graphical icons represent program structures and text in the icons represents user-supplied parameters attached to those structures. The two representations are coupled, so that modifications entered using either one automatically generate the appropriate update in the other. Although not all of the C language is yet supported, C² is not a toy system. Textual files that contain C programs serve as input and output. Graphical representations serve merely as internally-generated aids to the programmer, and are not stored between runs.

---

*First author's present address: New York State Office of Mental Health, 44 Holland Avenue, Albany, NY 12228.

Introduction

The primary goal of research in the field of interactive graphical programming environments, or visual programming as it is often called, is to discover improved and more easily accessible techniques for programming through the use of graphics in the human-computer interface. To this end, investigators have incorporated numerous visual representations for programs into a variety of environments [1,2,3,4]. Some people erroneously seem to believe that work in this area is an attempt to replace text with graphics and so return us to the age of hieroglyphics. Actually, most recent visual systems make use of both graphics and text [5,6,7]. The importance of visual programming, and of graphical human-computer interfaces in general, has been steadily growing in recent years. This trend will surely accelerate in the future, as use of supercomputers possessing the ability to overwhelm us with a flood of numerical output becomes more widespread.

Most of the visual environments completed to date have been experimental prototypes which support program composition by means of some single (graphical) representation. This is undesirable, because no one such representation has as yet been accepted as superior over all others for all tasks [8]. What we really want are production quality environments which support simultaneous program composition/editing in any of several representations, both textual and graphical, with correspondence among all views of the program being automatically maintained by the system. (Indeed, in the best of all possible worlds the programming environment would be user extensible, to allow easy incorporation of experimental program representations at will, complete with appropriate syntax and semantics.) Such environments would have significant advantages over those in use today. For one thing, they would allow programmers to work on each part of a program using the most natural means. Furthermore, they would smooth the migration from traditional textual programming to graphical program composition (for experts), or from the graphical to the textual (for novices), or between alternative graphical representations (for all users), by allowing each user to program using his/her personal interface of choice while assimilating the other.

In this paper, we describe the C^2 programming environment for a subset of the C language. The environment concurrently supports two fully modifiable views of a program. One view is for programming according to the traditional textual method with the aid of a built-in screen editor. The other view allows programming by means of a hybrid textual/graphical representation patterned after Glinert's recently-introduced BLOX methodology [9,10], in which planar objects called tiles are connected to one another via protrusions and matching indentations which interlock in a manner similar to that employed in jigsaw puzzles. Individual tiles represent the building blocks from which statements are formed. Groups of tiles represent statement schemas, text inserted into tiles and/or substructures encapsulated within them represent actual statement components, and the connections indicate flow of control (when appropriate). BLOX tiles are at once real and imaginary, for unlike their counterparts in the physical world they can hide (lower level) substructures which they encapsulate. BLOX tiles are also dynamic rather than static, in that their visible features (e.g., size, color, and edge contour or shape) may all change under appropriate circumstances – say, when elements are repositioned on the screen (location/context induced change), or as sundry events transpire (temporally induced change).

One reason the BLOX approach is promising is that it supports various hierarchies, or "vocabularies" as some authors have called them [11], of graphical clues to facilitate user selection of elements which may be joined. A simple hierarchy of this type, in which color supplements the information imparted by shape, might include: (*a*) background color or image; (*b*) edge color or pattern; and (*c*) edge contour. This latter attribute can be used to designate subfamilies of compatible elements through use of a master key concept; the arc length of appropriate edges is subdivided into segments (by the system designer), one or more of which remain identical for all members of the family while the contours of the others are varied. Depending upon the applications domain, the system designer could, if appropriate, impose additional constraints on which tiles

or blocks may be joined. For example, the images on the tiles might have to be compatible in some sense.

PC–TILES, a previously implemented BLOX-based programming environment on the IBM/PC for a subset of Pascal, provided users with just a single view of their programs [12,13]. Our C^2 environment represents a significant advance over this first effort.

A Guided Tour Through C^2

C^2 is coded in C, and runs under the UNIX[†] operating system within the SunTools[‡] environment on Sun Microsystems monochromatic workstations. The C^2 environment is *not* a toy system! Textual files that purport to contain C programs serve as input; their validity is checked, and errors flagged for user correction. Output consists of normal UNIX text files that contain C programs whose syntactical correctness is guaranteed. Although the environment provides graphical representations alongside the textual, these serve merely as internally generated aids to the programmer and are not stored between runs in the UNIX file system. A built-in *HELP* facility guides users in the operation of the graphics window's menu buttons (see below), and

also provides information regarding the syntax of C statements. The subset of C supported by C^2 is sufficiently rich to allow the use of conventional "structured" programming techniques such as sequence, iteration, decision and blocks. Data types supported include integers, reals and characters. #DEFINE and #INCLUDE are supported. Comments are allowed, and will in certain circumstances display in the graphics window (they will always display in the textual window, of course).

As alluded to in the preceding paragraph, the C^2 user interface consists of two windows running processes which interact under the SunTools umbrella. A shell window houses a traditional textual working environment, in which a built-in (full screen) text editor supports a subset of the commands familiar to users of the UNIX *vi* program. The C^2 editor's command repertoire is augmented with facilities for checking C syntax, and for communication with the graphics window. The graphics window, which is created at program initialization, provides a surface for composing BLOX representations for C programs. This window naturally employs the iconic mode of interaction, in which operations are selected by pointing at small images with the mouse. The operations available are analogous to the commands supported by the textual window.

The BLOX world is implemented as five panes, or subwindows:

1. *The main display pane*, located in the center of the graphics window, where BLOX structures are created and manipulated.

2. *The message pane*, located at the top of the window, where (textual) informational and syntax-error messages may be displayed by the system.

[†]**UNIX** is a registered trademark of AT&T Corporation.

[‡]**SunTools** is a registered trademark of SUN Microsystems, Inc.

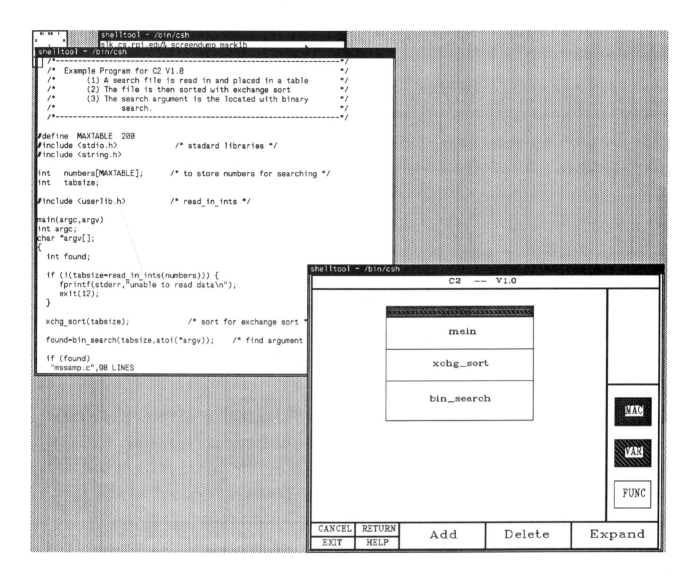

```
                    shelltool - /bin/csh
                    slk.cs.rpi.edu% screendump mark1b
 shelltool - /bin/csh
 /*-------------------------------------------------*/
 /*  Example Program for C2 V1.0                     */
 /*      (1) A search file is read in and placed in a table  */
 /*      (2) The file is then sorted with exchange sort      */
 /*      (3) The search argument is the located with binary  */
 /*               search.                            */
 /*-------------------------------------------------*/

#define MAXTABLE 200
#include <stdio.h>          /* stadard libraries */
#include <string.h>

int   numbers[MAXTABLE];    /* to store numbers for searching */
int   tabsize;

#include <userlib.h>        /* read_in_ints */

main(argc,argv)
int argc;
char *argv[];
{
    int found;

    if (!(tabsize=read_in_ints(numbers))) {
       fprintf(stderr,"unable to read data\n");
       exit(12);
    }

    xchg_sort(tabsize);           /* sort for exchange sort

    found=bin_search(tabsize,atoi(*argv));    /* find argument

    if (found)
    "mssamp.c",90 LINES
```

C2   --   V1.0

main

xchg_sort

bin_search

MAC

VAR

FUNC

CANCEL RETURN   Add   Delete   Expand
EXIT   HELP

Figure 1: Initial Screen Presented To Users Upon Invocation of C^2.

3. *The global overview pane*, in the upper right-hand corner, which shows a "fish-eye" map [14] of the entire program being edited.

4. *The BLOX tile menu*, directly below the global overview pane, which at any instant shows all of the icons which can be joined to (plugged into) the structure currently on display in the main display pane.

5. *The operations menu pane*, along the bottom, which provides buttons for all of the actions that can be performed on the structure in the main display pane. Four of these buttons, located at the left of the pane, are common across all screens; the others depend upon the current contents of the main display pane.

A typical work session in C^2 starts with the user specifying the name of a file that contains a conventional (textual) C program he/she wishes to edit. This program (which may be empty) is first checked for syntactical validity. Any errors are noted, and must be corrected before the file can be loaded into the system and full two-view programming can proceed. This phase is necessary in order to provide compatibility with program files which may have been generated using other environments (e.g., a "dumb" editor).

After input program syntax is correct, a data structure which embodies a global representation of the program is transmitted to the graphics process. This process in turn constructs a global overview diagram in the main display pane which, although simple, nevertheless affords a useful

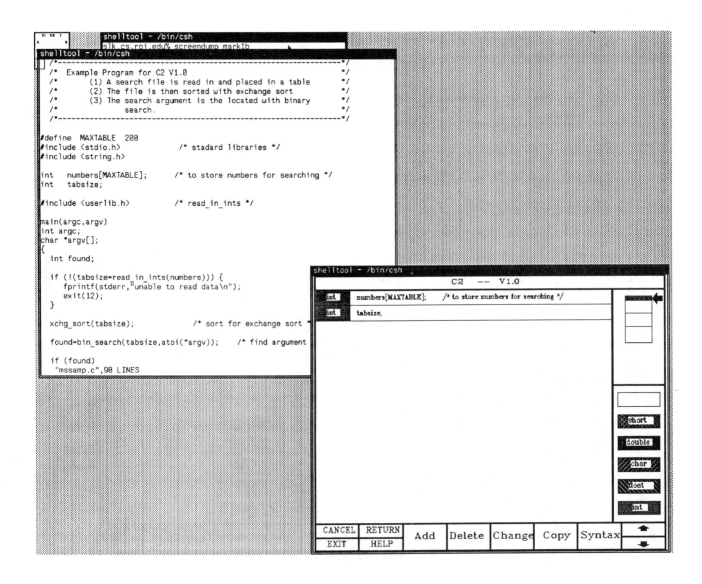

```
          shelltool - /bin/csh
          slk.cs.rpi.edu% screendump mark1b
shelltool - /bin/csh
   /*-------------------------------------------------------------*/
   /*   Example Program for C2 V1.0                               */
   /*       (1) A search file is read in and placed in a table    */
   /*       (2) The file is then sorted with exchange sort        */
   /*       (3) The search argument is the located with binary    */
   /*              search.                                        */
   /*-------------------------------------------------------------*/

#define MAXTABLE  200
#include <stdio.h>             /* stadard libraries */
#include <string.h>

int   numbers[MAXTABLE];       /* to store numbers for searching */
int   tabsize;

#include <userlib.h>           /* read_in_ints */

main(argc,argv)
int argc;
char *argv[];
{
  int found;

  if (!(tabsize=read_in_ints(numbers))) {
     fprintf(stderr,"unable to read data\n");
     exit(12);
  }

  xchg_sort(tabsize);                      /* sort for exchange sort

  found=bin_search(tabsize,atoi(*argv));    /* find argument

  if (found)
  "mssamp.c",90 LINES
```

Figure 2: Textual vs. Graphical Declaration and Commenting of Variables in C^2.

visual organizational tool whose importance increases with program size; cf. Fig. 1, which shows a portion of a program for sorting and searching a sequence of values. This diagram, which is a segmentation of the program according to global variables, macros and functions, will later be displayed in the global overview pane as the work session progresses. The relative size of each diagram segment is determined by the number of lines of code in the textual source. Global segments have internal structure, which may be revealed by means of the Expand operation.

When the global overview is presented in the main display pane of the graphics window, the user can elect to edit an existing global segment (e.g., to revise a function or to add a new macro to an existing group of macros). Al-

ternatively, he/she might choose to create a new segment, or to delete one that is no longer needed. To add a new segment, for example, the user would first select the Add button from the operations menu. Then, the MAC, VAR or FUNC button would be selected from the menu on display in the BLOX tile pane. The third and last step is to point to the location in the main display pane where the user wishes to place the new program component. The C^2 system will respond by displaying a new image in the main pane, as explained below, into which the user can insert elements that will comprise the new global segment. The only system-imposed restriction is that two global macro or variable segments of the same type cannot be consecutively defined.

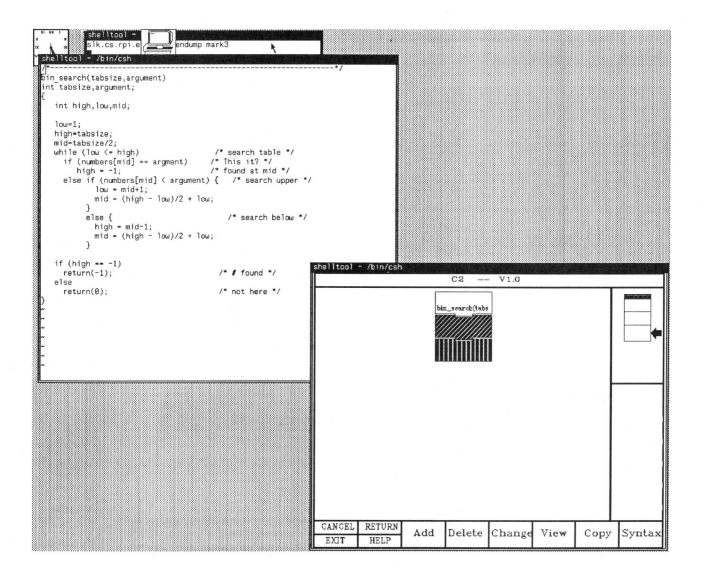

```
/*------------------------------------------------------*/
bin_search(tabsize,argument)
int tabsize,argument;
{
    int high,low,mid;

    low=1;
    high=tabsize;
    mid=tabsize/2;
    while (low <= high)               /* search table */
        if (numbers[mid] == argument)    /* This it? */
            high = -1;                     /* found at mid */
        else if (numbers[mid] < argument) {   /* search upper */
                low = mid+1;
                mid = (high - low)/2 + low;
            }
            else {                          /* search below */
                high = mid-1;
                mid = (high - low)/2 + low;
            }

    if (high == -1)
        return(-1);                    /* # found */
    else
        return(0);                     /* not here */
}
```

Figure 3: Root Level Graphical Display of a Function in C².

Variable and Macro Displays

The internal structures used for both global variable and macro segments are quite similar in C²'s subset of C, as is the manner in which the user manipulates them. A single discussion will therefore suffice to describe both of them.

Both of these types of segment are displayed in a format similar to that shown in Fig. 2, which is for global variables (these will serve as our example from here on). As the Figure indicates, the global view has been moved to the global overview pane, with an arrow pointing to the current position. Each variable definition is represented by an instance of an icon from the BLOX tile menu which represents a variable keyword (e.g., INT or CHAR), together with a user-supplied variable name which is input from the keyboard. An open line (that is, one containing no variable icon) is available for comments or extension of variables to another line. Operations available for the manipulation of definitions in the graphics window now include Add, Delete, Change, Copy and Syntax checking. A scrolling facility is also provided.

Updates carried out by the user in either window set a system flag that prevents changes in the opposing window until correspondence has been re-established. The system could try to do this automatically from time to time. However, the result would in most cases be expenditure of unnecessary effort at too fine a granularity, and a consequen-

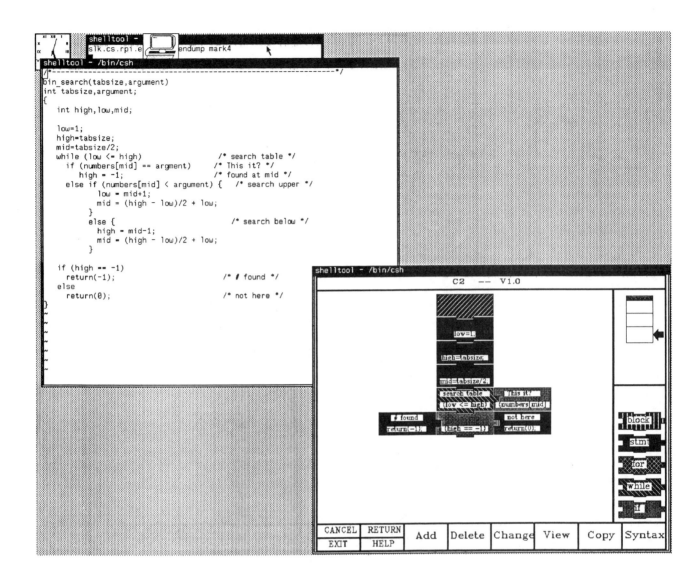

```
/*------------------------------------------------*/
bin_search(tabsize,argument)
int tabsize,argument;
{
    int high,low,mid;

    low=1;
    high=tabsize;
    mid=tabsize/2;
    while (low <= high)              /* search table */
        if (numbers[mid] == argment)     /* This it? */
            high = -1;                   /* found at mid */
        else if (numbers[mid] < argument) {   /* search upper */
            low = mid+1;
            mid = (high - low)/2 + low;
        }
        else {                           /* search below */
            high = mid-1;
            mid = (high - low)/2 + low;
        }

    if (high == -1)
        return(-1);                      /* # found */
    else
        return(0);                       /* not here */
}
```

Figure 4: Graphical Display of the Executable Body of a Function in C^2.

tial detection of spurious syntax errors. The alternative approach adopted in C^2 is to have the user expressly force correspondence of the textual representation from the graphics window by selecting the **Syntax** button with the mouse. When this is done syntax errors, if any, are noted one by one in the message pane and the error location is identified and positioned for correction. When no further syntax errors are detected, new/revised conventional C statements are generated and inserted at the appropriate points in the textual window's display. The user can now proceed with additional changes to this segment, using the BLOX world as before. Alternatively, he/she may move to the textual window and continue to work there for awhile, eventually selecting the syntax checking option to update the BLOX window.

Function Displays

One aspect of the C^2 environment where good design and implementation were felt to be particularly critical is how one uses the BLOX window to construct a C function. This is because refinement and decomposition of a program into constituent subprograms lies at the heart of so-called structured programming, so that the visual approach may potentially have its greatest impact here.

Function manipulation is carried out using a special display that is presented to the user after he/she has selected an existing function from the root level (global) view in the main pane, or added a new function to this root level display, or selected a function from the textual window. As illustrated in Fig. 3, the initial function display is now generated and the textual window is scrolled to the start of the appropriate function.

Functions are created by connecting C statement icons found in the BLOX tile menu. Each icon within the function display possesses both an internal structure and a set of valid connection points, which are represented by protrusions and indentations according to the standard BLOX lock and key (jigsaw puzzle) metaphor. Connection points are dynamic attributes of an icon. Those shown in the BLOX tile menu denote all possible potential connections; the actual connection points available are determined only upon attachment of an instance of the icon to the structure in the main pane.

Internally, each icon may have user-supplied (textual) data and a (textual) comment associated with it. Permissible data values are dependent upon the icon at hand (for example, Boolean conditionals for IF icons). In some cases, no data are allowed (e.g., in the case of the block icon, which represents statements between brackets "{" and "}"). Comments are considered to be attached to a C statement when they occur on the same line as the end of that statement (in the case of a block, when they occur at the beginning of the block). The comment in an icon provides a useful documentation tool, serving as a brief summary of a statement or block while concealing the details of the implementation. The block icon affords detail-hiding by allowing the user to join and encapsulate multiple icons within a single icon; this, in turn, facilitates top down program development by the method of stepwise refinement.

Upon entry to the function display, the structure in the main pane would, at a minimum, be a function icon showing the function's name coupled with a block icon which represents the C statements in the highest level block. In addition, if this function accepts parameters, a data icon (which encapsulates data definition statements) would be included for data definitions.

From this initial display, the user can edit the text within any icon on the main pane, or expand the block or data icon for greater detail. Expansion proceeds for a local data icon in a manner analogous to that for global variables discussed previously. Expansion of a block icon causes the current display to be cleared, and statements on the next level to be displayed instead (a zoom in, as it were).

The next level of detail is the actual C statements. The encapsulation which we have chosen allows the user to group statements either vertically or horizontally; cf. Fig. 4. Vertically placed icons denote sequential execution. Horizontally placed icons represent code within the bodies of FOR and WHILE statements, or the "then" and "else" clauses associated with IF statements. Up to five icons can be placed horizontally in a single row, while ten icons can be placed vertically before icons at the bottom are clipped from the main pane. Nesting of IF statements is allowed to any depth. When nesting occurs, the current level is shown in the middle of the pane, and the next level down only is shown offset to the left or right. Expansion of the next level

clears the display, moves the lower level icon to the middle of the pane, and displays the statements associated with this new (lower) level, if any, etc.

Operations at the function level include mouse-selectable icon insertion (Add), Delete, Change and Copy. UNIX *vi* commands to manipulate the text within an icon by using the keyboard are also provided. Icon expansion and contraction (zoom in and zoom out) are considered analogous to indentation in the textual world, but can provide a cleaner View by removing excess screen clutter. Syntax checking again fulfills a dual role, in that the function being edited is validated and new/revised C statements are transmitted to the textual window where they are displayed with appropriate indentation to show block structure and levels of nesting.

Internal System Organization

Conceptually, C^2 consists of three components: a data management process; a textual window process; and a graphics window process. The data management process maintains user program code in textual form and sends portions of it to the other processes upon request. This process also handles syntax checking upon demand, sending appropriate error notifications (including error type and location) to the client process. The duty of the textual and graphics processes is to maintain their respective windows; they communicate directly with the data manager process only (so that this process must act as intermediary when requests or data must be forwarded to the other window). Optimally, this configuration should allow different modules to be plugged in as needed in place of those presently supplied. Thus, the simplistic BLOX representation now provided could be replaced with another, if desired, or a version of EMACS might be substituted for the editor that comes with the system.

In reality, C^2 V1.0 is implemented as just a pair of interacting processes. The functionality of the data management process has been split between and incorporated into the textual and graphics window processes. The textual process always maintains the entire user program. The graphics process, on the other hand, maintains at any instant just the information currently relevant to its display. The graphics data structure for function statements is composed of what may be visualized as square nodes, with each side having a pointer to another node, and with each node representing a connection point. Top and bottom pointers represent sequential previous and sequential next, respectively. Side pointers are valid only on branch and loop statements, and correspond to "then" and "else" clauses and to loop bodies. Data kept at each node include the C statement type, user data, and the start and end line number (which helps to correlate data with the data manager).

Discussion

The end product of programming in the C^2 environment is a conventional C program. We believe that an environment such as this should allow programs to be developed faster, and with fewer bugs, than would be the case were either a conventional textual environment or a purely graphical environment employed. This is because the programmer can choose on the fly the best of both worlds at his/her option. Graphical interaction appears too cumbersome a means for entering and correcting simple data structures and macro statements; we find the textual approach is preferable for this purpose. However, with increased complexity this (subjective) observation could well be reversed.

Since every programming environment must ultimately be judged by the people who use it, we eagerly anticipate comments from both experienced and novice programmers. However, before eliciting user reactions we plan to incorporate enhancements such as the following into an expanded C^2 V2.0:

- Expansion of the subset of C supported by the environment to include both structures and files.

- Incorporation of color:
  - To assist the user in differentiating among icons.
  - To draw the user's attention to system messages.
  - To highlight the boundaries of graphics window panes from which the user is expected to make selections.

- Provision of an editor to allow users to redefine the edge contours of tiles.

- Support of dragging as a technique for icon placement.

- Provision of a "toggle" to allow the user to suppress display of comments and thereby increase the capacity of the textual window, as measured in terms of the number of lines of source code that can be displayed at one time.

Furthermore, we note as a general observation that we found the encapsulation mechanism and emphasis on top down programming embodied in the BLOX methodology, as presently implemented, particularly useful for clarifying the logical structure of programs through the elimination of a large amount of screen clutter. However, we also found this implementation of BLOX cumbersome for nesting of decision and loop statements beyond two levels. Thus, our implementation has been designed to facilitate experimentation with alternative graphical representations, in that just those routines that write the chosen structure on the graphics window would need to be changed.

Acknowledgment and Note on Software Distribution

The second author was supported, in part, by the DoD VHSIC program under contract #F33615-87-C-1435, by the IBM Corporation, and by the Xerox Corporation while this research was being carried out.

To obtain a copy of the experimental environment described in this paper for personal, not-for-profit use, please contact the second author (e-mail: *glinert@turing.cs.rpi.edu*).

References

[1] D. C. Smith. *PYGMALION: A Creative Programming Environment.* PhD thesis, Dept. of Computer Science, Stanford University (Technical Report STAN-CS-75-499), 1975.

[2] M. C. Pong and N. Ng. PIGS: A System for Programming with Interactive Graphical Support. *Software – Practice and Experience*, 13(9):847–855, September 1983.

[3] E. P. Glinert and S. L. Tanimoto. PICT: An Interactive, Graphical Programming Environment. *IEEE Computer*, 17(11):7–25, November 1984.

[4] S. P. Reiss. PECAN: Program Development Systems that Support Multiple Views. *IEEE Trans. on Software Engineering*, SE-11(3):276–285, March 1985.

[5] M.-J. Chung, E. P. Glinert, M. Hardwick, E. H. Rogers, and K. Rose. Toward an Object-Oriented Iconic Environment for Computer Assisted VLSI Design. In *Proc. 2nd Israel Conf. on Computer Systems and Software Engineering, Tel Aviv*, May 6-7, 1987.

[6] M. P. Stovsky and B. W. Weide. STILE: A Graphical Design and Development Environment. In *Proc. COMPCON '87*, pages 247–250, IEEE Computer Society Press, 1987.

[7] S. P. Reiss. Working in the GARDEN Environment for Conceptual Programming. *IEEE Software*, 4(6):16–27, November 1987.

[8] Ben Shneiderman. *Software Psychology: Human Factors in Computer and Information Systems.* Winthrop, Cambridge, MA, 1980.

[9] E. P. Glinert. Towards "Second Generation" Interactive, Graphical Programming Environments. In *Proc. 2nd IEEE Computer Society Workshop on Visual Languages, Dallas*, pages 61–70, June 25-27, 1986.

[10] E. P. Glinert. Out of Flatland: Towards Three-Dimensional Visual Programming. In *Proc. 2nd ACM/IEEE Fall Joint Computer Conference, Dallas*, pages 292–299, October 25-29, 1987.

[11] G. F. McCleary Jr. An Effective Graphic "Vocabulary". *IEEE Computer Graphics and Applications*, 3(2):46–53, March/April 1983.

[12] C. D. Smith and E. P. Glinert. *PC-TILES: A Visual Programming Environment for Personal Computers Based on the BLOX Methodology.* Technical Report 86-21, Dept. of Computer Science, Rensselaer Polytechnic Institute, 1986.

[13] E. P. Glinert, J. Gonczarowski, and C. D. Smith. An Integrated Approach to Solving Visual Programming's Problems. In *Cognitive Engineering in the Design of Human-Computer Interaction and Expert Systems (G. Salvendy, editor) — Volume 2, Proc. 2nd Int. Conf. on Human-Computer Interaction, Honolulu*, pages 341–348, August 10-14, 1987.

[14] G. W. Furnas. Generalized Fisheye Views. In *Conf. Proc., CHI'86: Human Factors in Computing Systems*, pages 16–23, April 13-17, 1986.

USING A PICTORIAL REPRESENTATION TO COMBINE DATAFLOW AND OBJECT-ORIENTATION IN A LANGUAGE INDEPENDENT PROGRAMMING MECHANISM

P.T Cox   T. Pietrzykowski

Technical University of Nova Scotia
PO Box 1000, Halifax, Nova Scotia, CANADA B3J 2X4
BITNET: PCOX@TUNS

Abstract

The standard textual representation of programming languages has many shortcomings, such as the abstract syntax inherited from Indo-European languages, enforced sequentiality, the necessity for variables, and the confusion between lógical and mnemonic information. The AI languages Lisp and Prolog are improvements over the standard Algol-like languages, but still suffer from some of their drawbacks. The use of a pictorial representation for programming is proposed as a means for overcoming all of these shortcomings, incorporating the powerful features of AI languages and removing the bias towards Indo-European languages, making programming equally accessible to users whose natural language relies on ideograms, such as Chinese. The language PROGRAPH 2 is described using extensive examples, and the environment provided by the present implementation is briefly discussed.

Key words and phrases

Pictorial programming; textual programming; variable; Chinese computing; AI languages; editor/interpreter; dataflow; object-orientation.

1 Introduction

The idea of pictorial programming is as old as programming, and first manifested itself in the form of control flow charts, which are closely related with Algol-like languages. Later, dataflow diagrams provided a more significant and direct contribution to programming because of their connection with dataflow architectures and functional programming. Independently, functional programming rose to significance as an alternative to Algol-like languages, represented initially by Lisp [19]. Since then the functional programming paradigm has received much attention [1]. The next major development of non Algol-like languages was Prolog [22]. Because of their clarity, expressive power and the ease with which they allow programs to be developed in a top-down fashion, Lisp and Prolog have become the main AI programming languages. They are also becoming more widely used in education and general software development.

The proliferation of microcomputers in the last decade has highlighted an important problem in the production of software, a problem normally referred to as "Chinese computing". Existing Algol-like programming languages, for long time the primary tool of software development, are intimately connected with the linguistic roots of Indo-European languages, based on a small symbolic alphabet and intricate syntax using punctuation symbols. Such languages are alien to programmers whose natural languages are rooted in the Chinese ideographic language paradigm. Lisp and Prolog rely less heavily on the syntactic conventions of Indo-

European languages, however, they do rely fundamentally on the concept of "variable", a meaningless symbol that represents some unknown object. Languages based on ideograms can express only meaningful concepts, so variables are unnatural in such languages.

In this paper we describe a pictorial formalism which combines the main features of AI languages with the object-oriented programming paradigm, while completely avoiding variables and the symbolic syntax inherited from Indo-European languages. The result is a powerful universal programming language which equally accessible to users from all linguistic backgrounds.

Research on PROGRAPH originated in 1982, and in its original form was similar to the independently developed GPL [15]. Although this early language employed dataflow control, it also relied heavily on nested Algol-like control structures (if-then-else, while-do) [11,12,18]. Pictorial programming languages have since become a topic of intense research [16, 17]. Experience with this early version of PROGRAPH [9,12,20] made it clear that nested Algol-like control structures are not suited to pictorial representation. Further research has led to replacement of these control structures by a "case" structure and control decisions based on failure. This is similar to Prolog, however PROGRAPH 2 provides a much finer, more precise control over failure.

In this paper we give a comprehensive overview of the language, and a cursory report on the implementation which will be dealt with in detail in another publication.

2 AI languages as a model for general programming

It is well known that the first radical departure from the traditional Algol-like programming was made by the programming languages for AI, Lisp and Prolog. Lisp [19] was the first such language and introduced a completely new paradigm for specifying a problem solution, based on the lambda calculus rather than procedures based on the underlying architecture. Among its major contributions was the introduction of lists as a primitive data structure, removal of declarations of variables, removal of assignment (reintroduced in limited form later), and simplification of syntax. Lisp has only recently become accepted as a language suitable for general purpose programming (software production), owing to extensions to the language (assignment, iteration), advances in user interface, and improvements in efficiency, compilation etc. Prolog [22], which arrived ten years later, went further in the revolution against programming based on von Neumann architecture, by introducing a paradigm based on limited first order predicate calculus. Like Lisp it provided lists as a basic datatype. But the computational paradigm subsumes that of Lisp, and is based on unification and backtracking as the main mechanisms. Further advances in this direction include attempts to combine Prolog and Lisp [2], extend the datastructure of Prolog to infinite trees [7], and extend the computational model of Prolog to deal with parallelism [6]. The acceptance of Prolog outside the AI

This research was supported by Natural Sciences and Engineering Research Council of Canada Operating Grants

community is still limited, however, mostly due to the fact that efficiency of compiled code is still not comparable to that of Lisp.

Although Prolog and Lisp are important in that they provide a different model for computing in general, they lack certain essential features. Neither Prolog nor Lisp have a convenient mechanism for constructing compact structures of records and pointers, a necessary part of most large computing tasks. Such structures can obviously be simulated using list structures, however, this is counter to the intuition of most real-world objects where attributes should have names which can be used to refer to their values. This is the point where real side effects are necessary and intuitive. This leads to an important development which has taken place recently, based on the observation that the focal point for certain kinds of computing tasks is more naturally the data involved rather than the algorithms. This has lead to the development of object-oriented languages [8] starting with Simula [13], and further developed in Smalltalk and others [14]. These languages, however, are all based on the traditional Algol-like structure, with all their attendant problems. Recently Lisp has been extended to include object orientation [3], and research is under way to add it to Prolog [23].

Both Lisp and Prolog provide mechanisms for recording persistent values, however, because of the lack of pointers, database manipulation is awkward or expensive since pointers can be simulated only by identifying atoms.

It is also well known that certain computing tasks are most naturally expressed as iterations. Neither Lisp nor Prolog in their pure forms accommodate iteration, requiring it to be simulated by tail recursion. Later versions of both languages have control structures for iteration, which are adapted from Algol-like languages, and fit only poorly with the basic computational paradigms.

In both Lisp and Prolog, control is accomplished by reacting in some way to Boolean values, explicit T and F in Lisp, and implicit success and failure in Prolog. The possible control reactions to these values are extremely limited in both languages. In Lisp they are used only to control selection of a case in a COND. In Prolog, failure causes backtracking which may be restricted by cut, and failure may be inverted via not. The primitiveness of control in Prolog is a well known problem which has received much attention.

The designs of Lisp and Prolog are both based on the underlying assumption of a sequential architecture. Consequently, both languages are completely sequential, although in Prolog the order of literals in clauses and the order of clauses themselves is sometimes unimportant. With the advent of parallel machines, research has been undertaken to modify these languages to accommodate parallelism, but clearly the task is difficult in view of their inherent sequential structure [6]. The nested functional nature of Lisp makes the expression of parallel algorithms particularly difficult, and although Prolog is based on first order logic which imposes no ordering, its execution paradigm makes parallel execution of literals extremely complex, since these executions are dependent on one another via variable bindings.

As mentioned above, compiled Prolog code is inherently inefficient because of the fact that the possibility of backtracking must be accommodated, even in code which does not use this feature. When backtracking occurs, variables must be unbound, so a complete storage management history must be maintained. Although many ingenious mechanisms have been devised to optimise this, it cannot be avoided because it is a consequence of the computational model of the language [4].

3 Using pictures to express programming concepts

The structure of Algol-like programming languages is based on the structure of Indo European languages like English, which we will refer to as "text based". Its conditional statements, block structure, punctuation and sequentiality are all inherited from such natural languages. Hence these programming languages have complex constructs such as "if-then-else" and "while-do", requiring an equally complex syntax with a multiplicity of punctuation symbols such as comma, semicolon, **begin**, and **end**. Furthermore, control constructs can be deeply nested; therefore significant associated parts of a program can become widely separated. The result is that such programs are difficult to read, and correspondingly error-prone. Lisp and Prolog are based on mathematical formalisms and are therefore less dependent on text based natural languages, but have nevertheless inherited many of their characteristics such as sequentiality and horizontal left-to-right order.

The greatest shortcoming of all text based programming languages, with perhaps the exception of Backus' FP, are variables. Variables used to represent data in programming languages originated from logic, which again stems from Indo-European languages. The special property of a variable is that it is a symbol used to represent some unknown object. This concept is most natural in languages in which new entities can be constructed from smaller meaningless symbols (alphabet) that impose no meaning on the new entity. By contrast, languages based on ideograms can express only meaningful concepts, so it is impossible to introduce a new symbol that represents some unknown object. The existence of variables therefore make programming languages much less intuitive for those whose natural language is ideographic, such as Chinese, Japanese and Korean [5].

Variables also have a number of other technical shortcomings, making them one of the major sources of programming errors [1]. They serve two contradictory purposes: first, they link points in a program where data is produced and used; and second, their names provide information about the intended use of the data. For the first use, short variable names are obviously the best, since long ones are prone to typographical error, but for the second, long names may be necessary to convey mnemonic information. Furthermore, the mnemonic use of variables is confused by the fact that different occurrences of the same variable sometimes require different explanations. Declarations of variables, required in traditional languages, add to the syntactic burden on the programmer and provide an additional opportunity for errors.

A solution to the above problems is to use pictures as the primary form of expression for programming, and relegate text to the syntax-free role of providing identifiers and optional explanatory remarks. The use of pictures in programming is well known: for example, they have always been used for flowcharts and datastructure diagrams. Recently, the advent of low cost graphical microcomputers has provided the impetus to use pictures more directly in the computing process [16, 17]. Using pictures as the form of expression is a complete departure from the linear sequential style of programs, thereby allowing the natural expression of parallelism of independent computations [21]. Variables can be eliminated by using pictorial means to indicate all the points in a program where the same data item occurs. Using pictures obviates the need for complex punctuation and nested control structures. In addition the expressive power of pictures gives the opportunity for introducing a number of powerful and concise control annotations, which would be extremely awkward to express in linear textual form.

4 The PROGRAPH 2 language

The purpose of the research reported here was threefold. The first was to design a general purpose programming language not biased towards any existing class of natural languages. Our second aim was to combine in this language the important features of AI languages with essential new features, while omitting features, such as backtracking and unbound variables, which are detrimental to the efficiency of compiled code. The third purpose of this research was to provide a program development environment in complete harmony with the design of the language; an environment that would provide integrated editing and debugging facilities for homogeneous top down design and development. It was decided to use a pictorial representation to accomplish these aims.

4.1 The dataflow features of PROGRAPH 2

In this section we present the dataflow features of the PROGRAPH 2 language, which are theoretically sufficient for any programming task. We will introduce the language by means of examples.

Our first example is an implementation of the topological sort algorithm on a directed graph represented by adjacency lists. In this representation a graph is specified as a list of lists, each of which corresponds to one node. A list representing a node consists of the name of the node followed by the names of all nodes at the heads of outedges from this node. Figure 1 depicts a graph and its adjacency list representation. In PROGRAPH 2, lists are a simple datatype as in Prolog and Lisp.

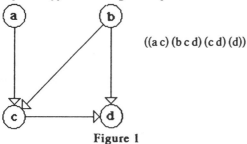

((a c) (b c d) (c d) (d))

Figure 1

Figure 2 shows the *methods* involved with solving this problem. The method **CALL** is the top level one to be executed to run the program. It consists of two *cases* also shown in figure 2.

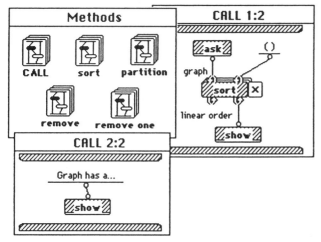

Figure 2

Each case of a method consists of an acyclic directed hypergraph, the nodes of which are called *operations*. Each hyperedge is a tree with its *root* at the bottom of an operation and its leaves, called *terminals* at the top of other operations. Roots are the origins of data, while terminals are the recipients, and the hyperedges define the distribution of data from roots to terminals. Every operation represents a call to either a *system-defined* method or a *user-defined* method. The system-defined methods in this example are the *primitives* **ask** and **show**, the constant () (the empty list), and two special operations *input* and *output* at the top and bottom of

the case respectively. The operation **sort** is a call to a user-defined method. Execution of a case follows the data driven, dataflow paradigm. In case 1 of **CALL**, the first operation to be executed is either **ask** or the constant (). **ask** obtains input from the user which becomes the value of its root. After both **ask** and the constant are executed, their results are passed to **sort** which is the next operation to be executed. Note that the operation **sort** is accompanied by a *control* called *next-on-failure*, represented by the icon to the right of the operation. The call to **sort** will *fail* if the given graph has a cycle (see the explanation below). If the **sort** operation *succeeds*, it produces a linearly ordered list of names of nodes which is displayed by the execution of the **show** operation. If **sort** fails, however, the control causes the execution of case 1 to halt, and case 2 is executed, producing a message about the cyclic nature of the graph. Note that the string constant containing this message is abbreviated so as not to obscure the program. The editor allows the user to inspect the complete value, however.

In case 1 of **CALL**, the operation **sort** is a *multiplex*, in this example, an *iterative multiplex*. A multiplex is pictorially distinguished from a simple operation by being drawn in a three dimensional fashion to emphasize the fact that it represents many executions of a method. A multiplex always has at least one *annotated* root or terminal. The one in figure 2 has *loop* annotated terminals, which are matched by loop roots. These annotations indicate that the operation will be repeatedly executed, and the output values on the loop roots will be passed to the loop terminals as input values for the next iteration. In the example, the leftmost loop terminal and root maintain the intermediate value of the still unsorted part of the graph, while the other pair holds the sorted part.

The reader should note that in figure 2, case 1 of **CALL** contains two *comments*, "graph" and "linear order". A comment is arbitrary text that can be associated with a program element, serves purely as information to the reader of the program and has no logical sigificance.

Figure 3 depicts the single case of the method **sort**. The input and output have respectively two roots and two terminals. In general the input has no terminals and the output has no roots. Execution of the input copies the input data from the calling operation, while executing the output copies values to the roots of the calling operation.

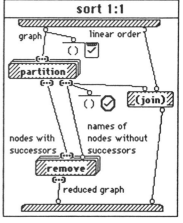

Figure 3

The first operation to be executed in this case is the constant (), which here has a terminal but no root. Such a constant, called a *matching*, tests the value on its terminal. If this value is the same as the value of the constant, the matching succeeds, otherwise it fails. In the event of success, the accompanying control, *terminate-on-success* causes the execution of the case to be immediately halted and the multiplex to terminate, producing as its outputs the results of the previous iteration. If the match succeeds, the incoming graph has no nodes left, and is therefore sorted. If the match fails, execution of the case continues with the operation **partition**, which is a *parallel multiplex*. A parallel multiplex has at least one root or terminal annotated as *list* and no loop annotated terminals or roots. Such a multiplex expects a list as input to each list annotated terminal, and applies the called method to corresponding elements of these input lists. The outputs of these applications are assembled as lists on the list annotated roots of the multiplex. In the case where such a multiplex has more than one list annotated terminal, the number of applications of the method is equal to the length of the shortest input list at most, although execution of the multiplex may be earlier terminated by the activation of some control. In our example, the left root of the **partition** multiplex produces the list of nodes of the graph which have at least one outedge, while the right root produces the list of names of nodes that have no outedges. The latter output is matched with the constant () accompanied by the control *fail-on-success*. If this control is activated, then **partition** did not find a node with no outedges, implying that the graph is cyclic. In this situation, the control causes the execution of the case to be immediately halted and the calling operation, **sort**, to fail. Otherwise, either the operation (**join**) or the multiplex **remove** will be executed next. The parallel multiplex **remove** completes the pruning of the graph by removing all outedges ending at nodes which already have no outedges. (**join**) is a primitive that concatenates lists, and in this instance adds to the already sorted part of the graph the names of the newly removed nodes. Finally, execution of the output operation copies values to the roots of the calling operation.

Figure 4 shows the two cases of the method **partition**. Note that the banners of cases indicate the case number and the total number of cases. In case 1, the primitive (**length**) finds the length of a list: in this example this equals the number of outedges of the node plus 1. If this number is 1, then the node has no outedges and should be removed from the graph. **unpack** is a primitive that expects a list as input and returns its individual elements on corresponding roots. Here **unpack** converts a node into its name. Note that the left terminal of the output is not connected to any root: during execution such a terminal produces the value NONE, which is suppressed from the list assembled on the corresponding list root of the calling multiplex. The second case of **partition** is executed only if the node has outedges, in which case it is passed to the first terminal of output, while the second terminal gets the value NONE.

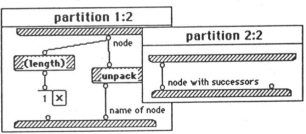

Figure 4

Figure 5, shows the single cases of **remove** and **remove one**. **remove** deletes from a node all the outedges ending at the most recently detected nodes with no outedges. To do this it executes **remove one** as a *mixed multiplex*, which has both list and loop annotations. Such a multiplex iterates values on loop terminals and roots as explained above, and in each iteration consumes one element from each list terminal and attaches one

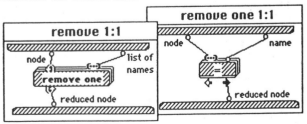

Figure 5

element to each list root. In **remove one**, the first root of the input is a node of the graph from which are to be removed outedges named by the second root of the input. This task is accomplished by a *separate multiplex* which applies a boolean operation to every element of the list on its list terminal, separating this list into lists of elements that produce TRUE and those that produce FALSE. These lists are output on the left and right roots of the muliplex respectively.

4.2 Control of execution

As mentioned earlier, PROGRAPH 2 programs are executed according to the data flow, data driven paradigm. Consequently, since a case is a directed, acyclic hypergraph, the operations can be executed according to any acceptable total order of this hypergraph. A total order is *acceptable* iff for every pair of operations A and B such that B has an associated control and A does not, if A occurs before B then there is a path from A to B.

The examples discussed above have employed various controls to modify the execution of methods. In general PROGRAPH 2 refines the control provided by Prolog using failure, but unlike Prolog allows intended failure to be distinguished from failure due to programming errors. For example, in Prolog if a literal calls a predicate of different arity where all clauses for the predicate have the same arity, the call simply fails, but obviously such failure could not be intentional.

The execution of an operation can have only three possible outcomes, *failure, success* and *error*. We will first discuss failure. First, failure can be generated only by certain primitives: for example, any boolean primitive which normally produces TRUE or FALSE on its root may also be used with no root, in which case its execution will either succeed or fail. Second, a matching generates failure if the incoming data is not equal to the constant. Finally, an operation which calls a user-defined method will fail if a *fail* control in one of the cases of the method is activated.

Error is generated in six ways. First primitives can produce error: for example if an arithmetic operation receives string inputs. Second, a call to a user-defined method will produce error if the last case of the method contains a *next* control which is activated. Third, a call to a user-defined method will produce error if the execution of an operation in the method fails, but has no associated control. Fourth the execution of an operation generates error if there is no corresponding method. Fifth, the execution of a multiplex with no list terminals produces an error if the called method contains no finish or terminate control. Finally, executing a simple operation which calls a method containing finish or terminate controls will generate error.

The execution of any operation succeeds iff it neither fails nor produces error.

The following table summarises the controls. Each control must contain an *activation mark*, either *on-success* or *on-failure*, indicated respectively by a check or cross, as in the above

Control	Name	Action
☐	next	halt execution of current case: start execution of next case
◯	fail	halt execution of current case: fail call to method
☐	terminate	halt execution of current case: end execution of calling multiplex
☐	finish	continue execution of current case: end execution of calling multiplex

examples. If a control is marked on-success (on-failure) it will be activated iff the associated operation succeeds (fails). If a control is not activated, execution proceeds. In the table, the controls are shown without activation marks.

Any control can be associated with any operation with the exception of finish-on-failure, which can be attached only to operations with no roots.

Activating a control which halts execution of the case overrides the effect of any previously activated control in the same case.

4.3 Class system and database of PROGRAPH 2

In the preceding sections we have presented the dataflow features of PROGRAPH 2. Here we will discuss mechanisms for constructing and manipulating complex data, modularisation and managing persistent side effects. To incorporate these features, we adopted the object-oriented paradigm based on the class hierarchy system. As before we will use examples for illustration.

Our first example implements the well known alpha-beta procedure for searching AND/OR game trees. Figure 6 depicts the hierarchy of *classes* for this example. In general the class structure is a forest where each node is a class. Every class consists of a set of methods, a set of *class attributes* and a set of *instance attributes*. Each tree represents an inheritance hierarchy: that is, every class inherits the methods and attributes of its parent class.

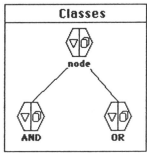

Classes

Figure 6

Figure 7 shows the attributes of the class **node**. This class has no class attributes; these would normally appear above the grey line. The instance attributes provide a template for constructing *instances* of the class, which are analogous to records in Pascal. Attributes have no type restrictions and have default values used to initialise instances. In this example all attributes have a default value NULL. The classes AND and OR have attributes identical to class **node**, and are therefore not displayed. The attribute **state** contains the state of the game; **value** contains the backed-up value assigned to the node; **maxor** (**minand**) contains the maximal (minimal) backed-up value of the OR ancestors (AND ancestors) of the node; **best child** indicates the successor node corresponding to the current backed value; and **depth** is an integer indicating the distance from the root node. It is important to note that our program deals only with instances of the classes AND and OR, which represent nodes of the game tree: the only reason for introducing the class **node** is to provide useful inheritance of methods for the successor classes.

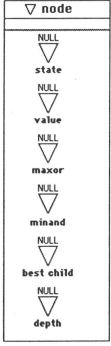

Figure 7

In figure 8 are shown the methods of class **node**, and their cases. Note that the names of cases of methods in classes are

prefixed by the class names. Such methods are called *class* methods in contrast to methods dicussed in the prevoius section which are called *universal* methods.

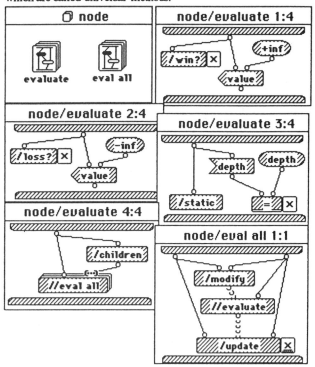

Figure 8

The method **node/evaluate** is used to find the backed-up value of any node, and the corresponding best child, indicating the move that should be played in the game. Case 1 of **node/evaluate** checks whether the node represents a winning game position, and if so, assigns a large positive value to it. Here the operation **/win?** represents a call to a class method **win?**, the **/** indicating that the method should be chosen according to the instance that arrives as the leftmost input to the operation (in this case, the only input). In this application, whether or not a node represents a win depends not only on the state of the game but also on which player has the next move. Therefore there are two methods called **win?**, one in each of the classes AND and OR. The operation **+inf** in case 1 of **node/evaluate** is graphically distinguished from a simple operation by having oval ends, indicating that it is a *database* operation referring to a *persistent* of the same name.

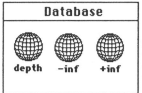

Figure 9

Persistents are used to store any data, can be accessed or modified during execution of a program, and are maintained between executions. Here we use three persistents, as shown in figure 9. Note that the database operation **+inf** in case 1 of **node/evaluate** has a root: execution of this operation will produce on this root the current value of the persistent **+inf**, which in this program is a positive value larger than any produced by static evaluation.

The third operation, **value**, in case 1 of **node/evaluate** is also pictorially distinct from simple operations. Its pointed left end shows that it is an *attribute assignment* operation, which assigns the value on its right terminal to the attribute of the instance on its left terminal specified by the name of the operation. Executing **value** sets the **value** attribute of the incoming node to the value obtained from the persistent +inf. It is important to note that an attribute assignment causes a side effect which will persist even if the execution of the case containing it is later abandoned. The root of the attribute assignment receives the modified instance. This is unnecessary since the instance is available elsewhere in the case, but is provided as an aid to simplifying the layout of cases.

Case 2 of **node/evaluate** in figure 8 deals with a node which is a loss. It is dual to case 1 and therefore requires no further explanation. Case 3 of **node/evaluate** applies to a node which is as deep in the game tree as the search should go. The value of the **depth** attribute of the node is extracted by the operation **depth** with the concave left end, an *attribute extraction* operation. Attribute extraction operations perform the dual action to that performed by attribute assignments. The allowable depth of the search is specified by the value stored in the persistent **depth** (figure 9). If the value of the **depth** attribute of the node is equal to this maximum depth, the static evaluation function for the game being played is applied to the node, placing a value in its **value** attribute. This evaluation function is realised by two methods called **static**, defined in the classes **AND** and **OR**. The final case of **node/evaluate** generates the children of the node using the methods **children** defined in **AND** and **OR**, and applies the method **node/eval all**. Note that the name of the operation that applies this method is preceded by //, indicating that the relevant method is the one which holds in the current class. A method is said to *hold in* a class if it is defined in the class or holds in the parent class. **node/eval all** is applied to each of the children of the node as a parallel multiplex.

The method **node/eval all** consists of one case containing three operations, all of which cause side effects. The operation **/modify** modifies the attribute **minand (maxor)** of the child node. The operation **//evaluate** computes a backed-up value for the child. The operation **/update** updates the backed-up value of the parent, and fails if the search should be cut off. This failure activates the control finish-on-failure, which discontinues the execution of the **//eval all** multiplex. It is important to note that the order in which the operations in this case are performed is significant. **/modify** sets the **minand (maxor)** attribute of the child, used for cutoffs in lower levels of the search by **//evaluate**. Also, **/update** computes the backed-up value of the parent using the value of the child computed by **//evaluate**. Clearly, therefore, **/modify** must be executed before **//evaluate**, and **//evaluate** before **/update**. This order would not normally be guaranteed by the dataflow paradigm, but here is enforced by *synchros*. A synchro is an edge between two operation represented by a sequence of rounded arrowheads, and is an edge of the case hypergraph.

Figure 10 lists the methods of class **AND**, and shows details of those which are independent of the game being played. Clearly **win?**, **loss?**, **static** and **children** must be defined for each specific game. The reader is invited to investigate the methods **AND/modify** and **AND/update** in detail, however, we will point out some features. First, the operation **min** in case 1 of **AND/modify** is a primitive that computes the minimum of its two

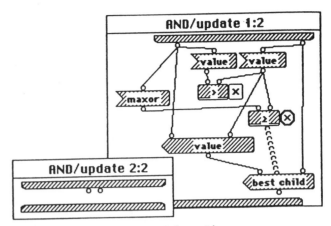

Figure 10 (contd.)

inputs. Second, the synchro in case 1 of **AND/update** is necessary to ensure that the **best child** attribute of the parent node is assigned before cutoff is detected. If the synchro were not present, the operation ≥ would be executed before **best child** because of its associated control.

The methods of class **OR** are strictly dual to those of **AND** and are presented in figure 11 below.

Clearly the class structure allows many methods of the same name to be defined, an essential feature of the object-oriented paradigm. As shown in the above example, the name of any operation which refers to a class method must have a *prefix* to indicate which method to apply. The prefix / indicates that an instance is expected on the leftmost terminal of the operation, and the method to be applied is the one that holds in the class to which the instance belongs. The prefix // indicates that the method is the

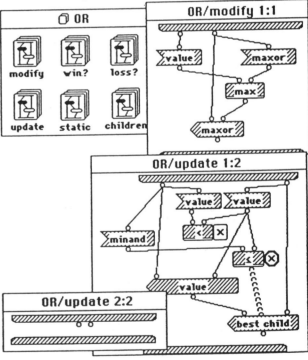

Figure 11

one that holds in the current class, that is the class containing the method in which the operation occurs. Finally, a prefix of the

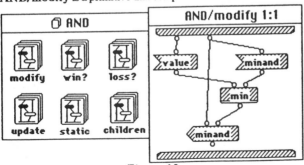

Figure 10

form <class>/ indicates that the method is the one that holds in the class named <class>. The // prefix is clearly an abbreviation which allows the class name to be omitted because of the context.

Our last example, presented to illustrate further advanced features, is a program that builds and queries a simple database of instances of different classes. For brevity, our commentary on this example will concentrate only on features of the language not previously discussed. Figure 12 shows the persistents, the class hierarchy, and the attributes of the two classes **person** and **employee**. Note that the attributes of the class **employee** have two different pictorial representations: the two inherited from **person** contain an arrow to distinguish them from those defined in **employee**. Note also that **employee** has a class attribute **best paid**, the value of which is always the instance of **employee** with the largest value of **salary** attribute. The persistent **people** is used to maintain a list of instances of **employee** and **person**.

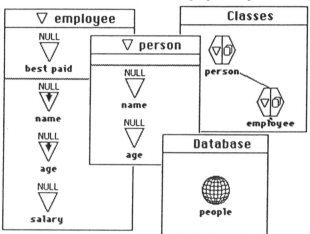

Figure 12

This example has one universal method **average**, which finds the average of any nonempty list of numbers, and is used by class methods to find average age and average salary of instances in the database. This method is shown in figure 13 following. If the input to this method is the empty list, the control fail-on-success will cause the calling operation to fail.

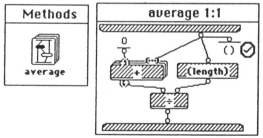

Figure 13

Figure 14 lists the methods of class **person**, and shows details of the methods **person/new** and **person/add**. Executing **person/add** constructs a number of new instances of **person**, adding them to the list of instances stored in the persistent **people**. The operation **person** in case 1 of **person/add** is an *instance generator*, indicated by its pointed ends. Executing an instance generator named <classname> makes an instance of the class <classname>, which beomes the value of the root of the operation. In our example, the instance generator **person** is a parallel multiplex with a list root, so it will produce a list of instances of **person**. The actions performed by an instance generator for a class can be extended by defining in the class a method called **new**, with input and output arity both 1. When an instance

generator for the class is executed, this method is then implicitly called with the newly generated instance as input. In our example, the method **person/new** prompts the user for values for the attributes **name** and **age**, assigns these values to the attributes, and

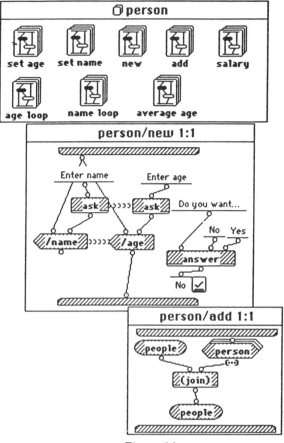

Figure 14

asks whether the user wishes to add another person. Note that the names of the two attribute assignments are preceded by a /, indicating that, instead of using the standard attribute assignment, methods supplied by the user should be executed. The attribute assignments /age and /name will call methods **person/set name** and **person/set age** respectively. This general mechanism allows the simple, uncontrolled attribute assignment to be replaced by any actions of the user's choice, for example to check validity of the data to be assigned. Similarly, standard attribute extractions may be overridden by creating a method with name of the form **get** <attribute name>. Executing the primitive **answer** displays a dialogue with a prompt specified by its first input: the user responds by selecting between replies specified by the other inputs. The value on the root is the selected reply. Here a reply of "No" will activate the control finish-on-success, stopping execution of the multiplex **person** in case 1 of **person/add**.

Figure 15 gives the details of the methods **person/set age** and **person/age loop**. In this example, **person/set age** calls the method **person/age loop** in an iterative multiplex in which the value being assigned is looped. Case 1 of **person/age loop** checks that the data is a number, using the primitive **number?**, then that this number is nonnegative. Note that the synchro is necessary to ensure that these tests occur in the correct order. If both tests succeed, the attribute assignment is performed. If the assignment is performed in case 1, the control finish-on-success on the output will cause execution of the multiplex /age loop in the method **person/set age** to end. Case 2 of **person/age loop** is

319

executed if the data did not pass the tests in case 1. In this event, the user is asked to supply a new value.

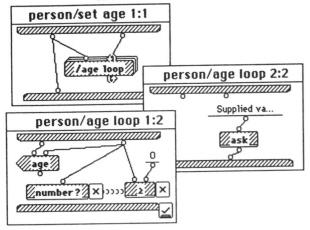

Figure 15

In figure 16 are shown the methods **person/set name** and **person/name loop**. These are analogous to the methods **person/set age** and **person/age loop** and will not be further explained.

Figure 16

In figure 17 we illustrate the single case of the method **person/average age**. We leave the reader to examine this method, commenting only on the fact that if the execution of the operation **average** fails, then so will the call to **person/average age**. If the operation **average** was not accompanied by a control, its failure would produce an error. The method **person/salary** will be explained later.

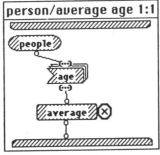

Figure 17

The methods of class **employee** are listed in figure 18. In the following, for the sake of brevity we will show will show only

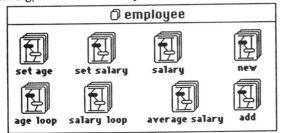

Figure 18

certain parts of the program. The methods set **age**, **age loop**, **salary loop**, **new**, and **add** in class **employee** are all analogous to methods in class **person** already discussed, so we will not present them.

Figure 19 illustrates the methods **salary**, **average salary** and **salary** from class **employee**, as well as **person/salary**. In the first case of **employee/set salary** the operation **/salary loop**

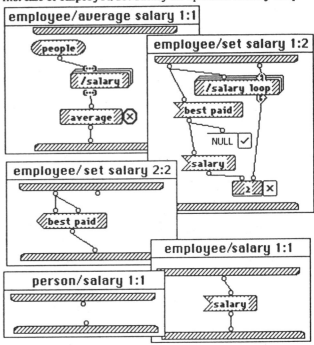

Figure 19

assigns a value to the **salary** attribute in an analogous fashion to the method **person/age loop** in figure 15. Then, if the current value of the attribute **best paid** is NULL, or the salary of the best paid **employee** is smaller than salary of the current **employee**, the second case is executed, assigning the current **employee** to the class attribute **best paid**. The method **employee/average salary** cannot directly extract the value of attribute **salary** because the list may contain instances of **person** which have no **salary** attribute. Instead it uses the methods **salary**, defined in classes **person** and **employee**. The method **employee/salary** simply applies the attribute extraction, while **person/salary** produces NONE.

5 Environment

In this section we discuss the current implementation of PROGRAPH 2. A more thorough treatment can be found in [10]. PROGRAPH 2 is at present implemented on the Macintosh computer, and all our discussions below refer to this implementation. However, most of our comments apply to any graphics workstation that provides similar interface capabilities.

The most important role in the PROGRAPH 2 environment is played by the *editor* which provides a true top down development system in which the design is progressively refined, eventually resulting in a completed program. This editor, therefore, provides a working example of the celebrated problem reduction approach to problem solving.

In keeping with the conventions of the host computer, the Macintosh, the main parts of a program, methods, cases, classes, attributes, and persistents, are all depicted in their own windows, simplified forms of which were shown in above examples above.

The main guiding principle in the design of the editor was that it should be as intelligent as possible, using all the available information to the user's advantage. Mouse actions are the main events which drive the editor. In order that the smallest possible number of actions should be required from the user to obtain a desired effect, these events are interpreted according to their context. A single click in an unoccupied part of a window creates an appropriate object. For example, in the **Class** window such a click produces a new class, while in a **Case** window it produces a new operation; or if the click is close to the top or bottom of an existing operation, produces a new terminal or root, respectively. Connections between roots and terminals, between classes and between operations (synchros) are created by the same protocol: if a suitable icon is selected, pressing the option key creates a "rubber band" from the icon to the cursor, and a single click on a suitable icon then makes the connection. As mentioned above, actions with an established meaning in the host computer have the same meaning in the PROGRAPH 2 editor. For example, a double click on an icon opens a window on the structure the icon represents, and a single click on an icon selects it. It is well known that using menus is an impediment; the editor's context sensitive processing of clicks makes the use of menus unnecessary for most editing actions. Menus are used only for less frequent actions, such as invoking the interpreter, deleting or annotating program elements.

The editor uses its knowledge of names in the system to minimise the need for typing, thereby avoiding typographical errors. The names of all primitives, persistents and methods are available to be copied and pasted elsewhere, so that no name needs to be typed more than once in a program.

Another principle in the design of the editor was that the user should be protected from syntactic errors. First, menu items are disabled to prevent their inappropriate application. For example, if an operation with any terminals or more than one root is selected, the menu item **constant** which transforms operations into constants will be disabled. Second, the context sensitive interpretation of mouse clicks, described above, ensures that only appropriate program elements can be created. For example, only operations, roots, terminals and synchros can be created in a **Case** window. Third, attempts to make incorrect connections are intercepted and disallowed. The editor therefore refuses to connect two roots together, to connect two terminals, or to build cycles of operations or classes (remember that the case hypergraph is acyclic, and the class hierarchy is a tree). Finally, whenever a program element is deleted, all associated elements are deleted as well, to maintain syntactic correctness. In every case where the user attempts to violate the syntax, the editor refuses to perform the action in question, and issues an explanatory message if requested.

A further mechanism, provided to help prevent logical errors and to improve readability of programs, is the transfer of terminals, roots and associated comments. When an operation is created and given the name of an existing method, either user defined or a primitive, terminals and roots are automatically created if the return key is pressed to terminate the typing of the name. The numbers of terminals and roots correspond to the input and output arities of the corresponding method. Similarly, a method created by double clicking on an existing operation will inherit the arity from the operation. Furthermore, in each of these situations any comments attached to roots and terminals are transferred along with the arity.

An important consideration in the design of the PROGRAPH 2 editor was to allow the user creative freedom, unhampered by the strict rules of structure and layout enforced by traditional textual programming environments. The user can arrange icons to suit his or her own aesthetic or perceptual preferences, alleviating the monotony of conventional programming. Rearranging icons is performed by the familiar "dragging".

The second major component of the PROGRAPH 2 environment is the *interpreter*, which illustrates the process of computation, and gives the information necessary for debugging. The interpreter shows the state of the execution stack in a special window and can also illustrate the process of execution through the individual cases of methods, using windows that depict the structure built during editing. In figure 20 below we show the execution of the topological sort program presented earlier. The **Stack** window depicts all the active methods as method icons with superimposed integers giving the case number. This stack grows from top to bottom and scrolls automatically as new elements are pushed on to it. The other windows show the details of the stack elements. In each of these windows there is exactly one selected operation which is the next to be executed. The operations drawn normally are those that have been executed. The other operations are drawn in a grey pattern.

An execution in progress can be halted and all the details of the execution history examined. For example, a window can be opened on to any icon on the stack, and values associated with any roots in any of these windows can be examined. This is done by opening a window on to the root. If the associated operation has not been executed, the root will have no value and no window will open on it. When a window is open on to a root, the user may be able to change the value. Note that all windows associated with execution have a dotted background to distinguish them from editing windows.

It is also possible to edit a PROGRAPH 2 program which is under execution, while this execution is halted. To do so an edit window on to a case must be opened. This can be done in the usual way by opening a window from a method icon, but can also be accomplished by double-clicking the background of a **Case**

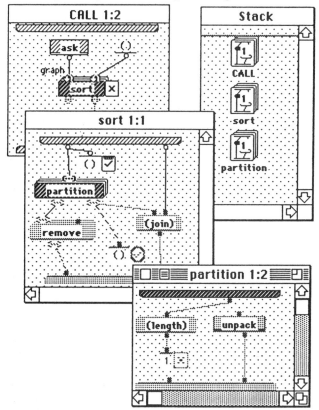

Figure 20

window corresponding to a stack element. Editing changes do not cause the suspended execution to be abandoned: instead the execution is modified in such a way that the parts unaffected by the changes do not have to be re-executed.

One of the most important principles in the design of PROGRAPH 2 is that errors should be either prevented or should be detected as early as possible, and when errors do occur, recovery should be simple and expedient. As mentioned above, no syntactic errors are permitted. To help the user to remove logical errors, the interpreter halts when execution of an operation produces an error. The interpreter opens the window containing the operation in question, flashes the icon and generates an explanatory message. When this occurs, the user may immediately invoke the corresponding editing window as described above, fix the error and resume executing. Even seemingly major changes, like adding a forgotten class, persistent or method, can be made without destroying the execution in progress.

6 Concluding remarks

We will now summarise what appear to be the major contributions of PROGRAPH 2.

It is well known that existing textual programming languages depend heavily on the conventions of Indo European languages, in which abstract symbols are combined according to some linear symbolic syntax to form meaningful strings. This is a severe restriction and does not appeal naturally to people whose languages are based on a different paradigm, for example Chinese. The alternative is to free programming from the constraints imposed by any natural language. PROGRAPH 2 does this by using a pictorial representation of data flow and class hierarchies. There is still a limitation to pictures, however, in that they are two dimensional. This limitation is at present imposed by the communication media such as paper and video screen. In PROGRAPH 2, however, a third dimension is available by means of windows that can be opened to explore the details of program elements.

Another consequence of the pictorial representation of PROGRAPH 2 is the ease with which certain characteristics of computations can be expressed. Independent operations in particular, are not arbitrarily restricted to some total order, parallel array and list processing can be directly represented, and clearly distinguished from inherently iterative array and list processing.

PROGRAPH 2 refines the concept of failure in Prolog to distinguish between intended failure and error. This could be accomplished in a linear textual language, however, it would necessitate the introduction of eight different operators to apply to procedure calls, even further degrading the readability. In contrast, such controls are clear and unobtrusive in PROGRAPH 2.

Our comments so far have been directed towards PROGRAPH 2 as a language. It is important, however, to consider the programming process in its entirety, and to observe how well the language and its features integrate with the environment. Again, the pictorial nature of PROGRAPH 2 is a key factor. First, the layout of the elements of a program is flexible, so that to a large extent the programmer can arrange them to enhance the clarity of the program. Second, comments, instead of being interspersed with logically meaningful parts as in a textual program, can in PROGRAPH 2 be placed wherever necessary to provide information without obscuring the logic of the algorithm. Finally, all the expressive power of pictures can be brought to bear on the process of testing programs. A complete display is given to illustrate the progress of execution, and the location of errors indicated in the pictures.

The PROGRAPH 2 language and environment frees the user from the usual tedious chores associated with unnecessary attention to details required by conventional languages. First the need for attention to the usual syntactic details is removed, while the intelligent editor prevents the construction of any unacceptable or ambiguous programs. Second, typographical errors are minimised by the fact that text is used only for names, and typing of names is reduced by the ease with which they can be transferred.

Because of the pictorial representation, variables, a subject of continued controversy in computing [1], and a concept alien to such languages as Chinese [5], are eliminated from PROGRAPH 2. The informational role of variable names is performed by comments on terminals and roots, a more flexible mechanism with no logical consequences. A result of the elimination of variables is that there are no declarations for the types of local data. This lack of type declaration is extended to persistents and attributes of classes. By redefining attribute assignments, however, the user has complete control over the data assigned to attributes.

It should be quite clear that the structure of the PROGRAPH 2 language presents no obstacle to compilation into efficient code. A compiler is in an advanced stage of development.

7 Acknowledgements

The authors wish to acknowledge helpful discussions with Qingshi Gao and Heng-Da Cheng.

8 References

[1] Backus, J., Can programming be liberated from the von Neumann style?, *Communications of ACM* 21, (1978), 613-641

[2] Barbuti, R.; Bellia, M.; Levi, G.; Martelli, M., On the integration of Logic Programming and Functional Programming, Proc. of International Symp. on Logic Prog. (1984), 160-166.

[3] Bobrow, D.G. et al., CommonLoops: Merging Lisp and Object Oriented Programming, *Proc. OOPSLA 86* (1986), 17-29.

[4] Campbell, J.A. (Ed), *Implementations of Prolog*, Ellis-Horwood (1984).

[5] Cheng H-D., *Private Communication* (1988)

[6] Clark, K.L.; Gregory, S., PARLOG: ParallelProgramming in Logic, *ACM Transactions on Programming Languages and Systems 8(1)* (1986), 1-49.

[7] Colmerauer, A., Prolog-II manuel de reference et modelle theoretique, Groupe d'Intelligence Artificielle, Universite d'Aix- Marseille (1982).

[8] Cox, B., *Object-oriented Programming, an Evolutionary Approach*, Addison-Wesley (1986).

[9] Cox, P.T.; Mulligan, I.J., Compiling the graphical functional language PROGRAPH, *Proceedings of ACM Sympos. on Small Systems*, Danvers, Mass. (1985), 34-41.

[10] Cox, P.T.; Pietrzykowski, T., *PROGRAPH 2: a visual, dataflow, object-oriented software engineering environment*, Tech. Rept., School of Computer Science, Technical University of Nova Scotia (1988).

[11] Cox, P.T.; Pietrzykowski, T., Advanced programming aids in PROGRAPH, *Proceedings of ACM Sympos. on Small Systems*, Danvers, Mass. (1985), 27-33.

[12] Cox, P.T.; Pietrzykowski, T., Matwin, S., Concurrent editing and executing in PROGRAPH on graphical microcomputers, *ISMM International Journal of Mini and Microcomputers v.6, no.1*, (1985), 1-3.

[13] Dahl, O.J.; Mihrhang, B.; Nygaard, K., *Simula67 Common Base Language*, Norwegian Computing Centre, S-22 (1970).

[14] Goldberg, A.; Robson, D., *Smalltalk-80: the Language and its Implementation*, Addison-Wesley (1983).

[15] *GPL Programming Manual*, Research Report, Computer Science Department, University of Utah (1981).

[16] IEEE, Proceedings of 1986 Workshop on Visual Languages, IEEE (1986)

[17] Linkoping University, Proceedings of 1987 Workshop on Visual Languages, (1987)

[18] Matwin, S.; Pietrzykowski, PROGRAPH: a preliminary report, *Comput. Lang. v.10, no.2*, (1985), 91-126.

[19] McCarthy, J. et al., *Lisp 1.5 Programmers Manual*, MIT Press, Cambridge (1965).

[20] Pietrzykowski, T., PROGRAPH as an Environment for Prolog Database Applications, *Proc. of Logic Programming Workshop*, Portugal (1983), 371-388.

[21] Pong, M-C., A Graphical Language for Concurrent Programming, *Proc. IEEE Workshop on Visual Languages*, (1986), 26-33.

[22] Roussell, P., *Prolog Manuel de Reference*, Groupe d'Intelligence Artificielle, UER de Luminy, Universite de Marseille (1975).

[23] Zaniolo, C., Object Oriented Programming in Prolog, Proc. International Symp. on Logic Programming (1984), 265-271

□□□ 5 □□□   Case Study: From **PECAN** to **GARDEN** and Beyond

S.P. Reiss. "PECAN: Program Development Systems That Support Multiple Views." *IEEE Trans. on Software Engineering*, SE–11(3):276–285, March 1985.

S.P. Reiss. "Working in the GARDEN Environment for Conceptual Programming." *IEEE Software*, 4(6):16–27, November 1987.

S.P. Reiss, S. Meyers and C. Duby. "Using GELO to Visualize Software Systems." In *Proc. 2nd Annual Symp. on User Interface Software and Technology (UIST'89)*, Williamsburg, Va., pages 149–157, November 13-15, 1989. ACM Press, New York.

Reprinted from *IEEE Transactions on Software Engineering*,
Volume SE-11, Number 3, March 1985, pages 276-285.

PECAN: Program Development Systems that Support Multiple Views

STEVEN P. REISS, MEMBER, IEEE

Abstract—This paper describes the PECAN family of program development systems. PECAN supports multiple views of the user's program. The views can be representations of the program or of the corresponding semantics. The primary program view is a syntax-directed editor. The current semantic views include expression trees, data type diagrams, flow graphs, and the symbol table. PECAN is designed to make effective use of powerful personal machines with high-resolution graphics displays and is currently implemented on APOLLO workstations.

Index Terms—Incremental compilation, multiple views, program development systems, programming environments, syntax-directed editors.

I. INTRODUCTION

THE availability of powerful personal computers and the desire for increased programmer productivity have led to the recent development of interactive programming environments for algebraic languages. In this paper we describe the PECAN family of program development environments developed at Brown University. PECAN differs from other systems in its use of the graphical facilities of personal workstations and its support for multiple concurrent views. PECAN provides views of the program, its semantics, and its execution.

A. Objectives

Out objective is to study environments that make full use of the computing power and graphics available on the new generation of personal machines. These environments will be used by both the experienced and the novice programmer. They will be easy and fast to use, offer immediate feedback to the user, and allow the user to visualize his program. PECAN is the prototype system we have developed to illustrate the potentials of these environments. Its support of multiple views and its modularity provide an execellent vehicle for experimentation.

PECAN contains many of the best features of other, similar systems. These include

• immediate feedback of semantic and syntactic errors while the user is editing

• an undo facility whereby the user can undo and redo any action back to the beginning of his session

• structured templates for building the program, available as command

• the flexibility to type text at any time instead of using templates

Manuscript received January 31, 1984. This work was supported in part by the National Science Foundation under Grants MCS-7905992, MCS-8200670, SER-8004974, and MCS-8121806, by the Office of Naval Research under Contracts N00014-78-C-0396 and N00014-83-K-0146, and by the Defense Advanced Research Projects Agency under Order 4786.

The author is with the Department of Computer Science, Brown University, Providence, RI 02912.

• the use of on-screen and pop-up menus as alternatives to typing most commands

• a multiple window display to make effective use of the screen

• incremental semantics that allow the program to be compiled as it is edited

• a framework that handles a variety of (algebraic) programming languages with the same commands.

B. Views in PECAN

The system differs from other program development systems in its use of multiple views of shared data structures. The program is represented internally as an abstract syntax tree. The user does not see this tree directly, but instead sees views or concrete representations of it. One such view is a syntax-directed editor. This view displays the tree by pretty-printing it with multiple fonts. Another view of the program is a Nassi-Shneiderman structured flowchart. A third view would be a module interconnection diagram showing how the program is organized. Each of these views may be read-only or modifiable. They all display the abstract syntax tree, and update their display automatically as the tree changes. Modifiable views also support changing the tree using the displayed representation.

PEACAN provides more than program views. In addition to the data structure representing the syntax of programs, the incremental compiler supports semantic data structures for the symbol table, the set of data types, expression trees, and control-flow graphs. PECAN supports incremental views of these data structures. The symbol table view provides a graphical drawing of the current symbol table and highlights the current symbol. The expression view provides a tree picture of the current expression. The data type view shows a data structure diagram for the current type. The flow view shows a flowchart of the current program.

PECAN supports program execution. Such support is based on the BALSA system that provides multiple dynamic views of a fixed program's data structures while the program is executing [1]. PECAN provides a user-controlled movie of the execution of an arbitrary program through its own displays and through displays of the user's data structures.

PECAN supports multiple vews concurrently with automatic updating. There can be several views of the same abstract syntax tree. If any one of them modifies the tree, PECAN sends messages to inform each view that it should be updated. The incremental compiler is treated as an invisible view and is called whenever a tree changes. In turn, as the compiler updates the semantic representation, views of the semantics are notified of the change so that they can update their displays. The same philosophy is used for execution views. As a variable or the stack or the location counter changes, any views that are displaying these items are notified to update their display.

PECAN is currently being developed at Brown University on APOLLO workstations. The first version is designed with experimentation in mind and with the goal of supporting student programming. The system design is flexible so that new views may be easily tried and so that a resonable combination of views can be found. The system design is highly modular. Components such as the incremental compiler can be changed without affecting other views or modules.

III. RELATED WORK

There are several efforts aimed at building interactive programming environments for personal machines. While PECAN borrows from many of these systems, it is differentiated by its use of multiple views, its target languages, and its reliance on graphics. In this section we briefly relate the more well-known systems.

The Cornell program synthesizer [2] provides a full system for PL/C including a syntax-directed editor and an interpreter. Its editor is template-based, but provides text editing for fixed constructs such as expressions. It has recently been implemented as a generator, so that it is possible to create synthesizers for different languages using attribute grammars to describe the output and semantics for each production of the abstract syntax. The COPE system [3], also developed at Cornell, provides another approach based on an intelligent parser. The editor in this system is a text editor tied to an error-correcting parser. The parser is able to insert missing keywords and tokens to get about the same effect as templates do in the synthesizer. This scheme has the advantage that the user can type his program at any time. It has the disadvantage that the user is not shown what templates are currently valid. The current PECAN editor is a compromise between these two schemes. It provides templates at every position, but allows the user to type at any point. Moreover, the parser has some error-correcting capabilities. COPE also includes the important concept of being able to undo and redo both editing and execution. PECAN provides a similar capability.

The GANDALF effort at Carnegie-Mellon University is an incremental programming environment generator currently working for several algebraic languages [4]. It includes the ALOE syntax-directed editor generator [5]. The abstract syntax descriptions and print specifications used by PECAN are derived from those defined for ALOE. ALOE produces general structure editors not geared toward programming languages. Thus, the semantics for the language in question have to be described procedurally. ALOE also is a template-based editor in that it provides templates for all productions in the tree and does not automatically allow parsing. It is possible, however, for the user to write his own parser and to use it for limited text editing. Much effort in GANDALF has been aimed toward programming in the large, an issue not addressed by PECAN. GANDALF has not, until recently, been targeted for personal machines with graphics capabilities.

Several programming environments have been developed at the Xerox Palo Alto Research Center. The Smalltalk system [6] is an interpreter for an object-oriented language based on message passing. It makes heavy use of windows and the capabilities of the graphical display, but is language dependent. The Interlisp environment [7] provides a good example of what can be done with an interpreted language and a high-resolution display. The Mesa [8] environment, and more recently CEDAR [9], apply many of the ideas from Smalltalk and Interlisp to an algebraic, compiled language. Many of the ideas proposed for CEDAR can be found in PECAN. CEDAR is designed as a production programming environment. PECAN differs in its emphasis on interaction and on showing the user multiple views of his program. PECAN is designed to be interactive and to support graphical programming.

III. THE DESIGN OF PECAN

The structure of PECAN emphasizes modularity and ease of change. The design is layered, with limied communication occurring between the layers, and with most communication being done with message passing. This structure is exhibited in Fig. 1. The lowest level of the design consists of the common support environment being developed at Brown. The next level contains common service modules. These are the PLUM data management facility and the ASPEN tree manager described later in this section. The next level includes the service modules that provide common services to other modules and to the user. These include the command manager, the parser, and the incremental compiler. These are described in Section III. The topmost layer contains the various views. Views supported by ASPEN are program views and currently include only the syntax-directed editor. The views that are supported by the semantic representations maintained by the compiler are the semantic views. These are described in Sections IV and V, respectively.

A. The Basic Environment

PECAN is based on an extensive underlying support environment being built at Brown to serve as a basis for graphics work on personal workstations [10]–[12]. This environment assumes a powerful processor, a high-resolution graphics display, a UNIX operating system, and a locator device such as a mouse or data tablet. It provides the primitives necessary for making full use of the hardware. The basic components are ASH, VT, SGP, MAPLE, and WILLOW. ASH is a screen and window management facility capable of supporting text and graphics in multiple overlapping windows [13]. VT is a virtual terminal package that provides a semiinfinite quarter-plane of multiple-font text with an intelligent terminal interface [14]. SGP is a graphics package that is modeled on a version of CORE that includes raster capabilities [15]. MAPLE is a general-purpose menu-based input facility that supports a wide variety of graphical input techniques and simplifies the standardizes program input throughout the environment [16]. WILLOW is a user-interface to the window manager that allows the user to create and manipulate the windows on the screen [17].

B. PLUM

Data structure support in PECAN is provided by PLUM [18].

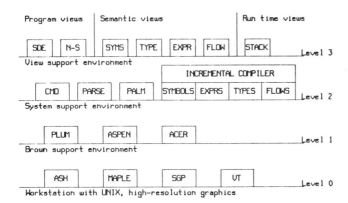

Fig. 1. Module hierarchy of PECAN.

PLUM supports data manipulation and database management operations such as auditing and printing. It is based loosely on the interface description language (IDL) developed to support the ADA intermediate representation [19], [20]. PLUM supports data structures throughout the PECAN system. Each module defines its data structures in a IDL-like syntax that is preprocessed into C declarations and macros. In addition, PLUM will be used to support the data structures of the user's program. PLUM supports operations on the data structures it knows about. These include

- data allocation, field reference, and deallocation
- file storage and retrieval of structures containing arbitrary pointers and of arbitrary complexity
- printing a readable representation of an arbitrary data structure
- recording changes to data structures, and allowing these changes to be undone and redone.

In addition, PLUM provides the tools that are used to support multiple independent views of a shared data structure. These include the following.

- Significant event management. Views can express their interest in knowing when a particular significant event occurs. PLUM keeps track of which modules are interested in wheich events. When an event is triggered (e.g., by ASPEN for a change in the syntax tree), PLUM sends an appropriate message to the interested views.
- Data structure monitoring. A routine can be registered with PLUM to be called whenever a node of a particular data type is changed. The routine is told the node that changed, what was done to it, and what the original values were. This routine can take any appropriate action, either by directly updating a view of the data structure, or, more likely, by issuing appropriate significant events.

PLUM is being used by projects other than PECAN.

C. ASPEN

ASPEN provides the data abstraction of abstract syntax trees for the program representation. Abstract syntax trees are used in many program development systems, since they are a convenient halfway point between a concrete syntax and a real semantics. ASPEN provides a forest of named trees. It allows the various views and service modules to ask relevant queries, such as the arity or type of any node of any of these trees. It

provides tree editing operations including deleting a subtree, copying a subtree to a given name, or expanding a meta node using the given abstract syntax rule.

ASPEN extends the facilities of PLUM for managing multiple views of shared data structures by making them specific to abstract syntax trees. It provides a significant event facility that announces when a node is about to change and when it has changed. A similar faciltiy sends messages when a named tree will be or has changed. The program views and the incremental compiler use these messages.

ASPEN extends the undo facilities of PLUM and simplifies them for its clients. ASPEN uses PLUM to record all changes to the underlying forest of trees. When the user makes an undo request through PLUM, ASPEN restores the forest to the desired state. While doing so, it sends out messages that make it appear to the various views as if the user were editing the forest to this state. In this way, program views and the incremental compiler automatically support the undo capabilities of PECAN.

D. Program Development System Generation

An important feature of PECAN is language independence. A PECAN program development system is generated for a particular language from descriptions of the syntax and semantics of the language. These descriptions are used to produce tables and code to direct the language-dependent modules of the system. The motivation for language independence is several fold.

- Many of the facilities provided in PECAN are appropriate to a wide range of languages.
- Different languages will modtivate different views that we will want to experiment with.
- One of our eventual goals is to develop graphical interfaces to programming, and since most programming languages are designed for textural use, it might become necessary to develop a new language.
- Different users prefer different languages and the system should not *a priori* dictate the ones they can use.
- To experiment with new languages, one would like to get a full environment working as quickly as possible. We are aiming for being able to generate a PECAN environment in about a week.

The language description for PECAN is given in four parts. The principal part describes the abstract syntax trees that are used by ASPEN. It includes the semantics of each abstract syntax production as well as information to control ASPEN, the parser, the editor, and other modules. This is preprocessed by the program READER into appropriate tables and definitions. The remaining parts of the description are more detailed semantic information about the use of symbols, data types, and expressions in the language. These are preprocessed by separate programs. This representation should allow an initial program development system to be generated for a language with a week's work. The representation is based on our previous work on the ACORN compiler production system [21], [22]. A variety of modern programming languages, including ADA, were described using the ACORN formalisms, and are the basis for this estimate. We plan to provide PECAN systems for languages other than Pascal, once the prototype implementation is complete and stable. The representation also allows easy experimentation with language modifications.

IV. SUPPORT MODULES

Much of the work of a PECAN program development system occurs in the background under the control of the support modules. The three principle support packages are the command facility, the parser, and the incremental compiler.

A. The Command Facility

The command module, CMD, provides the user interface for the global undo/redo facility, provides for executing selected commands, and provides for duplicating a run of the system by reexecuting the same commands again. It works with PLUM by maintaining a transcript of the commands the user has executed.

This transcript is kept in two parts. The first part is a list of primitive commands that were issued by the user through MAPLE. The second part is a list of user-oriented commands, each representing one or more primitive commands. A menu button is typically both a primitive and a user-oriented command. Text typed by the user would consist of a primitive command for each character, but a single user-oriented command up to a control character. The CMD facility correlates these lists with PLUM so that it knows the location in the PLUM history record for each executed command. If requested by the user, the CMD routine makes a file transcript of all the primitive commands. The session can be rerun from this transcript.

Most of the functionality of CMD derives from an editable view of the user-level commands. The commands are displayed in a window where the user can scroll back and forth to determine what has been done. The last command issued is highlighted. An example of this display is shown in Fig. 2. There are five menu buttons that allow the user to undo the last command, redo the next command on the display, scroll backwards and forwards through the display, and skip over the next command (i.e., delete it from the display and the corresponding transcript). The user can point with the locator device at a particular command, to cause the system to undo or redo to the chosen point. Using either the puck or the keyboard, the user can delete commands that have not been executed, and can pick old or new commands and place them in the command list at any point in the future. By editing the command list as it appears on the display, the user can control the system. This also provides a primitive global macro facility that will be extended in the future.

B. The Parser

PECAN provides a general purpose parser. The PARSE module is a table-based parser that uses a variation of the Earley parsing algorithm [23]. The tables for the parser are generated by the READER preprocessor and consist of a tabular representation of a syntax graph along with a lexical analyzer generated by LEX. The parser is called with either a string or a file name along with the meta node in an abstract syntax tree

Fig. 2. Command display.

that is to be replaced. It parses the text and produces a tree that can be substituted for that meta node.

The parser includes several useful features. It allows priorities to be associated with various rules to disambiguate a parse. The technique used here is to modify Earley's parsing algorithm to take priority into account, as is done for LR parsing in YACC [24]. The parser also allows a special token to represent an appropriate meta variable. The user can just type a '?' for an unknown part of the statement or expression, and the parser will substitute the appropriate construct. If the parser detects an error, it supplies an appropriate error message and associates the erroneous text with the original meta variable. It places a marker at the error location, and returns an appropriate message.

The tables that drive the parser are generated by READER from the print specifications associated with the abstract syntax tree. In this way, the implementer of a PECAN system only has to specify the concrete syntax once. Moreover, the input syntax and the output syntax are guaranteed to be consistent. In addition to the print strings, the definition includes the lexeme definitions and the priorities that are associated with the various rules. The disadvantage of this scheme is that it requires a general parser that is not particularly efficient. However, because the parser is used primarily for short text strings entered one line at a time, and because we have a good implementation of an Earley parser, performance is adequate.

V. THE INCREMENTAL COMPILER

The largest support component of PECAN consists of the incremental compiler. The incremental compiler is divided into a control module (SEMCOM), and special-purpose modules for symbol processing, data type processing, expression processing, and control-flow processing.

The control module, SEMCOM, is the portion of the compiler that interfaces to the rest of the system. SEMCOM accepts ASPEN events indicating that the abstract syntax trees have changed. For each syntax tree that represents a complete program fragment, such as a program or module in Pascal, it maintains a program of semantic actions. It calls the special-purpose modules to execute to undo each of these actions as needed. A change in the syntax tree causes it to recompute the list of actions for the changed node, find the ones that have changed, undo the old ones, and execute the new ones. Because ASPEN makes a user's undo request look like a normal command, SEMCOM handles such undo requests automatically.

The specifications for SEMCOM consist of short program fragments for each abstract syntax rule that specify the semantic actions to be performed. The READER preprocessor provides a special-purpose language that allows these to be both simple and straightforward. For example, a single statement in the language looks up a name, and resolves it by scope and expected class. Another statement creates an object and associates it with a name in the current scope. Statements exist for beginning and ending scopes, for constructing new data types, for using data types associated with names, for building control flow graphs, and for building expression trees. Our semantics for Apollo Pascal are mostly two to four statements long.

Interpreting the semantic actions is left to the special-purpose modules. The symbol module provides an incremental symbol table with calls to define, undefine, find, and resolve objects. It handles most of the complexities of symbol processing in modern programming languages, since it is derived from the symbol processing portion of the ACORN system [22]. This module is language dependent, since the types of scopes in the language, the types of names and constants to be looked up, and the rules for resolving ambiguities and overloadings differ from one language to another. Most of its code is either generated or is table-driven. The generated code and tables are created by a preprocessor that takes a listing of the classes of names, objects, and scopes, and a list of the name-resolution rules as input.

Modules similar to the incremental symbol processing portion of the compiler also exist for data types, expression, and contolflow. The data type module supports the built-in and constructed types of the language as well as handling all type conversions and coercions. It is also derived from a simple language-dependent specification by a preprocessor based on our earlier work. The expression module incrementally builds expression trees over source operators. It resolves these trees to use internal operators, using data types and other information pertinent to the particular language. The necessary language-dependent definitions are again provided by a simple specification and an appropriate preprocessor. Finally, a control flow module supports the incremental construction (and destruction) of flow graphs based on the contour model [25]. Statements exist in the semantic language to create and link nodes. These nodes can be computations, conditional branches, gotos, labels, variable allocations, and contour entries and exits.

VI. PROGRAM VIEWS

Program views are visual representations of abstract syntax trees. They can be either read-only views or modifiable views. In either case they are automatically updated as the trees they represent are changed, whether they initiated the change or not. In the current, initial implementation of PECAN, two different program views are available, and the user can have any number of any combination of these active at a time. The two views are a syntax-directed editor and a Nassi–Shneiderman flow gaph representation.

A. The Syntax-Directed Editor

The syntax-directed editor, SDE, is an example of modifiable view. It contains two independent parts, one that provides a user interface for editing, and one that provides a formatted display of the abstract syntax trees. Except for correlating a point on the display with a node in the syntax tree for a command and echoing text input on the display, these two parts interact only through ASPEN. The editor updates the display by making a change in the abstract syntax tree using ASPEN. ASPEN then sends out messages indicating that a node has changed. These messages are read by the output half of the editor and any other program views. The views then update their displays accordingly.

The front end of the syntax-directed editor is a cross between a traditional text editor and a structure editor. It allows the user to move to any point in the program, and do whatever text editing operations are appropriate. The editor would then parse the result, put it into its internal representation, and reformat the display. Portions of the text editor are currently under development, and this only works for program units that fit on one line. The freedom to treat a textual representation of the program as text is important, since many of the changes a programmer makes are textual ones, such as correcting typing errors. Moreover, when there are many corrections to a program, the programmer is likely to want to treat the program as a large textual object and make the corrections, and not to worry about its structure. Several systems, including COPE [3] and POE [26], use a textual approach to syntax-directed editing.

At the same time SDE provides a complete set of templates that allow the programmer to make full use of the structure of the underlysing syntax tree. The current location is not a single character, but is a tree node, and all the text for this node is placed in a box on the display. The user has available simple commands to climb around the syntax tree and to pick and put nodes of the tree. Whenever the current node is a meta variable or a leaf node, the editor provides a special menu that lists the possible expansions or contents. For meta nodes, these are the templates associated with such syntax-directed editors as ALOE [5] or the Cornell program synthesizer [2]. For leaf nodes, they are a list of the appropriate condidate names from the symbol table. Editing with templates is often easier for novice programmers and can save considerable typing on program entry.

While trying to compromise between structured editing and text editing, the syntax-directed editor also makes heavy use of the facilities of the graphical display and the pointing device. Fig. 3 shows a view of the editor window on a typical tree. The editor uses multiple fonts to distinguish between keywords, meta symbols that have yet to be expanded, text for identifiers, and text that contains semantic errors. The user is free to choose any of the available fonts for these purposes. The ed-

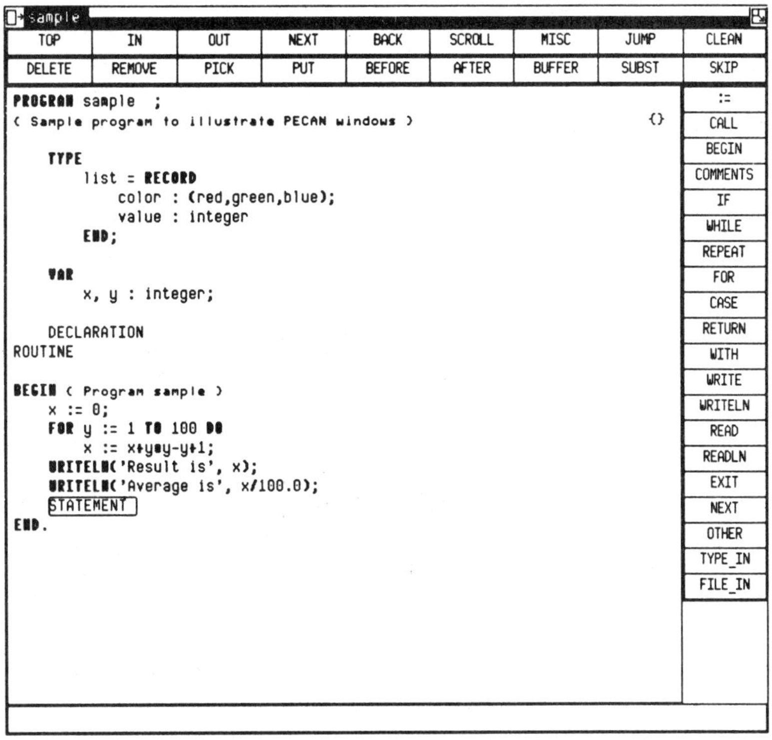

```
sample
 TOP  |  IN  | OUT | NEXT | BACK | SCROLL | MISC | JUMP | CLEAN
DELETE| REMOVE| PICK| PUT | BEFORE| AFTER | BUFFER| SUBST| SKIP

PROGRAM sample  ;                                                      :=
( Sample program to illustrate PECAN windows )                {}      CALL
                                                                     BEGIN
    TYPE                                                            COMMENTS
        list = RECORD                                                 IF
            color : (red,green,blue);                               WHILE
            value : integer                                         REPEAT
        END;                                                         FOR
                                                                     CASE
    VAR                                                             RETURN
        x, y : integer;                                             WITH
                                                                    WRITE
    DECLARATION                                                    WRITELN
ROUTINE                                                             READ
                                                                   READLN
BEGIN ( Program sample )                                            EXIT
    x := 0;                                                         NEXT
    FOR y := 1 TO 100 DO                                           OTHER
        x := x+y*y-y+1;                                           TYPE_IN
    WRITELN('Result is', x);                                      FILE_IN
    WRITELN('Average is', x/100.0);
    STATEMENT
END.
```

Fig. 3. Syntax-directed editor windows.

itor uses line drawing to place a box of whatever shape is necessary around the text, corresponding to the current node.

The interface to the editor uses the pointing device and the keyboard. The pointing device can select any of the menu buttons that are seen in Fig. 3. These provide the basic editing commands, and, for meta nodes and appropriate leaf nodes, the relevant templates and name alternatives. The pointing device is also used with the displayed tree. The user can change the current node by pointing at the desired location. Other buttons on the puck allow the user to pick, put, delete, and insert into the tree. Multiple clicks at the same location allow the user to move about the tree structure.

The keyboard is used primarily for text editing, but also can be used for many of the editor commands. The user is free to type text or text-editing commands. When the user is done text editing, he issues a command not involving text-editing or an explicit done command, and the editied text is parsed and the result is put into the tree. Control and function keys on the keyboard provide most of the tree-editing commands (delete, insert, pick, put), as well as tree movement and view scrolling commands. This makes it possible for the user to edit without continually having to move his hands from the keyboard to the pointing device and back again.

B. Nassi–Shneiderman View

A second program view is a graphical one based on Nassi–Shneiderman flow charts. These are a form of structured flow charts that use different types of blocks for different program constructs and use the nesting of blocks to represent the nesting of the program. With this view, the user sees the complete structured form of his program drawn as a structured flow graph.

The view is based on a pretty-print notation that describes how each abstract syntax construct should be represented graphically using a simple print rule. The rule shows the nesting and the creation of new blocks in the flow graph. These blocks are either rectangular blocks that indicate simple processing, decision blocks with a test on top and the alternative paths in subboxes beneath, iteration boxes that contain the loop body and the tests on the outside, and a separate box type to indicate scoping.

The view is tied into the system and is automatically updated as the user changes his program. We are currently working on adding basic editing operations to this view to allow the user to edit his program graphically.

C. Other Program Views

There are other program views that could be supported by PECAN and that we hope to see implemented some time in the future. These include a data-flow view, a module-level abstraction view, and a declaration view that allows the user to pick off menus to declare objects and prompts the user to declare undefined objects.

VII. Semantic Views

PECAN supports multiple views of arbitrary data structures. While abstract syntax trees representing user programs are the most logical data structure to view, it is often useful to provide the user with specialized views of the internal forms supported by PECAN. During program editing, the relevant forms are

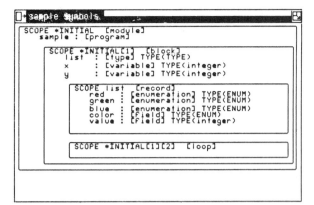

Fig. 4. Symbol table display.

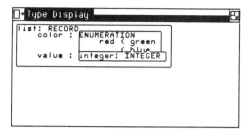

Fig. 5. Data type display.

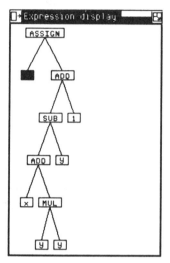

Fig. 6. Expression display.

the semantic representations of the program: the symbol table, data type definitions, expression trees, and control flow graphs.

A. The Symbol Table View

The compiler builds and incrementally maintains a scoped symbol table of all built-in and user-defined symbols. The corresponding view displays the scopes and symbols that are defined for a particular syntax tree. Fig. 4 shows a sample view. The boxes display the nesting of the various scopes. Each box contains a brief description of the scope and a list of all the names defined by the user program in that scope. Each name is displayed with its class, such as variable, type, or label, and other pertinent information such as the data type of a variable. If the current node in a program view is a variable, then this variable is highlighted in the symbol display. Pointing at a name or scope in the symbol display causes the appropriate program view to make the definition node for that scope or name the current location.

B. The Data Type View

The compiler maintains information on built-in and user-defined data types. A semantic view displays the current data type based on this information. If the user is editing a type definition, then the type being edited is displayed. If the current editing node is a variable, then the type of the variable is displayed. If the current node is an expression, then the type of the expression is displayed. Fig. 5 shows a sample display for a data type. The top line of a type display contains the class of the type, such as RECORD, POINTER, ARRAY. The following lines show the parameter values for this class. Where these parameters are also types, the display is recursive. To avoid infinite displays, the recursion typically stops after one level. However, the user is free to choose an unexpanded type and ask that it be expanded, either within the display or by making it the only type displayed. Pointing at a type definition causes the appropriate editor to make that definition its current location.

C. The Expression View

The third component of the compiler maintains expression trees for each expression in the program. The corresponding view draws these trees, affoding the user a different perspective of the expressions. The tree that is drawn is the one that is the current focus for editing operations. The node being edited is highlighted on the display. A typical expression tree display is shown in Fig. 6. The user may pan over the expression tree when the tree is too large to fit in the window assigned for expression display. He can also point at the tree to make the corresponding node the current location for editing.

D. The Flow View

The final component of the incremental compiler builds and maintains graphs that describe the flow of control for an abstract syntax tree. The corresponding view provides a flowchart of the program that is dynamically updated as the program changes. Nodes of the flowchart represent expression evaluations, gotos, and labels. Fig. 7 shows a sample flow graph view. The user can pan over a complex flowchart to view the currently relevant portion. He can also point at a given block and cause the corresponding code to become the focus for editing operations.

VIII. EXECUTION VIEWS

One goal of PECAN is to provide a wide variety of execution views based on experiences with the BALSA system [1]. These will include data views that render a graphical representation of a user's data structure, such as a tree that is automatically updated as the program executes. This work will be based on

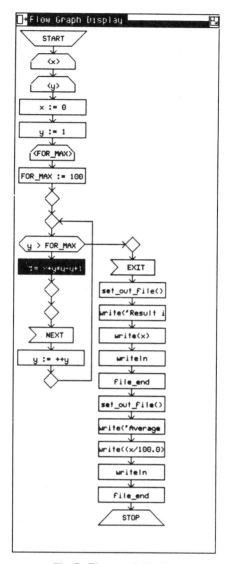

Fig. 7. Flow graph display.

an extensive library of possible graphical representations and is the subject of current research. Other data views would provide the user with more classical representations of the stack or of a selected set of variables. These will again be updated as the program executes. Execution views will also show the program in action. Simple program views will highlight each statement as it is executed. Other views will provide performance information such as execution counts in various graphical forms.

The interpreter of PECAN is only now beginning to work. The execution views currently supported include simple program feedback and a stack view. The program feedback is provided by the syntax-directed editor and the flow graph view, both of which highlight each statement as it is executed. The stack data view shows the current state of the execution stack, including each current stack frame, the variables in that frame, and their values. It allows the user to request more information on a value, such as the contents pointed to by a pointer variable using the pointing device as with the BLIT debugger [27]. These can be seen in Fig. 8.

IX. CONCLUSION

We have described PECAN and its family of program development systems. These systems use the concept of multiple views of shared data structures. This provides the user with multiple displays that concurrently show different aspects of the program in a natural way. The user is free to select the program views and semantic displays that are appropriate to the current editing or debugging activity. This allows him to select and vary his programming methods and to adjust the system to fit his immediate needs.

The underlying support for multiple views that makes it easy to add new views allows us to experiment with new ways of looking at a program and with new approaches to programming. Experiments that are being pursued at Brown with PECAN and related systems involve methods and languages for graphical programming.

The PECAN system currently is comprehensive only in its support for program construction. We are working on complet-

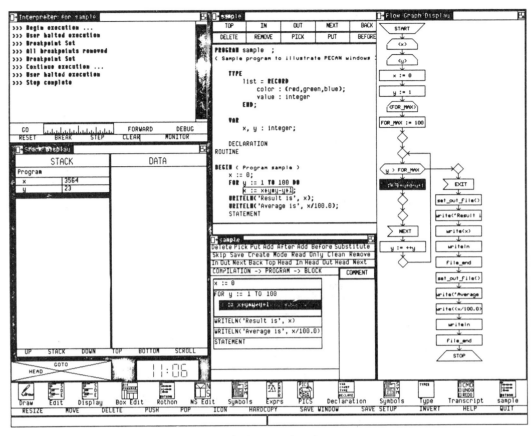

Fig. 8. An execution view.

ing the incremental compiler. We are also developing an interpreter for the internal representation that again runs in a window and provides easy methods for the user to control (including undo) execution. Along with the interpreter will be support for multiple views of the program's data structures. These views will be dynamically maintained during execution so that the user can see his program in action. This work will make use of the efforts currently underway at Brown on algorithm animation with BALSA and on data structure rendering.

ACKNOWLEDGMENT

The effort that has gone into PECAN has been supported by much of the environment activity at Brown. M. Brown is largely responsible for the MAPLE package. J. Pato and M. Vickers developed the virtual device interface for the Apollos. J. Pato also did the SGP graphics package. M. Vickers wrote a preliminary version of ASH. M. Brown and M. Strickman did the core of the BALSA implementation. R. Rubin and J. Hung are currently working on the Nassi-Shneiderman view. G. Sitzmann and G. Tsacnaris are currently working on the text editor.

REFERENCES

[1] M. Brown, N. Meyrowitz, and A. van Dam, "Personal computer networks and graphical animation: Rationale and practice for education," Dep. Comput. Sci., Brown Univ., Providence, RI, 1982.

[2] T. Teitelbaum and T. Reps, "The Cornell program synthesizer: A syntax-directed programming enviornment," Cornell Univ., Ithaca, NY, Tech. Rep. TR 80-421, May 1980.

[3] J. Archer, Jr. and R. Conway, "COPE: A cooperative programming environment," Cornell Univ., Ithaca, NY, Tech. Rep. TR81-459, June 1981.

[4] A. N. Habermann, "The Gandalf research project," Comput. Sci. Res. Rev., Carnegie-Mellon Univ., Pittsburgh, PA, 1979.

[5] R. Medina-Mora and D. S. Notkin, "ALOE users' and implementors' guide," Carnegie-Mellon Univ., Pittsburgh, PA, CMU-CS-81-145, Nov. 1981.

[6] A. Goldberg, "The influence of an object-oriented language on the programming environment," in Proc. ACM Comput. Sci. Conf., Feb. 1983.

[7] W. Teitelman, Interlisp Reference Manual. XEROX, 1974.

[8] J. G. Mitchell, W. Maybury, and R. Sweet, "Mesa language manual," Xerox Rep. CSL-79-3, Apr. 1979.

[9] L. P. Deutsch and E. A. Taft, "Requirements for an experimental programming environment," Xerox Rep. CSL-80-10, June 1980.

[10] "An integrated experimental environment for research in computer science," Dep. Comput. Sci., Brown Univ., Providence, RI, proposal submitted to Nat. Sci. Foundation, Sept. 1981.

[11] 'Ideographics—A DARPA/ONR research project," Dep. Comput. Sci., Brown Univ., Providence, RI, Sept. 1982.

[12] J. N. Pato, S. P. Reiss, and M. H. Brown, "The Brown workstation environment," Brown Univ., Providence, RI, Oct. 1983.

[13] S. P. Reiss, "A screen handler," Brown Univ., Providence, RI, Nov. 1982.

[14] —, "Virtual terminal package," Brown Univ., Providence, RI, Sept. 1982.

[15] D. B. Nanian and J. N. Pato, "Simple graphics package," Brown Univ., Providence, RI, Sept. 1982.

[16] M. H. Brown and S. P. Reiss, "MAPLE reference manual," Brown Univ., Providence, RI, Dec. 1982.

[17] S. P. Reiss, "WILLOW: A window manager," Brown Univ., Providence, RI, Sept. 1983.

[18] —, "PLUM: A data structure management package," Brown Univ., Providence, RI, Dec. 1982.

[19] J. R. Nestor, W. A. Wulf, and D. A. Lamb, "IDL—Interface description language: Formal description," Carnegie-Mellon Univ., Pittsburgh, PA, Feb. 1981.

[20] G. Goos and W. A. Wulf, "Diana reference manual," Carnegie-Mellon Univ., Pittsburgh, PA, Mar. 1981.

[21] S. P. Reiss, "Automatic compiler production: The front end," Brown Univ., Providence, RI, Res. Rep. 66, 1981.

[22] ——, "Generation of compiler symbol processing mechanisms from specifications," *ACM TOPLAS*, vol. 5, pp. 127-163, Apr. 1983.

[23] S. L. Graham, M. A. Harrison, and W. L. Ruzzo, "An improved context-free recognizer," *ACM TOPLAS*, vol. 2, pp. 415-462, July 1980.

[24] S. C. Johson, "YACC–Yet another compiler compiler," Bell Lab., Murray Hill, NJ, CSTR 32, 1974.

[25] J. B. Johnston, "The contour model of block structured processes," *SIGPLAN Notices*, vol. 6, pp. 55-82, Feb. 1971.

[26] C. N. Fischer, G. Johnson, and J. Mauney, "An introduction to Editor Allen Poe," Univ. Wisconsin–Madison, TR 451, Oct. 1981.

[27] T. A. Cargill and D. Barstow, "Knowledge-based program construction," *SIGPLAN Notices*, vol. 18, no. 8, pp. 190-200, 1979.

Steven Reiss (M'77) received the A.B. degree from Dartmouth College, Hanover, NH, in 1972, and the Ph.D. degree from Yale University, New Haven, CT, in 1977.

He is an Associate Professor of Computer Science at Brown University, where he has been a member of the faculty since 1977. His research interests include programming environments, graphical programming, database implementation, statistical database security, and computational geometry. His recent work involved the PECAN program development system.

Reprinted from *IEEE Software*, November 1987, pages 16-27.
Copyright © 1987 by The Institute of Electrical and Electronics
Engineers, Inc. All rights reserved.

Working in the Garden Environment for Conceptual Programming

Steven P. Reiss, *Brown University*

Program designers use a variety of techniques when creating their systems. This automated design system conforms to the programmer.

One important problem in automating the software development process is providing an environment for designing software systems. Most of the approaches for automated design environments provide one or two design methods and force the programmers to design with only these methods. Examples of such approaches include automated versions of SADT,[1] SREM,[2] and dataflow-based design.

Most program designers, however, naturally use a variety of techniques when designing their systems.[3] They draw pictures of their data structures, describe a control-oriented module with an automaton or a decision table, and illustrate the system structure with a module-interconnection diagram and a dataflow diagram. These techniques are selected to closely fit the system being designed. Moreover, designers modify the techniques to fit the problem better and develop new strategies or languages to simplify the description of an otherwise complex design.

Rather than force the programmer to conform to particular design methods, an automated design system should provide an environment that conforms to the programmer. Such an environment must provide many design paradigms. These range from traditional dataflow diagrams, pseudocode, and finite-state automata to logical specifications, object-oriented programming, or whatever language the designer developed to best describe the problem approach. These paradigms must be presented to the programmer in their most natural form. This form can be textual for pseudocode or logical specifications, a standard type of diagram for dataflow or automata, or something designed by the developer (textual or graphical or some combination of the two).

As well as providing a multiparadigm environment for program design, a good design-automation system should provide a framework for evaluating the resulting design. The simplest approach is to allow design-level prototyping. The system

EH0324-4/90/0000/0334/$01.00 © 1987 IEEE

should let the design itself act as the prototype program and let the developer evaluate the design by running it. The eventual goal is to make the design itself be the program, thus allowing system debugging and especially maintenance to be done directly in terms of the design. This goal is not realistic with current technology, but faster machines and better compilers could make it a reality in the future.

Finally, an automated design system should provide more than just a variety of design languages that can be consistently combined. It must give the designer a complete environment, including facilities for creating, modifying, recalling, and displaying designs. The system must also support browsing and automated analysis of the designs, plus cooperative design within a team of designers.

Garden is such a programming system. It is designed to support the concurrent use of a variety of languages that represent different programming paradigms. It tries to provide equal support to both textual and graphical languages and to support a wide spectrum of programming paradigms. In Garden, you define a conceptual language by giving its visual and textual syntax and its semantics in terms of an object basis. The language is then used through views of the objects that represent its programs.

Designers developing systems typically build system models in their heads. These models consist of the languages or paradigms used in the design. This is the conceptual system model that the programmers must understand and work with while implementing, debugging, and maintaining the system. The type of automated design system outlined above lets designers work directly with the model. Moreover, it turns the model into the program. A system that supports this type of effort — called conceptual programming — with an automated environment is a conceptual programming environment.

Requirements

A system that supports conceptual programming must be both flexible and powerful. The requirements for such a system are divided between those supporting multiple paradigms and those providing an appropriate environment.

A conceptual programming environment must simplify the definition and use of new languages. These languages can be visual or textual and can be completely new or derived from an existing language. The requirements here include:

• A consistent support framework. The environment's framework must let languages be freely mixed to form the proper conceptual model. This mixing will generally follow a hierarchy, for example, either with dataflow actions referenced by the

> **A system that supports conceptual programming must be both flexible and powerful.**

nodes of a control-flow graph or with control-flow actions assigned to the arcs of a finite-state automaton. More sophisticated mixing would not be restricted to such a hierarchy. For example, a single framework would let a piece of a program be viewed and edited as both a data diagram and a control-flow diagram.

• Equal support for visual and textual languages. Many languages used for design are visual languages. The environment should offer visual languages all the facilities normally offered to textual languages, including syntax definition, editing, file-based storage, program sharing, and browsing. This prevents worthwhile languages from being ignored because of inadequate support.

• Multiple views of a single language form. The system should let programmers view a complex design many ways. The

environment should support this (by allowing multiple views of the design languages) to give programmers different perspectives on the underlying design. For example, one view of a design diagram might show only the dataflow information while another might show both the dataflow and the control flow. Such views can provide different levels of abstraction and accommodate slight variations in formatting (especially graphical formatting) that different users might want.

• Facilities to simplify language definition. The environment must provide a rich set of support functions so the semantics of new languages can be defined with minimal effort. There should be a rich set of built-in data types and corresponding operations. There should also be specialized support for common but difficult-to-implement design-language features, such as dataflow, concurrency, and constraints. Finally, it should be easy to reuse and modify existing language definitions.

As well as providing a usable framework for incorporating multiple languages, a conceptual programming environment must provide substantial environmental support for design. In particular, it should provide:

• Prototype evaluation. One key idea of conceptual programming is that the design should be an executable prototype so designers can experiment directly with designs as they work on it. The environment must support this by providing a general interpreter that can evaluate programs in any language that can be defined in the system. Additional support can be provided by letting these languages be compiled to yield a more efficient evaluation.

• An experimental framework. Design prototyping should be encouraged by providing an interactive environment with immediate feedback. The advantages of such an environment are shown by the success of such systems as Lisp and Smalltalk.

The environment should have facilities that let designers understand the program as it executes. These facilities might include various execution views, profiling tools, debugging aids, and dynamic display of the program's data structures.

• A multiwindow, user-oriented front end. The environment should run on a workstation where different views and different languages can be displayed with multiple windows. These views should provide the functionality needed to do the design: They should be editors for the underlying design that support browsing and documentation as it is written. Multiple windows should also give programmers system-control functions such as the ability to execute and interact with the prototype designs.

• General environmental support. The environment should provide the tools needed for software design in a moderate-sized project, including design storage and retrieval with version control. This lets new ideas be tried without modifying a stable system. There should be support for cooperative design so a group of programmers sharing a common design can safely work on different pieces of it. While the system should provide a good interactive environment, it should also be able to produce a readable printout of the resulting design.

Garden overview

Garden is an attempt to meet many of these requirements for a conceptual programming environment. It consists of a programming system designed to support multiple languages, a set of tools that provide a multiwindow user interface, and an underlying database system to provide environmental support.

Object-oriented framework. Garden uses an object-oriented programming system to provide the necessary control abstraction.[4] Object-oriented systems view all their data in terms of objects: data blocks that are instances of a particular class or type. Associated with each class is a set of operations that can be applied to the object. The classes are arranged in a hierarchy so subclasses can inherit the properties, data, and operations of their

parents. Experience with Smalltalk[5] has shown that object-oriented systems are good for prototyping because they provide a high degree of reusability and encourage the use of data abstraction.

Garden uses objects to represent programs as well as data. The result is a system that is good for prototyping and encourages the use of both data and control abstraction. You build programs by putting together collections of objects, define new languages by defining new types of objects that represent programs, and use the class hierarchy to reuse existing languages when defining new ones.

The object-oriented Garden system is good for prototyping and encourages the use of both data and control abstraction.

Objects form a consistent basis for supporting multiple languages — any language can be defined in terms of its underlying constructs. In Garden, the differing constructs are represented by different classes of objects; the relationships among the constructs are represented as other objects referred to by the objects. For example, an automaton is represented as an object of class Fsa and includes objects of class State for each state of the automaton and each object of class Arc for each arc.

Garden uses these object constructs as the actual program. One operation it provides for an object class defines what it means to evaluate an object of that class. For example, evaluating an Fsa object with a value causes the automaton to move to the next state using that value. Since this operation is defined for all program objects, different program abstractions and hence different languages can be freely mixed hierarchically. Garden lets you define an operation for any object by providing another object that describes the operation. Thus you can use any currently defined language when describing the evaluation semantics of a new language.

Garden provides an interpreter and a corresponding compiler to yield efficient execution of object-based programs.

Because objects represent programs, Garden has no bias toward any syntactic form; it lets the syntax of an object-based language be defined textually or graphically, or both ways. The current implementation allows wide latitude in the selection of graphical displays for such languages. While Garden's goal is to let the system provide a natural representation using the underlying objects of most languages, the system now provides only a single textual, Lisp-like representation that is not suitable for all languages, particularly those with cyclic underlying structures.

Garden supports the definition of semantics for object-based languages by providing a rich underlying set of programming primitives, including strings, lists, and tables (indexed relations in the database sense) with a full range of operations. It provides primitives for concurrent processing using lightweight processes, including monitors and semaphores.

A general dependency mechanism can handle constraint-based programming as well as event-triggered demons. It gives full access to the system's underlying naming, typing, and evaluation mechanisms. These facilities can be used with any defined languages to define the semantics of a new language.

Multiwindow environment. Garden's programming environment lets you create and modify the objects that represent their programs and data. Objects can be viewed or modified in any of three editors. One editor displays the textual form of the object and allows normal text editing. The second provides an object-based browser on the object, letting you select, view, and modify an object's contents or one of its component objects on a field-by-field basis. The third displays a visual representation of the objects and lets you interact directly with this form.

The system coordinates these different editors with a multiwindow display on a Unix-based workstation. Each editor runs in a window on the display; you can set up these windows with a window manager or nest them in another editor or tool. Garden lets multiple instances of each editor be active simultaneously. It also lets you put up multiple editors, of the same or different types, on the same objects simultaneously. In this multiple view, the system keeps the various windows consistent: When you change the underlying object with any editor, all the other views update automatically.

The object editors can view data as well as enter and work on programs. The various editors can be brought up under program control as sophisticated input mechanisms or output displays. You can

put up views of the data structures the program is working on. Garden automatically updates such views as the program changes the underlying objects at a user-controllable granularity.

The multiwindow display provides other programming tools. One or more interactive windows can provide a read-eval-print loop with the textual language interface. A variety of system browsers can be defined that let you select an object with a variety of criteria such as the scope in which it is defined, its class, its name, and its fields. A documentation editor lets you quickly find and create textual documentation for any object in the system. In addi-

tion, windows can be defined for both graphical and textual program input and output.

Figure 1 shows a sample of a complete Garden screen. The sequence of Gothic letters and icons at the bottom represents the windows available. The windows displayed include a type editor in the upper left, a browser editor in the upper right, a read-eval-print loop window in the lower left, and a graphical editor in the lower right. Each window contains a title bar, move and resize icons in the corners, and a blank bar at the bottom to move the window. Hidden beneath the title bars are buttons to remove the window and to pop

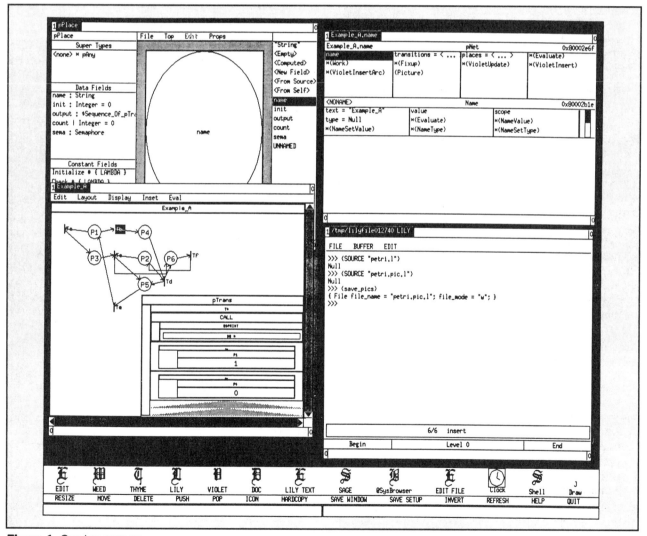

Figure 1. Garden screen.

Petri net example

The example in Figure A is specified in the textual language currently provided by Garden. The language is defined to look and feel like Lisp so first-time users have a degree of familiarity when they start using Garden. However, it is only a Lisp-like syntax that Garden uses to define objects. The basic form of a Lisp S-expression serves several purposes. If the first component is a type name, it is a definition of an object of that type where the latter components contain the field values for the object. If the first component is a field access object (identified by an initial open single quote [']), it is an invocation of the corresponding message applied to the second component; if the field object refers to a data field, the corresponding message just returns the field's value. If the first component is neither a type or a field access object, the S-expression is translated into a Call object where the first component is the object to evaluate and the latter components are composed into an argument list.

The language provides other extensions to simplify textual Garden programming. Objects can be defined with a named representation rather than the positional representation inherent in S-expressions. Quoting occurs as in Lisp, with a quotation mark (") followed by an expression actually yielding a Quote object containing that expression. Local scopes and local names can be defined with the separators {* and }* containing a list of names and one or more evaluatable objects. The result is either a Block object or an appropriate type of Lambda object with the initial list of names as local variables defined in a new scope and a Seq object containing the sequence of actions as the body.

The first part of the example in Figure A defines the type structure used for Petri nets. Each type is defined as a string containing its name and then a list of its fields inside braces ({ }). The fields are defined with a name, a separator, and a type. The separator can be a colon (:) indicating a data field, a vertical bar (|) indicating a structural field, or a caret (^) indicating a dynamic field. In general, data fields are descriptive; structural fields include the other components of the language; and dynamic fields are used for runtime values.

The second portion contains the definition of the Lambda objects associated with the messages used in evaluating the objects composing a Petri net. The function De takes three arguments: a name, a list of parameters, and a body. It creates a Lambda object with the list of parameters and the body and binds this to the given name. The parameters are defined in a local scope for this particular definition.

```
--
--    Type definitions
--
(TYPE_DEFINE "pNet{name:Name,transitions|#pTrans,places|#-
pPlace}")
(TYPE_DEFINE "pTrans{name:String,eval:Any,input:#pPlace,out-
put:#pPlace,"&
      "active^Boolean,sema^Semaphore}")
(TYPE_DEFINE "pPlace{name:String,init:Integer,output:#pTrans,"&
      "count^Integer,sema:Semaphore}")


--
--    Evaluation definitions
--

(DE pNet_EVAL <pnet:pNet>
   {* <>
      (LISTLOOP ('places pnet) 'Initialize)
      (LISTLOOP ('transitions pnet) 'Initialize)
      (LISTLOOP ('transitions pnet) 'NewThread)
      (LISTLOOP ('transitions pnet) 'Check)
      (THREAD_WAIT_FOR_CHILD)
   *}
)

(DE pTrans_THREAD <ptrans:pTrans>
   (THREAD_NEW_CHILD (BUILD CALL "Work (LIST_NEW (QQUOTE
ptrans))) 0 0) )

(DE pTrans_WORK <ptrans:pTrans>
   {* <>
      (LOOP True True (SEQ
         (SEMA_P ('sema ptrans))
         (EVAL ptrans)
         (LISTLOOP (LIST_PERM ('output ptrans)) 'Add)
         (FIELD_SET False ptrans 'active)
         ('Check ptrans)))
   *}
)

(DE pTrans_CHECK <ptrans:pTrans>
   {* <ok:Boolean>
      (COND ('active ptrans) (RETURN Null))
      (SETQ ok (LISTLOOP ('input ptrans) 'Check BOOL_AND True))
      (COND ok (LISTLOOP ('input ptrans) 'Use))
```

```
      (LISTLOOP ('input ptrans) 'Release)
      (COND ok (SEQ
         (FIELD_SET True ptrans 'active)
         (SEMA_V ('sema ptrans))))
   *}
)

(DE pTrans_EVAL <ptrans:pTrans> (EVAL ('eval ptrans)))

(DE pTrans_INIT <ptrans:pTrans>
   {* <>
      (FIELD_SET False ptrans 'active)
      (FIELD_SET (SEMAPHORE 0) ptrans 'sema)
   *}
)

(DE pPlace_INIT <pplace:pPlace>
   {* <>
      (FIELD_SET (SEMAPHORE 1) pplace 'sema)
      (FIELD_SET ('init pplace) pplace 'count)
   *}
)

(DE pPlace_CHECK <pplace:pPlace>
   {* <>
      (SEMA_P ('sema pplace))
      (INT_GTR ('count pplace) 0)
   *}
)

(DE pPlace_USE <pplace:pPlace>
   (FIELD_SET (INT_SUB ('count pplace) 1) pplace 'count))

(DE pPlace_ADD <pplace:pPlace>
   {* <>
      (SEMA_P ('sema pplace))
      (FIELD_SET (INT_ADD ('count pplace) 1) pplace 'count)
      (SEMA_V ('sema pplace))
      (LISTLOOP (LIST_PERM ('output pplace)) 'Check)
   *}
)

(DE pPlace_RELEASE <pplace:pPlace> (SEMA_V ('sema pplace)))
```

Figure A. Example of a Petri net in the Garden language.

(uncover) and push (cover) it on the display. General window-management commands and a prompt window are at the very bottom of the screen.

Garden provides a consistent menu and mouse-oriented interface to most windows. Apple Macintosh-style pull-down menus provide editing and control-oriented options in the editors. Complex parameters are entered in each window via dialogue boxes. A base editor with a common set of editing operations is used for all textual displays and editing. It can cut and paste text among displays. All these facilities are available for user programs from within the Garden system. They are implemented using the tools of the Brown Workstation Environment.[6]

Garden also provides a consistent set of mouse utilities to select and define objects. A common routine provides a series of dialogue boxes that prompt you to define an object of a given type. This dialogue is modified on the basis of the expected type to simplify your task as much as possible. For example, when a string object is required, you must type only the contents of a string. In general, this dialogue prompts you for access to an object or for the type of a new object; in the latter case, it prompts you for the various fields. You can control the dialogue on newly created objects of your own types by identifying the expected field types and noting which fields should not be prompted for.

In addition, Garden provides a common facility for selecting objects and reusing them anywhere on the display. All editors let an object be selected by pressing the right mouse button. The selected object is stored in a common buffer as the current object. All dialogue boxes let you choose this current object as an alternative to entering all the box's fields with generic types for the object.

Environmental support. Garden's object-oriented database system provides many environment facilities.[7] The database system is designed to store all objects in use. Because objects are used to represent programs and data — as well as the semantics for evaluating object-based programs and the syntax rules for drawing and editing objects textually and visually

— this facility saves your complete environment.

You can use the external database several ways. In its pure form, Garden provides a persistent environment where everything you do is stored in the database. Because the underlying database system is a real database system, many programmers can share the same object space with appropriate consistency checking and access control. The database system also provides version control, letting you create and restore versions of your whole environment.

You can access the database as if it were a workspace facility — taking an APL-like or Lisp-like approach to development, independent of whether it is done on one or several databases. You can open a data-

---

A conceptual environment first requires a workable underlying model that can support a wide variety of languages.

---

base as read-only to access a set of languages, an environment, and the current system state. Then, as new facilities are added to this workspace, they can be saved in the workspace in a separate database that can in turn be used as the starting point for a later run.

Partitioning the system this way uses the inherent similarities between environmental support and database technology, providing such features as version and access control consistently across systems and among users. However, it does place an efficiency burden on both Garden and the database system since an environment will consist of many (typically 20,000 to 100,000) relatively small (40-byte average) objects that must be rapidly accessed when evaluating the program and displaying object structures.

Garden attacks this problem by providing an in-core database system to interface to the external database and by having the in-core system cache as many objects as possible. The in-core system provides

additional environmental support, including background garbage collection over all objects not known to the database system in an effort to eliminate as many temporary objects as possible. It also provides a nested transaction mechanism with both fast and abortable transactions. This mechanism provides the basis for the general dependency mechanism that Garden offers; it could also be used as the basis for an undo facility because it lets you set marks in a transaction and partially abort the current transaction back to a previously defined mark.

Defining languages

The first problem in building a conceptual programming environment is to develop a workable underlying model that can support a wide variety of languages. This variety must include textual languages, visual languages, nonexecutable design languages, and languages that are now only a figment of someone's imagination. The key to solving this problem is the choice of an underlying representation through which languages can be defined.

Objects as a basis. Today's languages are usually defined formally in terms of their abstract syntax. This abstract syntax is represented as a tree where the internal nodes represent constructs such as statements and subprograms and where the leaf nodes represent semantically relevant terminals such as names and constants. A mapping from the concrete syntax (the textual form of the language) to the abstract syntax is provided either formally (by using a context-free grammar) or informally (by stating what the concrete form of each abstract construct is). The semantics of such languages are defined as mappings from the abstract syntax trees to some semantic form. This can be a program for operational semantics, a set of mathematical functions that show how the state changes for denotational semantics, or a set of logical rules for axiomatic semantics.

While abstract syntax trees work well for hierarchical, textual languages, they are not a natural representation for the nonhierarchical languages that arise in conceptual programming. In particular, two-dimensional languages such as finite-state automata and dataflow diagrams have a natural representation that is a general cyclic graph rather than a simple tree. Using an unnatural representation here would complicate language definition beyond what is desirable in conceptual programming.

Garden addresses this problem by generalizing the abstract syntax tree model of semantics into an object-based model. Objects represent programs directly. The instance data (fields) associated with an object are used three ways in specifying a program: (1) Some fields are structural, specifying an underlying graph of objects that replaces the abstract syntax tree. (2) Other fields are static attributes, containing data about the program instance relevant to the static semantics and corresponding to the attributes that would be attached to the abstract syntax tree to store the static semantics. (3) Still other fields are dynamic values, those that reflect the execution semantics, since Garden actually runs object-based programs.

Defining a language in Garden is a three-step process: (1) The type structure that serves as the object basis is developed. (2) The semantics for these types is defined. (3) The syntax, both textual and visual, is specified.

Defining the object basis. The first step is to define the set of types that describe program objects in the new language. This requires that you understand and characterize the language's components. You should create a type for each component. The type should have fields to contain both the structural information needed to describe the corresponding program structure and any state information needed to evaluate this object.

For example, suppose you wanted to develop a language based on Petri nets.[8] A Petri net is composed of places that can store markers and transitions that use markers and generate new ones. Typically, the markers are used for concurrency control while actions are associated with the transitions. Figure 2 shows an example Petri net. The object basis for Petri nets contains three types of objects: pNet objects represent complete Petri nets, pTrans objects represent transitions, and pPlace objects represent places.

A pNet object contains three fields, one holding the name of the Petri net and the others lists of transitions and places.

A pTrans object contains six fields. The first holds an identifying string that names the transition. The second field holds the associated action, an arbitrary object that Garden will evaluate when the transition is triggered so this Petri-net language can be associated naturally with any other Garden language. The next two fields contain the list of input places and the list of output places for the transition. The remaining fields hold a flag during execution indicating that the transition is currently active and a semaphore associated with the transition.

A pPlace object contains fields with the identifying name and the number of markers that should initially be at the place. It also contains a field with the list of transitions it is connected to, a field for the current count of the number of markers stored at the place, and a field containing the semaphore controlling access to the place.

Defining the semantics. The second step in defining a Garden language is to define the semantics of the types. You do this by associating evaluation functions with the types. Sometimes an evaluation function is defined only for the top-level type (for example, a flowchart or an automaton). In other cases, it is convenient to define the evaluation of an object of this type with the evaluation of its component objects, and it is thus necessary to define semantics for the component types.

Evaluation of a Petri net occurs when the pNet object is evaluated. The code associated with evaluating a pNet object first initializes the net and starts a control thread for each transition. It then tries to execute each transition by sending each one a Check message. After this, the Petri net will continue executing on its own until one of the transitions terminates.

Each transition evaluates in its own control thread. The message NewThread starts the control thread and sends a Work message to the transition. The code associated with this message is a simple loop that waits for the transition to be activated by doing a P operation on the transition's semaphore; it then evaluates the transition object itself to evaluate the associated action. When the action completes, an Add message is sent to each output place and the transition sends itself a Check message to see if it should fire again.

When a transition gets a Check message, it must check if it should fire and, if so, enable its semaphore. It first checks if the transition is active and, if so, returns immediately. It then loops through the input places, sending each a Check message. This message does a P operation on

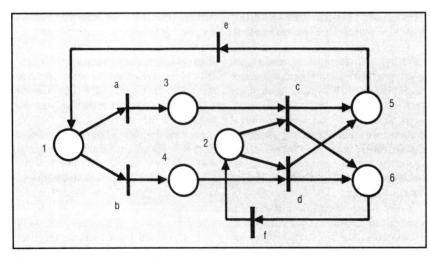

Figure 2. Petri net example.

IEEE Software

the corresponding place's semaphore and returns a Boolean value indicating whether there is a marker at the place. If all markers are present, each input place is sent a Use message to decrement its marker count. Next, each input place is sent a Release message to do a V operation on its semaphore. Finally, if the transition should fire, it does so by setting its active flag and doing a V operation on its semaphore. (This example is simplified so that multiple connections from a place to a transition are not handled. In a more practical framework, a link object would represent the connection between a place and a transition.)

pPlace objects must respond to five messages: (1) Initialize, (2) Check to lock and check if there is a marker, (3) Use to remove a marker, (4) Add to add a marker, and (5) Release to unlock their semaphore. The only complexity here involves adding a marker to a place when all transitions connected to the place must be sent a Check message.

Defining the language syntax. The final step in developing a conceptual language in Garden is providing a syntax for the language. Garden offers several syntactic forms that can be defined for the new language. These reflect the different ways that the language can be displayed and input.

Garden provides a textual interface to objects (this interface is a Lisp-like language). In the language, objects are defined by putting the object type and values for the fields in braces ({ }). The field values can be named or be provided positionally, where the first value is the first field. Omitted fields are initialized to a default value. In addition, parentheses can be used instead of braces when only positional fields are given.

Currently, you can make only small variations in the textual forms allowed for an object. For input, you can define reasonable default values for fields and can determine the fields' order. If you want more complex manipulations, you can define an explicit Build or Instance operator for the type. The Build operator takes the type and the set of initial field values and builds the correct instance; the Instance operator

Visual programming environments

The Garden effort draws on past research in several areas. Garden is a general-purpose visual programming system, providing many of the capabilities of visual programming languages. At the same time, Garden is an interactive programming environment in the flavor of the many versions of Lisp. Garden, being an object-oriented system, is closely related to previous work in this area, in particular to interactive systems such as Smalltalk and Lisp with types. And Garden is a programming environment designed for use with multiple windows on a powerful personal workstation and shares features of other such environments.

A multilanguage approach to conceptual programming such as Garden's differs considerably from the extensive body of work in visual languages.[1] Much of this work uses a single visual representation as a programming language. This work extends from flowchart programming to simulating finite-state automata, graphical dataflow representations, graphical data-structure representations, graphical programming-by-demonstration, and functional programming. Other work has concentrated on using visual representations to support design languages such as SADT, SREM, and the Yourdon method, or to provide machine-checkable documentation as a design aid. All these efforts are single-view systems. They do not support the wide range of views necessary for conceptual programming to be a practical approach to large-scale programming.

While Garden has a lot in common with interactive object-oriented environments such as Smalltalk, there are significant differences. Some of these are apparent at a finer level of detail than is presented in the main article, notably in the underlying model of objects. The basic difference, however, is the use of objects throughout the system to represent both programs and data. This, along with the lack of any preferred programming language or methodology, makes Garden an ideal testbed for working with several paradigms concurrently. Moreover, the heavy emphasis on the graphical display of objects provides a visual component that would have to programmed explicitly for each structure in other systems.

Garden's approach to producing a complete programming environment also differs from the multiview program-development systems for workstations developed over the past 10 years. These include the Cedar Mesa environment from Xerox PARC, the Magpie system from Tektronics, and the Pecan program-development system at Brown University. These systems are based on a single textual programming language. The Pecan system and PV try to provide alternative graphical representations to the textual programming language, but the experience with Pecan has shown that such graphical views have limited power and usefulness when they are tied to syntax. The syntactic basis forces you to treat these two-dimensional representations one-dimensionally, and the graphics provide no significant advantage over text. Because the wide range of graphical views that people use do not conveniently fall in the confines of a single language, it seems unlikely that a system based on a single programming language can effectively support them all.

Reference

1. G. Raeder, "A Survey of Current Graphical Programming Techniques," *Computer*, Aug. 1985, pp. 11-25.

must build an initial instance with no defined fields.

You have some control over the textual output form used to display the object. You can control the basic display form (whether to use the braced form with explicit field names or the parenthesized form).

Garden also gives you control over which fields are normally displayed. You can indicate fields that should not be displayed when showing a particular object type textually. Different fields can be indicated for objects that are displayed explicitly versus objects that are compo-

nents of another object, a facility that provides readable displays of cyclic structures. In this case, all fields are displayed at the top level, but only identifying fields are displayed at lower levels.

Finally, if you need more control over the object's textual display, you can provide a message handler that is invoked when the object is to be displayed that will display a substitute object. This message handler can differ for objects displayed at the top level and those displayed inside other objects.

In addition to a textual syntax, Garden provides a general facility for interactively requesting an object definition. This facility builds an instance of an object of the designated type and then uses a sequence of dialogue boxes to get field values for the component fields. You can customize this process to some extent for each object type you define. For example, you can order the fields so values are requested in a given order and abort the sequence of dialogue boxes to use default values for the remaining fields, or you can designate fields for which the system will not request values (these fields thus will hold the default value).

Additional control is provided through the typing of the fields, since values of different types are prompted for differently. For example, if a string is expected, you can enter the string without having to type quotes around it; if a type is expected, you are given dialogue-box buttons for the most common types.

You can also provide a message handler for the type to be invoked when you finish providing the fields. This function is then responsible for cleaning up the initial object and maintaining consistency of the data structures. Such functions are normally used to set up complex structural fields of objects with minimal user information. For a doubly linked list, for example, this function could set up the proper back links once you defined the forward links.

Defining the visual syntax. Defining the visual syntax of the new language is the final part of the language specification. This process has two parts: defining the visual display of the language's objects and defining the interpretation of graphical editing operations on this display. Garden tries to make this complex process as simple as possible by using a graphics package explicitly designed for drawing data structures. This package includes an editor that lets you interactively describe different ways to draw objects of a given type and a graphical editor that lets you modify the objects being displayed.[9]

Garden's general layout package, Gelo, is designed to be a flexible and powerful interface for drawing pictures of data structures or, in Garden, structures of objects representing programs and data. It provides a simple interface for designing the graphical representation for the structure and can lay out arbitrarily complex structures without programming the layouts.

Gelo's layouts are based on a hierarchy of graphical objects that are loosely related to the various components of the original data structure. Initially, four different types of objects are provided:

• Basic objects. These display simple user data, fields of more complex user data, and constants such as the name of the data type. They contain a text string representing their value. This string can be enclosed inside a rectangle, circle, or other figure, which can be filled and colored as desired.

• Tiled objects. These display fixed composites and recursive structures. They

---

Defining the visual syntax of the new languages is the final part of the language specification.

---

consist of a rectangle split into tiled regions. Each region contains another type of object to be drawn. You can impose some constraints on the regions' sizes and have some control on the tiles' sizes.

• Layout objects. These display more complex or variable structures. They consist of a rectangular region into which nodes and arcs are placed. Gelo uses heuristics to automatically lay out the resulting graph. It chooses the amount of space between the nodes, the method for laying out the nodes, and the method for routing the arcs between the nodes.

• Arc objects. These represent arcs in layouts. They allow a characterization of how the arc is drawn and of the labels that can be placed on the arc.

This simple framework is powerful enough to handle a wide variety of data-structure displays. Moreover, the system supports a general mechanism for these blocks, letting new block types be added as needed.

Visual languages in Garden are characterized by mappings from the Garden object types of the language to Gelo objects. These mapping are defined through a set of stylized examples of the display for the types and are used to build the hierarchy of Gelo objects that correspond to a particular Garden structure. You can display and edit this hierarchy.

Figure 3 shows the stylized mappings for the Petri-net language. A pNet object, the top level of the net, is drawn as a simple tiling with two tiles, one on top to hold the name and one below to hold the Petri net's picture. The layout used in the editor for this mapping is shown in Figure 3a.

Two mappings are shown for pTrans objects.

The first is used when the object is drawn inside a layout. This is the form used in the picture of the Petri net; it is a vertical line labeled with the identifying string of the transition. The mapping itself, shown in Figure 3b, specifies that both the input and output fields should be used, with arcs drawn from the objects denoted by the input fields and arcs drawn to the objects denoted by the output fields.

The second mapping, the default mapping for pTrans objects shown in Figure 3c, is used when the object occurs outside a layout. This is a tiling containing the type name on top, an indentation bar on the left, and then the fields in the order in which they occur in the type definition. The mapping for pPlace objects in the picture of a Petri net (Figure 3d) is a basic type shaped as a circle with the identifying string displayed.

The result of these mappings is the Petri net example of Figure 2 displayed by Garden in Figure 4. Garden lets you use this visual form to create and edit objects as well as for simple display. The editor uses Gelo to put up a display and then lets you apply graphical editing operations to modify it. Each graphical editing operation must map to a change of the underlying object. This change is made and the display is then updated for the modified object.

To support consistent graphical editing for a variety of structures, the graphical structure editor translates your editing request into requests to change values or

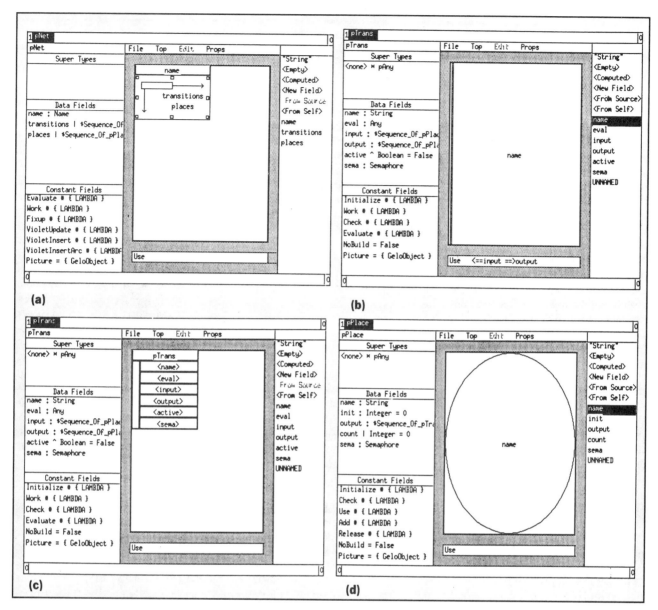

Figure 3. Stylized mappings for Petri-net objects: **(a)** layout for pNet object, **(b)** pTrans object mapping when drawn in a layout, **(c)** default pTrans object mapping, and **(d)** pPlace object mapping.

to add or delete elements from a layout. These requests are mapped by Garden into messages sent to the displayed objects. Garden's default facility for handling these messages is usually sufficient.

But one instance where it is insufficient is when the mapping from Garden objects to Gelo types is so complex that the facility cannot determine where a node or arc can be added or should be deleted. It also fails when nodes or arcs are added several times but actually appear only once. And it will succeed but yield inconsistent object structures if the Garden objects contain redundant information that was not used in the drawing, such as doubly linked lists. In these cases, you must provide message handlers that perform the correct operation on the particular data types.

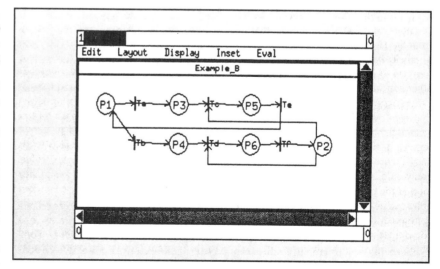

Figure 4. Garden's Petri-net display.

For the Petri net example, you would have to provide several message handlers to ensure that the editor worked correctly. In particular, handlers must be defined for inserting and deleting both nodes and arcs. These are necessary both because the underlying objects contain redundant information (the transitions point to their input places and the places point to the transitions in which they are used) and because adding nodes is ambiguous since a layout node can be a place or a transition.

The definition of these editing functions completes the introduction of a Petri-net language into Garden. The work involved is quite small: It takes a day or two for someone familiar with the Garden system.

Using the new language. Once the Petri-net language is defined in Garden, you can use it as one of the basic conceptual languages in your repertoire. Petri nets can be used to define the asynchronous control aspects of a more complex system. Petri net examples can be created and used easily. Moreover, programs using Petri nets can be freely mixed with all other Garden languages.

The conceptual programmer would create Petri-net objects with the graphical editor described above. The Petri net would be created and modified by adding places and transitions to the drawing of the net. When a new object is to be inserted, the system uses dialogue boxes to prompt for the object type and then for the fields of this new object. Places and transitions can be connected in the editor by dragging arcs from one to the other. The various values — labels, initial settings, and evaluation routines — can be changed using this or other editors.

Evaluation of the Petri net begins with the top-level pNet object. Garden's general debugging and monitoring facilities are available for the new language, and, if there is an error during evaluation, you would be placed in a read-eval-print loop at the point of the error so the variables can be queried and execution can be continued if requested. Similarly, you could trace and suspend execution of any object composing the Petri net.

In addition to these standard debugging facilities, the Garden graphical editor can automatically animate the Petri-net programs. The editor highlights each object that it displays when that object is evaluated. Because Petri nets evaluate by evaluating their transition objects, a graphical view of the pNet object being evaluated will show the evaluation by successively highlighting each transition as it fires.

There is nothing special about the Petri net example discussed here. Garden can and has been successfully used to define a wide variety of languages, including functional dataflow languages, finite automata, flowcharts, dataflow design languages, a CSP-like ports language, a programming-by-demonstration language, and language facilities provided by Paisley, Linda, and Multilisp.

The Garden prototype currently runs on Digital Equipment Corp. VAX workstations and on Sun workstations. It is being used both for general experimentation and as the basis for several research projects at Brown University. The implementation runs at about the speed of a Lisp interpreter and includes a compiler that produces C code to give a tenfold improvement in performance over interpreted code.

The work on the Garden system is only half done, and the system is just now becoming really usable. As the system becomes more stable and as my colleagues at Brown University and I get more experience with it, we hope to test out the promises of conceptual programming and see if this is a viable approach to design that improves programmer productivity as we hope it will. Such experiments will at first be informal, based on the experience of the initial users, but we hope be more rigorous later when the system can handle a controlled experiment.

We are working in several areas related to this system and its concepts because Garden is by no means perfect or complete. Significant work remains to be done

not only to get experience with the system but also to improve its interfaces and to make it into a real environment.

The graphical interface is weak in two respects. First, the layouts are produced completely automatically and often are not aesthetically pleasing. We are looking into using better heuristics for layouts and finding ways of letting programmers control the layout to some extent. Second, the graphical editor is essentially a structured editor for the underlying object. We would prefer, in many cases, that this editor be a simple drawing package to let users simply draw the program and then parse the result.

The textual interface also needs improvement. Currently, you must map your conceptual language into Garden's Lisp-like notation. While this isn't as detrimental in the textual case as it is in the graphical one, it is a drawback we want to eliminate. A more serious disadvantage is that the current language is not suitable for defining complex object structures, especially those that are not trees.

Although Garden is designed and implemented to sit on top of an object-oriented database system, we have had little experience with the actual use of the system, primarily because its initial implementations has not had the performance needed for an interactive system. The performance problem is being addressed and may be resolved in the next year.

We are also looking at the very difficult problem of semantics that the current implementation of Garden tries to avoid. Ideally, a multiparadigm system should have a consistent internal semantics. Such a semantics provides a basis for compilation, for consistency checking between views, and for view mapping. View mapping is important if the several programming paradigms are to be applied to the same portion of the program, a situation that arises when you want to see and use both a dataflow and a control-flow view of the same module. In this case, the system must be able to map changes in either view to appropriate changes in the other. With a broad spectrum of views, the simplest way of allowing such mappings is to have a common semantic basis and to generate the views from this basis.   ✧

Acknowledgments

This research was supported in part by the Office of Naval Research and the Defense Dept.'s Advanced Research Projects Agency under contract N00014-83-K-0146 and ARPA Order No. 4786, by National Science Foundation grant SER80-04974, by a contract with IBM, by a grant from AT&T Foundation, and by a grant from Digital Equipment Corp. Partial equipment support was provided by Apollo Computer, Inc.

References

1. D.T. Ross, "Applications and Extensions of SADT," *Computer*, April 1985, pp. 25-35.

2. M. Alford, "SREM at the Age of Eight: The Distributed Computing Design System," *Computer*, April 1985, pp. 36-46.

3. F.P. Brooks, Jr., "No Silver Bullet: Essence and Accidents of Software Engineering," *Computer*, April 1987, pp. 10-19.

4. S.P. Reiss, "An Object-Oriented Framework for Graphical Programming," *SIG-Plan Notices*, Oct. 1986, pp. 49-57.

5. A. Goldberg and D. Robson, *Smalltalk-80: The Language and Its Implementation*, Addison-Wesley, Reading, Mass., 1983.

6. J.N. Pato, S.P. Reiss, and M.H. Brown, "An Environment for Workstations," *Proc. IEEE Conf. Software Tools*, CS Press, Los Alamitos, Calif., 1985, pp. 112-117.

7. A.H. Skarra, S.B. Zdonik, and S.P. Reiss, "An Object Server for an Object-Oriented Database System," *Proc. Workshop Object-Oriented Database Systems*, CS Press, Los Alamitos, Calif., 1986, pp. 196-204.

8. J.L. Peterson, "Petri Nets," *Computing Surveys*, Sept. 1977, pp. 223-252.

9. S.P. Reiss and J.N. Pato, "Displaying Programs and Data Structures," *Proc. 20th Hawaii Int'l Conf. System Sciences*, CS Press, Los Alamitos, Calif., 1987

Steven P. Reiss is an associate professor of computer science at Brown University. His research interests include programming environments, graphical programming, database implementation, statistical database security, and computational geometry. Before working on Garden, he developed the Pecan program-development system.

Reiss received a BA in mathematics from Dartmouth College and a PhD in computer science from Yale University.

Address questions about this article to Reiss at Computer Science Dept., Brown University, Providence, RI 02912.

Using GELO to Visualize Software Systems*

Steven P. Reiss
Scott Meyers
Carolyn Duby

Department of Computer Science
Brown University, Box 1910
Providence, RI 02912

Abstract

GELO is a package that supports the interactive graphical display of software systems. Its features include built-in panning and zooming, abstraction of objects too small to see, pick correlation, windowing, and scroll bars. GELO creates a hierarchy of graphical objects that correspond to the components of the structure being displayed. Five flavors of graphical objects are supported, including those for simple structures, tiled layouts, and graph-based layouts. This framework is powerful enough to handle a wide variety of graphical visualizations, and it is general enough that new object flavors can be smoothly integrated in the future.

GELO is easy to learn and to use, and is presently employed in two software development environments. Among its current applications are a variety of visual languages, an interactive display of call graphs, an interactive display of data structures, and a graphical representation of module dependencies.

Introduction

Some aspects of software systems are most naturally depicted graphically. Programs are drawn as dataflow diagrams or as flowcharts, data structures are drawn as trees or as linked lists of records, call graphs and module dependencies are drawn as directed graphs, etc. Unfortunately, most software development environments provide little support for these graphical representations of software systems. This paper describes GELO, a package that makes it easy to produce complex pictures of programs, data structures, and other software components. GELO is a constraint-based system that automatically handles all aspects of picture layout, and it provides pick-correlation and other services so that its pictures can be used for input as well as for output.

A number of research projects have worked on incorporating graphical displays into programming environments. The PECAN system [Rei84] provided a predefined set of graphical views of programs that complemented the textual views. The systems PV [BCH+85], BALSA [Bro87], and TANGO [Sta89] allow programmers to write animations for algorithms, programs, and data structures. Incense [Mye83] provides displays of simple data structures in the Cedar programming environment [Tei84], and Amethyst[MCS88] does the same for Pascal in the MacGNOME programming environment[Cha85]. These systems, however, are limited in both the breadth and extensibility of their displays. PV provides a single program representation and several predefined data representations that can only handle simple data. PECAN provides three different structured flowchart representations of programs, but provides no mechanisms for user-defined displays. Incense and Amethyst offer predefined representations for the basic data structures in Cedar (Incense) and Pascal (Amethyst), but Incense requires hand-coded graphics for customized views of data structures, and Amethyst does not offer such customized views at all.[1] BALSA provid s a variety of different data structure and program views, but each one is hand-coded and involves considerable effort. TANGO is easier to use than

---

*Support for this research was provided by the NSF under grant DCR 8605567; by DARPA under contract N00014-83-K-0146, ARPA order 6320; and by the Digital Equipment Corporation under agreement 393.

---

[1] The designers of Amethyst are aware of this limitation, and they are in the process of allowing users to specify custom representations of data structures.

BALSA, but still calls for users to hand-code their displays. Many of these systems (e.g., BALSA, TANGO, Amethyst) also differ from GELO in that they do not allow the graphical images to be edited; for example, it is not possible to change the value of data structures by editing their graphical images.

GELO

GELO is a package that supports the interactive graphical display of software systems. Its features include built-in panning and zooming, abstraction of objects too small to see, pick correlation, windowing, and scroll bars. Unlike graphics packages where each primitive has a position in world coordinates, GELO pictures are placed by satisfying constraints.

GELO graphical representations are made up of different types of objects, each of which has a *flavor*. Each flavored object has a corresponding graphical representation. The simplest type of objects are the *data-flavored* objects. These are displayed as a simple geometric shape, possibly including text. For example, figure 8 shows the states of an FSA displayed as circles with the state names inside them. *Tile-flavored* objects are a collection of GELO objects that are drawn as a rectangle with non-overlapping subdivisions called *tiles*. Examples of tile-flavored objects can be seen in figure 2. *Layout-flavored* objects are used to display graphs, where the graph nodes can be a data-flavored or tile-flavored GELO object connected by arcs, which can be represented by *arc-flavored* objects. Finally, *empty-flavored* objects are represented by empty boxes on the display. They are used to represent objects that will not fit within the parameters of the window.

Each GELO object has a *minimum size* and a *desired size*, which are constraints on its dimensions along both the X and Y axes. The minimum size of an object specifies its smallest possible instantiation on the screen; if it cannot be displayed at least as large as its minimum size, it will be automatically converted into an empty-flavored object and displayed as an empty rectangle. An object's desired size is that size that best accommodates its associated text and outline. Each object also has a *priority* along each axis, a value that is used to control the relative sizes of different objects when displayed. Priorities play a role similar to glue in TeX [Knu84].

Since objects in GELO are not assigned positions in a world coordinate system by the user, the method for producing a picture from GELO objects is different from conventional graphics packages. A graphical representation in GELO can be thought of as a tree with data-flavored, arc-flavored, and empty-flavored objects as leaf nodes, and with tile-flavored and layout-flavored objects as interior nodes. This is the representation created by the application. A GELO display is produced

from flavored objects by making three passes over the display tree. The first pass is a combination top-down and bottom-up pass that determines the minimum size requirement of each object in the tree. The maximum extent is passed down and the minimum size is passed back up. This combination pass allows GELO to prune complex trees based on what can fit on the display. The second pass determines the placement of the objects on the screen. This entails having each object recursively position its immediate descendants. If the minimum size requirement of an object cannot be met during this second pass, it is converted to an empty-flavored object and its descendants are ignored. The third pass simply draws the objects. The user can pan and zoom over the resulting display.

GELO flavors are like abstract data types. Each flavor defines attributes and a set of operations that can be performed on it. Attributes represent the information that is specific to a flavor. For example, the attributes of a data-flavored object are shape, fill-style, and associated text.

The primary operations for GELO flavors are size, layout, and draw. These operations correspond to the three passes of displaying a GELO object. Other operations exist for highlighting an object when it is selected, correlating input from the mouse and keyboard, determining the source and destination locations of arcs associated with a flavored object, etc. Because of the flexibility of GELO's implementation, we can easily define a new flavor by specifying its attributes and by implementing the operations that can be performed on it. We are considering, for example, adding a new flavor for arrays.

Data-flavored objects are represented graphically by simple shapes filled with a color, a pattern, and text. The font size for the associated text is based on the size of the window that the GELO picture is displayed in. The size operation defines a minimum size and desired size based on font dimensions and exterior shape. Since data-flavored objects are leaves in the display tree, the layout operation does not do anything. The draw operation places the shape on the screen, fills it with the desired pattern and/or color, and places any associated text inside it.

Tile-flavored objects are displayed as rectangular regions composed of nonoverlapping subdividing rectangles. Each tile contains other GELO objects, which can be of any flavor. The tiles may be connected by lines or arrows. For example, binary trees can be displayed as tilings, with the tree root and each of its children displayed in their own tiles, and with lines connecting the root to its children (see figure 9). Each tile of a tiled object has a *priority*, an *expansion factor*, and a *fixed flag*, each of which affects its size. The priority and expansion factor of a tile determines its size relative to other tiles. The priority is meant to be a transient property, allowing the user to zero in on a particular node. The fixed flag sets the minimum size equal to the desired size, hence the object will always be represented in its desired size. Other constraints can be defined to control the proportions of an object. For example, the user can force a tile to be represented as a square by constraining its height to be equal to its width. The constraints are translated into a system of linear equations whose solution, found by a modified form of Gaussian elimination, defines a legal tiling for the object. The expansion factors provide additional constraints in the usual case that the system is underconstrained. The layout operation for tile-flavored objects finds a tiling within the given constraints. The draw operation calls the draw operation for each of the tiles, encases the tiles within a box, and then produces any specified connecting lines between tiles.

Layout-flavored objects consist of a rectangular border enclosing nodes of any GELO flavor connected by arcs of arc-flavored objects. The FSA shown in figure 8 is an example of a layout object. The size of the entire layout-flavored object is determined by finding the sizes and relative positions of all the nodes. First, each of the components of the layout-flavored object is placed on a grid, where each box on the grid holds at most one object. Placement can use one of several possible traversals of the display tree and several layout heuristics – see figure 7. Each row and column of the grid has a minimum and desired size, which is determined by the sum of the sizes of its components. The amount of space between rows and columns is user-defined and is expressed as a fraction of the space used by the components. The overall minimum size and desired size of the layout-flavored object is the sum of the area taken up by the components plus the amount of white space between them.

The layout operation for layout objects scales the components of the rows and columns of the layout according to their priorities. The higher the priority of a node, the larger it will appear in comparison to the other objects. The paths of the arcs connecting the nodes are also calculated in the layout operation. First, the location of the connecting points on the arc's source and destination nodes is determined. The path of the arc is calculated in one of three ways: direct from source to destination; routed and channeled through white space between source and destination; or drawn directly if it would not pass through another node and directed through white space if it would. The draw operation of a layout-flavored object consists of drawing a rectangle around the layout area, drawing all of the nodes, and then drawing the connecting arcs.

APPLE and PEAR

APPLE is a package that works with GELO to allow the user to define the relationship between the data structures of a program and their graphical representations. Without APPLE, the user would have to re-specify GELO objects each time the data structures changed. In general, APPLE serves to map data structures of a strongly typed language into GELO objects. Data structures can have different mappings under different conditions. For example, accepting and nonaccepting states of an FSA may be represented differently.

The mappings that can be defined range from simple to complex. A simple one would be a mapping from a program data structure to a data-flavored object; a more complex would be from program data structures to tile-flavored and layout-flavored objects. Later in this paper we show how APPLE can be used to interactively specify the mappings between program objects and GELO objects.

The APPLE-GELO interface creates a mapping between GELO objects and user data structures and types. It also specifies user-defined functions for operations that APPLE requires. Since APPLE is language independent, it relies on the application to provide functionality where information about the underlying language is necessary. For instance, APPLE needs to know type names and field names, how to access fields of user data, as well as how to load and store mappings. The application provides APPLE with pointers to functions which perform the necessary language-dependent operations.

PEAR is another package associated with GELO. It provides a user interface to the graphical capabilities of GELO, allowing the user to pan and zoom, selectively display objects or parts of objects, change display priorities, etc. It also provides the basis for a visual editor, allowing the user to graphically request changes to the displayed picture. These visual edits are mapped by PEAR into calls to the underlying application to make corresponding changes in the displayed data. There are two classes of edits: general edits that apply to any flavor of object, and layout-specific edits that can be used only on layout-flavored objects. The general editing capabilities include changing the value of an object, deleting an object, and creating a new object. The layout-specific editing operations consist of adding or deleting a node or arc in a layout-flavored object.

The interface between graphical editing and internal structure editing is done in two steps. The first step is to associate the components of the user structure to the GELO flavored objects. This is done using the information stored by APPLE. The second part of the PEAR interface is the mapping between graphical edits and underlying structure edits. PEAR takes care of the actual graphical edits, but it is language-independent like APPLE, so PEAR passes on the information about

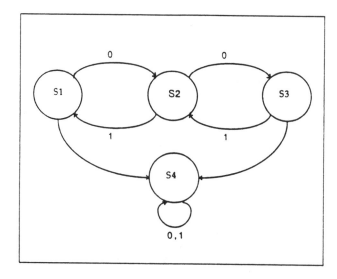

Figure 1: A Customary FSA Diagram

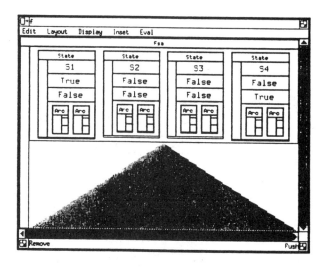

Figure 2: Default Display for f

graphical edits by calling routines provided by the application. These routines handle the edits on the underlying program structures.

Example: An FSA Language

GELO was originally developed for use in the Garden environment for conceptual programming [Rei87a, Rei87b, Rei87c]. Garden is a fully object-oriented system, and it uses GELO to allow users to interact with graphical representations of arbitrary objects. Such objects may correspond to both programs and data. Garden's interface to APPLE is called Thyme; Thyme is used to specify how Garden object types are to be displayed. Garden's interface to PEAR is called Violet; Violet allows users to graphically edit objects in the system. In this section, we show how GELO supports the development of a graphical programming language for Finite State Automata in Garden[2].

FSAs have many uses in programming, including user interface design and control logic. Let us suppose that we wish to create a new graphical programming language, one that allows us to create FSA programs by drawing and editing the customary diagrams, such as the one shown in figure 1. Let us further suppose that we have already defined the data structures and semantics of FSAs. In those definitions, an object of type *Fsa* consists of a list of states (the states of the FSA) and a current state (the state the FSA is currently in). An object of type *State* consists of a name, a list of arcs going out of the state, and flags that indicate whether the state is a start state or an accepting state. An *Arc*

object consists of an object to match in order to enable the arc, a state to move to if the match is successful, and an action to be taken if the arc is followed. Finally, let us suppose that we have defined an example FSA object f that is equivalent to the FSA depicted in figure 1.

The default Garden display for f is shown in figure 2. By default each object is displayed as a GELO tiling, with separate tiles for each of the fields of the object, a tile at the top for the type of the object, and an empty tile on the left to indent the fields. Hence f shows its states in the large upper tile, and its current state (null – depicted by a filled triangle) in the large lower tile. Note that each of the states is also drawn as a recursively tiled object, as are the arcs within the states.

Unfortunately, this doesn't look much like our conceptualization of an FSA, so we need to define new graphical representations for the object types *Fsa, State*, and *Arc*. We would like to view an FSA as a graph showing the structure of the automaton, plus a field telling us the current state of the FSA. The graph naturally corresponds to a GELO layout object, and the current state can be easily displayed as a data object, so we use Thyme to define the display of an *Fsa* as a tiling, with the top tile a data-flavored object containing the name of the current state, and the bottom tile a layout containing the states of the FSA.

We next turn our attention to the graphical representation for *State* objects. *State* objects are natural candidates for GELO data objects, because they are a simple shape (a circle) with text inside (their name). GELO supports a wide variety of options for data-flavored objects, including variations in the shape, the line style, and the font used if text is to be displayed inside the shape. Figure 3 shows the options available when defining a data-flavored object, and in-

---

[2] A more complete presentation of this example may be found in [RM89], which presents a step-by-step description of how a user creates a graphical language in Garden.

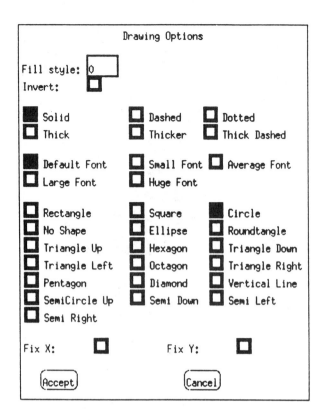

Figure 3: Thyme Options for Data-Flavored Objects

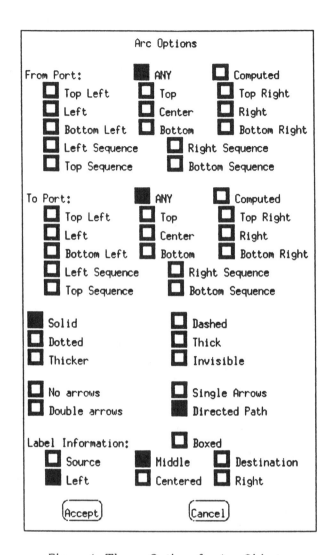

Figure 4: Thyme Options for Arc Objects

dicates which ones were chosen in our example to get a *State* object to be drawn as a circle.

Figure 5 shows how Garden displays *f* after editing the graphical representation of *State* objects. We can see that we have eight arc objects in the view, which is the number of arcs in *f*, and that each arc object contains a state depicted as a circle[3] with the name of a state inside. In addition, if we emphasize one of the small rectangles next to the arc objects, we see that it is actually a *State* object drawn in the way we expect; it is seen as a rectangle in figure 5 only because it is too small to display as a circle[4].

This still doesn't look much like our conceptualization of an FSA. Our problem is that the FSA's arcs aren't being drawn as we're used to seeing them; they're

being drawn in the same tiled format that Garden assigns as its default for most types. For our arcs to be drawn correctly, we need the source of the arc to be the object containing the arc (the state it comes from), the sink of the arc to be the arc's *next* field, and the label of the arc to be its *match* field. Using Thyme, we specify that *Arc* objects are to be drawn as GELO arcs, and we make the appropriate assignments for the source, sink, and label of the arcs.

GELO can draw arcs in a great number of formats, with the user given control over where the arc source and sink attach to their respective objects, how the arc line is drawn, what kind of arrowhead it should have, and where the label should be located. Figure 4 shows the options available when defining an arc, and indicates which ones were chosen in our example to get an *Arc* object to be drawn as a solid single-headed arrow with its attachment points automatically computed by GELO. The effect this has on *f*'s display is shown in figure 6.

---

[3] In this paper, all the "circles" appear as ovals because the aspect ratio of the surrounding windows isn't 1:1. GELO automatically scales drawings independently in X and Y so as to use the entire window area available to it. This behavior can be overridden by the user so that objects that are defined to be circles will always be drawn as true circles.

[4] GELO automatically elides information that is too small to display. In this case, an oval of the correct size looks just like a rectangle, and the state name is elided. Violet allows individual objects to be emphasized (enlarged) or deemphasized (reduced) under user control by simple menu choices and mouse clicks, however, so it is easy to emphasize the small rectangles in figure 5 and verify that they are really *State* objects.

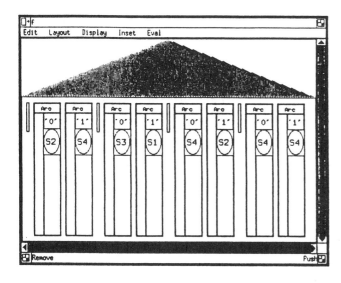

Figure 5: Display of *f* after Editing *State*

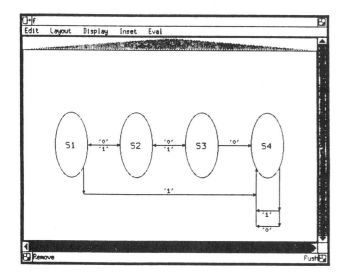

Figure 6: Display of *f* After Editing *Arc*

This is much closer to our conceptualization – the diagram is unmistakably an FSA. Still, the layout could be improved: it's not entirely obvious that there is an arc from S1 to S4. Fortunately, GELO gives us some control over the heuristics used when drawing layout objects. If we go back and edit the layout tile of the graphical representation for type *Fsa*, we are presented with the set of options shown in figure 7. Setting the options as shown there gives us the drawing for *f* shown in figure 8, which is our final program.

It is important to remember that the result of our efforts is not just a way of viewing the program *f*, but is instead a complete *graphical programming language*. We can now use Violet to create new FSA programs by drawing nodes and arcs and connecting them together. We can edit existing *Fsa* objects graphically, even if

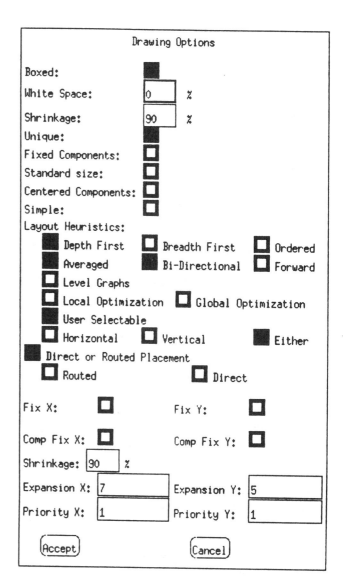

Figure 7: Thyme Options for Layout Objects

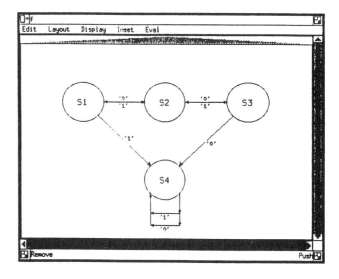

Figure 8: Display of *f* After Setting Layout Options

they were defined textually. We can also execute our *Fsa* objects and watch the execution graphically, since Garden uses GELO features to automatically highlight the object currently being evaluated.

Other Applications

As we have seen, GELO can be used as a basis for a graphical language. It is also flexible enough to support the creation of a wide variety of such languages. Among the other languages already defined within Garden are those for programming in Petri Nets[Rei87c], Flowcharts[Rei86], Data Flow Diagrams[Rei86], and a CSP-like parallel language[Rei87b].

GELO is also an integral component of the FIELD programming environment [Rei89]. For example, it has been used to display a dynamic view of the call graph of a program. Such a call graph highlights the currently executing function as the program runs. It also allows the user to pick nodes (functions) and arcs (calls) when s/he wishes to view or edit the functions or call sites. Figure 10 shows a call graph generated within FIELD. A similar facility allows the user to view the module dependencies in a software system. Another application of GELO in FIELD is to display the dependency graph in the configuration management tool.

GELO, APPLE, and PEAR are also used in FIELD to display arbitrary user data structures. An example of this kind of application can be seen in figure 9, which shows a snapshot of a dynamically changing binary search tree. This display is dynamic and editable. FIELD uses GELO and PEAR to provide fast, minimal updates to the visualization as the underlying data changes during program execution. The FIELD interface also translates graphical edits into appropriate debugger commands to change the underlying variables.

Discussion

GELO is a powerful and flexible system, but there is much room for improvement. One shortcoming is that the displays produced by GELO are developed entirely automatically and are sometimes not aesthetically pleasing; there is no way for a programmer to "tweak" the pictures to make them look just the way s/he wants. For example, the FSA *f* has overlapping arcs between nodes in figure 6, but the original conceptualization in figure 1 doesn't. Our attempts to solve this problem focus on a search for better automatic layout heuristics and on finding ways to let programmers have some direct control over layouts. In particular, we have been experimenting with algorithms developed by Di Battista and Tamassia [BT88].

Another problem is that GELO is designed to work best on hierarchical drawings; software systems with graphical relationships between different parts of the layout hierarchy can be difficult or impossible to specify. We intend to redesign GELO so that it accommodates such systems more easily.

Finally, graphical editing via PEAR can be uncomfortable. This grows out of the fact that PEAR must immediately reflect all editing operations in the underlying object being edited, and this causes PEAR to act as a structure editor, with all the attendant disadvantages of a structure editor. Eric Golin [GR88] has developed methods for general-purpose graphical parsing, however, and this should make it possible to allow more flexible graphical editing of GELO pictures.

Status

GELO is currently in use in a number of projects at Brown University, including the Garden and FIELD programming environments. GELO is available for public distribution as part of the Brown Workstation Environment (BWE)[RS89], a collection of graphics tools built atop the X Window System[5]. Inquiries about BWE should be addressed to the Software Librarian at the Brown University Computer Science Department.

References

[BCH+85] Gretchen P. Brown, Richard T. Carling, Christopher F. Herot, David A. Kramlich, and Paul Souza. Program Visualization: Graphical Support for Software Development. *IEEE Computer*, 18(8):27–35, August 1985.

[Bro87] Marc H. Brown. *Algorithm Animation*. PhD thesis, Brown University Computer Science Department, April 1987.

[BT88] Giuseppe Di Battista and Roberto Tamassia. Algorithms for Plan Representations of Acyclic Digraphs. *Theoretical Computer Science*, 61(3), 1988.

[Cha85] R. Chandhok *et al.* Programming Environments Based on Structure Editing: The GNOME Approach. In *Proceedings of the National Computer Conference*, 1985.

[GR88] Eric J. Golin and Steven P. Reiss. Parsing in a Visual Language Environment. Technical Report CS-89-06, Brown University Computer Science Department, November 1988.

[Knu84] Donald E. Knuth. *The TEXbook*. Addison-Wesley, Reading, Massachusetts, 1984.

[MCS88] Brad A. Myers, Ravinder Chandhok, and Atul Sareen. Automatic Data Visualization

---

[5] *X Window System* is a trademark of the Massachusetts Institute of Technology.

for Novice Pascal Programmers. In *Proceedings of the 1988 IEEE Workshop on Visual Languages*, pages 192–198, October 1988. Held in Pittsburgh, Pennsylvania, USA.

[Mye83]   Brad A. Myers. Incense: A System for Displaying Data Structures. *Computer Graphics*, 17(3):115–126, July 1983.

[Rei84]   Steven P. Reiss. Graphical Program Development with PECAN Program Development Systems. Technical Report CS-84-04, Brown University, 1984.

[Rei86]   Steven P. Reiss. Visual Languages and the GARDEN System. In P. Gorny and M. J. Tauber, editors, *Lecture Notes in Computer Science 282*, pages 178–198. Springer-Verlag, May 1986. Proceedings of the 5th Interdisciplinary Workshop in Informatics and Psychology, held in Schärding, Austria. Also available as Brown University Computer Science Department Technical Report No. CS-86-16, September 1986.

[Rei87a]   Steven P. Reiss. A Conceptual Programming Environment. In *Proceedings of the 9th International Conference on Software Engineering*, pages 225–235. Computer Society Press of the IEEE, April 1987. Held in Monterey, California, USA. Also available as Brown University Computer Science Department Technical Report No. CS-86-20, August 1986.

[Rei87b]   Steven P. Reiss. An Object-Oriented Framework for Conceptual Programming. In Bruce Shriver and Peter Wegner, editors, *Research Directions in Object-Oriented Programming*, pages 189–218. The MIT Press, 1987.

[Rei87c]   Steven P. Reiss. Working in the Garden Environment for Conceptual Programming. *IEEE Software*, pages 16 – 27, November 1987.

[Rei89]   Steven P. Reiss. Connecting Tools using Message Passing in the FIELD Program Development Environment. *IEEE Software*, 1989. Also available as Brown University Computer Science Department Technical Report CS-88-18, "Integration Mechanisms in the FIELD Environment," 1988.

[RM89]   Steven P. Reiss and Scott Meyers. Creating Graphical Languages in Garden. Technical Report CS-89-02, Brown University Computer Science Department, January 1989.

[RS89]   Steven P. Reiss and John T. Stasko. The Brown Workstation Environment: A User Interface Design Toolkit. In *Proceedings of*

the *Working Conference on Engineering for Human Computer Interaction*, August 1989.

[Sta89]   John Thomas Stasko. *TANGO: A Framework and System for Algorithm Animation*. PhD thesis, Brown University, 1989.

[Tei84]   Warren Teitelman. A Tour through Cedar. *IEEE Software*, April 1984.

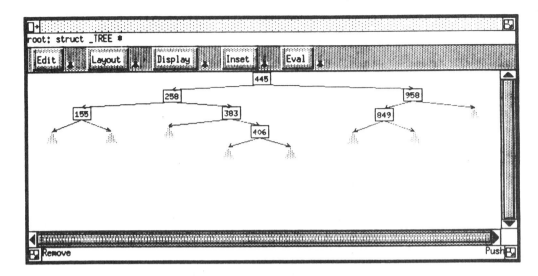

Figure 9: FIELD Display of Binary Search Tree

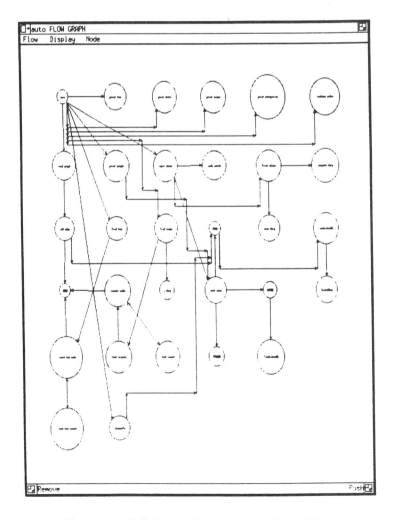

Figure 10: Call Graph Generated within FIELD

□□□ 6 □□□ Environments III: Using Data–Flow, Actors and Agents

W. Finzer and L. Gould. "Programming by Rehearsal." *Byte*, 9(6):187–210, June 1984.

S.L. Tanimoto and M.S. Runyan. "PLAY: An Iconic Programming System for Children." In *Visual Languages* (S.-K. Chang, T. Ichikawa and P.A. Ligomenides, editors), pages 191–205, 1986. Plenum, New York.

B.A. Myers. "Creating Interaction Techniques by Demonstration." *IEEE Computer Graphics and Applications*, 7(9):51–60, September 1987.

R.B. Smith. "Experiences with the Alternate Reality Kit: An Example of the Tension between Literalism and Magic." *IEEE Computer Graphics and Applications*, 7(9):42–50, September 1987.

T.D. Kimura, J.W. Choi and J.M. Mack. "Show and Tell."

F. Ludolph, Y-Y. Chow, D. Ingalls, S. Wallace and K. Doyle. "The FABRIK Programming Environment." In *Proc. Workshop on Visual Languages*, Pittsburgh, Penn., pages 222–230, October 10-12, 1988. IEEE Computer Society Press, Los Alamitos, Calif.

PROGRAMMING BY REHEARSAL

BY WILLIAM FINZER AND LAURA GOULD

*An environment for developing
educational software*

PROGRAMMING BY REHEARSAL is a visual programming environment that nonprogrammers can use to create educational software. It combines many of the qualities of computer-based design environments with the full power of a programming language. The emphasis in this graphical environment is on programming visually; only things that can be seen can be manipulated. The design and programming process consists of moving "performers" around on "stages" and teaching them how to interact by sending "cues" to one another. The system relies almost completely on interactive graphics and allows designers to react immediately to their emerging products by showing them, at all stages of development, exactly what their potential users will see.

The process is quick, easy, and enjoyable; a simple program may be constructed in less than half an hour. The beginning set of 18 primitive performers, each of which responds to about 70 cues, can be extended as the designers create new composite performers and teach them new cues.

We were motivated to undertake this project by our desire to give programming power to those who understand how people learn; we wanted to eliminate the need for programmers in the design of educational software. Programming by Rehearsal is implemented in the Smalltalk-80 programming environment and runs on a large, fast, personal machine: the Xerox 1132 Scientific Information Processor (the Dorado).

COMPUTERS AND INTUITION

In the spring of 1980 our attention was focused on a topic we called Computers and Intuition. It seemed to us that newly available, high-resolution computer images, combined with interactive control over these images, constituted a new medium for the presentation of information and concepts. We were particularly concerned with the implications that this interactive computer graphics medium might have for education.

We were also thinking about how paradoxical it was that the computer was often viewed as an engine for improving cognitive and analytical skills, while it might turn out that because of its

....

William Finzer is a consultant with the System Concepts Laboratory at the Xerox Palo Alto Research Center and an instructor and curriculum developer in the mathematics department at San Francisco State University (1600 Holloway, San Francisco, CA 94132).

Laura Gould has been a member of the Smalltalk group at the Xerox Palo Alto Research Center for the past seven years. She is now National Secretary of Computer Professionals for Social Responsibility (POB 717, Palo Alto, CA 94301).

superlative dynamic graphics, its main new contribution to education might be in the enhancement of nonanalytical, intuitive thought.

Such ideas were certainly not new. Even 15 years ago, a few farseeing people proposed that computer graphics would have a profound effect on human learning. As Brown and Lewis wrote in 1968, "In the same way that books support man's linear and verbal thinking, machines will support his graphic and intuitive thought processes." (See reference 1.) Similarly, in 1969 Tony Oettinger wrote "Computers are capable of profoundly affecting science by stretching human reason and intuition, much as telescopes or microscopes extend human vision." (See reference 2.) It seemed that now we had both the software and hardware to realize these visions.

From these ruminations grew the design and implementation of a system called TRIP, which attempted to give students an intuitive understanding of algebra word problems through the manipulation of high-resolution pictures. (See reference 3.) TRIP, implemented in the Smalltalk-76 system (see reference 4) on research hardware, a Xerox Alto, took about two months to design and four months to implement. It was structured in the form of a kit so that

In the Rehearsal World, only things that can be seen can be manipulated

teachers could add new time-rate-distance problems fairly easily; it included a diagram checker, an animation package, an expression evaluator, and an extensive help system. Members of the computing profession were impressed that we were able to bring to life such a complex, general, graphical, yet robust and helpful system in such a short time. Educators, however, were usually aghast that so much time and effort were needed to produce a single system and that the result was, in their view, so limited.

After we had pilot-tested TRIP and were thinking about what project to take on next, we realized that our interest had shifted up one level, from the actual design of educational software to the design of a "design environment" for educators. As our colleagues were busy building the Smalltalk-80 environment (see references 5, 6, 7, and 8), we undertook the task of extending and reifying that environment to allow curriculum designers who did not program to implement their own creative ideas.

DESIGNER CONTROL

The work described here is based on the belief that it should be possible to place the control of interactive computer graphics in the hands of creative curriculum designers, those with an understanding of the power of such systems but not necessarily with the ability or willingness to write the complex programs that are necessary to control the systems.

Design and implementation constitute two phases of a feedback loop. In most design situations, in which programming is a separate and specialized skill, the designer must somehow convey embryonic ideas to a programmer, perhaps by sketching on paper or talking. Then the programmer goes away to write a program so that something shows on the screen to which the designer can respond. This process introduces inter-

ruption, distortion, and delay of creative design.

In the creation of educational software it is particularly important that the design decisions be made by someone who understands how students learn and what they enjoy rather than by someone whose expertise is in how computers work. Too much of the educational software we see today has a lot of fancy graphics but little real learning content. We hope that if educators have more direct control of the computer, they will create high-quality software.

In the environment we describe here, the designer begins by sketching the description, not in words or on paper, but directly on the computer screen. This sketching is not free-form but is done with the aid of specially provided graphical entities. If the designer's ideas are rather vague, the process of sketching may help to define them; if the ideas are well defined, they can be quickly accepted, rejected, or improved. In either case, nothing is lost in the translation process, as the only intermediary between the designer and the product is a helpful, graphical computer system that gives immediate response. Since there is no waiting, the designer is involved in a collaborative, creative process in which there is minimal investment in the current production; thus a poor production can be rejected quickly and easily, and a good one pursued and improved.

THE REHEARSAL METAPHOR

A large, supportive design environment needs a potent metaphor in which the unfamiliar concepts of programming will have familiar, real-world referents. Our goal was that the metaphor would serve as a guide to the designers without getting in their way.

Smalltalk is an object-oriented language. This means that all the basic elements of programming—strings, numbers, complex data structures, control structures, and procedures themselves—are treated as objects. Objects interact with other objects by sending messages. Logo is an example of a programming language with one object, a Turtle, which can be sent a limited number of messages such as FORWARD 20. Smalltalk has many kinds of objects that respond to a wide variety of messages.

Our immersion in Smalltalk led us to

extend the object-message metaphor to a theater metaphor in which the basic components of a production are performers; these performers interact with one another on a stage by sending cues. We call the design environment the Rehearsal World and the process of creating a production Programming by Rehearsal.

Everything in the Rehearsal World is visible; there are no abstractions and only things that can be seen can be manipulated. Almost all of the designer's interactions with the Rehearsal World are through the selection (with a mouse) of some performer or of some cue to a performer. Assuming that a designer has the germ of an idea, the creation of a Rehearsal World production involves:

• Auditioning the available performers by selecting their cues and observing their responses to determine which are appropriate for the planned production. If a production involves getting the student to write stories using pictures, the designer might choose a text performer and a picture performer because the former responds to the cues *setText:* and *readFromKeyboard* and the latter responds to *growBy:* and *followTheMouse*.
• Copying the chosen performers and placing them on a stage.
• Blocking the production by resizing and moving the performers until they are the desired size and in the desired place.
• Rehearsing the production by showing each performer what actions it should take in response either to student (user) input or to cues sent by other performers.
• Storing the production away for later retrieval.

A SCENARIO

Static words and pictures on paper are a poor substitute for direct experience with a dynamic, interactive, computer design environment. Nevertheless, we shall try to give the flavor of what it is like to use the Rehearsal World through a simple scenario involving two novice designers, Laura and Bill. Suppose that these designers are interested in language curriculum and would like to

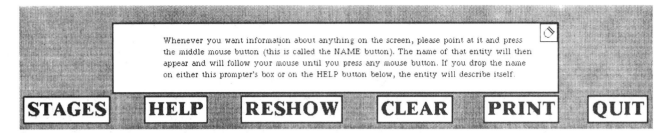

Figure 1: *The control panel and the prompter's box, showing an initial help message. The icon in the corner is an eraser.*

make some sort of word game. We'll follow their efforts, skimming over many of the details of their interactions with the Rehearsal World, with an eye to understanding some of the design decisions of Programming by Rehearsal itself. Although one person can manage both mouse and keyboard quite well, we'll assume that Laura is in charge of the mouse and Bill is typing on the keyboard. In what follows, the paragraphs describing the action of the designers have been italicized.

Bill and Laura know from their brief introduction to the Rehearsal World that all of the performers are clustered together in troupes waiting to be auditioned for parts in a production. They know also that the Rehearsal World includes a help facility that gives assistance and descriptive information about how to proceed.

Laura starts by selecting the HELP button from the control panel at the bottom of the screen (see figure 1). Selection of the HELP button causes the "prompter's box" to fill immediately with "procedural help" suggesting something that the designers might want to do next. When they select HELP initially, the procedural help message that appears explains that they can always obtain "descriptive help" about anything that they can see on the screen.

The fact that everything that can be seen is capable of self-description is an important component of the Rehearsal World and one that makes it accessible to nonprogrammers.

When they ask for descriptive help about the STAGES button, they learn that if they select the STAGES button, they will get a menu of troupes and productions. Laura selects the STAGES button which presents her with a menu of troupes and productions (see figure 2).

She finds a Text performer in the Basic Troupe that she wants to audition to learn what it can do. Laura starts by asking it to describe itself and is told by the help system that if she selects the Text performer, she can edit the text that it displays. This editing is the default action of the Text performer. Laura and Bill spend a minute becoming familiar with the simple editor that the Text performer provides.

The Rehearsal World uses a three-button mouse for pointing at things on the screen. The SELECT mouse button causes a performer to execute its default action. The NAME button always causes the name of the entity to appear at the cursor point; if this name is dropped in the prompter's box, a description of the entity appears. Finally, the MENU button raises a pop-up menu for the performer, enabling the designer to send cues to it. In interacting with a finished production, only the SELECT button is used; that is, the NAME and MENU buttons are not needed by the student user.

Laura uses the MENU mouse button to see the category menu for the Text performer (see figure 3). Certain commonly used cues are at the top of this menu in lowercase, while others are grouped under categories in uppercase. Most of the cues and categories are shared by all performers. Only the

(text continued on page 192)

PROGRAMMING BY REHEARSAL

Figure 2: *The entire Rehearsal World theater, showing the STAGES menu at the left, all the available Troupes, and a descriptive help message about the BasicTroupe.*

Figure 3: A BasicTroupe, containing a Text, a Number and a Counter, and a category menu for the Text performer.

categories at the bottom of the menu (in bold) are particular to the Text performer.

In its current prototype form, the Rehearsal World contains 18 primitive performers, each of which responds to a standard set of 53 cues and an average of 15 cues particular to that performer. To understand what this means, imagine a BASIC with a thousand reserved words. This complexity would be intolerable without a hierarchical organization and a simple way for the designer to browse that organization. The Smalltalk-80 system provides a window, called a Browser (see figure 4), whose visual structure reflects the hierarchical organization of the objects and methods in the system. In the Rehearsal World, functionality is organized around performers grouped together into troupes; the cues that each performer understands are grouped into categories. The result is that designers never have to scan too much information at a time, and, because each level in the hierarchy has a different screen appearance, they never lose track of where they are in that hierarchy.

Our novice designers proceed to rehearse the Text performer by sending it various cues. Laura tries move and resize and gets a pleasant surprise when the fonts change so that the text always fits within the performer's borders. She selects the SET category and gets a cue sheet showing the list of cues that have

to do with setting text (see figure 5). Some cues, like setText:, take parameters that are indicated by parameter lines next to the cue. They use the help system to discover that they can type any string as a parameter to the setText: cue. Bill types 'goodbye' on the parameter line. When Laura selects the cue, "goodbye" appears in the Text performer.

They discover through rehearsal that the setJumbled cue produces a random permutation of the characters in the text. They enjoy looking at the different bizarre configurations that jumbling a word can produce and decide to explore no more, but to make a jumble game as their first design exercise. As often happens, interaction with the design environment itself leads to a creative idea.

One would not expect jumbling of text to be a basic capability of a programming language. A programmer who encountered a need for such a function would expect to write a simple routine. In a design environment, however, we expect to find a great deal of high-level functionality, chosen with care by the implementors of the environment, so that the designer's attention is not diverted from the design task itself.

Laura and Bill's initial idea for their simple production is to use two Text performers, one to be placed above the

other on the stage. The top Text is to contain the word to be jumbled and the bottom one is to act as a soft button (a button on the screen which, when the student selects it with the mouse, causes something to occur). In this case its action will be to cause the jumbling of the top Text (see figure 6). Laura uses the copy cue to put a Text performer on an empty stage.

Any existing performer can be copied. Thus each performer acts as a prototype from which other performers can be generated; each new copy will have exactly the same characteristics as its prototype.

Laura and Bill use the resize cue to make the Text performer fill most of the top half of the stage, and then they copy it to make a second Text performer (exactly the same size as the first) in the bottom half of the stage. Bill types the word JUMBLE into it, as this is what they want the user to see. With the blocking thus completed, they decide to give each of their performers a mnemonic name that describes its purpose; they call the performers JumbledWord and JumbleButton. Now they are ready to define the action of the bottom Text, which they want to act as a button.

Any performer can become a button. By turning a performer into a button,

(text continued on page 194)

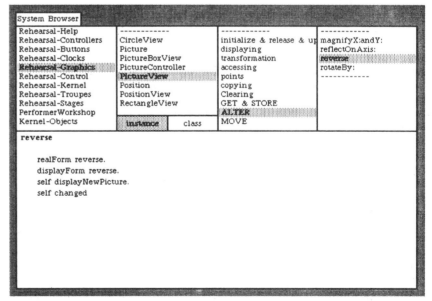

Figure 4: A Smalltalk browser showing the **Rehearsal-Graphics** category, the **Picture-View** class, its **ALTER** category, the message named reverse from that category, and the method associated with that message.

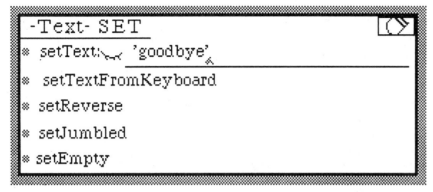

Figure 5: *A cue sheet for the* SET *category of a* Text *performer. The string 'goodbye' has been typed on the parameter line of its first cue.*

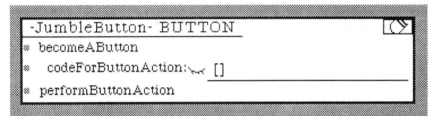

Figure 7: *The cue sheet for the* BUTTON *category of the performer named* JumbleButton. *The square brackets on the parameter line indicate that the designer should write some code between them.*

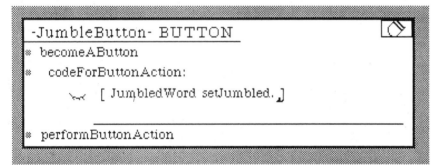

Figure 8: *The code, written by watching, which indicates what the* JumbleButton *should do whenever it is selected by the user.*

Figure 6: *A stage containing two* Text *performers, the top one showing a jumbled word and the bottom one acting as a button which the user can select to cause the jumbling to occur.*

indicate that the system is indeed watching. Then Laura sends the *setJumbled* cue to the *JumbledWord* by selecting it. The code *JumbledWord setJumbled* appears within the square brackets of the *codeForButtonAction:||* cue of the *Jumble-Button*, and the eye closes again (see figure 8).

Two significant obstacles to learning a programming language are mastering the language's syntax and learning the vocabulary. In the Rehearsal World, the designers rarely have to know either the syntax or the vocabulary as most writing of code is done by watching. While the eye is open, the designers rehearse a performer and the system makes a record of this rehearsal. The Rehearsal World's ability to watch, in combination with a mouse-driven interface, means that the designers do remarkably little typing. The designers know whether or not the code is correct not so much by reading it but by observing whether the effect produced on the stage is the desired one.

Immediately after Laura sends the codeForButtonAction:|| cue, she can select the newly defined button to see if it behaves as expected. Each time she selects the **JumbleButton**, *it flashes and the* **JumbledWord** *jumbles its text.*

In a traditional programming environment, the programmer moves back and forth between programming mode, in

---

the designers get to decide what will happen when the user selects that performer. One of the categories on every category menu is BUTTON; its cue sheet contains the cue *becomeAButton* (see figure 7).

After Laura sends the becomeAButton is cue to the **JumbleButton**, *it no longer responds to selection by providing an editor; instead, it simply flashes. It is now a soft button on the screen, but it has no action. They must show it what to do.*

They do this by using the cue codeFor- ButtonAction:|| *to which every performer responds. Bill and Laura understand that they are expected to provide a block of code between the square brackets to describe the action that should occur when the user selects* **JumbleButton**. *The action they want is very simple; they just want the* **Jumbled-Word** *to receive the setJumbled cue. Bill knows that he does not have to type the code; instead the Rehearsal World will "watch" while they show it what to do.*

To the left of each parameter line is a tiny icon representing a closed eye. When Laura selects it, the eye opens to

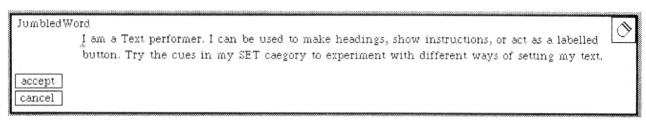

(9a)

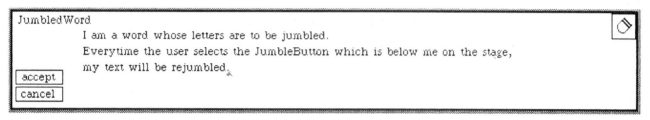

(9b)

Figure 9: *The default comment associated with every Text performer (9a) and the edited comment to be associated only with the performer named* JumbledWord (9b).

which typing code is the dominant activity, and running mode, in which testing takes place. In Programming by Rehearsal, the designer does not feel any shift from one mode to another.

Even though their production is very simple, Laura and Bill decide to document it. They have already given the two Text performers appropriate names: JumbledWord *and* JumbleButtton. *They use the help system to get the default comment for the* JumbledWord *and edit it to be more specific (see figure 9).*

As a designer creates new productions and new performers, the Rehearsal World becomes more complex. The default descriptive help messages can be changed by the designer by simply editing what appears in the prompter's box and selecting the ACCEPT button. This provides a quick and pleasant method for providing descriptive comments for productions, performers, and cues.

It takes our two designers less time to produce their first jumble game than it takes to read about it. Although they have some ideas about how to make the game more interesting and educationally worthwhile, they decide to store what they have implemented so far. It is the stage itself that must be instructed to do the storing. The stage has its own category menu and one of its categories is STORE. They store their efforts under the name Jumble1 *(see figure 10).*

No fixed set of functions provided in a design environment will ever be satisfactory; the designers will always run up against the limits of that set and wish for more capabilities. The fact that stages understand cues suggests one of the mechanisms for extensibility in the Rehearsal World: every stage can be

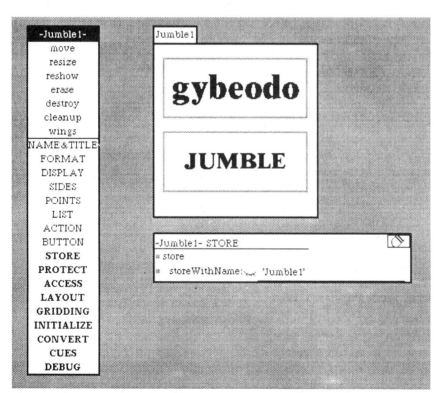

Figure 10: *A stage named* Jumble1; *it's a category menu and cue sheet for its* STORE *category.*

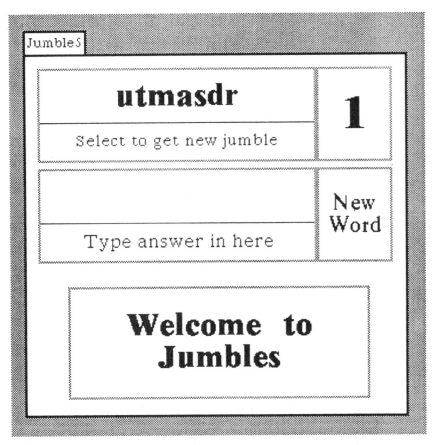

Figure 11: *An improved game named* Jumble5, *which evolved from* Jumble1.

converted into a new performer and every stage can be taught new cues. A designer who needs a new kind of performer can construct one by aggregating existing performers on a stage, teaching that stage some appropriate new cues, and converting the result into a new performer.

There are many circumstances in which the designers may wish to aggregate performers: several performers belong together as a logical and spatial unit; a group of performers are to be used repeatedly within a production or in several different productions; a production is very complex, and creating a new performer allows a factorization of the entire problem into smaller ones.

Bill and Laura's jumble game goes through four revisions until it finally becomes the one shown in figure 11. This improved game contains four Text performers and a Number performer. The large Text at the bottom is used simply to give feedback to the student.

The Text labeled "New Word" has been turned into a button; its button action is to cause a new secret word to be chosen from a List and presented in jumbled form in the top Text performer. This performer has also been turned into a button; its button action is to rejumble itself. The number of rejumblings is shown by the Number performer next to it. The Text performer in the center of the stage is to be edited by the student who will type the answer there. Every time that Text is changed, it will cause the answer to be checked against the secret word and suitable feedback to be provided. It does this by means of its change action.

When a performer changes in some fundamental way, as when a Number performer changes its value or a Text performer changes its text, it executes its change action. The default change action of a performer is to do nothing, but the designer can define this action for any performer. Certain other performers have additional possible ac-

tions: the Repeater performer has a repeat action, the List performer has a selection action, and the Traveler performer has a move action.

In the Jumble5 game, Laura and Bill use a List performer to keep a list of secret words. Since they don't want the user to see the List, they place it in the wings (see figure 12).

While everything should be visible to the designers, not everything should be visible to the user of the production. Wings can hold performers waiting to appear on stage, data structures like the List of secret words, or temporary variables used in computations.

A very simple game grew and prospered as our designers implemented it, changing in response to their new understanding of what they were doing, and to the needs and interests of users and other designers who experimented with it. It became something real that people wish to play with and from which they can get some increased intuitive understanding of the rules underlying English orthography.

BENEATH THE REHEARSAL WORLD — THROUGH THE TRAPDOOR

The Rehearsal World in some ways may be thought of as a visible Smalltalk. Although our original intention was to remove the need for programming at the Smalltalk level, it is paradoxically true that the Rehearsal World provides an excellent entry point for an incipient Smalltalk programmer. Designers may drop through the trapdoor of the Rehearsal World; beneath they will find all the tools of the Smalltalk-80 programming environment. A Rehearsal World tool found there is called the Performer Workshop. It looks like a simplified Smalltalk browser and provides a mid-level mechanism for creating new primitive performers and defining new cues.

For each kind of performer there is a corresponding Smalltalk class that is a subclass of class **Performer**. The inheritance mechanism of Smalltalk allows the subclass to inherit the message interface of class **Performer**. Each production corresponds to a subclass of class **Stage**. When designers store a production, the Rehearsal World defines a new subclass of class **Stage**. Interestingly, a stage is so much like a performer that class **Stage** is actually a subclass of class **Performer**.

When designers create new performers, the Rehearsal World defines a new subclass of **Performer** and writes the code for the appropriate additional methods that the class will need for layout and for cues. Because the code written by the Rehearsal World is indistinguishable from code written by a programmer, one can inspect it and modify it in either a Performer Workshop or a Smalltalk browser (see figure 4).

There are two important features of Smalltalk that are not present in the Rehearsal World. The first is the ability to create a hierarchy of objects. In Smalltalk, when one constructs a new kind of object—that is, a class—one usually con-

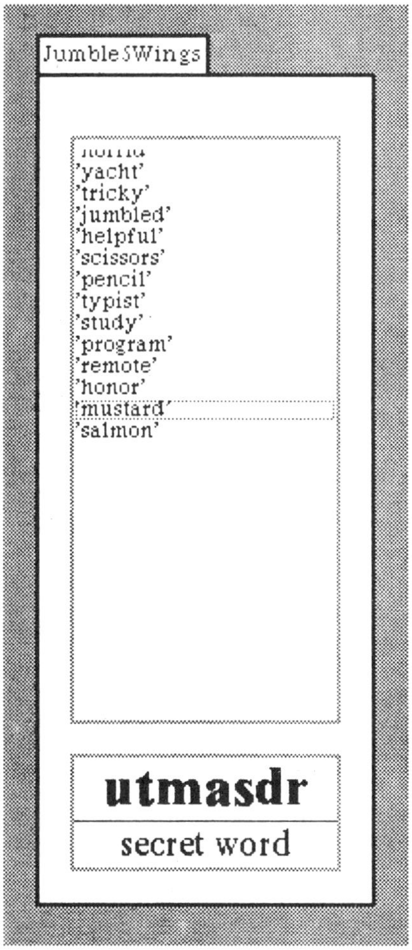

Figure 12: *The wings of the* **Jumble5** *game, showing a List performer in which the current secret word is selected.*

structs it by defining a subclass of the existing class that is most like the new class. In that way the new class can inherit a great deal of the desired behavior. In the Rehearsal World, there is no concept of class. A designer who wants a new production that is similar to an existing one can modify the existing production and store it under a different name. A major weakness of this method is that modifications made to the first production will not be automatically reflected in the modified one. In contrast, a modification made to a Smalltalk class will be automatically reflected in its subclasses.

The second difference between Smalltalk and the Rehearsal World is that in Smalltalk there is a distinction between a class and an instance of that class. The class is the abstraction; an object is always an instance of some class. A class may have any number of instances. Any changes to the class will be immediately reflected in all its instances. In the Rehearsal World, there are no abstractions, thus no classes. Everything is visible. Any performer can serve as a prototype and one gets new performers through copying. What is lost is the ability to have changes made to the original reflected automatically in the copies.

DEBUGGING

Ordinarily, the sooner a program gives evidence that something is wrong, the easier it is for the programmer to diagnose the problem. Designers in the Rehearsal World find that bugs manifest themselves very quickly because nearly all state information is visible and because the flow of control from performer to performer is fairly obvious to the eye. Even so, a situation will occasionally arise in which the designer cannot easily account for some behavior on a stage.

It seems appropriate in Programming by Rehearsal that help should come in the form of another performer, the Debugger performer (see figure 13). A Debugger, when placed on a stage, intercepts all the actions that performers execute, shows their code, and waits for the designer to tell it to go on. While the actions of the production are thus halted, the designers can investigate the cause of a problem using any of the normal Rehearsal World activities such as

opening up cue sheets and sending cues. Additional actions that may be initiated are placed in the Debugger's queue for later execution.

ANIMATION AND MULTIPLE PROCESSES

An intuitively pleasing, though incorrect, model for the Rehearsal World would be that each performer goes about its business independently of the others except when it needs another performer to answer a question or do something. Performers would be like people in the real world, capable of independent action but interacting through requests. Animation, you might think, would be easy because each performer would have its own rules for moving around on the screen. In this model, which we call the one-process-per-performer model, each performer would essentially have its own processor for its private use. Trouble comes when performers have to share resources and coordinate that sharing. Several schemes for dealing with these problems have been developed over the years.

Our own solution to the problems introduced by having one process per performer was to allow each user action to initiate a single independent process that either runs to completion or, as with animation, continues in an infinite loop. A single production can, at any given time, have any number of different processes running in it. (Beyond that, there can be several stages on the screen at a time, each running its own processes.) This one-process-per-user-action model has so far proven to be both intuitive and powerful, though we see it as an area where further research is necessary.

DESIGNERS AT WORK

Since the Rehearsal World is a prototype system, very few designers have had a chance to experiment with it. The first one to actually use the system was Joan Ross, a curriculum designer from the University of Michigan. Joan created many interesting productions using the Picture and Turtle performers. She helped us to debug the system and to understand how to improve it on all levels as we prepared for a pilot study.

We spent a month responding to the

issues that Joan raised as a result of her experiences and then invited Dan Fendel and Diane Resek, curriculum designers and faculty members of the Mathematics Department at San Francisco State University, to visit for three days to see what they could create in the Rehearsal World. They are very experienced designers, familiar with the power of interactive computer graphics, but they are not programmers.

We gave them a tour of the system and within 45 minutes Dan and Diane had taken over and were using the Rehearsal World themselves. They started by investigating a simple production we had made about probability and soon

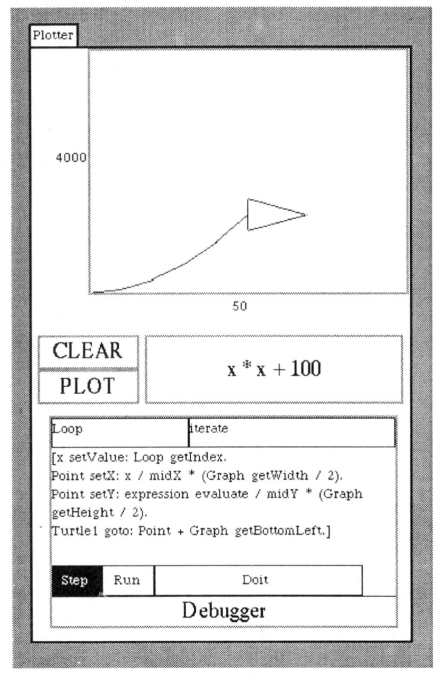

CLEAR
PLOT

$$x * x + 100$$

Loop	iterate

```
[x setValue: Loop getIndex.
Point setX: x / midX * (Graph getWidth / 2).
Point setY: expression evaluate / midY * (Graph
getHeight / 2).
Turtle1 goto: Point + Graph getBottomLeft.]
```

Step	Run	Doit

Debugger

Figure 13: *A stage on which a Debugger performer has been placed temporarily so that the designer may observe the code for each successive action.*

suggested and implemented some improvements. They found out how it worked by looking at the button actions and change actions of the performers, both on stage and in the wings. By the end of the first afternoon, they had turned it into a game that bore only a slight resemblance to our original exploratory activity. In the process, they had auditioned Texts, Numbers, Lists, and Repeaters to discover their capabilities, dealt some with the blocking of the stage, written a fair amount of code by watching, and understood about button actions, change actions, and repeat actions.

Dan and Diane spent an hour the next morning away from the machine, designing with words and a pencil. In the course of this design session, they refined their embryonic ideas for a fraction game through discussion of both the pedagogical issues and the fantasy through which they should be transmitted. They also considered which Rehearsal World performers they would need in their proposed game. The fantasy involved a cave filled with gold dust. They envisioned the ceiling of the cave as an irregular set of stalactites; they saw the floor as tiled. The student's problem would be to sweep a vertical broom through this cave, one floor tile at a time, trying to collect as much gold dust as possible without ever allowing the broom to touch the ceiling. The broom would stretch or shrink by a certain fractional amount which the student would specify before each move. For example, if the student edited the fraction to read 2/1, the broom would become twice as tall when it moved.

They had other design criteria as well. They wanted the game to configure itself differently every time the START button was selected, and they also wanted to make it easy for a designer to specify an easy cave, with broad floor tiles and very little variation in the ceiling, or a hard one. They wanted to have a score that was expressed as a percentage of the available gold dust; they wanted some sort of disaster to occur if the student made the fraction too large and the broom touched the ceiling. They decided to call their production GoldRush (see figure 14).

We found this description quite overwhelming for an initial project, as we

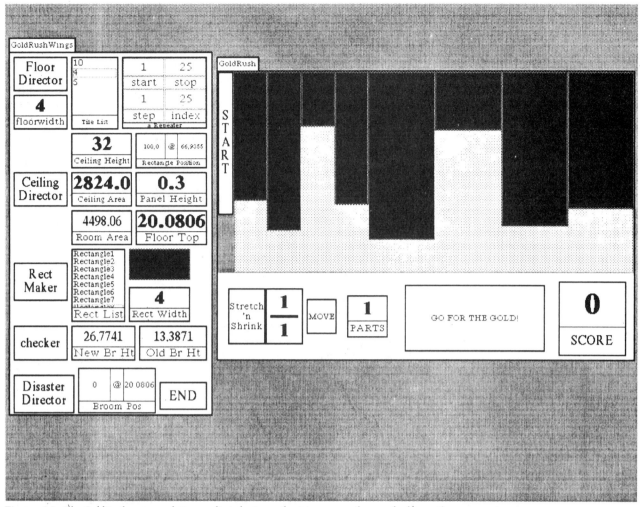

Figure 14: The GoldRush game and its complicated wings, showing more performers backstage than are on stage.

had expected them to embark on something at the level of the Jumble Game described earlier. Rather than starting with a toy example for practice, they were embarking on a real-world task after only one day's experience. We worried that they had chosen something too difficult for them to accomplish in the remaining two days.

By lunch time they had figured out how to use the Turtle to draw the floor. They said, "We need a Floor Director to be in charge of drawing the floor," and placed a button in the wings labeled FloorDirector for that purpose. They used this same strategy to make a CeilingDirector, a Checker to test whether or not the broom was touching the ceiling, and a DisasterDirector in charge of what should happen when it did. Certain performers had become, if you will, visible procedures. They invented this strategy on their own, led to it by the Rehearsal World's emphasis on buttons.

Next to these directors in the wings,

they placed the performers that would be needed by the directors to accomplish their tasks. These performers fulfil the role of variables; since everything in the Rehearsal World must be visible, all variables must be represented by performers. By grouping their performers in a logical manner, they could debug their program easily by selecting a button, like the CeilingDirector, and simply watching what happened, both on stage and in the wings.

Their next task was to implement the broom (for which they used a Rectangle), the START button, and the MOVE button. The action of the START button was simply to cause the FloorDirector and the CeilingDirector to perform their button actions. The action of the MOVE button was first to move the broom and then to ask the Checker to determine whether or not the broom was touching the ceiling. If it was, it asked the DisasterDirector to perform its action; if it wasn't, the Checker computed the score. That they had not yet

even designed the disaster didn't matter; they were using top-down programming techniques, realizing that they could return later and replace the empty code block of the DisasterDirector with whatever they wanted.

By the end of the day, the FloorDirector and the CeilingDirector were both working properly and they could move the broom through the cave. They started to plan the randomness that they wanted to build into the button action of the START button.

The next day they made a fraction to be edited by the user, creating it from two Numbers and two Rectangles, one to act as the line between the Numbers, the other to act as a frame. This looked and worked fine, but they soon discovered that it was a great disadvantage to be dealing with four independent performers instead of a single unified one: whenever they decided that their fraction was the wrong size or in the wrong place, they had to resize or move four performers commensurately.

Consequently they felt the need to create a new Fraction performer, which they did by placing two Numbers and a Rectangle for the central line on an otherwise empty stage. Since other performers would need to use the values of the numerator and denominator of this Fraction performer, they taught this stage the new cues *getNumerator*, *getDenominator*, and *getValue*. Then they told it to convert itself into a new performer named Fraction and promptly used it in their production.

By the end of the third day, they had a game that worked, that they could respond to, that they liked, and that still needed improvement.

An extra day of work was devoted to adding new features. A Number performer called Parts was added that could be edited by the user; its change action was to show the broom divided into the number of parts indicated. This additional piece of design arose from their interaction with the production; had they been working entirely from a paper sketch, this improvement might not have occurred to them.

They then invited others in our research center to play. Although it had been designed for third-graders, our colleagues found the game interesting and fun to play. They were impressed with the quality of the game and especially with the fact that the designers were nonprogrammers, yet had implemented something so complicated in only a few days.

Eventually we found some children of an appropriate age to be students; they also enjoyed playing the game and spent many hours trying to make a perfect score. Diane now plans to reimplement GoldRush at San Francisco State using the Rehearsal World design as a prototype but changing it to run on different hardware, which might include color and have a different pointing mechanism.

RESEARCH QUESTIONS

Our experiences with designers have given us confidence that our general ideas about how to make the power of computers accessible to nonprogrammers are correct. We believe that interactive, graphical programs could and should be built inside an interactive, graphical programming environment. We believe that for such programs, some sort of visual, spatial programming will eventually supplant the current process of writing lines of textual code. Nevertheless, we have many unanswered questions about the nature of visual programming.

An important aspect of the Rehearsal World is that everything is made visible; only things that can be seen can be manipulated. Thus, rather than thinking abstractly, as is necessary in most programming environments, a designer is always thinking concretely, selecting a particular performer, then a particular cue, then observing the cue's instant effect. We know that much of the initial accessibility of the system is due to this concrete, visual, object-oriented approach. What we don't know are its shortcomings.

As designers create increasingly large and sophisticated productions, they may find it a nuisance to have to instantiate everything (even temporary variables) in the form of a performer. There are problems with space on the screen and with visual complexity. Some of these problems are addressed by the ability to collapse a large set of performers into a single new one, which can be made very small while still retaining its original functionality. This helps not only with space but with factoring the production into significant pieces.

While beginning designers benefit from the concreteness, more experienced ones will benefit from being able to think in more general and abstract terms. They are led to think in general terms by the fact that all performers respond to a large set of common cues; they are led to think in abstract terms through the manipulation of Lists and Repeaters. Still, it may be difficult to build productions, for example, that need to access large amounts of data. At some point, the concreteness may become a barrier rather than an advantage.

We know that the "watching" facility is very important to beginners and makes it possible for them to "write" code without learning a language. But it's really very simple and is in no way "programming by example"; it employs no generalizations but merely makes a textual record of a performer being sent a cue, perhaps with parameters. Again, advanced designers might be led to think abstractly rather than specifically if the Rehearsal World provided a more powerful watching facility that was capable of some form of generalization.

In the Rehearsal World, button action and change action are the major mechanisms for expressing the interactions of all performers; a few performers, like the Repeater, the List, and the Traveler, have other special actions as well. Designers find these actions very natural and so far have had no difficulty describing their needs in these terms. However, the Rehearsal World does not provide designers with the facility to create new types of actions for new performers, and this may become a problem in the future.

The Rehearsal World supports multiple processes in such a natural way that our designers are not surprised by the existence of this facility as they interrupt whatever they're doing to do something else. However, we have little experience with designers using multiple processes in some production and expect a variety of conceptual and mechanical difficulties to arise.

Designers express actions in a procedural fashion, instructing a performer to send a cue under certain conditions. We are curious about how designers would deal with a constraint-based Rehearsal World in which the relationships between performers were expressed in terms of conditions that should always hold true (for example, that the value of a Number should always be twice that of another Number). We hope that researchers working on similar design environments will explore these questions. ■

REFERENCES
1. Brown, Dean, and Joan Lewis. "The Process of Conceptualization." Educational Policy Center Research Note EPRC-6747-9. SRI Project 6747. December, 1968.
2. Oettinger, Anthony, with Sema Marks. *Run, Computer, Run*. Cambridge, MA: Harvard University Press, 1969.
3. Gould, Laura, and William Finzer. "A Study of TRIP: A Computer System for Animating Time-Rate-Distance Problems." *International Journal of Man-Machine Studies* (1982) 17, 109–126.
4. Ingalls, Daniel H. H. "The Smalltalk-76 Programming System: Design and Implementation." *Conference Record of the Fifth Annual ACM Symposium on Principles of Programming Languages*. Tucson, AZ: 1978.
5. BYTE, August 1981.
6. Goldberg, Adele. *Smalltalk-80: The Interactive Programming Environment*. Reading, MA: Addison-Wesley, 1984.
7. Goldberg, Adele, and David Robson. *Smalltalk-80: The Language and its Implementation*. Reading, MA: Addison-Wesley, 1983.
8. Krasner, Glenn, ed. *Smalltalk-80, Bits of History, Words of Advice*. Reading, MA: Addison-Wesley, 1983.

PLAY

AN ICONIC PROGRAMMING SYSTEM
FOR CHILDREN

STEVEN L. TANIMOTO AND
MARCIA S. RUNYAN

1. Introduction

Children are commonly introduced to computers through games.
Games have been successful this way because they can reduce the amount
of expertise required to operate a computer to a few simple operations
(such as moving a joystick) while they provide sensory stimulation and
understandable goals.[5] However, games are usually very limited in the
kinds of interaction they encourage, and in the degree of intellectual challenge they offer children.

Another approach to getting young people involved with computers
is to teach them appropriate parts of a programming language such as
LOGO or BASIC. With the help of "turtle graphics," this approach has been
successful with children as young as six years.[6] Programming microworld
activities with LOGO can be even more effective than turtle graphics in some
situations.[4] These methods, however, also have important limitations.
Text-based programming languages require a relatively high degree of
sophistication with text, and in some cases they require intuition about
process and arithmetic, as well. These requirements pose an obstacle to
many children who nevertheless should be able to successfully interact with
computers in deep and meaningful ways. The Pict system[2] eliminated
dependence upon text; however, Pict limited the user to arithmetic and
list-structure operations, and these are unsuitable for young children. A
system that allowed drawings to control the dynamics of animation of
other drawings was the Genesis system[1]; this system provided relatively
little, however, to support longer sequences of animated events.

PLAY comprises a graphical language and an animation environment,
and it is designed to provide a means of easy, natural, and enjoyable communication between young people and computers. It combines the sensory
output and simplicity of games with some of the depth and richness of
programming languages, to provide for many children a more meaningful
experience than typical games can. In addition to its use of the iconic language, PLAY differs from the above-mentioned systems in being implemented on a popular microcomputer.

This paper describes the rationale behind the PLAY system, its design,
and the general features of its present implementation on an IBM PC.

We envision PLAY as part of an educational program divided into five
curricular levels. Level 1 would provide a very elementary facility for children to interact with a computer using a graphical mode of input and output. Levels 2 and 3 would provide additional steps in the conceptual lad-
der leading to level 4. In level 4 (which is the portion currently

STEVEN L. TANIMOTO and MARCIA S. RUNYAN • Department of Computer Science,
University of Washington, Seattle, Washington 98195.

implemented), the child has facilities at his/her disposal for creating pictorial "scripts" which describe stories, and for viewing performances based upon those scripts.

"PLAY" stands for "Pictorial Language for Animation by Youngsters." The PLAY system employs a drama metaphor (as does the "Programming by Rehearsal" system[3], which helps make the system understandable to parents and teachers as well as to children. There is a *stage* (an area of the screen in which the performances take place), and there are various backdrops and characters which can be designed and programmed to perform a play. The child becomes alternately a *playgoer* (watching a performance of a pre-programmed script), a *director* (adjusting certain aspects of a performance), and a *playwright* (composing a script, and/or designing characters and backgrounds).

Level 4, while a reasonably consistent and complete system itself, could be extended to produce a level-5 system which would include features by which the flow of program execution could be controlled. Having mastered level 4, in level 5 a child could begin to explore rich possibilities in *control* that are available in computer programming languages but not found in traditional plays. For example, loops, found in music (often indicated using a *repeat* sign) are seldom found in drama, yet they may add interest. Conditional branching in a play can allow a playgoer to alter the course of a play in midperformance or perhaps even throughout a performance. A child who has fully mastered level 5 of PLAY would be able to use the language to produce animated descriptions of simple computer algorithms or to produce a fully interactive computer game in which, for example, the playgoer controls one of the characters in a play, and all the other characters and the environment are programmed to react appropriately.

The following section describes the overall structure of PLAY levels 4 and 5.

2. System Overview

The PLAY system permits the user to watch animated productions (as a playgoer), adjust the performance (as a director), and compose plays (as a playwright). In the course of developing a script, the playwright may also create or edit character profiles and actions. In order to support these various activities, the PLAY system is divided into modules. Each module works with one or more kinds of PLAY data objects. Before we describe each of the modules, we describe these data objects. Both the modules and the types of data objects they manipulate are represented schematically in Figure 1.

2.1. Data Objects

There are three principal kinds of data objects in PLAY. They are:

1. The script, which gives the overall description of a story, telling who does what when;
2. Character profiles, which describe not only the appearance of characters in various positions, but also how they look in the course of performing various movements; and
3. Backgrounds (PLAYgrounds), which consist of large "mural" images.

Character profiles can describe inanimate objects as well as animate characters; thus they handle stage properties ("props") as well as the cast. Any character or prop is sometimes called a PLAYthing.

2.2. Program Modules

Whereas data objects can be edited and changed in order to have different animations, program modules are fixed in PLAY. There are four general kinds of program modules in PLAY. There are *animators,* which compute how various moving things should be displayed; there are *editors,* which help the playwright design his/her cast of characters and backgrounds and design his/her script. There is also an *interpreter* for the scripts, which controls the execution of performances, and there is a *dis-*

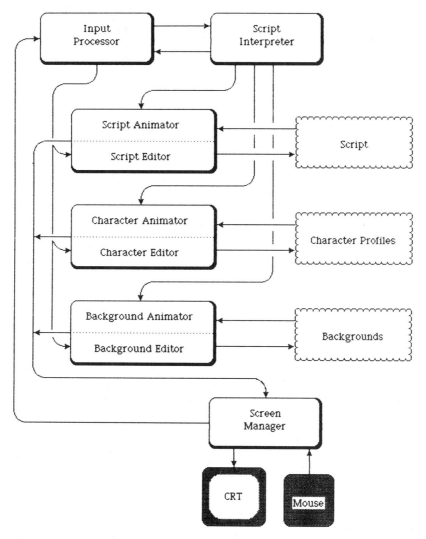

FIGURE 1. PLAY system structure showing program modules, the classes of data objects they manipulated, and the graphics devices.

play-screen manager, which keeps the various display areas in good order. Let us now describe the program modules in more detail.

The script animator (SA) determines how the script itself is to be displayed and moved on the screen as a performance or editing process progresses. It moves the script and highlights the currently important parts of it according to what the script interpreter is doing or what is being edited in the script editor. The SA sends commands to the screen manager; for example, it may tell the screen manager to shift the contents of the script window one cell to the left.

The script editor (SE) allows interactive design and modification of scripts. The script is organized as a horizontal sequence of "iconic sentences," each of which describes either some character doing something or a background change. The SE invokes the display of several menus:

1. A character menu, which contains a representative sample profile for each of the characters defined;
2. An action menu containing an icon for each of the defined actions; and
3. A menu of action modifiers, including eight directions, and appearance and disappearance commands.

An "insert" operation consists of two steps: (a) selecting the point in the script where the insertion is to be made, and (b) composing an iconic sentence by choosing items from the various menus to fill a template (e.g., character and action).

The character animator (CA) keeps track of the locations of characters on the stage and it computes their motions and appearances according to commands from the script interpreter. If the script interpreter processes an iconic sentence that has the meaning "Dragon breathes fire," then the script interpreter makes the CA retrieve pictorial information from the character profile of the dragon in order to show it breathing fire. An iconic sentence meaning "Jack walks left" would cause the character Jack to walk to the left for a fixed distance.

The character editor (CE) permits the user to draw images of the story characters and props, and it allows the design of the motions that those PLAYthings can undergo. The motions are associated with action icons. Standard actions include walking and jumping. A "default walk" is a short walk to the right. Other walks are specified by adding modifiers in the iconic sentence. A walking motion is typically effected by alternately displaying two character profiles in succession across the stage.

3. The Iconic Language

The language portion of the PLAY system is intended to provide a means of expression accessible to preliterate children. As a consequence, text must play at most a secondary role in the system. The iconic language itself does not involve text, although some of the icons in the system are almost as symbolic as text. Because of the avoidance of text, the language should appeal equally to children with different linguistic backgrounds, e.g., English, French, Chinese.

We make an assumption that dynamic ideas (such as a story, since it unfolds in time) are more easily created and edited if given a static, pictorial representation. In systems that require the user to program by demonstrating a sample execution (e.g., Ref. 8), it is difficult to modify the program because one cannot see but an execution snapshot at one time, and in order to find a particular place in the program, it may be necessary to wait through an execution from the start. Given that one wants a static representation, one may choose among such methodologies as flow-graphs, production rules, and constraints.[2] For PLAY, we chose a variation of flow-graph representation. A story is represented in PLAY in a comic-strip-like form. The story is divided into a sequence of events, each of which is described by a small picture. The pictures are necessarily stylized, since the playwright needs to be able to create them efficiently. A slightly more formal description of the iconic language is described in the next paragraph.

Expressions in the iconic language are used to describe animated stories. The largest structures in the languages are *scripts*. A script is a sequence of *iconic sentences*. An iconic sentence has one of two forms: (1) an action sentence, or (2) a background-loading command. An action sentence consists of three parts: (1) an icon designating a PLAYthing, (2) an icon designating an action, and (3) a modifier which normally specifies a direction. These three components of an action sentence are juxtaposed and placed in a box when the iconic sentence is formed by the playwright. The three components are shown in Figure 2. They form a stylized picture representing the event.

A background-loading command consists of a copy of the background icon, which appears in the main menu. (In a future implementation, we would like to have each background-loading command be an icon which is a miniature of the background image to be loaded. At present, the particular background image to be loaded is specified with a textual filename, typed by the playwright when the sentence is created, and subsequently hidden from view.)

FIGURE 2. An iconic sentence.

An action sentence describes an event in a story in which a PLAYthing appears, moves, or disappears. Looking at the visual display of an action sentence, one can see what PLAYthing is involved, what action is involved, and what the modifier is. There remain, however, some details of the event which are not explicitly displayed with the action sentence. These details are the following: (1) the sequence of frames used to produce the animation (these are specified in the character profile), and (2) the starting and ending points on the stage for the action (these are specified by the playwright when the iconic sentence is created, but are only seen when a performance takes place).

It would have been possible to make the language more flexible and to offer more ways of viewing iconic specifications. We did not do this for two reasons: (1) we wished to keep the system simple so that young children would be able to understand it, and (2) there was not adequate time to explore these possibilities.

4. A Sample Session

4.1. The PLAY Screen

During a session with PLAY, the screen of the computer is normally divided into four parts. This may be seen in Figure 3. At the top of the screen is the "script window," in which a portion of the current script is displayed. Below it is a menu (in iconic form) which may be used to enter various modes and during script editing and editing character profiles. Below that is the large window, the stage, in which animation is normally performed. The stage is also used during the editing of character profiles, and especially, the association of actions with characters. At the bottom of the screen are some icons for controlling the PLAY system. The extra space there is used for the display of certain error messages.

---

*It is a limitation of our prototype implementation that textual input is necessary in this function. We would like to have scripts themselves represented in the library by icons.

4.2. Performance

The new user can best find out what kinds of animations are possible in the PLAY system by adopting the role of a *playgoer*. An existing script may be loaded from the disk by first selecting the library icon, then selecting the script icon, and then typing a filename for the desired script.* Once a script is loaded, a performance may be started by selecting the "Take 1" icon at the bottom of the screen.

FIGURE 3. The normal display screen during a PLAY performance. The script can be seen at the top of the screen, and characters and a background are involved in a performance on the stage.

The performance proceeds in the stage window. Simultaneously, the script itself is animated in the script window; this animation consists of highlighting the currently active event and scrolling the script to the left to bring new portions onto the screen. When the end of the script is reached, the performance terminates and the PLAY system awaits another command from the user. While the performance is running, it can be interrupted by selecting the "Stop" icon. The execution can then be resumed by selecting the "Go" icon.

4.3. Designing Character Profiles

In order to have one's own story animated, it is necessary to develop not only the script but the images and actions for the characters and any other PLAYthings needed in the story.

To create a new character, edit an image of an existing character, or add an image for an existing character, the character-image editor is used. To begin, the user selects the "Character icon" from the main menu, and then a list of the defined characters is displayed (in the stage area) as a row of character images. Such a display may be seen in Figure 4. There is a special question-mark icon displayed to the right of the last character image, and the user selects it to enter character-definition mode (in order to define a new character). If the number of defined characters is more than ten, then they are not all shown on the stage at once, but may be called up using the double-arrow scrolling icon at the left side of the stage.

372

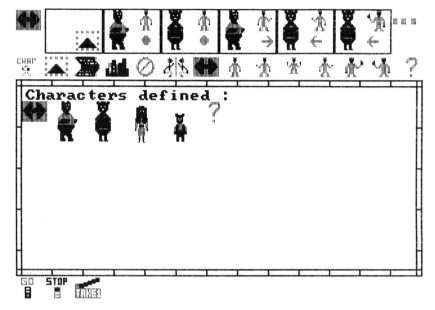

FIGURE 4. Display of the characters currently defined, with scrolling icon at the left and question-mark icon (for defining new characters) at the right. Here four characters have been defined.

If the user selects an existing character, a list of the profile images for the character is displayed, and the actions currently defined for the character are also displayed. If one of the profile images is then selected, the character-image editor is started, and the old screen contents are hidden. The character-image editor allows a 28-row by 24-column image to be drawn or modified. The image may use up to four colors, which are provided by one of the IBM PC color graphics adapter's palettes. The size of the rectangular paintbrush may be easily adjusted by the user. Images may be saved to and loaded from diskette files. During the drawing or editing, a blown up version of the image is displayed, as well as an actual-sized version (in the upper left corner of the screen). This is illustrated in Figure 5.

Once an adequate collection of images has been provided for a character, one may define a new action for the character. If an action icon already exists for the action, the user selects the question-mark icon which follows the list of actions defined for the character (i.e., the last icon in the

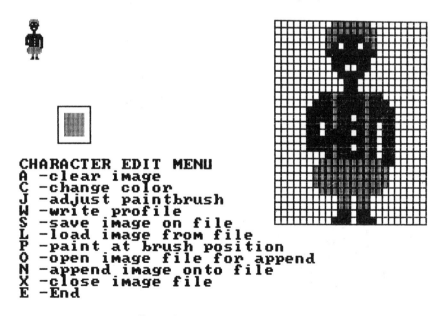

CHARACTER EDIT MENU
A -clear image
C -change color
J -adjust paintbrush
W -write profile
S -save image on file
L -load image from file
P -paint at brush position
O -open image file for append
N -append image onto file
X -close image file
E -End

FIGURE 5. The character-image editor.

stage area in Figure 4). It is also possible to define a new action icon, using an image editor similar to that for editing character-profile images (however, action icons are smaller than character images). After the action icon is selected, the manner in which the current character is to execute the action must be specified. The user does this by selecting a sequence of character images from those that have been drawn. A display of such a sequence is given in Figure 6. The character images in a sequence such as this are displayed successively in a series of cycles when the animation appears in a performance. At the same time, the position of the character is moved across the screen in accordance with information entered by the playwright when the iconic sentence is created.

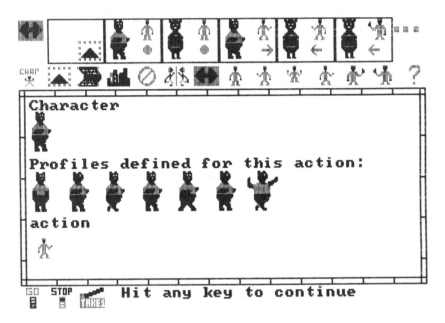

FIGURE 6. Display of the walking action for the "papa-bear" character.

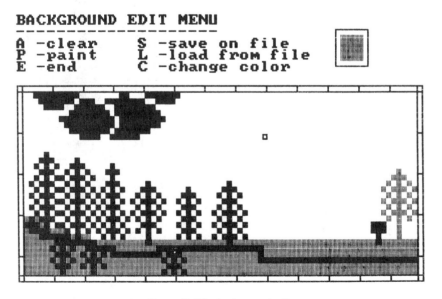

FIGURE 7. The background editor.

4.4. Designing Backgrounds

In order to create or modify backgrounds, the user selects the background-editor icon (which appears as a miniature mountain image). A rudimentary painting program is then called up which permits the user to draw or edit four-color images that have the same size as the stage. Background images must be stored as disk files, and like scripts, they are referred to using textual filenames (in the present version of PLAY). A sample screen from a background-editor session may be seen in Figure 7.

4.5. Writing a Script

In order to create or edit a script, the user (in the role of playwright) selects the script icon. The system responds by replacing the top-level menu with a sequence of direction symbols which are only needed in script mode. Let us describe the sequence of selections the playwright needs to make in order to create an iconic sentence and insert it into the current script. First, an insertion point is selected in the current script by pointing to the iconic sentence after which the new one is to be inserted. Next (unless a background-loading command is being created), a character is chosen for the sentence by pointing to one of the images that are displayed in the stage area. The user then selects either a direction icon from the menu underneath the script or an "appearance" or "disappearance" icon from the same menu. The "X" (disappearance icon) indicates that the character is to be removed from the stage, whereas the last icon in the menu (the appearance icon) signifies that the character is to be placed on the stage. If a direction icon has been selected, then the iconic sentence will denote a movement event. In this case, the playwright is prompted for starting and ending positions on the stage. The background may be loaded by the playwright to assist in positioning. After the starting and ending positions for the movement have been specified, the system displays the action icons that designate legal actions for the character that has been selected. The playwright selects one of these, and then the iconic sentence is complete.

The script is built up by adding iconic sentences in this manner, one at a time. Some of the iconic sentences may be background-loading ones, rather than action sentences. In order to specify a background-loading sentence, the playwright selects the background icon, and then the system prompts for the textual filename of a background image. The playwright types this information, and although hidden from view, it remains associated with the background-loading command in the script.

5. Summary, Discussion, and Future Work

5.1. Summary

A computer system that permits children to write and watch animated sequences has been described. Unlike commercially available software, our system called PLAY uses a pictorial language to represent the animation, and we feel that this is important if preliterate children are to use such systems, or if children speaking different languages are to use them. Additional details of the current PLAY level 4 implementation are described in Ref. 7.

5.2. Experience with PLAY

Several children have used PLAY. These children were introduced to PLAY by one of the authors (Runyan); for about 20 min, each child was shown animations and given guidance in operating the program. They were then encouraged to design a character of their own and to incorporate it into an existing script. Although time-consuming because of the details of drawing the many necessary images, children found it very satisfying to see their creations animated.

5.3. Future Work

There are many ways in which the present implementation of PLAY level 4 is limited. The speed of the system could be improved; currently implemented using the DeSmet C language compiler, additional speed could be achieved by coding more of PLAY in assembly language. More promising is the prospect of implementing PLAY on a system with a faster processor and better graphics.

The quality of animation in PLAY is adequate for telling a story. However, it is not aesthetically very pleasing. At present, character images are overlaid onto the background in such a way that an entire rectangle of the background is hidden, even if the character only occupies a fraction of that rectangular area. The speed at which animations take place is sometimes too fast and sometimes too slow. While it would not be difficult to provide the user a means for slowing down animated actions, additional processor speed or software efficiency would be necessary to speed up the slow sections.

The editing facilities for character images, other icons, and background images are complete in the sense that they allow any image to be created that is compatible with the rest of the system. However, their features are minimal, and it would be more convenient to have all of the features typically found in microcomputer painting programs. Additionally, a large library of characters, backdrops, scripts and various icons should be provided to stimulate children to develop interesting stories and remove some of the tedium of producing new images.

Our current implementation requires that scripts and backgrounds be referred to by MS-DOS filenames. For uniformity, as well as to avoid text for the reasons mentioned earlier, these files should be represented to the user by icons.

It would be useful to have additional display modes. For example, if the script is long, it would be convenient to be able to allocate the entire screen to it, especially when selecting an insertion point for a new event. It would also be nice to be able to test a character's action animations within the editor for character profiles, so that the details of actions could be adjusted without going back to the whole script each time.

As described in the introductory section, a system for PLAY level 5 would incorporate all the essential features of the present implementation, and would also include control-flow constructs and means of testing for conditions that would allow scripts to describe some simple computer algorithms. Such a system would make use of a more refined system of positioning objects on the stage, using a coordinate system, and would use a somewhat richer iconic language. PLAY-like systems may become arbitrarily sophisticated if the animations on the stage are to be done with three-dimensional graphics and realistic PLAYthings. Facilities for clearly representing and efficiently performing simultaneous animation of more than one character offer another challenge.

In spite of the limitations of our implementation, the response to PLAY has been sufficiently favorable that we feel additional work in this direction is justified.

Acknowledgment

This research was supported in part by NSF grant No. IST-8411831.

References

1. R. M. BAECKER, Interactive computer-mediated animation. Ph.D. thesis, Department of Electrical Engineering, Massachusetts Institute of Technology, Cambridge, Massachusetts, 1969.
2. E. P. GLINERT and S. L. TANIMOTO, Pict: An interactive graphical programming environment. *IEEE Comput.* **17** (11), 7–25 (1984).
3. L. GOULD and W. FINZER, Programming by rehearsal. *Byte* **9**(6), 187–210 (1984).
4. R. W. LAWLER, Designing computer-based microworlds. *Byte* **7**(8), 138–160 (1980).
5. T. W. MALONE, What makes things fun to learn: A study of intrinsically motivating computer games. Ph.D. dissertation, Department of Psychology, Stanford University, Palo Alto, California, 1980.
6. S. PAPERT, *Mindstorms: Children, Computers and Powerful Ideas,* Basic Books, New York, 1980.
7. M. S. RUNYAN, Unpublished Master's degree thesis. Department of Computer Science, University of Washington, Seattle, Washington, 1985.
8. D. C. SMITH, Pygmalion: A creative programming environment, Ph.D. thesis, Department of Computer Science, Stanford University, 1975.

Reprinted from *IEEE Computer Graphics and Applications*,
September 1987, pages 51-60. Copyright © 1987 by The Institute
of Electrical and Electronics Engineers, Inc. All rights reserved.

Creating Interaction Techniques by Demonstration

Brad A. Myers
University of Toronto*

When creating highly interactive, direct-manipulation interfaces, one of the most difficult design and implementation tasks is handling the mouse and other input devices. Peridot, a new user interface management system, addresses this problem by allowing the designer of the user interface to demonstrate how the input devices should be handled by giving an example of the interface in action. The designer uses sample values for parameters, and the system automatically infers the general operation and creates the code. After an interaction is specified, it can be executed immediately and edited. This promotes extremely rapid prototyping, since it is very easy to design, implement, and modify mouse-based interfaces.

Peridot also supports such additional input devices as touch tablets, as well as multiple input devices operating in parallel (for example, one in each hand) in a natural, easy-to-specify manner. All interaction techniques are implemented using *active values,* which are like variables except that the objects that depend on active values are updated immediately whenever they change. Active values are a straightforward and efficient mechanism for implementing dynamic interactions.

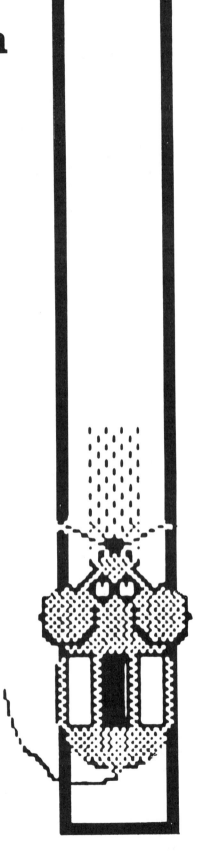

Peridot is an experimental user interface management system, or UIMS, that can create graphical, highly interactive user interfaces. A previous article[1] presented an overview of Peridot, concentrating on how the static displays (the presentation) of the user interfaces are created. This article describes how the dynamics of the user interface can be specified by demonstration. The full description of Peridot and the research that led to its development is also available.[2] Peridot, which

---

*The author is now with Carnegie Mellon University.

stands for programming by example for real-time interface design obviating typing, is implemented in Interlisp-D on a Xerox DandeTiger (1109) workstation.

The central approach of Peridot is to allow the designer of the user interface to design and implement direct-manipulation user interfaces[3,4] in a direct-manipulation manner. The designer need not do any programming in the conventional sense, since all commands and actions are given graphically. The general strategy of Peridot is to allow the designer to draw the screen display that the end user will see, and then to perform actions just as the end user would—for example, by moving a mouse, pressing its buttons, turning a knob, or toggling a switch. The results are immediately visible and executable on the screen and can be edited easily. The designer gives examples of typical values for parameters and actions, and Peridot automatically guesses (or infers) how they should be used in the general case.

Because any inferencing system will occasionally guess wrong, Peridot uses three strategies to ensure correct inferences. First, Peridot always asks the designer if guesses are correct. Second, the results of the inferences can be seen and executed immediately. Finally, the inferences can be undone if they are wrong. The interface can be edited easily, and the changes will be visible immediately. In addition, Peridot creates efficient code so that the final interface can be used in actual application programs.

As shown in a previous paper,[1] this technique allows the presentation aspects of the interface to be created by nonprogrammers in a very natural manner. Peridot may even be simple enough for end users to modify their user interfaces with. This article describes how these ideas have been extended to allow the dynamics of the interaction to be programmed by demonstration, which is harder because of the dynamic and temporal nature of the interactions.

To control the dynamics, all parts of the interaction that can change at runtime are attached to active values. These are like variables except that the associated picture is updated immediately when the value changes. Input devices and application programs can set active values at any time to modify the picture. Active values also form the link between the application program and the user interface.

Throughout this article the term "designer" is used for the person creating user interfaces (and therefore using Peridot). "User," or "end user," means the person using the interface created by the designer.

Background and related work

Because programming user interfaces is difficult and expensive, there has been a growing effort to create tools, called user interface management systems,[5-7] to help with the task. Many early (and some current) UIMSs require the designer to specify the interfaces in a textual, formal programming-style language. This procedure proved useful and appropriate for textual command languages[8] but difficult and clumsy for graphical, direct-manipulation interfaces,[9] and designers have been reluctant to use it.[10] Therefore, a number of UIMSs allow the designer to use more graphical styles. Examples include Menulay,[11] Trillium,[12] and GRINS.[13] These are, for the most part, still limited to using graphical techniques for specifying the placement of pieces of the picture and interaction techniques (for example, where menus are located and what type of light button to place where). Some systems, such as Squeak,[14] allow interaction techniques to be specified textually; but as far as we know, no previous system attempts to allow the dynamics of the actual input devices and the interaction techniques themselves to be programmed in a graphical, nontextual manner.

In trying a new approach to these problems, Peridot uses techniques from visual programming and example-based programming with plausible inferencing.[15] "Visual programming" refers to systems that allow the specification of programs using graphics. Some of these systems, such as Rehearsal World,[16] have succeeded in making programs more visible and understandable and therefore easier for novices to create.

Example-based programming systems allow the programmer to use examples of input and output data during programming. Some of these systems use "plausible inferencing," which means that they try to guess generalizations or explanations from specific examples.[17] Systems of this type are generally called "programming by example."[15] Some systems that allow the programmer to develop programs using specific examples do not use inferencing.[18-20] For example, SmallStar[18] allows users to write programs for the Xerox Star office workstation by simply performing the normal commands and adding control flow afterward. Peridot uses inferencing to try to make some of the complex parts of interface design automatic, such as specifying the control flow.

Another important component of Peridot is constraints, which are relationships among objects and data that must hold even when the objects are manipulated. Peridot uses two kinds of constraints. Graphical constraints, the kind used in ThingLab[21] and related systems,[22,23] relate one graphic object to another. Data constraints ensure that a graphical object has a particular relationship to a data value; these are used in the Process Visualization System,[24] which was influenced by "triggers" and "alerters" in database management systems.[25] They are also similar to the "control" values in GRINS[13] except that they are programmed by example instead of textually and can be executed immediately without waiting for compilation.

In Peridot, data constraints are associated with active values, which have been used in artificial intelligence simulation environments.[26,27]

IEEE CG&A

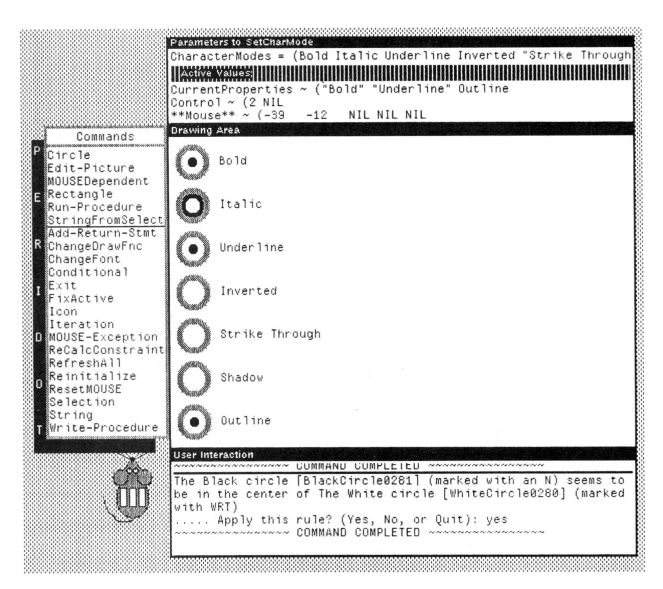

Figure 1. The three Peridot windows (the parameter window at the top is divided into two parts) and the Peridot command menu (left).

Peridot in action

A concrete example is the best way to demonstrate how easy creating a user interface is with Peridot. Space limitations require that some of the details be left out, but further explanations of the process appear in subsequent sections and in other articles.[1,2]

When creating a procedure by demonstration using Peridot, the designer first types in the parameters to the procedure, any active values needed, and an example of a typical value for each. Peridot then creates three windows and a menu and puts the parameters and active values in the upper window (see Figure 1). The menu, at the left, is used to give commands to Peridot. The window in the center shows what the user will see as a result

of this procedure (the end-user interface), and the window at the bottom is used for messages and prompts.

Figure 2 shows the steps for creating a scroll bar that displays both the part of a file that is visible in a window and the percentage of the file visible. First, in (a) the background graphics are created. In (b) the designer creates a grey bar that is as tall as the surrounding rectangle. This will be used to indicate that the entire file is visible, and the designer gives a Peridot command to have the height remembered. Then in (c) the designer makes the bar two pixels high and uses the same command to tell Peridot that this height is the other extreme. Peridot prompts for the active value that the height change should depend on (*ScrollPercent* in this case) and then asks the designer for the values that correspond to the two graphical extremes

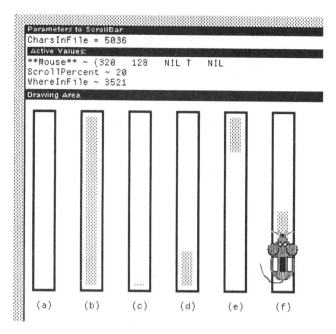

Figure 2. Steps during the creation of a scroll bar using Peridot. In (a) the background graphics have been created. The grey bar will represent percentage of file visible in the window. The two extremes of the full file (b) and none of the file (c) are demonstrated. The height of the bar will depend on the active value *ScrollPercent*, which ranges from 100 to 0. Next, two other extremes are demonstrated—the end of the file visible (d) and the beginning of the file visible (e). The active value *WhereInFile* controls this indicator. The designer then uses the simulated mouse (f) to demonstrate that the bar should follow the mouse when the middle button is down.

(here, 100 and 0). Peridot then automatically creates a linear interpolation that modifies the height of the bar on the basis of the value of *ScrollPercent*, as shown in (d). Similarly, the designer moves the grey box to the bottom of the bar (d) and then to the top (e) and specifies that this corresponds to the active value *WhereInFile* showing the position in the file. When asked, the designer specifies that *WhereInFile* varies from the value of the parameter *CharsInFile* down to 1. These two active values can then be set independently or at the same time by an application.

Next, the designer moves the simulated mouse (which represents the real mouse) over the grey box and presses the middle button (Figure 2f). Since the box has already been defined to move in *y* with an active value, Peridot infers that the mouse should control this action while its middle button is down. Of course, for this and all other inferences, the designer is queried to ensure that the guess is correct. If it is not, Peridot investigates other pos-

sibilities. When the mouse is used to update the graphics, the active values are also set and an application will be notified if appropriate. Now this piece of the interaction can be executed immediately with either the real or simulated mouse.

Overview

All UIMSs are restricted in the forms of user interface they can generate.[28] Peridot is aimed only at graphical, highly interactive interfaces that do not use the keyboard. It is clear, however, that Peridot will not be able to create every possible mouse-based type of interaction. Nevertheless, it does have sufficient coverage to create interfaces like those of the Apple Macintosh[29] as well as some entirely new interfaces, and it is much easier to create these interfaces using Peridot than with other existing methods.

Peridot tries to let the designer specify the input device actions mostly by demonstration. The goal is to let the designer simply move the devices the same way the end user would, and Peridot will create the code to handle the actions. For this to work, the system must infer how the specific actions on the example data should be generalized to handle any appropriate end-user data. In addition, exceptions and error cases must be handled.

An important consideration for any demonstrational system is how much should be done by demonstration and how much by conventional specification. It is usually much easier to implement the specification technique in UIMSs, and in some cases demonstration may actually be harder for the designer to use. This happens when the designer knows how the system should act and believes it would be much easier simply to specify the actions than laboriously demonstrate them. For example, to demonstrate by example whether an action should *toggle, set,* or *clear* a value, the designer must demonstrate the action twice. The first demonstration, over a set value, will cause the value to be cleared for the function *toggle,* stay set for *set,* and be cleared for *clear.* The second demonstration, over a cleared value, will cause the value to be set for the function *toggle,* be cleared for *set,* and stay cleared for *clear.* To specify which should happen, the designer need only choose *toggle, set,* or *clear,* which will probably be much quicker. In other cases, however, the number of possible choices is so large that it would be more difficult to use specification. This has been the case for most aspects of the presentation of user interfaces (the static pictures).[1]

To make Peridot as easy to use as possible, the specification method is allowed whenever there is a small number of easily delineated choices. Demonstration is considered the primary method, however, since it is more novel and difficult to provide, and thus more interesting in a research context. Demonstrational methods are more difficult for the dynamic interactions than for static pictures, since issues of *when* operations should happen are involved (not just *what* should hap-

IEEE CG&A

pen), and the ephemeral nature of the actions makes it harder to select the ones to which operations apply.

Active values

The key to easy specification of the way input devices are handled is to provide appropriate communication mechanisms between them and the graphics displays they manipulate. Peridot uses *active values* for this control, and they have proved powerful, efficient to implement, and easy for the designer to use. Active values are also used to connect the user interfaces with application programs.

Active values are like variables in that they can be accessed and set by any program or input device. They can have arbitrary values of any type. Whenever they are set, all objects that depend on them are immediately updated. The user interface designer can create as many active values as needed and give them arbitrary names. Typically, each part of the interface that can change at runtime will be controlled by an active value, as shown in Figure 2, where *ScrollPercent* and *WhereInFile* vary continuously in a specified range.

Different kinds of control using active values are shown in Figures 1 and 3. In Figure 1 the active value *CurrentProperties* contains a list of the names that are designated by a dot. In Figure 3 seven active values control a window that can scroll vertically or horizontally, move, or change size.

An important advantage of active values is that they allow the application to deal in its own units (0 to 100 and 1 to *CharsInFile* in Figure 2, and the string names of the font properties in Figure 1) and remain totally independent of how these values are represented graphically or how they are set by input devices. The graphics can be changed arbitrarily, and the application code is not affected.

Exceptional values

An important consideration is what to do when an active value is set outside its expected limits. This is obviously most important when the active value is set by an input device, but it can also have a hand in preventing application programs from setting values incorrectly. An application can supply a procedure that will support gridding and more complex types of semantic feedback (where the application must be involved in the inner feedback loop). Alternatively, one of Peridot's built-in range-checking routines can be used. The designer chooses what to do when the value is out of range:

1. Raise an error exception.
2. Peg the value to the nearest legal value (MIN or MAX).
3. Wrap the value around to the other extreme (MOD).
4. Allow the value to go outside the range.

Peridot lets the designer explicitly specify what happens

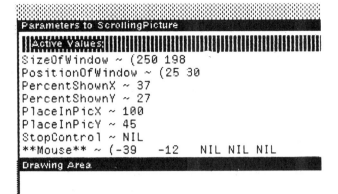

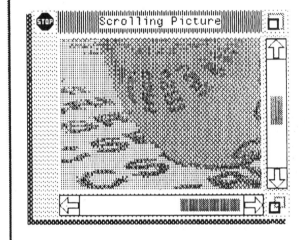

Figure 3. A complex interface created entirely by Peridot. The window can move or change size, and the picture can scroll either vertically or horizontally. This is controlled by seven active values. An application procedure is called to display the picture and calculate the percentage displayed in the window, but all other manipulations are handled by Peridot and were defined by demonstration.

(the default is "allow") and, in some cases, automatically infers the constraint.

Application notification

Another important consideration is when to notify an application program if an active value changes. This comes into play mainly when the value is changed by input devices, but an application procedure can also be used to tie certain active values together to provide semantic feedback. As an example, Figure 4 shows a graphical potentiometer for setting grey shades. The end user can move the diamond with the mouse. The position of the diamond and the number in the left box are tied directly to the active value *SliderValue* using linear interpolation, but the halftone representation of the cor-

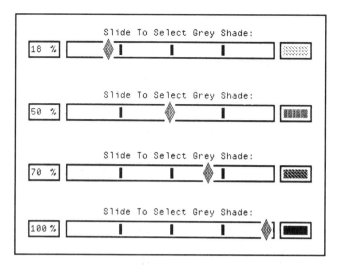

Figure 4. Multiple views of a graphical slider. The diamond and the numerical percentage (left) depend on one active value. The box on the right is shaded automatically on the basis of the halftone color calculated by an application procedure attached to the active value.

every increment during mouse tracking or other input device handling.

Peridot provides several options for when an application is notified:

1. Whenever the value is set (including when it is set to its existing value); this is useful as a trigger.
2. Whenever the value changes.
3. Whenever the value changes by more than some threshold.
4. When an interaction is complete (for example, when the mouse button is released after moving the diamond in Figure 4).
5. Never.

These choices are specified explicitly. The threshold choice (number 3) is useful for increasing efficiency (so that the application is not notified too often), and it is useful for controlling animations using the system-provided active value for the clock (for example, blinking or moving at a specific speed).

Application procedures attached to active values are also used to extend the operations that Peridot supports. If some kind of interaction or special effect is not provided, then a very short procedure can usually be written to perform the action by querying and setting active values.

The implementation of active values is very efficient[2] (the affected objects are computed at design time) and can be optimized for whatever operating system is in use. They do not require any complex constraint satisfaction techniques or much more computation than would be needed if the various actions were coded by hand.

Figure 5. The simulated mouse with its left button down is being used to program a menu of strings by demonstration. The black rectangle (now over *Copy*) will follow the mouse while the left button is held down.

responding grey shade is calculated using an application-provided procedure. The conversion function is called whenever the *SliderValue* value changes, so the color in the box on the right will always be correct.

Note that this allows the application program to have fine-grain control over the interface. Most other UIMSs provide only coarse-grain control, so they cannot handle this type of semantic feedback. The application can control feedback, default values, and error detection and recovery at a low level, and active values are efficient enough to allow application procedures to be called for

Input devices

Each input device is attached to its own active value. For example, the mouse has an active value called *Mouse*, which is a list of five items: the x position of the mouse, the y position, and a Boolean for each of the three buttons.* A button box would be represented as a set of Booleans—one for each button.

---

*Of course, some systems may provide more or fewer items for the mouse. The connection between the hardware devices and their active values is written in conventional Lisp code.

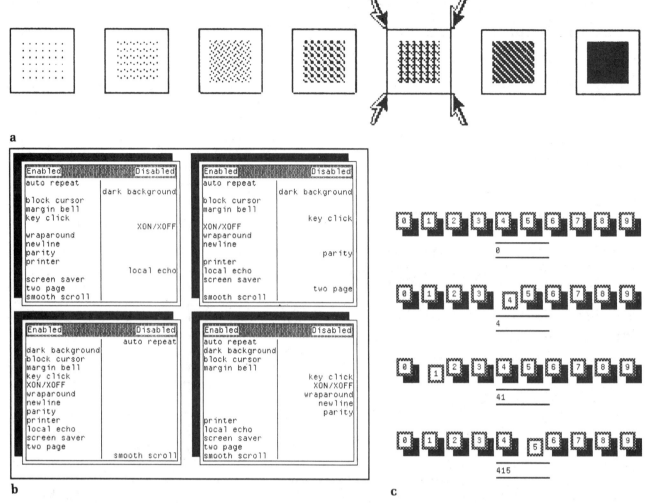

a

b

c

Figure 6. The response to the mouse action is limited only by the creativity of the designer. In (a) four arrows move with the mouse; in (b) text items move left and right; and in (c) number-pad buttons pretend to move in three dimensions.

Clearly, the mechanisms described in the previous section can be used to attach the input devices' active values to active values controlling the graphics. The techniques described under the subsection "exceptional values" are used to restrict the values to certain limits, and the application will be notified when appropriate.

If this were all that was provided, however, then code would have to be written for each mouse dependency to cover all the requirements. The main problem is that interaction techniques need to be activated only under certain conditions. For example, a typical menu has a black rectangle that follows the mouse (Figure 5), but only while the mouse button is held down over the menu. When the mouse button is released, the current value is returned.

When specifying interactions of this type, Peridot uses a postfix-style sequence. First, the designer creates the

graphics that should appear (the black rectangle in the menu, for example) and then specifies that it should depend on the mouse. The actual graphics that respond to the mouse actions are totally under the control of the designer. For example, in Figure 6a the four arrows move with the mouse; in Figure 6b the text items move left and right when the mouse button is pressed over them; and in Figure 6c the numbers appear to move in three dimensions.

The simulated mouse[1] is used to show what should happen, since the real mouse is used for giving Peridot commands. For the menu, the designer moves the simulated mouse over the black rectangle and shows the left button down. Peridot then confirms that the action should happen on left button down. On the basis of the position of the simulated mouse, Peridot next determines whether the action should happen when the mouse is

Figure 7. A menu in which some of the items are illegal. The grey items cannot be selected with the mouse.

(1) over a particular object (for example, the diamond in Figure 4), (2) over one of a set of objects (any of the strings in the menu—generalizing from Figure 5 where the mouse is over a particular item: *Copy*), or (3) anywhere on the screen. If the simulated button is down, Peridot assumes that the operation should happen continuously while the button is pressed. If the simulated button is pressed and released, the action will happen once when the button goes down. It is also possible to demonstrate that the action should happen once when the button is released, continuously while the button is up, or only after the mouse button has been pressed several times (for example, a double click).

Exception areas, where the interaction is not allowed, can be defined by demonstration. In Figure 7, for example, the black rectangle will not go over any of the names shaded in grey. Of course, the graphic presentation of the illegal items is determined totally by the designer and is independent of the exception mechanism. The value to use for the active value when the mouse is over an exception item, as well as the value used when the mouse goes outside the object's boundaries, can be specified by the designer.

The property-sheet interaction (Figure 1) is demonstrated much like the menu. The example value for the controlling active value is used to determine whether multiple items are allowed (as for the property sheet) or only one is allowed (as for the menu). The slider (Figure 4) is programmed the same way as the scroll bar (Figure 2). After each piece of the interaction is designed, it can be run immediately, using either the actual devices (by going into "run mode") or the simulated devices.

An interesting advantage of the demonstrational technique is that Peridot can infer what part of the object should be attached to the mouse during dragging on the basis of where the mouse was placed (Figure 8). Peridot checks to see if the designer placed the mouse in the center, at a corner, or in the middle of one side, and it asks the designer to confirm the inferred position.

Combining the clock active value and the above operations allows the designer to demonstrate that something should happen a certain amount of time after an action. For example, this can be used to specify the MacWrite-style scrolling, where the document starts scrolling continuously if the mouse button is held down for more than one second over an arrow. (A special feature of Peridot allows the wait interval to be demonstrated by pressing the mouse buttons rather than by specifying the time numerically, thus providing a demonstrational interface to time.)

Multiple mouse-button clicks (double click, triple click, etc.) and other input techniques can also be programmed by demonstration. If the designer presses the simulated mouse button several times, Peridot infers that multiple clicking is desired. To program a touch tablet or slider,[30] the designer simply attaches the desired object properties (size, for example) to the value from the input devices, possibly after filtering the values using a special application-defined procedure.

An important side effect of using active values for creating interactions is that multiple input devices operating in parallel[30] can be handled easily, whereas they are very difficult to implement in conventional systems. For example, the designer can easily tie the position of an object to the mouse, and its size to a knob operated with the other hand—allowing both to operate concurrently. In addition, it requires no extra effort to have multiple interactions that use the same device (such as multiple mouse menus) available to the end user at the same time, since Peridot ensures that all activated techniques are watching for their appropriate input.

Editing interactions

Editing static pictures is very easy, since they can be selected and respecified easily. Selecting dynamic and ephemeral things such as interactions is harder, however, because they typically do not have visual representations on the screen. Some systems have required the user to learn a textual representation for the actions to allow editing,[18] but this is undesirable.

Peridot allows interactions to be edited several ways. First, an interaction can be re-demonstrated, and Peridot will ask whether the new interaction should replace the old one or run in parallel. Since individual interactions

IEEE CG&A

are small, this should not be a large burden. A complex interaction, such as a menu or scroll bar, typically is constructed from a number of small interactions, each of which takes only a few seconds to define. The second way to edit interactions is to select an active value and request that the interactions affecting it be removed.

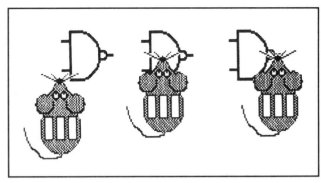

Figure 8. An object might be attached to the mouse in various places for dragging: bottom-left, center, or center of right side.

Evaluation

It is very difficult to quantify formally the range of user interfaces that Peridot can create, since there is no comprehensive taxonomy of interaction techniques. Informally, Peridot's range can be described by example: It can create menus of almost any form (with single or multiple items selected), property sheets, light buttons, radio buttons, scroll bars, two-dimensional scroll boxes, percent-done progress indicators, graphical potentiometers, sliders, iconic and title-line controls for windows, dynamic bar charts, and many other interfaces. Thus, Peridot can create almost all of the Apple Macintosh interface, as well as many new interfaces such as those using multiple input devices concurrently. Peridot also created its own user interface. The ideas in Peridot could be extended easily to handle the keyboard and other types of input devices.

To evaluate how easy Peridot is to use, 10 people used the system for about two hours each. Five were experienced programmers and five were nonprogrammers with some experience using a mouse. The results of this experiment were very encouraging. After about an hour and a half of guided use, the subjects were able to create a menu of their own design unassisted. This demonstrates that one basic goal of Peridot has been met: Nonprogrammers can use it to create user interfaces.

In addition, programmers will appreciate using Peridot to define graphical parts of user interfaces because it is so much faster and more natural than conventional programming. As a small, informal experiment, six expert programmers implemented a particular menu using their favorite hardware and software environments. Some wrote the menu by hand and others modified existing code. With Peridot, the time needed to create the menu ranged from 4 to 15 minutes, but programming took between 50 and 500 minutes.[2] Thus, using Peridot appears to be significantly faster.

with Peridot can be tried out immediately (with or without the application program), and the code generated is efficient enough to be used in actual end applications. This allows extremely rapid prototyping of direct-manipulation interfaces.

By providing the ability to use explicit specification and demonstrational methods, Peridot allows the designer to use the most appropriate techniques for creating the user interfaces. The novel use of demonstrational (programming-by-example) methods makes a large class of previously hard-to-create interaction techniques easy to design, implement, and modify. In addition, Peridot makes it easy to investigate many new techniques that have never been used before and in this way may help designers discover the next generation of exciting user interfaces. ∎

Acknowledgments

First, I want to thank Xerox Canada, Inc., for the donation of the Xerox workstations and Interlisp environment. This research was also partially funded by the National Science and Engineering Research Council of Canada. For help and support with this article, I would especially like to thank my advisor, Bill Buxton, and also Bernita Myers, Peter Rowley, and Ron Baecker.

Conclusions

Peridot successfully demonstrates that it is possible to program a large variety of mouse and other input-device interactions by demonstration. The use of active values supports multiprocessing and makes the linking to application programs straightforward, fast, and natural; and it supports semantic feedback easily. Interfaces created

References

1. B.A. Myers and W. Buxton, "Creating Highly Interactive and Graphical User Interfaces by Demonstration," *Computer Graphics* (Proc. SIGGRAPH 86), Aug. 1986, pp. 249-258.

2. B.A. Myers, *Creating User Interfaces by Demonstration*, doctoral dissertation, Dept. of Computer Science, Univ. of Toronto. Available as Tech. Report CSRI-196, Computer Systems Research Inst. Technical Reports, Univ. of Toronto, Ontario, Canada, M5S 1A1, May 1987.

September 1987

3. B. Shneiderman, "Direct Manipulation: A Step Beyond Programming Languages," *Computer*, Aug. 1983, pp. 57-69.

4. E.L. Hutchins, J.D. Hollan, and D.A. Norman, "Direct Manipulation Interfaces," in *User Centered System Design*, D.A. Norman and S.W. Draper, eds., Lawrence Erlbaum Associates, Hillsdale, N.J., 1986, pp. 87-124.

5. "Graphical Input Interaction Technique (GIIT) Workshop Summary," in *Computer Graphics*, J.J. Thomas and G. Hamlin, eds., ACM SIGGRAPH, Jan. 1983, pp. 5-30.

6. D.R. Olsen, Jr., et al., "A Context for User Interface Management," *CG&A*, Dec. 1984, pp. 33-42.

7. *User Interface Management Systems*, G.R. Pfaff, ed., Springer-Verlag, Berlin, 1985.

8. R.J.K. Jacob, "A State Transition Diagram Language for Visual Programming," *Computer*, Aug. 1985, pp. 51-59.

9. B. Shneiderman, "Seven Plus or Minus Two Central Issues in Human-Computer Interfaces," *Proc. SIGCHI 86: Human Factors in Computing Systems*, ACM, New York, 1986, pp. 343-349.

10. D.R. Olsen, Jr., "Larger Issues in User Interface Management," *Proc. ACM SIGGRAPH Workshop on Software Tools for User Interface Development*, reprinted in *Computer Graphics*, Apr. 1987, pp. 134-137.

11. W. Buxton et al., "Towards a Comprehensive User Interface Management System," *Computer Graphics* (Proc. SIGGRAPH 83), July 1983, pp. 35-42.

12. D.A. Henderson, Jr., "The Trillium User Interface Design Environment," *Proc. SIGCHI 86: Human Factors in Computing Systems*, ACM, New York, 1986, pp. 221-227.

13. D.R. Olsen, Jr., E.P. Dempsey, and R. Rogge, "Input-Output Linkage in a User Interface Management System," *Computer Graphics* (Proc. SIGGRAPH 85), July 1985, pp. 225-234.

14. L. Cardelli and R. Pike, "Squeak: A Language for Communicating with Mice," *Computer Graphics* (Proc. SIGGRAPH 85), July 1985, pp. 199-204.

15. B.A. Myers, "Visual Programming, Programming by Example, and Program Visualization: A Taxonomy," *Proc. SIGCHI 86: Human Factors in Computing Systems*, ACM, New York, 1986, pp. 59-66.

16. L. Gould and W. Finzer, "Programming by Rehearsal," Tech. Report SCL-84-1, Xerox Palo Alto Research Center, May 1984. A short version appears in *Byte*, June 1984.

17. A.W. Biermann, "Approaches to Automatic Programming," in *Advances in Computers*, Vol. 15, M. Rubinoff and M.C. Yovitz, eds., Academic Press, New York, 1976, pp. 1-63.

18. D.C. Halbert, *Programming by Example*, doctoral dissertation, Computer Science Division, Dept. of EE & CS, Univ. of California, Berkeley, 1984. Also available as Tech. Report TR OSD-T8402, Xerox Office Systems Division, Systems Development Dept., Dec. 1984.

19. H. Lieberman, "Constructing Graphical User Interfaces by Example," *Graphics Interface 82*, Canadian Information Processing Soc., Toronto, Ontario, 1982, pp. 295-302.

20. D.C. Smith, *Pygmalion: A Computer Program to Model and Stimulate Creative Thought*, Birkhauser, Basel, Switzerland, 1977.

21. A. Borning, "Thinglab—A Constraint-Oriented Simulation Laboratory," Tech. Report SSL-79-3, Xerox Palo Alto Research Center, 1979.

22. R.A. Duisberg, "Animated Graphical Interfaces," *Proc. SIGCHI 86: Human Factors in Computing Systems*, ACM, New York, 1986, pp. 131-136.

23. G. Nelson, "Juno, a Constraint-Based Graphics System," *Computer Graphics* (Proc. SIGGRAPH 85), July 1985, pp. 235-243.

24. J.D. Foley and C.F. McMath, "Dynamic Process Visualization," *CG&A*, Mar. 1986, pp. 16-25.

25. O.P. Buneman and E.K. Clemons, "Efficiently Monitoring Relational Databases," *ACM Trans. Database Systems*, Sept. 1979, pp. 368-382.

26. C.V. Ramamoorthy, S. Shekhar, and V. Garg, "Software Development Support for AI Programs," *Computer*, Jan. 1987, pp. 30-40.

27. M. Stefik, D.G. Bobrow, and K.M. Kahn, "Integrating Access-Oriented Programming into a Multi-Paradigm Environment," *IEEE Software*, Jan. 1986, pp. 10-18.

28. P.P. Tanner and W.A.S. Buxton, "Some Issues in Future User Interface Management System (UIMS) Development," in *User Interface Management Systems*, G.R. Pfaff, ed., Springer-Verlag, Berlin, 1985, pp. 67-79.

29. G. Williams, "The Apple Macintosh Computer," *Byte*, Feb. 1984, pp. 30-54.

30. W. Buxton and B. Myers, "A Study in Two-Handed Input," *Proc. SIGCHI 86: Human Factors in Computing Systems*, ACM, New York, 1986, pp. 321-326.

Brad Myers is a research computer scientist at Carnegie Mellon University. From 1980 until 1983 he worked at PERQ Systems Corporation, where he designed and implemented the Sapphire window manager and numerous PERQ demonstrations for the SIGGRAPH equipment exhibition. His research interests include user interface management systems, user interfaces, programming by example, visual programming, interaction techniques, window management, programming environments, debugging, and graphics.

Myers recently completed a PhD in computer science at the University of Toronto. He received the MS and BS degrees from the Massachusetts Institute of Technology while he was a research intern at Xerox PARC. He is a member of SIGGRAPH, SIGCHI, ACM, and the Computer Society of the IEEE.

Myers' address is Computer Science Department, Carnegie Mellon University, Pittsburgh, PA 15213-3890.

IEEE CG&A

Experiences with the Alternate Reality Kit: An Example of the Tension Between Literalism and Magic

Randall B. Smith

Xerox Palo Alto Research Center

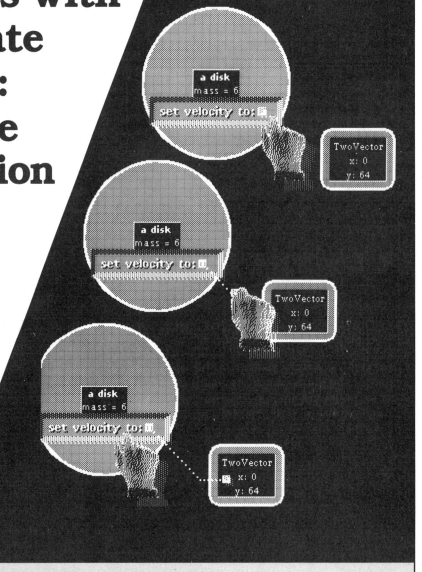

This article presents an overview of the Alternate Reality Kit, an animated environment for creating interactive simulations. ARK is built upon a physical-world metaphor: All objects have an image, a position, a velocity, and the ability to experience forces. Users manipulate objects with a mouse-operated "hand," which enables them to carry and throw objects, press buttons, and operate sliders.

The interface features are discussed in light of a general user interface tension between literalism and magic. Literal features—defined as those that are true to the interface's metaphor—enhance an interface's learnability. Magical features are defined as those capabilities that deliberately violate the metaphor in order to provide enhanced functionality. Discussion of each ARK feature includes informal observations of early ARK users, and an assessment of the feature's learnability, its usefulness, and its position on the magical-literal axis.

Despite ARK's magical features, applications-level users have been trained in a few minutes.

Although this article is about ARK, the tension between literalism and magic raises some interesting questions on its own. Some of these questions are presented briefly in the conclusion.

Reprinted from *IEEE Computer Graphics and Applications*, September 1987, pages 42-50. Copyright © 1987 by The Institute of Electrical and Electronics Engineers, Inc. All rights reserved.

T he designer of a system for use by novices can gain great advantage by basing the interface on a known metaphor. If the computer behaves like a system already understood by the user, the learning time will be greatly reduced. Interface features that are true to the designer's metaphor might be called *literal*. The learnability of literalism makes it beneficial.

However, the designer can always provide the user

Figure 1. The screen as seen by a user of the Alternate Reality Kit. Each window and the objects it contains represent an alternate reality. The mouse-operated hand (center) is casting a shadow that indicates it is "above" the alternate realities. The hand, used for picking up and carrying objects, and for pressing buttons, is the user's means of interacting with the system. Two interactors are present in the alternate reality under the hand. One, labeled "gravity," creates a gravitational force field; the other, labeled "motion," causes objects to change position according to their velocity. (The windows shown here are considerably smaller than those typically used in ARK.)

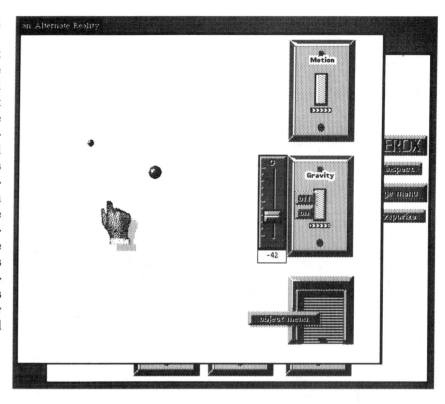

with enhanced capabilities, assuming there is a willingness to break out of the metaphor. These features might allow the user to do wonderful things that are far beyond the capabilities of literal features. Capabilities that violate the metaphor to provide enhanced functionality might be called *magical*. The power of magic is also beneficial.

Admittedly, literalism and magic are not part of conventional computer science parlance. However, I find them particularly appropriate for discussing ARK, where even the name Alternate Reality Kit suggests both the literal real world and the magical ability to choose between or modify realities.

There is a trade-off[1] between the learnability of literalism and the power of magic. I employ this tension to present my experiences in designing and observing users of the Alternate Reality Kit, a metaphor-based system being developed for nonexpert computer users. The Alternate Reality Kit is intended to allow users to play in their own simulated worlds and to create new ones. ARK is based on a close analogy to the physical world. Many of the important capabilities of ARK are literal: They are transcriptions into the computer of physical-world behavior. Even though the system is designed for inexperienced users, ARK has certain magical characteristics. Observations of ARK users suggest that novices are not significantly hampered by a small amount of magic. Although each magical feature requires a brief explanation, ARK's basic functionality can still be taught in a few minutes.

This article is a brief introduction to the ARK user interface in terms of the magic-literalism dimension. A more complete description of the functionality and philosophy behind ARK has been published elsewhere.[2] I will not offer a general discussion of the tension between magic and literalism; I simply employ this tension to help analyze the central features of ARK's interface. However, ARK does serve as an example of a magic-versus-literalism trade-off, which I believe is present in all user interfaces that are firmly grounded in a single metaphor.

Literalism versus magic in ARK

The Alternate Reality Kit[2] is a system for creating interactive animated simulations. ARK simulations are intended to facilitate an intuitive understanding of the simulation's interaction rules by making these rules appear as accessible physical objects called *interactors*. ARK also supports the creation and modification of new simulations from within the animated ARK environment.

The interface is quite faithful to a physical-world metaphor: All objects have a visual image, a position, a velocity, and the ability to experience forces. One of the objects is a hand, which the user controls with a mouse. The hand can be used to carry and throw objects, press buttons, and operate slider controls (see Figure 1). As in the real world, many things are happening simultaneously: A pendulum can swing while numbers change on a control box in response to the operation of a slider. The

Figure 2. Manipulation of buttons. In (a) the user is preparing to pick up the on/off button from the surface of the "vertical launcher." In (b) the button is carried over to the simulated photograph, and in (c) it has been released. Since the photograph does not "understand" how to turn on or off, the button has fallen through.

intent is for the user to conclude very quickly that the screen depicts a physical world and that the user is manipulating physical objects directly. This is the advantage of literalism: Interfaces based on a well-known metaphor require very little explanation.[3-5]

However, sticking completely to a metaphor can cripple a system's functionality.[6,7] For example, an ARK user may wish to connect a simulated push button to some ARK device, perhaps for turning the device on and off. Both the button and the device are depicted as physical objects that can be directly manipulated with the hand. Should the user be required to connect the button by drilling a hole in the device and cutting into metaphorical electrical work? Something like this would

be required if ARK were perfectly analogous to the everyday physical world. In the design of ARK, I found that perfectly literal ways of connecting buttons were too tedious. Instead, the ARK user connects the button simply by dropping it onto the device. Buttons have the message they send stamped on the surface; if the device does not understand the button's message, the button will fall right through the object (see Figure 2). If the button's message is meaningful, it will stick to the object's surface. An invisible connection is established automatically, and the button is immediately functional. Furthermore, buttons can be created that cause nonphysical effects, such as doubling an object's size and mass or causing the object to vanish. Features like these are called magical because they enable the user to do powerful things that are outside the possibilities of the metaphor.

Although ARK is more literal than most systems, it does contain certain magical features that are useful where literalism would be limiting. But one of the lessons of ARK is that the literal aspects of the interface are often obvious, while magical capabilities are harder to learn. In ARK, the time needed to explain the basics is actually measured in seconds. Every piece of added magic is relatively "expensive" because it requires its own explanation. Unlike literalism, with its easily understood physical metaphor, magic does not come for free. In designing ARK, therefore, I am faced with a tension between the limitations imposed by literalism and the obscurity of magic—or, in positive terms, between the power of magic and the learnability of literalism.

Overview of ARK

ARK is a project under development in the System Concepts Laboratory of the Xerox Palo Alto Research Center; it is being implemented in the Smalltalk-80 programming environment.[8] The system described here has already evolved under the influence of user feedback and will continue to do so. The six kinds of objects mentioned in this article are shown in the box on the next page.

The system consists of a collection of "physical" objects that can be manipulated with a simulated hand. Except for rare use of the keyboard for typing text, the hand is the user's sole means of interacting with the system. The ARK user can do three kinds of things with the hand: directly change an object's position or velocity (by carrying or throwing), send an object a message (by pressing a simulated button), and introduce a new object or button into the environment (by selecting from popup menus). The user can query objects or change their state by sending them messages, which are represented by buttons. Examples of button messages are "velocity," "set mass to [some parameter]," and "describe yourself." One special button, the message-menu button, causes a highly magical effect: Attaching it to an object and press-

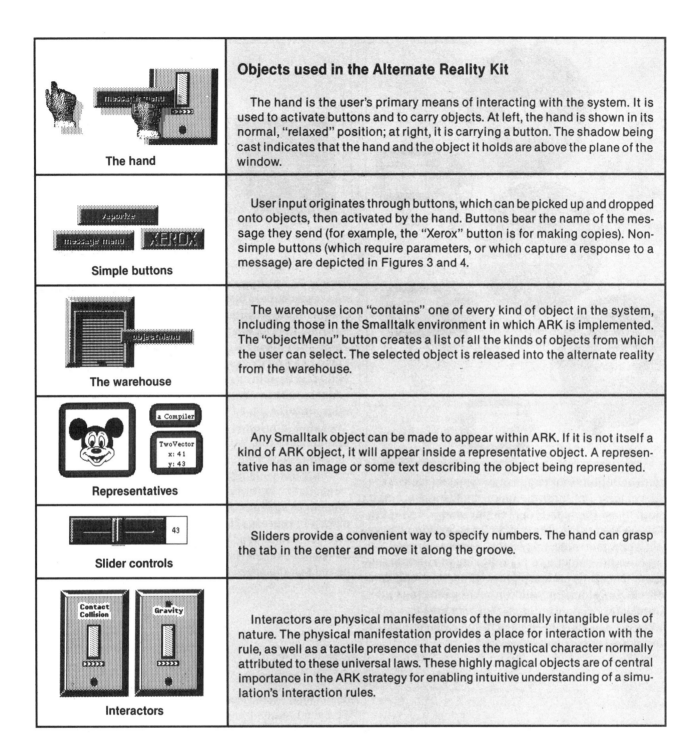

Objects used in the Alternate Reality Kit

The hand

The hand is the user's primary means of interacting with the system. It is used to activate buttons and to carry objects. At left, the hand is shown in its normal, "relaxed" position; at right, it is carrying a button. The shadow being cast indicates that the hand and the object it holds are above the plane of the window.

Simple buttons

User input originates through buttons, which can be picked up and dropped onto objects, then activated by the hand. Buttons bear the name of the message they send (for example, the "Xerox" button is for making copies). Non-simple buttons (which require parameters, or which capture a response to a message) are depicted in Figures 3 and 4.

The warehouse

The warehouse icon "contains" one of every kind of object in the system, including those in the Smalltalk environment in which ARK is implemented. The "objectMenu" button creates a list of all the kinds of objects from which the user can select. The selected object is released into the alternate reality from the warehouse.

Representatives

Any Smalltalk object can be made to appear within ARK. If it is not itself a kind of ARK object, it will appear inside a representative object. A representative has an image or some text describing the object being represented.

Slider controls

Sliders provide a convenient way to specify numbers. The hand can grasp the tab in the center and move it along the groove.

Interactors

Interactors are physical manifestations of the normally intangible rules of nature. The physical manifestation provides a place for interaction with the rule, as well as a tactile presence that denies the mystical character normally attributed to these universal laws. These highly magical objects are of central importance in the ARK strategy for enabling intuitive understanding of a simulation's interaction rules.

---

ing it will cause the object to create a menu listing all messages the object understands. When a message is selected from this menu, a corresponding button is created and attached to the object, ready for use.

Buttons that send an unparameterized message with no response are called "simple" buttons and are illustrated in the box above. Buttons requiring parameters or representing an object's reply to a message are called "nonsimple" and are shown in Figures 3 and 4. The "warehouse" object contains one copy of every kind of

object in the system, including one of each type from the underlying Smalltalk environment. By pressing the appropriate button, the user can cause the warehouse to display a menu listing all of the objects it contains. Selecting from the menu causes a copy of the named object to be introduced into the alternate reality.

There are buttons that allow the user to create new kinds of objects and store them in the warehouse. Ways to combine existing buttons into new kinds of buttons are still being explored.

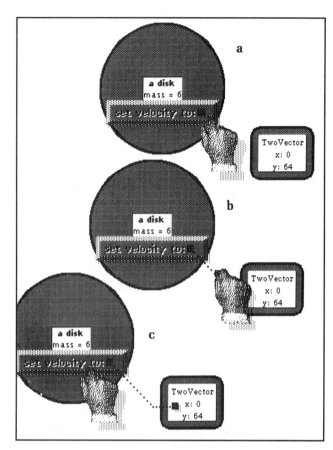

Figure 3. Buttons that require a parameter (such as the "set velocity to" button shown here) have a small "plug" used for specifying the parameter. In (a) the user reaches for the plug, and in (b) is carrying it over to the parameter object. In (c) the user has dropped the plug onto the object and is preparing to activate the button. Once the parameter is specified, the small dots start moving along the path connecting the plug to the button. (Only simple buttons, shown in the box on the previous page, have been used in the experiments in which users have been observed.)

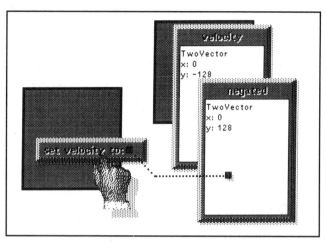

Figure 4. Buttons that elicit a response from their message-send are large objects that have a "view" rectangle for representing the result. Both the "velocity" button and the "negated" button shown here receive answers to the messages they send. The answer is displayed as text or graphics within the view rectangle and is accessible as an object present within the view. Objects within the view rectangle can be accessed with buttons just like any other object. Here the "negated" button is attached to the TwoVector object displayed in the "velocity" button's view. Similarly, the plug specifying the parameter to the "set velocity to" button is specifying the TwoVector object in the "negated" button's view. Buttons that capture responses are somewhat magical, especially in their ability to represent objects that are "really there" in the view rectangle. (Buttons that represent responses have not been part of the experiments in which users have been observed.)

Types of ARK user

ARK, like some other visual programming environments,[9,10] is intended for more than one kind of user. The applications-level user might typically be a student carrying out a simulated lab experiment. At a lower level, the simulation builder is the creator of a particular application. There may be a role for another layer below that, populated by individuals who create tools for use by simulation builders.

So far, I have observed about 50 applications-level users and two simulation builders. Most of the applications-level users are part of an experiment studying people's reactions to the violation of physical laws.[11] These users

do not have to create new objects, or new kinds of objects. The accumulated empirical evidence enlightens only certain portions of the interface: The applications-level users made no use of menus and the nonsimple button types illustrated in Figures 3 and 4.

Every user comes to the computer with certain expectations. Some sophisticated users take slightly more time to learn the literal features of the interface—they seem to expect more magic than ARK contains. On the other hand, extremely naive users (young children) have sometimes expected the interface to be more literal, apparently expecting *less* magic. ARK's balance between literalism and magic seems about right for computer novices above the age of ten. However, the effect of user sophistication is not great, and misunderstandings have always been correctable with one or two sentences.

Figure 5. Various aspects of the ARK interface as they relate to learning time and functionality. The easier-to-learn aspects are toward the right, and very useful aspects are toward the top. Notice how the interface aspects tend to lie on a line, with magical features in the upper left and literal features in the lower right. The void in the upper right is a sign of the fundamental tension between literalism and magic: Interface designers can always provide more powerful functionality at the price of violating the metaphor. Sometimes a broken metaphor is not particularly enabling, as evidenced by ARK's occasionally slow animation rate and use of the mouse. (Menus have been included here even though they have rarely been used as part of the user experiments with the system.)

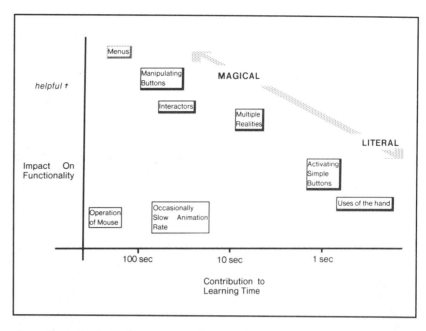

Limitation of the analogy: external factors

This presentation of the Alternate Reality Kit depicts the designer as violating a metaphor only to provide enhanced functionality (magic). But sometimes designers encounter factors beyond their control. Input devices, computer performance limitations, or other constraints can cause the metaphor to be violated in a way that does not necessarily enhance functionality. These fixed requirements are called "external" factors because they are imposed upon the designer. That is not to say that external factors are unimportant: Successfully presenting external factors to the user can be absolutely crucial.

I have found external factors difficult to present as either literal features or magical enhancements to the ARK interface. In ARK, external factors typically degrade learnability without enhancing functionality, and I consider them to be neither literal nor magical.

For example, when an alternate reality contains a very large number of extensively interacting objects, the animation rate (frames per second) drops, and it can become noticeably harder to grab and throw objects. Their jerky motion makes them look less like real-world things and makes them harder to interact with. This external factor has broken the metaphor in a way that degrades functionality. This behavior is clearly not literal, and even though it is outside the real world's behavior, I prefer not to use a sense-of-wonder term like magic for this odd and annoying visual phenomenon.

A second example is the mouse, which is used to operate the hand. The use of an indirect input device such as the mouse breaks the real-world metaphor without providing enhanced functionality. As a pointing device, the mouse is known to take a small but finite amount of time to learn.[12] Furthermore, one mouse button is used to make the hand grab objects, another to make the hand activate the simulated buttons. Every observed user has at some point confused these two functions.[13,14] Not only does the mouse take a while to learn, it also fails to enable users to do things that their physical-world hands can do.

Observations of the system's users indicate that these external factors are its most troubling aspects. As indicated in Figure 5, the operation of the mouse and the occasionally slow animation rate are neither enhancements to the functionality nor aids to ARK's learnability. In the ideal system, everything, including external factors, would fit along the magical-literal spectrum. But because of unfortunate constraints, I believe metaphor-based interfaces will usually have some features that are neither literal nor magical.

Selected interface aspects

Now we look in greater detail at aspects of the interface that have been used by applications-level users. This is not intended to be a complete list but rather a sample of the more important aspects of the interface. For each feature listed, I evaluate the magic content, discuss the power-versus-learnability trade-off, and note user experiences. The more literal aspects are listed first. This information is summarized in Figure 5.

Use of the hand

The user can pick up any object with the simulated hand. As the grasped object is carried about, it casts a shadow on the alternate reality beneath it. When a grasped object is released, it falls back into the alternate reality and maintains any velocity imparted by the hand's motion. In this way the user playing in the gravity simulation depicted in Figure 1 can throw the moon into orbit around the planet.

This feature is literal.

Power versus learnability

The hand has only limited abilities. It enables users to change the position and velocity of objects and establish physical contact between objects. However, it contributes quite a bit to the user's understanding of the system's basics. Users need only be told, "This mouse moves the hand on the screen. The left mouse button enables you to grab hold of an object. Try throwing something."

Some of this information is about the mouse. The remainder of this brief explanation is about the use of the hand, from which most users infer the following:

1. The objects on the screen are physical entities.

2. Physical proximity has semantic content. (Only one subject, an experienced mouse-user, has asked if it was necessary for the hand to be over an object to pick it up.)

3. The hand can carry an object and drop it at a new location, thus changing its position.

4. The hand can change an object's velocity. (After being invited to throw an object, some users ask how throwing is done. When asked to go ahead and guess, most have guessed correctly: Start the hand moving and release the object. Experienced mouse-users have sometimes asked if throwing is accomplished by pressing a special mouse button.)

5. The use of shadow to indicate that an object is "above" the reality has been only moderately successful. For a few users, an additional sentence or two of explanation is required. ("See the shadow? That indicates that the object in the hand is hovering over the objects in the window.")

Activation of simple buttons

A user playing in the planetary orbit simulation of Figure 1 may wish to suspend gravity temporarily. On the right side of the figure is a kind of controller device labeled "gravity" with an *off* button on its surface. All buttons are stamped with the name of the message they send. The user activates a simulated button by positioning the hand over it and pressing the middle mouse button. Only simple buttons (as shown in the box on page 45) have been used by applications-level users; buttons that require parameters (Figure 3) or that send messages

and represent responses (Figure 4) have not yet been used in ARK experiments.

This feature is literal.

Power versus learnability

Buttons are moderately useful, enabling users to send a message to an object. They are fairly easy to explain; users seem to understand immediately what buttons are for. The only training time required is for pointing out the characteristic visual presence of a button. It is simply assumed that an object responds to the press of a button in a way suggested by the name stamped on the button. Thus, without explicit instruction, the user adopts a model consistent with the picture of a button as a thing that sends a message. The button builds on the importance of physical contact in establishing relationships between objects.

Manipulating buttons

A simulated button can be picked up from the surface of an object and put down anywhere—even on top of certain other objects. A button will stick to the surface of any object that can respond to its message. If a button is dropped on an object that does not understand its message, the button will "fall through" the object. Many buttons can be attached to an object simultaneously. Sometimes a button will be larger than the object upon which it rests. Thus an object may have a button hanging off its edge or even completely covering it.

This feature is moderately magical.

Power versus learnability

Buttons are easily connected and removed, enabling the user to communicate with objects in a flexible way. It is not uncommon to have several generally useful buttons lying about. The "selective sticking" of buttons prevents a certain class of semantic errors. (For example, if we were able to send the message *cube root* to some text, an error would result.)

While the ability to manipulate the buttons is useful, this aspect requires a few sentences of explanation. A user must understand that a button will "stick to" or "fall through" an object, depending on the object's ability to respond to the button's message. Uninformed users have sometimes discovered accidentally that buttons can be picked up from an object, and they have been slightly startled. Some of these users wonder if a button will still work when removed from the surface of an object and dropped off to the side. Some have dropped the button onto the surface of a large "nonunderstanding" object, only to have the button disappear. (Actually, the button is lying underneath the object, having fallen through.)

Interactors

In ARK, an interaction law of the simulated universe (Newton's law of gravity, for example) is represented by a "physical" object called an interactor. Interactors form an interface between the user and the fundamental laws of the simulation. This feature is highly magical.

Power versus learnability

Interactors are the physical embodiment of normally intangible abstractions, and thus they exemplify how the design of ARK attempts to facilitate intuition by making things concrete. By enabling the user to change physical laws, interactors provide capabilities fundamentally beyond those suggested by the real-world metaphor. Most users have no trouble accepting the idea of a "control center" for gravity, for example. However, they do need to be explicitly introduced to the idea that an interactor object represents some abstraction. On occasion, users have had difficulty understanding exactly what abstraction is being controlled. These users may require a minute or two of discussion to clarify the interactor's role in the simulation. While this is a short time in absolute terms, it is much longer than the time required to explain any literal feature.

> *ARK's limited use of magic does not prove too confusing for novices, and the total teaching time remains quite short.*

Multiple realities

Looking at the computer screen, the ARK user sees one or more possibly overlapping rectangular windows. Each window represents a separate alternate reality. To move between alternate realities, the user simply moves the hand over the exposed portion of the window. The entire window will be automatically exposed, moving to the top of the stack of "overlapping worlds." The user can carry objects from one alternate reality to another.

This feature is highly magical.

Power versus learnability

The use of overlapping windows offers the usual advantage of enlarging the virtual screen area. The provision of multiple realities enables users to organize their ARK tasks. For example, one world can be used for building new objects, another for trying them out; or two side-by-side windows could facilitate comparison of separate worlds, each with its own speed of light. Users understand the idea quite readily. A brief description and one or two trials are required before most users are comfortable with their ability to go "reality hopping." However,

users who accidentally bring a buried alternate reality to the top are startled.

In certain applications, objects may drift off the window, disappearing under the edge. Users are sometimes concerned or amused at this; it is not always clear what has happened to the object. Can it be retrieved? Does it still exist? (In fact, the coordinate system for each window world is indefinitely large, and an object can go as far as is allowed by the computer's ability to allocate new words for storing its growing x and y coordinates.) As with interactors, the absolute time to teach the use of overlapping worlds is short, although it is longer than for teaching a typical literal interface feature.

Overall ARK learnability

The preceding list of features demonstrates the inverse correlation between power and learnability. Literal interface aspects are easily understood; in fact, some important parts of the literal functions are simply assumed by the user. Magical aspects are quite useful but require the majority of the training time. ARK's limited use of magic does not prove too confusing for novices, and the total teaching time remains quite short. After a few minutes of explanation, most novices are able to use the capabilities outlined above.

Conclusions and questions

I have used the magic-literalism tension to discuss some of the central features of the Alternate Reality Kit because it is a useful way to analyze some of ARK's design issues and user experiences. With a large portion of ARK at the literalism end of the spectrum, many of the important aspects do not need much explanation. Furthermore, although each magical aspect requires its own explanation, limited use of magic in ARK keeps the total teaching time short. User experiences indicate that applications-level functionality can be taught in a few minutes. Features that are neither magical enhancements nor literal adherents to the metaphor are the most troubling.

The magic-versus-literalism trade-off may offer an interesting perspective on other systems whose interfaces revolve around a single metaphor (other graphical programming environments or desktop-like window systems, for example).

Some questions are raised by this way of viewing metaphorical user interfaces. How does the designer decide when to implement a capability magically instead of literally? Since literalism can be carried too far, when does an interface become so literal that it surprises even novice users? Building systems with both literal and magical ways of doing the same task may enable users to gain proficiency smoothly; how is this best done? What is the minimum set of magical capabilities that will allow users to create their own magic features? Is there a metaphor that can put all external factors along the literalism-magic spectrum?

Questions like these can lead to interesting discussions of ways to control the release of the magic latent in computers. ■

Acknowledgments

The following individuals provided stimulating discussions and thoughtful comments: Sara Bly, Adele Goldberg, George Goodman, Laura Gould, Jane Laursen, Tim O'Shea, Dave Robson, and Frank Zdybel.

References

1. D.A. Norman, "Design Principles for Human-Computer Interfaces," *Proc. Conf. Human Factors in Computer Systems*, ACM, New York, 1983, pp. 1-10.

2. R.B. Smith, "The Alternate Reality Kit: An Animated Environment for Creating Interactive Simulations," *Proc. 1986 IEEE Computer Soc. Workshop on Visual Languages*, CS-IEEE, Los Alamitos, Calif., pp. 99-106.

3. J.M. Carroll and R.L. Mack, "Metaphor, Computing Systems, and Active Learning," *Int'l J. Man-Machine Studies*, Jan. 1985, pp. 39-57.

4. J.M. Carroll and J.C. Thomas, "Metaphor and the Cognitive Representation of Computing Systems," Tech. Report No. RC 8302, IBM Watson Research Center, Yorktown Heights, N.Y., 1980.

5. D. Gentner, "The Structure of Analogical Models in Science," Tech. Report 4451, Bolt, Beranek, and Newman, Cambridge, Mass., July 1980.

6. D. Gittins, "Icon-Based Human-Computer Interaction," *Int'l J. Man-Machine Studies*, June 1986, pp. 519-543.

7. F. Halasz and T.P. Moran, "Analogy Considered Harmful," *Proc. Conf. Human Factors in Computer Systems*, ACM, New York, 1982.

8. A.J. Goldberg and D. Robson, *Smalltalk-80: The Language and its Implementation*, Addison-Wesley, Reading, Mass., 1983.

9. A.H. Borning, "The Programming Language Aspects of ThingLab, a Constraint-Oriented Simulation Laboratory," *ACM Trans. Programming Languages and Systems*, Oct. 1982, pp. 353-387.

10. L. Gould and W. Finzer, "Programming by Rehearsal," Tech. Report SCL-84-1, Xerox Palo Alto Research Center, Palo Alto, Calif., May 1984. A short version appears in *Byte*, June 1984.

11. T. O'Shea and R.B. Smith, "Violating the Laws of Nature: Experiments in Understanding Physics by Exploring Alternate Realities," (in progress).

12. S.K. Card, T.P. Moran, and A. Newell, *The Psychology of Human-Computer Interaction*, Lawrence Erlbaum Associates, Hillsdale, N.J., 1983.

13. W.L. Bewly et al., "Human Factors Testing in the Design of Xerox's 8010 'Star' Office Workstation," *Proc. Conf. Human Factors in Computer Systems*, ACM, New York, 1983, pp. 72-77.

14. L.A. Price and C.A. Cordova, "Use of Mouse Buttons," *Proc. Conf. Human Factors in Computer Systems*, ACM, New York, 1983, pp. 262-266.

Randall B. Smith is a member of the System Concepts Lab at the Xerox Palo Alto Research Center. He spent a year at Atari Research before joining Xerox in 1984, and before that he taught physics at the University of California at Davis for two years. His interests include educational simulation environments, computer languages, graphics, and computer-human interfaces. He received his PhD in theoretical physics from the University of California at San Diego in 1981.

A 16-minute videotape demonstrating the Alternate Reality Kit is available from the author at a nominal charge.

Smith can be contacted at the Xerox Palo Alto Research Center, 3333 Coyote Hill Rd., Palo Alto, CA 94304.

Show and Tell: A Visual Programming Language*

Takayuki Dan Kimura†, Julie W. Choi††, and Jane M. Mack††

†Department of Computer Science
Washington University
St. Louis, Missouri 63130

††AT&T Bell Laboratories
Naperville, Illinois 60566

Introduction

Show and Tell™ (ST) is a visual programming language for school children, and is designed for the Apple© Macintosh™ personal computer. Using icons consisting of boxes and arrows, ST requires no keyboarding except for textual data entry. The subroutine, iteration, recursion, and concurrency functions are represented by two-dimensional graphic patterns. The immediate goal of ST is to enable school children to develop programming skills and knowledge through the use of visual, or keyboardless programming.

Figure 1 illustrates an ST program created to send a picture home through a modem, and to receive an acknowledgement that concurrently is shown in a window and spoken. The visual programming increases and reinforces the programming learning process.

In this paper, we will discuss the semantic model of the ST language, focusing on two features of ST: the consistency concept and the iteration box construct. Both features allow the selection (if-then-else) and iteration (while-do) control structures without resorting to the notions of Boolean value and loop. An overall description of the ST language is given in references [10] and [13].

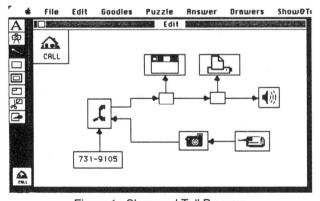

Figure 1: Show and Tell Program

The semantic model of ST integrates three application areas in the school environment: communication, database, and computation. The model is based on the concepts of *dataflow* and *completion*. Dataflow [3] was chosen for its understandability and intrinsic concurrency. A dataflow language is easier for school children to understand for two reasons: its two-dimensional syntax and value-oriented computation. By the principle of direct object manipulation [12], a graphic object is more acceptable to school children than text. For the same reason, direct manipulation of values in a dataflow language, rather than indirect manipulation through variables, reinforces the learning process. The notion of variable, or equivalently, the notion of state, is a difficult concept for school children to master [14]. Dataflow's intrinsic concurrency is an important concept for the ST semantic model because modelling communication requires concurrency. Parallel programming is more intuitive and natural than sequential programming for novice computer users.

The dataflow model also has shortcomings as a computation model for school children. A cycle (loop) in a dataflow graph presupposes the notion of state, and multiple cycles may cause a deadlock. Secondly, there is no abstraction mechanism inherent in the model by which complex computations can be broken down into simpler ones. There is no construct similar to the block structure of ALGOL, well-known for its effectiveness in program structuring. Thirdly, the dataflow switching operations, such as distributors and selectors, are inadequate for children. A data token representing a logical value is counter-intuitive, and introduces an element of control flow into dataflow, which confuses novice programmers. Finally, there is no encapsulation mechanism by which error propagation can be controlled and modular programming can be exercised.

To overcome the above difficulties, the ST semantic model eliminates cycles and Boolean values from the dataflow model and introduces the block structure and the logical *consistency* in place of Boolean values. A formal definition of the ST semantic model and its properties are given in [9]. The elimination of cycles and Boolean values creates a new technical problem: how to represent the iteration (while-do) and the selection (if-then-else) control structures in the new dataflow model. We will describe the ST solution to the problem following the next section. First, we will outline the concept of completion.

Completion

The notion of completion is well-known in psychology but little known in computer science [8]. A completion problem is defined as the filling-in of missing portions of a partially hidden pattern in such a way that the completed pattern satisfies a set of consistency rules. In ST, completion is used to unify the concepts of communication, computation, and data query. To school children, the ST system is presented as a tool for defining and solving a certain kind of puzzle. A Show and Tell *puzzle* consists of boxes connected by arrows. The arrows define the neighborhood relationship among the boxes. Some boxes may be empty in the beginning. The puzzle is solved when the empty boxes are filled with data satisfying the constraints imposed by neighboring boxes. An ST puzzle defines a logical completion problem in the same way a jig-saw puzzle defines a physical completion problem. The puzzle is solved when it is completed.

Figure 2 illustrates the various completion problems. Figure 2(a) is a perception completion problem; in (b), the constraint is the physical shape; (c) shows a computation as a completion problem; in (d), the constraint is the content of the database; and in (e), the constraint is the connectivity of the network.

The ST system solves puzzles by computation or by a database search. A puzzle is solved by computation (and communication) when empty boxes are filled by the transfer of data objects from neighboring boxes. A database search in ST consists of selecting a record in the database that contributes to a completion of the puzzle. Both methods may be used to complete a single ST puzzle. Examples of such puzzles are given in [11] where database applications of ST are discussed.

Box-Graphs

A computation in ST is specified by a *box-graph*, a set of boxes connected by a set of arrows. No cycle or loop is allowed in a box-graph. Each box may be empty or may contain a data value or another box-graph. A data value may consist of a number, a text, or a bit-map image. Boxes can be nested, but they never intersect with each other. An arrow directs the data flow from one box to

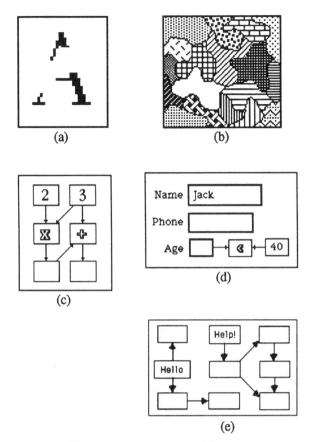

Figure 2: Completion Problems

another, and defines the consistency relationship between the boxes. Each arrow has one starting box and one destination box. Arrows do not branch out. Formally, a box-graph is a directed acyclic multi-graph in which a node represents a box and may contain another box-graph.

Consistency: A Box-graph is *inconsistent* if there is no conflict, directly or indirectly, between the contents of the boxes; otherwise it is *inconsistent*. A box-graph has a conflict, i.e., it is inconsistent, if there are two boxes in the box-graph containing different data values and directly connected by an arrow. A computation functions to complete a box-graph with empty boxes into a consistent box-graph. It involves finding data with which to fill the empty boxes and testing the consistency of the completed box-graph. Once an empty box is filled, the content of the box never changes during the computation.

A box containing a box-graph is called a *complex* box. A complex box can be *open*, represented by a dash-line rectangle, or *closed*, represented by a solid-line rectangle as illustrated in Figure 3 on the next page. If an open box contains an inconsistent box-graph, the box-graph containing the open box is also inconsistent by definition, i.e., consistency spreads through the boundary of an open box into the larger context. In a sense, an open box broadcasts the exceptional condition (i.e., inconsistency) of its components toward the members of its community, while a closed box delimits the boundary of such broadcasting. The effect of inconsistency is, by definition, to make the inconsistent closed box non-communicative and non-existent when viewed from the outside, i.e., the closed box and all intersecting arrows can be deleted from the box-graph without changing the consistency property of the box-graph. Any dataflow passing through an inconsistent complex box is considered to be terminated at the box.

Figure 3 illustrates the differences between an open box and a closed box, as well as the switching capability of box-graphs. In Figure 3(a), the complex box is inconsistent because one constant 2 crashes with one constant 3, i.e. 2 cannot flow into 3; therefore, the data value 1 cannot reach the destination box. Note that the ST system hatches all inconsistent complex boxes during the execution time. In (b), the inconsistency is contained inside the smaller closed box, and the larger complex box is consistent. Therefore, the constant 1 can reach the destination. In (c), the inconsistency propagates out of the smaller open box, and the larger complex box becomes inconsistent as in (a). This switching capability of box-graphs replaces the Boolean data value of traditional dataflow models.

Subroutine: A box-graph can be identified by an icon, and a complex box may contain the icon in place of

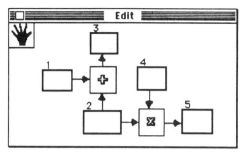

(a) Ordering of Base Boxes

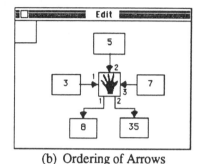

(b) Ordering of Arrows

Figure 4: Positional Binding Rule

the box-graph itself. In Figure 4(a), the icon of a hand at the upper-left corner represents the box-graph which consists of seven boxes. The icon is used in the consistent box-graph of (b). Figure (a) corresponds to a subroutine declaration, and (b) corresponds to a subroutine call in a traditional programming language. A

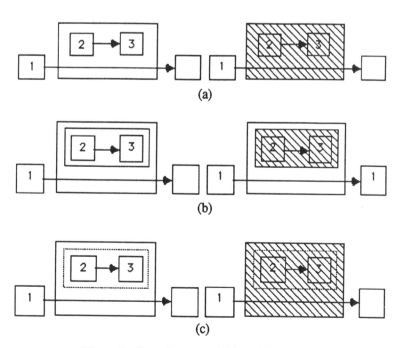

Figure 3: Open Boxes and Closed Boxes

recursive definition of a box-graph is also allowed. In (a), the thickly framed boxes are designated the base boxes, and correspond to the formal parameters of a subroutine. The actual parameters in (b) are determined by the arrows intersecting with the complex box containing the icon. Base boxes are made darker or wider so they will be more clearly understood.

Binding Rule: The association between the base boxes of (a) and the arrows in (b) is established by a *positional* binding rule. All base boxes are ordered by the lexiconigraphical ordering of the (x,y) coordinate of the left-upper corner of each box. Boxes 1,2, and 4 are input base boxes because no arrows enter them, and boxes 3 and 5 are output base boxes. Similarly, all arrows in (b), incident with the complex box, are ordered by the (x,y) coordinates of the intersection point of an arrow and the complex box. The ST binding rule associates the first input base box with the first incoming arrow and the output base box with the first outgoing arrow, and so on. If the number of base boxes (the number of formal parameters) is different from that of intersecting arrows (one number of actual parameters), the complex box containing the box-graph will be evaluated as inconsistent.

There are other possible binding rules for visual programming languages. For example, a base box and the corresponding arrow could be identified by the same label. However, this type of name-based binding rules tend to congest the screen space, which is the most valuable resource in visual programming.

Function and Predicate: As the box-graph of Figure 4 demonstrates, a box-graph can be used to represent a function or a predicate of traditional programming languages. However, to represent a function, there must be only one way of filling the empty boxes to produce a consistent box-graph after its input base boxes are filled with of actual parameters. In [9], it has been demonstrated that the box-graph computation model is deterministic, and that the model is deadlock-free.

There are system defined box-graphs represented by system-defined icons. The box-graph icons are stored in the three system-defined directories (or *drawers* in the ST terminology), as shown in Figure 5. The user can create new drawers and save user-defined box-graphs in them. To open a user-defined box-graph, the user simply uses a mouse to double-click the icon in a drawer. Each drawer represents a separate Macintosh file.

Examples: In summary, we will demonstrate the logical switching and subroutine capabilities of ST by constructing a full adder without using any arithmetic operations.

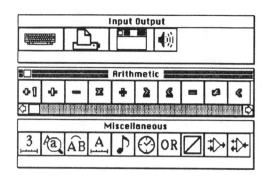

Figure 5: System Defined Drawers

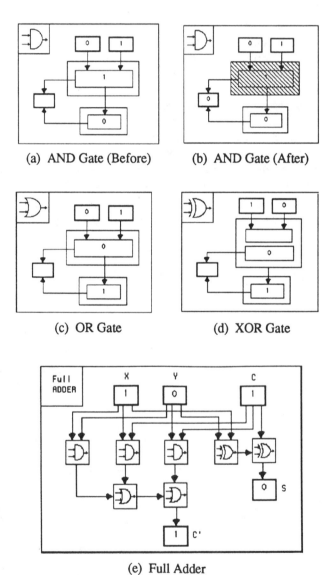

(a) AND Gate (Before)   (b) AND Gate (After)

(c) OR Gate   (d) XOR Gate

(e) Full Adder

Figure 6: Switching Capabilities

Figure 6(a), (c), and (d) define a standard set of Boolean operations. The name icons are selected from the standard symbols for corresponding gate circuits. The Boolean values are represented by the integers 1 and 0, though T and F would do as well. Figure (b) is the result, demonstrating how the and operation works with the inputs 1 and 0. Figure 6(e) defines a full-adder using the previously defined functions (subroutines). Crossing arrows have no effects on dataflow.

Iteration Box

The previous section has demonstrated how the selection control structure (if-then-else) is constructed in the ST language without using Boolean data values. In this section we will show how the iteration control structure (while-do) is incorporated into the acyclic dataflow model of ST.

Complexity: A box-graph can be arbitrarily complex. There is no theoretical limit on the number of boxes in a box-graph. Furthermore, each part of a box-graph may contain a box-graph that is arbitrarily complex. We differentiate two types of complexity associated with a box-graph: the number of boxes and the maximum depth of nesting. The former represents the *horizontal* complexity, while the latter represents the *vertical* complexity. Figure 7 compares two box-graphs with similar functions showing different complexity profiles.

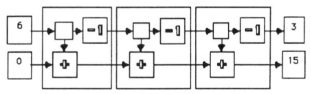

(a) Horizontally Complex Box-graph

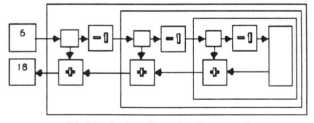

(b) Verticallly Complex Box-graph

Figure 7: Complexity Profile

For managing such complexities, ST provides two abstraction mechanisms: *folding* and *naming*. Each mechanism is used to reduce the horizontal and vertical complexity, respectively.

Naming: By naming, we mean to represent an arbitrarily complex box-graph by a name (an icon) of fixed size, as illustrated in Figure 4. Using the naming abstraction, the box-graph of Figure 7(b) can be approximately represented by Figure 8(a), where the name is defined by Figure 8(b) in the ST syntax. The representation is approximate because the box-graph of Figure 8(a) represents an unbounded nesting of the same box-graph, while Figure 7(b) has a bounded depth of nesting.

An example of naming a bounded nesting, a recursive definition of the factorial function, is given in Figure 9. When this puzzle is solved, the ST system not only completes the puzzle with the output value 120, but also speaks words "one," "two," "six," "twenty-four," and "one hundred twenty," tracing the dynamic expansion of the nested box-graph.

To make recursion easier for school children to understand, ST has a set-break-point operation enabling the user to mark a box containing a box-graph name for later run-time inspection. When the ST system stops prior to evaluating the marked box, the user has the option to open a new window, called a *peek window*, to display the named box-graph itself, or to continue the computation. When a peek window is opened next to the current window, the user can see the results of

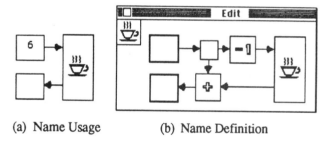

(a) Name Usage   (b) Name Definition

Figure 8: Naming Abstraction

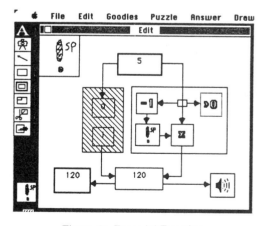

Figure 9: Factorial Function

computation in both windows simultaneously. Because this option is available at any level of nesting, each level of recursion can be displayed on the screen side-by-side at once.

Folding: By folding, we mean to collect a spatially (or horizontally) spreading array of similar box-graphs into one place. It is syntactically represented by an *iteration box* in ST. For example, the box-graph in Figure 7(a) can be folded into the form shown in Figure 10(a), and the corresponding ST syntax is given in Figure 10(b). Note that the iteration box of Figure 10(b) specifies a folding of an unspecified number of components, rather than a limited number of components as in (a). Methods of limiting the number of components in a folding will be explained later.

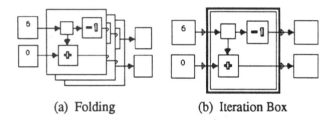

(a) Folding   (b) Iteration Box

Figure 10: Folding Abstraction

In ST, there are three different forms of interaction (communication) among the folded components and their shared environment: *serial*, *parallel*, and *global*. Parallel iteration is used to represent a *database* as an array of records, and a *data query* as an array of query, each accessing records in parallel. Due to the space limitation, however, parallel iteration will not be discussed here. Database applications in ST are described in [11].

Sequential iteration: A folding with a sequential iteration provides a serial communication between the components. Sequential iteration is represented by a pair of *sequential ports* (small triangles) attached to the iteration box. Figure 11 shows the general syntax and semantics of sequential iteration, where α is an arbitrary box-graph. There may be more than one sequential port on a single iteration box, as illustrated by Figure 10(b), but only one arrow may pass through each sequential port.

When the ST system executes an iteration box such as the one in Figure 11(a), the system unfolds the array by dynamically creating a new copy of *a* and transferring the data from the existing most recent component to the new one. The unfolding terminates when the newly created box-graph component is evaluated as inconsistent. For example, the unbounded iteration box of Figure 10(b) can be bounded as shown in Figure 12. The box-graph computes 6+5+4+3+2+1 = 21.

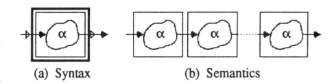

(a) Syntax   (b) Semantics

Figure 11: Sequential Iteration

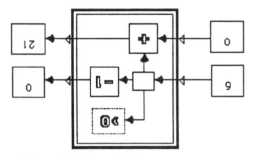

Figure 12: Bounded Sequential Iteration

Note that the data transfer from one component to the next is synchronized at the boundary of the component, limiting the degree of parallelism existing inside the array. However, within each component, dataflows are still asynchronous and potentially parallel. Also note that the array components can communicate with each other only through sequential iteration.

Global input: An iteration box can receive a data value from an incoming arrow when the arrow does not pass through any communication port. The value will be transferred to every component of the iteration corresponding to a global variable in a traditional programming language. The syntax and semantics are given in Figure 13.

For example, the puzzle in Figure 14 defines the square-root function using the Newton's method and is equivalent to the following sequential program where the variable *a* is a global input to the repetitive construct:

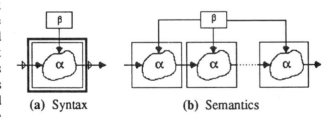

(a) Syntax   **(b) Semantics**

Figure 13: Sequential Iteration with Global Inputs

```
read(a);
x := a;
repeat
        y := x;
        x := (a/y + y)/2;
until  y - x ≤ 0.001;
write (x).
```

Visual programming (VP) is a new research area of importance. The first fundamental issue in VP is the visualization of programming concepts, i.e., how to represent data structures and algorithms so that a user can closely and efficiently interact with a computation through high resolution graphics. We have introduced *keyboardless programming* as a goal of VP, assuming that if we minimize the usage of a keyboard, we will maximize the visualization of programming concepts. Show and Tell[tm] was designed and implemented to investigate to what degree we can achieve this goal. We conclude that successful programming can be performed without keyboarding, unless desired.

At the outset of the ST project in 1983, we made a fundamental judgement that dataflow is a more suitable model of computation for school children than that of the von Neumann machine model. Recently, more visual programming languages have adopted the use of dataflow rather than control flow, as their semantic foundation [4,6,7]. Our experiences with the ST system confirm our judgement.

Folding and propagation of inconsistency in ST are examples of programming concepts that are unique to visual programming. These concepts are unique because they are spatial concepts, and the notion of space is not well established in traditional programming languages. Future investigation of various spatial programming concepts is more urgent in visual programming than in textual programming.

Another challenge necessitated by VP is a formal study of two-dimensional languages. There is no known formal grammar for ST puzzles. Some of our efforts to construct formal syntax for two-dimensional languages are described in [1] and [5]. In [1], we have demonstrated that a two-dimensional systolic array can detect cycles in an ST box-graph using linear time. In [5], we show that a major subset of ST box-graphs can be formally specified by an index grammar. In [10], we use a pseudo BNF grammar assisted by English to specify the syntax of ST. In this informal two-dimensional grammar, the shape and type of a figure are significant, while the size and geographic location are not. Our basic idea behind the grammar is our realization that two-dimensional grammars require two composition operations, *concatenation* and *superposition*, while one-dimensional grammars require only the concatenation operation.

The current version of the ST system is interpreter based. The performance consideration was secondary to the conceptual feasibility of keyboardless programming. After having established the feasibility, we designed and implemented a prototype ST compiler. See [2] for the detail.

The declarative semantics of ST in [9] encourages us to investigate the relationship between ST and other declarative languages. One such investigation can be pursued by extending ST into *Picture LISP* and *Picture Prolog*. While basic components of LISP are already incorporated into ST by design, it is not the case for

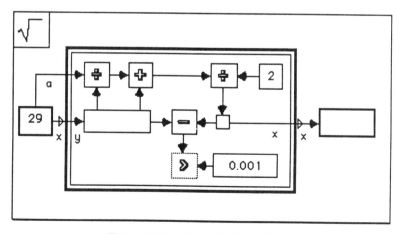

Figure 14: Iteration with Global Inputs

Prolog. A visual language for logic programming will require new ideas beyond those provided in ST.

Finally, a design and implementation of an ST system drawer for *Picture Logo* will demonstrate a contribution of ST in educational application, which was, after all, the initial motivation for developing a visual programming language.

6. References

[1]   Bojanczyk, A.W. and Kimura, T.D., "A Systolic Parsing Algorithm for a Visual Programming Language," Proceedings of *Fall Joint Computer Conference*, 1986, pp. 48-55.

[2]   Choi, J.W. and Kimura, T.D., "A Compiler for a Two-dimensional Programming Language," Proceedings of ACM Conference on Personal and Small Computers, ACM, N.Y., Dec. 1986

[3]   Davis, A.L. and Keller, R.M., "Data Flow Program Graphs," *IEEE Computer*, Vol. 15, No. 2, Feb. 1982, pp. 26-41.

[4]   Gerasch, T.E., Rice, M.D., and Seidman, S.B., "Graphical Programming Languages for MIMD Computation," *TR-10-87*, Center for Parallel Computation, George Mason University, Fairfax, VA., Sept. 1987.

[5]   Gillett, W.D. and Kimura, T.D., "Parsing Two-dimensional Languages," *Proceedings of Tenth International COMPSAC '86*, IEEE Computer, 1986, pp. 472-477.

[6]   Haeberli, P.E., "ConMan: A Visual Programming Language for Interactive Graphics," *Computer Graphics*, Vol. 22, No. 4, Aug. 1988, pp. 103-111.

[7]   Ingalls, D., Wallace, S., Chow, Y.Y., Ludolph, F., and Doyle, K., "Fabrik: A Visual Programming Environment," *Proceedings of OOPSLA Conference*, ACM, N.Y., 1988.

[8]   Kimura, T.D., "Completion Problem and Its Solution for Context-Free Languages (Algebraic Approach)," Ph.D. Thesis, *Moore School Report 72-09*, University of Pennsulvania, Philadelphia, Penn., May 1971.

[9]   Kimura, T.D., "Determinacy of Hierarchical Dataflow Model: A Computation Model for Visual Programming," *Technical Report WUCS-86-5*, Department of Computer Science, Washington University, St. Louis, MO., March, 1986.

[10]   Kimura, T.D., Choi, J.W., and Mack, J.M., "A Visual Language for Keyboardless Programming," Technical *Report WUCS-86-6*, Department of Computer Science, Washington University, St. Louis, MO., March 1986.

[11]   Kimura, T.D., "Relational Completeness of Visual Programming Language," *Technical Report WUCS-88-15*, Department of Computer Science, Washington University, St. Louis, MO., Sept. 1988.

[12]   Shneiderman, B., "Direct Manipulation: A Step Beyond Programming Languages," *IEEE Computer*, Vol. 16, No. 8, Aug. 1983, pp. 57-69.

[13]   Shu, N.C., *Visual Programming*, Van Nostrand Reinhold Company, N.Y., 1988.

[14]   Private conversation with Seymour Papert.

The Fabrik Programming Environment

Frank Ludolph, Yu-Ying Chow, Dan Ingalls, Scott Wallace, Ken Doyle

Apple Computer Inc.
20525 Mariani Avenue
Cupertino, CA 95014

Abstract

Fabrik is an experimental interactive graphical programming environment designed to simplify the programming process by integrating the user interface, the programming language and its representation, and the environmental languages used to construct and debug programs. The programming language uses a functional, bidirectional data-flow model that trivializes syntax and eliminates the need for some traditional programming abstractions. Program synthesis is simplified by the use of aggregate and application-specific operations, modifiable examples, and the direct construction of graphical elements. The user interface includes several features designed to ease the construction and editing of the program graphs. Understanding of both individual functions and program operation are aided by immediate execution and feedback as the program is edited.

Keywords: visual programming, data-flow, direct manipulation, programming-with-example, user interface

Introduction

Fabrik is designed to simplify programming, a difficult task requiring large investments of time and effort. Lewis and Olson [1] summarize many of the difficulties associated with programming, among them the concepts of control-flow and variables, the use of multiple abstract representations, and the complexity of program synthesis. Their analysis of the spreadsheet programming paradigm suggests that its success is a result of many factors including a familiar, concrete, visible representation, suppression of the inner world of computation, automatic consistency maintenance, aggregate and high-level operations, and immediate feedback. They state that the features that make spreadsheets relatively easy to use are applications of some of the principles of cognition, such as the use of familiar representations and analogies to aid understanding, and the use of immediate feedback to aid problem-solving.

BASIC was the first widely used end-user programming environment. It achieved this status, in part, because it too contained features that were applications of those cognitive principles, e.g. immediate statement execution, easy access to the inner world of computation, a more concrete representation of variables, a few aggregate operations, and a simplified edit-compile-execute-debug cycle.

The developers of spreadsheet and BASIC programming environments also recognized that programming involves more than just the programming language. Both integrated to some extent the environmental languages used to construct, debug and modify programs and spreadsheets virtually eliminated the edit-compile-link-execute-debug cycle.

While BASIC and spreadsheets have taken significant steps to simplify programming, more needs be done. Generally speaking, spreadsheets have little support for creation and use of high-level, user-defined functions, and BASIC has only a simple subroutine facility. Debugging is still difficult in spite of the inner world suppression because the control-flow, multi-assignment properties of BASIC require the programmer to know the execution history in order to interpret the current state of the program, and neither spreadsheets nor BASIC provides for a broad, visible, concrete presentation of program relationships.

Fabrik is a visual environment that attempts to make programming more accessible to the casual and novice programmer by supplementing and extending the concepts that made spreadsheets and BASIC successful. The remainder of this paper describes elements of the Fabrik language and programming environment that could significantly simplify the programming task. A companion paper addresses the topics of synthetic graphics and compilation, and provides a more detailed discussion of the language elements described in the next section [2].

Language Overview

Fabrik is an interactive environment based on an augmented structural data-flow model. Programs are represented as data-flow graphs of interconnected function icons, called *components*. This basic approach, used by many other systems [3-8], was chosen because a graphical representation presents the programmer with a concrete view of the relationships between data and functions. Data-flow graphs provide good support for user-defined abstractions because they can be hooked together and nested. On the other hand, control-flow graphs, e.g. flow charts, usually treat the access of data stored in variables as a side-effect, and side-effects make the merging of graphs more difficult. In fact, the need for variables to store temporary results disappears altogether from data-flow graphs.

The two prevailing models of data-flow are the token and structure models [3]. In the token model, data is viewed as a token that is absorbed by a node, transformed, and passed on to downstream nodes. Iteration is accomplished by creating loops in the graph to recycle tokens. In the structural model the data is not absorbed but remains for the lifetime of the execution. Nodes generate new output data based on the inputs. Streams of data are treated as a structure, e.g. lists or trees. Iteration is accomplished without loops by aggregate or recursive functions that operate on an entire structure. The maintenance of the execution history and the elimination of loops remove much of a program's dynamic operation and gives the structural model and, as a result, Fabrik a "timelessness" that makes program operation easier to understand and simplifies debugging.

Bidirectional Data-flow

Fabrik enhances the traditional data-flow model with bidirectional data-flow. Components have connection points or *pins* around their periphery. Input and output pins are shown as triangles that point toward or away from the component respectively. Bidirectional components have diamond-shaped pins which may function either as input or output depending on the direction of the dataflow. This extension permits the construction of components that combine several related functions, typically a function and its inverse, within a single package.

The direction of the data-flow through a bidirectional pin is established by the modality of the pins to which it is connected. For example, if a bidirectional pin is connected to an output-pin, it will function as an input pin. The actual function performed by the component is the one whose input and output specification matches the data-flow. The packaging of multiple functions in a single package results in a fewer number of system components.

Bidirectional diagrams result from the use of bidirectional components. Input entering a component at the left of a diagram, such as through a type-in box, may flow through the diagram left-to-right, while input entering a component at the right may flow right-to-left through the same diagram components and connections. This bidirectionality provides a simple local constraint mechanism [9] and results in diagrams with fewer components and connections.

Syntax

The syntax of text-based languages is always problematical for the inexperienced or casual programmer. The syntax for graphs is very simple, node-arc-node. Using a mouse, Fabrik components are dragged from a parts bin onto the Fabrik diagram and released. The mouse is then used to draw connections between the pins of different components. Potential syntax errors are limited to attempts by the user to connect incompatible pins, e.g. input to input, graphic to numeric, and connections that result in loops. If the programmer attempts such a connection, Fabrik refuses to make the connection and informs the user of the incompatibility. Thus every Fabrik diagram is always syntactically correct.

Diagrams that have unconnected pins may still execute. A component with one or more unconnected input pins may be able to generate output value(s) either because an unconnected input pin might have a defined default value, or because some function of the component can compute without using the pin's value. If a component cannot compute, the values on the output pins are invalid and this invalidity is passed on to the connected input pins, overriding any default value defined for the pin. Connections that carry an invalid value is shown as a dashed line.

This section described techniques that Fabrik uses to simplify the programming language. The structural data-flow model promotes understanding of program operation with its timelessness and simplified model of iteration. The use of diagrams rather than linear text simplifies the syntax and makes the program relationships visible and concrete. And bidirectionality reduces both system and program component counts and the number of program connections.

Building A Simple Analog Clock

The Fabrik programming environment includes a basic set of predefined components. The components perform arithmetic, string and graphic manipulation, file access, and generate common graphical elements such as rectangles, ovals, lines, polygons and bitmaps. Additional sets or *kits* of application specific components can be added as needed. For example, a modern application program has many idiomatic graphic elements that make up its user interface. A user interface kit might contain components such as views, panels with editable text, lists of selectable items, choice buttons, scroll bars, and menus that can be combined in various ways when building new applications.

Some of the components are *primitive*, implementing system-defined functions. The rest are *built* from primitive and possibly other built components, and they can be altered by the user. Primitive and built components are essentially indistinguishable from each other in appearance and use.

In this section, we illustrate the Fabrik programming process and the support for browsing, constructing, testing and packaging a complete application by building a simple analog clock. Figure 1a shows a Fabrik Parts Bin window (above) and a Fabrik Construction Window (below). At the bottom of the

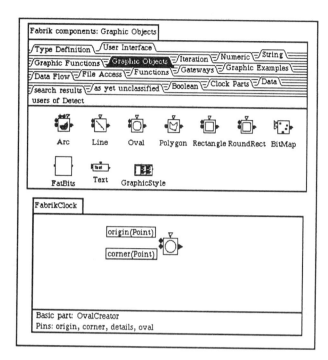

Figure 1a. An Oval Creator has been dragged from the Parts Bin (above) to a new Construction Window (below).

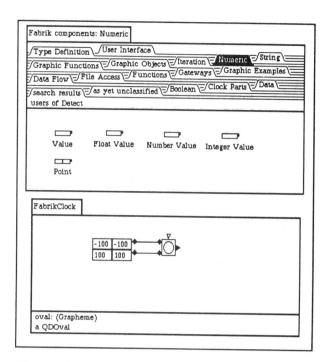

Figure 1b. Two Points have been connected to the Oval Creator and locations of the top-left corner and bottom-right corner have been entered. The oval grapheme is waiting at the output pin of the Oval Creator.

Construction Window is a *status panel* that displays information about the selected component, pin, or vertex, and feedback about editing activity such as error messages about attempts to connect incompatible pins. The operation of the Parts Bin is described below under *Finding Components*.

To build a Fabrik application, the user drags components from the Parts Bin into a Construction Window, and connects their pins together. In the first figure, an Oval component has been copied from the Graphic Objects category of the Parts Bin to the Construction window to be used as the clock face. The Oval has two pins on the left, for the locations of the top-left and bottom-right corners of a box that would contain the oval, and a pin on top for specifying border width, border pattern and inside pattern. The oval grapheme of the specified size and appearance is output from the pin at the right.

In figure 1b, the author has dragged two Point components from the Numeric category of the Parts Bin and connected them to the Oval. During connection, a pin's name and type (as shown in figure 1a) automatically pops-up when the cursor is over the pin. In this figure the author has entered two points for the top left corner and the bottom right corner of the clock face, i.e. the clock face will have a radius of 100 pixels.

In figure 1c, the author has dragged both Group and ScalableDisplay components from the Graphic Functions category of the Parts Bin. A Group can merge any number of graphemes. When the Group was copied, the user specified that it should have four input pins, although pins can be added and deleted at

any time. As soon as the Oval output was connected to the Group input and the Group output connected to the ScalableDisplay input, the clock face was displayed. The ScalableDisplay, one of several graphic viewers in the library, automatically scales the input grapheme to the size of the viewer.

In figure 1d, a ClockHand component has been copied from the Clock Parts category of the Parts Bin three times and the output of each connected to input pins on the Group. The three ClockHand components will produce the second, minute and hour hand graphemes. Inputs to a ClockHand component are two

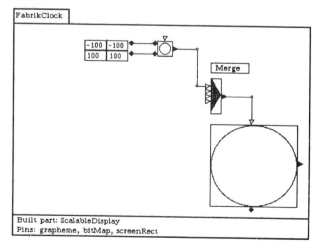

Figure 1c. A Group and a ScalableDisplay have been installed and attached to view the clock face.

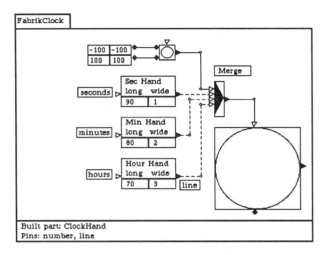

Figure 1d. Three ClockHand generators have been laid down and connected to the Group to produce second, minute and hour hands.

type-in boxes to customize the length and width of its hand display and an input number between 0 and 59. In the clock example, the second hand (the top one) will display as 90 pixels long and 1 pixel wide, the minute hand 80 long and 2 wide, and the hour hand 70 long and 3 wide. The connections between the ClockHand outputs and the Group appear dashed at this point in the construction because, with no hands produced yet, the values are invalid. Fabrik tracks invalidity so that no component executes with invalid input data.

In figure 1e a Time component has been added and connected to the Second ClockHand and Minute ClockHand. Activated by the connections to their inputs the Second and Minute ClockHands generate their graphical clock-hand outputs and the dashed output connection lines become solid. The clock-hands are merged with the clock face and displayed. Our clock is running and the clock hands are moving as the time

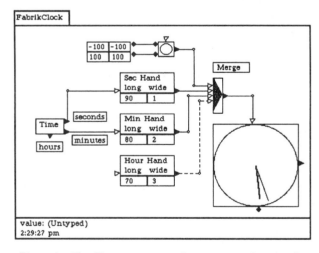

Figure 1e. The Time component that generates the seconds, minutes and hours has been hooked up to produce the display of the second and minute hands.

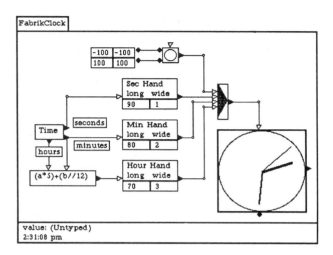

Figure 1f. To show the hour hand in proper position a Formula has been attached that converts the hours in between 0 and 11 to between 0 and 59 depending the minutes value.

changes. Only the hour hand remains to be added.

Figure 1f shows a Formula component added to convert the hours from the Time component, an number between 0 and 11, to a number between 0 and 59 for the Hour ClockHand. It also adds in an offset for the number of elapsed minutes. The Formula component evaluates an expression (currently in Smalltalk-80 syntax) typed-in by the user. Here the first argument pin ('a' in the expression) is connected to the hour output pin from the Time component and the second argument pin ('b') is connected to the minutes pin. The hour-hand grapheme propagates and is displayed.

The desired application has been programmed and is now fully functional. However, the clock display is surrounded by the computational components and their connections. Fabrik allows a subregion of a diagram to be designated as the *user frame*. This has been done with the ScalableDisplay in figure 1f, and the user frame is shown as a heavy border around its periphery. Once the user frame has been designated, a menu command is used to *enter* the frame. This command instructs Fabrik to restrict the view to only

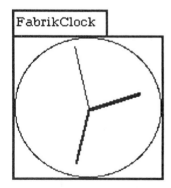

Figure 1g The connection diagram has been hidden and the clock can be launched and its window can be resized just like a normal application.

the designated components, and to make the result visible in a standard application window. Figure 1g shows our clock after entering the user frame and being enlarged for better viewing.

An application such as this can easily be assembled in a short amount of time. Moreover all of the original scaffolding can later be retrieved for documentation or as the basis for a revision. This ease of "opening the hood" adds to the potential reusability of Fabrik software and provides the end user with the ability to tailor an application to his specific needs.

The Fabrik Environment

The Fabrik environment has many elements: a component library, library management functions, file system interface, a graphical language-based editor, an interactive run-time system with change-triggered recomputation, and a set of debugging tools. Each element has some user interface aspects.

User Interface Guidelines

The intended Fabrik user interface was to be generally Macintosh-like though the experimental nature of the Fabrik project, implementation in Smalltalk-80, and the requirements specific to the programming task encouraged us to try new alternatives. The interface was to be single-handed, mouse-based, visible, concrete, and direct. Many alternatives were tried. Often competing approaches were implemented and made switchable by a flag setting in order to understand each alternative better and discover personal preferences. Although the experience is anecdotal, we feel it has value and some of the more interesting alternatives are described below.

One-Handed and Two-Handed Input

Since the early days of the mouse, there has been a continuous debate between those that prefer to use keyboard-based interfaces and those that prefer mouse-based interfaces. But there is also a more muted discussion on the mouse side about one- and two-handed input. The most common forms of two-handed input are the use of command-keys as an alternative to menus and the use of modifier keys to alter the function of the mouse button. In addition, Buxton [11] and others suggest the use of additional devices, such as the touch pad, to be controlled by the alternate, "non-mouse" hand. The reasoning behind two-handed input is that it can increase the bandwidth from person to machine, alleviating a common performance bottleneck caused by today's faster machines and user-event driven applications.

Fabrik was initially designed to be run single-handed and, to that end, techniques not common to the Macintosh, e.g. the gesture menus described below, have been used. The occasional new operation that seemed to require the use of a second-hand was always augmented with single-handed alternatives soon afterward.

More than one user, shown only the single-handed methods, complained of having to "sit on their left hand." An apparently conflicting experience of the implementation group, who were all quite familiar with the two-handed alternatives, was that even those that pressed most for two-handed input tended toward single-handed use. Subsequent observation showed that there was only limited opportunity during editing to use the second hand and that it tended to move away from the keyboard to more relaxed positions when not used for a period of time.

As a result of this experience, the user interface goals have been modified to provide a two-pronged approach to mouse use: design a single-handed interface which is complete, visible, and as efficient as possible, and augment it with two-handed alternatives that focus on improved performance and continuous use. Where modifier keys are used in conjunction with the mouse button, there has been an attempt to define a consistent set of modifier operations that can be applied to all objects. For example, the shift key is used for multiple selection and to constrain drawing operations, the command key is used with alpha keys to issue commands and with the mouse button to pop-up a menu appropriate to the object under the cursor, and two other keys are used for moving and drawing.

Building Programs

Program synthesis, the process of constructing a program from component parts, is difficult. The programmer must have full knowledge of what each of the parts does, how the parts interact, and plans for combining parts to perform common functions such as counting, traversing data structures, etc. Most languages also require the programmer to translate from "what" is to be done to "how" to do it. In spite of the difficulties, synthesis is used to write programs because decades of use have demonstrated its extraordinary flexibility.

Fabrik provides support to ease many of the inherent difficulties. Structural data-flow reduces the "how" by relieving the programmer of the need to specify much of the arbitrary sequencing associated with control-flow. Built-in high-level and aggregate components reduce the need for the programmer to learn and remember plans. Immediate execution gives rapid feedback about the in-diagram operation of components. And on-line support for locating, documenting, and examining in-diagram use of components aid in component selection.

Fabrik also supports alternatives to synthesis: modification and programming-with-example. Given a large library of working components, it might often be easier to find and modify a similar component rather than build a new one from scratch. Important to this approach is support for rapidly locating the potential base component. When a suitable, modifiable example cannot be easily located, the user might construct a (portion of a) new program by giving examples as when defining the programs graphic elements and their behavior [12]. In Fabrik the programmer draws graphical elements within a Draw component which automatically generates the corresponding Fabrik diagram as the elements are drawn. (See "The Draw Component" below.)

Finding Components

The Parts Bin is divided into sections indicated by folder tabs. Fabrik maintains two permanent folders, "search results" and "as yet unclassified." The user can add, delete, and rename other folders at will. All components are kept in the Parts Bin and appears in at least one folder. The user can put copies of a component in additional folders or delete a component from a folder.

Fabrik currently supports three kinds of searches: partial-name, keyword, and content. Each places copies of the selected components in the "search results" folder. The results remain in the folder until the next search is performed. The partial-name search is a simple form that all components that contain the given string anywhere in their names. The keyword search selects all components that include any of the given keywords anywhere in component's on-line text description or within comment blocks in the built component's diagram.

The content search selects built components that use a specified component, either primitive or built. (This is similar to opening a browser on a method's "senders" in Smalltalk-80 [15].) The content search is an important form of on-line documentation about a component. The user can open the diagrams of components found by a content search to see how the component of interest is used and, since Fabrik is interactive, what the component actually does within the diagram.

The Parts Bin provides an adequate organizing scheme for about 100 components. The current search facilities work reasonably well for this quantity, but for larger quantities additional facilities such as alphabetical and chronological listings, multiple parts bins, and a pin-type based topological search will be necessary.

Editing

A complete set of efficient techniques for editing diagrams does not yet exist, but it is useful to remember that editing text programs has not always been easy. Over the years sequence numbers have disappeared, simplifying statement insertion, and tools like group select, indent, and move have made it easier to coordinate logical organization and visual layout. As program interfaces become more complex, new tools are being developed that serve as learning and memory aids because, ultimately, the program text still must be accurately typed-in.

Drawing and CAD systems will likely be a rich source of new techniques during the next few years. There is some expectation that automatic aids, e.g. the routing of connections, will be important. They may

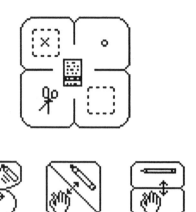

Figure 2. Gesture Menus. The lower three show alternatives menus for the same function.

well be, but it is interesting to note that the widely used editing aids for text-based languages today are the ones that provide efficient and precise manual control with minimal automated support.

The individual techniques used in Fabrik are not generally unique. Two not in common use, relocatable pins and directional gestures, are described below.

Pin Positioning

Fabrik components have pins that are used as connection points around their periphery. In many other diagram-based systems the connection points are invisible, fixed, or position dependent [4-8]. In Fabrik, the user can reposition a component's pins. This freedom of pin placement allows components to be placed directly adjacent to each other, as when creating a user frame, and enables the user to simplify a diagram's wiring by moving pins to reduce the number of twists and turns a connection must take. Although a pin that has been moved cannot be recognized by its location, identification by this means is only marginally useful given a large number of components. Moving the cursor over the pin gives immediate positive identification.

Directional Gestures

Fabrik uses simple directional gestures to increase the number of commands associated with the mouse button. The user initiates a gesture-based operation by positioning the cursor over an object, pressing the button and moving in a specific direction. Once the initial direction, hence operation, is established, the mouse may then be moved in any direction to complete the operation. If no significant cursor movement occurs within a half-second after the mouse button is pressed, a pop-up "gesture menu," such as those shown in figure 2, appears under the cursor. The short delay prevents flashing during normal editing but provides prompting for less commonly used operations.

For example, a gesture menu is used to both move and connect pins and vertices because their small, eight-pixel-square size is not large enough to allow separate areas to be designated for each operation. A connection is initiated by clicking on the pin/vertex and moving in one direction, while relocation is initiated by clicking and moving is a different direction. An additional set of gestures is defined for the editing window background and includes operations such as group select and delete.

The intent was to create a very fast form of command invocation using just one hand and is somewhat different from both pie menus [13] and full gestures [14]. Gestures require more complex movements that are difficult to perform with a mouse and are slow compared to a directional gesture. Pie and other forms of pop-up menus require the mouse button to be released over specific area to invoke the command, an action inappropriate for certain actions such as moving and drawing. There is also a visual feedback loop from eye to hand that slows command invocation.

Although no formal user-testing has been performed, experience suggests that the design of gesture menus is fairly critical. Four unique directions seems the maximum for fast error-free operation using a mouse, though wedges as small as 45 degrees may have acceptably low error-rates. The near-reflex response of learned movements to pre-conscious intent requires that common operations appearing on more than one menu must use the same direction regardless of context or high error rates will occur. And the asymmetric movement of the human wrist means that left-hand/right-hand differences should be considered.

User reception to gestures used in this way has been mixed. While established Fabrik users have few complaints, new users split about 50-50 initially until they learn to first establish the operation, then the direction. Even among some experienced users the feeling persists that other approaches might be more appropriate for operations that inherently include arbitrary direction, e.g. moving and drawing.

Running and Debugging

A Fabrik diagram is always active, that is, every time a connection or value is changed, the related subgraph recomputes its values. This immediate feedback after each action promotes understanding of both the function of individual components as they are added to the diagram and the operation of the diagram as a whole. The edit-compile-execute-debug cycle is greatly simplified since the process of editing automatically includes "compiling" and execution. (Fabrik is interpretive at diagram level, but built components are compiled when placed in the parts bin.)

Fabrik's structural data-flow model and graphical representation do much to simplify debugging. As mentioned above, the input and output values of each component persist following execution. Connections that have no value are shown as dashed lines (see figure 1d), immediately indicating to the the user inactive portions of the diagram. The user can click on any pin or vertex and see its value in the status panel at the bottom of the construction window. In addition, small value display boxes can be attached to pins and vertices to monitor values continuously at several points simultaneously.

Should the monitored values cause the user to suspect a faulty user-built subcomponent, it can be opened into an active edit view of its own to permit both monitoring values during operation and direct editing of the subcomponent. Edits are immediately reflected in the execution of the program. The changes may be saved, either as an updated version of the component or as a different component.

Encapsulation and the User Frame

When a Fabrik diagram has been completed the user places a user frame around the part of the diagram that is to be visible in its component/application form, as described in the Clock example above, and saves the diagram thus encapsulating its function as a reusable component that is available in the parts bin. If the user frame includes components that accept keyboard input or display components, they will be active in the component form, that is, the user can type in to them or they will display the results of their internal computation as appropriate.

An alternative to the user frame adopted by other systems [7] is the use of a second window that displays only the user visible elements of the diagram while the first window holds the entire diagram. This approach allows components to be arranged for display in an arbitrary fashion without impacting the diagram layout but at the cost of additional windows and a mechanism to relate visible components in the display view to the corresponding component in the diagram. We felt that these costs added too much complexity and so chose the simpler user frame, an approach we are comfortable with but do not yet have sufficient experience to validate.

The Draw Component

The Draw component is a special component that automatically generates the program diagram for graphical display while the user draws the graphical objects in the Draw component. It frees the user from having to find, place, and connect the corresponding graphic components and operations. It allows users to design graphical displays in a very natural way, much as a normal drawing program. Adjustments to the location and size of the graphic objects in the Draw component are immediately reflected in the diagram. Alternatively, the ability to enter specific values into the diagram using the keyboard gives the user the precise control that can be difficult using just the mouse. The Fabrik diagram generated is identical in structure to one assembled from scratch so the user can edit it directly to add additional components and

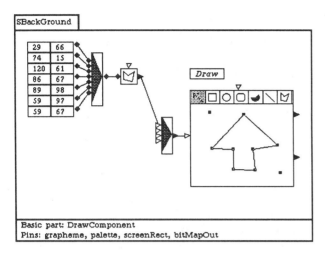

Basic part: DrawComponent
Pins: grapheme, palette, screenRect, bitMapOut

Figure 3a. A Draw component has been laid down and the polygon tool selected, and the sketch of an arrow has been drawn in the Draw component.

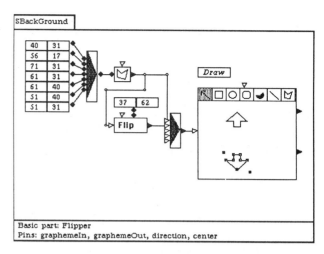

Basic part: Flipper
Pins: graphemeIn, graphemeOut, direction, center

Figure 3b. The arrow has been adjusted and a Flip component has been laid down to generate the down arrow.

connections that are not possible via the Draw component.

We demonstrate the Draw component by creating a scroll bar background that can later be combined with the thumbing logic for a usable scroll bar. The complete scroll bar diagram and the discussion of synthetic graphics and mouse sensitivity are in a companion paper [2].

The Draw component has a palette at the top for selecting the graphical objects to be drawn. In the example of figure 3a, the only component the user actually laid down was the the one marked "Draw". A scroll bar contains an upward-arrow, a downward-arrow and some rectangles. The polygon tool (the rightmost one in the palette) was selected first and a rough sketch of the up-arrow drawn. When the arrow drawing was finished, the rest of the diagram was automatically constructed by Fabrik. The selection tool (the leftmost one in the palette) was then selected. The control points for further adjusts are shown in the figure.

In figure 3b the author has adjusted the up-arrow to get the correct shape, size and location. To produce the down-arrow, Flip and Point components were dragged from the parts bin and connected as shown. The Point was connected to the "center" pin (top right one) of the Flip component, but no values were entered. (By default a grapheme is flipped vertically about its center.) When the output of the Flip was connected to the second input pin of the Group, the down-arrow appeared on top of the up-arrow. Then the down-arrow was dragged downward to the location shown in the figure which automatically updated the Point value to the corresponding value for the center of the Flip.

In figure 3c a rectangle tool (the second one from left in the palette) is selected first to create the rectangle (the Rectangle above "Up Arrow Rect") that surrounds the up-arrow. Then the same logic for flipping the up-

arrow is copied to flip this rectangle so that a second rectangle is created to surround the down-arrow. At this point, the order of the Group inputs is such that the arrows are displayed under their bounding rectangles. To reverse this ordering the author invokes a menu command in the Group component to rotate the connections downward twice. The corresponding portions of the diagram were manually rearranged using a group-move for neatness.

The the gray area (the Rectangle next to "Gray Area") was generated by creating another rectangle in the Draw component in between the two arrows' bounding rectangles. Under the area marked "Style", the color specification of this rectangle was generated with a GraphicStyle component, selecting '1' for the border width, 'black' for the border color and 'light gray' for the inside color, and then connecting its output pin to the graphic style pin (top) of the Rectangle.

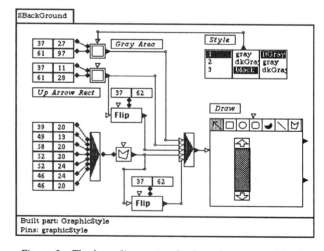

Built part: GraphicStyle
Pins: graphicStyle

Figure 3c. The bounding rectangles have been created in the Draw component and another Flip component was added for the down arrow's rectangle.

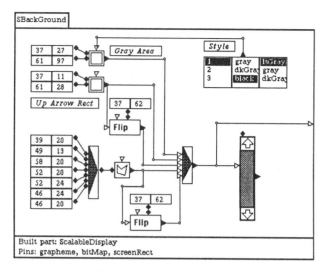

Built part: ScalableDisplay
Pins: grapheme, bitMap, screenRect

Figure 3d. The Draw component has been replaced by a ScalableDisplay so that the scroll bar will be automatically scaled to the viewer size. An output gateway has been added, and the diagram is ready to be used to build a scroll bar.

To complete the scroll bar for use with the thumbing logic, the author replaced the Draw component with a ScalableDisplay as shown in the figure 3d. An output gateway was added to the right side of the window and connected to provide the scroll bar grapheme to the user of this component. Now with a user frame around the ScalableDisplay, this component is ready to be stored into the parts bin for use with other components.

History and Experience

Fabrik began with an attempt to mix arbitrary layout and cell types in an object-oriented spreadsheet. The spreadsheet approach broke down with the complex expressions needed for synthetic graphics and other generative structures. Graphical layout, as described above, addressed this problem and also opened the way for bidirectional dependence.

The initial Fabrik prototype was developed in Smalltalk within the Advanced Technology Group of Apple in 1985, and was demonstrated widely within Apple in Spring of 1986. Two more feature-laden and library-rich versions were made available to a limited audience by Spring of 1987. The type system was added during the Winter of 1987 and compilation was completed in the Spring of 1988.

Rapid system evolution and poor performance have limited experience with the programming environment to the implementation of demonstration programs, e.g. the clock, configurable analog gauges, and simple animated simulations, simple parsers, bar charts, and the full set of relational database operators. Now that the system is more stable and compilation has improved the performance, it is possible to attack more interesting problems.

An important next step in this investigation is to assemble a library of components sufficient to accommodate a large class of applications, and to support networking of this library so that many people can borrow from, and experiment with, each other's work. This broader group of users and programs will help to test the ideas expressed above, investigate solutions to the problems of diagram complexity, and evolve the user interface more rapidly.

References

[1] C. Lewis and G.M. Olson, "Can Principles of Cognition Lower the Barriers to Programming?" in *Empirical Studies of Programmers (Vol 2)*, Ablex, 1987.

[2] D. Ingalls, S. Wallace, Y-Y. Chow, F. Ludolph, K. Doyle, "Fabrik: A Visual Programming Environment," to appear in *1988 OOPSLA Conference Proceedings*.

[3] A.L. Davis and R.M.Keller, "Data flow Program Graphs," *IEEE Computer*, Feb. 1982, pp 26-41.

[4] P. McLain and T.D Kimura, *Show and Tell™ User's Manual*. Tech. Report WUCS-86-4, Dept. of Computer Science, Washington University, St. Louis, March, 1986.

[5] I. Yoshimoto, N. Monden, M. Hirakawa, M. Tanaka, T. Ichikawa, "Interactive Iconic Programming Facility in Hi-Visual," *1986 IEEE Workshop on Visual Languages*, pp 34-41.

[6] ProGraph™, on-line documentation, 1988.

[7] *LabVIEW™ Demonstration Manual*, National Instruments, Corp. Austin, Texas, 1987.

[8] D.N. Smith, "InterCONS: Interface CONstruction Set," Tech. Report RC 13108, IBM T.J.Watson Research Center, September 1987.

[9] A.H. Borning, "ThingLab -- A Constraint-Oriented Simulation Laboratory," Tech. Report SSL-79-3, Xerox Palo Alto Research Center, July, 1979.

[10] D.C. Smith, *Pygmalion*, ISR 40, Birkhauser Verlag Basel, 1977.

[11] W. Buxton and B.A. Myers, "A Study in Two-Handed Input," *Proc. CHI'86 Human Factors in Computer Systems*, pp 321-326.

[12] B.A. Myers, "The State of the Art in Visual Programming and Program Visualization," Tech. Report CMU-CS-88-114, Computer Science Department, Carnegie Mellon University, Pittsburg, PA. 1988.

[13] J. Callahan, D. Hopkins, M. Weiser, B. Shneiderman, "An Empirical Comparison of Pie vs. Linear Menus," *Proc. CHI '88 Human Factors in Computer Systems*, pp. 95-100.

[14] M. Lamb and V. Buckley, "New Techniques for Gesture-Based Dialog," *Human-Computer Interaction - INTERACT '84*, North-Holland, Amsterdam, 1984, pp. 135-138.

[15] A. Goldberg, *Smalltalk-80, The Interactive Programming Environment*, pp 178-179, Addison-Wesley, 1984

□□□ 7 □□□ Case Study: The Evolution of ThingLab

A.H. Borning. "The Programming Language Aspects of ThingLab, a Constraint Oriented Simulation Laboratory." *ACM Trans. on Programming Languages and Systems*, 3(4):353–387, October 1981.

A.H. Borning. "Graphically Defining New Building Blocks in ThingLab." *Human–Computer Interaction*, 2(4):269–295, 1986.

A.H. Borning, R. Duisberg, B. Freeman-Benson, A. Kramer and M. Woolf. "Constraint Hierarchies." In *Proc. OOPSLA '87*, Orlando, Fla., pages 48–60, October 4-8, 1987. ACM Press, New York.

The Programming Language Aspects
of ThingLab, a Constraint-Oriented
Simulation Laboratory

ALAN BORNING
Xerox Palo Alto Research Center

The programming language aspects of a graphic simulation laboratory named ThingLab are presented. The design and implementation of ThingLab are extensions to Smalltalk. In ThingLab, *constraints* are used to specify the relations that must hold among the parts of the simulation. The system is object-oriented and employs *inheritance* and *part-whole* hierarchies to describe the structure of a simulation. An interactive, graphic user interface is provided that allows the user to view and edit a simulation.

Key Words and Phrases: constraints, constraint satisfaction, object-oriented languages, inheritance, part–whole hierarchies, Smalltalk, ThingLab
CR Categories: 3.69, 4.22, 8.1, 8.2

1. INTRODUCTION

This paper describes the programming language aspects of a simulation laboratory named ThingLab. The principal research issue addressed is the representation and satisfaction of *constraints*. A constraint specifies a relation that must be maintained. For example, suppose that a user desires that the value of some integer always be displayed as a piece of text at a certain location on the screen. In a conventional language, one must remember to update the text whenever the value of the integer is changed, and to update the integer if the text is edited. In a constraint-oriented system such as ThingLab, the user can specify the relation between the text and the integer and leave it to the system to maintain that relation. If additional constraints are placed on the integer or the text, the system takes care of keeping these satisfied as well.

The notion of an *object* provides a basic organizational tool; in particular, the modularity gained by the use of object-oriented programming techniques is important for constraint satisfaction, where it is essential to know what is affected by a given change. Nonprimitive objects are constructed hierarchically from *parts*, which are themselves other objects. As is shown below, constraints provide a natural way to express the relations among parts and subparts. Methods are

This work was supported in part by the Xerox Corporation.
Author's present address: Department of Computer Science, FR-35, University of Washington, Seattle, WA 98195.
© 1981 ACM 0164-0925/81/1000-0353 $00.75

also described for integrating the use of constraints with *inheritance hierarchies*, allowing new kinds of objects to be described in terms of existing ones. Finally, an interactive, graphic user interface is described that is integrated with the constraint, part–whole, and inheritance mechanisms, allowing a user to view and edit objects conveniently.

The concept of constraints, combined with inheritance and part–whole hierarchies, is one that could add significant power to programming languages. While ThingLab is not a general-purpose language, many of the concepts and techniques described here would be useful in such a context. A promising direction for future research is to explore the design of a full constraint-oriented programming language.

ThingLab is an extension to the Smalltalk-76 programming language [6, 7] and runs on a personal computer. This paper is based on the author's Stanford Ph.D. dissertation [2].

1.1 The ThingLab System

The original question addressed by the research described in this paper is as follows: "How can we design a computer-based environment for constructing interactive, graphic simulations of experiments in physics and geometry?" Examples of the sorts of things that a user should be able to simulate are simple electrical circuits and mechanical linkages. However, the underlying system should be general. Rather than a program with knowledge built into it about electrical circuit components and linkages, we envisioned a sort of kit-building kit, in which environments tailored for domains such as electrical circuit simulations or geometric figures could be constructed. There would thus be two kinds of users of the system. The first kind would employ ThingLab to construct a set of building blocks for a given domain; for example, for use in simulating electrical circuits, such a user would construct definitions of basic parts such as resistors, batteries, wires, and meters. The second kind of user could then employ these building blocks to construct and explore particular simulations.

Another requirement on the system was that it have an appropriate user interface, particularly for the second kind of user working in a particular domain. For example, to create a geometric object such as a triangle, the user should be able simply to draw it on the screen, rather than having to type in its coordinates or (worse) write some code. Similarly, making changes to an object should also be natural. To move a vertex of the triangle, the user should be able to point to it on the screen and drag it along with a pointing device, seeing it in continuous motion, rather than pointing to the destination and having the triangle jump suddenly, or (again, worse) typing in the coordinates of the destination.

As specified in the above problem description, ThingLab provides an environment for constructing dynamic models of experiments in geometry and physics, such as simulations of constrained geometric objects, simple electrical circuits, mechanical linkages, and bridges under load. However, the techniques developed in ThingLab have wider application and have also been used to model other sorts of objects, such as a graphic calculator, and documents with constraints on their layout and contents. Examples of the system in operation are presented in Section 2.

ACM Transactions on Programming Languages and Systems, Vol. 3, No. 4, October 1981.

1.2 Constraints

The range of relations that can be specified in ThingLab using constraints is broad. Some examples of constraints that have been defined by various users are

(1) that a line be horizontal;
(2) that the height of a bar in a bar chart correspond to an entry in a table;
(3) that one triangle be twice as big as another;
(4) that a resistor obey Ohm's law;
(5) that a beam in a bridge obey Hooke's law;
(6) that the gray-scale level of an area on the computer's display correspond to a number between zero and one;
(7) that a rectangle on the display be precisely big enough to hold a given paragraph.

The representation of constraints reflects their dual nature as both descriptions and commands. Constraints in ThingLab are represented as a *rule* and a set of *methods* that can be invoked to satisfy the constraint. The rule is used by the system to construct a procedural test for whether or not the constraint is satisfied and to construct an error expression that indicates how well the constraint is satisfied. The methods describe alternate ways of satisfying the constraint; if any one of the methods is invoked, the constraint will be satisfied.

It is up to the user to specify the constraints on an object, but it is up to the system to satisfy them. Satisfying constraints is not always trivial. A basic problem is that constraints are typically multidirectional. For example, the text–integer constraint mentioned above is allowed to change either the text or the integer. Thus, one of the tasks of the system is to choose among several possible ways of locally satisfying each constraint. One constraint may interfere with another; in general, the collection of all the constraints on an object may be incomplete, circular, or contradictory. Again, it is up to the system to sort this out.

Further, the user interface as specified in the problem description demands that constraint satisfaction be rapid. Consider the case of the user continuously moving some part of a complex geometric figure. Every time the part moves, the object's constraints may need to be satisfied again. To meet this speed requirement, constraint satisfaction techniques have been implemented that incrementally analyze constraint interactions and compile the results of this analysis into executable code. When possible, the system compiles code that satisfies the constraints in one pass. Constraint satisfaction thus takes place in two stages: there is an initial planning stage, in which a constraint satisfaction plan is formulated and compiled; then at run time this compiled code is invoked to update the object being altered.

Constraint representation is described in Section 4; constraint satisfaction is discussed in Section 5.

1.3 Object-Oriented Language Techniques

Smalltalk, in which ThingLab is written, is a language based on the idea of objects that communicate by sending and receiving messages. This object-centered factorization of knowledge provides one of the basic organizational tools.

For example, in representing a geometric construction, the objects used in the representation are things such as points, lines, and triangles. This provides a natural way of bundling together the information and procedures relevant to each object. Each object holds its own state and is also able to send and receive messages to obtain results.

Object descriptions and computational methods are organized into *classes*. Every object is an *instance* of some class. In broad terms, a class represents a generic concept, while an instance represents an individual. A class holds the similarities among a group of objects; instances hold the differences. More specifically, a class has a description of the internal storage required for each of its instances and a dictionary of messages that its instances understand, along with *methods* (i.e., procedures) for computing the appropriate responses. An instance holds the particular values that distinguish it from other instances of its class.

A new class is normally defined as a subclass of an existing class. The subclass inherits the instance storage requirements and message protocol of its superclass. It may add new information of its own and may override inherited responses to messages.

One of the important features of Smalltalk is the sharp distinction it makes between the inside and the outside of an object. The internal aspects of an object are (1) its class and (2) its instance fields and their contents; the external aspects are the messages that it understands and its responses. Since other parts of the system and the user interact with the object by sending and receiving messages, they need not know about its internal representation. This makes it easier to construct modular systems. For example, the class Rectangle defines the message *center*. It makes no difference to the user of this message whether a rectangle actually has a center stored as one of its instance fields or whether the center is computed on demand (in fact, it is computed on demand).

ThingLab extends Smalltalk in a number of respects. The principal extension is the inclusion of constraints and constraint satisfaction mechanisms. The other significant extensions are provision for multiple superclasses rather than just a single superclass; a part–whole hierarchy with an explicit, symbolic representation of shared substructure; the use of *paths* for symbolic references to subparts and *prototypes* for the representation of default instances; and a facility for class definition by example. The latter extensions are discussed in Section 3.

Object-oriented languages generally emphasize a very localized approach to interaction within a program: an object interacts with other parts of the system only by sending and receiving messages to other objects that it knows about. On the other hand, it is very difficult to do constraint satisfaction in a purely local way: there are problems of circularity and the like that are better spotted by a more global analysis. There is consequently a tension between the object and constraint metaphors; the integration of these approaches in ThingLab is one of its points of interest.

1.4 The User Interface

Considerable effort has been spent on designing a good user interface to the system. Some quite general graphic editing tools are provided, and purely graphic

ACM Transactions on Programming Languages and Systems, Vol. 3, No. 4, October 1981.

objects, such as a triangle, can be constructed using graphic techniques only. The user interface allows objects to be viewed in other ways as well, for example, as a structural description or as a table of values.

The user interface allows smooth access to the constraint mechanism and to the inheritance and part–whole hierarchies. Thus, when the user edits an object, say by selecting a point and moving it with the cursor, the constraint satisfaction mechanism is invoked automatically to keep all the constraints satisfied. New classes may be defined by example, that is, by constructing a typical instance. The structural descriptions provided by the interface present the part–whole hierarchy, the constraints, and so forth.

1.5 Relation to Other Work

One of the principal influences on the design of ThingLab has been Sketchpad [16], a general-purpose system for drawing and editing pictures on a computer. In Sketchpad the user interacts directly with the display, using a light pen for adding, moving, and deleting parts of the drawing. ThingLab has adopted much of Sketchpad's flavor of user interaction, and the Sketchpad notions of constraints and of recursive merging have been central to its design. ThingLab has extended Sketchpad's constraint mechanism in a number of respects, most notably by integrating it with an inheritance hierarchy, by allowing local procedures for satisfying a constraint to be included as part of its definition, and by incrementally compiling the results of constraint satisfaction planning into Smalltalk code.

The other principal ancestor of ThingLab is Smalltalk. Not only is ThingLab written in Smalltalk, but the important ideas in Smalltalk—objects, classes and instances, and messages—are all used directly in ThingLab. As prevously described, ThingLab adds a number of new features to the language. Smalltalk has proved to be an excellent language to support research of this sort, in terms of both linguistic constructs and programming environment.

ThingLab is also related to some very interesting work on constraint languages done at M.I.T. by Guy Steele and Gerald Sussman [13]. The ThingLab representation of an object in terms of parts and subparts, with explicit representation of shared parts, is nearly isomorphic to the representation independently developed by Steele and Sussman. Their system has a built-in set of primitive constraints, such as adders and multipliers, from which compound constraints can be constructed. This is similar to the method used in the ThingLab calculator example described in Section 2.2. To handle constraints that cannot be satisfied using a one-pass ordering, they employ multiple redundant views that can cooperate in solving the problem; in their previous work, symbolic algebraic manipulation techniques were employed. Their use of multiple views has been adopted in ThingLab. Among the differences between the two systems is that Steele and Sussman's language retains dependency information, that is, a record of the justifications for each conclusion, for producing explanations and for implementing efficient backtracing when search is needed (dependency-directed backtracking). On the other hand, their system has no graphics capabilities. Also, ThingLab has two significant advantages in regard to efficiency. First, it compiles plans into the base language, whereas in Steele and Sussman's system constraint satisfaction is done interpretively. Compilation is essential if constraint languages are to

ACM Transactions on Programming Languages and Systems, Vol. 3, No. 4, October 1981.

become practical tools. Second, ThingLab has a class-instance mechanism, including multiple inheritance, that allows information common to several objects to be factored out, while their system uses a macro facility for abstraction, which has the disadvantage that a complete copy of the constraint network is required for each instance.

Steele's recent Ph.D. dissertation [12], completed after the work described above and the author's own dissertation, gives a clear statement of design goals for a complete, general-purpose language organized around constraints and describes further progress toward implementing such a language. The system deals explicitly with the problem of behaving properly in the presence of contradictions, which is important for the interactive construction of large systems, and further develops the notions of assumptions and defaults. While its usual mode of operation is interpretive, it also includes a constraint compiler like that used in ThingLab.

Other related work on languages includes SIMULA [3], which is one of the principal ancestors of Smalltalk. The distinction that Smalltalk makes between the inside and the outside of an object is also closely related to the data-abstraction mechanisms in languages such as MESA [10], CLU [9], and AL-PHARD [17]. These languages separate the interface specification of a type from its internal implementation, just as Smalltalk distinguishes the external message protocol of an object from its internal aspects. Thus, in programs in these data-abstraction languages, changes to the implementation of a type (but not its interface) do not affect the users of that type; so more modular systems result.

ABSET [4] is a set-oriented language developed at the University of Aberdeen with a number of constraint-like features; for example, given the statement $A + B = 3$ AND $A = 1$, it can deduce B's value. Also, it emphasizes the avoidance of unnecessary ordering restrictions in the statement of a program. The ACTOR languages [5] use and extend the notion of objects that communicate by passing messages. Representation languages for artificial intelligence work, such as KRL [1], develop the notion of multiple inheritance. ThingLab's facility for class definition by example is related to work on programming by example [8, 11].

There is a large body of work in artificial intelligence on reasoning and problem-solving systems of various kinds. Most of these systems are concerned with more complex problem-solving tasks than those tackled in ThingLab. By contrast, in ThingLab much of the emphasis has been on finding ways of generalizing plans and compiling them as procedures so that they may be used efficiently in a graphic environment. However, the problem-solving techniques developed in these other systems may well prove useful if ThingLab's constraint satisfaction abilities are to be strengthened.

This artificial intelligence work includes a number of systems that use constraints and constraint satisfaction as such. Steels [14] has constructed a reasoning system, modeled on a society of communicating experts, that uses propagation of constraints in its reasoning process. Unlike either ThingLab or Steele and Sussman's system, Steels' system is description-oriented and does not require that constraint satisfaction yield a unique value. Stefik [15] uses the technique of constraint posting in MOLGEN, a system for planning experiments in molecular genetics. His system uses hierarchical planning and dynamically formulates and propagates constraints during its planning process.

2. SOME EXAMPLES

Before plunging into a technical discussion of the system, it is useful to present some examples of its operation. A brief description of the operation of the ThingLab user interface is needed first. The user interacts with ThingLab via a *window*, a rectangular area on the computer's display. The window notion is central to Smalltalk's user interface philosophy. The ThingLab window described here is typically one of several windows on the screen, with other windows being available for debugging, editing system code, freehand sketching, and so on.

The ThingLab window is divided into five panes: the *class pane*, the *format pane*, the *messages pane*, the *arguments pane*, and the *picture pane*. The class pane is a *menu* of names of classes that may be viewed and edited. Once a class has been selected, a menu of formats in which it can display itself appears in the *format pane* immediately to the right. The class shows itself in the chosen format in the large *picture pane* at the bottom of the window.

The two remaining panes, messages and arguments, contain menus used for graphic editing of the class' prototype. All editing operations are performed by sending a message to the object being edited; the ThingLab window allows us to compose and send certain kinds of editing messages graphically. The messages pane contains a list of message names, such as *insert* and *delete*, while the arguments pane contains a list of possible classes for the message argument. The argument itself will be an instance of that class, either newly created or selected from among the parts in the picture.

The user communicates with the system primarily by means of a *mouse* and secondarily by use of a keyboard. The mouse is a small box-shaped object that can be moved about on the user's desk top; as it moves, its relative position is tracked by a cursor on the screen (the arrow in the illustrations). If some graphic object on the screen is "attached" to the cursor, that object moves as well. The mouse also has three buttons on it, which serve as control keys.

In the menu panes, a black stripe indicates a selected item. Thus, in Figure 1, *Triangle* and *prototype's picture* have been selected. Since a menu may be too long to fit in its pane, all the menus can be *scrolled* up or down so that the user can view and select any of the items. To make a selection, the user positions the cursor over the item to be selected and pushes a button on the mouse.

2.1 A Geometric Example

As an introductory example, we use ThingLab to construct a quadrilateral and to view it in several ways. We then use the system to demonstrate a theorem about quadrilaterals.

2.1.1 *Defining the Class of Quadrilaterals.* First, we define the class of quadrilaterals. New classes are always defined as a subclass of some more general class; if nothing better is available, they can be made subclasses of class Object, the most general class in the system. In this case, we create the new class Quadrilateral as a subclass of GeometricObject.

One of the important features of the ThingLab environment is that the user can define classes by example. To be more precise, the structural aspects of a class (its part descriptions and constraints) may be specified incrementally by editing its prototypical instance. We define the class Quadrilateral in this way.

ACM Transactions on Programming Languages and Systems, Vol. 3, No. 4, October 1981.

Class Pane   Format Pane   Messages Pane   Arguments Pane

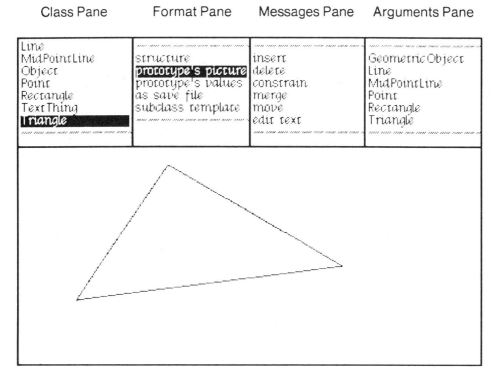

Picture Pane

Fig. 1.   Panes of the ThingLab window.

First, we ask to view the picture of the prototype Quadrilateral. So far, the prototype has no parts, and so its picture is blank. We now edit the prototype by adding and connecting four sides. Using the mouse, we select the word *insert* in the messages pane and the word *Line* in the arguments pane. When we move the cursor into the bottom pane, a blinking picture of a line appears, attached to the cursor by one of its endpoints. As the cursor is moved, the entire line follows. When the endpoint attached to the cursor is in the desired location, we press a button. This first endpoint stops moving, and the cursor jumps to the second endpoint. The second endpoint follows the cursor, but this time the first endpoint remains stationary. We press the button again to position the second endpoint (Figure 2).

We insert another line in the same way. To connect the new line to the first, we position the endpoint attached to the cursor near one of the endpoints of the first line. When the two points are close together, the moving point locks onto the stationary point, and the line stops blinking. This indicates that the two points will merge if the button is pressed. We press the button and the points merge. The two lines now share a common endpoint. Also, a record of the merge is kept by the class Quadrilateral. Similarly, we position the other endpoint and insert the remaining two lines (Figure 3).

During this editing session, the system has been updating the structure common to all quadrilaterals that is stored in the class Quadrilateral, as well as saving the

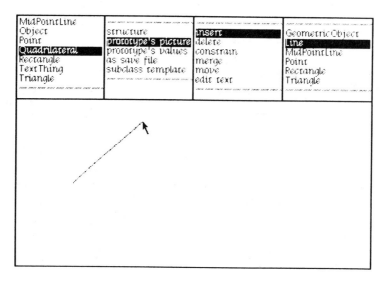

Fig. 2.   Positioning the second endpoint of a line.

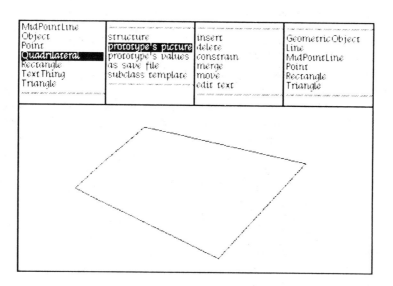

Fig. 3.   The completed quadrilateral.

particular locations of the prototype's sides. To see the structure of the class Quadrilateral, we select *structure* in the menu of formats. The class responds by listing its name, superclasses, part descriptions, and constraints (Figure 4). We may also view the values stored in the prototype by selecting *prototype's values* (Figure 5).

2.1.2 *Demonstrating a Geometry Theorem.* We may now use the new class in demonstrating a geometry theorem. The theorem states that, given an arbitrary quadrilateral, if one bisects each of the sides and draws lines between the adjacent midpoints, the new lines form a parallelogram.

To perform the construction, we make a new class named *QTheorem.* As before, we create it as a subclass of GeometricObject and define it by example. We first add an instance of class Quadrilateral as a part. We select *insert* and *Quadrilateral.* As we move the cursor into the bottom pane, a blinking picture of a quadrilateral, whose shape has been copied from the prototype, appears. We position the quadrilateral and press a button.

The next step is to add midpoints to the sides of the quadrilateral. To do this, we use four instances of the class MidPointLine. This class specifies that each of its instances has two parts: a line and a point. In addition, it has a constraint that, for each instance, the point be halfway between the endpoints of the line. As we insert each instance of MidPointLine, we move it near the center of one of the sides of the quadrilateral and merge the line part of the MidPointLine with the side of the quadrilateral (Figure 6). The last step is to add four lines connecting the midpoints to form the parallelogram.

Once the construction is complete, we may move any of the parts of the prototype QTheorem and observe the results. In general, it is not enough for the system simply to move the selected part; because of the constraints we have placed on the object, other parts, such as the midpoints, may need to be moved as well to keep all the constraints satisfied. Suppose we want to move a vertex. We select the message *move* and the argument *Point.* A blinking point appears in the picture that is attached to the cursor. We position it over the vertex to be moved and hold down a button. The vertex follows the cursor until the button is released (Figure 7). (The first time we try to move the vertex, there will be a long pause as the system plans how to satisfy the constraints.) We notice that indeed the lines connecting the midpoints form a parallelogram no matter how the quadrilateral is deformed. The theorem remains true even when the quadrilateral is turned inside out!

2.1.3 *Constraint Satisfaction.* The user described how QTheorem should behave in terms of the midpoint constraint and the various merges, but not by writing separate methods for moving each part of QTheorem. The midpoint constraint (as defined by an experienced user) describes methods that can be invoked to satisfy itself. Three such methods were specified: the first asks the midpoint to move to halfway between the line's endpoints; the second asks one of the line's endpoints to move; and the third asks the other endpoint to move. It was up to QTheorem to decide which of these methods to invoke, and when and in what order to use them.

In general, the constraints on an object might specify its behavior incompletely or redundantly, or they might be unsatisfiable. QTheorem, for example, is

ACM Transactions on Programming Languages and Systems, Vol. 3, No. 4, October 1981.

425

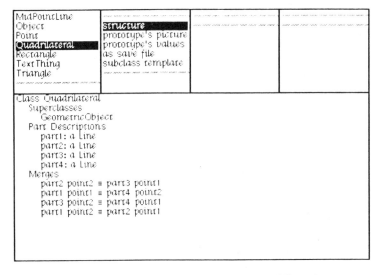

Fig. 4. Structure described by the class Quadrilateral.

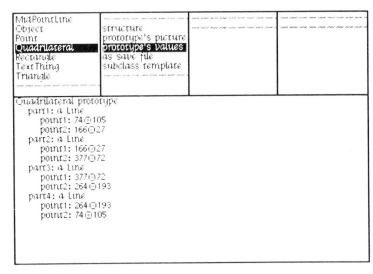

Fig. 5. Values of the prototype Quadrilateral.

•   Alan Borning

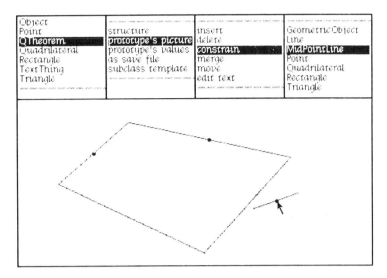

Object	structure	insert	Geometric Object
Point	prototype's picture	delete	Line
QTheorem	**prototype's picture**	**constrain**	**MidPointLine**
Quadrilateral	prototype's values	merge	Point
Rectangle	as save file	move	Quadrilateral
TextThing	subclass template	edit text	Rectangle
Triangle			Triangle

Fig. 6.   Adding a midpoint.

underconstrained. The behavior we observed was only one way of moving the vertex while satisfying the constraints. Two other possibilities would have been for the entire object to move, or for the midpoints to remain fixed while the other vertices moved. Neither of these responses would have been as pleasing to us as human observers. (If we had wanted the entire object to move, we would have specified *move QTheorem* instead.) Therefore, besides the more mathematical techniques for finding *some* way of satisfying its constraints, or for deciding that they are unsatisfiable, an object can also take the user's preferences into account in deciding its behavior. In this case, the midpoint constraint specified that the midpoint was to be moved in preference to one of the endpoints of the line.

We might override the preference specified in the midpoint constraint by anchoring the midpoints, as in Figure 8. (Anchor is a subclass of Point, with an added constraint that its instances may not be moved during constraint satisfaction.)

2.2 Constructing a Program for a Graphic Calculator

In this second example, we construct some graphic programs for a simulated calculator. In the process, we use a number of classes from a "calculator kit." One simple but important class is NumberNode. An instance of NumberNode has two parts: a real number and a point. Its purpose is to provide a graphic representation of a register in the calculator. Another class is NumberLead, consisting of a number node and an attached line. As with leads on electrical components, it is used to connect parts of the calculator. Also, classes that represent the various arithmetic operations have been defined. There is a general class Number-Operator, whose parts are a frame containing the operator's symbol and three number leads that terminate on the edges of the frame. Four subclasses of NumberOperator are defined, namely, Plus, Minus, Times, and Divide. Plus, for example, has three number leads with number nodes at the ends, which are inherited from NumberOperator (Figure 9). It has an added constraint that the

ACM Transactions on Programming Languages and Systems, Vol. 3, No. 4, October 1981.

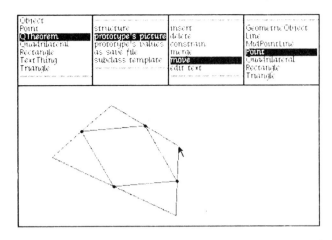

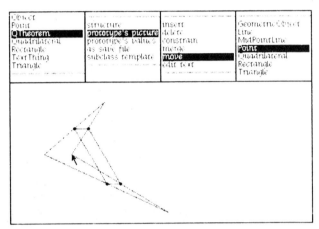

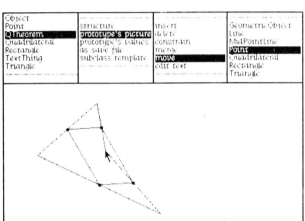

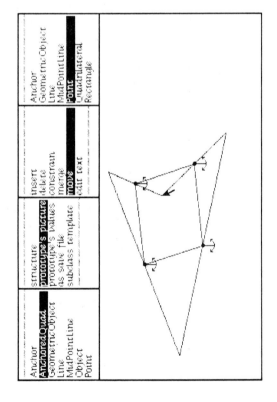

Fig. 7. Moving a vertex of the quadrilateral.

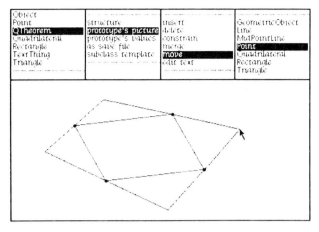

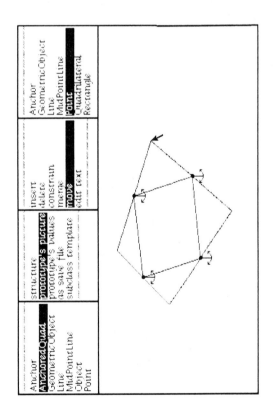

Fig. 8. A quadrilateral with anchored midpoints.

428

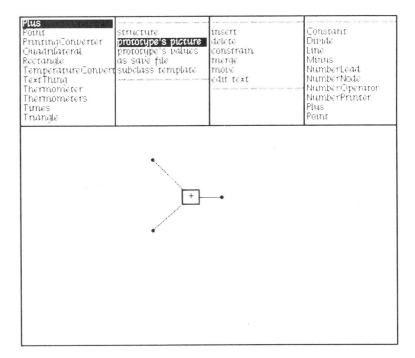

Plus			
Point	structure	insert	Constant
PrintingConverter	prototype's picture	delete	Divide
Quadrilateral	prototype's values	constrain	Line
Rectangle	as save file	merge	Minus
TemperatureConverter	subclass template	move	NumberLead
TextThing		edit text	NumberNode
Thermometer			NumberOperator
Thermometers			NumberPrinter
Times			Plus
Triangle			Point

Fig. 9.   Picture of the prototype for Plus.

number at the node on the right always be the sum of the numbers at the leads on the left. The classes for Minus, Times, and Divide prototypes have been defined analogously.

To view and edit a number at a node, the class NumberPrinter has been constructed. Its parts are a number lead and an editable piece of text. Also, it has a constraint that the number at its node correspond to that displayed in the text. If the node's number changes, the text is updated; if the text is edited, the node's number is changed correspondingly. A special kind of NumberPrinter is a Constant. For constants, the constraint is unidirectional. The text may be edited, thus changing the number; but the number may not be changed to alter the text.

2.2.1 *Constructing a Celsius-to-Fahrenheit Converter.* Using these parts, let us construct a Celsius-to-Fahrenheit converter. After creating a new class, TemperatureConverter, we select *insert* and *Times.* As we move the cursor into the picture pane, a blinking picture of an instance of the class Times appears. We position the frame that holds the multiplication symbol, and then the three nodes. Next, we insert a Plus operator in the same manner, connecting its addend node to the product node of the times operator. (The connection is made by merging the nodes, in the same way that the endpoints of the sides of the quadrilateral were connected.) Finally, we insert two instances of Constant, connecting them to the appropriate nodes of the operators. We then invoke the *edit text* message and change the constants to 1.8 and 32.0. The result is shown in Figure 10.

Once the converter has been defined, we may use it as a part of other objects (i.e., as a subroutine). As an example, we define a new class PrintingConverter. We add an instance of TemperatureConverter as a part, and also two instances

ACM Transactions on Programming Languages and Systems, Vol. 3, No. 4, October 1981.

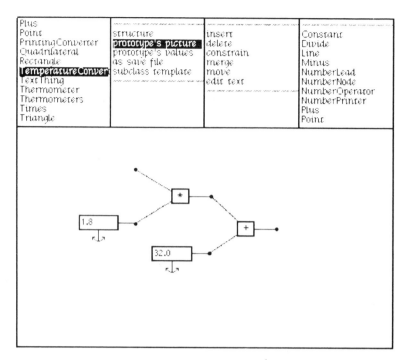

Fig. 10. Picture of the completed Celsius-to-Fahrenheit Converter.

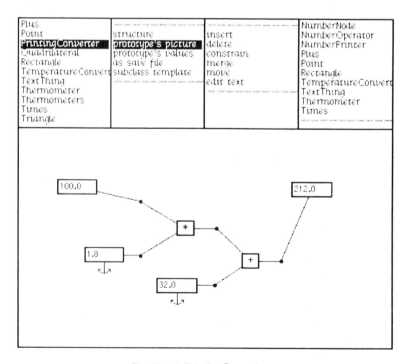

Fig. 11. A PrintingConverter.

of NumberPrinter to display the Celsius and Fahrenheit temperatures (Figure 11). If we edit the Celsius temperature, the PrintingConverter satisfies its constraints by updating the numbers at its nodes and the Fahrenheit temperature displayed in the frame on the right.

However, because of the multiway nature of the constraints, the device works backward as well as forward! Thus, we can edit the Fahrenheit temperature, and the Celsius temperature is updated correspondingly (Figure 12). This demonstrates the need for the special class Constant: without it, the system could equally well have satisfied the constraints by changing one of these coefficients rather than the temperatures.

We may also connect the converter to other types of input/output devices, for example, a simulated thermometer. We can select *move* and *Point* and grab either of the columns of mercury with the cursor. When we move one of the columns up or down, the other column moves correspondingly (Figure 13).

2.2.2 *Solving a Quadratic Equation.* After experimenting with the converter, we might try building a more complex device, such as the network for solving quadratic equations shown in Figure 14.

When we edit any of the constants, the value in the frame on the left changes to satisfy the equation. In the picture, the coefficients of the equation $x^2 - 6x + 9 = 0$ have been entered, and a solution, $x = 3$, has been found. This case is unlike the temperature converter examples: the system was unable to find a one-pass ordering for solving the constraints and has resorted to the relaxation method. Relaxation will converge to one of the two roots of the equation, depending on the initial value of x.

Now let us try changing the constant term c from 9 to 10. This time, the system puts up an error message, protesting that the constraints cannot be satisfied. Some simple algebra reveals that the roots of this new equation are complex; but the number nodes hold real numbers, and so the system was unable to satisfy the constraints.

A better way of finding the roots of a quadratic equation is to use the standard solution to the quadratic equation $ax^2 + bx + c = 0$, namely, $x = (-b \pm (b^2 - 4ac)^{\frac{1}{2}}) / 2a$. The system can be told about this canned formula by defining a class QuadraticSolver whose parts include four NumberNodes a, b, c, and x and a constraint that $x = (-b + (b^2 - 4ac)^{\frac{1}{2}}) / 2a$. (Since the class NumberNode does not allow multiple values, in the QuadraticSolver's constraint one of the roots has been chosen arbitrarily as the value for x. A more general solution would be to define a class MultipleRoots and set up the constraint so that it determined both the number of roots and their values.)

We can insert an instance of QuadraticSolver into the network, merging its number nodes with the appropriate existing nodes in the network (Figure 15). Now, the system can find a simple one-pass ordering for satisfying the constraints and does not need to use relaxation.

In inserting an instance of QuadraticSolver into the network, we have added another view of the constraints on x. In the sense that the permissible values of x are the same with or without it (ignoring the multiple-root problem), the new constraint adds no new information. However, QuadraticSolver's constraint is computationally better suited to finding the value of x. This technique of

ACM Transactions on Programming Languages and Systems, Vol. 3, No. 4, October 1981.

431

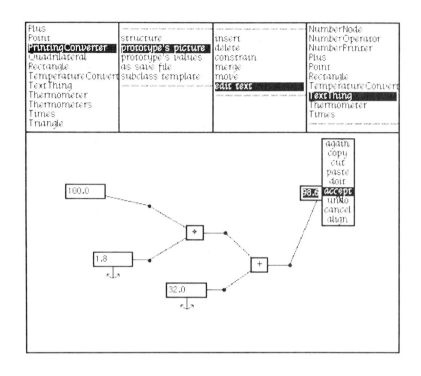

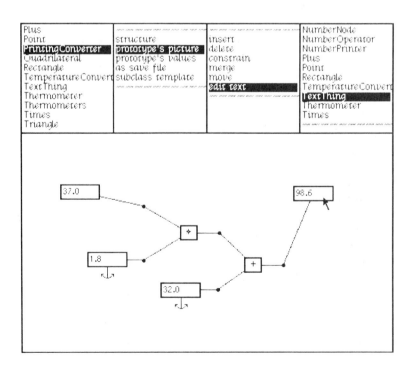

Fig. 12.   Editing the Fahrenheit temperature.

432

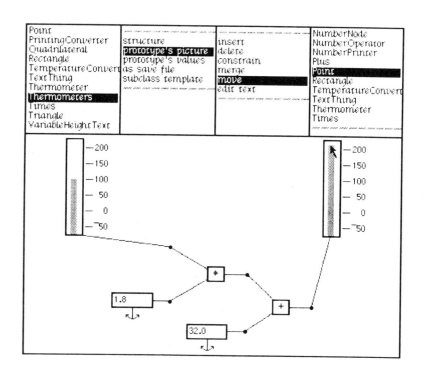

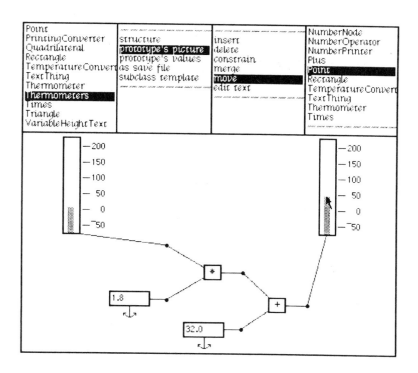

Fig. 13.   The temperature converter with thermometers for input and output.

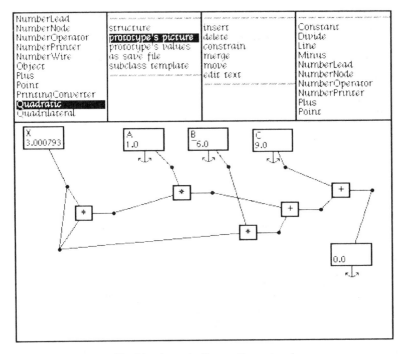

Fig. 14.   A quadratic equation network.

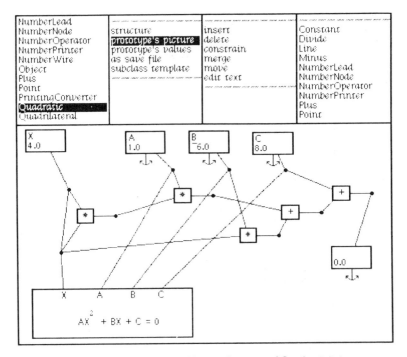

Fig. 15.   The network after adding an instance of QuadraticSolver.

introducing multiple redundant constraints on an object is an important way of dealing with circularity.

3. OBJECTS

3.1 The Part–Whole Relationship

In ThingLab, an object is composed of named parts, each of which is in turn another object. The parts are thus composed of subparts, and so on. The recursion stops with primitive objects such as integers and strings. Consider a line:

Line
  point1: a Point
    x: 50
    y: 100
  point2: a Point
    x: 200
    y: 200.

The line is composed of two parts that are its endpoints. Each endpoint is in turn composed of an *x* and a *y* value; these are primitive objects (integers). An object is sometimes referred to as the *owner* of its parts. For example, the above line owns its endpoints.

3.1.1 *Part Descriptions.* A *PartDescription* is an object that describes the common properties of the corresponding parts of all instances of a class. Every class has a list of part descriptions, one for each part owned by its instances. The following things are associated with each part description:

name   an identifier;
constraints the set of constraints that apply to the corresponding part of each instance;
merges   the set of merges that apply to the corresponding part of each instance;
class   the class of the corresponding part of each instance. This is more restrictive than in Smalltalk, where the class of the contents of an instance field is not declared. Imposing this restriction makes the job of constraint satisfaction easier.

When a part description is added to a class, messages are compiled automatically in the class' message dictionary to read and write the part.

For example, the class Line has two part descriptions that describe the parts of each instance of Line. The first part description has the name *point1*. It has no constraints or merges, and it specifies that the *point1* part of each line be an instance of class Point. The other part description is defined analogously. For a class that specifies some constraints, for example, the class HorizontalLine, the *point1* part description would also indicate that there was a constraint that applied to the *point1* part of each of its instances.

3.1.2 *Insides and Outsides.* As described in Section 1.3, one of the important features of Smalltalk is the sharp distinction it makes between the inside and the outside of an object. In ThingLab, the notion of having a part has implications for both the internal and external aspects of the object that owns the part.

ACM Transactions on Programming Languages and Systems, Vol. 3, No. 4, October 1981.

Internally, the object must have an instance field in which the part is stored, as well as a corresponding part description in its class; externally, the object should understand messages to read and write the part. However, these internal and external aspects are separate. A *virtual part*, as proposed in [2], is an example of the use of this separation. Such a part would have all the external manifestations of a part, that is, messages to read and write it. Internally, however, there would be no corresponding field; rather, the part would be computed as needed. (Smalltalk already has virtual parts; the proposed mechanism would add the necessary declarative superstructure so that the constraint satisfaction mechanism could know about them.)

3.1.3 *Paths.* A *path* is a ThingLab object that represents a symbolic reference to a subpart. Each path is a hierarchical name, consisting of a list of part names that indicates a way to get from some object to one of its subparts. The path itself does not own a pointer to the object to which it is applied; this must be supplied by the user of the path. Thus the same path can be used to refer to the corresponding subpart of many different objects. For example, *point*1 x is a path to get to the x value of the first endpoint of any line. Typically, the path as such is used only during compilation; this path would compile code that sent the message *point*1 to a line and then sent the message x to the result.

While the definition of a path is simple, the idea behind it has proved quite powerful and has been essential in allowing the constraint- and object-oriented metaphors to be integrated. As mentioned above, Smalltalk draws a distinction between the inside and the outside of an object. The notion of a path helps strengthen this distinction by providing a protected way for an object to provide external references to its parts and subparts. For example, if a triangle wishes to allow another object to refer to one of its vertices, it does so by handing back a path such as *side*2 *point*1, rather than by providing a direct pointer to the vertex. If this other object wants to change the location of the vertex, it must do so by routing the request through the triangle, rather than by simply making the change itself. This allows the triangle to decide whether or not to accept the change; if it does accept it, it knows what has been altered, so that it can update its other parts as necessary to satisfy all its constraints.

In addition to these semantic considerations, a major pragmatic benefit of this discipline is that no backpointers are needed. (If the triangle did hand out a direct pointer to its vertex, the vertex would need a pointer back to the triangle so that it could inform the triangle when it changed.) Access to parts is somewhat slower using this technique, since each access involves following a path. However, an access via a path can often be moved out of the inner loops by the constraint compiler. Another pragmatic consideration is that constraints and merges can be represented symbolically using paths, so that they apply to all instances of a class, rather than to a particular instance. This allows the system to compile constraint satisfaction plans in the form of standard Smalltalk methods.

ThingLab's constraint satisfaction techniques all depend on noticing when one constraint applies to the same subpart as another. Paths are used to specify which parts or subparts of an object are affected by the constraint. Two paths *overlap* if one can be produced from the other by adding zero or more names to the end of the other's list. The following paths overlap the path *side*1 *point*1:

*side*1 *point*1 *x*
*side*1 *point*1
*side*1
(*the empty path*)

The following paths do not overlap *side*1 *point*1:

*side*1 *point*2
*side*2

To test if two constraints apply to the same subpart, the system checks to see if any of their paths overlap.

3.2 Inheritance

A new class may be defined as a subclass of one or more existing classes. The subclass inherits the part descriptions, constraints, merges, and message protocol of its superclasses. It may add new information of its own, and it may override inherited responses to messages. Every class (except class Object) must be a subclass of at least one other class.

The superclasses of an object are represented by including an instance of each superclass as a part of the object. The field descriptions for such parts are instances of SuperclassDescription, a subclass of PartDescription. These parts may have constraints and merges applied to them in the usual way; among other things, this allows the user to indicate that parts inherited from several super-classes are in fact to be represented by only a single part in the subclass. The only difference between these instances of superclasses and ordinary parts is that messages are forwarded to them automatically. (The actual implementation is somewhat more arcane, to take advantage of the efficient single-superclass mechanism built into Smalltalk. However, the effect is as described, and the reader should think of it in this way.)

3.2.1 *Class Object.* The most general class in both Smalltalk and ThingLab is class Object. As part of the ThingLab kernel, a large number of methods have been added to this class. These methods provide defaults for adding or deleting parts, merging parts, satisfying constraints, showing in a ThingLab window, and so on. In general, these methods treat an object as the sum of its parts. For example, to show itself, an object asks each of its parts to show; to move itself by some increment, the object asks each of its parts to move by that increment. This strict hierarchy is, however, modified by the object's constraints and merges. Thus, when an object decides exactly how to move, it must watch for overlap between its parts due to merges, and it must also keep all its constraints satisfied.

3.2.2 *Message Behavior.* When an object receives a message, the object's class first checks its own message dictionary. If a corresponding method is found, that method is used. If not, the class asks each of its superclasses if any of them has an appropriate method. In turn, each superclass, if it does not itself define the method, will ask *its* superclasses, and so forth, thus implementing inheritance through multiple levels of the hierarchy. If there is a single inherited method for that message, then that method is used. If there is no method, or if there are several conflicting inherited methods, an error occurs. Note that the overriding of inherited methods is still allowed; it is an error only if a class with no method of its own inherits different methods via two or more of its immediate superclasses. If the user wants to choose among conflicting messages, or to combine them somehow, an appropriate method for doing this should be defined in the subclass. To avoid this search the next time the message is received, the class automatically compiles a *message forwarder* that will intercept that message in the future and relay it directly to the appropriate superclass part.

As an example of the use of multiple superclasses, suppose that a user has available a class of horizontal lines and another class of lines of constant length. The class of horizontal lines of constant length may then be defined as a subclass of both of these.

Multiple superclasses also provide a way of implementing multiple representations of objects. For example, suppose the user desires to represent a point in both Cartesian and polar forms. This may be done as follows:

Class CartesianPoint
   Superclasses
     GeometricObject
   Part Descriptions
     x: a Real
     y: a Real
Class PolarPoint
   Superclasses
     GeometricObject
   Part Descriptions
     r: a Real
     theta: a Real
Class MultiplyRepresentedPoint
   Superclasses
     C: CartesianPoint
     P: PolarPoint
   Constraints
     $C = P\ asCartesian$
     $C \leftarrow P\ asCartesian$
     $P \leftarrow C\ asPolar$

The constraint on MultiplyRepresentedPoint keeps the parts representing the two superclasses in coordination. It makes use of an auxiliary message to PolarPoint that returns its Cartesian equivalent, and of an analogous message to CartesianPoint.

3.2.3 *Prototypes.* For a given class, a prototype is a distinguished instance that owns default or typical parts. All classes understand the message *prototype* and respond by returning their prototypical instance. If the user does not specify otherwise, the prototype has nil in each of its instance fields. However, if the user has defined the class by example, the prototype holds the particular values from the example. These values may also be set by writing an initialization message.

Prototypes provide a convenient mechanism for specifying default instance values. Thus, in the introductory example, when a new line was being inserted into the quadrilateral, its initial length and orientation were copied from the prototype Line. Such defaults are essential in graphic editing, since every object needs *some* appearance.

ACM Transactions on Programming Languages and Systems, Vol. 3, No. 4, October 1981.

More important, a prototype serves as a representative of its class. ThingLab distinguishes between messages that have no side effects for the receiver (read-only messages), messages that alter the values stored in the receiver, and messages that alter the receiver's structure. Any instance accepts read-only or value-altering messages, but only prototypes accept structure-altering messages. The reason is that this latter type of message affects the class. The prototype is in charge of its class and is willing to alter it, but, for instances other than the prototypical one, the class is read-only. Requests to move a side of a polygon, or even turn it inside out, are examples of value-altering messages. On the other hand, requests to add or delete a side, edit a constraint, or merge two points are structure-altering messages.

3.2.4 *Defining Classes by Example.* When the user defines a class by example, the editing messages are always sent to the prototype, rather than sometimes to the class and sometimes to one of its instances. The prototype takes care of separating the generic information that applies to all instances of its class from the specific information that applies only to the default values that it holds in its fields. With its class it associates the number and class of the parts, the constraints, and the merges. With its own instance fields it associates the default values for its parts.

It is not possible to define all classes by example; some, such as classes for new constraint types and abstract classes like GeometricObject, must be entered by writing an appropriate Smalltalk class definition. In general, there are many possible classes that could be abstracted from a given example; which one *should* be abstracted depends on the user's purposes. The ThingLab facility for definition by example provides a reasonable default, but it is not a general solution to this problem. If the user wants some other sort of class, he or she should write an appropriate definition.

4. CONSTRAINT REPRESENTATION

This section describes the representation of ThingLab constraints. To support constraints, some new kinds of objects were implemented. In Smalltalk, objects communicate by sending and receiving messages; an object's response to a message is implemented by a method (i.e., a procedure). ThingLab objects are described that stand for Smalltalk messages and methods. The purpose of this additional mechanism is to provide tools for reasoning about messages and methods, and in particular about the interactions among messages and constraints.

4.1 Message Plans

A message plan is an abstraction of the Smalltalk notion of sending a message. A message plan does not stand for a particular act of sending a message; rather, it is a template for any number of messages that might be sent. A message plan is itself an object: an instance of class *MessagePlan*. The parts of a message plan include a *receiver*, a *path*, an *action*, and zero or more *arguments*. The receiver is normally a particular object, although for some uses it may be nil or may be a prototype representing any instance of a class of objects that might receive the message. The path tells how to get to one of the receiver's subparts, which will be called the *target* of the message plan. The action is a *selector* for a Smalltalk method understood by the target. The arguments may be either actual or symbolic. Actual arguments are pointers to other objects; symbolic arguments are simply names (strings). The arguments correspond to the arguments passed at run time to the Smalltalk method invoked by the action. For example, here is a message plan asking a triangle to move one of its vertices right by ten screen dots:

triangle side1 point2 moveby: 10@0.

The receiver is *triangle*, the path is *side1 point2*, the action is *moveby:,* and the argument is the point 10@0.

An important use of message plans is to describe the methods for satisfying a constraint. If a message plan is used in this way, the plan will have several Boolean flags and a pointer to the constraint that generated it, in addition to the parts listed above. The flags are the following:

uniqueState	true if there is only one state of the target that will satisfy the constraint (given that all other parts of the receiver are fixed). See Section 4.3.2 below;
referenceOnly	true if the action described by the message plan only references its target, rather than altering it;
compileTimeOnly	true if the message plan is used only during constraint satisfaction planning and not in producing executable code.

4.2 Methods

In ThingLab, an explicit class *Method* has been defined. The parts of a method are a list of *keywords*, a matching list of symbolic *arguments*, a list of *temporaries*, and a procedural *body*. The selector for the method is constructed by concatenating the keywords. These parts are the same as those of a Smalltalk method, the only difference being that in Smalltalk the method is stored as text, and the parts must be found by parsing the text. One reason for defining an explicit class in ThingLab is to simplify access to the parts of a method. This is useful because methods are often generated by the system rather than being entered by the user, with different parts of the method coming from different parts of the system. Also, some methods have their own special properties. For example, all the methods that an object has for showing itself are indexed in a table used by the ThingLab user interface.

After a ThingLab method has been constructed, it is usually asked to add itself to some class' method dictionary. In the implementation, the method does this by constructing a piece of text and handing it to the regular Smalltalk compiler. The Smalltalk compiler in turn produces a byte-coded string for use at run time and indexes it in the class' method dictionary.

4.3 The Structure of a Constraint

As described in Section 1, a constraint represents a relation among the parts of an object that must always hold. Constraints are themselves objects. New kinds of constraints are defined by specifying both a *rule* and a set of *methods* for satisfying the constraint. Adding or modifying a constraint is a structural change; so only prototypes accept new constraints or allow existing ones to be edited.

ACM Transactions on Programming Languages and Systems, Vol. 3, No. 4, October 1981.

Constraints are indexed in several tables in the prototype's class for easy retrieval during constraint satisfaction.

The constraint's methods describe alternate ways of satisfying the constraint; if any one of the methods is invoked, the constraint will be satisfied. These methods are represented as a list of instances of class Method. The constraint also has a matching list of instances of MessagePlan. Each message plan specifies how to invoke the corresponding method and describes its effects. When the constraint satisfier decides that one of the methods will need to be invoked at run time, the message plan that represents that method is asked to generate code that will send the appropriate Smalltalk message to activate the method. Exactly which methods are used depends on the other constraints and on the user's preferences as to what should be done if the object is underconstrained.

The rule is used to construct a procedural test for checking whether or not the constraint is satisfied and to construct an error expression that indicates how well the constraint is satisfied. Both the test and the error expression are instances of class Method. These methods are constructed in a fairly simple-minded way. If the constraint's rule equates numbers or points, the test checks that the two sides of the equation are equal to within some tolerance; the error will be the difference of the two sides of the equation. If the constraint is nonnumerical, the rule is used directly to generate the test; the error will be zero if the constraint is satisfied and one if it is not. If the user wants to override these default methods, he or she can replace them with hand-coded Smalltalk methods.

4.3.1 *Example of a Constraint.* Consider the structure described by the class MidPointLine used in the quadrilateral example.

Class MidPointLine
  Superclasses
    Geometric Object
  Part Descriptions
    line: a Line
    midpoint: a Point
  Constraints
    midpoint = (line point1 + line point2)/2
      midpoint ← (line point1 + line point2)/2
      *line point1 ← midpoint * 2 − line point2*
      *line point2 ← midpoint * 2 − line point1*

The class MidPointLine has a constraint that the midpoint lie halfway between the endpoints of the line. The constraint has three alternate ways of satisfying itself, as described by the methods listed under the rule. The first method alters the midpoint, the second one alters one endpoint of the line, and the third alters the other endpoint.

The user may want one method to be used in preference to another if there is a choice. This is indicated by the order of the methods: if the system has a choice about which method to use to satisfy the constraint, the first one on the list is used. In the case of the midpoint, the user preferred that the constraint be satisfied by moving the midpoint rather than by moving an end of the line.

4.3.2 *Relations Among the Parts of a Constraint.* The relations among the parts of a constraint are fairly rigidly defined. Each of the methods, if invoked,

ACM Transactions on Programming Languages and Systems, Vol. 3, No. 4, October 1981.

441

must cause the constraint to be satisfied. For every part that is referenced by the rule, there must be either a method that alters that part or a dummy method referencing it. Currently, it is up to the user to see that these requirements are met; none of this is checked by the system.

As has been previously discussed, Smalltalk makes a strong distinction between the inside and the outside of an object. A method for satisfying a constraint is internal to the constraint and its owner, while the message plan that describes the method is the external handle of that method. It is the message plan that is used by the constraint satisfier in planning how to satisfy an object's constraints.

In particular, the path of a message plan describes the side effects of its method. The constraint satisfier uses this information to detect overlap in the parts affected by the various methods. Therefore, the more precisely one can specify which subparts are affected by the method, the more information the constraint satisfier has to work with. Also, the constraint satisfier can do more with a method if it is known that there is only one state of the subpart affected by the method that satisfies the constraint, given the states of all other parts. This is described by the Boolean variable *uniqueState* listed previously; in the example above, *uniqueState* is true.

This way of describing constraints allows the representation of relations that are not very tractable analytically. Any sort of relation can be expressed as a constraint, if a procedural test exists and some algorithm can be specified for satisfying the relation. In the most extreme case of analytical intractability, the constraint has a single method that affects the entire object that owns the constraint, and this message is not *uniqueState*. However, in such a case, the constraint satisfier has little to work with, and only one such constraint can be handled.

4.4 Merges

An important special case of a constraint is a *merge*. When several parts are merged, they are constrained to be all equal. For efficiency, they are usually replaced by a single object, rather than being kept as several separate objects. The owner of the parts maintains a symbolic representation of the merge for use by constraint satisfiers, as well as for reconstruction of the original parts if the merge is deleted. There are two principal uses of merging, both of which were illustrated by the introductory example in Section 2.1. The first use is to represent connectivity, for example, to connect the sides of the quadrilateral. The other is for applying predefined constraints, as was done with the midpoint constraint. As with constraints, adding or modifying a merge is a structural change; so only prototypes allow their merges to be edited. The process of merging is the same for both these uses. The object that owns the parts to be merged (e.g., QTheorem) is sent the message *merge: paths*, where *paths* is a list of paths to the parts to be merged.

When it can be done, the replacement of several merged objects by a single object yields a more compact storage format and speeds up constraint satisfaction considerably, since information need not be copied back and forth between the parts that have been declared equal. It does not result in any loss of information, since the owner of the parts keeps a symbolic representation of the merge that contains enough information to reconstruct the original parts. On the other hand, it is slower to merge or unmerge parts, since more computation is required; so, for applications in which the structure of the object changes frequently, equality constraints would be more efficient. Another efficiency consideration is that a single merge can apply to an indefinite number of objects, while constraints have built into them the number of objects to which they apply. Thus, it is simple to make five separate points be equal using merges. To do this with equality constraints would require either that four separate constraints be used or that a special equality constraint be defined for use with five objects.

The most difficult parts of the ThingLab system to program and debug were those that deal with adding and deleting merges, due especially to interactions among merges at different levels of the part–whole hierarchy. For example, in the quadrilateral construction presented in Section 2.1, when merging the line part of the MidPointLine with the side of the quadrilateral, the system not only had to substitute a new line for the two line parts, but because of the merges connecting the sides of the quadrilateral it also had to substitute a new endpoint for the two connecting sides. In fact, at one point the author gave up in disgust and always represented merges by using equality constraints; but he eventually backtracked on this choice because it made things too slow for typical uses of ThingLab. Future implementers of systems using merges are hereby warned!

5. CONSTRAINT SATISFACTION

5.1 Overview

Constraint satisfaction is divided into two stages: planning and run time. Planning commences when an object is presented with a message plan. This message plan is not an actual request to do something; rather, it is a declaration of intent: a description of a message that might be sent to the object. Given this description, the object generates a plan to be used at run time for receiving such messages, while satisfying any constraints that might be affected. The results of this planning are compiled as a Smalltalk method. Directions for calling the compiled method are returned as a new message plan.

Consider the quadrilateral example described in Section 2.1. When the user selects *move Point* and first positions the cursor over a vertex of the quadrilateral, the ThingLab window composes a message plan and presents it to the quadrilateral. The quadrilateral decides how to move its vertex while still keeping all the midpoint constraints satisfied and embeds this plan in a compiled Smalltalk method. It then returns another message plan that gives directions for invoking that method. As the user pulls on the vertex with the cursor, the window repeatedly sends the quadrilateral a message asking it to update its position. This message invokes the Smalltalk method that was just compiled.

During planning, the object that is presented with the message plan creates an instance of ConstraintSatisfier to handle all the work. The constraint satisfier gathers up all the constraints that might be affected by the change and plans a method for satisfying them. The constraint satisfier first attempts to find a one-pass ordering for satisfying the constraints. There are two techniques available for doing this: propagation of degrees of freedom and propagation of known states. If there are constraints that cannot be handled by either of these techniques, the constraint satisfier asks the object for a method for dealing with circularity. Currently, relaxation is the only such method available. If relaxation is used, the user is warned, so that perhaps some other redundant constraints can be supplied that eliminate the need for relaxation. Relaxation is described in Section 5.2.3.

5.2 Constraint Satisfaction Methods

The constraint satisfaction methods used in ThingLab are now described in more detail. To illustrate the operation of the methods, an electrical circuit example is used (Figure 16). Briefly, the classes involved are as follows. Instances of class Node are connection points. The parts of a node are a voltage and a set of currents flowing into that node; there is also a constraint that the sum of the currents be zero. (This is Kirchhoff's current law.) A subclass of Node is Ground, which has an additional constraint that its voltage be zero. Instances of Lead, like their physical counterparts, are used to connect devices. The parts of a lead are a node and a current; there is a constraint that the current belong to the node's set of currents flowing into it. Leads are connected by merging their nodes. There is a general class TwoLeadedObject, whose parts are two instances of Lead, and which has a constraint that the currents in the lead be equal and opposite. A number of subclasses of TwoLeadedObject are defined, including Resistor, Battery, Wire, and Meter; Meter in turn has subclasses Ammeter and Voltmeter. All these objects have appropriate constraints on their behavior: a resistor must obey the Ohm's law constraint relating its resistance, the current flowing through it, and the voltage across it; an ammeter must display the current flowing through it; and so forth. A complete listing of the ThingLab classes for building electrical circuit simulations is given in [2].

5.2.1 *Propagation of Degrees of Freedom.* In propagating degrees of freedom, the constraint satisfier looks for a part with enough degrees of freedom so that it can be altered to satisfy all its constraints. If such a part is found, that part and all the constraints that apply to it can be removed from further consideration. Once this is done, another part may acquire enough degrees of freedom to satisfy all its constraints. The process continues in this manner until either all constraints have been taken care of or no more degrees of freedom can be propagated.

Because of the difficulty of giving a precise definition of degrees of freedom for nonnumeric objects, the constraint satisfier uses a simpleminded criterion for deciding if a part has enough degrees of freedom to satisfy its constraints: it has enough degrees of freedom if there is only one constraint that affects it. It does not matter whether or not the constraint determines the part's state uniquely (removes all its degrees of freedom).

In deciding when a constraint affects a part, the part–whole hierarchy must be taken into account. The set of constraints that affect a given part is found by checking whether the path to the part overlaps the paths of any of the message plans generated by the constraints. Thus, a constraint on the first endpoint of a line affects the line as a whole, the first endpoint, and the x coordinate of the first endpoint; but it does not affect the line's second endpoint.

ACM Transactions on Programming Languages and Systems, Vol. 3, No. 4, October 1981.

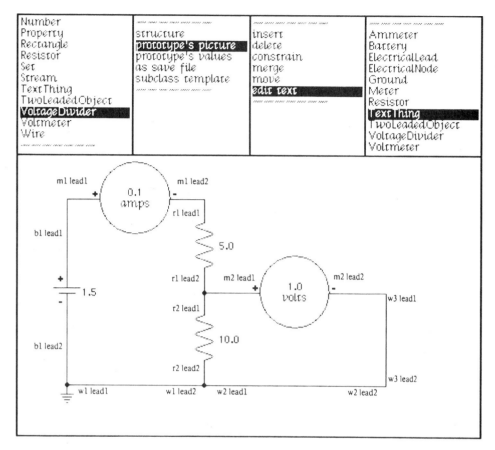

Number			
Property	─── ─── ─── ─── ─── ───	─── ─── ─── ─── ─── ───	─── ─── ─── ─── ─── ───
Rectangle	structure	insert	Ammeter
Resistor	**prototype's picture**	delete	Battery
Set	prototype's values	constrain	ElectricalLead
Stream	as save file	merge	ElectricalNode
TextThing	subclass template	move	Ground
TwoLeadedObject		**edit text**	Meter
VoltageDivider	─── ─── ─── ─── ─── ───	─── ─── ─── ─── ─── ───	Resistor
Voltmeter			**TextThing**
Wire			TwoLeadedObject
─── ─── ─── ─── ─── ───			VoltageDivider
			Voltmeter

Fig. 16.   A voltage divider.

In the voltage divider example, the text that displays the voltmeter's reading has only a single constraint on it: that it correspond to the voltage drop between *m2 lead1 node* and *m2 lead2 node*. Similarly, the text in the ammeter is constrained only by its relation to *m1 lead1 current*. Therefore, these pieces of text can be updated after the voltage drop and current are determined, and their constraints can be removed from further consideration. In this case, there are no propagations that follow.

5.2.2 *Propagation of Known States.* This method is very similar to the previous one. In propagating known states, the constraint satisfier looks for parts whose state will be completely known at run time, that is, parts that have no degrees of freedom. If such a part is found, the constraint satisfier looks for one-step deductions that will allow the states of other parts to be known at run time, and so on recursively. For the state of part A to be known (in one step) from the state of part B, there must be a constraint that connects A and B and that determines A's state uniquely. This is indicated by the *uniqueState* flag on the message plan whose target is A. When propagating known states, the constraint satisfier can use information from different levels in the part–whole hierarchy: if

ACM Transactions on Programming Languages and Systems, Vol. 3, No. 4, October 1981.

the state of an object is known, the states of all its parts are known; if the states of all the parts of an object are known, the state of the object is known.

If the state of a part is uniquely determined by several different constraints, one of the constraints is used to find its state, and run-time checks are compiled to see if the other constraints are satisfied.

In the example, this method would be used as follows. By the constraint on the ground, at run time *b1 lead2 node voltage* is known. (Actually, it was already known during planning, but the constraint satisfier does not use this information.) Also, by the battery's constraint, *b1 lead1 node voltage* is known, and it is the same as *m1 lead1 node voltage*. The ammeter has a constraint that there be no voltage drop across it, and so *m1 lead2 node voltage* is known. Similarly, the voltmeter has a constraint that it draw no current, and so the current in its leads and connecting wires is known. Finally, by the constraint on the wires, *w1 lead2 node voltage*, *w2 lead2 node voltage*, and *w3 lead1 node voltage* are all known.

The voltage at the node between the resistors, and all the other currents, are still unknown.

5.2.3 *Relaxation.* If there are constraints that cannot be handled by either of these techniques, the constraint satisfier asks the object for a method for dealing with circularity. Currently, relaxation is the only such method available (unless the user supplies more information; see below). Relaxation can be used only with objects that have all numeric values; also, the constraints must be such that they can be adequately approximated by a linear equation.

When relaxation is to be used, a call on an instance of Relaxer is compiled. At run time, the relaxer changes each of the object's numerical values in turn so as to minimize the error expressions of its constraints. These changes are determined by approximating the constraints on a given value as a set of linear equations and finding a least-mean-squares fit to this set of equations. The coefficients of each linear equation are calculated by noting the initial error and by numerically finding the derivative of the error expressions with respect to the value. Relaxation continues until all the constraints are satisfied (all the errors are less than some cutoff), or until the system decides that it cannot satisfy the constraints (the errors fail to decrease after an iteration).

Often, many more parts would be relaxed than need to be. To help ease this situation, a trick is used during planning. The trick is to try assuming that the state of one of the parts to be relaxed, say P, is known. This part P is chosen by looking for the part with the largest number of constraints connecting it to other still unknown parts. P is placed in a set S. Then the method of propagation of known states is invoked to see if the states of any other parts would become known as a result. All the parts which would become known, along with P itself, are eliminated from the set of parts to be relaxed. The process is repeated until the set of parts to be relaxed is empty. At run time, only the parts in S are relaxed. As each part P in S is relaxed, the system also computes the new states of the parts which had become known as a result of assuming that P was known. In computing the error in satisfying the constraints on P, the system considers the errors in satisfying the constraints on both P itself and also these other parts.

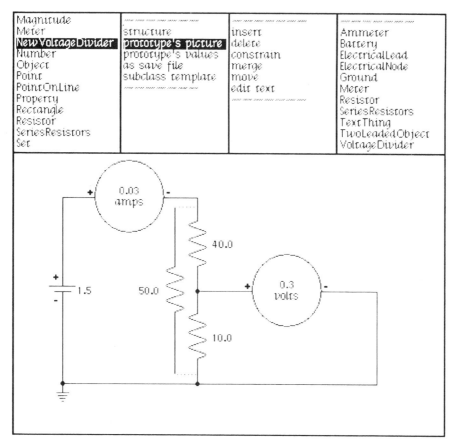

Magnitude			Ammeter
Meter		insert	Battery
NewVoltageDivider	prototype's picture	delete	ElectricalLead
Number	prototype's values	constrain	ElectricalNode
Object	as save file	merge	Ground
Point	subclass template	move	Meter
PointOnLine		edit text	Resistor
Property			SeriesResistors
Rectangle			TextThing
Resistor			TwoLeadedObject
SeriesResistors			VoltageDivider
Set			

Fig. 17.   The voltage divider with an added instance of SeriesResistors.

In the voltage divider, *r2 lead1 current* has three constraints connecting it to other unknowns: the Ohm's law constraint on *r2*, *r2*'s constraint inherited from TwoLeadedObject, and the Kirchhoff's law constraint on *r2 lead1 node*. No other unknown has more constraints, and so the system tries assuming that it is known. Given its value, *r2 lead1 node voltage* and all the other currents would be known. Therefore, at run time, only *r2 lead1 current* is relaxed.

5.2.4 *Using Multiple Views to Avoid Relaxation.* Using the method employed by Steele and Sussman [13], another view of the voltage divider may be added that obviates the need for relaxation. First, a new class SeriesResistors is defined that embodies the fact that two resistors in series are equivalent to a single resistor. An instance of SeriesResistors has three parts: resistors *rA* and *rB*, which are connected in series, and an equivalent single resistor *rSeries*. There is a constraint that the resistance of *rSeries* be equal to the sum of *rA*'s resistance and *rB*'s resistance.

To add this new description to the voltage divider, an instance of Series-Resistors is inserted in the circuit (call it *series*), and the resistors *rA* and *rB* of *series* are merged with the existing resistors *r1* and *r2* in the circuit (Figure 17).

ACM Transactions on Programming Languages and Systems, Vol. 3, No. 4, October 1981.

・ Alan Borning

Using this additional description, all the constraints can be satisfied in one pass. As previously described, *m1 lead2 node voltage* and *w1 lead2 node voltage* are both known. These are the same as *series rSeries lead1 node voltage* and *series rSeries lead2 node voltage*, respectively. Thus, by the Ohm's law constraint on *series rSeries*, *series rSeries lead1 current* is known. But this is the same current as *series rA lead1 current* and also the same as *r1 lead1 current*. Again by Ohm's law, the voltage at the midpoint, *r1 lead2 node voltage*, is known. All the other currents are also known.

It is appropriate to apply this redundant view to a pair of resistors in series only if there is no significant current flowing from the center node of the resistors. If this is not the case, then some of the constraints are not satisfiable, and the user is notified. However, in the present implementation there is no explicit representation of the fact that a redundant description has been provided; the system could do a better job of describing the reason that the constraints could not be satisfied if it knew about the use of such descriptions.

6. CONCLUSION

This paper has described ThingLab, a simulation laboratory. The system uses a number of concepts and techniques (in particular, constraints) that could add significant power to programming languages. A promising direction for future research is to explore the design of a full constraint-oriented programming language; work on this topic is underway, both by the author and by other researchers. Constraints will be taking an increasingly prominent position in our paradigms for programming in the years to come.

ACKNOWLEDGMENTS

Among the many people who have helped with this research, I would particularly like to thank all the members of the Learning Research Group at Xerox Palo Alto Research Center and my dissertation advisor, Terry Winogard. Thanks also to the referees for their useful comments.

REFERENCES

1. BOBROW, D., AND WINOGRAD, T. An overview of KRL, a Knowledge Representation Language. *Cognitive Sci. 1*, 1 (Jan. 1977), 3–46.
2. BORNING, A. ThingLab—A Constraint-Oriented Simulation Laboratory. Ph.D. dissertation, Dep. Computer Science, Stanford Univ., Stanford, Calif., March 1979 (revised version available as Rep. SSL-79-3, Xerox PARC, Palo Alto, Calif., July 1979).
3. DAHL, O.-J., AND NYGAARD, K. SIMULA—An ALGOL-based simulation language. *Commun. ACM 9*, 9 (Sept. 1966), 671–678.
4. ELCOCK, E.W., FOSTER, J.M., GRAY, P.M.D., McGREGOR, J.J., AND MURRAY, A.M. ABSET, a programming language based on sets: Motivation and examples. In *Machine Intelligence*, vol. 6, B. Meltzer and D. Michie (Eds.). Edinburgh University Press, Edinburgh, Scotland, 1971, pp. 467–492.
5. HEWITT, C. Viewing control structures as patterns of passing messages. *Artif. Intell. 8*, 3 (June 1977), 323–364.
6. INGALLS, D.H.H. The Smalltalk-76 programming system: Design and implementation. In Conf. Rec., 5th Ann. ACM Symp. Principles of Programming Languages, Tucson, Ariz., Jan. 23–25, 1978, pp. 9–16.
7. KAY, A., AND GOLDBERG, A. Personal dynamic media. *Computer 10*, 3 (March 1977), 31–42.

ACM Transactions on Programming Languages and Systems, Vol. 3, No. 4, October 1981.

448

8. LIEBERMAN, H., AND HEWITT, C. A session with TINKER: Interleaving program testing with program design. In Proc. 1980 LISP Conf., Stanford Univ., Stanford, Calif., Aug. 1980, pp. 90–99.
9. LISKOV, B., SNYDER, A., ATKINSON, R., AND SHAFFERT, C. Abstraction mechanisms in CLU. *Commun. ACM 20*, 8 (Aug. 1977), 564–576.
10. MITCHELL, J., MAYBURY, W., AND SWEET, R. Mesa language manual. Rep. CSL-79-3, Xerox PARC, Palo Alto, Calif., April 1979.
11. SMITH, D. PYGMALION: A creative programming environment. Rep. AIM-260, Dep. Computer Science, Stanford Univ., June 1975.
12. STEELE, G. The Definition and Implementation of a Computer Programming Language Based on Constraints. Ph.D. dissertation, Dep. Electrical Engineering and Computer Science, M.I.T., Cambridge, Mass., Aug. 1980 (available as MIT-AI TR 595, Aug. 1980).
13. STEELE, G.L., JR., AND SUSSMAN, G.J. Constraints. MIT AI Lab. Memo 502, M.I.T., Cambridge, Mass., Nov. 1978. Also in APL '79: Conf. Proc., *APL Quote Quad* (ACM SIGPLAN/STAPL) *9*, 4 (June 1979), part 1, pp. 208–225.
14. STEELS, L. Reasoning modelled as a society of communicating experts. MIT-AI TR 542, M.I.T., Cambridge, Mass., 1979.
15. STEFIK, M. Planning with constraints (MOLGEN: part 1). *Artif. Intell. 16*, 2 (May 1981), 111–139.
16. SUTHERLAND, I. Sketchpad: A Man–Machine Graphical Communication System. Ph.D. dissertation, Dep. Electrical Engineering, M.I.T., Cambridge, Mass., 1963.
17. WULF, W.A., LONDON, R., AND SHAW, M. An introduction to the construction and verification of Alphard programs. *IEEE Trans. Softw. Eng. SE-2*, 4 (Dec. 1976), 253–264.

Received August 1980; revised April 1981; accepted May 1981

ACM Transactions on Programming Languages and Systems, Vol. 3, No. 4, October 1981.

449

Graphically Defining New Building Blocks in ThingLab

Alan Borning
University of Washington

ABSTRACT

ThingLab is a constraint-oriented, interactive graphical system for building simulations. A typical problem in ThingLab (and in systems like it) is that, to define an object with a new kind of constraint, the user must leave the graphical domain and write code in the underlying implementation language. This makes it difficult for less experienced users to add new kinds of constraints or to modify existing ones. As a step toward solving this problem, the system described here allows the graphical definition of objects that include new kinds of constraints. This is supported by an interface in which a user can open two views on an object being defined, a use view and a construction view. The use view shows the object's normal appearance; the construction view contains additional objects and constraints, which serve to graphically specify the new constraints on the defined object.

CONTENTS

Author's present address: Alan Borning, Department of Computer Science, FR-35, University of Washington, Seattle, WA 98195.

1. INTRODUCTION

A constraint specifies a relation that must be maintained; for example, that a line be horizontal, that a resistor obey Ohm's law, or that the digits in an editable paragraph correspond to the height of a bar in a chart. In general, constraints are multidirectional: A constraint that $A = B + C$ can be used to determine the value of A, given B and C, but can also be used to find B, given A and C, or C, given A and B. When used as part of an interactive graphical system, constraints are a powerful tool for constructing such things as simulations, dynamic documents, and manipulable geometric objects. In such a system, the relations to be satisfied are separated from the process by which they are satisfied. All the constraints on an object can be specified independently of one another. It is up to the system to decide whether or not they can all be satisifed simultaneously, and if so, how to satisfy them.

A problem in previous constraint-oriented systems is that, to define an object with a new kind of constraint, the user typically must leave the graphical domain and write code in the underlying implementation language. This makes it difficult for less experienced users to add new kinds of constraints or to modify existing ones. The system described here addresses that problem by allowing the graphical definition of objects with new kinds of constraints.

The remainder of this section describes in more detail the problem being addressed and outlines the proposed solution. Section 2. describes the user interface to the system and gives examples of its use, and Section 3. describes the underlying model of multiple views in more detail. Section 4. outlines related work, and Section 5. describes the current status of the system and plans for future research.

1.1. ThingLab

The system is an extension to ThingLab, a constraint-oriented simulation laboratory (Borning, 1979, 1981). ThingLab provides an environment for constructing dynamic models of experiments in geometry and physics, such as simulations of constrained geometric objects, simple electrical circuits, mechanical linkages, and bridges under load. Using the techniques developed for these domains, the system has also been used to model other sorts of objects, such as a graphical calculator, and documents with constraints on their layout and contents. ThingLab is currently implemented using the Smalltalk-80 system (Goldberg & Robson, 1983), and runs on a variety of machines, including Xerox Dorados, Tektronix 4400 series workstations, and SUN workstations.

ThingLab is a kind of kit-building kit. The kernel ThingLab system consists of an extension to the Smalltalk language that is used in all ThingLab simulations. The kernel system doesn't have any knowledge about specific domains in which ThingLab can be used, such as geometry or electrical circuits; rather, it provides tools that allow the construction of objects that contain such knowledge. There would thus be two sorts of users of ThingLab (or a system like it). The first sort would use ThingLab to construct a set of building blocks for a given domain. For example, for simulating electrical circuits, such a user would construct definitions of basic parts such as resistors, batteries, wires, and meters. The second sort of user could then employ these building blocks to construct and explore particular simulations.

One of the kits that has been constructed using ThingLab contains parts for making geometric constructions, and includes objects such as points, lines, horizontal lines, and so forth. The kit may be used in illustrating the following geometric theorem: Given an arbitrary quadrilateral, if one bisects each of the sides and draws lines between the adjacent midpoints, the new lines will form a parallelogram. The object depicted in Figure 1 contains four instances of **MidPointLine**. Each **MidPointLine** consists of a line and a point, along with a constraint that the point lie halfway between the endpoints of the line. In addition to the four **MidPointLines**, the object in Figure 1 contains the four lines that form the parallelogram in the middle. The user can drag one corner of the quadrilateral with the cursor, and the system will adjust other parts of the figure to keep all its constraints satisfied.

1.2. The Problem

The interface provided for the second sort of user of ThingLab (who employs predefined building blocks to construct and explore particular simulations) is intuitive and graphical. However, the interface for the first sort of user (who constructs the building blocks) involves writing bits of Smalltalk code. Figure 2, for example, shows the definition of **MidPointLine** in the original version of ThingLab. This way of doing things is not completely satisfactory: Anticipating all the kinds of building blocks that might be needed is impractical, but requiring users to be programmers is also undesirable.

Another problem with defining new constraints concerns the amount of information that the user must provide. Constraints in ThingLab consist of a predicate, which can be used to test whether the constraint is satisfied, and one or more methods, which can be used to alter some part or subpart of the constrained object to make the constraint hold. In the original ThingLab the user must provide both the predicate and the methods; it is left up to the user to ensure that running one of these methods will in fact satisfy the constraint.

1.3. A Proposed Solution

To help with these problems, a facility that allows the graphical definition of new kinds of constraints has been constructed. Only the constraint's predicate is given, either explicitly or implicitly. The system will automatically derive the various methods for satisfying the constraint, so that less information need be provided by the user, and a possible source of error is eliminated. In addition to constraints, some other information is usually provided when defining new building blocks; namely, a list of the object's parts, a list of its inserters, and sometimes a specialized method for showing its picture. (An object's inserters designate parts that are to be positioned when a new copy of the object is inserted in a thing being constructed. For example, the two endpoints of a line are its inserters.) Except for some kinds of specialized picture methods, this other information can now also be specified graphically at the same time the object's constraints are given.

Two different views are shown of an object being defined: a *use view* and a *construction view*. The use view is the object's normal appearance (i.e., as it will appear whenever it is used as a part in some larger object). The construction view includes additional "scaffolding" to give the object its desired behavior. More precisely, the construction view will always include the parts from the use view and may contain any other sorts of parts. The use view must obey all the constraints of the parts which have been attached in the construction view. To ensure this, the system synthesizes a new constraint that applies to the use view, and which enforces all the constraints and relations given in the construction view. When additional copies of the object are made, these copies will contain only the parts specified in the use view, and not the additional parts in the construction.

In the examples in the following section, three different styles of definition are illustrated: constraint networks, constraint expressions, and purely graphical definitions. A constraint network is "wired together" from more primitive elements, such as adders and multipliers. Constraint expressions look like standard two-dimensional algebraic notation. Finally, purely graphical definitions are similar to the geometric constructions of Euclidean geometry. The same underlying mechanisms are used for all three modes of definition. All three styles coexist peacefully within the object definer; further, a single defini-

Figure 1. A demonstration of a theorem about quadrilaterals.

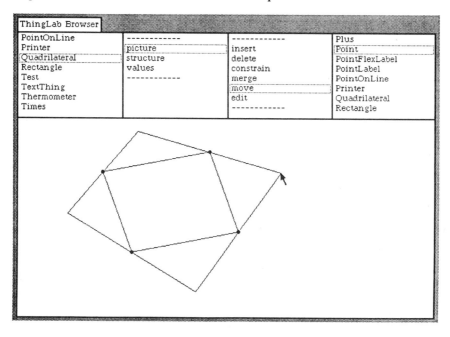

Figure 2. Defining a MidPointLine by writing Smalltalk code.

```
/u1/borning/thinglab/st/things/MidPointLine.st
    ThingLabObject subclass: #MidPointLine
        instanceVariableNames: 'line point '
        classVariableNames: ''
        poolDictionaries: ''
        category: 'Prototypes'!

    MidPointLine prototype parts: 'line point'.
    MidPointLine prototype field: 'line' replaceWith: (40@40 line: 100@20).
    MidPointLine prototype field: 'point' replaceWith: 70@30!

    MidPointLine prototype inserters: #('line point1'  'line point2').
    MidPointLine prototype constrainers: #('line')!

    Constraint owner: MidPointLine prototype
        rule: 'point = ((line point1 + line point2) // 2)'
        error: 'line location dist: point'
        methods: #('self set.point: (line point1 + line point2) //2'
            'line set.point2: line point1 + (point-line point1*2)'
            'line set.point1: line point2 + (point-line point2*2)' )!
```

tion can employ an arbitrary mixture of styles. These styles are in no way built in to the underlying system; by adding different sets of building blocks, other styles can be supported as well.

Constructing a new set of building blocks remains a more complicated activity than using predefined parts to assemble a particular simulation. Care is needed in selecting a set of parts that can be fitted together in many useful ways, and the specification of the building blocks may require some knowledge of algebra. However, the information that must be provided is mostly of the sort that a user with knowledge about the specific domain will have, rather than general programming knowledge or knowledge about ThingLab's internal workings.

Another potential advantage of the approach presented here is that it may aid users who want to modify some existing definition rather than construct a definition from scratch. In general, it is easier to modify some existing description (of whatever kind) than to build a new one. For users who want to customize some existing object, a graphical definition should be easier to comprehend than Smalltalk code, and a concrete manipulation system such as this one will give more immediate feedback during the modification process.

2. EXAMPLES

To support the graphical definition of objects with new kinds of constraints, a new sort of ThingLab window has been added to the system: an *object definer* window. It is similar to the ThingLab browser shown in Figure 1, except that there are two panes at the bottom of the window: a *construction pane* and a *use pane*. These two panes show the construction and use views, repsectively, of the object being defined.

2.1. Geometric Examples

Figure 3 shows a graphical definition of a **MidPointLine,** using the constraint network style. The use view simply contains the line and the midpoint. These appear in the construction view as well. In addition, the construction view includes labels for the line's endpoints and midpoint, so that they can be referred to symbolically. The network to the right of the line constrains the value of the midpoint to be equal to the average of the values of the two endpoints of the line (i.e., to be equal to the vector sum of the endpoints divided by 2). Based on this information in the construction view, the system will synthesize a new constraint that each **MidPointLine** must obey; the construction view thus includes a graphical specification of a new kind of constraint. Finally, the two "inserter" labels specify that, when a new instance of **MidPointLine** is inserted in a diagram, first one endpoint of the line should be positioned, and then the other.

The construction and use views are assembled in much the same way as other objects in ThingLab (see Borning, 1981, for a general description of the ThingLab user interface). For example, to assemble the **MidPointLine** definition, the user first indicates that a new object named "MidPointLine" is to be defined. Next, a line is inserted into the use view by selecting *insert/ LineSegment* in the two rightmost panes at the top of the window, and positioning the line in the use view shown in the bottommost pane. (It will then automatically appear in the construction view as well.) Similarly, a point that will be the midpoint is inserted by selecting *insert/Point* and positioning the point approximately at the line's center. Following this, the plus and divide constraints, the labels for the points, and the inserter tags are inserted into the construction view.

In building some kinds of constraint networks, it may be necessary to refer to parts that don't have a graphical image in the definition pane. To allow this, a constraint network in the definition may include paths to subparts of an object. Figure 4, for example, shows the definition of a vertical line; its constraint simply specifies that *x* values of its endpoints be equal. To refer to these *x* values, which aren't directly visible, each of the two label references in the definition pane includes a path from an endpoint to its *x* value. Connecting the output leads of these two label references constrains the *x* values to be equal.

In addition to networks of algebraic constraints, the construction view can contain other kinds of objects that specify the behavior of the object. For example, the MidPointLine can also be defined in terms of a point-on-line and an equal-length-lines constraint (Figure 5), thus resulting in a purely graphical definition.[1] In this version, the use view again contains only a point and a line. The construction view, in addition, contains a PointOnLine object, which requires the midpoint to lie somewhere on the line, and an EqualLengthLines object, which requires the midpoint to be equidistant from the line's endpoints. Figure 5 shows this definition under construction. The line and midpoint have already been inserted in the use view, and an EqualLengthLines object has been inserted in the construction view and connected appropriately to the line and midpoint. Because constraints are satisfied immediately, the Equal-LengthLines constraint has forced the midpoint to be equidistant from the endpoints of the line (although not necessarily on the line). The user is in the process of inserting the PointOnLine object into the construction view. After the PointOnLine object has been inserted, the midpoint also will need to lie on the line.

After the definition is completed, the parts in the use view will simply be a line and a point. The parts in the construction view will be the line and point from the use view, a PointOnLine object (whose parts are a line and a point) and EqualLengthLines object (whose parts are two lines). However, all four lines will be collinear, so one can see only a single line. The definition also has a set of merges, which are automatically generated during the construction process. (A merge is an equality constraint among two or more objects; merges play a fundamental role in the ThingLab user interface.) The user can ask to see a tabular, textual view of the object, in which all of the connectivity is explicit (see Figure 6).

2.2. A Bar Graph

Figure 7 shows a bar graph, such as might be included in a dynamic document. Each bar graph includes a bar (a rectangle) and a text object displaying a number. The height of the bar is constrained to be proportional to the number displayed in the text. If the text is edited, the height of the bar will change; conversely, if the top of the bar is moved with the mouse, the text will be updated. In addition to the bar and text from the use view, the construction view includes a reference value (100.0 in the figure), and a reference line (which appears to the right of the bar). When the value shown in the text is equal to the reference value, then the height of the bar is to be equal to the height of the reference line, and proportionately for other values. The constraint network to the right sets up the desired relation. The subnetwork *b1 y − b2 y* constrains the value of its output lead to be equal to the height of the bar; similarly, the network *r1 y − r2 y* finds the height of the line. The ratio of the height of the bar to the height of the line is then constrained to be equal to the ratio of the text number to the reference number.

When the system updates the bar object to satisfy its constraints, we want it to do so by changing either the value of the text or the *y* value of the top of the bar, rather than, for example, by changing the length of the reference line. The anchors in the construction view on the reference value, the bottom of the bar,

---

[1] The code that ThingLab generates in this case will be less efficient due to current limitations of its constraint satisfaction strategies. This alternate definition is not intrinsically less efficient, but for it to equal the efficiency of that shown in Figure 3, the constraint satisfier would need some symbolic algebra capabilities.

Figure 3. Defining a MidPointLine using a constraint network.

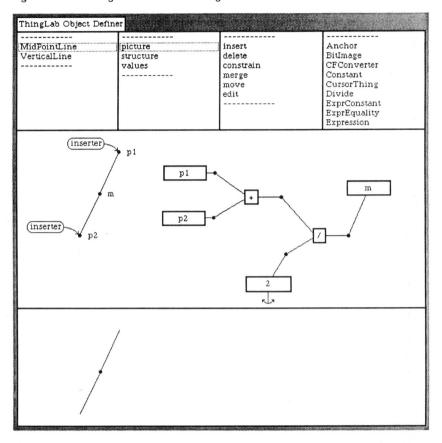

Figure 4. A vertical line definition.

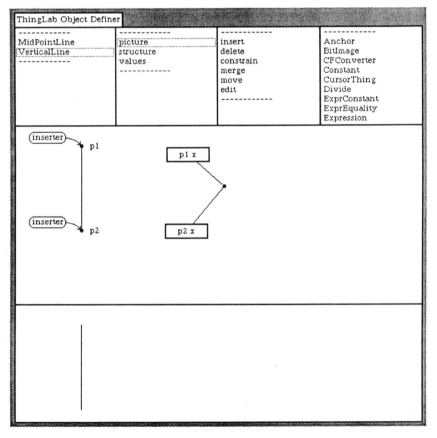

and the two endpoints of the reference line enforce this requirement, by telling the system that it may not alter these parts to satisfy the constraints.

2.3. A File List Browser

The next example is a graphically constructed file list browser, similar in functionality to the file list browser provided in the Smalltalk-80 environment (Goldberg, 1984). The graphical construction of such a file list was inspired by a similar construction in the Ariel system, designed and written by Dan Ingalls.

The object shown in the use pane in Figure 8 is the file list browser itself. It is a three-paned window: In the top pane is a pattern used to match file names, in the middle is a menu of file names matching the pattern, and in the bottom is a text editor in which the contents of the selected file are displayed. In the figure, the pattern is *thing*.cm. Three files match that pattern; the file thinglab.cm is selected. The bottom pane displays the contents of that file.

The construction view includes constraints to give the file list browser the desired functionality. To allow these constraints to be applied graphically in the definition, connector objects have been merged with each of the file list panes, making connection leads available. Thus the pattern has a lead coming out of it that makes the text of the pattern available, the menu has two leads that make the list of menu items and the selection available, and the text editor at the bottom again has a text lead. The pattern lead and the output from the All-FileNames object are connected to a filter object, which selects the set of file names matching the pattern. This set of matching file names is in turn connected to the list lead of the menu. The menu selection is then connected to a FileContents object, which extracts the contents of the named file. Finally, the file contents is connected to the bottom text pane.[2]

Constraints are also used to make all the panes have the same width, and to make them line up vertically. This is accomplished by merging in two UpDown objects into the panes in the construction view. Each UpDown object consists of two rectangles, constrained to have equal widths and to lie one on top of the other. (Figure 9 shows one UpDown object in place, with a second being inserted.) This example, incidentally, demonstrates that the construction pane can contain an arbitrary mixture of constraint network objects, such as the Filter object, and purely graphical objects, such as the UpDown objects.

There are a number of limitations in the current file list browser that make it merely a toy; for example, it can be used only within the ThingLab browser and not as an ordinary Smalltalk window. Also, the menu has no scrolling mechanism, so that long lists of files result in a tall menu. However, this way of constructing user interface applications is promising as a means of significantly reducing the length of time needed to assemble an application.

2.4. Examples Using Constraint Expression Objects

For simple constraints, networks such as those shown in several of the previous figures are satisfactory, and have the benefit of making clear the multi-directional nature of constraints. More complex networks, however, take up considerable space and are difficult to understand. To help with this problem, a collection of building blocks for two-dimensional constraint expressions has been implemented, thus allowing a more standard algebraic notation. Figure 10, for example, shows a MidPointLine definition using constraint expression objects.

---

[2] The filter constraint is unidirectional. Given a pattern and a list of all file names, it will find the set of file names matching the pattern. However, the pattern and list of all file names are reference only; the constraint will not attempt to find a pattern or a list of all file names that would make the constraint hold. The FileContents constraint is bidirectional: It will extract the contents of a given file, or if the displayed text is edited, the constraint will be used in the other direction so that the file is updated.

Figure 5. **A purely graphical definition of the MidPointLine.**

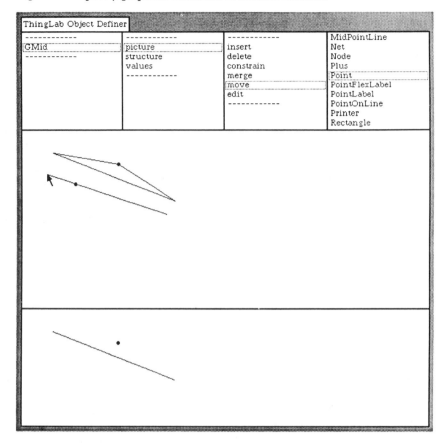

Figure 6. **Showing the structure of the purely graphical definition.**

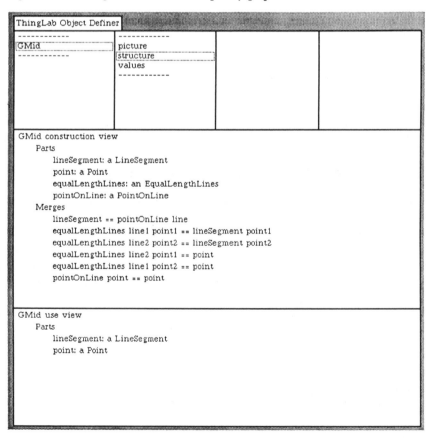

Figure 7. **A bar graph definition.**

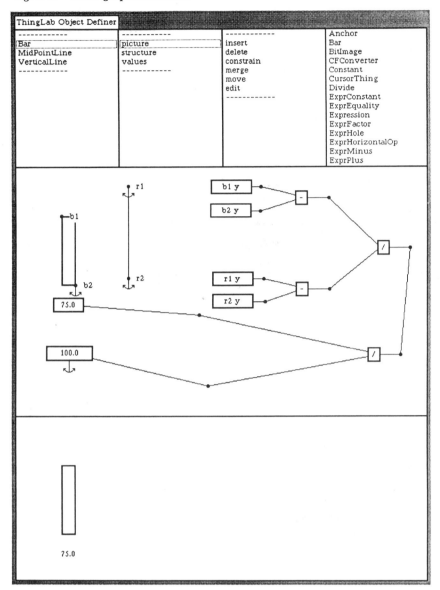

An interesting feature of these expression objects is the use of constraints in describing the layout of the expressions as well as their value. For example, the **Divide** object has the obvious constraint that the value of the entire expression is equal to the numerator divided by the denominator; in addition, it has constraints that the numerator be centered over the denominator, and that the length of the horizontal bar be the maximum of the widths of the numerator and denominator. If either the numerator or the denominator is edited, the layout of the **Divide** object will thus be updated appropriately. The standard ThingLab editing operations (*insert, delete,* and so forth) are used to build up expressions. Figure 11 shows the constraint expression for the **MidPointLine** under construction. The boxes represent holes in the expressions (i.e., non-terminals in the expression grammar). The user is about to insert the **Plus** object into the numerator of the **Divide** object. After this is done, variables *p* and *q* will be inserted into the holes in the **Plus** object to complete the construction.

Finally, Figure 12 shows a definition of the bar graph object using constraint expressions. Note that the expressions used in this definition include paths to subparts of the object, similar to the paths used in the vertical line definition in Figure 4. For this more complex constraint, the expressions are clearly easier to understand than the network version of the bar graph definition.

Figure 8. **A file list browser.**

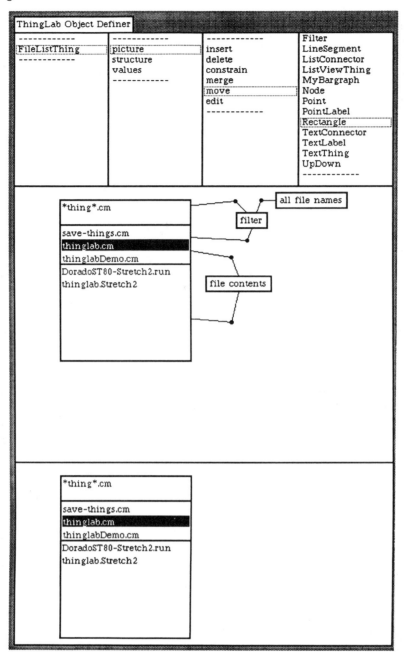

3. ON MULTIPLE VIEWS

As previously discussed, the construction and use panes of the object definer window show two views of the object being defined. Support for these particular views is hardwired into the current implementation. However, we envision the object definer as making use of a more general mechanism for coordinating multiple views, which is currently being designed. The relation between the construction and use views is most clearly explained in terms of this mechanism.

In general, an object will be able to make available an arbitrary number of alternate views of itself. Each alternate view is itself another object, The relations among these alternate views is described by constraints among the views. Each of the alternate views may also have internal constraints, and an object must obey all the constraints specified for all its alternate views.

460

For example, one view of a screen rectangle might specify the location and dimensions of the rectangle by its upper-left and lower-right corners. Another view might specify the location and dimensions by a center, width, and height. These two views would be kept in coordination by an appropriate set of constraints. Letting "cornerView" name the upper-left/lower-right view and "centerView" the center-width/height view, these constraints are:

```
centerView center = (cornerView lowerRight −
                          cornerView upperLeft) / 2
centerView width = cornerView lowerRight x −
                          cornerView upperLeft x
centerView height = cornerView lowerRight y −
                          cornerView upperLeft y
```

Given a rectangle so defined, we might add an additional constraint requiring the rectangle to be a square, by constraining the width to be equal to the height in the center-width/height view. The upper-left/lower-right view would have to obey this constraint as well.

There is a simple relation between this multiple-view mechanism and the standard ThingLab mechanism for part–whole hierarchies. An object and all its alternate views can be regarded as parts of an enclosing container object. The constraints relating the views can then be regarded as constraints owned by the container object.

An object behaves as if all its alternate views were present. However, there is room for cleverness in the implementation. For a given alternate view, one

Figure 9. **UpDown objects used to align the window panes.**

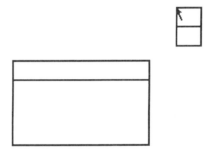

strategy is to create the view at the same time the original object is created; another is to create the view on demand. A third strategy is never to create the view; rather, when an attribute of the view is needed, to compute that attribute on the fly, and whenever a change to an attribute is requested, to make the necessary changes to the original object instead.

3.1. Current Status

As noted previously, only a specialized implementation of the view mechanism currently exists; namely, for the construction and use views of an object. The parts of the use view are always constrained to be equal to corresponding parts in the construction view. When a construction view is created, a use view is always created at the same time. However, when a use view is created, the construction view is *not* created at the same time; rather, it is created only on demand. However, the use view is required to act as if the construction view exists at all times (i.e., to obey the constraints in the construction). This is implemented by synthesizing a new constraint that the use view must obey, and which has the same effect on the use view as the constraints in the construction. For the **MidPointLine** example, this synthesized constraint has the same effect

Figure 10. An expression-oriented definition of the MidPointLine.

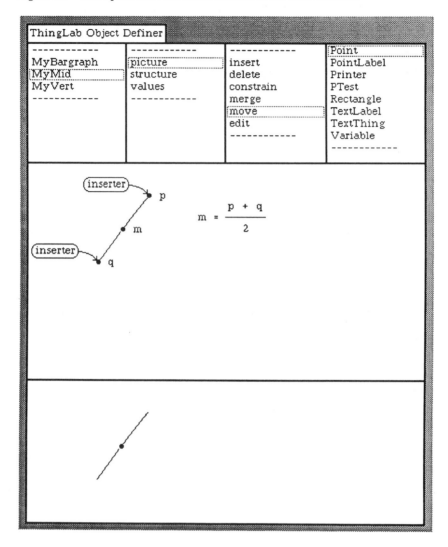

Figure 11. Building an expression.

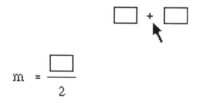

as the one defined by hand that it is shown in Figure 2. (In future implementations it should be the same as the constraint defined by hand; at the moment, the methods it generates are less efficient, due to expediencies taken in the implementation.)

These methods in the synthesized constraint are produced using the standard ThingLab constraint satisfaction techniques of propagating known values, propagating degrees of freedom, and so forth. For example, the method that computes a new value for the first endpoint of the line *p1*, given values for the other endpoint *p2* and for the midpoint *m*, is constructed as follows. Because the value of *m* and of the constant 2 are both known, at run time the value of the dividend for the divide constraint will be known. Now the plus constraint can determine the value for *p1*, because *p2* and the sum are known.

3.2. Abstraction and Multiple Views

Nearly all programming languages contain an abstraction mechanism that allows new functions or procedures to be defined using existing ones. The object definer plays an analogous role in ThingLab. As the examples show, given an existing set of objects, one can define a new kind of object in terms of them. A more standard programming example will illustrate the analogy more clearly. Figure 13 shows the definition of a **Squarer** object, which can be used in one direction to compute the square of a number, or in the other direction to compute a square root. The use view of the **Squarer** simply includes a placeholder function box. In the construction view, this function box is wired to a times constraint, giving it the appropriate behavior. In Figure 14, an instance of **Squarer** has been connected to two printers. The number **2** has been entered in the printer on the right, and to satisfy the constraint, the square root of 2 has been computed and displayed in the printer on the left. (Because the definition was simply given in terms of a times constraint, ThingLab resorts to relaxation to compute the square root.)

This mechanism is more than simply a macro facility; it is a true abstraction mechanism. For example, one can define recursive constraints, such as a recursive factorial, using the object definer. This would not be possible with a macro facility, because a recursive definition would result in an infinite structure. The relation of the object definer mechanism to programming languages is discussed in more detail in Borning, 1987, which includes examples of recursive constraint definitions, higher-order constraints, and so forth.

Figure 12. **An expression-oriented definition of the bar graph.**

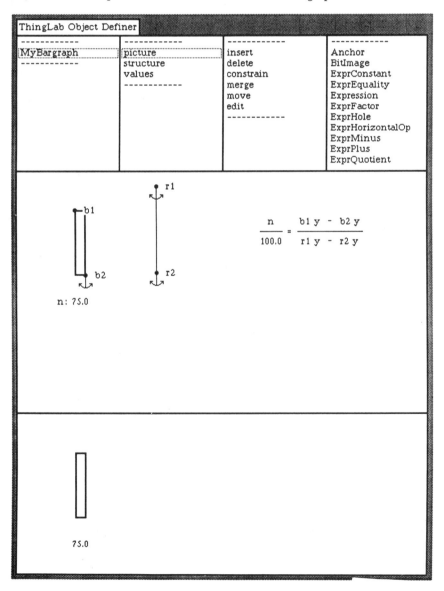

4. RELATED WORK

There are two main bodies of related work: on constraints and on graphical programming.

In constraints, related work includes Sutherland's (1963) Sketchpad program, a pioneering system in both constraints and computer graphics; Steele's (1980) work on constraint languages (see also Sussman & Steele, 1980); the IDEAL system for typesetting graphics (Van Wyk, 1980, 1982); Gosling's (1983) dissertation on algebraic constraints; Nelson's (1985) graphics system JUNO; Duisberg's (1986a, 1986b) Animus system for constraint-based animation; and Leler's (1986) Bertrand, a general-purpose constraint language that uses rewrite rules to solve constraint systems. Levitt (1984) surveyed constraint languages and described his own work on a jazz composition system.

The system described here is a kind of graphical programming system. (Other work in this area, however, has generally concerned procedural rather than declarative languages.) Early work includes Sutherland's (1966) system for constructing graphical procedures, based on an electronic circuit metaphor; the GRAIL language, developed at RAND Corporation for programming using flowcharts (Ellis, Haefner, & Sibley, 1969); and the AMBIT languages (Christensen, 1966). Smith's (1975) PYGMALION and Curry's (1978) PAD both use programming by example with a strong graphical interface. Recent systems include Glinert's (1985) PICT program, which uses a graphical interface for constructing programs using flowcharts; Gould and Finzer's (1984a, 1984b) graphical system for Programming by Rehearsal, which employs a theatrical metaphor, with performers, troupes, and stages; Halbert's (1984) Programming by Example system; Tinker by Lieberman (Lieberman & Hewitt, 1980); and Trillium (Henderson, 1986), an environment for simulating and experimenting with machine interfaces. Scofield (1985) described a system, Voodoo, in which the editing of graphical or textual images is used as the paradigm for interacting with systems. Meyers (1986) provided a taxonomy of systems for visual programming, programming by example, and program visualization. In his taxonomy, the system reported here is interactive, a visual programming system, and a system that uses programming by example. (Meyers's article also has numerous other references to systems of these sorts.)

An earlier version of this article is published in the *Proceedings of the CHI '86 Conference on Human–Computer Interaction* (Borning, 1986). The system described in the earlier version is extended in several ways, and the article contains a discussion of the general multiple-view mechanism, as well as a number of new examples, including those using expression-oriented constraints and the file list browser.

5. FUTURE RESEARCH

The system described here is still under development, and many issues remains to be explored. Several of these are outlined in this section.

5.1. Using the Object Definer Throughout ThingLab

At present, the object definer has been used to define only a subset of the building blocks that have been constructed for ThingLab. We plan to enhance the definer in a number of ways, and to use it routinely for all ThingLab building blocks. This project will include a bootstrapping operation, in which the objects that are used in the definitions (e.g., the arithmetic expression objects) are replaced with objects built using the object definer.

Some improvements are needed before this an be done. First, the constraint code generated by the system contains some inefficiencies, and it should be improved so that it is equal or close in efficiency to that written by hand by a hu-

Figure 13. A definition of a Squarer object.

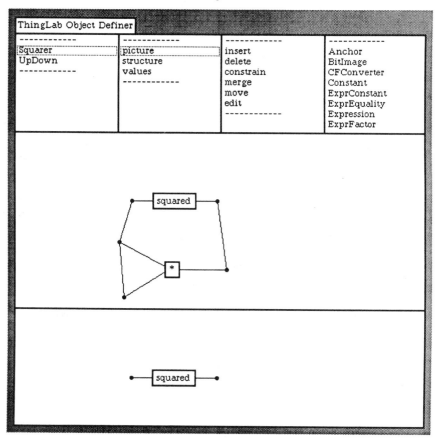

Figure 14. Using the Squarer.

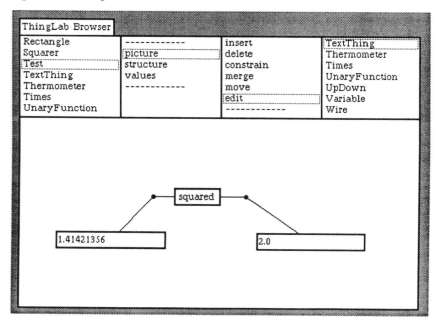

man programmer. Second, constraints defined by hand contain a series of alternate methods for satisfying the constraint. In the current object definer, these methods are constructed automatically. When this can be done, it is clearly an improvement, but sometimes ThingLab will be able to find only an inefficient inverse (e.g., for the inverse of the **Squarer** constraint), or won't be able to find one at all. A facility will be added for expressing alternate methods if necessary.[3] The third improvement is relatively minor. In constraints that are constructed by hand, the order in which the methods are listed indicates the programmer's preference as to which quantity is to be changed to satisfy the constraints, if there is a choice. A facility will be added so that such preferences can be specified, using labels similar to the "inserter" labels shown in Figure 3.[4]

5.2. Generalizing Multiple Views

Another current activity is to complete the design and implementation of the general multiple-view mechanism. In addition to allowing a cleaner implementation, this mechanism will support greater flexibility in showing and hiding information. As an example of its usefulness, consider the bar graph example (Section 2.2.). Users who want to change the reference number or the reference line must go to the construction view to do so. If they want to change these attributes for only some bar graph instances, copies of the entire definition must be made and edited. In place of this awkward situation, what one would like is to provide a third view of the bar that shows the reference line and number and allows them to be edited, but that hides the full constraint network. A convenient way should be provided for a user to open this alternate view edit an attribute, and then close the view.

5.3. Empirical Questions

At this point, nobody but the author has used the system. Once it is more stable, there are many empirical questions to be explored and improvements to be made to the user interface. For example, it is not clear which of the three definition styles is most appropriate: the constraint network style of defintion (as in Figure 3), the purely graphical style (as in Figure 5), or the constraint expression style (as in Figure 10). The author's hypothesis is that no single one of these styles is the best for all kinds of definitions. In general, the network notation makes clear the multidirectional nature of the constraints and is useful in making connections among parts of the object more vivid. Constraint expressions look like standard two-dimensional algebraic notation. As such, they are familiar and concise. However, the use of symbolic names to express connectivity may not be as clear to naive users as wires. Also, the expressions have an implied directionality, which may sometimes be misleading. Purely graphical definitions can be intuitive for constructing geometric objects, but are much more limited in their range of applicability than are the other two styles. A more general characterization of the strengths and weaknesses of the different notations should be made, and experiments should be designed and performed to test this characterization.

---

[3] This problem can almost be handled at present by connecting in alternate, redundant views (e.g., in the **Squarer** by wiring in a square root function along with the times constraint.) However, ThingLab doesn't know that satisfying either the times or the square root constraint is enough to ensure that the other constraint will be satisfied, and so the constraint satisfaction code that it generates will be suboptimal.

[4] At the moment, the object definer decides this preference information based on the preferences built into the components. For example, for the network or expression **MidPointLine** definitions, the divide constraint has a preference that the quotient be changed before the divisor or dividend. Because midpoint is connected to the quotient, the system will change the midpoint in preference to the other points. Although it works in this case, it is only a temporary solution.

Regarding the specific examples shown in this article, for the **MidPointLine** it seems that the constraint expression definition is the easiest to understand, but for the file list browser the network form is best, because it makes the connections between the panes more vivid. The purely graphical definition of the **MidPointLine** is somewhat hard to comprehend, because all of the lines end up being collinear and the structure of the definition isn't visible in the picture. One can ask to see a tabular, textual view of the structure, as in Figure 6. However, a better alternative (suggested by one of the *HCI* referees) would be to support in addition a kind of "exploded parts" view, in which all of the merged parts could be shown slightly separated, with dotted lines to indicate the connectivity.

5.4. Further Applications of the Object Definer

Duisberg's (1986a, 1986b) Animus system, which was cited in Section 4., is built on top of ThingLab and includes several new kinds of constraints needed for animation, including constraints on trajectories, constraints that describe responses to events, and constraints involving derivatives. Another research direction is thus to use the object definer in defining the sorts of constraints needed by Animus. This is clearly possible — if nothing else, we can use textual expressions in the construction pane — but it will be interesting to see whether more graphical depictions are possible and useful. This will probably involve mapping time onto one of the spatial dimensions, as is done, for example, in standard musical notation.

Spreadsheet programs are extremely useful, and can be regarded as simple constraint systems in which the constraints are all one way.[5] Incorporating the convenient and intuitive interface provided by spreadsheets into ThingLab would allow more general sorts of relations to be defined among elements of the spreadsheet, and would also allow the spreadsheet to be connected to graphical objects. The object definer might be useful in this context in defining the analog of spreadsheet macros.

The expression objects described in Section 2.4. provide a structure editor[6] for algebraic constraint expressions without additional programming effort. It would be straightforward to add other objects (square roots, summations, products, ceilings, floors, etc.), so that a rich set of mathematical operators is available for building expressions that follow standard mathematical typographic conventions. One interesting direction for future research would be to implement constraint-based expression objects (and hence structure editors) for other sorts of languages, such as programming languages. These expression objects need not be restricted to one-dimensional text, so that one could explore a variety of two-dimensional representations. A related project would be to analyze the relation between constraints and attribute grammars, which have in previous work been a standard mechanism for propagating information in structure editors.

One of the lessons learned from the research on structure editors is that it sometimes becomes tedious for expert users to build programs using only a structure editor; for arithmetic expressions and the like, they would sometimes rather just type in some text and have the machine parse it (Waters, 1982). A similar facility should be provided in ThingLab. This can be handled within the multiple view framework: For a mathematical expression, one view is in its two-dimensional form, another is as a linear text string.

---

[5] TK!Solver (Konopasek & Jayaraman, 1984, 1985) is a commercial constraint language descended from spreadsheet programs that can handle true multiway constraints.

[6] Structure editors for programming languages have been the subject of considerable research (see Delisle, Menicosy, & Schwartz, 1984; Notkin, 1985; Reiss, 1984; Teitelbaum & Reps, 1981).

Acknowledgments. Thanks to Peter Deutsch, Rob Duisberg, Adele Goldberg, Robert Henry, Dan Ingalls, David Notkin, Dave Robson, and Randy Smith for comments and suggestions. Thanks also to the *HCI* referees; one of the referees in particular gave extremely detailed and useful recommendations.

Support. This research was sponsored in part by Xerox Corporation, in part by National Science Foundation Grants MCS-8202520 and IST-8604923, and in part by an equipment grant from Tektronix, Inc.

REFERENCES

Borning, A. H. (1979). *ThingLab — A constraint-oriented simulation laboratory.* Doctoral dissertation, Stanford University, Stanford, CA. (A revised version is published as Xerox Palo Alto Research Center Report SSL-79-3, July 1979.)

Borning, A. H. (1981). The programming language aspects of ThingLab, a constraint-oriented simulation laboratory. *ACM Transactions on Programming Languages and Systems, 3,* 353–387.

Borning, A. H. (1986). Defining constraints graphically. *Proceedings of the CHI '86 Conference on Computer-Human Interaction,* 137–143. New York: ACM.

Borning, A. H. (1987). Constraints and functional programming. *Proceedings of the Sixth Annual IEEE Phoenix Conference on Computers and Communications,* 300–306. New York: IEEE Computer Society.

Christensen, C. (1966). On the implementation of AMBIT, a language for symbol manipulation. *Communications of the ACM, 9,* 570–573.

Curry, G. A. (1978). *Programming by abstract demonstration.* Doctoral dissertation, University of Washington, Department of Computer Science, Seattle. (Published as University of Washington, Department of Computer Science, Technical Report No. 78-03-02.)

Delisle, N. M., Menicosy, D. E., & Schwartz, M. D. (1984). Viewing a programming environment as a single tool. *Proceedings of the ACM SIGSOFT/SIGPLAN Software Engineering Symposium on Practical Software Development Environments,* 49–56. (Issued as *Sigplan Notices, 19*(5) and *Software Engineering Notes, 9*(3). New York: ACM.)

Duisberg, R. A. (1986a). Animated graphical interfaces using temporal constraints. *Proceedings of the CHI '86 Conference on Computer-Human Interaction,* 131–136. New York: ACM.

Duisberg, R. A., (1986b). *Constraint-based animation: The implementation of temporal constraints in the animus system.* Doctoral dissertation, University of Washington, Department of Computer Science, Seattle. (Published as University of Washington, Department of Computer Science, Technical Report No. 86-09-01.)

Ellis, T. O., Haefner, J. F., & Sibley, W. L. (1969). *The GRAIL Project: An experiment in man–machine communication* (Tech. Rep. No. RM-5999-ARPA). Santa Monica, CA: the Rand Corporation.

Glinert, E. P. (1985). *PICT: Experiments in the design of interactive, graphical programming environments.* Doctoral dissertation, University of Washington, Department of Computer Science, Seattle.

Goldberg, A. J. (1984). *Smalltalk-80: The interactive programming environment.* Reading, MA: Addison-Wesley.

Goldberg, A. J., & Robson, D. (1983). *Smalltalk-80: The language and its implementation.* Reading, MA: Addison-Wesley.

Gosling, J. (1983). *Algebraic constraints.* Doctoral dissertation, Carnegie-Mellon University, Pittsburgh. (Published as Carnegie-Mellon University Computer Science Department Technical Report No. CMU-CS-83-132.)

Gould, L., & Finzer, W. (1984a). *Programming by rehearsal* (Tech. Rep. No. SCL-84-1). Palo Alto, CA: Xerox Palo Alto Research Center.

Gould, L., & Finzer, W. (1984b). Programming by rehearsal. *Byte, 9*(6), 187–210.

Halbert, D. (1984). *Programming by example.* Doctoral dissertation, University of California, Berkeley. (Published as Technical Report No. OSD-T8402, Office Systems Division, Xerox Corporation, Palo Alto, CA.)

Henderson, D. A. (1986). The Trillium user interface design environment. *Proceedings of the CHI '86 Conference on Computer-Human Interaction,* 221–227. New York: ACM.

Konopasek, M., & Jayaraman, S. (1984). *The TK!Solver book.* Berkeley, CA: Osborne/McGraw-Hill.

Konopasek, M., & Jayaraman, S. (1985). Constraint and declarative languages for engineering applications: The TK!Solver contribution. *Proceedings of the IEEE, 73,* 1791–1806.

Leler, W. (1986). *Specification and generation of constraint satisfaction systems using augmented term rewriting*. Doctoral dissertation, University of North Carolina, Chapel Hill.

Levitt, D. (1984). Machine tongues X: Constraint languages. *Computer Music Journal, 8*, 9–21.

Lieberman, H., & Hewitt, C. (1980). A session with TINKER: Interleaving program testing with program design. *Proceedings 1980 LISP Conference*, 90–99. Redwood Estates, CA: LISP Conference.

Meyers, B. A. (1986). Visual programming, programming by example, and program visualization: A taxonomy. *Proceedings of the CHI '86 Conference on Computer-Human Interaction*, 59–66. New York: ACM.

Nelson, G. (1985). Juno, a constraint-based graphics system. In B. A. Barsky (Ed.), *SIGGRAPH '85 Conference Proceedings* (pp. 235–243). New York: ACM.

Notkin, D. (1985). The GANDALF Project. *The Journal of Systems and Software, 5*(2), 91–105.

Reiss, S. (1984). Graphical program development with PECAN program development systems. *Proceedings of the ACM SIGSOFT/SIGPLAN Software Engineering Symposium on Practical Software Development Environments*, 30–41. Issued as *Sigplan Notices, 19*(5) and *Software Engineering Notes, 9*(3). New York: ACM.

Scofield, J. A. (1985). *Editing as a paradigm for user interaction*. Doctoral dissertation, University of Washington, Department of Computer Science, Seattle. (Published as University of Washington, Department of Computer Science, Technical Report No. 85-08-10.)

Smith, D. C. (1975). *PYGMALION: A creative programming environment*. Doctoral dissertation, Stanford University, Stanford, CA. (Published as Stanford University, Computer Science Department, Report No. STAN-CS-75-499.)

Steele, G. L. (1980). *The definition and implementation of a computer programming language based on constraints*. Doctoral dissertation, Massachusetts Institute of Technology, Cambridge. (Published as MIT-AI TR 595, August 1980.)

Sussman, G. J., & Steele, G. L. (1980). CONSTRAINTS—A language for expressing almost-hierarchical descriptions. *Artificial Intelligence, 14*, 1–39.

Sutherland, I. (1963). *Sketchpad: A man-machine graphical communication system*. Doctoral dissertation, Massachusetts Institute of Technology, Cambridge.

Sutherland, W. (1966). *On-line graphical specifications of computer procedures*. Doctoral dissertation, Massachusetts Institute of Technology, Cambridge.

Teitelbaum, T., & Reps, T. (1981). The Cornell program synthesizer: A syntax-directed programming environment. *Communications of the ACM, 24*, 563–573.

Van Wyk, C. J. (1980). *A language for typesetting graphics*. Doctoral dissertation, Stanford University, Stanford, CA.

Van Wyk, C. J. (1982). A high-level language for specifying pictures. *ACM Transactions on Graphics, 1*, 163–182.

Waters, R. C. (1982). Program editors should not abandon text-oriented commands. *ACM SIGPLAN Notices, 17*(7), 39–46.

HCI Editorial Record. First manuscript received April 29, 1986. Revision received January 5, 1987. Accepted by Thomas Malone. — *Editor*

Constraint Hierarchies

Alan Borning, Robert Duisberg, Bjorn Freeman-Benson,
Axel Kramer, and Michael Woolf[1]

Abstract. Constraints describe relations that must be maintained, and provide a useful tool for such applications as interactive simulations, algorithm animation, and graphical user interface construction. We describe a major overhaul and extension to the constraint satisfaction mechanism in ThingLab, a constraint-oriented simulation laboratory written in the Smalltalk-80 language. First, a specification is presented of *constraint hierarchies*. Such hierarchies include both required constraints and default constraints of differing strengths, thus adding considerable expressive power to the system. Second, an algorithm for satisfying constraint hierarchies is described. The new satisfier is substantially faster than the previous version, even though it also includes new functionality.

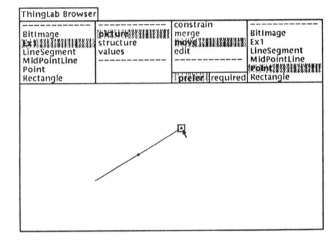

Figure 1: A MidPointLine being stretched by the mouse.

1 Introduction

Constraint-based languages and systems have a demonstrated utility for a wide variety of applications including geometric layout, physical simulations, user interface design, document formatting, algorithm animation, design and analysis of mechanical devices and electrical circuits, and even jazz improvization [2,3,4,7,9,10,11,12,13,14,15,16,17]. They allow a set of declarative relations to be transformed into executable procedures to maintain the specified relationships. Constraints separate the conditions to be satisfied from the process by which it is done, leaving it up to system to decide whether a set of constraints can

all be satisfied simultaneously, and if so, how to go about it. Due to space limitations, a complete survey of constraints and their relation to object-oriented languages and systems is beyond the scope of this paper, but such a survey may be found in [1].

A problem arises when an object is under- or over-constrained; one would like the system to behave reasonably in such cases. Consider the example of a MidPointLine (Figure 1), a line segment with a point on it constrained to lie at the midpoint. Upon moving one endpoint, the user would probably expect the midpoint to move to keep the constraint satisfied, rather than the opposite endpoint, and certainly not both. Here the user's expectations and the Principle of Least Astonishment imply some preferential ordering of defaults. Conversely, if one were to anchor an endpoint of a horizontal line, and then move the other endpoint, an over-constrained object would result. The user's manipulation is considered to be a constraint that the point being moved is equal to the mouse position. But if the user moves the mouse vertically, then all the constraints cannot be met. To handle the situation gracefully, the system must decide which constraint it will leave unsatisfied (either the anchor or the mouse constraint). This implies the need for some ordering

[1] Robert Duisberg is with the Computer Research Laboratory, Tektronix, Inc. MS 50-662, P.O. Box 500, Beaverton, Oregon 97077. All others are with the Department of Computer Science, FR-35, University of Washington, Seattle, Washington 98195.

of constraints with respect to their relative strengths.

Previous implementations in ThingLab and its extension in Animus relied on special purpose notions of defaults and preferences. For example, mouse input and time were given special handling. Unspecified values remained unchanged by default, but as an artifact of the constraint satisfaction algorithms used rather than by explicit declaration. Overconstrained systems resulted in an error being signaled unless the conflict arose from mouse input, in which case the value moved by the mouse would be overwritten by values determined by constraints.

The primary impetus for the research reported here comes from the "filters" project, in which we are using ThingLab as a base on which to build a system for the declarative, graphical construction of user interfaces [6]. The filters project requires a number of additions to ThingLab's repertoire of constraint types, and in addition would benefit greatly from faster constraint satisfaction planning. In designing a faster and enhanced constraint satisfaction algorithm, it became obvious that it was necessary to have a clear specification of what it means to satisfy constraints in the presence of defaults. The present paper thus presents both a theory of hierarchies of constraints of varying strengths, as well as an algorithm for satisfying such hierarchies. This provision for constraints of different strengths adds significant new flexibility to the system.

2 Specification of a Constraint Hierarchy

A constraint consists of a *predicate*, an *error function*, and a set of *methods* for making that constraint hold. The predicate can be used to test whether or not the constraint is satisfied. The error function indicates how nearly the constraint is satisfied by mapping the state of an object to a vector of real numbers. The constraint error for the constraint c and value x is denoted by $e(x, c)$; its magnitude must be 0 whenever x satisfies c. Each of the constraint's methods allows values for one or more parts of an object to be determined, given values of other parts. For example, the midpoint constraint (Figure 1) has three methods: one to determine the midpoint given the two endpoints of the line, another to determine one endpoint of the line given the midpoint and the other endpoint, and a third to determine the other endpoint. Methods may determine values for more than one part, and may optionally have a precondition that must hold if the method is to be used. For example, an integer divide method

can determine both the quotient and remainder, with a precondition that the divisor not be 0. The following relation must hold between each method and the constraint's predicate: if the precondition holds, and if the parts of the object are set to the values determined by the method, then the constraint will be satisfied. The methods will be used in the constraint satisfaction algorithm described in Section 3, but are not employed further in the specification.

A constraint hierarchy H is a list of sets $C_0 \ldots C_n$ of constraints. We wish to define the set S of objects that best satisfy H. The constraints in C_0 are required: all objects in S must satisfy the constraints in C_0. The remaining constraints $C_1 \ldots C_n$ are weak: we prefer but do not require that the objects in S satisfy them. The constraints in each successive set C_i are weaker than the constraints in the preceding set C_{i-1}. Constraints within a given set C_i are of equal strength. Constraints at a given level C_i completely dominate those at weaker levels, even if a constraint at a weaker level has an extremely large error for a given solution preferred by the stronger levels.[2]

Ideally, we would find successive sets S_i of objects that best satisfied all the constraints up to and including those at the ith level, until one was found that contained a single object. This object would then best satisfy the constraints in the hierarchy. However, for many hierarchies there will be several objects that satisfy all the constraints through level $i-1$, and then no objects that completely satisfy the constraints at level i. For this reason, the definition given below employs a predicate $better(x, y, H)$, which we will call the *comparator*. (Read this as "object x better satisfies the constraints in hierarchy H than does object y".) The *better* predicate will allow us to discriminate among competing solutions; it is used to discard potential solutions that are worse than some other potential solution.

We first define the set S_0 of objects that satisfy the required constraints. Then, using S_0, we define the desired set S by eliminating all potential solutions that are worse than some other potential solution.

$$
\begin{aligned}
S_0 &= \{x \mid \forall c \in C_0 \; x \; satisfies \; c\} \\
S &= \{x \mid x \in S_0 \land \forall y \in S_0 \neg better(y, x, H)\}
\end{aligned}
$$

---

[2]In many design problems one wishes to balance various competing goals, e.g. to minimize cost, space, power requirements, and to maximize reliability. In our specification of constraint hierarchies, these preferences would all need to be at the same level in the hierarchy if they were to interact. One could also include weighting factors to weight the errors (or costs), but we have not added such a capability to our system so far.

Note that this is purely a specification of the set S—in many cases, S_0 will be infinite, so the definition does not provide an effective means for computing S. An algorithm is described in Section 3.

2.1 Comparators

There are a number of different, useful definitions of the comparator $better(x, y, H)$. We will insist that $better$ be irreflexive and transitive:

$$\forall x \forall H \neg better(x, x, H),$$

$$\forall x \forall y \forall z \forall H \, better(x, y, H) \wedge better(y, z, H) \rightarrow$$

$$better(x, z, H).$$

From irreflexivity and transitivity it immediately follows that:

$$\forall x \forall y \forall H \, better(x, y, H) \rightarrow \neg better(y, x, H).$$

Note that, in general, $better$ will not provide a total ordering—there may exist x and y such that x is not better than y and y is not better than x.

We also insist that $better$ respect the hierarchy—if there is some object in S that completely satisfies all the constraints through level k, then all objects in S must satisfy all the constraints through level k:

$$\text{if } \exists x \in S \wedge \exists k \in 0 \ldots n \text{ such that}$$

$$\forall i \in 1 \ldots k \; \forall p \in C_i \quad (x \text{ satisfies } p)$$

$$\text{then } \forall y \in S \; \forall i \in 1 \ldots k \; \forall p \in C_i \quad (y \text{ satisfies } p)$$

2.2 Kinds of Comparators

We can categorize comparators as either *local* or *global*, and orthogonally as either *predicate-only* or *error-measuring*. A local comparator just looks at each constraint in H individually, while a global one looks at some aggregate measure that applies to all the constraints at some level C_i. A predicate-only comparator just involves checking whether or not constraints are satisfied, and ignores the error associated with the constraints, while an error-measuring comparator does look at the constraint errors.

We define four comparators, as listed in the following table:

	predicate-only	*error-measuring*
local	locally-predicate-better	locally-error-better
global	satisfied-count-better	least-squares-better

locally-predicate-better x is better than y if it satisfies each constraint that y does at each level through some level k, and at least one more constraint at level k. More formally,

$$locally\text{-}predicate\text{-}better(x, y, H) \equiv$$

$\exists k \in 1 \ldots n$ such that

$\forall i \in 1 \ldots k \; \forall p \in C_i \; (y \text{ satisfies } p \rightarrow x \text{ satisfies } p)$

$\wedge \; \exists q \in C_k \; (x \text{ satisfies } q \wedge \neg y \text{ satisfies } q).$

locally-error-better x is better than y if for each constraint through some level k the magnitude of the error for x is at least as good as for y, and if the error magnitude is strictly better for at least one constraint at level k. (Recall that $e(x, p)$ denotes the error in satisfying constraint p for object x.)

$$locally\text{-}error\text{-}better(x, y, H) \equiv$$

$\exists k \in 1 \ldots n$ such that

$\forall i \in 1 \ldots k \; \forall p \in C_i \; |e(x, p)| \leq |e(y, p)|$

$\wedge \; \exists q \in C_k \; |e(x, q)| < |e(y, q)|.$

satisfied-count-better x is better than y if for each level through some level $k - 1$ it satisfies at least as many constraints as does y, and if at level k it satisfies a greater number. Let

$$count(x, C) \equiv \# \{p \mid p \in C \wedge x \text{ satisfies } p\}$$

Then

$$satisfied\text{-}count\text{-}better(x, y, H) \equiv$$

$\exists k \in 1 \ldots n$ such that

$\forall i \in 1 \ldots k - 1 \; count(x, C_i) \geq count(y, C_i)$

$\wedge \; count(x, C_k) > count(y, C_k).$

least-squares-better x is better than y if for each level through some level $k - 1$ the sum of the squares of the magnitudes of the errors for x is less than or equal to that for y, and at level k it is less.

$$least\text{-}squares\text{-}better(x, y, H) \equiv$$

$\exists k \in 1 \ldots n$ such that

$$\forall i \in 1 \ldots k - 1 \; \sum_{p \in C_i} |e(x, p)|^2 \leq \sum_{p \in C_i} |e(y, p)|^2$$

$$\wedge \; \sum_{p \in C_k} |e(x, p)|^2 < \sum_{p \in C_k} |e(y, p)|^2.$$

It is easy to show that each of these comparators satisfies the criteria of irreflexivity, transitivity, and hierarchy correctness. There are a number of interesting relations that hold among them:

Lemma. $\forall x \, \forall y \, \forall H \; \textit{locally-error-better}(x, y, H) \rightarrow \textit{least-squares-better}(x, y, H)$

Proof. Suppose $\textit{locally-error-better}(x, y, H)$ holds. Then $\exists k \in 1 \dots n$ such that

$$\forall i \in 1 \dots k \; \forall p \in C_i \; |e(x, p)| \leq |e(y, p)| \, .$$

We first square each of the error magnitudes

$$\forall i \in 1 \dots k \; \forall p \in C_i \; |e(x, p)|^2 \leq |e(y, p)|^2$$

and then sum the magnitudes of the errors at each level C_i:

$$\forall i \in 1 \dots k \; \sum_{p \in C_i} |e(x, p)|^2 \leq \sum_{p \in C_i} |e(y, p)|^2 \, .$$

Furthermore, for the same k:

$$\exists q \in C_k \; |e(x, q)| < |e(y, q)| \, .$$

Squaring the error magnitude:

$$\exists q \in C_k \; |e(x, q)|^2 < |e(y, q)|^2 \, .$$

And summing with other errors at C_k:

$$\sum_{p \in C_k} |e(x, p)|^2 < \sum_{p \in C_k} |e(y, p)|^2 \, .$$

Corollary. Let LE denote the set of objects that best satisfies a hierarchy H using the $\textit{locally-error-better}$ comparison, and LS the set for $\textit{least-squares-better}$. Then $LS \subseteq LE$.

Lemma. $\forall x \, \forall y \, \forall H \; \textit{locally-predicate-better}(x, y, H) \rightarrow \textit{satisfied-count-better}(x, y, H)$.

Proof. Suppose $\textit{locally-predicate-better}(x, y, H)$ holds. Then $\exists k \in 1 \dots n$ such that

$$\forall i \in 1 \dots k \; \forall p \in C_i \; (y \text{ satisfies } p \rightarrow x \text{ satisfies } p) \, .$$

Thus the $count(x, C_i)$ for each level through k is at least as large as $count(y, C_i)$:

$$\forall i \in 1 \dots k \; count(x, C_i) \geq count(y, C_i) \, .$$

Furthermore,

$$\exists q \in C_k \; (x \text{ satisfies } q \wedge \neg y \text{ satisfies } q) \, .$$

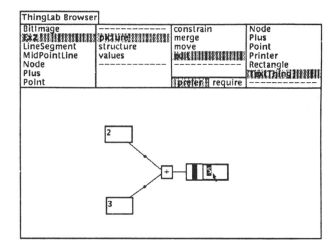

Figure 2: Editing the sum connected to a plus constraint.

And so the $count(x, C_k)$ will be greater than $count(y, C_k)$:

$$count(x, C_k) > count(y, C_k) \, .$$

Corollary. Let SC denote the set of objects that best satisfies a hierarchy H using the $\textit{satisfied-count-better}$ comparison, and LP the set for $\textit{local-predicate-better}$. Then $SC \subseteq LP$.

Note that the converse of each of the lemmas and corollaries does not hold: for example, $\textit{least-squares-better}$ does not imply $\textit{locally-error-better}$.

2.3 An Example

The different behaviors yielded by various comparators may be seen in the plus constraint example shown in Figure 2. For reference, let us call the left hand values A and B and the right hand value C. Suppose that C were edited to be 7. The plus constraint, along with the user's edit, specifies an infinite set of pairs of values for A and B whose sum is 7. However, in addition we have default constraints that the left hand values remain unchanged. Both of the predicate-only comparators would leave one value unchanged while adding 2 to the other. The admissible object states are therefore $(A = 2, B = 5, C = 7)$ and $(A = 4, B = 3, C = 7)$. The least-squares-better comparator splits the difference, yielding a single solution $(A = 3, B = 4, C = 7)$. Locally-error-better, however, yields a range of values for A and B, namely $A \in [2, 4]$ and $B \in [3, 5]$ such that $A + B = 7$. This is so because the definition of S makes use of $\neg better$, and there is no pair of values in these ranges that yields a larger error for *each* constraint than any other pair. The set of values satisfying the constraint by the least-squares comparator is clearly a subset of those that are found with the locally-error-better comparator, in keeping with the first corollary above. Note that in no case will any of these comparators admit unexpected, deviant values such as $(A = 1000, B = -993, C = 7)$.

2.4 Existence of Satisfying Objects

If S_0, the set of objects that satisfies the required constraints, is empty, then clearly S will be empty as well. One would prefer that if S_0 were non-empty, then S would be non-empty as well, since there would be *some* objects that satisfy the required constraints. Unfortunately, this is not always the case, as illustrated by the following hierarchy.

> Let C_0 consist of the constraint $x > 0$ on some real number x, and let C_1 consist of the constraint $x = 0$. Then S_0 is the open interval $(0, \infty)$, but S will be empty for any reasonable error-measuring comparator, since for any potential solution one can find another potential solution that better satisfies the constraint in C_1.

However, the desired property does hold if S_0 is finite:

Theorem. If S_0 is non-empty and finite, then S is non-empty.

Proof. Suppose to the contrary that S is empty. Pick an element x_1 from S_0. Since $x_1 \notin S$, there must be some $x_2 \in S_0$ such that $better(x_2, x_1, H)$. Similarly, since $x_2 \notin S$, there is an $x_3 \in S_0$ such that $better(x_3, x_2, H)$, and so forth for $x_4, x_5, \ldots$ Since *better* is transitive, it follows by induction that for all positive integers i and j that if $i > j$ then $better(x_i, x_j, H)$. However, since S_0 is finite, there must be positive integers i and j such that $i > j$ and $x_i = x_j$. But the irreflexivity property of *better* implies that $\neg better(x_i, x_j, H)$, a contradiction.

2.5 Choosing a Comparator

There are at least two relevant criteria in choosing a comparator: one psychological and the other computational. From the psychological standpoint, we want answers that aren't surprising to the user: for example, when moving a figure, it shouldn't start wildly gyrating about the screen. Much of this lack-of-surprise requirement can be handled by placing constraints at different levels in the hierarchy, but some of it needs to be handled by the comparator. For example, if a constraint cannot be completely satisfied, we will nevertheless want an object that satisfies it as well as possible; this argues for an error-measuring comparator rather than a predicate-only one. From the computational standpoint, we are particularly interested in algorithms that use local propagations, that is, in which first one constraint is satisfied, and then another, and so forth. (This is in contrast to algorithms which satisfy constraints using some more global techniques.) This then suggests that a local measure will be more appropriate than a global one. For these two reasons, we choose *locally-error-better* as our comparator. As an artifact of our algorithm, when it is able to satisfy the constraints in one pass, the solution will also satisfy *local-predicate-better*; when relaxation is used, it will often satisfy *least-squares-better*.

3 An Algorithm

In this section we present an algorithm for satisfying a hierarchy of constraints by producing a solution $s \in S$. In an interactive graphics environment such as that provided by ThingLab, constraint satisfaction should be rapid, since, for example, as the cursor is used to move some part of an object, each time a picture is refreshed the constraints must be re-satisfied. For this reason we divide constraint satisfaction into two stages. In the initial planning stage, the constraints are analyzed and a Smalltalk method is composed that will keep the constraints on an object satisfied as some part is moved or edited. Then, during the actual moving or editing, this precompiled method is repeatedly invoked by sending a change request to the object.

3.1 Algorithm Overview

In overview, the algorithm operates as follows. First the required constraints at level C_0 are inspected to see if, at runtime, values for any parts can be determined using one of the methods of a C_0 constraint. If so, other C_0 constraints may allow other values to be determined, and so forth. If a value is determined by more than one required constraint, one of the methods will be used and runtime checks will be compiled to check that the other required constraints are satisfied. The algorithm then processes the default constraints, beginning at level C_1 and working down the hierarchy to weaker levels. Again, the algorithm attempts to make one-step deductions, determining that the values of more and more parts can be found. Weaker constraints are, of course, not allowed to determine values for parts whose value has already been determined by some stronger constraint. Also, unlike the required constraints, it is not an error if some weaker constraint is not satisfied, and so for such constraints no run-time checks need be included.

After all the levels in the hierarchy have been processed, ideally the algorithm will have found constraint methods that can be used (in the proper order) to determine values for all parts of the object. However, sometimes circularities in the constraint network do not allow this; if the constraints apply to numeric objects, the algorithm instead compiles a call to an iterative technique (relaxation), which can in some cases be used to solve the constraint network. If there are circularities involving non-numeric objects, our current implementation will be unable to satisfy the constraints, and will notify the user.

There are a number of complications that the algorithm must handle—for example, often one or more strong constraints will apply to some part, but none of the strong constraints has enough information to determine that part's value uniquely. In such a situation, the algorithm must ensure that any value determined for the part by a weaker constraint is consonant with the stronger constraints. Also, some constraint methods are *non-unique-state*: that is, even if all the inputs to the method are known, there is not enough information to uniquely determine values for the outputs, as in the AnchoredConstantLengthLine example in Section 4.2. These complications are discussed in the detailed description that follows.

3.2 Details of the Algorithm

The algorithm is called when a modification to an object is performed for which no Smalltalk method exists. The modification is requested by sending an appropriate message to the object pursuant to direct manipulation by the user; if no such message is defined, Smalltalk will trap the request at *Object messageNotUnderstood:* and invoke the planner.

The current ThingLab objects only use levels $C_0, \ldots, C_4$, but nothing precludes the use of additional levels. These levels are by convention used as follows:

C_0 **Require** the constraints that must hold

C_1 **Strongly Prefer** these constraints will typically be anchors[3]

C_2 **Prefer** these constraints correspond to normal user editing requests, e.g. dragging and editing

C_3 **Default** the usual level for stay constraints, e.g. constraints that keep an object unchanged

C_4 **Weak Default** stay constraints on derived values, e.g. the midpoint on a MidPointLine

Once invoked, the planner first builds two inter-related graphs to hold information about the object structure and the constraint hierarchy. The two graphs are the Object Structure Graph (OSG) and the Constraint Hierarchy Graph (CHG). The Object Structure Graph is a directed acyclic graph of the structure of the object. It differs from the usual ThingLab object in that it contains backpointers from parts to parent substructures. The Constraint Hierarchy Graph is a list ordered by constraint priority containing the constraint hierarchy H, i.e. a list of the sets $C_0, \ldots, C_n$. These two graphs have pointers, backpointers, and various flags to facilitate quick access and efficient computation of certain values. The two graphs also have interconnections for efficient searching and traversing. For example, each MethodNode (in the CHG) contains pointers to GraphNodes (in the OSG) for all objects referenced and assigned (inputs and output to the method). Also, each GraphNode has pointers to each ConstraintNode that could potentially modify it.

Next the planner perturbs the graphs slightly by adding ConstraintNodes and GraphNodes. This pertubation represents the outside influence upon the object, usually the result of editing some part of the object or moving a part with the mouse. At run time this would result in the object no longer being consistent with its constraints, and so the third step is to traverse the two graphs and plan a sequence of messages to satisfy the constraint hierarchy. The fourth and last step is to compile the plan into a Smalltalk method that can be used to repeatedly satisfy the hierarchy for the given modification.

3.3 Perturbation

These two graphs initially represent the object in its static, satisfied state. The second stage of the algorithm augments the graphs with the outside influences, and produces a representation of the object that needs resatisfying.

---

[3]We use "strongly prefer" rather than "require" for anchors, since otherwise there would be no way to move an anchor once it was in place, short of deleting or deactivating it.

The usual outside influences consist of dragging a part of the object with the mouse, editing a piece of text, or advancing the simulation clock in an animation involving temporal constraints. To represent this, one or more additional ConstraintNodes are added to the CHG at the priority given to the mouse, the editor, or the simulation clock. In the ThingLab browser the mouse can be given one of two levels: C_0 (Require) or C_2 (Prefer), with Prefer being the usual level. (The level is selected with the switch at the bottom of the third browser pane, as shown in the figures.)

Adding ConstraintNodes to the CHG requires that GraphNodes be added to the OSG so that the MethodNodes will have objects to refer to as their inputs. (These added nodes represent the current mouse position, the new text to be substituted for some old text, or the like.) Any number of these augmentations can be made before the actual planning starts, since each simply adds constraints to the hierarchy.

3.4 Planning

After the two graphs have been built and augmented, the algorithm traverses them to build a plan—a sequence of Smalltalk messages that satisfy the hierarchy. The algorithm proceeds as follows:

- Traverse the CHG until a useable or an unuseable constraint is found.

- If that constraint is useable then add the code for the appropriate method to the message list.

- If the constraint is unuseable then discard it.[4]

- Restart at the top of the hierarchy.

- When C_n is reached, a call to the Relaxer may be needed to handle any circularities encountered in the object's constraints.

3.4.1 Useability and Accomodation

An *unuseable constraint* is a constraint $c \notin C_0$ such that for each of c's methods at least one output is known. These will be default constraints that have been overruled by stronger constraints, and usually are the weak "stay" constraints that keep objects in the same place. A *useable constraint* is one that has a method for which all inputs are known, no outputs are

known, and all outputs can accomodate a change. A *known object* is one for which, at compile time, it can be determined that a unique value will be assigned at run time. If there is more than one useable constraint at a constraint level C_i, then the constraints considered first are those that are useable and will produce a candidate value for some previous non-unique method (Section 3.4.2), followed by those that are just useable.

A part p can *accomodate* being changed by a constraint $c \in C_i$ if all the constraints in $C_0, \ldots, C_{i-1}$ that affect p can accomodate the change. A constraint can accomodate a change to a part p if it has a method for which p is an input, p is not an output, and all outputs can accomodate a change in $C_0, \ldots, C_{i-1}$.

The definition of accomodate is recursive and is implemented by a recursive search of the OSG. Each ConstraintNode and GraphNode is marked as potentially known when it is encountered so the planner does not go into an infinite loop. The search halts when either accomodation is verified or a circularity prevents accomodation. In the later case a call to the Relaxer will be needed to uniquely determine the value for some of the objects.[5]

3.4.2 Generating code for methods

There are two types of methods: those that uniquely specify a value for their output objects and those that do not. When a method does not uniquely determine a value, by the formal specification, it should determine a set S of valid values. This set would be intersected with one or more other sets to determine a single value s that satisfies the hierarchy H. Most of these sets are infinite, and the efficient implementation of general infinite sets is non-trivial, so ThingLab uses an alternative form to determine s given $c \in C_i$:

- Some constraint $d \in C_j, j > i$ is used to generate a *candidate value*, t. Typically C_j is a default constraint that a value remain unchanged.

- Then the non-unique method from c uses t to find an object x such that $e(x, d)$ is minimized; in other words, x is chosen to satisfy c completely, and to satisfy d (a weaker constraint) as well as possible.

---

[4]Note that C_0 constraints will never be discarded; see the definition of "unuseable" in Section 3.4.1.

[5]This concept of accomodation is descended from the propagation-of-degrees-of-freedom method in previous implementations of ThingLab. Here, however, rather than serving to plan how to satisfy constraints, it serves the auxiliary role of determining when the primary propagation-of-known-states technique may be safely used.

In the implementation, when a non-unique method is encountered, the output GraphNodes are marked as *needs-a-candidate-value*. When a second constraint generates a method for the same object one of two things happens:

- If the second method is a unique method, its code is used to generate a candidate value, which is then passed to the original non-unique method's code (as described above).

- If the second method is a non-unique method, then x is the intersection of two or more non-singular sets and, if the constraints are numeric, will be solved for by relaxation.

3.5 An Optimization

During the implementation and testing of the new algorithm, we discovered that although many of the constraints in levels $C_0, \ldots, C_n$ are satisfied, most them end up doing no effective work due to the many "stay in the same place" constraints. For example, in an object built from two separate, unconnected MidPoint-Lines, the mouse can only modify one line at a time. However, the planning would produce code to resatisfy the other MidPointLine constraint—unneeded code that could be left out.

To improve the code we added an additional flag to the GraphNodes to keep track of whether they were known to be fixed in place or not. An object is *known-to-be-fixed* when it is known because of a "stay in the same place" constraint, or it is known because it was an output of a unique-state method for which all the inputs are known-to-be-fixed. Note that this optimization is only valid because of the assumption that the initial OSG and CHG represent an object for which all the constraints were satisfied.

A method fragment that is about to be generated as Smalltalk code can be ignored if all the inputs are known-to-be-fixed. Additionally, if the method is being generated using a candidate value as described in Section 3.4.2, then the candidate value must be considered as an input, and thus it must also be known-to-be-fixed.

4 Two Examples of Satisfying Constraint Hierarchies

4.1 MidPointLine

As a first simple example, consider the MidPointLine object in Figure 1. It has two parts, a line and a point, and the line has two further sub-parts (its endpoints). There is one C_0 constraint, which ensures that the point lies at the midpoint between the two endpoints. The constraint has three methods that can satisfy it: move one endpoint, move the other endpoint, or move the midpoint. There are three additional constraints used to keep the points in the same place: one for each endpoint at C_3 and one for the midpoint at C_4. The midpoint stay is at C_4 and the endpoints at C_3, since we prefer that the midpoint move rather than the endpoints; however, neither endpoint is favored over the other.

When the mouse grabs onto one endpoint, a message is sent to the object requesting the change. The object does not understand the message and so asks ThingLab to build a method for it. First the OSG and the CHG are built, and an additional constraint is added at C_2 constraining the endpoint of the line to equal the mouse location.

Then the actual planning starts. The hierarchy is traversed:

[point = midpoint of line] is not useable because neither of the endpoints nor the midpoint is known, so none of the methods can be used.

[endpoint1 = mouse] is useable because the mouse location is known, the endpoint is not, and the endpoint can accomodate a change as follows:

1. endpoint1 can change if endpoint2 or the midpoint can change to satisfy all the constraints through level C_1,
2. endpoint2 can change to satisfy all the constraints through level C_1.

Thus the code for moving endpoint1 to the mouse location is put into the plan and endpoint1 is marked as known.

The hierarchy is traversed again:

[point = midpoint of line] is still not useable because although one endpoint is known, all the methods require two points to determine the third.

[endpoint1 stay] is unuseable because endpoint1 is already known.

[endpoint2 stay] is useable because it has no inputs (so they are all known), endpoint2 is not known, and it can accomodate a change due to:

1. endpoint2 can change if endpoint1 or the midpoint can change to satisfy all the constraints through level C_2,
2. endpoint1 is already known and cannot change,
3. but the midpoint can change to satisfy all the constraints through level C_2.

Due to the optimization described in Section 3.5 no code is added to the plan, but endpoint2 is marked as known and as known-to-be-fixed.

The hierarchy is traversed again:

[point = midpoint of line] is now useable because one of the methods uses endpoint1 and endpoint2 (both known) to determine the midpoint. The midpoint can accomodate a change to satisfy all the constraints in C_0, as there are no other C_0 constraints on it.

The code for determining the midpoint is added to the plan, and the midpoint is marked as known.

The planner has now satisfied the hierarchy, and does not need to call the Relaxer, so the complete plan is compiled into a Smalltalk method:

```
moveby.prefer.line.point1: t1
    line point2 primitiveMoveby: t1.
    self primitiveSet.point:
        line point1 + line point2 // 2
```

When the mouse grabs and moves the endpoint, the other endpoint will stay fixed and the midpoint will adjust to remain halfway between the two endpoints.

4.2   AnchoredConstantLengthLine

This second example demonstrates how non-unique methods are satisfied. The AnchoredConstantLength-Line (shown in Figure 3), has two parts: an Anchor and a ConstantLengthLine. The ConstantLengthLine

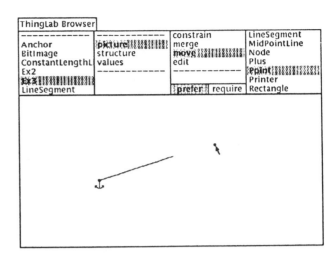

Figure 3: Manipulating the free end of an Anchored-ConstantLengthLine

has three parts: two points and a length, and four constraints: a C_0 constraint that the length stay fixed, a C_0 constraint that the length be the same as the distance between the points, and two C_3 constraints that the endpoints stay fixed. The Anchor has just a single C_1 constraint that it stay fixed.

The planner builds the OSG and the CHG, adding an additional C_2 constraint that endpoint2 of the line be equal to the mouse location. The first useable constraint is the C_0 "length stay fixed". Thus the length is marked as known and known-to-be-fixed. The next useable constraint is the Anchor C_1 "stay fixed". Thus endpoint1 is marked as known and known-to-be-fixed.

The third constraint to be useable is the C_0 "distance between endpoints equals length". This constraint has two non-unique methods, each taking one endpoint and a candidate value for the other and producing the best resulting point. When this method is considered, the length and endpoint1 are known, so endpoint2 is marked as needs-a-candidate-value, but no code is added to the plan.

The next constraint considered is the C_2 "endpoint2 equals mouse location". This constraint is useable and so its code is added to the plan. This causes endpoint2 to be known and to be the candidate value needed by the previous method. Thus the previous method's code is also added to the plan.

The final plan is:

```
moveby.prefer.constLine.line.point:   t1
    constLine line point2
        primitiveMoveby: t1.
    constLine line primitiveSet.point2:
```

```
constLine line point1 +
   (constLine line point2
    - constLine line point1
    * constLine length
    / constLine line length)
```

This resulting code causes the ConstantLengthLine to point at the mouse as a compass points to a magnet.

5 Relaxation

If the constraint satisfaction planner is unable to find a one-pass solution, it will ask the object for a method that will satisfy its constraints using some iterative technique. The only such method currently available is relaxation. Relaxation is a general algorithm for minimizing the value of a function by iteratively modifying each of its parameters in turn [2,16].

The algorithm described here is an extension of the relaxation algorithm used in the old version of ThingLab. The principal changes allow relaxation to find a solution in the context of constraint hierarchies; the algorithm was also modified slightly to guarantee stability (the old version sometimes went into infinite loops).

5.1 Errors and Solvers

Three kinds of error measures are used by the relaxer. These are the constraint errors mentioned above, *object errors*, and the *total error*. The object error for the object x is denoted by $oe(x)$ and is defined as

$$oe(x) \equiv \sum_{c \in C(x)} |e(x,c)|^2$$

where $C(x)$ is the set of all constraints applying to x. The total error is simply the object error for the top-level object.

The relaxer knows how to modify some kinds of objects so as to reduce their object errors. An object of this kind is called a *relaxable object*, and the corresponding technique is the object's *solver*. Some solvers assume that the constraint error functions have properties other than just having magnitude 0 when the constraint is satisfied. If, for instance, a solver is based on Newton's method, then $e(x,c)$ should be differentiable with respect to x. Note that it is vital to the relaxation algorithm that the solvers never increase the object errors at any time. (The solvers in the old relaxer did not have this property, leading to the infinite loops mentioned earlier.)

5.2 The Relaxation Algorithm

The relaxer needs the following information at run time:

1. a constraint hierarchy of constraint errors and tests,

2. the objects to be relaxed,

3. a table specifying which constraints are affected by each object,

4. a solver for each object, and

5. a method for each object that should be run whenever that object is modified. Each of these methods must cause all constraints on the objects modified by the method to be satisfied.

The code invoking the relaxer with this information is produced in the planning stage. This code also guarantees that all constraints not in the constraint hierarchy are satisfied by the methods in item 5 above.

The relaxation algorithm used is as follows:

1. While the constraint hierarchy is not empty and some of the constraints in it are unsatisfied, relax the objects. If some of the constraints in the hierarchy are still unsatisfied after the objects are relaxed, remove the weakest level of the hierarchy. Continue removing levels until either all the remaining constraints are satisfied, or until the hierarchy is empty. After the loop terminates, if the hierarchy is empty and there were formerly constraints in the required level C_0, then stop and notify the user that no solution could be found.

2. If some levels were removed in step 1, then add back just the last level that was removed but no others, and remove from the set of relaxable objects those objects affected by constraints at higher levels than the current one. Relax the objects in this new set. Note that this step does not modify any of the objects affected by the constraints satisfied in step 1.

The phrase "relax the objects" means all of the relaxable objects' solvers should be invoked repeatedly until all of the constraints in the current hierarchy are satisfied, or the total error changes by less than some tolerance *minChange* from one iteration of invoking the solvers to the next.

5.3 Correctness

The relaxation algorithm detailed above does eventually halt. This can be seen by noting that each cycle of invoking the object solvers does not increase the total error. If the decrease were always greater than *minChange*, then the total error would eventually become negative, which is impossible. So the decrease in total error must eventually be less than *minChange*, at which point the algorithm halts. Note that the test for satisfaction of the constraints is not necessary to the algorithm, though it does prevent an unnecessary relaxation cycle in some cases.

The solution found by the relaxer is almost admissible using the least-squares-better criterion. This solution satisfies all the constraints down to some level n and (with the exceptions mentioned in the next paragraph) minimizes the sum of the squares of the errors at level $n+1$, given the values of the objects affecting the constraints in the first n levels. Since it is possible that the errors at level $n + 1$ could be reduced further if the objects affecting the higher levels were modified (still maintaining the stronger constraints), it is not strictly admissible by the definition given in Section 2. Unfortunately, relaxation does not necessarily find the absolute minimum of the total error function. The inner loops relaxing the objects will stop not only when the constraints are satisfied, but also when an approximately flat part of the total error function is found. This could be near a saddle point, a horizontal asymptote, a local minimum, or even a local maximum (in rare cases).

For future research, an iterative technique is needed that is guaranteed to find an admissible solution. Both problems mentioned above seem to stem from the fact that relaxation is a local hill-climbing algorithm. It only tries to modify one object at a time and treats the others as constants. An admissible algorithm will probably need to look at more of the search space or at least look in more directions at once than does relaxation.

6 Performance

There are a greatly increased number of constraints for any one object, since all the constraints in the hierarchy are explicit, including the stay fixed constraints, whereas in the old ThingLab most constraints were implicit, with only the C_0 and C_1 constraints explicit. Nevertheless, the new planner is significantly faster than the old version.

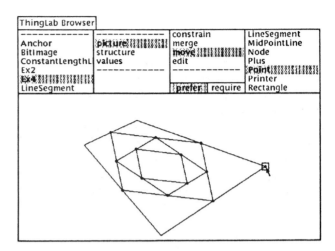

Figure 4: A Quadrilateral four levels deep.

The preliminary timings given below are for two different objects: an AnchoredConstantLengthLine (Figure 3) and a FourLevelQuadrilateral (Figure 4). The times obtained include the overhead from the ThingLab browser and the Smalltalk compiler, and are measured from the time the object is grabbed with mouse until the time the object moves, i.e. the time to build, compile, and execute a plan. (All times are measured in seconds on a Tektronix 4406 Smalltalk system.)

	old	*new*	*speedup*
AnchoredLine	1.5	1.1	1.4x
FourLevelQuad	57.6	7.4	7.8x

These numbers indicate that larger, more complex objects can be satisfied in a reasonable amount of time, and still behave according to the Principle of Least Astonishment. Further, we have not yet done extensive performance tuning of our algorithm, and so further improvements can be expected.

One of the reasons for this increased performance is that a multitude of special cases have been replaced by the hierarchical constraints, and do not need to be considered separately in the planning. Another reason is that the old version of ThingLab did not effectively use the relationship between the known objects and the constraints, but rather performed time-consuming linear searches to find the next constraint to satisfy.

7 Future Work

The work described here is quite recent, and the increased performance it will provide will support further investigation into a number of interesting areas, some of which are outlined below.

There is a need for the implementation of conditional and iterative constraints, particularly to support the filters project mentioned earlier [6]. A conditional constraint includes a predicate to be evaluated at runtime, and two sets of constraints, one set that must be satisfied if the predicate is true, the other if it is false. An iterative constraint allows multiple instantiations of a prototype constraint to be produced, each parameterized by some loop variable.

The Animus system extended ThingLab by implementing constraints involving time. These proved useful for building dynamic simulations of physical processes and animations of algorithms. Animus is being updated so that it becomes reintegrated with the new ThingLab constraint satisfier. In addition, new exploratory work on a "gestural interface" [5] for declaring new temporal constraints will be included. The system will support "animation by demonstration" by capturing the user's gestures involved in direct mouse manipulation of a picture in the environment of a drafting program, and by allowing such gestures to be related to specific events in the text of a program, again by gestural indication.

The satisfier needs more alternative solution methods when circularities are encountered in the constraint network, for example, for constraints on non-numeric objects. Also, algebraic and other transformations could be used on the constraint graph to remove circularities, perhaps by applying tree manipulation and pattern matching techniques derived from compiler technology [8].

The order-of-magnitude improvement in compile-time performance opens the possibility of handling large constrained structures with hundreds of objects. In such cases it would be fruitful to provide for incremental recompilation, so that when small changes are made to the structure the system can avoid invalidating all methods for the entire structure. This would involve keeping track of dependencies, so that the system can infer what parts are unaffected by the change. One can also envision the system being able to partition constraint networks into modules with well-defined interfaces and local recompilation.

In a context of rapid prototyping, when an object and its constraints are under development with much editing and replanning being performed, it may be useful to implement interpreted as well as compiled constraint satisfaction. In addition, while in our current implementation the two graphs, the OSG and the CHG, are built on demand for each new plan, one or both of them could be retained between planning sessions.

Acknowledgements

Thanks for useful discussions and comments to Raimund Ege, Jacob Gore, Richard Ladner, David Maier, to the members of the Architectures for Interactive Systems Working Group, and to members of the System Concepts Laboratory and the Knowledge Systems Area at Xerox PARC. The project is sponsored in part by the National Science Foundation under Grant No. IST–8604923, and in part by Tektronix, Inc. The ThingLab system on which we are building was sponsored in part by the Xerox Corporation.

References

[1] Alan Borning. Constraint-Oriented Programming. In Kristen Nygaard and Peter Wegner, editors, *Object-Oriented Programming*, Addison-Wesley, 1988. In preparation.

[2] Alan Borning. The Programming Language Aspects of ThingLab, A Constraint-Oriented Simulation Laboratory. *TOPLAS*, 3(4):353–387, Oct 1981.

[3] Alan Borning and Robert Duisberg. Constraint-Based Tools for Building User Interfaces. *ACM Transactions on Graphics*, 5(4), October 1986.

[4] Robert Duisberg. *Constraint-Based Animation: The Implementation of Temporal Constraints in the Animus System*. PhD thesis, University of Washington, 1986. Published as U.W. Computer Science Department technical report No. 86-09-01.

[5] Robert Duisberg. *Visual Programming of Program Visualizations*. Technical Report 87-20, Computer Research Laboratory, Tektronix, Inc., Feb 1987.

[6] Raimund K. Ege, David Maier, and Alan Borning. The Filter Browser—Defining Interfaces Graphically. In *Proceedings of the European Conference on Object Oriented Programming*, Association Française pour la Cybernétique Économique et Technique, 1987.

[7] James Gosling. *Algebraic Constraints*. PhD thesis, Carnegie-Mellon University, May 1983. Published as CMU Computer Science Department technical report CMU-CS-83-132.

[8] Robert Henry and Peter Damron. *Code Generation Using Tree Pattern Matchers.* Technical Report 87-02-04, Computer Science Department, University of Washington, 1987.

[9] M. Konopasek and S. Jayaraman. *The TK!Solver Book.* Osborne/McGraw-Hill, Berkeley, CA, 1984.

[10] William Leler. *Specification and Generation of Constraint Satisfaction Systems Using Augmented Term Rewriting.* PhD thesis, University of North Carolina at Chapel Hill, 1986.

[11] David Levitt. Machine Tongues X: Constraint Languages. *Computer Music Journal*, 8(1):9–21, Spring 1984.

[12] Sanjay Mittal, Clive L. Dym, and Mahesh Morjaria. PRIDE: An Expert System for the Design of Paper Handling Systems. *Computer*, 102–114, July 1986.

[13] Greg Nelson. Juno, A Constraint-Based Graphics System. In B.A. Barsky, editor, *SIGGRAPH '85 Conference Proceedings*, pages 235–243, ACM, San Francisco, July 1985.

[14] Guy Steele. *The Definition and Implementation of a Computer Programming Language Based on Constraints.* PhD thesis, MIT, August 1980. Published as MIT-AI TR 595, August 1980.

[15] Gerald Sussman and Guy Steele. CONSTRAINTS—A Language for Expressing Almost-Hierarchical Descriptions. *Artificial Intelligence*, 14(1):1–39, January 1980.

[16] Ivan Sutherland. Sketchpad: A Man-Machine Graphical Communication System. In *Proceedings of the Spring Joint Computer Conference*, pages 329–345, IFIPS, 1963.

[17] Christopher J. van Wyk. A High-level Language for Specifying Pictures. *ACM Transactions on Graphics*, 1(2):163–182, April 1982.

□□□ 8 □□□   Environments IV: More Constraint–Based Systems

R.A. Duisberg. "Animation Using Temporal Constraints: An Overview of the ANIMUS System." *Human–Computer Interaction*, 3(3):275–307, 1987/88.

G. Nelson. "JUNO: A Constraint–Based Graphics System." *ACM Computer Graphics* (*Proc. SIGGRAPH'85*, San Francisco, Calif.), 19(3):235–243, July 1985.

R. Yeung. "MPL: A Graphical Programming Environment for Matrix Processing Based on Logic and Constraints." In *Proc. Workshop on Visual Languages*, Pittsburgh, Penn., pages 137–143, October 10-12, 1988. IEEE Computer Society Press, Los Alamitos, Calif.

C. Lewis. "NoPumpG: Creating Interactive Graphics with Spreadsheet Machinery."

Animation Using Temporal Constraints: An Overview of the Animus System

Robert Adámy Duisberg

Computer Research Laboratory
Tektronix, Inc.

ABSTRACT

Algorithm animation has a growing role in computer-aided algorithm design, documentation, and debugging, because interactive graphics is a richer channel than text for communication. Most animation is currently done laboriously by hand, and it often has the character of canned demonstrations with restricted user interaction. Animus is a system that allows for easy construction of an animation with minimal concern for lower-level graphics programming. Constraints are used to describe the appearance and structure of a picture as well as how those pictures evolve in time. The implementation and support of temporal constraints are substantive extensions to previous constraint languages that had only allowed for the specification of a static state. Use of the Animus system is demonstrated in the creation of animations of dynamic mechanical and electrical circuit simulations, sorting algorithms, problems in operating systems, and geometric curve drawing algorithms.

This article is based on the author's PhD thesis in Computer Science at the University of Washington, 1986.

Author's present address: Robert A. Duisberg, Computer Research Laboratory, Tektronix, Inc., P.O. Box 500, Mail Station 50–662, Beaverton, OR 97077.

CONTENTS

Reprinted with permission from *Human-Computer Interaction*, Volume 3, Number 3, 1987/88, pages 275-307. Copyright © 1988 by Lawrence Erlbaum Associates, Inc. All rights reserved.

1. INTRODUCTION

Animation can be a valuable addition to the interface of a program. As Knuth (1973) put it, "an algorithm must be seen to be believed, and the best way to learn what an algorithm is all about is to try it" (p. 4). The perceptual endowments of people are strongly optimized for real-time image processing, and interactive graphics can immediately communicate multidimensional information about the internal state of a complex dynamic process. Data structures, for example, are almost invariably represented by two-dimensional diagrams in texts and documentation with the implication that the structures are more easily understood in this spatial form than, say, through a textual description or an algebraic specification. By extension, understanding of the often obscure algorithms operating on data structures can be assisted through dynamic motion in such diagrams. Animated pictures make some dynamic aspects of a system easily visible, which would be difficult to infer from an execution trace. As computer technology matures, it is becoming possible and increasingly important for new systems to accommodate their users' idiosyncrasies, as opposed to the traditional situation that required users to assimilate all the peculiarities of the system. In this respect, animation can be seen as an integral part of a software design and development environment where an interactive interface is important (Duisberg, 1986a) particularly for debugging, process monitoring, and documentation (London & Duisberg, 1985), as well as for applications in education (Brown & Sedgewick, 1984) and skill development (Chi, 1984).

This article includes some of the research presented in my dissertation (Duisberg, 1986b) describing a prototype system named *Animus,* which seeks to present appropriate dynamic imagery by which to understand a program and through which to interact with it. Animus provides facilities for the construction of such images and demonstrates the feasibility of using constraints to allow the animator to write executable specifications for animated components. The animator may be relieved of the task of writing detailed graphics code in an imperative style. This article describes the ways in which a user can build and interact with an animation by presenting a number of examples followed by a brief discussion of the implementation.

1.1. The Difficulties of Animation

Animations are laborious to construct by hand. Research has shown that about 80% of the code in an animation is involved in just doing the graphics, even in a system like Smalltalk[1] (Goldberg & Robson, 1983) which offers a powerful, high-level graphics interface. The difficulties are further magnified if we wish for more than just a passive movie, but rather more interactive access to the executing objects through their pictures. A fully interactive animation must interpret user input in relation to screen images, in addition to creating those images in the first place. The user should be able to point to a part of the picture as the animation is in progress and effectively say, "What is that?" or "Do this to that over there." Clearly, the overhead and mechanism to provide such interaction is much more involved than for just transferring bits to the screen.

In applications to algorithm design and development, it is important that it be relatively easy to construct new animations. It is unacceptable if much more effort must be spent bringing up an animation than the algorithm itself, which the animation is supposed to test or provide insights about. For purposes of debugging, for example, the user might like to build a quick "throw away" animation to see a particular detail of passing interest. Animus

---

[1] In this article, "Smalltalk" is used to mean "Smalltalk-80," which is a registered trademark of the Xerox Corporation.

shows the feasibility of building animations quickly from a kit of components with graphical and temporal behavior built in. The animator is provided with composable parts, and the interactions involved in such composition are controlled by constraints. The fundamental problem for the system is to organize its responses in view of the interactions of the parts so composed. This is achieved by the mechanisms of *constraint satisfaction*.

1.2. Constraints

One may think of an animation as the creation of a picture that bears some specified relation to the state of the object being animated. This need for consistency of state and representation suggests the use of constraints to implement animations. Constraint languages allow the programmer to state relations that the system must satisfy. Furthermore, the statement of constraints is a declarative task in which the user expresses what he wants to see and how it should move, and it is the job of constraint satisfaction algorithms to find a way to satisfy the specified relationships. This declarative character is attractive because it tends to be simpler than writing out detailed graphics instructions in an imperative language.

Constraints in ThingLab (Borning, 1979, 1981), which is the base system upon which Animus is built, are implemented as objects that represent some relation as a predicate and that contain a variety of methods as code fragments that can be used to establish the relation under different circumstances, depending on what is known. For example, a constraint that $a = b + c$ would contain the expressions $a \leftarrow b + c$, $b \leftarrow a - c$, and $a - b$, any one of which may be used. But depending on what values are known or have just been changed, only one may be appropriate. The goal of constraint satisfaction techniques is to choose and order appropriate methods so that relations throughout the network of constraints are reestablished after a change. The system is thus like a novice programming environment (see, e.g., Glinert & Tanimoto, 1984) in which much of the code to execute the user's wishes is generated by the system itself in response to the user's manipulation of high-level objects and icons.

But, no constraint system to my knowledge, explicitly models time. Time requires special treatment and cannot simply be inserted as another variable in a constraint relation. Time is a distinguished variable in at least two respects. First, it is in some sense global to a simulation; all component parts of a simulation exist at the same time (simulations of relativistic mechanics notwithstanding), and yet temporal dependencies should be specified as local to the components. This means that temporal constraints must be satisfied globally, in contrast to the normal local satisfaction of static constraints. Second, normal constraint relations have the property of satisfying themselves in multiple directions depending on computational circumstances. When applied to time, this could result in setting the clock forward and backward erratically because of changes occurring to values dependent on time, unless time were given special treatment to insure its relentlessly monotonic advance. Also, there is a disjunction between the discrete frame-by-frame, time-slice character of computation and the kinds of continuum statements one would like to make in describing rates of change (e.g., $v = dx/dt$). One must consider how to get the system to construct discrete approximations of continuous processes and how to treat the errors inherent in these approximations.

Animus contributes to constraint technology by implementing temporal constraints and their associated mechanism. New classes of constraints have been constructed which address the difficulties just described and provide a means to specify temporal behavior, both continuous evolution and discrete event-driven causes and effects. Simulation components are provided with constraints built in that insure not only internal consistency of instantaneous state but also proper evolution between states and responses to events. The specification tools provided lead to a variety of "scripting" mechanisms from program-driven animation to giving an equation to describe the time variation of a particular value, and to providing an explicit stream of scripted events.

2. WORK IN RELATED FIELDS

Animation, of course, has its roots in cinema, and the computer-generated instructional movie about sorting algorithms, *Sorting Out Sorting* by Baecker (1981), has been an inspiration for some of our work. Earlier, Baecker (1975) had produced two small real-time animation systems called *mini-LOGO* and *micro-PL/1,* which had built-in, hard-coded animation controls and did not allow user interaction with program during execution. Perhaps the most ambitious algorithm animation project to date is the Brown University ALgorithm Simulation and Animation (BALSA) system (Brown & Sedgewick, 1984), developed in effort to create "a dynamic book in an electronic classroom." An auditorium containing 60 Apollo work stations provides a teaching environment in which animated courseware may be broadcast to the network from the professor's work station. BALSA has an extensive library of animated representations, but animations are still essentially hand crafted in the system. The Program Visualization (PV) system (Brown, Carling, Herot, Kramlich, & Souza, 1985) is a production environment, developed at the Computer Corporation of America, intended to support and help visualize large systems. The visualizations provided are usually block diagrams, but the system has the ability to zoom in to provide more detail within hierarchical structures. What all these systems have in common is the need for a great deal of low-level graphics coding on the part of the animator. The techniques of constraint-based animation tend to alleviate this situation by offering a cleaner separation between the algorithmic code and the description of the animation, which in turn may be specified in a declarative style.

In constraint systems, related work includes Sutherland's (1963) Sketchpad program, which was a pioneering system in both constraint satisfaction and computer graphics. Sketchpad was not widely used because its requirements for processor cycles and communication bandwidth were beyond the time-sharing systems of the day. Sketchpad uses propagation of degrees of freedom to satisfy constraints and numerical relaxation when that fails. Hard coding of a limited set of graphics and constraint primitives (e.g., points, lines, circles; vertical, horizontal, parallel, perpendicular) and some special purpose hardware with switches and dials for manipulating these resulted in an interactive graphics interface with a fluid facility that has scarcely been equaled on the economical graphics work stations of today. Sussman and Steele (1980) implemented several constraint languages, which are distinguished by their ability to produce explanations for how values were derived, but the mode of interaction is strictly textual and infused with LISP syntax. Gosling (1983) produced a constraint-based graphical layout system called *Magritte,* which is implemented in Lisp. Magritte's constraint system operates on only simple numeric scalars, the only primitive data type. However, the user may define new structures and compound constraints to operate on these structures. The graphics system JUNO (Nelson, 1985) allows constraints to be specified graphically by selecting icons and points. These constraints relate the elements of a picture to a textual program that will draw the picture. The domain of the system is limited to line drawing; its only data object is the point with lines as simple pairs of points, and there are only four primitive geometric constraints. Levitt (1984) surveyed constraint languages and described his own work on a jazz composition system. Essentially, the use of constraints in the musical context consists in specifying harmonic and scale structures from which a stochastic process may select pitches, as though it was "improvising." The Bertrand system (Leler, 1986) is a constraint language that uses term rewriting to solve systems of constraints, tantamount to algebraic transformations of the given relations. In commercially available systems, the many spreadsheet programs can be viewed as simple but very useful kinds of constraint systems. TK!Solver (Konopasek & Jayaraman, 1984) is a more powerful commercial constraint language descended from these spreadsheet programs. TK!Solver can handle true multiway constraints, unlike most spreadsheet programs which only provide one-way propagation of values.

The design of the behavior of **Responses** in Animus was influenced by the approach taken by Dannenberg (1984) in his functional language, Arctic, designed for real-time signal processing. Arctic values are implicitly functions of time, and thus concurrently varying values are handled succinctly. For example, an amplifier running in real-time may be specified simply as:

$$output \,=\, input * gain$$

in which all three variables are real valued functions of time. Arctic programs are functional in that they have no state or imperative commands; order of execution is driven by data flow, obviating the need for explicit synchronization primitives. Expressions in Arctic denote what are called *prototypes* (conceptually distinct from prototypes in ThingLab), which are regarded as specifications for responses to classes of events. The major difference is that Arctic is a language whose semantics assume that values are continuous functions of time, whereas Animus must produce a discrete frame animation, hence the realization of a **Response** is a stream of discrete **Events** instead of a continuous function.

3. APPLICATIONS

Within both Animus and ThingLab, the notion of "programming" takes a number of different forms. At the highest level, which resembles a novice programming environment, a user may find the components he or she needs to build the application already made in the kit. The act of programming then consists of picking such pieces out of the kit and hooking them together in allowable ways. This mode involves virtually no typing at the keyboard or coding, but it is certainly programming, because the user may create new structures with new behaviors. The system is left to generate the code that implements that behavior. This is the mode in which one builds the circuits and mechanical examples that follow.

If the desired component is not available in the kit, however, it can be manufactured at another programming level. The user is free to "drop through the trap door" and generate a new building block by typing Smalltalk code using ThingLab and Animus syntax for constraint declarations. When this text is loaded and compiled, it will then generate the new desired prototype. There is no other provision in Animus for programming at this level, unlike recent extensions to ThingLab (Borning, 1986) in which new prototypes and constraints can be defined graphically. In our recent work at Tektronix, we have been experimenting with a "gestural" interface for generating animations, along the lines of "animation by demonstration," with graphical means for expressing what amount to temporal constraints (Duisberg, 1987).

4. CONSTRUCTING AN ANIMATION

During construction and execution, interaction with an animation is through the browser. The style of interaction emphasizes direct manipulation of the pictures representing objects, but the effects of such manipulations is determined by selections made in the upper panes. Though this browser has the same appearance and layout as the standard Smalltalk browser, the meaning of the various panes is quite different. It is convenient to think of the four upper panes as constituting the parts of a sentence indicating the action to be associated with mouse gestures in the bottom pane. The first two panes are a noun phrase for the subject, the third pane is a verb, and the direct object is chosen from the final pane, that is, "NewRC/picture/ insert/Capacitor" as shown in Figure 1.

Figure 1. **Building an RC circuit by merging the ends of leads of a capacitor and resistor.**

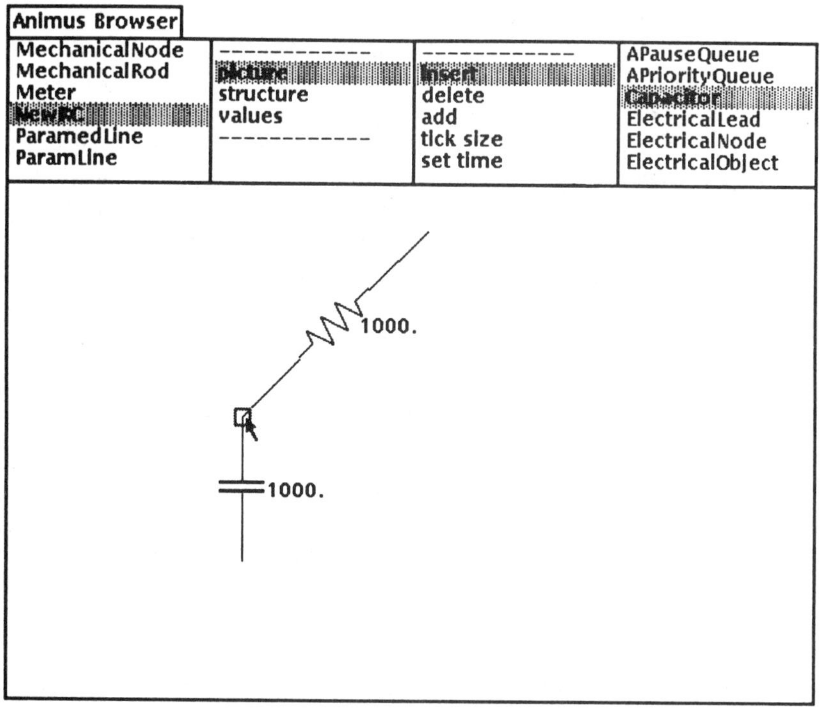

Animated simulations of physical systems provide a relatively simple and concrete introduction to the animation task. Continuous physical processes are describable by differential equations, for example, the equations of motion of a mechanical system. Animus provides the class TimeDifferentialConstraint, which allows the user to write such differential equations as constraints on the system's behavior. The mechanism contained in a TimeDifferentialConstraint satisfies the constraint by automatically generating and executing a finite difference approximation to the behavior so specified. For example, in the definition of a MechanicalNode, one finds the constraint that $v = dx/dt$.[2] That is, the prototypical instance of MechanicalNode has an instance variable representing its position whose value is constrained, as time advances, to be derived from the value of the instance variable for velocity.

Temporal constraints make possible extensions to the electrical circuit

---

[2] The actual syntax of the code used to define these constraints is given in Section 5. Here, emphasizing the meaning of the relations expressed, only the standard mathematical notations for the constraint relations are given.

examples of ThingLab where the only circuits that were modeled were steady state, direct current circuits. The electrical components available in Animus include such things as capacitors, inductors, oscilloscopes, and wave generators, with time-dependent behavior built in. For example, the prototype capacitor contains the constraint that $i = dq/dt$, the prototype inductor has $\Delta V/L = di/dt$, a sine wave generator obeys $\Delta V = A \sin \omega t$, and so on, where ΔV indicates the difference in voltage between the two leads of the component.

Suppose we wished to demonstrate or investigate the behavior of a capacitor discharging through a resistor. We would begin by defining a new prototype class, as in the current version of ThingLab, which is accomplished by selecting "define new thing" from the menu that pops up with a button click in the first pane of the window shown. A prompt window then comes up and asks for the name of the new prototype, to which we might respond "RC." Now "RC" will appear in the list of prototypes where we may select it and begin to build the prototypical RC graphically by selecting "picture" in the second pane and "insert" in the third pane listing operations, and then by selecting the objects we wish to insert from the last pane such as a capacitor. A flashing image of the capacitor will follow the cursor and allow us to place it where we like. We then insert a resistor and find that the endpoints of leads are "sticky" and will merge when brought close to the capacitor leads, as shown in Figure 1 by the gray box around the merged node.

We connect a wire and ground similarly. Once the circuit has been assembled, we may probe it with an oscilloscope to view the voltage as in Figure 2. The beam of the oscilloscope is constrained so that its y-position is proportional to the voltage difference between its leads and its x-position is constrained to track with the value of time modulo the width of the scope. Finally, to start the animation going, we simply select "go" in the third pane, which begins to send messages to advance the clock.

But when the clock is sent the message to increment the time, the constraint requires that this can only be done maintaining $i = dq/dt$ in the capacitor. A new method becomes compiled which, in addition to incrementing time, enqueues a message to be sent upon the next tick of the clock which adjusts the charge on the capacitor.[3] This planned change to the charge in turn triggers other constraints that change the voltage on the capacitor (because $V = q/C$), propagate voltages and currents along wires, change the text that displays the charge on the capacitor, move the beam on the oscilloscope, and change the current through the resistor. The exponential decay seen on the scope is not the result of any analytical calculation of exponentials, but occurs as a result of the finite-difference approximations embodied in these new methods generated by the system to satisfy the specified **TimeDifferentialConstraint**. This planning and compilation phase takes a little time, about 15 sec for this circuit, running on a Tektronix 4405, a M68020-based work station. After the methods are compiled (just once), clock ticks come with a satisfying swiftness, and the motion attains a reasonable degree of smoothness.

The capacitor comes in the kit with an initial charge, but after a while it discharges. To reinitialize the charge, the user can edit the capacitor directly and simply assign a new value to the charge whereupon the animation may proceed. To perform the edit we would select "edit" in the third pane, and in the fourth select the kind of object we want to edit, in this case "Capacitor." We then get a flashing image of a capacitor that will stick to any capacitor we select and show us the selection by displaying a box around the selected element. Clicking the button on the selection now brings up a standard Smalltalk **Inspector** window in which values of the instance variables of the selection may be examined and edited, as shown in Figure 3. We select the text for the magnitude of the charge, edit it, accept it, close the window, and we may resume the execution by shifting back to the "go" position.

---

[3] See Section 5 for a description of the event queue mechanism in the temporal kernel.

Figure 2. An RC circuit with an oscilloscope attached.

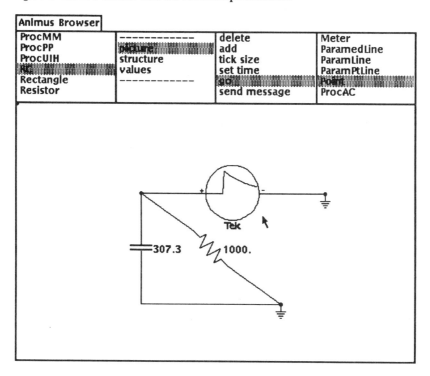

Figure 3. Selecting the capacitor in order to edit its properties.

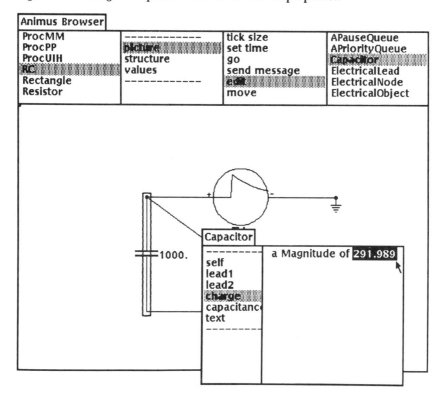

This demonstrates an important feature of the system: The pictures of objects on the screen offer direct access to their underlying representations. It is this property which justifies the claim that such animations may provide an interactive graphical interface to executing processes.

As another example, we may build an electrical oscillator by connecting an inductor with a capacitor to build the circuit shown in Figure 4. Now the inductor also contains a TimeDifferentialConstraint that $\Delta V/L = di/dt$, where L is the inductance and ΔV is the voltage across the inductor. When the circuit is told to "go," both temporal constraints must be satisfied. The method to increment time now enqueues two messages, one to adjust the charge on the capacitor and another to adjust the current in the inductor, and these messages again trigger other constraints so that a reasonable set of finite-difference functions are effectively generated. The oscilloscope shows (see Figure 4) that the voltage varies in a smooth sinusoid, and again, no sines are being calculated!

A mechanical analog to the electrical oscillator may also be built. A spring containing a constraint modeling Hooke's Law $\mathbf{F} = -k\mathbf{x}$ (where $\mathbf{F}$ indicates a *vector* force and $\mathbf{x}$ indicates a distance *vector*) is provided in the kit. Hooke's Law is expressed as a static constraint between the spring's extension and the force it contributes. A mass containing constraints expressing Newton's Law $\mathbf{F} = m\mathbf{a}$ and the basic kinematic relations $\mathbf{v} = d\mathbf{x}/dt$ and $\mathbf{a} = d\mathbf{v}/dt$ may be attached to the end of the spring where these kinematics appear as TimeDifferentialConstraints as just mentioned. When the system is told to "go," methods are compiled that solve the vector constraints, as can be seen in Figure 5. If we do a graphical edit of the mass's position by selecting "move" and "MechanicalNode" and thereby reach in and pull the mass over to the side, it will subsequently continue to oscillate in two dimensions.

We could convert this example to a *driven* oscillator by introducing another important element, namely, a hand to drive the system at a fixed sinusoidal frequency as shown in Figure 6. This enables the observation of the transient behavior of a driven oscillator and demonstrates resonance phenomena. This building block introduces a kind of scripting constraint, a TimeFunctionConstraint in which the value of a variable is determined by evaluating some function of time. That is, the hand prototype definition constrains an instance variable, verticalOffset, by a sine function, *A sin ωt*. When time is incremented, constraint satisfaction enqueues a message that assigns the value of the function at the current time into the constrained variable, the vertical offset of the hand from its initial position.

A general purpose animation system should provide a set of sliders and gauges to provide direct access to particular variables and a graphical way of connecting such things onto variables to be monitored. There are a number of conceivable ways of doing this, for example, one could insert a version of the sliders used in ThingLab. But a graphically explicit point should appear so that the slider could be attached to in order to indicate what value the "mercury level" in the slider is to reflect. To accomplish this we may textually edit the file defining the Hand prototype and change a primitive value such as "frequency" to be, instead, an instance of NumberNode. Now this number node can be constrained to appear as a point near the hand icon, and with a little more effort could even be labeled and print the value. As shown in Figure 6, a slider can now be connected to that point and by manipulating the mercury level (i.e., by selecting "move" and "Point" in the third and fourth browser panes and pointing at the top end of the bar in the slider) we can directly change the value of the driving frequency, which will be reflected in the value printed by the label and immediately resume execution with the new driving frequency by switching back to "go." An alternative approach might obviate the need for this bit of textual programming. One could imagine the implementation of a special subclass of Inspector which could be opened on an object that, while listing the instance variables of the object, would allow

Figure 4. An oscillating circuit.

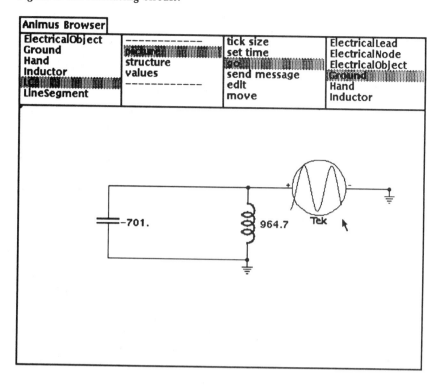

Figure 5. A mechanical oscillator.

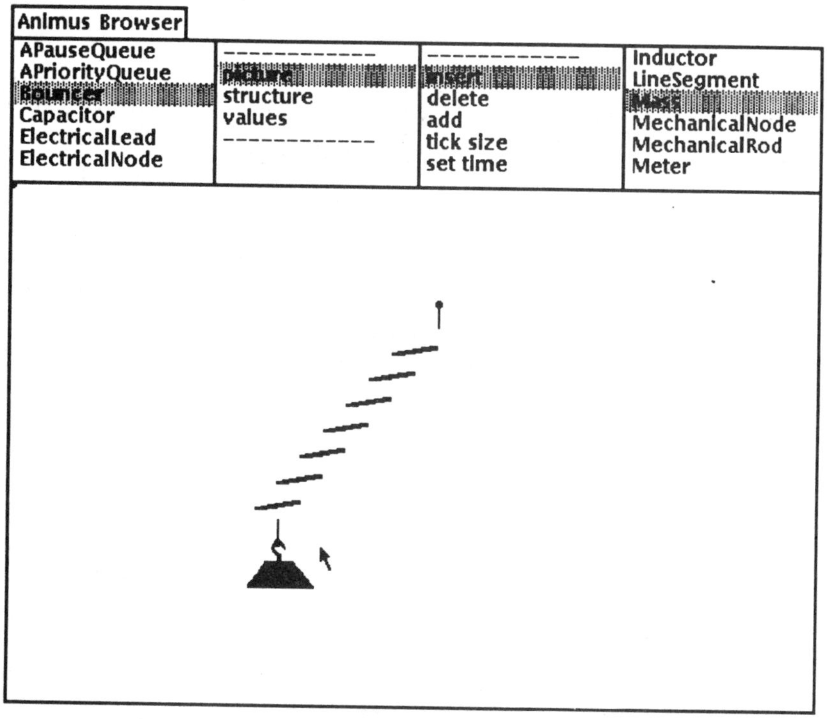

Figure 6. Manipulating the mercury level to change the driving frequency of the hand.

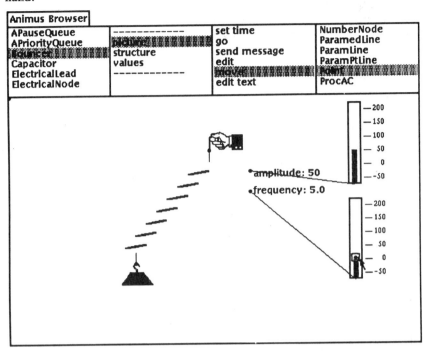

Figure 7. Adding elements to a queue to be sorted.

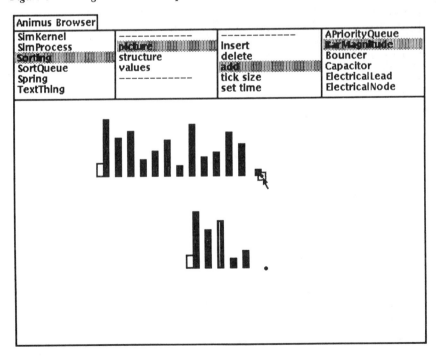

the user to point to these variables in order to hook up sliders and probes instead of requiring the user to redefine the prototype so it will show the variables that can be probed. Such interaction and probing techniques, although not implemented in Animus, are the subject of ongoing research at Tektronix.

4.1. Algorithms and Discrete Simulations

The transition to the animation of discrete processes such as algorithms poses a whole new set of problems. Here it is no longer so easy to write mathematical descriptions of temporal evolution, but rather one encounters event-driven causes and effects. The principle means for describing responses to events is provided by the mechanism of **TriggerConstraints**, which are like the guarded commands of CSP (Hoare, 1985). A **TriggerConstraint** allows the animator to specify certain graphical responses to the occurrence of particular events.

Sorting algorithms are a standard testbed for algorithm animation techniques. To build a sorting animation in Animus we are able to select an item from the kit called a **SortQueue**, and place it in the lower window. This representation of a linear array is a fairly general component and is also used, with slight alterations, in other examples.

We first select and insert a **SortQueue** into a new prototype. We may then graphically add elements, each an instance of **BarMagnitude**. A bar's corner will stick to the point to the right of the queue symbol, as shown in Figure 7, and then the bar may be stretched vertically to the desired magnitude. The magnitude represented by the bar is constrained to be proportional to the bar's height. The queue may be sent a message to sort itself through the graphical means of selecting "send message" in the third pane, and "SortQueue" in the fourth, and then pointing to the particular receiver as in Figure 8. (Note that there may be several queues in the structure from which to choose as in the operating system animation.)

The system looks to see what messages the queue can understand and presents the user with a menu from which to choose. The queue in the kit comes equipped to respond to **selectionSort** or a **bubbleSort** messages, so we select one from the menu in Figure 8 and the sort begins, displaying both of the comparisons by flashing the bars (as in Figure 9) and the swapping by smoothly and simultaneously interchanging the respective bars representing the values on the screen.

Notice also that, whereas many standard animation techniques (e.g., subroutine calls) typically show the swap of elements as a pair of moves in sequence (London & Duisberg, 1985), the swaps here show the moves simultaneously as a single event because responses become automatically interleaved in the event queue. This is described in greater detail in Section 5.

It is significant that the code in which the sorting algorithms are written is exactly the same as if it were unanimated. There are no graphics procedure calls or broadcast messages inserted interlinearly into the algorithmic code. All that the animator has to do is state a pair of trigger constraints, one on the message selector **compare:with:** and one on **swap:with:** entailing responses that flash the bars being compared and move the bars being swapped. This feature is particularly important in applying animation to algorithm design efforts because it makes the technique "transparent" or "nonintrusive." A transparent technique becomes most important when the system being animated grows large. Then this style provides considerable code-size reduction for the animator, because a single declaration of the trigger constraint may serve to trigger on many uses of the chosen message name. Also, in large applications the animator and algorithm designer are likely to be different people, and it is better if their jobs are separate. In particular, the animator

Figure 8. Selecting a message to send.

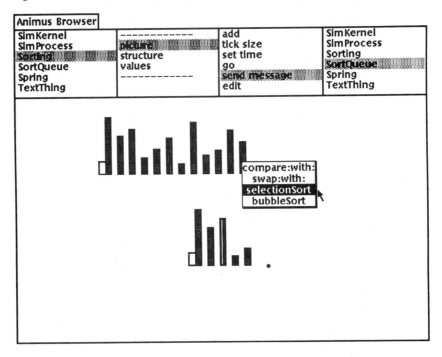

Figure 9. A queue comparing two elements.

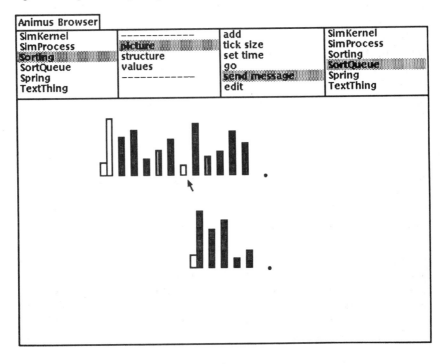

Figure 10. An operating system animation.

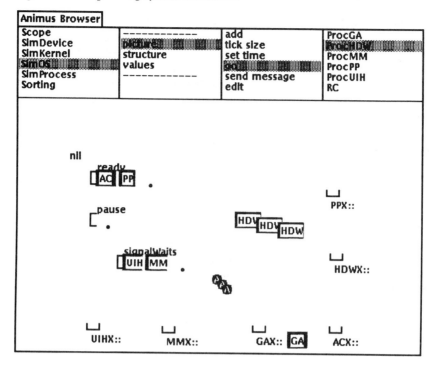

Figure 11. A Menu Manager process with its priority being edited in the middle of execution.

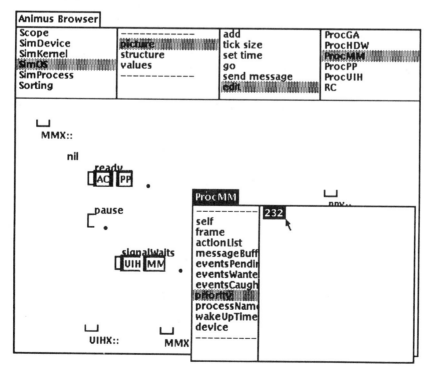

should not have to achieve a deep understanding of the algorithm in order to animate it.

This has been the case in the application of animation to aid in the design and tuning of a real-time operating system before it is used in a Tektronix instrument under development. The system implementor (Dickey) made animation his "method of choice" to test the operating system design and to experiment with the effects of altering time slice size, process priorities, and behaviors before committing the design to firmware. As the animator, I was simply given a large body of operating system simulation code, which by using the techniques described here, was animated with few changes to that code.

The operating system animation is constructed primarily of the kernel, which in turn consists of three queues of processes: a priority queue of those processes ready to run, those waiting on a signal, and those that are pausing for a time-out. Notice that the queues themselves are like the **SortQueue** of the earlier sample. This is an example of how new building blocks can be easily constructed by cloning them from other similar components and just adding refinements to their behavior such as priority insertion, time-out facility, and so on. To start the animation in a particular configuration, processes of various types are added into the queues in the same way that bars were placed into the sorting queue, and then "go" is selected. In Figure 10, hardware process (HDW) is proceeding from the ready list to wait on its message exchange, and a message is being sent to the process General Accounting (GA). Each process in the real system also has an associated message exchange (shown in the animation by a "bucket" labeled with the process name with "X::" appended), which is also placed by the user. Each process actually contains a hollow shell of a program consisting of clock ticks consumed, followed by kernel requests, with conditional branches on the content of messages picked up at the process's message exchange.

The kernel contains the simulation code for handling kernel requests from processes. The most substantial thing that was needed to animate the system was to state trigger constraints on the selectors of two messages to the kernel: **moveProcess:fromQueue:toQueue:withTimeOut:** and **sendMessage:to Exchange:**. The responses to these triggers are to create **Trajectories** that move the process and message icons from place to place.

The ability to edit the process priorities and programs in the middle of execution, as described in Section 4 and as shown in Figure 11, was crucial for the utility of the animation as a tool for design exploration. We are grateful to have had the opportunity to address this design problem, because it provides a dramatic demonstration of the potential of animation in the real world as a design tool in computer-aided software engineering.

4.2. Curve Generation by Parameterized Bounding Polygons

The field of computer-aided geometrical design is concerned with the computational generation of curves and surfaces with industrial applications in design and manufacturing, as when a modeling or milling machine might be driven under numerical control. Certain classes of curves (e.g., Bezier curves and B-Splines and their geometrical construction) are well known.[4] But a subject of active investigation by DeRose (professor at the University of Washington) and others, is the nature of curves generated when the geometric constructions are generalized by different parameterizations of the generating polygons.

DeRose approached me looking for the means to visualize these curves as they are generated and to be able to experiment with the effects of changing parameterizations. The necessary experimental tools were provided, as shown in Figure 12, by modifying the standard **MidPointLine** definition from ThingLab so that the position of the point of the line was constrained so that:

Figure 12. The de Casteljau construction of Bezier Curves.

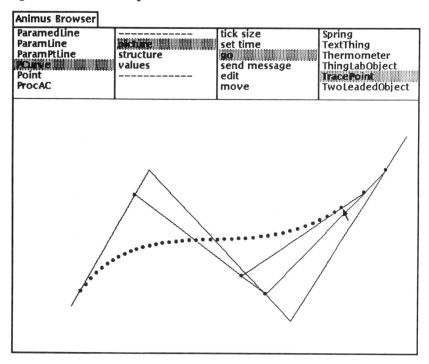

Figure 13. Editing the parameters of a line segment.

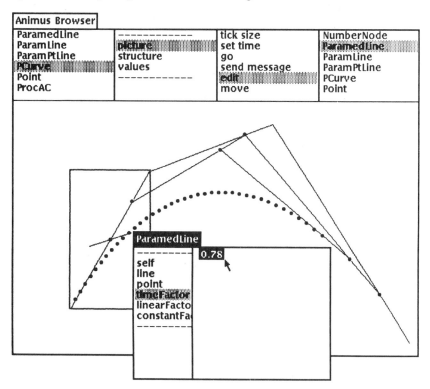

$$position = (line\ point2 - line\ point1) * (linearFactor * t + constantFactor) + line\ point1$$

where linearFactor and constantFactor are editable parameters, and the parameter t has been bound to animation time.

Of course, the most important capability is being able to edit the parameterization of any given line segment, as shown in Figure 13, in order to perform experiments. This work is very recent and exploratory and it is yet to be seen what results may come of it. It is rewarding, however, to see how, with relatively little effort, tools could be generated using Animus which may provide insights into problems of theoretical interest.

5. THE TEMPORAL KERNEL (THE ANIMA)

All time management protocols and controls for compiling temporal constraints are implemented as instance methods in a class called Anima. The anima, of whose presence the user is generally unaware, is in some sense the "soul" of the animation. The simulation time as well as the eventQueue are instance variables of and are managed by the single instance of the Anima subclass associated with each animation. When the user defines a new prototype in the browser, say a "Circuit," Animus automatically defines a new class called CircuitAnima as a subclass of Anima into which methods for the response and temporal behavior of this particular circuit are compiled. An anima that is an instance of this new subclass is automatically created when the user constructs a new prototype and is initialized and assigned as the value of the instance variable anima of that prototype when time first advances. Any instance of Anima responds to the message tick: dt, by first checking to find all events in the eventQueue with time-stamps less than or equal to the current value of time, sends off the messages represented by the events, and finally increments the value of time by dt.

The eventQueue is implemented in the style of event queues in Simula (Birtwistle, Dahl, Myhrhaug, & Nygaard, 1979), where an instance of class Event is a representation of a Smalltalk message along with a time-stamp specifying a clock time at which that message will be sent. A message in Smalltalk semantics consists of an object designated as the receiver, a symbol serving as the message selector, and an array of arguments. The time-stamp serves to defer the action until the simulation clock reads a value greater than or equal to the time stamp. Upon the occurrence of a designated trigger event, Responses are realized as a stream of Events, which become placed in the eventQueue.

Because events are explicitly time-stamped and management of all events and responses occurs in one time-ordered queue, there is no need for synchronization primitives. An arbitrary degree of concurrency may be handled by the queue, because any number of events may be stamped to occur at the same time. In particular, the interleaving of complex responses consisting of sequences of events occurs for free. If two responses, such as Trajectories of icons moving across the screen, consisting of series of single-step events are specified to begin at specific times with durations that overlap, the constituent events will be inserted time-ordered in the queue and executed in that order, thus interleaved. When events are time-stamped to occur at the same time, they are executed in the order in which they were enqueued before the clock advances.

---

[4] For further details on the construction due to de Casteljau, see Boehm, Farin, and Kahmann (1984).

5.1. Temporal Constraint Satisfaction

A temporal constraint is a relation that is required between the existence of a stimulus event and a response in the form of a stream of new events. The statement of a temporal constraint must include a description of the stimulus event and some representation of the abstract response from which the response stream of events can be generated at a particular time. The stimulus event may simply be a tick of the clock, or it may be the receipt of some specified message by a particular object.

As in ThingLab, temporal constraints are expressed locally in the components that exhibit the specified behavior, and these components are then combined so that the constraints interact in a network. But unlike ThingLab where constraints are satisfied more locally (in the least common ancestor of the affected parts), in Animus time is considered global, and the single clock as well as the single event queue are managed by the single instance of **Anima** which is contained in the ancestor to all parts of the animated structure. Therefore, at the time of initialization the animated structure must be traversed and all temporal constraints caused to migrate up to the anima, because the anima is the owner of the constrained variable, time. Any message that would increment time must consider the constraints on time, and a new method is compiled to respond to that message which in addition to incrementing time guarantees that the constraints are satisfied.

One can imagine applications that would like time to be managed in a more distributed way, for example, in modeling distributed systems of asynchronous processors or in simulating experiments in relativistic mechanics. Such an implementation would require a distributed set of animae, each managing the clock local to it and presumably communicating with each other through synchronization messages. Such a distributed scheme was not implemented in the Animus prototype, but is included in the new design of an updated system.

The satisfaction of a temporal constraint requires the realization of a response. Responses in Animus are implemented by subclasses of the abstract superclass **Response**. **TimeDifferentialConstraints** that model continuum processes cause instantiation of **ImmediateResponses**, which are the closest thing to the instantaneous reactions of the continua being modeled. **TriggerConstraints** often cause more elaborate responses such as instances of **Flasher** or **Trajectory**, which cause an extended sequence of graphical events to occur. An instance of class **Response** is an object that represents an abstraction of the event sequence. The particular sequence is generated when the **Response** is realized by sending it the message **enqueueEvents**. All instances of response classes understand this message and react by generating an event stream and placing it time-ordered into the event queue. Responses can also be realized given parameters such as the object whose image is to be moved, time delays, or time dilation factors. Maintaining descriptions of responses in relatively abstract terms in these classes, rather than concretely instantiated, allows greater flexibility. For example, a simple parameter may determine whether an icon is to move along a trajectory in constant time or at a constant velocity.

Finally, a **TriggerConstraint** may be created without the convenience of abstract **Responses**, but rather the **causes:** field may be filled with a string of arbitrary Smalltalk expressions. This is the means by which an arbitrary algorithm may be specified as in the sorting examples.

In a continuum process described by a differential equation such as $i = dq/dt$, increments are infinitesimal and continuous. In the digital world, this must be modeled by a sequence of assignments and a finite time granularity. So the satisfaction of a **TimeDifferentialConstraint**, which must be assured at every increment of the clock, involves the instantiation of an **ImmediateResponse**. An instance of **ImmediateResponse** enqueues a single event to cause the change specified by the constraint, such as decrementing the charge on the capacitor by $i\Delta t$ in the RC circuit. Note that because the increment to the charge calculated at t_o, namely $\Delta q = i \, \Delta t$, is assigned in the next instant, $t_o + \Delta t$, the essential feature of the approximation has been achieved; that is, the "derivative" value (the current) has been considered good for the duration of the time interval in order to get a first approximation to the new value of the differential variable (the charge) after other values are adjusted according to the constraints for static consistency. This serves to break the instantaneous circular dependency implied in the constraint equation, that is that the charge depends on the current which in turn depends on the charge.

The implementation of this approach in Animus occurs in several stages. First the programmer of the **Capacitor** prototype includes in its definition the simple declaration:

```
TimeDifferentialConstraint owner: Capacitor prototype
    timeDerivativeOf: 'charge' equals: 'lead1 current'.
```

When this declaration is compiled, a parse tree is generated and stored in the constraint representing the code fragment:

```
delta.charge: t1
    | delta |
    delta ← lead1 current * t1.
```

The value of the time increment is not known until run time and, therefore, is expected to be a parameter. Notice that this fragment by itself does nothing. However, when the capacitor has been incorporated into a larger structure and the constraint is activated by an attempt to advance the clock, the fragment is compiled into a larger **Response** method reflecting the context. That is, when the item "go" is selected, the browser sends **tick:** messages to the prototype's anima, which inherits from the abstract superclass, **Anima**, the following protocol:

```
tick: dt
    | eventsToDo |
    eventsToDo ← eventQueue check: time.
    eventsToDo do: [:anEvent | anEvent happen].
    self incrementby: dt.
```

That is, the anima checks the eventQueue for events whose time stamps are less than or equal to the current time, causes those events to happen (i.e., sends the messages the events represent), and finally sends itself the message **incrementby: dt**.

Initially the **incrementby:** message is not understood. But the constraint satisfier traps the **doesNotUnderstand:** message, recognizing that it should be able to compile a response and then resend the message. The structure of the RC prototype is searched for temporal constraints, and the following method is compiled into class **RCAnima**.

```
incrementby: t1
    time primitiveIncrement: t1.
    events enqueue:
        (Array with:
        (Event new
            atTime: time value + t1
            receiver: self
            selector: #delta.rc.capacitor1.charge:
            arguments: (Array with: t1))).
```

This method advances the clock while placing an event in the queue to occur in the next instant, constituting an invocation of the differential constraint's response. The response has been given the name **delta.rc.capacitor1.charge:**, which is another system-generated method derived from the code fragment in the constraint, recompiled in the current context.

```
delta.rc.capacitor1.charge: t1
   | delta |
   delta ← rc capacitor1 lead1 current * t1.
   rc capacitor1chargeprimitiveIncrement: delta.
```

Notice that references to subparts and the selector itself have been "relocated" (described in the next section), that is, they have been extended with a path of variable names identifying the new context. Also, the local **delta** is now passed to the system generated "primitive" increment method that ensures static constraint satisfaction in the circuit in order to make things consistent once the charge has been set. This method, finally, looks like:

```
capacitor1chargeprimitiveIncrement: t1
   capacitor1 charge primitiveIncrement: t1.
   ground6 node set.voltage: 0.0.
   wire5 lead1 node set.voltage: wire5 lead2 node voltage.
   capacitor1 lead1 node set.voltage:
   capacitor1 lead2 node voltage +
   capacitor1 charge value / capacitor1 capacitance.
resistor2 set.resistance: resistor2 text text asNumber.
resistor2 lead1 set.current:
   resistor2 lead1 node voltage −
   resistor2 lead2 node voltage / resistor2 resistance.
capacitor1 lead1 set.current:
   0.0 − ((capacitor1 lead1 node currents applyTo: self)
         excluding: capacitor1 lead1 current) sum.
capacitor1 lead2 set.current: 0.0 − capacitor1 lead1 current.
wire5 lead1 set.current:
   0.0 − ((capacitor1 lead2 node currents applyTo: self)
         excluding: wire5 lead1 current) sum.
wire5 lead2 set.current: 0.0 − wire5 lead1 current.
resistor2 lead2 set.current:
   0.0 − ((resistor2 lead2 node currents applyTo: self)
         excluding: resistor2 lead2 current) sum.
```

Such system generated code is neither highly optimized (note the unnecessary resetting of the ground voltage to zero) nor very clear, but it is correct. The user may simply be grateful to avoid having to write or even read such a code.

The abstraction of the function of moving icons across the screen in animations is implemented by another subclass of **Response**, namely **Trajectory**. An instance of class **Trajectory** is created by specifying at least the object whose image is to be moved and the place to where it is to go. Additional instance creation messages may specify how it is to move, say at constant velocity, or along the path of a spline. But the default is that the icon will be moved in constant time, that is, in a constant number of steps, along a straight line between the original position and the destination. **Trajectories** with as many as 10 steps and as few as 4 have been used. More steps, of course, create smoother movements, but interestingly using just four steps seems adequate to provide the illusion of smooth motion, the eye seeming to do the interpolation on its own, with only the barest suggestions of intervening positions. The motivation for using fewer steps is that in some cases where a single triggered constraint causes the instantiation of four or five trajectories interleaved at the same time, there is a noticeable delay while 40 or 50 events are created, initialized, and inserted time-ordered into the event queue.

Also class **Flasher** provides another common animation response in exactly the same way that **Trajectory** does. A **Flasher** is instantiated by simply specifying the region of the screen, a rectangle, that is to flash. An instance of **Flasher** then responds to the message **enqueueEvents** by creating and enqueuing a series of events that will flash the region on the screen. This is the response that is used to show the comparisons as they are made in the sorting algorithm example discussed in Section 4.1.

5.2. Method Relocation

Crucial to the implementation of temporal constraints is the process of reinterpretation of messages. New methods must be compiled in which actions are taken to satisfy the constraints, that is, to enqueue the appropriate responses, while executing the received message. In the larger context of the structure the user has assembled, this involves reinterpretation of the method fragments declared locally in constraints. Furthermore, all temporal constraints defined in subparts of the structure must be migrated in order to be owned and managed by the anima, which has **time** as an instance variable. Hence the process is known in the system as *method relocation*.

Suppose, for example, that one wishes to send a message to change the value of the current through a capacitor in an RC circuit, as discussed in Section 4. Access to the object representing the current would be via the path **rc capacitor1 lead1 current**. Each path name is both the name of an instance variable and the selector of an automatically generated access function that simply returns the value of the named variable. Thus, the path is in fact an executable message or sequence of messages that will return the desired part. During the process of relocation and after a component is inserted into a structure (e.g., the capacitor into the RC circuit) the paths to its parts must be extended to reflect its position in the structure. Thus, for example, in constraint methods defined local to the capacitor, there may be references to **lead1 current**, and all such references will have to be extended as previously discussed to **rc capacitor1 lead1 current**.

Trigger selectors are similarly treated upon relocation in that they are extended by the path names to the part where the trigger is defined. The purpose of this is to provide a unique selector in the anima for that trigger. The system then compiles a new method for that selector into the anima, which performs the specified animation and then executes the unaltered method. For example, assume that one wishes to animate the swap of two elements in a list that is part of a larger structure, say the readyList of a simulated operating system kernel as cited in the example shown in Section 4.1. To accomplish this one would state a trigger constraint in the readyList object, triggering on the selector **swap:with:**, which is defined in the standard Smalltalk system in class SequenceableCollection. If the path to the readyList is, say, **os simKernel1 readyList1 list**, then a new method will be compiled into the anima with the unwieldy selector **ossimKernel1readyList1listswap:with:**, which instantiates a pair of trajectories asking them to enqueue their events and then performs the primitive **swap:with:** method on the list. Once methods have been relocated, the selectors that have been designated triggers in **TriggerConstraints** require special treatment. The point is that without any special treatment, a message such as **list swap: t1 with: t2** would relocate into something like **ossimKernel1 readyList1 list swap: t1 with: t2**, which is to say that the reference to the variable **list** will have been relocated, but nothing is done to the selector. But because this selector will trigger a response, that response has recompiled into the anima under a new selector, such as **ossimKernel1readyList-**

504

1list.swap:with: which does the swap as well as enqueuing the required responses (shown in the next section). Thus, during the process of relocation, a list is kept of all designated trigger selectors and the paths to the objects in which those selectors will trigger responses. When these selectors are encountered, they are replaced by new selectors generated by "compressing" the path into the original selector, so that the proper method, including the responses, is executed.

In order to summarize and clarify this discussion, it may help to present the results of method relocation for the sorting example shown in Section 4.1. The algorithmic code contained in the kit component SortQueue is coded in a straightforward manner in Smalltalk.

```
selectionSort
    | least |
(1 to: list size) do: [:i |
    least ← i.
    (i + 1 to: list size)
    do: [:j | (list compare: least with: j)
        ifTrue: [least ← j]].
    least = i
      ifFalse: [list swap: i with: least]]
```

In addition the SortQueue component defines the constraint.

```
TriggerConstraint owner: SortQueue prototype
  to: 'list' trigger: #swap:with: causes:
    '(Trajectory with: (list at: a1)
       destination: (list at: a2)) enqueueEvents.
    (Trajectory with: (list at: a2)
       destination: (list at: a1) ) enqueueEvents'
```

When a SortQueue is inserted as a part of a structure, and the anima of that structure is initialized, there will come to be defined in the class of that anima the method

```
sortingsortQueue3list.selectionSort
    | least |
(1 to: sorting sortQueue3 list size)
    do: [:i |
      least ← i.
      (i + 1 to: sorting sortQueue3 list size)
        do: [:j |
          (self sortingsortQueue3list.compare: least with: j)
            ifTrue: [least ← j]].
          least = i
          ifFalse:
            [self sortingsortQueue3list.swap: i with: least]].
    self controlToAnima.
    ↑ nil
```

There are three significant differences between this and the original version. First, all references to instance variables (the variable list in this example) have been extended to reflect the context. Second, uses of the trigger selector swap:with: have been replaced by an extended selector for a new method defined in the anima, as shown in the following. And finally, a controlToAnima message has been added to turn control back to the animation kernel so that the newly enqueued events are executed forthwith.

The new method called by the method just mentioned will be defined in the anima so that they include the specified responses:

```
sortingsortQueue3list.swap: t1 with: t2
    (Trajectory with: (sorting sortQueue3 list at: t1)
        destination: (sorting sortQueue3 list at: t2)) enqueueEvents.
    (Trajectory with: (sorting sortQueue3 list at: t2)
        destination: (sorting sortQueue3 list at: t1)) enqueueEvents.
    self controlToAnima. '
    ↑ sorting sortQueue3 list swap: t1 with: t2
```

In comparing the relocated method **sortingsortQueue3list.selectionSort** with the original **selectionSort** method shown here, it is evident that the code to perform the sort within the context of the construction is more lengthy and obscure. One immediate observation is that the programmer is spared this incremental complexity. Also the ability to state the **TriggerConstraints** just once, although the selector triggered may be used quite often in many methods within the object owning the **TriggerConstraints**, potentially constitutes a considerable code reduction when compared to in-line insertions of animation procedure calls. This proved to be the case in the larger operating system example (see Section 4.1).

But the real advantage of using **TriggerConstraints** is the transparency of the technique. There is something aesthetically pleasing about being able to write the algorithm cleanly as though no animation were being done and then being able to state the animation triggers externally and have the system take care of all the contextual reinterpretation, macro expansion, and additional methods compiled to perform the animation, all in code that the user need never see.

6. FURTHER RESEARCH

The Animus prototype has demonstrated the feasibility and power of using constraints to specify behavior in time-dependent simulations and animations. Ongoing research involves investigating alternative designs and algorithms to implement constraint satisfaction (Borning, Duisberg, Freeman-Benson, Kramer, & Woolf, 1987). The structure might include back-pointers, removing the restriction that the animated structure be represented by a directed acyclic graph. In particular, parts could have back-pointers to the constraints on them. (In ThingLab there are only pointers from the constraints to the objects they constrain.) In this way, access to objects could trigger a more localized set of constraints greatly simplifying the job of the constraint satisfaction planner compared with access from the root, which can cause a spreading activation throughout the structure.

Although Smalltalk is congenial as a language and an environment in which to construct a prototype system, it poses certain problems as a language in which to construct animations and as a language in which to express algorithms to be animated. An important part of constructing a system like this involves writing code that writes code. The system automatically generates methods that incorporate context and interaction among the method fragments defined locally in constraints, as described in Section 5.2. It so happens that this is fairly awkward to do in Smalltalk. A method that constructs another system generated method must build a parse tree for the method node by node. This may be simpler, say, in Lisp where data and programs have the same form. Also algorithm designers do not usually express their designs in Smalltalk syntax, but rather, in some sort of pseudo-Algol. There is considerable research performed at the Computer Research Lab at Tektronix that implements multilingual environments (see

Delisle & Schwartz, 1986). Technology that facilitates building such environments is that Tektronix Smalltalk runs as a process under a Unix-like operating system and further provides a set of classes that provide Unix domain pipes and sockets to subtasks and background processes. Thus, Smalltalk can act as the main process forking off processes coded in any other language supported by the operating system. A later implementation of an animation system could be designed to take advantage of such multiligual facilities so that animations could be constructed in a Smalltalk interface while being triggered from a program running, say, in C.

An important direction of ongoing research is into a graphical or "gestural" interface for the description of temporal constraints, allowing, as it were, "animation by demonstration." This work has yielded some promising early results reported in Duisberg (1987), which describes a system in which a user's gestures may be recorded, parameterized, and triggered by a program where even the binding of gestures to program events is indicated graphically.

7. CONCLUSION

In summarizing this work, it should be seen again in the larger context of the motivating problem: representation. It has been argued by Simon (1981) that solving a problem is simply a matter of representing it so that the solution is transparent. Mathematical derivations, for example, may be viewed as mere changes in representation, making evident what was implicit, though obscure, in the premises. In short, the way a problem is represented has a major influence on our understanding and ability to solve it, and researchers in human factors emphasize the suggestive power of visual representations (Raeder, 1985). Further, in discussions of the current "software crisis" we hear that:

> machines must be designed so that the . . . user [is] accommodated in a way that supports his or her mental abstraction of the process taking place in the machine. . . . A key factor is the degree to which these programs can be made to hide the details of operation from the users. (Birnbaum, 1985, p. 1227)

The Animus system addresses these issues at a number of levels. On the surface, the system provides some useful imagery for thinking about and interacting with the examples to which it has been applied. But perhaps more important, it has provided some tools for generating such imagery, and the emphasis has been on providing high-level abstractions to the animator in the form of abstract response prototypes, equational descriptions, and composable building blocks. The use of constraints to describe animations also bears directly on these issues, because their declarative style frees the animator to some degree from concerns about the details of operation of the graphics engine. The compilation of the detailed imperative code to carry out the graphics may be left to the system.

Needless to say, this work is a long way from Birnbaum's "domesticated microelectronics." But whatever that might be, interactive graphical interfaces involving imagery at a high-level of abstraction would almost certainly be a part of it in some form or other. Animus contributes a gesture in that direction.

Acknowledgments. This work would have been impossible without the foundations provided by ThingLab, and many thanks are due to Alan Borning for his guidance and encouragement in helping to bring up this extension. I am grateful, too, for the interest, encouragement, and advice of the Smalltalk community at Tektronix Laboratories, especially Ralph London, as a collaborator, mentor, and friend. Thanks are also due to Ken Dickey and Tony DeRose for providing the impetus of "real-world" applications.

Support. This research was supported in part by National Science Foundation grants numbered DCR 82 02520 and IRI-8604923. Further support and equipment were provided by the Computer Research Lab at Tektronix, Inc. I also appreciate the generous support and recognition of the ARCS Foundation, Inc., of Seattle.

REFERENCES

Baecker, R. (1975). Two systems which produce animated representations of the execution of computer programs. *ACM SIGCSE Bulletin, 7*(1), 158–167.

Baecker, R. (1981). *Sorting out sorting* [16 mm, color sound film, 25 min]. Toronto, Ontario: University of Toronto.

Boehm, W., Farin, G., & Kahmann, J. (1984). A survey of curve and surface methods in CAGD. *Computer Aided Graphics Design 1*(1), 1–60.

Borning, A. H. (1979). *ThingLab—A constraint-oriented simulation laboratory.* Doctoral thesis, Stanford University, Stanford, CA. (A revised version is published as Xerox Palo Alto Research Center Report SSL-79-3, July 1979.)

Borning, A. H. (1981). The programming language aspects of ThingLab, a constraint-oriented simulation laboratory. *ACM Transactions on Programming Languages and Systems, 3*(4), 353–387.

Borning, A. H. (1986). Graphically defining new building blocks in ThingLab. *Human–Computer Interaction, 2,* 269–295.

Borning, A. H., Duisberg, R. A., Freeman-Benson, B., Kramer, A., & Woolf, M. (1987). Constraint hierarchies. *Proceedings of the OOPSLA '87 Conference on Object Oriented Programming Systems Languages and Applications,* 48–60. New York: ACM SIGPLAN.

Birtwistle, G. M., Dahl, O., Myhrhaug, B., & Nygaard, K. (1979). *Simula begin.* New York: Van Nostrand Reinhold.

Birnbaum, J. S. (1985). Toward the domestication of microelectronics. *Communications of the ACM, 28*(11), 1225–1235.

Brown, G., Carling, R., Herot, C., Kramlich, D., & Souza, P. (1985). Program visualization: Graphical support for software development. *IEEE Computer, 18*(8), 27–37.

Brown, M. H., & Sedgewick, R. (1984). A system for algorithm animation. *Computer Graphics, 18*(3), 177–186.

Chi, U. H. (1984). *Formal specification of user interfaces* (Tech. Rep. No. 84-05-01). Seattle, WA: Computer Science Department, University of Washington.

Dannenberg, R. B. (1984). Arctic: A functional language for real time control. *Proceedings of the Symposium on LISP and Functional Programming,* 96–103. New York: ACM.

Delisle, N., & Schwartz, M. (1986). *Neptune: A hypertext system for CAD applications* (Tech. Rep. No. CR-85-50). Beaverton, OR: Computer Research Laboratory, Tektronix, Inc.

Duisberg, R. A. (1986a). Animated graphical interfaces using temporal constraints. *Proceedings of the CHI '86 Conference on Human Factors in Computing Systems,* 131–136. New York: ACM.

Duisberg, R. A. (1986b). *Constraint-based animation: The implementation of temporal constraints in the Animus system.* Doctoral thesis, University of Washington, Seattle, WA. (Published as the University of Washington, Computer Science Department, Tech. Rep. No. 86-09-01.)

Duisberg, R. A. (1987). *Visual programming of program visualizations* (Tech. Rep. No. 87-20). Beaverton, OR: Computer Research Laboratory, Tektronix, Inc.

Gosling, J. A. (1983). *Algebraic constraints.* Doctoral thesis, Carnegie-Mellon University, Pittsburgh, PA. (Published as Carnegie-Mellon University, Computer Science Department, Tech. Rep. No. CMU-CS-83-132.)

Goldberg, A., & Robson, D. (1983). *Smalltalk-80: The language and its implementation.* Reading, MA: Addison-Wesley.

Glinert, E. P., & Tanimoto, S. L. (1984). Pict: An interactive graphical programming environment. *Computer, 17*(11), 7–25.

Hoare, C. A. R. (1985). *Communicating sequential processes.* London: Prentice-Hall International.

Knuth, D. E. (1973). *The art of computer programming, Vol. 1.* Reading, MA:

Addison-Wesley.

Konopasek, M., & Jayaraman, S. (1984). *The TK!Solver book.* Berkeley, CA: Osborne/McGraw-Hill.

Leler, W. (1986). *Specification and generation of constraint satisfaction systems using augmented term rewriting.* Doctoral thesis, University of North Carolina at Chapel Hill.

Levitt, D. (1984). Machine tongues x: Constraint languages. *Computer Music Journal, 8*(1), 9–21.

London, R. L., & Duisberg, R. A. (1985). Animating programs using smalltalk. *IEEE Computer, 18*(8), 61–71.

Nelson, G. (1985). Juno, a constraint-based graphics system. *SIGGRAPH '85 Conference Proceedings,* 235–243. New York: ACM.

Sussman, G. J., & Steele, G. L., Jr. (1980). Constraints—A language for expressing almost-hierarchical descriptions. *Artificial Intelligence, 14*(1), 1–39.

Sutherland, I. (1963). Sketchpad: A man-machine graphical communication system. *Proceedings of the Spring Joint Computer Conference,* 329–347. Detroit: American Federation of Information Processing Societies.

HCI Editorial Record. First manuscript received March 16, 1987. Revision received December 22, 1987. Accepted by Tim O'Shea. —*Editor*

"JUNO: A Constraint-Based Graphics System" by G. Nelson from
ACM Proceedings Computer Graphics (SIGGRAPH), Volume 19,
Number 3, July 1985, pages 235-243.   Copyright 1985,
Association for Computing Machinery, Inc., reprinted with
permission.

Juno, a constraint-based graphics system

Greg Nelson

Xerox Palo Alto Research Center*

Abstract. Juno is a system that harmoniously integrates a language for describing pictures with a what-
you-see-is-what-you-get image editor. Two of Juno's
novelties are that geometric constraints are used to
specify locations, and that the text of a Juno program
is modified in response to the interactive editing of the
displayed image that the program produces.

Introduction

Connect a computer to a marking engine, and you get a
drawing instrument of revolutionary precision and versatility. Already some graphic artists have abandoned their
T-squares and pens for the new world of bit-mapped displays, mice, and laser printers. But they face a serious
problem: to harness the power of a computer, artists must
become programmers.

Of course, the artist's business is art, not bits: someone else should deal with floating-point numbers and raster
ops. But an artist using a computer must somehow provide
a precise constructive specification for the (often complicated) image in his mind. And in an important sense, to
give a precise constructive specification for any complicated
thing is a programming problem.

The first key to any programming problem is to approach it at the right level of abstraction, which often boils
down to choosing the right language. One language designed for the artist-programmer is D. E. Knuth's META-
FONT [6]. Three of its key features are that the positions
of points are specified by declarative constraints, that the
image is rendered by imperative painting commands parameterized by these points, and that procedural abstraction is provided. Let us call a language with these features a "METAFONT-style language". METAFONT-style
languages are well-suited for producing images with a constrained and hierarchical structure.

From the language designer's point of view, artists are
unusual programmers in that they like to specify free-form,
unconstrained shapes, relying on their hand-eye coordination and on repeated adjustments to get the shape right.
This is best done under the control of a what-you-see-is-
what-you-get (WYSIWYG) image editor, by which I mean
a system that continuously displays an image while the user
interactively modifies it by pointing into it. Patrick Baude-

laire's Draw program [1] for the Xerox Alto is an example
of such an editor.

Several years ago I used METAFONT and Draw to
produce figures for my thesis. These figures contained hierarchical structure, constrained positions, and free-form
shapes, so that neither program by itself was quite right.
Draw has no constraints and is not programmable. META-
FONT can be driven interactively, a command at a time,
but it is not WYSIWYG, since you cannot point into the
image and modify it.

The contrasting virtues of these two programs inspired
me to design Juno, a system that integrates a programming
language like METAFONT with a WYSIWYG image editor
like Draw. I implemented Juno in the Cedar programming
system [9] at Xerox PARC. Figure 1 shows some examples
of images produced with Juno.

Two techniques greatly contributed to the harmony of
Juno's integration of WYSIWYG editing with programmability: *geometric specification*, or the use geometric constraints to specify locations, and *implicit editing*, or the
modification of the text of a Juno program in response to
the interactive editing of the displayed image that the program produces.

As an example of geometric specification, a Juno user
might specify that points a, b, and c be collinear, and that
the distance from a to b be equal to the distance from b
to c. The Juno interpreter will translate these geometric
constraints into numerical constraints on the coordinates
of the points, and solve them by numerical methods. Less
trivially, a regular pentagon is easily constructed by specifying equality of length for its sides and for three of its
chords.

The use of declarative specifications for positioning
points derives from METAFONT. But METAFONT allows
only constraints that are algebraically linear, and this precludes the important geometric predicates of parallelism
and congruence, which correspond to quadratic equations.
The pentagon example hints at the extra power of nonlinear specification, but more important than this extra power
is the fact that a user of a WYSIWYG interface can specify geometric constraints simply by selecting the constraint
and the points it is to be applied to. By contrast, the speci-

* Author's present affiliation: DEC Systems Research Center

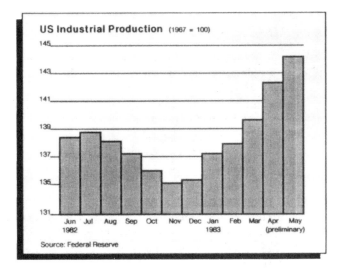

Figure 1.

fication of linear algebraic constraints on the coordinates of points requires naming the points and typing the equations, which does not fit well into a WYSIWYG interface.

Going from linear to nonlinear constraints is more ambitious than going to the "slightly nonlinear" constraints of Chris Van Wyk's Ideal [10], but less ambitious than going all the way to open-ended, client-defined constraint types, as in Alan Borning's Thinglab [2]. The nonlinear constraints pose two dangers: the solver might become too slow, or the solver might become too unpredictable to the user.

In regard to the first danger, the Juno constraint solver uses Newton-Raphson iteration (described in most standard texts in numerical analysis, for example, Conte and de Boor [3]) to solve constraints. On the powerful Xerox Dorado, my first crude implementation was fast enough. Bruce Lucas programmed a variant of Juno called "Banzai" for a Sun workstation at CMU [7]; he reported acceptable performance only after including some standard optimizations. Derivative-based methods like Newton-Raphson iteration are reputed to be faster than relaxation methods, like those employed in Ivan Sutherland's Sketchpad [8]. Of course, if all the constraints in a complicated image had to be solved together, the asymptotically slow behavior of the constraint solver would bring the system to a halt. But an appropriate hierarchy can avoid this, and is desirable regardless of whether nonlinear constraints are allowed.

In regard to the second danger, a nonlinear solver behaves quite predicatably provided that the initial configuration is not too far from the solution. Therefore, in using the WYSIWYG editor, the user must lay out the points of the image in roughly the right positions, and rely on the

constraint solver only to align them accurately, not to rearrange them drastically. Similarly, when a running Juno program invokes the constraint solver, it must supply "hints" for the initial positions of the unknown points.

The implicit editing technique is more novel. It is almost dictated by the integration of programmability with WYSIWYG editing: if an image produced by a program were "touched up" by interactive editing, then the touching up would have to be repeated if the program were modified; this is unacceptable. It follows that the interactive editing operations must be considered to modify not the displayed image, but the underlying program that produces the image.

For example, consider the following command of the Juno language (a little liberty has been taken with the syntax):

```
LET p, q | p = (0, 0) AND q = (100, 124)
  IN DRAW (p, q)
END ,
```

which draws a line segment slightly steeper than 45 degrees by introducing two point variables p and q at specified positions and connecting them with a line segment. When this command is "current", the line segment is displayed on the screen. If the user then points at the higher end of the segment and moves it, the coordinate pair (100, 124) in the program text will change to reflect the new position of the endpoint q. In addition to moving points, interactive editing commands may add or delete points, constraints, or painting commands; each such operation is most properly understood as a syntactic operation on the current command. After each operation, the screen is updated by re-

Figure can be found printed in color on page 656.

executing the current command.

In a general WYSIWYG editor, the user modifies a data structure d by interacting with an image $I(d)$. Implicit editing is the special case in which d is a program text and I is an interpreter. Any WYSIWYG editor must solve the *pointing problem*: if the user points at a position p in the image $I(d)$, but two or more components of the data structure d affect the rendering of the image in the vicinity of p, then the user's image position does not translate into a unique component of the underlying data structure. For example, if a user points near the intersection of two edges, there will be an ambiguity about which edge is meant. Happily, it is fairly easy to avoid the pointing problem in the implicit editing of METAFONT-style languages, since in these languages variables denote only points; shapes like edges are created as the side-effect of procedures parameterized by points.

The two main sections of this paper describe the Juno language and interactive editor. To smooth the exposition, Juno is sometimes described as it ought to be instead of as it is. Each such liberty will be accompanied by a footnote like this[0] that points to a terse caveat at the end of the paper.

Programming Juno

The Juno programming language is a version of the calculus of guarded commands described in E. W. Dijkstra's *Discipline of Programming* [5]. This is natural, because guarded commands are defined formally as predicate transformers, and "predicate" is just another word for "constraint". Dijkstra's language is a collection of predicate transformers acting upon the predicates of a theory of integers and arrays. The Juno programming language is essentially the same collection of predicate transformers acting upon the predicates of Euclidean geometry. But this section's description is conventional and operational.

A Juno command can be considered to act upon an "abstract Juno machine". The state of this machine is determined by:

- an indefinite number of named *point registers*, each of which contains a value representing a point in the Cartesian plane.
- a single anonymous *image*, to be imagined as a map from the Euclidean plane to the set of colors, but represented as a map from a fine discrete grid to the set of colors.
- three *mode registers*, the color register, width register, and endsType register, whose contents will be described later.

Painting commands. The painting commands will be described first; these are used only after the point registers have been set by commands yet to be described. Here is a list of them:

A;B: Execute A, then execute B. (Composition)

FILL p: Change the color of every image point entwined by the path p to the current contents of the color register. (A path entwines a point if the winding number

of the path with respect to the point is non-zero.)

STROKE p: Draw a stroke along the path p whose color is the contents of the color register, whose width is the contents of the width register, and whose ends are finished off in a style determined by the contents of the endsType register.

c PAINT A: Set the color register to c, execute A, restore the old contents of the color register.

e ENDS A: Set the endsType register to e, execute A, restore the old contents of the endsType register.

p, q WIDTH A: Set the width register to the distance between points p and q, execute A, restore the old contents of the width register.

r WIDTH A: Set the width register to r millimeters,[1] execute A, restore the old contents of the width register.

DRAW p: This is short for ROUND ENDS BLACK PAINT 1 WIDTH STROKE p.

The basic marking commands have the form FILL p and STROKE p, where p is a *path*, that is, a connected sequence of edges and arcs. An edge is specified by its two endpoints; an arc is specified by its four Bezier control points.

The semicolon has higher binding power than PAINT, ENDS, or WIDTH; for example, e ENDS A;B means e ENDS (A;B) rather than (e ENDS A); B.

For example, Figure 2 shows the result of executing the command

```
GREY PAINT BUTT ENDS 8 WIDTH
STROKE (a, b), (b, c);
STROKE (d, e); STROKE (e, f);
ROUND ENDS STROKE (g, h);
BUTT ENDS STROKE (i, j);
SQUARE ENDS STROKE (k, l);
FILL (n, m, o, p), (p, n);
BLACK PAINT 3 WIDTH
STROKE (n, m, o, p), (p, n);
o, q WIDTH ROUND ENDS STROKE (q, q)
```

Figure 2.

in a state in which points a through q have the locations labeled in the figure.

Here is the syntax of these commands (the ellipses in the first production indicate that the syntax for a Command will be extended further):

```
Command ::= FILL Path | STROKE Path
          | DRAW Path | ModeChange
          | Command ; Command | ...

ModeChange ::= Color PAINT Command
             | EndsType ENDS Command
             | Number WIDTH Command
             | Point, Point WIDTH Command

EndsType ::= BUTT | SQUARE | ROUND

Color ::= BLACK | WHITE | GREY | RED | BLUE
        | GREEN | YELLOW | CYAN | MAGENTA | ...

Path ::= Patch | Path , Patch

Patch ::= (Point, Point)
        | (Point, Point, Point, Point)

Point ::= a symbolic name

Number ::= a decimal numeral
```

Juno also includes a primitive for painting a text string at a given position in a given font, but it will not be described.

Constraint commands. Juno's constraint command is a special case of the general construct from the guarded command calculus, which has the form[2]

LET Variables | Constraints IN Command END ,

where Variables is a list of local variables to be introduced, Constraints is a conjunction of constraints on the values of the variables, and Command is what is to be executed in the scope of the local variables. If no values for the variables satisfy the constraints, the command is equivalent to *Abort*. If the constraints do not determine the values of the variables uniquely, then the command is non-deterministic, which means that the implementation is allowed to introduce any values that do satisfy the constraints.

As an example, let us translate Euclid's proposition I.1 into guarded commands: "*On a given line to construct an equilateral triangle.* Let ab be the given line; thus it is required to describe on the line ab an equilateral triangle. With center a and distance 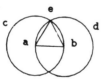 ab let the circle c be described; and with center b and distance ba let the circle d be described; and let the circles c and d cut one another at e. Now I say that the triangle abe is equilateral. For, since b and e both lie on the circle c, ab is equal to ae ..." [4]. Euclid went on to prove what would today be called the partial correctness of his construction.

Here is the construction expressed using guarded commands:

```
LET c, d
   | Circle(c) AND Center(c) = a AND On(b, c)
AND Circle(d) AND Center(d) = b AND On(a, d)
 IN LET e | Point(e) AND On(e, c) AND On(e, d)
    IN Draw (a, b), (b, e), (e, a)
    END
END
```

which not only constructs the point e, but also draws the sides of the triangle. The predicates Circle, Point, and On are used with their obvious meanings.

The construction above is not a legal Juno program, since firstly, variables in Juno range only over points, and secondly, the only four constraint types allowed in Juno are the following:

(x, y) CONG (u, v): the distance from x to y equals the distance from u to v.

(x, y) PARA (u, v): the direction from x to y parallels the direction from u to v.

HOR(x, y): the direction from x to y is horizontal

VER(x, y): the direction from x to y is vertical

Note that any constraint expressible in the Euclidean theory of geometry can be expressed in terms of CONG and PARA. In particular, the collinearity of a, b, and c can be expressed (a, b) PARA (b, c). At least one additional constraint type is needed to orient images on the output pages, since these are not circular. Both HOR and VER were added, since to choose one of them would be asymmetric.

Euclid's construction can still be succinctly expressed with the limited predicates available in Juno:

```
LET e | (a, e) CONG (a, b) AND (b, e) CONG (a, b)
   IN DRAW (a, b), (b, e), (e, a)
END
```

But we still don't have a legal Juno program, since we still have to settle the important issue: which of the two solutions for e will be introduced? The semantics of guarded commands say that either may be introduced; this is unacceptable, since the programmer must be given control over which triangle is to be drawn.

One solution to this problem (the first that I tried) is to allow a fifth predicate, CC(x, y, z), which asserts that points x, y, and z are counter-clockwise. Then the constraints on e in the last command could be extended with CC(a, b, e) (to get the triangle shown in the illustration of Euclid's construction), or with CC(a, e, b) (to get the other triangle). Unfortunately, while the predicates CONG, PARA, HOR and VER translate into polynomial equality constraints on the coordinates of the points, the predicate CC translates into a polynomial inequality constraint. I tried to use a hybrid of the simplex and Newton-Raphson methods to handle these inequalities, but it didn't work very well.

Here is a better solution: since the behavior of a numerical solver depends on the initial trial solution, Juno allows the program to give the solver a hint about where to look for the solution. The syntax LET x == u | P IN A END means the same thing as LET x | P IN A END, but it hints to the solver that the solution for x is likely to be in the vicinity of u. The "==" may be read "approximately equal to". No formal semantics can be given without describing the detailed behavior of the constraint solver, but from an operational point of view this is an obvious interface to a numerical solver.

The notation (x, y) can be used to specify an absolute position in the Cartesian plane, but it is almost always better to specify a position relative to a coordinate system determined by given image points. So, the notation (x, y) REL (p, q) denotes the point whose coordinates are the real numbers x and y in the coordinate system determined by the points p and q as follows: p is the origin of the coordinate system and q is the point (1, 0), that is, the tip of the unit x-vector. The rest of the coordinate system is determined by the condition that it be orthonormal and right-handed. Using complex arithmetic, (x, y) REL (p, q) can be defined to be p + (x + iy)(q - p).

Putting this all together, we finally obtain the following Juno program for drawing an equilateral triangle on the segment ab, such that the new vertex e will make abe counterclockwise:

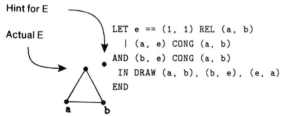

```
        LET e == (1, 1) REL (a, b)
           | (a, e) CONG (a, b)
        AND (b, e) CONG (a, b)
           IN DRAW (a, b), (b, e), (e, a)
        END
```

If "(1, 1)" were changed to "(1, -1)" (or to any point in the bottom half-plane), then the triangle abe would come out clockwise.

In summary, here is the syntax for constraint commands, in which the quotes in the first production are intended to prevent "such that" from being read as the BNF "or":

```
Command ::= ...
   | LET LocalList "|" Constraints
     IN Command
     END
   | ...

LocalList ::= Local | LocalList , Local

Local ::= Point == (Number, Number)
                REL (Point, Point)

Constraints ::= Constraint
              | Constraints AND Constraint

Constraint ::= HOR (Point, Point)
             | VER(Point, Point)
             | (Point, Point) CONG (Point, Point)
             | (Point, Point) PARA (Point, Point)
             | TRUE
```

Any state solves the constraint TRUE; hence if it is the only constraint, the hints will become the initial positions of the local variables. For example, here is a program to draw a square on ab:

```
LET c == (1, 1) REL (a, b)
   , d == (0, 1) REL (a, b)
   | TRUE
   IN DRAW (a, b), (b, c), (c, d), (d, a)
END
```

Procedures. No complications are created by Juno procedures, since the only data-type is point, and there are no side-effects on points. (All side-effects are on the anonymous global image.) The syntax is:

```
Command ::= ... | ProcName(PointList)

ProcDef ::= ProcName(PointList): Command

ProcName ::= a symbolic name
```

For example, here is a Juno procedure for trisecting an angle. More precisely, given points b and e equally distant from a given point a, the procedure draws two segments ac and ad which trisect the angle bae and have the same length as ab and ae:

```
Trisect(b, a, e):
   LET c == (.3, 0) REL (b, e)
     , d == (.6, 0) REL (b, e)
      | (b, c) CONG (c, d) AND (c, d) CONG (d, e)
   AND (a, c) CONG (a, b) AND (a, d) CONG (a, b)
     IN DRAW (a, c); Draw (a, d)
   END
```

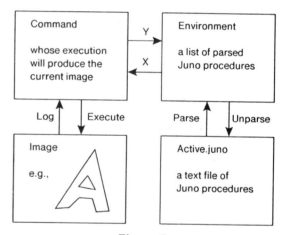

Figure 3.

The interactive system

The overall structure of the Juno system is shown in Figure 3. The state of the system is determined by the *procedural context*, which is a list of parsed Juno procedures (called the environment in the figure), and the *current command*, which is a Juno command of a particular form to be described later. The user views this state through two windows on the display screen; one (the *text window*) contains the pretty-printed (or "unparsed") text for each of the procedures in the environment, and the other (the *image window*) displays the image that results from executing the current command. The user changes the state by pointing into the windows with a mouse and clicking or typing.

The text window is essentially a conventional what-you-see-is-what-you-get editor. After editing the text, the user triggers the "Reparse" command with the mouse, which regenerates the internal list of parsed procedures from the current text and simultaneously pretty-prints the procedures in the window. Caching at the procedure level is used to speed up the reparsing. If a parse error occurs, the region of the error is highlighted on the display.

The image window is used for implicit editing: the user specifies editing operations in terms of the displayed result, and the system translates them into modifications to the text of the current command. Eventually, the current command can be installed in the environment as a procedure.

```
LET c == (.6, .6) REL (SW, SE)
  , a == (.1, .5) REL (SW, SE)
  | TRUE
  IN LET b == (.2, 0) REL (SW, SE)
       , d == (.7, .1) REL (SW, SE)
       | (a, c) PARA (b, d)
    AND (a, c) CONG (b, d)
    AND (a, d) CONG (b, c)
    AND (a, c) CONG (c, d)
     IN Circle(c, d)
      ; DRAW(c, d, a, b)
      ; DRAW(b, d)
      ; YellowSubmarine(a, c)
    END
END
```

Figure 4.

For example, Figure 4 shows a current command on the right and the corresponding image on the left. The four labeled dots in the image are for reference purposes only and would not appear on the screen. The conventional variables SW and SE represent the southwest and southeast corners of the window in which the image is to be drawn.[3]

Note the constraints of the command in Figure 4:

that (a, c) is parallel to (b, d), i.e., that acdb is a trapezoid;

that (a, c) is congruent to (b, d), i.e., that the trapezoid is a parallelogram;

that (a, d) is congruent to (b, c), i.e., that the parallelogram is a rectangle;

that (a, c) is congruent to (c, d), i.e., that the rectangle is a square.

The two calls to DRAW produce the straight and curved lines that appear in the image. We assume that the procedural context includes the procedure Circle(c, d), which draws a circle centered at c through d, and YellowSubmarine(a, c), which draws a yellow submarine with its snout at a and its tail at c.

The general syntax for the current command is:

```
CurrentCommand
  ::= LET LocalList "|" TRUE
      IN LET LocalList "|" Constraints
      IN CommandList
      END
  END

CommandList ::= PaintingCommand
              | PaintingCommand ; CommandList

PaintingCommand ::= DRAW Path | ProcCall
```

The points in the outer LocalList are called "independent points"; the points in the inner LocalList are called "dependent points". This is because the positions of the independent points are fixed by the outer LET; the positions of the dependent points are set by the inner LET to satisfy the constraints. Note that the syntax of the current command excludes mode changes; this restriction simplifies implicit editing. In summary, the current command is determined by a list of independent points, a list of dependent points, a conjunction of constraints, and a list of painting commands.

When the system needs to update the image on the display, it clears the image and executes the current command. There is a wrinkle: the solution found by the solver is used to replace all the hints, so if the current command is executed again, the hints will specify an exact solution. Note that this only changes the hints for the dependent points. Thus the update operation establishes a state in which the hints satisfy the constraints.

From an n-dimensional geometric point of view, the solution set of the constraints is a real variety (a generalized curve or surface) in Cartesian n-space, the hints specify a point in n-space, and the update operation moves the point onto the variety, without changing any coordinate of any independent point. The hint for a point is sometimes called its "current position".

As in many drawing programs, different cursors are used for different operations. Figure 5 lists the Juno cursors and their functions. A user editing operation begins when the user "picks up" one of the cursors by pointing at its icon on the screen.

The user then specifies the argument list for the operation, which is a PointList: a sequence of point variables occurring in the current command. This is done by pointing and clicking. A click with the middle mouse button adds to the argument list the name of the point closest to the cursor; a click with the left button creates a new point at the position of the cursor and includes this new point in the argument list. In other words, a new name is chosen and inserted into the dependent point list of the current command, with the cursor's position as its hint. The name of the point is not displayed in the image, although this feature would sometimes be useful.

Finally, the user hits the escape key to apply the operation associated with the current cursor to the sequence of arguments specified. An n-ary operation is applied to the most recent n arguments specified. For example, if the last four arguments specified were p, q, r, and s, with s the most recent, then the effect of hitting escape while holding the various cursors is:

Horizontal T-square. Add HOR(r, s) to the constraint of the current command.

Vertical T-square. Add VER(r, s) to the constraint of the current command.

Compass. Add (p, q) CONG (r, s) to the constraint of the current command.

Parallel bars. Add (p, q) PARA (r, s) to the constraint of the current command.

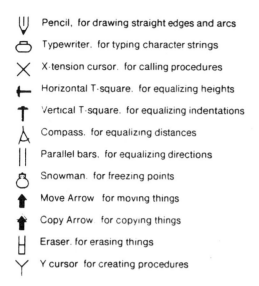

‖	Pencil, for drawing straight edges and arcs
⊖	Typewriter. for typing character strings
✕	X-tension cursor. for calling procedures
⊢	Horizontal T-square. for equalizing heights
⊤	Vertical T-square. for equalizing indentations
⋀	Compass. for equalizing distances
‖	Parallel bars. for equalizing directions
⛄	Snowman. for freezing points
↑	Move Arrow. for moving things
⬆	Copy Arrow. for copying things
⊟	Eraser. for erasing things
Y	Y cursor. for creating procedures

Figure 5.

Pencil. If no escapes have been typed since the user entered the argument q, then add DRAW(p, q, r, s) to the current command. Otherwise add DRAW(r, s) to the current command. (Although this is complicated to describe, it is simple to use.)

X cursor. This cursor is used to add to the current command a call to any procedure in the context. To pick up this cursor, the user must specify one of the procedures in the current context. The number of arguments of the procedure determines the number of arguments the X cursor will use from the sequence.

Move arrow. Change r's position to coincide with s's position, then replace all occurrences of s with r in the constraints and commands, and eliminate the point s from whichever LocalList it occurs in. (This can be used to "weld" two existing points together, but more commonly r is an existing point and s is a new point created by left-clicking, and it is desirable to eliminate it after r has been moved.)

Snowman. If s is independent, make it dependent, and vice versa.[4] (The cursor is a snowman because independent points were originally called frozen points. While the user holds the snowman, the independent points are highlighted.)

For example, to produce the image of Figure 4 starting from a blank screen, the user would execute the following instructions (in which $ means hit escape, x means click near point x with the middle button, X means click near point x with the left button, and [P] means click the procedure P in the text window):

- With the Pencil: DBACd
- With the X: [Circle] cd$ [YellowSubmarine] ac$
- With the Parallel bars: acbd$
- With the Compass: acbdcdadbc$
- With the Snowman: ca

Note that a point is left-clicked at its first occurrence (to create it) and middle-clicked thereafter. Note also how the last argument(s) of an operation are re-used as the first argument(s) of the next operation, in the case of the pencil and compass.

It is remarkable how much easier it is to construct procedures by "drawing" them in this way than by typing them. Fewer user actions are required (in this case, 40 clicks or keystrokes instead of more than 300 keystrokes), but the important factor is avoiding the burden of names. **For example, to constrain four points to bound three equal arcs of a circle centered about a fifth point is easy when the points are laid out before you and the constraints are applied by pointing.** But if the points are named b, c, d, e, and a respectively and the constraints must be specified in terms of the names, as was the case when this problem came up in the Trisect procedure, then more concentration is required to avoid errors.

Operations performed by the user with the Pencil and X cursor are reflected immediately in the image, because they can be executed incrementally. (Note that the commands inserted by these cursors are added at the end rather than the beginning of the command list in the current command.) The Move operation also causes the screen to be updated, although this cannot be done incrementally. Operations that add constraints do not cause the image to be updated unless the user explicitly requests it, by typing escape twice instead of once. This is because constraints are conveniently entered in batches.

To adjust the size, position, and orientation of the image on the screen, the Move arrow is used to move the independent points to whatever positions are desired, say, X and Y:

- With the Move arrow: aXbY ...

The move commands are repeated until the image looks right.

It is also possible to select a group of points by drawing a balloon around them, and then to erase, move, copy, or transform the group by a linear transformation. But these operations will not be described.

Another example is shown in Figure 6. The sequence of clicks shown in the right of the figure produces the image; it takes an experienced user only a few seconds. The independent points are a, c, l, and m: moving a up and down will adjust the height of the letter, moving m left and right will adjust the width of the letter, and moving l left and right will adjust the boldness of the letter, that is, the width of its strokes.

Figure 7 illustrates a common kind of construction: two cubic Bezier arcs are constrained to be symmetric around a vertical axis, by the obvious constraints on their control points. After entering the constraints, the control points are adjusted interactively until the curve looks right. The instructions in the figure call for adjusting u, leaving it to the solver to move its mirror image q. Alternatively, the user could freeze q, u, r, t, and s and adjust v, leaving it to the solver to move p; or freeze the upper four points and move t, leaving it to the solver to move both r and s.

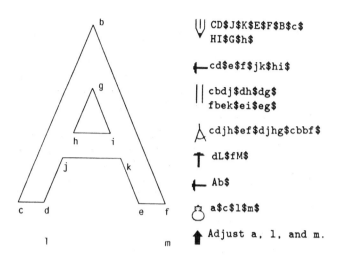

CDJKEFBc$
HIGh$

cd$e$fjkhi$

cbdjdhdg$
fbekeieg$

cdjhefdjhg$cbbf$

dLfM

Ab$

aclm

Adjust a, l, and m.

Figure 6.

Using a WYSIWYG constraint solver is effective and fun, but there are several pitfalls that an uninitiated user can fall into. Two examples: If b and c are near one another and far from a, then the constraint (a, b) PARA (a, c) is more stable than (a, b) PARA (b, c), even though they are equivalent geometrically: if the user makes a long segment parallel to a short segment, the solver tends to collapse the short segment to a point. Also, redundant constraints, though usually harmless, will sometimes prevent the solver from converging. I learned this when, miscounting degrees of freedom, I tried to make a regular pentagon by specifying equality of length for its sides and for four (rather than three) of its chords. These pitfalls are easily learned and avoided; perhaps both of them would go away if more attention were paid to the solver.

For simple images like those in Figures 6 and 7, the update operation is immediate (less than a second). Since the cost of solving a system of equations is very roughly proportional to the cube of the number of constraints, the only hope for handling large images is to introduce a hierarchy, making lots of small problems instead of one big one. The Juno language provides a satisfactory hierarchy. For example, the constraint solving problem in Figure 4 has four constraints on the two unknown points b and d; a simple system. Dozens of other constraint problems must be solved inside the procedures Circle and YellowSubmarine, but neither the local variables of these procedures nor the constraints that initialize them are of any relevance to the outer-level problem of determining b and d.

(An interesting programming problem is to somehow employ caching to further speed the update process. For complicated images, this might improve performance dramatically.)

Since the instructions for drawing Figure 4 require that the environment already contain procedures for drawing circles and yellow submarines, hierarchical drawings must be built from the bottom up. The Y cursor is used to in-

sert the text of the current command into the environment as a procedure, whence it can be invoked by the X cursor. The independent points of the current command become parameters to the procedure, and the hints for the positions of the dependent points are expressed in a coordinate system determined by the independent points, instead of in the (SW, SE) coordinate system.

For example, if the Y cursor were used to make a procedure called P out of the current command illustrated in Figure 4, the result would be

```
P(a, c):
    LET b == (0, -1) REL (a, c)
      , d == (1, -1) REL (a, c)
    | ...
    IN ...
```

The constraints and painting commands are as before. The introduction of hints for b and d that are relative to a and c is crucial, since if, in a future call to P(a, c), the constraints were solved with randomly initialized b and d, the nonlinear solver might fail to find the solution.

In order that there be no ambiguity about the coordinate system, the Y cursor won't create a procedure with more than two parameters. Thus to "draw" the Trisect procedure, the user would create it with the two arguments b and e, since it is most natural and stable to specify the hints for c and d in the be coordinate system. After creating the procedure with the Y cursor, the user would edit the procedure in the Juno text file, inserting a as an argument and deleting it from the list of locals. This awkwardness should have been avoided by enriching the interactive editing system with a command that specifies, for a dependent point, the pair of independent points relative to which the point's hint is to be specified.

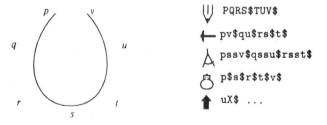

PQRS$$TUV$

pvqurs$t$

pssv$qssu$rsst$

psrtv$

uX$ ...

Figure 7.

Conclusions

Since the Cedar system is not widely available, Juno has been used only by a few researchers. Also, the Juno project was interrupted when I left PARC. However, even from this unconcluded project, the general conclusion can be drawn: implicit editing with geometric constraints is a workable technique for constructing a programmable WYSIWYG system. Perhaps the best way to be more specific is to describe the things that a Juno user comes to yearn for.

Juno allows the abstraction of commands into parameterized procedures, but not the abstraction of constraints into parameterized predicates, which would also be useful. For example, instead of using twelve clicks to constrain abc to be a right angle, it would be convenient to apply a predicate defined by some expression such as

```
      Right(a, b, c)
  == (EXISTS d == (1, 1) REL (a, b, c)
         : (a, b) CONG (c, d)
      AND (b, c) CONG (d, a)
      AND (a, c) CONG (b, d))
```

(The triple (a, b, c) is used to denote the skewed coordinate system in which b = (0, 0), a = (1, 0), and c = (0, 1).) As another example, consider the constraint that a point e lie on the cubic spline with Bezier control points a, b, c, and d. Although the geometric form of this constraint is well-known, it is rather challenging to click it into Juno; John Warnock was the first to do it. It is unthinkable that it would be used frequently unless it were abstracted into a parameterized predicate. (Both of these examples suggest the interesting problem of optimizing predicates by symbolic algebraic transformations to eliminate unnecessary existentially quantified variables.)

The greatest inconvenience in using Juno is that there is no way to select a procedure body from the environment and install it as the current command for editing in WYSI-WYG mode. (There is no good reason for this restriction.) Note, however, that many procedure bodies do not satisfy the syntax for current commands, and liberalizing this syntax requires rethinking the implicit editing user interface. For example, if the nesting level of LETs is n instead of two, then instead of independent and dependent points there is a general hierarchy of dependence; this cannot be controlled by the simple snowman interface. Ideally, a natural user interface would be found for implicit editing of an arbitrary command.

There would be great leverage in extending Juno's universe of values. For example, the graph in Figure 1 required a procedure BarGraph12, which drew a 12-bar graph given two points to determine a baseline and twelve points to determine the heights of the bars. After calling BarGraph12 from the current command, the heights of the bars were adjusted in WYSIWYG mode. It would be nicer to write a procedure BarGraphN, taking a list of points, but this would require extending Juno's universe of values to include lists of points.

Some reflection suggests that the appropriate universe is the smallest set containing the real numbers and closed under the formation of ordered pairs, since this includes points, lists of points, and more; and the natural class of primitive constraints on the set is easy to solve. However, the implicit editing problem for this universe seems completely open-ended.

Acknowledgements

To the programmers of Cedar and Cedar graphics, for making the marvels that Juno needed; to Jim Sasaki, for programming Juno's special parser generator; to Donna Auguste, for programming the interpreter for the first version of the language; to Rick Beach, Hania Gajewska, Lyle Ramshaw, Maureen Stone, and the many others who helped in this long, drawn-out project; my heart-felt thanks.

Caveats

1. The actual units are screen pixels.
2. The actual syntax uses IF, ->, and FI instead of LET, IN, and END.
3. Instead of SW and SE, absolute coordinates are used at the outer level.
4. Since the snowman takes only one argument, hitting escape is not necessary.

References

[1] P. C. Baudelaire. Draw Manual. *Alto User's Handbook*, Xerox Corp., Palo Alto, CA, 1979. Referenced by [10].

[2] Alan Borning. Thinglab — a constraint-oriented simulation laboratory. SSL-79-3, Xerox PARC, Palo Alto, CA, July 1979.

[3] S. D. Conte and Carl de Boor. *Elementary Numerical Analysis*. McGraw-Hill, 1972.

[4] Euclid. *The Thirteen Books of the Elements*. Tr. by Thomas L. Heath, Dover, 1956.

[5] Edsger W. Dijkstra. *A Discipline of Programming*. Prentice-Hall, 1976.

[6] Donald E. Knuth. TeX and METAFONT. Digital Press, 1979.

[7] Bruce Lucas. Private communication, February 1985.

[8] Ivan Sutherland. *Sketchpad, A Man-Machine Graphical Communication System*. PhD thesis, MIT, January, 1963.

[9] Warren Teitelman. The Cedar Programming Environment: A Midterm Report and Examination. SL-83-11, Xerox PARC, Palo Alto, CA, June 1984.

[10] Christopher J. Van Wyk. A high-level language for specifying pictures. *Transactions on Graphics*, v. 1 no. 2, April 1982.

Reprinted from *IEEE Proceedings Workshop on Visual Languages*, 1988, pages 137-143. Copyright © 1988 by The Institute of Electrical and Electronics Engineers, Inc. All rights reserved.

MPL—A Graphical Programming Environment for Matrix Processing Based on Logic and Constraints

Ricky Yeung

Department of Computer Science
University of Washington
Seattle, WA 98195

Abstract

The matrix is a commonly used two-dimensional data structure. On a two-dimensional display, 2-D data structures are more suitable for visualization than other linear structures such as lists. This paper describes a graphical programming environment for processing matrices, called MPL, in which matrices are integrated graphically as parts of the program. The system demonstrates that several ideas from programming language research—constraints, logic programming, and functionals—can be combined with visual programming techniques to form an efficient mixed graphical-textual notation. It also provides a new framework for expressing and prototyping matrix related algorithms.

1 Motivation

Graphics has a growing role to play in programming. Many different paradigms have been proposed, such as text-free and/or keyboardless iconic programming (e.g. Pict [1], HI-VISUAL [2], and MSTL [3]), programming by demonstrative examples (e.g. PAD [4], Programming by Rehearsal [5], and ThinkPad [6]), and direct manipulation interfaces [7]. It is not unfounded to predict that in the end, many things done today will be replaced by direct manipulation systems [8], programming by demonstration interfaces (e.g. [9]), text-free and/or keyboardless iconic systems, etc. But one thing for sure is that we will still have conventional programming. It is a challenge to the visual programming researchers to incorporate graphics into the existing programming languages. In fact, two of the six open problems facing graphical programming environments raised by Glinert [10] are: "Establishment of a 'graphical vocabulary' for interactive graphical programming environments" and "development of novel and uniform representations of a mixed textual-graphical nature for programs, data types and structures." While designing such graphical notations, we should also take into consideration of the ideas from programming language research (e.g. constraints and logic programming) because they will have significant impact on programming languages and should be reflected.

First, let us look at some of the general problems with the existing visual programming systems.

Some Problems with Existing Systems

One of the purposes of using graphics in programming is to substitute some of the text with some more natural, easy-to-understand means of expression. However, as pointed out by Myers [11], many visual programming systems employ visual representations that are physically much larger than the text they replace. For example, some systems require the user to draw several boxes and arrows to express a simple arithmetic expression. Many programmers (not end-users) will find it too tedious for any real work. This can be viewed as the problem of inefficient graphical notation. Another common problem is that many systems offer very hard to understand static representations, such as flowcharts, diagrams with excessive use of arrows or crossing lines, and so on. Moreover, most of the existing systems have no place for graphical comments.

Readable representations and efficient graphical notations are the main concerns of our study.

Control and Data Structures

A program is mainly composed of two parts: control and data. Many efforts have been stressed on making the control structures visible, for examples, SDD [12], GreenPrint [13], PIGS [14], PECAN [15], and PC-TILES [16]. There are relatively few attempts to integrate data structures into textual programs graphically, with few exceptions such as AMBIT/L [17] and PLAN2D [18]. They both are for the description and manipulation of pointers. Arrow lines are employed to show the pointers. For program segment involved with many pointers, the picture could get complicated. That is probably the reason why Myers [11] says their static representations are hard to understand. Nonetheless, from the recent success in program animation and visualization research (e.g. Animus [19], VIPS [20], BALSA [21], PV [22], Incense [23], and VISAL [24]), we have learned that making the data structures visible is one of the keys to the understanding of programs. Our approach is to concentrate on data visualization: properly present the graphical representations of the data structures to the programmers throughout the programming cycle.

However, many data structures like lists are linear in nature; displaying them in 2-D fashion may not benefit the programmers. On the other hand, data structures like matrices that are truly two-dimensional (have unique properties such as random access) may be more suitable to express on the 2-D display.

We will restrict our focus on integrating the 2-D structure matrix into a textual programming system. We wish to develop an efficient graphical notation while not sacrificing the readability. Through this study, we hope to develop some methodology or techniques that will lead to the answers to some of the funda-mental issues.

2   Description of MPL

MPL is an integrated programming environment which includes an editor, an interpreter and a debugger. It provides a set of graphical notation for the description and manipulation of matrices. One of its design goals is to provide a high level efficient graphical notation for the programmer to express matrix related algorithms. It is efficient in the sense that many attributes, relationships, and structures can be readily seen from the two-dimensional graphics.

In the current implementation, MPL is fully integrated into a constraint logic programming system called CLP [25] [26]. CLP of Heintze et. al. is a superset of Prolog capable of solving arithmetic constraints (e.g. a set of simultaneous linear equations).

The main ideas employed by MPL are:

1. Unification (pattern matching + logical variables).

2. Positional constraints.

3. Structural graphical clues.

4. Non-procedural graphical iterators.

5. Associating structures with graphical textures.

2.1   Extending the Prolog Ideas

The first three ideas are borrowed from Prolog and extended to the matrix structures.

In the Prolog list [27], say [a,b|T] (it is a short-hand notation for (a.(b.T))), T denotes a logical variable which can be unified (matched) with the rest of the list. a is the first element, b is the second, and T represents a list which contains either zero elements or elements from the third to the last one in the list. One can find out these pieces of information by looking at the positions of those elements in the list. These are referred to as positional constraints.

Let us consider another list [H|T]. H and T represent an element and a list, respectively. They both are variables but have different meanings. One can tell by the graphical clues provided: a variable to the left of the vertical bar in the list denotes a unit element, while a variable immediately following a "|" represents a structure. These structural graphical clues provide the means to distinguish structures from unit elements.

These ideas together permit the programmers to manipulate the data structures without explicit selectors or constructors, such as CAR, CDR, and CONS in LISP. Warren and Pereira [28] have argued that pattern matching is a better way to pass parameters. When extending these ideas into matrices, we will see their argument is further supported.

2.2   The Basic Building Blocks

In MPL, a matrix consists of one enclosing rectangle and any number of non-overlapping sub-rectangles (sub-rect for short). Each sub-rect can have an optional label (can be constant, variable, or arithmetic expression as permitted by CLP) and an optional graphical texture. There are three kinds of sub-rects: the solid line sub-rects (solid sub-rects), the dotted line sub-rects (generic sub-rects), and the diagonal sub-rects. A solid sub-rect denotes a unit element, while a generic and diagonal sub-rect denote structures (can be empty). In Figure 1, S is a solid sub-rect, G is a generic sub-rect, and D is a diagonal sub-rect. Normally in a diagonal sub-rect, the super-diagonal and sub-diagonal are not drawn. The label of a solid sub-rect represents the value of the unit element. If the label of a generic sub-rect or a diagonal is a logical variable, it represents that sub-structure, in a manner similar to that of the logical variable T in the Prolog list example in the previous section; if it is not a variable, then every element in the sub-structure will be unified with this value (it is possible to represent this value by a variable: in the diagrams, a variable in bold face means it is a structural variable; otherwise it means every element in the sub-structure will have the value of that variable).

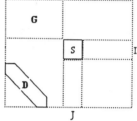

Figure 1: Example of an MPL Matrix

Each sub-rect has four index attributes: starting row (RS), ending row (RE), starting column (CS), and ending column (CE). For a sub-rect r, we will use $r.RS$ to denote its starting row, and so on. For the solid sub-rect $r, r.RS = r.RE$, and $r.CS = r.CE$. Besides, these four attributes are governed by the relative position of the sub-rect, or positional constraints. For example, in Figure 1, the sub-rect G is on the left-upper most corner in the matrix; therefore $G.RS = 1$ and $G.CS = 1$. The right-bottom corner of G touches the left-top corner of S, so $G.RE+1 = S.RS$, and $G.CE + 1 = S.CS$. Other situations are similar.

If any side of a generic or solid sub-rect overlaps with some side of its bounding matrix, an index label (*side index*) could be given. Side indices are displayed outside the matrix to distinguish from the sub-rect labels. If a sub-rect a has a north or south side index j, then $a.CS = a.CE = j$; if it has an east or west side index i, then $a.RS = a.RE = i$. For instance, the south side index of the sub-rect right below S in Figure 1 is J. Note that the 2-D nature of matrices allows us to directly address the elements in the graphical notation, for instance, in Figure 1, we can tell that S is on the I-th row, J-th column in the matrix. Linear structures like lists do not offer this convenience.

Optional labels and textures can be given to the sub-diagonal and super-diagonal in a diagonal sub-rect.

Let us give a simple MPL example. Shown in Figure 2 is a program to test if two row vectors are the reverses of each other.

The first clause says if both matrices are 1×1 and contain the same element, then *reverse* is true. The second clause says two matrices are reverse of each other if the first element of the first matrix is equal to the last element of the second matrix, and the reverse of the sub-rect T is R. Notice that for the sub-rect T, $T.RS = T.RE = 1$, $T.CS = 2$, and $T.CE = $ *number of columns in the matrix*. A similar relationship holds for R. These relations can be readily seen from the graphics.

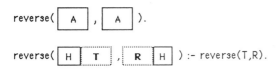

Figure 2: Reverse a Row-Vector.

2.3 Iteration

Specification for repetition of operations and data is an important part of a computer program. Most programming languages provide looping constructs to achieve repetition of operations. Quite often, however, loops are used mainly to accomplish the following two tasks:

- assigning values to a specific set of elements in a structure;

- selecting (accessing) a set of elements in a structure.

By providing graphical means to do these tasks, explicit looping constructs (recursion in Prolog) can be avoided in many cases.

Graphical textures and/or colors can be used for expressing associations of sub-rects into groups (textures are used in the current implementation of MPL). Different sub-rects could be painted with the same graphical texture and grouped together to form a new sub-structure. A value label can be used to achieve the first kind of repetition.

Other kinds of looping are permitted through two types of non-procedural graphical iterators. The first kind is similar to the apply-to-all operator in a functional language [29]. You can specify a predicate relationship to be tested over all the elements inside a sub-structure. During execution, the predicate will receive the entire matrix as a parameter along with the information to tell which sub-rect is of current interest. This differs from the normal apply-to-all operator which always applies the operation to all the elements in the structure. However, predicates such as that to find the maximum element or that to sum all the values in a matrix cannot be easily implemented by this kind of iterator.

A second category of iterators is needed which could provide the capability to do accumulation. It could be similar to the first kind of iterator, but the programmer needs to specify the relationship between the old and the new values of the accumulation variable. This would be roughly equivalent to the reduction operator in a functional language [29].

2.4 The Environment

A programmer creates programs (Prolog clauses) with a modified text editor, in which matrices can be manipulated like ordinary text objects. Consequently, their graphical representations can be included in the comments just like text. Inside the matrix, one can draw, move, resize, delete, duplicate, paint, and label the sub-rects. Having created the program, the programmer calls up the MPL translator to compile the diagrams into first-order Prolog predicates. Since Prolog distinguishes input and execution mode, after the translation, the programmer needs to set up an inquiry clause for the execution. The output is shown in the Output window. Figure 3 shows a scenario of the execution (see the next section for more detail). In the figure, the debugger is being called and the programmer is stepping through his program. For the output lines with the heading ' m n >TRY ...', the first number tells which rule the system is trying, and the second number tells the level of the current execution. The matrices are displayed graphically and the current *iterating* element is in reverse-video. We will take a closer look at MPL by presenting some examples in the next section.

3   More MPL Examples

Pascal Triangle

Figure 3 shows an example which uses the graphical iterator mentioned in the previous section. This program computes the Pascal (or binomial coefficients) triangle (for us it is actually a square since we zero-fill the other half). It is not hard to see that the following relationship will be true for all the elements from the second row, second column to the last row, last column: the value of each element is equal to the sum of the element above it and the one in the previous row and the previous column. Let us call this relationship *sumUp2*. The first clause in the *biCo2* window in Figure 3 shows this predicate written in MPL. The sub-rect X is blackened to denote the element of interest. This is a hint to instruct the system to unify the current *iterating* element with X. The sub-rect in the second clause with a scanning icon means the predicate *sumUp2* will be tested on those elements row by row, from left to right, and each of them will become the *iterating* element. Although the order of iteration does not affect the logical meaning of the program, the programmer can specify the order of iteration (e.g. from bottom to top, column by column, etc.) to gain extra efficiency. The diagram tells us that the first column of A contains all 1's (because the north-side index forces it to be a single-column sub-rect), and the first row starting from the second through the last columns contains all 0's. The 'A:' tells the system that the following matrix is actually the matrix A.

To execute, we have to set up an inquiry. It is shown on the small window at the lower-left corner. From the diagram we can tell the matrix is 4×4 because the last row, last column element has both east and south side indices 4. The elements of the matrix in the inquiry are initially unbounded. The Output window shows the output produced by the debugger.

Computing Determinants

The next example is on computing the determinant of a matrix. We first compute the cofactor for each element in the first row,

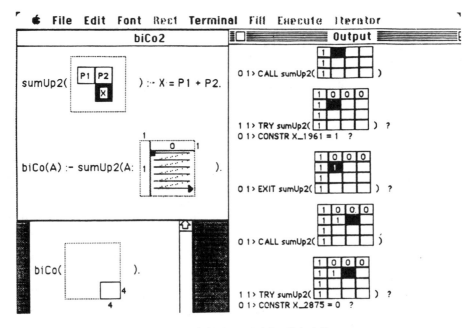

Figure 3: Execution of the Binomial Coefficient Program.

and then sum them up to get the determinant (see Figure 4). The cofactors are stored in the array C. In the third clause (*cofactor* in Figure 4) we can see that $S1$ and $S2$ are combined together to form a new matrix. This is done graphically without calling any explicit selection or construction procedures. Figure 5 shows a snapshot of the execution (running under the debugger) with the query clause in the *Untitled 1* window.

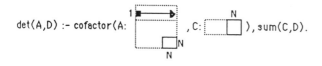

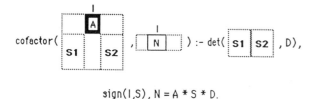

sign(I,S), N = A * S * D.

Figure 4: The Determinant Program.

The N-Queens Problem

The last example is the N-Queens problem which states that we

want to place N queens on an $N \times N$ chess-board such that every queen is safe, that is, no two queens are on the same row, same column or same diagonals. We use a 'q' to represent a queen, and an 'x' to denote an unoccupied space on the board. Figure 6(a) shows a possible MPL solution to the problem. The *safe* predicate says that for the row of current interest, there exists an element which has the value 'q' and all other elements in the same row, same column and same diagonals have the value 'x'. The added column is just for iteration purpose because we are only interested in the current row. Since the iterator we are using is from top to bottom, we can take advantage of it to save the system some effort in the matching process by omitting all the sub-structures below the row of current interest in the *safe* predicate (Figure 6(b)). This example also demonstrates the use of graphical textures.

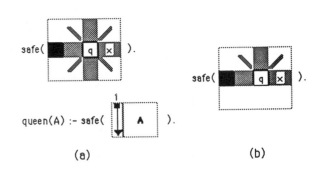

(a)　　　　　　　(b)

Figure 6: (a) The N-Queens Problem Solution. (b) Taking Advantage of the Order of Iteration.

If one were to rewrite the MPL examples in another language

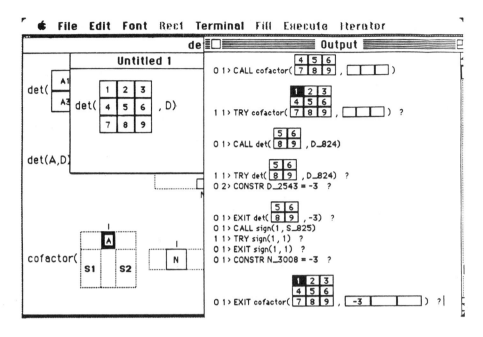

Figure 5: Execution of the Determinant Program.

(for instance, straight Prolog), one could expect to see that MPL saves quite a few lines of code. More importantly, MPL programs maintain the declarative characteristics as straight Prolog programs do. The "reversible programming" property [27] is preserved, too. For example, a matrix multiplication predicate, $times(A, B, C)$, can be used to compute the inverse of the matrix A, by making C equal to the identity matrix and B unbound.

The MPL notation is intended to allow the programmer to easily translate the problem specification to an executable program. This is particularly useful for rapid prototyping.

4   Implementation Notes

In this section, we will briefly describe the current implementation of MPL. The current MPL is built as an extension to the constraint logic programming system CLP [26]. MPL is implemented on the Macintosh Plus [1] computer and written in Lightspeed Pascal[2]. It communicates with the CLP system (which runs on a VAX with ultrix[3]) through the serial port. The implementation of diagonals and reduction iterators are not yet complete.

A matrix is implemented as a list of lists. We have developed a Prolog library to support the predicates that allow accessing individual elements, rows, columns, or sub-matrices of a matrix, assigning (unifying) values to sub-structures, etc. They can take unbound parameters; therefore reversible computation such as the matrix multiplication example can be performed. The MPL translator generates these predicates to simulate the two-dimensional unification. Furthermore, the existing Prolog debug-

[1] Macintosh Plus is a trademark of Apple Computer, Inc.
[2] Lightspeed Pascal is a trademark of THINK Technologies, Inc.
[3] ultrix is a trademark of Digital Equipment Corporation

ger and tracer are modified to handle them and produce output recognizable by the MPL system for the display of the matrices.

MPL does not parse the diagrams because the interactive editor ensures the correctness of the input graphical syntax and stores the sub-rects in some appropriate internal format. During the translation, for each matrix, a directed acyclic graph is constructed from the sub- rects, and then a topological sort is performed to identify the indices of each sub-rect. The translator only needs to generate codes for the labeled sub-rects or sub-rects with the iterators as textures. A built-in constraint solver is used to solve the trivial constraints found during the indices identification process. As a result, the produced codes are more compact than they would otherwise be.

5   Summary and Future Directions

The MPL project demonstrates that several ideas from programming language research—constraints, functionals, and logic programming— can be combined with visual programming techniques to provide an efficient graphical notation for writing declarative programs. It also provides a visual framework for expressing matrix related algorithms. MPL is intended to shorten the gap between the specification and the coding processes so that prototyping can be done more rapidly.

The current implementation of MPL is not yet complete. Currently, attention is being paid to (1) development of a novel graphical representation for the graphical reduction operation, and (2) completion of the diagonal implementation.

Due to the non-overlapping nature of the sub-rects, some patterns are quite hard or awkward to construct, for example, the tridiagonal matrix in Figure 7(a). Therefore, a macro facility is being planned. It will allow the programmers to create their own sub-rects such as the one in Figure 7(b).

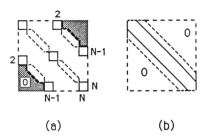

Figure 7: (a) A Tridiagonal Matrix. (b) A Possible Macro for (a).

Efficiency of MPL programs could be improved if true arrays were used to implement the matrices. That may require the development of a non-linear unification algorithm. In addition, the structure-sharing technique [28] might need to be extended to efficiently handle matrix composition and decomposition at run-time.

Another possible direction is to integrate the MPL notation into the existing spreadsheet systems. The MPL notation could be an alternative approach to the one described by Ambler [30].

Presently, MPL only displays the matrices graphically during the debugging phase. Other aspects such as the execution tree and the unification of arguments should also be visualized (as in the Transparent Prolog Machine of Eisenstadt and Brayshaw [31]) in coordination with the MPL matrices.

One interesting extension is to rewrite the MPL translator to generate codes for an imperative programming language like Modula-2, or Ada.

We intend to look into the possibility of applying the MPL ideas to other data structures, such as graphs.

References

[1] E. P. Glinert and S. L. Tanimoto. Pict: An Interactive Graphical Programming Environment. *IEEE Computer*, 17(11):7–25, 1984.

[2] M. Hirakawa, S. Iwata, I. Yosimoto, M. Tanaka, and T. Ichikawa. An Environment for HI-VISUAL Programming. In *1987 Workshop on Visual Languages*, pages 305–314, Linköping, Sweden, 1987.

[3] T. D. Kimura, J. W. Choi, and J. M. Mack. A Visual Language for Keyboardless Programming. Technical report, Computer Science Department, Washington University, St. Louis, March 1986.

[4] G. A. Curry. *Programming by Abstract Demonstration*. PhD thesis, Computer Science Department, University of Washington, 1978.

[5] W. Finzer and L. Gould. Programming by Rehearsal. *Byte*, 9(6):187–210, 1984.

[6] R. V. Rubin, E. J. Golin, and S. P. Reiss. ThinkPad: A Graphical System for Programming by Demonstration. *IEEE Software*, 2(2):73–79, 1985.

[7] B. Shneiderman. Direct Manipulation: A Step Beyond Programming Languages. *IEEE Computer*, 16(8):57–69, 1983.

[8] E. L. Hutchins, J. D. Hollan, and D. A. Norman. Direct Manipulation Interfaces. *Human-Computer Interaction*, 1:311–338, 1985.

[9] B. A. Myers. Creating Interaction Techniques by Demonstration. *IEEE Computer Graphics and Applications*, pages 51–60, 1987.

[10] E. P. Glinert. Interactive, Graphical Programming Environments: Six Open Problems and a Possible Partial Solution. In *COMPSAC '86*, pages 408–410. IEEE Computer Society, 1986.

[11] B. A. Myers. Visual Programming, Programming by Example, and Program Visualization: A Taxonomy. In *CHI'86 Conference Proceedings*, pages 59–66, Boston, April 1986.

[12] Y. Kanda and M. Sugimoto. Software Diagram Description: SDD and Its Application. In *Proceedings: Computer Software and Applications Conference*, pages 300–305, 1980.

[13] L. A. Belady, C. J. Evangelisti, and L. R. Power. Greenprint: A Graphic Representation of Structured Programs. *IBM Systems Journal*, 19(4):542–553, 1980.

[14] M. C. Pong and N. Ng. PIGS—A System for Programming with Interactive Graphical Support. *Software—Practice and Experience*, 13(9):847–855, 1983.

[15] S. P. Reiss. PECAN: Program Development Systems that Support Multiple Views. In *Proc. of the 7th International Conference on Software Engineering*, pages 324–333, 1984.

[16] E. P. Glinert and C. D. Smith. PC-TILES: A Visual Programming Environment for Personal Computers Based on the BLOX Methodology. Technical report, Rensselaer Polytechnic Institute, 1986.

[17] C. Christensen. An introduction to AMBIT/L, a diagrammatic language for list processing. In *Proceeding of the 2nd Symposium on Symbolic and Algebraic Manipulation*, pages 248–260, Los Angeles, 1971.

[18] E. Denert, R. Franck, and W. Streng. PLAN2D—Towards a Two-Dimensional Programming Language. In *Proceedings of the 4th Annual Meeting of the Gesellschaft fur Informatik, Berlin*, pages 202–213, 1974. Published by Springer-Verlag, Berlin, as Vol. 26 in the series "Lecture Notes in Computer Science".

[19] R. A. Duisberg. *Constraint-Based Animations: Temporal Constraints in the Animus System*. PhD thesis, Computer Science Dept., University of Washington, September 1986.

[20] S. Isoda, T. Shimomura, and Y. Ono. VIPS: A Visual Debugger. *IEEE Software*, pages 8–19, May 1987.

[21] M. H. Brown and R. Sedgewick. A System for Algorithm Animation. *Computer Graphics*, 18(3):177–186, 1984.

[22] C. F. Herot, G. P. Brown, R. T. Carling, and D. A. Kramlich. Program Visualization: Graphics Support for Software Development (The Final Report). Technical report, Computer Corporation of America, 1984.

[23] B. A. Myers. Incense: A System for Displaying Data Structures. *Computer Graphics*, 17(3):115–125, 1983.

[24] M. Caboara, E. I. Giannotti, and F. Ricci. An Interactive System for Displaying Data Structures on Personal Computers. In *Proceedings of the 8th ACM International Computing Symposium ICS-85*, March 1985.

[25] J. Jaffer and J. L. Lassez. Constraint Logic Programming. In *1987 Principles of Programming Languages Conference*. ACM, 1987.

[26] N. Heintze, J. Jaffar, C. S. Lim, S. M., P. Stuckey, R. Yap, and C. N. Yee. The CLP Programmer's Manual, Version 1.0. Technical report, Monash University, Australia, 1986.

[27] W. F. Clocksin and C. S. Mellish. *Programming in Prolog*. Springer-Verlag, New York, 1981.

[28] D. H. D. Warren, L. M. Pereira, and F. Pereira. Prolog - the Language and its Implementation compared with Lisp. In *Proceedings of ACM Symposium on Artificial Intelligence and Progamming Languages*, pages 109–115, New York, 1977.

[29] C. Ghezzi and M. Jazayeri. *Programming Language Concepts*. Wiley, New York, 1982.

[30] A. L. Ambler. Forms: Expanding the Visualness of Sheet Languages. In *1987 Workshop on Visual Languages*, pages 105–117, Linköping, Sweden, 1987.

[31] M. Eisenstadt and M. Brayshaw. The Transparent Prolog Machine (TPM): An Execution Model and Graphical Debugger for Logic Programming. Technical Report Technical Report No. 21a, Human Cognition Research Laboratory, The Open University, Milton Keynes, U.K., October 1987.

NoPumpG: Creating Interactive Graphics with Spreadsheet Machinery

Clayton Lewis

Department of Computer Science and
Institute of Cognitive Science
Campus Box 430
University of Colorado
Boulder, CO 80309
(303) 492-6657

Abstract

The spreadsheet has made computing power widely accessible to nonprogrammers. By adding a small number of new concepts to the basic spreadsheet framework, NoPumpG can create interactive graphics without the need for programming. The graphics can even incorporate animation, as seen in physics and geometry tutorial demonstrations. While not as powerful as other similar systems, NoPumpG offers a favorable balance between power and conceptual simplicity.

Introduction

Graphical representations of program structure may provide the flexible control of computing that programming provides, at less expense. We also must consider what underlying models of computation can do to provide the foundation for more accessible programming. There is a class of system which provides a graphical, or at least a two-dimensional, program representation, while embodying a comprehensible model of computation: the spreadsheet.

Spreadsheets have been given major credit for the microcomputer revolution by permitting non-literate computer-users to customize and use their own applications. Horowitz and Munson [1], addressing software engineers, note that the spreadsheet has brought many new users to computers, and it has produced a large gain in productivity. The spreadsheet possibly has done more to increase the accessibility of computing to the general public than any other development since FORTRAN.

The success of the spreadsheet and the robustness of its underlying concepts have made possible a number of extensions [2]. Businesses can readily produce a variety of graphics for reports and publications using spreadsheet programs. Extensions to provide access to database functions are available in a number of systems. The ASP system [3], is a spreadsheet that can operate on any Smalltalk data object, including bit images. Van Emden, Ohki, and Takeuchi [4] describe a spreadsheet interface to logic programming. Lewis [5] describes a spreadsheet capable of manipulating approximate quantities and relationships.

This paper describes extensions designed to permit a user to create and manipulate graphical objects by using a spreadsheet framework, capitalizing on the empirically proven success of the basic spreadsheet concept. The paper also demonstrates that the time and effort required to produce interactive graphics in traditional programming approaches can be reduced by the use of the spreadsheet framework.

The design of these extensions has been guided by the following principles:

Add as little as possible to the basic spreadsheet paradigm: The market shows that people can understand and use spreadsheets.

Provide low-level primitives from which larger structures can be built: Graphical toolkits, such as Pinball Construction Set [6], provide easy access only to specialized graphical components that can be used for specific functions (e.g. to build pinball machines).

Strive to support a wide range of sample applications: The examples presented in this paper are drawn from a number of different domains, including geometry and physics. Other potential applications, such as a simple flight simulator, have influenced the design. Features have been added to the design to support a sample application, provided the features appear to be of general value and to be easy to understand.

Don't try to do everything: The original spreadsheet represents a successful compromise between simplicity and power, delivering less power than available with traditional programming but with greater simplicity. In Gerhard Fischer's words, the "subjective computability" of spreadsheets is often greater than that of a traditional programming language, even if its "objective computability" is limited because people can understand what they are doing. Some problems encountered in extending the spreadsheet into new domains may prove resistant to any sufficiently simple approach and should not be attempted.

The extensions previously referred to are embodied in a prototype system called NoPumpG. While the interactions supported by the prototype are quite general, the practical applications to which they are most suited are tutorial demonstrations that permit students to view and manipulate physical or geometrical systems. A number of additional extensions for other applications, such as rapid development of user interfaces, are contemplated.

What are Spreadsheets, and What are Their Advantages?

For our purposes, a *spreadsheet* is a collection of cells, each of which can contain a value and a formula. A *formula* refers to one or more other cells and specifies how to compute a *value* using the values of those cells as arguments. The computed value becomes the value of the cell containing the formula. The value of a cell that has no formula can be entered or edited by the user. When the value of any cell changes, the values of any cells containing formulae referring to that cell are recomputed.

The simple scheme of a spreadsheet has profound

advantages, discussed more fully in Lewis and Olson [7]. The automatic propagation of changes permits the user to state dependencies among quantities without being concerned how the dependencies are enforced. The user also does not have to detect when changes occur, to decide what to do about them, or specify the order in which actions responding to changes will be taken, all of which are essential concerns in conventional programming.

Because the spreadsheet user does not need to specify how changes are processed, many of the concepts and mechanisms of procedural languages, such as flow of control, parameter passing, recursion, and similar difficult notions, are not needed.

The facts that values are always visible (or can be made visible by simple actions such as scrolling), and that values entered by the user can be modified at any time, eliminate the need to *pump* data back and forth across an opaque barrier separating the user from the program. Consider a program that adds numbers, written in a traditional language. The part of the program that does the desired computing, adding up numbers, is trivial. But the program has to include much more code to be useful. The user has data that must somehow be conveyed to the program. The user cannot simply give the program data and see results; rather, the program must include input and output code to do the required pumping. Further, once data have been conveyed to the program they are inaccessible to the user, unless more pumping code is provided.

None of this pumping code, which permits you to enter your numbers, to see the result, and to edit the numbers if desired, is needed in a spreadsheet. The spreadsheet implements a form of inter-referential i/o [8] in which objects are shared between the user and the system can be seen and operated on by both. Avoidance of pumping code is a key objective in NoPumpG, and contributed to the name of the system (the 'G' is for 'Graphics').

Extending the Spreadsheet to Control Graphics

The characteristic strengths of the spreadsheet can be extended to specify and control interactive graphics with a bidirectional linkage between certain cells in the spreadsheet, called control cells, and graphical entities.

Consider a line segment as an example of a graphical object. The four coordinates specifying its end points are held in four control cells simultaneously created with the line. If the value of any of these cells is changed, the line is automatically redrawn. If the line is moved with the mouse, the values of the corresponding controls are updated automatically to reflect the new coordinates.

This picture is oversimplified in one respect; that is, if a formula is placed in a control cell, it will be evaluated as usual in a spreadsheet, and the line will be redrawn as described. However, if the line is moved with the mouse, the coordinate corresponding to the control cell will not change, because it is determined by its formula, and the line will only move in such a way as to leave the coordinate unchanged.

This simple extension to the spreadsheet paradigm produces a simple but expressive tool for building graphical interactions, as illustrated later.

The NoPumpG Prototype

This extension, together with a few ancillary extensions described later, have been implemented in a prototype system for the Apple Macintosh using Turbo Pascal. This prototype, which uses a generally Macintosh-like interaction style to permit the user to perform the following operations, was used to produce all of the examples presented later. An extended version of the system is described in [9].

Create and Modify Cells

Figure 1 shows examples of cells. Each cell has a name, an optional formula, and a value. When the user creates a cell, he or she provides it with a name, and it has initial value of zero. The cell contains no formula. The user can enter a new value by clicking on the old value and typing a new value, provided the cell contains to formula. Formulae are entered by clicking on the formula portion of a cell, selecting an operator from a pull-down menu, and by clicking on one or more other cells to act as operands. A variety of arithmetic and trigonometric operators, together with some special operators described later, are provided.

The syntax of formulae in the prototype is restricted and results in some visible awkwardness in the examples. Formulae can contain only one operator and arguments must be cells, so that constants must be referred to by being placed in cells. A more convenient syntax has been provided in later versions of the prototype.

Because cells can quickly clutter the screen, a simple means is provided to conceal and redisplay cells. Cells and graphical objects coexist in the same screen area to permit the user to drag a cell to any desired location on the screen. Thus NoPumpG cells are not locked into a grid arrangement, unlike cells in typical spreadsheets.

Create Graphical Objects

The prototype provides line segments and small bitmaps called '*sketches*, created by using a simple bitmap editor and fixed text strings. When objects are created, control cells for them are created and automatically displayed. Control cells can be modified in the same manner as user-created cells. A line is associated with four control cells, one for each coordinate of each end. Sketches and text strings are associated with two control cells that define the horizontal and vertical position of the object. Additional control cells that determine the visibility of these objects are described later.

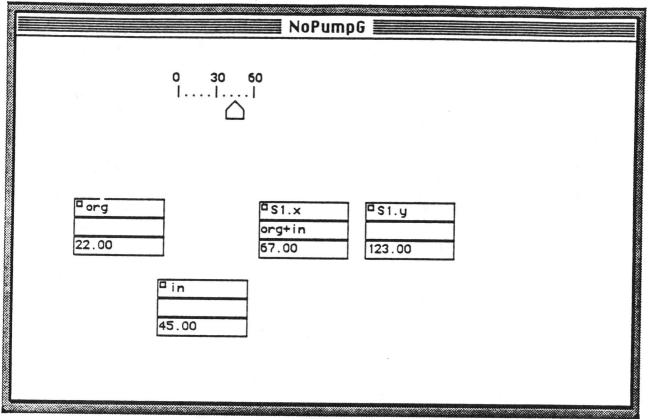

Figure 1: A simple output device. The pointer moves horizontally to a position determined by the cell 'in.' Normally these cells would not be visible.

Move Graphical Objects

The ends of a line, the middle of a sketch, and the beginning of a text string are all mouse sensitive. Placing the mouse cursor on any of these points and holding the mouse button down while moving the mouse will send a request to the object to move with the mouse. This request will be honored to the extent that it does not conflict with formulae placed in the control cells for the point. If a point has a formula in its X control cell, but none in its Y control cell, it moves vertically but not horizontally when dragged. If an object is moved, its control cells are automatically updated.

Additional features of the prototype permit the user to delete objects, to control the visibility of graphical objects, to create and manipulate pens that leave a visible trace on the screen, and to export and import objects. Where relevant, these additional features will be described later.

The implementation of the prototype follows a message-passing discipline, although it is not written in an object-oriented language. Graphical objects respond to mouse actions by sending update requests to their control cells. A cell will be updated unless it contains a formula. When any cell changes its value, it notifies any other cells or graphical objects that are associated with it; these objects then reevaluate themselves.

Although no special effort has been devoted to tuning the implementation, this simple computational mechanism performs quite adequately on the Macintosh. Responses to user actions are immediate, although sometimes insufficiently smooth for more complex structures. Animation, as described later, varies in smoothness with the number of moving or changing objects and the speeds of their motions. One animation shows an orbiting satellite, allowing the user to vary its initial position and velocity. It produces an adequate depiction of the motion if the speed of the satellite is not too great, and there are not too many cells that must be updated as the satellite moves left visible on the screen.

Graphical Output

Figure 1 shows how graphical output from the spreadsheet can be accomplished in NoPumpG. The pointer is a sketch and cells S1.x and S1.y contain and control its position. Cell S1.x, which controls the horizontal position of the pointer, contains a formula making its value the sum of the values of cells 'in' and 'org.' Cell 'in' holds the value to be displayed, and cell 'org' sets the origin of the pointer. Cell S1.y contains no formula since the pointer is intended to move horizontally. Whenever the value of 'in' is changed, by editing or by evaluation of a formula placed in 'in,' the pointer moves to the appropriate position. In this and most of the other examples to be shown, cells are left exposed on the screen to show some of the formulae used. In practice, only cells for which the user might wish to supply new values remain visible.

Figure 2 shows a more elaborate output device in which the mercury is formed from three lines tied together by formulae in their control cells. Cells L1.y2 and L2.y2 are shown: the formula in the latter indicates that its value will always be a copy of the value of L1.y2. Thus as Line L1, forming the left side of the mercury, moves up, the upper end of line L2, forming the right side of the mercury, moves up with it. As the cell 'in' is changed, the value of L1.y2, which controls the position of the top of the mercury, changes accordingly. Other formulae in cells not shown keep the pieces of the mercury tied together as required.

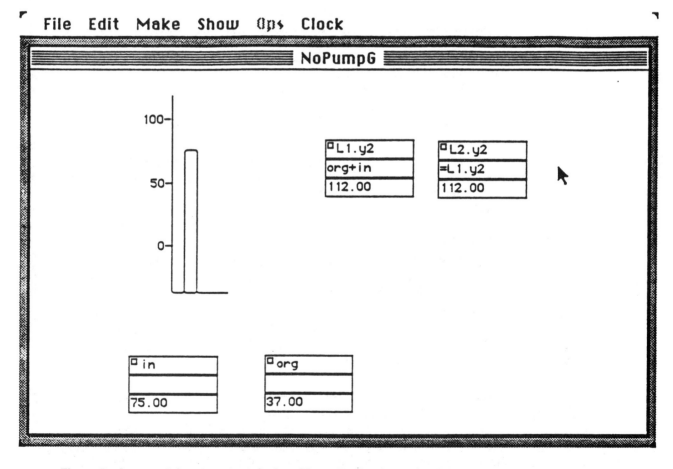

Figure 2: A more elaborate output device. The cells shown on the right show how the height of the upper end of Line L1, forming the left side of the mercury, depends on the value in 'in,' and how the top of line L2, forming the right side of the mercury, is tied to L1.

The treatment of the parts of the mercury illustrates another effect of the linkage between control cells and graphical objects: It is possible to set up constraints between objects. By placing formulae in control cells that refer to other control cells, graphical objects can be attached to one another, as shown here, or constrained to move in concert. Parts of the same object can be constrained in the same manner. The sides of the mercury are kept vertical by making the x coordinate of one end equal to the x coordinate of the other.

The same principles can be used to produce other kinds of output devices. A needle dial can be constructed by fixing one end of a line segment and by computing the coordinates of the other end as trigonometric functions of the input cell.

Graphical Input

Since control cells and graphical objects are linked bidirectionally, graphical input to the spreadsheet can be contrived as easily as output. Figure 3 shows the indicator of Figure 1 modified to act as a slide controller. Since cell S1.x now contains no formula, the pointer can be dragged horizontally. To keep the pointer from straying vertically, cell S1.y is given the dummy formula 'const.' The formula in the cell 'out' dictates that it will contain as its value the distance between the pointer and 'org,' wherever the pointer is dragged.

Coordinated Input and Output

Figure 4 shows an example drawn from Borning [9]. The outer lines in the first panel form an arbitrary quadrilateral, while the inner lines connect the midpoints of adjacent sides. No matter how the quadrilateral is distorted, the inner lines always form a parallelogram.

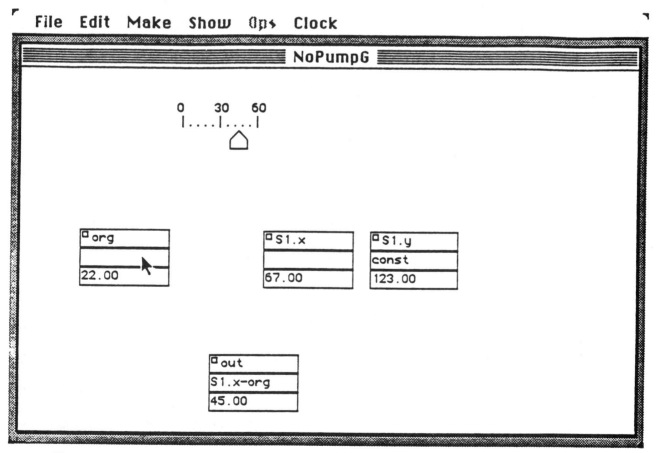

Figure 3: A simple slide controller. Because the control cell for the 'x' coordinate of pointer S1.x contains no formula, the pointer can be dragged horizontally. The cell 'out' is updated automatically to reflect the position of the pointer.

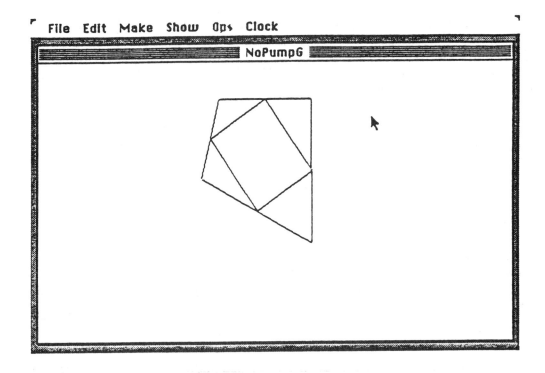

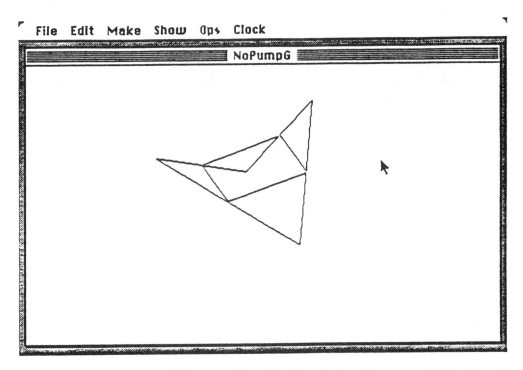

Figure 4: Two views of a quadrilateral with midpoints of its sides connected. The midpoint connectors are updated as the vertices of the figure are dragged, and always form a parallelogram.

This example is easy to construct in NoPumpG. The four lines of the quadrilateral are connected by placing formulae, such as those shown in the upper right portion of Figure 5, in the cells controlling one end of each line. Cells, such as those shown in the lower portion of the figure, contain formulae that compute the sums of the end coordinates of each line. Dividing these sums by two produces the coordinates of each midpoint. Formulae to this effect are simply inserted into the control cells of four new lines, as illustrated in the left-hand portion of the figure. The unconstrained line ends of the original quadrilateral can now be dragged at will and the coordinates of the midpoint connectors will be continuously recomputed, and the associated lines redrawn, accordingly.

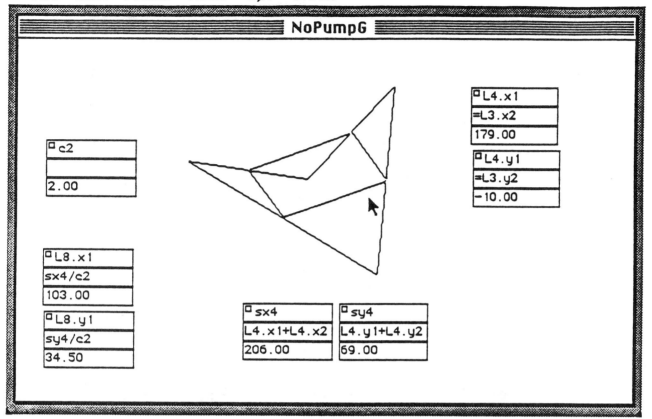

Figure 5: Some of the cells used to build the structure in Figure 4. The cells in the upper right illustrate how the lines forming the quadrilateral are tied together at the corners. The cells in lower center show how the sums of the coordinates for the ends of the sides are computed, and the cells in the lower left show how these sums are used to compute the coordinates for the ends of the midpoint connectors.

This example demonstrates how a dynamic, responsive display can be constructed by linking control cells and graphical objects in both directions within the same structure. Changes to the position of the quadrilateral cause recomputation within the spreadsheet, and the midpoint connectors are displayed in new positions.

Animation by Time-Dependent Positions

Because graphical objects are redisplayed whenever their control cells are changed, and control cells can be given formulae that depend on arbitrary computations, animation can be obtained by simply permitting time-dependent formulae. This is accomplished in NoPumpG by including a *clock* cell whose value is automatically updated by the system. Means are provided for stopping and starting the clock as desired. A formula in a control cell can be made to depend directly or indirectly on the clock, thus moving the corresponding graphical object.

Figure 6 shows two snapshots of a simple of this form of animation. The cells x, controlling the position of the butterfly sketch, S1.x and S1.y, contain formulae that depend on the clock. The advance of the clock between the two panels of the figure has caused the sketch to move up and to the right.

This form of animation can be used with more complex structures because any objects whose positions are related to an object tied to the clock will also be updated automatically. For example, it would be easy to tie one vertex of the quadrilateral in Figure 4 to the clock. As it moved in the manner specified, the parallelogram would be automatically adjusted.

Note that this kind of animation is accomplished in NoPumpG without any further extensions to the spreadsheet framework. Once a cell containing a clock is provided, animation becomes possible without

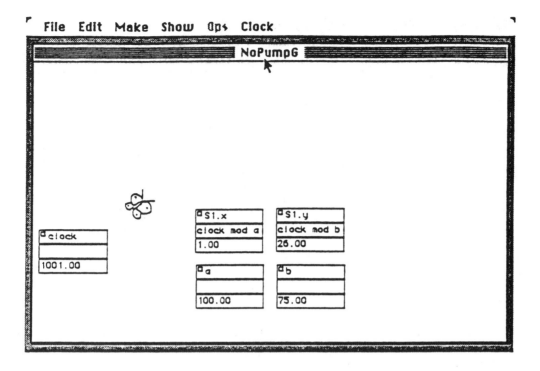

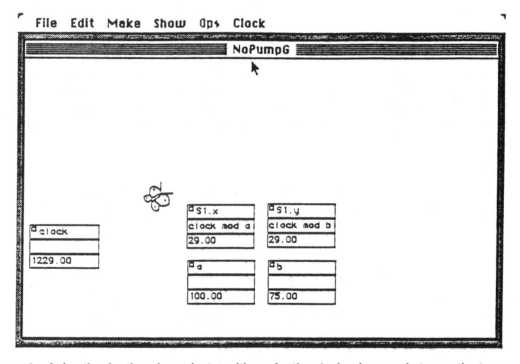

Figure 6: Animation by time-dependent position. As the clock advances between the two panels, the values of the control cells for the position of the butterfly, S1.x and S1.y are updated, causing the butterfly to move up and to the right.

requiring users to master any additional concepts. The basic spreadsheet evaluation mechanism, together with the linkage between cells and graphical objects, does the work.

Integration

In many physical systems, it is not possible to specify the positions of objects as simple functions of time, because these functions are determined dynamically. Consider an object that is to move with a velocity determined by a user-adjustable control. Because the settings of the control and how they change are not known in advance, it is impossible to express the position of the object as a simple function of time.

One approach to this problem would be to express the new position of the object at a given instant as the sum of its old position and its current velocity, scaled in an appropriate way. However, placing a formula of this kind in a spreadsheet leads to an immediate loop with the position dependent directly upon itself.

To deal with this problem, NoPumpG provides an integral operator. If F is a cell 0 placing the formula *F dt* in another cell 0, C produces the following behavior. When the clock is started and has a zero value, the value of C also is set to zero. When the clock is updated, the value of C is augmented by the product of the time occurring since the last update and the current value of F. Even though F is an argument in the formula for C, C is not updated when F changes, but only when the clock is updated.

This integral operator makes it easy to specify the motion of objects in a physically reasonable way. Figure 7 shows a demonstration of the motion of a mass suspended by an elastic cord. The position of the

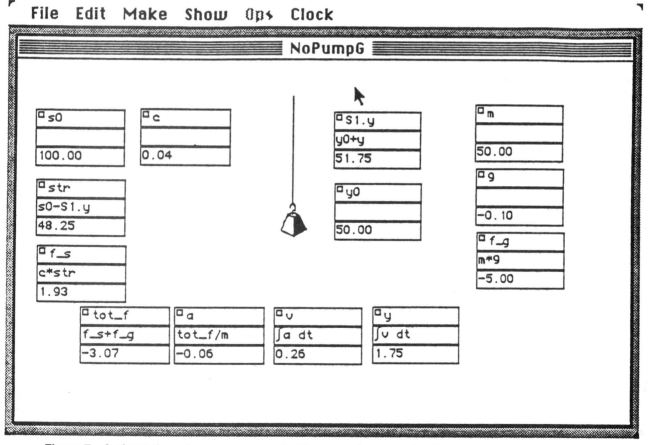

Figure 7: A simulation of a mass suspended from an elastic cord. The formulae in the cells show how the position of the mass is specified from basic physical principles, with the force due to the cord calculated on the left, the force due to gravity on the far right, and the change in position due to these forces at the bottom. The control cell S1.y, which determines the vertical position of the mass, contains a value obtained by adding the change in position to an initial height of the mass. When the clock runs, time integrals in some of the formulae cause the mass to oscillate up and down.

mass is expressed in a physically meaningful manner as the sum of an initial position and its integrated velocity, where the velocity is obtained by integrating the acceleration, and the acceleration is the quotient of the mass and the total force on the weight. The total force is the sum of a gravitational force and a force produced by the spring, and so on. The parameters of the model, including the mass and the spring constant, can be varied, even while it is running, simply by placing new values in the associated cells. The demonstration can easily be elaborated upon by providing graphical controllers for these parameters, such as those shown in Figure 3.

Animation by Visibility Control

While time-varying positions can accomplish animation adequately in many situations, some motions are too complex to be conveniently described in this manner. Figure 8 shows two views of a butterfly in flight. The transition between these views would be tedious to describe in terms of the motions of smaller graphical objects and would tax the performance of the system.

NoPumpG deals with this problem by permitting different views of an object to be displayed cyclically in the same location, producing animation by a succession of images. Doing this requires only one new feature--additional control cells that determine whether a graphical object appears on the screen or not. Figure 9 shows these cells and their use in animating the butterfly. Objects are visible just when their visibility control cells are positive. In the first panel, control cell S1.v, which controls the visibility of sketch 1, has the value '1,' while S2.v, which controls sketch 2, is '0.' Thus, sketch 1 is shown and sketch 2 is not. In the second panel, the clock has advanced and the contents of the visibility control cells has changed so that sketch 1 is hidden and sketch 2 is shown. This alternation continues as the clock runs. Because the position control cells for the two sketches have the same values, the sketches alternate in the same position on the screen.

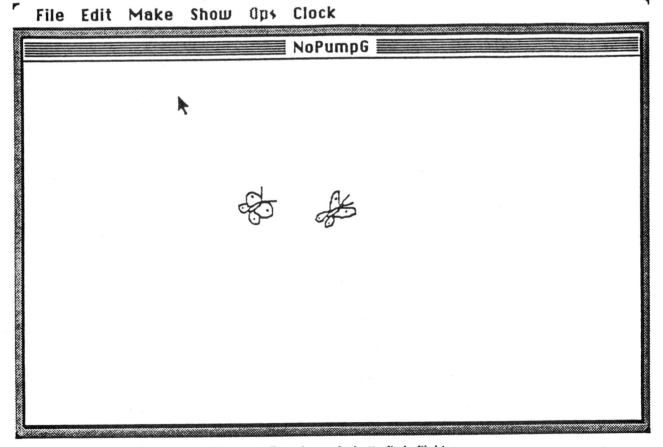

Figure 8: Two views of a butterfly in flight.

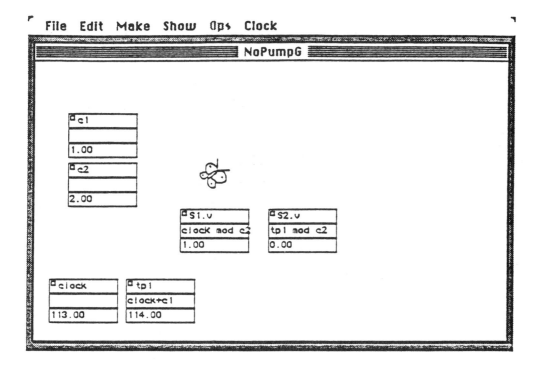

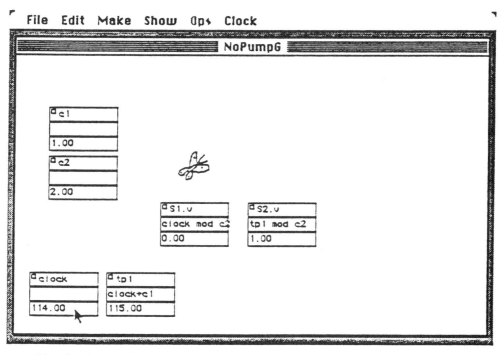

Figure 9: Showing how animation can be obtained by alternating the views shown in Figure 8. The cells S1.v and S2.v control the visibility of the two views. The formulae in these cells are tied to the clock in such a way that they are displayed alternately as the clock advances.

Concurrent Processes

As the clock advances, any objects whose positions depend on the clock are updated automatically by the system. Simultaneously, dragging of the mouse by the user is detected and any resulting changes in the display are made. No special techniques are required to model situations in which several activities, including user input, are going forward concurrently.

Handling Bidirectional Relationships
in a Simple Evaluation Model

The system described has an important limitation most easily understood by considering a position control cell for an object. If the cell has a formula, it can change the position of the object; but the object cannot be dragged by the user to provide a new value for the cell. If the cell has no formula, the object can be dragged; but the cell cannot change the position of the object. Thus, a single graphical object can provide input to, or output from, the spreadsheet, but not both.

An example drawn from Borning [9] illustrates the problem. Suppose we wish to illustrate the relationship between Celsius and Fahrenheit temperatures. A natural way to do this would be to provide two thermometers, such as shown in Figure 2, but arranged so that we can drag either mercury column to a new level and have the other column move to the equivalent level on the other scale. We cannot accomplish this with the features previously described because the level of the mercury is either determined by a formula, in which case we cannot drag it, or it can be dragged, in which case it cannot be adjusted by the spreadsheet to respond to changes in the other thermometer.

Borning's ThingLab does not have this problem because it uses a more powerful type of constraint than that supported by the basic spreadsheet system. ThingLab constraints are specifications of relationships among quantities or objects, with mechanisms to modify these entities to satisfy their relationships. These modification methods can change any of the entities in the constraint. In the thermometer example, the mercury columns are constrained to show corresponding temperatures. In contrast to what happens in a simple NoPumpG model, this constraint would be satisfied by the *other* column moving when the user modifies the first.

NoPumpG handles this problem with one added feature, which does not require any modification of the simple spreadsheet evaluation mechanism. The 'lc' operator, standing for 'last changed,' works as follows: If 'lc' is used in a formula in an ordinary cell, it takes two other cells as arguments. The value of the formula is the value of the more recently changed argument. When placed in a control cell, the value takes only one cell as argument, with the position of the associated object playing the role of the second argument. Thus a control cell with an 'lc' operator in its formula will respond to dragging as if it contained no formula, but also will respond to changes in its argument cell.

Figure 10 demonstrates how the temperature conversion problem is dealt with by using the 'lc' operator. Cell L2.y2, which controls the position of the top of the mercury in the thermometer on the left, can be set either by dragging, or by a temperature computed (ultimately) from the position of the mercury on the right. Similar arrangements provide for the mercury on the right to be dragged or to move when the mercury on the left is dragged.

As this example shows, the last-changed operator can be used to implement bidirectional constraints, without changing or extending the underlying spreadsheet model of computation. Unfortunately, the operator brings problems with it that make it uncertain that the extension is, all things considered, desirable. First, most applications of last changed involve circular dependencies, in which the value of a cell depends on the value of another cell, which, in turn, depends on it. Some such dependencies, such as those in the thermometer example, are innocuous, but as a general principle, they should be avoided. Second, and more serious, the behavior of some of these circular dependencies is determined not by the formulae alone but by the order *in which changes are propagated* in the implementation. This is clearly bad. If last changed is retained as an operator, it will need an accompanying warning.

Abstraction

In building complex structures, abstraction (the ability to identify and reuse substructures) is essential. Subroutines in conventional programming languages are a good example of abstraction, as are class definitions in object-oriented programming. NoPumpG supports abstraction through its export and import facilities. The content of a model being built in NoPumpG can be stored at any time. Any stored model

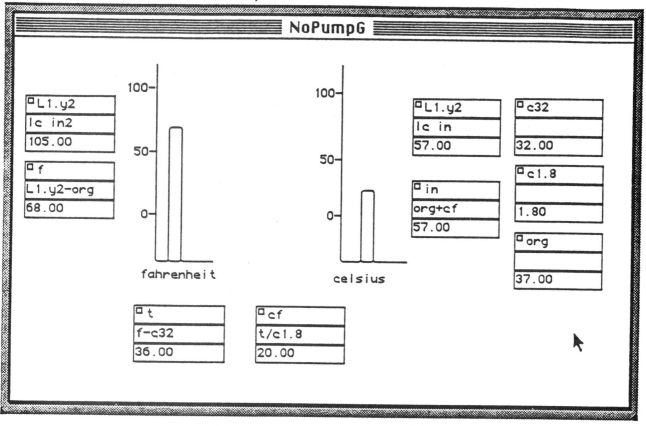

Figure 10: Coupled thermometers. When one mercury column is dragged, the other registers the corresponding temperature on its scale. The 'lc' operators in the two cells L1.y2, which specify the heights of the mercury in the two columns, permit these heights to be controlled either by dragging, or by a calculation driven by the height of the other column. The calculation that drives the Celsius thermometer can be traced in the cells shown. The Fahrenheit mercury has been dragged to an absolute height of 105, which corresponds to a scale reading of 68°, as shown in the cell 'f.' This Fahrenheit scale value is converted to Celsius in the cells 't' and 'cf.' The resulting Celsius value of 20° is converted to an absolute height of 57 in the cell 'in,' and this value determines the height of the Celsius mercury in the cell L1.y2 at upper left. If the Celsius mercury were to be dragged, the value of L1.y2 would be replaced by the result of the drag, and a similar computation, not shown, would adjust the Fahrenheit mercury.

can then be retrieved and merged with the current model. By repeating this merge operation, many copies of a stored model can be incorporated in the current model.

The thermometers in Figure 10 were built in this way, starting with the thermometer in Figure 2. It was not necessary to repeat the work of tying the pieces of mercury together, or building the scale.

Notice that Figure 10 shows two cells called L1.y2. These cells arise from bringing together two thermometers, each possessing an L1.y2 cell. Since references to cells are established by pointing rather than by using the names, no ambiguity results. The user does, however, need to keep track of which L1.y2 goes with which thermometer, placing them appropriately.

This abstraction facility serves NoPumpG's commitment to minimize the proliferation of concepts. The idea of copying is familiar and concrete, and does not require such additional concepts as the distinction between classes and instances, as may be required in other approaches (see Lieberman [10] and Ungar and Smith [11]).

However, not all repeated operations can be abstracted by copying only. To build a structure in which a large number of text strings are to be tied to a like number of sketches, in pairs, one needs to place appropriate formulae in the control cells of each text string. Copying would not avoid the necessity of performing this operation manually for each pair if the strings and sketches already exist.

A further limitation of simple copying is that changes to a substructure are not automatically reflected wherever the substructure is used. If an improvement were made to the thermometer in Figure 2, corresponding changes would have to be made to each copy of it in Figure 10. In more complex abstraction schemes, this problem is dealt with by separating the definitions of objects from instances of the definition. Changing the definition of the thermometer would change any instances subsequently created from it (although instances created previously may give trouble). The example in Figure 10 would be handled by reinstantiating the definition each time the model is set up for execution.

Comparison with Other Approaches

How does NoPumpG, with its spreadsheet foundations, compare with other systems with similar application goals? I group other systems according to the central idea of each. I will emphasize the way a programmer must specify and control the interactive graphics in each system, with secondary attention to the interface provided to the end user.

Procedural Languages

CT Tutor [12] produces graphics by executing procedural commands embedded in a language designed to support tutorial interactions. Procedural languages do not normally support creation and modification of graphics by direct manipulation, but CT Tutor implements an elegant linkage that provides some of the benefits of direct manipulation. The program instructions that draw graphics contain specifications of points in the graphics output area. If one of these point specifications is selected for editing and the mouse is clicked in the graphics area, the clicked point replaces the previously specified point. The same machinery can be used to add new point specifications to a program, so the code that produces a drawing can be produced largely by clicking points in the output area.

While this innovation gives it some important advantages over other procedural graphics systems, CT Tutor is still a procedural language. Users must organize the presentation of material and interactions with the user, in procedural form.

The Boxer system [13, 14] provides an innovative and economical conceptual framework in which such diverse operations as text editing and programming can be performed. As with CT Tutor, the expressive medium for graphics in Boxer is a procedural language, but some important facilities have been added. The Boxer language supports moving entities called sprites which have speed and heading attributes. Because sprites move autonomously according to their heading and speed attributes, animations involving multiple objects moving at once can be obtained in a natural way.

Programming by Rehearsal [15] is a simplified object-oriented programming system in which objects (called performers, in a theatre metaphor for programming) are controlled by messages (called cues). While message-passing permits more convenient programming than the standard procedural languages, the language is still procedural at bottom in that the response of an object to a message is specified as a procedure. The programmer must specify the order in which actions will occur in response to a message.

Programming by Rehearsal includes an elegant method for easing the burden of this procedural programming on people not accustomed to it. Rather than writing out code to specify how a performer should respond to a cue, the programmer can put the system in an observation mode and then can demonstrate manually how the performer should respond. The system captures the actions in the demonstration and writes the corresponding code automatically.

Simple procedural approaches are ill suited for describing highly dynamic situations where one or more objects are in motion and where user actions or other operations must be catered for simultaneously. The difficulty is that the programmer must indicate how control is to be distributed among several activities, such as moving an object or waiting for user input. Boxer deals with this problem with its sprite mechanism, which lets the user specify the behaviors of multiple sprites and leave it up to the system to manage them. Programming by Rehearsal uses a form of multiprocessing in which user actions can spawn new processes. In both cases, new concepts are required to adapt the procedural framework to handle concurrent activities; no new concepts are needed in NoPumpG's spreadsheet framework.

Constraint Systems

Borning's ThingLab [9] permits graphical interactions to be programmed without specifying procedures directly. ThingLab is implemented in an object-oriented, and hence procedural, framework. Once a suitable collection of primitive objects has been defined, a programmer works with objects whose behavior is specified by constraints that they and their parts obey, rather than by responses to messages. As mentioned earlier, constraints in ThingLab are relationships that the system will enforce as objects are moved or changed, together with methods of enforcing the relationships. For example, the midpoint of a line segment is constrained to lie on the segment equidistant from its ends, no matter how the segment is moved or stretched.

ThingLab's primitives include objects whose behavior cannot be replicated in NoPumpG. For example, elements which can be graphically connected on the screen by direct manipulation are provided. These elements can be used to build dataflow diagrams or models of electronic circuits.

Borning [16] describes extensions to the original ThingLab that permit constraints to be specified graphically, rather than by writing Smalltalk code, as in the original version. In some applications, this method works in a manner similar to NoPumpG. For example, the midpoint constraint can be expressed by showing how the coordinates of the midpoint can be computed from the coordinates of the ends of the segment, as in NoPumpG. However, constraints in ThingLab are ordinarily bidirectional, in that changes to either of two mutually constrained objects affect the other, not unidirectional as in NoPumpG. Having constrained a point to be the midpoint of a segment, one could move the point. ThingLab would respond by redrawing the segment so that the point is still its midpoint. In NoPumpG, the natural way to specify the midpoint constraint is unidirectional; only the segment, not the midpoint, could be changed by the user. The bidirectional constraint could be constructed by using the last-changed operator; however, this would be considerably more complicated than the unidirectional one.

Duisberg [17] describes how constraints involving time can be used to produce animation. The principle is the same as employed in NoPumpG. If the position of an object is made to depend on time, the object will move, thus avoiding the perplexities of procedurally specifying concurrent activities. The embodiment of this idea is more sophisticated and complex in Duisberg's system than in NoPumpG, however. A class of specialized objects, called responses, is provided; these generate streams of screen update events that the implementation interleaves to produce smooth animation.

With the extensions mentioned above, ThingLab offers much more functionality than NoPumpG, representing an expected tradeoff between power and complexity. Some of ThingLab's greater power comes from additional primitives, implemented through SmallTalk. Analogous extensions to NoPumpG are possible (and probably desirable), but would increase the complexity of the system.

More fundamentally, ThingLab's notion of constraint is more powerful than, but also more complex than the simple notion of computation that NoPumpG inherits from the spreadsheet. The key difference is in how constraint maintenance is described. A typical algebraic constraint, such as $d = rt$, does not define uniquely what will happen when we change one of the quantities concerned. The definition of this constraint in ThingLab must include, for example, indications of which quantities (if any) are fixed and (if the situation is still ambiguous) how any modifiable quantities are to be modified. For example, if none of d, r, and t are fixed, the effect of a change in d on r and t must be spelled out.

NoPumpG does not attempt to represent general constraints directly. Rather, it provides natural support only for the simple special case in which quantity is to be computed from others. The equation $d = rt$ has only the limited interpretation that d is to be computed from r and t. As indicated above, more general constraints must be handled by the last-changed operator.

Smith's Alternate Reality Kit (or ARK) [18, 19] provides a constraint-like mechanism to control the movement of simulated physical objects. Objects called 'interactors,' when turned on, produce influences on and interactions among other objects. For example, a 'gravity' interactor produces attractive forces between objects. This interaction can be turned off or modified, allowing the user to view the effect of various gravitational forces on the movement of objects.

ARK is implemented in and provides access to Smalltalk. It uses a message-passing model of computation in addition to the constraint-like facility provided by interactors. Users can create and control objects by placing them and pressing graphical pushbuttons that represent Smalltalk methods.

Some features of ARK would be difficult to provide in NoPumpG. For example, a mouse-controlled hand is used in ARK to pick up and move objects. The mouse-controlled hand imparts velocity to the object so that it is possible to throw objects across the screen. A similar effect could be contrived in NoPumpG but it would be complicated and unnatural. There is no simple way to determine just when an object starts and stops being dragged.

On the other hand, some of the objectives of ARK can be achieved in NoPumpG through its simpler conceptual framework. It is easy to set up gravitational attractions between a small number of objects, and to permit a user to experiment with different force laws. The same approach demonstrated in Figure 7 can be used. ARK makes physical laws concrete by representing them as visible objects (or interactors) that can be placed in a space or removed. It would be difficult to bundle NoPumpG's alternate gravity specifications in a similar manner.

Dataflow

Hookup [20] is a system primarily intended for control of a music synthesizer. The system supports interactive graphics at the same level of conceptual complexity as NoPumpG. Hookup allows the user to build a dataflow diagram whose nodes are chosen from a collection of primitives that include slide controls, clocks, sprites, x-y graphs, storage devices, and others. For example, by interconnecting the nodes of the diagram through direct manipulation, the user can specify that the X coordinate of a sprite will be the value of a clock, and that its Y coordinate will be provided by a slide control. An auxiliary input to a sprite selects one of a number of prepared views to be displayed at the sprite's current position, making animation by alternation of views easy.

Hookup does not provide primitives at as low a level as NoPumpG, so it is less flexible. For example, because there is no line segment primitive, building animated linkages is not possible. On the other hand, Hookup provides a variety of specialized nodes whose functions cannot easily be replicated in NoPumpG. These include push buttons, which produce transient signals, and nodes, which respond to such signals by starting clocks, by storing or deleting data, and the like. Hookup could be extended to provide the level of primitives that NoPumpG offers, while retaining the additional features.

If Hookup were extended in this way, the two systems would offer interesting competing metaphors. Hookup's dataflow metaphor, in which nodes communicate by sending values along paths, in much the way electronic components do, might not be as readily comprehensible to nontechnical users as NoPumpG's spreadsheet model. On the other hand, the spreadsheet model may not be extensible to deal with events such as button-presses as naturally as the dataflow model.

Limitations and Extensions

As previously stated, NoPumpG aims to provide broad functionality while adding as little as possible to the conceptual framework of the spreadsheet. It is inevitable that the resulting design--like the spreadsheet itself--will solve some problems poorly or not at all. In this section, I will evaluate NoPumpG's deficiencies and remedies for them. In some cases, simple extensions to the implementation, not requiring much in the way of new conceptual overhead, should suffice. In other cases, it is not clear what should be done or whether any sufficiently comprehensible extension is possible.

Some Simple Extensions

Additional Graphical Primitives

Some form of parametrized curve should be provided in the same manner as line segments. Provisions could easily be made to permit such curves to have an indefinite number of parameters (and hence control cells).

Text I/O

NoPumpG's current text objects are fixed and thus cannot be used to enter text or to display text computed from other information. Enhanced text objects whose value would be held in a control cell could be provided. The text could be edited if this cell contained no formula, or could be computed if the cell contained a formula. Appropriate operations on text, such as concatenation, would be needed.

Graphical Operations

Tying the ends of two lines together by placing formulae in control cells is workable but tedious. A purely graphical shortcut could be provided so that selecting two points would cause formulae to be placed in the control cells for one point that copies the coordinates of the other point. Similar graphical operations could place formulae in such a way as to locate one point in a given position relative to another, or could fix a point in place by placing the 'const' operator in its control cells.

Access to the Mouse

If NoPumpG were to be useful as a tool for building user interfaces, it would need to support a much wider range of mouse actions. As it is, the mouse can be accessed only when the user chooses to drag an object: actions such as clicking a button, or simply moving the mouse without depressing the button, cannot be handled. It is possible to provide cells that always contain the position of the mouse and the state of the mouse button. This makes more flexible use of the mouse possible, though using such low-level information would be tedious. Determining whether the mouse is on a particular object when the button is pressed, for example, is possible but complicated. Higher-level support for some common operations is desirable. For example, one might associate a new control cell with a sketch that would toggle between '1' and '0' when the mouse is clicked on the sketch.

More Difficult Issues

Aggregates

NoPumpG has not inherited from spreadsheets the desirable ability to specify operations such as 'total' or 'average' on groups of cells because its cells are not placed in a grid of rows and columns. Means could, however, be provided to allow the user to select a group of cells as an argument.

There are deeper issues in handling aggregates for which the basic spreadsheet mechanism provided no solution, such as how a new cell can be added to an aggregate at runtime, or how to refer to such a cell once it is created. Some spreadsheets provide a macro language that can deal with these matters as discussed later. These languages, however, add a great deal of procedural machinery to the basic spreadsheet paradigm. Such problems could possibly be avoided by permitting aggregates of data to appear as values of single cells, rather than as scalar values situated in a group of cells. Such an approach may be difficult to understand.

Andreas Lemke has pointed out that some of these same issues arise in NoPumpG in connection with graphical objects. How could one create a new line segment dynamically? How would one refer to its control cells? One could imagine an operator with suitable arguments that would build a new line or other object with specified position and with specified formulae in its control cells and another that would permit new formulae to be constructed and inserted in specified cells. But this machinery would involve many concepts alien to the basic spreadsheet framework.

Relative Copying of Formulae

Spreadsheets provide a very useful shortcut by permitting formulae to be copied from cell to cell so that the arguments in the formula are adjusted to suit the context wherever it is placed. Thus, if a formula refers to a cell one place to the right and two up, the copy will refer to the cell relative to the copy position. This relative copying saves much work if (as often happens) several groups of cells are related computationally (e.g. if several rows of a table are to be totalled at the end of each row).

Because NoPumpG cells are not placed in a grid, this facility cannot be provided in a straightforward way. A user could conceivably group cells into local grid arrangements on the screen, thus permitting relative copying between cells.

Collisions

Many problems involve detecting and responding to collisions between objects, such as a ball and a wall, or two simulated vehicles. Such interactions cannot be easily handled in NoPumpG. There are two aspects of the problem: First, determining when a collision occurs involves tedious computation of coordinates. Second, taking action when a collision is detected requires special handling of an event, discussed more generally below.

General Issues with Events

Suppose a problem requires a change in behavior when a button is pressed, or when a collision occurs, that persists after the button is released or the collision ends. In the simplest spreadsheet model, such behavior is impossible. Formulae can have different values when the button is down than when it is up, assuming the state of the button is reflected in some cell. When the button goes back up, these formulae will revert to their former values.

NoPumpG has two ways to get around this apparent restriction. First, suppose some cell contains the integral of the button state cell, and suppose the button state is '0' when the button is up and '1' when it is down. If the button is pressed, the integral will become positive and will stay positive even after the button is released. Thus, formulae that depend on this integral can change their output permanently when the button is pressed.

NoPumpG provides an if-then-else operator that can be used to produce this desired latching behavior in a more straightforward way, as pointed out by David Kieras. The operator takes three arguments, examines the value of its first argument, and chooses the value of its second or third argument as its value depending on whether the value of the first argument is positive or not. Suppose the cell BUTTON_BEEN_PRESSED contains the formula IF BUTTON_STATE THEN 1 ELSE BUTTON_BEEN_PRESSED. Whatever the initial value of this cell, it will become '1' and stay '1' when the button is pressed. The apparent loop in this formula is harmless because BUTTON_BEEN_PRESSED only propagates an update notice to itself when its value actually changes as the button is pressed. More elaborate formulae can be used to perform more complex operations such as storing the value of the clock whenever an event occurs.

Connectable Components

While the NoPumpG user can construct objects from cells, lines, and other primitives and can then interconnect these objects by placing appropriate formulae in the cells, there is no graphical way to accomplish this interconnection. The kind of dataflow diagram that can be constructed in ThingLab or Hookup can be built statically in NoPumpG but cannot be built or modified dynamically without manually manipulating formulae.

Providing a graphical operation that would interconnect two cells would permit simple dataflow diagrams to be built dynamically in NoPumpG but it is not adequate for all situations. Some interconnections of objects require several cells to be linked between the same two objects requiring several connections to be placed manually in this scheme. A more general solution would require the ability to encapsulate and place under simple graphical control arbitrary actions, including placing numbers of connections and entering new formulae.

More Powerful Abstraction

As mentioned earlier, NoPumpG's sole abstraction mechanism permits the user to export objects and to reimport copies of them. This allows the internal structure of object (such as the thermometer in Figure 2) to be specified once and used many times. Two limitations were mentioned: It does not permit operations on objects to be abstracted and it does not accommodate changes to multiple copies of an original.

The first limitation can be solved by incorporating a procedural language in which operations such as formula entry can be specified. A device such as that sued in Programming by Rehearsal might be used to lessen the learning requirement of the language.

Such an approach represents a major departure from NoPumpG's philosophy of hewing as closely as possible to the spreadsheet computational model. While spreadsheets often provide a macro language in this spirit, the language does not use the basic spreadsheet execution model. It thus involves such difficult issues as control flow and the use of variables found in standard programming languages. For example, users of the macro facility in Microsoft's EXCEL spreadsheet [21] may encounter the following notions: dereferencing, goto, input, and return (with and without a returned value).

Another direction to explore would be the use of analogy. It might be possible to permit the user to identify two groups of objects and to ask the system to modify the second so that it resembles the first. If two objects in the first group are connected in a particular way, the system would place analogous formulae in corresponding objects in the second group. This can be seen as an extension of the idea of relative copying discussed earlier. How correspondences between objects in the two groups should be established is not clear; one approach is to rely on relative position.

The second limitation of NoPumpG's abstraction mechanism, accommodating changes to multiple copies on an original, can be solved by replacing NoPumpG's simple copy operation with a more sophisticated operation using *prototypes* [10, 11]. In such a scheme, full copying is not done; rather, a "copy" of an object contains a reference to the original or prototype. Only information unique to a copy, such as the values of cells, would be kept in it, while information shared by all copies would be held in the prototype and accessed through the reference to the prototype in each copy. Thus, changes to the prototype would be reflected in all copies.

Conclusion

NoPumpG provides flexible support for interactive graphics and animation by building on the basic concepts of the spreadsheet. The main added concept is a bidirectional linkage between graphical objects and cells in the spreadsheet. Additional features such as the presence of a clock in a spreadsheet cell, control of the visibility of graphical objects through the value of cells, the use of an integral operator, and an operator that permits a cell to reflect values from more than one source, all serve to increase the power of NoPumpG.

This design goal is open to challenge. It may be that in the long run, users will benefit more from systems that are conceptually less minimal. Possibly this will provide a setting in which to learn concepts such as recursion, complex data structures, message passing, or constraints. There are two arguments against this: First, market success demonstrates unequivocally that people at large have embraced the spreadsheet despite its limited power and flexibility. Second, our understanding of computation generally is too immature to permit us to make reliable judgments about how people "should" think about it. Any of today's programming paradigms may seem inappropriate for the future, as more disposable computational power, possibly organized into massively parallel systems, becomes commonplace.

Acknowledgements

My ideas about spreadsheets and the desirability of extending them were strongly influenced by Robert Balzer, Gerhard Fischer, Thomas Green, Donald Norman, and Gary Olson, who had participated in a workshop held in Boulder, Colo. in 1986, on new approaches to programming. This discussion owes much to their insights. Andreas Lemke, David Kieras, Jakob Nielsen, and Beth Richards have also made useful suggestions about the work. Richard Young, Randall Smith, and two anonymous reviewers provided many valuable comments on an earlier version of this paper. I thank the Air Force Human Resources Laboratory and the Institute of Cognitive Science for financial support.

References

[1]   E. Horowitz and J.B. Munson, "An Expansive View of Reusable Software," *IEEE Transactions on Software Engineering*, Vol. SE-10, No. 5, Sept. 1984, pp. 477-487.

[2]   A. Kay, "Computer Software," *Science American*, Vol. 251, 1984, p. 52.

[3]   K.W. Piersol, "Object Oriented Spreadsheets: The Analytic Spreadsheet Package," *OOPSLA '86 Proceedings*, ACM, New York, 1986, p. 385.

[4]   M.H. van Emden, M. Ohki, and A. Takeuchi, "Spreadsheets with Incremental Queries as a User Interface for Logic Programming, *New Generation Computing*, Vol. 4, 1986, p. 287.

[5]   C.H. Lewis, "Extending the Spreadsheet Interface to Handle Approximate Quantities and Relationships," *Proc. CHI '85 Human Factors in Computing Systems*, ACM, New York, 1985, p. 55.

[6]   B. Budge, "Pinball Construction Set (Computer program)," *Electronic Arts*, San Mateo, Calif., 1983.

[7]   C.H. Lewis and G. Olson, "Can Psychology Lower the Barriers to Programming?" *Proc. of the Second Workshop on Empirical Studies of Programmers*, Ablex, Norwood, N.J., 1987.

[8]   S.W. Draper, "Display Managers as the Basis for User-Machine Communication," *User Centered System Design: New Perspectives on Human-Computer Interaction*, Edited by D.A. Norman and S.W. Draper, Erlbaum, Hillsdale, N.J., 1986, p. 339.

[9]   N. Wilde and C. Lewis, "Spreadsheet-Based Interactive Graphics: From Prototype to Tool," *Proc. CHI '90, Human Factors in Computing Systems*, ACM, New York, 1990, pp. 153-159.

[10]   A. Borning, "The Programming Language Aspects of ThingLab, A Constraint-Oriented Simulation Laboratory," *ACM Transactions on Programming Languages and Systems*, Vol. 3, 1981, p. 353.

[11]   H. Lieberman, "Using Prototypical Objects to Implement Shared Behavior in Object-Oriented Systems," *OOPSLA '86 Proc.*, ACM, New York, 1986, p. 214.

[12]   D. Ungar and R.B. Smith, "Self: The Power of Simplicity," *OOPSLA '87 Proc.*, ACM, New York, 1987, p. 227.

[13]   B.A. Sherwood and J.N. Sherwood, "The CT Language and Its Uses: A Modern Programming Tool, The *Conference on Physics Instruction Proc.*, Edited by E.F. Redish and J.S. Risley, Addison Wesley, Redwood City, Calif., 1990, pp. 445-453.

[14]   A.A. diSessa, "A Principled Design for an Integrated Computational Environment," *Human-Computer Interaction*, Vol. 1., 1985, p. 1

[15]   A.A. diSessa and H. Abelson, "Boxer: A Reconstructible Computational Medium," *Communications of the ACM*, Vol. 29, 1986, p. 859.

[16]   W. Finzer and L. Gould, "Programming by Rehearsal," *Byte*, Vol. 9, 1984, p. 187.

[17]   A. Borning, "Defining Constraints Graphically," *Proc. CHI '86 Human Factors in Computing Systems*, ACM, New York, 1986, p. 137.

[18]   R.A. Duisberg, "Animated Graphical Interfaces," *Proc. CHI '86 Human Factors in Computing Systems*, ACM, New York, 1986, p. 131.

[19]   R.B. Smith, "The Alternate Reality Kit," *Proc. CHI '87 Human Factors in Computing Systems*, ACM, New York, 1987, p. 99.

[20]   R.B. Smith, "Experiences with the Alternate Reality Kit: An Example of the Tension Between Literalism and Magic," *Proc. CHI '87 Human Factors in Computing Systems*, ACM, New York, 1987, pp. 61.

[21]   D. Levitt, "Hook Up: An Iconic, Real-Time Data-Flow Language for Entertainment," Unpublished Technical Note, MIT Media Lab., Cambridge, Mass., 1986.

[22]   Microsoft Corp., *Microsoft EXCEL: Arrays, Functions, and Macros*, Microsoft Corp., Bellevue, Wash., 1985.

□□□ 9 □□□   Environments V: Parallel and Distributed Computing

L. Snyder. "Parallel Programming and the POKER Programming Environment." *IEEE Computer*, 17(7):27–36, July 1984.

P.D. Stotts. "The PFG Language: Visual Programming for Concurrent Computation." In *Proc. Int. Conf. on Parallel Processing*, University Park, Penn., Volume 2: Software, pages 72–79, August 15-19, 1988, Pennsylvania State University Press, University Park, Penn.

M.P. Stovsky and B.W. Weide. "Building Interprocess Communication Models Using STILE." In *Proc. 21st Hawaii Int. Conf. on System Sciences (HICSS-21)*, Kailua Kona, Haw., Volume 2: Software Track, pages 639–647, January 5-8, 1988. IEEE Computer Society Press, Los Alamitos, Calif.

A. Giacalone and S.A. Smolka. "Integrated Environments for Formally Well–Founded Design and Simulation of Concurrent Systems." *IEEE Trans. on Software Engineering*, SE–14(6):787–802, June 1988.

M. Graf. "VERDI: The Architecture of a Visual Environment for Distributed System Design."

Parallel programming with Poker is far less chancy than drawing to an inside straight. This comprehensive system serves for writing and running programs for CHiP computers.

Parallel Programming and the Poker Programming Environment

Lawrence Snyder, University of Washington

Since there are few parallel computers in existence, programmers who have written and run a parallel program are rare.* Yet, as parallel computers become more widely available in response to recently recognized critical needs, [1-2] the number of programmers developing parallel programs is sure to grow.

Although parallel programming is quite different from the familiar sequential programming, it is nonetheless straightforward and understandable. To demonstrate this, we begin by establishing what the programmer must accomplish in parallel programming and then analyze how programs might be developed in a particular parallel programming environment. [†]

This article presents an overview of the Poker parallel programming environment that has been developed to support the Configurable, Highly Parallel, or CHiP, computer. [3] The Poker environment runs on a front-end sequential computer (Vax 11/780) and serves as a comprehensive system for writing and running parallel programs. Poker is sufficiently general that, with minor modification, it could be a parallel programming environment for any of a half-dozen recently-proposed ensemble parallel computers. [4]

The parallel programming activity

Before building a parallel programming environment, one must analyze the programming activity to determine what can be included to simplify programming and what must be excluded to avoid making it hard.

*In fact, it was possible to track down virtually everyone who ever programmed the Illiac IV. [5]

[†] A parallel programming environment is the collection of all language and operating system facilities needed to support parallel programming integrated together into a single system.

What do programmers do? Programming, either sequential or parallel, is the conversion of an abstract (machine independent) *algorithm* into a form called a *program,* that can be run on a particular computer. The algorithm is an abstraction describing a process that could be implemented on many machines. The program is an implementation of the algorithm for a particular machine. Programming is a conversion activity and, as such, will be easy or difficult depending on whether the algorithmic form is similar or dissimilar to the desired program form. But what are the sources of dissimilarity between algorithm and program?

First, algorithms are abstractions whose generality is intended to transcend the specifics of any implementation. As a result, when an algorithm is specified in the technical literature, many details are purposely omitted or, at best, merely implied because they have little or no bearing on the operation of the algorithm. The omitted details must be defined in the course of programming since the computer only follows explicit instructions. There seems not to be much point (or much possibility) in trying to develop a software support system to reduce this source of dissimilarity. It is inherent.

Consider a sequential programming example in which the mechanism of recursion is used; further, imagine that the programming activity is performed in a nonrecursive programming language. In this case, programming would be difficult because one must, in effect, implement a support package for recursion within the existing mechanisms of the language. Any programming environment will reduce dissimilarity due to mechanism mismatch when the form required of its programs is similar to the form the algorithms already have, that is, when there is a minimum amount of conversion to be done. Consequently, this source of dissimilarity is not inherent; it can be removed.

The ideal programming environment, then, cannot make parallel programming effortless, since there will always be some dissimilarity due to the inherent properties of abstraction. It could greatly simplify the programming task, however, by supporting a specificational form close to that used in the technical literature to describe display algorithms. Although such a form would seemingly be unattainable since algorithms are presented in a form unencumbered by any preordained syntax or semantics and are intended for thinking readers rather than computers, common characteristics of parallel algorithm specification can be identified. From these properties, parallel programming mechanisms can be developed.

Parallel algorithm specification. In order to illustrate the common characteristics of a parallel algorithm specification, we begin by giving two parallel algorithms. These examples are not intended to suggest any particular form for specificational mechanisms; they simply provide the essential aspects of two "typical" algorithms.

Example I. Kung and Leiserson[6] describe their systolic band-matrix multiplication algorithm with the picture shown in Figure 1 together with the explanation that each processor repeatedly executes a three-step cycle, two of which are idle steps and the third, an "inner product" step defined by the text:

$$\text{read } A, B, C$$
$$C \leftarrow C + AB$$
$$\text{write } A, B, C$$

Processors of every third (horizontal) row execute their inner product step simultaneously while the other processors are idle. The A band-matrix enters through the upper left edge, the B band-matrix enters through the upper right edge, and the result is emitted along the top edge.

Example II. Schwartz[7] presents an algorithm in which the maximum of $n \log n$ values is found in time proportional to $\log n$ (where the n processes are interconnected to form a complete binary tree, and each process initially has

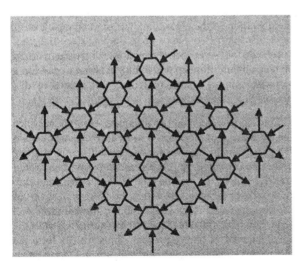

Figure 1. A Communication graph for a band-matrix multiplication algorithm.[6]

$\log n$ of the values). All processes begin by finding the local maximum of their values. Then, leaf processes pass their local maxima to their parents and halt while each interior process, after awaiting the arrival of maxima from each of its two descendants, reads the two values, compares them with its local maximum, and passes the largest of these three values to its parent. The global maximum is ejected by the root.

Common characteristics. There are at least five characteristics commonly exhibited by the descriptions of parallel algorithms for the nonshared memory model of parallel computation:

A graph $G = (V, E)$ whose vertex set V represents processors, and whose edge set E represents the communication structure of the algorithm;

A process set P describing the types of computational activity to be found in the algorithm;

An assignment function $\pi: V \rightarrow P$ giving to each processor a process;

A synchronization statement describing the interaction of the separate computational elements; and

An input/output statement describing the assumed form of the data, and the format of the results.

There is nothing surprising about the entries on this list. They arise all the time in parallel algorithm descriptions; let us see how they were used in the two preceding examples.

In the case of the band-matrix multiplication algorithm, the graph G is given in Figure 1.* For the maximum-finding algorithm, the graph is a complete binary tree. It is significant that the information describing the communication structure of the algorithm was, or could have been, given by a picture. Notice that in both cases the graph is really a representative for a graph *family*. Problems of different input size will require graphs of different size; for example, the structure in Figure 1 is appropriate for matrices with bands that are four values wide; matrices with bands of width five would require 25 processors. The way in which the graph family is defined, the way in which a particular input size determines a particular graph family member, and the way to handle the cases where the graph has more vertices than the available number of processors, are examples of those "commonly omitted details" previously cited as the first source of dissimilarity. These details are omitted because they are obvious, their effect is inconsequential, or they are irrelevant. The graph, by contrast, is fundamental, as is the fact that its size is determined by the problem's input size.

The process set P for the systolic algorithm contains three elements: one with the inner product step first followed by the two idle steps, one with the inner product between the idles, and one with it following the idles. The maximum finding algorithm has two elements in its process set: an interior node process that receives descendant inputs and a leaf process that does not. Notice that the size

*Strictly speaking, this is not a graph, but the edges around the perimeter are intended to be connected to I/O "vertices."

of the process set is fixed, independent of the size of the graph.

The assignment function π is given in the case of the systolic array by describing which horizontal rows are performing the inner product step and which are idling. The fact that processing is performed on every third row and that the outputs of an inner product step are obviously transmitted to processes that will read the values on the next step is sufficient information to assign the processes to processors. For the binary tree algorithm, the assignment is implicit in the use of the phrases "leaf process" and "interior process" (that is, we know which nodes are leaf nodes and they obviously get leaf processes).

The synchronization specification may not be very recognizable in either algorithm, but it is there. The processes of the systolic algorithm operate in lock step, since the time of an idle step equals the time of an inner product step. This means that the question of when processes read and write is determined in this case simply by the explicit use of the idle. In the tree algorithm, the phrase "after waiting for the arrival" implies that the process operation is "data-driven" (that is, the process executes until it needs data and then it idles until the data has been read).

The input/output statement is curious in that it must be known to program the process set, it can influence the synchronization, and it is critical to demonstrating the correctness of the algorithm. However, it seems to enter the process explicitly only after the program is written and is ready to be run. Since its indirect influence permeates the programming activity and is hard to extract, we will not mention I/O much after the following two points. First, the I/O for the band-matrix product algorithm was given pictorially in the original description,[6] offering another example of the role of pictures. Second, the data in both examples can be viewed as streams, since it is unstructured.

Although there might be other characteristics commonly exhibited by parallel algorithm specifications, this set of five properties is sufficiently comprehensive to serve as our "standard algorithmic form." It summarizes the things that computer scientists describe about an algorithm when they explain it to each other. Making the program form of our parallel-programming environment close to this standard algorithmic form will contribute to reducing dissimilarity due to mechanism mismatch. We should, therefore, consider the extent to which this has been achieved in the Poker environment.

The mechanisms of Poker

The statement that the communication structure of a parallel algorithm can be, and frequently is, given as a graph is simply a comment on the nature of computation in the nonshared memory model of parallelism. It does not, by itself, indicate a convenient mechanism for expressing such a graph. The graph could be given by a pointer structure or by an adjacency matrix.[8] It could also be defined implicitly by a routine that computes packet addresses or in any of a dozen other ways. The choice will affect the degree of mechanism mismatch between program and algorithm, of course, and again one should be guided by what is actually used in the technical literature. The

mechanisms selected for the Poker system represent one way to balance the convenience of "user-friendly" mechanisms and the pragmatics of efficient implementation.

The first property for which a mechanism must be selected is the graph used to define the communication structure of the algorithm. The most convenient way to express a graph is evidently with a picture, judging from how frequently they are used to describe graphs. Thus, the Poker environment provides an interactive graphics system as the mechanism for defining the graph. The graph is not drawn free-form, but rather it is laid out on a stylized two-dimensional medium called a *lattice* (see Figure 2). Potential vertex positions (squares) can be connected by line segments that can bend and cross over one another at certain sites (circles)—to define graph edges. Line segments are drawn by moving a cursor from circle to circle along the path of the intended edge. Such a drawing is called an *embedding* of the graph into the lattice.

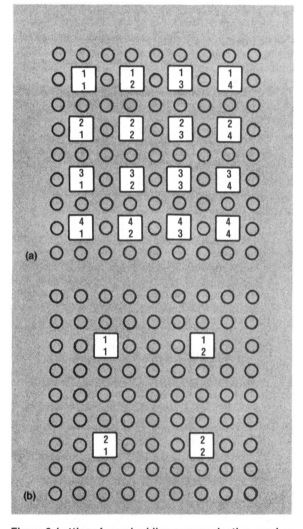

Figure 2. Lattices for embedding communication graphs: (a) corridor width = 1, (b) corridor width = 3. Squares represent potential vertex positions that can be connected by line segments to define edges. The circles provide sites where line segments can bend and cross over one another.

Figure 3 shows how to program the communication structures for the graphs of the example algorithms. The hexagonal mesh is, except for a 45° rotation, a direct implementation of Figure 1. The binary tree must be deformed to fit in the particular lattice medium, but the embedding is still a mechanical process in general.[3]

Notice that the embedding activity is graphical programming rather than symbolic programming. Since graphs tend to be given graphically rather than symbolically, this probably represents a reduction in dissimilarity over the symbolic alternatives.

The next step is to specify the sequential code segments of the processes, that is, to define the elements of the process set P. This is conventional symbolic programming and could be done in any sequential language such as C or Pascal. For this purpose, the Poker environment uses a primitive language, called XX, and the mechanism is to define a set of independent procedures. Two sample process codes are

```
code inner;
ports Ain, Aout, Bin, Bout, Cin, Cout;
begin
    real A, B, C;
    while true do
```

```
begin
    A←Ain; B←Bin; C←Cin;
    C := C + A * B;
    Aout←A; Bout←B; Cout←C;
    end
end                                                    (1)
```

```
code inode (logofn);
ports lchild, rchild, parent;
begin
    integer logofn, i;
    real big, temp, vals[logofn];
    big := vals[1];
    for i := 2 to logofn do
        if big<vals[i] then big := vals[i];
    temp←lchild;
    if big <temp then big := temp;
    temp←rchild;
    if big<temp then big := temp;
    parent←big
end                                                    (2)
```

When compared with the logical process presented in *Example I*, the code shown in code sample (1) is seen to differ in two ways. First, there are the syntactic features such as key words and declarations that are characteristic

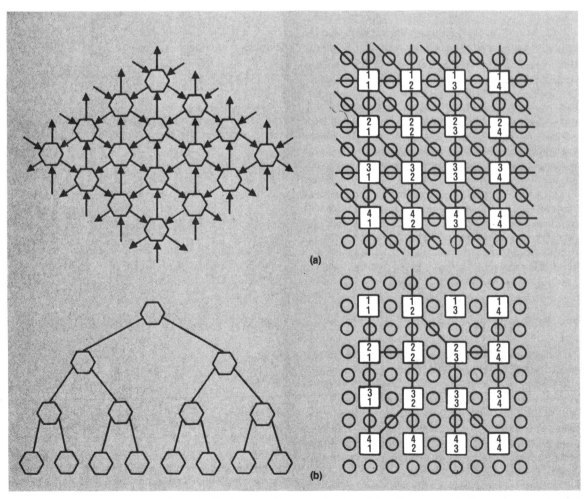

Figure 3. Embedding of the band-matrix (Figure 1) and tree graphs describing the communication structures for the band-matrix multiplication algorithm of *Example I* (a) and the maximum-finding algorithm of *Example II* (b).

of standard programming languages; second, there is the explicit mention of "ports." Ports provide a means for a process to refer to the processes with which it communicates: To read from another process, it assigns from a port name (for example, $A \leftarrow Ain$), and to write to another process, it assigns to a port name (for example, $Aout \leftarrow A$). Which processes these will be and how they are specified cannot be addressed until port names are defined.

The mechanism for specifying the assignment of a process to each vertex $\pi: V \rightarrow P$ is to display the graph embedding and request that the user assign process names (the name following **code** in the procedure definition) to each vertex. Figure 4 shows the assignment for the sample programs.

For the band-matrix product systolic array, one might expect three different process types in the set P, one corresponding to each of the three positions of the inner product step in a pair of idles, as described in *Example I*. However, the XX code of code samples (1) and (2) does not have any idle instructions, since the XX programming language uses a data-driven semantics to define the synchronization of processes: The reads wait for the arrival of the data. The three process types mentioned in *Example I* reduce to one type when data-driven semantics are used.

How, then, is synchronous communication achieved in Poker?

Automatically. After the whole program specification is complete, a code optimization facility, called *coordination*, analyzes the program and converts it to a synchronously communicating program, if possible.[9] In this respect, programming an algorithm with Poker is somewhat easier than defining the algorithm in the first place.

It must be emphasized that not all Poker programs can be efficiently coordinated. XX has an idle instruction for those cases when synchronous execution is desired, but automatic coordination is not possible. The user could always decide to do his own coordination, but this is probably not advisable since coordination, like code optimization, is better done by machine. For example, automatic coordination can produce a better algorithm than the one with the explicit idles described in *Example I*.*

With four of the mechanisms defined, the programming is nearly complete. All that remains is to interface the graphical communication structure with the symbolic code segments. This is accomplished by a mechanism that assigns port names to the edges of the graph that meet at a vertex so that the process assigned to that vertex can refer to its logical neighbors (see Figure 5). The port name assignment is a feature of Poker programming with no direct analog in the conceptual discussion of parallel programming given previously. It can be viewed as an explicit means of establishing a vocabulary with which to describe communication. Terms like "parent" and "left neighbor" have no intrinsic meaning; they must be specified to the computer. Thus, port-naming is a type of declaration.

At this point the Poker program is finished. It can now be compiled, coordinated, assembled, and linked. To run the program, we must give the input/output specification. This is done with a mechanism that labels the edges connecting to the perimeter of the lattice with the names of the streams that flow in or out of them. In this way, the edges are ports to the lattice. The data, of course, moves to and from the lattice in a data-driven manner.

To program an algorithm, Poker supplies the mechanism to draw a picture of a graph representing the communication structure, define a set of sequential procedures, label a picture of the graph with process names in one case and port names in the other, and it furnishes data-driven semantics with coordination for synchronization; to run the program, the I/O is specified as named streams of data.

Poker also provides the phase construction mechanism. Informally, a *phase* is an algorithm (in the sense we've been using) with a single communication graph. Each of

*This observation was made by Janice E. Cuny, University of Massachusetts.

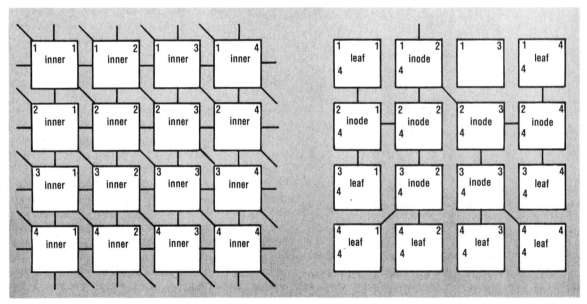

Figure 4. Process assignments for *Example I* (a), and *Example II* (b). The actual parameter for the tree program of *Example II* is given on the line following the name.

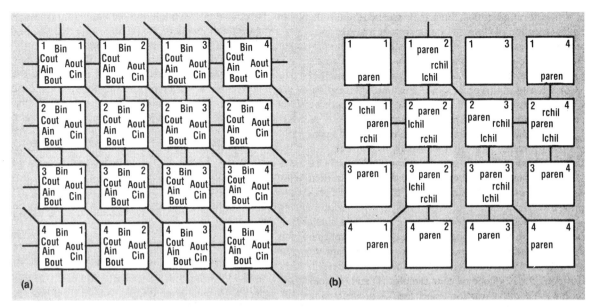

Figure 5. Port name declaration for *Example I* (a), and *Example II* (b). Names are abbreviated to the first five characters.

our example algorithms is a phase, since each is based on a single communication graph. Moreover, algorithms found

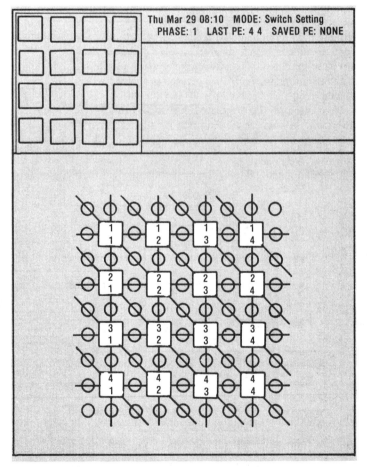

Figure 6. A typical primary display form, showing a 16 processor switch settings display. The exact form of the representation changes (compare Figure 6 with Figure 7) depending on whether the programmer is performing such operations as graph embedding, process assignment, or port declaration.

in the technical literature frequently qualify as phases. (See the Thompson and Kung[11] sorting algorithm for an example of a multiphase, that is, multiple interconnection structure, algorithm.) "Real-world" problems—the complicated, ill-defined, exception-prone programming situations that application programmers will be solving when they use the programming environment—tend not to be so tidy. Solutions to real-world problems will presumably be developed by dividing them into parts that can be solved either directly by a phase or further subdivided until their constituents can be solved by phases. The consequence of this strategy is that phases must be composed, that is, put together, to form more complicated algorithms. For example, the conjugate gradient method of solving partial differential equations can be handled in four phases: an input phase, a "grid" phase for matrix multiplication, a "tree" phase for summation and broadcast, and an output phase.[12] The grid and tree phases are executed iteratively in an alternating schedule. Poker has been designed to support phases and their composition.

Description of the Poker environment

After considerable discussion of various concepts and abstractions, it is time to get down to the details of the Poker system. Perhaps the first question to be asked following the discussion of the Poker mechanisms is what does a whole Poker program look like? Answer: It cannot be seen *in toto*. Unlike "regular" programs, Poker programs are not monolithic pieces of program text. Instead, they are databases. To see the communication structure, one displays a picture of the graph that is stored in the database. To see the assignment function, one displays a picture of the graph* labeled with process names.[13] To make changes to the program, one simply changes the picture or the labeling, which causes the database to be

---

*This picture is not actually stored directly in the database. It is constructed by the Poker system from the database relations. How this is done is interesting, but beyond the scope of this article.[13]

changed. But we are ahead of ourselves; let's go back and start at the beginning of a Poker session.

Displays. The Poker environment uses two displays, primary and secondary, one of which must be a high-resolution (1024×768 pixel), bit-mapped display. Two displays are used simply to increase the amount of information available to the programmer at any one time. Most activity takes place on the primary display; XX programming is usually done on the secondary display.

The primary display has the form illustrated in Figure 6. The bottom square region, called the *field*, is where most of the programming activity takes place. The field always displays some schematic representation of the lattice being programmed. The exact form of the representation changes (compare Figure 6 with Figure 7) depending on whether the programmer is performing such operations as graph embedding, process assignment, or port declaration. Status information, diagnostics, and miscellaneous data are given in the upper right region of the display, called the *chalkboard*. (The upper left region gives a map of the lattice marked with that portion being displayed in the field; this is useful only for problems larger than the one shown in Figure 6.) The bottom line of the chalkboard

is the *command line*, used for specifying the few textual commands required by Poker,* such as reading library files.

Facilities. The logical structure of the Poker environment is shown in Figure 8. It provides an integrated set of facilities to

- define architectural characteristics (CHiP parameters),
- embed communication graphs (switch settings),
- program process set codes, (XX language),
- declare port names (port naming),
- assign processes to processors (code naming),
- compile, coordinate, assemble, load, and define I/O (command request),
- execute, trace, peek, and poke (trace values).

Although the facilities have been listed in the order in which they might be used when writing a program, notice in Figure 8 that no order is actually enforced; programmers can, and typically do, jump back and forth between the different facilities.

---

* Poker is extremely interactive; most actions are given as a single keystroke and have immediate effect.

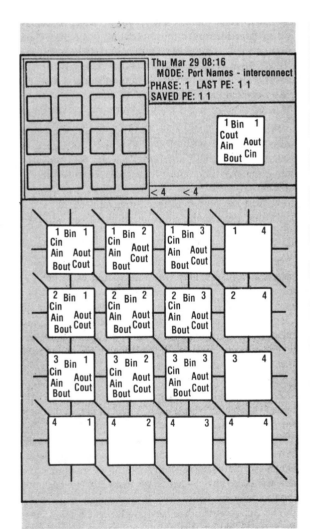

Figure 7. A 16 processor port names display.

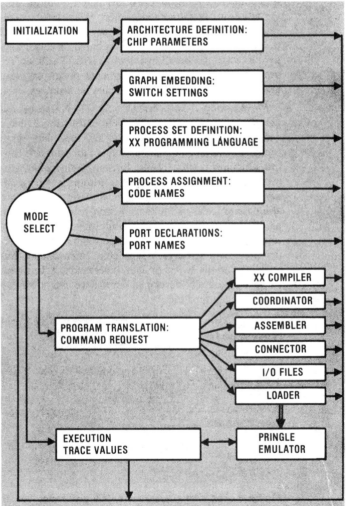

Figure 8. The logical structure of the Poker environment.

Next, we briefly describe the kinds of information displayed with each facility and the service provided. The reader should be cautioned that much is being left out in the interest of brevity, though full details are available,[14] and that the dynamic, interactive character of the system is completely lost in this presentation.

Architectural definition. Because Poker is intended to support CHiP programming, it has been designed to accommodate a number of CHiP family architectures. Programs can be written for logical CHiP machines with four to 4096 processors. All these logical machines can be emulated with a software emulator. (The emulated instruction set is the Pringle parallel computer,[15] a hardware emulator of the 64 processor members of the CHiP family.) Consequently, the programmer begins using Poker by specifying the characteristics of the underlying logical architecture. These include the number of processing elements and the amount of routing capability needed for the lattice (corridor width[3]). The default parameters match the machine defined in the previous session or, if there was no previous session, the parameters of the Pringle hardware.

Embedding communication graphs. The field of the primary display shows the lattice of the current architecture, as illustrated in Figure 2. The programmer defines the communication structure of the algorithm by drawing the graph in the lattice that defines the structure. This chiefly involves connecting processors with line segments to define edges. Graphics primitives based on cursor keys permit edges to be drawn and erased. Facilities are available for such activities as managing the display, saving embeddings, and reading in library embeddings.

Programming the process set codes. The XX sequential programming language is a simple scalar language for defining processes. The language has four data types (Boolean, character, integer, and real), the common control structures (such as **while**, **for**, and **if-then-else**), vectors, and the usual supply of scalar arithmetic and logical operators. In addition to data type declarations, one can also declare scalar variables to be port names, procedure parameters, or variables to be traced. Input/output is performed by assigning from or to a port name. The semantics are "data-driven": Writes occur immediately and reads wait on the arrival of data, if necessary. XX process codes are generally developed on the secondary display using a standard editor.

Process assignment. The processors are assigned processes with a field display on the primary terminal, like the

two shown in Figure 4. The programmer enters the name of the process procedure on the first line of the box symbolizing the processor. If the process has formal parameters, values for the actual parameters can be entered on the following (four) lines. For example, the formal parameter *logofn* in code sample (2) is assigned the value 4 in Figure 4b. Facilities are provided to avoid tedious typing. One can buffer the contents of a box, then automatically deposit the contents of the buffer into processors in whole regions of the processor array. For example, if the programmer buffers a box, then typing <4<4 followed by the insert key causes the processors whose indices are both <4 to receive the contents of the box. (The same mechanism for port declarations is shown in Figure 7.) Standard facilities, such as screen management and library access facilities, are available.

Port declarations. The field of the primary display has the same form as the two examples shown in Figure 5. Each processor has up to eight incident edges as a result of the graph embedding, and it has received a process that refers to up to eight port names. These names are matched by means of the port declaration. The processor box is divided into eight windows (see Figure 9). The programmer enters the names used by the assigned process code into the window for that edge. The names are clipped to the first five characters. Facilities are provided for displaying unclipped names in the chalkboard. Like the process assignment, it is possible to buffer port assignments and deposit them automatically in whole regions of the processor array (Figure 7). Screen management and other ancillary commands are available.

Program translation. The preceding facilities provide a means of specifying a Poker database containing the elements of a parallel program. They are then converted into executable form. The XX compiler converts each process into assembly code. The coordinator[9] then attempts to convert the process assigned to each processor into a form that permits the entire program to run with synchronous (not data-driven) execution. (This step can be by-passed and the processes can be run in data-driven form.) If coordination is successful, the processors may all have different assembly codes associated with them. In any event object code is produced. The connector "compiles" the graphical representation of the communication graph into a symbolic object form. The object code and the object graph as well as the actual parameter values are loaded into the emulator (or the Pringle). Finally, the I/O files are specified.

Execution. The resulting program is executed. The traced variables are displayed in a field similar to that used for process assignment. The execution can proceed for a given number of steps or until a displayed value changes. When the execution is suspended, any of the displayed values can be changed. When execution resumes, these new values are poked—hence, the name Poker—back into the processor memories.

The Poker system has been implemented as a C program (~40,000 lines) to run on a Vax 11/780 under the Unix operating system.

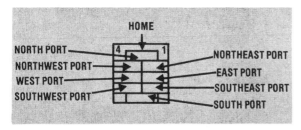

Figure 9. For port declarations, the processor box is divided into eight windows; each processor has up to eight incident edges as a result of graph embedding.

Program performance

How do programs written in the Poker environment perform on the CHiP computer? Since there is no CHiP computer implementation and only scant experience with the Pringle, it is not possible to support our claims with copious evidence. But claims can be made nevertheless.

Generally speaking, Poker introduces little inefficiency. Its graphical programming facilities—switch settings, port names, and code names—do not introduce inefficiency. The latter two facilities are only definitional. The switch settings are directly translated into source-target pairs for the Pringle and will be literally translated for the CHiP computer. The XX language is so simple that every efficient compilation of phase encoded code is possible. (The language could be richer and still be efficient; replacement with another sequential language, such as Pascal, is a simple change.) There is only one XX feature with noticeable execution time inefficiency, the data-driven I/O, and even this is only occasionally a liability.

Data-driven I/O is both a luxury and a necessity. It is a luxury in that certain programs capable of being run synchronously need not be written using the tedious process of inserting explicit idles. They can be written with data-driven communication, then be run through the coordination phase[9] to be converted into synchronous form. Some programs, however, cannot be coordinated. Others cannot be run synchronously without introducing superfluous I/O, or "chattering," in which the processors communicate back and forth at regular intervals whether or not there is actually any data to be sent[9] These programs ought to be written using data-driven communication because it is easier and substantially more efficient than the chattering. In such cases, data-driven I/O is a necessity. To the extent that a program could be run with synchronous I/O but is not—either because it is not coordinated at all or the coordinator fails to find a synchronous variant—there is a small loss in performance. As an example of the case where coordination is not used, we know that the Kung-Leiserson band-matrix product algorithm[6] takes 1.16 times longer with uncoordinated data-driven than with coordinated data-driven communication.* Since data-driven I/O is necessary for the nonsynchronously executable programs anyway, the inefficiency arises only when the coordinator phase fails to find an existing synchronous variant. This failure is analogous to criticizing sequential languages because their optimizers occasionally fail to find an optimization.

As a result, the Poker environment is a very efficient programming system for the CHiP computer. But how well does it support other ensemble machines?[4]

Since the processor element of the CHiP computer and the Pringle are similar to other ensemble machines and an XX compiler for them would be similarly efficient, the inefficiencies will arise in expressing the communication structure. Suppose that we have an ensemble machine with a fixed interconnection structure S and want to use Poker

First, we can configure the lattice once and for all to be the interconnection structure S. Then, if the algorithm uses a different communication structure than S, the programmer must encode the appropriate routing actions in the processor element codes. In this case, the burden of mapping the communication structure onto the architecture is entirely on the programmer. Poker's switch-setting facility would be of little help. Second, the programmer could use Poker switch settings to express the algorithm's communication structure just as if the target machine were the CHiP computer. Then, if that structure did not match S, either an automatic or a manual scheme for embedding the graph into S could be used. This embedding might take the form of packet address encoding, if it were appropriate for the architecture. The advantage would be that the interconnection graph mechanism would still be convenient for the programmer. The disadvantage would be the possible inefficiencies in the runtime implementation of the processor-to-processor communication, but these inefficiencies would be caused by the architecture, not Poker.

Starting from first principles, we have descended from a high-level abstract idea of what is required for parallel programming to the basic details of a particular parallel-programming environment. Although each step was more specific and brought us closer to the realities of everyday parallel programming, we realized our original goals to utilize five common properties of parallel algorithm specification: a graph describing the communication structure, a finite process set defining the activities, an assignment function giving processes to processors, a synchronization statement, and I/O information. These properties motivated mechanisms that were illustrated by the Poker environment. *

Acknowledgments

The Poker environment represents the ideas and hard work of many people. Dennis B. Gannon and Janice E. Cuny contributed to many of the concepts as well as to the design of XX. Version 1.0 of Poker[13,14] was implemented almost entirely in the summer of 1982 at Purdue University by a delightful and committed group of gentlemen: Steven S. Albert, Carl W. Amport, Brian B. Beuning, Alan J. Chester, John P. Guaragno, Christopher A. Kent, John Thomas Love, Eugene J. Shekita, and Carleton A. Smith (coauthors on the technical report[12]); significant enhancements have since been made by Steven J. Holms. The presentation of Poker in this article benefitted from helpful comments by the referees. The Poker effort is part of the Blue CHiP Project which has been funded by the Office on Naval Research under Contracts N00014-80-K-0816, N00014-81-K-0360 (SRO-100), and N00014-84-K-0143. All of this help is deeply appreciated.

References

1. P. B. Lax, *Report of the Panel on Large Scale Computing for Science and Engineering,* National Science Foundation, GPO, Washington, D.C., 1982.

*This result is due to Janice E. Cuny, University of Massachusetts.

2. R. F. Cotellessa, *Report of the Information Technology Workshop,* National Science Foundation, GPO, Washington, D.C., 1983.

3. L. Snyder, "Introduction to the Configurable, Highly Parallel Computer," *Computer,* Vol. 15, No. 1, Jan., 1982, pp. 47-56.

4. C. L. Seitz, "Ensemble Architectures for VLSI—A Survey and Taxonomy," in P. Penfield (ed.), *Proc. Conf. Advanced Research in VLSI,* Artech House, 1981, pp. 130-135.

5. R. H. Perrott and D. K. Stevenson, "User's Experience with the Illiac IV System and Its Programming Languages," *Sigplan Notices,* Vol. 16, No. 7, July, 1981, pp. 75-81.

6. H. T. Kung and C. E. Leiserson, "Algorithms for VLSI Processor Arrays," in C. Mead and L. Conway, *Introduction to VLSI Systems,* Addison-Wesley, Reading, Mass., 1980, pp. 271-292.

7. J. T. Schwartz, "Ultracomputers," *ACM Trans. Programming Languages and Systems,* Vol. 2, No. 4, Oct., 1980, pp. 484-521.

8. A. V. Aho, J. E. Hopcroft, and J. D. Ullman, *The Design and Analysis of Computer Algorithms,* Addison-Wesley, Reading, Mass., 1974.

9. J. E. Cuny and L. Snyder, "Conversion from Data Driven Programs for Synchronous Execution, " in *Proc. 10th Principles of Programming Languages,* ACM, 1983, pp. 197-202.

10. C. D. Thompson and H. T. Kung, "Sorting on a Mesh-Connected Parallel Computer," *Comm. ACM,* Vol. 20, No. 4, Apr., 1977, pp. 263-271.

11. D. B. Gannon, L. Snyder, and J. Van Rosendale, "Programming Substructure Computations for Elliptic Problems on the CHiP System," in A. K. Noor (ed.), *Impact of New Computing Systems on Computational Mechanics,* The American Society of Mechanical Engineers, 1983, pp. 65-80.

12. L. Snyder et al., "The Poker Programming Environment and Its Implementation," Purdue University, tech. report CSD-TR-410, 1982.

13. L. Snyder, "Poker Programmers Guide," Purdue University, tech. report CSD-TR-434, 1983.

14. A. A. Kapauan et al., "The Pringle Parallel Computer," in *Proc. 11th Int'l Symp. Computer Architecture,* 1984.

Lawrence Snyder is professor of computer science at the University of Washington. He was formerly professor of computer science at Purdue and associate professor of computer science at Yale. He has authored papers on process synchronization, data structures, parallel computation, VLSI, theory of graph embeddings, capability-based protection systems, and programming language semantics. In addition to serving on program committees for the ACM Symposium on the Theory of Computation, Snyder has been program chairman for IEEE Symposium on Foundations of Computer Science. He is associate editor for *Journal of Computer and Systems Science, Journal of the Association for Computing Machinery,* and *Journal of Parallel and Distributed Computing.*

Snyder received his BA degree in mathematics and economics from the University of Iowa and his PhD degree in computer science from Carnegie-Mellon University, Pittsburgh, Pa.

Questions about this article can be addressed to the author at Dept. of Computer Science, FR-35, University of Washington, Seattle, WA 98195.

The PFG Language:
Visual Programming for Concurrent Computation

P. David Stotts

*Department of Computer Science and
Institute for Advanced Computer Studies
University of Maryland
College Park, MD 20742*

Abstract

PFG (Parallel Flow Graphs) is a language for expression of concurrent, time-dependent computations. Its syntax is graphical and hierarchical to allow construction and viewing of realistically-sized programs. Its execution semantics are defined by a mathematical model of concurrent computation based on timed Petri nets and hierarchical graphs. The PFG language and underlying computation paradigm serves as the foundation of a development and analysis environment for real-time software systems under development at the University of Maryland.

PFG is rich enough to express many of the common concurrent control structures found in parallel languages, as well as some less common ones. Each syntactic structure in PFG has a direct translation into a portion of a timed Petri net model. The net created by legally combining PFG structures is guaranteed to be well-formed, in the sense that each Petri net is in the *free-choice* class and has a clear interpretation in terms of a hardware/software system. Several techniques have been defined which allow the model produced from a PFG program to be analyzed for concurrency properties, such as deadlock freedom and proper mutual exclusion on shared data structures.

1. Visual programming and concurrency

Though graphical languages are not a new idea, they have not caught on particularly well, especially in comparison to the popularity of textual languages. Part of this failure up until now may have been from the relative lack of high-resolution, bit-mapped screens for display of graphical programs. The widespread availability of desk-top workstations now eases this problem considerably. Icon-based tools, offering a pictorial style of user-interface, are now very popular and should presage a renewal of interest in graphical programming as well.

Many researchers have designed and experimented with graphical languages. Representative projects include the PICT system [3], which uses flowchart-like diagrams constructed by the user interactively, and the PROGRAPH language [5,6] which allows interactive construction of functional dataflow programs. Earlier work on dataflow languages also used graphical program representations [2], though the user interfaces were not as visually rich as those of the more recent projects due to hardware limitations. The Poker programming environment [8] is another language that allows visual programming. It supports concurrent computations for the CHiP parallel processor architecture, but its visual interface is limited to the grid-based specification of a graph showing communication paths among the parallel processes in a program.

Though PFG is graphical in its syntax, it differs from previous visual languages in two aspects: it is intended for the expression and analysis of concurrent computations (PROGRAPH and Poker are among the few others), and its semantics are formally defined by a mathematical model based on timed Petri nets and hierarchical graphs. In essence the graphical syntax for PFG is just a convenient method for a user to specify the mathematical model of his computation. Previous graphical languages with mathematical semantic models, like FGL [4] and GPL [1], have been confined to the dataflow paradigm.

The HG model of concurrent software systems, which defines the formal semantics of PFG, is explained in section 2. This theory forms the basis for both static program analyses and dynamic analyses (in the form of execution simulation using the Petri net execution rules). Section 3 contains the definition of a parallel flow graph and and an explanation of the syntax of PFG. Section 4 then discusses the timing aspects of a PFG program. A description of the translation from PFG into the HG model is presented in section 5, and the general utility of the language is then illustrated in section 6 by giving the PFG representations of several well known concurrent control structures, and discussing several analysis techniques that have been developed for concurrent computations in PFG. Section 7 concludes with a brief discussion of future research plans using PFG.

2. The formal semantics of PFG

The formal semantic definition of the PFG language is provided by the *HG software system model*. This theory is intended for the representation and analysis of concurrent, time-dependent systems composed of a combination of software (applications, operating system, language support, etc.) and hardware (host machine). The mathematical details are presented fully elsewhere [9,10], but for ease of discussion we present here a summary of the theory, with emphasis on the issues of concurrency.

The HG formalism separates the major aspects of concurrent computation into three distinct model components.

- The *data model* is a formal representation, using h-graphs, of the structure and interrelationships among collections of data that are to be transformed by the computation under study. The h-graphs provide enough leverage to detect overlapping access to different parts of data structures by concurrently executing code segments.

- The *static program model* is a representation of all the operations on data (procedure calls) required by a computation as a set of non-overlapping *basic blocks*. Execution of the procedure calls in each block is necessarily sequential, but blocks can execute concurrently with each other. Each procedure during execution has its own local data area, and the procedure call semantics require copy-in, copy-out argument passing. The formalism for expressing basic blocks works in conjunction with the h-graph formalism to allow complete determination of operations which alter (as opposed to simply viewing) portions of data structures.

- The model component of greatest interest here is the *control flow model*. It expresses the possible parallel execution threads of a concurrent computation. A thread is a sequence of basic blocks from the static program model, the execution of which produces the portion of the total computation contributed by that thread. The control flow model is a timed Petri net together with a (somewhat complex) interpretation of the net structure in terms of the other model components.

2.1. Data modeling

Representation of data in PFG is done with an extension to the theory of *hierarchical graphs*, or *h-graphs*, first developed by Pratt [7]. The extended theory presupposes two universal, finite base sets: the set Φ of *nodes*; and the set Ξ of *characters*. An *atom* is a finite sequence of characters from Ξ. The set of all atoms is denoted Δ, and $\Delta = \Xi^*$. The atom # denotes the null, or empty, string. An *extended directed graph* (or simply *graph*) over Φ and Δ is the standard notion of directed graph with atoms appearing as labels on the arcs. Given these, the following definition presents the concept of an h-graph, the basic model of data in this theory:

Definition 1: H-graph
An *h-graph* over Φ and Δ is a triple, $h=\langle G,V,r\rangle$, in which

$$G=\{g_1,\cdots,g_k\}, k\geq 1, \text{ is a finite subset of } \Omega,$$
$$\text{such that each } g_i=\langle M_i,E_i\rangle$$
$$V: \bigcup_{i=1}^{k} M_i \rightarrow G\cup\Delta$$
$$r\in G$$

G is termed the *graph set* of h; V is the *immediate value function*; r is the *root graph* of h. We assume that $r=g_1$ and write $h=\langle G,V\rangle$.
Related terms:

  a. $\bigcup_{i=1}^{k} M_i$ is the *nodeset* of h, written $\overline{M}(h)$.
  b. If $m\in\overline{M}(h)$, $V(m)$ is the *value* of m in h.
  c. If $V(m)\in G$ then m is a *graph-valued node*

of h; otherwise $V(m)\in\Delta$ and m is an *atom-valued node* of h.

  d. The set of all h-graphs over Φ and Δ is denoted Γ.
  e. The set $\Psi=\Gamma\cup\Delta$ is termed the set of *values*.

An h-graph is essentially a collection of directed graphs and atoms, and a function which maps the nodes in the graphs into these entities, thus creating a structural hierarchy among the graphs. Figure 1 illustrates these concepts.

Selection of a node from the hierarchical structure of an h-graph is performed by an *h-graph selector*, or simply *selector*. H-graph selectors are syntactically the concatenation of one or more graph path designations, with embedded indications of when the hierarchy of graphs is delved into more deeply. Semantically, a node is selected by repeating for each path designation this procedure:

- apply the path designation to the target graph, obtaining a node;
- apply the h-graph value function of the target graph to the node, obtaining a new target graph.

The selection is started by using the root graph of the h-graph as the first target graph. Considering the entire h-graph h in Figure 1, some sample h-graph selectors and their respective function values are shown in Figure 2. As in the previous selector example, the value of each selector application is the *node* designated by the outer brackets. Node values are indicated for clarity. Note that the single "/" selector denotes the top level node in the h-graph, and that the value in that node is another graph. Also, note that a selector produces a *node*; the value function must then be invoked if the value of that node is desired.

Selectors provide the link between the control flow model and the data model. At decision points in the control flow, one or more paths are selected from a set of alternatives according to the value found in nodes of the data state, as indicated by specific selectors.

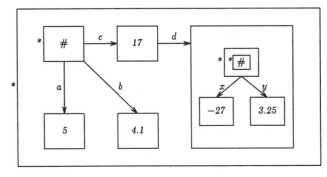

* = initial node of a graph

Figure 1 Example h-graph.

```
selector      node selected

/        →  [ [ # ]
               -a-> [ 5 ]
               -b-> [ 4.1 ]
               -c-> [ 17 ] -d-> [ [ [ # ] ]
                                    -x-> [ -27 ]
                                    -y-> [ 3.25 ]
                                 ]
            ]

//a       →  [ 5 ]
//c.d/x   →  [ -27 ]
//c.d//   →  [ # ]
```

Figure 2 Sample selectors for h-graph in Figure 1.

2.2. Control flow modeling

Both the structure and the semantics of Petri nets have been enhanced for modeling software. First, deterministic times have been added, one per place in the net, with each place time being an integer greater than zero. As discussed more completely later, a place represents one of the basic blocks of procedure calls in the static program model, and the time associated with a place represents the execution duration of that code block. Secondly, to model code block execution, the notion of *token aging* is included in the net execution semantics. A token arriving at a place p with time τ_p cannot participate in enabling the transitions following p until τ_p *time units* have expired, at which point the token is said to be *fully aged*. A time unit can have several definitions; the most convenient for our purpose is simply one state change of the entire Petri net. Thus the interpretation for this situation is that τ_p state changes occur in the modeled system while the software associated with p is executing.

Thirdly, to mesh token aging with the rest of the net semantics, we employ a *concurrent transition firing rule*. This allows a single state change to be effected by the firing of more than one transition. A transition is *enabled* when a fully aged token resides in each of the places that are inputs to it. A transition is *data-enabled* (in the case of two or more transitions sharing input places) if the state of the data model specifies it over the others in conflict with it. From the current state (net marking) all data-enabled transitions are identified, and some subset of them is fired. The effects of these firings are accumulated to produce the next state.

The concurrent firing rule allows state changes in the net to be equated with ticks of a wall clock. This in turn allows modeling and analysis of time-dependent computations on parallel hardware. There may be state changes in which no transitions fire, due to a lack of fully aged tokens in the net. The entire effect of such a state change is to age all tokens one "tick." The length of the Petri net state sequence produced by concurrent net execution, then, gives

the duration of the modeled computation.

The data state is transformed in lock-step with the state changes in the control flow model. The control state transition rule dictates which code blocks are to be executing at any particular instant. The data state transition rule provides semantics for creating local data regions for procedures when called, passing arguments via copy-in, copy-out semantics, and effecting the function calculated by each procedure on its local data. The two rules are coordinated in that one data state change occurs for each control state change.

A word is in order here about our interpretation of these nets in terms of the hardware that is intended to host the modeled computation. Our working assumption is that each place in a Petri net is mapped to one (unique) processor in some parallel architecture; the mapping is one-to-one, but not necessarily onto. Because of the association of code blocks with places, then, each basic block executes on it own processor. While this may be unrealistic for large computations on today's machines, it may not be so for machines in the near future. It also makes analysis easier, and so is a reasonable assumption for a first look at the utility of this model. Tokens may, under this view, be thought of as requests for the hardware processor to execute its associated code block. Only one request is handled at a time, which means that only one token at a place is allowed to age. Any others arriving while this is happening simply wait their turn, in "limbo." The same code block is executed to fulfill each request. Thus, tokens have no identity, and there is no need to queue them to preserve their arrival order. Finally, a transition with a fully aged input set of tokens must fire as soon as the subset selection allows it to do so. No arbitrary waiting is allowed as in the original Petri net execution semantics. This restriction is made to ease the problems associated with timing analyses. With one processor per net place, it seems reasonable to insist that when one block execution request is satisfied, the processor not "idle", but get right to handling any other of its outstanding requests (tokens).

3. The syntax of PFG: parallel flow graphs

The control flow model, as presented, is largely a general Petri net with some additions that enhance its suitability for time-dependent analysis. The PFG language offers a technique for controlling the acceptable structure of these nets, that is, limiting the software modeler to using only a subset of the general timed Petri nets. The restrictions serve the same purpose in our theory that structured programming does for the creation of manageable algorithms--they limit achievable complexity but not expressive power.

To accomplish the goal of modeling concurrent computation with a Petri net structure of limited complexity, we view the static program model and the control flow model as a unified entity, represented in a graphical notation termed a *parallel flow graph*. A PFG program is constructed as a hierarchical collection of parallel flow graphs, and then each can be dissected into the two component models for analysis. The components of a Petri net produced from PFG are easily associated with portions of the modeled software, thus ensuring that analysis is attempted only for HG models with reasonable interpretations.

The following definition describes the mathematical structure of a parallel flow graph.

Definition 2: Parallel flow graph

Let W be a set of procedure calls, S be a set of selectors, and $\mathbb{Y}$ be a distinguished node value. A *parallel flow graph* ϕ over W, S, and $\mathbb{Y}$ is a tuple $\phi = \langle g, K, V, \hat{t} \rangle$ in which

a. $g = \langle \eta, E_\phi, \eta' \rangle$ where

   η is a finite set of nodes,

   $\eta' \in \eta$ is the *initial node*, and

   E_ϕ is a finite set of arcs, each $e_{\phi_i} \in E_\phi$ of the form $\langle \eta_j, \eta_k, a \rangle$ with $\eta_j, \eta_k \in \eta$ and $a \in \Delta$, indicating that an arc labeled with atom a exists from node η_j to node η_k; the arcs in E_ϕ are subject to the restrictions stated below.

b. $K: \eta \rightarrow \{$ pcall, cbranch, nbranch, join $\}$ is a function mapping each node in g into one of four types, termed respectively *procedure call*, *concurrency branch*, *nondeterministic branch*, and *join*.

c. $V: \eta \rightarrow S \cup W \cup \{\mathbb{Y}\}$ is a function mapping each node in g into either a selector, a procedure call, or the distinguished value $\mathbb{Y}$. The value $\mathbb{Y}$ only serves to make the function total.

d. $\hat{t}: \eta \rightarrow \{1, 2, \cdots\} \cup \{\infty\}$ is a function that associates a positive, integral execution time, or the value ∞, with each node in the PFG.

Visually, a parallel flow graph is drawn with different icons to represent the four node types. A *concurrency branch* is denoted by a base-down triangular icon. A *nondeterministic branch* is denoted by a base-down half-circle icon. A *join* node is denoted with a base-up triangular icon. We employ a syntactic shorthand in the case of procedure call nodes. Rather than explicitly picture each node, we represent an entire sequence of them as a single rectangular icon, termed a *basic block* node. The underlying mathematical entity still contains a sequence of individual "pcall" nodes. The node icons in a parallel flow graph are connected with arrows. The PFG prototype allows an icon to be "clicked" open to reveal its contents (value), either a selector expression or a block of procedure calls, in a viewing window. At the outer syntactic level, nodes are numbered; branch nodes are indicated by notation such as "s4", and basic blocks are indicated with notation like "b7." Join nodes are pictured with $\mathbb{Y}$ on them.

We now describe restrictions on the general structure prescribed in the definition of a parallel flow graph. Because each procedure begins with a single control path,

the initial node η' may not be of type "join." The arcs between nodes represent the flow of control from one action in an algorithm to the next, and each arc has an atomic label associated with it. To ensure connectivity, each node in the graph must be on a directed path from the initial node. Obviously at least one arc, then, must enter each node (other than the initial node), but we place no upper limit on this number. The initial node may possibly have no arcs entering it.

Arcs leaving a node are governed by several constraints. A node containing a procedure call or a join may have no arcs leaving it, or it may have a single arc leaving it with the label on that arc being *null*, written #[1]. Each of the two types of *branch node* contains a selector, and may have any positive number of arcs leaving it. The label on each of these arcs may be any atom from Δ, and they need not be unique, *i.e.*, an atom may serve as label for two or more of the out-arcs of a branch node. Figure 3 illustrates this synthesis with a portion of a PFG in which each s_i represents a selector and each b_i represents a basic block node.

As stated earlier, the formal semantics of PFG are fully defined by the HG computation model. Informally, this model prescribes the following computational behavior for a parallel flow graph. Execution proceeds from the initial node, and nodes are executed in the order they are encountered by following arcs. Such a sequence is termed a

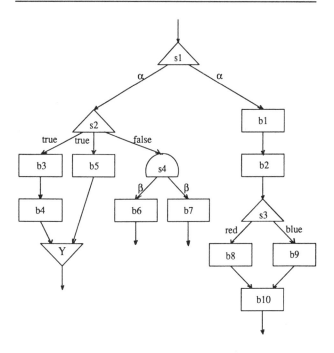

Figure 3 Parallel flow graph.

---

[1]By default, an arc with no written label has the *null* label.

control thread. An initial data state, represented by an h-graph, is assumed. The effects of executing a node are dependent on its type. If a node contains a procedure call, then the data state is altered as specified by the function of the called procedure. If a node contains a selector, then the data state is consulted at the node selected and a choice of next node (or nodes) is made based on the value found there. For a node of type "cbranch", two or more parallel control threads can be created. All arcs bearing the atom label found as the value of the selected node are concurrently followed. For a node of type "nbranch", the selector is evaluated to get an atom; then, *one* of the perhaps several arcs bearing that atom as label is chosen *nondeterministically* and followed. If a node contains a join ⅄, then synchronization of the potentially many incoming concurrent control paths is performed, and a single control path continues from the node. If no arc leaves a node, or if none bears the selected atom, then the control path through that node expires; execution does not continue from the node. Execution of the entire PFG terminates when all individual control paths expire.

Since a PFG has a single initial node, the execution of a PFG always begins with one control path. When a branch node selector produces an atom that labels several out arcs, then concurrent control paths come into being. Since branch nodes are the only nodes allowed to have multiple out-arcs, they are the only points in a PFG at which concurrent control paths can be created. Subsequently, the progression of actions along each parallel control path is considered to be executing asynchronously and concurrently with the other parallel paths. Though the synchronization and merging of parallel paths is possible with ⅄ nodes, it is not required. Two or more parallel paths may come together in a common segment of a PFG without being joined. Each path retains its separate identity and proceeds in turn to execute the PFG nodes in the common section. This feature, coupled with the fact that PFGs may be cyclic, allows a potentially unbounded number of parallel paths to be created in a computation. The number of such paths that can actually be executing at any time (as opposed to activated but waiting) is bounded, however, since the number of nodes in a PFG is finite.

Note that sequential computation is represented by a special form of parallel flow graph, one in which labels on arcs leaving a concurrency branch node must be unique. Under this restriction, at most one control thread may proceed from any node in a sequential PFG. With only one initial node, no concurrent activity can then be generated. This simple and succinct restriction adds to the attractiveness of the theory as a unified computation model.

4. Procedure timing in PFG

While timing information is an insignificant part of PFG syntax, it is an important part of the HG software system model, and hence of the semantics of PFG programs. All data transformation in PFG is accomplished via procedure calls (expression evaluation, the only other operation

on the data model, is read-only and enables branching and parameter passing). A basic block in the HG model is a sequence of procedure calls unbroken by any branches. These procedures are of two kinds: *primitive*, and not. A primitive procedure in a PFG program has no parallel flow graph to represent its structure; it has only a duration (a timing) and a data transformation specified by a function. A non-primitive procedure, on the other hand, has a parallel flow graph representation of its structure. Its timing is then recursively derivable from the structure of the procedures called, with the primitive procedures providing the base timings that cause the recursion to terminate. Its function is also derivable, as the composition of the functions of the called procedures, in one of the possibly many orders specified by the control flow model.

The Petri nets employed in the HG model are determinately timed. Software is often not determinate in its behavior, that is, a block of procedure calls will often have an execution duration that varies with the input data. PFG is intended for the expression of computations in a way that will allow verification of adherence to absolute timing constraints, such as "module X must finish in under 10

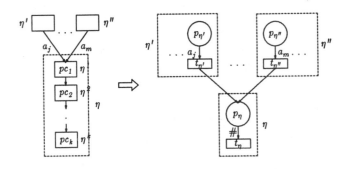

Figure 4 Translation of a basic block node.

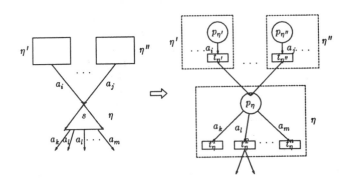

Figure 5 Translation of a cbranch node.

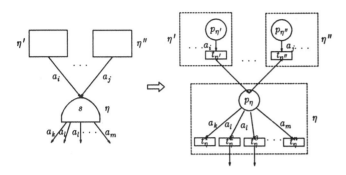

Figure 6 Translation of an nbranch node.

milliseconds," or "module Y can be no longer than 3 seconds behind module X in completion of execution."

Timing of procedures under the determinate semantics, then, is accomplished by constructing two models for each-- a minimum timed model and a maximum timed model. These execution bounds are obtained by path analysis on the concurrent reachability tree [11], for the Petri net in the control flow model. This graph is a state-space structure that reflects the difference between regular Petri net semantics and the concurrent firing rule employed in PFG semantics. It is constructed in such a way that duration of a block is reflected by the length of the state sequence (path in the graph) in which it is active. With some restrictions on its structure, such as breadth-first node generation, the concurrent reachability tree can be searched for the longest and shortest paths, and the leaves of those paths can be checked for repetition of earlier states (indicating a potentially infinite duration). Naturally, for cyclic procedures, either one of these bounds can be infinite, and the duration of ∞ will propagate to procedures which call it. Thus each PFG program is analyzed as a dual-system model for timing.

5. Translation of PFG into timed Petri nets

Each structure in a parallel flow graph has a translation specified into the HG modeling formalism. Figures 4, 5, 6, and 7 illustrate the Petri net components of the control flow model, and the connections among them, created for each type of PFG structure that can be encountered in a program. The details of this translation are fully specified in [9]. In summary, an unbroken sequence of PFG procedure call nodes is coalesced into a single entity (a basic block in the static program model) and represented by a single place connected to a single transition in the Petri net (termed a *P/T* component). A branch node in a PFG program has multiple arcs leaving it, perhaps several labeled with the same atom. For a cbranch, a Petri net structure s created having a single place connected to several transitions, one for each unique atomic arc label (termed a *P/nT* component). The same number of arcs leave each transition as there are bearing its atomic label leaving the PFG branch node. For an nbranch, the translation is similar, except that one transition is created for each arc, with one arc leaving each transition. A join node in PFG has multiple arcs entering it that must be synchronized and coalesced. It becomes a Petri net structure having one place for each arc entering the join node, and a single transition to which the places are all connected (termed an *nP/T* component). A single arc then exits this transition. Once created, the Petri net components have the same interconnectivity as the PFG nodes have. The timing on a PFG node is the timing given each place in the Petri net component created from it.

The Petri nets that are created from PFG programs by this translation form a subclass of general Petri nets, termed *free-choice* nets. Their structure is simplified in that if any place serves as input to several transitions, then it is the only input place for those transitions. The transitions that share the input place are said to be in conflict. Hack [12] has

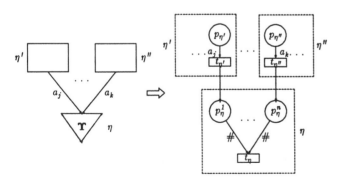

Figure 7 Translation of a join node.

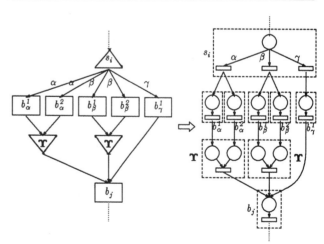

Figure 8 Multi-way fork-and-join (cobegin).

shown necessary and sufficient conditions to guarantee liveness and safeness of free-choice nets.

6. Utility of PFG

Many common concurrent control structures can easily be expressed in PFG. Figures 8 and 9 show examples along with the Petri net components created from them. Programs written to use such semantics can then be analyzed for concurrency problems using the HG model. In addition, the syntax of PFG allows expression of some concurrent control structures which have no well-known names, as exemplified in Figure 10.

Several analysis techniques have been developed for PFG programs. The dual-model method for timing of systems has been previously mentioned. It allows verification of adherence of procedures to execution time bounds. Details of this method are presented in [9].

Another analysis technique allows the detection and correction of improper accesses to shared data structures [10]. The analysis is based on the concurrent reachability tree mentioned earlier. Since a code block is associated with each place, a state (net marking) showing a token in a place indicates that a code block is executing in that

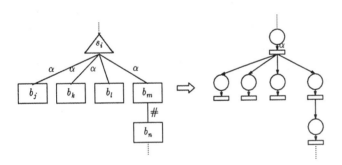

Figure 9 Spawn concurrent threads.

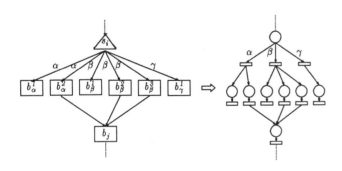

Figure 10 Arbitrary concurrent control structure.

state. The concurrent reachability tree, then, shows in its markings which pairs of code blocks may possibly execute concurrently. The data structures accessed by these code blocks are checked for improper accesses, such as one procedure reading twice consecutively from a datum, and another procedure concurrently writing to the same datum. The h-graphs used to model the data provide the ability to detect conflicts on portions of structured data rather than simply on variable names. When identified, these potential improper accesses can be prevented during execution by automatic insertion of synchronizing places into the Petri net models representing the calling procedure. As small an involved portion as possible of each code block is identified, and each block is restructured into two or more new, smaller blocks. These new blocks are then given Petri net places and transitions in the control flow model. For each block pair an extra place, marked with a single token, is connected into the model to create mutual exclusion on the conflicting sequences of procedure calls.

A third analysis for the HG model is detection of some deadlocks, which appear in the concurrent reachability tree as partial markings of places that are portions of join components. The semantics of a join are such that if any one of the places entering it are marked (indicating that the software represented by that place is executing) then all of the other places must eventually be marked as well in the same state, or the following transition can never fire, blocking progress at that point. Further, the fully marked state must be reachable from the partially marked ones. For example, consider a join component having three incoming arcs in a PFG program. The join is represented in the Petri net of the control flow model by three places entering a single transition. If some state μ appears in the reachability tree having tokens in one of these places, then there must be a state μ' on a path from μ that has all three places marked. If no such μ' exists, then a potential deadlock exists in the original PFG program.

In addition to these concurrency analyses, aliasing detection in the data model has been developed by Wilson [13] for sequential computations (a special case in PFG syntax).

7. Future research

PFG is interesting both for its graphical syntax and for its formal concurrent computation semantics. The language allows expression of time-dependent concurrent computations; the underlying semantic model allows incorporation of the behavior of the host machine into analysis of the system. An initial implementation of the language is just now underway, in conjunction with the development of the PFG programming environment. The PFG environment is a unified construction and analysis toolset for concurrent, time-dependent computations. It has the HG software system model as a formal basis for all activity in the environment: static analysis, dynamic simulation, and code generation. The PFG language serves as the primary program source. Programming in other languages, such as Ada or Modula-2, is possible in the PFG environment, with source programs being translated directly into the HG model. After creation, the model can then be viewed as a PFG program. Various target machines will have HG representations stored in a modelbase so that time-dependent analyses can be done on a software system for a particular host. Once an HG model has been analyzed and is correct, executable code for the host can be generated from the model. The system is being developed for a Sun workstation.

References

1. A. L. Davis and S. A. Lowder, "A Sample Management Application Program in a Graphical Data-Driven Programming Language," *Digest of Papers, Compcon Spring 81*, pp. 162-167 (February 1981).

2. A. L. Davis and R. M. Keller, "Data Flow Program Graphs," *Computer*, **15**(2), pp. 26-41 (February 1982).

3. E. P. Glinert and S. L. Tanimoto, "Pict: An Interactive Graphical Programming Environment," *Computer*, **17**(11), pp. 7-25 (November 1984).

4. R. M. Keller and W.-C. J. Yen, "A Graphical Approach to Software Development Using Function Graphs," *Digest of Papers, Compcon Spring 81*, pp. 156-161 (February 1981).

5. T. Pietrzykowski, S. Matwin, and T. Muldner, "The Programming Language PROGRAPH: Yet Another Application of Graphics," *Graphics Interface '83*, Edmonton, Alberta, pp. 143-145 (May 1983).

6. T. Pietrzykowski and S. Matwin, "PROGRAPH: A Preliminary Report," Technical Report TR-84-07, University of Ottawa (April 1984).

7. T. W. Pratt, "Formal Specification of Software Using H-Graph Semantics," pp. 314-332, in *Lecture Notes in Computer Science #153: Graph Grammars and Their Application to Computer Science*, ed. H. Ehrig, M. Nagl, and G. Rozenberg, Springer-Verlag, Berlin (1983).

8. L. Snyder, "Parallel Programming and the Poker Programming Environment," *Computer*, **17**(7), pp. 27-36 (July 1984).

9. P. D. Stotts, Jr., "A Hierarchical Graph Model of Concurrent Real-Time Software Systems," Ph. D. Dissertation (TR-86-12), Department of Computer Science, University of Virginia, Charlottesville, Virginia (August 1985).

10. P. D. Stotts, Jr. and T. W. Pratt, "Hierarchical Modeling of Software Systems With Timed Petri Nets," *Proceedings of the International Workshop on Timed Petri Nets*, Torino, Italy, pp. 32-39 (July 1985).

11. P. D. Stotts and T. W. Pratt, "Petri Net Reachability Trees for Concurrent Execution Rules," *Journal of Parallel and Distributed Computing* (accepted, to appear).

12. M. Hack, "Analysis of Production Schemata by Petri Nets," *M.S. thesis*, Cambridge, Massachusetts, Department of Electrical Engineering, Massachusetts Institute of Technology (February 1972).

13. J. N. Wilson, "Data Types and Aliasing in Program Specification and Verification," Ph. D. dissertation (TR-86-13), University of Virginia, Department of Computer Science, Charlottesville, Virginia (May 1985).

BUILDING INTERPROCESS COMMUNICATION MODELS USING STILE

Michael P. Stovsky and Bruce W. Weide

Department of Computer and Information Science
The Ohio State University
Columbus, Ohio 43210
(ARPANET/CSNET: stovsky@ohio-state.edu, weide@ohio-state.edu)

Abstract

STILE provides a graphical environment for describing logical relationships among components of systems. The syntax of the graphs produced using STILE is separate from the semantics which are supplied by a post-processor. A major advantage of this approach is the ability to address different models of computation, especially different concurrency models, using the same graphical environment. This paper describes how to create primary building block parts for analog computing and data flow computing from parts defined in a different model of computing. Composing parts in this fashion eliminates the need to build post-processors for these additional models of computation, thereby overcoming one of the major problems introduced by separating graphical syntax from semantics.

1. Introduction

STILE (STructure Interconnection Language and Environment) is a general-purpose computer-based graphical design and development system for describing logical relationships among components of systems. Software systems created using STILE can be compiled into runable code by a post-processor. STILE allows software engineers to construct systems bottom-up by defining component parts and combining them. Similarly, systems may be constructed top-down, outside-in, or inside-out. Because parts are easily composed from other parts, hierarchical systems engineering is supported and reusability is facilitated.

The STILE environment follows the classical engineering design metaphor: each part has a catalog page containing specifications describing *what* the part does and a blueprint detailing *how* the part is constructed. A text editor is used to create and modify catalog page specifications. A syntax-sensitive graphical editor is used to construct blueprints describing part implementation details. The graphical editor does not allow the construction of syntactically invalid blueprints. However, the editor knows nothing about the meaning of blueprint contents. Semantic interpretation of blueprints is performed by a post-processor whose input is the structural description maintained by STILE. This separation of blueprint syntax from semantics allows STILE to be used to describe systems for a variety of computational models. STILE can be customized to address new models of computation either by constructing new post-processors or by combining parts from currently used models of computation so the resulting parts behave like those in the new one.

Previous papers on STILE concentrated on the philosophy, engineering design metaphor, syntax of STILE graphs, and the "STILE Basic interpretation" — an abstract concurrency model that separates data and control[1,2,3]. This paper describes how to assemble parts that behave like parts from analog computing and data flow computing. These models of computation are built from parts in the STILE Basic interpretation and, therefore, do not require their own post-processors.

Section 2 introduces the notion of an "interpretation," the context for supplying meaning to STILE graphs. Sections 3 and 4 concentrate on two useful interpretations corresponding to analog and data flow computation, respectively. Section 5 briefly discusses future work.

2. Interpretations

Each blueprint has an external and an internal section. The external section describes the part's connection points for communicating with the outside world. The internal section contains the part's implementation details. Each section has an associated *interpretation* that determines which semantic rules should be applied by the post-processor. In addition, parts with a particular external interpretation can only be instantiated in blueprints with that internal interpretation. For example, if the part being constructed has an external interpretation of Analog and an internal interpretation of STILE Basic, only parts with an external interpretation of STILE Basic can be instantiated in the internal section of the new part's blueprint. Similarly, the new part can only be instantiated in blueprints whose internal interpretation is Analog. As this example suggests, the two interpretations need not be the same. Hence, changing interpretations at the external/internal boundary serves as an abstraction mechanism. (Figure 10, explained in section 3.4.3, uses this capability.)

Reprinted from *IEEE Proceedings of the 21st Hawaii International Conference on System Sciences (HICSS-21)*, Volume 2: Software Track, pages 639-647. Copyright © 1988 by The Institute of Electrical and Electronics Engineers, Inc. All rights reserved.

The primary building-block parts for a new model of computation and, consequently, a new interpretation of STILE graphs, can be created by an expert programmer from existing parts as described in this paper. Once these parts have been created, they are available to the community of programmers as "primitive" parts in the new interpretation. In other words, people using these parts to create graphs in the new model of computation are not aware the parts are compositions; they are not allowed to examine the blueprints created by the expert, as enforced by system administration policy. They may only see the catalog pages (specifications) for these parts. Aside from the obvious information hiding this provides, programmers are (unknowingly) using abstraction since they are describing graphs in the new model of computation by assembling parts composed in a different model of computation.

By exploiting STILE's part composition, abstraction, and information hiding capabilities, trees of the models of computation supported by each post-processor can be constructed. Engineers designing and constructing systems are able to select models of computation that precisely match the problem domain at each level of system decomposition. Because each part within STILE has an external interpretation and an internal interpretation which may differ, the interpretation applied to parts within a system may change as different levels of the system hierarchy are encountered.

As each new interpretation is added to STILE, its position in the tree of interpretations is specified. Figure 1 is the interpretation tree for the post-processor supporting the models of computation described in this paper. Arrows emanating from a node describe which interpretations are candidates for the internal portion of a blueprint whose external interpretation is the node value. For example, a graph whose external interpretation is Analog may have either Analog or STILE Basic as its internal interpretation.

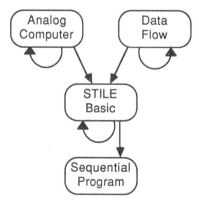

Figure 1: Interpretation Tree

3. Analog Interpretation

Digital computers use clocks to synchronize the activities necessary to carry out computations. The functional units of a digital computer are activated by clock pulses. Real numbers are approximated using finite-precision floating point numbers. On the other hand, in an analog computer the functional units (devices) operate continuously. There is no concept of a clock "tick" or device synchronization. At any time, the output of a device is a function of its input(s) and time. Furthermore, all numeric quantities in analog computers are proportional to voltage levels. These levels are free to vary within the circuits' electrical limits; they are not limited to discrete levels.

Ideally, the wires used to connect the units in an analog computer provide instantaneous transmission of voltage changes. In addition, an output wire may be connected to several inputs, thereby exhibiting fan-out. Since the output of an analog device is often fed back into the device's input, analog outputs may be dependent on the computation's history; i.e., analog computers have "memory".

This section explains how software based on the analog computing model can be built from more primitive parts using STILE.

3.1. Composition and Reusability

From a software perspective, analog computing has interesting properties related to reusability. Analog computers have been used to solve complex problems by combining existing circuits to form more powerful ones[4]. For example, as shown in Figure 2, multiplier, inverter, and operational amplifier circuits can be combined to form a square root circuit. (An inverter negates its input. The output of an operational amplifier is a very large constant times the sum of its inputs.) This square root circuit can be considered a new part which may be used independently or as a building block in more powerful circuits.

The ability to construct such hierarchies of parts within an interpretation is captured by the *composition property*[5]. This property can be summarized as follows. A compound agent should behave abstractly like a primitive agent; it should communicate and be composed just like primitive agents; and the composition operations should be independent of the internal structure of the agents to which they are applied. Finally, the meaning or function of a compound agent should be uniformly definable in terms of its constituents. Analog computer components satisfy this property, which makes them interesting from the standpoint of studying reusability.

Historically, analog computers have served as the basis for real-time controllers. Figure 3 is a simple model of a feedback control system. In such a system, the setpoint is the desired value of the controlled variable. For example, the temperature setting on a thermostat is a setpoint. A control engineer synthesizes a control algorithm to

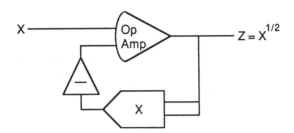

Figure 2: Square Root Circuit Built from Simpler Parts

influence the system to insure the value of the controlled variable tracks the setpoint. In order to synthesize a stable control algorithm, the engineer must account for the dynamics of the controlled system. Inability to correctly account for system dynamics can result in an unstable system which may exhibit wild fluctuations of the controlled variable's value.

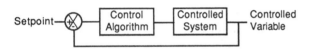

Figure 3: Feedback Control System

STILE's three part types can be mapped to analog computer components in a straightforward fashion. Specifically, STILE boxes denote functional units, links denote wires, and ports denote electrical terminals. This informal semantic assignment is called the *Analog* interpretation. We have found this interpretation to be useful for designing real-time control software[4,6,7]. Constructing a STILE interpretation for analog computing provides a vehicle for exploring software reusability as well as an environment to solve real-time software problems.

The Analog interpretation provides a framework with which a control engineer can build software simulations of analog systems. However, processing delays involved in this software are analogous to bandwidth limitations of the analog components, have a similar impact on stability, and must be analyzed using feedback control theory. STILE supplies the syntactic and semantic constructs needed to design these systems, but does not insure their stability. Stability, an independent property, must be verified by the control engineer.

3.2. A Sample Analog System

Figure 4 is a blueprint (implementation) for the software control of a Heating Control System (HCS). (Each caption in this paper specifies the external and internal interpretations as follows: (external interpretation/internal interpretation). The internal interpretation is not revealed in a figure if it is not revealed to the user of the system, as in catalog pages.) The Dial box reads the desired

room temperature (the setpoint). Temp is a thermometer returning the actual temperature (the controlled variable). The Subtract box computes the difference between these two quantities. Furnace turns on the heating element and fan if the room temperature is too far below the setpoint. Once the temperature is high enough, Furnace turns the heating element and fan off.

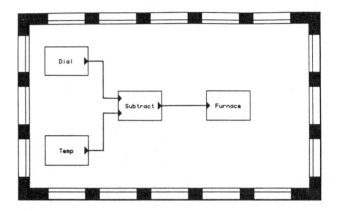

Figure 4: Heating Control System (Analog/Analog)

Figure 5 is the catalog page (specifications) for the Furnace box and Figure 6 is its blueprint. The Range box exhibits hysteresis so the heating element and fan do not oscillate on and off. Constants supplies the Range box with a sensitivity value. If the difference between the desired and actual temperatures is greater than this value, the heater and fan are turned on. Similarly, when the room temperature exceeds the setpoint plus this sensitivity value, the heater and fan are turned off.

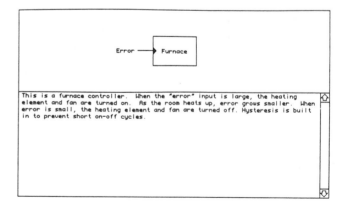

Figure 5: Furnace Catalog Page (Analog)

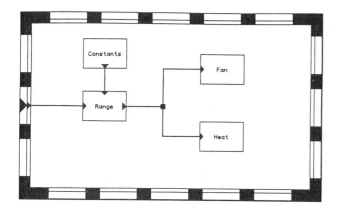

Figure 6: Furnace Blueprint (Analog/Analog)

3.3. The STILE Basic Interpretation

Since the objective is to show how Analog interpretation semantics can be "created" from STILE Basic interpretation parts, this section briefly summarizes the STILE Basic interpretation. A previous paper contains a detailed explanation of the STILE Basic interpretation[3].

In the STILE Basic interpretation, the internal section of a box may contain text which describes sequential computations in a typical sequential programming language, or it may contain a STILE Basic interpretation graph, thereby allowing hierarchical design. The interpretation of a box containing a graph is as though its internal section were substituted for its icon wherever the box is used. Each box in a completely expanded (flat, or single-level) graph represents a single sequential process. Each process operates concurrently and communicates with the other processes via its ports and according to its link bindings.

Ports are of two major types: data ports and control ports. Data ports are used to communicate data with other boxes. An input data port is like a register that can be read by the box. It keeps its current value until it is overwritten by another box writing to an output data port connected to the input port by a link. Control is communicated through input and output control ports. An input control port is like a single flip-flop. Each box has a monitor that keeps track of the states of its input control ports. An input control port is set when a box "pokes" an output control port connected to it by a link. The monitor continually checks to see if any control input ports are set. If so, it selects one of the set input ports arbitrarily, resets the port, runs a corresponding sequential code segment to completion, and resumes monitoring the input control ports. Internal communication among separate code segments of a box is by shared data. All communication between separate boxes is by communication protocols and data transmission via ports and links. Links in the STILE Basic interpretation are simply extension cords which bind together the ports of boxes.

3.4. Implementing the Analog Interpretation in STILE

In the STILE Basic interpretation, data and control are transmitted as discrete entities and boxes compute only when their control inputs are poked. On the other hand, wires in analog computers continuously carry meaningful values to functional units which continuously compute with them. Despite these differences, STILE Basic interpretation parts can be arranged to simulate analog computer parts, as described below.

3.4.1. Analog Ports

Figure 7 shows a STILE port in the Analog interpretation, called "Pin." A Pin represents an electrical terminal to which wires can be connected. The Pin is composed of a data port and a control port. When a box computes a value, it writes the value to the data port of the Pin and pokes the Pin's control port, thus signalling a fresh value has been computed.

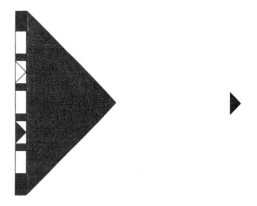

Figure 7: Pin Blueprint (Analog/STILE Basic) and Icon

3.4.2. Analog Links

Figure 8 is the blueprint of a STILE link in the Analog interpretation, called "Wire." The Wire part consists of a Pin at each end with the data and control ports connected to their duals. Wire forwards the data and control signals from the source to the destination, exactly what is needed. The values produced by a box may be transmitted to several other boxes, but "wired ORs" are not allowed. Consequently, a Wire may exhibit fan-out but not fan-in. This syntax rule is described in Wire's catalog page by allowing multiple output connections, but not multiple input connections, as shown in Figure 9.

3.4.3. Analog Functional Units

Figure 10 is the blueprint of a typical STILE box in the Analog interpretation, called "Subtract." It is constructed from a STILE Basic Subtract box. When either of the Analog Subtract box's input

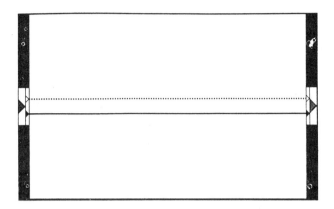

Figure 8: Wire Blueprint (Analog/STILE Basic)

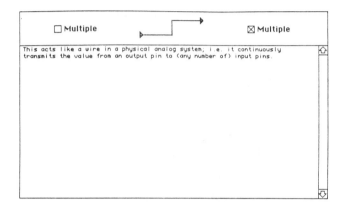

Figure 9: Wire Catalog Page (Analog)

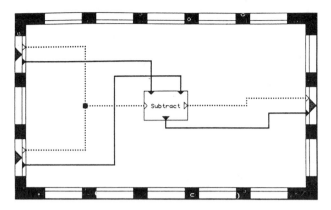

Figure 10: Subtract Blueprint (Analog/STILE Basic) and Icon

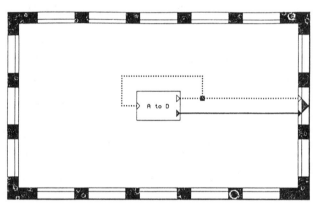

Figure 11: Dial Blueprint (Analog/STILE Basic)

Pins has a new value (i.e., the control input port is poked) the subtrahend is subtracted from the minuend and the difference is available on the output Pin (i.e., the difference is written to the output data port, and the output control port is poked). Note the box performing the subtraction is a STILE Basic Subtract box which has not been altered in any way. It has been instantiated in Analog Subtract's blueprint and connected to the Pins on the box's periphery using STILE Basic control and data links. Once created, the Analog Subtract box can be instantiated wherever it is needed without further modification, as in Figure 4. Other Analog functional units are similarly constructed from their STILE Basic cousins.

For some Analog boxes, such as Dial in Figure 4, there are no input Pins. Hence, there is no external triggering mechanism to serve the function of the control port of an input Pin. This kind of Analog box is triggered internally. For example, Dial might be constructed from a STILE Basic box that samples an A/D converter whenever its input control port is poked, and whose output control port is fed back into its input control port. Figure 11 is the blueprint for this implementation of Dial. Alternatively, the stimulus for sampling may come from a STILE Basic "Clock" box that periodically pokes its output control port[7].

3.5. An Improved Implementation

Figure 12 is the blueprint for an improved Wire. The STILE Basic "Change" box propagates control and data signals it receives only when the new data value differs from the value last written to the output data port. The blueprint for the Change box is shown in Figure 13. Substituting the improved Wire link for the original Wire has no effect on the functionality of an Analog system, but reduces the computation load in a nearly-quiescent system by preventing a box from recomputing its outputs when no inputs have changed. In a real-time control application this may be an important factor in responsiveness and in keeping hardware costs to a minimum[1].

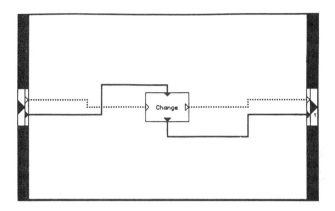

Figure 12: Improved Wire Blueprint (Analog/STILE Basic)

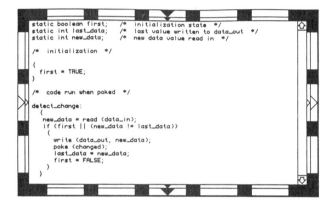

```
static boolean first;      /*  initialization state */
static int last_data;      /*  last value written to data_out */
static int new_data;       /*  new data value read in  */

/*  initialization  */

{
  first = TRUE;
}

/*  code run when poked  */

detect_change:
{
  new_data = read (data_in);
  if (first || (new_data != last_data))
  {
    write (data_out, new_data);
    poke (changed);
    last_data = new_data;
    first = FALSE;
  }
}
```

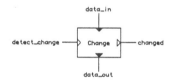

Figure 13: Change Blueprint (STILE Basic /STILE Basic) and Icon

4. Data Flow Interpretation

Data flow graphs are useful computational models[8] as well as an analysis and design tool[9,10]. This section explains how to construct the parts necessary to assemble data flow graphs, using STILE Basic parts, based on Dennis' data flow model of computation.

In this model, data tokens flow along arcs connecting functional units. A unit may perform its function as soon as all of its input data tokens have arrived. Once the function is computed, output token(s) are created, and the unit awaits a new set of input tokens. At no time can an arc have more than one token on it. Hence, a unit cannot output a new token until its previous output has been consumed (by a downstream unit) *and* all inputs are available.

An example data flow graph is shown in Figure 14. It computes the area and volume of a sphere, given its radius r:

$$Area = 4 \pi r^2 \qquad Volume = 4 \pi r^3 / 3$$

Squares represent data inputs and outputs which provide or remove the indicated values. Circles represent functional units which perform the indicated operations. In this example, all functional units happen to multiply their inputs together.

Figure 15 shows an equivalent STILE graph, using the *Data Flow* interpretation. STILE boxes represent functional units, links represent the arcs along which data tokens flow, and ports represent the input and output connections on the functional units.

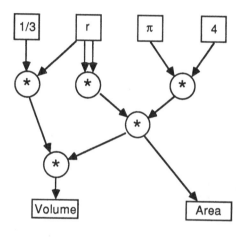

Figure 14: Data Flow Solution for Volume and Area of Sphere

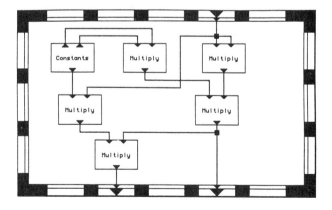

Figure 15: Sphere Blueprint (Data Flow/Data Flow)

4.1. Implementing the Data Flow Interpretation in STILE

It is possible to construct data flow elements from STILE Basic interpretation parts to capture the semantics of data flow graphs in much the same way as these STILE Basic parts were combined to build the Analog interpretation in Section 3. The parts created include data flow ports, data flow links, and data flow boxes.

4.1.1. Data Flow Ports

Figure 16 is a data flow port. In order to be faithful to the data flow paradigm, it is necessary to insure there can never be more than one token on a link at a time. This is accomplished by "handshaking" involving the control ports. When a data value (the value carried by a data token) is written to a data port, the corresponding control port is poked. This informs the recipient a token is available. When this box consumes the data token, it pokes the return control port, informing the token generator it may generate a new token.

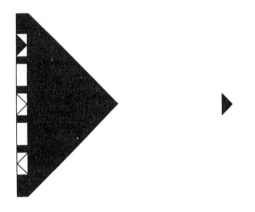

Figure 16: Port Blueprint (Data Flow/STILE Basic) and Icon

4.1.2. Data Flow Links

Externally, a data flow link appears to be an extension cord which can connect data flow ports. Further, the link allows fan-out to occur so multiple token recipients may be connected to a single token generator. The protocol described above works only if there is no fan-out from any data token generators, however. When there is fan-out, all copies of the token must be consumed before a new token can be generated. Even in the simple area and volume evaluation example, several token generators exhibit fan-out. Consequently, the data flow port has to be augmented to model a data flow computation correctly. This modification occurs within data flow links. Figure 17 is the blueprint for such a link.

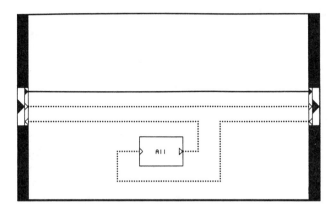

Figure 17: Link Blueprint (Data Flow/STILE Basic)

Fan out capability is due to the presence of the STILE Basic "All" box. When all the control ports connected to an All box's input control port have been poked, the All box pokes its output control port. Hence, all downstream data boxes must consume their data tokens before the data source can generate another token.

The All box is crucial to correct operation of data flow links. The input control port of All is a vector port. The size of the vector depends upon the degree of fan-in (i.e., the degree of fan-out from the data flow link). The STILE Basic interpretation processor expands the single port into as many distinct ports as there are connections to it in the graph. These distinct ports can be accessed individually by the code inside the All box.

By using an input control port which is a vector port, only one versatile All box need be constructed. Figure 18 shows the blueprint of such an All box.

Figure 18: All Blueprint (STILE Basic/Sequential Program) and Icon

The "in" port is a vector port. A boolean state vector is maintained to remember which input control ports have been poked. The first chunk of code is initialization code, run only when the system starts up. The "size" function returns the number of output control ports connected to the All box's input control port (i.e. the length of the vector). This information is used to allocate storage for the state vector. The state vector is then cleared since no ports have been poked. Once all of the constituents of the vector port have been poked, the All box pokes its output control port and resets the state vector.

Notice vector ports are not created by graphical means, but by cues in the text of parts whose internal interpretation is Sequential Program. Processing of the STILE graph structure in conjunction with this text provides the vector port feature. Recall data flow programmers cannot see the blueprint for a data flow link since they believe such links are primitive and need not be concerned with such details of the STILE Basic interpretation.

4.1.3. Data Flow Functional Units

In Dennis' model of data flow, a functional unit cannot proceed with its computation until its output tokens have been consumed and all input tokens are available. Boxes must be designed so this rule is not violated. Figure 19 is the blueprint of the Data Flow "Multiply" box. An All box is used to insure the computation cannot proceed until all input tokens have been generated and previous output tokens have been consumed. Once the appropriate tokens have been generated and consumed, the All box pokes its output control port which activates the STILE Basic Multiply box. Upon completion of its computation, Multiply pokes its output control port which informs the downstream units a token has arrived. The same poke is used to inform the upstream units their tokens have been consumed.

4.1.4. System Initialization

Upon system start up, each box needs to request tokens from upstream units. This is accomplished by initializing the data flow link's return control port to "poked" when the data flow link part is created. As a result, engineers instantiating links need not be concerned with this aspect of start up.

5. Future Work

We continue to look for new areas of application for STILE. One goal of this work is to learn more about reusability, composition, and hierarchical systems design and apply this knowledge to software. In addition, we are trying to find and define the limits of the STILE approach to systems design and development. Areas currently being investigated include creating interpretations for image processing, module interconnection, processor assignment, and general software design. In the future we plan to use STILE to create parametrically configured parts for discrete event simulation, computer graphics, and computer music. By using the STILE environment we hope

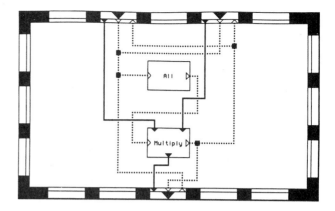

Figure 19: Multiply Blueprint
(Data Flow/STILE Basic)

to create software platforms of reusable parts from which to build systems for a variety of problem domains.

6. Summary

STILE is a general-purpose design and development environment. By separating graph syntax from semantics, STILE provides a rich environment which can be applied to many problem domains. New models of computation can be introduced to the system by either building new post-processors to interpret the graphs differently or by assembling existing parts so the result behaves like a part in a different model of computation. Engineers creating systems using parts from these new models of computation need not be aware the parts are composed from other parts. Consequently, information hiding and abstraction are strongly supported. In this paper we have illustrated how to build basis parts for Analog computing and Data Flow computing from STILE Basic parts. The fundamental parts for other models of computation can be similarly constructed.

Acknowledgements

We would like to thank Mark Brown, Douglas Harms, Peter Maurath, Robert McGhee, William Ogden, Karsten Schwan, Sanjiv Taneja, Gregor Taulbee, and Stuart Zweben for their ideas and valuable contributions to this work.

Generous support for this project from The Ohio State University and the Department of Computer and Information Science are gratefully acknowledged.

References

[1]   Brown, M.E., and Weide, B.W.,
       "Automating Process-to-Processor
       Mapping Under Real-Time Constraints,"
       in *Proc. 1984 Real-Time Systems
       Symposium*, IEEE, Austin,TX, December,
       1984, pp. 145 - 150.

[2]   Taneja, S., and Weide, B.W., "Graphical
       Description and Run-Time Environments
       for Real-Time Software," in *Proc. ACM
       Computer Science Conference*, ACM,
       Cincinnati, February 1986, pp. 205 - 211.

[3]   Stovsky, M.P., and Weide, B.W., "STILE: A
       Graphical Design and Development
       Environment (Extended Abstract)," in
       Digest of Papers, Spring COMPCON 87,
       IEEE, San Francisco, February, 1987, pp.
       247 - 251.   Full report available from
       Department of Computer and Information
       Science, The Ohio State University,
       Columbus, Ohio, OSU-CISRC-86TR1BWW,
       October 1986.

[4]   Jackson, A.S., *Analog Computation*,
       McGraw-Hill Book Company, 1960.

[5]   MacQueen, D.B., "Models for Distributed
       Computing," Rapport de Recherche No.
       351, April 1979, Institut de Recherche
       d'Infromatique et d'Automatique (IRIA),
       Le Chesnay, France.

[6]   Ogata, K., *Modern Control Engineering*,
       Prentice-Hall, Inc., 1970.

[7]   Brown, M.E., and Weide, B.W.,
       "Preliminary Design of a Highly Parallel
       Architecture for Real-Time Applications,"
       in *Proc. 18th Anual Allerton Conf.
       Communications, Control, and
       Computing*, October 1980, pp. 534 - 543.

[8]   Dennis, J.B., "First Version of a Data Flow
       Procedure Language," *Lecture Notes in
       Computer Science*, Springer-Verlag,
       Heidelberg, 1974, pp. 362 - 376.

[9]   Yourdon, E., and Constantine, L.L.,
       Structured Design, Yourdon Press, 1978.

[10]   DeMarco, T., *Structured Analysis and
       System Specification*, Prentice-Hall, 1979.

Reprinted from *IEEE Transactions on Software Engineering*, Volume SE-14, Number 6, June 1988, pages 787-802. Copyright © 1988 by The Institute of Electrical and Electronics Engineers, Inc. All rights reserved.

Integrated Environments for Formally Well-Founded Design and Simulation of Concurrent Systems

ALESSANDRO GIACALONE AND SCOTT A. SMOLKA

Abstract—We describe an ongoing project concerned with the systematic development of environments that support the specification and design of concurrent systems. The project has two key aspects: an existing and working system, Clara, that supports Milner's CCS as a specification and design language; and the development of general techniques for computer-aided generation of Clara-like environments for other concurrent languages. In this paper, we focus on the Clara environment.

The Clara environment has two main components: 1) support for the usage of formal techniques in the design process, and 2) a rich and highly interactive simulation facility. A further distinguishing feature is the environment's graphical user interface which is based on a pictorial version of CCS.

CCS is one of the most promising formalisms for defining concurrent systems and has been used successfully in many practical applications. This makes an environment that supports the calculus attractive in its own right. Moreover, the semantics of CCS is defined nonprocedurally in two phases: an operational semantics given as a set of inference rules, and then an algebraic semantics represented by a set of equational rules. This nonprocedural representation of formal semantics constitutes the foundation of our strategy for exporting the functionalities of Clara to its "clone environments."

Index Terms—Concurrency, CCS, formal reasoning, graphical user interfaces, programming environments, simulation.

(. . .) A central commitment to a double thesis: that the design of computing systems can only properly succeed if it is well grounded in theory, and that the important concepts in a theory can only emerge through protracted exposure to application. If we take this commitment seriously, then we must make an organised attempt to unite the development of theory with its experimental application. (*Robin Milner—from his inaugural lecture of The Laboratory for Foundations of Computer Science, University of Edinburgh, 1986*)

I. Introduction

CONCURRENT systems are attracting more and more interest, largely because of the availability of powerful parallel machines, such as Connection [24], NCUBE [37], and Encore Multimax [15]. At the same time, concurrent systems tend to be more complex to conceive, understand, and design than their sequential counterparts.

Deadlocks and race conditions, for example, are problems peculiar to concurrent systems. This added complexity has been a driving force behind an intense theoretical investigation of concurrency, although this work has not yet matured into a set of practical tools supporting system development.

An ongoing project at SUNY Stony Brook is concerned with the generation of interactive environments that support the *specification* and *design* of concurrent systems. The basic idea is that each environment is built around and supports a given specification/design formalism. Ideally, all the environments will have the same functionalities and similar user interfaces, i.e., the language-independent features. The project is experimental in nature and explores a variety of issues. For example, what type of support should a design environment for concurrent systems provide; how should this support be implemented; what role should formal semantics play; what is a suitable user interface; and how can graphics be used effectively in the user interface.

This paper describes the first result of the Stony Brook project, the *Clara* environment.[1] Clara supports Milner's *Calculus of Communicating Systems* (CCS) [32], [33] and is a model environment in that it already includes many of the functionalities we plan for our family of environments. The ultimate goal of the project is the development of general techniques for the systematic and computer-aided generation of Clara-like environments for other concurrent languages. These long term developments are discussed in the concluding section of the paper.

In the remainder of the introduction, we highlight several key aspects of the Clara environment in particular, and the Stony Brook project in general.

A. Support for Formally Well-Founded Design and Simulation

A major goal of the Stony Brook project is to provide powerful support for designing systems within a formally well-founded framework. The other main goal is to enable system designers to simulate executions at any stage of development, based on a well-defined semantics.

The Clara environment includes a highly interactive simulation facility. Simulation can provide valuable sup-

Manuscript received January 15, 1988. The work of A. Giacalone was supported by the National Science Foundation under Grant NSF CCR-8704309. The work of S. A. Smolka was supported by the National Science Foundation under Grants NSF DCR-8505873 and NSF CCR-8704309.

The authors are with the Department of Computer Science, SUNY at Stony Brook, Stony Brook, NY 11794.

IEEE Log Number 8820964.

[1]The name "Clara" was chosen for a number of reasons that include its Latin meaning of "things that are clear," and the fact that it is the name of the first author's daughter.

port for one's intuition about the behavior of a system and, in any case, constitutes the only viable support for debugging it. Moreover, simulation of specifications and designs can be viewed as rapid prototyping: a design that can be simulated *is* a prototype, with the more detailed the design, the more realistic the prototype. Conversely, a ''good'' prototype may well be considered a specification.

Because of the diversity of existing parallel and distributed architectures, it is often difficult to design portable concurrent software that can execute on different machines. Also, the design of concurrent algorithms is often hindered by having to pay too much attention to the details of the underlying model of parallel computation. The Clara environment addresses these problems by allowing users to design and ''run'' their systems in a target-architecture-independent way.

Simulation can even by exploited to obtain useful and intelligible information about the system's performance. As observed in [7], ''simulation models offer advantages over analytical ones when the performance of a system under design and development is not very predictable. Concurrent systems to be executed on multiprocessors are examples of systems whose performance is perhaps better analyzed and understood through simulation.''

As for formally well-founded design, it is advisable that properties of *any* complex system be formally verified, and is especially important for concurrent systems. A significant obstacle to the practical application of formal techniques is the absence of adequate tools to assist the user. Working without such tools is analogous to programming without, e.g., a debugger. We view these tools as not only aiding the designer in verifying properties of complex systems, but also supporting activities that may be considered more immediately practical. A goal of the Clara project can be viewed as one of embedding formal development techniques within tools, which are then integrated in the ''natural'' design process. The tools that result have a well-defined behavior and constrain the user to proceed in a correct manner, without requiring intimate knowledge of the underlying theory. We will see in Section III a major application of this approach, involving the usage of equational rules as the basis for *semantics-directed* editing.

B. An Integrated Environment

An important feature of Clara (and one to be maintained in our future Clara clones) is that the environment is built around a unique descriptive formalism—CCS in the case of Clara. In particular, the same formalism is used for both specification and design, and all tools operate on the expressions of the formalism. We thus view specification and design as the same process, the only difference being the degree of detail provided. In fact, a primary purpose of the environment is to assist its users in carrying out their chosen design strategies: from ''ideal'' top-down design, where abstract (and possibly incomplete) specifications are iteratively refined into detailed and complete designs, to ''prototype-based'' design, where an initial design is pieced together from preexisting components. The environment is thus *integrated*, in that it ensures a certain conceptual consistency, but it is also integrated in a more interesting sense. The functionalities of its tools are conceptually consistent with the meanings of the constructs on which the tools operate. In fact, often tools are *defined* in terms of the constructs of the supported formalism. For example, we will see that in the simulation environment the user communicates with executing processes by opening *ports*, a basic construct of CCS.

C. A Graphical User Interface

Anyone working with CCS, or with any complex textual description of a system, has most likely found it helpful, if not inevitable, to visualize its constructs in some pictorial form. This is especially true when dealing with distributed systems, where it is important to understand the *structure* of a system and the interfaces between modules.

A major aspect of the Clara environment is that it provides a highly visual support for designing systems. In particular, its user interface is based on a two-dimensional representation of CCS syntax called IDCCS [17]. With IDCCS, we attempt to provide an *ideographic* syntax for CCS expressions: expressions are represented as pictures which are self-explanatory or, at least, have shapes that can be clearly identified with their meanings. The user interface is described in more detail in Section III-A.

D. CCS as a Design Formalism

As mentioned, Clara is an environment that supports CCS as a specification and design language. CCS has been used successfully in many practical applications, including concurrent programming languages [21], [22], [48], operating systems [14], user interfaces [10], communication protocols [29], [47], fault-tolerant systems [43], and VLSI [9]. In Section IV, we describe our experiences in using CCS within the Clara environment, commenting on how the environment facilitated our use of the calculus, and pointing out where Clara's support for CCS might be improved.

CCS is at the same time a language for defining concurrent systems and a formal system. Its *behavior expressions* define the structure and behavior of systems in terms of processes that execute concurrently and communicate via *ports*. Behavior expressions can be interpreted both *operationally*, as concurrent programs, and *algebraically*, as terms in an algebra. This dual nature of CCS expressions allows the Clara user to view an expression as the algebraic specification of a concurrent system, and also as a program that can be run in simulation. CCS is discussed further in Section II-C.

E. A Nonprocedural Approach to Building Design Environments

Our approach to building design environments is nonprocedural. As we explain in Section II-C, Clara's knowl-

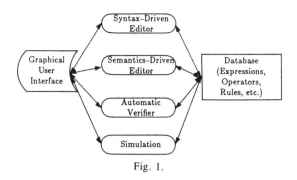

Fig. 1.

edge of CCS is given totally in terms of rules: syntax rules for syntax-directed editing, equational rules for semantics-driven editing, and derivation rules for simulation. Each activity is thus achieved within the environment through rule-based transformations of expressions. This nonprocedural approach, described further in Section IV, is key to our effort in developing techniques for systematic and computer-aided generation of environments to support other concurrent languages.

Fig. 1 depicts the general architecture of Clara and thus the architecture of any design environment built following the nonprocedural approach we advocate. Note that the functionality of such an environment is fixed (according to our present conception of what this functionality should be); only the environment's knowledge of the syntax and semantics of the underlying descriptive formalism changes.

F. Structure of the Rest of the Paper

Section II briefly describes background and related work, in particular programming environments, structural operational semantics, and CCS. Section III, the main section of the paper, provides a description of Clara, including its graphical user interface, support for formal reasoning, and simulation facility. Section IV discusses a number of applications of the Clara environment, as well as ongoing and future work.

II. BACKGROUND AND RELATED WORK

A. Environments

Programming environments have become a mainstream area of research in computer science since the late 1970's. Most work to date has concentrated on environments for sequential programming. Currently, several conferences are devoted entirely to environments, for example [2], [12], [19], [20]. A collection of important papers, which cover the early Lisp environments on up to modern day environments such as Smalltalk and UNIX®, can be found in [3].

Recent work that has been influential to our project concerns environments for visual programming (e.g., [18], [35], [44], [45]), and the generation of environments

®UNIX is a registered trademark of AT&T Bell Laboratories.

(e.g., [46] and [1]). The work of [1] is particularly relevant. It describes a system for generating the language specific parts of an interactive programming environment from a definition of the language semantics. The generated environment includes an interpreter derived from a denotational definition.

Programming environments for concurrent languages have received less attention. One of the larger projects is the MUPPET environment [4], [30], [36], an environment that supports concurrent programming in Modula-2. Here users can run their programs on various simulated machine architectures. Several environments provide direct support for the multitasking facilities of DoD's Ada programming language [50]. For example, CAEDE [6] generates Ada multitasking code from pictorial specifications. Arcadia [11] provides support for the testing and debugging of Ada multitasking programs in the form of static and dynamic concurrency analysis.

Finally, some work has centered on environments for the *specification* and *design* of concurrent programs. IDEOSY [18] constitutes an early version of the Clara environment presented in Section III, whose primary purpose was to experiment with graphical languages in user interfaces. In [13], an environment for Hoare's CSP [26] is described which provides a CSP editor and simulator. A number of design systems based on Petri nets have been developed. One of particular note is SARA [16] which allows the integration of place transition nets (for control flow) with data flow models.

B. Operational Semantics

Operational semantics was one of the first approaches to formal semantics. Examples of proposed methods include the Vienna Definition Language [51] and, for concurrent computation, Petri nets [40]. Early operational methods were each based on some fixed abstract machine, and all the constructs of the language being defined had to be mapped onto the constructs of that machine. This mapping was not always natural. Definitions and especially formal proofs had to deal with too many details of the abstract machine. In this sense, the operational approach was considered by many not sufficiently abstract. Approaches that followed, namely, axiomatic and denotational, attempted to achieve greater abstraction in definitions.

For concurrent systems the operational approach has proven more adequate, since an operational definition expresses more directly the structure of the system being defined. This is especially important when dealing with systems composed of independent interacting computing agents. Moreover, relatively recent work has shown that greater abstraction can be achieved in operational definitions by following a structural approach [32], [33], [41], [42]. Here the notion of a fixed abstract machine is replaced by the notion of an arbitrarily abstract transition system based directly on the structure of the expressions in the language/system being defined. In the CCS case, this structural approach is fully exploited. The "configurations" of the transition system are CCS expressions themselves. Transitions, in turn, become defined in terms of pure "symbol pushing."

C. An Overview of CCS

We briefly describe CCS, the formalism on which Clara is based; applications of the calculus have been discussed in Section I. CCS *behavior expressions* define systems in terms of processes communicating through *ports*. Communication is synchronized: two processes must coordinate at some point in time in order to communicate. Moreover, communication can take place only over *complementary* ports—ports with the same name and opposite directions. By convention, barred port names are output ports, and unbarred ones are input ports (e.g., p and $\bar{p}$).

CCS exists currently in two versions, an asynchronous version [32] in which processes can evolve asynchronously, and a synchronous version [33] in which executions of processes are synchronized by a global clock.

CCS is a small language with constructs for specifying sequential composition, nondeterministic choice, concurrent composition, port restriction and relabeling, conditional behavior, and recursion. As an introduction, we present a simple example that is used in Section III to demonstrate the capabilities of Clara.

Consider two processes $PROC1$ and $PROC2$ desiring mutually exclusive access to a shared variable, modeled in CCS by a "register" process with output port $\overline{read}$ and input port $write$:

$$REG(x) <= \overline{read}(x) . REG(x) + write(v) . REG(v)$$

where REG is a parametric process, "." separates actions executed sequentially, and "+" is an exclusive or operator: we can either write the register (thereby updating its contents) or read its current value.

A semaphore process SEM with two ports p and v is used to implement the necessary synchronization. SEM continually offers communications at p and v. In CCS this process may be defined as:

$$SEM <= p . v . SEM$$

For a process to be able to enter its critical section, it must first succeed in communicating with SEM over port p; after finishing its critical section, the process communicates with SEM over port v to complete the protocol.

Assume that $PROC1$ continually decrements the value of the shared variable, while $PROC2$ increments the variable's value. Both processes obey the semaphore protocol:

$$PROC1 <= \bar{p} . read(x) . \overline{write}(x-1) . \bar{v} . PROC1$$
$$PROC2 <= \bar{p} . read(x) . \overline{write}(x+1) . \bar{v} . PROC2$$

The system consisting of the concurrently executing $PROC1$, $PROC2$, SEM, and REG is:

$$SYS <= (PROC1 \mid PROC2 \mid SEM \mid REG(0))\backslash\{p, v\}$$

where "$\mid$" is the *composition* operator and "$\backslash$" denotes the *restriction* operator. In this case, restriction limits the use of ports p and v to the processes of SYS.

The formal semantics of CCS is defined in two steps. First, a set of axioms and inference rules (*derivation rules*) defined inductively on the structure of expressions, provide the language with an operational semantics. Derivations define the atomic computational events and correspond to synchronized communications between processes at ports. In Clara, we exploit this "operational" interpretation of expressions as the basis for an interpreter which in turn constitutes the heart of the simulation environment. Secondly, a notion of equivalence between expressions is defined which assigns meanings to expressions in terms of their equivalence classes. Properties of the equivalence relation, expressed as equational rules, allow one to reason equationally about the expressions in the calculus. The semantics-directed editing capabilities of Clara (described in length in Section III-B) are driven by such equational rules.

What follows are some representative derivation rules of CCS's structured semantics. The axiom:

$$a.P \xrightarrow{a} P$$

defines the semantics of "sequential" computation. Albegraically, it states that an expression of the form $a . P$ can derive P, through the binary relation $\xrightarrow{a}$. Operationally, the axiom states that a process defined by the expression $a.P$ can perform a communication action at port a and then continue with whatever behavior is defined by expression P.

Next consider the CCS derivation rules below that define the semantics of composition:

$$\frac{P \xrightarrow{a} P'}{P \mid Q \xrightarrow{a} P' \mid Q} \quad \frac{Q \xrightarrow{b} Q'}{P \mid Q \xrightarrow{b} P \mid Q'}$$

$$\frac{P \xrightarrow{a} P', Q \xrightarrow{\bar{a}} Q'}{P \mid Q \xrightarrow{\tau} P' \mid Q'}$$

They state that two processes in composition may autonomously offer communication actions to the outside world (the two top rules), or agree to communicate via *complementary* actions (the bottom rule) to produce a hidden internal transition (τ-move). Derivation rules like these allow the behavior of complex systems of processes to be inferred from the behaviors of the components.

Regarding the equational part of CCS semantics, various equivalence relations have been defined over the expressions of the calculus, starting with observational equivalence and strong congruence [32], among others. Roughly, two expressions are considered equivalent when they have the same derivations, i.e., when they define systems that can "simulate" each other in all possible contexts. Alternative equivalence relations were later proposed, e.g., [5], [23], [25], [31], [38].

III. Clara: An Environment for CCS

Clara is an experimental environment built to support Milner's CCS. It represents a major step toward making CCS evolve from an extremely interesting conceptual framework for reasoning about concurrency into a full-blown language for designing, verifying, and testing concurrent systems. Throughout the environment we attempt to make the conceptual model and the simplicity of Milner's calculus coexist with a rich and flexible set of tools.

As mentioned in the introduction, Clara is an integrated environment in which CCS expressions are the central objects. It appears to its users as an "expert" aid which is quite knowledgeable about CCS syntax and semantics, and can assist them in manipulating CCS expressions in various ways. All tools operate on expressions, and different types of manipulations can be performed by switching between sets of tools. For example, an expression can be constructed and edited using a syntax-driven editor, or can be transformed using semantic rules. The latter feature can be viewed as syntax-driven editing under the further constraint that all transformations are semantics-preserving. Even simulation, as we will see, can be viewed in terms of expression transformation, as users view execution steps in terms of derivations. All tools interact with the user through a highly graphical user interface subsystem. In particular, a pictorial version of CCS, described in detail in [17], is used in Clara.

The heart of the environment is a database of internal representations of CCS expressions, operators, and rules. Internal representations are maintained, essentially, in "abstract syntax" form. Clara's tools manipulate abstract syntax trees representing CCS expressions. The tools are subdivided into three main sets, which can be viewed as determining subenvironments: tools for syntactial manipulation, tools for semantic manipulation and verification, and tools for simulation. The description that follows reflects this subdivision. We begin in Section III-A by overviewing the pictorial syntax for CCS used in the environment and the syntactical editing facilities. Section III-B describes the type of semantics-directed editing of specifications currently supported by Clara and the support for formal verification. Section III-C describes the simulation environment and underlying concurrent abstract machine.

A. An Ideographical User Interface

As mentioned in the introduction, with IDCCS we attempt to provide an *ideographic* syntax for CCS expressions. IDCCS pictures are built out of a few basic symbols, which are pictorial versions of CCS primitive operators. The rules for constructing pictures are provided by a two-dimensional context-free grammar. The syntax is designed to permit a picture representing a given construct to retain an easily identifiable outside shape, even when, e.g., embedded within complex expressions, distorted, or greatly reduced in dimensions. In summary, it is conceived to use expressions as ideograms. Furthermore, IDCCS expressions render the structure of the systems they define much more evident than their textual counterparts.

IDCCS expressions are not just "passive" entities manipulated by tools of the environment. They form an integral part of the user interface and can themselves be viewed as tools: each symbol in an IDCCS expression is a "button of a menu" which activates some function of the environment. Any expression, from the environment's viewpoint, is thus an object with capabilities that the user can activate. The basic user/system interaction in Clara can be summarized in three steps: 1) the user identifies an object and the environment proposes functions applicable to that object; 2) the user selects a function and provides further parameters (if any); 3) finally, the environment applies the function.

We describe IDCCS and Clara's editor with the help of some examples. The editor can be used in two basic ways: 1) in a "classical" top-down fashion to replace a nonterminal symbol with the right-hand side of a grammar production, and 2) to modify an expression by replacing one subexpression with another. This latter operation is permitted by the editor only if the replacement yields a syntactically correct expression. The text that appears in IDCCS expressions (e.g., action or process names) is parsed as it is typed in; there is no syntax-driven editing for text.

We illustrate the top-down approach by considering the IDCCS version of the semaphore example of Section II-C. Fig. 2 shows what the screen looks like while editing an expression. The editing tools are the row of buttons at the bottom left of the screen, which represent grammar rules, and the small set of buttons on the right, labeled *replace*, *insert*, *delete*, etc. The IDCCS expression we are currently working on appears in the larger area at the center of the display (the *expression area*).

Fig. 2 represents a composition of four processes (*PROC*1, *PROC*2, *SEM*, *REG*) whose behaviors are defined by the four pictorial expressions appearing inside the large box. The large box itself is the IDCCS syntax for CCS composition and the area it encloses represents its scope. The smaller box enclosing the two names p and v on the top right corner is the IDCCS version of CCS port restriction. Note that with two-dimensional syntax, one has much more freedom in assigning positional meanings to symbols. Three of the four processes in our composition consist of diagonal arrangements of action symbols terminated by process identifiers. In IDCCS, diagonally arranged actions define a sequential execution of the actions. The symbols for actions are:

which stand, respectively, for an input action at port p, an output action at port p, and the unobservable τ action[2]

---

[2]The two symbols for input and output actions are often used in flowchart-like languages—for example, in the *SDL* formalism (Specification Description Language [8]), an international standard for specification of telecommunication systems. They "fit" together naturally to form the τ action symbol.

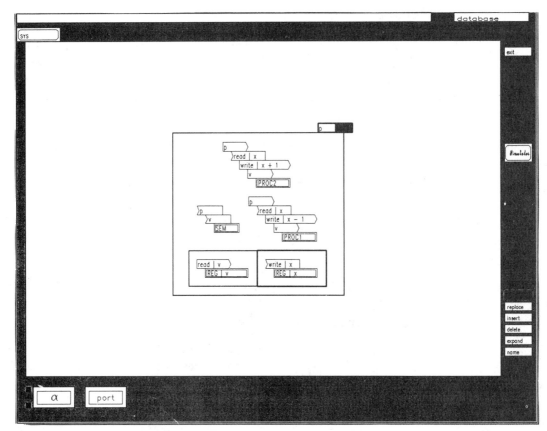

Fig. 2.

(see Section II-C). The fourth process (*REG*) is defined by an *or*, whose IDCCS syntax consists of juxtaposed boxes each enclosing one alternative.

Syntax-Driven Editing of Pictorial Expressions: Let us assume that we want to construct the expression of Fig. 2 by first constructing separately the four processes *SEM*, *PROC*1, *PROC*2, and *REG*, and then combining them into a restricted composition. We start with process *SEM*. Upon informing the environment that we intend to define a new process (by picking the rectangular symbol at the top left of the expression area), the editor prompts us for a name. Once the name (*SEM*) is provided, it displays the picture below:

The "bowl" symbol is the distinguished symbol of the grammar and represents a complete process. At this point, a row of buttons appear at the bottom of the screen, labeled by icons representing the grammar rules that are applicable to the bowl. Since we intend to construct a sequential process, we pick the corresponding rule and obtain:

In this expression, the rectangle is the nonterminal symbol for an action. The bowl placed diagonally represents the rest of the sequential process, which, syntactically, is

a process. When several nonterminals appear in an expression, the editor chooses one by default as the one to be expanded next, but, obviously, we can explicitly select one by pointing at it. Let us assume that the editor now expects us to define the action. It then replaces the previous grammar rules with those for actions (input with and without parameters, output with and without values, and τ). We pick the rule for an input action without parameters, provide the name *p* when prompted, and obtain:

We now need to expand the bowl symbol again. We create the second action *v* of the sequence similarly, after which we obtain:

We then complete the recursive definition of the *SEM* process by replacing the bowl with a process identifier option from the grammar and by providing the name *SEM* when prompted. The result is the complete expression for *SEM*.

We can define the behaviors of *PROC*1, *PROC*2, and *REG* in a similar fashion. At this point, the four agents are known to Clara, and at any time we are able to replace their identifiers with their definitions. To construct the restricted composition of *PROC*1, *PROC*2, *SEM*, and *REG* we inform the editor that we are defining a new system of processes, called *SYS*, and select the "restricted composition" alternative of the grammar. We obtain the picture:

We expand the restriction part by providing names p and v, then "split" the initial bowl three times to obtain a composition of four processes in the box.

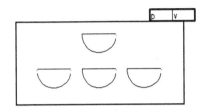

We can now point at each of the four bowls in turn and replace them with process identifiers for our processes, thereby obtaining:

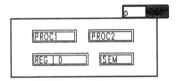

Finally, we obtain the desired expression (Fig. 2) by asking the editor to replace each identifier with its definition.

The replacement of a nonterminal symbol in an expression with the right-hand side of a grammar rule is, within the editor, a special case a general replacement operation. Any syntactical construct may be replaced by a construct of the same syntactical class. For example, an action symbol may be replaced by another action symbol, a process by another process, etc. This strategy allows for a quite acceptable degree of flexibility in manipulating expressions, while ensuring that the expressions are always syntactically correct.

To replace a construct with another, one must identify the construct to be replaced (possibly the whole expression), pick the *replace* command, and finally identify the new construct. The new construct may be one of the following:

1) another construct appearing in the expression on the screen;

2) an expression in the database (identified by name). The user may at any time assign a name to a subexpression and put it into the database;

3) the right-hand side of a grammar rule. In this case the editor treats the expression to be replaced as if it were a nonterminal and expands the grammar rule as if the expression were "bound" to the nonterminals of the same syntactical type in the grammar rule. When a grammar rule is used, it is not necessary to pick the *replace* button.

Other special cases of replacement are represented by

the *insert* and *delete* commands. *Insert* operates on every construct that has a variable number of operands (e.g., action sequences or compositions). Its effect is to insert another operand. As for *delete*, its effect is the opposite of *insert* for constructs for which *insert* is defined. For all the others (e.g., a whole restricted process or a whole action sequence), it replaces the construct with the highest level nonterminal from which it was derived. This can be a bowl symbol (for processes) or a nonterminal action symbol.

B. Support for Formal Development

The syntactical editing capabilities described in the previous section are driven by IDCCS syntactical rules. Clara also allows users to edit IDCCS specifications in a semantics-driven fashion. In the context of Clara, semantics-driven editing is syntax-driven editing with further semantic constraints imposed in the form of *equational rules*. Equational rules are theorems induced by equivalence and congruence relations defined over expressions. They can be viewed as equivalence relations defined for specific classes of expressions, i.e., for expressions having specific syntactical structures. Examples of (simple) equational rules derivable from the CCS notion of strong congruence are:

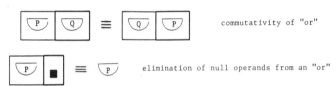

Juxtaposed boxes are the IDCCS syntax for the *exclusive or* operator of CCS, and the small black square is the IDCCS version of *NIL*. Below, is an example of the "τ-laws," equational rules based on CCS observation equivalence that allow one to eliminate hidden actions from expressions.

Equational rules are very useful in complex formal proofs, where they may be used to "simplify" expressions (e.g., to prove an induction step). Taking a more general and perhaps more immediately practical view, equational rules can be considered as specifying structural transformations of expressions that preserve the expressions' semantics. For example, in designing a system one may notice through simulation that parts of the design are inefficient and that the inefficiency is due to structural problems. Equational editing rules may be useful in transforming the design to obtain a more efficient system which is also guaranteed to be equivalent in external behavior.

Clara supports the usage of equational rules by performing all the repetitive and error-prone work involved in their use. In particular, the environment can acquire rules from the user incrementally, can advise the user about what rules are applicable to a given syntactical context, and can apply the rules to transform an expression. Finally, it keeps track of what rules are applied and when, to allow backtracking. Below we show, with the help of a few examples, how new rules are inserted into the environment, how the environment keeps track of them, and how it uses them to assist users.

Acquiring New Equational Rules: In IDCCS syntax, rules are pairs of expressions which generally include named nonterminal symbols of the grammar. Named nonterminals are considered as syntactical variables and stand "for every" construct derivable from them. For example, the expression:

denotes all systems in which port α is restricted.

Suppose we want to insert the rule that defines the commutativity of the *or* operator shown above. In defining a rule, we interact with a modified version of the editor. First, we tell the environment that we intend to define a rule by selecting the appropriate button from a *menu* of the various objects that can be defined (expressions, operators, rules). The environment prompts for the "type" of equivalence used in the rule. Assuming that we have selected strong congruence, the following picture will be displayed:

At this point, we can edit separately the two sides of the rule as if they were expressions, the only difference being that we can place variables in expressions in the form of named nonterminals. In our example, we expand each of the two bowls as an *exclusive or* of processes, and then appropriately assign the names P and Q to obtain the rule below.

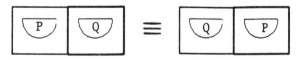

Once the rule is acquired, it is associated by the environment with all the terminal symbols and syntactical constructors occurring within the rule. For example, the commutativity rule is associated with the *or* constructor only, while the *NIL* elimination rule is associated with both the *or* constructor and the *NIL* symbol. Rules are interpreted by Clara as properties of syntactical constructors and are represented in abstract syntax form. Thus the rule above is applicable wherever an *or* appears in an expression. The applicability of rules may be further constrained by subcontexts. Consider, for example, the rule below, which defines the associativity of composition.

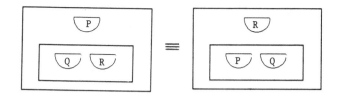

Although the rule is considered a property of *composition*, it is applicable only within the context of "nested composition."

Applying Equational Rules: If in the course of using Clara we decide to transform an expression, we can ascertain which rules are applicable to any of its subexpressions E by simply identifying E. The environment then scans the rules associated with the syntactical constructors appearing in E and attempts to unify E with the left side of each rule. (This unification is actually term matching since only rules contain variables.) For each rule that unifies successfully, a *substitution* is constructed in which the syntactical variables present in the two sides of the rule are bound to subexpressions of the expression selected from the screen (E, in this case). Each successfully unified rule is then displayed in the form of an icon. At this point we can select one of the rules and ask the environment to apply it. Clara instantiates the right side of the chosen rule with the bindings set up during unification, thereby obtaining a new expression. The expression previously identified on the screen is then replaced by the new expression.

One of the most important equational rules is the so-called *expansion theorem*[3] of [32]. Given a restricted composition of processes, the expansion theorem allows us to transform the expression into an equivalent one in which the observable behavior of the system as a whole is rendered "one step more explicit." To illustrate, consider our example of Fig. 2 without the register process. The resulting system is a composition of three processes that can evolve in one of two mutually exclusive ways—in each alternative, one of the two processes $PROC1$, $PROC2$ succeeds in performing its p-communication with the SEM process. Each such evolution generates a τ-action, and there are no other possible evolutions, since the ports p and v are restricted. This behavior is captured by the *exclusive or* expression (Fig. 3), which we can obtain from the previous one by asking Clara to apply the expansion theorem.

Each of the two alternatives can now be expanded separately in order to further explore the possible evolutions of our system. For example, after a number of expansion steps, we will obtain the expression of Fig. 4, which defines explicitly its observable behavior.

Note that our system exhibits a cyclic "finite state" behavior. In simple cases like this one, but also in significantly more complex ones, the environment can effec-

---

[3]The formulation of the expansion theorem is significantly more complex than the simple rules we presented above and will not be shown here. For pragmatic reasons, in Clara, the rule is currently "hard-wired."

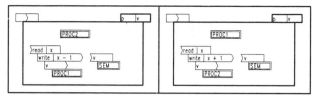

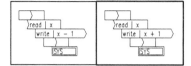

Fig. 3.

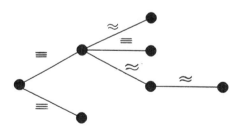

Fig. 4.

tively assist the user in verifying "by inspection" properties of the system being designed.

In complex expressions which involve compositions of several components, each expansion step may produce a large number of alternatives, many of which can be pruned by using equational rules as simplification rules. Typical rules used to simplify expressions include the *NIL* elimination mentioned above, the so-called *absorption* rules, and the various τ-elimination rules. Clara can be directed to attempt to simplify an expression as far as possible using a given set of rules. The rules in the set are applied repeatedly until no more rules are applicable. Rules can also be organized as specific sequences. When requested, the environment will apply the whole sequence in the specified order. Sequences can be viewed as "macros" and can be defined "by example."

Besides performing all the transformation work, Clara can also keep track of the user's activity in transforming expressions and displays the "history" of such activity in the form of a tree.

Each node of the tree represents a stage in the transformation work reached by applying rules. Every time a new rule is applied, the environment creates a new node which is a child of the current node, and labels the arc between the two nodes with the identifier of the type of equivalence used in the transformation. Any previous stage of transformation can be retrieved by simply pointing to a node of the tree.

Automatic Verification Tools: Certain concurrent systems, such as our semaphore example of Fig. 2, exhibit finite behavior: their derivations can lead them to a finite number of system states only. The equivalence problem for such systems is decidable, and procedures for deciding strong congruence, observational equivalence, and

failure equivalence [5] appear in [28]. These procedures are present in Clara as tools which can be used, for example, to automatically verify that a concurrent system meets its specification.

It should be noted that, unlike trace equivalence (the classical notion of equivalence based on language acceptance) and failure equivalence, strong congruence and observational equivalence can be decided in time polynomial in the size of the processes being tested.

C. The Simulation Environment

At any point while working on a system specification on the screen, we can decide to consider the expression constituting the specification as a concurrent program and execute it within a rich, interactive simulation environment. The simulation environment allows us to view the evolution of the simulated system in graphical form, to influence it, and even to participate in the interprocess communication as processes. The simulator can handle complete expressions as well as expressions that contain nonterminals, i.e., which are not fully specified. It stops whenever it finds an incomplete or undefined construct. This provides a way to test specified parts of incomplete specifications.

Executions are expressed in terms of expression *derivations* (see Section II-C) and are thus perceived by the user as sequences of state transitions of the executing system of processes. Transitions are due to communications between processes at ports, and states are represented by expressions. The simulation environment is thus especially suited for (but not restricted to) executions of highly distributed "data-flow-like" systems, in which each individual process performs locally only trivial computations, and in which the communication structure is preeminent.

As a simple example of simulation, consider the expression of our previous example (Fig. 2). In the system defined by the expression, one of the two processes *PROC*1 and *PROC*2 will nondeterministically succeed in communicating with the *SEM* process, and thus in accessing the register. In such cases, the simulator selects randomly one alternative; however we can always inspect all the alternatives and determine which one should be followed. Note that a graphical user interface is of particular value here. In CCS nondeterminism can manifest itself as the availability of more than one complementary action for a given action in a given state. Through a button labeled *next* (on the right of the screen in Fig. 5), we can ask the simulator to show successively all the alternatives, by highlighting the corresponding actions, and then to proceed with one of these. Assuming that *PROC*1 succeeds, our system will perform a transition to the state depicted in Fig. 5 below. Fig. 5 also shows the simulation environment screen, with the available commands on the right.

*PROC*1 and *SEM* have now performed a transition, while *PROC*2 is unchanged. The simulator has now highlighted the new actions it proposes to execute (those

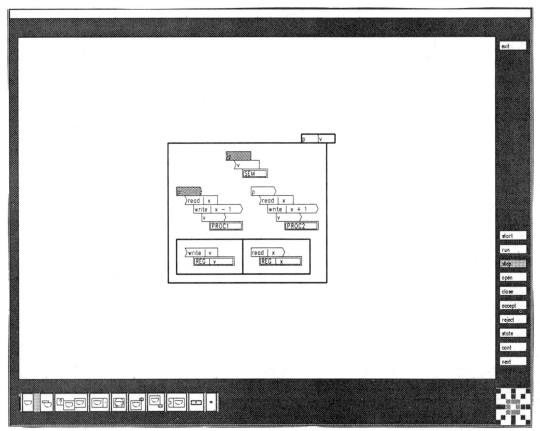

Fig. 5.

named *read* in *PROC*1 and *REG*). Note that the expression above represents exactly one of the alternatives of the *or* in Fig. 3, which was produced by applying the *expansion theorem* to the initial expression. The expansion theorem is an equational rule and, as such, produces an *equivalent* expression which includes *all* the possible evolutions. The simulator follows only one such evolution at a time. Figs. 6(a)–(c), which show only the expression, represent the further transitions that bring our example system back to its initial state. The first two transitions are due to the execution of the *read* and *write* actions by *PROC*1 and *REG*, while the last one is due to a *v*-communication between *PROC*1 and *SEM*.

The execution can proceed in *step* mode or *run* mode. In *step* mode the simulator stops after completing each communication and displays the system state as an IDCCS expression. In *run* mode the execution is continuous and can be stopped by inserting *breakpoints* in the expression. These are special actions that can be placed wherever an input, output, or τ action is legal. When the simulator encounters a breakpoint, it interrupts the execution, reconstructs the IDCCS expression corresponding to the current state, and displays it.

Both the asynchronous and the synchronous versions of CCS (see Section II-C) can be simulated. Accordingly, the simulator can be instructed to operate in asynchronous or synchronous mode. In asynchronous mode, every execution step involves a communication between *one* pair of processes at complementary ports so that, as users, we

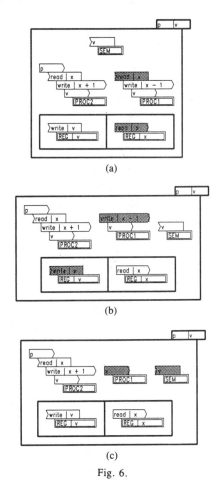

(a)

(b)

(c)

Fig. 6.

will see at most two processes changing state at every step (as in the example above). A scheduler chooses the pair randomly among those existing in the current state, but we can influence the choice, as described above. In synchronous mode, every execution step involves a communication between *all* the pairs of complementary ports which are enabled to communicate in a given state. In this mode, we view the executing system as ruled by a clock which, at every *tick*, enables all actions appearing at the head of an action sequence. We will thus see all the processes in the system perform a transition at every step. Note that in synchronous mode all the actions that are available *must* be executed, i.e., must have complementary actions available. If this is not the case, the simulator aborts the execution. A process that does not wish to communicate should have an "idling" (i.e., a τ) action as an alternative.

Finally, states of the execution, i.e., expressions, can be saved and given names. At any point, any previously saved state can be recalled and the execution restarted from it, possibly following another alternative in a nondeterministic situation.

Communicating with Executing Processes: The User as a Process: The facilities described so far allow us to view and influence the execution of a system "from the outside." We can also communicate with executing processes through their ports, thus becoming *observers* of the processes in the CCS sense. Consistently, the user is viewed by the processes as yet another process. In fact, we will see below that the user is actually represented as a process in the simulator. In this way, the CCS model of concurrency based on port-to-port communication is also applied to the user/system interaction.

To communicate with processes through their ports, we *open* complementary ones on the screen. A port can be opened or closed whenever the execution is stopped. We can have virtually any number of ports open at the same time. Suppose, for example, that we wanted to behave like our register process in order to observe the behaviors of *PROC*1 and *PROC*2. Then, like the *REG* process, we could open an output port named *read* and an input port named *write*. Ports appear in the simulation environment as small windows at the bottom of the screen (see Fig. 5). Fig. 7 shows them magnified.

The simulator treats a user port as an action which is always being attempted by the user, and competes with all actions of the same name and direction attempted by the other processes. However, user actions are treated somewhat asymmetrically. When the action is selected for execution, the simulator lets the user decide whether or not the communication will actually take place. If we "accept" then one of two things happens: 1) for output ports, we are asked for a value, if the receiving process is expecting one; 2) for input ports, a value appears in the *value field*, if a value is being sent. If we reject the communication, the simulator tries to find another partner for the process, and failing this looks for another communication possibility.

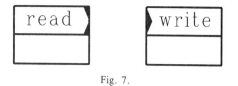

Fig. 7.

A Concurrent Abstract Machine: The simulator is based on a *concurrent abstract machine* (CAM). The CAM "architecture" consists of a collection of *processors* and a collection of *memoryless communication channels*. The number of both processors and channels is unbounded, in the sense that we assume that a processor and a channel are always available when we need to allocate one.

Processors execute independently and in parallel. They are created to execute sequential processes and "disappear" when their processes terminate. In effect, in our CAM a process and the processor on which it runs are really the same thing and we will use the two terms interchangeably. Processes do not share data and can exchange values with other processes by accessing communication channels. Thus, processes that communicate share communication capabilities in the form of accesses to channels.

Channels are abstract communication devices which do not imply any particular realization (e.g., shared memory, physical devices). They can be viewed as specialized processors that implement a *rendezvous* (i.e., synchronized) communication discipline between processes. Processes send their requests for communications to channels. Each channel collects them and maintains two sets of pending requests, for *send* and *receive*, respectively. When enabled, it selects two complementary requests (i.e., one *send* and one *receive*) and informs the two processes that they can communicate. A centralized scheduler decides which channels should be enabled at each step of the CAM execution. Roughly speaking, a channel at a time is enabled to simulate asynchronous executions, while all channels are enabled simultaneously to simulate synchronized (i.e., clocked) executions.

The external user is represented in the CAM by a *user-process* which is assumed to be always executing. When the user has an open port, a request is always present in the corresponding channel. When the channel decides to satisfy a request and realizes that the request comes from the user-process, the CAM execution stops and the control is assumed by the interactive part of the simulation environment. The latter implements the above mentioned dialog with the user about whether or not the communication should take place.

Executing CCS Expressions: A CCS expression is executed by translating it into a configuration of the CAM, letting the machine run, and by stopping it in configurations that can be translated back into CCS expressions. Users thus view executions in terms of expression derivations. The machine stops its executions and displays the execution's state in the following cases:

- at the completion of every derivation, if it is running in step mode;
- when a breakpoint is found as the next action to be executed;
- when all the executing processes terminate;
- when a *deadlock* occurs, that is, when some processes are still attempting to execute communications, but no attempted action has a complementary one.

In order to simulate the execution of a CCS expression, CCS operators are interpreted in their operational meaning. The rules for such interpretation can be summarized as follows.

- Sequential expressions are obviously translated into sequential executions of processes.
- *NIL*, having no actions, provokes the termination of the process in which it appears.
- The *composition* operator is interpreted as a "create process" primitive. The processes in the composition execute concurrently in an environment in which they can communicate through complementary ports. A channel is allocated for every port name; thus a CAM channel actually models several connections between CCS ports, one per pair of complementary ports. The appearance of a process identifier at the end of a sequential expression is considered a special case of composition involving only one operand.
- *Relabeling* of ports is interpreted in its literal meaning. Since relabeling in CCS is applied recursively to all the descendents of a process, each process carries with it a *relabeling table*. The table is passed on to all descendant processes.
- *Restriction* of port visibility is implemented as a variation of relabeling. New, unique port names are created, and restricted ports are renamed into these. This implies the creation of new channels reserved for the new ports. Like relabeling, restriction is transmitted to all descendants.
- The *or* operator is perhaps the most complex, in that its semantics states that the execution of one alternative excludes the others. This, in turn, implies that channels cannot operate independently. When a process tries to execute an *or*, the first action of each alternative is associated to a channel. When one of these actions is selected for execution, all the actions initiating the other alternatives must be removed from the corresponding channels.

IV. Conclusions

In this section we conclude by examining the past, present, and future of the Clara project at Stony Brook.

A. Experience with Clara and Examples

The Clara environment has been "stable" for less than a year and has been used so far on small to medium size applications. The environment has already proven effective in teaching CCS to neophytes and in enabling researchers to gain deeper insight into various concurrency issues. In summary, it is one thing to reason about concurrent systems in the abstract; it is another to be able to quickly construct systems and run them.

At present, the Clara environment has attracted the attention of researchers in diverse areas at Stony Brook: from neural networks to distributed databases, to parallel algorithms and architectures. It is interesting to note that these applications may be used to study different issues. For example, a goal of the neural networks application is to study execution patterns in order to, e.g., "tune" numeric threshold parameters. Database applications, on the other hand, seem to be concerned with problems like correctness, synchronization, and race conditions. As for algorithms, performance is a major issue. In the context of algorithms, the combination of CCS and the concurrent abstract machine provides an interesting framework for studying different parallel architectures. As noted in Section III-C, the CAM has a quite unstructured architecture which assumes the conceptual topology of the CCS system it executes. By appropriately naming CCS ports, we can induce on the CAM different configurations, such as pipelines, meshes, or hypercubes. We will see in the next section that this feature has pleasant repercussions in performance evaluation.

Below, we briefly describe three widely varying example applications of Clara, which should give an idea of the environment's flexibility. Also, in the next section we discuss ongoing developments that were in part suggested by these applications. The examples concern the modeling of data-flow machines, communication protocols, and man/machine interaction.

A Data-Flow Machine: The data-flow machine defined by the CCS expression in Fig. 8 [32] inputs from the user an integer n and outputs 2^n. The basic idea here is that the behavior is obtained by putting together a number of very primitive components (gates, switches, etc.). The machine includes two compound subsystems, plus four small components whose tasks are to start the machine and to interact with external processes (e.g., the user). The two subsystems appear in the picture as the two restricted compositions of processes inside the main composition box. One is the "control part" (on the left), which counts how many times the basic operation (multiplication by 2) is performed. The other one performs one iteration every time it is triggered by the control. The two subsystems execute independently and in parallel. They need to synchronize on the trigger and on the "done" signals sent by the control (the actions called *goon* and *done*, respectively).

Communication Protocols: Our second example concerns communication protocols. In particular, we have used Clara to model and simulate the alternating bit protocol and the CSMA/CD protocol for common bus transmission medium. Our models of these protocols were derived from the CCS representations given in [39]. For example, the alternating bit protocol as it appears to the Clara user is given in Fig. 9.

The protocol consists of the sender and receiver processes plus two communication media, both of which are also modeled as processes. The alternating bit protocol must ensure successful transmission of data despite unreliable behavior by the media. In particular, the media

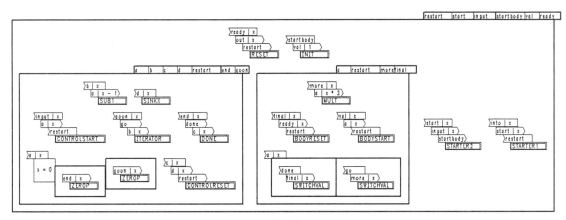

Fig. 8.

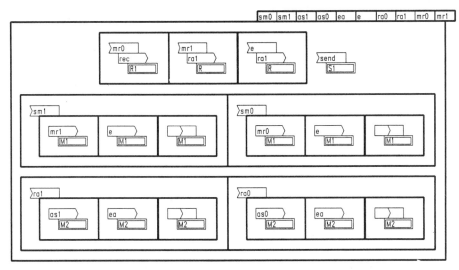

Fig. 9.

can garble and lose messages, the latter causing the sender process to time out (take one of its τ-transitions). We found the graphical syntax for CCS and the degree of control over simulation offered by Clara to be very helpful in studying the behavior of the protocol under the variety of anomalous conditions.

Man/Machine Interaction: A slightly modified version of the editor and the simulation environment are being used by the first author in a project concerned with the generation of user interfaces for interactive systems from abstract specifications. The system, currently under implementation, will allow user interface designers to specify user/system dialogs graphically, by using a subset of IDCCS. The dialog is thus specified as a system of independent, communicating processes. Communications can take place between processes, or between a process and the external user via some I/O device, abstracted in the system by a communication channel. A variation of the Clara simulation environment will provide a dialog debugging environment which enables one to debug the interaction at the same level at which it was specified, and while the interaction takes place (in "real" time). The debugging system will show, simultaneously and in two separate windows, the actual "end-user" screen and the state of the dialog.

B. Ongoing Developments

Support for Engineering: Applications like the dataflow machine of Section IV-A reveal the need for more extensive support for what we call the *engineering aspects* of system design. In particular, our data-flow machine consists of a composition of several components, which can be obtained as instances of more general computing agents by applying operators that are well defined in CCS. For example, the machine contains several instances of a *gate* process whose general behavior is defined by the expression below:

The *gate* repeatedly inputs a value (at port *in*), outputs the same value (at $\overline{out}$), then waits for a signal (*s*) and repeats. The various gates present in the machine can be obtained by *relabeling* port names. Other examples are the various processes which simply input a value and out-

587

put a (simple) function of the input (e.g., *SUB*1 and *MULT*). These can be obtained from a general parametric agent whose parameter is the function.

CCS favors this assembly of complex behaviors from basic components, a process that can be viewed as prototyping with "off the shelf" components. We are currently integrating into the editing facilities of the environment various operations that allow the instantiation of components mentioned above. These include renaming the ports, parametric processes, and the definition of indexed families of processes. In this way, CCS operators support not only the definition of systems but also the process of assembling them. What we gain are two important characteristics. First, the process of generating components is well defined, being based on CCS operators. Second, every time we can use the same language to define systems and in constructing the definitions themselves, we take one more step toward a truly *integrated* environment.

Toward an Environment for Programming in the Large: We believe that an interesting aspect of Clara is that the model of concurrency based upon processes communicating via ports is a useful paradigm for designing systems at the module level. A popular term for this activity is "programming in the large." For example, the programming language NIL was conceived specifically to support the design of very large systems [49]: the basic unit of abstraction is the process and interfaces between processes are defined in terms of ports. We thus expect that many of the ideas and techniques developed in the course of the Clara project will be applicable to environments for programming in the large.

We are developing a version of the Clara environment for a specification/design language that combines features of CCS, Occam [27], and ML [34]. The goal of this effort is to obtain a language and environment in which one can treat a given module as a function or, interchangeably, as a system of processes. The functional style plays a dual role within this combination of programming paradigms: it allows the user to shift naturally between the "small" and the "large" during system development. On one hand, a functional program can define the internal sequential behavior of a process in a clear and precise manner. On the other hand, a functional definition can be used as an abstract substitution for a system of processes.

Performance Evaluation: We are presently extending the simulation environment of Clara to include capabilities for evaluating the performance of the system under development. Within Clara, the basic computational event is that of a communication between two processes at complementary ports. The simulation environment can keep track of various types of events, such as the number of communications 1) occurring in the system as a whole; 2) at a given port or group of ports; and 3) by a given process or group of processes.

A typical usage of these statistics is to locate communication bottlenecks in the system under simulation. Once these statistics have been obtained, other measures of system performance become possible:

- *Processor Utilization*—number of communications performed by a process divided by number of communications requested (or enabled) by the process;
- *Memory Utilization*—CCS can be used to model systems with local memories. Essentially, each memory cell is represented as a CCS register behavior. As such, memory utilization becomes the number of communications to distinct memory cells divided by the total number of memory cells;
- *System Execution Speed*—by running the simulator in synchronous mode, communications occur at regular intervals corresponding to the ticks of a global clock. The performance of a system with regard to execution speed can then be measured by counting the number of elapsed clock ticks.

C. Generation of Design Environments

The ultimate goal of the Clara project is the development of what can be viewed as a laboratory for the computer-assisted construction of interactive design environments for concurrent systems (the *Clara-Lab*). In particular, the Clara-Lab should enable one to quickly build an environment prototype by assembling a collection of reusable modules and providing them with appropriate knowledge about the language to be supported.

The Clara environment for CCS described in Section III constitutes, at present, the experimental part of the project. Clara serves as a model and a prototype for the type of environments we want to develop. The environments whose construction is supported by the Clara-Lab will reproduce Clara's structure and functionalities. In addition, Clara's current manual but systematic implementation is gradually formalizing an implementation model for code-generating tools.

As is thematic of our project, our environments are built around specification/design languages. What changes across environments is thus the supported language. An environment is viewed as a collection of parametric modules which implement the environment's functionalities. The parameters define the various aspects of syntax and semantics of the supported language, as well as various aspects of the user interface.

A fundamental point that supports our strategy is the operational/algebraic approach to the formalization of language semantics (see Section II-B), which in the CCS case allowed us to consider an expression interchangeably as a program and as a term in a formal system. A major part of our ongoing work consists thus of "exporting" this method to other languages.

The process can be viewed as one of breaking down the semantics of a language into an operational part and an algebraic part. Inference rules of the type described for CCS provide the operational part, in the sense that they define the form computations take in the language. Equational rules define the algebraic semantics of computations and, at the same time, can be used as practical tools for semantics-driven editing. They can be obtained incrementally given that the supporting environment has the ability to acquire new rules from the user.

ACKNOWLEDGMENT

We gratefully acknowledge the contributions of E. Murray, who implemented most of the initial version of Clara and assisted in the preparation of the figures for the final version of the paper, and S. Goellner who implemented the tools needed to generate the user interface of Clara. We are also appreciative of the valuable comments provided by the anonymous referee.

REFERENCES

[1] R. Bahlke and G. Snelting, "The PSG system: From formal language definitions to interactive programming environments," *ACM Trans. Prog. Lang. Syst.*, vol. 8, no. 4, pp. 547–576, Oct. 1986.

[2] J. Barnes and J. Fischer, Eds., *Proc. IEEE Int. Conf. Ada Applications and Environments*, Paris, France, May 1985.

[3] D. R. Barstow, H. E. Shrobe, and E. Sandewall, Eds., *Interactive Programming Environments*. New York: McGraw-Hill, 1984.

[4] P. M. Behr, W. K. Giloi, and H. Muhlenbein, "SUPRENUM: The German supercomputer architecture—Rationale and concepts," in *Proc. 1986 Int. Conf. Parallel Processing*.

[5] S. D. Brooks, C. A. R. Hoare, and A. W. Roscoe, "A theory of communicating sequential processes," *J. ACM*, vol. 31, no. 3, pp. 560–599, July 1984.

[6] R. Buhr, "CAEDE: An iconic Prolog-based design environment approach for Ada," Carleton Univ., Ottawa, Ont., Canada, Jan. 1985.

[7] J. M. Butler and A. Y. Oruc, "Euclid: An architectural multiprocessor simulator," in *Proc. 6th Int. Conf. Distributed Computing Systems*, Cambridge, MA, May 1986, pp. 280–287.

[8] CCITT, "Functional specification and description language (SDL)," Document AP VII, No. 20-E, Geneva, Switzerland, Document AP VII, No. 20-E, June 1980.

[9] L. Cardelli, "An algebraic approach to hardware description and verification," Ph.D. dissertation, Univ. Edinburgh, Dep. Comput. Sci., Rep. CST-16-82, Apr. 1982.

[10] L. Cardelli and R. Pike, "Squeak: A language for communicating with mice," *Comput. Graphics*, vol. 19, no. 3, pp. 199–204, July 1985.

[11] L. Clarke, J. C. Wileden, R. N. Taylor, M. Young, and L. J. Osterweil, "ARCADIA: A software development environment research project," in *Proc. IEEE Second Int. Conf. Ada Applications and Environments*, Miami Beach, FL, Apr. 1986.

[12] P. Degano and E. Sandewall, Eds., *Integrated Interactive Computing Systems: Proc. European Conf. Integrated Interactive Computing Systems (ECICS 82)*. Amsterdam, The Netherlands: North-Holland, 1983.

[13] N. Delisle and M. Schwartz, "A programming environment for CSP," in *Proc. ACM SIGSOFT/SIGPLAN Symp. Practical Software Development Environments*, Palo Alto, CA, Dec. 1986.

[14] T. W. Doeppner, Jr. and A. Giacalone, "A formal description of the UNIX operating system," in *Proc. 2nd ACM SIGACT/SIGOPS Symp. Principles of Distributed Computing*, Montreal, P.Q., Canada, Aug. 1983.

[15] "Multimax technical summary," Encore Computer Corp., May 1985.

[16] G. Estrin, R. S. Fenchel, R. R. Razouk, and M. K. Vernon, "SARA (system architects apprentice): Modeling, analysis, and simulation support for design of concurrent systems," *IEEE Trans. Software Eng.*, vol. SE-12, no. 2, Feb. 1986.

[17] A. Giacalone and I. D. Kovacs, "IDCCS: An ideographic syntax for CCS," Dep. Comput. Sci., Brown Univ., Tech. Rep. CS-83-05, Feb. 1983.

[18] A. Giacalone, M. C. Rinard, and T. W. Doeppner, Jr., "IDEOSY: An interactive and ideographic program description system," in *Proc. ACM SIGSOFT/SIGPLAN Symp. Practical Software Development Environments*, Pittsburgh, PA, Apr. 1984, pp. 15–20.

[19] P. B. Henderson, Ed., *Proc. ACM SIGSOFT/SIGPLAN Symp. Practical Software Development Environments*, Pittsburgh, PA, Apr. 1984.

[20] P. B. Henderson, Ed., *Proc. ACM SIGSOFT/SIGPLAN Symp. Practical Software Development Environments*, Palo Alto, CA, Dec. 1986.

[21] M. C. B. Hennessy, W. Li, and G. Plotkin, "A first attempt at translating CSP into CCS," in *Proc. 2nd IEEE Int. Conf. Distributed Computing*, 1981.

[22] M. C. B. Hennessy and W. Li, "Translating a subset of Ada into CCS," in *Proc. IFIP Conf. Formal Description of Programming Concepts-II*, 1983, pp. 227–247.

[23] M. C. B. Hennessy, "Acceptance trees," *J. ACM*, vol. 34, no. 4, pp. 896–928, Oct. 1985.

[24] W. D. Hillis, *The Connection Machine*. Cambridge, MA: MIT Press, 1985.

[25] C. A. R. Hoare, "A model for communicating sequential processes," Programming Research Group, Oxford Univ., Comput. Lab., Tech. Rep. PRG-22, 1981.

[26] —, *Communicating Sequential Processes*. Englewood Cliffs, NJ: Prentice-Hall, 1985.

[27] C. A. R. Hoare, Ed., *Occam Programming Manual*, INMOS Ltd. Englewood Cliffs, NJ: Prentice-Hall, 1984.

[28] P. C. Kanellakis and S. A. Smolka, "CCS expressions, finite state processes, and three problems of equivalence," in *Proc. 2nd ACM Symp. Principles of Distributed Computing*, Montreal, P.Q., Canada, Aug. 1983, pp. 228–240.

[29] C. J. Koomen, "A structure theory for communication network control," Ph.D. dissertation, Delft Univ. Technology, 1982.

[30] O. Kramer and H. Muhlenbein, "Mapping strategies in message based multiprocessor systems," in *Proc. Conf. Parallel Architectures and Languages Europe (PARLE)*. Eindhoven, The Netherlands: Springer-Verlag, June 15–19, 1987.

[31] K. G. Larsen, "Context-dependent bisimulation between processes," Ph.D. dissertation, Dep. Comput. Sci., Univ. Edinburgh, Tech. Rep. CST-37-86, May 1986.

[32] R. Milner, *A Calculus of Communicating Systems (Lecture Notes in Computer Science*, Vol. 92). New York: Springer-Verlag, 1980.

[33] —, "Calculi for Synchrony and Asynchrony," *Theoret. Comput. Sci.*, 25, (1983), 267–310.

[34] —, "The standard ML core language," Dep. Comput. Sci., Univ. Edinburgh, Internal Rep. CSR-168-84, 1984.

[35] M. Moriconi and D. Hare, "The PegaSys system: Pictures as formal documentation of large programs," *ACM Trans. Prog. Lang. Syst.*, vol. 8, no. 4, pp. 524–546, Oct. 1986.

[36] H. Muhlenbein, O. Kramer, F. Limburger, M. Mevenkamp, and S. Streitz, "Design and rationale for MUPPET: A programming environment for message based multiprocessors," Gesellschaft fur Mathematik und Datenverarbeitung mbH, Sankt Augustin, West Germany, Tech. Rep., Feb. 1987.

[37] "NCUBE/ten: An overview," NCUBE Corp., 1986.

[38] R. D. Nicola and M. C. B. Hennessy, "Testing equivalences for processes," *Theoret. Comput. Sci.*, vol. 34, no. 1, pp. 83–133, 1984.

[39] J. Parrow, "Fairness properties in process algebra with applications in communication protocol verification," Ph.D. dissertation, Dep. Comput. Syst., Uppsala Univ., Sweden, 1985.

[40] C. A. Petri, "Kommunication mit automaten," Bonn Institut fur Instrumentelle Mathematik, Schriften des IIM No. 2, 1962.

[41] G. Plotkin, "A structural approach to operational semantics," Dep. Comput. Sci., Aarhus Univ., Internal Rep. DAIMI FN-19, Sept. 1981.

[42] —, "An operational semantics for CSP," Dep. Comput. Sci., Univ. Edinburgh, Internal Rep. CSR-114-82, May 1982.

[43] K. V. S. Prasad, "Specification and proof of a simple fault tolerant system in CCS," Dep. Comput. Sci., Univ. Edinburgh, Int. Rep. CSR-178-84, 1984.

[44] S. P. Reiss, "PECAN: Program development system that support multiple views," in *Proc. 7th Int. Conf. Software Engineering*, Orlando, FL, Mar. 1984, pp. 45–54.

[45] —, "Visual languages and the garden system," Dep. Comput. Sci., Brown Univ., Providence, RI, Tech. Rep. CS-86-16, 1986.

[46] T. Reps and T. Teitelbaum, "The synthesizer generator reference manual," Dep. Comput. Sci., Cornell Univ., Aug. 1985.

[47] M. W. Sheilds and M. J. Wray, "A CCS specification of the OSI network service," Dep. Comput. Sci., Univ. Edinburgh, Tech. Rep. CSR-136-83, Aug. 1983.

[48] S. A. Smolka and R. E. Strom, "A CCS semantics for NIL," in *Formal Description of Programming Concepts-III*, M. Wirsing, Ed. Amsterdam, The Netherlands: North-Holland, 1987.

[49] R. E. Strom, S. Yemini, and P. Wegner, "Viewing Ada from a process model perspective," in *Proc. 1985 AdaTec Conf.*, Paris, France, 1985.

[50] *Reference Manual for the Ada Programming Language*, U.S. Dep. Defense, Rep. MIL-STD 1815A, Feb. 1983.

[51] P. Wegner, "The Vienna definition language," *ACM Comput. Surveys*, vol. 4, no. 1, Mar. 1972.

Alessandro Giacalone graduated from the University of Pisa, Italy, in 1977, and received the M.S. and Ph.D. degrees in computer science from Brown University, Providence, RI, in 1982 and 1984, respectively.

From 1978 to 1980 he was a Software Engineer at the ITALTEL Research Laboratory in Milano, Italy. From 1983 to 1984 he was Director of Research at IKAN Systems Corporation, in Providence, RI. He is currently an Assistant Professor in the Department of Computer Science of the State University of New York at Stony Brook. His research interests are in the design, verification, and simulation of concurrent systems and in the generation of graphical user interfaces.

Scott A. Smolka received the B.A. and M.A. degrees in mathematics from Boston University, Boston, MA, in 1975 and 1977, respectively, and the Ph.D. degree in computer science from Brown University, Providence, RI, in 1984.

Since 1983, he has been an Assistant Professor at the State University of New York at Stony Brook. His current research interests include the formal analysis of communicating processes and related computational complexity issues, design environments for concurrent systems, and distributed algorithms.

VERDI: The Architecture of a
Visual Environment for Distributed System Design

Mike Graf
MCC and NCR Corporation
Austin, Texas

Introduction

The modest original goal of VERDI, which is a visual environment for designing in distributed systems, was to demonstrate visual language concepts. Soon, VERDI became a vehicle for exploring the features required in professional design tools and a platform for further research into distributed computing theory. The key to meeting these diverse needs was the development of a sound implementation architecture. VERDIs architecture is designed to be easily extended, to be highly portable, and to be connectable to downstream code generation. In this paper, we present an overview of the VERDI architecture.

VERDI: A Brief Look

In VERDI, a designer creates a distributed system design by constructing system control flow diagrams and by specifying the points of interprocess communication and synchronization. This is done by creating primitive visual elements and aggregating them into composite elements that together represent complete system designs. There are specific visual representations for each of the primitives and the allowable composites. Figure 1 shows the primitive elements and an example of a complete system design. Figure 2 is a photograph of a VERDI worksurface containing a design under development and several design fragments.

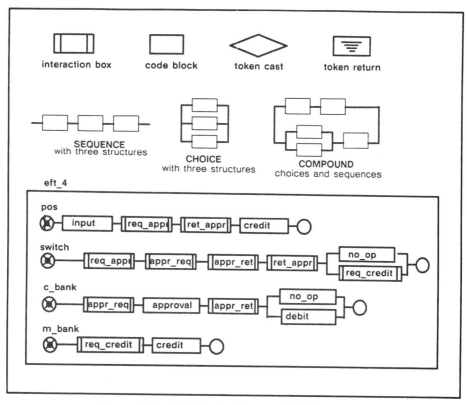

Figure 1: The VERDI primitives and a VERDI design

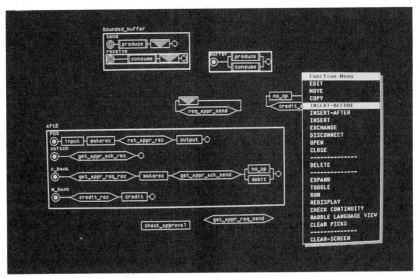

Figure 2: The VERDI work surface

For the purposes of this paper, it is not necessary to understand the complete functionality of VERDI. Those system characteristics that are relevant to understanding the design goals of the VERDI architecture are as follows:

- *Design visualization:* The designer interacts with VERDI through a visual presentation of the design under development. Input is received from both a keyboard and a locator/selector device (usually a three-button mouse). The highest level of any design is presented as a composition of primitive icons. VERDI includes a visual editor to manipulate these compositions.

- *Embedded computational language:* Normal computations (assignments, evaluation of expressions, etc.) are specified in a standard computational language that is embedded in VERDI. The selection of this language is essentially arbitrary. The current VERDI implementation uses a C subset. A textual editor is used to specify computations in this language as well as other textual components of the design. The textual editor interacts with an embedded parser to ensure syntactic correctness.

- *Design execution:* One of the most distinctive features of VERDI is its ability to interpretively execute designs. Executions are displayed to the user by animating VERDI visual designs.

For those readers desiring a more detailed discussion about VERDI and its functionality, see references 1 and 2.

Raddle: The Foundation for VERDI

The most critical element of any visual programming system is the existence of a unifying principle, which is the foundation of the entire system. VERDI's unifying principle is Raddle.

Raddle is a distributed system design specification language under development at MCC.[3,4] In Raddle, a user designs concurrent processes by using a new high-level communication abstraction called N-party interaction to specify synchronization and communication. Designers using Raddle are able to specify an interaction among N of the processes. All processes enter the interaction simultaneously and, during the interaction, a temporary global state is established among the interacting parties to exchange data. The execution semantics also feature nondeterministic resolution of conflict.

VERDI's visual programming language is derived from Raddle, providing a two-dimensional representation of concurrent systems. Horizontally connected elements represent sequences of computations and vertically connected elements indicate a choice among alternative actions. Disconnected elements indicate concurrency.

Design Goals for this Architecture

An earlier VERDI prototype was distributed to users in several MCC shareholder companies for evaluation. The initial feedback included requests for improving and expanding the functionality. These improvements were made

Figure can be found printed in color on page 659.

and accepted, but further feedback indicated that VERDI needed to execute on other more widely available computer configurations than the one on which it was delivered. This was followed by a requirement that alternate design visualizations, such as performance and data flow, be added. It was decided to build a new prototype based upon a new architecture. The primary objectives of the new architecture were the following:

- *Flexibility:* Since VERDI is an on-going research project, the new architecture needs to accommodate a constant infusion of new concepts and theories. The architecture also needs to accommodate new user requirements.

- *Portability:* The VERDI architecture needs to be easily portable to a variety of popular systems and configurations. This is especially important to reach a diverse user community, most of whom already have a personal workstation.

- *Choice of embedded language:* The systems designed in VERDI must eventually be implemented in some computer language. When connecting an upstream design environment to a downstream code-generating system, the choice of language may be critical. Because there are many of these in common use, VERDI needs to be able to specify computation in a variety of languages.

An important secondary goal of VERDI's architecture is that it facilitate the transfer of VERDI to research and development organizations in the MCC shareholder companies. These receptor organizations will evolve and modify VERDI to suit their local environments. Thus, the architecture needs to be easy to document and to understand.

Overview of the Architecture

At the top level, VERDI's architecture consists of a non-visual system and a visual system. Each is a collection of subsystems that communicate with each other through grammar-based protocols. The use of clearly specified protocols allows the subsystems to be easily replaced or augmented by other subsystems that follow those protocols. Conceptually, the subsystems may be located on distributed processors in a client/server relationship. Such a configuration is being considered for future implementation. Figure 3 shows the VERDI architecture.

The Non-Visual System

The non-visual system maintains a representation of all designs and design fragments in VERDI. Designs under development are kept in memory and are manipulated by the internal design manager. Stored designs are kept in the design archive. The design execution machine is used to execute designs to investigate their behavior. An embedded language server is utilized to execute computational expressions.

Internal Design Manager

The internal design manager maintains developing designs as a collection of internal data structures. Each structure represents a primitive Raddle syntactic element. These elements combine to form composite syntactic elements through parent, child, and sibling relations. Textual components of the design, such as declarations, computations, and comments, are attached to the syntactic elements.

A design session begins with a message to the internal design manager to create a VERDI element or to load an existing VERDI design. Each element is assigned a unique id for future reference. The subsequent messages in the editing session add or delete VERDI elements, form composite elements, edit the textual components, query the current design, and direct interactions with the archive system.

Design Execution Machine

When a design is sufficiently specified, the designer may execute it to observe its behavior. A message is sent to the design execution machine to begin the execution. This spawns messages to the internal design manager and the design archive to load the selected design for execution.

During execution, state change messages and control messages are exchanged with the visual system and dialogues are established with the embedded language server for executing computational expressions in the design.

Embedded Language Server

As stated earlier, VERDI is based on the Raddle model of distributed system specification, which includes the notion of an embedded computational language. The choice is somewhat arbitrary and various VERDI prototypes have embedded partial implementations of Pascal, Lisp, and C. The embedded language server performs syntactic analysis of embedded language code during design editing and interprets expressions to maintain the state of declared variables in the designs during execution.

Design Archive

The VERDI design methodology is dependent on building a repository of reusable design fragments that are stored in the design archive. The internal design manager or the design execution machine retrieves them as needed. VERDI currently stores the designs and design fragments in standard Unix files. A planned future system enhancement will replace this simple approach with a full-featured design reuse facility.

Visual System

The visual system presents the internal design representation in the VERDI visual language. The design view appearing in the visual system is controlled by the visual

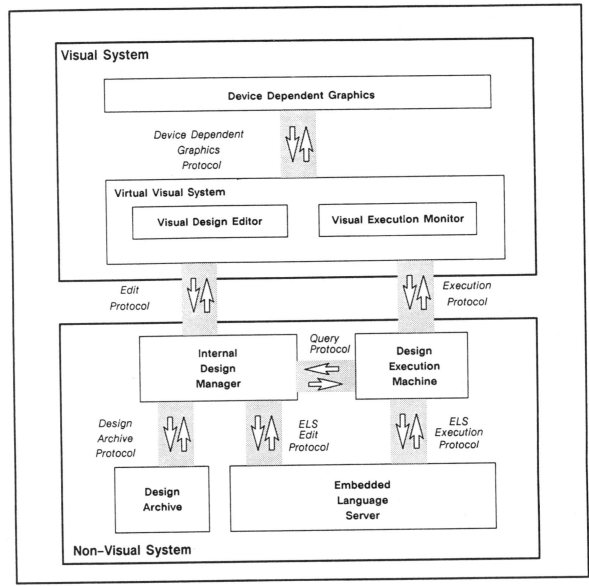

Figure 3: Architectural block diagram

design editor and the visual execution monitor. In the future, these will be complimented by additional subsystems that provide other views, such as performance and data flow. The interface to the physical graphics i/o system is managed by the device-dependent graphics subsystem.

Visual Design Editor

A visual language for distributed systems design has been formulated for VERDI. The visual design editor allows the design to specify a distributed system's functionality in this visual language. Usually a VERDI designer starts by building a simplified, highly abstracted solution to a design problem. This is followed by successively transforming the design into increasingly detailed solutions. These visual editing operations cause messages to be exchanged with the internal design manager where a virtual (non-visual) representation of the current design is maintained. During editing, the visual design editor ensures syntactic correctness of the design.

Visual Execution Monitor

When a design is selected for execution in the VERDI worksurface, the visual execution monitor takes control over the user interface. During execution, the visual execution monitor receives the state change messages from the design execution machine and presents visual changes to the designer. In Figures 4a and 4b, we see two successive snapshots of a VERDI design during execution. The red dots are tokens which move through the design indicating the loci of control. The primitive icons change color to indicate changes of state with respect to execution. Communicating processes are joined by gold lines during communication. The visual execution monitor also provides for a number of run-time control and analysis functions, such as deadlock detection, setting break points, interrogation of internal state and the ability to change parts of the design during pauses in the execution.

Device-Dependent Graphics

One of the most difficult problems in porting a visual system from one computer to another is the vast differences that exist in graphics systems. From the beginning, VERDI has been designed to minimize the porting effort by utilizing only those graphics features that were most likely to appear in other graphics software packages. In the new architecture, all of the interfaces to the graphics software is gathered into a single, simple subsystem, the device-dependent graphics.

The device-dependent graphics is limited to routines that draw lines, circles, and text, and to routines that define and

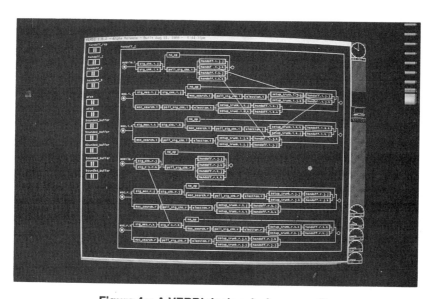

Figure 4a: A VERDI design during execution

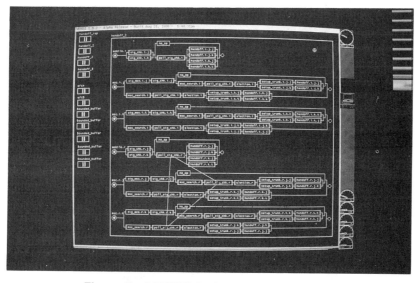

Figure 4b: A VERDI design during execution

Figures can be found printed in color on page 659.   595

```
Device-Dependent Graphics Set-Up Protocol
      worksurface_message
            : CREATE_WS
            ; INIT_WS ws_id top left height width title font
            ; RUN_WS ws_id
            ;
      top    : integer
            ;
      left   : integer
            ;
      height : integer
            ;
      width  : integer
            ;
      title  : string
            ;
      font   : string
            ;
      ws_id  : integer
            ;
      worksurface_create_reply
            : Ok ws_id
            ; ERROR
            ;
```

Device-Dependent Graphics Set-Up Semantics

The CREATE_WS message causes the graphics system to prepare a VERDI worksurface. If this is successful, the reply returns an OK token and the integer ws_id, referring to this worksurface. Else, an ERROR token is returned.

The INIT_WS message specifies the ws_id, position, size, title, and font to be used in the execution of the worksurface. Any or all of these may be ignored by the implementation of the device-dependent graphics.

The device-dependent graphics is in passive mode while receiving the set-up messages. Once the RUN_WS message is received, the device-dependent graphics enters the active mode, which monitors mouse events, such as the selection of visible objects and menu items.

Figure 5: Device-dependent graphics—set up protocol

manage menus and routines that monitor mouse activity. In porting VERDI to another computer configuration, the interfaces to these functions in the target graphics system will have to be rewritten.

The Inter-System Protocols

The VERDI subsystems communicate with each other through a set of protocols. The input and output messages are specified as a simple BNF grammar, in a form compatible with YACC.[5] For brevity, certain well understood types, such as *integer*, are left unspecified. Types presented as capitalized words indicate unique tokens. The device-dependent graphics protocol is presented as an example.

Device-Dependent Graphics Protocol

The device-dependent graphics protocol consists of messages that direct changes in the worksurface display. VERDI requires that a worksurface be created before any design work occurs. The device-dependent graphics are initially in passive mode, listening for messages. Once properly initialized, a run message causes the device-dependent graphics to enter the active mode. When a button event is noticed, a message describing the event is issued and the passive mode is reentered until another run message is received.

Figure 5 shows the set-up protocol. This protocol is used to initialize the work surface and to begin its execution.

After creating the VERDI worksurface, menus may be specified. Whenever the worksurface is in the passive mode, the menu messages may be received by the device-dependent graphics. Once a run message is received, the worksurface is in the active mode and the mouse is monitored for motion and button depressions. Mouse motion is tracked by a visible cursor on the worksurface. When a button depression occurs, a button event message is sent from the device-dependent graphics and the worksurface reenters the passive mode. These messages are presented in Figure 6.

A button event message usually results in a design change that is reflected in the visual worksurface. These changes are caused by a series of draw messages sent to the device-dependent graphics from the graphics management subsystem. This sequence ends with a run message to reinstate the active mode. The draw messages are described in Figure 7.

Implementation of the Inter-System Protocols

The implementation of the VERDI protocols has taken two forms. In one configuration, the device-dependent graphics is implemented on a remote graphics subsystem with a separate computer hosting all other modules. In this configuration, the protocol is implemented as a series of ASCII messages, with send/receive modules servicing the transmission. The reason for choosing ASCII is to simplify implementation and debugging, at the expense of some performance. At a later time, an implementation with a more efficient message format will be implemented.

In the other configuration, VERDI is implemented by using an integrated graphics system and color monitor. In this configuration, it was determined to be more efficient to use direct subroutine calls rather than passing messages.

```
Device-Dependent Graphics Menu/Mouse Protocol
      menu_message
           ; MENU_CREATE ws_id
           ; MENU_TITLE ws_id menu_id
           ; MENU_ITEM ws_id menu_id item_no item_string
           ; MENU_ATTACH ws_id menu_id button_id
           ;
      menu_create_reply
           : OK menu_id
           : ERROR
           ;
      menu_id
           : integer
           : NULL_MENU
           ;
      item_no : integer
           ;
      item_string : string
           ;
      button_id
           : LEFT
           : MIDDLE
           : RIGHT
           ;
      button_event
           ; button_id ws_id item_no x y
           ;
Device-Dependent Graphics Menu/Mouse Semantics
      A MENU_CREATE message responds with an OK token followed by an integer id for a newly created menu,
      or an ERROR token for a creation failure. Once created, the menu content is defined with MENU_TITLE and
      MENU_ITEM messages.

The menu protocols interact with a three-button mouse. The graphics management subsystem directs that particular
menus be attached to particular mouse buttons. When a button is depressed, the device-dependent graphics sends a
button_event message to the graphics management subsystem. Alternative graphics systems may utilize other
selecton devices, for instance, a one-button mouse with pull-down menus may be used to simulate a three-button
mouse.
```

Figure 6: Device-dependent graphics—menu mouse protocol

Device-Dependent Graphics Drafting Protocol
    draw_message
        : DRAW_LINE ws_id x1 y1 x2 y2 color
        : DRAW_BOX ws_id top left height width color
        : DRAW_CIRCLE ws_id x y radius color
        : DRAW_FILLED_CIRCLE ws_id x y radius color
        : DRAW_STRING ws_id x y text color

Device-Dependent Graphics Drafting Semantics
    The draw_messages may be sent any time after a mouse event message is received. Usually the response to a mouse event consists of sending several draw_messages to change the visual display. This sequence is terminated by sending a run_worksurface message.

Figure 7: Device Dependent Graphics—Drafting Protocol

```
# include "menu.h"

reply = menu_create(ws_id)
        MENU_REPLY *reply;
        int ws_id;

menu_sts = get_menu_sts(reply)
        int menu_sts;

menu_id = get_menu_id(reply);
        int menu_id;

menu_title(ws_id, menu_id, title)
        char *title;

menu_item(ws_id, menu_id, item_no, item_text)
        int item_no;
        char *item_text;

menu_attach(ws_id, menu_id, button_id)
        int button_id;

button_event(ws_id, button_id, item_no, x, y)
        int x, y;
```

Usage

The call to menu_create returns a pointer to a MENU_REPLY structure. The contents of the status and id slots in the structure can be extracted by using the get_menu_sts and get_menu_id macros. If the menu creation was successful, the status slot will hold the value OK and the id slot will contain the reference id for future menu calls. If the menu was not created, the status field will hold ERROR and the contents of the id field will be meaningless.

The menu_title and menu_item routines specify information about a menu. The menu_attach routine associates a defined menu with a mouse button. The possible values for button_id (as defined in the menu.h file) are LEFT, MIDDLE, RIGHT.

Calls to button_event provide the x and y coordinates of the cursor at the time the mouse button is depressed. The item_no is the index of the selected menu item. If no item is picked or if no menu is attached to the button, the value of item_no is NULL_ITEM.

Figure 8: Device-Dependent Graphics Menu Protocol: C Equivalent

Figure 8 shows the equivalent C specification of the device-dependent graphics menu protocols of Figure 6. In this example, the button event routines reside in the internal design manager and are called by the device-dependent graphics when an event is noticed.

Building on the New Architecture

The VERDI architecture has been implemented and we are expanding it as well as integrating VERDI with other systems. With respect to the stated objectives of the VERDI architecture, we are achieving the following successes:

- *Portability:* VERDI has been successfully implemented on a Sun Workstation using the SunViews graphics routines. It has also been successfully ported to a PC with MicroSoft Windows graphics. A generic UNIX implementation with X-Windows is underway.

- *Flexibility:* We have started integrating a performance modelling view based on CSIM[6] and we are formulating a joint project with a shareholder company to provide a data view. Integration of the distributed computing research concepts of quorum interaction[7] and super-imposition[8] is being specified.

- *Choice of embedded language:* The concept of an embedded language server has made it possible to extend VERDI to include several computational languages. We have begun extending the VERDI visual language to include additional communications primitives, with an eye to producing an environment for specifying concurrent Ada systems.

We have been very encouraged by these early results with the new architecture. Systems designers, who have used VERDI, feel it improves their productivity, particularly because it is able to build and execute the designs in the visual form. We expect wider use of VERDI in the shareholders, both in their laboratories and in product development.

References

1. Graf, M., "Building a Visual Designer's Environment," in *Principles of Visual Language Systems*, Chang, S.K. (Ed.), Prentice-Hall, Englewood Cliffs, N.J., 1990

2. Graf, M., "A Visual Environment for the Design of Distributed Systems," in *Visual Programming and Visual Languages*, Korfhage, R. (Ed.), Plenum Press, New York, 1990.

3. Attie, P., "Raddle87 Reference Manual," *STP-340-87*, Microelectronics and Computer Technology Corp., Austin, Tex., Nov. 1987

4. Evangelist, M. et al., "Using Raddle to Design Distributed Systems," in *Proceedings of the 10th International Conference on Software Engineering*, IEEE Computer Society Press, Los Alamitos, Calif., 1988, pp.

5. Johnson S., "YACC—Yet Another Compiler Compiler," *CSTR-32*, Bell Laboratories, 1975.

6. Schwetman, H., *CSIM Reference Manual (Revision 13)*, Microelectronics and Computer Technology Corp., Austin, Tex., 1988.

7. Evangelist, M., Francez, N., and Katz, S., Multiparty Interactions for Interprocess Communication and Synchronization," to appear in *IEEE Transactions on Software Engineering*, 1989.

8. Katz, S., "A Superimposition Control Construct for Distributed Systems," *STP-268-87*, Microelectronics and Computer Technology Corp., Austin, Tex., Aug. 1987.

9. Shen, V.Y., "Using Superimposition to Add Fault Tolerance to an EFT System," *STP-386-87*, Microelectronics and Computer Technology Corp., Austin, Tex., March 1988.

# □□□ □□□ Selected Readings

Despite the length of the two volumes which comprise this tutorial, there is much interesting material that unfortunately could not be included. The citations on the following pages are intended to remedy this shortcoming insofar as possible by providing access to additional research results. We apologize in advance for the many relevant papers which have undoubtedly been omitted by mistake.

A second objective in compiling this bibliography has been to provide an alternative sort order to assist in locating specific papers in these volumes. Within chapters, papers are grouped according to topic. Here, on the other hand, the organization is:

MAJOR KEY: Lexicographic order.
MINOR KEY: Date of publication.

Those entries that correspond to papers that are reproduced in this tutorial are indicated by means of a special symbol:

♠ if the paper is in *Visual Programming Environments: Paradigms and Systems*.
♣ if the paper is in *Visual Programming Environments: Applications and Issues*.

The appropriate symbol is followed by the number of the chapter where the paper may be found. So, for example, "♣ 6" denotes Chapter 6 of *Visual Programming Environments: Applications and Issues*.

— E.P.G.

References

[1] H. Abelson and A.A. DiSessa. *Turtle Geometry: The Computer as a Medium for Exploring Mathematics.* MIT Press, Cambridge, Mass., 1981.

[2] A.L. Ambler and M.M. Burnett. "Influence of Visual Technology on the Evolution of Language Environments." *IEEE Computer*, 22(10):9–22, October 1989. ♠ 1

[3] M. Aoyama, K. Miyamoto, N. Murakami, H. Nagano and Y. Oki. "Design Specification in Japan: Tree–Structured Charts." *IEEE Software*, 6(2):31–37, March 1989. ♣ 10

[4] A. Arblaster. "Human Factors in the Design and Use of Computer Languages." *Int. J. of Man–Machine Studies*, 17(2):211–224, August 1982.

[5] R. Arnheim. *Visual Thinking.* University of California Press, Berkeley, Calif., 1971.

[6] Y. Artsy and R. Finkel. "Designing a Process Migration Facility: The CHARLOTTE Experience." *IEEE Computer*, 22(9):47–56, September 1989.

[7] M. Azuma, T. Tabata, Y. Oki and S. Kamiya. "SPD: A Humanized Documentation Technology." *IEEE Trans. on Software Engineering*, SE–11(9):945–953, September 1985. ♠ 2

[8] R.M. Baecker and W.A.S. Buxton. *Readings in Human–Computer Interaction: A Multidisciplinary Approach.* Morgan Kaufmann, Los Altos, Calif., 1987.

[9] B.R. Baker. "Using Images to Generate Speech." *Byte*, 11(3):160–168, March 1986. ♣ 8

[10] R. Beach and M. Stone. "Graphical Style: Towards High Quality Illustrations." *ACM Computer Graphics (Proc. SIGGRAPH'83*, Detroit, Mich.), 17(3):127–135, July 1983. ♣ 6

[11] L.A. Belady, C.J. Evangelisti and L.R. Power. "GREENPRINT: A Graphic Representation of Structured Programs." *IBM Systems Journal*, 19(4):542–553, 1980. ♠ 2

[12] M. Beretta, P. Mussio and M. Protti. "Icons: Interpretation and Use." In *Proc. Workshop on Visual Languages*, Dallas, Tex., pages 149–158, June 25-27, 1986. IEEE Computer Society Press, Los Alamitos, Calif. ♣ 5

[13] A. Berztiss. "Formal Specification Methods and Visualization." In *Principles of Visual Programming Systems* (S.-K. Chang, editor), pages 231–290, 1990. Prentice Hall, Englewood Cliffs, N.J.

[14] M.M. Blattner, D.A. Sumikawa and R.M. Greenberg. "Earcons and Icons: Their Structure and Common Design Principles." *Human–Computer Interaction*, 4(1):11–44, 1989. ♣ 10

[15] R.A. Bolt. "PUT–THAT–THERE: Voice and Gesture at the Graphics Interface." *ACM Computer Graphics (Proc. SIGGRAPH'80*, Seattle, Wash.), 14(3):262–270, July 1980.

[16] J.G. Bonar and B.W. Liffick. "A Visual Programming Language for Novices." In *Principles of Visual Programming Systems* (S.-K. Chang, editor), pages 326–366, 1990. Prentice Hall, Englewood Cliffs, N.J.

[17] A.H. Borning. "The Programming Language Aspects of THINGLAB, a Constraint Oriented Simulation Laboratory." *ACM Trans. on Programming Languages and Systems*, 3(4):353–387, October 1981. ♠ 7

[18] A.H. Borning. "Defining Constraints Graphically." In *Conference Proceedings, CHI'86: Human Factors in Computing Systems*, Boston, Mass., pages 137–143, April 13-17, 1986. ACM Press, New York.

[19] A.H. Borning. "Graphically Defining New Building Blocks in THINGLAB." *Human–Computer Interaction*, 2(4):269–295, 1986. ♠ 7

[20] A.H. Borning, R. Duisberg, B. Freeman-Benson, A. Kramer and M. Woolf. "Constraint Hierarchies." In *Proc. OOPSLA'87*, Orlando, Fla., pages 48–60, October 4-8, 1987. ACM Press, New York. ♠ 7

[21] J.B. Brooke and K.D. Duncan. "An Experimental Study of Flowcharts as an Aid to Identification of Procedural Faults." *Ergonomics*, 23(4):387–399, April 1980.

[22] J.B. Brooke and K.D. Duncan. "Experimental Studies of Flowchart Use at Different Stages of Program Debugging." *Ergonomics*, 23(11):1057–1091, November 1980.

[23] R.E. Brooks. "Studying Programmer Behavior Experimentally: The Problems of Proper Methodology." *CACM*, 23(4):207–213, April 1980.

[24] G.P. Brown, R.T. Carling, C.F. Herot, D.A. Kramlich and P. Souza. "Program Visualization: Graphical Support for Software Development." *IEEE Computer*, 18(8):27–35, August 1985. ♠ 4

[25] M.H. Brown. "Exploring Algorithms Using BALSA–II." *IEEE Computer*, 21(5):14–36, May 1988. ♣ 3

[26] M.H. Brown. "Perspectives on Algorithm Animation." In *Conference Proceedings, CHI'88: Human Factors in Computing Systems*, Washington, D.C., pages 33–38, May 15-18, 1988. ACM Press, New York. ♣ 3

[27] M.H. Brown and R. Sedgewick. "A System for Algorithm Animation." *ACM Computer Graphics (Proc. SIGGRAPH'84, Minneapolis, Minn.)*, 18(3):177–186, July 1984. ♣ 3

[28] M.H. Brown and R. Sedgewick. "Techniques for Algorithm Animation." *IEEE Software*, 2(1):28–39, January 1985. ♣ 3

[29] M.L. Brown, S.L. Newsome and E.P. Glinert. "An Experiment into the Use of Auditory Cues to Reduce Visual Workload." In *Conference Proceedings, CHI'89: Human Factors in Computing Systems*, Austin, Tex., pages 339–346, April 30-May 4, 1989. ACM Press, New York. ♣ 10

[30] R.J.A. Buhr. *System Design with Ada*. Prentice Hall, Englewood Cliffs, N.J., 1984. ♠ 2

[31] W. Buxton, M.R. Lamb, D. Sherman and K.C. Smith. "Towards a Comprehensive User Interface Management System." *ACM Computer Graphics* (*Proc. SIGGRAPH'83*, Detroit, Mich.), 17(3):35–42, July 1983.

[32] J. Callahan, D. Hopkins, M. Weiser and B. Shneiderman. "An Empirical Comparison of Pie vs. Linear Menus." In *Conference Proceedings, CHI'88: Human Factors in Computing Systems*, Washington, D.C., pages 95–100, May 15-18, 1988. ACM Press, New York.

[33] S.K. Card, W.K. English and B.J. Burr. "Evaluation of Mouse, Rate–Controlled Isometric Joystick, Step Keys and Text Keys for Text Selection on a CRT." *Ergonomics*, 21(8):601–613, August 1978.

[34] S.K. Card, T.P. Moran and A. Newell. *The Psychology of Human–Computer Interaction*. Lawrence Erlbaum Associates, Hillsdale, N.J., 1983.

[35] L. Cardelli. "Two–Dimensional Syntax for Functional Languages." In *Integrated Interactive Computing Systems—Proceedings of a Conference held in Stresa, Italy* (P. Degano and E. Sandewall, editors), pages 107–119, 1983. North Holland, Amsterdam, The Netherlands. ♠ 2

[36] S.-K. Chang. "Icon Semantics—A Formal Approach to Icon System Design." *Int. J. of Pattern Recognition and Artificial Intelligence*, 1(1):103–120, 1987.

[37] S.-K. Chang. "Visual Languages: A Tutorial and Survey." *IEEE Software*, 4(1):29–39, January 1987. ♠ 1

[38] S.-K. Chang, editor. *Principles of Visual Programming Systems*. Prentice Hall, Englewood Cliffs, N.˙, 1990.

[39] S.-K. Chang. "Principles of Visual Languages." In *Principles of Visual Programming Systems* (S.-K. Chang, editor), pages 1–59, 1990. Prentice Hall, Englewood Cliffs, N.J.

[40] S.-K. Chang, T. Ichikawa and P.A. Ligomenides, editors. *Visual Languages*. Plenum, New York. 1986.

[41] S.-K. Chang, Q.-Y. Shi and C.-W. Yan. "Iconic Indexing by 2–D Strings." *IEEE Trans. on Pattern Analysis and Machine Intelligence*, PAMI-9(3):413–428, May 1987.

[42] S.-K. Chang, M.J. Tauber, B. Yu and J.-S. Yu. "A Visual Language Compiler." *IEEE Trans. on Software Engineering*, 15(5):506–525, May 1989. ♣ 9

[43] C. Christensen, M.S. Wolfberg and M.J. Fisher. "AMBIT/G, Final Report—Task Area I for the Project 'Research in Machine Independent Software Programming'." *Technical Report AD–720–313*, NTIS, 1971.

[44] B.E.J. Clark and S.K. Robinson. "A Graphically Interacting Program Monitor." *Computer Journal*, 26(3):235–238, August 1983.

[45] E.K. Clemons and A.J. Greenfield. "The SAGE System Architecture: A System for the Rapid Development of Graphics Interfaces for Decision Support." *IEEE Computer Graphics and Applications*, 5(11):38–50, November 1985. ♣ 2

[46] J.-C. Corbeil. *Visual Dictionary*. Facts On File Publications, New York. 1986.

[47] P.T. Cox and T. Pietrzykowski. "Using a Pictorial Representation to Combine Data–Flow and Object Orientation in a Language–Independent Programming Mechanism." In *Proc. Int. Computer Science Conference, Hong Kong*, pages 695–704, 1988 (available as *Tech]nical Report TR–3–1988*, School of Computer Science, Technical University of Nova Scotia, Halifax, Canada). ♠ 4

[48] G.A. Curry. *Programming by Abstract Demonstration*. PhD Thesis, Dept. of Computer Science, University of Washington (*Technical Report 78–03–02*), Seattle, Wash., 1978.

[49] B. Curtis, editor. *Tutorial: Human Factors in Software Development*, Second Edition. IEEE Computer Society Press, Los Alamitos, Calif., 1981.

[50] E.G. Davis and R.W. Swezey. "Human Factors Guidelines in Computer Graphics: A Case Study." *Int. J. of Man–Machine Studies*, 18(2):113–133, February 1983.

[51] S.P. DeJong. "The System for Business Automation (SBA): A Unified Application Development System." In *Information Processing '80* (S.H. Lavington, editor), pages 469–474, 1980. North Holland, Amsterdam, The Netherlands.

[52] N.M. Delisle, D.E. Menicosy and M.D. Schwartz. "Viewing a Programming Environment as a Single Tool." In *Proc. ACM SIGSOFT/SIGPLAN Symposium on Practical Software Development Environments*, April 1984. ACM Press, New York.

[53] E. Denert, R. Franck and W. Streng. "PLAN2D: Towards a Two Dimensional Programming Language." In *Proc. 4th Annual Meeting of the Gesellschaft Fur Informatik, Berlin*, pages 202–213, 1974. Springer Verlag, Berlin, West Germany (published as Volume 26 in the series 'Lecture Notes in Computer Science').

[54] F. DeRemer and H.H. Kron. "Programming–In–The–Large vs. Programming–In–The–Small." *IEEE Trans. on Software Engineering*, SE–2(2):80–86, June 1976.

[55] J.L. Diaz–Herrera and R.C. Flude. "PASCAL/HSD: A Graphical Programming System." In *Proc. COMPSAC'80*, Chicago, Ill., pages 723–728, 1980. IEEE Computer Society Press, Los Alamitos, Calif. ♠ 4

[56] M.E. Dickover, C.L. McGowan and D.T. Ross. "Software Design Using SADT." In *Proc. ACM Annual Conference*, Seattle, Wash. pages 125–133, October 17-19, 1977. ACM Press, New York.

[57] W.C. Donelson. "Spatial Management of Information." *ACM Computer Graphics* (*Proc. SIGGRAPH'78*, Atlanta, Ga.), 12(3):203–209, August 1978.

[58] M. Dragomirecky, E.P. Glinert, J. Jasica, D.A. Duff, W.D. Smith and M.A. D'Abreu. "High–Level Graphical User Interface Management in the FACE Synthesis Environment." In *Proc. 26th Design Automation Conference*, Las Vegas, Nev., pages 549–554, June 25-29, 1989. ACM Press, New York.

[59] R.A. Duisberg. "Animated Graphical Interfaces Using Temporal Constraints." In *Conference Proceedings, CHI'86: Human Factors in Computing Systems*, Boston, Mass., pages 131–136, April 13-17, 1986. ACM Press, New York.

[60] R.A. Duisberg. "Visual Programming of Program Visualizations." In *Proc. Workshop on Visual Languages*, Linkoping, Sweden, pages 55–66, August 19-21, 1987. University of Linkoping Press.

[61] R.A. Duisberg. "Animation Using Temporal Constraints: An Overview of the ANIMUS System." *Human–Computer Interaction*, 3(3):275–307, 1987/88. ♠ 8

[62] M. Edel. "The TINKERTOY Graphical Programming Environment." In *Proc. COMPSAC'86*, Chicago, Ill., pages 466–471, 1986. IEEE Computer Society Press, Los Alamitos, Calif. ♠ 4

[63] A.D.N. Edwards. "SOUNDTRACK: An Auditory Interface for Blind Users." *Human–Computer Interaction*, 4(1):45–66, 1989.

[64] T.O. Ellis, J.F. Haefner and W.L. Sibley. "The GRAIL Project: An Experiment in Man-Machine Communications." *RAND Report RM–5999–ARPA*, The RAND Corporation, 1969.

[65] W. Finzer and L. Gould. "Programming by Rehearsal." *Byte*, 9(6):187–210, June 1984. ♠ 6

[66] G. Fisher. "An Overview of a Graphical Multilanguage Applications Environment." *IEEE Trans. on Software Engineering*, SE–14(6):774–786, June 1988. ♣ 1

[67] M.J. Fitter. "Towards More 'Natural' Interactive Systems." *Int. J. of Man–Machine Studies*, 11(3):339–350, May 1979.

[68] M.J. Fitter and T.R.G. Green. "When Do Diagrams Make Good Computer Languages?" *Int. J. of Man–Machine Studies*, 11(2):235–261, March 1979.

[69] J.D. Foley and C.F. McMath. "Dynamic Process Visualization." *IEEE Computer Graphics and Applications*, 6(3):16–25, March 1986. ♣ 1

[70] H.P. Frei, D.L. Weller and R. Williams. "A Graphics–Based Programming–Support System." *ACM Computer Graphics (Proc. SIGGRAPH'78*, Atlanta, Ga.), 12(3):43–49, August 1978. ♠ 3

[71] G.W. Furnas. "Generalized Fisheye Views." In *Conference Proceedings, CHI'86: Human Factors in Computing Systems*, Boston, Mass., pages 16–23, April 13-17, 1986. ACM Press, New York.

[72] W.W. Gaver. "Auditory Icons: Using Sound in Computer Interfaces." *Human–Computer Interaction*, 2(2):167–177, 1986.

[73] W.W. Gaver. "The SONICFINDER: An Interface That Uses Auditory Icons." *Human–Computer Interaction*, 4(1):67–94, 1989. ♣ 10

[74] D. Gentner and A. Stevens, editors. *Mental Models.* Lawrence Erlbaum Associates, Hillsdale, N.J., 1982.

[75] M. Gerstendorfer and G. Rohr. "Which Task in Which Representation on What Kind of Interface?" In *INTERACT'87, Proc. 2nd IFIP Conf. on Human–Computer Interaction*, Stuttgart, West Germany, pages 513–518, September 1-4, 1987. North Holland, Amsterdam, The Netherlands. ♣ 7

[76] S.L. Getz, G. Kalligiannis and S.R. Schach. "A Very High–Level Interactive Graphical Trace for the Pascal Heap." *IEEE Trans. on Software Engineering*, SE–9(2):179–185, March 1983.

[77] A. Giacalone and S.A. Smolka. "Integrated Environments for Formally Well–Founded Design and Simulation of Concurrent Systems." *IEEE Trans. on Software Engineering*, SE–14(6):787–802, June 1988. ♠ 9

[78] D.J. Gilmore and H.T. Smith. "An Investigation of the Utility of Flowcharts During Computer Program Debugging." *Int. J. of Man–Machine Studies*, 20(4):357–372, April 1984.

[79] E.P. Glinert. *PICT: Experiments in the Design of Interactive, Graphical Programming Environments.* PhD Thesis, Dept. of Computer Science, University of Washington (*Technical Report 85–01–01*), Seattle, Wash., 1985.

[80] E.P. Glinert. "Towards 'Second Generation' Interactive, Graphical Programming Environments." In *Proc. Workshop on Visual Languages*, Dallas, Tex., pages 61–70, June 25-27, 1986. IEEE Computer Society Press, Los Alamitos, Calif.

[81] E.P. Glinert. "Interactive, Graphical Programming Environments: Six Open Problems and a Possible Partial Solution" (panel position paper). In *Proc. COMPSAC'86*, Chicago, Ill., pages 408–410, 1986. IEEE Computer Society Press, Los Alamitos, Calif.

[82] E.P. Glinert. "Out of Flatland: Towards Three–Dimensional Visual Programming." In *Proc. 2nd Fall Joint Computer Conference*, Dallas, Tex., pages 292–299, October 25-29, 1987. IEEE Computer Society Press, Los Alamitos, Calif. ♣ 10

[83] E.P. Glinert. "Toward Software Metrics for Visual Programming." *Int. J. of Man–Machine Studies*, 30:425–445, 1989.

[84] E.P. Glinert. "Nontextual Programming Environments." In *Principles of Visual Programming Systems* (S.-K. Chang, editor), pages 144–232, 1990. Prentice Hall, Englewood Cliffs, N.J.

[85] E.P. Glinert and J. Gonczarowski. "A (Formal) Model for (Iconic) Programming Environments." In *INTERACT'87, Proc. 2nd IFIP Conf. on Human–Computer Interaction*, Stuttgart, West Germany, pages 283–290, September 1-4, 1987. North Holland, Amsterdam, The Netherlands. ♣ 9

[86] E.P. Glinert, M.E. Kopache and D.W. McIntyre. "Exploring the General–Purpose Visual Alternative." *J. Visual Languages and Computing*, 1(1):3–39, March 1990.

[87] E.P. Glinert and D.W. McIntyre. "The User's View of SUNPICT, an Extensible Visual Environment for Intermediate–Scale Procedural Programming." In *Proc. 4th IEEE Israel Conference on Computer Systems and Software Engineering*, Tel Aviv, Israel, pages 49–58, June 5-6, 1989. IEEE Computer Society Press, Los Alamitos, Calif.

[88] E.P. Glinert and S.L. Tanimoto. "PICT: An Interactive, Graphical Programming Environment." *IEEE Computer*, 17(11):7–25, November 1984. ♠ 3

[89] E.J. Golin and S.P. Reiss. "The Specification of Visual Language Syntax." In *Proc. Workshop on Visual Languages*, Rome, Italy, pages 105–110, October 4-6, 1989. IEEE Computer Society Press, Los Alamitos, Calif. ♣ 9

[90] M. Graf. "A Visual Environment for the Design of Distributed Systems." In *Proc. Workshop on Visual Languages*, Linkoping, Sweden, pages 330–344, August 19-21, 1987. University of Linkoping Press.

[91] M. Graf. "Building a Visual Designer's Environment." In *Principles of Visual Programming Systems* (S.-K. Chang, editor), pages 291–325, 1990. Prentice Hall, Englewood Cliffs, N.J.

[92] M. Graf. "VERDI: The Architecture of a Visual Environment for Distributed System Design." In *Tutorial: Visual Programming Environments: Paradigms and Systems* (E.P. Glinert, editor), 1990. IEEE Computer Society Press, Los Alamitos, Calif. ♠ 9

[93] M. Graf. "Visual Programming and Visual Languages: Lessons Learned in the Trenches." In *Tutorial: Visual Programming Environments: Applications and Issues* (E.P. Glinert, editor), 1990. IEEE Computer Society Press, Los Alamitos, Calif. ♣ 7

[94] T.R.G. Green, M.E. Sime and M.J. Fitter. "The Problems the Programmer Faces." *Ergonomics*, 23(9):893–907, September 1980.

[95] S.H. Gutfreund. "Maniplicons in THINKERTOY." In *Proc. OOPSLA '87*, Orlando, Fla., pages 307–317, October 4-8, 1987. ACM Press, New York. ♣ 1

[96] P.E. Haeberli. "CONMAN: A Visual Programming Language for Interactive Graphics." *ACM Computer Graphics (Proc. SIGGRAPH'88*, Atlanta, Ga.), 22(4):103–111, August 1988. ♣ 2

[97] S. Hanata and T. Satoh. "COMPACT CHART: A Program Logic Notation with High Describability and Understandability." *ACM SIGPLAN Notices*, 15(9):32–38, September 1980.

[98] D. Harel. "On Visual Formalisms." *CACM*, 31(5):514–530, May 1988. ♠ 2

[99] E.S. Helfman. *Blissymbolics: Speaking Without Speech.* Elsevier Nelson, New York, 1981.

[100] D.A. Henderson Jr. "The TRILLIUM User Interface Design Environment." In *Conference Proceedings, CHI'86: Human Factors in Computing Systems*, Boston, Mass., pages 221–227, April 13-17, 1986. ACM Press, New York. ♣ 1

[101] D.A. Henderson Jr. and S.K. Card. "ROOMS: The Use of Multiple Virtual Workspaces to Reduce Space Contention in a Window–Based Graphical User Interface." *ACM Trans. on Graphics*, 5(3):211–243, July 1986. ♣ 6

[102] C.F. Herot. "Spatial Management of Data." *ACM Trans. on Database Systems*, 5(4):493–513, December 1980.

[103] N. Hirakawa, S. Iwata, I. Yoshimoto, M. Tanaka and T. Ichikawa. "HI–VISUAL Iconic Programming." In *Proc. Workshop on Visual Languages*, Linkoping, Sweden, pages 305–314, August 19-21, 1987. University of Linkoping Press.

[104] N. Hirakawa, J.-I. Miyao, T. Kikuno and N. Yoshida. "An Approach to Form Creation Based on And/Or Tree." In *Proc. 21st Hawaii Int. Conf. on System Sciences (HICSS-21)*, Kailua Kona, Haw., Volume 2: Software Track, pages 655–661, January 5-8, 1988. IEEE Computer Society Press, Los Alamitos, Calif.

[105] N. Hirakawa, N. Monden, I. Yoshimoto, M. Tanaka and T. Ichikawa. "HI–VISUAL: A Language Supporting Visual Interaction in Programming." In *Visual Languages* (S.-K. Chang, T. Ichikawa and P.A. Ligomenides, editors), pages 233–259, 1986. Plenum, New York.

[106] K.-T. Huang. "Visual Interface Design Systems." In *Principles of Visual Programming Systems* (S.-K. Chang, editor), pages 60–143, 1990. Prentice Hall, Englewood Cliffs, N.J.

[107] *Human Factors in Computer Systems.* Proceedings of a Conference Held at Gaithersburg, Maryland, March 15-17, 1982. Institute for Computer Sciences and Technology, National Bureau of Standards, United States Dept. of Commerce, Gaithersburg, Md.

[108] T. Ichikawa and M. Hirakawa. "Visual Programming: Toward Realization of User–Friendly Programming Environments." In *Proc. 2nd Fall Joint Computer Conference*, Dallas, Tex., pages 129–137, October 25-29, 1987. IEEE Computer Society Press, Los Alamitos, Calif. ♣ 1

[109] D. Ingalls, S. Wallace, Y.-Y. Chow, F. Ludolph and K. Doyle. "FABRIK: A Visual Programming Environment." In *Proc. OOPSLA'88*, San Diego, Calif., pages 176–190, September 25-30, 1988. ACM Press, New York.

[110] P.R. Innocent. "Towards Self–Adaptive Interface Systems." *Int. J. of Man–Machine Studies*, 16(3):287–299, April 1982.

[111] L.A. Iverson, E.S. Cohen and E.T. Smith. "Constraint–Based Tiled Windows." *IEEE Computer Graphics and Applications*, 6(5):35–45, May 1986.

[112] R.J.K. Jacob. "A State Transition Diagram Language for Visual Programming." *IEEE Computer*, 18(8):51–59, August 1985. ♠ 2

[113] S.L. Jarvenpaa and G.W. Dickson. "Graphics and Managerial Decision Making: Research Based Guidelines." *CACM*, 31(6):764–774, June 1988. ♣ 7

[114] Y. Kanda and M. Sugimoto. "Software Diagram Description: SDD and Its Application." In *Proc. COMPSAC'80*, Chicago, Ill., pages 300–305, 1980. IEEE Computer Society Press, Los Alamitos, Calif.

[115] H. Kangassalo. "CONCEPT D: A Graphical Language for Conceptual Modelling and Data Base Use." In *Proc. Workshop on Visual Languages*, Pittsburgh, Penn., pages 2–11, October 10-12, 1988. IEEE Computer Society Press, Los Alamitos, Calif. ♣ 4

[116] T.D. Kimura. "Visual Programming by Transaction Network." In *Proc. 21st Hawaii Int. Conf. on System Sciences (HICSS-21)*, Kailua Kona, Haw., Volume 2: Software Track, pages 648–654, January 5-8, 1988. IEEE Computer Society Press, Los Alamitos, Calif. ♠ 2

[117] T.D. Kimura, J.W. Choi and J.M. Mack. "Show and Tell." In *Tutorial: Visual Programming Environments: Paradigms and Systems* (E.P. Glinert, editor), 1990. IEEE Computer Society Press, Los Alamitos, Calif. ♠ 6

[118] M.E. Kopache and E.P. Glinert. "C²: A Mixed Textual/Graphical Programming Environment for C." In *Proc. Workshop on Visual Languages*, Pittsburgh, Penn., pages 231–238, October 10-12, 1988. IEEE Computer Society Press, Los Alamitos, Calif. ♠ 4

[119] R.R. Korfhage and M.A. Korfhage. "Criteria for Iconic Languages." In *Visual Languages* (S.-K. Chang, T. Ichikawa and P.A. Ligomenides, editors), pages 207–231, 1986. Plenum, New York.

[120] D. Kurlander and S. Feiner. "Editable Graphical Histories." In *Proc. Workshop on Visual Languages*, Pittsburgh, Penn., pages 127–134, October 10-12, 1988. IEEE Computer Society Press, Los Alamitos, Calif. ♣ 6

[121] R. Kurzweil. "The Technology of the Kurzweil Voice Writer." *Byte*, 11(3):177–186, March 1986.

[122] R.E. Ladner. "Public Law 99–506, Section 508: Electronic Equipment Accessibility for Disabled Workers" (panel position paper). In *Conference Proceedings, CHI'88: Human Factors in Computing Systems*, Washington, D.C., pages 219–222, May 15-18, 1988. ACM Press, New York. ♣ 8

[123] F.H. Lakin. "A Structure From Manipulation for Text–Graphic Objects." *ACM Computer Graphics (Proc. SIGGRAPH'80*, Seattle, Wash.), 14(3):100–107, July 1980.

[124] F.H. Lakin. "Computing with Text–Graphic Forms." In *Conf. Record of the 1980 LISP Conference*, Stanford, Calif., pages 100–106, August 25-27, 1980.

[125] J.A. Larson, editor. *Tutorial: End User Facilities in the 1980's*. IEEE Computer Society Press, Los Alamitos, Calif., 1982.

[126] J.A. Larson. "A Visual Approach to Browsing in a Database Environment." *IEEE Computer*, 19(6):62–71, June 1986.

[127] R.W. Lawler. "Designing Computer–Based Microworlds." *Byte*, 7(8):138–160, August 1980.

[128] C. Lewis. "NoPumpG: Creating Interactive Graphics with Spreadsheet Machinery." In *Tutorial: Visual Programming Environments: Paradigms and Systems* (E.P. Glinert, editor), 1990. IEEE Computer Society Press, Los Alamitos, Calif. ♠ 8

[129] H. Lieberman. "A Three–Dimensional Representation for Program Execution." In *Proc. Workshop on Visual Languages* Rome, Italy, pages 111–116, October 4-6, 1989. IEEE Computer Society Press, Los Alamitos, Calif. ♣ 10

[130] H. Lieberman and C. Hewitt. "A Session with TINKER: Interleaving Program Testing with Program Design." In *Conf. Record of the 1980 LISP Conference*, Stanford, Calif., pages 90–99, August 25-27, 1980.

[131] K.N. Lodding. "Iconic Interfacing." *IEEE Computer Graphics and Applications*, 3(2):11–20, March/April 1983. ♣ 5

[132] H.C. Lucas and N.R. Nielsen. "The Impact of Information Presentation on Learning and Performance." *Management Science*, 26(10):982–993, October 1980.

[133] F. Ludolph, Y-Y. Chow, D. Ingalls, S. Wallace and K. Doyle. "The FABRIK Programming Environment." In *Proc. Workshop on Visual Languages*, Pittsburgh, Penn., pages 222–230, October 10-12, 1988. IEEE Computer Society Press, Los Alamitos, Calif. ♠ 6

[134] J. MacKinlay. "Automating the Design of Graphical Presentations of Relational Information." *ACM Trans. on Graphics*, 5(2):110–141, April 1986. ♣ 6

[135] N. Magnenat–Thalmann and D. Thalmann. "Introducing Programming Concepts with Graphical Objects." *ACM SIGCSE Bulletin*, 12(1):105–109, February 1980.

[136] N. Magnenat–Thalmann and D. Thalmann. "A Graphical Pascal Extension Based on Graphical Types." *Software—Practice & Experience*, 11(1):53–62, January 1981.

[137] N. Magnenat–Thalmann and D. Thalmann. "The Use of High–Level 3–D Graphical Types in the MIRA Animation System." *IEEE Computer Graphics and Applications*, 3(9):9–16, December 1983.

[138] T.W. Malone. *What Makes Things Fun to Learn? A Study of Intrinsically Motivating Computer Games*. PhD Thesis, Dept. of Psychology, Stanford University,, Stanford, Calif., 1980. ♣ 6

[139] F. Mavaddat. "An Experiment in Teaching Programming Languages." *ACM SIGCSE Bulletin*, 8(2):45–59, June 1976.

[140] F. Mavaddat. "Another Experiment with Teaching of Programming Languages." *ACM SIGCSE Bulletin*, 13(2):49–56, June 1981.

[141] R.E. Mayer. "The Psychology of How Novices Learn Computer Programming." *ACM Computing Surveys*, 13(1):121–141, March 1981.

[142] G.F. McCleary Jr. "An Effective Graphic 'Vocabulary'." *IEEE Computer Graphics and Applications*, 3(2):46–53, March/April 1983. ♣ 5

[143] D.W. McIntyre and E.P. Glinert. "The Design and Implementation of SUNPICT, A User–Extensible Visual Environment for Intermediate–Scale Procedural Programming." In *Designing and Using Human-Computer Interfaces and Knowledge Based Systems* (G. Salvendy and M.J. Smith, editors)—*Volume 2, Proc. 3rd Int. Conf. on Human–Computer Interaction*, Boston, Mass., pages 338–345, September 18-22, 1989. North Holland, Amsterdam, The Netherlands.

[144] D.W. McIntyre and E.P. Glinert. "The Design and Evolution of an Object–Oriented Graphics Library for Creating User Interfaces for VLSI Design Tools." *Technical Report 90-13*, Dept. of Computer Science, Rensselear Polytechnic Institute, Troy, N.Y., 1990.

[145] G.A. Miller. "The Magic Number Seven Plus or Minus Two: Some Limits on Our Capacity for Information Processing." *Psychological Review*, 63(2):81–96, 1956. ♣ 6

[146] L.H. Miller. "A Study in Man–Machine Interaction." In *Proc. National Computer Conference*, pages 409–421, 1977. AFIPS Press, Reston, Va.

[147] T.G. Moher. "PROVIDE: A Process Visualization and Debugging Environment." *IEEE Trans. on Software Engineering*, SE–14(6):849–857, June 1988. ♣ 2

[148] F.S. Montalvo. "Diagram Understanding: Associating Symbolic Descriptions with Images." In *Proc. Workshop on Visual Languages*, Dallas, Tex., pages 4–11, June 25-27, 1986. IEEE Computer Society Press, Los Alamitos, Calif.

[149] M. Moriconi and D.F. Hare. "Visualizing Program Designs Through PEGASYS." *IEEE Computer*, 18(8):72–85, August 1985. ♠ 2

[150] T.S. Moyer and E.P. Glinert. "Reducing Line Clutter in Software Engineering Diagrams." *Technical Report 90-2*, Dept. of Computer Science, Rensselear Polytechnic Institute, Troy, N.Y., 1990.

[151] M.A. Musen, L.M. Fagan and E.H. Shortliffe. "Graphical Specification of Procedural Knowledge for an Expert System." In *Proc. Workshop on Visual Languages*, Dallas, Tex., pages 167–178, June 25-27, 1986. IEEE Computer Society Press, Los Alamitos, Calif.

[152] B.A. Myers. "INCENSE: A System for Displaying Data Structures." *ACM Computer Graphics (Proc. SIGGRAPH'83*, Detroit, Mich.), 17(3):115–125, July 1983.

[153] B.A. Myers. "The User Interface for SAPPHIRE." *IEEE Computer Graphics and Applications*, 4(12):13–23, December 1984.

[154] B.A. Myers. "The Importance of Percent–Done Progress Indicators for Computer–Human Interfaces." In *Conference Proceedings, CHI'85: Human Factors in Computing Systems*, San Francisco, Calif., pages 11–17, April 14-18, 1985. ACM Press, New York.

[155] B.A. Myers. "Visual Programming, Programming by Example and Program Visualization: A Taxonomy." In *Conference Proceedings, CHI'86: Human Factors in Computing Systems*, Boston, Mass., pages 59–66, April 13-17, 1986. ACM Press, New York. ♠ 1

[156] B.A. Myers. "Creating Interaction Techniques by Demonstration." *IEEE Computer Graphics and Applications*, 7(9):51–60, September 1987. ♠ 6

[157] I. Nassi and B. Shneiderman. "Flowchart Techniques for Structured Programming." *ACM SIGPLAN Notices*, 8(8):12–26, August 1973. ♠ 2

[158] G. Nelson. "JUNO: A Constraint–Based Graphics System." *ACM Computer Graphics (Proc. SIGGRAPH'85*, San Francisco, Calif.), 19(3):235–243, July 1985. ♠ 8

[159] N. Ng. "A Graphical Editor for Programming Using Structured Charts." *IBM Research Report RJ2344(31476)9/19/78*, September 1978.

[160] C.D. Norton and E.P. Glinert. "A Visual Environment for Designing and Simulating Execution of Processor Arrays." *Technical Report 90–18*, Dept. of Computer Science, Rensselear Polytechnic Institute, Troy, N.Y., 1990.

[161] D.W. Olson and L.E. Jasinski. "Keyboard Efficiency." *Byte*, 11(2):241–244, February 1986.

[162] H.L. Ossher. "GRIDS: A New Program Structuring Mechanism Based on Layered Graphs." In *Conf. Record of the 11th Annual ACM Symposium on Principles of Programming Languages*, pages 11–22, January 1984. ACM Press, New York.

[163] S. Papert. *Mindstorms: Children, Computers and Powerful Ideas*. Basic Books, New York, 1980.

[164] G. Pearson and M. Weiser. "Of Moles and Men: The Design of Foot Controls for Workstations." In *Conference Proceedings, CHI'86: Human Factors in Computing Systems*, Boston, Mass., pages 333–339, April 13-17, 1986. ACM Press, New York.

[165] G. Pearson and M. Weiser. "Exploratory Evaluation of a Planar Foot-Operated Cursor-Positioning Device." In *Conference Proceedings, CHI'88: Human Factors in Computing Systems*, Washington, D.C., pages 13–18, May 15-18, 1988. ACM Press, New York.

[166] E. Petajan, B. Bischoff, D. Bodoff and N.M. Brooke. "An Improved Automatic Lipreading System to Enhance Speech Recognition." In *Conference Proceedings, CHI'88: Human Factors in Computing Systems*, Washington, D.C., pages 19–25, May 15-18, 1988. ACM Press, New York.

[167] M.C. Pong and N. Ng. "PIGS: A System for Programming with Interactive Graphical Support." *Software—Practice & Experience*, 13(9):847–855, September 1983. ♠ 3

[168] K. Potosnak. "Do Icons Make User Interfaces Easier to Use?" *IEEE Software*, 5(3):97–99, May 1988. ♣ 7

[169] R.L. Potter, L.J. Weldon and B. Shneiderman. "Improving the Accuracy of Touch Screens: An Experimental Evaluation of Three Strategies." In *Conference Proceedings, CHI'88: Human Factors in Computing Systems*, Washington, D.C., pages 27–32, May 15-18, 1988. ACM Press, New York.

[170] G. Raeder. "A Survey of Current Graphical Programming Techniques." *IEEE Computer*, 18(8):11–25, August 1985.

[171] H.R. Ramsey, M.E. Atwood and J.R. Van Doren. "Flowcharts vs. Program Design Languages: An Experimental Comparison." In *Proc. 22nd Annual Meeting, The Human Factors Society*, pages 709–713, 1978. The Human Factors Society.

[172] P. Reisner. "Formal Grammar and Human Factors Design of an Interactive Graphics System." *IEEE Trans. on Software Engineering*, SE–7(2):229–240, March 1981.

[173] S.P. Reiss. "PECAN: Program Development Systems That Support Multiple Views." *IEEE Trans. on Software Engineering*, SE–11(3):276–285, March 1985. ♠ 5

[174] S.P. Reiss. "An Object–Oriented Framework for Graphical Programming." *ACM SIGPLAN Notices*, 21(10), October 1986.

[175] S.P. Reiss. "Working in the GARDEN Environment for Conceptual Programming." *IEEE Software*, 4(6):16–27, November 1987. ♠ 5

[176] S.P. Reiss, E.J. Golin and R.V. Rubin. "Prototyping Visual Languages with the GARDEN System." In *Proc. Workshop on Visual Languages*, Dallas, Tex., pages 81–90, June 25-27, 1986. IEEE Computer Society Press, Los Alamitos, Calif.

[177] S.P. Reiss, S. Meyers and C. Duby. "Using GELO to Visualize Software Systems." In *Proc. 2nd Annual Symp. on User Interface Software and Technology (UIST'89)*, Williamsburg, Va., pages 149–157, November 13-15, 1989. ACM Press, New York. ♠ 5

[178] C.F. Reynolds. "The Use of Colour in Language Syntax Analysis." *Software—Practice & Experience*, 17(8):513–519, August 1987.

[179] G.-C. Roman and K.C. Cox. "A Declarative Approach to Visualizing Concurrent Computations." *IEEE Computer*, 22(10):25–36, October 1989. ♣ 2

[180] D.T. Ross. "Structured Analysis (SA): A Language for Communicating Ideas." *IEEE Trans. on Software Engineering*, SE–3(1):16–34, January 1977.

[181] D.T. Ross. "Applications and Extensions of SADT." *IEEE Computer*, 18(4):25–34, April 1985. ♠ 2

[182] D.T. Ross and K.E. Schoman. "Structured Analysis for Requirements Definition." *IEEE Trans. on Software Engineering*, SE–3(1):6–15, January 1977.

[183] D.A. Scanlan. "Structured Flowcharts Outperform Pseudocode: An Experimental Comparison." *IEEE Software*, 6(5):28–36, September 1989.

[184] D.A. Scanlan. Letter and author's reply concerning "Structured Flowcharts Outperform Pseudocode: An Experimental Comparison." *IEEE Software*, 6(6):4, November 1989.

[185] S.C. Schaffner and M. Borkan. "SEGUE: Support for Distributed Graphical Interfaces." *IEEE Computer*, 21(12):42–55, December 1988. ♣ 6

[186] M.D. Schwartz, N.M. Delisle and V.S. Begwani. "Incremental Compilation in MAGPIE." In *Proc. ACM SIGPLAN Symposium on Compiler Construction*, June 1984. ACM Press, New York.

[187] S.A.R. Scrivener. "The Interactive Manipulation of Unstructured Images." *Int. J. of Man–Machine Studies*, 16(3):301–313, April 1982.

[188] M. Shaw. "An Input–Output Model for Interactive Systems." In *Conference Proceedings, CHI'86: Human Factors in Computing Systems*, Boston, Mass., pages 261–273, April 13-17, 1986. ACM Press, New York. ♣ 9

[189] S.B. Sheppard and E. Kruesi. "The Effects of Symbology and Spatial Arrangement of Software Specifications in a Coding Task." In *Trends and Applications 1981: Advances in Software Technology*, pages 7–13, 1981. IEEE Computer Society Press, Los Alamitos, Calif.

[190] S.B. Sheppard, E. Kruesi and B. Curtis. "The Effects of Symbology and Spatial Arrangement on the Comprehension of Software Specifications." In *Proc. 5th Int. Conf. on Software Engineering*, pages 207–214, 1981. IEEE Computer Society Press, Los Alamitos, Calif.

[191] B. Shneiderman. *Software Psychology: Human Factors in Computer and Information Systems*. Winthrop, Cambridge, Mass., 1980.

[192] B. Shneiderman. *Designing the User Interface: Strategies for Effective Human–Computer Interaction*. Addison Wesley, Reading, Mass., 1986.

[193] B. Shneiderman. "Direct Manipulation: A Step beyond Programming Languages." *IEEE Computer*, 16(8):57–69, August 1983. ♣ 6

[194] B. Shneiderman, D. McKay R. Mayer and P. Heller. "Experimental Investigations of the Utility of Detailed Flowcharts in Programming." *CACM*, 20(6):373–381, June 1977.

[195] N.C. Shu. "FORMAL: A Forms–Oriented, Visual–Directed Application Development System." *IEEE Computer*, 18(8):38–49, August 1985.

[196] N.C. Shu. "Visual Programming Languages: A Perspective and a Dimensional Analysis." In *Visual Languages* (S.-K. Chang, T. Ichikawa and P.A. Ligomenides, editors), pages 11–34, 1986. Plenum, New York. ♠ 1

[197] N.C. Shu. "A Visual Programming Language Designed for Automatic Programming." In *Proc. 21st Hawaii Int. Conf. on System Sciences (HICSS-21)*, Kailua Kona, Haw., Volume 2: Software Track, pages 662–671, January 5-8, 1988. IEEE Computer Society Press, Los Alamitos, Calif. ♣ 4

[198] N.C. Shu. *Visual Programming*. Van Nostrand Reinhold, New York, 1988.

[199] M. Singh. "Tools for Good Design: Modeling Power Plants." *IEEE Spectrum*, 24(5):56–57, May 1987.

[200] D.C. Smith. *PYGMALION: A Creative Programming Environment*. PhD Thesis, Dept. of Computer Science, Stanford University, Stanford, Calif., 1975. ♠ 3

[201] D.C. Smith, B. Verplank C. Irby, R. Kimball and E. Harslem. "Designing the STAR User Interface." *Byte*, 7(4):242–282, April 1982.

[202] R.B. Smith. "The Alternate Reality Kit: An Animated Environment for Creating Interactive Simulations." In *Proc. Workshop on Visual Languages*, Dallas, Tex., pages 99–106, June 25-27, 1986. IEEE Computer Society Press, Los Alamitos, Calif.

[203] R.B. Smith. "Experiences with the Alternate Reality Kit: An Example of the Tension between Literalism and Magic." *IEEE Computer Graphics and Applications*, 7(9):42–50, September 1987. ♠ 6

[204] L. Snyder. "Parallel Programming and the POKER Programming Environment." *IEEE Computer*, 17(7):27–36, July 1984. ♠ 9

[205] P.D. Stotts. "The PFG Environment: Parallel Programming with Petri Net Semantics." In *Proc. 21st Hawaii Int. Conf. on System Sciences (HICSS-21)*, Kailua Kona, Haw., Volume 2: Software Track, pages 630–638, January 5-8, 1988. IEEE Computer Society Press, Los Alamitos, Calif.

[206] P.D. Stotts. "The PFG Language: Visual Programming for Concurrent Computation." In *Proc. Int. Conf. on Parallel Processing*, University Park, Penn., Volume 2: Software, pages 72–79, August 15-19, 1988, Pennsylvania State University Press, University Park, Penn. ♠ 9

[207] M.P. Stovsky and B.W. Weide. "STILE: A Graphical Design and Development Environment." In *Proc. COMPCON'87*, San Francisco, Calif., pages 247–250, 1987. IEEE Computer Society Press, Los Alamitos, Calif.

[208] M.P. Stovsky and B.W. Weide. "Building Interprocess Communication Models Using STILE." In *Proc. 21st Hawaii Int. Conf. on System Sciences (HICSS-21)*, Kailua Kona, Haw., Volume 2: Software Track, pages 639–647, January 5-8, 1988. IEEE Computer Society Press, Los Alamitos, Calif. ♠ 9

[209] I.B. Sutherland. "SKETCHPAD, A Man–Machine Graphical Communication System." In *Proc. Spring Joint Computer Conference*, pages 329–346, 1963. AFIPS Press, Reston, Va. ♠ 3

[210] W. Sutherland. *On–Line Graphical Specification of Computer Procedures*. PhD Thesis, Massachusetts Institute of Technology, Cambridge, Mass., 1966.

[211] S.L. Tanimoto. "An Iconic/Symbolic Data Structuring Scheme." In *Pattern Recognition and Artificial Intelligence*, 1976. Academic Press, New York.

[212] S.L. Tanimoto. "Stylization as a Means of Compacting Pictorial Databases." *J. of Policy Analysis and Information Systems*, 3(2):67–89, December 1979. ♣ 5

[213] S.L. Tanimoto. "Visual Representation in the Game of Adumbration." In *Proc. Workshop on Visual Languages*, Linkoping, Sweden, pages 17–28, August 19-21, 1987. ♣ 5

[214] S.L. Tanimoto and E.P. Glinert. "Designing Iconic Programming Systems: Representation and Learnability." In *Proc. Workshop on Visual Languages*, Dallas, Tex., pages 54–60, June 25-27, 1986. IEEE Computer Society Press, Los Alamitos, Calif. ♣ 6

[215] S.L. Tanimoto and M.S. Runyan. "PLAY: An Iconic Programming System for Children." In *Visual Languages* (S.-K. Chang, T. Ichikawa and P.A. Ligomenides, editors), pages 191–205, 1986. Plenum, New York. ♠ 6

[216] W. Teitelman. "A Display Oriented Programmer's Assistant." *Int. J. of Man–Machine Studies*, 11(2):157–187, March 1979.

[217] W. Teitelman. "A Tour Through CEDAR." *IEEE Software*, 1(2):44–73, April 1984.

[218] G. Tortora and P. Leoncino. "A Model for the Specification and Interpretation of Visual Languages." In *Proc. Workshop on Visual Languages*, Pittsburgh, Penn., pages 52–60, October 10-12, 1988. IEEE Computer Society Press, Los Alamitos, Calif. ♣ 9

[219] L.L. Tripp. "A Survey of Graphical Notations for Program Design: An Update." *ACM SIGSOFT Software Engineering Notes*, 13(4):39–44, 1988. ♠ 2

[220] E.R. Tufte. *The Visual Display of Quantitative Information*. Graphics Press, Cheshire, Conn., 1983.

[221] E.R. Tufte. *Envisioning Information*. Graphics Press, Cheshire, Conn., 1990.

[222] F.L. Van Nes, J.F. Juola and R.J.A.M. Moonen. "Attraction and Distraction by Text Colors on Displays." In *INTERACT'87, Proc. 2nd IFIP Conf. on Human–Computer Interaction*, Stuttgart, West Germany, pages 625–630, September 1-4, 1987. North Holland, Amsterdam, The Netherlands. ♣ 7

[223] A.R. Vener and E.P. Glinert. "MAGNEX: A Text Editor for the Visually Impaired." In *Proc. 16th Annual ACM Computer Science Conference*, Atlanta, Ga., pages 402–407, February 23-25, 1988. ACM Press, New York. ♣ 8

[224] C. Ware and H.H. Mikaelian. "An Evaluation of an Eye Tracker as a Device for Computer Input." In *Conference Proceedings, CHI+GI'87: Human Factors in Computing Systems*, Toronto, Canada, pages 183–188, April 5-9, 1987. ACM Press, New York.

[225] A.I. Wasserman. "User Software Engineering and the Design of Interactive Systems." In *Proc. 5th Int. Conf. on Software Engineering*, pages 387–393, 1981. IEEE Computer Society Press, Los Alamitos, Calif.

[226] A.I. Wasserman. "Extending State Transition Diagrams for the Specification of Human–Computer Interaction." *IEEE Trans. on Software Engineering*, SE–11(8):699–713, August 1985. ♠ 2

[227] A.I. Wasserman, P.A. Pircher and R.J. Muller. "The Object–Oriented Structured Design Notation for Software Design Representation." *IEEE Computer*, 23(3):50–63, March 1990.

[228] C.J. Watson and R.W. Driver. "The Influence of Computer Graphics on the Recall of Information." *MIS Quarterly*, 7(1):45–53, March 1983.

[229] G. Weber. "Gestures as a Means for the Blind to Interact with a Computer." In *INTERACT'87, Proc. 2nd IFIP Conf. on Human–Computer Interaction*, Stuttgart, West Germany, pages 593–595, September 1-4, 1987. North Holland, Amsterdam, The Netherlands.

[230] R.W. Witty. "Dimensional Flowcharting." *Software—Practice & Experience*, 7:553–584, 1977.

[231] P.C.S. Wong and E.R. Reid. "FLAIR: User Interface Dialog Design Tool." *ACM Computer Graphics (Proc. SIGGRAPH'82, Boston, Mass.)*, 16(3):87–98, July 1982.

[232] W.T. Wood and S.K. Wood. "Icons in Everyday Life." In *Social, Ergonomic and Stress Aspects of Work with Computers* (G. Salvendy, editor)—*Volume 1, Proc. 2nd Int. Conf. on Human–Computer Interaction*, Honolulu, Haw., pages 97–104, August 10-14, 1987. North Holland, Amsterdam, The Netherlands. ♣ 5

[233] L. Yedwab, R.L. Rosenberg C.F. Herot and C. Gross. "The Automated Desk." *ACM SIGSMALL Newsletter*, 7(2):102–108, October 1981.

[234] R. Yeung. "MPL: A Graphical Programming Environment for Matrix Processing Based on Logic and Constraints." In *Proc. Workshop on Visual Languages*, Pittsburgh, Penn., pages 137–143, October 10-12, 1988. IEEE Computer Society Press, Los Alamitos, Calif. ♠ 8

[235] B.W. York and A.I. Karshmer. "Tools to Support Blind Programmers." In *Proc. 17th Annual ACM Computer Science Conference*, Louisville, Ken., pages 5–11, February 21-23, 1989. ACM Press, New York. ♣ 8

[236] N. Yoshida, T. Kikuno, J.-I. Miyao and N. Hirakawa. "Advanced Functions in a Form System based on a Formal Form Model." In *Tutorial: Visual Programming Environments: Applications and Issues* (E.P. Glinert, editor), 1990. IEEE Computer Society Press, Los Alamitos, Calif. ♣ 4

[237] R.M. Young. "The Machine Inside the Machine: Users' Models of Pocket Calculators." *Int. J. of Man–Machine Studies*, 15(1):51–85, January 1981.

[238] M.V. Zelkowitz. "An Editor for Program Design." In *Proc. COMPCON'87*, San Francisco, Calif., pages 242–246, 1987. IEEE Computer Society Press, Los Alamitos, Calif.

[239] T.G. Zimmerman, J. Lanier, C. Blanchard, S. Bryson and Y. Harvill. "A Hand–Gesture Interface Device." In *Conference Proceedings, CHI+GI'87: Human Factors Computing Systems*, Toronto, Canada, pages 189–192, April 5-9, 1987. ACM Press, New York.

[240] M.M. Zloof. "A Language for Office and Business Automation." In *Office Automation Conf. Digest*, pages 249–260, March, 1980. AFIPS Press, Reston, Va. ♣ 4

Index

□□□   □□□

The entries on the following pages serve as a unified index for the two volumes which together constitute this tutorial. Entries which refer to "*Visual Programming Environments: Paradigms and Systems*" are set in Roman type, while those which refer to "*Visual Programming Environments: Applications and Issues*" are set italics. Names of authors of papers included in the tutorial are followed by a special symbol to indicate this fact: ♠ if the paper is in "*Visual Programming Environments: Paradigms and Systems*" and ♣ if it is in "*Visual Programming Environments: Applications and Issues.*"

636

MIDI (musical instrument digital interface) *573*

Miller, G.A. *276* ♣

Miller, L.H. 278

Mills, H. 73

Milner, R. 190, 585

minimal icon *264*

MIRA–3D 269

Mitroff, I.I. *450*

mixed language program *47*

Miyamoto, K. *550* ♣

Miyao, J.–I. *198* ♣

ML 598

MLP *49*

modality *623*

model

    activity 148, 149

    actor 124

    class–instance pair (CLIP) *505, 507, 512, 561*

    contour 78

    data 148

    data flow 124

    Entity–Relationship (E–R model) *188*

    form *198*

    input–output *492*

    state transition 92

    support 149

    visual *332*

model archivist *74*

modeler, chained *155*

modeling

    conceptual *188*

    concrete *25*

    statistical *25*

    symbolic *26*

modeling environment *26*

modeling language *72*

modeling package *71*

modeling transformation matrix (MTM) *20*

MODULA/2 *46*

modular programming 115, 252

modularization *59*

module, program *59, 72, 97*

module hierarchy *59*

module interconnection *158*

MODVUE *17*

Moher, T.G. *95* ♣

MOLGEN 431

monitor, event *101*

monitoring

    process *17, 22*

    program *17*

monitoring system *15, 83*

Montalvo, F.S. 14

Montessori, M. *323*

Moonen, R.J.A.M. *435* ♣

Moore, E.F. 210

Moore's algorithm 210

Moriconi, M. 26, 38, 59, 157 ♠, 170

Morrison, J. *241*

Mosier, J. *460*

MOTIF *594, 601, 603*

motion *14*

motivational aspects of games *292*

mouse 393, *9, 51, 63, 97, 107, 114, 136, 180*

    Braille *483, 484*

movable icon *54*

movement, eye *436*

movie *115, 127, 133*

MPL 529

MPROLOG *196*

MRS *363*

MSTL 529

MTM (modeling transformation matrix) *20*

multicolor display *435*

MULTICS *317*

multilanguage debugger *46*

multilanguage interpreter *46*

multilanguage programming *46*

multilanguage system *51*

multilevel undo *431*

multimodal workstation *617, 624*

multiple interfaces 113

multiple meaning *477*

multiple resource theory *618*

multiple views 470, *10, 16*

multiple virtual workspaces *369*

multiprocessor, hypercube class *84*

multitasking 47

multivariate statistical analysis *34*

MUMPS 101

Munsell, G.F. *241*

Munson, J.B. 536

MUPPET 587

music *296*

Figure 1. Example data definition header for an NSD

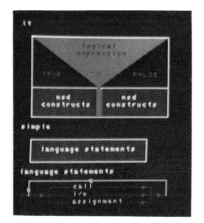

Figure 2. NSD syntax

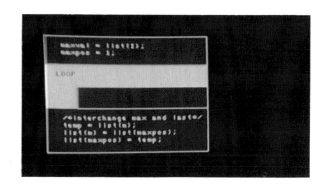

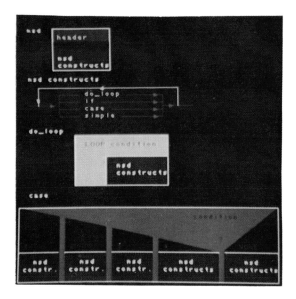

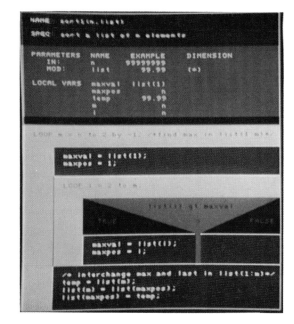

Figure 3. A sample NSD

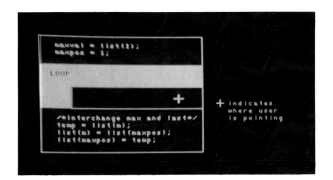

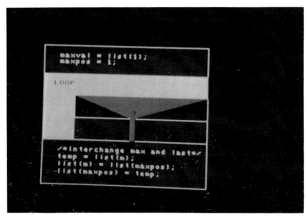

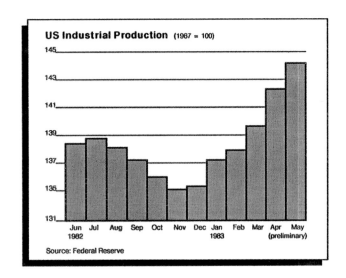

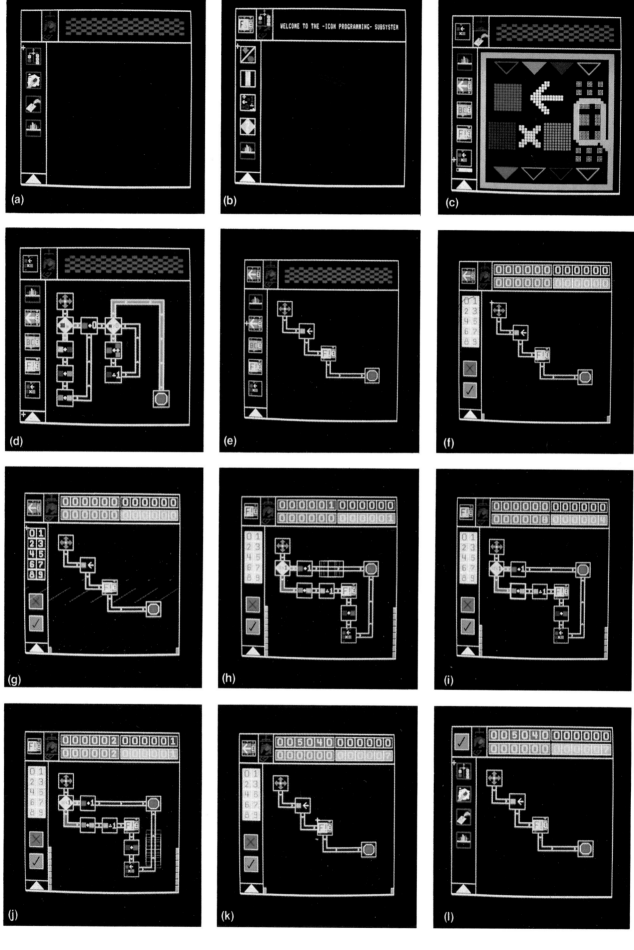

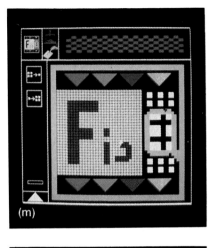

(m)

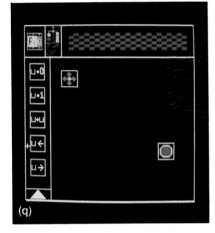

(n)

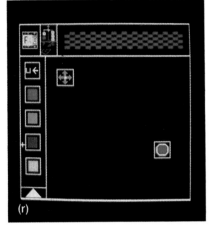

(o)

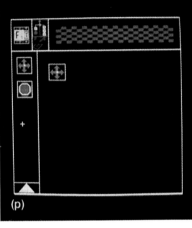

(p)

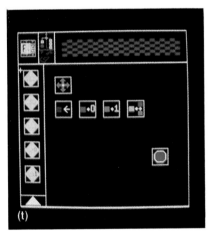

(q)

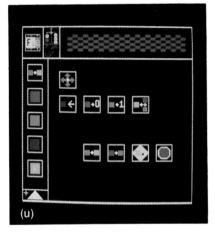

(r)

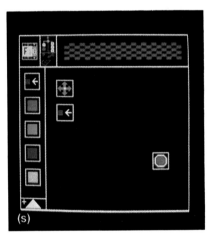

(s)

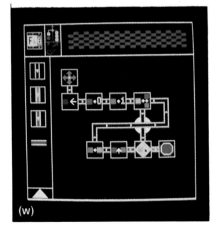

(t)

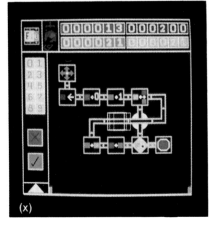

(u)

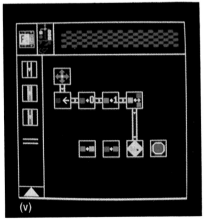

(v)

(w)

(x)

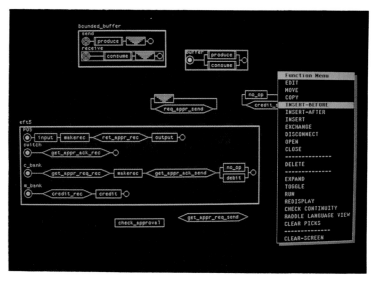

Figure 2: The VERDI work surface

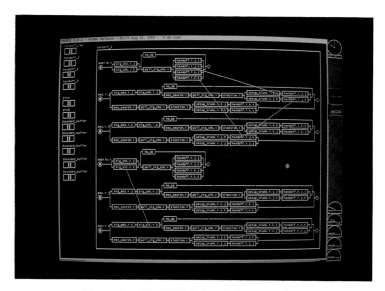

Figure 4a: A VERDI design during execution

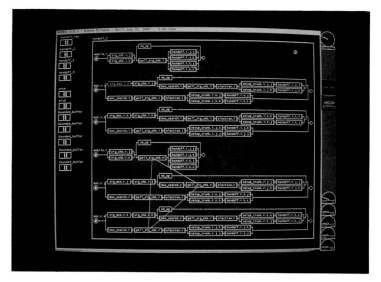

Figure 4b: A VERDI design during execution

659

□□□ □□□ About the Editor

Ephraim P. Glinert is with the Computer Science Department at Rensselaer Polytechnic Institute. Together with his graduate students, he has designed and implemented numerous visual systems, including PICT, SUNPICT, PC–TILES and C² (four experimental visual environments for procedural programming), NOVIS (an experimental visual environment for parallel/distributed programming), a Large Font Virtual Terminal Interface to UNIX* and the MAGNEX text editor (two systems to assist visually handicapped computer users), the user interface and graphics library for OOCADE (a CAD system for VLSI design), and the GLASSBOARD (a CASE tool for large–scale system development and maintenance).

Dr. Glinert holds the Ph.D. and M.Sc. in computer science from the University of Washington, Seattle, where he was an IBM graduate fellow for two years, and the M.Sc. and B.Sc. in mathematics from the Technion, Israel Institute of Technology, Haifa. In addition to lecturing widely on his research both within the United States and abroad, he has presented tutorials[†] at CHI'89 in Austin, SIGGRAPH'89 in Boston and CHI'90 in Seattle, and an intensive graduate level course in the Department of Computer Engineering at National Chiao Tung University, Taiwan (R.O.C.) in the summer of 1987. The notes for this latter course were later reworked to become the chapter "Nontextual Programming Environments" in the volume *"Principles of Visual Programming Systems"* edited by S.–K. Chang (Prentice Hall, 1990).

Dr. Glinert's current research interests include visual and multiparadigm programming environments, multimodal human–computer interfaces, computers and the physically handicapped, CASE tools for large–scale systems, and CAD environments for VLSI design. He is a member of the ACM and the IEEE Computer Society. He currently serves as Associate Editor of the Journal of Visual Languages and Computing, published by Academic Press, and as Vice Chair of the ACM's Special Interest Group for Computers and the Physically Handicapped (SIGCAPH), a position to which he was elected in 1987.

---

*UNIX is a trademark of Bell Labs.

†Together with Brad A. Myers of CMU and Marc H. Brown of DEC.

⏚ IEEE Computer Society

IEEE Computer Society Press Publications

Monographs: A monograph is an authored book

Tutorials: A tutorial is a collection of original materials prepared by the editors and reprints of the best articles published in a subject area. They must contain at least five percent original material (15 to 20 percent original material is recommended).

Reprint Books: A reprint book is a collection of reprints divided into sections with a preface, table of contents, and section introductions that discuss the reprints and why they were selected. It contains less than five percent original material.

(Subject) Technology Series: Each technology series is a collection of anthologies of reprints, each with a narrow focus on a subset of a particular discipline, such as networks, architecture, software, robotics.

Submission of proposals: For guidelines on preparing CS Press Books, write Editor-in-Chief, IEEE Computer Society, P.O. Box 3014, 10662 Los Vaqueros Circle, Los Alamitos, CA 90720-1264 (telephone 714-821-8380).

Purpose

The IEEE Computer Society advances the theory and practice of computer science and engineering, promotes the exchange of technical information among 100,000 members worldwide, and provides a wide range of services to members and nonmembers.

Membership

Members receive the acclaimed monthly magazine *Computer*, discounts, and opportunities to serve (all activities are led by volunteer members). Membership is open to all IEEE members, affiliate society members, and others seriously interested in the computer field.

Publications and Activities

Computer. An authoritative, easy-to-read magazine containing tutorial and in-depth articles on topics across the computer field, plus news, conferences, calendar, interviews, and new products.

Periodicals. The society publishes six magazines and four research transactions. Refer to membership application or request information as noted above.

Conference Proceedings, Tutorial Texts, Standards Documents. The Computer Society Press publishes more than 100 titles every year.

Standards Working Groups. Over 100 of these groups produce IEEE standards used throughout the industrial world.

Technical Committees. Over 30 TCs publish newsletters, provide interaction with peers in specialty areas, and directly influence standards, conferences, and education.

Conferences/Education. The society holds about 100 conferences each year and sponsors many educational activites, including computing science accreditation.

Chapters. Regular and student chapters worldwide provide the opportunity to interact with colleagues, hear technical experts, and serve the local professional community.

Lights! Camera! **Action!**

IEEE Computer Graphics and applications

How do you keep up with the latest in computer graphics?

The hardware is changing. The software is changing. The standards that get the hardware and software to work together are changing.

But your need to keep up with the progress of computer graphics never changes.

Science, art, engineering, architecture, medicine, education, — all of these appear in the four-color pages of *IEEE Computer Graphics and Applications*.

We help you keep in touch with the latest changes in animation, scientific visualization, multimedia, and computer aided design and engineering.

IEEE Computer Graphics and Applications is as colorful, diverse and precise as the field it covers. We offer you the insight, the color, the lights, and the camera.

All you need to do is take action. Subscribe today.

 **IEEE COMPUTER SOCIETY**

 **THE INSTITUTE OF ELECTRICAL AND ELECTRONICS ENGINEERS, INC.**

Other IEEE Computer Society Press Texts

Monographs

Analyzing Computer Architecture
Written by J.C. Huck and M.J. Flynn
(ISBN 0-8186-8857-2); 206 pages

Desktop Publishing for the Writer: Designing, Writing, Developing
Written by Richard Ziegfeld and John Tarp
(ISBN 0-8186-8840-8); 380 pages

Integrating Design and Test: Using CAE Tools for ATE Programming
Written by K.P. Parker
(ISBN 0-8186-8788-6 (case)); 160 pages

JSP and JSD: The Jackson Approach to Software Development (Second Edition)
Written by J.R. Cameron
(ISBN 0-8186-8858-0); 560 pages

National Computer Policies
Written by Ben G. Matley and Thomas A. McDannold
(ISBN 0-8186-8784-3); 192 pages

Physical Level Interfaces and Protocols
Written by Uyless Black
(ISBN 0-8186-8824-6); approximately 272 pages

Protecting Your Proprietary Rights in the Computer and High Technology Industries
Written by Tobey B. Marzouk, Esq.
(ISBN 0-8186-8754-1); 224 pages

Tutorials

Advanced Computer Architecture
Edited by D.P. Agrawal
(ISBN 0-8186-0667-3); 400 pages

Advanced Microprocessors and High-Level Language Computer Architectures
Edited by V. Milutinovic
(ISBN 0-8186-0623-1); 608 pages

Advances in Distributed System Reliability
Edited by Suresh Rai and Dharma P. Agrawal
(ISBN 0-8186-8907-2); 352 pages

Computer Architecture
Edited by D.D. Gajski, V.M. Milutinovic, H. Siegel, and B.P. Furht
(ISBN 0-8186-0704-1); 602 pages

Computer Communications: Architectures, Protocols, and Standards (Second Edition)
Edited by William Stallings
(ISBN 0-8186-0790-4); 448 pages

Computer Graphics (2nd Edition)
Edited by J.C. Beatty and K.S. Booth
(ISBN 0-8186-0425-5); 576 pages

Computer Graphics Hardware: Image Generation and Display
Edited by H.K. Reghbati and A.Y.C. Lee
(ISBN 0-8186-0753-X); 384 pages

Computer Graphics: Image Synthesis
Edited by Kenneth Joy, Max Nelson, Charles Grant, and Lansing Hatfield
(ISBN 0-8186-8854-8); 384

Computer and Network Security
Edited by M.D. Abrams and H.J. Podell
(ISBN 0-8186-0756-4); 448 pages

Computer Networks (4th Edition)
Edited by M.D. Abrams and I.W. Cotton
(ISBN 0-8186-0568-5); 512 pages

Computer Text Recognition and Error Correction
Edited by S.N. Srihari
(ISBN 0-8186-0579-0); 364 pages

Computers for Artificial Intelligence Applications
Edited by B. Wah and G.-J. Li
(ISBN 0-8186-0706-8); 656 pages

Database Management
Edited by J.A. Larson
(ISBN 0-8186-0714-9); 448 pages

Digital Image Processing and Analysis: Volume 1: Digital Image Processing
Edited by R. Chellappa and A.A. Sawchuk
(ISBN 0-8186-0665-7); 736 pages

Digital Image Processing and Analysis: Volume 2: Digital Image Analysis
Edited by R. Chellappa and A.A. Sawchuk
(ISBN 0-8186-0666-5); 670 pages

Digital Private Branch Exchanges (PBXs)
Edited by E.R. Coover
(ISBN 0-8186-0829-3); 400 pages

Distributed Computing Network Reliability
Edited by Suresh Rai and Dharma P. Agrawal
(ISBN 0-8186-8908-0); 368 pages

Distributed Control (2nd Edition)
Edited by R.E. Larson, P.L. McEntire, and J.G. O'Reilly
(ISBN 0-8186-0451-4); 382 pages

Distributed Database Management
Edited by J.A. Larson and S. Rahimi
(ISBN 0-8186-0575-8); 580 pages

Distributed-Software Engineering
Edited by S.M. Shatz and J.-P. Wang
(ISBN 0-8186-8856-4); 304 pages

DSP-Based Testing of Analog and Mixed-Signal Circuits
Edited by M. Mahoney
(ISBN 0-8186-0785-8); 272 pages

Fault-Tolerant Computing
Edited by V.P. nelson and B.D. Carroll
(ISBN 0-8186-0677-0 (paper) 0-8186-8667-4 (case)); 432 pages

Gallium Arsenide Computer Design
Edited by V.M. Milutinovic and D.A. Fura
(ISBN 0-8186-0795-5); 368 pages

Human Factors in Software Development (2nd Edition)
Edited by B. Curtis
(ISBN 0-8186-0577-4); 736 pages

Integrated Services Digital Networks (ISDN) (Second Edition)
Edited by W. Stallings
(ISBN 0-8186-0823-4); 404 pages

For Further Information:

IEEE Computer Society, 10662 Los Vaqueros Circle, P.O. Box 3014,
Los Alamitos, CA 90720-1264

IEEE Computer Society, 13, Avenue de l'Aquilon, 2,
B-1200 Brussels, BELGIUM

IEEE Computer Society,
Ooshima Building, 2-19-1 Minami-Aoyama,
Minato-ku, Tokyo 107, JAPAN

Interconnection Networks for Parallel and Distributed Processing
Edited by C.-L. Wu and T.-Y. Feng
(ISBN 0-8186-0574-X); 500 pages

Local Network Equipment
Edited by H.A. Freeman and K.J. Thurber
(ISBN 0-8186-0605-3); 384 pages

Local Network Technology (3rd Edition)
Edited by W. Stallings
(ISBN 0-8186-0825-0); 512 pages

Microprogramming and Firmware Engineering
Edited by V. Milutinovic
(ISBN 0-8186-0839-0); 416 pages

Modeling and Control of Automated Manufacturing Systems
Edited by A.A. Desrochers
(ISBN 0-8186-8916-1); 384 pages

Modern Design and Analysis of Discrete-Event Computer Simulations
Edited by E.J. Dudewicz and Z. Karian
(ISBN 0-8186-0597-9); 486 pages

New Paradigms for Software Development
Edited by William Agresti
(ISBN 0-8186-0707-6); 304 pages

Object-Oriented Computing--Volume 1: Concepts
Edited by Gerald E. Peterson
(ISBN 0-8186-0821-8); 214 pages

Object-Oriented Computing--Volume 2: Implementations
Edited by Gerald E. Peterson
(ISBN 0-8186-082108); 214 pages

Office Automation Systems (Second Edition)
Edited by H.A. Freemand and K.J. Thurber
(ISBN 0-8186-0822-6); 324 pages

Parallel Architectures for Database Systems
Edited by A. R. Hurson, L.L. Miller, and S.H. Pakzad
(ISBN 0-8186-8838-6); 478 pages

Programming Productivity: Issues for the Eighties (Second Edition)
Edited by C. Jones
(ISBN 0-8186-0681-9); 472 pages

Recent Advances in Distributed Database Management
Edited by C. Mohan
(ISBN 0-8186-0571-5); 500 pages

Reduced Instruction Set Computers (Second Edition)
Edited by W. Stallings
(ISBN 0-8186-8943-9); 448 pages

Reliable Distributed System Software
Edited by J.A. Stankovic
(ISBN 0-8186-0570-7); 400 pages

Robotics Tutorial (2nd Edition)
Edited by C.S. G. Lee, R.C. Gonzalez, and K.S. Fu
(ISBN 0-8186-0658-4); 630 pages

Software Design Techniques (4th Edition)
Edited by P. Freeman and A.I. Wasserman
(ISBN 0-8186-0514-0); 736 pages

Software Engineering Project Management
Edited by R. Thayer
(ISBN 0-8186-0751-3); 512 pages

Software Maintenance
Edited by G. Parikh and N. Zvegintzov
(ISBN 0-8186-0002-0); 360 pages

Software Management (3rd Edition)
Edited by D.J. Reifer
(ISBN 0-8186-0678-9); 526 pages

Software-Oriented Computer Architecture
Edited by E. Fernandez and T. Lang
(ISBN 0-8186-0708-4); 376 pages

Software Reusability
Edited by Peter Freeman
(ISBN 0-8186-0750-5); 304 pages

Software Risk Management
Edited by B.W. Boehm
(ISBN 0-8186-8906-4); 508 pages

Standards, Guidelines, and Examples on System and Software Requirements Engineering
Edited by Merlin Dorfman and Richard H. Thayer
(ISBN 0-8186-8922-6); 626 pages

System and Software Requirements Engineering
Edited by Richard H. Thayer and Merlin Dorfman
(ISBN 0-8186-8921-8); 740 pages

Test Generation for VLSI Chips
Edited by V.D. Agrawal and S.C. Seth
(ISBN 0-8186-8786-X); 416 pages

VSLI Technologies: Through the 80s and Beyond
Edited by D.J. McGreivy and K.A. Pickar
(ISBN 0-8186-0424-7); 346 pages

VLSI Testing and Validation Techniques
Edited by H. Reghbati
(ISBN 0-8186-0668-1); 616 pages

Reprint Collections

Dataflow and Reduction Architectures
Edited by S.S. Thakkar
(ISBN 0-8186-0759-9); 460 pages

Expert Systems: Software Methodology
Edited by Peter Raeth
(ISBN 0-8186-8904-8); 476 pages

Logic Design for Testability
Edited by C.C. Timoc
(ISBN 0-8186-0573-1); 324 pages

Microprocessors and Microcomputers (3rd Edition)
Edited by J.T. Cain
(ISBN 0-8186-0585-5); 386 pages

Software (3rd Edition)
Edited by M.V. Zelkowitz
(ISBN 0-8186-0789-0); 440 pages

VLSI Technologies and Computer Graphics
Edited by H. Fuchs
(ISBN 0-8186-0491-3); 490 pages

Artifical Neural Networks Technology Series

Artificial Neural Networks: Concept Learning
Edited by J. Diederich
(ISBN 0-8186-2015-3); 140 pages

Artificial Neural Networks: Electronic Implementation
Edited by Nelson Morgan
(ISBN 0-8186-2029-3); approximately 192 pages

Artificial Neural Networks: Theoretical Concepts
Edited by V. Vemuri
(ISBN 0-8186-0855-2); 160 pages

Software Technology Series

Computer-Aided Software Engineering (CASE)
Edited by E.J. Chikofsky
(ISBN 0-8186-1970-8); 110 pages

Communications Technology Series

Multicast Communication in Distributed Systems
Edited by Mustaque Ahamad
(ISBN 0-8186-1970-8); 110 pages

Robotic Technology Series

Multirobot Systems
Edited by Rajiv Mehrotra and Murali R. Varanasi
(ISBN 0-8186-1977-5); 122 pages